JEWISH AMERICAN FICTION WRITERS

GARLAND REFERENCE LIBRARY
OF THE HUMANITIES
(VOL. 972)

JEWISH AMERICAN FICTION WRITERS
An Annotated bibliography

Gloria L. Cronin
Blaine H. Hall
Connie Lamb

GARLAND PUBLISHING, INC. • NEW YORK & LONDON
1991

Library of Congress Cataloging-in-Publication Data

Cronin, Gloria L., 1947–
    Jewish American fiction writers : an annotated bibliography /
Gloria L. Cronin, Blaine H. Hall, Connie Lamb.
        p. cm. — (Garland reference library of the humanities ; vol.
972)
    ISBN 0–8240–1619–X (alk. paper)
    1. American fiction—Jewish authors—History and criticism—
Bibliography. 2. American fiction—20th century—History and
criticism—Bibliography. 3. Jewish fiction—United States—History
and criticism—Bibliography. I. Hall, Blaine H. II. Lamb, Connie.
III. Title. IV. Series.
Z1229.J4C76   1991
[PS153.J4]
016.813'5098924—dc20   91–20634
                                                              CIP

Printed on acid-free, 250-year-life paper
Manufactured in the United States of America

Contents

Individual Authors

Entries for individual authors
are categorized as follows:

Primary Sources
 Novels
 Collected Works
 Short Fiction in Anthologies
 Short Fiction in Periodicals
Secondary Sources
 Books
 Articles and Chapters
 Interviews
 Biographical Sources
 Bibliographies
 Dissertations

Acknowledgments

The authors would like to thank the Brigham Young University English Department and the Harold B. Lee Library for allowing us the time, money, and personnel to complete this bibliography. We give particular thanks to the Interlibrary Loan Department and the Copy Center of the Lee Library, without whose efforts in obtaining and copying thousands of articles and books this project would not have been possible. We also appreciate the contributions of Julene Butler, who spent a year working on the project before leaving to pursue a doctoral program. In addition we gratefully recognize the technical support of Barbara Carlson, Tessa Meyer Santiago, and Alan Sevison and the many student assistants and typists who assisted in the research and preparation of the manuscript during the nearly four years required for its completion.

Introduction

From the beginning of Jewish immigration into the United States in the years 1881-1924 the Jewish presence in American letters began to be felt. Even before our century began Jews had found their way as characters into contemporary fiction, and a large number of Jewish immigrants were writing in Yiddish. However, as the twentieth century dawned the number of Jewish writers writing in English increased dramatically. During the period between the Great Depression of the 1930s and World War II, their influence began to be felt in drama, criticism, and poetry, but even more particularly in fiction. However, it was in the post-war period that Jewish writers entered the mainstream in overwhelming numbers. As Louis Harap describes it in *Creative Awakening*, Vol 1. (1987) p. 2, it is the story of this journey from the periphery to the center of American literature where Jewish American writers were accepted by the American reading public as well as by a literary audience, and thereby achieved full citizenship. This bibliography bears witness to the complexity of this movement from periphery to mainstream, and, more particularly, to its sheer volume, range and quality.

We have made no attempt to add to the current debates among Jewish American writers and critics, namely Bellow, Malamud, Philip Roth, Chametsky, Walden, Fiedler, Pinsker,

Shechner and many others, as to what constitutes a Jewish American author or work of fiction. We do not subscribe to any prescriptive definition of "Jewishness," "Jewish writer," or "the Jewish American" literary tradition, but have identified the sixty-two writers included here as marked by a Jewish American acculturation, which in no way diminishes the stature and universality of their work. We recognize also that though Jewishness is a multi-faceted ethnic identification, there is nevertheless a distinctive ethnicity which is Jewish and which stems from such sources as historical tradition, theology, family life, religious observance, world view, generational patterns, customs, foodways, values, sociological traits, and characterological identifiers. As Mark Shechner points out:

> Though terms like "Jewish fiction" and the "Jewish novel" are not useful as literary categories, like "The Elizabethan sonnet," or national catchalls like "The Russian novel," they do merit a place in *social* history. The most accessible collective facts about Jewish novelists in America are demographic: their sheer numerical presence among the ranks of American novelists and their insistent upward mobility. Not only are so many American novelists Jews, more or less, but the work of these writers includes some of the most acclaimed fiction written in this country since World War II. The postwar era has seen Saul Bellow, Norman Mailer, Isaac Bashevis Singer, Philip Roth, and Bernard Malamud take their place among the most celebrated of our writers, and to mention them together is to be conscious of both their place in our literature and the enormously varied terrain they occupy collectively. And to their names can be added others from that vast penumbra of Jewish fiction writers who have also

earned some measure of national recognition. ("Jewish Writers," *Harvard Guide to Contemporary American Writing*, pp. 191-92).

It is part of the "vast penumbra" of lesser but not unimportant lights in the Jewish American tradition of fiction writing that we have documented in this annotated bibliography. The selection of writers to be included was made by consulting reference works, reading widely in the literature on Jewish American fiction, and by consulting with leading scholars in the field. Finally, we looked at the quantity and quality of the secondary source materials about them. We hope that the sheer size of this work, which includes sixty-two writers of the nineteenth and twentieth centuries and was compiled during the last decade of this century, will contribute to a general awareness of the enormous contribution of Jews to American literature, because this is one of the great stories in the development of American cultural history.

This bibliography includes references to primary and secondary sources obtained through searching numerous bibliographic and indexing sources through 1988, with many additional works from 1989 to 1991. By intent, except for the primary sources, we have not included everything we have found, choosing to include only secondary sources with substantive content. Undoubtedly, in spite of our best efforts, some items have eluded us, since many of these authors have been written about in many little-known or local publications over more than a century when, particularly in the earlier years, the bibliographic and indexing sources were nonexistent or incomplete.

While many of the authors wrote in other literary genres, we have listed only their fiction and works about their fiction except for biographical sources and interviews that shed light on the creative process and their literary careers. However, since the distinction between fiction and memoir, reminiscence, and autobiography often becomes blurred for some authors, such as Antin and Yezierska, we have included these types of writings as primary sources for these two authors. Finally, we have excluded all foreign language publications and did not search foreign language bibliographic and indexing sources.

The book reviews were taken primarily from nationally recognized magazines, journals, and newspapers published in major cities and indexed in standard book review indexes, but not exclusively so. Brief book notices or plot summaries have generally been omitted. With few exceptions, however, any review or article with substantive critical commentary has been listed and annotated.

As much as possible, the bibliographic citations have been verified from the source documents. However, because copies of articles from interlibrary loan often came without full bibliographic information on the source itself, we have assumed the citation's correctness when its use brought us the requested item. We also attempted to obtain all the items included here to verify the bibliographic data, including the various editions of the novels and collected works. However, some sources were not available even through interlibrary loan. When we felt confident that the publication information was correct and could verify it in two or more sources, we have included them. References to multiple publishing dates for paperback editions of the novels were impossible to verify, and some of these dates may refer to printings rather than different editions. Notations such as "Pag. not available," or "Cited in PBIP" have also been inserted to indicate our inability to obtain the required information.

For each author we have arranged the entries under two main headings: **Primary Sources** and **Secondary Sources**. The primary sources are categorized as **Novels, Collected**

Works, Short Fiction in Anthologies, and **Short Fiction in Periodicals.** The primary sources appear without annotations except for listing the individual stories published in each of the collected works.

In the listings for novels, collected works, and anthologies, we have tried to discover and list all editions of each work both hardbound and paperback. These listings have been compiled from the *Library of Congress National Union Catalog, Cumulative Book Index, Books in Print, Paperbound Books in Print, British Books in Print, British Museum Catalog, British National Bibliography,* and *Short Story Index,* with additional information from the RLIN (Research Libraries Information Network) and OCLC (Online Computer Library Center) online bibliographic databases.

The secondary sources are categorized as **Books, Articles and Chapters, Interviews, Biographical Sources, Bibliographies,** and **Dissertations.**

All secondary sources have been annotated except for General Sources, books, dissertations and book-length biographies and autobiographies. In the annotations we have taken care to reflect the author's tone and choice of language. Annotations contain main ideas or summarize directions of thought but do not attempt to paraphrase the course of the article or its argument. Some articles, of course, lend themselves better to this approach than do others. Generally, the annotations are descriptive rather than evaluative, but occasionally we have noted major articles. The length of the annotation does not necessarily reflect the title's importance.

During our research we discovered a number of articles and books on the subject of Jewish American literature and culture that gave useful information on Jewish American fiction and fiction writers. Some of these have been cited in reference to specific authors in the individual authors section of the bibliography, but many have not. Users will find these listed in a **General Sources** section at the beginning.

In citing author's names we have not standardized a single form for those with multiple citations but have given the form used in the published sources.

The citations follow *The MLA Style Manual* (1985). Within each section and subsection the arrangement is alphabetical. To facilitate data entry on the word processor, we have arbitrarily eliminated all diacritics in names and titles. We have tried hard over the nearly four years we have been working on this bibliography to avoid omissions and errors, but inevitably a few may have slipped through. For these we apologize.

Gloria L. Cronin
Blaine H. Hall
Connie Lamb

Brigham Young University
May 1991

JEWISH AMERICAN
FICTION WRITERS

General Sources

General Articles and Chapters

Adler, Ruth. "Mothers and Daughters: The Jewish Mother as Seen by American Jewish Women Writers." *Yiddish* 6.4 (1987): 87-92.

Alexander, Edward. "The Holocaust in American Jewish Fiction: A Slow Awakening." *The Resonance of Dust: Essays on Holocaust Literature and Jewish Fate.* Edward Alexander. Columbus: Ohio UP, 1979. 121-46.

Alter, Robert. "Jewish Dreams and Nightmares." *Commentary* Jan. 1968: 48-54. Rpt. in *After the Tradition: Essays on Modern Jewish Writing.* Robert Alter. New York: Dutton, 1969. 17-34; *Contemporary American-Jewish Literature: Critical Essays.* Ed. Irving Malin. Bloomington: Indiana UP, 1973. 58-77.

Bellman, Samuel I. "Sleep, Pride, and Fantasy: Birth Traumas and Socio-Biologic Adaptation in the American-Jewish Novel." *Costerus* 8 (1973): 1-12.

Bernstein, Melvin. "Jewishness, Judaism and the American-Jewish Novelist." *Chicago Jewish Forum* 237 (Sum. 1965): 275-82.

Bradbury, Malcolm. "Liberal and Existential Imaginations: The 1940s and 1950s." *The Modern American Novel.* Malcolm Bradbury. Oxford: Oxford UP, 1984. 126-55.

Chenetier, Marc. "Charting Contemporary American Fiction: A View from Abroad." *New Literary History* 16.3 (1985): 653-69.

Daiches, David. "Some Aspects of Anglo-American Jewish Fiction." *Jewish Quarterly* 21.1-2 (1973): 88-93.

Donald, Miles. "Minorities: The Jewish-American Novel." *The American Novel in the Twentieth Century*. London: David; New York: Barnes, 1978. 160-75.

Fiedler, Leslie A. "The Breakthrough: The American Jewish Novelist and the Fictional Image of the Jew." *Midstream* 4.1 (1958): 15-35.

Fiedler, Leslie A. "Genesis: The American-Jewish Novel Through the Twenties." *Midstream* 4.3 (1958): 21-33. Rpt. in *Jewish-American Literature: An Anthology of Fiction, Poetry, Autobiography, and Criticism*. Ed. Abraham Chapman. New York: Mentor-NAL, 1974. 570-86.

Fiedler, Leslie A. "The Two Memories: Reflections on Writers and Writing in the Thirties." *Proletarian Writers of the Thirties*. Ed. David Madden. Crosscurrents/Modern Critiques. Carbondale: Southern Illinois UP, 1968. 3-25.

Fiedler, Leslie A. "Zion as Main Street." *Waiting for the End: The Crisis in American Culture & A Portrait of 20th Century Literature*. Leslie A. Fiedler. New York: Stein, 1964. 65-117.

Field, Leslie. "Israel Revisited in American Jewish Literature." *Midstream* Nov. 1982: 50-54.

Fine, David M. "Immigrant Ghetto Fiction, 1885-1918: An Annotated Bibliography." *American Literary Realism 1870-1910* 6.3 (1973): 169-95.

Fineman, Irving. "The Image of the Jew in Our Fiction." *Tradition* 8.4 (1966): 19-47.

Friedman, Alan Warren. "The Jew's Complaint in Recent American Fiction: Beyond Exodus and Still in the Wilderness." *Southern Review* ns 8.1 (1972): 41-59.

Friedman, Melvin J. "Dislocations of Setting and Word: Notes on American Fiction Since 1950." *Studies in American Fiction* 5.1 (1977): 79-98.

Fuchs, Daniel. "The Jewish Writer and the Critics." *Contemporary Literature* 15.4 (1974): 562-79.

Girgus, Sam B. "A Poetics of the American Idea: The Jewish Writer and America." *Prospects* 8 (1983): 327-48.

Glicksberg, Charles I. "A Jewish American Literature?" *Southwest Review* 53 (Spr. 1968): 196-205.

Goldsmith, Arnold L. "'A Curse on Columbus': Twentieth-Century Jewish-American Fiction and the Theme of Disillusionment." Yiddish 4.1 (1979): 47-55. Joint Issue with *Studies in American Jewish Literature* [Univ. Park, PA] 5.2 (1979): 47-55.

Gollin, Rita K. "Understanding Fathers in American Jewish Fiction." *Centennial Review* 18.3 (1974): 273-87.

Guttmann, Allen. "The Conversions of the Jews." *Wisconsin Studies in Contemporary Literature* 6.2 (1965): 161-76. Rpt. in *Contemporary American Jewish Literature: Critical Essays*. Ed. Irving Malin. Bloomington: Indiana UP, 1973. 39-57.

Harrison, Walter L. "Six-Pointed Diamond: Baseball and American Jews." *Journal of Popular Culture* 15.3 (1981): 112-18.

Hatcher, Harlan H. "The Proletarian Novel." *Creating the Modern American Novel*. Harlan H. Hatcher. New York: Farrar, 1935. 262-74.

Howe, Irving. "The Stranger and the Victim: The Two Jewish Stereotypes of American Fiction." *Commentary* Aug. 1949: 147-56.

Jaher, Frederic Cople. "The Quest for the Ultimate *Shiksa*." *American Quarterly* 35.5 (1983): 518-42.

Kahn, Lothar. "American-Jewish Literature After Bellow, Malamud and Roth." *Jewish Book Annual* 45 (1987-1988): 5-18.

Kazin, Alfred. "The Jew as Modern American Writer." *The Commentary Reader*. Ed. Norman Podhoretz. New York: Atheneum, 1966. xv-xxv.

Lainoff, Seymour. "American Jewish Fiction Before the First World War." *Chicago Jewish Forum* 24 (1966): 207-12.

Lelchuck, Alan. "The Death of the Jewish Novel." *New York Times Book Review* Nov. 25, 1984: 1, 38-39.

Levin, Meyer. "What Is an American Jewish Writer?" *Congress Bi-Weekly* 19 May 1972: 22-24.

Levine, Paul. "Recent Jewish-American Fiction: From *Exodus* to Genesis." *Contemporary American Fiction*. Eds. Malcolm Bradbury and Sigmund Ro. Stratford-upon-Avon Studies. 2nd Series. London: Arnold, 1987. 71-86.

Lewis, Stuart A. "The Jewish Author Looks at the Black." *Colorado Quarterly* 21.3 (1973): 317-30.

Lewisohn, Ludwig. "A Panorama of a Half-Century of American Jewish Literature." *Jewish Book Annual* 9 (1950-1951): 3-10.

Malin, Irving, and Irwin Stark. Introduction. *Breakthrough: A Treasury of Contemporary American-Jewish Literature*. Eds. Irving Malin and Irwin Stark. New York: McGraw, 1964. 1-24. Rpt. in *Jewish-American Literature: An Anthology of Fiction, Poetry, Autobiography, and Criticism*. Ed. Abraham Chapman. New York: Mentor-NAL, 1974. 665-89.

Mersand, Joseph E. "Jewish Novelists Portray the Jew, 1867-1939." *Traditions in American Literature: A Study of Jewish Characters and Authors*. Joseph Mersand. New York: Modern Chapbooks, 1939; Essay and General Literature Index Reprint Series. Port Washington: Kennikat, 1968. 83-92.

Nilsen, Helge Normann. "Trends in Jewish-American Prose: A Short Historical Survey." *English Studies* 64.6 (1983): 507-17.

Pinsker, Sanford. "The Rise-and-Fall of the American-Jewish Novel." *Between Two Worlds: The American Novel in the 1960s*. Sanford Pinsker. Troy: Whitston, 1980. 29-57.

Ribalow, Harold U. Introduction: The Jewish Short Story in America. *This Land, These People.* Ed. Harold U. Ribalow. New York: Beechhurst, 1950. 1-10.

Ribalow, Harold U. Introduction. *The Tie That Binds: Conversations with Jewish Writers.* Harold U. Ribalow. San Diego: Barnes, 1980. 3-23.

Rideout, Walter B. "'O Workers' Revolution . . . The True Messiah': The Jew as Author and Subject in the American Radical Novel." *American Jewish Archives* 11.2 (1959): 157-75.

Rosenfeld, Alvin H. "Inventing the Jew: Notes on Jewish Autobiography." *Midstream* Apr. 1975: 54-67.

Rosenfeld, Alvin H. "The Progress of the American Jewish Novel." *Response* 7.1 (1973): 115-30.

Scholnick, Sylvia Huberman. "Money Versus Mitzvot: The Figure of the Businessman in Novels by American Jewish Writers." *Yiddish* 6.4 (1987): 48-55.

Schwarz, Leo W. "Mutations of Jewish Values in Contemporary American Fiction." *Tradition and Change in Jewish Experience.* Ed. A. Leland Jamison. The B. G. Rudolph Lectures in Judaic Studies. Syracuse: Syracuse UP, 1978. 184-97.

Shechner, Mark. "Jewish Writers." *Harvard Guide to Contemporary American Writing.* Ed. Daniel Hoffman. Cambridge: Belknap-Harvard UP, 1979. 191-239.

Smith, Allan Lloyd. "Brain Damage: The Word and the World in Postmodernist Writing." *Contemporary American Fiction.* Eds. Malcolm Bradbury and Sigmund Ro. Stratford-Upon-Avon Studies. 2nd Series. London: Arnold, 1987. 38-50.

Sochen, June. "Identities Within Identity: Thoughts on Jewish American Women Writers." *Studies in American Jewish Literature* 3 (1983): 6-10.

Syrkin, Marie. "Jewish Awareness in American Literature." *The American Jew: A Reappraisal.* Ed. Oscar I. Janowsky. Philadelphia: Jewish Pub. Soc. of America, 1967. 211-33.

Tuerk, Richard. "Jewish-American Literature." *Ethnic Perspectives in American Literature: Selected Essays on the European Contribution.* Eds. Robert J. DiPietro and Edward Ifkovic. New York: MLA, 1983. 133-62.

Waxman, Meyer. "American Jewish Literature" and "Anglo-Jewish Literature." *A History of Jewish Literature from the Close of the Bible to Our Own Days.* Meyer Waxman. 4 vols. New York: Bloch, 1936. 4: 956-95.

Zanger, Jules. "On Not Making It in America." *American Studies* 17.1 (1976): 39-48.

General Books

Baumgarten, Murray. *City Scriptures: Modern Jewish Writing.* Cambridge: Harvard UP, 1982.

Bilik, Dorothy Seidman. *Immigrant-Survivors: Post-Holocaust Consciousness in Recent Jewish American Fiction.* Middletown: Wesleyan UP, 1981.

Fiedler, Leslie A. *The Jew in the American Novel.* Herzl Inst. Pamphlet 10. New York: Herzl Inst., 1959. Rpt. in *To the Gentiles.* Leslie Fiedler. New York: Stein, 1971; *The Collected Essays of Leslie Fiedler.* Leslie Fiedler. 2 vols. New York: Stein, 1971. 2:65-117; *To the Gentiles.* New York: Stein, 1972. 65–117.

Fried, Lewis, Ed. *Handbook of American-Jewish Literature: An Analytical Guide to Topics, Themes, and Sources.* New York: Greenwood, 1988.

Gittleman, Sol. *From Shtetl to Suburbia: The Family in Jewish Literary Imagination.* Boston: Beacon, 1978.

Guttman, Allen. *The Jewish Writer in America: Assimilation and the Crisis of Identity.* New York: Oxford UP, 1971.

Harap, Louis. *Creative Awakening: The Jewish Presence in Twentieth-Century American Literature, 1900-1940s.* Contributions in Ethnic Studies 17. New York: Greenwood, 1987.

Harap, Louis. *The Image of the Jew in American Literature from Early Republic to Mass Immigration*. Philadelphia: Jewish Pub. Soc. of America, 1974.

Harap, Louis. *In the Mainstream: The Jewish Presence in Twentieth-Century American Literature, 1950s-1980s*. Louis Harap. Contributions in Ethnic Studies 19. New York: Greenwood, 1987.

Liptzin, Sol. *The Jew In American Literature*. New York: Bloch, 1966.

Malin, Irving. *Jews and Americans*. Crosscurrents/Modern Critiques. Carbondale: Southern Illinois UP, 1965.

Sanders, Ronald. *The Downtown Jews: Portraits of an Immigrant Generation*. New York: Harper, 1969.

Schulz, Max F. *Radical Sophistication: Studies in Contemporary Jewish-American Novelists*. Athens: Ohio UP, 1969.

Sherman, Bernard. *The Invention of the Jew: Jewish-American Novels (1916-1964)*. New York: Yoseloff, 1969.

Wisse, Ruth R. *The Schlemiel as Modern Hero*. Chicago: U of Chicago P, 1971.

Yudkin, Leon I. *Jewish Writing and Identity in the Twentieth Century*. London: Helm, 1982.

Walter Abish

1931 –

Primary Sources

Novels

Alphabetical Africa. New York: New Directions, 1974.

How German Is It. New York: New Directions, 1980; Manchester: Carcanet, 1982; London: Faber, 1983.

Collected Works

In the Future Perfect. New York: New Directions, 1977; London: Faber, 1984.
Contents: The English Garden, Parting Shot, Ardor / Awe / Atrocity, Read-Only Memory, Access, In So Many Words, Crossing the Great Void.

Minds Meet. New York: New Directions, 1975.
Contents: Minds Meet, Life Uniforms, This Is Not a Film This Is a Precise Act of Disbelief, The Istanbul Papers, Frank's Birthday, With Bill in the Desert, The Second Leg, A Stake in Witches, More by George, How the Comb Gives a Fresh Meaning to the Hair, Crossing Friends, Non-Site.

99, The New Meaning Providence: Burning Deck, 1990.

Contents: What Else; Inside Out; Skin Deep; Reading Kafka in German; 99, The New Meaning.

Short Fiction in Anthologies

"Alphabet of Revelations." *New Directions in Prose and Poetry 41*. Ed. J. Laughlin. New York: New Directions, 1980. 66-78; *Contemporary American Fiction*. Ed. Douglas Messerli. Washington, DC: Sun & Moon, 1983. 145-61.

"Auctioning Australia." *Text-Sound Texts*. Ed. Richard Kostelanetz. New York: Morrow, 1982. 27-30.

"The Idea of Switzerland." *The Best American Short Stories, 1981*. Eds. Hortense Calisher and Shannon Ravenel. Boston: Houghton, 1981. 1-28.

"Life Uniforms: A Study in Ecstasy." *Statements: New Fiction from the Fiction Collective*. Ed. Jonathan Baumbach. New York: Venture-Braziller, 1975. 9-18.

"Parting Shot." *Statements 2: New Fiction*. Eds. Jonathan Baumbach and Peter Spielberg. New York: Fiction Collective, 1977. 11-29.

Short Fiction in Periodicals

"Crossing the Great Void." *Transatlantic Review* 60 (1977): 16-30.

"Happiness." *Parenthese* (1979): 107-12.

"House on Fire." *Antaeus* 64-65 (1990): 146-60.

"The Idea of Switzerland." *Partisan Review* 47.1 (1980): 57-81.

"Inside Out." *Personal Injury* 4 (1978): 57-68.

"99, The New Meaning." *Renegade* 1 (1979): pag. not available.

"Read-Only Memory." *Fiction* 4.3 (1976): 21-22.

"The Second Leg." *Paris Review* 14.55 (1972): 103-25.

"What Else." *Conjunctions* (Wint. 1981-82): 105-19.

Secondary Sources

Articles and Chapters

Abish, Walter. "The Writer-To-Be: An Impression of Living"
Abish discourses to great length about what is implied in wanting to be a writer, exploring from numerous angles the question, "But why write?" Useful for insights into his own motives for trying to become a writer. Implicit throughout is the idea that one never becomes a writer, but is always a writer-to-be.

Arias-Misson, Alain. "The 'New Novel' and TV Culture: Reflections on Walter Abish's *How German Is It.*" *Fiction International* 17.1 (1987): 152-64.
Argues that *How German Is It* will be read for the feverish, brittle life of its characters, and for the faint, radioactive glow of their activities and urbane settings—unsettling and distinctive in the entire panorama of new American fiction. Claims, however, that all is not what it appears to be in this remarkable novel: behind, within its surface scintillae, it betrays and reveals the symptoms which threaten the heart of fiction today; not merely fiction, but language itself. A major article which deals exhaustively with the experimental surfaces of the novel and the vision of modern life it portrays.

Arias-Misson, Alain. "The Puzzle of Walter Abish: *In the Future Perfect.*" *SubStance* 27 (1980): 115-24.
Describes how Walter Abish fabricates puzzles of sex, minds, death, words, images, letters, and numbers. Claims that he displays a virtuoso's command of articulation, phonetics, syntax, semantics, and structuring. *In the Future Perfect* reveals an enrichment of the alphabetical instrumentarium with numbering-cogs and wheels, and a tightening of the humor to a razor cutting edge. Concludes that the puzzle, or peculiar interest of an examination of his work is the ultra-violet light it sheds on contemporary fiction.

Baker, Kenneth. "Restricted Fiction: The Writing of Walter Abish." *New Directions: An International Anthology of Prose and Poetry.* New York: New Directions, 1977. 48-56.

Points out that in the Abish story the construction is the telling narrative substance. Argues that this subversion of realism is only the beginning of his achievement. Claims that Abish's writing demands that we know the meanderings of activity—all of which reflects a view of language with definite ethical implications. Concentrates primarily on *Alphabetical Africa.*

Butler, Christopher. "Skepticism and Experimental Fiction." *Essays in Criticism* 36.1 (1986): 47-67.

Comments that in the context of an essay on the techniques and style of experimental fiction that people like Abish, Faulkner, Barth, Barthleme, Coover, Federman, and Gass centered their work around representational and moral aims to do with a skeptical epistemology.

Butler, Christopher. "Walter Abish and the Questioning of the Reader." *Facing Texts: Encounters Between Contemporary Writers and Critics.* Ed. Heide Ziegler. Durham: Duke UP, 1988. 168-85.

Argues that a book like *How German Is It* can show us how this disruptive relationship of the text to our assumed knowledge of the world can still have a moral effect over which we might be able to agree. Claims that Abish convicts us of harboring prejudices which he seems positively to encourage us to hold—a dangerously Swiftian and experimental game with few parallels. Discusses the work as a metafiction full of metajokes.

Caramello, Charles. "On the Guideless Guidebooks of Postmodernism: Reading *The Volcanoes from Puebla* in Context." *Sun & Moon* 9-10 (1980): 59-99. Rpt. in *The Avant-Garde Tradition in Literature.* Ed. Richard Kostelanetz. Buffalo: Prometheus, 1982. 348-77; as *"The Volcanoes from Puebla* and Other Reflections." *Silverless Mirrors: Book, Self, and Postmodern American Fiction.* Tallahassee: UP of Florida, 1983. 143-73.

Argues that, while Sorrentino and Barthes use the alphabet as a neutral principle for organizing content, the alphabet as an organizing principle both issues from and largely determines the content of Butor's and Abish's books. Claims that the alphabet circumscribes authorial choice and produces highly de-subjectivized guidebooks not only to places, but also to the problematics of constructing discourses about places.

Durand, Regis. "The Disposition of the Familiar (Walter Abish)." *Representation and Performance in Postmodern Fiction.* Ed. Couturier, Maurice. Montpellier: Delta, 1983. 73-83. Rpt. from Proceedings of Nice Conference on Postmodern Fiction, Apr. 1982. Argues that Abish's very fine point lies in the complexity and ambiguities of the relations between the self and the other, the very idea of otherness.

Hornung, Alfred. "Recollection and Imagination in Postmodern Fiction." *Representation and Performance in Postmodern Fiction.* Ed. Maurice Couturier. Montpellier, FR: Delta, 1983., 57-70.

Discusses the treatment of the themes of recollection and imagination and such postmodern fiction as that written by Pynchon, Doctorow, Coover, Barth, Vonnegut, Abish, and Federman. Reviews the significant philosophical and literary instances in the development of these twin themes, and traces the re-emergence of a recollective imagination which affects contemporary narrative practices. Discusses Federman's *The Voice in the Closet,* and Abish's *How German Is It.*

Jardine, Alice A. "Feminist Tracks." *Gynesis: Configurations of Woman and Modernity.* Ed. Alice A. Jardine. Ithaca: Cornell UP, 1985. 50-52.

Discusses "Crossing the Great Void" from a feminist perspective, noting the device of the guilty mother introduced into the narrative only to provide an enigma and a rather obvious case of Oedipal anxiety.

Karl, Frederick R. "Somewhat Experimental: Abish, Sorrentino, Doctorow." *American Fictions 1940-1980: A Comprehensive History and Critical Evaluation.* Frederick R. Karl. New York: Harper, 1983. 551-55.

Describes Abish the man, his cultural and historical place in 1970s American fiction, his major works, and his typical themes and characters. Provides a critical analysis of *How German Is It.*

Klinkowitz, Jerome. "Avant-garde and After." *The Practice of Fiction in America: Writers from Hawthorne to the Present.* Jerome Klinkowitz. Ames: Iowa State UP, 1980. 114-28. Rpt. in *SubStance* 27 (1980): 125-38.

Describes the postmodernist challenge to conventional realism, and the response of a variety of postmodernist writers to the movement. Includes Abish briefly in this general discussion.

Klinkowitz, Jerome. "Experimental Realism in Recent American Painting and Fiction." *Representation and Performance in Postmodern Fiction.* Ed. Maurice Couturier. Montpellier: Delta, 1983. 149-62. Rpt. from Proceedings of Nice Conference on Postmodern Fiction, Apr. 1982.

Traces the evolution of experimental realism out of the visual arts and into writing. Accounts for Abish and others in this paradigm by arguing that it incorporates within its vision both the new technology in our lives and the equally new modes of perception within which we see. Organizes his comments under the headings "All Over," "Anti-Hierarchal," "Materiality: Hard and Flat," "Color Field," and "Surface."

Klinkowitz, Jerome. *The Self-Apparent Word: Form as Language/Language as Form.* Carbondale: Southern Illinois UP, 1984. 81-83, 87-95, 128-31.

Comments that Abish uses the alphabet and other conventions of experimental fiction energetically: his characters, plot, theme, and action wend their way through his alphabetically titled chapters, albeit within the confines of a discipline more rigorous than any of his colleagues. A major chapter discussing each of his works and their particular stylistic experiments.

Klinkowitz, Jerome. "Walter Abish." Jerome Klinkowitz. *The Life of Fiction.* Urbana: U of Illinois P, 1977. 59-71.

An extensive description of Abish, his life and his fiction-making methods, interspersed with samples from his various novels and short fiction. Mostly presented in the first person from interview material.

Klinkowitz, Jerome. "Walter Abish and the Surfaces of Life." *Georgia Review* 35.2 (1981): 416-20.

Describes Abish's method of narration in treating the materials of fiction as objects in themselves—not as familiar cues to the reader (which trigger conventional responses and so set formulaic narrative to action), but rather as semiotic integers within the syntax of human behavior. Traces this method through several of his works.

Kuehl, John. "The Ludic Impulse in Recent American Fiction." *Journal of Narrative Techniques* 16.3 (1986): 167-78.

Discusses the propensity of modern fiction to use games as metaphor, and turns to Abish's *Alphabetical Africa* which uses anagrams, acrostics, and experimentation with letters. Argues that such devices furnish Abish with the most restrictive forms yet practiced by any contemporary, antirealist, American novelist. Provides an extensive treatment of the novel in the context of the larger discussion.

Martin, Richard. "Walter Abish's Fictions: Perfect Unfamiliarity, Familiar Imperfection." *Journal of American Studies* 17.2 (1983): 229-41.

Considers Abish's high-spirited inventiveness as growing out of the self-set limitations of a predetermined system, and in part as a response to the craft of writing. A major article primarily discussing *Alphabetical Africa*.

Messerli, Douglas. "The Role of Voice in Nonmodernist Fiction." *Contemporary Literature* 25.3 (1984): 281-304.

A major article on the emergence of voice in modernist fiction which somewhat incidentally deals with Abish's contribution to the movement.

Pearce, R. A. "Riding the Surf: Raymond Federman, Walter Abish, and Ronald Sukenick." *The Novel in Motion: An Approach to Modern Fiction.* R. A. Pearce. Columbus: Ohio State U P, 1983. 118-30.

A major chapter discussing postmodernist technique in Federman, Abish, and Sukenick. Discusses the influence of Robbe-Grillet and the French literary movements. Deals with Abish in this larger context.

Peterson, James. "The Artful Mathematicians of the Avant-Garde." *Wide Angle* 7.3 (1985): 14-23.

Compares Abish's novel *Alphabetical Africa* to J. J. Murphy's film *Print Generation* in overall structure, theme, and technique and in response from critics. Pays particular reference to the perceptual schemata and the numerical schema.

Saalmann, Dieter. "Walter Abish's *How German Is It*: Language and the Crisis of Human Behavior." *Critique* 26.3 (1985): 105-21.

Argues that in this novel the stylistic asceticism inherent in such an approach represents a conscious desire on the part of the author to avoid the traditional pathetic fallacy of sentimental identification between reader and text. Claims instead that he allows the inner dynamics of the verbal structure full reign, letting the recipient of his fictional realm become a direct participant in the emerging signification of the textual grid.

Siegle, Robert. "On the Subject of Walter Abish and Kathy Acker." *Literature and Psychology* 33.3-4 (1987): 38-58.

Argues that Abish's works carry forward a rethinking of contemporary subjective reality, the illusion of self, behavior as a complex of systems and structures, and the encounter between history, systems, and subjectivity.

Tanner, Tony. "Present Imperfect: A Note on the Work of Walter Abish." *Granta* ns 1 (1980): 65-71.

Primarily an essay on the implications of the Lacanian contention that we are *serfs du language* applied to *In the Future Perfect*.

Varsava, Jerry A. "Walter Abish and the Topographies of Desire." *Thought* 62.246 (1987): 295-310.

Describes *How German Is It* as a novel that does not permit playful distortions of historical fact. Claims that "Abish realizes that life is full of moral quandaries, of inexplicable situations, yet, at the same time he acknowledges that these aporias elicit from us interpretive responses. His fictions are his response to these aporias, and though they refuse to tell us how to live, they certainly tell us how *not* to."

Wotipka, Paul. "Walter Abish's *How German Is It*: Representing the Postmodern." *Contemporary Literature*. 30.4 (1989): 503-17.

Claims that the question implicit in the title of this novel immediately alerts us to problems of history, for any contemporary meditation on Germanness elicits stories of infamy, forcing Germans to simultaneously forget and recollect. Discusses how Abish identifies Nazi stereotypes of Germany which trigger dangerous strings of disturbing associations, reducing history to a fixed and familiar image of a past unmediated by an understanding of the present.

Reviews

Balliett, Whitney. "Yes!" Rev. of *How German Is It. New Yorker* 21 Dec. 1981: 143-44.

Calls this novel a trick book full of pretensions and loaded with two-ton ironies. Finds all kinds of typographical hijinks and very little narrative; instead Abish tells us that Germany today is full of rot, sham, arrogance, and cupidity. Concludes that, while this may be so, the book is so repellent itself it makes us impatient with what he has to say. Ends with the comment that this is the sort of book that wins awards, and it did.

Broyard, Anatole. "Writer's Experiment." Rev. of *In the Future Perfect. New York Times Book Review* 13 Nov. 1977: 14, 75.

Describes in detail the contents of *In the Future Perfect,* and concludes that it is less well-structured than earlier pieces and contains too much aimless posturing. Argues that the dozen or so devices used such as free association, motiveless acts, hackneyed incongruities, predictable discontinuities, sensationalism, coyness, self-consciousness, obscurantism, negativism, and pretension finally become boring.

Clemons, Walter. "What Is Germany?" Rev. of *How German Is It? Newsweek* 4 May 1981: 80, 81A.

Claims that *How German Is It* demands an inquiry into present-day German identity conducted in biting, crystal-clear snapshot pictures. Provides a generous account of the contents of the novel, and concludes that, while this is not exactly an American novel, we are nevertheless stung by it.

Condini, Nereo E. "The Edge of Forgetfulness." Rev. of *How German Is It. National Review* 29 May 1981: 620.

Primarily a plot summary, but calls the novel a peculiar mix of extremely controlled diction and raw objectivity.

Deveson, Richard. "Scrabble." Rev. of *In the Future Perfect. New Statesman* 20 Apr. 1984: 26-27.

Explains that *In the Future Perfect* is experimental in technique with its italics, alphabetized lists, epigraphs, and other signs suggesting literature is primarily created out of language. Nevertheless, claims that despite all this self-reflexivity, the story keeps breaking through.

Falkenberg, Betty. "Literary Games." Rev. of *How German Is It. New York Times Book Review* 4 Jan. 1981: 8-9.

Calls *How German Is It* a rabble-rousing book about Germany that is less convincing than startling. Comments on Abish's delight in human thought and action. Sees the whole book as an assault on the familiarity of everyday things. Digs deeply into unassimilated terrors of the German past, probing the unease and guilt beneath the surface of German prosperity and well-being.

Hayman, Ronald. "How German Is It?" Rev. of *How German Is It. Books and Bookmen* June 1982: 12-13.

Argues that *How German Is It* provides a critical treatment of the Federal Republic of Germany while trying not to provide a "thrillerish" suspense. Considers Abish as showing sufficient technical prowess to shape this rich and difficult material into a story that is eminently worth reading.

Describes his prose as taut, ironical self-parodying, despite his acrobatic swings from particular to general. Concludes that we never stop caring what will happen next to his characters.

Hofmann, Michael. "Letting Down Daddy." Rev. of *How German Is It. Times Literary Supplement* 2 Apr. 1982: 395.

Shows how *How German Is It* reveals traces of a tight mechanical organization that is formal and conceptual rather than sheerly alphabetical. Briefly describes style and contents.

Howard, Richard. "The Dark Continent A to Z." Rev. of *Alphabetical Africa. New York Times Book Review* 29 Dec. 1974: 19.

Describes the novel as a lively piece of legerdemain by a poet influenced by Gallic magicians Robbe-Grillet, Henri Roussel, and Raymond Queneau. Calls the text a kind of breviary of compulsive (masturbatory) gratification.

Josipovici, Gabriel. "Another Old Atrocity." Rev. of *In the Future Perfect. Times Literary Supplement* 25 May 1984: 598.

Sees this book as a collection of stories of uneven and often banal quality. Claims that Abish is never really easy with the given forms of narrative but doesn't know quite what to do about it. Concludes that this is mostly a collection of tedious stories about sex, unpleasant marital behavior, and blowing things up.

Kearns, George. "Fiction Chronicle." Rev. of *How German Is It. Hudson Review* 34.2 (1981): 303-6.

Calls *How German Is It* an ice-cold *tour de force*, in which Abish's vision is of contemporary Germany as the Air-Conditioned Nightmare. Shows how the narrative probes the characters and action with a thousand questions about past and future which are acutely embarrassing to Germans. Details contents and briefly discusses style.

Knowlton, James. "How German Is It?" Rev. of *How German Is It. American Book Review* Mar.-Apr. 1981: 12.

A lengthy review of *How German Is It* that talks of Abish's experimental prose, his unsettling view of modern Germany, the contents of the novel, and its style. Calls the novel a literary *tour de force* combining philosophical perspective with readability. Concludes that his sociology of Germany is haunted with flaws finding their origin in Abish's Austrian-born American prejudices against Germany.

Lemon, Lee T. "Bookmarks." Rev. of *Alphabetical Africa*. *Prairie Schooner* 49.3 (1975): 277-78.

Describes *Alphabetical Africa* structurally, speaks snidely of its language, and criticizes its storytelling potential. Concludes that this book is only for those who admire very simple practical jokes.

Levinson, Daniel. "Books." Rev. of *Minds Meet*. *Aspect* 66 (1976): 43-45.

Describes *Minds Meet* as a book in which Abish uses Africa not as a geographical entity but as a matrix of psychic and linguistic entanglements. Considers the stories deliberately unpredictable and emotionally charged, and the words familiar but unexpected.

Malin, Irving. "In So Many Words." Rev. of *In the Future Perfect*. *Ontario Review* 9 (1978-79): 112-14.

Describes *In the Future Perfect* as a subversive piece of writing in which barely recognizable individuals act in unbelievable ways. Provides a detailed textual explication of this thesis.

Samway, Patrick. "How German Is It: Wie Deutsch Ist Es." Rev. of *How German Is It*. *America* 12 Sept. 1981: 123-24.

Details the plot and then asserts that the style of this book is clinically cold and insistent, while its content raises serious moral questions about modern-day Germany.

Sullivan, Walter. Rev. of *How German Is It*. *Sewanee Review* 90.3 (1982): 486-87.

Describes the plot, mechanics, style, and content of *How German Is It*.

Taubman, Robert. "Submission." Rev. of *How German Is It*. *London Review of Books* 20 May 1982: 18.

Claims that *How German Is It* is about the positive absence of meaning in the disconnected, anonymous features of modern German life—blocks of flats, cafe conversations, the loud noise that may or may not be a terrorist bomb. Provides an elaborate account of the contents.

Updike, John. "Through a Continent, Darkly." Rev. of *Alphabetical Africa*. *New Yorker* 24 Mar. 1975: 109-15. Rpt. in *Picked Up Pieces*. John Updike. New York: Knopf, 1975. 349-51.

Finds *Alphabetical Africa* a remarkable and ludicrously programmatic verbal safari. Mostly details the verbal pyrotechnics in the novel.

Concludes that, in the finish, this is not a novel about Africa but an invitation to the realms of the imagination.

West, Paul. "Germany in the Aftermath of War." Rev. of *How German Is It. Washington Post Book World* 9 Nov. 1980: 4, 9.
Argues that, like snow, *How German Is It* accumulates delicately, lulling the mind with an inaudible dream. Discusses the verbal effects, details the contents, and concludes that Abish writes with meticulous, philatelic obsessiveness.

Interviews

Klinkowitz, Jerome. "Walter Abish: An Interview." *Fiction International* 4-5 (1975): 93-100.
In this interview Abish discusses: his fascination with the idea of fiction exploring itself, *Alphabetical Africa*, his methods of writing, his disbelief in psychologically developed characters, early career activities, childhood spent in China, encounters with American culture, discovering Wittgenstein, the move away from simple humanism, his interest in the way ideas are formed, various of his works, and his future writing projects.

Biographical Sources

Abish, Walter. "The Writer-to-Be: An Impression of Living." *SubStance* 27 (1980): 104-14.
Discusses impressionistically the impulse of the desire to be a writer, answering in various ways the question: Why write? Uses others as well as himself as examples. Useful for the insights it gives into the development and purposes of Abish's own writing career.

Dissertations

Pestino, Joseph Francis. "The Reader/Writer Affair: Instigating Repertoire in the Experimental Fiction of Susan Sontag, Walter Abish, Rejean Ducharme, Paul West and Christine Brooke-Rose." Diss. Pennsylvania State U, 1986.

Robertson, Mary Frances. "Language as Hero in Post-Modern Formalist Fiction." Diss. U of Wisconsin - Madison, 1979.

Charles Angoff
1902 – 1979

Primary Sources

Novels

Between Day and Dark. New York: Yoseloff, 1959.

The Bitter Spring. New York: Yoseloff, 1961.

In the Morning Light. New York: Beechhurst, 1953.

Journey to the Dawn. New York: Yoseloff, 1951, 1962; New York: Beechhurst, 1951.

Memory of Autumn. South Brunswick: Yoseloff, 1968.

Mid-Century. South Brunswick: Barnes, 1974.

Season of Mists. New York: Yoseloff, 1971.

Summer Storm. New York: Yoseloff, 1963.

The Sun at Noon. New York: Beechhurst, 1955.

Toward the Horizon. South Brunswick: Barnes, 1980.

Winter Twilight. Cranbury: Yoseloff, 1970.

Collected Works

Adventures in Heaven. New York: Akerman, 1945; Short Story Index
   Reprint Series. Freeport: Books for Libraries, 1970.

Contents: God Repents, God is Encouraged, One Woman to Another,
Three Dolls and a Woman, Two Women, The Wisdom of Woman, The
Doctors in Heaven, The Road to Heaven, Jesus and the Little Girl, God's
Felicity, The Substance of Things Hoped For, Love's Greatest Reward,
Sacred and Profane Love, The Painter and the Little Boy, Man's Work,
Where Heaven Is.

The Man from the Mercury: A Charles Angoff Memorial Reader.
   Rutherford: Fairleigh Dickinson UP, 1986; London: Associated
   University Presses, 1986.

Contents: Laura, Henry, Yetta, Sidney, Willie, Jerry, Harrele-mit-the-Pants.

Something about My Father, and Other People. New York: Yoseloff, 1956.

Contents: Something about My Father, Goldie Tabak, Mother and I See
Anna Pavlova, Curly, Simche der Chochem, Beryl der Croomer, The
Ostrovskys, The Original Sam, Natalie and John, Phyllis, Chatzkel,
Barnet Rosenberg, Thelma, S.A., Lapidus, Louis, Benny, Minuet in G,
Rabbi Sharfman.

When I Was a Boy in Boston. New York: Beechhurst, 1947; N.p.: Jewish
   Book Guild, 1947; Short Story Index Reprint Series. Freeport: Books
   for Libraries, 1970.

Contents: Zayde Tzalel, Laura, Henry, Yetta, Sidney, Willie, Jerry,
Disillusionment, Bertha, Mr. Harmon, Zalmon the Wise, Tante Bessie,
Harrele-mit-the-Pants, Lodge Doctor, Alte Bobbe.

Short Fiction in Anthologies

"Alte Bobbe." *This Land, These People.* Ed. Harold U. Ribalow.
   Beechhurst, 1950. 32-39. *"The Safe Deposit" and Other Stories about
   Grandparents, Old Lovers, and Crazy Old Men.* Ed. Kerry M.
   Olitzky. New York: Wiener, 1989. 283-91.

"Azriel and Yolanda." *My Name Aloud: Jewish Stories by Jewish Writers.*
   Ed. Harold U. Ribalow. South Brunswick: Yoseloff, 1969. 19-26.

"Chatzkel." *Yisroel: The First Jewish Omnibus*. Ed. Joseph Leftwich. New York: Yoseloff, 1963. 188-95.

"Grandfather Tzalel." *Feast of Leviathan*. Ed. Leo W. Schwarz. New York: Rinehart, 1956. 70-75.

"Jerry." *The Best American Short Stories, 1946*. Ed. Martha Foley. Boston: Houghton, 1946. 1-12.

"The Steamer." *Modern Stories from Many Lands*. Ed. Clarence Raymond Decker. 2nd ed. New York: Manyland Books, 1972. 402-09.

Short Fiction in Periodicals

"Azriel and Yolanda." *Literary Review* 4.1 (1960): 16-23.

"Big Jim Gordon." *University of Kansas City Review* June 1955: 275-80.

"Cop on the Beat." *Prairie Schooner* 15.1 (1941): 124-29.

"The Cultured One." *Literary Review* 4.1 (1960): 24-31.

"Femme Fatale." *University of Kansas City Review* Mar. 1957: 173-80.

"The Future Faces Us." *Literary Review* 14.2 (1970-71): 211-17.

"Goldie Tabak." *Prairie Schooner* 26.4 (1952): 392-99.

"Helen." *Literary Review* 18.3 (1975): 366-75.

"It Don't Add Up." *North American Review* 247.2 (1939): 312-17.

"Jerry." *Prairie Schooner* 19.1 (1945): 15-21.

"Liberalism in the Upper Brackets." *University Review* Dec. 1964: 143-46.

"Life of Letters." *Literary Review* 14.4 (1971): 420-34.

"Lost Eden." *Literary Review* 12.1 (1968): 5-16.

"Lost Opportunity." *Prairie Schooner* 15.2 (1941): 277-79.

"Reuben." *Antioch Review* 13.1 (1953): 371-78.

"Sidney." *Prairie Schooner* 20.4 (1946): 271-76.

"The Steamer." *Literary Review* 12.4 (1969): 505-11.

Secondary Sources

Articles and Chapters

Angoff, Charles. "The Origins and Aims of the Polonsky Saga." *Chicago Jewish Forum* 25 (1966): 32-41.

A lengthy article outlining his own autobiographical background and its relation to the genesis of the Polonsky Family chronicles in his ten novels focusing on them. Suggests origins of actual families, individuals, and events.

Angoff, Charles. "Why I Wrote a Jewish Novel." *Congress Weekly* 26 Nov. 1951: 21-22. Rpt. in *Mid-Century: An Anthology of Jewish Life and Culture in Our Times*. Ed. Harold U. Ribalow. New York: Beechhurst, 1955. 323-26.

Discusses how he came to write *Journey to the Dawn*, pointing out that the theme selected him more than he selected it. Argues that the characters are only the "remotest cousins" of the real people in his life. Also discusses the critical reception of his book, and concludes that this is just the first of a trilogy or tetralogy about Jewish people and situations.

Farber, Frances. "Yiddish Voices in American Jewish Fiction." *Yiddish* 5.4 (1984): 22-41.

A major article which discusses how Roth, Angoff, Gold, and Bellow reconstruct the experiences of Yiddish-speaking Jews in America and evoke the tensions and conflicts brought from the *shtetl* in the lives of these immigrants and their children. Describes each author's highly individualized style, employing specific techniques in representing the language of the Jew and in creating what Alfred Kazin has called "the classic bitterness of Jewish dialogue."

Greenfield, Louis. "Charles Angoff." *University of Kansas City Review* 17.3 (1951): 205-12.

Calls Angoff an individual of puzzling and astonishing character because of his versatility, vast production, and social criticism. Details his life and career. A major biographical essay that discusses many of his works, his publishing history, and his personal life.

Ribalow, Harold U. "Charles Angoff: A Literary Profile." *Chicago Jewish Forum* 20.1 (1961): 21-23.

Commends Angoff for maturity, optimism, compassion, ease with his own Jewish identity, unaffected style, graceful dealing with Jewish issues, and chronicling of the assimilation of the Jewish-American family. Regrets that his reputation for being an old-fashioned writer has kept him from the pages of the current and fashionable literary journals.

Ribalow, Harold U. "Charles Angoff and Jewish-American Fiction." *The Old Century and the New: Essays in Honor of Charles Angoff.* Ed. Alfred Rosa. Rutherford: Fairleigh Dickinson UP, 1978. 94-110.

A literary appreciation of Angoff's career and works. Considers his primary place in Jewish-American fiction of the early modern period, and provides an account of his force as a chronicler of the assimilation of the Jewish family and the cost to the Jewish community and its individual members. Discourses generally on a number of topics common to the field of Jewish studies, and then spends the rest of the article discussing individual works in terms of theme, character, and setting. Contains some biographical material.

Sherman, Bernard. "The David Polonsky Series." Bernard Sherman. *The Invention of the Jew: Jewish-American Education Novels (1916-1964).* New York: Yoseloff, 1969. 206-11.

Calls this series the greatest venture into nostalgia in the Jewish novel of this type. Characterizes it as an old-fashioned, Victorian narrative with solid characterization, leisurely pace, and the realistic recreation of immigrant life with all its social currents and recurring themes. Describes religion and immigrant life in the novels.

Yoseloff, Thomas, and Harold U. Ribalow. "The Importance of Charles Angoff." *Literary Review* 4.1 (1960): 37-48.

In part 1, Yoseloff, Angoff's publisher, appraises his writing, provides biographical details about their relationship through the years, and then gives an almost novel-by-novel synopsis of content and characters. Sees him as a Proustian writer, introspective, mannered, and poetic. Defends Angoff against the accusation that he only produces "good" people. Discusses his modesty and quiet nature as the chief contributing factor to the quiet tone of the novels. Sees him as a writer of considerable stature. In part 2, Ribalow reviews the recent flood of Jewish novels, and discusses Angoff's gargantuan effort to capture the essence of Jewish living in the United States. Concludes that he tells a great story and is producing a brilliant group of books.

Reviews

Barach, Gloria. "An Honest Novel About Immigrants." Rev. of *In the Morning Light. New Leader* 9 Mar. 1953: 20.

Describes *In the Morning Light* as being about what America means to its Jewish characters. Calls it a powerful and robust story told with compassion and admirable attention to the truth. Concludes that Angoff's characterization is his strong suit, along with his superb knowledge of the social milieu.

Bell, Lisle. "Family Album." Rev. of *When I Was a Boy in Boston. New York Times Book Review* 7 Dec. 1947: 56.

Describes *When I Was a Boy in Boston* as a collection of warmly recollected and vividly told anecdotes—charming memories—which add up to an altogether charming album.

Greenberg, Eliezer. "The New World." Rev. of *Journey to the Dawn. Nation* 10 Mar. 1951: 236-37.

Details the contents of the novel and argues that the book suffers from occasional overwriting, while some of its characters seem unsubstantial.

Grusd, Edward E. "The Saga Goes On." Rev. of *Memory of Autumn. National Jewish Monthly* Oct. 1969: 43.

Finds the novel refreshing—low-keyed, slow in pace, thoughtful, and full of substance, unlike most recent novels filled with violence, sex, sadism, and assorted mayhem. Complains that sometimes he slows the narrative by overdoing the social and economic background. Concludes that the book is about real Jews, not the unbelievable saints or sinners presented in so many other so-called 'Jewish' novels.

Kreiter, Samuel. Rev. of *Season of Mists. Jewish Frontier* June 1972: 29-30.

Describes *Season of Mists* as a monumental saga of a Jewish immigrant family through which the author intersperses religious, ideological, political, philosophical, and social concerns of the community. Calls Angoff an incontestably eloquent and incisive chronicler of the Jewish-American scene, and praises the book for its Proustian scope. Concludes that the stories and the characters are completely engrossing if occasionally overextended.

Levin, Meyer. "David Polansky [sic] Marches On." Rev. of *Summer Storm. New York Times Book Review* 15 Dec. 1963: 23.

Describes *Summer Storm* as a tender story of the decline of the American world and *The American Mercury* during the depression, and with it the decline of H. L. Mencken.

Levin, Meyer. "Life of David Polansky [sic]." Rev. of *Memory of Autumn. Hadassah Magazine* Mar. 1968: 21.

Describes this as the seventh work in a series of autobiographical novels that violate every fashion in today's writing, but argues that Angoff is closer than Saul Bellow, and truer than Philip Roth, to the core of American Jewish thought and experience.

Levin, Meyer. "Polonsky Saga Continued." Rev. of *Winter Twilight. Hadassah Magazine* Sept. 1970: 23.

An intelligent review of *Winter Twilight* commending the novel for its warmth, emergence out of bitterness, and subtle characterization of protagonist, David Polonsky. Laments that, for all his skill, Angoff is not among the stylish writers of the moment.

McGrory, Mary. "Quiet Glance Backward." Rev. of *When I Was a Boy in Boston. New York Times Book Review* 3 Aug. 1947: 5.

Describes *When I Was a Boy in Boston* as an album of family portraits perfectly in focus. Calls it a restrained approach, somber at times, and even elegiac or Saroyanesque. The stories all convey family loyalty, pride in racial heritage, and consistency of point of view.

"Other New Novels." Rev. of *Winter Twilight. Times Literary Supplement* 21 Aug. 1970: 919.

Describes *Winter Twilight* as Angoff's eighth novel about the Polonsky family, and as a choked, sentimental, periphrastic, self-indulgent work with appallingly sticky dialogue and endless monologues. Concludes that besides all this, the characters systematically diminish until they become little more than an audience themselves.

Ribalow, Harold U. "Art and Real Life." Rev. of *Summer Storm. Congress Bi-Weekly* 13 Jan. 1964: 17.

Describes *Summer Storm* as a book written in the leisurely style of the Russian masters. Comments that far from being contemporary in style, the novel is warm and sentimental, but unfortunately likely to lapse into superfluous detail which makes it seem more sociological and historical than literary.

Ribalow, Harold U. "Books." Rev. of *Memory of Autumn. Chicago Jewish Forum* 27.2 (1968-69): 132-33.

Asserts that in *Memory of Autumn* Angoff has produced a work literally drenched in Judaism. Details the contents of the book and concludes that perhaps the intense Jewishness of the novel accounts for the fact that he has not yet broken through to a mass audience.

Ribalow, Harold U. "Broad Canvas of Jewish Life." Rev. of *Between Day and Dark. Congress Bi-Weekly* 13 Apr. 1959: 19.

Describes *Between Day and Dark* as the fourth novel in a series describing Jewish life in America. Concedes, despite the fact that the book is crowded with characters, that they are generally treated in depth. Details the contents as having to do with the frequent disintegration of marriages of many who succumb to the tempo of American life, its cruel pressures, its depressions, its business ethics, and communal problems.

Ribalow, Harold U. "An Enduring Jewish Chronicle." Rev. of *The Sun at Noon. Congress Weekly* 24 Jan. 1955: 13.

Describes *The Sun at Noon* mainly in terms of its successful characterization and depiction of the American Jewish milieu. Calls the characters rich and varied, the situations rich and true, and the documentation of minority integration unusually lucid.

Ribalow, Harold U. Rev. of *Memory of Autumn. Jewish Frontier* Jan. 1969: 27.

Finds little plot in this novel or in any of Angoff's fiction. Feels his strength is in creating character and in showing the problems Jews face.

Ribalow, Harold U. "Jews in Short Stories." Rev. of *When I Was a Boy in Boston. Congress Weekly* 10 Jan. 1949: 16.

Characterizes *When I Was a Boy in Boston* as a collection of nostalgic stories told by a sensitive writer through the eyes of a young boy. Calls them timeless, beautiful, humorous stories, some of them full-fledged sketches of friends, aunts, maïden aunts, grandparents, and others. Concludes that though they have little narrative interest and seem like extended essays, they are readable and penetrating.

Ribalow, Harold U. "Jews in America." Rev. of *Something About My Father and Other People. Saturday Review of Literature* 12 May 1956: 40-41.

Calls *Something About My Father and Other People* a collection of stories introducing dozens of characters who do not appear in the novels. Claims that the focus here is on undramatic, lonely, forever seeking men and women who find that life casually and cruelly passes them by. Details this as the place to see the undramatic American Jew.

Ribalow, Harold U. "Life's Stuff." Rev. of *The Sun at Noon. Saturday Review of Literature* 15 Jan. 1955: 34.

Describes *The Sun at Noon* as an extremely readable narrative and a remarkable fictional world which delves more deeply than the previous books into the lives of the men and women Angoff has so clearly brought into being. Details plot and characters and concludes with a high commendation.

Ribalow, Harold U. "A Memorable Jewish Novel." Rev. of *Journey to the Dawn. Congress Weekly* 5 Feb. 1951: 13-14.

Finds this novel convincing evidence that those critics who insist that no "real" Jewish fiction can be written in any language but Yiddish and Hebrew are wrong. Finds this novel warm, alive, smoothly flowing, informed, and written with sympathy and compassion. Asserts that Angoff has thrown off the non-Jewish intellectual influences and written out of the Jewish source of being and traditions. Describes the hero and other characters and some memorable scenes showing the blend of dream and reality that characterize this novel.

Ribalow, Harold U. "The Saga of Jewish Life in America." Rev. of *The Bitter Spring*. *Congress Bi-Weekly* 29 May 1961: 18, 20.

Describes *The Bitter Spring* as the work of a potentially major writer, and the series of which this is the fifth novel as a prodigious achievement. Claims that though this novel does not stand on its own as strongly as did its predecessors, it is still a fine portrait of Jews in this century. Provides a detailed formalistic account of the novel.

Ribalow, Harold U. "Search for Identity." Rev. of *Mid-Century*. *Congress Bi-Weekly* 21 June 1974: 20.

Describes this as the tenth novel about the Polonsky clan by Angoff, in which he is concerned with character and religious commitment, or indifference to faith. Calls it 'old-fashioned' writing, dense and detailed, with observation piled upon observation.

Ribalow, Harold U. "Tales of Many Jews." Rev. of *Something About My Father and Other People*. *Congress Weekly* 23 July 1956: 18.

Notes that *Something About My Father and Other People* contains thirty-five stories about Jews who are "innocent, lovely, nice folks" depicted in a friendly, shrewd, lyric manner. Comments that the stories are laden with conflict on the small neighborhood scale, and that the entire book affirms Angoff's love of Judaism and Jewish people.

Roskolenko, Harry. "Zionism as a Moral and Religious Movement." Rev. of *Winter Twilight*. *New York Times Book Review* 8 Feb. 1970: 33.

Calls this a naturalistic, continuous chronicle inclusive in its history of Zionism. Notes that it misses the depths of a Farrell novel, but that Angoff is a thorough scholar and fictioneer. Claims that this novel will infuriate hippies and lefties—and critics—for different reasons. Concludes that the pace is staggering and the book loaded with zany characters.

Rothchild, Sylvia. "Freedom's Deadly Fruit." Rev. of *In the Morning Light*. *Commentary* June 1953: 632-34.

Describes *In the Morning Light* as sentimental, awkwardly written, and not entirely honest. Asserts that older women get the most sensitive treatment, the men are more real when angry, and the children are flat. Finds there are foolish people, but no wicked ones; the gentiles are never anti-Semitic and the Jewish types, only types. Calls the use of Yiddish in the book unfortunate. Concludes that this book has the value of a family photograph album.

Rubin, Philip. "Angoff's Jewish Boston." Rev. of *In the Morning Light*. *Congress Weekly* 23 Feb. 1953: 14-15.

Discusses *In the Morning Light* in terms of the history of Boston Jewry and its immigration patterns. Claims that *Morning Light* teems with episodes from the lives of the Polonskys, all written in Angoff's unmistakable vigor and style. Concludes that, though it could be shorter and is generally lacking in humor and overloaded with sentiment, the book is a work of solid merit which the Jews of Boston should long remember and cherish.

Sackler, Howard O. "Nostalgia Is Not Enough." Rev. of *Journey to the Dawn*. *Commentary* Apr. 1951: 402-04.

Describes *Journey to the Dawn* as a painful case of a memory sent forth to wander through a novel with only warmth, sympathy, and nostalgic prejudice to direct it. Comments that the writing is awkward, and Angoff's good-natured attitude extended so uncritically that the reader must either extend a reciprocal amount of goodwill or submit to his own impatience. Adds that the characters are childlike, and that the whole book has an aura of unreality. Details the contents.

Spiegel, Moshe. Rev. of *Summer Storm*. *Chicago Jewish Forum* Fall (1965): 54-55.

Describes *Summer Storm* as Angoff's sixth chronicle of the Polonsky family, a book which covers the transition from the bogus prosperity of the Twenties into the bleakness of the early Depression years and the limping revival of the early New Deal period. Commends Angoff for what his lifelike and realistic characters have to teach us about our history.

Stern, Daniel. "Editor's Last Stand." Rev. of *Summer Storm*. *Saturday Review* 4 Jan. 1964: 82.

Argues that *Summer Storm* provides the atmosphere and occurrences of the 1930s featuring the demise of a vital magazine. Calls this an enormous and valuable task of interpreting American life from a Jewish angle of refraction. Concludes, however, that compassion alone is not enough.

Weiss, Carol. "Old and New." Rev. of *In the Morning Light*. *Commonweal* 27 Mar. 1953: 632-33.

Describes the stories, themes, and characters of this "warm-hearted interpretation of the Jewish immigrant." Notes that unfortunately the book is built around David, the son, but the story is his parents'.

Yezierska, Anzia. "Outside the Algonquin Looking In." Rev. of *The Bitter Spring. New York Times Book Review* 18 June 1961: 26.

Calls *The Bitter Spring* an evocation of the literary life of New York in the Twenties. After describing its contents and relation to previous Polonsky family chronicles, Yezierska comments that it would have been better if it had been condensed to half its length, despite the fact that it is a memorable portrait of a memorable era.

Yezierska, Anzia. "The Polanskys [sic] of Boston." Rev. of *In the Morning Light. New York Times Book Review* 1 Feb. 1953: 22.

Calls *In the Morning Light* a book which would have been more integrated if it had been cut in half, but which nevertheless, brings to fulfillment much of the promise of Angoff's early work, and clearly demonstrates the author's power to make the reader participate in his own discovery: that love in extended personal relationships gives life dignity.

Yezierska, Anzia. "A Search for Solace." Rev. of *The Sun at Noon. New York Times Book Review* 16 Jan. 1955: 4.

Considers *The Sun at Noon* as memorable in places, lit with flashes of quiet humor, redolent with folklore, and full of lyrical sweep and power.

Interviews

Ribalow, Harold U. "A Conversation with Charles Angoff." *Congress Bi-Weekly* 8 Nov. 1974: 15-18. Rpt. in an expanded version in *The Old Century and the New: Essays in Honor of Charles Angoff.* Ed. Alfred Rosa. Rutherford: Fairleigh Dickinson UP, 1978. 35-68; *The Tie That Binds: Conversations with Jewish Authors.* Harold U. Ribalow. San Diego: Barnes; London: Tantivy, 1980. 25-45.

The interview gives a vivid portrait of Angoff and discusses his reasons for writing fiction, his handling of Jewish issues, his readership, the future of the Jewish novel, his writing habits, and his relationships with other writers such as H. L. Mencken.

Biographical Sources

Benton, Juliette T. "The World of Charles Angoff on the Occasion of His 75th Birthday." *Jewish Book Annual* 35 (1977-78): 128-35.

A review of Angoff's immigrant history, childhood, youthful experiences, attachment to his great grandmother, Americanization, the

Polonsky saga, his association with Mencken and the Algonquin group, his positive Jewishness, and his views on the rapidly changing contemporary American scene. Contains useful biographical information.

Fuller, Muriel. "Charles Angoff." *Wilson Library Bulletin* June 1955: 746.
A two column biographical sketch of Angoff's education at Harvard, his editing career, and his literary works.

Green, Martin. "Charles Angoff, 1902-1979." *Literary Review* 22 (1979): 380, 492.
A brief biographical sketch written at the time of his death.

Wagniere, Harriet Helms. "Behind the scenes: Charles Angoff and *The American Mercury.*" *The Old Century and the New: Essays in Honor of Charles Angoff.* Ed. Alfred Rosa. Rutherford: Fairleigh Dickinson UP, 1978. 79-93.
A detailed biographical account of Angoff's rise to stature on the staff of *The American Mercury*, his manifold duties as outlined by Mencken, and the course of his career there until 1933.

Mary Antin
1881 – 1949

Primary Sources

Short Fiction in Anthologies

"The American Miracle." *Jubilee: One Hundred Years of the Atlantic.*
Eds. Edward Weeks and Emily Flint. Boston: Little, 1957. 247-53.

"The Life." *Atlantic Narratives: Modern Short Stories.* Ed. Charles
Swain Thomas. 2nd Series. Boston: Atlantic, 1918. 1-28; *The Jewish
Caravan: Great Stories of Twenty-Five Centuries.* Ed. Leo W.
Schwarz. New York: Farrar, 1935; Philadelphia: Jewish Pub. Soc. of
America, 1935; Rev. ed. New York: Holt, 1965; Rev. ed. New York:
Schocken, 1976.

Short Fiction in Periodicals

"The American Miracle." *Atlantic* Jan. 1912: 52-67.

"Amulet." *Atlantic* Jan. 1913: 31-34.

"First Aid to the Alien." *Outlook* 29 June 1912: 481-85.

"The House of Bondage." *Atlantic* Nov. 1911: 593-613.

"The Immigrant's Portion." *Atlantic* Apr. 1912: 518-25.

"A Kingdom in the Slums." *Atlantic* Mar. 1912: 368-79.

"The Lie." *Atlantic* Aug. 1913: 177-90.

"The Making of a Citizen." *Atlantic* Feb. 1912: 211-26.

"Malinke's Atonement." *Atlantic* Sept. 1911: 300-19.

"The Promised Land." *Atlantic* Dec. 1911: 785-97.

"The Soundless Trumpet." *Atlantic* May 1937: 560-69.

"Within the Pale." *Atlantic* Oct. 1911: 433-53.

Secondary Sources

Articles and Chapters

Antin, Mary. "How I Wrote *The Promised Land.*" *New York Times Book Review* 30 June 1912: 392.

Says that the story of her life wrote itself with the chapters naming themselves. Also notes that living one's life over again through writing it is the real thing, not a metaphor, but she warns that once a life is put on paper, it is like a mounted butterfly, a dead carcass.

Avery, Evelyn. "Oh My 'Mishpocka'! Some Jewish Women Writers from Antin to Kaplan View the Family." *Studies in American Jewish Literature* 5 (1986): 44-53.

Discusses the effects of Americanization on the structure of the family as reflected in the works of a number of Jewish-American writers. Of Antin and Yezierska she notes that their depiction of *shtetl* women as chained to housework, obligated to fathers and brothers, subjugated, and deprived of an education. Details the contents of *The Promised Land* and *Bread Givers* as well as describing their respective heroines.

Cohen, Sarah Blacher. "Mary Antin's *The Promised Land*: a Breach of Promise." *Studies in American Jewish Literature* [University Park, PA] 3.2 (1977-78): 28-35. Joint issue with *Yiddish* 3.1 (1977).

Begins with an account of the privations of Antin's experience growing up in the Pale of Settlement, isolated from the rest of Russia. Also details her immigration to America at age 13 and subsequent experience of upward mobility in the ghetto. Cohen attributes Antin's nervous breakdown to her abandonment of her Judaism and her eager assimilation of American patriotism. Concludes: "As a model of Jewish-American literature by a Jewish-American woman, Mary Antin's *The Promised Land* is a breach of promise. The task still remains for a Jewish-American woman to write her *Memories of a Jewish Girlhood*, or, if you will, her *Portrait of a Meydl*, and out of this exploration her novel of the grown-up Jewish woman."

Handlin, Oscar. Foreword. *The Promised Land*. 2nd ed. Boston: Houghton, 1969. x-xv.

Outlines the social attitudes to the American experiment prevailing at the time *The Promised Land* was published. Discusses the national doubts over the policies of unlimited immigration and the fears that the nation could not assimilate more European immigrants as an historical backdrop to the appearance of the book. Moves then to a discussion of Antin's life and marriage to Grabau, a cosmologist. Also discusses the influence of Emma Lazarus' denial of traditional Judaism upon Antin and Antin's emotional decline toward the end of her life.

Homberger, Eric. "Charles Reznikoff's Family Chronicle: Saying Thank You and I'm Sorry." *Charles Reznikoff: Man and Poet*. Ed. Milton Hindus. Orono: National Poetry Foundation, U of Maine at Orono, 1984. 327-42.

Contains a brief account of Antin's family life and her subsequent chronicling of it in *Promised Land*. Classes the work as a classic "liberation-from-slavery memoir" favored by Jewish women writers of the era.

Lewisohn, Ludwig. "A Panorama of a Half-Century of American Jewish Literature." *Jewish Book Annual* 9 (1950-51): 3-10.

Discusses *The Promised Land* as a facile and superficial book when viewed alongside *The Rise of David Levinsky*. Sees Antin degrading herself and raging against her residual Judaism. A very brief reference in the context of a general discussion of other second generation Jewish-American writers.

McKee, Rose L. *"Brother Will" and the Founding of Gould Farm.* Great
Barrington: William Gould Corp., 1963. 51, 67-68, 73-76.

Details the attachment Antin had to her spiritual mentor, Brother William
Gould, and her commitment to the Gould Farm as a source of spiritual
inspiration and healing.

Neidle, Cecyle S. "Real Truth versus Artistic Truth." *America's
Immigrant Women.* The Immigrant Heritage of America Series.
Boston: Twayne, 1975. 256-59.

Calls *The Promised Land* a classic biography which details the spiritual
meaning of America from the point of view of the immigrants.

Parkman, Mary R. "The Making of a Patriot: Mary Antin." *Heroines of
Service.* Mary R. Parkman. New York: Century, 1917. 185-208.

A tribute from one patriot to another extolling Antin's wholehearted
assimilation into the American experience. Several brief and superficial
references to *The Promised Land* reveal how non-Jewish readers reacted
to her story.

Rosenfeld, Alvin H. "Inventing the Jew: Notes on Jewish
Autobiography." *Midstream* Apr. 1975: 54-67.

Begins with some theoretical observations that Jews do not invent themselves, history does; however, perhaps Jews invent history to some
extent. Then proceeds to discuss Antin's autobiography showing the process by which she divested herself of her Jewish identity and cancelled
all claims to the past.

Zangwill, Israel. Foreword. *From Plotzk to Boston.* Boston: Clark, 1899.
7-9.

Descibes Antin's remarkable sensitivity and perceptiveness as an observer, the vivid descriptiveness of her writing, and her ability to handle
English after only a short time in America.

Reviews.

Bicknell, Percy F. "How One Immigrant Girl Discovered America." Rev.
of *The Promised Land. Dial* 1 May 1912: 348-50.

Reviews *The Promised Land* by discussing Antin's early life, general
biography, the style of the book, its contents, and its background.

"From Russia to America." Rev. of *From Plotzk to Boston*. *New York Times Saturday Review of Books and Art* 27 May 1899: 341.

Describes the contents of *From Plotzk to Boston*, and comments that it is guileless, appealing, warm, human and will doubtless appeal to readers Jewish and non-Jewish. Contains a note on the title change (due to printing error) from first to second printing.

"The Immigrant." Rev. of *The Promised Land*. *New York Times Book Review* 14 Apr. 1912: 228.

Calls *The Promised Land* a simple narrative of a woman's life which is both moving and vividly interesting. Provides a detailed account of the contents.

Maxwell, William H. "Reviews of New Books." Rev. of *The Promised Land*. *Literary Digest* 15 June 1912: 1261-62.

Provides mostly a biography of Antin and a plot summary of *The Promised Land*. Commends the book to a historian as containing both accurate and valuable information. Concludes that, while the book is an autobiography of surpassing interest, it is a treatise on sociology of which education is the dominant feature.

Middleton, George. "Ten Books of the Month." Rev. of *The Promised Land*. *Bookman* June 1912: 419-21.

A brief commendation of the patriotic and human value of *The Promised Land* which designates it as a sociological novel. Contains excerpts from the novel, and comments on content only.

Monmouth, Geoffry. "Twelve Books of the Month." Rev. of *They Who Knock at Our Gates*. *Bookman* June 1914: 458-59.

Says of *They Who Knock at Our Gates* that it possesses depth, lyricism, faulty structure, high compression of feeling, strong political views, and passion.

"The New Books." Rev. of *The Promised Land*. *Outlook* 29 June 1912: 501-02.

Claims that this work is deeply moving in the rapid utterance and intense purpose that informs its self-revelation. Comments on the social implications of the book and its effect on the Gentile reader. Concludes that readers should look forward to future books from a writer of such eloquence.

"New Books Reviewed." Rev. of *They Who Knock at Our Gates. North American Review* July 1914: 159-60.

Calls this work a charmingly written, earnest plea for altruism in the formation of national immigration policy. Provides a detailed analysis of Antin's position in the social theory debate on immigration. Asserts that in this book we are only listening to one side of the debate, but that Antin stirs our interest because of her authority on the immigrant's perspective.

Parkhurst, Charles H. "The Book of the Month." Rev. of *The Promised Land. Hearst's Magazine* Sept. 1912: 107-12.

An admiring summary of the contents of the novel laced with large excerpts from the novel itself.

"A Plea for the Poor Immigrant." Rev. of *They Who Knock at Our Gates. Dial* 1 June 114: 470-71.

Provides a social commentary on the issue of Jewish immigration and Antin's critique of it in *They Who Knock at Our Gates.*

Rev. of *The Promised Land. Nation* 23 May 1912: 517.

Considers the style of *The Promised Land* direct, vivid, a little embarrassing, and rather over-enthusiastic. Details the contents and commends the book to sociologists and patriots.

"Sensibility in Economics." Rev. of *They Who Knock at Our Gates. New York Times Book Review* 12 July 1914: 305.

Calls *They Who Knock at Our Gates* a book which fails to discuss the economic problems from a background in economic studies, and fails to make a serious historical study of immigration. Argues that what she has written is a popular gospel on the theme for those who are already convinced.

Woodbridge, Elizabeth. "Book Reviews." Rev. of *The Promised Land. Yale Review* 2.1 (1912): 175-76.

Describes *The Promised Land* along with the society it portrays. Applauds the politics of the volume, and excuses many of its literary shortcomings in light of its honesty and pain.

Biographical Sources

Bates, E. Stuart. *Inside Out: An Introduction to Autobiography*. New York: Sheridan House, 1937. 30-33, 78-80, 109, 251-53.

Contains much autobiographical commentary about Antin's first seven years from her autobiography, *The Promised Land*, interspersed with biographical commentary.

Beard, Annie E. S. *Our Foreign Born Citizens: What They Have Done for America*. Rev. and enl. ed. New York: Crowell, 1932. 30-38.

A brief tribute and autobiographical account of the life and contribution of Mary Antin.

Cronbach, Abraham. "Autobiography." *American Jewish Archives* Apr. 1959: 3-4, 40-43.

Contains a brief account of Cronbach's memories of Mary Antin in which he tells of the effect *The Promised Land* had on him and of his first meeting with her on a train bound for Scarsdale. Also mentions an evening in the home of Antin and Grabau, her husband. Discusses at length the illness and end of Antin's life as a far cry from the ringing optimism of the last passage of her autobiography.

Guttmann, Allen. "The Rise of a Lucky Few: Mary Antin and Abraham Cahan." *The Jewish Writer in America: Assimilation and the Crisis of Identity*. Ed. Allen Guttmann. New York: Oxford UP, 1971. 25-28.

Biographical commentary on autobiographical passages from Antin's writings. Discusses whether or not she might have regretted what she gave up at Ellis Island for what she purchased in Brooklyn and Brownsville because of her lapse from traditional Judaism.

Koppelman, Susan. "Mary Antin." *Dictionary of Literary Biography Yearbook: 1984*. Ed. Jean W. Ross. Detroit: Gale, 1984. 225-32.

More than mere details of her life, this is a career biography tracing the development of her works, describing their contents and themes, evaluating her reputation, and placing her in the larger context of American literary history. Includes lists of primary and secondary sources as well as illustrations.

Liptzin, Solomon. *"The Promised Land." The Jew in American Literature*. Solomon Liptzin. New Jersey: Bloch, 1966. 123-33.

Contains a general account of her early life in Russia, her immigration to America, her apostasy from traditional Judaism, her marriage, career as a writer, and final lapse into ill health when her spiritual idealism about the American promise failed to materialize for her generation.

Proefriedt, William A. "The Education of Mary Antin." *Journal of Ethnic Studies* 17.4 (1990): 81-100.

Discusses the writings of immigrants and marginal members of American society about their educations and the issues of nurturing the old self while forging the new. Considers Antin's experiences in *The Promised Land* one of the richest of these examples. A major treatment which covers her educational experiences from her childhood in Russia to her girlhood and adulthood in America.

Sedgwick, Ellery. "Mary Antin." *American Magazine* Mar. 1914: 64-65.

Describes Antin's early life in an Old Testament Russia; her life as an immigrant to America; the dramatic changes made by education; and her supreme achievement, *The Promised Land*.

Stewart, Jane A. "Attractive Biographies: Mary Antin." *Journal of Education* 28 Jan. 1915: 91-92.

Using quotes from Antin's autobiographical works, Stewart describes Antin's life in Russia and the U.S., her education in the two distinct systems, her curiosity and desire to know, and her contribution to our understanding of the Jewish immigrant experience.

Wade, Mary H. "Mary Antin: A Pilgrim from Russia." *Pilgrims of Today*. Mary H. Wade. Boston: Little, 1916. 112-41.

Considers this almost a child's account of the life of a Jewish immigrant child and woman. Clearly designed to cause non-Jewish readers to applaud Antin's patriotism and assimilation into the American mainstream.

Dissertations

Greenberg, Abraham Herbert. "The Ethnocentric Attitudes of Some Jewish American Writers: Educational Implications." Diss. Yeshiva U, 1956.

Max Apple
1941 –

Primary Sources

Novels

The Propheteers. New York: Harper, 1987; New York: Perennial, 1987; London: Faber, 1987.

Zip: A Novel of Left and Right. New York: Viking, 1978; New York: Warner: 1986.

Collected Works

Free Agents. New York: Harper, 1984; New York: Colophon-Harper, 1985; London: Faber, 1986.

Contents: Walt and Will, Bridging, Small Island Republics, The Eighth Day, Child's Play, Stranger at the Table, Carbo Loading, Pizza Time, Free Agents, Momma's Boy, The National Debt, Business Talk, Post¬Modernism, Eskimo Love, The Four Apples, Help, Kitty Partners, An Offering, Blood Relatives

The Oranging of America. New York: Grossman, 1976; Penguin-Viking, 1976; New York: Bantam, 1978; Harmondsworth: Penguin, 1981, 1987; London: Faber, 1986.

Contents: The Oranging of America; Selling Out; Vegetable Love; Inside

Norman Mailer; The Yogurt of Vasirin Kefirovsky; Understanding Alvarado; Gas Stations; My Real Estate; Noon; Patty-Cake, Patty-Cake . . . a Memoir.

Three Stories. Dallas: Pressworks, 1983.
Contents: Safe at Home, Meyerland, Free Agents.

Short Fiction in Anthologies

"Bridging." *The Norton Book of American Short Stories*. Ed. Peter S. Prescott. New York: Norton, 1988. 692-700.

"Carbo Loading." *Junk Food*. Eds. John Farago and others. New York: Dell, 1980. Pag. not available.

"My Real Estate." *Southwest Fiction*. Ed. Max Apple. New York: Bantam, 1981. 21-33; *Necessary Fictions: Selected Stories from "The Georgia Review."* Eds. Stanley W. Lindberg and Stephen Corey. Athens: U of Georgia P, 1986. 19-31.

"The Oranging of America." *Many Windows: 22 Stories from American Review*. Ed. Ted Solotaroff. New York: Harper, 1982. 210-24.

"Paddycake, Paddycake . . . a Memoir." *Prize Stories 1978: The O. Henry Awards*. Ed. William Abrahams. New York: Doubleday, 1978. 76-86.

"Safe at Home." *Texas Stories & Poems*. Eds. Walter McDonald and James P. White. Dallas: Texas Center for Writers, 1978. 33-49.

"Small Island Republics." *The Best American Short Stories, 1981*. Eds. Hortense Calisher and Shannon Ravenel. Boston: Houghton, 1981. 29-43.

Short Fiction in Periodicals

"Bridging." *Short Story International*. Feb. 1986: 146-56; *Atlantic* Apr. 1984: 93-96.

"Business Talk." *Mademoiselle* Sept. 1977: 126, 128, 130, 132.

"Carbo-Loading." *Michigan Quarterly Review* 21.1 (1982): 146-51.

"Disneyad." *American Review* 26 (1977): pag. not available. Publ. as "Walt and Will" in *Free Agents*.

"Eskimo Love." *Esquire* Apr. 1984: 216-18, 220, 223-24, 226.

"The Filling Station." *Esquire* Dec. 1975: 104-05, 220, 223.

"Four Apples." *Paris Review* 20.74 (1978): 101-03.

"Free Agents." *Iowa Review* 8.4 (1977): 42-51.

"Heart Attack." *TriQuarterly* 35.1 (1976): 20-22.

"Inside Norman Mailer." *Georgia Review* 30.2 (1976): 278-89.

"Kitty Partners." *Antaeus* 49-50 (1983): 59-67.

"Momma's Boy." *Forthcoming* 5 (Spr. 1984): 54-57.

"My Real Estate." *Georgia Review* 30.3 (1976): 595-608.

"The Oranging of America." *American Review* 19 (1974): pag. not available

"Paddycake, Paddycake . . . A Memoir." *Ohio Review* 17.3 (1976): 66-76.

"Peace." *Harper's* Feb. 1989: 56-61.

"Post-Modernism." *Harper's* Sept. 1984: 31-32.

"Research." *Harper's* Jan. 1987: 66-71.

"Stepdaughters." *Esquire* Sept. 1984: 286-91.

"Stranger at the Table." *Esquire* Feb. 1984: 74-77.

"This Land is Meyerland." *Antaeus* 29 (1978): 88-92.

"Understanding Alvarado." *New American Review.* 22 (1975): 258-72.

"A Visit with Our National Debt." *Nation* 11 Feb. 1984: 157-58.

"Yoghurt of Vasirin Kefirovsky." *Georgia Review* 29.3 (1975): 594-609.

Secondary Sources

Articles and Chapters

Glausser, Wayne. "Spots of Meaning: Literary Allusions in Max Apple's *Vegetable Love.*" *Studies in Short Fiction* 20.4 (1983): 255-63.

Claims that Apple's allusions are chosen from primal texts, especially the Old and New Testaments, mythology, and Shakespeare. Claims that he also thrives on materials provided by popular culture, hence a high and low culture mix in his allusions. Concludes that *Vegetable Love* is a particularly helpful story for studying allusiveness and the issue of multiple influence.

McHale, Brian. "Some Postmodernist Stories." *Postmodern Fiction in Europe and the Americas.* Eds. Theo D'haen and Hans Bertens. Amsterdam: Rodopi, 1988. 13-25.

Discusses Apple's dissatisfaction with postmodernist theory and subsequent recourse to exemplary or *diegetic* stories. Suggests that his definition includes world weariness, cleverness, the gnomic, and suspensive irony. Mostly an essay on the characteristics of postmodernist fiction which incorporates many of Apple's ideas.

Vannatta, Dennis. "Satiric Gestures in Max Apple's *The Oranging of America.*" *Studies in Contemporary Satire* 7 (1980): 1-7.

Discusses the satire of the American dream in this collection of stories, pointing out that these are not "pure" satire, but "near-satire," with comic and romantic elements undercutting the harshness. Also finds that Apple does not satirize an individual character, but "a foible or issue or obsession or exaggerated dogma." Discusses each of the stories, and concludes that Apple "rejects satiric scorn and ends in understanding, and forgiving."

Wilde, Alan. "Dayanu: Max Apple and the Ethics of Sufficiency."
Contemporary Literature 26.3 (1985): 254-285.

Focuses on the short stories in *Free Agents* by discussing its heteroge-
neous contents, styles, and effects on various readers. Develops the thesis
that the book is intended to subvert traditional notions of aesthetic and
psychological order.

Wilde, Alan. "Irony in the Postmodern Age: Toward a Map of
Suspensiveness." *Boundary 2* 9.1 (1980): 4-58. Rpt. as "A Map of
Suspensiveness" in *Horizons of Assent: Modernism, Postmodernism,
and the Ironic Imagination*. Alan Wilde. Baltimore: Johns Hopkins
UP, 1981. 127-65.

Discusses the relationship between modernism's attempts to describe the
character of its own still nascent enterprise, and those same dislocations,
mythical paradigms, and aesthetic reflexiveness addressed by the post-
modernists. Within the context of this major essay, Wilde discusses
Apple's *The Oranging of America* in considerable detail. Discusses
prose, tone, events, characters, postmodernist strategies, protest, sympathies, suspensiveness, and irony.

Wilde, Alan. "Max Apple and the American Nightmare." *Critique*. 30.1
(1988): 27-47.

Argues with the prevailing political clichés that Apple's work is animated
by tenderness and mildness. Claims instead that such entrenched, uncritical opinion obscures and thus discounts the progression from his early to
late works. Traces Apple's progressive engagement with American nightmare and the deleterious effects it has on his protagonists.

Wilde, Alan. "'Strange Displacement of the Ordinary': Apple, Elkin,
Barthelme, and the Problem of the Excluded Middle." *Boundary 2*
10.2 (1982): 177-99.

Begins with elaborate theorizing about self-reflexive fiction, surfiction,
and postmodernist strategies before elaborating on the work of Apple,
which he identifies as a kind of "midfiction" existing between the old
realism and the new surfiction.

Reviews

Allen, Bruce. "Crackpot Comedy, Baldfaced Parody." Rev. of *Zip: A Novel
of the Left and the Right. Chicago Tribune Book World* 10 Sept. 1978: 3.

Appreciates Apple's capacity for delight and spinning tall tales. Details the adventures of Ira, the major protagonist, and his Portnoyan family. Argues that the story charms with offbeat wit and defies meaning making. Concludes that it is a book full of zany throwaway lines and inventions, all of which contribute to the ungainly comedy of the piece.

Bellamy, Joe David. "Howard Johnson in Person." Rev. of *The Oranging of America and Other Stories. New York Times Book Review* 13 Feb. 1977: 8.

Considers *The Oranging of America* a remarkable debut with its peculiar combination of resourcefulness, fanaticism, greed, and dumb luck. Concludes that, the book, for all its satire, is mellow, charming, and nostalgic in its potshots at the ravaged American dream.

Betsky, Celia. Rev. of *The Oranging of America and Other Stories. Saturday Review.* 22 Jan. 1977. 40.

Claims *The Oranging of America and Other Stories* takes American obsessions and fads, myths and habits, and explodes them into ingenious symbols with a life all their own. Notes that here is much comic intelligence, and that his real brilliance lies in the versatile range of voices he is able to assume and a talent for punning that leaps into a wonderful realm of linguistic hijinks and buffoonery.

Broyard, Anatole. "Books of the Times." Rev. of *Free Agents. New York Times* 8 June 1984: C28.

Calls *Free Agents* a collection of stories, satires and essays which constitute another piece of friendly criticism of American culture, full of tender wit, patient, amused, and saintly. It is a strange mixture of postmodernism in the arts, primal therapy, the national debt, race relations, and Eskimo love.

Charyn, Jerome. "Jane Fonda Does a Cameo." Rev. of *Zip: A Novel of the Left and the Right. New York Times Book Review* 16 July 1978: 8.

Describes *Zip* as a laughing look, or a blink, at loony American culture. Finds it full of humorous accounts of psychosis, sad old men, Disneyland, Fidel Castro, and Howard Johnson's private ice cream scoop. Concludes that it is a tender and crazy book without an ounce of savagery.

Clemons, Walter. "Apple Blossoms." Rev. of *Free Agents. Newsweek* 25 June 1984: 68.

Mostly a description of the zanier contents of the book. Claims that "Bridging" is one of the best stories anybody has ever written.

Clemons, Walter. "Up from Junk." Rev. of *Zip: A Novel of the Left and the Right. Newsweek* 10 July 1978: 72, 74.

Briefly reviews the plot, but concludes that while the boxing aspects are delicately and lovingly done, the book comes apart when it moves to the political fantasies of the 1960s. States that the appearance of "real" people—J. Edgar Hoover and Jane Fonda—doesn't work, but that the ending has an incontrovertible mythic power.

Cook, Carole. "Fiction and Mock Fact." Rev. of *The Oranging of America and Other Stories. Nation* 15 Jan. 1977: 59-60.

Describes *The Oranging of America* as full of vestiges of the mythic mind—an endangered species. Briefly reviews its contents. Concludes that our pleasure in the book is due to our familiarity with kitsch artifacts—our self-deprecating recognition of mid-cult America. Concludes that, unfortunately, Apple has not thought hard enough about paying back with interest into the collective fund of better cultural ideas.

Delbanco, Nicholas. Rev. of *Zip: A Novel of the Left and the Right. New Republic* 24 June 1978: 35-36.

Argues that Max Apple has a real comic talent and an eye for incongruity. Claims that the cast of characters teeters between the imagined and the real. Details the contents of several of the stories and concludes that Apple's humor and prose are sprightly throughout. Describes the dialogue as excellent and the whole effect as a sweet read.

Eder, Richard. Rev. of *The Propheteers. Los Angeles Times Book Review* 8 Mar. 1987: 3.

Calls this an amusing fantasy about national change and decay that is written like a three-legged parable whose style and light manner are reminiscent of Doctorow.

Frank, Sheldon. "Can a Satirist Out-Parody Mad Ave?" Rev. of *The Oranging of America and Other Stories. National Observer* 5 Feb. 1977: 19.

Wonders how Apple can successfully parody a culture which is already a parody in his *The Oranging of America*, because, to begin with, a satirist must love what he/she satirizes and Apple does not. Concludes that most of the stories are predictable and only a few are inspired.

Fremont-Smith, Eliot. "Brontosaurus Country." Rev. of *Zip: A Novel of the Left and the Right. Village Voice* 7 Aug. 1978: 62.

Finds that Apple has new "gentleness; he hoists his victims, but in love." Considers that *Zip*, his first novel, lacks enough anger. Briefly describes the story, and concludes that it has energy, but no directed force and that it spreads sunshine, but doesn't become magic.

Fremont-Smith, Eliot. "Making Book." Rev. of *The Oranging of America and Other Stories*. *Village Voice* 14 Feb. 1977: 79.

Describes the novel as funny, revelatory, and moving, always declining anger and choosing tenderness.

Gray, Paul. "Legends." Rev. of *The Propheteers*. *Time* 23 Feb. 1987: 78.

The Propheteers is described as a gentle fable as fabulous as truth. Details content and characters generously.

Heller, Amanda. "Short Reviews." Rev. of *The Oranging of America*. *Atlantic* Feb. 1977: 96.

Calls Apple extraordinarily entertaining because of his mischievous wit and generosity. Describes the volume as a delightful romantic fantasy and his characters as lean, whimsical types pursuing a series of harmless passions. Concludes that the book overflows with vitality, charm, and good humor.

Horne, Philip. "Life and Work." Rev. of *Free Agents*. *London Review of Books* 8 May 1986: 16-17.

Describes *Free Agents* as a collection of stories which are urbane, well-crafted, convincing, likable, and ingenious. Details several of the stories. Praises Apple's prose, and complains about his handling of the point of view, as well as his cloying, smart-sentimental Jewish humor.

Kakutani, Michiko. "Books of the Times." Rev. of *The Propheteers*. *New York Times* 4 Feb. 1987: C25.

Calls the novel a satire that conveys not anger, but amused reverence and tenderness for the inanities of the human race. Claims that this mythic picture of America results in a kind of children's cartoon, artfully outlined with sharp brush strokes and inked in with bright primary colors. Contains a detailed description of contents.

Kaveney, Roz. "Cash of Titans." Rev. of *The Propheteers*. *Times Literary Supplement* 9 Oct. 1987: 1106.

Claims that *The Propheteers* is a novel preoccupied with demystifying the very rich by showing them as compulsive neurotics. Finds many felicitous scenes at once picturesque and drily amusing. Concludes that, unfortunately, the novel fails to follow those steely wills through to a convincing conclusion.

Kotzwinkle, William. "The Father As Girl Scout, and Other Wonders." Rev. of *Free Agents*. *New York Times Book Review* 17 June 1984: 11.

Describes *Free Agents* as vintage Max Apple, irresistible and charming. Details the contents.

LeClair, Tom. "Brief Review." Rev. of *Free Agents*. *New Republic* 22 Oct. 1984: 46, 48.

Complains of the narcissism of *Free Agents*, yet admits the appeal of Apple's kindliness, humor, and guilts. Argues that many of the stories seem designed for magazine space. Concludes that, if Apple can lay off speed and miniaturization, he won't have to be in his own joke in his next work.

Leonard, John. "Books of the Times." Rev. of *Zip: A Novel of the Left and the Right*. *New York Times* 17 July 1978: C15.

Describes *Zip* as a wonderful collection of short stories which never nag. Sees Apple's cartoons as real people tenderly treated. Attributes to him a fine comic intelligence and a brilliant command of slapstick. Discusses tone and contents in detail.

Leonard, John. "Dream Along With Them." Rev. of *The Oranging of America and Other Stories*. *New York Times* 20 Nov. 1976: 23.

Describes *The Oranging of America* as the work of a clearly minor writer who nevertheless invests his stories with compassion and regard for his characters. Claims that the stories reflect an author interested in dreaming, identity crisis, food, idiosyncratic behavior, and the ironies of unfulfillment and the absurd.

Luria-Sukenick, Lynn. "Four Novels." Rev. of *Zip: A Novel of the Left and the Right*. *Partisan Review* 47.2 (1980): 292-93.

Calls *Zip* a novel which mates the *schlemiel* of the 1950s with the whimsy and politics of the pop novels of the 1960s. Calls Apple a good, funny novelist with a rich imagination but no larger vision.

Maurer, Robert. "Books in Brief." Rev. of *Zip: A Novel of the Left and the Right*. *Saturday Review* 22 July 1978: 49.

Argues that this is a novel of fictional playfulness because Apple has no particular convictions. It has narrative drive, all the embellishments of a quick wit, and a runaway imagination.

McDonald, Peter. "Between Kisses." Rev. of *The Propheteers. London Review of Books* 1 Oct. 1987: 12.

Claims that *The Propheteers* is a novel in which post-war American society is caricatured with remorseless precision and its values inflated into religious terms that seem ludicrous only at first. Details the contents and concludes that it is an original, shockingly far-fetched parable of the sad success of a profit-society in which everyone, even among the winners, ends up losing.

McFadden, Cyra. "Love Among the Orange Roofs." Rev. of *The Propheteers. New York Times Book Review* 15 Mar. 1987: 13-14.

Describes the contents and discusses Apple's style and his blending of fact and fiction in this novel whose protagonists are true prophets inspired by the profit motive—Howard Johnson, Walt Disney, and Margery Post Merriweather.

Prescott, Peter S. "Faith, Hope and...Fiction." Rev. of *The Propheteers. Newsweek* 23 Feb. 1987: 77.

Describes how Apple uses Old Testament imagery in distinctly secular ways in order to write obliquely about religious issues. Calls him the sweetest of satirists, the gentlest of wits, who inflates the banalities of American consumerism to mythic dimensions. Details the contents of *Propheteers*.

Prescott, Peter S. "What So Proudly We Hail." Rev. of *The Oranging of America and Other Stories. Newsweek* 6 Dec. 1976: 90.

Sees the ten stories in *The Oranging of America* as charming, optimistic, and built around the metaphors of America's excesses. Argues that Apple is original, witty, even startling. His principal asset is his battering of our cultural cliches and his charming humor.

Shack, Neville. "Front Line of a Phoney War." Rev. of *Free Agents* and *The Oranging of America. Times Literary Supplement* 10 Oct. 1986: 1130.

Describes both *Free Agents* and *The Oranging of America* as books that make a stylistic virtue out of uncertainty, while enriching the rhythm and tempo, and also letting the awkward authorial voice grate. Finds Apple more convincing than entertaining when he controls the nervousness in the prose and manages to blacken the humor a little. Concludes that both fictions belabor their sense of absurdity, trying too hard to project clever, wacky, skittish touches.

Sipper, Ralph B. "Surrealism Plus Wild Invention: Apple-core Humor." Rev. of *Free Agents. Los Angeles Times Book Review* 26 Aug. 1984: 3.

Argues that like Woody Allen, Max Apple tilts at the establishment windmills with charming quips, autobiographical asides, and much cultural criticism. Details several of the stories.

Stevick, Philip. "Napalm and M&M's." Rev. of *Zip: A Novel of the Left and the Right. Nation* 19-26 Aug. 1978: 153-54.

Describes the demise of the novel of manners, and then details the use Apple makes of this form in *Zip*. Comments on the book's wonderful moments, wonderful sense of verbal play, keen eye for the styles of the 1960s, and less imaginative power than Apple's earlier works.

Wincelberg, Shimon. "Delightfully Rearranging Our World." Rev. of *Free Agents. New Leader* 9-23 July 1984: 15-16.

Describes *Free Agents* as full of overtly autobiographical stories, sweet-natured, and magical. Concludes that these stories make us laugh out loud with pleasure and give us a new way of looking at the world.

Winch, Terence. "Down for the Count." Rev. of *Zip: A Novel of the Left and the Right. Washington Post Book World* 6 Aug. 1978: F3.

Calls *Zip* a self-mocking piece which belongs firmly to the tradition of the Jewish-American novel. Details the contents of the collection, admires the poise of Apple's prose, and complains that he has taken on too much in too brief a novel.

Wolff, Geoffrey. "Apple Unzipped." Rev. of *Zip: A Novel of the Left and the Right. New Times* 21 Aug. 1978: 66.

Calls *Zip* a kind of Jewish-American novel—a running monologue of wisecracks—so cute it could squeak. Argues that it is perhaps a homage to Friedman, Richler, Markfield, Malamud, and half a dozen others, but unfortunately, compared to his earlier fiction, this book seems sweaty, an exhausted clinch, a time on the ropes, or the slow unwinding of a warm-up match rather than the main event.

Interviews

Hundley, Patrick D. "Triggering the Imagination: An Interview with Max
    Apple." *Southwest Review* 64.3 (1979): 230-37.

Here Apple discusses: his academic training, publishing history to date,
his use of historical figures in *The Oranging of America*, his interest in
sports, the impetus to individual pieces, his treatment of death, stylistic
relationship to Barthleme and Coover, philosophy of the short story,
modernism and postmodernism, and writing plans for the future.

Vorda, Allan. "An Interview with Max Apple." *Michigan Quarterly
    Review* 27.1 (1988): 69-78.

Here Apple discusses: his enjoyment of old-fashioned fiction, Schwartz,
Conrad, Eliot, his views on postmodernism, his teenage ambition to be a
writer, the influence of E.L. Doctorow, his apprenticeship, his own narrative style, earlier works, the theory of the novel, his views on American
fiction, and the art of telling a story.

Biographical Sources

Apple, Max. "The Making of a Writer: My Love Affair with English."
    New York Times Book Review 22 Mar. 1981: 9, 24-25.

Apple describes his growing up and formative years in Grand Rapids
speaking Yiddish and reading in English, the influence of his parents and
grandparents on his life, his love affair with words, and his struggle to
make the sentences carry the breath of life.

Apple, Max. "On Persisting as a Writer." *Michigan Quarterly Review*
    21.1 (1982): 21-25.

Talks about what is needed by writers, the success of writers of popular
fiction, the perseverance of writers of serious literature and their role as
revolutionaries. Insists that serious fiction will persist, will endure, even
though bad writing may drive the good out of circulation. Good readers
who know how to value words and feelings still exist. Useful for its
insight into his reasons for writing.

Dissertations

Wilson, Lucy Ann. "A Study of Technical Innovations and Thematic
    Concerns in the Short Prose Fiction of Barthelme, Gass, Coover, and
    Apple." Diss. Temple U, 1982.

Sholem Asch

1880 – 1957

Primary Sources

Novels

The Apostle. New York: Putnam, 1943; Toronto: Allen, 1943; London: MacDonald, 1949; New York: Pocket, 1957; New York: Carroll, 1985.

The Calf of Paper. London: Gollancz, 1936, 1938; Toronto: Ryerson, 1936. Publ. as *The War Goes On.* New York: Putnam, 1936.

East River. New York: Putnam, 1946; Toronto: Allen, 1946; London: MacDonald, 1948; New York: Carroll, 1983, 1986.

Kiddush Ha-Shem: An Epic of 1648. Trans. Rufus Learsi (Isaac Goldberg). Jewish Publication Society Series 9. Philadelphia: Jewish Pub. Soc. of America, 1912, 1926; New York: Meridian, 1959; The Modern Jewish Experience. New York: Arno, 1975.

Mary. New York: Putnam, 1949, 1951; Toronto: Allen, 1950; London: MacDonald, 1950; New York: Cardinal-Pocket, 1957; New York: Carroll, 1985.

Moses. New York: Putnam, 1951; London: MacDonald, 1952; New York: Pocket, 1958.

The Mother. New York: Liveright, 1930; New York: Putnam, 1937; Toronto: Allen, 1937; London: Routledge, 1937; New York: Grosset, 1940; Garden City: Sun Dial, 1950; New York: AMS, 1970.

Mottke, the Thief. New York: Putnam, 1935; London: Gollancz, 1935, 1936; Toronto: Ryerson, 1936; Westport: Greenwood, 1970; Originally publ. as *Mottke the Vagabond.* Boston: Luce, 1917.

The Nazarene. New York: Putnam, 1939; Toronto: Allen, 1939; London: Routledge, 1939, 1941, 1949, 1956; New York: Pocket, 1947, 1956; New York: Carroll, 1984.

One Destiny: An Epistle to the Christians. New York: Putnam, 1945; Toronto: Allen, 1945.

A Passage in the Night. New York: Putnam, 1953; Toronto: Allen, 1953; London: MacDonald, 1954.

The Prophet. New York: Putnam, 1955; Toronto: Allen, 1956, 1957; London: MacDonald, 1956; New York: Giant Cardinal-Pocket, 1957; New York: Pocket, 1958.

Salvation. New York: Putnam, 1934, 1951; Toronto: Ryerson, 1934; London: Gollancz, 1934; Toronto: Allen, 1951; Rev. and enl. ed. London: MacDonald, 1953; New York: Schocken, 1968.

Song of the Valley. New York: Putnam, 1939; Toronto: Allen, 1939; London: Routledge, 1939.

Uncle Moses. New York: Dutton, 1920; London: Unwin, 1922; New York: Putnam, 1936.

The War Goes On. New York: Putnam, 1936. Publ. as *The Calf of Paper.* London: Gollancz, 1936; Toronto: Ryerson, 1936.

Collected Works

Children of Abraham: The Short Stories of Sholem Asch. New York:
Putnam, 1942; London: Routledge, 1944; Short Story Index Reprint
Series. Freeport: Books for Libraries, 1971.

Contents: The Boy Saint; Yoshke the Beadle; The Song of Hunger; The
Mother's Reward; The Lucky Touch; God's Bread; The Carnival
Legend; From the Beyond; My Father's Greatcoat; The Rebel; Young
Years; All His Possessions; De Profundis; The Stranger; The Footsteps;
Sanctification of the Name; A Letter to America; The Heritage; A
Peculiar Gift; The Last Jew; White Roses; The Magic of the Uniform;
Dust to Dust; The Quiet Garden; Fathers-in-Law; "Heil, Hitler!"; A
Royal Table; The Pull of the City; His Second Love.

From Many Countries: The Collected Short Stories of Sholem Asch.
London: MacDonald, 1958.

Contents: The Boy Saint, My Father's Greatcoat, The Mother's Reward,
The Last Jew, The Quiet Garden, The Heritage, The Rebel, The Dowry,
A Divorce, His Second Love, Tricked, From the Beyond, A Royal Table,
The Magic of the Uniform, Dust to Dust, Sin, Yiskadal v' Yiskadash,
The Song of Hunger, A Child Leads the Way, Jewish Eyes, The Duty to
Live, Eretz Israel, Mama, Christ in the Ghetto, The Finger, A Peculiar
Gift, The Carnival Legend, God's Bread, Sanctification of the Name, The
Stranger, The Footsteps.

Tales of My People. New York: Putnam, 1948; Toronto: Allen, 1948;
Short Story Index Reprint Series. Freeport: Books for Libraries, 1970.

Contents: The Little Town, Tricked, A Divorce, The Dowry, Yiskadal v'
Yiskadash, A Child Leads the Way, The Duty to Live, Jewish Eyes,
Eretz Israel, Mama, The Finger.

Three Cities, a Trilogy. New York: Putnam, 1933, 1943; Toronto:
Ryerson, 1933, 1937; London: Gollancz, 1933, 1934, 1937; London:
MacDonald, 1955; New York: Bantam, 1967; New York: Carroll,
1983.

Contents: Petersburg, Warsaw, Moscow.

Three Novels. New York: Putnam, 1938; Toronto: Allen, 1938, London:
Routledge, 1938.

Contents: Uncle Moses, Chaim Lederer's Return, Judge Not—.

Short Fiction in Anthologies

"Abandoned." *Great Short Stories of the World: A Collection of Complete Short Stories from the Literature of All Periods and Countries*. Eds. Barrett H. Clark and Maxim Lieber. New York: McBride, 1925, 1928; Boston: Heath, 1925; Garden City: Halcyon, 1925; Cleveland: World, 1925; New York: Boni, 1925, 1931, 1933; New York: World, 1947, 1962; Garden City: Garden, 1947. 740-43.

"The Duty to Live." *Mothers: A Catholic Treasury of Great Stories*. Ed. Ann J. Fremantle. New York: Daye, 1951; New York: Ungar, 1951. 200-17; *Feast of Leviathan*. Ed. Leo W. Schwarz. New York: Rinehart, 1956. 139-52.

"Eretz Israel." *A Treasury of Jewish Sea Stories*. Ed. Samuel Sobel. New York: David, 1965. 201-06; *Jewish Sea Stories*. Ed. Samuel Sobel. Middle Village: David, 1985. 201-06.

"Exalted and Hallowed." *Jewish Frontier Anthology, 1934-1944*. New York: Jewish Frontier, 1945. 395-407.

"First Day in School." *A Union for Shabbos and Other Stories of Jewish Life in America*. Ed. Max Rosenfeld. Philadelphia: Sholom Aleichem Club, 1967. Pag. not available; *Pushcarts and Dreamers*; *Stories of Jewish Life in America*. Ed. Max Rosenfeld. South Brunswick: Yoseloff, 1969. Pag. not available.

"I Will Send Thee." *The Ways of God and Men*. Ed. R. Selden. New York: Daye, 1950. 372-85.

"A Jewish Child." *Yiddish Stories*. Ed. Helena Frank. Philadelphia: Jewish Pub. Soc. of America, 1912. 506-13; *Great Stories of All Nations*. Eds. Maxim Lieber and Blanche Williams. New York: Brentano, 1927. 882-87.

"Kola Road." *An Anthology of Modern Yiddish Literature*. Ed. Joseph Leftwich. The Hague: Mouton, 1974. 27-41; *Yisroel: The First Jewish Omnibus*. Ed. Joseph Leftwich. London: Heritage, 1933. 633-51; Rev. ed. London: Clarke, 1945. 482-96; Rev. ed. New York: Beechhurst,

1952. 482-96; Rev. ed. New York: Yoseloff, 1963. 456-70. Titled "Kola Street." *A Treasury of Yiddish Stories*. Eds. Irving Howe and Eliezer Greenberg. New York: Viking, 1954; New York: Meridian, 1958. 260-75. [Clarke ed. titled *Yisroel: The Jewish Omnibus*.]

"Mama." *To Mother with Love: A Tribute in Great Stories*. Ed. Frederick Ungar. New York: Daye, 1951. 91-106.

"A Peculiar Gift." *The Seas of God: Great Stories of the Human Spirit*. Ed. Whit Burnett. Philadelphia: Lippincott, 1944. 129-35; *Jewish Short Stories*. Ed. Ludwig Lewisohn. New York: Behrman, 1945. 42-53.

"A Quiet Garden Spot." *A Treasury of Yiddish Stories*. Eds. Irving Howe and Eliezer Greenberg. New York: Viking, 1954; New York: Meridian, 1958. 519-23.

"Sanctification of the Name: A Legend." *A Treasury of Yiddish Stories*. Eds. Irving Howe and Eliezer Greenberg. New York: Viking, 1954; New York: Meridian, 1958. 255-60.

"A Scholar's Mother." *Yiddish Tales*. Ed. Helena Frank. Philadelphia: Jewish Pub. Soc. of America, 1912. 514-28.

"A Simple Story." *Yiddish Stories*. Ed. Helena Frank. Philadelphia: Jewish Pub. Soc. of America, 1912. 493-505.

"The Sinner." *Yiddish Stories*. Ed. Helena Frank. Philadelphia: Jewish Pub. Soc. of America, 1912. 529-39; *The Jewish Caravan: Great Stories of Twenty-Five Centuries*. Ed. Leo W. Schwarz. New York: Farrar, 1935; Philadelphia: Jewish Pub. Soc. of America, 1935. 336-42.

"The Stranger." *The Questing Spirit*. Eds. H. E. Luccock and Francis Brentano. New York: Coward, 1947. 119-25.

"A Union for Shabbos." *A Union for Shabbos and Other Stories of Jewish Life in America*. Ed. Max Rosenfeld. Philadelphia: Sholom Aleichem Club, 1967. Pag. not available; *Pushcarts and Dreamers: Stories of Jewish Life in America*. Ed. Max Rosenfeld. South Brunswick: Yoseloff, 1969. Pag. not available.

Short Fiction in Periodicals

"At the Shore of Eretz Isroel." *Jewish Mirror* (Wint. 1962): 9-12.

"Exalted and Hallowed." *Jewish Frontier* Nov. 1942: 17-25.

"I Adopt An Ancestor." *American Mercury* Jan. 1943: 47-53.

"The Red Hat." *Esquire* Apr. 1934: 48-49, 100.

"Through the Wall." *Current Literature* Oct. 1910: 461-63.

"Village Tsaddik." *Slavonic and East European Review* July 1934: 41-45.

"The Wiles of Destiny." *Nation* 18 July 1923: 59-61.

Secondary Sources

Books

Lieberman, Chaim. *The Christianity of Sholem Asch: An Appraisal from the Jewish Viewpoint.* Trans. Abraham Burstein. New York: Philos. Lib., 1953.

Siegel, Ben. *The Controversial Sholem Asch: An Introduction to His Fiction.* Bowling Green: Bowling Green U Popular P, 1976.

Articles and Chapters

"The Apostle." *1,300 Critical Evaluations of Selected Novels and Plays.* Ed. Frank N. Magill. 4 vols. Englewood Cliffs: Salem, 1978. 1: 94-95.

Briefly describes the contents, characterization, and style of this chronicle of the lives of Peter and Paul. Finds it particularly valuable for the information it provides about the Judeo-Christian heritage of Western civilization.

Ashkenazi, Touvia. "Sholem Asch." *National Jewish Monthly* Feb. 1958: 8-9.

Discusses the widespread debate in Jewish circles about Asch's commitment to Judaism after the debut of his so-called Christian novels. Reviews his life, career, politics, Judaism, and his death. Concludes that he was a good Jew, and urges that his remains be buried in Israel.

Bludworth, Rosa. "Sholem Asch and His Plea for Reconciliation." *Religion in Life* 27.1 (1957-58): 85-94.

Provides a detailed critical description of Asch's three New Testament novels—*The Nazarene, The Apostle,* and *Mary*. Argues that they represent an eloquent plea for mutual understanding between Jews and Christians because their faiths are so rooted in one another, and because such a sympathetic understanding will bring increased goodwill between the two religions.

Cargill, Oscar. "Sholem Asch: Still Immigrant and Alien." *English Journal* Nov. 1950: 483-90;. *College English* Nov. 1950: 67-74.

Discusses the American habit of not accepting as American writers *emigrés* like Asch who did not write in English. Touches briefly on Peretz's influence on young Asch, categorizing his works into three groups: (1) plays, short stories, and novels on the plight of the Jews in Europe, (2) short stories and novels on Jewish life in New York City, and (3) tracts and a fictional trilogy to establish the common cultural and moral matrix of the Jewish and Christian faiths. Discusses each work briefly.

Charnes, Gloria L. "Commemorating a Controversial Literary Figure." *Christian Century* 19 Nov. 1980: 1130-31.

A brief tribute to Asch on the centenary of his birth.

Cournos, John. "Three Novelists: Asch, Singer and Schneour." *Menorah Journal* Jan. 1937: 81-91.

Discusses *Three Cities* as an epic of great descriptive and imaginative power, and full of historical types striving against circumstance during what is the eternal *Diaspora*. Refutes the idea Jewish writers have produced nothing that is universal. Amplifies its point by ranging through several of Asch's works for evidence of the universality of character and theme in the novels and stories.

George, Ralph W. "Sholem Asch—Man of Letters and Prophet." *Religion in Life* 20.1 (1950-51): 106-13.

A brief overview of Asch's life and reputation which praises him for his subtle humor, consciousness of his people's tragedies, elfish sense of delight, clever use of materials unfamiliar to the reader, colorful settings, and exalted style. Briefly touches on some of the major works, and finally commends him for his avoidance of modern faithlessness and vulgarity, such as found in Hemingway. Sees Asch as part of the classic tradition of the novel of Dickens, Scott, and Thackeray.

Gittleman, Sol. *From Shtetl to Suburbia: The Family in Jewish Literary Imagination.* Boston: Beacon, 1978. 94-101, 134-36.

Discusses Asch as one of several second and last generation Yiddish writers. Describes him as controversial and condemned as an apostate for his Christological novels. Notes his glorification of the working classes and his themes of Jewish determination, Jewish communal values, eroticism, family issues, and the intergenerational conflict within the Jewish-American family.

Goldberg, Isaac. "New York's Yiddish Writers." *Bookman* Feb. 1918: 684-89.

Discusses the renaissance in Yiddish literature during the latter part of the nineteenth century and the movement of the center of Yiddish culture from Warsaw to New York City. Characterizes Asch as the Yiddish Mark Twain, and mentions the revolutionary strain in much of the writing. Discusses the Yiddish stage, a large number of briefly mentioned writers residing in New York City, and a variety of their works. Pays particular attention to Asch, whom he characterizes as an individualist. Calls him the successor of Perez and Pinski. Reviews Asch's individual works.

Golden, Harry. "Sholem Asch and Anne Frank." *Carolina Israelite* May-June 1959: 8-9.

Describes the inception of the Christian trilogy in the early work of Asch, such as *Three Cities*. Tries to explain some of Asch's own ambivalence about Christ as Jew and prophet, himself as Yiddish writer-prophet, and his inadequate art. Claims that not until Anne Frank are some of these issues of the Holocaust in relation to the crucifixion and the courage of the Jews resolved. Concludes that it will be Frank's book that remains and Asch's that will become lost to history.

Gorman, Herbert S. "Yiddish Literature, and the Case of Sholom Asch." *Bookman* June 1923: 394-400. Rpt. in *The Procession of Masks.* Herbert S. Gorman. New York: Brimmer, 1923. 139-54.

Discusses the insistent voice of Jewish nationality emerging from Asch's works. Also contains anecdotes of the meetings between Gorman and Asch. Comments that the Yiddish language is unstable and will inevitably pass out of use. Contains random biographical information.

Greenwood, A. K. "Storm Over *The Nazarene." Jewish Digest* Oct. 1940: 65-68.

Discusses *The Nazarene* as a best seller, describes its publishing history, and the objections to it from both Christian and Yiddish quarters.

Klein, A. M. "The Thirteenth Apostle?" *Canadian Jewish Chronicle* 18 Feb. 1944. Rpt. in *Literary Essays and Reviews.* Eds. Usher Caplan and M. W. Steinberg. Collected Works of A. M. Klein. Toronto: U of Toronto P, 1987. 37-39.

An explanation regarding the fury of comments in the Yiddish press about an interview with Asch given to *The Christian Herald.* Primarily a defense of Asch's right to write on Christian subjects, since he does so for material synthesis and not for spiritual analysis. Concludes that "the spiritual meanderings of Sholom Asch are a purely personal affair, and certainly have neither historic nor religious significance."

Liptzin, Sol. "Sholem Asch." *The Flowering of Yiddish Literature.* Sol Liptzin. New York: Yoseloff, 1963. 178-89.

An introductory chapter on Asch covering his early life and work, travels, middle-period works, characters, style, his Christological works, and his influence in pouring the Yiddish word into the mainstream of European and American culture as the first Yiddish writer of truly international vogue.

Lookstein, Joseph H. "Why Did Sholem Asch Write *The Nazarene?"* *Jewish Outlook* Mar. 1940: 4-6.

A review essay on *The Nazarene* commenting on the acclaim the book received from Christian commentators and the sharp criticism it drew from the Yiddish press from such people as Abraham Cahan, Dr. Mukdoni, and Ephraim Kaplan. Condemns the construction of the novel, dismissing it as poor history because of its numerous biblical misquotations, serious defections in rabbinic interpretation, and the not-too-clear treatment of some of the debated events in the life of the Nazarene. Applauds Asch for the magnificent description of the temple and the detailed reconstruction of the Jerusalem of the day. Explores Asch's probable motives of the quest for intellectual certainty. Sees Asch as a secularized, frustrated intellectual who, realizing Utopia has not come to Europe, becomes an admirer of Christianity. Accuses Asch of preaching anti-Semitism to the Christians and reclamation of Christianity to the Jews. Quarrels with the ending of the book that suggests a *rapprochement* between the young generation of Jews and Christians.

Madison, Charles A. "Notes on Sholem Asch, Novelist." *Chicago Jewish Forum* 16.3 (1958): 174-79.

A tribute to Asch on the occasion of his recent death. Provides a general overview of his life, fiction, and artistic achievements. Repeats critical comments made in earlier articles.

Madison, Charles A. "Scholom Asch." *Poet Lore* Dec. 1923: 524-31.

Calls the imagination of Asch "primitively exuberant, poetically naive," "earthbound," and "sensuous." Discusses the archetypal Eve figure who appears so often in the novels in the form of Jewish peasant women. Also comments on his implicit faith in the goodness of nature, and wonders if, in fact, he has pantheistic tendencies. Discusses the ingeniousness of the majority of Asch's characters, and then notes his constant characterization of women as born to serve men. Accuses him of frequently producing moralistic endings that mar the books. Condemns him as a poor stylist, for his sentimentality and characterizations of children who are psychologically unreal. Finally commends him for artistic intensity and lyrical fervor.

Madison, Charles A. "Sholem Asch." *Poet Lore* 46.4 (1940): 303-37. Shortened version rpt. in *Books Abroad* 15.1 (1941): 23-29.

A detailed account of Asch's life and major works with a brief plot summary of each. Concludes that the works are marked by Asch's depictions of women as nudes, as instinctive peasants, and as totally absorbed mothers, while all other types of women are depicted as anomalous. Claims that, in contrast, his men are either sexually assertive or mystically filial. Accuses Asch of being a poor stylist who is spontaneous rather than polished and precise. Finds his strength is his lyric intensity and creative vigor.

Madison, Charles A. "Sholem Asch: Novelist of Lyric Intensity." *Yiddish Literature: Its Scope and Major Writers.* Charles A. Madison. New York: Ungar, 1968; Schocken, 1971. 221-61.

A major essay covering Asch's early education in Kutno, Poland; his youth; sudden rise to fame at twenty; early works; his play, *The God of*

Vengeance; the seven novels of 1913; his life on the eve of WWI; his descriptions of the Lower East Side of New York City and works about this experience; the pogroms of Eastern Europe after WWI; the subsequent works of exalted spiritual faith; the 1920-22 sojourn in Europe; the works that followed in the thirties; the trilogy about Jesus; the carping criticism that followed him all his life; and the novels that occupied him during the last decade of his life.

"The Nazarene." *1,300 Critical Evaluations of Selected Novels and Plays.* Ed. Frank N. Magill. 4 vols. Englewood Cliffs: Salem, 1978. 3: 1552-53.

Briefly discusses characterization, particularly that of Yeshua ben Joseph, and comments on his mastery of evocative description.

"The Prophet." *Survey of Contemporary Literature.* Ed. Frank N. Magill. 12 vols. Englewood Cliffs: Salem, 1977. 9: 6091-94.

Describes the theme, contents, and characterization, and comments that this is the least effective of Asch's biblical novels.

Rogoff, Harry. "Sholom Asch: An Appreciation." *Nine Yiddish Writers* N.p.: np, n.d. 95-107. Rpt. from *East and West* Dec. 1915.

An early admiring introduction to Sholem Asch which describes his life, writing career, thematic interests, influence, reputation, Jewishness, and sense of suffering. Concludes with a prediction of great future success.

Roskies, David G. "Jews on the Cross." *Against the Apocalypse: Responses to Catastrophe in Modern Jewish Culture.* Cambridge: Harvard UP, 1984. 264-65.

Briefly discusses Asch's treatment of the "Crucifix Question" in his story "In a Carnival Night." Notes that his point was "that Jewish-Gentile antagonism was a thing of the past and that enlightened Jews now recognized the essential humanity of the dominant Christian culture."

Rothenberg, Joshua. "Yiddish Literature and Jewish History." *Yiddish* 2.1 (1975): 1-8.

Compares Asch to Mendele in his reflection of contemporary Jewish history. Sees Asch reflecting a later period, and as a writer who, though not representative of his time, broadened the thematic horizons of Yiddish literature to include all strata and classes of Jews in his literary work.

Smertenko, Johan J. "Sholom Asch." *Nation* 14 Feb. 1923: 180-82.

A brief commentary pointing out Asch's popularity, his works, and his political and ethnic affiliations. Doubts Asch will be properly appreciated by American readers, disparages the quality of the English translations, and briefly mentions his plays.

Werfel, Franz. "In Praise of Schalom Asch." *Living Age* Feb. 1931: 596-99.

The transcription of a speech of praise and welcome given at a banquet honoring Asch by the Penn Club in Vienna published originally in Yiddish in the *Neue Freie Presse*, a Vienna liberal daily. Calls him a realist, a poet, a seer, and an epic writer of considerable stature.

Reviews

Adelberg, Julius. "Sholem Asch Proclaims the War Goes On." Rev. of *The War Goes On. Boston Evening Transcript* 7 Nov. 1936: 3.

Describes *The War Goes On* as detailing the recent tragic period of inflation in Germany. Details the plot, characters, and themes, and provides a clear account of the contents of the novel.

Angoff, Charles. "In the Christological Vein." Rev. of *The Prophet. Congress Weekly* 5 Mar. 1956: 14.

Describes *The Prophet* as being written with lushness of imagery and language, submission to childish credulity, and big fat globs of hope that the redeemer is watching over all sinners. Condemns the Isaiah character as a motion picture construction smeared with celluloid cheapness and devoid of all spirituality.

Bates, Ernest Sutherland. "The Gospel in a Modern Version." Rev. of *The Nazarene. Saturday Review of Literature* 21 Oct. 1939: 5.

A detailed one-page book review discussing the content, style, and characters of the novel. Pays particular attention to Asch's ending in which Jesus is claimed for the Jews, not the Christians.

Bullock, Florence Haxton. "The East Side as a Land of Living Religion." Rev. of *East River. New York Herald Tribune Weekly Book Review* 27 Oct. 1946: 5.

Claims that the novel gives an intimate account of living Judaism, very poor portraits of women, and a relatively convincing social history of New York Jews at the turn of the century.

Caswell, Wilbur Larremore. "A New Life of Jesus." Rev. of *The Nazarene. Churchman* Dec. 1939: 19, 39.

Describes the plot and characters of *The Nazarene* and comments on how historically authentic the settings and incidents are in relation to New Testament Christian scriptures. Concludes with amazement at the author's reverence for his character.

Chworowsky, Karl M. "Jesus the Jew." Rev. of *The Nazarene. Christian Century* 7 Feb. 1940: 179-80.

Describes *The Nazarene* as Asch's greatest novel. Calls its structure and effects symphonic, and details each of its four parts. Admires the beautiful descriptions and regrets the book has been denounced as a poorly disguised attempt to exonerate the Jews for the guilt of the Crucifixion.

Colum, Mary M. "Re-creation of New Testament History." Rev. of *The Nazarene. Forum* Dec. 1939: 261-62.

Asserts that the novel sees the world in which Jesus moved as a man does in a clear vision. Claims that Asch is helped to this vision by his knowledge of Hebrew poetry, custom, and character.

Cournos, John. "The Atlantic Bookshelf." Rev. of *The Nazarene. Atlantic* Nov. 1939: [n.p.].

Claims that judged purely as a novel, *The Nazarene* is a superb achievement. Sees the portraits of the women as touchingly human, and argues that Asch clearly thinks Jesus the finest Jew ever to have lived. Concludes that the subject is treated with tenderness and reverence.

Cournos, John. "From the Yiddish." Rev. of *Three Novels. New York Times Book Review* 2 Oct. 1938: 21.

Claims that *Three Novels* betrays Asch's Dickensian bent, as well as the influence of Tolstoy and the other prophetic, nineteenth-century novelists. Describes the faults and strengths of each of the novels.

Cournos, John. "Mr. Asch's Stories." Rev. of *Children of Abraham. New York Times Book Review* 26 Apr. 1942: 6.

Describes *Children of Abraham* as containing twenty-nine short stories and sketches written over a long period of years. Describes several of the pieces and concludes that Asch is a powerful writer: these stories are scarcely less distinguished than his longer narratives.

Cournos, John. "A Novel of Palestine." Rev. of *Song of the Valley. New York Times Book Review* 2 Apr. 1939: 26.

Describes *Song of the Valley* as a novel of Jewish colonization in Israel. Comments on the tone of exultation in the work, and the impossibility of deciding whether this is a fact or a fiction chronicle.

D., H. "New Books." Rev. of *The Nazarene. Catholic World* Dec 1939: 362-64.

Argues that *The Nazarene* confirms the suspicion that most writers see Jesus as they wish to see him. Concludes, nevertheless, that its careful reading will prove interesting to every student of religious thought and history.

Easton, Burton Scott. "Sholem Asch's Great Book." Rev. of *The Nazarene. Living Church* 20 Dec. 1939: 12.

Describes *The Nazarene* in detail and admires its historical authenticity. Applauds the moral qualities of the Nazarene as depicted here and catalogues the minor characters.

Fadiman, Clifton. "Recreation of a Dean—Sholem Asch's Masterpiece." Rev. of *The Nazarene. New Yorker* 21 Oct. 1939: 76-77.

Considers this a "major opus . . . a work of detailed historical reconstruction without the smell of archaeology." Briefly describes the three mouthpieces who tell the story and discusses the difficulty of reviewing a book based on the New Testament. Finds it flawed by the narrative frame in which Asch encased his story.

Feld, Rose. "St. Paul, Great Prophet, Great Politician." Rev. of *The Apostle. New York Herald Tribune Weekly Book Review* 19 Sept. 1943: 3.

Calls *The Apostle* an erudite and reverent account of the life of St. Paul which should stand along with the earlier *The Nazarene*. Argues that it is composed of a tremendous wealth of fact, color, and characters. Concludes that the whole pageantry of an ancient world and ancient religions and cultures unfold under his pen.

Fiedler, Leslie A. "Exodus: Adaptation by Sholem Asch." Rev. of *Moses. Commentary* Jan. 1952: 72-75.

Sees the novel as historical-religious with loose linear form, sentimentality toward the past, exotic sexiness and broad comic relief. Argues that by succeeding in popularizing the religious legend Asch may have filtered out that which gives it its religious significance. Accuses Asch, the intellectual, for apologizing for the story by toning it down and cleaning it up, as well as by explaining away the marvelous.

Fineman, Irving. "A Tower of Babel in Jewish Poland." Rev. of *Salvation. Saturday Review of Literature* 29 Sept. 1934: 142.

Provides a thorough description of the contents of the novel. Complains of the quality of the translation, but concludes that it is still a moving and significant story.

Fuller, Edmund. "Mother of Christ." Rev. of *Mary. Saturday Review of Literature* 8 Oct. 1949: 19-20.

Describes *Mary* as the third in Asch's trilogy on Christ's life. Commends him for almost avoiding sentimentality and sectarianism, for the better unity and more lyrical prose in this volume, and for the rich fabric of folklore in the novel. Complains of some of the repetition from previous volumes and concludes that, for fictional accounts of Christ, Asch towers over other such writers as Lloyd Douglas. Sees his finished trilogy as epic in the grand tradition of Mann.

Fuller, Edmund. "Portrait of the Lawgiver." Rev. of *Moses. Saturday Review of Literature* 22 Sept. 1951: 16.

Highlights the epic dimensions of the character of Moses and his mystical identification with his Hebrew people. Claims that Asch quickly identifies such themes as Israel's separatism, the failure of the people to rise to their leadership, and the God of wrath portrayed here.

"Germany in 1923." Rev. of *The Calf of Paper. Times Literary Supplement* 17 Oct. 1936: 831.

Describes *The Calf of Paper* as a work showing a certain vehemence and talent for drawing historical portraits. Claims that, remarkably, there is a certain impartiality about its picture of the "Jewish Problem" in the Germany of the day. Provides a plot summary.

Goldin, Grace. "Moses, Manna and Miracles." Rev. of *Moses. New Leader* 11 Feb. 1952: 17.

Provides a generally negative review of *Moses* by accusing the author of baking the cake with a few too many eggs in it. Argues that the book is tedious in its inclusion of absolutely everything and particularly unconvincing in terms of its characterizations of Biblical passages.

Howe, Irving. "Sholem Asch: The Inner Loss." Rev. of *The Prophet*. *Midstream* 2.3 (1956): 81-87.

Argues that Asch, in writing the Christological novels, has deeply betrayed himself and his Jewish culture. Describes *The Prophet* in considerable detail. Complains that, in avoiding the problematics of Jewish history, he has reduced the whole sweep to pageant with as little message or meaning as a Cecil B. DeMille movie *The Ten Commandments*. Provides a sweeping item-by-item critique of the novel.

Jack, Peter Monro. "A Nobly Conceived Novel of the Life of Jesus." Rev. of *The Nazarene*. *New York Times Book Review* 29 Oct. 1939: 3, 30.

Describes *The Nazarene* as a superbly told story by a man of courage and simple-heartedness. Gives a detailed account of the narrative strategy and supporting characters in the story. Concludes that, within its large and noble conception, it is amazingly interesting.

"Jesus: A New Imagination." Rev. of *The Nazarene*. *Times Literary Supplement* 4 Nov. 1939: 643.

Considers *The Nazarene* remarkably alive history which gives the reader the impression of having really met characters long since heard about. Concludes that, unfortunately, the author has so carefully balanced points of view between the narrators that his own views are hard to discern.

Kahn, Sholom J. "Two Latter-day Gospels." Rev. of *Mary*. *Commentary* Dec. 1949: 607-08.

Calls *Mary*, Asch's third novel about Christianity, a fascinatingly complex document composed of many diverse elements which simply fail to jell into any aesthetic unity. Identifies much straight historical analysis, straight preaching, painstaking realism, and a selection of all of Asch's former themes.

Kapp, Isa. "Pious Tearjerker." Rev. of *Tales of My People*. *Commentary* Jan. 1949: 99.

Describes *Tales of My People* sarcastically in terms of its melodramatic folk contents. Accuses Asch of taking the Jewish religion into his service and rewarding it with a foggy and filial devotion. Complains particularly of the Holocaust stories that they must have been written in a kind of willful blindness, dealing as they do with subhuman facts of the Nazi program in terms of a regressive and tasteless supernaturalism.

Kazin, Alfred. "Rabbi Yeshua ben Joseph." Rev. of *The Nazarene. New Republic* 1 Nov. 1939: 375-76.

Calls *The Nazarene* artificially constructed and typically bombastic. Argues that it is not a Jewish interpretation of Jesus; it is a biography of a rabbi whose fervor, like his education, was drawn from the profound intellectual democracy of Jerusalem. Concludes that Yeshua makes his place in the Hebrew martyrology, a Jew betrayed by Judah is Kariot, and not the first Jew to perish on the cross.

Kronenberger, Louis. "Profound Compassion." Rev. of *Salvation. New York Times Book Review* 7 Oct. 1934: 7.

Views *Salvation* as having a much different scope than *Three Cities,* composed on altogether another scale, and making another kind of appeal. Argues that it has the affecting power of a parable as it reveals the tensions of the ritual expectations of Jewish ghetto life of the last century and the emergence of a practitioner of brotherly love.

Kronenberger, Louis. "Sholem Asch's Novel of a Thief's Career." Rev. of *Mottke the Thief. New York Times Book Review* 27 Oct. 1935: 8, 24.

Explains that, in *Mottke the Thief,* Asch has written a picaresque novel which remains within the same milieu. Concludes that, despite what has been inevitably lost in translation, this is a book which stares out at us full of life and meaning.

Kronenberger, Louis. "Sholem Asch Dramatizes Germany's Years of Inflation." Rev. of *The War Goes On. New York Times Book Review* 15 Nov. 1936: 4.

Claims that *The War Goes On* dramatizes the inflation years in Germany on an impressive dramatic scale. Finds Asch a moralist rather than a propagandist, and his novel a burning protest, intense, often tragic, and well above sectarianism. Complains that, unfortunately, the characters are often far from convincing.

Kronenberger, Louis. "Sholom Asch's Great Trilogy." Rev. of *Three Cities: A Trilogy. New York Times Book Review* 22 Oct. 1933: 1.

Describes the book as a work demonstrating Asch's mastery of milieu, narrative technique, history, and epic scope as he describes the Jews of St. Petersburg, Warsaw, and Moscow. Details some of the plots and main characters. Concludes that this is a densely packed and unsurpassed picture of these three cities at this point in time.

"Latest Works of Fiction." Rev. of *Mottke the Vagabond*. *New York Times Book Review* 23 Dec. 1917: 570.

Describes *Mottke the Vagabond* as a book that never leaves the confines of Russia. Primarily a plot and character summary. Concludes that the story avoids stereotypes, has moments of genuine pathos and tragedy, contains a sense of fate, and is written with a natural grace.

Lee, Lawrence. "A Novel of Man and His Destiny." Rev. of *East River*. *New York Times Book Review* 20 Oct. 1946: 1, 36.

Calls *East River* a novel of the American spirit, not just a novel of the Jews. Commends Asch for his beautiful and enduring values, for his veneration of what America was supposed to represent, and calls the book a mirror in which we may look to rediscover our innocence, our energy, and our faith.

Lee, Lawrence. "Stories by Sholem Ash." Rev. of *Tales of My People*. *New York Times Book Review* 14 Nov. 1948: 11.

Says of *Tales of My People* that its stories are awkward, poetic, simple, sentimental, moving, and full of compassion and interest.

Levin, Meyer. "A Haunting Guilt." Rev. of *A Passage in the Night*. *New York Times Book Review* 18 Oct. 1953: 5.

Describes *A Passage in the Night* as impregnated with religio-moral themes and written with good old-fashioned narrative technique. Concludes that there are many eloquent passages, but, in the end, everyone has the feeling of a patriarch tenderly patting everyone on the head.

Levin, Meyer. "Prophet of the Return." Rev. of *The Prophet*. *New York Times Book Review* 6 Nov. 1955: 4.

Calls *The Prophet* the culminating book in Asch's series on biblical personages. Admires its religious fervor, and points out its controversiality for Jews. Criticizes what he calls the author's excessive delight in masochistic detail, and concludes that, novelistically, the book is the weakest of the series.

Lipsky, Eleazar. "Folk Living & Dying." Rev. of *Tales of My People*. *Saturday Review of Literature* 4 Dec. 1948: 33.

Prefaces his discussion of this collection of stories by noting Asch's difficulties in satisfying either Christians or Jews with his "hybrid" conception of Jesus, Paul, and other Jewish characters. Finds the earlier stories characterized by "a moral certitude that there was a God in Heaven," but complains that the post-Holocaust stories "cannot satisfy a thirst for an adequate summation of an entire people's tragedy."

Lowenthal, Marvin. "What Is Man That Thou Art Mindful of Him?" Rev. of *Three Cities. New York Herald Tribune Books* 15 Oct. 1933: 7.

Describes the contents of *Three Cities*, Nathan Asch's trilogy about the three cities, and comments that though cast in the form of a novel, this is really an ongoing drama. Concludes that they constitute a sensitive barometer of social change in Russia.

Mehring, Walter. "The Story of a Fighter for Freedom." Rev. of *Moses. New York Times Book Review* 23 Sept. 1951: 5, 32.

Argues that *Moses*, while being "Bible true" in all its episodes, reads like the novel of a Victorian social revolutionary of the Fourth Estate, a contemporary Turgenev's *Fathers and Sons*. Sees it as based in part on Asch's reading of Freud's reading of the Moses story. Concludes that it imparts many humanist lessons worth taking to heart, but claims that its modernization reveals the inadequacy of up-to-date Biblical novels and movie scripts.

"Miriam & Yeshua." Rev. of *Mary. Time* 7 Nov. 1949: 100, 102, 104.

Describes the plot, the author's borrowing from Christian and Jewish sources and traditions, and his purpose of demonstrating the interdependence of the two faiths in hopes of bringing about a better world. Concludes that these ingredients do not make a satisfying novel. Finds Christ's childhood unconvincing, which may send thousands of readers back to the Bible for the story told there.

Moody, Charlotte. "Chaotic Lives." Rev. of *The War Goes On. Saturday Review of Literature* 31 Oct. 1936: 6-7.

Argues that this novel about finance and the Jewish problem is primarily a picture of a despairing people with their values turned upside down, and starving, while food rots in speculator's cellars. Claims that the novel works best when history is told through his characters, but concludes that the chapters on financiers, food speculators, etc., while fascinating reading, are "thorns in the side of the novel."

Peretz, Maya. "From Sholem Asch to Nathan Zach." Rev. of *Three Cities. Jewish Spectator* 49 (Fall 1984): 55-58.

Reviews the plot of Asch's trilogy and concludes that it is "a work of sensitivity and original thinking." Also comments generally on several Hebrew writers and a smattering of their works.

Peters, E. H. "New Books." Rev. of *The Apostle. Catholic World* Oct. 1943: 98-99.

Considers *The Apostle* to be greatly superior to *The Nazarene*, following as it does the structure of *Acts of the Apostles*. Claims that it attempts to clarify the Jewish-Christian relations by presenting a vivid picture of the world, especially the world of the Spirit, in which Christ and the apostles lived.

"Pioneers of Zion." Rev. of *Song of the Valley. Times Literary Supplement* 22 Apr. 1939: 231.

Primarily recounts the contents of *Song of the Valley* and finds not a novel but a hymn of praise for the rebirth of Israel. Concludes that, as a study of Zionist pioneering in Palestine, the book is full of interest, though perhaps a little repetitive.

Podhoretz, Norman. "The Interfaith Temperament." Rev. of *A Passage in the Night. Commentary* Nov. 1953: 492, 494-95.

Claims that *A Passage in the Night* is not a good novel, but that it does make all the talk heard for years about Asch's apostasy seem mere partisan claptrap. Sees this book as a fable and its plot as a vehicle for reflections on human destiny and the nature of God. Finds it has the interest of a well-told anecdote. Traces the central character and the story and concludes that the book is so obviously an artistic failure that it is pointless to dwell on its faults. Discusses Asch's disgust with materialism and his religious views.

Rahv, Philip. "The Healing of a Wound." Rev. of *The Nazarene. Nation* 28 Oct. 1939: 470.

Sees *The Nazarene* as a novel of unnecessary bulk, though amazingly convincing in its recreation of the historical period. Describes the contents and political agenda of the novel and concludes that, in its evocation of the past, it also recreates the present for us.

Rich, J. C. "Maudlin Morality Tale." Rev. of *A Passage in the Night. New Leader* 16 Nov. 1953: 24-25.

Calls *A Passage in the Night* turgid, somber, and tractlike, and another of his studies in comparative religion. Describes the story-line of the novel, and then concludes sarcastically by noting that everything winds up on a happy and pious note with "the old man hamming it up well and truly." Concludes that Asch is still obsessed with religiosity and has produced a dull, boring, theological tract which bears little resemblance to a novel.

Roberts, R. Ellis. "Sholem Asch's Story of Paul." Rev. of *The Apostle*. *Saturday Review of Literature* 18 Sept. 1943: 17.

Considers this novel a good omen for peace in the world because it demonstrates Pope Pius XI's assertion that Christians can never be anti-Jewish because they are "spiritually Semites." Comments on the quality of Asch's characterizations and briefly describes the plot and vividness of incidents. Also sees him hesitating between "a modernist and traditional treatment of Christian origins" and wonders about the pedantry seen in the use of Bar Naba for Barnabas, Silo for Silas, for example.

Rosenberg, Harold. "What Love Is Not." Rev. of *East River*. *Commentary* June 1947: 592-94.

Calls the novel a melodrama of love and religious differences replete with street scenes and an undergirding social vision. Views that what divided and made these polyglot immigrants so cruel to one another was their failure to see that love was the underlying true meaning of both Judaism and Christianity. Accuses Asch of applying the screws to the divisive aspects of Jewish and Roman Catholic orthodoxy. Sees the novel as a mixture of bathos meditation, descriptive talent, theatrical "corn," and social concern and contempt.

Rothman, Nathan L. "Asch . . ." Rev. of *Children of Abraham*. *Saturday Review of Literature* 9 May 1942: 11.

Wonders at the unity of effect created by stories so diverse in time, place, mood, and treatment. Briefly describes the individual stories, their treatment, and impact. Concludes that, collectively, they all flow together into their real integration: a narrative poem of the children of Abraham.

Rothman, Nathan L. "The Earlier Asch." Rev. of *Mottke the Thief*. *Saturday Review of Literature* 12 Oct. 1935: 6.

Finds Asch in these stories a vigorous, humorous, sentimental spinner of lively tales who gives the folk-figure, "Mottke ganniff" (the thief) its final and enduring expression. Concludes that the atmosphere of that little Russian village is reproduced in the most vital and evocative coloring writing can afford.

Rothman, Nathan L. "A Man's Conscience." Rev. of *A Passage in the Night*. *Saturday Review of Literature* 17 Oct. 1953: 27.

A fairly detailed account of the novel, referencing its affinity with parable, its spiritual essence, and its moral complexity.

Rothman, Nathan L. "Mr. Asch's Ambitious Novel." Rev. of *East River*. *Saturday Review of Literature* 19 Oct. 1946: 18-19.

Provides a vivid description of the style and content of the novel, its philosophical idealism, its subtle depiction of the battle between the desire for life and the desire for death on the part of the Lower East Side dwellers, and its rich concrete detail.

Rugoff, Milton. "A Great Novel About the Life of Jesus Christ." Rev. of *The Nazarene*. *New York Herald Tribune Books* 22 Oct. 1939: 3.

Calls *The Nazarene* the kind of book only a continental writer would write. Claims that it bears a great burden of lore and wisdom, covering as it does numerous cities, characters, cultures, and religions. Concludes that, ultimately, it is a book of spiritual sensitivity and imagination.

Rugoff, Milton. "In a Fantastic Post-War World." Rev. of *The War Goes On*. *New York Herald Tribune Books* 1 Nov. 1936: 6.

Asserts that in *The War Goes On* Asch sets a mighty stage and all the outcome is tragedy. Describes the conditions of post-war Germany outlined in the book, as well as the political and personal forces which govern their tragic lives.

"Saga of Jewish Migration: Griefs and Joys in Palestine Depicted by Sholem Asch." Rev. of *Song of the Valley*. *Newsweek* 27 Mar. 1939: 36.

Recognizes that this little book cannot compare with Asch's major works, but argues that it shouldn't be dismissed because it describes the trials, sorrows, and strength of faith of the city-bred Jews who settled the valleys of Palestine.

"Salvation." Rev. of *Salvation*. *Times Literary Supplement* 13 Sept. 1934: 618.

Argues that a peculiarly fervid religious sense pervades *Salvation*, which has the defect of its qualities and which, although it turns to dramatic use a great deal of Talmudic knowledge, seems to be rather narrowly preoccupied with problems of Jewish teaching and rabbinical interpretation.

Strauss, Harold. "An Early Indiscretion." Rev. of *The Mother*. *Nation* 25
    Dec. 1937: 724.

Argues that, unfortunately, Asch skips blithely over the whole question of
economics in the melting pot to chronicle the breaking away of the
younger generation from rigid religious customs and close family life.
Calls it generally a weak performance as a novel: the mother's devotion
fails to gain our sympathy, gross melodrama intrudes, and genuine pathos
also appears. Concludes that this novelist has struck other more vital notes.

T., E. M. "Among the New Books." Rev. of *Salvation*. *San Francisco
    Chronicle* 15 Apr. 1951: 24.

Claims that *Salvation* gives us a picture of an alien, almost vanished,
society through which he traces the spiritual depths possible in Judaism.
Sees it as the Judaism of Jesus, the Pharisees, and Paul filled with mystery and light that attracts him. Details the story and characters.

T., M. I. Rev. of *The Apostle*. *Canadian Forum* Nov. 1943: 191.

Views *The Apostle* as a novelistic history of St. Paul's life and teaching,
and as such is complementary to his earlier work, *The Nazarene*.
Discusses the elements of mysticism, erudition, and feeling in the book.
Concludes that this book should give those not of the Jewish faith a deeper appreciation of our indebtedness to Israel.

Teller, Judd L. "Unhistorical Novels." Rev. of *The Prophet*. *Commentary*
    Apr. 1956: 393-96.

Provides a good description of the novel in Arthur Saul Super's English
translation. Describes it as a neo-Christian novel and criticizes its
baroque style. Commends it for its "primordial effect." Comments on the
colorful visual style and the spiritual sentiment.

"Three Cities." Rev. of *Three Cities*. *Times Literary Supplement* 9 Nov.
    1933: 769.

Calls *Three Cities* an immensely long book in which the author often
achieves his effects through the piling on of detail. Finds it a fascinatingly
vivid and impartial view of main aspects of social existence during the reign
of Nicholas II and on the turmoil of the first months of the Revolution.

Untermeyer, Louis. "An Intimate Saga." Rev. of *The Mother*. *Saturday
    Review of Literature* 30 Oct. 1937: 15.

Details the plot of *The Mother,* and concludes that the characters are too much like automata, never breaking through established patterns. Nevertheless, describes them, as well as the descriptions in the book, as moving. Concludes that the book has warmth, humor, and a teasing tenderness.

van Paassen, Pierre. "Asch's Uninspired Moses." Rev. of *Moses. Congress Weekly* 5 Nov. 1951: 14.

Describes *Moses* as having stopped short imaginatively of the heights arrived at in *The Nazarene* and *The Apostle.* Claims that this book will not recompense the disillusion of the Jewish audience with his Christian books because Asch has signally failed to live up to his rich Jewish heritage and tradition which his publishers alone now attribute to him. Critiques the contents and characterization of the novel in considerable detail.

Wagenknecht, Edward. "A Dramatic Novel-Biography of the Apostle Paul." Rev. of *The Apostle. New York Times Book Review* 19 Sept 1943: 3.

Details the particular difficulties presented Asch by writing this story, and comments on how well Asch has met each one of them. Describes the characterization of Paul, the adherence of the novel to *Acts* and his own epistles. Predicts this book will take its place in the great tradition of the heroic novel.

Wagenknecht, Edward. "A Novel of Mary." Rev. of *Mary. New York Times Book Review* 9 Oct. 1949: 5.

Calls *Mary* a book which is richly imaginative and draws widely on the Biblical knowledge of its subject. Doubts the non-virgin birth theory will offend anyone, but wonders if the wedding at Cana orgy will. Concludes that, like other biblical novels, this one too fails to compete with the scriptures themselves.

Walton, Eda Lou. "A Prophet Arises in Israel." Rev. of *Salvation. New York Herald Tribune Books* 23 Sept. 1934: 2.

Describes the contents of *Salvation* as a political look at life in a completely isolated town in Poland. Calls it a beautifully written and detailed study of Jewish religion. Concludes that it is also a book of violence, pathos, poetic beauty, humor, and terror.

Wilson, P. W. "Epistle to Christians." Rev. of *One Destiny. New York Times Book Review* 7 Oct. 1945: 8.

Asserts that *One Destiny* is full of eloquent descriptions of almost unreadable horror about Polish atrocities to the Jews. Finally describes the book as "an epistle to the Christians."

Bibliographies

Cohen, Libby Okun. "Shalom Asch in English Translation: A Bibliography." *Bulletin of Bibliography* 22.5 (1958): 109-11.

Lists all of Asch's works published in English, including all editions and reprints, excluding transliterations of Yiddish titles even if translated.

Biographical Sources

Asch, Nathan. "My Father and I." *Commentary* Jan. 1965: 55-64.

A remarkable series of impressions and anecdotes about Sholem given by his son. Also contains much biographical material about Nathan Asch's life as a young writer.

Girson, Rochelle. "The Author: Sholem Asch." *Saturday Review of Literature* 8 Oct. 1949: 20.

Briefly describes Asch's early childhood in Poland, his *cheder* schooling and his lifelong interest in Christ as Jew and everlasting sufferer, his sojoun in Jerusalem, and his life and works in the U.S. Concludes with Asch's assertion that his interest in Christianity, in spite of his increasing piety as a Jew, has been "to demonstrate the interdependence of the two faiths."

Hutchens, John K. "Mr. Asch at 75: Prophet with Honor." *New York Herald Tribune Book Review* 6 Nov. 1955: 2.

A tribute to Asch, recounting his life and literary accomplishments. Contains some interview and biographical material reproduced in Asch's own words.

Hutchens, John K. "On an Author: Sholem Asch." *New York Herald Tribune Book Review* 15 Apr. 1951: 2.

A tribute to Asch on his seventieth birthday which provides some first-hand commentary by Hutchens about his life and career.

van Gelder, Robert. "Asch Returns from the Past." *New York Times Book Review* 28 Apr. 1940: 16. Rpt. in *Writers and Writing*. New York: Scribners, 1946. 49-51.

Describes Asch's sources of ideas for novels, some difficulties encountered in writing *The Nazarene*, his writing habits, and details of his
upbringing in Russia.

Dissertations

Alexander, Cheryl Amy. "Major Themes in Selected American Novels
by Sholem Asch." Diss. East Texas State U, 1984.

E. M. Broner

1930 –

Primary Sources

Collected Works

Journal-Nocturnal, and Seven Stories. New York: Harcourt, 1968.
Contents: Journal-Nocturnal, The Woman Who Lived for Ten, A Magic Thing That Fixes, The Enemies, The Schva, Each Face Extinct, The Lone Ranger, The New Nobility.

Novels

Her Mothers. New York: Holt, 1975; Medallion Book. New York: Berkley, 1976; Bloomington: Indiana UP, 1985.

A Weave of Women. New York: Holt, 1978; Toronto: Bantam, 1982; Midland Book ed. Bloomington: Indiana UP, 1985.

Short Fiction in Anthologies

"The New Nobility." *Prize Stories 1968: The O. Henry Awards*. Ed. William Abrahams. Garden City: Doubleday, 1968. 18-49.

Short Fiction in Periodicals

"The Dancers." *Ms* Nov. 1983: 68-70, 114.

"Forget Me Not, O Jerusalem." *National Jewish Monthly* Oct. 1973: 28-33.

"The Freaks Speak." *North American Review* 257.3 (1972): 66-72.

"Is Fred Dead?" *Mother Jones* Jan. 1983: 35-41.

"Love and Ulpan in Jerusalem." *National Jewish Monthly* Mar. 1973: 12-14, 16, 18.

"Remember, Daughter, Remember the Tale." *Midstream* Aug.-Sept. 1969: 29-36.

"Saga of Great Men." *Commentary* Dec. 1971: 59-66.

"The Sheller." *New Letters* 50.2 (1984): 11-28.

"Traveler and His Telling." *Commentary* Sept. 1970: 69-73.

Secondary Sources

Articles and Chapters

Burstein, Janet. "Jewish-American Women's Literature: The Long Quarrel with God." *Studies in American Jewish Literature* [Kent State] 8.1 (1989): 9-25.

In this general article Burstein argues that while some Jewish women writers treat Jewish tradition as an adversary, others see it as a source of nurturance, some ignore it, and still others tell of a search for substitute commitments. Nonetheless, all seem to engage in a one-sided quarrel with God. Discusses briefly Jong, Kaufman, Shulman, Greenberg, Olsen, Rosen, Paley, Yezierska, and Broner.

Duncan, Erika. "The Hungry Jewish Mother." *The Lost Tradition: Mothers and Daughters in Literature*. Eds. Cathy N. Davidson and E. M. Broner. New York: Ungar, 1980. 231-41.

Argues the thesis that the underside of the nag and Yenta of Jewish fiction who devours the soul with every cup of chicken soup she gives is a woman who is asked almost from birth to give a nurturance she never receives. Illustrates the theme through the example of *Her Mothers*.

Kamel, Rose Yalow. "'I'm Pregnant with a Girl, Mother.' Gender and Self-Fragmentation in Broner's Fiction." *Aggravating the Conscience: Jewish-American Literary Mothers in the Promised Land*. Rose Yalow Kamel. American University Studies: Ser. 4, English Language and Literature 64. New York: Lang, 1988. 151-85.

A major chapter on *Her Mothers* as well as an introduction to Broner's background, life, and writing. Using the female affiliation theory, this essay argues that this is the paradigm of development for understanding the female children in the novel. A lengthy interpretive essay on women's relationships within the novel.

Reviews

Crain, Jane Larkin. "Three Novels." Rev. of *A Weave of Women. New York Times Book Review* 13 Aug. 1978: 26.

Sees the novel demanding readers to accept a vision of Everywoman as shackled by the chains of cultural oppression, with an emphasis on the particular degradations she finds inherent in Jewish traditions. Admits it has a certain narrative drive, but concludes that it is essentially silly and stuffed with all the cant of contemporary sexual politics.

Dalton, Elizabeth. "Books in Review." Rev. of *Journal/Nocturnal and Seven Stories. Commentary* Apr. 1969: 72.

Briefly describes the experimental columnar layout of *Journal/Nocturnal,* and praises the novel for its translation of the public atmosphere generated by the Vietnam War—the hatred and impotence and poisoned feelings—into private emotional conflict.

Frakes, James R. "Density Clarified." Rev. of *Journal/Nocturnal and Seven Stories. New York Times Book Review* 29 Sept. 1968: 56.

Praises *Journal/Nocturnal* for its escape from traditional form, yet calls the form ultimately irritating despite its being neither tricky nor self-indulgent.

Franks, Lucinda. "On the Arts." Rev. of *A Weave of Women*. *Ms.* July
  1978: 34.

Traces the healing women's rituals which operate in this community of
outcast women from all over the world which make up *A Weave of
Women*. Concludes that we are left in the end with a vivid impression of
the myths that have lead generations of women to instill a sense of inferiority and powerlessness into their daughters.

Kotker, Zane. "Fiction." Rev. of *A Weave of Women*. *Hadassah
  Magazine* Oct. 1978: 26.

Finds this "comic-poignant novel full of blood, beauty, hatred and
praise" a weave of "midrash-like tales." Briefly describes the stories and
concludes that Broner's "audacious tone is quite perfect."

Leonard, John. "Books of the Times." Rev. of *A Weave of Women*. *New
  York Times* 25 July 1978: C6.

Outlines Broner's newly elaborated myth of nurture and the epic rhythms
of a circular, sinuous, and ceremonial female consciousness. Warns readers not to expect a narrative sprint, but rather a series of weavings of
Bach repetitions.

McGrashan, Zena Beth. Rev. of *A Weave of Women*. *Studies in American
  Jewish Literature* [University Park, PA] 5.1 (1979): 73-74.

Identifies Broner's theme that women all over the world live on the thirteenth floor. Calls her writing exquisitely painful and sometimes
soaringly funny. Considers the prose lean and subtle and her knowledge
of love, legend, and language remarkable. Concludes that this is an
important book and not easily forgotten.

Napolin, Leah. "Demons Tweaking Her Funny Bone." Rev. of *Her
  Mothers*. *Ms.* July 1976: 105-06.

Calls the novel a bitter, fearless, and uproariously funny work about
birth, nurturance, the rebirth of all women, and the shaping and misshap-
ing of the people we are. Illuminates the plot, feminist ideology, and the
power of the novel. Identifies the book as Broner's answer to Lawrence's
Sons and Lovers, and Turgenev's *Fathers and Sons.*

Sachs, Susan Hersh. "The Mothers We've Had and the Mothers We
  Are." Rev. of *Her Mothers*. *Lilith* (Spr.-Sum. 1977): 40.

Describes *Her Mothers* as an experimental novel about female role models. Details the many types of women in the novel, and finally affirms that a woman must be unafraid despite being deprived of the ideal female role models.

Schwartz, Sheila, and Nancy Lynn Schwartz. "The House of Women." Rev. of *A Weave of Women. Nation* 4 Nov. 1978: 481-82.

Provides a detailed account of the characters, plot, and themes of the novel. Describes the novel as mystical and surreal, epic, and classic.

Silver, Adele Z. "Parched Souls and Full Hearts." Rev. of *Journal/Nocturnal and Seven Stories. Saturday Review* 23 Nov. 1968: 66.

Describes the contents and experimental form of *Journal/Nocturnal.* Complains that the irritating namelessness of the characters and the topicality of the plot smother the story's real artistic interest and the "parched soul of the wife." Praises its supple style and natural handling of poetic images. Accuses Broner of barely avoiding the trap of such well-worn subject matter as campus life and the Jewish heart.

Zeitlin, Leora. "Everything Being Equal." Rev. of *A Weave of Women. Present Tense* 6.1 (1978): 60-62.

Sees the novel as giving voice to Jewish-feminist issues such as why women are excluded from most rituals, why they are subservient to their husbands, why the tradition of slapping girls on the occasion of their first menses, etc. Calls the novel enjoyable, sensuous, poetic, and ceremonial.

Interviews

Hoy, Nancy Jo. "Of Holy Writing & Priestly Voices: A Talk with Esther Broner." *Massachusetts Review* 24.2 (1983): 254-69.

In interview, Broner describes her novels in terms of the changing roles of women, the female pilgrimage, the search for the mother, and the rediscovery of runaway daughters. She describes the search for a prose style to deify gender and for the shape of the spiritual quest. Also discusses her play and her short stories. Primarily elaborates her personal vision and celebration of women.

Robson, Ruthann. "A Conversation with E. M. Broner." *Kalliope: A Journal of Women's Art* 7.1-2 (1985): 51-57.

In this conversation with Robson, Broner discusses her work in the historical novel since the publication of *A Weave of Women*. Broner likens the speaking out of women to the discovery of their own exodus, a speaking of plagues, a singing of women's songs, a reaching out to absent prophets and friends in a circle of holiness. Contains a great deal of valuable personal anecdote and biography.

Windstone, Shebar. "Lilith Interview: Esther Broner." *Lilith* 1 (Fall-Wint. 1977-78): 32-36.

In a conversation with Windstone, Broner discusses the origins of her first work, *Summer Is a Foreign Land*; her grandmother, one of the novel's main characters; the necessity of the young writer to make a legend of herself or her family; her treatment of Black-Jewish relations in her stories; her attachment to Israel; her six-months teaching in Israel; *Her Mothers* as a work in progress; and her feelings about being female. She talks also of the place of women in rabbinic rites in Reform Judaism, women writers, and being female.

Biographical Sources

Broner, E. M. "Participant in the UNITAR Conference on 'Creative Women in Changing Societies.'" *Lilith* 8 (1981): 31.

Briefly describes Broner as being "de-legitimized as one of the member nations of the earth" at the conference because she was a Jewish/Israeli woman. No literary comments.

Davidson, Cathy N. "E. M. Broner." *Twentieth-Century American-Jewish Fiction Writers*. Ed. Daniel Walden. Detroit: Gale, 1984. Vol. 28 of *Dictionary of Literary Biography*. 94 vols. to date. 1978- . 26-28.

More than details of her life, this is a career biography, tracing the development of the author's canon, describing the contents and themes of her works, evaluating her reputation, and placing her in the larger context of American literary history. Includes a list of primary sources and illustrations.

Abraham Cahan

1860 – 1951

Primary Sources

Novels

The Rise of David Levinsky. New York: Harper, 1917; New York: Grosset, 1917; Novels of Distinction. New York: Grosset, 1928; New York: Smith, 1951; The Academy Library. New York: Torchbooks-Harper, 1960; New York: Colophon-Harper, 1966; Gloucester: Smith, 1969. Serialized in *McClure's* Apr. 1913: 92-106; May 1913: 73-85; June 1913: 131-52; July 1913: 116-28.

The White Terror and the Red; A Novel of Revolutionary Russia. New York: Barnes, 1905; London: Hodder, 1905; The Modern Jewish Experience. New York: Arno, 1975.

Yekl; A Tale of the New York Ghetto. New York: Appleton, 1896.

Collected Works

The Imported Bridegroom and Other Stories of the New York Ghetto. Boston: Houghton, 1898; The American Short Story Series 7. New York: Garrett, 1968; New York: Irvington, 1972.

Contents: The Imported Bridegroom, A Providential Match, A Sweat-Shop Romance, Circumstances, A Ghetto Wedding.

Yekl and The Imported Bridegroom and Other Stories of the New York Ghetto. New York: Dover, 1970.

Contents: Yekl, The Imported Bridegroom, A Providential Match, A Sweatshop Romance, Circumstances, A Ghetto Wedding.

Short Fiction in Anthologies

"A Ghetto Wedding." *Jewish-American Literature: An Anthology.* Ed. Abraham Chapman. New York: Mentor-NAL, 1974. 3-16.

Short Fiction in Periodicals

"Apostate of Chego-Chegg." *Century Illustrated Monthly Magazine* Nov. 1899: 94-105.

"Back to Dear Old Russia—the Disillusionment of Sonia Rogova." *Commercial Advertiser* 15 Apr. 1899: sec. 2: 1.

"Circumstances." *Cosmopolitan* Apr. 1897: 628-40.

"Daughter of Reb Avrom Leib." *Cosmopolitan* May 1900: 53-64.

"Dumitru and Sigrid." *Cosmopolitan* Mar. 1901: 493-501.

"A Ghetto Wedding." *Atlantic* Feb. 1898: 265-73.

"A Marriage By Proxy: A Story of the City." *Everybody's Magazine* Dec. 1900: 569-75.

"A Providential Match." *Short Stories* Feb. 1895: 191-213.

"Rabbi Eliezer's Christmas." *Scribner's* Dec. 1899: 661-68.

"A Sweat-Shop Romance." *Short Stories* June 1895: 129-43.

"Tzinchadzi of the Catskills." *Atlantic* Aug. 1901: 221-26.

Secondary Sources

Books

Chametzky, Jules. *From the Ghetto: The Fiction of Abraham Cahan.* Amherst: U of Massachusetts P, 1977. Excerpt rpt. as "The Father of American-Jewish Literature" in *Jewish Digest* Nov. 1977: 46-50.

Articles and Chapters

Angoff, Charles. "Dusting Off the Bookshelf." *Congress Weekly* 30 Jan. 1950: 14-15.

Comments that in the past decades there have been numerous books about Jews, their past, customs, New York lives, foibles, sociology, and religion. Yet few have provided the insights of *The Rise of David Levinsky*. Takes the reader slowly through the contents of the book pointing out its artistry and veracity. Considers David Levinsky, the character, as Cahan's single most important creation. Details some of the defects of the novel and concludes that it should be put back into print.

Bilik, Dorothy Seidman. "Backgrounds: Literary and Nonliterary." *Immigrant-Survivors: Post Holocaust Consciousness In Recent American Fiction.* Dorothy Seidman Bilik. Middletown: Wesleyan UP, 1981. 11-35.

Reviews the Jewish immigration to America up to the end of World War II. Discusses Cahan's *The Rise of David Levinsky* and Roth's *Call It Sleep*. Reissued in 1960, these two novels have created renewed interest in the Jewish American immigrant past and a post-Holocaust awareness. Discusses these novels in detail, relating the experiences of their protagonists to the social realities of Jews in American society. Also discusses Rosenfeld's *Passage from Home* as an example of Jewish writers such as Bellow and Schwartz, who show Jewish writing moving from adolescence to maturity but with their protagonists alienated both from their own Jewish roots and from the dominant culture.

Carlin, M. M. "The Rise of David Levinsky." *University of Capetown Studies in English* 9 (1979): 54-70.

Claims that Cahan exhibits unusual mastery of English in *The Rise of David Levinsky* due to his prior grasp of Russian, Hebrew, and Yiddish. Argues the particular value of his work because he is a Russian Jew of the revolutionary period, an American of the period of vast capitalist expansion, a commentator on Jewish life in New York City, and an inside observer of Jewish family life and psychology. Provides a recapitulation of the plot, a character study of David, and commentary on a series of events from the novel likely to yield such historical and sociological insights.

Chametzky, Jules. "Focus on Abraham Cahan's *The Rise of David Levinsky*: Boats Against the Current." *American Dreams, American Nightmares*. Ed. David Madden. Crosscurrents/Modern Critiques. Carbondale: Southern Illinois UP, 1970. 87-93. Rpt. in part in *From the Ghetto: The Fiction of Abraham Cahan*. Jules Chametzsky. Amherst: U of Massachusetts P, 1977. 125-44.

Discusses *The Rise of David Levinsky* as offering a paradigm for the fulfillments and horrors of fighting for and attaining the American Dream. Talks about Cahan's attempt to rid himself of Old World backwardness and his inevitably being forced back to a recognition of his own Jewishness. Also discusses his intention to accommodate the American and the East European Jewish immigrant to each other as the intent of this and other novels.

Chametzky, Jules. "Immigrant Fiction as Cultural Mediation." *Yiddish* 5.4 (1984): 14-21.

Discusses first the concept of mediation from a Marxist perspective, and argues that consciousness and its products are integral and constitutive elements of "reality," not mere reflections of some other more basic, primary reality. Notes that American immigrant culture produced such various forms and modes in profusion that it is valuable to see its function as mediator and creator of culture. Discusses *Yekl* and *Jews Without Money* from this perspective.

Chametzky, Jules. "Notes on the Assimilation of the American Jewish Writer: Abraham Cahan to Saul Bellow." *Jahrbuch fur Amerikastudien* 9 (1964): 173-180. Rpt. in part in *From the Ghetto: The Fiction of Abraham Cahan*. Jules Chametzky. Amherst: U of Massachusetts P, 1977. 57-74.

Chametzky claims that there have been three distinct phases of acculturation and adjustment for American Jewry, beginning with the familiar traumas of the early immigrants, proceeding to the stage of aggressive-defensiveness, and culminating in the 1950s with a secure sense of

American tolerance. This three-generation process is illustrated with reference to Abraham Cahan, Michael Gold, Clifford Odets, and Saul Bellow.

Chametzky, Jules. "Our Decentralized Literature: A Consideration of Regional, Ethnic, Racial,and Sexual Factors." *Jahrbuch fur Amerikastudien* 17 (1972): 56-72. Rpt. in part in *From the Ghetto: The Fiction of Abraham Cahan.* Jules Chametzky. Amherst: U of Massachusetts P, 1977. 57-74; *Our Decentralized Literature: Cultural Mediations in Selected Jewish and Southern Writers.* Jules Chametzky. Amherst: U of Massachusetts P, 1986. 21-45.

States "The considerable reputation that George Washington Cable, Abraham Cahan, Charles W. Chestnutt, and Kate Chopin enjoyed toward the end of the century was (and often still is) based on their being classified as regional or local color writers. This designation, however, served to ignore or minimize their true concerns, which went to the heart of a changing America's dilemmas: the racial grounds of the Southern tragedy, the stakes involved in the acculturation of immigrant populations, the assertion of black ethos, and the terms of women's entrapment within cultural assumptions." Discusses the role W. D. Howells played in promoting Cahan. Accuses Howells of harboring contradictory impulses toward a realist's establishment view of American literature and a more specific view of ethnic conflicts, an attitude which influences his reception of Cahan. Comments in considerable detail on Howells' glowing reception of *Yekl* in 1896.

Chametzky, Jules. "Regional Literature and Ethnic Realities." *Antioch Review* 31.3 (1971): 385-96. Rpt.in a longer version as "Our Decentralized Literature: A Consideration of Regional, Ethnic, Racial and Sexual Factors." *Jahrbuch fur Amerikastudien* 17 (1972): 56-72.

Contains a summary of materials already commented on at length in his previously published articles "Notes on the Assimilation of the American-Jewish Writer: Abraham Cahan to Saul Bellow," in *Jahrbuch fur Amerikastudien* Band 9, 1964. and "Our Decentralized Literature: A Consideration of Regional, Ethnic, Racial, and Sexual Factors," in *Jahrbuch fur Amerikastudien* Band 17, 1972.

Chametzky, Jules. "The Yiddish Fiction of Abraham Cahan." *Yiddish* 2.2-3 (1976): 7-22.

Provides a detailed account of the publication and reception of Cahan's Yiddish fiction. Also comments on Cahan's growth as a fiction writer and his response to his own success. Contains useful summaries of plot and character in each of these works along with thematic commentary.

"Chronicle and Comment." *Bookman* Jan. 1900: 428-30.

Discusses the negative reactions of some Jews to Cahan's depiction of ghetto life in New York in *Yekl* and the cultural chasm existing between the East Side Talmudic Jews and the more prosperous German-American Jews.

Dembo, L. S. "Levinsky and the Language of Aquisition." *The Monological Jew: A Literary Study.* L. S. Dembo. Madison: Wisconsin UP, 1988. 84-92.

Tries to answer the question of why Cahan in *The Rise of David Levinsky* omitted the struggles of the Jewish socialist movement in America to concentrate instead on the personal problems of a single, bourgeois man—to take as his central concern not class struggles, but the vicissitudes of life of an ambitious, but essentially non-political Russian immigrant. Uses Buber's theories of language as a valuable tool for examining the relationship between extreme individualism and language in this novel.

Engel, David. "The Discrepancies of the Modern: Reevaluating Abraham Cahan's *The Rise of David Levinsky.*" *Studies in American Jewish Literature* [University Park, PA] 5.2 (1979): 68-91. Joint issue with Yiddish 4.1. (1979). Rpt. in slightly expanded form as "The 'Discrepancies' of the Modern: Towards a Revaluation of Abraham Cahan's *The Rise of David Levinsky*" in *Studies in American Jewish Literature* [Albany] 2 (1982): 36-60.

Attributes Cahan's success in the novel to his capturing the "discrepancies" in his life that contribute to Levinsky's particular failures. Claims that this evocation of the failure of the halves of David's life (European/American, traditional/modern, faithful/apostate) creates the disturbing impression of Levinsky as a man somehow absent from his own life and self-estranged. Engel also argues that the novel is richly descriptive of that situation in time and history and feeling called "modernity," as well as being a useful chronicle of a phase of Jewish-American history.

Fiedler, Leslie A. "Genesis: The American-Jewish Novel Through the Thirties." *Midstream* 4.3 (1958): 21-33. Rpt. in *The Jew in the American Novel.* Leslie Fiedler. Herzl Institute Pamphlets 10. New

York: Herzel, 1959. 16-19; A Seven Star Book 5. 2nd ed. New York: Herzl, 1966. 16-19; "The Jew in the American Novel," *The Collected Essays of Leslie Fiedler*. 2 vols. New York: Stein, 1971. 2: 75-79; *To the Gentiles*. New York: Stein, 1972. 75-79.

Describes the main business of the marginal writing of American Jews in the 1920s to be the assertion that it is possible to establish an image of the Jew which is satisfying to both Jew and Gentile. Claims that the writing of the American-Jewish novel is essentially an act of assimilation, and that this effort on the part of the writers of the 20s fails to impress mainstream American readers for whom the images of the overgrown boy scout and hangdog lover projected by Hemingway's Cohn are the images that prevail in the imagination. Traces the historical evolution of images of the anti-Jewish stereotype from early to contemporary American literature. Details the work of Henry Harland-Luska as providing the basic conflicts of the Jewish-American novel, and then describes *The Rise of David Levinsky* as indicative of the erotic desire, latent in the newly emerging tradition, to become a Don Juan or to marry a *shiksa*. Sees its ultimate subject as the loneliness of the immigrant Jew among the philistinism of the prevailing culture and its delusive bourgeois values. Describes David's moral failure in terms of his failing on repeated occasions throughout the novel to find love and a woman. These, says Fiedler, are the failures of a Jew in love with love and with money.

Fine, David M. "Abraham Cahan, Stephen Crane, and the Romantic Tenement Tale of the Nineties." *American Studies* 14.1 (1973): 95-107.

Discusses *The Rise of David Levinsky* and *Maggie: A Girl of the Streets* as works which demonstrate the marketability of fiction about slum and tenement life of the period. Sees both novels in the context of ideological battles about the true nature of literary realism and in the context of both authors' relationships to W. D. Howells. Points out that while most of the tenement literature was reported through the eyes of a bourgeois commentator with whom the reader can identify, Crane and Cahan provide the uncomfortable moral insights of the insider whose loyalty is with the urban slum dweller, not the bourgeois reader. Hence, at the height of interest in tenement romances these writers "brazenly defied the conventional attitudes which characterized these tales. In these two novels poverty is not ennobling, women not inviolable, men not always hardworking, stoical and uncomplaining. Poverty does affect character and not for the best. Moreover, in these works . . . there is no middle-class narrator between us and the slums, no kindly guide leading us through the exotic netherworld of the city, interpreting for us, moralizing, justifying."

Fisch, Harold. "The Pact with the Devil." *Yale Review* 69.4 (1980): 520-32.

In a discussion of the myth of the pact with the devil in literature, Fisch briefly discusses *The Rise of David Levinsky* and finds it similar to Dreiser's Cowperwood trilogy in that Levinsky succumbs to the same sexual temptations and responds to the same urge for wealth and power. But for Levinsky, the demon is America itself. Concludes with Rosenfeld that this is not a Jewish novel, but "an exemplary treatment of one of the dominant myths of American capitalism."

Fletcher, John. "Comparing the Literatures: Or, What Happens When the American Dream Is Celebrated on Opposite Sides of the Fence." *Comparative Literature Studies* 13.2 (1976): 116-31.

Provides a theoretical discussion of whether comparative literature can properly sponsor comparisons between British and American literature. Fletcher then gives a brief reference to Cahan in the context of a discussion on the form of the American Dream in the American literary tradition.

Girgus, Sam B. "A Convert to America: Sex, Self, and Ideology in Abraham Cahan." *The New Covenant: Jewish Writers and the American Idea*. Sam B. Girgus. Chapel Hill: U of North Carolina P, 1984. 64-91.

Describes the phenomenon of Jewish radical socialists who, while critical of American culture and politics, were also great adherents to principles of the American Idea. This shift in Jewish intellectual life in America toward viewing America as an ideology, and toward seeing themselves as Jeremiahs working within an American tradition, is best illustrated in Cahan's *The Rise of David Levinsky*. Notes a split between Cahan's Yiddish and English writings, his development of a theory of realism in literature, and also his careful separation of propaganda and art. Traces his supposed conversion from socialism to Americanism. Accuses him of falling victim to Americanism as an ideology, and then compares the demonic progress of this dream with the failed dream of *The Great Gatsby*. Finally sees Levinsky as a symbol of impotence masked as power, and discusses his sexual attitudes, including his ambivalence toward women which results in making him an outcast. Traces this psychological maladjustment from David's earliest conceptions of himself as alien among aliens in Russia, his problematic relationship with his mother, and on down to the ending of the novel. Concludes that this novel exposes the underside of the American Dream.

Goldberg, Mark F. "Books: the Jew as lover: Exemplified by David Levinsky, Moses Herzog and Alex Portnoy." *National Jewish Monthly* Nov. 1969: 64, 66-67.

Provides a brief, comparative treatment of the characters David Levinsky, Moses Herzog, and Alex Portnoy as examples of the "raging, blunted or thwarted neurotic, surrounded by a constellation of urgent romantic and sexual difficulties," stemming from the tensions inherent within Jewish family relationships.

Greenspan, Ezra. *The Schlemiel Comes to America.* Metuchen: Scarecrow, 1983. 30-43, passim.

A general literary history of Cahan's life and contribution to American literature, with an emphasis on the character of the *schlemiel* in his works. Includes discussion on *The Rise of David Levinsky*.

Guttmann, Allen. "The Rise of a Lucky Few: Mary Antin and Abraham Cahan." *The Jewish Writer in America: Assimilation and the Crisis of Identity.* Allen Guttmann. New York: Oxford UP, 1971. 28-33, passim.

Provides a brief account of Cahan's life and writings, including an account of the plot and themes in *The Rise of David Levinsky*. Emphasizes the issue of assimilation in each work.

Harap, Louis. "Fiction in English by Abraham Cahan." *The Image of the Jew in American Literature: From Early Republic to Mass Immigration.* Louis Harap. Philadelphia: Jewish Publication Society of America, 1974. 485-524.

Provides a detailed socio-historical treatment of Cahan and his works touching upon nearly every theme and idea expressed up to this point in time. A useful summary article focusing on the image of the Jew in American literature and Cahan's contribution to the tradition.

Higham, John. Introduction. *The Rise of David Levinsky.* New York: Torch-Harper, 1960. v-xii.

A useful, condensed summary of plot, character, background history, biography, and immigrant sociology concerning the novel. Provides also a short account of the reception of *The Rise of David Levinsky*.

Hindus, Milton. "Abraham Cahan: Early American Realist." *Jewish Heritage* (Fall 1964): 38-44.

Details the important relationship between W. D. Howells and Cahan referred to in Cahan's memoirs and Howells's championing of *The Rise of David Levinsky*. An important historical source document.

Kahn, Lothar. *"The Rise of David Levinsky*: Fifty Years After." *Chicago Jewish Forum* 26.1 (1967): 2-5.

Gives a brief account of the strengths and weaknesses of *The Rise of David Levinsky* after fifty years and re-introduces the novel. Claims it to be a minor classic which has passed the test of time. Concludes that the novel is an important social document with some remarkable socio-historical parallels with contemporary issues such as materialism.

Kress, Susan. "Women and Marriage in Abraham Cahan's Fiction." *Studies in American Jewish Literature* [Albany] 3 (1983): 26-39.

Provides a very detailed treatment of women and marriage in the novels of Cahan, commenting on the institution of marriage in the lives of Jewish-American immigrants, the anxiety of the unmarried, the claustrophobia of the married, and related topics. Focuses primarily on the short fiction, pointing out how Cahan avoids period stereotypes, and presents the limitations of the marital arrangement from the perspectives of women. Sees this body of fiction challenging the assumptions of romantic fiction. Claims that the fiction offers poignant and compassionate portraits of women transcending circumstance.

Levenberg, Diane. "David Levinsky and His Women." *Midstream* Aug./Sept. 1980: 51-53.

Sees the novel's central incident as the death of David Levinsky's mother, an event that leaves the gaping psychological hunger that motivates all his future efforts to nurture and nourish his emotional needs. Comments also on the guilt and frustration the young Talmudic scholar feels when he realizes his mother died for him, and he was powerless to save her. Much is made of the sustaining role his mother has played and her desires for him to be a famous Talmudic scholar. Describes America as the woman he substitutes, a woman he will woo, seduce, and ultimately rape. Hence, what has been called his metaphysical loneliness by other critics is really this drive. The women like Dora, with whom he falls in love, are all women who live in the same house and temporarily fill in for his mother. Concludes that everything else he does is mere distraction from this original pain.

Lyons, Bonnie. "David Levinsky: Modern Man As Orphan." *Tulane Studies in English* 23 (1978): 85-93.

Sees David Levinsky as a Stephen Daedelus wandering through America in search of his father and the novel as a central exploration of the modern condition of alienation. Emphasizing this aspect of the novel, Lyons claims, gives focus and coherence to "the disparate and superficially connected aspects, particularly the seemingly unrelated business pursuits and abortive love life. Second, it clarifies the novel's genuine significance for the modern reader by allowing us to see the novel as more than a dusty, rambling period piece interesting only in terms of literary history or nostalgia."

Macy, John. "Abraham Cahan." *The Critical Game.* John Macy. New York: Boni, 1922. 227-33.

An early general commentary on Cahan and the novel. Comments on the strong feeling expressed in the book and then on its absence of eloquence. Locates it stylistically as a "Russian" novel, thus calling it a singular and solitary performance in American fiction.

Marovitz, Sanford E. "The Lonely New Americans of Abraham Cahan." *American Quarterly* 20.2 (1968): 196-210.

Explores the element of the "Americanized," secularized Jew in Cahan's ghetto fiction by tracing it through his novels and tales. Attempts to prove that it was not the sweatshop that defeated Cahan's soul-racked immigrants, but an essential weakness or flaw in the characters themselves. Those who traded their faith for the gospel of materialism suffered the pangs of loneliness regardless of their wealth, prestige, or position; those, however, who clung to their heritage, despite poverty and hard work, avoided the constant sting of isolation, disillusion, and despair.

Marovitz, Sanford E. "The Secular Trinity of a Lonely Millionaire: Language, Sex and Power in *The Rise of David Levinsky*." *Studies in American Jewish Literature* [Albany] 2 (1982): 20-35.

Sees *The Rise of David Levinsky* as centering on three intricately interrelated themes: language, sex, and power. The initial discussion focuses on Levinsky's attraction/repulsion to his own sexuality, his relationship with his mother, and later adult debauchery. Notes the role power and language play in the courtships. Discusses Levinsky's intense drive for both material power and sexual power as being linked with his dual view of women as inferior in the workplace and superior in the chivalric arena of love and courtship. Notes that as a lover, he pays much attention to the kinds of language spoken on the street by young men. Concludes that his final state is one of control over words, women, and wealth—his central goal throughout the book.

Marovitz, Sanford E. *"Yekl*: The Ghetto Realism of Abraham Cahan." *American Literary Realism, 1870-1910* 2.3 (1969): 271-73.

Discusses how the ghetto realism of *Yekl* at first failed to appeal to his readers. Locates Cahan with the literary realism of Howells, Garland, and Norris. Claims that the realistic detail of *Yekl* is emotionally charged and impressionistic; Cahan's East Siders rise above their limitations as Russian immigrants. The book succeeds because of its "happy conjunction of objectivity, sentiment, and universality."

Michel, Sonja. *"Yekl* and *Hester Street*: Was Assimilation Really Good for the Jews?" *Literature/Film Quarterly* 5.2 (1977): 142-46.

Primarily a comparison between Cahan's *Yekl* and Silver's film version of it in *Hester Street*. Pays considerable attention to the depictions of old world and new world women in both works. Sees some overtly feminist inclinations in the film direction. Concludes that the world the immigrants entered was not one of unmitigated opportunity, as both book and film show.

Miller, Gabriel. "Jews Without Manners." *Screening the Novel: Rediscovered American Fiction in Film*. Gabriel Miller. New York: Ungar, 1980. 1-18.

Claims that in *Hester Street*, Joan Micklin Silver has transformed *Yekl* into a vibrant, amusing study of manners and morals in transition—in effect translating Cahan's period piece into the timeless language of comedy, which embraces both the old and the new worlds. A detailed treatment of both the novel and the film version.

Pinsker, Sanford. "Sixty Years of David Levinsky: An Abiding Presence." *Reconstructionist* Nov. 1977: 13-20.

Argues that the novel is written in confessional mode and that it tries to create its own kind of expiation. "The pendulum which presumably swings from the sacred to the profane [in the novel] is complicated by the very psychodynamics of a confessional mode. Levinsky labors under the grand illusion that candor is a conscious and, therefore, controllable matter. He pulls it out like a checkbook, paying off guilts both real and imagined." Pinsker goes on to discuss honesty and subterfuge, Freudian overtones, the psychic costs of upward mobility, assimilation, and related issues.

Richards, Bernard G. "Introduction: Abraham Cahan Cast in a New Role." *Yekl* and *The Imported Bridegroom and Other Stories of the New York Ghetto*. Abraham Cahan. New York: Dover, 1970. iii-viii.

Describes the background and history of Abraham Cahan, in particular his contribution as editor of *The Jewish Daily Forward*, as a thrilling public speaker, and as a writer.

Rosenfeld, Isaac. "America, Land of the Sad Millionaire." *Commentary* Aug. 1952: 131-35. Rpt. in *Breakthrough: A Treasury of Contemporary American-Jewish Literature*. Eds. Irving Malin and Irwin Stark. New York: McGraw, 1964. 259-66; as "David Levinsky: The Jew as American Millionaire" in *An Age of Enormity: Life and Writing in the Forties and Fifties*. Isaac Rosenfeld. Cleveland: World, 1962. 273-81; *Jewish American Literature: An Anthology of Fiction, Poetry, Autobiography, and Criticism*. Ed. Abraham Chapman. New York: Mentor-NAL, 1974. 618-25, and as "The Fall of David Levinsky" in *Preserving the Hunger: An Isaac Rosenfeld Reader*. Ed. Mark Shechner. Detroit: Wayne State UP, 1988. 152-59.

A brief evaluation of the novel praising it as one of the best fictional studies of the Jewish character available in English, and at the same time, as an intimate and sophisticated account of American business culture.

Sanders, Ronald. "The American Dream: Abe Cahan as the East Side Maggid." *Jewish Heritage* 12.3 (1970): 14-17.

Claims that what *The Jewish Daily Forward* has in common with Cahan's fiction is the consistently didactic purpose of both. Traces briefly the convergence of Cahan's socialism with mainstream Jewish-American attitudes in the 1930s. Discourses generally on the subject of Cahan and the American Dream.

Sherman, Bernard. "First Generation: The Socialist Imagination." *The Invention of the Jew: Jewish-American Education Novels (1916-1964)*. Bernard Sherman. New York: Yoseloff, 1969. 43-48, passim.

Provides a brief account of *The Rise of David Levinsky* as a Jewish-American *bildungsroman* or novel of education. Also briefly discusses his socialism.

Singer, David. "David Levinsky's Fall: A Note on the Liebman Thesis."
  American Quarterly 19.4 (1967): 696-706.

Singer first cites the Liebman theory that the Eastern European Jewish
immigrants were not nearly as orthodox as historians and literary critics
have supposed. Then he argues that early criticism of *The Rise of David
Levinsky*, which assumes the myth that they were largely religious and
orthodox, has distorted a proper interpretation of the book. David's break
with orthodoxy came before he arrived in America because of the series
of blows to his world view he sustains before he leaves Antomir.
Concludes that in Antomir he finds an island of modernism that seriously
undermines his faith.

Sollors, Werner. "Some Tales of Consent and Descent." *Beyond
  Ethnicity: Consent and Descent in American Culture*. New York:
  Oxford UP, 1986. 149-73.

Discusses *Yekl* and other late nineteenth-century novels as they reveal
how Americans perceive, feel, and conceptualize the harmony or conflict
between ethnic and national loyalties, showing how the stories support
theories, and how theory functions as a form of storytelling.

Strout, Cushing. "Personality and Cultural History in the Novel: Two
  American Examples." *New Literary History* 1.3 (1970): 423-38. Rpt.
  in *The Veracious Imagination: Essays on American History,
  Literature, and Biography*. Cushing Strout. Middletown: Wesleyan
  UP, 1981. 245-62; *Ourselves/Our Past: Psychological Approaches to
  American History*. Ed. Robert J. Brugger. Baltimore: Johns Hopkins
  UP, 1981. 244-56.

Argues that literary sources can be of specific value to historians as they
reveal the author's private life, a people's conflicts, and their prevailing
attitudes. Hence, the article analyzes Cahan's Jewish immigrant world in
late nineteenth-century New York City with regard to ethnic identity,
social mobility, the psychic costs of living in a pluralistic society, and so
on. Strout begins with such a consideration of *Esther* by Henry Adams,
and then deals with *The Rise of David Levinsky*. The common thread in
the latter essay seems to be an interpretation of American capitalism
based on Cahan's novel.

Syrkin, Marie. "Jewish Awareness in American Literature." *The
  American Jew: A Reappraisal*. Ed. Oscar I. Janowsky. Philadelphia:
  Jewish Pub. Soc. of America, 1964. 211-26.

Describes Jewish awareness in American literature under the general headings: The Twenties and Thirties—Taking Stock; The Forties: Reaction to Catastrophe; Integration or Assimilation; and The Drama. A major historical survey which deals in particular depth with the early contributions of Cahan and the influence of *The Jewish Daily Forward*.

Vogel, Dan. "Cahan's *Rise of David Levinsky*: Archetype of American Jewish Fiction." *Judaism* 22.3 (1973): 278-87.

Portrays the story of *The Rise of David Levinsky* as archetypal of the Jewish-American novel, not in the sense of racial memory, but in the sense of community experience during the three generations since the flood of East European Jewish immigration in the 1880s. Claims that Levinsky is the prototype whose features of personality and career, whether ill or for good, are reborn in later protagonists of this genre.

Walden, Daniel. "The American Yiddish Writer: From Cahan to Singer." *Ethnic Literatures Since 1776: The Many Voices of America, Part 2*. Eds. Wolodymyr T. Zyla and Wendell M. Aycock. Proceedings, Comparative Literature Symposium, Texas Tech U 9. Lubbock: Texas Tech P, 1978. 591-604.

In an article discussing the role of writers in helping Jews move from the *shtetl* into the mainstream of life, Cahan is considered the major influence in America through his tremendously popular Yiddish newspaper *The Forward* and his novels, particularly *The Rise of David Levinsky* with its essential message of adaptation to the new conditions. Describes the Americanization of David and its implications for the immigrant Jews, including Cahan himself, undergoing a similar process.

Walden, Daniel. "Urbanism, Technology and the Ghetto in the Novels of Abraham Cahan, Henry Roth, and Saul Bellow." *American Jewish History* 73.3 (1984): 296-306.

Discusses the socio-historical role of the urban ghetto as portrayed in the works of Cahan, Roth, and Bellow. Provides an account of the power of the American experience to transform the newly arrived Eastern European masses as revealed in the writings of Cahan.

Weinstein, Bernard. "Cahan's David Levinsky: An Inner Profile." *MELUS* 10.3 (1983): 47-53.

Discusses the inner life revealed in the account of David Levinsky's life, eschewing former interpretations concentrating on the novel as mere critique of capitalism or a thinly disguised social history. Claims the novel to be archetypal in its dimensions and a work of intense psychological realism.

Yudkin, Leon I. "The Immigrant Experience in America." *Jewish Writing and Identity in the Twentieth Century.* Leon I. Yudkin. London: Helm, 1982. 27-44.

Discusses the Jewish immigration to America as the most remarkable demographic event in Jewish history and shows its impact on America as it emerged as a great world power. Also sees the Jewish writers Cahan, Lewisohn, Hecht, Fuchs, Michael Gold, and Henry Roth as expanding the range of an exotic consciousness in America but also showing the "Jew on the outside trying to get in, or perhaps coming to terms with his outsider status." Discusses the major works of each of these writers and how they demonstrate the struggles, the conflicts, and the costs of their Jewish protagonists to become assimilated.

Zanger, Jules. "David Levinsky: Master of Pilpul." *Papers on Language and Literature* 13.3 (1977): 283-94.

Concentrates on presenting the case that *The Rise of David Levinsky* is more than an immigrant novel, it is a coherent work of art. Defends the novel against charges that its syntax and episodic structure disqualify it as good art. Argues that it is much more than transcribed personal history. Sees the central artistic tensions as being the dualities between the spiritual and the material, the mystical and the rational modes of perception, selflessness and selfishness, relations between man and God, and relations between man and man. David's engagement in *pilpul* or legalistic hairsplitting provides the unifying aspect of his characterization that is a developed personality theory in the novel.

Zlotnick, Joan. "Abraham Cahan, A Neglected Realist." *American Jewish Archives* 23.1 (1971): 33-46.

Explores several facets of Cahan's realism in a variety of his works of fiction: complex characters; modification of happy endings and the demand for poetic justice; international themes; socio-political issues; vernacular, colloquial, and dialectal speech; commonplace characters; comic tone; and contemporary settings.

Reviews

"Abraham Cahan and David Levinsky." Rev. of *Rise of David Levinsky*. *New York Call* 7 Oct. 1917: 15.

Primarily a recounting of Cahan's personal history and the correspondences between his own life and that of his hero, David Levinsky. Considers the novel *The Rise of David Levinsky* to have been written with a socialist purpose, but to have maintained high aesthetic standards as well.

B., R. "Americans in the Making." Rev. of *The Rise of David Levinsky*. *New Republic* 2 Feb. 1918: 30-32.

Claims that this novel is written with insight and power, and sets a new standard for the subject matter of the Jewish immigrant in the promised land.

Banks, Nancy Huston. "The New York Ghetto." Rev. of *Yekl: A Tale of the New York Ghetto. Bookman* Oct. 1896: 157-58.

Yekl is described mainly in the light of the background and setting it establishes. Describes the characters, and complains that the book has too much journalistic familiarity and too little literary reserve. Concludes that this is not realism in its best and widest sense.

Bellow, Saul. "Up From the Pushcart." Rev. of *The Rise of David Levinsky. New York Times Book Review* 15 Jan. 1961: 10.

Describes his pleasure in discovering that *The Rise of David Levinsky* is a tough book written by a tough-minded man, and not the kind of Yiddish daily romance his mother used to weep over. Concludes that Cahan was not a doctrinaire Socialist, nor simple-minded, nor a great literary artist, but that he had the instincts of a fine novelist with none of the false piety of later generations of Jewish writers.

Claghorn, Kate Holladay. Rev. of *The Rise of David Levinsky*. *Survey* 1 Dec. 1917: 260, 262.

Describes the contents of *The Rise of David Levinsky*, and complains that, had it been written anonymously, it might have been taken for a cruel satire of a hated race by an anti-Semite. Deplores the crude, selfish, sensual, tasteless, foolish, ignorant, ambitious, and egotistical characters.

"An East Side Romance." Rev. of *Yekl: A Tale of the New York Ghetto. New York Times* 12 July 1896: 31.

Describes the contents of *Yekl* and a little of Cahan's background. Commends Cahan's truthful reporting of the ghetto and his avoidance of sensationalism.

"Glimpses of Reality." Rev. of *The Rise of David Levinsky*. *Nation* 18 Oct. 1917: 431-32.

The Rise of David Levinsky is described here as a naturalistic novel, appalling, spontaneous, and sincere. Calls it a study in the Yiddish character. Describes a little of the story.

Hapgood, Hutchins. "A Realistic Novel." Rev. of *The White Terror and the Red*. *Critic* Jun. 1905: 560-61.

Commends Cahan for his background knowledge of Jewish history and life as evident in *The White Terror and the Red*. Calls it a sweet and fully realized piece of fiction which stands out in seriousness, meaning, and genuine interest from the mass of hastily digested and flimsily written novels. Details contents.

Howells, William Dean. "New York Low Life in Fiction." Rev. of *Yekl: A Tale of the New York Ghetto*. *New York World* 26 July 1896: 18.

A lengthy essay on the New York Jewish ghetto and the first literary attempts to present the life of the streets. Commends Crane in *The Red Badge of Courage* and Cahan in *Yekl* for presenting the truest pictures of East Side life. Provides a general essay on Cahan's virtues as a realist. Commends *Yekl* for being a story well told, and for having such a strong sense of character.

Howells, William Dean. "Some Books of Short Stories." Rev. of *The Imported Bridegroom and Other Stories of the New York Ghetto*. *Literature* 31 Dec. 1898: 629.

Describes these Russian stories of Yiddish life as very important. Sees Cahan's art as naturalistic, his knowledge of Hebrew perfect, and his humor unsparing.

"In Darkest Russia." Rev. of *The White Terror and the Red*. *American Monthly Review of Reviews* June 1905: 763.

Calls the novel a fair, competent, and powerful book about revolutionary Russia. Characterizes it weak as a novel but strong as a sociological study.

Kessner, Carole S. "*Hester Street*: Film and Fiction." Rev. of *Hester Street*. *Reconstructionist* Jan. 1976: 18-22.

Reviews the bicentennial-year film *Hester Street* based on Cahan's novel *Yekl: A Tale of the New York Ghetto*.

"Latest Works of Fiction." Rev of *The Rise of David Levinsky*. *New York Times Book Review* 16 Sept. 1917: 341-42.

Calls *The Rise of David Levinsky* a vividly convincing depiction of the rag trade. Details the contents of the book. Sees its major themes as the vivid portrayal of the eternal struggle between materialism, idealism, and business.

LeFevre, Edwin. "Abraham Cahan's *The White Terror and the Red*." Rev. of *The White Terror and the Red*. *Bookman* Apr. 1905: 186-88.

Discusses the depiction of Underground Russia in *The White Terror and the Red*. Notes that this book has sensational episodes, a gallery of interesting types, a vivid picture of history in the making, and is a work of high art. Calls Cahan a master Russian realist. Provides an elaborate account of the contents.

"Literature." Rev. of *Yekl: A Tale of the New York Ghetto*. *Critic: An Illustrated Weekly Review of Literature* 25 July 1896: 53.

Calls Cahan a local-color writer who feels he can expose his sordid and unpleasant observations of life in the ghetto. Finds these "neither pleasing nor delightful" and details a distraction to the touching story of a family destroyed by incompatibility created by the immigration from Russia to America. Also objects to his "phonetic fidelity" to the mixture of English and Yiddish speech of his characters. Concludes that this book provides matter for thought for those interested in social and ethnological problems of Jewish immigrants.

Macy, John. "The Story of a Failure." Rev. of *The Rise of David Levinsky*. *Dial* 22 Nov. 1917: 521-22.

Considers this story of the vanity of great riches one of the most searching and sincere. Praises Cahan for his moral sense and accurate portrait of both the Jewish business world and, by extension, that of America generally. Admires the philosophical distance the author maintains and what might be considered a lack of emphasis. Sees this novel's antecedents in the great nineteenth-century Russian novel with its vast, impartial, yet sympathetic panoply of character types.

Marcosson, J. F. "Love in the Ghetto." Rev. of *The Imported Bridegroom and Other Stories. Bookman* Aug. 1898: 513-14.

Describes *The Imported Bridegroom and Other Stories* primarily in terms of its contents and particularly its characters.

"A Revolutionary Novel of Russia." Rev. of *The White Terror and the Red. New York Times Saturday Review of Books and Art* 22 Apr. 1905: 258.

Describes *The White Terror and the Red* as a sad, graphic, fictional account of life in Russia during the period of the revolution, and of the underground experience. Commends the novel for the quality of its information.

Sanders, Ronald. "Up the Road to Materialism." Rev. of *The Rise of David Levinsky. New Republic* 6 Mar. 1961: 17-18.

Sees the novel as a classic American success story. Excellent plot summary.

"Stories of the Ghetto." Rev. of *The Imported Bridegroom and Other Stories of the New York Ghetto. New York Times Saturday Review of Books and Art* 14 May 1898: 321.

Describes these stories of the ghetto as evidencing keen sympathy and observation which make a fine contribution to the story of the foreign Hebrew in America.

Ware, Ella Reeve. "Literature of the Ghetto." Rev. of *The Imported Bridegroom and Other Stories of the New York Ghetto. New York Times Saturday Review of Books and Art* 2 July 1898: 442.

Calls these stories vivid character sketches whose relation to life in the ghetto are remarkable. Details the contents of nearly all the stories.

Biographical Sources

Cahan, Abraham. *The Education of Abraham Cahan.* Trans. Leon Stein, Abraham P. Conan and Lynn Davison. Philadelphia: Jewish Pub. Soc. of America, 1969. Vols. 1 and 2 of *Bleter Frun mein Leben.*

Chametzky, Jules. "Abraham Cahan." *Twentieth-Century American-Jewish Fiction Writers.* Ed. Daniel Walden. Detroit: Gale, 1984. Vol. 28 of *Dictionary of Literary Biography.* 94 vols. to date. 1978- . 28-35.

More than details of his life, this is a career biography, tracing the development of the fiction, describing the contents and themes of his works, evaluating his reputation, and placing him in the larger context of American literary history. Includes lists of primary and secondary sources and a character portrait.

Engel, David. "Abraham Cahan." *American Novelists 1910-1945, Part 1: Louis Adamic-Vardis Fisher*. Ed. James J. Martine. Detroit: Gale, 1981. Vol. 9 of *Dictionary of Literary Biography*. 94 vols. to date. 1978- . 117-22.

More than details of his life, this is a career biography, tracing the development of the author's canon, describing the contents and themes of his works, evaluating his reputation, and placing him in the larger context of American literary history. Includes lists of primary and secondary sources and a portrait.

Gollomb, Joseph. "Interesting People: Abraham Cahan." *American Magazine* Oct. 1912: 672-74.

A tribute to Cahan describing him as "editor, family advisor, lay preacher, comrade, critic, *litterateur*, teacher, and political leader all in one" to people of the East Side. Goes on to describe the contents of *The Forward* and its social power.

Hindus, Milton. "Abraham Cahan." *The Old East Side: An Anthology*. Ed. Milton Hindus. Philadelphia: Jewish Pub. Soc. of America, 1969. 17-21.

A traditional biographical tribute and essay detailing Cahan's life and work.

Kirk, Rudolf, and Clara M. Kirk. "Abraham Cahan and William Dean Howells: The Story of a Friendship." *American Jewish Historical Quarterly* 52.1-4 (1962): 27-43.

A detailed historical account of the seminal friendship between Howells and Cahan.

Poole, Ernest. "Abraham Cahan: Socialist-Journalist-Friend of the Ghetto." *Outlook* 28 Oct. 1911: 467-78.

An early account of both Cahan's life and achievements, depicting him as a great friend and aid to the immigrant populations. Written in the first person, this is a delightful, firsthand account of the author's meeting with Cahan. Interspersed are passages of direct reportage in Cahan's own voice telling of his childhood and later life.

Sanders, Ronald. "How a Publicist Became a Man of Letters." *The Downtown Jews: Portraits of an Immigrant Generation*. Ronald Sanders. New York: Harper, 1969. 181-204.

A detailed critical and interpretive account of the life, beliefs, contributions, and myth of Cahan.

Schack, William, and Sarah Schack. "The Schooling of Abraham Cahan." *Commentary* Nov. 1954: 457-65.

A biographical account of Cahan based on the first volume of his five-volume Yiddish autobiography, then not yet translated into English.

Strother, French. "Abraham Cahan, A Leader of the Jews." *World's Work* Aug. 1913: 470-74.

A sketch of and an admiring tribute to the life and accomplishments of Cahan.

Waldinger, Albert. "Abraham Cahan and Palestine." *Jewish Social Studies* 39.1-2 (1977): 75-92.

Contains a detailed account of Cahan's visit to Israel in 1925.

Wexelstein, Leon. "Abraham Cahan." *American Mercury* Sept. 1926: 88-94.

An early biographical account of the life of Cahan and the progress of his career as journalist and writer.

Bibliographies

Jeshurin, Ephim. *Abraham Cahan Bibliography*. New York: United Vilner Relief Committee, 1941.

Includes both primary and secondary sources, and English and Yiddish citations.

Marovitz, Sanford E., and Lewis Fried. "Abraham Cahan (1860-1951): An Annotated Bibliography." *American Literary Realism, 1870-1910* 3.3 (1970): 197-243.

Dissertations

Gartner, Carol Blicker. "A New Mirror for America: The Fiction of the Immigrant of the Ghetto, 1890-1930." Diss. New York U, 1970.

Gitenstein, Rose Barbara. "Versions of the Yiddish Literary Tradition in Jewish-American Literature: Isaac Bashevis Singer, Abraham Cahan, and Saul Bellow." Diss. U of North Carolina at Chapel Hill, 1984.

Goldman, Irene Carolyn. "Captains of Industry and Their Mates: A New Look at the American Business Novel from Howells to Dreiser." Diss. Boston U, 1986.

Gordon, Nicholas K. "Jewish and American: A Critical Study of the Fiction of Abraham Cahan, Anzia Yezierska, Waldo Frank and Ludwig Lewisohn." Diss. Stanford University, 1968.

Laufer, Pearl David. "Between Two Worlds: The Fiction of Anzia Yezierska." Diss. U of Maryland, 1981.

In addition to discussing Yezierska, Laufer also discusses *The Rise of David Levinsky* as a novel that deals with the Jewish immigrant experience.

Pollock, Theodore Marvin. "The Solitary Clarinetist: A Critical Biography of Abraham Cahan, 1860-1917." Diss. Columbia U, 1959.

Tewarie, Bhoendradatt. "A Comparative Study of Ethnicity in the Novels of Saul Bellow and V. S. Naipaul." Diss. Pennsylvania State U, 1983.

Includes a brief discussion of *The Rise of David Levinsky*.

Waldinger, Albert. "Abraham Cahan as Novelist, Critic, and Folk Advocate." Diss. Boston U, 1971.

Hortense Calisher

1911 –

Primary Sources

Novels

Age. New York: Weidenfeld, 1987; Large print ed. Thorndike: Thorndike, 1988.

The Bobby-Soxer. Garden City: Doubleday, 1986.

Eagle Eye. New York: Arbor, 1973; New York: St. Martin, 1975.

False Entry. Boston: Little, 1961; London: Secker, 1962; New York: Weidenfeld, 1988.

Journal From Ellipsis. Boston: Little, 1965; London: Secker, 1966.

Mysteries of Motion. New York: Doubleday, 1983.

The New Yorkers. Boston: Little, 1969; London: Cape, 1970; New York: Avon [Cited in PBIP, 1970]; New York: Weidenfeld, 1988.

On Keeping Women. New York: Arbor, 1977; New York: Berkley, 1979.

Queenie. New York: Arbor, 1971; New York: Dell [Cited in PBIP, 1972]; London: Allen, 1973.

The Railway Police, and The Last Trolley Ride. Boston: Little, 1966.

Standard Dreaming. New York: Arbor, 1972, 1983; New York: Dell, 1974.

Textures of Life. Boston: Little, 1963; London: Secker, 1963.

Collected Works

The Collected Stories of Hortense Calisher. New York: Arbor, 1975, 1977, The Arbor House Library of Contemporary Americana. New York: Arbor, 1984.

Contents: In Greenwich There Are Many Gravelled Walks; Heartburn; The Night Club in the Woods; Two Colonials; The Hollow Boy; The Rehabilitation of Ginevra Leake; The Woman Who Was Everybody; A Christmas Carillon; Il Ploe:r Da Mo Koe:r; If You Don't Want to Live I Can't Help You; A Wreath for Miss Totten; Time, Gentlemen!; May-ry; The Coreopsis Kid; A Box of Ginger; The Pool of Narcissus; The Watchers; The Gulf Between; The Sound of Waiting; Old Stock; The Rabbi's Daughter; The Middle Drawer; The Summer Rebellion; What a Thing, to Keep a Wolf in a Cage!; Songs My Mother Taught Me; So Many Rings to the Show; One of the Chosen; Point of Departure; Letitia, Emeritus; The Seacoast of Bohemia; Mrs. Fay Dines on Zebra; Saturday Night; Little Did I Know; Night Riders of Northville; In the Absence of Angels; The Scream on Fifty-Seventh Street.

Extreme Magic, a Novella and Other Stories. Boston: Little, 1964; London: Secker, 1964.

Contents: Il Ploe:r Da Mo Koe:r, Two Colonials, A Christmas Carillon, The Rabbi's Daughter, Little Did I Know, The Gulf Between, Songs My Mother Taught Me, If You Don't Want To Live I Can't Help You, Extreme Magic.

In the Absence of Angels: Stories. Boston: Little, 1951; London: Heinemann, 1953; Toronto: Little, 1963.

Contents: In Greenwich There Are Many Gravelled Walks; Point of

Departure; One of the Chosen; The Woman Who Was Everybody; Heartburn; A Wreath for Miss Totten; Letitia, Emeritus; Night Riders of Northville; In the Absence of Angels; A Box of Ginger; The Watchers; The Sound of Waiting; The Pool of Narcissus; Old Stock; The Middle Drawer.

Saratoga, Hot. Garden City: Doubleday, 1985.

Contents: Gargantua; Real Impudence; The Library; The Sound Track; The Passenger; The Tenth Child; Survival Techniques; Saratoga, Hot

Tale for the Mirror, a Novella and Other Stories. Boston: Little, 1962; London: Secker, 1963.

Contents: The Rehabilitation of Ginevra Leake; So Many Rings to the Show; The Night Club in the Woods; The Seacoast of Bohemia; Time, Gentlemen!; May-ry; Saturday Night; What a Thing, to Keep a Wolf in a Cage!; The Hollow Boy; Mrs. Fay Dines on Zebra; The Coreopsis Kid; The Scream on Fifty-Seventh Street; Tale for the Mirror.

Short Fiction in Anthologies

"A Christmas Carillon." *Prize Stories 1955: The O. Henry Awards.* Eds. Paul Engle and Hansford Martin. Garden City: Doubleday, 1955. 68-84.

"Heartburn." *American Short Stories since 1945.* Ed. John Hollander. New York: Harper, 1968. 73-84.

"Il Ploe:r Da Mo Koe:r." *The Shape of Fiction.* Eds. Leo Hamalian and Frederick Karl. New York: McGraw, 1967. 449-56.

"In Greenwich There Are Many Gravelled Walks." *The Best American Short Stories, 1951.* Ed. Martha Foley. Boston: Houghton, 1951. 45-59; *Great American Short Stories.* Ed. Wallace Stegner. New York: Dell, 1957: 493-511. *Mid-Century.* Ed. Orville Prescott. New York: Washington Square, 1957. 173-89; *Fifty Best American Short Stories, 1915-1965.* Ed. Martha Foley. Boston: Houghton, 1965. 438-52.

"In the Absence of Angels." *Writer's Choice.* Ed. Rust Hills. New York: McKay, 1974. 37-48.

"The Middle Drawer." *55 Short Stories from the New Yorker*. New York: Simon, 1949. 86-95; *Full Measure: Modern Short Stories on Aging*. Ed. Dorothy Sennett. St. Paul: Graywolf, 1988. 300-11.

"One of the Chosen." *These Your Children*. Ed. Harold U. Ribalow. New York: Beechhurst, 1952. 243-53.

"The Scream on 57th Street." *Stories from the Sixties*. Ed. Stanley Elkin. Garden City: Doubleday, 1971. 107-36; *Nightwalks: A Bedside Companion*. Ed. Joyce Carol Oates. Princeton: Ontario Review, 1982. 23-50.

"Time, Gentlemen!" *The Uncommon Reader*. Ed. Alice S. Morris. New York: Avon, 1965. 84-95.

"A Wreath for Miss Totten." *The Best American Short Stories, 1952*. Eds. Martha Foley and Joyce F. Hartman. Boston: Houghton, 1952. 61-70; *40 Best Stories from Mademoiselle 1935-1960*. Eds. Cyrilly Abels and Margarita G. Smith. New York: Harpers, 1960. 141-51; *The Secret Sharer and Other Great Stories*. Eds. Abraham Lass and Norma Tasman. New York: Mentor-NAL, 1969. 79-91.

Short Fiction in Periodicals

"Box of Ginger." *New Yorker* 16 Oct. 1948: 31-34.

"A Christmas Carillon." *Harper's* Dec. 1953: 32-41.

"The Evershams' Willie." *Southwest Review* 72.3 (1987): 298-335.

"Heartburn." *New American Mercury* Jan. 1951: 30-39.

"Hollow Boy." *Harper's* Oct. 1952: 49-57.

"If You Don't Want to Live I Can't Help You." *Mademoiselle* Oct. 1954: 110-11, 132-41.

"In Greenwich There Are Many Gravelled Walks." *New Yorker* 12 Aug. 1950: 20-27.

"In The Absence of Angels." *New Yorker* 21 Apr. 1951: 29-35.

"Little Did I Know." *Saturday Evening Post* 8 June 1963: 46-51.

"May-ry." *Reporter* 30 Mar. 1961: 37-40.

"The Middle Drawer." *New Yorker* 10 July 1948: 16-20.

"Mrs. Fay Dines on Zebra." *Ladies' Home Journal* Oct. 1960: 78-79, 119-21, 123-24.

"Night Riders of Northville." *Harper's* Sept. 1951: 84-91.

"Old Stock." *New Yorker* 30 Sept. 1950: 26-32.

"One of the Chosen." *Harper's* Dec. 1948: 56-60.

"Pool of Narcissus." *New Yorker* 25 Sept. 1948: 33-36.

"So Many Rings to the Show." *New Yorker* 16 May 1953: 31-36.

"Stead." *Yale Review* 76.2 (1987): 169-77.

"Textures of Life." *Redbook* Mar. 1963: 139-70.

"What a Thing, to Keep a Wolf in a Cage!" *Mademoiselle* Apr. 1957: 126-27, 164-71.

"A Wreath for Miss Totten." *Mademoiselle* July 1951: 48-49, 94-96.

Secondary Sources

Articles and Chapters

Hahn, Emily. "In Appreciation of Hortense Calisher." *Contemporary Literature* 6.2 (1965): 243-49.

Contains critical commentary, biographical materials, excerpts from the author, and a brief publishing history.

Kirby, David K. "The Princess and the Frog: The Modern American Short Story as Fairy Tale." *Minnesota Review* 4 (1973): 145-49.

Describes in three paragraphs the fairy tale element of Calisher's "Heartburn."

Mittleman, Leslie B. Rev. of *The Collected Stories of Hortense Calisher*. *Survey of Contemporary Fiction*. Ed. Frank N. Magill. Rev. ed. 12 vols. Englewood Cliffs: Salem, 1977. 3: 1413-15.

A standard reference article that discusses settings, characteristic themes, symbols, characters, and style. Also discusses individual stories and the autobiographical elements of Calisher's fiction.

Murphy, Christina. "Hortense Calisher." *Critical Survey of Short Fiction*. Ed. Frank N. Magill. 8 vols. Englewood Cliffs: Salem, 1981. 3: 1034-40.

A standard reference article that discusses Calisher's birthplace, principal short fiction, influences, story characteristics, biography, and major publications. Analyzes her themes and style.

Peden, William. *The American Short Story: Continuity and Change, 1940-1975*. 2nd ed. Boston: Houghton, 1975. 56-57.

Provides a brief sketch of Calisher's collections of short stories. Identifies her favorite subject matter as the Jewish family, their defeats in relationships in a fragmented world, their fallibility, and the author's compassion in portraying them.

"*Tale for the Mirror*." *Survey of Contemporary Literature*. Ed. Frank N. Magill. Revised. 12 vols. Englewood Cliffs: Salem, 1977. 11: 7386-88.

A standard reference article covering background, influences, themes, characters, style, and plot and references to individual stories in *Tale for the Mirror*.

Reviews

Abrahams, William. "Out of Sight." Rev. of *Herself: An Autobiographical Work* and *Standard Dreaming. Saturday Review* 14 Oct. 1972: 75-76.

Provides a review of *Herself* mixed with praise and reservations about the style and content of the novel. Sees the book as both stylistically mannered and simple at the same time. Wishes Calisher had written an outright autobiography rather than an autobiographical novel. Concludes that the book is a mishmash of materials and somewhat tedious in places.

Allen, Bruce. "Books." Rev. of *Saratoga, Hot. Saturday Review.* July-Aug. 1985: 76-77.

Calls this collection of short stories "densely written" and full of inner music. Considers the content impressive in its variety with absorbingly dramatic prose and rhetorical splendor.

Allen, Bruce. "More Than an Adventure, This Ambitious Novel Deserves Attention." Rev. of *Mysteries of Motion. Christian Science Monitor* 18 Jan. 1984: 22.

Describes Calisher's previous works, comments on the strain of imaginative brilliance in her novels, and sees her formal education in philosophy and education as contributing to her mandarin style. Calls her prose either sonorously rich or else terse, crabbed, and urgent.

Auchincloss, Eve. "Good Housekeeping." Rev. of *Extreme Magic. New York Review of Books* 25 June 1964: 17-18.

Calls *Extreme Magic* a remarkably uneven collection of stories which are feminine in the pejorative sense. Considers the talent diaphanous for the most part but points out a couple of limpid and moving stories. Describes the writing as sometimes skillfully evocative, sometimes depressingly glib. Concludes that it is sad the author of stories as civilized and scrupulous as the best in the book should stoop to posturing and Jamesian pretentiousness in others.

Berricault, Gina. Rev. of *False Entry. San Francisco Chronicle This World.* 29 Oct. 1961. 33.

Calls *False Entry* a profoundly penetrating first novel focussing on the human condition of solitude. Details the plot and character of *Pierre.*

Blakeston, Oswell. "Hortense Calisher." Rev. of *Queenie. Books and Bookmen* May 1973: 104-05.

Details the contents of the novel, and comments that Calisher has given an atmospheric picture of a circle of aging ladies in New York who sincerely believe in spending men's money. Argues that Part 1 of this three-part novel is superior to the disintegrations pictured in parts 2 and 3.

Bolger, Eugenie. "Endangered Species." Rev. of *The Collected Stories of Hortense Calisher. New Leader* 19 Jan. 1976: 18-19.

Praises the collection for its firm structures and plots, along with its wealth of detail and ability to evoke mood and place. Describes the prose as leisurely, cadenced, and sparkling with poetic images. Identifies the Elkin stories as the most successful. Concludes that the stories are symmetrical, polished, conclusive, and deeply steeped in human drama.

Boroff, David. "The Saving Remnants of Grace." Rev. of *Extreme Magic: A Novella and Other Stories. Saturday Review* 2 May 1964: 36-37.

Describes the stories as firm in integrity of purpose and scrupulously crafted. Sees the stories as vignettes of grace under pressure rather than of existentialist travail. Claims that Calisher, belonging to the humanistic tradition, includes anecdotes, spoofs, and a patchwork of human relationships which reverberate in the mind long after the reading has ended.

Brooks, John. "Judge Mannix Comes Home to Adultery and Matricide." Rev. of *The New Yorkers. New York Times Book Review* 13 Apr. 1969: 5, 36.

Describes *The New Yorkers* as a strange, melodramatic novel full of surprisingly leisurely descriptions and ruminations, long interior monologues, and social scenes built up at painstaking and exhausting length. Considers its bulk awesome and its lyric philosophical flights often impressive.

Brophy, Brigid. "Consequential Marriages." Rev. of *Textures of Life. New Statesman* 13 Sept. 1963: 326. Rpt. in *Don't Never Forget: Collected Views and Reviews*. Brigid Brophy. New York: Holt, 1966. 160-62.

Claims that *Textures of Life* pulls off something like *The Golden Bowl*. Identifies her material as the American bourgeois home. Calls the work Jamesian in structure and density. Details the contents.

Brophy, Brigid. "Solitaries." Rev. of *Tale for the Mirror: A Novella and Other Stories. New Statesman* 21 June 1963: 942. Rpt. in *Don't Never Forget: Collected Views and Reviews.* Brigid Brophy. New York: Holt, 1966. 159-60.

Describes *Tale for the Mirror* as written with taut artistry bespeaking a major talent. Claims that Calisher cuts a figure of stylish eccentricity and modishness. Briefly discusses the contents.

Brown, Rosellen. "Trying for the Life." Rev. of *Saratoga, Hot. New York Times Book Review* 26 May, 1985: 10.

Calls this a collection of stories rather than a novel. Reviews the contents of each of the stories, and concludes that the whole thing is subtle and clotted to the point of obscurity, but nevertheless remains suggestive, lively and entertaining.

Broyard, Anatole. "Family Situations." Rev. of *On Keeping Women. New York Times Book Review* 23 Oct. 1977: 14.

Calls the novel an anthology of all the impulses, ideas, and reflections about marriage and love which might conceivably occur to a modern woman. Reviews the contents of the book, and concludes that this is less a slick novel than it is an experimental one.

Broyard, Anatole. "How Big Is An Apocalypse?" Rev. of *The Collected Stories of Hortense Calisher. New York Times* 13 Oct. 1975: 27.

Describes *The Collected Stories of Hortense Calisher* as full of stories representing an apocalypse in a small tea cup. Calls some mocked-up demonstrations of what a short story should be like. Claims that the most difficult stories to read are those about adolescence, but that the best are those that unfashionably affirm love.

Buckman, Gertrude. "Unfulfilled Yearnings." Rev. of *In the Absence of Angels. New York Times Book Review* 18 Nov. 1951: 46.

Calls the novel intelligent and full of feeling. Considers Calisher to be a thoughtful and conscientious writer whose language lies somewhere between science and inspiration.

Burgess, Anthony. "Report From Janice." Rev. of *Journal from Ellipsia. New York Times Book Review* 7 Nov. 1965: 62.

Describes *Journal from Ellipsia* as a book whose style fails to match the title because the book is far from elliptical, very explicit, and luxuriant in its post-Jamesian prose. Finds "an excessive blowing-up of pretty fancy language of positively Debussyan impressionism, though spiked with bits of hard science; "there is also a small clinker-like residue of something, to ponder over."

Capouya, Emile. "Writers and Artists." Rev. of *The Railway Police and The Last Trolley Ride*. *New York Herald Tribune Book Week* 1 Jan. 1967: 8.

Calls *The Last Trolley Ride* a novella showing the power of Calisher's literary imagination and genuine artistry. Comments on the modest story outline and her excellent ear for speech. Concludes that these stories give us poetry.

Cassill, R. V. "Feminine and Masculine." Rev. of *The Railway Police* and *The Last Trolley Ride*. *New York Times Book Review* 22 May 1966: 4-5.

Discusses the novelettes as formed from well nigh perfect syntheses of language, symbol, narrative, and theme. Details the contents of each, and concludes that in both works there is precision in the rise and fall of emotion.

Cavell, Marcia. "Pondering a Family Mystery." Rev. of *The Bobby Soxers*. *New Leader* 16 June 1986: 20.

Describes *The Bobby Soxers* as about the haunted provincialism of American life. Complains, unfortunately, that the narrative is not compelling because we are often in the dark about things we haven't been moved to see. Details plot and character, and then concludes that the writing lacks a sure sense of key that allows one to keep the beginning in mind, to sense where one is going, and yet be surprised.

Cooper, Arthur. "Woman in a Manly Sport." Rev. of *Herself: An Autobiographical Work* and *Standard Dreaming*. *Newsweek* 16 Oct. 1972: 110, 112.

Reviews her autobiography and her fifth novel, seeing them charged with intelligence, texture, rich imagery, and symbolism. Finds them deserving of a larger readership than previous works have drawn. Contains commentary and biographical insight into Calisher's work.

Davenport, John. "Exoticisms." Rev. of *Journal from Ellipsia*. *Observer* 24 Apr. 1966: 27.

Describes *Journal from Ellipsia* as coolly running against the stream because it is a cerebral fantasy and "devilishly difficult to read." Describes plot, setting, and characters, and calls this an exciting but overwritten book.

Davis, L. J. "Auntie Was a Hooker." Rev. of *Queenie. Washington Post Book World* 28 Mar. 1971: 5.

Sees *Queenie* as a kind of mulligatawny stew written in the reminiscent fashion of the old Algonquin crowd dimly overheard through layers of cheesecloth. Laments that once upon a time Calisher was a real short story writer; one wonders what has happened to her.

Davis, Robert Gorham. "Questions at Dawn." Rev. of *Tale for the Mirror: A Novella and Other Stories. New York Times Book Review* 28 Oct. 1962: 5.

Calls Calisher a superb raconteur who presents the reader with pauses, interruptions, nostalgia, expected sidelights, and suddenly broadened perspectives. Commends her for the narrative pleasure she takes in the stories in this collection, especially in her finding the exact phrase to define a mood or gesture. Details the contents of individual stories.

Dickstein, Morris. "Learning about Life from Aunt Leo." Rev. of *The Bobby-Soxer. New York Times Book Review* 30 Mar. 1986: 5.

Sees the work as a departure from the transparent well-made novel. Concludes that this novel grips us not as objective story, but as personal projection, a piece of made-up autobiography.

Drake, Sylvie. "Charting the Frontier Called Age." Rev. of *Age. Los Angeles Times Book Review* 13 Dec. 1987: 11.

Calls *Age* a slender, fragile, paradoxical novella. Describes its style as idiosyncratic, eccentric, affected, and uneven.

Eder, Richard. Rev. of *Mysteries of Motion. Los Angeles Times Book Review* 9 Oct. 1983: 1.

Sees this novel as an ambitious book chronicling many of the sicknesses of our time. Concludes that, while the prose finally becomes a fidgety form of lethargy, this is a novel whose ideas count for much even if the prophecy does not.

Elstob, Peter. "Wholly Modern." Rev. of *The New Yorkers. Books and Bookmen* Mar. 1970: 26-27.

Calls *The New Yorkers* a big family chronicle crammed with busy characters and a slowly developing story. Calls Calisher a writer's writer with dazzling skills and deep psychological insight. Notes her subject matter in this novel to be about Jewishness and the East Coast American writers. Concludes that all who think literary form is still important should read this book.

"Family Secrets." Rev. of *The New Yorkers*. *Times Literary Supplement* 15 Jan. 1970: 49.

Claims that in *The New Yorkers* Miss Calisher has shown that she knows how to create the pattern of blood relationships which tug and strain to keep a family together. Concludes that her novel has the grandeur which helps to make sense not only of established institutions, but of how much we still rely on the Mannixes in the world to put into practice the public rites of dignity, loyalty, and self-sacrifice which even the dedicated revolutionary must admire.

Freedman, Richard. "Literary Leftovers and a Consolatory Tale." Rev. of *Herself: An Autobiographical Work* and *Standard Dreaming*. *Washington Post Book World* 1 Oct. 1972: 9.

Calls *Herself* a hodge-podge of literary, political, and biographical leftovers which definitely do not pass for art. Concludes that it is self-indulgent *chutzpah*.

Fuller, Edmund. "Aristocratic New York." Rev. of *The New Yorkers*. *Wall Street Journal* 9 June 1969: 16.

Asserts that this novel has links with Henry James and Edith Wharton. Describes the family saga it develops with all the sociological links provided.

Grumbach, Doris. "One of the Few on Whom Nothing Is Lost." Rev. of *The Collected Stories of Hortense Calisher*. *New York Times Book Review* 19 Oct. 1975: 3-4.

Discusses the volume as an achievement worth celebrating. Describes the stories as slow and decorous in form, enriched by complex and decorative language. Claims that they make everyday life seem lyrical and rich with implication. Concludes that the stories take us to the private depths of lives we know almost nothing about, and that we enter because she has shown us life, or at least the ashes of it, in her very small cup.

Grumbach, Doris. "A Yule Feast: Fiction Seasoned With Biography." Rev. of *Standard Dreaming* and *Herself: An Autobiographical Work*. *America* 23 Dec. 1972: 553.

Comments on both *Standard Dreaming* and *Herself* as formidable achievements by an elitist writer. Considers both intensely interesting, self-revealing, written in delicately layered prose, and full of fast telegraphic scenes and brilliant narration. Calls her talent little short of disturbing.

Hale, Nancy. "After the Wedding, Brr-r-r." Rev. of *Textures of Life. New York Times Book Review* 12 May, 1963: 5.

Shows how the novel explores the antagonism between a mother and daughter, and evaluates the beat way of life of the young couple. Feels the story to have been rendered with compelling depth of conviction.

Hall, Joan Joffe. "Two Tickets to Tomorrow." Rev. of *The Railway Police* and *The Last Trolley Ride. Saturday Review* 18 June 1966: 39-40.

Discusses *The Railway Police* and *The Last Trolley Ride* as both highly idiosyncratic novels full of convolutions of sentences, fake suspense about who is telling the story, and much coyness. Claims that Calisher keeps jazzing things up and obscuring the narrative line, trying to create a mystery where there is none. Concludes that, at her best, she is witty, ripe with insights, and competent with language.

Hartt, J. N. "New Books in Review." Rev. of *False Entry. Yale Review* 51.2 (1961): 302-03.

Describes *False Entry* as a beautifully written novel whose style and disclosure is vivid and luminous, and whose powerful moral argument is given an expression as dramatic as it is poetic because it evokes terror, noise, and public crises.

Hicks, Granville. "The Gentle Imposter." Rev. of *False Entry. Saturday Review* 28 Oct. 1961: 17.

Calls Calisher a producer of distinguished stories for a number of years. Claims that in *False Entry* she uses an unmannered style, involved, not allusive, and beautifully suited to her style. Details the plot of the novel, showing how she uses all the traditional arts of the novelist. Concludes that this book rewards the closest reading, but can give a more casual kind of pleasure too.

Hicks, Granville. "The Quiet Desperation." Rev. of *Tale for the Mirror: A Novella and Other Stories*. *Saturday Review* 27 Oct. 1962: 22.

Sees Calisher as primarily a short story writer rather than a novelist, who most often sees the pathos in life, joining it at times with humor. Decides she is "not a great talent," but "a fine one."

Hilton, James. "Caustic, Disciplined Pity." Rev. of *In the Absence of Angels*. *New York Herald Tribune Book Review* 18 Nov. 1951: 4.

Describes *In the Absence of Angels* as covering a wide range of people and exploits. Calls some stories minor masterpieces and others remarkable for their compassion. Describes several of the stories.

Isaacs, Susan. "Exercises in Style." Rev. of *Saratoga, Hot*. *Washington Post Book World* 9 June 1985: 8.

Describes the novel as an appeal to the intellect, not to the heart. Comments on the wordplay, self-conscious imagery, and large numbers of emotionally deadened characters. Concludes that occasionally the writing is sprightly or incisive, but that it has all the humanity and emotional resonance of a well-constructed double acrostic.

J., L. Rev. of *Mysteries of Motion*. *West Coast Review of Books* Jan. 1984: 41.

Compares *Mysteries of Motion* to Porter's *Ship of Fools* but set on a passenger space shuttle instead. Addresses the question of how life in space affects the body, including the emotions and appetites. Claims that this kind of book had better be left in the hands of sci-fi writers who know the territory. Concludes that Calisher seems out of her milieu.

Johnson, Lucy. "High Polish." Rev. of *False Entry*. *Progressive* Jan. 1962: 49-50.

Calls *False Entry* an immensely accomplished and fascinating first novel, that, through its ornate style and the obsession of its major character and narrator, engulfs the reader in its world.

Kapp, Isa. "The Sag of the Heart." Rev. of *In the Absence of Angels*. *Commentary* Mar. 1952: 298-99.

Asserts that *In the Absence of Angels* is written by a writer notable for her clarity and explicitness about her own origins and those of her characters. Argues that, thoroughly imbued with a sense of her own class and vocation, her stories satisfy at best that curiosity one normally feels about another's home, source of money, and style of expenditure. A detailed critical analysis of the whole collection of stories.

Kendall, Elaine. Rev. of *Saratoga, Hot. Los Angeles Times Book Review* 21 July 1985: 5.

Considers *Saratoga Hot* an acutely observed love story full of nostalgic commentary in its accounts of the run-down elegance of the horse-owning world of the day.

Kiely, Robert. "On the Subject of Love." Rev. of *Textures of Life. Nation* 25 May 1963: 442-43.

Describes *Textures of Life* as delicate in expression, subtle in its psychology, and rooted in commonplace events. Complains about the kind of biological determinism which seems to govern the depressing life of the central female protagonist. Objects to Elizabeth Pagani as a modern Everywoman on the grounds she is too pinched and narrow even for this petty century.

Kiely, Robert. "A Sort of Memoir, a Sort of Novel." Rev. of *Herself: An Autobiographical Work* and *Standard Dreaming. New York Times Book Review* 1 Oct. 1972: 3, 20, 22.

Begins with a discussion of Calisher's life as refracted through the autobiography *Herself*. Describes also the contents of *Standard Dreaming*, which appeared simultaneously. Concludes that, while the first book is a sprawling artist's grab bag about the writing of fiction in postwar America, the novel is a short, controlled, imagistic nightmare of love and grief.

Lamport, Felicia. "Miss Calisher's Super-Intense Art." Rev. of *Textures of Life. New York Herald Tribune Books* 28 Apr. 1963: 4.

Commends the novel for its subtle modern tonalities, brilliant depiction of the mother-daughter relationship, graceful style, and its capturing of the nuances of complex relationships. Also castigates Calisher for preciousness, obscurity, and characters that "respire" rather than breathe.

Larkin, Joan. "Twice Over Heavily." Rev. of *Eagle Eye. Ms.* Jan. 1974: 39-40.

Describes *Eagle Eye* as a spare, skillful book, tightly controlled, and often as difficult as a poem. Details the initiation story of the male protagonist, and concludes that this is not Calisher's first attempt at working out the difficulties of parent-child, male-female, humanist-scientist relationship problems.

Lee, Charles. "People and Love." Rev. of *In the Absence of Angels*. *Saturday Review of Literature* 1 Dec. 1951: 37, 43.

Comments on Calisher's treatment of adult love, Jewish assimilation, the hungers of the young, and the tragedies of old age. Concludes that both the language and the fiction itself are commanding.

Lehmann-Haupt, Christopher. "Hortense Calisher Explains." Rev. of *Standard Dreaming* and *Herself: An Autobiographical Work*. *New York Times* 9 Nov. 1972: 45.

Describes the contents of *Herself: An Autobiographical Work* and *Standard Dreaming* as containing opacity, round-aboutness, and much of the author's leftover bits and pieces. Concludes that there is little room or vision in the telling and an altogether far too idiosyncratic definition of style.

Lehmann-Haupt, Christopher. "Scenes Without Intellect." Rev. of *The New Yorkers*. *New York Times* 18 Apr. 1969: 41.

Describes *The New Yorkers* as an arresting book with an endless smorgasbord of characters, subplots, themes, points of view, forward and backward leaps in time, social and psychological insights, physical and character detail, quirky dialogues, and fancy writing. Claims, over the long run, that the patternless stimuli induce boredom.

Levine, Paul. "Reviews." Rev. of *Textures of Life*. *Hudson Review* 16.3 (1963): 458-59.

Claims that, in this novel, Calisher fares better with the younger generation than the older, but is quite moving in a minor key. Argues that in her fictive world her subtle intimacy is her most endearing quality.

Levitas, Gloria. "Solitary Shadows of Driven Souls." Rev. of *Tale for the Mirror: A Novella and Other Stories*. *New York Herald Tribune Books* 4 Nov. 1962: 13.

Praises Calisher for her compassionate irony, skillful imagery, and ability to juxtapose the weird and the ordinary. Argues, however, that a melancholy sentimentality settles over this book of short stories blurring the acuity of Calisher's vision and reducing all of life's problems to lack of communication between people. Sees the collection as despairing, but imbued with a strange human dignity.

Levy, Francis. "Living in a World of Lies." Rev. of *Eagle Eye. New York Times Book Review* 11 Nov. 1973: 38-39.

Argues that this novel has an elusive texture that mirrors the protagonist's mind while creating the subtle process by which a sense of exclusion and isolation is achieved. Calls it a book about the solitude of knowing in a world of lies. Concludes, unfortunately, that her desultory and muddled style turn an imaginative idea into little more than a predictable stereotype.

"Life Among the Dreamers." Rev. of *Extreme Magic: A Novella and Other Stories. Cosmopolitan* May 1964: 10.

Claims that *Extreme Magic* spins a beguiling web which is amusing, strange, and terrifying. Thinks Calisher casts a special magic over all her work; like a medieval alchemist, she combines such potions as irony and contrast, wit, love, and death, and brings the pot to bubble. Concludes that, in this collection, she has produced pure gold.

"The Listener." Rev. of *False Entry. Times Literary Supplement* 27 July 1962: 537.

Calls *False Entry* a long, ruminative soliloquy covering life from birth to the prospect of marriage. Considers this book illuminated by flashes of intuition and keen perceptions. Yet complains that Calisher blurs her best images by overwriting, and that too often her style is clogged with affectations. Concludes that *False Entry* is an uneven novel with a strong ebb and flow of human emotions.

Longley, Edna. "Pilgrim Mothers." Rev. of *On Keeping Women. Partisan Review* 47.2 (1980): 309-10.

A brief review of a semi-satirical feminine-quest novel whose strongest element is "a comic awareness, alas too flickering."

Maddocks, Melvin. "The Ability to Play Any Role but Himself." Rev. of *False Entry. Christian Science Monitor* 2 Nov. 1961: 13.

Argues that Calisher apes the search for self in the Joycean novel, producing a circling, reverting, slowly advancing novel written in stylized sentences, throbbing similes, and ineffective aphorisms. Notes an unevenness in her attention to her story, and compact scenes juxtaposed against overblown episodes. Concludes that she is an excellent minor writer stretching beyond her own range.

Magid, Nora L. "Reviews." Rev. of *The New Yorkers*. *Kenyon Review* 31.5 (1969): 714-15.

Complains that Calisher's style has become increasingly convoluted; consequently, *The New Yorkers* is awash in possibly archetypal or mythic mysteries. Complains finally that the reader sinks under the weight of bizarre mechanism and cumulative paradox.

Maguire, Gregory. "'Outlook Tower." Rev. of *Mysteries of Motion. Horn Book Magazine* June 1984: 372-73.

Claims that the novel will prove sluggish, discursive, and difficult to follow for younger readers. Finds the picture of the rocket lift-off and details of space travel convincing for civilians. Details plot and central characters.

Malin, Irving. "Supremacy of Consciousness." Rev. of *Eagle Eye*. *New Republic* 3 Nov. 1973: 26-27.

Commends the novel for its depiction of private consciousness, even when it is obsessive and poetic. Notes Calisher's ability to observe social ills, the displacements of youth, and the futilities of the rich. Concludes that the novel is a stunning act of the imagination full of magic, sharp vision, and sudden leaps.

Mallon, Thomas. "To the One Left Behind." Rev. of *Age. New York Times Book Review* 18 Oct. 1987: 14.

Calls *Age* a technically complicated novella, narrated in an alternating set of diaries in progress. Details some of the characters, scenes, and stylistics.

Mannes, Marya. "A Difficult Act to Follow." Rev. of *Extreme Magic: A Novella and Other Stories. New York Herald Tribune Book Week* 10 May 1964: 13.

Calls *Extreme Magic* a book showing the wide range of Calisher's prose and interests. Considers this book a sleight of hand skillful enough to cause amazement and admiration, but also a sense of the knowledge that one has been tricked. Concludes that the magician had one too many cards up her sleeve. Describes some of the stories.

Martin, Jean. "Ways of Telling It." Rev. of *False Entry*. *Nation* 18 Nov. 1961: 411-12.

Sees *False Entry* as Jamesian and rococo in style, full of filigreed hair-splitting thought, every sentence a glittering jewel, and each piece of dialogue masterfully wrought.

McClenahan, Catherine L. "Genre and Mainstream Intersection." Rev. of *Mysteries of Motion*. *Fantasy Review* May 1984: 27.

Calls *Mysteries of Motion* a dramatic and almost sci-fi novel asking some important questions about colonizing space, while dealing with the issue of what it is like to journey through human life. Concludes that some will call this a great novel, while others will call it a tedious puzzle.

Merril, Judith. "Books." Rev. of *Journal from Ellipsia*. *Magazine of Fantasy and Science Fiction* Feb. 1968: 52-53.

Considers this novel funny, suspenseful, poignant, philosophical, and lots more. Describes setting and a little of the plot.

Mitchell, Adrian. "Finding What is Human." Rev. of *Extreme Magic: A Novella and Other Stories*. *New York Times Book Review* 17 May 1964: 4.

Sees *Extreme Magic* as a collection of eight stories and one novel alive with compassion and sophistication. Details the contents of several of the pieces.

"Mixed Fiction." Rev. of *False Entry*. *Time* 10 Nov. 1961: 102, 104.

Thinks *False Entry* leaves one feeling as if one had sipped gallons of weak mandarin-style tea from a fur-lined cup. Laments that, instead of a lion, this novel, six years in the making, is a mouse. Finds it all hem-stitched with the heaviest of embroidery.

Morgan, Edwin. "Unconcerned." Rev. of *Journal from Ellipsia*. *New Statesman* 15 Apr. 1966: 545.

Considers *Journal from Ellipsia* a metaphysical fantasy written in an archly witty, quacking, and garrulous fashion. Argues that its theme has to do with the limitations of the temporal life. Discusses the contents briefly.

Morgan, Edwin. "Violent Fruit." Rev. of *The New Yorkers*. *Listener* 15 Jan. 1970: 93.

Asserts that this is a long, massive, realistic, complex, and ambitious novel, which is often penetrating and represents a clear advance on her previous work. Complains that the book is eroded by the relentless concentration of its questioning. Observes that Calisher has learned not a little from Henry James. Details contents.

Morris, Alice S. "Sealed Within a Secret Self." Rev. of *False Entry. New York Times Book Review* 29 Oct. 1961: 4, 38.

Describes the novel as a work of subliminal craftsmanship and literary virtuosity. Considers this a brave and major book capable of throwing new light on life while providing a vicarious experience of human living, profound, revelatory, and enchanting.

Nightingale, Benedict. "Uptown and Downtown." Rev. of *The New Yorkers. Observer* 18 Jan. 1970: 33.

Calls Calisher's an attentuated muse. Notes that she rarely uses one word if she can use a hundred. Observes much empty lyricism and endless enervating analysis of mild affections and corruptions.

Nordell, Roderick. "New Novels by Iris Murdock and Hortense Calisher." Rev. of *Textures of Life. Christian Science Monitor* 9 May 1963: B8.

Calls *Textures of Life* silken, abrasive, and delicate by turns in its seamy weave. Notes the shameless coincidence, shuttlings of human events, dramatic imagery, and sharp analytical gaze.

Nordell, Roderick. "Words Like Bangles." Rev., of *Extreme Magic: A Novella and Other Stories. Christian Science Monitor* 30 Apr. 1964: 4.

Calls this novel a polished, smooth performance from a writer with a very sure touch. Concludes that Calisher's worldly stance never becomes a posture of despair.

"Notes on Current Books." Rev. of *Standard Dreaming. Virginia Quarterly Review* 49.2 (1973): viii.

Asserts that *Standard Dreaming* is a complex book written in surrealistic style about souls doomed to failure. Sees her theme as basically a classic one of search which Calisher pursues with unwavering diligence.

Oates, Joyce Carol. "The Citizen Courier in Outer Space." Rev. of *Mysteries of Motion. New York Times Book Review* 6 Nov. 1983: 7, 26.

Discusses the contents of the novel as apocalyptic and massively plotted. Calls the work subtle, ingenious, puzzling, and not always well integrated. An excellent account of the contents of the novel.

Oates, Joyce Carol. "Reviews." Rev. of *The New Yorkers. Hudson Review* 22.3 (1969): 534-35.

Claims that this novel reveals Calisher's primitive belief in magical powers, fantastic feats of consciousness, and the uncanny confusion between inner will and outer history. Finds nothing realistic in this novel apart from its concern with law and setting. Complains that everything is dense, weighed down, and slightly insane.

"The Occasional Victory." Rev. of *Tale for the Mirror: A Novella and Other Stories. Time* 16 Nov. 1962: 98.

Argues that *Tale for the Mirror*, a collection of short stories, demonstrates the precision of her language and the imaginative quality of her writing. Concludes that her characters are thought up, not noted down. Describes several of the stories.

"One Bird Too Many." Rev. of *In the Absence of Angels. Time* 10 Dec. 1951: 115-16.

Characterizes this as a book in which the author has fingered her characters, but not felt them, and does not make the reader feel them either. Calls the title story a bucketful of political satire hauled up from the deep, old Orwell. Likes the last six stories about quiet Jewish family life. Claims that the rest show her talent for diverting imitations.

Ozick, Cynthia. "Hortense Calisher's Anti-Novel." Rev. of *The New Yorkers. Midstream* Nov. 1969: 77-80.

Sees the work as "a miraculous novel that is equal to its ambitions." Considers it self-aware, full of internal allusions, echoes, murmurings, and obliqueness of method. Likens her concept of the novel to that of Nabokov's anti-novel. Considers the work intelligently designed. Points out that to read the novel for its sociology of Jewish assimilation patterns is to miss its essential psychology, biology, and comments on fate.

Penner, Jonathan. "One Foot in the Quicksand." Rev. of *On Keeping Women. Washington Post Book World* 6 Nov. 1977: 8.

Sees the novel as giving domestic lamentation a circumambient medium in which the characters play out their futile gestures. Concludes, however, that this is really an overwritten novel about language.

Perera, Padma. Rev. of *On Keeping Women* and *The Collected Short Stories. American Book Review* Apr. 1978: 4.

Calls *On Keeping Women* a novel which, despite some superb things in it, doesn't quite come off. Argues that the loss in this novel is that it seems more like a brilliant thesis reacting to social trends than a work of fiction. Laments that all arguments are forestalled and all the bases covered.

Peterson, Virgilia. "Many Questions, Few Answers." Rev. of *False Entry. New York Herald Tribune Books* 29 Oct. 1961: 10.

Calls *False Entry* dashing, mystifying, and tantalizing because Calisher foregrounds the mystery of human motivation, modern psychology notwithstanding. Details the contents, and concludes that few writers have her sense of place, time, and image.

Peterson, Virgilia. "Mystery Stories." Rev. of *The Railway Police* and *The Last Trolley Ride. Reporter* 17 Nov. 1966: 66-67.

Calls Calisher's manipulation of language "brilliant," and the language sustaining the work "sulphurous." Identifies her persistent theme as the burden of private shame and the enigmas and mystery of the private consciousness. Provides a plot and character description of both books.

Phillips, Robert. Rev. of *The Collected Stories of Hortense Calisher. Commonweal* 7 May 1976: 317-19.

Provides a descriptive review of the contents of the collection, calling it formidable in the best tradition of the short story. Describes her inner settings as "psychscapes," and praises her insight and language, which Phillips compares to that of Elizabeth Bowen and Henry James. Commends Calisher's range, covering as it does the urban, the suburban, the adolescent, the male, the female, the historical past, and the hysterical present. Describes her persistent themes as the failure of love, of marriage, of communication, and of identity. Concludes that the work is full of sensibility, grace, compassion, and insight.

"Pi in the Sky." Rev. of *Journal from Ellipsia. Time* 22 Oct. 1965: 128.

Calls *Journal from Ellipsia* a prodigious intellectual plonk—the autobiography of an Hegelian monad. Describes the style as combining the least admirable prose qualities of Joyce and Henry James with

Hortenseness all of her own. Complains she writes about it for 375 pages and never explains why.

Pickrel, Paul. "The New Books." Rev. of *False Entry*. *Harper's* Nov. 1961: 118.

Describes the main events in the life of the protagonist that illustrate his "false entry" into life and his "role playing" as an adult. Comments that Calisher's style is "shot through with intelligence and perception," and concludes that the novel "bears the mark of singularity, of an effort to do something significant and to do it in its own way."

Pickrel, Paul. "Some Women Novelists." Rev. of *Textures of Life*. *Harper's* June 1963: 106-07.

Considers *Textures of Life* to be drawing on Calisher's lyric and descriptive powers. Claims that the story invites disaster because it is the threadbare standby of bourgeois comedy. Concludes, however, that Calisher does write prose of great delicacy, and that her solution is to point out that it is not rebellion itself which fails, but the sheer force of circumstance.

Poore, Charles. "There Are Fewer Listeners Than Talkers, You Know." Rev. of *Extreme Magic: A Novella and Other Stories*. *New York Times Book Review* 28 Apr. 1964: 35.

Explains *Extreme Magic: A Novella and Other Stories* as describing the human condition of struggle between poise and disquiet in the human heart. Considers this a humorous, unsparing cartoon. Details several of the stories.

Poore, Charles. "Two Tales of the Need To Be Unique." Rev. of *The Railway Police* and *The Last Trolley Ride*. *New York Times Book Review* 12 May 1966: 43.

Describes the contents of *The Railway Police* and *The Last Trolley Ride*, and calls the writer antic in her sense of humor. Concludes that she is a pleasure to read.

Prescott, Orville. "Books of the Times." Rev. of *False Entry*. *New York Times* 30 Oct. 1961: 27.

Describes *False Entry* as a novel in which the narrator's melancholy reflections are more important than any story which he has to tell. Claims that there are too many startling figures of speech and ambiguities.

Details the contents of several stories, and concludes that most of the collection is relatively static with almost no dramatic episodes. Complains that there are few emotions, only thoughts.

Prescott, Orville. "Books of the Times." Rev. of *Tale for the Mirror: A Novella and Other Stories. New York Times* 28 Nov. 1962: 37.

Describes *Tale For the Mirror* as a set of short stories demonstrating Calisher's uncanny skill in drawing a wide variety of characters. Complains, however, that the style is too clever, too smooth, and a little too precise. Concludes that she never writes about moral or physical squalor, but instead examines crucial moments in ordinary lives.

Prescott, Orville. "Books of the Times." Rev. of *Textures of Life. New York Times Book Review* 29 Apr. 1963: 29.

Describes *Textures of Life* as a more disciplined novel than *False Entry*, less richly carved and painted. Finds it lacking the verbal fancy work, i.e., mere decoration, characterizing *False Entry*. Details the contents.

Raban, Jonathan. "Tobacco Strands." Rev. of *The New Yorkers. New Statesman* 16 Jan. 1970: 89.

Confesses to having failed to finish *The New Yorkers* because of boredom and disappointment. Thinks the title sounds like a cross between Henry James and Harold Robbins. Complains that this middle-class epic rapidly descends into soap opera. Concludes that it is like attending a party full of very dull and very rich people.

Rabinowitz, Dorothy. "New Books." Rev. of *The Collected Stories of Hortense Calisher. Saturday Review* 18 Oct. 1975: 17-18.

A brief appreciation for the stories of one "among the most literate practitioners of modern American fiction."

Rennert, Maggie. "Great Terms and Small Mercies." Rev. of *Textures of Life. Saturday Review* 24 Aug. 1963: 49.

Sees *Textures of Life* as written in deft and lovely prose. Asserts that, like a fine and embroidered organdy, the texture is delicate and pleasing, and the craftmanship admirable. Concludes that life can only be seen through it, but never clearly enough.

Ridley, Clifford A. "A Reach for Totality in *The New Yorkers*." Rev. of *The New Yorkers. National Observer* 14 Apr. 1969: 21.

Argues that in *The New Yorkers* Calisher has created her most ambitious novel, a sprawling chronicle which is dense, elliptical, and touching by turns. Considers it full of facile half-irony and too-simple observation. Details the contents of the novel, and concludes that Miss Calisher seems something of a contradictory slave to her characters: like Simon, she appears determined to talk the universe to death; like Mirriam, she appears to plead "Life is movement. Tell me how to stop."

"A Ringing in the Third Ear." Rev. of *The New Yorkers*. *Time* 16 May 1969: 116.

Argues that this is a massive family chronicle initially impressive but then degenerating into authorish rhetoric and an obsessively circular kind of storytelling. Asserts that Calisher's straining for nuance distorts the prose. Concludes that this is not rightfully a psychological novel, but a strayed social one.

Rose, Ellen Cronan. Rev. of *The Collected Stories of Hortense Calisher*. *New Republic* 25 Oct. 1975: 29-30.

Describes the contents of several stories, commenting on their wry sophistication, well-bred sentimentality, superb knowing, and exquisite portraits.

Rosenthal, Lucy. "A Family in the Realm of Almost-Myth." Rev. of *The New Yorkers*. *Washington Post Book World* 27 Apr. 1969: 8.

Describes *The New Yorkers* as a self-contained novel dipping back into the same time and characters as *False Entry*. Considers this book sculptural, visual, tactile, psychological, stagey, full of dialogue, and full of characters in freizes.

Rosenthal, Lucy. Rev. of *Queenie*. *Saturday Review* 3 Apr. 1971: 34.

Discusses the plot, and praises the book for its ideas, sparkling aphorisms, ability to touch on the generation gaps, the sexual gap, and the communication gap. Sees Queenie as the embodiment of Everywoman's sexual fable. Concludes that the book is densely written and full of wit, ideas, and life.

Sayre, Nora. "The Heroine Is Not Queer for Herself." Rev. of *Queenie*. *New York Times Book Review* 28 Mar. 1971: 5, 26.

Describes *Queenie* as a novel which tilts at sexual language and mores with much skill. Claims that it resembles a pubescent narrator's description of female orgasm—somewhat like an underground explosion.

Concludes that, like an unzipped belch, this novel dispels old superstitions that men hunt experience and women let it come upon them.

Schmidt, Sandra. "Oval's Progress." Rev. of *Journey From Ellipsia*. *Christian Science Monitor* 11 Nov. 1965: 11.

Discusses the novel as a smoothly written piece setting up a tension between action and reflection. Provides an account of the contents of the novel.

Sklar, Robert. "Conflict of Generations." Rev. of *Textures of Life*. *Congress Bi-Weekly* 13 Jan. 1964: 18-19.

Calls *Textures of Life* a frail, thinly characterized novel with the slightest movement for a plot. Praises the charming and perceptive prose which makes the theme come alive when the characters cannot. Concludes, nevertheless, that this small family novel may turn out to be one of the truest expressions of the times.

"Something Recognizable." Rev. of *The Railway Police* and *The Last Trolley Ride*. *National Observer* 8 Aug. 1966: 21.

Describes *The Last Trolley Ride* and *The Railway Police* as written in wild, eclectic, Calisher prose. Sees the former as a brilliant piece of literary construction, strung upon a tenuous story, and full of buccolic idioms. Calls both stories brilliant in insight, humor, mood, and use of symbolic flashback. Concludes that Calisher is a welcome original.

Spacks, Patricia Meyer. "Reviews." Rev. of *Queenie*. *Hudson Review* 25.1 (1972): 163-64.

Complains that this is a futile novel that manipulates its readers while failing to express any significant feelings or ideas. Concludes that it raises the question of whether the women in this and other novels value themselves any differently from the way men value or devalue them.

Stowers, Bonnie. "'The Same World-Dwarfing Stories'." Rev. of *Eagle Eye*. *Nation* 29 June 1974: 829-30.

Calls the novel a durable masterpiece depicting a journey that is a perilous exploration of a man's head and heart. Adds that the plot is constructed on the return of the wandering son and concerns itself with how and whether the protagonist, Bunty, will make it in modern America.

"Sums and Scrubbers." Rev. of *Journal from Ellipsia*. *Times Literary Supplement* 14 Apr. 1966: 332.

Accuses Calisher of scattering abroad *Encyclopedia Britannica* learning by the random handful and indulging in pseudo-Joycean logopaidia of persistent and exasperating tedium. Adds that from all this hective welter of words and fidget of ideas there does emerge now and then an incontestable poetic power and vitality giving promise of a real achievement under steadier, sparer control.

Thwaite, Anthony. "Journeys of Discovery." Rev. of *Queenie. Observer* 18 Feb. 1973: 37.

Describes *Queenie* as a work of discovery about Queenie's New York penthouse existence. Adds that Calisher's tone is arch, withering, scatty, knowing, tangential, and shrill.

"To Nowhere and Back." Rev. of *The Railway Police* and *The Last Trolley Ride. Time* 6 May 1966: 110.

States that these two novellas leave the reader asking where are we going and did we get there? Describes the plot briefly.

"True or False." Rev. of *False Entry. Newsweek* 30 Oct. 1961: 79.

Shows how this first novel reveals Calisher as a novelist in the grand manner, luxuriating in rich imagery and rhetoric to show a "tragic and illumined vision of life." Discusses the theme and the skeleton of the story. Concludes that it is uneven with many parts better than the whole, but that it is also "an anguished and brilliant parable on truth and falsehood."

Tyler, Ann. "Apocalypse in a Teacup." Rev. of *The Collected Stories of Hortense Calisher. Washington Post Book* World 18 Sept. 1977: E3.

Describes *The Collected Stories of Hortense Calisher* as apocalyptic, brief, intense, fine, compact, beautifully timed, brilliantly characterized, and deceptively simple. Adds that each strikes the reader with an ache of recognition, and alters, in some indefineable way, our perceptions of the world.

Tyler, Anne. "Tales of Apocalypse Served up in a Tureen." Rev. of *The Collected Stories of Hortense Calisher. National Observer* 22 Nov. 1975: 21.

Describes *The Collected Stories of Hortense Calisher* as a warm, evocative, and delicately wrought collection providing a very distinctive sense of time which seals moments permanently. Details several of the stories, and describes several possible groupings and divisions.

W, C. Rev. of *The Bobby Soxer*. *West Coast Review of Books* Sept. 1986: 37.

Calls *The Bobby Soxer* a painting so detailed and intricate one could study for hours the patterns and brushstrokes without ever quite understanding who or what it is the artist has chosen to paint. Comments that Calisher has filled her palette with language instead of paint and created just this kind of work in this novel.

Weeks, Edward. "The Peripatetic Reviewer." Rev. of *Herself: An Autobiographical Work* and *Standard Dreaming*. *Atlantic* Oct. 1972: 132-33.

Details the contents of the autobiography, and identifies the prevailing theme of the novel as pity. Concludes with a detailed plot summary.

Wordsworth, Christopher. "Irritations." Rev. of *The New Yorkers*. *Manchester Guardian Weekly* 24 Jan. 1970: 18.

Calls *The New Yorkers* full of wedding cake tiers of numinous convolutions. Adds Calisher is unbearably oracular, not entirely guiltless of psychological mumbo jumbo, and unclear about her central, sibylline mystery. Concludes that these are mountains in labor trying to bring forth a mystic mouse.

Yoder, Edwin. Rev. of *Queenie*. *Harper's* Mar. 1971: 107.

States that *Queenie* is a story told in Portnoy-type, tape-recorded monologues to her dean, Miss Pirenesi. Adds that the moral of the story is that "Portnoy's Complaint is not yet epidemic." Describes contents briefly.

Interviews

Amory, Cleveland. "Trade Winds." *Saturday Review* 8 May 1971: 6, 12.

A brief interview following the publication of *Queenie*.

Bannon, Barbara A. "Authors & Editors." *Publishers Weekly* 21 Apr. 1969: 19-20. Rpt. in *The Author Speaks: Selected PW Interviews, 1967-1976*. New York: Bowker, 1977. 24-26.

Provides important biographical and first person interview commentary from Calisher on her life as a writer and her early years.

Gurganus, Allan, Pamela McCordick, and Mona Simpson. "The Art of Fiction C: Hortense Calisher." *Paris Review* 105 (1987): 156-87.

An interview with Calisher in which she discusses: her father's love of poetry and books, his desire to be a poet, her difficulties about how to begin a writing career when you have been raised in a home stocked with great books, her background as a member of a German Southern Jewish family born in the North, her fascination with language, the difficulties of fitting in New York City without any knowledge of Yiddish, the themes and styles of several of her works, her fascination with transportation as a theme, the metaphysical quality of several of the novels, her reading program as a teenager and later as an adult, and her conviction that American literary reviewers do not emendate women writers until they are firmly dead.

Ingersoll, Earl, and Peter Marchant. "A Conversation with Hortense Calisher." *Southwest Review* 71.2 (1986): 186-93.

Calisher discusses the autobiographical elements of her work, writing on her first novel, literary influences, form in the short story, her sense of the organic whole of the short story, reactions of reviewers, the moral implications of her work, her humanistic philosophy, and her feminism. Argues that she was one of the first to use domestic material in her fiction.

Newquist, Roy. "Hortense Calisher." *Conversations*. Roy Newquist. Chicago: Rand, 1967. 62-70. Rpt. in digest form as "An Interview with Hortense Calisher" in *Writers' Digest* Mar. 1969: 58-60, 94-96.

Contains information about Calisher's childhood notebooks, her late start with writing, her first published work, her opinions on the plight of the female and male author in America, her early work history, her young reading tastes, and her own mature works.

Biographical Sources

Calisher, Hortense. *Herself: An Autobiographical Work*. New York: Arbor, 1972.

Calisher, Hortense. *Kissing Cousins: A Memory*. New York: Weidenfeld, 1988.

Cooper, Arthur. "Woman in a Manly Sport." Rev. of *Herself: An Autobiographical Work* and *Standard Dreaming. Newsweek* 16 Oct. 1972: 110, 112.

Reviews her autobiography and her fifth novel, seeing them charged with intelligence, texture, rich imagery and symbolism, and deserving of a larger readership than previous works have drawn. Contains commentary and biographical insight into Calisher's work.

Gottesfeld, E. "WLB Biography: Hortense Calisher." *Wilson Library Bulletin* Mar. 1963: 599.

Hazard, Eloise Perry. "Eight Fiction Finds." *Saturday Review* 16 Feb. 1952: 16-18.
A brief biographical summary of Calisher's becoming a writer.

Matalene, Carolyn. "Hortense Calisher." *American Novelists Since World War II*. Eds. Jeffrey Helterman and Richard Layman. Detroit: Gale, 1978. Vol. 2 of *Dictionary of Literary Biography*. 94 vols. to date. 1978- . 75-81.
More than details of her life, this is a career biography tracing the development of the author's canon, describing the contents and themes of her works, evaluating her reputation, and placing her in the larger context of American literary history. Includes lists of primary and secondary sources and illustrations.

Bibliographies

Snodgrass, Kathleen. "Hortènse Calisher: A Bibliography, 1948-1986." *Bulletin of Bibliography* 45.1 (1988): 40-50.

Dissertations

Blustein, Bryna Lee Datz. "Beyond the Stereotype: A Study of Representative Short Stories of Selected Contemporary Jewish American Female Writers." Diss. Saint Louis U, 1986.

Islas, Arturo Jr. "The Work of Hortense Calisher: On Middle Ground." Diss. Stanford U, 1971.

Shinn, Thelma J. Wardrop. "A Study of Women Characters in Contemporary American Fiction, 1940-1970." Diss. Purdue U, 1972.

Snodgrass, Kathleen. "Rites of Passage in the Works of Hortense Calisher." Diss. U of Delaware, 1987.

Jerome Charyn

1937 –

Primary Sources

Novels

American Scrapbook. New York: Viking, 1969; New York: Collier-Macmillan [Cited in PBIP, 1970].

Blue Eyes. New York: Simon, 1975; New York: Avon, 1977; First Black Cat ed. New York: Grove, 1986.

The Catfish Man: A Conjured Life. New York: Arbor, 1980; New York: Bard-Avon, 1981.

Darlin' Bill: A Love Story of the Wild West. New York: Arbor, 1980; New York: Primus-Fine, 1980; New York: Bard-Avon, 1982; New York: Fine, 1985.

The Education of Patrick Silver. New York: Arbor, 1976; New York: Bard-Avon, 1977, 1981.

Eisenhower, My Eisenhower. New York: Holt, 1971, 1973.

Elsinore. New York: Warner, 1991.

The Franklin Scare. New York: Arbor, 1977; New York: Avon, 1978.

Going to Jerusalem. New York: Viking, 1967; London: Cape, 1968; New York: Holt, 1971.

The Good Policeman. New York: Mysterious, 1990.

Marilyn the Wild. New York: Arbor, 1976; New York: Bard-Avon, 1977, 1981.

On the Darkening Green. New York: McGraw, 1965.

Once Upon a Droshky. New York: McGraw, 1964.

Panna Maria. New York: Arbor, 1982.

Paradise Man. New York: Fine, 1987; London: Joseph, 1988.

Pinocchio's Nose. New York: Arbor, 1983.

Secret Isaac. New York: Arbor, 1978; New York: Bard-Avon, 1980.

The Seventh Babe. New York: Arbor, 1979; New York: Bard-Avon, 1980.

The Tar Baby. New York: Holt, 1973.

War Cries Over Avenue C. New York: Fine, 1985; Contemporary American Fiction Series. New York: Penguin, 1986; London: Abacus-Sphere, 1986.

Collected Works

Isaac Quartet: Marilyn the Wild, Blue Eyes, The Education of Patrick Silver and Secret Isaac. The Black Box Thriller. London: Zomba, 1984.

The Man Who Grew Younger, and Other Stories. New York: Harper, 1967.

Contents: 1944; Faigele the Idiotke; The Man Who Grew Younger; Imberman; "Farewell! . . . Farewell! . . ."; Race Day at Hiawatha; Sing, Shaindele, Sing.

Short Fiction in Anthologies

"Faigele the Idiotke." *The Young American Writers: Fiction, Poetry, Drama & Criticism*. Ed. Richard Kostelanetz. New York: Funk, 1967. 39-54.

"Farewell! . . . Farewell! . . ." *Tales of Our People—Great Stories of the Jew in America*. Ed. Jerry D. Lewis. New York: Geis, 1969. 193-210.

"from *King Jude*." *Statements 2: New Fiction*. Eds. Jonathan Baumbach and Peter Spielberg. New York: Fiction Collective, 1977. 78-86. Excerpt from an unpublished novel.

"The Man Who Grew Younger." *My Name Aloud: Jewish Stories by Jewish Writers*. Ed. Harold U. Ribalow. South Brunswick: Yoseloff, 1969. 40-48; *The Single Voice: An Anthology of Contemporary Fiction*. Ed. Jerome Charyn. New York: Collier, 1969. 310-19.

"Sing, Shaindele, Sing." *The Human Commitment: An Anthology of Contemporary Short Fiction*. Ed. Don Gold. Philadelphia: Chilton, 1967. 206-18; *Stories from the Transatlantic Review*. Ed. Joseph F. McCrindle. New York: Holt, 1970; London: Gollancz, 1970. 74-83; Harmondsworth: Penguin, 1974. 111-22.

Short Fiction in Periodicals

"The Changeling." *Transatlantic Review* 27 (1967): 81-92.

"Faigele the Idiotke." *Commentary* Mar. 1963: 220-31.

"God Bless Captain Freddy and Private Ming!" *Mademoiselle* Apr. 1964: 142-43, 202-06.

"Joel's Millions." *Fiction* 5.2-3 (1978): 167-76.

"The Man Who Grew Younger." *Paris Review* 10.37 (1966): 93-102.

"Monsieur Jerome." *Antaeus* 20 (1976): 69-83.

"On Second Avenue." *Commentary* July 1963: 26-33.

"The Pig-Eaters." *Fiction* 3.1 (1974): 9-10.

"Sing, Shaindele, Sing!" *Transatlantic Review* 22 (1966): 139-48.

"Two from Whalebone." *Fiction* 4.1 (1975): 24-27.

Secondary Sources

Articles and Chapters

Guerard, Albert. "Notes on the Rhetoric of Anti-Realist Fiction, A
   Representative Career: Jerome Charyn." *TriQuarterly* 30 (1974): 36-49.

In a lengthy piece discussing trends in writing careers in the postwar
period, Charyn's career is taken as representative of the 1960s. A
detailed and excellent overview of his life and career. Contains critical
commentary on many of his works.

Oriard, Michael. *Dreaming of Heroes: American Sports Fiction, 1868-
   1980*. Chicago: Nelson-Hall, 1982. 258-59.

In contrast to Roth's *The Great American Novel*, which "deflates myth as
myth," seemingly making sports fiction no longer possible, Charyn's *The
Seventh Babe* creates "a mythic baseball fantasy in which the sport is recognizable but everything about it is enchanted, in which historical facts
are embroidered with fantastic trappings." Briefly describes the plot and
concludes that this novel seems "the sort of oral tale that might have been
recited in a great hall a dozen centuries ago to a preliteratre audience who
still believed that magic was part of life."

Patten, Robert L. "Pinocchio Through the Looking Glass: Jerome Charyn's
   Portrait of the Artist as Mytholept." *Novel* 17.1 (1983): 67-76.

This major essay on Charyn's *Pinocchio's Nose* argues that the book is
charged by a personal, desperate hunt for an origin, a psychic and biolog-

ical family, and a social context, whose absence has kept the protagonist in thrall to a violated childhood. Claims that this novel rings so many changes on that theme and swallows so many correlative myths, that Charyn appears to be a lexical golem who lives a life in language that is foreclosed to him in life.

Solomon, Eric. "Counter-Ethnicity and the Jewish-Black Baseball Novel: The Cases of Jerome Charyn and Jay Neugeboren." *Modern Fiction Studies* 33.1 (1987): 49-63.

This major article provides a brief look at the sociology of baseball, a glance at the history of the baseball novel as genre, and a detailed examination of two novels by Neugeboren and Charyn that twist the genre into a postmodern, parodic, anti-realist form. Provides extensive discussion of Charyn's *The Seventh Babe*.

Woolf, Mike. "Exploding the Genre: The Crime Fiction of Jerome Charyn." *American Crime Fiction: Studies in the Genre.* Ed. Brian Docherty. New York: St. Martin's, 1988. 131-43.

Argues that as the American tradition has taken over the genre of the detective novel, it has been exploded to become the vehicle for exploring the profane and profound. Argues that, in Charyn, the radical potential within the genre is fully realized and the boundaries of the reader's expectations deeply altered by the manner in which he exploits and transcends the traditional preoccupations of the form.

Reviews

Bellman, Samuel I. "A Good Place to Grow Up Absurd." Rev. of *The Man Who Grew Younger and Other Stories. Saturday Review* 14 Jan. 1967: 85.

Describes these seven short stories of growing up in the Bronx as enormously effective, fresh, face-slapping, and artistically acceptable. Contains a lengthy description of contents.

Bellman, Samuel I. Rev. of *American Scrapbook. Saturday Review* 23 Aug. 1969: 40.

Calls this novel fresh and conventional in the positive sense, and a trip into the unfamiliar world of the Japanese-Americans interned in government camps during World War II. Adds that this is also an absorbing stream-of-consciousness narrative, and represents Charyn at his best.

Bellman, Samuel I. "Traveling Game." Rev of *Going to Jerusalem.*
   Saturday Review 9 Sept. 1967: 34-35.

Considers the novel a wild, zany melange of sketches, revelations, epistles far too disorganized for narrow, conventional taste. Adds that it calls
up moods and experiences at the threshold of experience, and promises
some big experience which it never actually delivers.

Bergonzi, Bernard. "New Fiction." Rev. of *On the Darkening Green.*
   New York Review of Books 22 Apr. 1965: 15-16.

Calls *On The Darkening Green* a sprawling, lively first person narrative,
exuberant, fantastic, Dickensian, and grotesque with many of the failings
of a Dickens or a Sterne.

Blackburn, Sara. "Four Novels—Two Up, Two Down." Rev. of *The Tar
   Baby. New York Times Book Review* 28 Jan. 1973: 7.

Describes this novel as written in the style of Nabokov and failing to
quite measure up. Complains that the whole thing ends up being pretentious and boring. Adds that its readers will be a limited few, and asks
why this frivolous exercise?

"Books." Rev. of *Secret Isaac. Time* 30 Oct. 1978: 128.

Claims that this is an energetic work that echoes rhythms of Bellow and
Joyce, but still manages to sustain its own peculiar tone, a unique amalgam of psychological insight and scatological farce. Calls it one of the
most unlikely and yet compelling fictions since *Gerontion* with its mixed
garlic and sapphires in the mud.

Boroff, David. "Heart-Breaking and Heartening." Rev. of *Once Upon a
   Droshky. American Judaism* (Sum. 1964): 12, 30.

Discusses this novel as one of several recent books preoccupied with the
recent Jewish past, written by "apple-cheeked boys fascinated by the
exotic appeal of the Lower East side," all with the result that the writing
is more picturesque than authentic. Briefly describes the characters,
whom Charyn treats as amusing relics of an almost irrelevant past.
Concludes that the Lower East Side, once the scene of extraordinary
intellectual and cultural vitality, still waits for its chronicler.

Boroff, David. "Stranded on Second Avenue." Rev. of *Once Upon a
   Droshky. Saturday Review* 29 Feb. 1964: 34.

Explains that *Once Upon a Droshky* tells of the Lower East Side in its melancholy decline at a time when Yiddish culture has receded. Details the contents, and concludes that Charyn lacks both the comic imagination and the poetic energy to do justice to his milieu. Complains that it reads like Damon Runyan with a Yiddish accent.

Brickner, Richard P. "Immigrant Slapstick." Rev. of *Panna Maria. New York Times Book Review* 27 June 1982: 12.

Asserts that *Panna Maria* (Virgin Mary in Polish), a whorehouse novel full of vigorous imagination, amatory, political and thuggish dealings, is made up of episodes that have no aggregate force. The style is manic and swollen, and in the right hands might have been a fiction of genius. Concludes that it could have been less effortful and more proportioned.

Brickner, Richard P. Rev. of *The Education of Patrick Silver. New York Times Book Review* 5 Sept. 1976: 5, 17.

States that this work concludes Charyn's trilogy of novels about New York cops and crooks. The language is ripe, reflecting the book's spicy stew and exoticism, but though this is talented, it is certainly mostly plumage.

Cassill, R. V. "Enough Already." Rev. of *Once Upon a Droshky. New York Herald Tribune Book Week* 16 Feb. 1964: 16.

Claims that this novel reminds us of the stereopticon charms of local colorism and dialect stories whose characters are like puppets with brightly painted faces, and whose dialect is entertaining in small doses but unvaried. Concludes that page after page, it sets up a shattering sympathetic vibrato in the nervous system that not every reader will be able to stand.

Clute, John. "The Haunted Forest of Manhattan." Rev. of *Panna Maria. Washington Post Book World* 18 July 1982: 5.

Panna Maria is described mostly in terms of plot and characters. This is a relentless Charyn universe created as much through style as content. It is a fabled world seen through childlike eyes. Calls the novel an ambitious mosaic of Charyn's telling of America. Argues that it is a brilliant, witty, and sumptuous centerpiece.

Cormier, Robert. "The Man Who Grew Younger." Rev. of *The Man Who Grew Younger and Other Stories. Commonweal* 21 Apr. 1967: 156-57.

Describes *The Man Who Grew Younger* as a collection of stories neither brilliant nor negligible. Shows several of them as wonderfully noisy with several undertones of pathos. Sees Charyn as obviously dedicated and writing the truth, though the stories fail to rise above the vernacular, thus revealing his impoverishment of expression.

Davis, Douglas M. "Imitation, Not Wit." Rev. of *Going to Jerusalem*. *National Observer* 25 Sept. 1967: 25.

Sees *Going to Jerusalem* as a "wouldn't it be funny if" novel. Adds that there is a lot more in this novel than plot and that like Nabokov, Charyn combines weighty themes with wit and force. Concludes that there is much here about manners and mores of heartland America, but that reading it is as much a strain as having to laugh at an evening full of bad jokes.

DeMott, Benjamin. "Charyn's Sally." Rev. of *Darlin' Bill: A Love Story of the Wild West*. *New York Times Book Review* 7 Dec. 1980: 11, 31.

Darlin' Bill is described as a comic, historical novel offering a wide variety of pleasures. Woven into the plot are several splendid reanimations of the tall tale—vivid description, delightful patois, and vivid narrative. Argues that ultimately it is shrewd, tough, funny, and triumphantly detailed.

Dolan, Paul. Rev. of *Secret Isaac*. *James Joyce Quarterly* (Fall 1979): 109-10.

Calls *Secret Isaac* a good, tough, New York detective novel about a central character bitten by conscience and perhaps James Joyce. In addition to being a tribute to Joyce, it is a novel about a modern city. Describes the plot and characters, and traces many parallels to the works of Joyce.

Eder, Richard. Rev. of *War Cries Over Avenue C. Los Angeles Times Book Review* 26 May 1985: 3.

Sees this novel as a superimposition of the Vietnam wasteland over the Lower East Side wasteland, built on the metaphor of titanic buying and selling of drugs and treasure as a representation of modern American life. Concludes that though the paradoxes are corrosive and witty, unfortunately, Charyn needs ballast, and a human sensibility or two.

Epstein, Seymour. "Weakness for Damaged Women." Rev. of *Secret Isaac. New York Times Book Review* 21 Jan. 1979: 14.

Describes the chaotic contents of *Secret Isaac,* and wonders whether or not the characters function in any conventional sense since they are really only names performing different aspects of frenzy—political, sexual, homicidal. Adds that the style seems to be literary abstract impressionism which is effective paragraph by paragraph, but not in the long run.

Feingold, Michael. "Tough Magic." Rev. of *Paradise Man. Village Voice* 26 May 1987: 65.

Calls *Paradise Man* a novel of magic realism, but complains that when everything is a thrilling revelation, the revelations don't thrill so much; and when the entire cast has the same line of tough talking actions and low motives, no one ends up seeming notably real. Describes contents in detail. Argues that though the consciousness of the novel is a shallow thing, the game Charyn plays to hook readers into it is brilliant, rich with potential, and skillfully played.

Fremont-Smith, Eliot. "Clapping Hands—If That's What You Came for." Rev. of *Going to Jerusalem. New York Times* 6 Sept. 1967: 45.

Describes *Going to Jerusalem* as ambitious, raucous, eccentric, clever, ironic, and nutty, and Charyn as gifted and inventive.

Gropman, Donald. "It Can Happen." Rev. of *American Scrapbook. Christian Science Monitor* 24 July 1969: 7.

American Scrapbook recounts the experiences of a group of American citizens and residents, the Japanese, who were deprived of their rights for the sin of national origin. Argues that for all those who shout, "It can't happen here!" Mr. Charyn coolly refreshes the memory.

Haber, Leo. "All Men Are Japanese." Rev. of *American Scrapbook. Midstream* Oct. 1969: 78-80.

Describes the contents of *American Scrapbook* and its politics. Comments that the novel is billed as comic, but only in the sense of a grand joke. Concludes that it is a book full of low-keyed narrative styles, contemporary politics, Jewish agendas, and much subtlety.

Haber, Leo. "An Important Young Writer." Rev. of *The Man Who Grew Younger and Other Stories. Jewish Frontier* June 1967: 28-29.

Reviews *The Man Who Grew Younger and Other Stories* as an extremely promising work by a different, urban Jewish writer. Commends the Jewishness of the works, describes their contents, and concludes that Charyn belongs close to Singer and Malamud in vision and style.

Harron, Mary. "Gateway To Myth." Rev. of *Metropolis. Manchester Guardian Weekly* 6 March 1988: 27.

Metropolis takes as its central theme the trauma of immigrants arriving in the concrete bunker of Ellis Island. Describes the contents of the novel. Concludes that ultimately it is not enough to present New York as a myth or magic land; one is left wanting to know more about the bankers, the market place, and the developers.

Howard, Maureen. "Books." Rev. of *Going to Jerusalem. Partisan Review* 35.1 (1968): 142, 143.

Calls this is a book full of Nabokovian devices, Pynchon-like ingenuity, and fine writing. Describes contents briefly.

Judell, Brandon. Rev. of *Panna Maria. Village Voice Literary Supplement* May 1982: 4.

Claims that *Panna Maria* is the work of a cult novelist still without a cult. States that the author juggles thirty nefarious characters like a Dickens. Argues that Charyn creates a world you have to work a little to enter, but once in, you don't mind the sweat.

Keller, Karl. "From Gepetto to a Ghetto and Old Giacomo Joyce." Rev. of *Pinocchio's Nose. Los Angeles Times Book Review* 10 July 1983: 2.

Calls *Pinocchio's Nose* a very silly novel, in a good sense. Complains about the shifting around of the plot; describes the contents, point of view, and humorous effects.

Larsen, Ernest. "Busy Boy." Rev. of *Catfish Man: A Conjured Life. Village Voice* 21 Apr. 1980: 43.

Sees *The Catfish Man* as an exercise in flaky exhilaration of the Natty Bumpo ilk. Concludes that it is the dilemma of the boy who never grows up—or the dilemma of the dilemma of the American writer.

Lask, Thomas. "World within World." Rev. of *The Man Who Grew Younger and Other Stories. New York Times* 4 Jan. 1967: 41.

Claims that this third collection of Charyn's short stories focuses on the world of immigrant Jews living in enclaves on the Lower East Side or the Bronx. Describes joy and grief as unconfined in these stories, and the world as one fenced in by language, religious tradition, folkways, and habits of speech.

Lask, Thomas. "End Papers." Rev. of *American Scrapbook. New York Times* 3 June 1969: 45.

Claims that in this novel Charyn has moved from the urban Jewish milieu, still showing traces of ghetto psychology and the nervousness of displacement, to the miseries and intramural divisions within the Japanese detention camp during WWII.

LeClair, Thomas. "Isaac the Pure, The Just, The Cop." Rev. of *Marilyn the Wild. New York Times Book Review* 2 May 1976: 54, 56.

Argues that in this novel Charyn sets up the father for a double fall—a stumble as man, a bumble as myth. Further notes that more than simply showing the hero's weakness, Charyn shows us his absorption in his own paternal myth. Complains that the plot is pure convention, full of coincidences, melodrama, and ritualized scenes, yet concludes that this is an exciting and clever work.

LeClair, Thomas. "Police Deals, an Anti-Utopia, Some Old Hollywood." Rev. of *Blue Eyes. New York Times Book Review* 9 Feb. 1975: 6.

Argues that Charyn blunts the search for the father theme in *Blue Eyes* by distributing point of view among numerous minor characters who surround Coen. Eccentricity is allowed to build vigor and colloquial vigor. Comments that they remind us of Stanley Elkin's authentic excess.

Lehmann-Haupt, Christopher. "Books of the Times." Rev. of *The Seventh Babe. New York Times* 18 June 1979: C15. Rpt. as "Two on Baseball" in *Books of the Times* 2.6 (1979): 286-88.

Sees the novel as an enactment of the American dream of baseball as a nightmare. Comments that readers brought up on the traditional baseball myths will find the novel irritating and disturbing.

Lehmann-Haupt, Christopher. "Fiction in the Melting Pot." Rev. of *Blue Eyes. New York Times* 23 Jan. 1975: 31.

Argues that *Blue Eyes* is a novel in which Charyn probably overindulges his taste for the ethnically obscure and the sexually bizarre. Complains that Charyn's knock-kneed prose, when at its best, forces one into his inimitable world of tough-talking freaks and fuzz. Provides lengthy plot summary.

Leonard, John. "Nostalgia of the Absurd." Rev. of *The Franklin Scare. New York Times* 17 Nov. 1977: 19.

Discusses *The Franklin Scare* as incredibly sympathetic to J. Edgar Hoover. Describes the plot as zany, and makes no literary judgments.

Levin, Beatrice. "Books." Rev. of *Once Upon a Droshky. Chicago Jewish Forum* 23.1 (1965): 320-21.

Describes the novel as an extraordinarily fascinating work based on the golden years of the Yiddish stage in New York. Details the contents of the plot, and concludes that the story is told in a rich, poetic tongue, neither Yiddish nor English, by a fine, young, promising writer.

Levin, Martin. "Before the Blintzes Were Frozen." Rev. of *Once Upon A Droshky. New York Times Book Review* 16 Feb. 1964: 37.

Describes the content and characters of *Once Upon A Droshky* as a local color exercise of superior literary quality and charm.

Lieber, Joel. "The Life and Wild Times of Toby Molothioon." Rev. of *Eisenhower, My Eisenhower. New York Times Book Review* 28 Mar. 1971: 4.

Calls *Eisenhower, My Eisenhower* a frantic, frown-making, fantastical, crazy book. Sees it as a definitely original and zany book whose "style matches syntax, time, the linear flow—in a scramble that parallels first-person narration." Concludes that it is impossible to tell whether the book succeeds or fails, only that it startles with its strange vision.

Maddocks, Melvin. "Chess Ploys." Rev. of *Going to Jerusalem. Christian Science Monitor* 5 Oct. 1967: 17.

Argues that *Going to Jerusalem* is not a special kind of whimsy found in Charyn's earlier works. It is black humor played with white chessmen—a dark game, but not without a lyrical upbeat. Claims that this book finally lets the air out of its own whimsy, and that Charyn does not have the heavily flogging gusto of a Barth. Attributes to him something more convincing, the quietly assured energies of a man who doesn't have to prove that life is more of a pleasure than otherwise.

Malin, Irving. "Books in Brief." Rev. of *The Franklin Scare. Hollins Critic* 14.4 (1977): 16-17.

Discusses the novel as a book that mixes categories, distorts and turns magical actual facts, and that is really all about how history is simply another story.

Malin, Irving. Rev. of *Blue Eyes*. *Commonweal* 26 Mar. 1976: 219-220.

Argues that in *Blue Eyes*, Charyn gives us urban craziness while he wrestles with questions of guilt, responsibility, and destiny. Concludes that this is much more than a grotesque, fast-moving picture of New York which offers an odd mixture of hope and absurdity. .

Malin, Irving. "Expect the Unexpected." Rev. of *The Catfish Man: A Conjured Life*. *Ontario Review* (Fall-Wint. 1980-81): 96-97.

Argues that *The Catfish Man* is a self-referential, grotesque, comic novel full of unlikely subject matter and wonderfully subversive. The novel shows conjured lives, a series of mirrors and illusions, as well as distortions.

Maloff, Saul. "Son of Bruno and Bathsheba." Rev. of *Pinocchio's Nose*. *New York Times Book Review* 17 July 1983: 11, 22.

Calls this novel difficult and garbled. Details the quixotic contents.

Marcus, Greil. "Seventh Son." Rev. of *The Seventh Babe*. *Rolling Stone* 18 Oct. 1979: 44.

Claims that *The Seventh Babe* is a long way from being a first-rate novel because incident merely follows incident, and the characters are made to jump through hoops. Describes some of the plot.

Morton, John. "Mr. Charyn Concocts a Culture, and Does It Have Its Problems." Rev. of *Eisenhower, My Eisenhower*. *National Observer* 24 May 1971: 17.

Sees *Eisenhower, My Eisenhower* as a book which orchestrates the terrors, longings, and frustrations of the dispossessed. Claims that to make readers believe in the invented culture of the Azazians requires skill, and that it is a testament to Charyn's talent that his invention stays aloft from first page to last.

"Other New Novels." Rev. of *Going to Jerusalem*. *Times Literary Supplement* 29 Aug. 1968: 929.

Calls *Going to Jerusalem* gothic in invention, and argues that it grapples with more layers of symbolism and meaning than he can control. Claims that along this headlong highway there are some pertinent sweeps at the horrors of American life, that the symbolism is so erratic we come up for consciousness only occasionally, and then mostly lapse back into drowsy incomprehension.

Plummer, William. "A Left-Handed Third Baseman." Rev. of *The Seventh Babe. New York Times Book Review* 6 May 1979: 12, 19.

Calls *The Seventh Babe* an ambitious, daring book which modulates into something more strange, wonderful, and south of the border. Claims that like earlier works Charyn takes recognizable genres and washes them in psycho-analytic ideas. Sees this novel as a departure for having been written not under the tutelage of Freud, but more likely that of Gabriel Garcia Marquez.

Pritchard, William. "The View From Crotona Park." Rev. of *The Catfish Man: A Conjured Life. New York Times Book Review* 20 Apr. 1980: 15, 35.

Describes *The Catfish Man* as strongest in its first block of chapters where the author is on home ground. After this it reads like a version of "can you top this." Complains there is too much relentless, wacky invention, and the narrative voice registers too limited a range of feeling and expressiveness.

Reynolds, Stanley. "Wierdies." Rev. of *Going to Jerusalem. New Statesman* 5 July 1968: 21.

Calls *Going to Jerusalem* a novel of hope; rich, comic invention; bizarre characters; flashes of insight; soulful touches; and black comedy.

Ricks, Christopher. "Convulsive Throes." Rev. of *Eisenhower, My Eisenhower. New York Review of Books* 22 July 1971: 12.

Asserts that Charyn's *Eisenhower, My Eisenhower* is full of gothic comics and futurist fantasy. Concludes that it manifests no natural imagination, but rather a hardened childishness.

Rosen, Richard. "The Hit Man With a Heart." Rev. of *Paradise Man. New York Times Book Review* 29 Mar. 1987: 11.

Considers that in *Paradise Man* there is enough material for three novels. Calls Charyn a genius at portraying the complexity of human alliances and low-life lethal types. Claims that although adept at several styles, he has trouble making them all cohere. Concludes that, unfortunately, the book's tone causes us not to sympathize with the central character—we watch the chess game without caring sufficiently which pieces get taken.

Scholes, Robert. Rev. of *Eisenhower, My Eisenhower. Saturday Review* 5 June 1971: 40. Edited version rpt. in *Fabulation and Metafiction*. Robert Scholes. Urbana: U of Illinois P, 1979. 133-35.

Addresses the lack of general popularity of Charyn's work, and the fact that reviewers tell a different tale than this would suggest. Argues that something important is lacking in Charyn's work, probably structurally. Concludes that there is insufficient coherent shape, intelligibility, and substance, not only in his work, but in that of the metafictionists generally.

Schorr, Mark. "Title Page." Rev. of *Paradise Man. Los Angeles Times Book Review* 8 Mar. 1987: 4.

Calls *Paradise Man* a wonderful tale of manipulation, murder, and a man trying to find himself as his world slowly unravels. Concludes that the characters are intriguing and larger than life.

Schott, Webster. "Van Buren vs. Kortzfleisch." Rev. of *Going to Jerusalem. New York Times Book Review* 17 Sept. 1967: 45.

Describes the novel as so loaded with explosives it ought to tick because of the kind of attack it makes on child-parent relationships. Also sees it as a broadside against human exploitation and a brazen assault on ideals dear to the heart of America—precocity, success, and moral righteousness. Concludes that for all this, the characters are as funny as monkeys—bearing about that much resemblance to human beings.

Schreiber, LeAnne. "A Terrible Beauty." Rev. of *Marilyn the Wild. Time* 19 Apr. 1976: 94, 96.

Argues that in *Marilyn the Wild,* father searching has become a bizarre and moving search-and-destroy mission. Calls this a brilliantly conceived and tortuously crafted novel flawed by its own rampaging vitality.

Simon, Roger L. "And Now, Comic Book Noire." Rev. of *The Magician's Wife. Los Angeles Times Book Review* 7 Feb. 1988: 5.

This novel seems to be a brave new genre of graphic novels, black and comic. Describes the contents, and comments that it is a mesmerizing experience.

Sokolov, Raymond A. "Ignoble Episode." Rev. of *American Scrapbook. Newsweek* 9 June 1969: 114, 116.

Describes the book as a novelistic treatment of life in the Japanese-American concentration camps and a concomitant lesson to blacks and other minorities. Briefly describes the contents.

Solotaroff, Theodore. "Jewish Camp." Rev. of *Once Upon a Droshky.* *Commentary* Mar. 1964: 76-78. Rpt. in *The Red Hot Vacuum and Other Pieces on the Writing of the Sixties.* Theodore Solotaroff. New York: Atheneum, 1970. 87-93.

Considers this first novel by Charyn a thin, improvised version of immigrant Jewish folkways that resulted from "the facile spell of Jewish camp" on which writers today place a literary premium. Further notes that unfortunately, "after a promising start the characters fall into a series of flat exotic types—the gentled ex-mobster, the crooked lawyer, the slovenly cafeteria owner, the superannuated chippy, the rich but obese widow." Concludes that Charyn has attempted to exploit Jewish folk material that "flickers intermittently and goes out."

Stern, Daniel. "The Day the Melting Pot Froze Up." Rev. of *American Scrapbook. Life* 6 June 1969: 24.

Argues that in order to discuss the racist attitudes of America and the precariousness of our innocence, *American Scrapbook* bypasses all the easy sociological approaches, and plunges into the guts and heart of a Nisei family named the Tanakas imprisoned in California. Concludes that this is an intense book which raises very deep questions.

Stern Daniel. "Mirrors of Memory." Rev. of *The Man Who Grew Younger and Other Stories. New York Times Book Review* 5 Feb. 1967: 46.

Calls *The Man Who Grew Younger* a book full of charms and terrors and remembered weathers. Sees it as deeply moving, and cites Charyn's gifts: his language sings, and he has a sense of wonder and the energy to communicate it.

"The Stuff of Which Novels are Made: Wayward Boys, a Cook, the Irish." Rev. of *On the Darkening Green. National Observer* 10 May 1965: 21.

Claims that *On the Darkening Green* faithfully recaptures the mood of a time when Charyn was younger. It is written with humor and pathos in just the right proportions. Claims that he takes great pains to hide the message—that a sensitive husband can't stay on the sidelines. Concludes that the novel's freshness makes up for any lack of freshness in its theme.

Theroux, Paul. "Field Day for Gypsies." Rev. of *Eisenhower, My Eisenhower. Washington Post Book World* 6 June 1971: 2.

Explains that *Eisenhower, My Eisenhower* is largely a fantasy about a society ruled by Anglos, the good folk, and hectored by muscular gypsies. Notes that the whole thing reads like a freakish cartoon with enough obscurities and flourishes to pass as serious writing. Claims that Charyn's fluency and humor are apparent, but are entirely a glib surface horror. Concludes that outrage is his watchword, but even this is diffused in a farrago of private jokes, graspings, and unrecognizable disorder that is rare even in the worst nightmares.

Interviews

Berkeley, Miriam. "PW Interviews Jerome Charyn." *Publishers Weekly* 26 Apr. 1985: 84-85.

In this interview Charyn discusses *War Cries Over Avenue C* and his previous books, his theory on the short story, his writing methods, and his future work.

Biographical Sources

Willis Michael A. "From Kerouac to Koch." *Columbia College Today* (Wint.-Spr. 1971): 46-51.

Discusses Charyn's life and writing career in the context of an article discussing the writers who have come out of Columbia University. Finds them some of the most exciting writers of the fifties and sixties.

Woolf, Michael. "Jerome Charyn." *Dictionary of Literary Biography Yearbook: 1983.* Eds. Mary Bruccoli and Jean W. Ross. Detroit: Gale, 1984. 194-201.

A general overview of Charyn's works, background, and critical reception, as well as a book-by-book explication. A major essay and excellent starting place for research on Charyn.

Dissertations

Woolf, M. P. "A Complex Fate: Jewish-American Experience in the Fiction of Leslie Fiedler, Edward Wallant, Chaim Potok, and Jerome Charyn." Diss. U of Hull, 1981.

Arthur A. Cohen
1928 – 1986

Primary Sources

Novels

Acts of Theft. New York: Harcourt, 1980; London: Secker, 1980; Chicago: U of Chicago P, 1988.

An Admirable Woman. Boston: Godine, 1983, 1987; Manchester: Carcanet, 1985; St. Albans: Paladin, 1987.

The Carpenter Years. New York: NAL, 1967; London: Rupert, 1967; New York: Signet-NAL, 1968.

A Hero in His Time. New York: Random, 1976; London: Secker, 1976; Chicago: U of Chicago P, 1988.

In the Days of Simon Stern. New York: Random, 1973; New York: Laurel-Dell, 1974; New York: Delacorte [Cited in PBIP, 1974]; London: Secker, 1974; Chicago: U of Chicago P, 1988.

Collected Works

Artists & Enemies; Three Novellas. Boston: Godine, 1987.

Contents: Hans Cassebeer and the Virgin's Rose, The Monumental Sculptor, Malenov's Revenge.

Short Fiction in Periodicals

"Hans Cassebeer and the Virgin's Rose." *TriQuarterly* 33 (1975): 79-111.

"Last Word from Berlin." *Present Tense* 10.4 (1983): 43-47.

"The Monumental Sculptor." *TriQuarterly* 41 (1978): 169-242.

"Truth Is Not Good Enough." *American Judaism* 16 (1967): 10-11, 37-39.

Secondary Sources

Articles and Chapters

Berger, Alan L. "Judaism as a Religious Value System." *Crisis and Covenant: The Holocaust in American Jewish Fiction*. Alan L. Berger. SUNY Series in Modern Jewish Literature and Culture. Albany: New York State UP, 1985. 42-49.

Discusses *In the Days of Simon Stern* as a rambling novel that creates a pastiche of Messianic, cabalistic, Talmudic, philosophical, and theological ruminations on various interpretations of Jewish theodicy, the Jewish vocation, the reciprocal nature of the divine-human relationship, and millennial Jewish endurance.

Bilik, Dorothy Seidman. "Cohen's Ultimate Diaspora." *Immigrant Survivors: Post-Holocaust Consciousness in Recent Jewish American Fiction*. Middletown: Wesleyan UP, 1981. 167-78.

A detailed explication of *In the Days of Simon Stern*, focusing on how the novel employs the specifics of Jewish history, tradition, theology, and philosophy to shatter the limits of realistic fiction. Discusses its narrative strategies, style, use of anachronisms, and development of Simon's character.

Gertel, Elliot B. "Visions of the American Jewish Messiah." *Judaism* 31.2 (1982): 153-65.

Sees the novel as messianic because Cohen has moved from explorations of the assimilationist mentality to dramatic accounts of recovered Jewish identity, and then to a messianic vision that is theologically unique. Describes Stern's community as a redemptive venture in the spirit of traditional prophetic and rabbinic theology, which addresses itself to Jew and non-Jew alike. Concludes that despite its mixture of disparate genres and its unnecessary length, this is the most successful and authentically Jewish of the messiah novels because its vision is a theological hope that, like fiction, must be believed in.

Jauss, David. *In the Days of Simon Stern. Survey of Contemporary Literature.* Ed. Frank N. Magill. Rev. ed. 12 vols. Englewood Cliffs: Salem, 1977. 6: 3678-81.

A standard reference article covering characters, background, influences, theme, and style.

Kaufman, William E. "Arthur A. Cohen and Jacob B. Agus: The Supernatural and the Absolute Self." *Contemporary Jewish Philosophies.* William E. Kaufman. New York: Reconstructionist, 1976. 217-50.

Focuses on the idea of transcendence as articulated by Cohen. Summarizes his theology and attitudes toward the question of Jewish identity. Attempts to understand his concept of the supernatural Jew representing his ultimate truth, including his conception of God. Concludes that Cohen's theology is more or less consistent if one is willing to grant his supernaturalist premises.

Kremer, S. Lillian. "Eternal Faith, Eternal People: The Holocaust and Redemption in Arthur A. Cohen's *In the Days of Simon Stern.*" *Witness Through the Imagination: Jewish American Holocaust Literature.* S. Lillian Kremer. Detroit: Wayne State UP, 1989. 279-99.

Argues that *In the Days of Simon Stern* is a rich, culturally textured, complex philosophical novel that incorporates biblical legend and theological, Talmudic, and Messianic redemptive theory to wrest instruction from the Holocaust. Discusses also Stern's theory that all Jews, whether the Holocaust maimed them physically or not, are psychologically survivors and inherit Holocaust knowledge.

Lask, Thomas. "Publishing: From Art Books to a Novel About Art." *New York Times* 22 Feb. 1980: C24.

Briefly describes Cohen's professional career as a publisher, bookstore owner, and writer, and notes his themes of art and myth, the nature of the creative act, and of the artist as a kind of confidence man, a thief, in his fiction. Quotes his defense of the intrusion of long parables, dialectical discussions, and dream sequences into his fiction as "something extra delivered by the novelist, a discipline delivered as a bonus about a subject not familiar to all readers." Readers fail to recognize that the mind is a generative force, not just "imagination acting as an immediate sensation."

Malin, Irving. "Acts of Faith." *Congress Monthly* 1980: 15-17.

Laments that so few critics have discussed the works of Arthur Cohen. Reviews the titles of the novels, the theology behind them, and then discusses the individual books, claiming that *Acts of Theft* is the best. Concludes that all of the novels fuse action and thought dramatically, and deserve to be read because they dare to explore acts of faith in provocative, subtle, extra-logical ways.

Rosenfeld, Alvin H. "Arthur A. Cohen's Messiah." *Midstream* Aug.-Sept. 1973: 72-75.

Claims that in turning to the novel, Cohen was attempting to effect a major turn of focus, language, and over-all address, even if not of thematic concern. Sees results as uneven but not unpromising. Discusses the story of Simon Stern and his messianic role, calling the novel a minor miracle of contemporary experimentation with form.

Stern, David. "Theology into Art: An Appreciation of Arthur A. Cohen." *Response* 21 (Spr. 1974): 63-71.

A major tribute which discusses the centrality of exile and unredemption to modern Jewish existence reflected in Cohen's theological works, as well as in his novels. Describes the contents of *In the Days of Simon Stern* in considerable depth, and treats its theology in the same manner. Sees the book as an anti-Christian novel in its depiction of a messiah whose mission is to prove the unredeemedness of the world. Discusses also the accuracy of his characterization of the Jew as a type.

Reviews

Bandler, Michael J. Rev. of *In the Days of Simon Stern*. *Commonweal* 28 Sept. 1973: 530-31.

Summarizes the plot of the novel that treats the themes of survival, endurance, and ultimate redemption in which Cohen chronicles the "life and times of a messiah—not necessarily a false messiah, not *the* Messiah, but a messiah nonetheless."

Bell, Pearl K. "Dead Endings." Rev. of *A Hero in His Time*. *New Leader* 22 Dec. 1975: 11.

Provides a brief overview of the novel, criticizing it for its ambivalence. Asks whether it is a satiric indictment of Soviet oppression, a contemptuous swipe at the Yevtushenko groupies in New York, an elegiac tribute to the masters of modern Russian poetry, or a lament for the Jews of Russia.

Bergonzi, Bernard. "Eat! Eat!" Rev. of *The Carpenter Years*. *New York Review of Books* 1 June 1967: 31.

Calls Cohen a serious writer who turns outward to an alien order outside the Jewish family, thus raising the fundamental question of what it means to be a Jew in twentieth-century America and how far a Jew can abandon his identity. His style is wooden and melodramatic, written in the gray no-style of standard commercial fiction.

Brenden, Piers. Rev. of *In the Days of Simon Stern*. *Books and Bookmen* Mar. 1976: 57.

Calls *In the Days of Simon Stern* less than deeply moving, full of impermeable textures, clotted and stilted with Jewish allusions and expressions, and less than metaphysically satisfying. Complains that the novel is vastly overblown and profoundly boring.

Broyard, Anatole. "Books of the Times." Rev. of *An Admirable Woman*. *New York Times* 17 Nov. 1983: C25.

Provides a plot summary and brief analysis of the major weakness—the heroine who achieves only a kind of dry, majestic remoteness—of the novel suggested to Cohen by the career of his friend Hannah Arendt.

Broyard, Anatole. "The Politics of Poetry." Rev. of *A Hero in His Time*. *New York Times* 5 Jan. 1976: 27.

Describes *A Hero in His Time* as a relatively unimaginative fictional reconstruction of the life of Yevtushenko as poet in the Soviet Union. Concludes, unfortunately, that whatever it is trying to say is too elusive to be grasped by the reader.

Cunningham, Valentine. "Death-Dealers." Rev. of *A Hero in His Time*. *New Statesman* 27 Feb. 1976: 264-65.

Compares and contrasts this novel with the Victorian novel. Provides an elaborate plot summary.

Daiches, David. "Symbolic Dimensions." Rev. of *The Carpenter Years*. *Commentary* Apr. 1967: 94-96.

A detailed account of the plot and characters of the novel, praising it for its skill and care, but criticizing it for not being clearly realistic or symbolic. Concludes that these two levels of probability destroy, instead of reinforce, each other.

Dirlam, Sharon. "The Homage Inside." Rev. of *An Admirable Woman*. *Los Angeles Times Book Review* 20 Nov. 1983: 10.

Calls this novel a treasure because of its chronicling of the life of a fictional character, Erika Hertz, based on the life of Hannah Arendt.

Duchene, Anne. "A Promising Apprentice." Rev. of *Acts of Theft*. *Observer* 23 Mar. 1980: 39.

Calls *Acts of Theft* a very earnest novel debating mythology as well as the weakened art of modern men without mythology in involuted paragraphs of Conradian complexity.

Elkin, Lillian. "The Cord of Memory." Rev. of *An Admirable Woman*. *Jewish Frontier* Jan. 1984: 24-25.

A review essay sketching the era depicted in the novel from Elkin's own experience, and summarizing the analogous events, details, and characters from the novel. Praises the novel for its craftmanship and sheer intelligence.

Elman, Richard M. "Edgar Morrison's Choice." Rev. of *The Carpenter Years*. *New York Times Book Review* 5 Feb. 1967: 45.

Sees the novel as a pretentious religious potboiler asserting archetypes as people and people as archetypes.

Fyne, Robert. "The Jewish Messiah." Rev. of *In the Days of Simon Stern*. *Christian Century* 28 Nov. 1973: 1177-78.

Calls *In the Days of Simon Stern* an outstanding novel concerned not with social criticism or reform, but with the destiny of the Jewish people.

Admires the dazzling techniques of metaphor, surrealism, fantasy, mysticism, and spiritualism, along with its incisive and lapidary style.

Gold, Arthur R. "What Makes Edgar Run?" Rev. of *The Carpenter Years. New York Herald Tribune Book Week* 12 Mar. 1967: 2.

Calls *The Carpenter Years* a good novel but not very technically satisfactory. Objects to the depiction of the main character and the general outcome of the plot.

Gold, Ivan. "Arthur Cohen (1928-1986)." Rev. of *Artists and Enemies: Three Novellas. Partisan Review* 55.1 (1988): 159-63.

Provides an account of Cohen's life, writing career, education, individual novels, literary techniques, and latest book, *Artist's and Enemies.*

Groner, Oscar. "To Endure Against God Himself." Rev. of *In the Days of Simon Stern. National Jewish Monthly* Sept. 1973: 22, 26-27.

Elaborates the plot and points out the similarities with I. B. Singer and the marriage of Simon Stern's parents, his birth, and their deaths. Describes Cohen's puzzling view of Messianism and the surrealistic mixture of time, events, and characters in the novel.

Grumbach, Doris. "Arthur Cohen Catches Fire." Rev. of *A Hero In His Time. Village Voice* 15 Mar. 1976: 45.

Provides a brief history of Cohen's writing career which covers each of his works in turn, including work in progress. Focuses primarily on the contents, style, and qualities of *A Hero In His Time.*.

"Hebrewing Up." Rev. of *In the Days of Simon Stern. Times Literary Supplement* 15 Mar. 1974: 269.

Finds Cohen giving us "a bulky slice of universal Jewish Experiences" in a novel in which the story line "can be ignored with somewhat unnerving convenience." This "traipse through the Diaspora, not assisted by pauses for italic meditation, is to destroy any narrative cohesion and to substitute intolerable pretentiousness for legitimate pretense." It is his facility with words that has thwarted his efforts at creating fiction in spite of his encyclopedic knowledge of the Jewish past.

Hochfield, Sylvia. "Create Like a God, But Work Like a Slave." Rev. of *Acts of Theft. Art News* Sept. 1980: 28, 30.

Calls *Acts of Theft* a triumphant exception to the generalization that novels about artists usually fail. Concludes that this is a book full of wisdom about art and art making.

Horchler, Richard. Rev. of *The Carpenter Years. Commonweal* 8 Sept. 1967: 558-59.

Commends the novel for its profound philosophy and ideas, but complains that they are hung on the characters rather than developed fictionally. Praises its concern with the spiritual meaning of modern American experience.

Jefferson, Margo. "Innocent Abroad." Rev. of *A Hero in His Time. Newsweek* 12 Jan. 1976: 65-66.

Summarizes the plot with no evaluation or critical comment.

Jonas, Gerald. Rev. of *A Hero in His Time. Present Tense* 3.3 (1976): 80.

Comments on plot, characters, and themes, spending considerable time on the character of Yuri Maximovich.

Kriegel, Leonard. "The Wondering Jew." Rev. of *The Carpenter Years. Nation* 3 July 1967: 23-24.

Sees the theme of the novel as an exploration of the very brittle heritage of both Jews and Christians, but claims that it is not quite successful because of Cohen's inability to make his religious consciousness decisive for the reader.

LeClair, Thomas. Rev. of *A Hero in His Time. America* 13 Mar. 1976: 215-16.

Says of *A Hero in His Time* that it features an unlikely hero who finally achieves enough stature to gain our respect as he finds his own private courage. Concludes that the book is a modest success with a large, worthy spirit.

Lehmann-Haupt, Christopher. "The Messiah Travels Uptown." Rev. of *In the Days of Simon Stern. New York Times* 5 June 1973: 39.

Claims that *In the Days of Simon Stern* is a book in which Cohen attempts to embrace the ancient tradition, transplant it whole into the new world, and thus astonishingly persuade us that the Jewish novelist's imagination need not be torn at all. Concludes that it bears a message about how the Jews ought to conduct their lives in the new world, and thus embraces Judaism in all its permutations.

Leonard, John. "Books of the Times." "Acts of Theft." Rev. of *Acts of Theft*. New York Times 12 Feb. 1980: C9. Rpt. in *Books of the Times*. Apr. 1980. 134-36.

Details the artistic career of the protagonist, Mauger, in *Acts of Theft*, and comments that the author's ability to make the reader believe in an art we cannot see, a space shaped in silence, and "essential things" through the piling on of words, is little short of remarkable.

Maddocks, Melvin. "'An Expert: Full of Interior Ghettoes.'" Rev. of *The Carpenter Years*. *Christian Science Monitor* 23 Feb. 1967: 11.

Claims that in this novel, Cohen cuts deeper than the issues of Jewish identity to discuss spiritual rootlessness and ethical confusion. Concludes that the novel is really a worthy failure, which is better than a cheap success.

Miller, Jim. "A Moveable Feast of Fiction." Rev. of *An Admirable Woman*. *Newsweek* 14 Nov. 1983: 114.

Briefly summarizes the plot, compares Erika with Hannah Arendt, her inspiration, but claims that she lacks Arendt's caustic wit and flair for philosophical fireworks. Concludes that it is the emotional world of the novel that rings true.

Mirsky, Mark Jay. "One Man's Messiah." Rev. of *In the Days of Simon Stern*. *Washington Post Book World* 29 July 1973: 5, 10.

Describes *In the Days of Simon Stern* as a frustration and a torment, for its content coincides and collides. Claims that the content is ultimately hollow and blunders about in sociology, psychology, philosophy, all gracelessly, but never tells a convincing story. Describes the contents.

Morgan, Edwin. "A Russian in New York." Rev. of *A Hero in His Time*. *Times Literary Supplement* 27 Feb. 1976: 213.

Sees *A Hero in His Time* as a thin story padded out with flashbacks and having very little capacity for delight. Outlines the story, and concludes that the novel is alternately entertaining, wry and savage, is too determined to labor its broad political points, but nevertheless has a serious as well as a maliciously topical interest.

Murray, Michele. "A Puzzling Fable Expands to Fill a Universe." Rev. of
  In the Days of Simon Stern. National Observer 28 July 1973: 23.

Calls *In the Days of Simon Stern* a quaint novel filled with quaint talk,
quaint characters, and bagels. Argues that it discusses evil, salvation, the
process of redemption, the role of each individual in the creation, and the
role of thought. Concludes that this is a book which talks of vertical relationships and takes seriously Martin Buber's "I and Thou" relationship.
This fable has weight and gravity.

Nordell, Roderick. "Undashing Poet—Yet Admirable." Rev. of *A Hero
  in His Time. Christian Science Monitor* 5 Feb. 1976: 22.

Describes the comic antics of the protagonist, the circumstances of living
in the Soviet Union described in the book, the strengths and weaknesses
of Cohen's prose, and the central thematic concerns of the novel.

Oliver, Roy. "Not-so-simple Simon." Rev. of *In the Days of Simon Stern.
  Jewish Quarterly* 22.2 (1974): 21-22.

Comments on the novel in detail, commending the narrative strategies,
describing the protagonist, and briefly discussing the theological perspectives of the novel.

Ozick, Cynthia. "Assimilation and Downward Mobility." Rev. of *The
  Carpenter Years. Congress Bi-Weekly* 6 Mar. 1967: 16-17.

Identifies the themes as questions of Jewish as opposed to Christian identity. Notes that curiously the smaller, sociological questions in the book
are the more interesting. Sees Cohen as making damning historical judgments on the quality of Jewish assimilation. Sees it as assimilation
towards the lower stratas of taste and values—a spectacularly plebeian
caste identity. Claims that, in America, Jewry stays in its "carpenter
years" like Christ during his preparatory ministry; there are no
"Jerusalem years." Though the novel is not very good, his thesis
demands examination and interpretation.

Ozick, Cynthia. "The Coming, not of a Messiah, but of the Messiah."
  Rev. of *In the Days of Simon Stern. New York Times Book Review* 3
  June 1973: 6.

Surveys the story, plot, and character. Discusses the embedded tales
within tales, letters, legend, ritual drama, meditations, and religious play
within the novel, commending it for being original, American, and
Jewish.

Perlberg, Mark. "Spiritual Bankruptcy." Rev. of *The Carpenter Years*. *Christian Century* 1 Mar. 1967: 275-77.

Describes *The Carpenter Years* as a book full of Eliotic hollow men who cannot put the pieces of inner and outer life together because they lack the vital principle around which to organize either. Details the contents.

Philipson, Morris. "Art Is Not Enough." Rev. of *Artists and Enemies: Three Novellas. New York Times Book Review* 12 Apr. 1987: 20.

Describes the contents of the novellas, and praises them for their sophistication, rich language, and lyrical celebrations.

Phillips, Robert. Rev. of *A Hero in His Time. Commonweal* 26 Mar. 1976: 215-16.

Considers the novel worthwhile reading because of its depiction of Russian history and because of the protagonist's rage for justice. Criticizes some of the satirical portraits in the book, particularly that of Stanley Kunitz, which he describes as gratuitous and unfortunate.

Plotkin, Frederick. "The Messiah Lives Downtown." Rev. of *In the Days of Simon Stern. Congress Bi-Weekly* 26 Oct. 1973: 20-22.

Calls this the most masterful Jewish novel of Cohen's generation because he has caught the inner and outer meaning of the Holocaust, of Jewish hope, and Jewish tragedy. Calls his thinking mystical and apocalyptic, and commends him for the constellation of old and new perspectives he is able to work within. Labels the novel allegorical, and praises it for its maturity of vision and humanistic sympathy.

Prescott, Peter S. "The Last Jew." Rev. of *In the Days of Simon Stern. Newsweek* 11 June 1973: 108.

Describes the protagonist Simon Stern as a messiah standing in for a god who "is to be honored, but not trusted again. Claims he is vain and weak, able only to weep for man." Finds the story intelligent, grave and ambitious and worth our attention and respect, but dislikes its "vagaries of pace" and Cohen's failure to develop his arguments before chasing another line of thought.

Riemer, Jack. "Parable of U.S. Today." Rev. of *The Carpenter Years*. *National Jewish Monthly* July-Aug. 1967: 34.

Briefly describes the two central characters—father and son—and the confrontation the story builds to. Finds this "a searing parable of religion—and the lack thereof—in the contemporary world."

Rovit, Earl. "American Fiction." Rev. of *In the Days of Simon Stern.*
     Contemporary Literature 15.4 (1974): 545-46.

Calls *In the Days of Simon Stern* large in ambition and equally large in its failure. Notes that naturalism is supplanted by tenuous fable allegory, while unbelievable characters invade the plot, and philosophical divagations from Nathan become wearisome.

Sage, Lorna. "Too Serious By Half?" Rev. of *A Hero in His Time.*
     Observer 22 Feb. 1976: 27.

Calls *A Hero in His Time* a lengthy appendix to his work on the history of Jewish thought. Claims that the best things in it are descriptions of the struggles in Russia to preserve names, manuscripts, and snatches of song against the bureaucratic machine.

Sage, Lorna. "When Silence is Golden." Rev. of *In the Days of Simon
     Stern. Observer* 10 Feb. 1974: 32.

Calls *In the Days of Simon Stern* a garrulous, shaky book that pretends to revere quiet and simplicity. Concludes that Mr. Cohen is an historian of Jewish thought, and writes like one here.

Shechner, Mark. "Graven Images and Other Temptations." Rev. of *Acts
     of Theft. New York Times Book Review* 9 Mar. 1980: 10.

Provides a good summary of plot and characters, but criticizes the novel for its failure to maintain its vividness, for its lecturing, and for its hopelessness with regard to language. Concludes that Cohen wants the sublime but can achieve only the breathless, which works in fiction about as well as it does in religion.

Shorris, Earl. "Not Hannah Arendt." Rev. of *An Admirable Woman. New
     York Times Book Review* 20 Nov. 1983: 9, 49.

Provides an overview of the characters and events, and concludes that, for all its thoughtfulness and knowing and sure-handed use of the writer's craft, the novel is flawed by the timidity of the scene of disagreement between Erika Hertz and Hannah Arendt over Arendt's use of the word "banality" in her famous treatise on evil in *Eichmann in Jerusalem.* Points out the parallels between Cohen's fictional Erika Hertz and Hannah Arendt.

Skow, John. "A Lyre for the KGB." Rev. of *A Hero In His Time*. *Time* 5 Jan. 1976: 66, 68.

Briefly describes the plot and concludes that the novel is "a delightful minor-key force" that sounds like "a U.S.S.R. satirist writing riskily for *Samizdat* circulation." Concludes that, unfortunately, the New York section is weakened by too many plot turns and satire of the academic community that lacks teeth.

Steiner, Deborah. "Crossing the Line." Rev. of *An Admirable Woman*. *Times Literary Supplement* 15 Mar. 1985: 283.

Argues that the novel fictionalizes Hannah Arendt by presenting her as an old woman dying and undergoing self-examination, while leaving out key events that would seem tailor-made for a novelist. Concludes that in the end the novel falls heavily between two stools—it is neither a good biography nor a good novel.

Tracy, David. "A Thoughtful Life." Rev. of *An Admirable Woman*. *Commonweal* 10 Feb. 1984: 92-93.

Calls *An Admirable Woman* a remarkable novel by a remarkable novelist and theologian. Describes the central character, Erika Hurst, and her dedication to a life of thought as a Jewish woman and committed politician in the public realm. Concludes that this is a great *bildungsroman*.

Ungar, Andre. "An American Messiah." Rev. of *In the Days of Simon Stern*. *Haddasah Magazine* Sept. 1973: 39-40.

Considers *In the Days of Simon Stern* to be a vastly ambitious, flawed, and astonishing triumph. Calls it a splendid fusion of fact and fantasy, abstract ideas, and flesh and blood people. Describes Cohen's attempt to avoid a naturalistic treatment by stylizing, using symbols, hinting, alluding, and circumscribing the events. Concludes that the results are devastating and cathartic.

Washburn, Martin. "Artifiction." Rev. of *Acts of Theft*. *Village Voice* 17 Mar. 1980: 39-40.

Sees this latest fiction as having turned away from the consciousness of the Jewish mind which characterized his earlier work. Details the contents of each piece, and concludes that it fails to account for the negative feelings held by the characters creating motivational implausibility. Concludes that it is also overwritten, hence frequently imprecise in its language.

Winegarten, Renee. "American Insiders and Outsiders." Rev. of *The Carpenter Years. Jewish Observer and Middle East Review* 19 May 1967: 15.

Briefly describes the story of Morris Edelman/Edgar Morison, the symbolic Jew who joins a de-Christianized society as a de-Judaized Jew, seeing it as "a negative picture, an ironic comment on the status-quo."

Wisse, Ruth R. "The Pen & the Sword." Rev. of *A Hero in His Time. Commentary* Oct. 1976: 93-94, 96.

Describes the novel as a politically and artistically complex work concerned with the poet's ancient obligation to keep an ear open for God. Calls it well-written with engaging ideas, but marred by the false bravado of its ending.

Wohlgelernter, Maurice. "Fathers - Artichokes, Choosers, Carpenters - and All Their Sons." Rev. of *The Carpenter Years. Tradition: A Journal of Orthodox Thought* 9.3 (1967): 136-40.

Claims that while Cohen does not fully achieve the symbolic dimension of his novel, it is nevertheless powerful. Argues that its flaws lie in the inadequately drawn character of Edgar, in its excessive contempt for mediocrity, and in its failure to succeed as fiction.

Wolff, Geoffery. "How Yuri Maximovich Isakovsky Survived." Rev. of *A Hero in His Time. New York Times Book Review* 25 Jan. 1976: 4.

Describes the protagonist Isakovsky as a shlemiel Russian poet, who in spite of his failure to gain notoriety remains true to his craft, "wanting the poem more than he wanted to please." Concludes that the novel is stately, funny, and, like its poet-hero, ragged at times but a "true article."

Zara, Louis. "Books." Rev. of *The Carpenter Years. Chicago Jewish Forum* 26.4 (1968): 306-07.

Describes the plot, structure, and characterization of the protagonist in this first novel. Admires the structure but finds the truncated ending puzzling, feeling the need for the sickly son to have been analyzed in greater detail to make him more understandable.

Zeitlin, Naomi. "Fathers and Sons." Rev. of *The Carpenter Years. World Jewry* Sept.-Oct. 1967: 30.

A brief comparison of the novel to Potok's *The Chosen* and Gold's *Fathers.* Claims that Cohen's character repudiates his Jewishness in contrast to the protagonists of the other two novels.

Interviews

Baker, John F. "Interview: Arthur A. Cohen." *Publishers Weekly* 19 Jan. 1976: 10-12. Rpt. in *The Author Speaks: Selected PW Interviews, 1967-1976.* New York: Bowker, 1977. 27-31.

A general review of Cohen's background as publisher, writer, and religious historian. Discusses several of the novels briefly, and describes the nature of the historical research done by Cohen while preparing a novel.

Biographical Sources

Cole, Diane. "Arthur A. Cohen." *Twentieth-Century American-Jewish Fiction Writers.* Ed. Daniel Walden. Detroit: Gale, 1984. Vol. 28 of *Dictionary of Literary Biography.* 94 vols. to date. 1978-. 35-41.

More than details of his life, this is a career biography, tracing the development of the author's canon, describing the contents and themes of his works, evaluating his reputation, and placing him in the larger context of American literary history. Includes lists of primary and secondary sources and illustrations.

Cole, Diane. "Profession: Renaissance Man; Profile of Arthur A. Cohen." *Present Tense* 9.1 (1981): 32-35.

Contains much biographical information about Cohen as publisher and intellectual, and brief critical remarks about his novels. Concludes with Cohen's first person response to questions about his religious orthodoxy and philosophy of life.

Stanley Elkin
1930 –

Primary Sources

Novels

Alex and the Gypsy. New York: Pocket, 1976. Originally publ. as *The Bailbondsman* in *Searches and Seizures.* New York: Random, 1973 and in *Eligible Men.* London: Gollancz, 1974.

A Bad Man. New York: Random, 1967; London: Blond, 1967, 1968; New York: Berkley, 1971; London: Panther, 1971; New York: Warner, 1980; New York: Obelisk-Dutton, 1984.

Boswell: A Modern Comedy. New York: Random, 1964; London: Hamilton, 1964; A Berkley Medallion Book. New York: Berkley, 1967; New York: Warner, 1980; New York: Dutton, 1986.

The Dick Gibson Show. New York: Random, 1971; London: Weidenfeld, 1971; New York: Pocket, 1972; New York: Warner, 1980; New York: Dutton, 1983.

The Franchiser. New York: Farrar, 1976; Boston: Nonpareil-Godine, 1980.

George Mills. Dallas: Pressworks, 1980; New York: Dutton 1982, 1983.

The Living End. New York: Dutton, 1979, 1985; New York: Warner, 1980; London: Cape, 1980; London: Virgin, 1981.

The Magic Kingdom. New York: Dutton, 1985; New York: Obelisk-Dutton, 1986.

The Making of Ashenden. Covent Garden Stories 2. London: Covent Garden, 1972.

The Rabbi of Lud. New York: Scribner, 1987, 1988.

Collected Works

Alex and the Gypsy: Three Short Novels. Harmondsworth: Penguin, 1977. Originally publ. as *Searches and Seizures.* New York: Random, 1973, and as *Eligible Men.* London: Gollancz, 1974. Original title of *Alex and the Gypsy* was *The Bailbondsman.*
Contents: *Alex and the Gypsy, The Making of Ashenden, The Condominium.*

Criers and Kibitzers, Kibitzers and Criers. New York: Random, 1966; London: Blond, 1967; New York: Berkley, 1968; New York: Plume-NAL, 1973; New York: Warner, 1980.
Contents: Criers and Kibitzers, Kibitzers and Criers; I Look Out for Ed Wolfe; Among the Witnesses; The Guest; In the Alley; On a Field Rampant; A Poetics for Bullies; Cousin Poor Lesley and the Lousy People; Perlmutter at the East Pole.

Early Elkin. Flint: Bamberger, 1985.
Contents: Where I Read What I Read, A Sound of Distant Thunder, The Party, Fifty Dollars, The Graduate Seminar.

Eligible Men: Three Short Novels. London: Gollancz, 1974; Publ. as *Searches and Seizures: Three Novellas.* New York: Random, 1973, and as *Alex and the Gypsy: Three Short Novels.* Harmondsworth: Penguin, 1977. Original title of *Alex and the Gypsy* was *The Bailbondsman.*
Contents: *The Bailbondsman, The Making of Ashenden, The Condominium.*

Searches and Seizures: Three Novellas. New York: Random, 1973; New York: Nonpariel-Godine, 1973, 1978, 1980. Publ. as *Eligible Men: Three Short Novels.* London: Gollancz, 1974, and as *Alex and the Gypsy: Three Short Novels.* Harmondsworth: Penguin, 1977. *The Bailbondsman* publ. as *Alex and the Gypsy.* New York: Pocket, 1976. Contents: *The Bailbondsman, The Making of Ashenden, The Condominium.*

Stanley Elkin's Greatest Hits. New York: Dutton, 1980; New York: Warner, 1981.

Contents: *The Making of Ashenden,* Feldman & Son, Bernie Perk, The Guest, The Transient, Mr. Softee, The Conventional Wisdom.

Short Fiction in Anthologies

"Among the Witnesses." *Accent: An Anthology 1940-1960.* Eds. Daniel Curley and George Scouffas. Urbana: U of Illinois P, 1973. 43-64.

"The Conventional Wisdom." *The Best American Short Stories, 1978.* Eds. Ted Solotaroff and Shannon Ravenel. Boston: Houghton, 1978. 223-48; *Matters of Life and Death: New American Stories.* Ed. Tobias Wolff. Green Harbor: Wampeter, 1983. 20-42.

"Criers and Kibitzers, Kibitzers and Criers." *The Best American Short Stories, 1962.* Eds. Martha Foley and David Burnett. Boston: Houghton, 1962. 51-80; *Fiction as Process.* Eds. Carl Hartman and Hazard Adams. New York: Dodd, 1968. 199-231; *My Name Aloud: Jewish Stories by Jewish Writers.* Ed. Harold U. Ribalow. South Brunswick: Yoseloff, 1969. 64-91; *The Norton Introduction to Literature: Fiction.* Ed. Jerome Beaty. New York: Norton, 1973. 254-74; *Jewish-American Stories.* Ed. Irving Howe. New York: Mentor-NAL, 1977. 333-60.

"The Guest." *The Single Voice: An Anthology of Contemporary Fiction.* Ed. Jerome Charyn. New York: Collier, 1969. 1-32; *Love Is the Theme.* Eds. Douglas Angus and Sylvia Angus. Greenwich: Fawcett, 1970. 247-76; *The Arbor House Celebrity Book of the Greatest Stories Ever Told.* Eds. Martin H. Greenberg and Charles G. Waugh. New York: Arbor, 1983. 169-98.

"I Look Out for Ed Wolfe." *The Best American Short Stories, 1963*. Eds. Martha Foley and David Burnett. Boston: Houghton, 1963. 140-65; *Contemporary American Short Stories*. Eds. Douglas Angus and Sylvia Angus. Greenwich: Premier-Fawcett, 1967; New York: Ballantine, 1983. 519-49; *How We Live: Contemporary Life in Contemporary Fiction*. Eds. Penney Chapin Hills and L. Rust Hills. New York: Macmillan, 1968; New York: Collier, 1972. 38-59; *Writer's Choice*. Ed. L. Rust Hills. New York: McKay, 1974. 127-51; *Great 'Esquire' Fiction: The Finest Stories from the First Fifty Years*. Ed. L. Rust Hills. New York: Penguin, 1983. 269-94.

"On a Field, Rampant." *The Human Commitment: An Anthology of Contemporary Short Fiction*. Ed. Don Gold. Philadelphia: Chilton, 1967. 280-325.

"A Poetics for Bullies." *New Sounds in American Fiction*. Ed. Gordon Lish. Menlo Park: Cummings, 1969. 173-90; *Collection: Literature for the Seventies*. Eds. Nancy Shingler Messner and Gerald Messner. Lexington: Heath, 1972. 284-97; *The Challenge of Conflict*. Eds. Paul C. Holmes and Anita J. Lehman. New York: Harper, 1976. 85-97; *American Short Story Masterpieces*. Eds. Raymond Carver and Tom Jenks. New York: Delacorte, 1987. 146-60; *The Norton Book of American Short Stories*. Ed. Peter S. Prescott. New York: Norton, 1988. 572-87.

"The Transient." *The Best American Short Stories, 1965*. Ed. Martha Foley. Boston: Houghton, 1965; New York: Ballantine, 1965. 57-91.

Short Fiction in Periodicals

"Alone Is Hurt Too." *Illini Writers* 4 (Spr. 1951): 11-19.

"Among the Witnesses." *Accent* 19.4 (1959): 179-200.

"Boswell Steps Out." *Esquire* July 1964: 64-69, 96, 98-99.

"The Bottom Line." *Antaeus* 28 (1978): 7-30.

"The Conventional Wisdom." *American Review* 26 (1977): 79-109.

"Corporate Life." *Chicago* Mar. 1985: 156+.

"Cousin Poor Lesley and the Lousy People." *Perspective* 11.1 (1959): 12-30.

"Criers and Kibitzers, Kibitzers and Criers." *Perspective* 12.2 (1961): 55-80.

"The Dodo Bird." *Iowa Review* 1.3 (1970): 28-47.

"The Dying." *Illini Writers* 4.1 (1950): 10-18.

"Everything Must Go." *Saturday Evening Post* 31 Jul 1965: 50-54, 56-57.

"Fifty Dollars." *Southwest Review* 47.1 (1962): 41-60.

"The First George Mills." *Antaeus* 40-41 (1981): 86-104.

"The Franchiser." *Fiction* 4.1 (1975): 32-35.

"George Mills." *Playboy* Nov. 1982: 96-98, 100, 108, 186-91.

"Garbage Dump." *Saturday Evening Post* 22 Apr. 1967: 60-62.

"The Graduate Seminar." *Fiction* 1 (1972): 16-18.

"The Great Sandusky." *Paris Review* 8.32 (1964): 78-91.

"The Guest." *Paris Review* 9.34 (1965): 43-77.

"I Look Out for Ed Wolfe." *Esquire* Sept. 1962: 112-17, 161-67.

"In the Alley." *Chicago Review* 13.4 (1959): 3-25.

"The Magic Kingdom." *Delta* 20 (1985): 37-55.

"The Making of Ashenden." *TriQuarterly* 26 (1973): 42-103.

"The Memory Expert." *Esquire* May 1970: 152-54, 175-78, 180.

"The Merchant of New Desires." *Saturday Evening Post* 6 May 1967: 70-72.

"On a Field, Rampant." *Perspective* 18.2 (1963): 67-100.

"The Party." *Views* 4 (1958): 37-51.

"Perlmutter at the East Pole." *Saturday Evening Post* 13 Feb. 1965: 46-49, 52, 54, 56-58, 60, 62-63.

"A Poetics for Bullies." *Esquire* Apr. 1965: 66-68, 128, 132.

"The Rabbi of Lud." *Chicago* Oct. 1986: 196+.

"A Sound of Distant Thunder." *Epoch* 8.1 (1957): 39-57.

"The State of the Art." *TriQuarterly* 44 (1979): 230-59.

"The Telethon." *Playboy* Sept. 1982: 102-03, 222.

"Three Meetings." *TriQuarterly* 63 (1985): 155-59.

"The Transient." *Saturday Evening Post* 25 Apr. 1964: 54-60.

Secondary Sources

Books

Bailey, Peter J. *Reading Stanley Elkin*. Urbana: U of Illinois P, 1985.

Dougherty, David C. *Stanley Elkin*. Twayne United States Authors Series 568. Boston: Twayne, 1991.

Articles and Chapters

Andrews, Larry. "The Dick Gibson Show." *Survey of Contemporary Literature.* Ed. Frank N. Magill. Rev. ed. 12 vols. Englewood Cliffs: Salem, 1977. 3: 1946-50.

Provides a detailed formalist plot summary, description, and appraisal of the style of *The Dick Gibson Show.*

Bailey, Peter. "M. S. as Metaphor." *Delta* 20 (1985): 57-71.

Begins with Sontag's observation that diseases whose origins are murky tend to be awash in moral interpretations and meanings that have a distinctly nineteenth-century ring. Claims that in *The Franchiser* Elkin creates meaning out of his own disease, M. S., along with the metaphorical associations which derive from the occupations mentioned in all of the novels. Argues that the ultimate theme in *The Franchiser* is that the self is always manifesting diseases of one sort or another.

Bailey, Peter. "Stanley Elkin's Tales of Last Resorts." *Mid-American Review* 5.1 (1985): 73-80.

Discusses "Among the Witnesses" and "The Condominiums" as two pieces of fiction that demonstrate the shift in Elkin's work over three decades. Details this shift with reference to style, subject matter, Jewishness, father/son relationships, and a host of other factors.

Bargen, Doris G. "The Orphan Adopted: Stanley Elkin's *The Franchiser.*" *Studies in American Jewish Literature [Albany]* 2 (1982): 132-43.

Discusses Elkin's use of orphanhood as a metaphor to dramatize the existential theme of the novel. Comments on the absence of conventional family relationships in the novel, and shows how orphanhood also provides the protagonist of the Elkin novel the chance to bond with the family of mankind.

Burnside, Gordon. "The Funniest Writer." Rev. of *Searches and Seizures. St. Louis* May 1983: 128.

A general article on Elkin's humor that construes itself as rival humor being neither book review, literary history, biography, or anecdote. Contains a couple of large excerpts from Elkin's *Searches and Seizures.*

Charney, Maurice. "Stanley Elkin and Jewish Black Humor." *Jewish Wry: Essays on Jewish Humor*. Ed. Sarah Blacher Cohen. Jewish Literature and Culture. Bloomington: Indiana UP, 1987. 178-95.

Documents Elkin's disavowal of affiliation with a school of Jewish writers, and insists that because of his particular use of black humor, he does indeed belong to this group. Deals in depth with *George Mills*, illustrating Elkin's use of the unheroic protagonist, the grotesque, the *schlemiel*, and alienation. Discusses several of the other novels from this perspective, concluding that style and choice of character types, black humor, themes of powerlessness, and comic religious attitudes definitely place Elkin as a Jewish writer.

Colbert, Robert Edward. "The American Salesman as Pitchman and Poet in the Fiction of Stanley Elkin." *Critique* 21.2 (1979): 52-58.

Provides a general overview of Elkin's life and individual works. Calls him a stunning verbal virtuoso, a black humor writer, and a gifted comic writer. A good introduction to Elkin that concentrates on major protagonists.

Connaughton, Michael E. "Stanley Elkin." *Critical Survey of Long Fiction*. Ed. Frank N. Magill. English Language Series. 8 vols. Englewood Cliffs: Salem, 1983. 3: 884-93.

A standard reference article covering Elkin's background, style, previous works, comedy, favorite theme of obsessive behavior as comedy, the interplay of reality and fantasy, and the use of narrative disruption as theme. Provides a brief insight into each novel.

Coover, Robert. Foreword. *Stanley Elkin's Greatest Hits*. New York: Dutton, 1980. ix-xii.

Calls Elkin a great tragicomic genius who shares with comedians a zest for bizarrely elaborated routines. Comments that the voice which sustains his composite tales is vivid, intense, singular, celebrative, and egocentric. Provides a general description of the ambience of Elkin's work.

Couturier, Maurice. "Elkin's *George Mills*, or How to Make an Ectoplasm Schmooze." *Delta* 20 (1985): 73-91.

Describes a central scene in the novel in which George is questioning the validity of the ectoplasm expert's premises from the perspective of its language strategies. Couturier then argues that this scene is actually an allegory of the reading process in which Imolatty must somehow make his text acceptable to the reader (George) who is constantly monitoring his statements, or supposed to be doing so. He expands his thesis to include "The Balloon" and then returns to *George Mills*, concluding with a series of assertions on the nature of Elkin's use of language.

Dillard, R. H. W. "Boswell." *Survey of Contemporary Literature*. Ed. Frank N. Magill. English Language Series. Rev. ed. 12 vols. Englewood Cliffs: Salem, 1977. 2: 856-58.

An outline of the characters, plot, and style of *Boswell*. Concludes with a brief formal description of the literary qualities of the text.

Ditsky, John. "'Death Grotesque As Life': The Fiction of Stanley Elkin." *Hollins Critic* 19.3 (1982): 1-11.

Claims that though Elkin has attained a loyal following, he has been denied the acclaim his gifts deserve. Describes the themes and styles of the various works to right this wrong. Pays particular attention to the ever-present theme of death that gives form and definition to life. Comments also on Elkin's splendid ear for the cadences of American speech, his humor used to disguise powerlessness, and his use of the grotesque. Discusses each of the works chronologically. An excellent overview of the novels.

Edinger, Harry G. "Bears in Three Contemporary Fictions." *Humanities Association Review* 28.2 (1977): 141-50.

Analyzes the use of first-person narratives and wealthy narrators, and brings in Elkin's "The Making of Ashenden," Davies' *The Manticore*, and Mailer's *Why Are We In Vietnam?* to show that the use of these "deep (hence profound) layers of folk-tale, folk-memory, fairy-tale, saga, epic, or tragedy from the old days when literature was receiving energy from the common man" can assure the survival of an author's works. Concludes by pointing out that it should not be surprising that modern fictions end with some purifying or revelatory encounter with the wild.

Gass, William. "Stanley Elkin's *The Franchiser*." *New Republic* 28 June 1980: 29-32. Rpt. as Introduction. *The Franchiser*. New York: Nonpareil-Godine, 1980. v-xv.

Describes how Elkin first places his imagination seed-like within a vocation, then proceeds to develop character and plot from these givens. Reviews this technique in the earlier novels. Praises *The Franchiser* for its language, detail, imaginative quality, use of pop culture, and what he calls Elkin's "rich topsoil of city asphalt." Calls Elkin a visionary writer who brings hope and celebrates all that the city has and has not become.

Graff, Gerald. "Babbitt at the Abyss: The Social Context of Postmodern
American Fiction." *TriQuarterly* 33 (1975): 305-37. Rpt. in *Literature
Against Itself: Literary Ideas in Modern Society*. Gerald Graff.
Chicago: U of Chicago P, 1979. 207-39.

Defines modern and postmodern literature by describing the postmodern
novel as that fiction which finally rejects bourgeois belief in the material
progress of civilization. Claims that fiction like that of Elkin's shows an
amorphous mass society that has lost contact with these earlier beliefs
and traditions. Only briefly mentions Elkin within this larger context.

Guttmann, Allen. "The Black Humorists." *The Jewish Writer in America:
Assimilation and the Crisis of Identity*. New York: Oxford UP, 1971.
79-85.

Says "it is high time Stanley Elkin's high jinks are noted." Sees him as a
gifted practitioner of the black humor genre. Notes his major works and
major themes, his style of comedy, and his gifts with language.

Guttmann, Allen. "Stanley Elkin's Orphans." *Massachusetts Review* 7.3
(1966): 597-600.

Comments on the fantastically comic people who inhabit Elkin's fictional world, all of whom seem to be orphans. Provides a fairly systematic
treatment of the orphans in fiction in general, and concludes that such a
phenomenon makes him tremble as a reader.

Hardaway, Francine O. "The Power of the Guest: Stanley Elkin's
Fiction." *Rocky Mountain Review of Language and Literature* 32.4
(1978): 234-45.

Provides a critical overview of the limited possibilities of the individual
in contemporary literature, and sums it up with Ellison's comment that
"humanity is won by continuing to play in the face of certain defeat."
This vision, Hardaway argues, is added upon by Elkin, who is perhaps
the best representative of contemporary existentialist fiction. Describes
him as a writer who can still create a character like Boswell to serve as a
model for this age's heroic possibilities. Provides a lengthy account of
Boswell and several other works, stressing the ironic humor and presence
of orphan characters, and illustrating Elkin's ability to see humor in second-rate existence. Concludes that though a reader unfamiliar with the
truncated possibilities of contemporary characters may despair over
them, Elkin himself does not take them too seriously: his characters are
not peering over into the void like their modernist predecessors, they are

companionably facing a random universe like tourists looking over into the Grand Canyon.

Kazin, Alfred. "The Absurd as a Contemporary Style." *Bright Book of Life: American Novelists and Storytellers from Hemingway to Mailer.* Alfred Kazin. Boston: Little, 1973. 258-59.

Groups Elkin along with Jerome Charyn, Joseph Heller, and Leonard Michaels as black humor novelists. Argues that Elkin's self-imposed task has been to assist his audience in throwing out its old moral baggage. Calls him harsh, derisive, and influenced by the post-Holocaust mentality of Jewish absurdity. Sees him as mocking the actuality of things, and mimicking guile and hysteria. Argues that Elkin's novels all contain a character making a last ditch act of madness, and dealing constantly with the phenomenon of death.

Kincheloe, Henderson. "*A Bad Man.*" *Survey of Contemporary Literature.* Ed. Frank N. Magill. Revised. 12 vols. Englewood Cliffs: Salem, 1977. 1: 521-23.

A standard reference article that lists the principal characters and provides a detailed account of its publishing history, sources, influences, plot, themes, symbolism, and style.

Lebowitz, Naomi. "Parody." *Humanism and the Absurd in the Modern Novel.* Naomi Lebowitz. Evanston: Northwestern UP, 1971. 123-36.

Argues that parody for the contemporary novelist is a serious matter because it clears the way for the heroism of language. "The old character, morality, and metaphysics are mere shadows with which substantially fleshed words can box." The novelist as hero uses language to parody social relationships or spiritual yearnings as a protest against aesthetic limitations. Discusses Elkin's Feldman, the protagonist in *Bad Man,* in this context.

LeClair, Thomas. "Hopes for American Writing." *New Republic* 22 Nov. 1980: 3.

A response to Alfred Kazin's "American Writing Now" (*New Republic,* Oct. 18, 1980) which identifies the novels of seven "achieved" writers of the 1970s, including Elkin's *The Dick Gibson Show.* Claims that Kazin ignores in his assertion that the novels of most contemporary leading novelists will not last.

LeClair, Thomas. "The Obsessional Fiction of Stanley Elkin."
Contemporary Literature 16.2 (1975): 146-62.

Develops the thesis that Elkin's characters are driven, that his fiction balances objectivity, ordinariness, compromise, obsession, intense desire, extravagant means, and the strange. Argues that the characters in the Elkin novel are obsessive in such a way as to illuminate multiplicity and create focus. Locates him with other absurdist writers and Jewish-American humorists. Introduces and analyzes Elkin's major works.

Lee, L. L. "The Anonymous American as Historian: Stanley Elkin's *Boswell.*" *Critique* 26.4 (1985): 185-91.

Sees Boswell as the quintessential American with his belief that life should be change, variety, and action. Claims that Boswell, while writing his own history, is inadvertently writing the history of America. Sees Boswell as a traditional picaro who lives by his wits, his body, and his ego, and who, rather than making history, makes experience, wishing to be in history as a kind of Sancho Panza or second team. Concludes that it is history that remains Boswell's true concern.

McCaffery, Larry. "Stanley Elkin's Recovery of the Ordinary." *Critique* 21.2 (1979): 39-51.

Discusses Elkin's ability to transform the ordinary through language; how his characters find their freedom in embracing the ordinary, unlike Bellow, and how they are moved by excesses because they are obsessively aware of death. Claims that as outcasts and outsiders, these men operate on the fringes of society even as they control it. Shows how death and bodily decay become dominant motifs along with the loss of literary and literal potency. Provides an extremely detailed exegesis of the character of Ben, and a detailed analysis of structure and style in the Elkin novel. Concludes with high praise for his prose.

Molesworth, Charles. "Stanley Elkin and 'Everything': The Problem of Surfaces and Fullness in the Novels." *Delta* 20 (1985): 93-110.

Describes Elkin as a "midfiction" writer who uses parable to enable him to suspend his irony between the poles of mimetic realism and the free-play of metafiction's self-reflexivity. Sees Elkin as employing the surface textures of realism: colloquial dialogue, standard exposition of spatial and temporal scenes, consistent characterology, and so forth. Shows that where he most clearly deviates from realistic canons is in his characters' implausible obsessions, the use of fairly frequent empirical impossibilities rather than a constant welter of juxtaposition, and an almost endless string of additional occurrences and details to the point of madcap exhaustiveness of an epistemological exhaustion. Goes on to discuss the full range of Elkin's comedy, humor, style, and metaphysics.

Moody, Hiram. "Stanley Elkin's New Novel." *Grand Street* 7.4 (1988): 196-201.

Discusses the ever-present theme of death in *The Rabbi of Lud*, *The Living End*, and *George Mills*. Comments also on the recurring themes and character types in all of his fiction. Discusses also Elkin's treatment of powerlessness, consumer culture, and class structure. Concludes with a strong, positive commendation of Elkin's worth as a writer.

Morace, Robert A. "George Mills." *Magill's Literary Annual 1983*. Ed. Frank N. Magill. 2 vols. Englewood Cliffs: Salem, 1983. 1: 273-77.

A formalist explication of Elkin's *George Mills* which details Elkin's general style, previous works, background, the methods of narrative disruption and phototechnic style, his affinities with other modernist writers, the contents of the novel, and its thematic implications.

O'Donnell, Patrick. "The Thicket of Writing: On Stanley Elkin's Fiction." *Facing Texts: Encounters Between Contemporary Writers and Critics*. Ed. Heide Ziegler. Durham: Duke UP, 1988. 32-44.

Analyzes Elkin's prose in detail by close exegesis of passages from several novels as allegories of language and authorship. Spends the remainder of the article discussing the prose in "What's In a Name?" Concludes that Elkin's writing continually wavers between the registers of ordinariness and otherness, the familiar and the alien. Argues that he uses the conventional and the anarchic to explode one another, and to parody the forms and intonations of conventional discourse, while at the same time, preserving these altered forms and accents in the metaphor, catalog, and speech.

O'Donnell, Patrick. "The Wor(l)d Made Flesh: Stanley Elkin's *The Franchiser*." *Passionate Doubts: Designs of Interpretation in Contemporary American Fiction*. Patrick O'Donnell. Iowa City: U of Iowa P, 1986. 116-36.

Provides a detailed discussion of the novel, arguing that what *The Franchiser* "franchises through the discontinuous voice of its talkative subject is language, but not molded, as in *Wiseblood*, into an assemblage of preemptive signs. Rather, the language of Elkin's novel implicates the 'more' of discourse that Foucault describes, the 'communications' of the cultural field or *arche* which, replete with its own discontent and the eruptions of the uncanny into the ordinary, conserves itself within the inscription of the human world as the conversation of that world. . . . The self here is 'unauthorized'; it is the mutable, groundless intersection of the languages that it speaks and is determined by."

Olderman, Raymond M. "The Fisher King Turns Warden." *Beyond the Waste Land: A Study of the American Novel in the Nineteen-Sixties.* Raymond M. Olderman. New Haven: Yale UP, 1972. 52-71.

Discusses *A Bad Man* from the perspective of the individual confronting an institution. Sees the wasteland as symbolized by the jail and as mad as any asylum. Claims that even its madness is outdone by the individual Feldman, or the "felled man." Sees the character of Warden Fisher as the "Fisher of bad men," and claims strong parallels between this novel and Kesey's *One Flew Over the Cuckoo's Nest.* Also sees the archetype of the Fisher King turned upside down in the character of Feldman as modern Grail Knight. Concludes that the novel employs three methods typical of 1960's fiction: black humor, a violent demonstration of humanity, and affirmation through the individual's purely symbolic gesture.

Olderman, Raymond M. "The Lighter Side of Conspiracy: A Note on Stanley Elkin's *Boswell.*" *Beyond the Waste Land: The American Novel in the Nineteen-Sixties.* Raymond M. Olderman. New Haven: Yale UP, 1972. 175-81.

Discusses the novel from the perspective that the drama of the isolated self offers one more argument in the ongoing dialogue about the powers that rule us and that are usually treated lightheartedly by the writers of the sixties. Claims that the novel establishes that age-old knowledge that man is trapped within himself, unable to move beyond the circle of his own limited experience, and tyrannized by the demands of the same impenetrable self that is the cause of his solitude. Concludes that this novel shows how the self's isolation has been made a usable property for the black humorist in the sixties.

Olderman, Raymond M. "The Politics of Vitality: On Stanley Elkin." *Fiction International* 2-3 (1974): 140-44.

An admiringly enthusiastic endorsement of Elkin's *Searches and Seizures.* Describes his catalogues, comic absurdity, Shakespearean compassion, metaphysical flights, vigorous descriptions, wonder, and mystery. Describes each of the novels, and concludes that Elkin is eminently worth reading.

Olderman, Raymond M. "The Six Crises of Dick Gibson." *Iowa Review* 7.1 (1976): 127-40.

Discusses Elkin's *The Dick Gibson Show* as an allegory of American history. Sees Dick Gibson, the protagonist, as the legal and spiritual representation of America's growth from The Great Depression to the Vietnam War. Demonstrates that he is a one-man cultural history and a history of a particular kind of American consciousness that learned its lessons by the end of WWII, and brought those lessons into full vapid literalization in the fifties and early sixties. Concludes that by the end of the novel, by the end of the sixties, Dick Gibson is forced to confront squarely the consequences of his own development. He is America in confrontation with itself.

Raff, Melvin. "Wyndham Lewis and Stanley Elkin: Salvation, Satire, and Hell." *Studies in Contemporary Satire* 8 (1981): 1-8.

Argues that *The Living End* is firmly in the tradition of Mennipean satire, and that the central premise of the novel, the depiction of events in the afterlife, has been a traditional premise for satire since Lucian's *Dialogues of the Dead*. Lists as evidence its catalogs, monolog curses, bathos, *non sequiturs*, displays of encyclopedic knowledge, coupling of high and low language, etc. until finally the novel itself overwhelms its author's verbal denial with its own profuse reality. Also points out many similarities between the satire of Wyndham Lewis and that of Elkin.

Sadkin, David. "Stanley Elkin." *Critical Survey of Short Fiction*. Ed. Frank N. Magill. 7 vols. Englewood Cliffs: Salem, 1981. 4: 1338-43.

Provides a standard reference book outline of Elkin under the headings "Born," "Principal Short Fiction," "Influence," "Story Characteristics," "Biography," "Analysis," "Major Publications," and "Bibliography."

Saltzman, Arthur M. "Ego and Appetite in Stanley Elkin's Fiction." *Literary Review: An International Journal of Contemporary Writing* 32.1 (1988): 111-18.

Argues that Elkin's fiction engages our appreciation most for its richly metaphorical, relentlessly clever, and unmistakably poetic narrative voice which enters by the ear. Notes his thematic trademarks—selling, scheming, the bizzare, the comic—and claims that it all evolves from the immediacy and primacy of voice. Relates matters of ego, food, and linguistic satisfaction.

Updike, John. "Cohn's Dream." Rev. of *God's Grace* by Bernard Malamud. *New Yorker* 8 Nov. 1982: 167-70.

In the context of a review of Malamud's *God's Grace*, Updike discusses *The Living End* as directing Elkin's Malamudian cadences, burlesque, and scorn against all popular manifestations of Christianity.

Watts, Emily Stipes. "The Businessman as Hero." *The Businessman in American Literature.* Emily Stipes Watts. Athens: U of Georgia P, 1982. 136-49.

Discusses Elkin's *The Bad Man* and *The Franchiser* as novels that depict the businessman as hero and use the traditional occupation of salesman to celebrate. Calls the vision informing both books puritanic because of its dark view of human sinfulness. Concludes that, nevertheless, both protagonists are presented as heroes.

Watts, Emily Stipes. "The Values of Capitalism." *The Businessman in American Literature.* Emily Stipes Watts. Athens: U of Georgia P, 1982. 150-60.

Examines the profile of values concerning capitalism found in (among many other writers) Elkin's works. Also examines the myths generated. Refers only generally to Elkin.

Wilde, Alan. "Irony in the Postmodern Age: Toward a Map of Suspensiveness." *Boundary 2* 9.1 (1980): 7-9, 36-39. Rpt. as "A Map of Suspensiveness" in *Horizons of Assent: Modernism, Postmodernism, and the Ironic Imagination.* Alan Wilde. Baltimore: Johns Hopkins UP, 1981. 127-65.

Provides a detailed examination of this entire phenomenon using Elkin's *The Bailbondsman* as one of many cases in point. Sees the novel as a critique of Elkin's own mythical method, a sardonic evaluation of its motive force and of its inadequacy in the face of the contemporary world. Also sees Elkins's attitude of suspensiveness as a ploy for freedom, a tolerance of the uncertainty about meanings. Concludes that the novel is a boisterous mock-heroic fable gone amok in the postmodern world.

Wilde, Alan. "Strange Displacement of the Ordinary: Apple, Elkin, Barthelme, and the Problem of the Excluded Middle." *Boundary 2*

10.2 (1982): 177-99. Rpt. in *Middle Grounds: Studies in Contemporary American Fiction.* Alan Wilde. Philadelphia: U of Pennsylvania P, 1987. 17-40.

In discussing the pros and cons of realistic and experimental writing and the problematics of definition, Wilde uses Elkin's *The Making of Ashenden* to continue his debate on the qualities and interchangeable categories of these artificially separated categories of fiction.

Reviews

Adams, Robert M. "The Story Isn't Over." Rev. of *The Magic Kingdom. New York Review of Books* 18 July 1985: 21-23.

Claims that the novel relies on straightforward, limited narrative. Sees its language as extraordinarily artistic, and its humor notable. Provides extensive plot summary.

Allen, Bruce. "Fiction Chronicle." Rev. of *Searches and Seizures. Hudson Review* 27.1 (1974): 129-31.

Provides a brief plot summary of the three short novels that make up this work. Claims that each comic story details a "search" that is rewarded with a painfully unanticipated revelation, a "seizure."

Apple, Max. "Having Their Last Good Time." Rev. of *The Magic Kingdom. New York Times Book Review* 24 Mar. 1985: 34-35.

Details the plot and characters of the novel and concludes that Elkin is a master of style who strips away sentimentality and replaces it with an honest look at the grotesque possibilities we all carry around with us. Claims that in this novel the lyrical merges with the clinical, the romantic motif of the journey couples with the vocabulary of the hospital ward, and people are incarnations of their diseases. Sees the comic vision of this book as both hysterical and profound. Concludes that part sick joke, part lyrical meditation on the nature of disease, the journey to this magic kingdom earns its place among the dark voyages that fiction must chronicle.

Bailey, Paul. "The Quick and the Dead." Rev. of *The Living End. Times Literary Supplement* 18 Jan. 1980: 54.

Provides a brief plot summary of the three-part novel with three settings—Heaven, Hell, and Minneapolis-St. Paul. Thinks this shortest of Elkin's novels his finest and is destined for survival. Concludes that it will surely be celebrated as a minor classic.

Bailey, Peter. "Stanley Elkin, *The Living End*." Rev. of *The Living End*. *Fiction International* 12 (1980): 274-76.

Calls the novel a book that takes on the received Christian vision of the afterlife and, among other things, has a rousing good time with it, pointing up its absurdities, deflecting its moral import, humanizing it, and ultimately transforming it from the authoritative Western myth into a lively and delightfully suggestive fiction.

Barrett, Mary Ellin. "Cosmo Reads the New Books." Rev. of *The Dick Gibson Show*. *Cosmopolitan* Mar. 1971: 10.

Describes *The Dick Gibson Show* as a book by a wild, wonderful American writer who should not be insulted with tags, but experienced directly for himself. Notes his subject to be the ego and the soul trying to rise above humdrum modern life. Concludes that while Elkin ridicules, even blackens, in the end he affirms.

Barton, Rick. Rev. of *The Living End*. *Cresset* Dec. 1979: 30.

Claims that *The Living End* contains one barely passable joke, much that is sacrilegious, more that is monotonous, and even more that is sophomoric.

Bell, Pearl K. "Slogging Through a Sahara." Rev. of *The Dick Gibson Show*. *New Leader* 5 Apr. 1971: 17-18.

Comments that *The Dick Gibson Show* is a bizarre, maniacally funny account of a perpetually apprenticed radio announcer whose elusive vision of success is one of perfect neutrality, the disembodied pseudonymity of the amplified human voice. Describes plot, characters, and the exciting freshness of its satiric laughter.

Bellman, Samuel Irving. "The Good & the Bad." Rev. of *A Bad Man*. *Congress Bi-Weekly* 11 Mar. 1968: 21-22.

Claims that he dislikes the novel because Elkin doesn't know what he is doing here, he horrendously overwrites, and he uses overworked symbols that lack impact.

Bellman, Samuel I. Rev. of *Searches and Seizures: Three Short Novels*. *Studies in Short Fiction* 11.4 (1974): 438-39.

Briefly describes the plot of the three novels, and excoriates Elkin for his inability to create stories that make sense or that have coherence and purpose. He concludes: "when Elkin's in good form [occurring only in flashes], he's really not bad at all!"

"Briefly Noted." Rev. of *The Living End. New Yorker* 25 June 1979: 105.

Describes the content of this fantasy, and calls it "a rare delight in this age of 'good reads' sold by the pound."

Bromley, Robin. "Book Briefs." Rev. of *Stanley Elkin's Greatest Hits. Saturday Review* Nov. 1980: 72.

Claims that this work contains excerpts from seven novels, pieces that are highly self-contained, and highly provocative short stories. Sees the characters as refreshingly intelligent people wrestling with a riotously out-of-joint world.

Brown, Robert. "Music When Soft Voices Die." Rev. of *The Living End. New York* 18 June 1979: 70-71.

Summarizes the plot of the novel and concludes that anyone who reads this book without admiration and delight does not really know how to read.

Ciardi, John. "Realism and Fantasy." Rev. of *Boswell: A Modern Comedy. Saturday Review* 15 Aug 1964: 6.

In the context of discussing John O'Hara's well-deserved receipt of the 1964 Award of Merit for the Novel for his tradition of realism, Ciardi is grateful for *Boswell* for its wacky satire. He briefly summarizes the plot, seeing the story as a "satirist's diary of the ego," and asserts that from Elkin, Boswell has "an intellect both learned and honed, a perception forever ready to burst into its own sort of wild and wacky poetry, and a well-mastered pen with which to keep his diary."

Clapp, Susannah. "The Lists of Lust." Rev. of *Eligible Men. Times Literary Supplement* 13 Dec. 1974: 1405.

Calls *Eligible Men* a collection of three novels, all about prosperous American men, more or less encumbered by wives, and all possessed of a certain swagger, ambition, and desire for style. Concludes that, unfortunately, the blurb on the cover is right in saying "it hardly matters what they are about." Sadly, it does not.

Conarroe, Joel. "Stanley Elkin's St. Louis Everyman." Rev. of *George Mills. Washington Post Book World* 10 Oct. 1982: 1, 11.

Briefly recites Elkin's previous works, and notes his relative obscurity as a writer's writer. Praises his use of language and storytelling, summarizes the novel, and concludes that Elkin is one of our essential voices in a class with Singer, Bellow, and Roth.

Crane, Milton. Rev. of *Boswell: A Modern Comedy. Chicago Tribune Books Today* 26 July 1964: 9.

Describes *Boswell* as evidence that a writer can become a *non pareil* easily enough if one sets one's sights low enough. Calls it the story of the preposterous misadventures of a celebrity-hunter on the make with occasional parallels to the Laird of Auchinlock.

Davis L. J. Rev. of *Searches and Seizures: Three Short Novels. Washington Post Book World* 28 Oct. 1973: 10-11.

Praises the brilliance of Elkin's language in these three novellas, but sees the first two as failed and the third as overwrought because the characters are artifacts whose gestures are frozen. Claims that the prose itself becomes the hero. Laments that Elkin has allowed himself to be taken prisoner by his own prodigious gift of language.

Des Pres, Terrence. "To Hell and Back with Stanley Elkin." Rev. of *The Living End. Washington Post Book World* 1 July 1979: 1, 4.

Calls the novel a comic fable of heaven, hell, and the last days. Sees Elkin as a master storyteller who has just the right blend of irreverence, care, and hard-core realism. Discusses his theme of death, his use of public domain cliche and information, and his stunning gifts with language.

Edelman, Lily. "The Seeing Eye: Three Writers and Their Tales of Home." Rev. of *Searches and Seizures: Three Short Novels. National Jewish Monthly* June 1974: 47-49.

Sees the novel as being about the alienation of father and son. Thoroughly summarizes plot. Concludes that the book deals primarily with a vision of the ambiguities of home and *mishpocha.*

Edwards, Thomas R. "Funny and Moving Assaults on the Reader's Habits of Sense and Manners." Rev. of *Searches and Seizures: Three Short Novels. New York Times Book Review* 21 Oct. 1973: 3.

Praises the three novellas for their style and humor, for the author's mastery of clashing tones and expectations, for his erratic imagination, and for his ability to write far more than just a series of comic novellas.

Galloway, David. "Vision of Life in Recent Fiction." Rev. of *Criers and Kibitzers, Kibitzers and Criers*. *Southern Review* 4.3 (1968): 859-60.

Considers this one of the most important collections of short stories published in recent years. Claims that an Elkin character moves in an "absurd, life-denying world . . . struggling to give the whole piece, and to assert, thereby, his own existence." Concludes that not all his characters survive, some lose heart and hope, but some do survive and assert themselves as human beings.

Gray, Paul. "Two Serious Comic Writers." Rev. of *Stanley Elkin's Greatest Hits*. *Time* 10 Nov. 1980: 102, 107.

Briefly reviews this reprinting of some of Elkin's works, admiring his set pieces and his ability to work with words.

Grumbach, Doris. "Fine Print." Rev. of *Criers and Kibitzers, Kibitzers and Criers*. *New Republic* 23 Mar. 1974: 32-33.

Briefly reviews the reprint edition of this collection of stories. Considers Elkin one of the giants of the English language short story.

Hamilton, Philip. "Stanley Elkin's *A Bad Man*." Rev. of *A Bad Man*. *MLA Quarterly* 29 (Sept. 1968): 237-38.

Calls *A Bad Man* a chronicle about a protagonist with superhuman dimensions. Claims that the book is a success built upon another unforgettable character whose origins lie somewhere in the mysterious recesses of history and artistic imagination.

Heilbut, Anthony. "Dregs Addicts and Cultural Illiterates." Rev. of *The Franchiser*. *Nation* 28 Aug. 1976: 151-52.

Claims that Elkin is one of the few writers whose new works can fill a reader with pangs of anticipation and alarm. Sees *The Franchiser* as stylistically elegant, not overtly experimental, but full of stylistic pyrotechnics. Provides a detailed account of the main events and characters of the novel, and his use of multiple sclerosis as a metaphor for the contemporary condition. Concludes that the novel is best read as a display of literary virtuosity.

Irving, John. "An Expose of Heaven and Hell." Rev. of *The Living End*. *New York Times Book Review* 10 June 1979: 7, 30.

Describes this as a novel that exposes the lives of the damned and the divine. Gives an excellent account of the novel, and discusses Elkin's preoccupation with death, the doomed, and the process of dying. Describes the prose as capable of love, scorn, pity, and cringing all at the same time.

James, Caryn. "Stanley Elkin's Deli Delight." Rev. of *George Mills.*
    Village Voice 26 Oct. 1982: 52.

Praises Elkin for his "life's not too bad" attitude, his ability to combine high art with pop culture, the density and dazzle of the language, and the complexity of meaning. Reviews the characters, plot, and style of the novel. Concludes that for Elkin, the greatest curse must be not having a sense of humor, since humor plays such a redeeming role in the novel's ending.

Kermode, Frank. "'Love and Do as You Please'." Rev. of *The Living
    End. New York Review of Books* 16 Aug. 1979: 45.

Basically a summary of the plot. Sees Elkin as "an original with his sour manic prose, and his cult of outrage." Claims that he takes the dirty joke to new heights, out of a horrified sense that the world is a plot largely made up of interwoven dirty jokes. Claims that Elkin deserves greater recognition, and that this novel "will stand a lot of attention from anybody who thinks he could get hooked on a taste so wild and bitter."

Klein, Marcus. "Fiction North and South." Rev. of *Boswell: A Modern
    Comedy. Kenyon Review* 26.4 (1964): 761-62.

Sees Boswell as having been borrowed from Bellow's *Augie March,* speaking a similar exuberant language and interested in metaphysical categories. Claims that the novel deals "cogently with Life and Death," but while "Death" is inevitable, "Life" is better.

Knickerbocker, Conrad. "Short Stories by a Pair of Young Masters." Rev.
    of *Criers and Kibitzers, Kibitzers and Criers. Life* 14 Jan. 1966: 8, 10.

Says these stories contain more art than 98 percent of the thousands of novels published in the previous five years. They are "fully realized expressions of the comic sense of tragedy, that uniquely American response to the weirdly dispersed, incongruous, contradictory, dislocated, sprung quality of modern life."

Koch, Stephen. "The Dark Side of Mickey Mouse." Rev. of *The Magic
    Kingdom. Washington Post Book World* 14 Apr. 1985: 9.

Argues that Stanley Elkin's *The Magic Kingdom* is a rich but macabre business—a comic novel about the death of children which manages to slide this most unendurably poignant subject along the whole razor's edge between realism and fantasy without once seeming to draw blood. Concludes that there is more obsession with life here than with the end. Claims that his imagination is redemptive: his magic—all irony and language.

LeClair, Thomas. Rev. of *The Franchiser. New Republic* 12 June 1976: 27.

Calls Elkins an eminent vulgarian and sensitive receiver at large in the access-road America. Claims that Elkin drills desire and plumbs how popular culture creates and satisfies need. Describes voice, characters, plot, and contents of the novel and concludes that its weaknesses are lack of cumulative effect and a waste of perception.

LeClair, Thomas. "Brief Reviews." Rev. of *George Mills. New Republic* 27 Dec. 1982: 37-38.

Comments on the "range of the strange" in the novel, along with describing the plot, characters, and obsessive quality of the novel. Concludes that *George Mills* is a "wonderful, grief-ridden . . . pure book."

LeClair, Tom. Rev. of *The Living End. Saturday Review* 13 Oct. 1979: 75.

Calls the novel a burlesque written with grace and art. It invents once more the last things, and in so doing, helps us invent our lives before our living end. Describes the contents.

Lehmann-Haupt, Christopher. "Books of the Times." Rev. of *The Living End. New York Times* 25 May 1979: C27. Rpt. in *Books of the Times* 2.5 (1979): 247-48.

Recounts the story and scenes from this three-part divine vaudeville comedy, the work of a man who is desperately trying to joke away death. Concludes that marvelously funny gags and sketches lie in wait around the next corner, but that one needs to read the whole book to appreciate them.

Lehmann-Haupt, Christopher. "Books of the Times." Rev. of *George Mills. New York Times Book Review* 20 Oct. 1982: C28.

Sees *George Mills* as a novel full of wonderful things because the writer is a stand-up vaudevillian comic. Claims that the novel is too surrealistically improvisational to warrant trying to read meaning into it. Concludes that it should not be taken too seriously.

Lehmann-Haupt, Christopher. "Books of the Times." Rev. of *The Magic Kingdom. New York Times* 18 Mar. 1985: C16.

Claims that *The Magic Kingdom* is a novel built on a brilliant idea and embellished with brilliant comic invention which pays unusual attention to a conventional plot line.

Lehmann-Haupt, Christopher. "A Gag and Two Ominous Words." Rev. of *Searches and Seizures: Three Short Novels. New York Times* 9 Oct. 1973: 45.

Sees *Searches and Seizures* as a book in which Elkin has finally put his game together. Concludes that he doesn't make up stories and plots any more to be stuffed with gags and jokes because now the gags become the plot.

Lehmann-Haupt, Christopher. "Killing for Fun and Games." Rev. of *A Bad Man. New York Times* 7 Oct. 1967: 27.

Describes *A Bad Man* as a book whose symbolism is gratifyingly unobtrusive, and whose story is an ominous evocation of the condition of the Jews in a totalitarian state. Shows how, in addition to this, Elkin sees the funny and peculiar almost everywhere, but that eventually his mad, wild, imaginative routines begin to clog the life of the story.

Lehmann-Haupt, Christopher. "Sobering Up." Rev. of *Criers and Kibitzers, Kibitzers and Criers. New York Times* 3 Jan. 1966: 25.

Argues that *Criers and Kibitzers, Kibitzers and Criers* is about life in which the odds look worse than equal, and about contests. Claims that it smells like a soap opera in which many have deserted the firing line for the bivouac, and in which black humor prevails. Concludes that Elkin is mischievous and versatile, writes in an evocative and taut style, and continually shocks, tickles, and surprises.

Lemon, Lee. "Bookmarks." Rev. of *The Rabbi of Lud. Prairie Schooner* 62.3 (1988): 133.

Describes *The Rabbi of Lud* as Elkin at his wonderful best. Sees the novel as a sumptuous, riotous, comic, tragic, mundane, miraculous rant, the kind of high-energy performance many attempt and only Elkin can sustain. Details the plot.

MacVicar, Bill. "Updated Dante in Minneapolis." Rev. of *The Living End." Maclean's* 20 Aug. 1979: 38.

Describes the novel as a fiendishly fast and clever rhapsody on the four last things—death, judgment, heaven, and hell (or rather on the ragbag of literal notions about them we all cart around). This book is divinely written, satanically funny, and celestially wise.

Marcus, Greil. "Real Life: San Francisco's Days of Rage." Rev. of *Living End. Rolling Stone* 12 July 1979: 50.

Argues that *The Living End* is an American update of the *Divine Comedy.* Declares that in different times he might be less unappreciative of the book, but hopes never to find it satisfying. Details the contents.

Maurer, Robert. "Shaggy Doggerel." Rev. of *Boswell: A Modern Comedy. New York Herald Tribune Book Week* 21 June 1964: 16.

Asserts that Elkin writes marvelously well, but this novel is "an overlong single joke, perhaps because most of us, having adjusted to both our mediocrity and our approaching death in less frantic (and less interesting) ways than Boswell has, will find it impossible to project ourselves into the spot of a man admittedly so uncommon."

McKinley, Maryann U. "A 'Spiffy' God in Man's (Distorted) Image." Rev. of *The Living End. National Catholic Reporter* 23 May 1980: 13.

Calls *The Living End* a religious triptych fashioned in prose, and a book which simultaneously nods to both Dante and Hieronymous Bosch. Claims that it provides a final comment on 20th century Judeo-Christianity. Concludes that there is no longer anything grand and mysterious about it.

Midwood, Barton. "Fiction." Rev. of *The Dick Gibson Show. Esquire* Apr. 1971: 30, 32.

Calls *The Dick Gibson Show* the work of a stylist—visceral, nervous, urban, and eclectic. Claims that the story is the servant of the voice, and that the reader is intrigued by the energy of the author. This book, part complaint and part cautionary tale, plunges wildly into wild exhibitionism. Concludes, however, that the forced burlesque and descriptions of cruel sexual aberrations succeed each other too quickly.

Milofsky, David. "The Fiction of Powerlessness." Rev. of *George Mills. Prairie Schooner* 57.2 (1983): 97-100.

Reviews the case for and against Elkin's fiction, and discusses why this latest novel is likely to continue the debate about his genius with language and his failure to provide significant content. Describes the plot and characters, and identifies the main theme of the novel as death. Points out how Elkin's characters never put up with their sense of the powerlessness of life without turning it into a black joke on humanity. Commends Elkin for portraying men and women who stand up and fight in a tragicomic world and "push against things." Concludes that *George Mills*, like Elkin's other recent fiction, is long, discordant, digressive, occasionally maddening, but the work of a master.

Mudrick, Marvin. Rev. of *Criers and Kibitzers, Kibitzers and Criers*. *Hudson Review* 19.2 (1966): 315-17.

Compares Elkin's novels favorably to other Jewish novels, which he refers to as "tedious regionalisms." Finds his narrative style as different as life to death. Considers him an important American writer whose "doubts are a happy change from dead certainties."

Murray, G. E. Rev. of *The Living End. Chicago* Sept. 1979: 114, 116, 118.

Calls Elkin a spiritual descendant of James Joyce and Lenny Bruce—all three visionary comics and Elkin in particular as America's leading specialist in black comedy and revelatory escapades. Sees *The Living End* as a triptych of three separate episodes that develop as one novel. Describes the contents of all three stories, and concludes that this is his most fulsome and effective fiction yet with its ultimately poetic language, informative irony, and delicate economy.

Murray, G. E. Rev. of *George Mills. Chicago* Dec. 1982: 134-36.

Describes *George Mills* as a hilarious novel written by a stand-up comedian. Shows how the complex narrative design flip-flops chronology and weaves a rich tapestry of past and present. Claims that the real story here is the manner in which Elkin accumulates the effects of ordinary circumstances into an outrageous vision of human frailty. Concludes that here we have Everyman in continual decline and disenchantment.

Murray, G. E. "Stanley Elkin *The Franchiser*." Rev. of *The Franchiser*. *Fiction International* 6-7 (1976): 152-53.

Sees *The Franchiser* as a typical word-heavy, borderline, surreal, jackhammer-action novel. Claims that it is the most difficult, comprehensive, satisfying fiction he has delivered so far.

Naughton, John. "Outrageous." Rev. of *The Living End. Listener* 14 Feb 1980: 222.

Sees this novel as a complete nonsense from start to finish, and no less enjoyable. Details the cast and antics of the story.

"Notable." Rev. of *Searches and Seizures: Three Short Novels*. *Time* 29 Oct. 1973: 122.

Briefly describes the three parts of the novel.

Owens, Brad. "History's Straight Man." Rev. of *George Mills*. *Christian Science Monitor* 19 Feb. 1983: 15.

Describes Elkin's anti-hero of the 1980s as blue-collar and uncommon. Argues that the book's energetic entertainment sometimes overpowers its more serious agendas, but notes that among all the wild and outrageous adventures and pure wit, there is also the dignity of particular human lives and insight into how we are all connected to one another.

Perrin, Noel. "Stanley Elkin Meets Mickey Mouse." Rev. of *The Magic Kingdom*. *USA Today* 22 Mar. 1985: 3D.

Sees *The Magic Kingdom* as a series of dark fantasies both sad and funny. Claims that this is a fairly good book containing several bravura performances with language and much self-indulgence.

Pinsker, Sanford. "Power of Language." Rev. of *Stanley Elkin's Greatest Hits*. *Reconstructionist* June 1981: 28-30.

Argues that Elkin is an essentially religious writer whose heroes are not pathetic victims dealing with failure of hope, but rather people who, if they cannot rise above the tragicomic world, at least can stand in it and laugh with compassion. Sees the fiction as a loving and very funny representation of this tragicomic world. Reviews the sample items contained in this anthology as a teasing collection of pieces taken from five novels and two collections of short stories. Concludes that Elkin's main theme is that the bizarre is not really as bizarre as it seems, a kind of affirmation that locates him squarely in the mainstream tradition of Jewish American writing.

Pinsker, Sanford. Rev. of *George Mills*. *Southern Humanities Review* 17.3 (1983): 276-78.

Argues that in *George Mills* Elkin unfortunately suffers the curse of being a writer's writer, and eludes most of his audience. Concludes that to the literature about beautiful losers and lovable *schlemiels* Elkin has added a thick, very funny milestone.

Plummer, William. "A Fall Harvest of Fiction." Rev. of *George Mills*.
    Newsweek 25 Oct. 1982: 117-18a.

Calls *George Mills* a wonderful novel which chronicles the hard times of
an endless succession of George Millses cursed with "blue collar blood,"
who embrace mediocrity as mythos. Notes that the book is a monument
to fictional invention got up as family saga. Concludes that the plot is so
unmeshed and the verbal hijinks so extravagant, that it requires a reader
with fortitude.

Plummer, William. Rev. of *The Living End* and *Searches and Seizures:
    Three Short Novels*. *New Republic* 23 June 1979: 33-35.

Calls Elkin a writer's writer. Compares his snappy dialogue with that of
Roth and Heller. Comments on his use of digressions, modern parables,
conventional wisdom, and ability to raise the cliche to sacral intensity.

Poore, Charles. "A Novel About a Wild Young Man in a Hurry." Rev. of
    Boswell: A Modern Comedy. *New York Times* 7 July 1964: 33.

Describes *Boswell* as a book that plunders the great resources of the
novel and doesn't know quite what to do with it. Complains that his storytelling methods are atrocious, his satire precarious, and his wearily
daring discussions of sex profit-motivated and tatterdemalion.

Prescott, Peter S. Rev. of *The Living End*. *Newsweek* 18 June 1979: 83, 86.

Briefly describes the three parts of the novel and concludes that Elkin's
blasphemy, stemming from a well-established tradition in Western literature, is "only the outsider's smart ass sneer." Yet shows how the book offers
numerous pleasures: much good writing and many sharp scenes. Claims
that Elkin, like his God, is a good dramatist despite the fact that they are
both estheticians with an inadequate sense of what it all ultimately means.

Pritchard, William H. "Stranger Than Truth." Rev. of *The Dick Gibson
    Show*. *Hudson Review* 24.2 (1971): 359.

Argues that even though this novel is touted for its dirty but funny scenes,
Elkin has reached a kind of yellow maturity in this book. Details the contents, and illustrates Elkin's experimental black humor with excerpts.

Pritchard, William. "Thank God for Rashes and Toothaches." Rev. of
    The Rabbi of Lud. *New York Times Book Review* 8 Nov. 1987: 12.

Describes *The Rabbi of Lud* as a piece of snappy writing with poor jokes
and no other act in town. Claims that the plot is of little interest, the elabo-

rate use of flashback is overdone, and the novel a perfectly closed system. Concludes that, unfortunately, he has the tendency to run on, making the book less amusing as a whole than its individual parts suggest.

Rev. of *Searches and Seizures: Three Short Novels. Playboy* Nov. 1973: 44-45.

Considers Elkin's storytelling ability in *Searches and Seizures* (three novellas) to fall somewhere between Vonnegut's "outer fantasies" and Roth's "inner frenzies." Labels Elkin a realist who stretches reality until it emits a sustained, unbearable, demonic shriek. Details the three plots and sets of characters.

Rovit, Earl. "American Fiction." Rev. of *The Dick Gibson Show. Contemporary Literature* 15.4 (1974): 547.

Argues that in *The Dick Gibson Show* the structure of the novel defines the increasing disillusionment which the narrator feels as he perceives the growing discrepancy between the sounds he sends out over his microphone and the echoes from the real world he gets back. Claims that the triumph of this novel is the voice. Concludes that in the end it has no place to go except to gather laughs and grow increasingly bitter.

Rubins, Josh. "Variety Shows." Rev. of *George Mills. New York Review of Books* 16 Dec. 1982: 46-47.

Sees *George Mills* as God's blue collar worker, an all-purpose chameleon-like character who moves through all of the novel's disorderly rooms without illuminating any of them. Concludes that he is finally an unconvincing time clock. Details the plot and the novel's flaws at considerable length.

S., M. "In Short Stories, Elkin Hits Funny Bone and Heart." Rev. of *Criers and Kibitzers, Kibitzers and Criers. National Observer* 10 Jan. 1966: 27.

Calls Elkin a masterful storyteller who doesn't posture, moralize, or embroider. Claims that *Criers and Kibitzers, Kibitzers and Criers* is a collection of nine stories of remarkably varied nature. Describes them as sad stories about dispossessed Jews written with black humor.

Seabrook, John. "Freaks." Rev. of *The Magic Kingdom. Nation* 1 June 1985: 681-82.

Calls *Magic Kingdom* a book full of characters who are diseases personified, sideshow freaks for whom Elkin is the barker. Claims that his purpose is primarily to amaze and appall. Claims that there is so little life in this book and so much disgust that even Elkin's exotic diction and comedy cannot quicken this morbid kingdom for long.

Sheppard, R. Z. "Birth of the Blue-Collar Blues." Rev. of *George Mills*. *Time* 1 Nov. 1982: 79.

Calls *George Mills* the work of a master literary pitch man. Notes that it is his longest and most complex novel which contains large autobiographical elements. Provides a detailed treatment of themes and characters.

Shrapnel, Norman. "Three Letter Worlds." Rev. of *A Bad Man*. *Manchester Guardian Weekly* 11 Apr. 1968: 11.

Calls *Bad Man* a novel about life, the biggest trap of all. Concludes that it is a moral fantasy of an appealing solid sort with gravely comic scenes.

Sternman, William. "Beyond the Badinage, Indifference." Rev. of *The Franchiser*. *National Observer* 12 June 1976: 21.

Calls *The Franchiser* proof that its brilliant author has yet to write a brilliant novel. Claims that we can feel very little for the Elkin hero or his predicaments.

Stokes, Geoffrey. "Short Circuits." Rev. of *The Living End*. *Village Voice* 20 Aug. 1979: 82.

Finds this novel a surprising evidence that Elkin can, after failing in most of his other novels, sustain a story over the longer form of the novel. Describes the character of God, and concludes that it is now "possible to forgive God, and unnecessary to forgive Stanley Elkin."

Sullivan, Walter. "'Where Have All the Flowers Gone?' Part II: The Novel in the Gnostic Twilight." Rev. of *A Bad Man*. *Sewanee Review* 78.4 (1970): 659-60.

Calls the novel not so much bigger than life but realer than real. Elkin takes new directions in this novel. Details the characters, plot, setting, and general contents. Concludes that the satire is finally shallow, Feldman grossly oversimplified, and the moments of vitality not well-sustained.

Taliaferro, Frances. "Lyricist of the Lunch Pail." Rev. of *George Mills*. *Harper's* Nov. 1982: 74-75.

Argues that the central message of this novel is history as random process. Sees George's life as accidental. Complains that Elkin spends his best energy on the digressions in the book, and concludes that it is the ultimately tiresome and rambling product of an eccentric virtuoso.

Towers, Robert. Rev. of *The Franchiser*. *New York Times Book Review* 13 June 1976: 5, 22, 24.

Sees the surface of the novel portraying the homogenized man-made surface of American life, a sort of coast-to-coast mall, or plastic horror, replete with motels and fast-food chains. Argues that for all its potential richness of character and situation, the novel never really mobilizes all its forces and therefore remains oddly static.

West, Paul. "The Many Voices of Stanley Elkin." Rev. of *The Six-Year-Old Man*. *Washington Post Book World* 29 Nov. 1987: 4-5.

One voice is Elkin's big gift along with his talents as a comedian. Describes the characters and the plot of *The Six-Year-Old Man*.

Wolcott, James. "Final Fling." Rev. of *The Magic Kingdom*. *Vanity Fair* Apr. 1985: 95.

The Magic Kingdom is described mainly in terms of its contents. Comments that finally the book becomes so wacky and untamed with its black absurdism that it lapses into hysteria and human sacrifice. Concludes that there is no denying the rhetorical power of the book, but that it is finally about death as boss.

Wolff, Geoffrey. "Books." Rev. of *The Dick Gibson Show*. *Newsweek* 19 Apr. 1971: 120, 123.

Provides a brief plot summary and comments on Elkin's humor and ability to fly in the face of fiction's decorums. The stories are arresting, the gags funny, and the language experimentation effective and demanding of attention.

Wolff, Geoffrey. "Hell and Superhell: Elkin's Vision of the Afterlife." Rev. of *The Living End*. *Esquire* 19 June 1979: 13-14.

Acclaims Elkin for his pyrotechnic display of language, and describes the contents of the book. Concludes that it is a counteroffensive and calculated revenge on pain, sickness, and mortality. Sees the novel as "a man-made miracle."

Wolff, Geoffrey. "Topping the Tank." Rev of *The Franchiser*. *New Times* 25 June 1976: 70.

Calls *The Franchiser* a noisy book full of bits and numbers, and based on the growth of a benign cancer—crazy and freakish. Details the contents, and describes the book as a black comedy full of bleak, comic improvisations, and high octane fuel.

Wood, Michael. "Flirting with Disintegration." Rev. of *Searches and Seizures: Three Short Novels*. *New York Review of Books* 21 Mar. 1974: 20-21.

Describes the three short novels, and finds that the real subject is a "complicated invention of character by means of snowballing language." Concludes that the writer invents characters who invent themselves as they talk and thereby invent him, the writer.

Interviews

Berkley, Miriam. "P. W. Interviews Stanley Elkin." *Publishers Weekly* 29 Mar. 1985: 74-75.

An interview that provides some background information, a smattering of his titles, and several descriptive comments on the contents and style of his novels and short stories.

Bernt, Phyllis, and Joseph Bernt. "Stanley Elkin on Fiction: An Interview." *Prairie Schooner* 50.1 (1976): 14-25.

Elkin discusses the absurdity of situation confronted by his characters, death as a universal experience, the pre-eminence of style, the beginning of his writing career, what writing does for him, his teaching of creative writing, reading, other Jewish writers, what makes a Jewish writer, reactions to the reviewers, and his notions of America.

Chenetier, Marc. "An Interview with Stanley Elkin." *Delta* 20 (1985): 15-35.

Elkin discusses his public success, his classification as a Jewish writer, his writing process, the germination of several of the novels, his use of the theme of powerlessness, the nature of contemporary self, his use of lists and catalogues, his agonized relation to realism, the influence of Bellow, his incorporation of pop culture into the novels, and his comments on the 1980s upsurge of realism.

Clayton, Jay. "An Interview with Stanley Elkin." *Contemporary Literature* 24.1 (1983): 2-12.

Elkin discusses his philosophical attitudes as manifested in his characters, his use of satire, the metaphorical implications of people's occupations, the illusion of destiny held by many of his characters, form, the use of cliche in the novels, the orphaned condition of many of the protagonists, and miscellaneous other topics.

Duncan, Jeffrey L. "A Conversation with Stanley Elkin and William H. Gass." *Iowa Review* 7.1 (1976): 48-77.

Both writers discuss the fashion of doing interviews, the responses of the audience to some of their work, individual scenes from their own and each other's work, their current works in progress, theories of language, their mutual disrespect for critics and reviewers who interpose themselves as morally superior new priests, the public expectation that writers be shamanistic, what can be learned from popular culture, their views on a variety of twentieth-century writers, the discovery of subject matter, movies, modern theater, and the primacy of language.

Earlywine, Robert. "An Interview with Stanley Elkin." *Webster Review* 8.1 (1983): 5-16.

Elkin begins by complaining about the reviewers, then discusses his attitude that the imagination should be free of conventions; his note-taking processes; his theory of the displacements of the ordinary; his work in progress; *Magic Kingdom*; his theory of plot; character development; the inner logic of the story; the future of fiction; his attitudes towards the term "new fiction;" and his reactions to negative reviews of his works. Concludes with the statement that *George Mills* is his best book.

Elkin, Stanley. "An Interview with Stanley Elkin." *MLA Quarterly* 29 (Sept. 1968): 217-22.

Elkin discusses the genesis of *Boswell*, how he characterizes himself as a writer, what changing his environment does for his writing, his views on the current status of the novel, getting published as a young novelist today, his experience with editors and little magazines, what he has done since *Bad Man*, whether or not a novelist's social concerns should manifest themselves in the novel, his high opinion of Norman Mailer, his response to the charge that his fictional characters are not realistic, and what qualities he admires most in human nature.

Gass, William. "Adventures in the Writing Life." *Washington Post Book World* 10 Oct. 1982: 1, 10-11.

Gass discusses with Elkin the death of John Gardner; Elkin's own preoccupation with death; the hazards of living the life of a writer; his latest novel, *George Mills*; and the actual process of writing.

LeClair, Thomas. "Stanley Elkin: The Art of Fiction." *Paris Review* 17 (1976): 54-86. Rpt. in edited version in *Anything Can Happen: Interviews with Contemporary American Novelists*. Eds. Tom LeClair and Larry McCaffery. Urbana: U of Illinois P, 1983. 106-25.

Elkin discusses his father, his early life, the autobiographical element in his fiction, the writing of *Boswell*, his beginning place with a character's occupation, his views on other writers (Barth, Gass, Faulkner), his fictive strategies, his philosophy of language, his perceived audience, his assessment of himself as a black humorist, how the writers energize their fiction, miscellaneous details about several of his novels, the origins of his characters' obsessions, how he researches the factual parts of his novels, and his theory and practice in teaching creative writing.

Plummer, William. "An Interview with Stanley Elkin." *Bookletter* 2 Aug. 1976: 13.

Elkin discusses his black humor, his roots in American literature, his episodic picaresque style, humor, the inception of *The Franchiser* and its symbolic significance, his own relationship to Ben Flesh, his expectations of the reader, language and good lines, the beginning research process, influences, his own reading, and views on the teaching of writing.

Renwick, Joyce. "Stanley Elkin: An Interview." *Mid-American Review* 5.1 (1985): 61-71.

Elkin comments that to be a good writer one must be a serious reader. Describes his daily work routine, his conscious use of myths, his preoccupation with getting the words right, his passion for movie-going, his vision of himself as a realist, his response to John Gardner's accusation that his fiction is ultimately hollow and lacking in love, and his refusal to accept the label of Jewish writer. Concludes by asserting that maturity should bring to the writer the attitude that it is time to cut your losses with life and move on from unrealistic expectations.

Sale, Richard B. "An Interview with Stanley Elkin in St. Louis." *Studies in the Novel* 16.3 (1984): 314-25.

Elkin discusses his vision of what comedy in the modern novel is, his kinds of novelistic affirmations, his use of myth, tidbits of background information on several of the books and major protagonists, the impulse to immortality in each of the characters, his views on Hawkes and Faulkner, and other random topics.

Sanders, Scott R. "An Interview with Stanley Elkin." *Contemporary Literature* 16.2 (1975): 131-45.

Elkin discusses why he is attracted to the extreme; his views on critics and reviewers; his thesis on Faulkner; his large number of con men, salesmen, and hustlers as protagonists; his belief in the power of rhetoric; his theory and practice in the classroom; the role of personality and language in fiction; his aversion to social issues, politics, and ideology in the novel, and the notion of selling anything to the audience except fiction; his defense of John Updike; his perceived audience of other writers; his dislike of the French *nouveau roman*; his admiration for Saul Bellow; his style of dialogue that mixes formal and vernacular elements; and other miscellaneous topics.

Ziegler, Heide, and Christopher Bigsby. "Stanley Elkin." *The Radical Imagination and the Liberal Tradition: Interviews with English and American Novelists*. Eds. Heide Ziegler and Christopher Bigsby. London: Junction, 1982. 93-110.

Begins with a brief biographical review, then proceeds to a discussion of the conflict between idealism and sensuality in the novels, and Elkin's deconstruction of the relationship between author and character in each. Details the contents of each novel. In the interview, Elkin discusses: the element of satire, central characters, issues in *Criers and Kibitzers, Kibitzers and Criers*, and several other works. Provides a good critical introduction and overview of Elkin's work and his personal attitudes towards his craft.

Biographical Sources

Bargen, Doris G. "Stanley Elkin." *Twentieth-Century American-Jewish Fiction Writers*. Ed. Daniel Walden. Detroit: Gale, 1984. Vol. 28 of *Dictionary of Literary Biography*. 94 vols. to date. 1978- . 47-50.

More than details of his life, this is a career biography, tracing the development of the author's canon, describing the contents and themes of his works, evaluating his reputation, and placing him in the larger context of

American literary history. Includes list of primary and second sources and illustrations.

Bargen, Doris G. "Stanley Elkin." *American Novelists Since World War II.* Eds. Jeffrey Helterman and Richard Layman. Detroit: Gale, 1978. Vol. 2 of *Dictionary of Literary Biography*. 94 vols. to date. 1978- . 131-36.

More than details of his life, this is a career biography, tracing the development of the author's canon, describing the contents and themes of his works, evaluating his reputation, and placing him in the larger context of American literary history. Includes list of primary and secondary sources and illustrations.

Bargen, Doris G. "Stanley Elkin." *Dictionary of Literary Biography Yearbook: 1980.* Eds. Karen L. Rood, Jean W. Ross, and Richard Ziegfeld. Detroit: Gale, 1981. 36-39.

An update to the article in Vol. 2 of *DLB*, concentrating on more recent developments in his career and providing analysis of *The Living End* (1979).

Gass, William. "Stanley Elkin: An Anecdote." *Washington University Magazine* (Spr. 1984): 12-14.

A rather fine portrait of Elkin based on Gass's long-time association with him spanning his own graduate student days to the present. Ends up being as much about Gass as Elkin.

Leonard, John. "Stanley Elkin, Nice Guy." *New York Times Book Review* 15 Oct. 1967: 40.

A brief biographical sketch with comments about some of his works, his writing habits, and his teaching.

Bibliographies

Chenetier, Marc. "Stanley Elkin: Bibliographie Selective." *Delta* 20 (1985): 207-14.

McCaffery, Larry. "Stanley Elkin: A Bibliography 1957-1977." *Bulletin of Bibliography and Magazine Notes* 34.2 (1977): 73-76.

Robins, William M. "A Bibliography of Stanley Elkin." *Critique* 26.4 (1985): 169-84.

Dissertations

Bailey, Peter Joseph. "Pattern and Perception in the Fiction of Stanley Elkin." Diss. U of Southern California, 1980.

Bargen, Doris G. "The Fiction of Stanley Elkin." Diss. U of Tubingen, 1978. Studien und Texte zur Amerikanistik, 8. Frankfurt: Lang, 1980.

Robins, William M. "Stanley Elkin: The Art of the Novel." Diss. U of South Carolina, 1986.

Richard Elman
1934 –

Primary Sources

Novels

The 28th Day of Elul. New York: Scribner, 1967; London: Hutchinson, 1967.

The Breadfruit Lotteries. New York: Methuen, 1980.

A Coat for the Tsar. Austin: U of Texas P, 1958.

Disco Frito. Salt Lake City: Peregrine Smith, 1988.

An Education in Blood. New York: Scribner, 1971.

Fredi & Shirl & the Kids: The Autobiography in Fables of Richard M. Elman. New York: Scribner, 1972.

Ill-at-Ease in Compton. Hastings-on-Hudson: Ultramarine, 1967.

Lilo's Diary. New York: Scribner, 1968.

Little Lives. Fred Jordan Books. New York: Grosset, 1978. Published under the pseudonym of John Howland Spyker.

The Menu Cypher. New York: Macmillan, 1982.

The Reckoning; the Daily Ledgers of Newman Yagodah, Advokat and Factor. New York: Scribner, 1969.

Taxi Driver. New York: Bantam, 1976; London: Corgi-Transworld, 1976.

Collected Works

Crossing Over, and Other Tales. New York: Scribner, 1973.
Contents: Crossing Over, Old Old Friends, The Ballad of the Long-Legged Ichthyologist, On Making Friends, Myself and the Tugoman, Eyes, I O U, Chamber Music, Who Killed Pretty Brilliant?, A Friend's Story, The Buffalo Hunter, Goldy, Playing with Mary, The Flirt, Have a Good Time, Tit for Tat, Timmy, Turn on Guatemala, Law 'n Order Day.

Short Fiction in Anthologies

"Timmy." *The American Judaism Reader: Essays, Fiction and Poetry from the Pages of American Judaism*. Ed. Paul Kresh. New York: Abelard, 1967. 188-200.

"Tit for Tat." *My Name Aloud: Jewish Stories by Jewish Writers*. Ed. Harold U. Ribalow. South Brunswick: Yoseloff, 1969. 92-100.

Short Fiction in Periodicals

"The Anvil of the Times." *Michigan Quarterly Review* 26.4 (1987): 673-76.

"A Brief Life Is Best in the End, I Suppose." *Atlantic* Dec. 1972: 62-66.

"Little Sharks." *Antaeus* 60 (1988): 87-92.

"Playing with Mary." *Transatlantic Review* 45 (1973): 79-85.

"Tit for Tat." *Transatlantic Review* 69 (1965): 65-76.

"Turnabout." *Michigan Quarterly Review* 24.5 (1987): 677-78.

Secondary Sources

Articles and Chapters

Berger, Alan L. "Symbolic Judaism." *Crisis and Covenant: The Holocaust in American Jewish Literature*. SUNY Series in Modern Jewish Literature and Culture. Albany: New York State UP, 1985. 160-64.

Describes *A Coat for the Tsar* as a novel dealing with the moral dilemma of a pre-Holocaust Russian Jew who was the sole survivor of a pogrom. Then describes his Holocaust trilogy *The 28th Day of Elul* (1967), *Lilo's Diary* (1968), and *The Reckoning* (1969) as a sustained treatment of the Holocaust. Complains this trilogy masquerades as a documentary piece of literature, but portrays stereotyped caricatures of Jews who are mostly self-hating. Concludes that it fails in its attempt at universalizing the Holocaust.

Delbanco, Nicholas. "Nicholas Delbanco on Richard Elman's *The 28th Day of Elul, Lilo's Diary*, and *The Reckoning*." *Rediscoveries II: Important Writers Select Their Favorite Works of Neglected Fiction*. Eds. David Madden and Peggy Bach. 1st Carroll and Graf ed. New York: Carroll, 1988. 71-77.

Primarily a good description of the contents of the three Elul novels with interspersed comparisons on the likenesses among them.

Kremer, S. Lillian. "The Trial of the Damned: Richard Elman's Holocaust Trilogy." *Witness Through the Imagination: Jewish American Holocaust Literature*. S. Lillian Kremer. Detroit: Wayne State UP, 1989. 142-80.

Concentrates primarily on the content of Elman's treatment of the plight of Hungarian Jewry in his Holocaust trilogy—Vol. One *The 28th Day of Elul* (1967); Vol. Two, *Lilo's Diary* (1968); Vol. Three, *The Reckoning* (1969). Concludes that this is a major historical and literary critical treatment.

Reviews

"After the Deluge." Rev. of *The 28th Day of Elul*. *Times Literary Supplement* 21 Sept. 1967: 833.

Describes *The 28th Day of Elul* as an ambitious undertaking because of its Eurocentric split. Claims that it is an exercise overwrought but never overplayed. Concludes that its moral restraint tells us more than many a head-on confrontation with the abyss.

Blackburn, Sara. "Diary of a Villain." Rev. of *The Reckoning*. *Washington Post Book World* 7 Sept. 1969: 12.

Claims that *The Reckoning* continues Elman's investigation into the lives of a family of Hungarian Jews at the brink of the Nazi destruction. Calls this a finely researched, fascinatingly detailed novel done with dash, craftsmanship, and sheer nerve considering its formidable protagonist.

Burg, Victor. "A Diary—and a Book of Judgment." Rev. of *The Reckoning*. *Christian Science Monitor* 9 Oct. 1969: 13.

Calls *The Reckoning* a novel peculiarly balanced, terse, initially cold, but finally striking. Concludes, however, that it lacks humor and in some respects is "small."

Dolan, Harry. "Lily-White No More." Rev. of *Ill-at-Ease in Compton*. *New York Times Book Review* 9 July 1967: 8.

Calls *Ill-at-Ease in Compton* a book in which Elman pulls no punches concerning the racial issues he raises about the Watts revolt, Martin Luther King, and the whole interracial situation during the sixties in Compton.

Ellin, Stanley. "Secret Agents." Rev. of *The Breadfruit Lotteries*. *New York Times Book Review* 2 Mar. 1980: 9.

Briefly describes the plot, and wishes the book were longer because it wastes not a word and is so entertaining.

Fremont-Smith, Eliot. "Desolation on Main Street." Rev. of *Ill-at-Ease in Compton*. *New York Times* 14 June 1967: 45.

Calls *Ill-at-Ease in Compton* a hideous look at a town like Compton, California. Concentrates on a detailed description of the contents of the novel.

Gilmore, Michael T. "The Moral Vacuum." Rev. of *The Reckoning*. *Congress Bi-Weekly* 23 Jan. 1970: 17.

Describes the protagonist of *The Reckoning* as an American of the 1960s living on the edge of the modern-day holocaust of Vietnam. Yet claims that Yagodah is a fleshed-out character whose elaborate lies and grotesque theorizing only mask a callous soul—a murderer. Argues that Elman's judgment is a stern one bristling with Old Testament severity. Concludes that if Yagodah has already gone to his reckoning, we as a society are still waiting for ours.

Goodman, Mitchell. "Nicaraguan Patchwork." Rev. of *Cocktails at Somoza's. Stony Hills* 4.2 (1982): 1, 13, 15.

Describes this novel as a patchwork muddle comprised of a contradictory authorial personna and much Hemingwayesque sex, blood, and tough talk. Details contents.

Hislop, Alan. "A Tough Act to Follow." Rev. of *Fredi & Shirl & The Kids. Washington Post Book World* 25 June 1972: 6.

Calls *Fredi & Shirl & The Kids* a book about a man who hates his family, whom he describes as monsters, and whose whole being is governed by monstrousness. Considers the book worth reading but basically off-putting like a reverse Pollyanna.

Hochman, Baruch. "The Jewish Vogue." Rev. of *The 28th day of Elul. Commentary* Sept. 1967: 107-10.

Calls *The 28th Day of Elul* an ambitious book that poses very real, very public questions, only to obscure them in a cloud of erotic irrelevance. Claims that Elman captures the guilt and the torment of a particular Holocaust survivor, then veers off into other subject matter.

Koch, Christopher. Rev. of *Lilo's Diary. Commonweal* 17 Jan. 1969: 504-05.

Sees *Lilo's Diary* as a book which explores the utter failure of middle-class presumptions to deal with their conditions. Calls the characters unlikable. Claims that Elman's real theme is the impingement of reality on the consciousness trained to abide by self-contained illusions.

Lekachman, Robert. "Good Boys, Bad Boys, Old Boys." Rev. of *The Breadfruit Lotteries. Nation* 26 Apr. 1980: 504-06.

Calls *The Breadfruit Lotteries* an enlightened and compassionate novel which is inventive and high-spirited, though full of uncertain tonal shifts from farce to serious politics and back again. Concludes that it does not exactly expand the genre of the espionage novel.

Leonard, John. Rev. of *Little Lives. New York Times* 1 Feb. 1979: C19. Rpt. in *Books of the Times* Feb. 1979: 57-58.

Reveals that *Little Lives* by John Howland Spyker is actually written by Elman himself. Provides a detailed examination of the contents, and designates it a minor masterpiece in the order of *Spoon River Anthology* and *Winesburg, Ohio.* Commends Elman for the creation of Spyker as a character and for his packed novels full of the politics of family and the tribal rites of academe.

Leonard, John. "Complicity and Consequences." Rev. of *Lilo's Diary*. *New York Times* 13 Sept. 1968: 45.

Calls *Lilo's Diary* a book about self-deception, cowardice, and hypocrisy, and centered on the same materials as his previous novel, *The 28th Day of Elul*, with even the same characters. Calls it a brilliant and closely textured narrative which abstains from rhetorical flamboyance. Concludes that it contains a sense of fateful pity, a sense of loss, and a conviction of consequences.

Leonard, John. "Two Novels." Rev. of *The Breadfruit Lotteries*. *New York Times* 7 Mar. 1980: C25. Rpt. in *Books of the Times* May 1980: 191-93.

Describes *The Breadfruit Lotteries* as a romp in which half of the characters are using cannabis, while the others are plotting assassinations. Concludes that it is as if Lenny Bruce had written James Bond—after such reading, who can look at another spy novel with a straight face.

Lieber, Joel. "The Bartered Bride." Rev. of *Lilo's Diary*. *Saturday Review* 7 Sept. 1968: 46.

Designates *Lilo's Diary*, despite some of its faults and shortcomings, a remarkable feat when one realizes the male author has to climb inside the head and feelings of a Hungarian girl half his age as she experiences the events of the last year of her life in 1944. Though mysterious, it is elliptical, and fragmented without first having read *The 28th Day of Elul*. Concludes that the novel is an examination of one particular tragic moment in a mad, tragic history.

Lieber, Joel. "Fiction." Rev. of *The Reckoning*. *Saturday Review* 11 Oct. 1969: 39-40.

Calls *The 28th Day of Elul* the diary-chronicle of a man approaching the end of his life, while *The Reckoning* bears the same unmistakable stamp of painful honesty that makes the reader squirm with discomfort. Argues that moving the point of view character to Newman Yagodah, the father, we are all reminded of the challenging Durrell-like approach Elman has undertaken. Concludes that out of all this, a real human being emerges in the book.

Lieber, Joel. "The Fruits of the Holocaust." Rev. of *The 28th Day of Elul*. *Saturday Review* 15 Apr. 1967: 36-37.

Claims that *The 28th Day of Elul* is the product of research and imagination, not personal experience. Concludes that it is an unequivocally honest book written with great skill. Describes the contents.

Maddocks, Melvin. "Reviewer's Choice." Rev. of *An Education in Blood. Life* 25 June 1971: 15.

Calls *An Education in Blood* too long, and Elman a sort of Grand Inquisitor novelist. Sees this as a flawed version of *Crime and Punishment*. Sums up the key idea of the book as "The world has not done me any particular injury and I am determined to get even with it."

Maddocks, Melvin. "A Survival Artist in a Time of Death." Rev. of *The Reckoning. Life* 19 Sept. 1969: 20.

Calls *The Reckoning* a Holocaust novel whose tone is quieter, and where concentration on the ordinary event is so convincing one might think he had forgotten the monstrous ending to his story. Concludes that though the concentration camp remains off-stage, death has been in our minds and hearts from the beginning of the novel's presence.

Mano, D. Keith. "Eastover Is and Isn't a Murderer." Rev. of *An Education in Blood. New York Times Book Review* 25 Apr. 1971: 7, 55.

Argues that *An Education in Blood* offers few easy pleasures and many profound speculations on man's condition. Details the plot and characters, and concludes that Elman is an excellent, sensuous writer.

Mano, Keith D. Rev. of *Crossing Over and Other Tales. New York Times Book Review* 4 Mar. 1973: 41.

Describes *Crossing Over* as inconsequential and disgruntling. Claims that the fiction seems copybook work. Shows how all but three are written in a tentative first person which excuses Elman from any descriptive or metaphorical responsibilities. Concludes that the personae are not very special, and nor are their words particularly distinguished.

Morse, J. Mitchell. "Fiction Chronicle: The Death of Love." Rev. of *An Education in Blood. Hudson Review* 24.3 (1971): 535-37.

Describes *An Education in Blood* as psychologically valid, and claims that it deserves to be taken seriously intellectually. Yet argues that beyond that, its rhythms are wrong and it doesn't work: There are poor pieces of dialogue and even worse falsities of language. Concludes that the book is ultimately a failure.

Morton, Frederic. "When Yagodah Glimpses His Fate, His Humanity
   Vanishes." Rev. of *The Reckoning. New York Times Book Review* 14
   Sept. 1969: 5, 20.

Considers that *The Reckoning* deals with a philistine Jew who ends up a
genuine human being. Contains mostly a plot summary. Concludes that,
in the end, Elman doesn't really bring it off. Though comic and heart-
breaking, he reaches the limits of the realistic novel and strains appear.
Claims that this author needs a reality that will speak the unspeakable.

Neugeboren, Jay. Rev. of *Ill at Ease in Compton. Washington Post Book
   World* 24 Sept. 1967: 11.

Argues that *Ill at Ease in Compton* is a brief, rather loosely put together
series of facts, impressions, speculations, descriptions, interviews, and
open-ended generalities concerning the city of Compton, California.
Describes the book's concentration on the increasing blackness of this
city with its corruption, racial feuds, and increasingly rootless lives.
Concludes that, though what is happening is terrible, Elman's vague
phrases and half-thoughts, since they evoke no sense of the specific, cannot evoke a sense of terror.

Riemer, Jack. "Three Tales of 'Madness.'" Rev. of *Lilo's Diary.
   Hadassah Magazine* Oct. 1968: 16.

Sees Elman's *Lilo's Diary* as a literary feat of the first magnitude considering he is an American male living in 1968, and yet he projects himself
into the psyche of a European girl growing up and dying in the 1940s.
Concludes that this book is an outcry of a man who knows that his contemporaries are dead children of the Europe past and Asia present.

Rothchild, Sylvia. "From the Book Reviewer's Shelf: A Survivor Lives
   With His Past." Rev. of *The 28th Day of Elul. Christian Science
   Monitor* 27 June 1967: 9.

Describes the plot and dilemmas faced by Alex Yagodah, a Hungarian
survivor of the Holocaust, as he tries to come to terms with the future
while obsessed with the past.

Schemering, Christopher. "The Spy Who Came from the Kitchen." Rev.
   of *The Menu Cypher. Washington Post Book World* 29 Aug. 1982: 6.

Calls *The Menu Cypher* a rip-snorter with its rhythmical, satirical jabs at
U.S. foreign policy done in poetic and subtly biting prose. Claims that,
reaching ingenious comic heights at times, the book has a surprisingly

cynical and violent denouement that is curiously flat and unaffecting. Concludes that what begins as a prodigiously funny flight-of-fancy dive bombs and crashes right on the coast of Missed Opportunity.

Sigal, Clancy. "Hell Came for a Visit." Rev. of *Lilo's Diary. New York Times Book Review* 25 Aug 1968: 4.

Describes *Lilo's Diary* as a re-creation of the thoughts of a young Jewish girl during one fatal summer in Hungary in 1944. Concludes that this novel is more than an act of protest—it is an extraordinarily, angry, and tender work of imagination.

Sokolov, Raymond A. "A Roundup of Recent Fiction." Rev. of *An Education in Blood. Newsweek* 19 Apr. 1971: 118, 120.

Describes the plot of the novel, and commends the book for being one of the most ambitious psychological novels written in years.

Stark, Irwin. "The Ledger of His Life." Rev. of *The Reckoning. Hadassah Magazine* Nov. 1969: 25.

Describes *The Reckoning* as both a work of art and a searing testimony. Calls the novel a shrewd, unsparing dissection of a middle-class "Jewish" mind but which finally lacks a strong enough bite. Concludes that it is to be regretted Elman could not find an effective technical method of presenting the world behind the mirror.

Sullivan, Mary. "Breathless." Rev. of *28th Day of Elul. Listener* 14 Sept. 1967: 344.

Argues that *The 28th Day of Elul* is so honest and serious it is tormenting not to know whether it is the initial situation, the narrative, or the conclusion which is real. Details contents.

Weinberg, Helen. "Before the Fatal Moment." Rev. of *The 28th Day of Elul. Congress Bi-Weekly* 22 May 1967: 22-23.

Describes the contents of the novel and notes that it is a family novel about a specific Jewish family. Comments on the intermixture of anguish and irony, the Holocaust material, and the large Jewish questions it raises. Concludes that Elman's subtle, urgent and imaginative novel is one more renewed effort to reveal the human complexity that our yearning for certainty, catered to in histories, conceals.

Weinberg, Helen. "A Sequel in the Present Tense." Rev. of *Lilo's Diary. Congress Bi-Weekly* 25 Nov. 1968: 21-22.

Describes *Lilo's Diary* as a novel concerned with middle-class Jewish ideas about complacency. Sees Lilo as the victim of these failed values. Details the contents, and urges that this novel be read in tandem with *The 28th Day of Elul*, which is the same story from a different point of view.

Weiss, Joseph I. "Honor Lost and Gained." Rev. of *The 28th Day of Elul*. *Dimensions* 3 (1968): 54.

Shows that in *The 28th Day of Elul* Elman writes of Hungary and of the rottenness and decadence that slowly seep into the town. Concludes that the book makes it plain that if ever there was beauty and honor in Europe, it will be hard to find it again.

West, Paul. "The Sorrows of Young Werther, Brooklyn-Style." Rev. of *Fredi & Shirl & the Kids: The Autobiography in Fables of Richard Elman: A Novel. New York Times Book Review* 25 June 1972: 4, 31.

Describes *Fredi & Shirl & the Kids* as a story about coming of age in Brooklyn presented in the worst possible light. Comments that the book alternately "barks and percusses," "yearns and confesses." Describes the contents briefly.

Wiesel, Elie. "Legacy of Evil." Rev. of *The 28th Day of Elul*. *New York Times Book Review* 28 May 1967: 4, 34.

Describes the contents and background of *The 28th Day of Elul*. Commends Elman and writers like him for dealing with the subject matter of the Holocaust, because the book touches upon the most important moral and philosophical issues of our time. Describes the plot.

Winegarten, Renee. "A Powerful, Imaginative Novel." Rev. of *The 28th Day of Elul*. *Hadassah Magazine* May 1967: 16.

Calls *The 28th Day of Elul* sometimes turgid in style, strikingly outspoken, and allegorical in thrust. Claims that Richard Elman's highly suggestive vision of the sordid interaction of supplanter and supplanted touches upon the raw place of our own secret misgivings.

Zeitlin, Naomi. "Strange Document." Rev. of *The 28th Day of Elul*. *World Jewry* Nov.-Dec. 1967: 29.

Argues that through the mouth of Yagodah, Elman has dealt with the issue of individual and universal responsibility for the slaughter of the Jews. Claims that he raises unanswerable questions, and that he has implemented his intent to shock and revive the brutality of the memory.

Howard Fast

1914 –

Primary Sources

Novels

Agrippa's Daughter. Garden City: Doubleday, 1964; London: Methuen, 1965; London: Mayflower, 1968.

The American; A Middle Western Legend. New York: Duell, 1946; London: Bodley Head, 1949; London: Lane, 1949; New York: Tempo Star-Ace, 1977; New York: Ace, 1981; New York: Tempo-Grosset, d. not available.

April Morning. New York: Crown, 1961; Large Print ed. New York: Watts, 1961; New York: Keith Jennison-Watts, 1961; London: Methuen, 1961; New York: Bantam, 1962; London: Panther, 1964; New York: Pathfinder-Bantam, 1967, 1979; New York: Falcon-Noble, 1970; New York: Bantam, 1976.

Before Dawn: A Story of Christmas 1942. New York: [Stores], 1942.

The Children. New York: Duell, 1947.

Citizen Tom Paine. New York: Duell, 1943; Bombay: International Book, 1943; New York; Overseas, 1944; New York: Random, 1945;

Cleveland: World, 1945, 1946; London: Lane, 1945; New York: Modern Library, 1946; New York: Blue Heron, 1953; New York: Bantam, 1959; New York: Evergreen-Grove, 1983.

Conceived in Liberty; A Novel of Valley Forge. New York: Simon, 1939; New York: Duell, 1939, 1947; New York: World, 1939; London: Joseph, 1939; Cleveland: Forum-World, 1944; New York: Penguin, 1945; New York: Signet-NAL, 1974.

The Confession of Joe Cullen. Boston: Houghton, 1989; New York: Dell, 1990; Large Print ed. Boston: Hall, 1990; London: Hodder, 1990; Sevenoaks: Coronet, 1990; Bath: Chiver, 1991.

The Dinner Party. Boston: Houghton, 1987; New York: Dell, 1987; Large Print ed. Boston: Hall, 1988.

The Establishment. Boston: Houghton, 1979; Large Print ed. Boston: Hall, 1979; New York: Amsco School, 1980; New York: Dell, 1980, 1982, 1987.

Fallen Angel. Boston: Little, 1951, 1952; Publ. as *Mirage.* Mayflower-Dell Paperbacks. London: Mayflower, 1967. Publ. under pseudonym of Walter Ericson.

Freedom Road. New York: Duell, 1944; New York: Book Find Club, 1944; New York: Crown, 1944, 1964, 1969; Amsco Literature Series. New York: Amsco School, 1944, 1970; New York: Eds. for the Armed Services, 1944; Cleveland: World, 1945; New York: Pocket, 1946; London: Lane, 1946; Cheaper ed. London: Lane, 1951; New York: Blue Heron, 1952; New York: Bantam, 1969; London: Futura, 1979; London: Severn, 1980.

The Hessian. New York: Morrow, 1972; Large Print ed. Boston: Hall, 1973; London: Hodder, 1973; New York: Bantam [Cited in PBIP, 1974]; London: Coronet, 1974; New York: Dell, 1980.

The Hunter and the Trap. New York: Dial, 1967.

The Immigrant's Daughter. Boston: Houghton, 1985; Book Club ed. Boston: Houghton, 1985; Large Print ed. Boston: Hall, 1986; London: Hodder, 1986; Sevenoaks: Coronet, 1986; Large Print ed. Bath: Chivers, 1986; New York: Dell, 1987.

The Immigrants. Boston: Houghton, 1977; Large Print ed. Boston: Hall, 1978; New York: Dell, 1978; London: Hodder, 1978; London: Prior, 1978; Sevenoaks: Coronet, d. not available.

The Last Frontier. New York: Duell, 1941; London: Bodley Head, 1948; New York: Signet-NAL, 1971.

The Legacy. Boston: Houghton, 1981; Book Club ed. Boston: Houghton, 1981; Large Print ed. Boston: Hall, 1981; New York: Dell, 1982; Sevenoaks: Coronet, 1982.

Max. Boston: Houghton, 1982; Book Club ed. Boston: Houghton, 1982; Large Print ed. Boston: Hall, 1982; New York: Dell, 1983; London: Hodder, 1983.

Moses, Prince of Egypt. New York: Crown, 1958; London: Methuen, 1959; London: Panther-Hamilton, 1961.

My Glorious Brothers. Boston: Little, 1948, 1949; Toronto: McClelland, 1948; London: Bodley Head, 1950; London: Lane, 1950; New York: Blue Heron, 1953; London: Panther-Hamilton, 1960; Greenwich: Premier-Fawcett [Cited in PBIP, 1972]; New York: Popular Library [Cited in PBIP, 1974]; Brooklyn: Bonim-Hebrew, 1977; Mattituck: Amereon, d. not available.

The Outsider. Boston: Houghton, 1984; Book Club ed. Boston: Houghton, 1984; Large Print ed. Boston: Hall, 1984; London: Hodder, 1984; New York: Dell, 1985; Sevenoaks: Coronet, 1985.

The Passion of Sacco and Vanzetti: A New England Legend. New York: Blue Heron, 1953; Toronto: McLeod, 1953; London: Lane, 1954; London: Bodley Head, 1954; Westport: Greenwood, 1972.

Place in the City. New York: Harcourt, 1937; Toronto: McLeod, 1937.

The Pledge. Boston: Houghton, 1988; Large Print Book Club ed. Boston: Houghton, 1988; New York: Dell, 1989; Large Print ed. Boston: Hall, 1989; Bath: Chivers, 1989; London: Hodder, 1989; Sevenoaks: Coronet, 1990.

Power. Garden City: Doubleday, 1962; London: Methuen, 1963; New York: Giant Cardinal-Pocket, 1964.

The Proud and the Free. Boston: Little, 1950; London: Bodley Head, 1952.

Second Generation. Boston: Houghton, 1978; Large Print ed. Boston: Hall, 1979; New York: Dell, 1979; Sevenoaks: Coronet, 1979.

Silas Timberman. New York: Blue Heron, 1954; London: Bodley Head, 1955; London: Lane, 1955.

Spartacus. New York: Printed privately, 1951, 1952; New York: Citadel, 1952; Toronto: McLeod, 1952; London: Bodley Head, 1952; London: Lane, 1952; New York: Crown, 1958, 1964; New York: Bonanza-Crown, 1958; London: Mayflower, 1959; London: Panther-Hamilton, 1959; New York: Bantam, 1960; Toronto: Ambassador, 1964; New York: Dell, 1979, 1980; Large Print ed. Boston: Hall, 1984; Mattituck: Amereon, d. not available.

The Story of Lola Gregg. New York: Blue Heron, 1956; London: Bodley Head, 1957; London: Lane, 1957; London: White Lion, 1972.

Strange Yesterday. New York: Dodd, 1934.

The Tall Hunter. New York: Harper, 1942, 1966.

Torquemada. Garden City: Doubleday, 1966; London: Methuen, 1967.

Two Valleys. New York: Dial, 1933; Toronto: McLeod, 1933; London: Dickson, 1933.

The Unvanquished. New York: Duell, 1942; New York: Book League of America, 1942; New York: Eds. for the Armed Services, 1942;

Cleveland: World, 1942, 1945; Toronto: Collins, 1942; Bombay: International, 1944; New York: Modern Library, 1945; New York: Penguin, 1946; Cleveland: Tower-World, 1946; London: Lane, 1947; Cheaper ed. London: Lane, 1951; New York: Popular Library, 1970.

The Winston Affair. New York: Crown, 1959; Toronto: Ambassador, 1959; New York: Bantam, 1960; London: Methuen, 1960; London: Panther-Hamilton, 1962.

Collected Works

The Call of Fife and Drum. Secaucus: Citadel, 1987.

Contents: *The Unvanquished, Conceived in Liberty, The Proud and the Free.*

Departure and Other Stories. Boston: Little, 1949; Culver City: Peace, 1980.

Contents: Departure, The Old Wagon, The Shore Route, Onion Soup, An Epitaph for Sidney, Where Are Your Guns?, Spoil the Child, The Little Folk from the Hills, Who Is He?, The Suckling Pig, The Rickshaw, The Gentle Virtue, Dumb Swede, The Gray Ship, Three Beautiful Things, The First Rose of Summer, Wake Up Glad, The Police Spy, Thirty Pieces of Silver.

The Edge of Tomorrow. New York: Bantam, 1961, 1966; London: Corgi-Transworld, 1962.

Contents: The First Men; The Large Ant; Of Time and Cats; Cato the Martian; The Cold, Cold Box; The Martian Shop; The Sight of Eden.

The General Zapped an Angel: New Stories of Fantasy and Science Fiction. New York: Morrow, 1970; New York: Ace, 1970.

Contents: The General Zapped an Angel, The Mouse, The Vision of Milty Boil, The Mohawk, The Wound, Tomorrow's *Wall Street Journal*, The Interval, The Movie House, The Insects.

The Howard Fast Reader. New York: Crown, 1960; Toronto: Ambassador, 1960.

Contents: The Man Who Looked Like Jesus; Rachel; Onion Soup; Three Beautiful Things; The First Rose of Summer; Where Are Your Guns?;

The Gentle Virtue; The Golden River; Neighbor Sam; Departure; The Gray Ship; The Suckling Pig; Old Sam Adams (Three Tales): Journey to Boston, The Ancestor, The Child and the Ship; The Vision of Henry J. Baxter; The Children; The Little Folk from the Hills; Coca Cola; The Cold, Cold Box; The Large Ant; Freedom Road; Spoil the Child.

The Last Supper, and Other Stories. New York: Blue Heron, 1955; London: Bodley Head, 1956; London: Lane, 1956.

Contents: The Last Supper, The Ancestor, The Vision of Henry J. Baxter, A Walk Home, Coca Cola, Christ in Cuernavaca, The Power of Positive Thinking, Dignity, Gentleman from Mississippi, Journey to Boston, The Child and the Ship, Sunday Morning, The Upraised Pinion, The Holy Child, My Father, Coda: The Poet in Philadelphia.

Patrick Henry and the Frigate's Keel, and Other Stories of a Young Nation. New York: Duell, 1945; New York: Book Find Club, 1945.

Contents: Patrick Henry and the Frigate's Keel, Rachel, The Pirate and the General, Neighbor Sam, Conyngham, The Brood, The Day of Victory, Amos Todd's Vinegar, Sun in the West, The Bookman, The Price of Liberty, Not Too Hard.

Time and the Riddle: Thirty-One Zen Stories. Pasadena: Ward Ritchie, 1975; Boston: Houghton, 1980.

Contents: UFO; The Hole in the Floor; General Hardy's Profession; Echinomastus Contentii; Tomorrow's *Wall Street Journal*; A Matter of Size; Show Cause; The Martian Shop; The Pragmatic Seed; The Trap; The Hoop; The Cold, Cold Box; The Talent of Harvey; The Wound; The General Zapped an Angel; The Price; The Vision of Milty Boil; Cato the Martian; Not with a Bang; The Movie House; Cephes 5; Of Time and Cats; The Interval; The Egg; The Insects; The Sight of Eden; The Mind of God; The Mohawk; The Mouse; The Large Ant; The Hunter

A Touch of Infinity: Thirteen New Stories of Fantasy and Science Fiction. New York: Morrow, 1973; Large Print ed. Boston: Hall, 1973; New York: Daw, 1974; London: Hodder, 1975; London: Coronet, 1976.

Contents: The Hoop, The Price, A Matter of Size, The Hole in the Floor, General Hardy's Profession, Show Cause, Not with a Bang, The Talent of Harvey, The Mind of God, UFO, Cephes 5, The Pragmatic Seed, The Egg.

Short Fiction in Anthologies

"The Mouse." *Zoo 2000: Twelve Stories of Science Fiction and Fantasy Beasts*. Ed. Jane Yolen. New York: Seabury, 1973. 119-36.

"The Large Ant." *Black Water: The Book of Fantastic Literature*. Ed. Alberto Manguel. New York: Potter, 1983. 783-91.

"The Price of Liberty." *Jewish Short Stories*. Ed. Ludwig Lewisohn. New York: Behrman, 1945. 142-57; *A Treasury of Jewish Sea Stories*. Ed. Samuel Sobel. New York: David, 1965. 116-28; *Jewish Sea Stories*. Ed. Samuel Sobel. Middle Village: David, 1985. 116-28.

"Where Are Your Guns?" *This Land, These People*. Ed. Harold U. Ribalow. New York: Beechhurst, 1950. 11-19; *Yisroel: The First Jewish Omnibus*. Ed. Joseph Leftwich. Rev. ed. New York: Yoseloff, 1963, 196-201.

Short Fiction in Periodicals

"Because He Trusted Me." *Good Housekeeping* July 1940: 36-37, 153-57.

"Beyond the War." *Ladies' Home Journal* Oct. 1937: 16-17, 127, 129-30.

"The Brood." *Good Housekeeping* Dec. 1939: 24-25, 200-02.

"The Children." *Story Magazine* Mar. 1967: pag. not available.

"The Day of Victory." *Woman's Home Companion* Feb. 1943: 22-23, 98, 101, 106, 108.

"The Man Who Looked Like Jesus." *Esquire* Dec. 1959: 316-27.

"A Man's Wife." *Ladies' Home Journal* Feb. 1939: 11-13, 79-80.

"Mister Lincoln." *Collier's* 15 Feb. 1947: 18-19, 49-52.

"Neighbor Sam." *American Magazine* Mar. 1942: 38-40, 102-06.

"A President's Wife." *Ladies' Home Journal* Aug. 1939: 16-17, 62-63.

"Stockade." *Ladies' Home Journal* Dec. 1936: 14-15, 122-26.

"Sun in the West." *Ladies' Home Journal* Oct. 1938: 26-27, 56, 58, 60.

"To Marry with a Stranger." *Ladies' Home Journal* July 1940: 16-17, 92-95.

"While They Dance." *Ladies' Home Journal* July 1937: 11-13, 89-92.

Secondary Sources

Articles and Chapters

Campenni, Frank. Introduction. *Time and the Riddle: Thirty-One Zen Stories.* Howard Fast. Pasadena: Ritchie, 1975. xi-xv.

Describes Fast's writing and political career, his earlier interest in science fiction and fantasy, and how Zen stories compare and contrast to sci-fi and fantasy fiction. Reviews Fast's major novels and his changing views and ideas. Briefly describes several of the stories.

Cohn-Sherbok, Lavinia. "Defaming Jewish Women." *Jewish Spectator* 48 (Sum. 1983): 58-59.

Describes Fast's portrayal of Jewish women in *Max*, and claims that since this and other novels like it have so little literary merit, they cannot do much harm. Concludes, however, that they do Jewish women a great wrong and contribute to anti-Semitism.

Collamore, Elizabeth. "False Starts and Distorted Vision in *April Morning*." *English Journal* Nov. 1969: 1186-88.

Provides an account of teaching *April Morning* to a class and the difficulties that emerge with various of the characters and the development of the themes. Argues that the road signs in the dialogue and metaphorical levels of the novel are thoroughly misleading.

Evans, John W. *"Freedom Road." Survey of Contemporary Literature.* Ed. Frank N. Magill. Rev. ed. 12 vols. Englewood Cliffs: Salem, 1977. 4: 2779-82.

A standard reference article on *Freedom Road* that covers principal characters, contents, themes, symbolism, style, social commentary, and impact.

Fast, Howard. "Reply to the Critics." *Masses & Mainstream* Dec. 1950: 53-64.

A hot response to Sterling North of the New York *World Telegraph and Sun* who criticized him for "treasonable distortion of fact." A lengthy, impassioned defense of his research for *The Proud and the Free.*

Gertel, Elliot B. "Two Recent Novels About Rabbis." *Jewish Spectator* 50 (Fall 1985): 54-6.

Calls *The Outsider* a book which looks beyond the curiosities of its readers to ask the question, what really makes a rabbi? Suggests that one does get the impression that Fast has woven together all the motifs and situations from other novels and rabbis in order to have the final word. Sees Hartman finally as a raging, angry old Jewish prophet. Concludes that, in the end, he becomes a joyless, forbidding character without compassion and thoughtfulness.

Hicks, Granville. "Howard Fast's One Man Reformation." *College English* Oct. 1945: 1-6.

Argues that in writing primarily in the genre of the historical novel, Fast has broken with its traditions and conventions by avoiding all swashbuckling heroes, unearthly female beauties, black-browed villains, and fiendish machinations. Claims that there are no important female characters and no romantic roles. Describes his early life, historical novels, and reformulation of the Victorian historical novel.

Lifka, Marion. "Howard Fast: Wool Puller?" *Catholic World* Sept. 1953: 446-51.

Details Fast's career and honors received, his treatment by the McCarthy tribunal, and his patriotic writings on U. S. history. Reviews the critical acclaim Fast has received and his powers of persuasion. The remainder of the article attempts to balance this picture with an account of the accolades he has received from communist sources and his former affiliations with the Communist Party. Examines the contents of his books and their dedications. Accuses him of debunking past presidents and political leaders.

Meisler, Stanley. "The Lost Dreams of Howard Fast." *Nation* 30 May 1959: 498-500.

Reviews Fast's personal history with the Communist Party, his early novels reflecting this mind set, his bent for American history, his utopian world view, each of the major books, how Fast differed from other American communists, his ultimate break with the party, and the themes of freedom in his later novels.

Polansky, Janet. "Howard Melvin Fast." *Beacham's Popular Fiction of America*. Ed. Walter Beacham. 4 vols. Washington: Beacham, 1986. 2: 423-35.

A standard reference article that covers Fast's publishing history, critical reception, analysis of *Spartacus* and *The Immigrants*, literary precedents, and related titles.

Rideout, Walter B. "The Long Retreat." *The Radical Novel in the United States: Some Interrelations of Literature and Society*. Walter B. Rideout. Cambridge: Harvard UP, 1956. 255-91.

This lengthy treatment of Fast contains references to all his novels, his political ideology, style, treatment of American history, and vision of American society. The best single account of Fast and the definitive critical treatment. Rideout is writing of the tradition of the radical novel in American literary history, and places Fast in this context.

Scheiber, Alexander. "A Tale of the Mother's Heart." *Journal of American Folklore* 68 (1955): 72, 86, 89.

Claims to have identified the source of the story told by Gracchus to Cicero in *Spartacus* as a Breton folksong. Includes a letter from Fast in which he indicates he didn't know where he got the story, but that others had written to him suggesting Italian, Indian, and Talmudic origin.

Sharma, K. N. "Spartacus: Variations on a Theme." *Modern Studies and Other Essays in Honour of Dr. R. K. Sinha*. New Delhi: Vika, 1987. 261-72.

Provides the historical background of the rebellion of Spartacus in Italy in 73-71 B.C. and compares the treatment of the same story by James Mitchell, Arthur Koestler, and Fast. Comments on Fast's Marxist beliefs, fervor, style of storytelling, and his enthusiasm.

Reviews

Alpert, Hollis. "Fiction Notes." Rev. of *Departure and Other Stories*. *Saturday Review of Literature* 24 Dec. 1949: 27-28.

Describes *Departure and Other Stories* as fluently readable, economical, full of delicate self-revelation; deep, biting irony; sentimentality; and political views.

Benet, Stephen Vincent. "Valley Forge." Rev. of *Conceived in Liberty*. *Saturday Review of Literature* 1 July 1939: 11.

Admires Fast's grasp of the dim facts of the Revolutionary War in *Conceived in Liberty*. Yet, complains that somehow this novel is a nightmare because of the curiously impressionistic quality of the prose. Notes that the dialogue is frequently unrealistic, and disagrees with the somewhat hysterical picture of Washington and the hectic overwriting. Concludes, however, that it is an honest attempt to tell a great story from the reverse of the conventional point of view.

"Books." Rev. of *The General Zapped an Angel*. *Magazine of Fantasy and Science Fiction* Sept. 1970: 18-19.

Complains that all these stories are parables with too obvious morals. Suggests that some are marginal science fiction and the rest fantasies.

Boroff, David. "Counsel for the Defense." Rev. of *The Winston Affair*. *Saturday Review* 19 Sept. 1959: 32.

Argues that *The Winston Affair* invites comparison with *The Caine Mutiny* because it is taut, hard-hitting, and focuses on a court martial during WWII. Comments that, unfortunately, Fast has little appetite for the complexities of human experience, for those grey spectral shapes that emerge from the collision of moral forces. Claims that he has written too long in an atmosphere of rarified heroism. Concludes that this is entertaining and readable, but lacks research documentation and resonance.

Boroff, David. "Keys to Corruption." Rev. of *Power*. *Saturday Review* 22 Sept. 1962: 30.

Describes *Power* as a barely disguised portrait of a labor leader, John L. Lewis, as well as an account of the tumultuous origins of the coal miners' union. Suggests that here Fast shows his natural storytelling ability and his lucid, sharp, compelling writing. Concludes that this novel explores an epic chapter in American experience.

Capouya, Emile. "Evil in the Name of Good." Rev. of *Torquemada*. *Saturday Review* 22 Jan. 1966: 43.

Calls *Torquemada* a brief, intense, and disappointing novel. Suggests that his treatment is heavy-handed, rigid, portentous, and abstract. Complains that the female characters are particularly bad.

"The Common Soldier at Valley Forge." Rev. of *Conceived in Liberty*. *Christian Science Monitor* 8 July 1939: 10.

Describes *Conceived in Liberty* as an example of the historical novel conspicuously lacking pomp and circumstance. Complains there is nothing in it of the noble commander and much of the common soldier freezing, quarreling, and living in rags and filth. Concludes that human nature rather than history is Howard Fast's field.

Conrad, George. "Leading Summer Fiction." Rev. of *Place in the City*. *New York Herald Tribune Books* 15 Aug. 1937: 6.

Describes the novel in terms of its characters, setting, plot, theme, and action. Concludes that it is a fine first novel by a young man with a pronounced gift for observation, style, and pace.

Conner, John W. "Book Marks." Rev. of *The Hessian*. *English Journal* Jan. 1973: 144-45.

Calls this novel a rare book that is of particular interest to adolescents. Commends it to English teachers.

Cook , Bruce. "Crimes Against Conscience: The McCarthy Era Fiction." Rev. of *The Pledge*. *Washington Post Book World* 23 Oct. 1988: 10.

Argues that *The Pledge* takes the "Red" witch hunt of World War II directly as its subject. Describes the plot and the characters. Concludes that the book has not been entirely honestly written and that those best prepared by experience to write such a novel seem least equipped as writers.

Cosgrave, Mary Silva. "Outlook Tower." Rev. of *The Hessian*. *Horn Book Magazine* June 1973: 296.

Calls this a novel about the Revolutionary War which details the sense-less death of a drummer boy. Considers it an exceptionally spare novel with strong implications of the effect of war on love and hate, good and evil, tolerance and bigotry, conformity and nonconformity.

Cowley, Malcolm. "The Death of Debunking." Rev. of *The Unvanquished. New Republic* 17 Aug. 1942: 203.

Sees the novel as true to historical facts, made human and credible. Considers it a book that restores dignity to our historical figures. Notes that Fast writes with a catch in his breath and succeeds in making his characters likeable and heroic. Concludes that if this book does not belong to the history of American literature, at least it will be important in the history of the popular mind.

Du Bois, William. "The Grand Inquisitor." Rev. of *Torquemada. New York Times Book Review* 6 Feb. 1966: 42.

Considers the book a romance for teenagers, for the first half at least. Suggests that later it becomes a tract for our times, and for all ages. Insists that the Grand Inquisitor is an attitude, not a character capable of change and complexity. Concludes that, unfortunately, the book insuffi-ciently dramatizes its moral postures.

Duhamel, P. Albert. "Between Conqueror and Conquered Was Berenice." Rev. of *Agrippa's Daughter. New York Times Book Review* 13 Sept. 1964: 52-53.

Describes *Agrippa's Daughter* as cinematic, scenic, epic with only inci-dental dialogue. Notes that it appears to have been built from a series of sketches rather than plotted.

Edwards, Willard. "Communism's Affair with the Intellectual." Rev. of *The Naked God. Chicago Sunday Tribune Magazine of Books* 29 Dec. 1957: 2.

Comments during a discussion of *The Naked God* that no American writ-er has been more honored by the Soviet Union than Howard Fast until his 1957 renunciation of the Communist Party. Suggests that this novel discusses the plight of the Soviet writer under communist domination. Concludes that Fast's portrayal of the agony of being bereft of the com-munist faith has clinical interest for students of the communist mentality.

Epstein, Bennett. "The Patriarch When Young." Rev. of *Moses, Prince of Egypt. New York Herald Tribune Book Review* 30 Mar. 1958: 5.

Describes *Moses, Prince of Egypt* as a fictional account of the life of Moses up to age twenty-three.

Fadiman, Clifton. "There Are No Nazis." Rev. of *Citizen Tom Paine. New Yorker* 1 May 1943: 70, 74-75.

Calls Fast one of America's most important historical novelists. Complains that this novel begins unskillfully but gathers strength as it goes along.

"Fast Shuffle." Rev. of *Torquemada. Time* 28 Jan. 1966: 91-92.

Calls *Torquemada* a bitter fictional parable about a detested inquisitor. Considers it a terrible and simple tale which raises more questions than it answers. Dismisses the book as a costume drama, minus the costume, designed to give the somnambulistic inevitability of real action. Concludes that it is hypnotic and tries hard only to use a child's vocabulary. Sees the book as not more than a *tua culpa* in which, in the person of Alvero, Fast seems to be trying to recover in the fifteenth century the innocence he lost in the twentieth.

"Fast Work." Rev. of *Freedom Road. Newsweek* 21 Aug. 1944: 83-84.

Describes the novel as a terrifying book with strength of characterization, moving honesty, and timeliness. Considers it a book that asks why the period of Reconstruction has been neglected, and what that means for modern democracy.

Fearing, Kenneth. "A Meeting at Concord." Rev. of *April Morning. New York Times Book Review* 23 Apr. 1961: 38.

Describes *April Morning* as a book whose events move swiftly along in a nimbus of historic color and detail. Calls Fast a veteran at this sort of historical recreation who has admirably recaptured the idioms, sights, sounds, religious and political attitudes, and military tactics and strategies of the day.

Feld, Rose. "Free Doom." Rev. of *The Last Frontier. New York Times Book Review* 27 July 1941: 6-7.

Describes the novel as austerely polished and poetic, yet complains Fast is less concerned with his characters as people than he is with what they stand for. Concludes that, despite its shortcomings, this is a rich American novel.

Feldman, Anita. "A Melodramatic Howard Fast Novel." Rev. of *Power*. *Commonweal* 2 Nov. 1962: 158-59.

Calls this novel dramatic, full of momentous events and vivid impressions. Yet, notes its disturbing static quality. Suggests that the story is like a tragedy where all the murders take place on the stage and all the questions, answers, revelations, and soliloquies happen somewhere in the wings between acts.

Felix, Herbert. "Intellectual in Search of Faith." Rev. of *Moses, Prince of Egypt*. *New Leader* 16 June 1958: 23-24.

Comments on the point of view, period of time, and vision of history which informs *Moses, Prince of Egypt*. Argues that Fast does violence not only to factual detail, but also to the Bible. Sees it as a novel full of haunted men of God. Concludes, however, that Fast is a superb story-teller-raconteur, making the narrative unfold with facility and felicity.

"Frontier America." Rev. of *Two Valleys*. *New York Times Book Review* 15 Oct. 1933: 9.

Discusses the contents of *Two Valleys*, and commends the author for successfully creating mood, lifelike characters, and settings. Above all, commends Fast for conveying the mood of optimism which characterized earlier frontier America.

Geismar, Maxwell. "A Rebel Prince Who Chose Exile." Rev. of *Moses, Prince of Egypt*. *New York Times* 23 Mar. 1958: 38.

Describes the contents of *Moses, Prince of Egypt* as a book whose message is often at variance with its aesthetic choices. Praises the descriptions of Egyptian architecture and the power and the savagery of Egyptian military might. Concludes that the book is weak in mythological and human interpretations.

Gelb, Alan. "In Short: Fiction." Rev. of *The Pledge*. *New York Times Book Review* 2 Oct. 1988: 26.

Calls *The Pledge* a novel which addresses the political and moral upheaval of the McCarthy era written in a dated, formulaic manner. Complains that Fast undercuts his story by making his hero a dolt.

Glauber, Robert H. "That Day at Lexington." Rev. of *April Morning*. *New York Herald Tribune Lively Arts and Book Review* 7 May 1961: 34.

Calls *April Morning* Fast's fictionalized history of the April 19, 1775, Battle of Lexington. Describes the plot briefly, and commends it as a sensitive, brief, and wonderful account of a young soldier's growing up. Considers it also a well-researched account of the battle itself.

"God's Underground?" Rev. of *Moses, Prince of Egypt*. *Time* 7 Apr. 1958: 101-02.

Describes *Moses, Prince of Egypt* in detail. Comments that Fast's Moses is reasonably convincing as a potential lawgiver who comes to believe the sun God Aton is really justice. But suggests that Howard Fast cannot get within miles of the God-inspired, prophetic Moses who stirred the souls and the genius of the Chosen People and marked out the history of civilized man.

Goldreich, Gloria. "Fiction." Rev. of *The Outsider*. *Hadassah Magazine* Aug.-Sept. 1984: 70.

Describes the contents of *The Outsider*, and then criticizes its major protagonist, David Hartman, as a cardboard ecumenical figure which Fast has clothed in the paper garments of his own naive political perspective and his disappointingly flimsy Jewish insight.

Grusd, Edward E. "Another Fine Howard Fast Story." Rev. of *Agrippa's Daughter*. *National Jewish Monthly* Dec. 1964: 49.

Considers *Agrippa's Daughter* to be a well conceived, beautifully written, and well-researched story describing one of the most significant periods of Jewish history, and filled with insights into human character.

Handlin, Oscar. "Fake." Rev. of *The American: A Middle Western Legend*. *Commentary* Sept. 1946: 295-96.

Comments that, unfortunately, *The American* will satisfy few discerning readers. Calls it undistinguished, unenlightening, remarkable for the opportunities it passes by, and interesting only for the techniques which animate best sellers. Complains that the characters are threadbare and unfurnished, speak a colorless language, and act without meaning or motivation. Concludes that this is a very poor historical novel.

Hardy, Melody. "Fiction." Rev. of *A Touch of Infinity*. *Best Sellers* 1 Sept. 1973: 239-40.

Calls *A Touch of Infinity* a collection of dessert stories, more fantasy than hard-core science fiction. Comments that each of the thirteen stories focuses on a sadly ironic view of the twentieth century, and is peopled by men and women caught in a tragic, misguided dilemma. Concludes, however, that too often he tells little more than tired, moralist tales. Suggests that this is a collection which lacks a main course.

Heath, Melville. "War of the Gladiators." Rev. of *Spartacus. New York Times Book Review* 3 Feb 1952: 22.

Calls *Spartacus* a tract rather than a novel. Asserts that his pages take on a brilliance that recalls his earlier work, but that the Q. E. D. he proposes simply does not square with the geometry of history.

Himmelfarb, Milton. "Fast and Loose." Rev. of *My Glorious Brother. Commentary* Dec. 1948: 584-85.

Considers *My Glorious Brother* a historical novel in which every gesture staggers under the weight of tragic symbolism, and in which the heroism of the heroes is only equalled by the villainy of the villains. Calls the document racist, and notes that there are large infusions of proletarian and revolutionary sympathies, love of violence, and other opinions on the corruption of the radical ideal.

"Historical Amnesia?" Rev. of *Freedom Road. Time* 21 Aug. 1944: 100, 102, 104.

Discusses *Freedom Road* as an expert and convincing novel which provides a view of Reconstruction that the history books have overlooked. Argues that Fast declares that the memory of the war expunged much of what some people considered Americans did not need to know about the war.

Hoopes, Alban W. Rev. of *The Last Frontier. Social Studies* Nov. 1941: 328-29.

Calls *The Last Frontier* historically accurate, dramatic, and worth the consideration of every student of the history of the American Indian.

Howes, Victor. "A Hard Flint Chip of a Story." Rev. of *The Hessian. Christian Science Monitor* 23 Aug. 1972: 11.

Calls *The Hessian* a shard preserved from the American Revolution. Sees it as a book full of conflict, authentic regional atmosphere, and dialogue as tight as a soldier's drum. Concludes that it is a parable that remains a hard chip from another age.

Huston, McCready. "Masterful Novel of the Rise of a Labor Union Czar." Rev. of *Power*. *San Francisco Chronicle* 14 Oct. 1962: 24.

Calls *Power* a masterful story of the rise of a labor union czar. Considers it a fictionalized version of the evolution of the United Mine Workers with another story embedded within it. Describes the story, and concludes that Fast is a writer of literary integrity because here he is a writer first and a philosopher second.

Hutchens, John K. "Oddments of History." Rev. of *Patrick Henry and the Frigate's Keel and Other Stories of a Young Nation*. *New York Times Book Review* 8 Apr. 1945: 6.

Suggests that *Patrick Henry and the Frigate's Keel* is a charming collection designed to stir the true patriot. Sees the stories as interesting, lively, but not expert renditions of history. Concludes that Fast's style is a rather plain instrument, and his reticence wise.

J., L. "Fiction." Rev. of *The Legacy*. *West Coast Review of Books* Feb. 1982: 34-35.

Describes *The Legacy* as a smooth, fast-moving, complex novel about movers and shakers from San Francisco to Beverly Hills.

Jackson, Joseph Henry. "An Important American Historical Novel." Rev. of *The Last Frontier*. *New York Herald Tribune Books* 27 July 1941: 3.

Labels *The Last Frontier* a book which economically chooses its incident and situation as it reveals the story of the Cheyenne. Calls it a dramatic and finely told story which may easily become a classic example of what to put in and what to leave out in the historical novel.

Jonas, Gerald. "Browsing." Rev. of *The Outsider*. *Present Tense* 12.1 (1984): 63.

Calls this an amiable novel dealing with all the major social upheavals of the past fifty years. Gives a detailed account of the contents, and concludes that this is an engaging and powerful book despite the fact the reader never gets a clear picture of the protagonist rabbi.

Kazin, Alfred. "Domestic Adventure." Rev. of *Place in the City*. *New York Times Book Review* 8 Aug. 1937: 7.

Calls *Place in the City* an astonishing achievement for a 23-year-old, but is disappointed that the novel is so exasperatingly soft. Argues that it is a nostalgic neighborhood piece full of wistful, lachrymose folktale. Concludes that it is really only a study in innocence, full of garlands, roses, and sighs.

Kiessel, William C. "Lexington in '75." Rev. of *April Morning. Saturday Review* 17 June 1961: 24.

Describes the plot and characters of *April Morning*, Fast's account of the battles of Lexington and Concord. Suggests that this is a gripping story told realistically through the actions of Adam Cooper. Concludes that it gives vibrant meaning to one of the great moments in the heritage of America.

Kondracke, Morton. "Uncle Sam Is the Heavy." Rev. of *The Confession of Joe Cullen. New York Times Book Review* 20 Aug. 1989: 24.

Calls *The Confession of Joe Cullen* a cops and spies thriller which might hold the reader's attention at the beach. Describes its contents, its political ideology, and its conspiracy theory about the CIA and the U.S. government.

La Farge, Oliver. "Flight of the Cheyennes." Rev. of *The Last Frontier. Saturday Review of Literature* 26 July 1941: 5.

Describes *The Last Frontier* as a novel that will set straight the slaughter of the Indians in the conquering of the American West, and yet which only tells us what white men saw. Complains that its references to Nazism seem anachronistic and forced, and that, frequently, Indian statistics are incorrect. Concludes that it is still, however, a finely written and moving story.

Lask, Thomas. "Mr. Fast and the Maccabbean Revolt." Rev. of *My Glorious Brothers. New York Times Book Review* 10 Oct. 1948: 4.

Sees *My Glorious Brothers* as another Fast novel about heroes who give their lives to a cause. Finds the Maccabean revolt against Syrian-Greek overlords is told with narrative skill and power. Praises the writing for being lean and uncluttered, and using the devices of the framing tale.

Lecierco, Diane. Rev. of *The Hessian. Books and Bookmen* Nov. 1973: 99-100.

Calls *The Hessian* a likeable, sentimental book. Details the contents and concludes that this is a very American book written in stiff upper lip and full of fine portraits and compelling narrative.

Leedom-Ackerman, Joanne. "Fast's Quick-Scene Novel: Grist for TV
     Drama Mill ?" Rev. of *The Immigrants*. *Christian Science Monitor* 7
     Nov. 1977: 18.

Details the contents of the novel and calls it "entertainment fiction"—not
profound or artistically remarkable, but a good, easy read. Comments
that at times the book becomes banal but that usually the storyteller saves
the situation.

"Lilo." Rev. of *The Naked God*. *Time* 2 Dec. 1957: 92, 95.

Describes *The Naked God* as Fast's disillusionment with communism,
and his tribute to the rank and file of the party. Concludes that Fast is
"very slow off Marx."

Lipsius, Frank. "Fiction." Rev. of *The Crossing*. *Books and Bookmen*
     Aug. 1972: 83.

Complains that this novel is written in generally flaccid prose and that
Fast has the annoying habit of imagining conversations, which he dic-
tates with a useless disclaimer just to separate fact from his pallid fiction.
Describes the contents.

Love, Paul. "Four in Midsummer." Rev. of *Place in the City*. *Nation* 14
     Aug. 1937: 177.

Sees *Place in the City* as a melodramatic cross-section of one alley in the
city, told swiftly and glibly, sometimes immaturely. Concludes that this
is light reading at best.

Lurie, Alison. "Realism and Sociology." Rev. of *The Children*.
     Commentary Aug. 1947: 199-200.

Argues that, although *The Children* is a story of slum children on the
Lower East Side, Fast limits his book to a sociological case study, thus
disregarding its further and wider implications although they are still
there for the reader. Suggests that the housing officials read the Preface.

Lynch, William S. "Altgeld of America." Rev. of *The American: A Middle
     Western Legend*. *Saturday Review of Literature* 20 July 1946: 6.

Calls *The American* a novel which presents challenging material with
restraint and dramatic effectiveness. Suggests that, within the limiting
framework of fictionalized biography, Fast demonstrates his own liberal
partisanship through his vivid drama.

MacBride, James. "Stories by Howard Fast." Rev. of *Departure and Other Stories. New York Times Book Review* 11 Sept. 1949: 8.

Comments that the stories in *Departure and Other Stories* range over much of the disputed area of the globe. Shows, however, the present stories, for all their promise, seldom come to grips with either their people or their suggested themes. Concludes that Fast's mind darts on to other fields after each warm-up—leaving both cast and reader dangling in midair.

Maurer, Robert. "Beautiful Dreamer." Rev. of *Agrippa's Daughter. New York Herald Tribune Book Review* 11 Oct. 1964: 20.

Describes the novel as a search through Jewish history that combines pure storytelling and vivid re-creations of earlier times. Also describes the implied social values and critique.

Mayberry, George. "Two Down." Rev. of *Freedom Road. New Republic* 14 Aug. 1944: 196-97.

Claims that there is neither confusion nor stylistic nonsense in *Freedom Road*, which has at once the virtues and defects of a cleanly written political tract. Yet, notes that Gideon Jackson's rise lacks depth and saturation in its materials. Calls this a useful democratic tract for the times. Suggests, also, that there is an imbalance in the manner in which Fast uses the Lincoln legend, since Lincoln's policies and his temper regrettably were poles apart from the cause.

McGuinness, Frank. "Selected Books." Rev. of *Power. London Magazine* Sept. 1963: 85.

Describes *Power* as a work of massive dreariness whose plot is marked by a dearth of imagination that is staggering in a writer of such a large reputation. Details plot and contents.

Moon, Bucklin. "Mr. Fast Surveys the 'Tragic Era.'" Rev. of *Freedom Road. New York Times Book Review* 27 Aug. 1944: 5.

Describes *Freedom Road* as a timely book about the true meaning of freedom and its cost. Suggests that though this is not one of Fast's best books, the subject matter is of great importance.

Nevins, Allan. "An Eagle Forgotten of the West." Rev. of *The American: A Middle Western Legend. New York Times Book Review* 21 July 1946: 4, 20.

Describes *The American* as polemic-type fiction written with verve, warmth, and narrative intensity. Considers, however, that he has written a bad book because he has surrendered to a conventionalized, pseudo-radical concept of Altgeld and his times which fits his own train of political thought. Concludes that Fast is ultimately an irresponsible historian and reconstructor of history.

Nevins, Allan. "Man of Reason with a Mission." Rev. of *Citizen Tom Paine*. *Saturday Review of Literature* 1 May 1943: 8.

Discusses *Citizen Tom Paine* as a good topic for a historical novelist. Comments that the portrait Fast gives is vigorous, vividly imagined, highly dramatic, swift-paced, lusty-spirited, and rhetorical. Also notes that it contains false facts and false taste on occasion. Concludes that it has power, but that it needs more restraint and more accuracy.

Newlove, Donald. "Three Novels." Rev. of *The Immigrants*. *New York Times Book Review* 2 Oct. 1977: 22, 24.

Recounts the story line. Argues that some overriding social purpose does not get in front of the relentless pace of events—that the reader can enjoy this novel without a thought in his or her head. Describes the story as covering forty years of French, Italian, Irish, and Chinese immigrants in turn-of-the-century San Francisco. Calls it one of Fast's best novels because each scene stands on firm detail.

R., D. H. "Fiction." Rev. of *Max*. *West Coast Review of Books* Nov. 1982: 32-33.

Describes *Max* as a palatable history, a tasty fiction, and a well-told tale of unflagging interest. Contains mostly an account of the contents of the novel.

Raven, Simon. "Holy Moses." Rev. of *Moses, Prince of Egypt*. *Spectator* 3 Apr. 1959: 484.

Characterizes this novel as dealing with Moses' youth, taking him from age ten to twenty-three, during all which time chambering, brawling, soldiering, and feasting, he behaves in a worldly, monied, and insouciant manner befitting a Prince-God of the Egyptian royal house.

Ribalow, Harold U. "Pointed Short Stories." Rev. of *Departure and Other Stories*. *Congress Weekly* 14 Nov. 1949: 15.

Suggests that these nineteen stories manage to convince readers that the world has much injustice, that life is hard, and that people with ideals and illusions are the best. Describes the stories, concluding that they all have meaning but can be read for pleasure.

Rice, Elmer. "Tom Paine, Prophet of Liberty." Rev of *Citizen Tom Paine. New York Times Book Review* 25 Apr. 1943: 1, 18.

Describes *Citizen Tom Paine* as a book full of straightaway narration which means a series of quick and vivid impressions with frequent changes of locale and sudden flashbacks to Paine's early life—in short, a kind of montage. Concludes that this is a timely and readable reincarnation of a forgotten man.

Rothman, Nathan L. "The Bumpy Road of Liberty." Rev. of *Freedom Road. Saturday Review of Literature* 23 Sept. 1944: 11.

Calls *Freedom Road* a real historical novel which provides historical vision and vitality, because it reaches out into the past and expands into the future.

Rothman, Nathan L. "The New Books." Rev. of *Place in the City. Saturday Review of Literature* 7 Aug. 1937: 20.

Calls this a novel about New York written with enthusiasm and fierce gesturing. Sees the picture as blurred by sentimentality and distorted by melodrama. Concludes that the characters strut stale stuff, and that even the better passages fail to become credible.

Schmitt, Gladys. "Statuary of Time." Rev. of *Moses, Prince of Egypt. Saturday Review* 29 Mar. 1958: 25-26.

Considers that *Moses, Prince of Egypt* develops deep and worthy themes, is strongly plotted, and yet fails to show Moses in the context of the time he lived in. Complains that, unfortunately, he is only shown as a young man. Sees the book's real failure as its use of historical archetypes which ultimately have no power to move us.

Shepard, Richard F. "Books: Jewish Life." Rev. of *The Outsider. New York Times* 24 Sept. 1984: C16.

Describes *The Outsider* as a straightforward easy-to-read story whose heroic maunderings can be skipped over quickly. Notes that it fills the gap in the novel-history of the Jewish people in the new land as they move out into the suburbs after WWII.

Sheppard, R. Z. "Reds to Riches." Rev. of *The Immigrants. Time* 7 Nov. 1977: 120-22.

Calls *The Immigrants* a pop epic which underscores the fact that there are second and third acts in the lives of American authors and citizens. Details Fast's writing career, and concludes that this book consolidates his talent for soap history. Suggests that it is a long way from Emma Lazarus' New York to Howard Fast's Beverly Hills, where descendants of immigrants cater to huddled masses yearning for TV.

Shoemaker, Elisabeth. "Mutiny Again." Rev. of *The Proud and the Free. New York Herald Tribune Book Review* 5 Nov. 1950: 21.

Calls *The Proud and the Free* a story of the American Revolution. Describes it in detail, and commends it for its fully drawn historical figures and accurate detail.

Spector, Robert. Rev. of *Power. New York Herald Tribune Book Week* 25 Nov. 1962: 13.

Argues that, in his own vague, romantic way, Fast is a social historian. Comments that *Power*, which is an historical account of the American labor movement, continues in the same vein as his earlier work on the Civil War. Accuses the book of a failure of characterization, didacticism, sentimentality, and mechanical faults. Yet concludes that, for all of these weaknesses, the book shows genuine compassion and truthful portraits.

Swados, Harvey. "Epic in Technicolor." Rev. of *Spartacus. Nation* 5 Apr. 1952: 331.

Wonders why *Spartacus* was rejected by publishers since it contains no ideas that could not be wholeheartedly accepted by all men of goodwill, and with no diminution of talent on Fast's part. Comments that the story, however, is diffused and scattered with regard to sequence, and calls Fast's sense of history not much different than that of Cecil B. DeMille. Concludes that his technicolor characters are banal and stubbornly refuse to speak in accents different from those of movie epics.

Terry, C. V. "Early Howard Fast." Rev. of *The Children. New York Times Book Review* 23 Mar. 1947: 10.

Describes *The Children* as dated, proletarian fiction which we can now only puzzle mildly at. Argues that within the stage set of a familiar tenement block, there is by now a very familiar microcosm. Concludes that, in a way, this is a king-sized pamphlet.

Terry, C. V. "Mr. Fast's Defense of the American Communist." Rev. of *Clarkton. New York Times Book Review* 28 Sept. 1947: 4.

Calls *Clarkton* continuously readable and even engrossing in spots, but argues that when you have closed it, it will seem rather a slim philippic, and you will wonder why you stayed with it so long. Concludes that Fast never really pauses to debate what it is the communists in the story want.

Tilden, David. "Valley Forge Now in Fiction." Rev. of *Conceived in Liberty*. *New York Herald Tribune Books* 25 June 1939: 2.

Claims that Fast's novel has the merits of energy, gusto, a quick visualization of men and episodes, and a strong feeling for the spirit of the common man in the revolution. Describes contents, characters, style, and quality of research. Concludes that this is a quick, nervous book with great promise.

Trilling, Diana. "Fiction in Review." Rev. of *Citizen Tom Paine*. *Nation* 8 May 1943: 676.

Heartily recommends this novel, and commends Fast for his ability to make the human connections between the present and the past which are so lacking in our teaching of history. Considers that, unlike other historical novelists, Fast works on the premise that even people who were born two hundred years ago were really people. Considers him in a class by himself among historical novelists for his taste and talent.

Wallace, Margaret. "A Novel of the American Revolution." Rev. of *Conceived in Liberty*. *New York Times* 25 June 1939: 7.

Describes *Conceived in Liberty* as a book which, while it shows little fumbling or uncertainty, does not yet show a major talent. Notes that the prose is clear and often moving, but ultimately fails to convey the grimness of the detail. Concludes that he lacks the poetry of a Crane and thereby misses the true pitch of effectiveness.

Wallace, Willard M. Rev. of *The Crossing*. *American Historical Review* 77.1 (1972): 203.

Calls *The Crossing* a fascinating little book written in a lively and colorful manner. Questions Fast's use of historical source materials about Washington, D.C. and some of the characterizations.

Weeks, Edward. "Black Hatred." Rev. of *Freedom Road*. *Atlantic* Sept. 1944: 127.

Respects Fast as one of the ablest and most patriotic of our novelists, but finds Fast the historian has sometimes been outmaneuvered by Fast the moralist. Concludes that sure narrative skill redeems the novel.

Weeks, Edward. "Peripatetic Reviewer." Rev. of *The Crossing. Atlantic*
    Feb. 1971: 125-26.

Describes the novel as graphic, sharply characterized, fast-paced, and a
fascinating historical portrayal of Washington's army.

West, Paul. "Uninquisitive." Rev. of *Torquemada. New York Herald*
    Tribune Book Week 23 Jan. 1966: 18.

Complains that *Torquemada* is curiously flavorless as a story about a
great mythomaniac and that subsidiary characters are mere props.
Discusses the timeless and insipid convolutions of Segovia, a general
aloofness, and general boredom.

Interviews

Baker, John F. "PW Interviews Howard Fast." *Publishers Weekly* 1 Apr.
    1983: 64-65.

Describes Fast's career, personality, present literary rediscovery, the
emotional quality of the novels, his publishing history, financial ups and
downs, his leftist politics, his interest in Buddhism, his functioning in the
direct tradition of the traditional American novel, and his neglect by the
critics.

Newquist, Roy. "Howard Fast." *Counterpoint.* Roy Newquist. Chicago:
    Rand, 1964. 179-85.

Provides an extensive history of Fast, reviews his major works and publishing career, contains a report of an extensive interview, and concludes
by attempting to place Fast historically. In the interview Fast discusses:
his early life of poverty, his joining the Communist Party, his favorite
books, his belief in novelistic storytelling, his denunciations of contemporary writing, his advice to young writers, his opinions of moviegoing,
his disappointment with the critical establishment, and his assessment of
himself as an honest workman, rather than a dilettante artist.

Biographical Sources

Dudar, Helen. "Howard Fast: 50 Stormy Years as an Author." *Chicago*
    Tribune Book World 13 Feb. 1983: 1, 5.

Reviews Fast's writing career, including the seventeen E. V. Cunningham
novels he produced as light entertainment. Repeats Fast's denial that he is
a "prolific" writer, usually a signal of a lack of literary talent.

Dunning, Jennifer. "Behind the Best Sellers." *New York Times Book Review* 11 Dec. 1977: 48.

A brief description of Fast's career written at the time of publication of *The Immigrants*, Fast's 56th book. Briefly reviews his writing career, his financial success as a writer, his writing family, his life in California, and his break with the Communist Party.

Fast, Howard. *Being Red.* Boston: Houghton, 1990.

Fast, Howard. "Something About My Life Briefly." *Zeitschrift fur Anglistik und Amerikanistik* 1 (1953): 13.

Briefly describes his impoverished childhood, his working from age eleven, and his beginning to write at sixteen with "a tremendous cascade of words."

Fast, Howard. "Under Forty." *Contemporary Jewish Record* Feb. 1944: 25-7.

A contribution to an article in which Jewish writers were asked to discuss the relationship of their writing to Jewish heritage. Explains his difficulty in understanding just what the term consists of, and says if it means "Jewish learning, Jewish tradition, Jewish religious influences, a Jewish historical memory, and a sense of my importance and insularity in this world as a Jew," then his works have no relationship to it. But agrees that if his work is related to the Jewish heritage of hate and persecution, chauvinism, race hatred, and attacks on individual rights, then he writes as an American and as a Jew, and finds no conflict between the two. Concludes that "a Jew is nothing special; I see him as no better, no worse than other human beings—no wiser, no more foolish."

"Howard Fast." *Wilson Library Bulletin* Oct. 1942: 82.

Describes Fast's series of menial jobs prior to becoming a writer, gives a brief description of his novels to *The Unvanquished*, and recounts some critical comments that led him to a lean and unweighted style, and to embark on a one-man reformation of the historical novel in America.

Lingeman, Richard R. "55 Books Later." *New York Times Book Review* 21 Aug. 1977: 39.

Reviews Fast's extremely long publishing career and comments that his latest book, *The Immigrants*, uses history not as philosophy, but as a backdrop for describing immigrant families in California in 1889.

Manousos, Anthony. "Howard Fast." *American Novelists, 1910-1945,*
Part I: Louis Adamic-Vardis Fisher. Ed. James J. Martine. Detroit:
Gale, 1981. Vol. 2 of *Dictionary of Literary Biography.* 94 vols. to
date. 1978- . 277-81.

More than details of his life, this is a career biography, tracing the development of his works, evaluating his reputation, and placing him in the
larger context of American literary history. Includes a list of primary
sources and a portrait.

McDowell, Edwin. "Behind the Best Sellers." *New York Times Book*
Review 22 Nov. 1981: 50.

Reviews Fast's writing career, present interests, and Californian trilogy
with particular reference to *The Establishment.*

Smilgas, Martha. "Howard Fast's Many Sides: A Born-Again Yankee,
Blacklisted Best-Seller." *People Weekly* 7 Apr. 1980: 119-21.

A biographical portrait of Fast that discusses most of his books, his work
habits and family, his politics, and his recreational habits.

Dissertations

Campenni, Frank. "Citizen Howard Fast: A Critical Biography." Diss. U
of Wisconsin, 1971.

Irvin Faust
1924 –

Primary Sources

Novels

The File on Stanley Patton Buchta. New York: Random, 1970; New York: Bard-Avon, 1973.

Foreign Devils. New York: Arbor, 1973; New York: Popular, 1976.

Newsreel. New York: Harcourt, 1980; New York: Pinnacle, 1982.

A Star in the Family. Garden City: Doubleday, 1975; New York: Ballantine, 1976.

The Steagle. New York: Random, 1966; New York: Bard-Avon, 1971, 1976.

Willy Remembers. New York: Arbor, 1971, 1983; New York: Avon, 1972; New York: Bard-Avon, 1977; New York: Priam-Arbor, 1980.

Collected Works

Roar Lion Roar, and Other Stories. New York: Random, 1965; London: Gollancz, 1965; New York: Bard-Avon, 1966.

Contents: Philco Baby, Jake Bluffstein and Adolph Hitler, Into the Green Night, Googs in Lambarene, The Madras Rumble, Miss Dorothy Thompson's American Eaglet, The World's Fastest Human, Justice for Ladejinsky, The Duke Imlach Story, Roar Lion Roar.

The Year of the Hot Jock and Other Stories. New York: Dutton, 1985.

Contents: The Year of the Hot Jock, Bar Bar Bar, Operation Buena Vista, The Dalai Lama of Harlem, The Double Snapper, Simon Girty Go Ape, Gary Dis-Dong, Melanie and the Purple People Eaters, Bunny Berigan in the Elephants' Graveyard.

Short Fiction in Anthologies

"Roar Lion Roar." *The Norton Anthology of Contemporary Fiction.* Ed. R. V. Cassill. New York: Norton, 1988. 141-55.

"The World's Fastest Human." *Stories from the Transatlantic Review.* Ed. Joseph F. McCrindle. New York: Holt, 1970; London: Gollancz, 1970. Pag. not available; Harmondsworth: Penguin, 1974. 252-63.

Short Fiction in Periodicals

"The Double Snapper." *Esquire* Dec. 1965: 180, 182, 304-08.

"Madras Rumble." *Saturday Evening Post* 14 Nov. 1964: 44, 46-47, 49, 52, 54.

"Melanie and the Purple People Eaters." *Atlantic* Dec. 1981: 70-77.

"Operation Buena Vista." *Paris Review* 9.35 (1965): 86-105.

"Philco Baby." *Paris Review* 8.31 (1964): 72-96.

"Simon Girty Go Ape." *Transatlantic Review* 21 (1966): 67-75.

"Wobbil-loggy Mobbays." *Transatlantic Review* 17 (1964): 18-21.

"The World's Fastest Human." *Transatlantic Review* 14 (1963): 45-55.

"The Year of the Hot Jock." *Confrontation* 29 (1985): 4-17.

Secondary Sources

Articles and Chapters

Darrow, Diane. *"Roar Lion Roar and Other Stories."* Survey of Contemporary Literature. Ed. Frank N. Magill. Rev. ed. 12 vols. Englewood Cliffs: Salem, 1977. 10: 6439-41.

A standard reference article covering background, influences, theme, characters, plot, and style in *Roar Lion Roar*.

Faust, Irvin. "Irvin Faust on His Novels." *American Writing Today*. Ed. Richard Kostelanetz. 2 vols. Washington: U.S. Intl. Communication Agency, 1982. 1: 277-85.

In this lengthy chapter, Faust discusses his origins as a writer, publishing history, critical reception, feelings about his Jewishness, the turmoil of the 1960s, and life as a writer.

Kostelanetz, Richard. "New American Fiction Reconsidered." *Tri-Quarterly* 8 (1967): 280-81.

Touts Faust's *The Steagle* as a perceptive and sustained portrait of a psychotic breakdown. States that barely aware of his impending fall, Harold Aaron Weissburg externalizes his fantasies, really believing that he is a movie star or a gruff Italian capable of making a stripper fall in love with him. Sees Faust's major achievement in this novel as the skillful blending of fantasy and reality. Describes the prose as a sort of elliptical shorthand that is singularly elegant. Criticizes the book's parochialism and falseness in certain key details. Concludes, however, that Faust is an accomplished craftsman in the field of fiction.

Mablekos, Carole. *"The File on Stanley Patton Buchta."* Survey of Contemporary Literature. Ed. Frank N. Magill. Revised. 12 vols. Englewood Cliffs: Salem, 1977. 4: 2580-83.

A standard reference article that lists principal characters and discusses contents, style, themes, symbols, social commentary, and impact.

Reviews

Bandler, Michael J. "A Novelist's View of 'the Ordeal of America.'"
   Rev. of *The File on Stanley Patton Buchta. Christian Science Monitor*
   29 Oct. 1970: 9.

Describes the contents of *The File on Stanley Patton Buchta* and calls it
a story of fear, power, and patriotism.

Bell, Pearl K. "Transient Pleasures." Rev. of *Foreign Devils. New
   Leader* 28 May 1973: 18.

Comments that *Foreign Devils* is a book about writing a book. Describes
the contents, and concludes that finally this book and others like it are
too much fun to read, and that most of the time their goals are transient,
undemanding, and wasteful.

Bone, Robert. "Book Reviews." Rev. of *Roar Lion Roar and Other
   Stories. Teacher's College Record* May 1965: 777.

Argues that these ten stories make Faust a serious contender on the New
York literary scene. Calls his inventive powers extraordinary, his language distinguished, his diction colloquial, and his surface humor
deceptive. Comments also on his preoccupation with ideological systems
that fail to make contact with reality.

Boyers, Robert. "The Legitimacy of Madness." Rev. of *The Steagle. New
   Leader* 10 Oct. 1966: 26-27.

Describes the novel in detail, and concludes that Faust is uncomfortably
groping for narrative continuities and a vital context that will lend significance to his broken train of associations. Claims that there are moments
of power, but that he must learn to resist humor and originality as ends in
themselves, at which point his talents will undoubtedly subserve the
more serious ends we know he admires.

"Captive Tribe." Rev. of *Roar Lion Roar and Other Stories. Newsweek* 1
   Feb. 1965: 78-79.

Describes *Roar Lion Roar* as a book filled with compassion, humor,
metropolitan speech rhythms, and a pop imagination.

Cassill, R. V. "Faust Let His Old-Young Willy Sing, Yawp and Growl."
   Rev. of *Willy Remembers. New York Times Book Review* 29 Aug.
   1971: 5, 26.

A review of *Willy Remembers* which describes the Joycean complexity, ambivalence, sense of place, "yawp and yowl" of Manhattan, and the general good humor of the novel. Describes Willy's monologue as protean, the narrative as crisp, and the content of the novel as being full of chants, reveries, vignetted histories, anecdotes, lists, bigotries, and exhalations. Concludes with the expectation that this book deserves the status of minor classic.

Catinella, Joseph. "Willy Remembers." Rev. of *Willy Remembers*. *Saturday Review* 11 Sept. 1971: 43-44.

Argues that in *Willy Remembers* Faust has produced a luscious novel of Americana which recreates a vernal period in the nation's history when war was believed to be a test of strength, courage, and manhood. Concludes that it is a boisterous, funny, and quiet novel written with breadth and dexterity.

Charyn, Jerome. "A Cop from Queens." Rev. of *The File on Stanley Patton Buchta*. *New York Times Book Review* 28 June 1970: 30.

Claims that Faust always lays bare the horrifying interior life of urban America. Discusses the contents of the book in detail and concludes that had Faust built his novel around the Alamos, shunted Stan Buchta aside, and expanded Danny Caruso, he would have given us a more convincing portrait of our national psychosis. He might then have written a remarkable novel.

Chubb, Thomas Caldecott. "The Enchanted Voyage." Rev. of *The Enchanted Voyage*. *North American Review* 242.2 (1936-37): 441.

Describes the contents of *The Enchanted Voyage,* and asserts that it is a brave fantasy wherein perplexed souls seek a sort of happiness. Concludes that it will be read, enjoyed, and quickly forgotten.

Cooper, Arthur. "To Myself Be True." Rev. of *The File on Stanley Patton Buchta*. *Newsweek* 10 Aug. 1970: 75-76.

Argues that *The File on Stanley Patton Buchta* exposes the hysteria that exists just beneath the apparent unconcern of urban America. Claims that this is not art concerned with reaffirmation. Concludes that there are no epiphanies, and that in the end Stanley watches through his binoculars as his city incinerates.

Corcoran, John H. "Faust." Rev. of *A Star in the Family*. *National Observer* 12 Apr. 1975: 21.

Claims that *A Star in the Family* is unfortunately unfunny. Complains that Goldwine is unconvincing as a comedian and as a character because he is neither clown nor klutz. Concludes that we are never convinced that Goldwine is anything better than a third-rate hack.

Corke, Hilary. "New Fiction." Rev. of *Roar Lion Roar and Other Stories. Listener* 22 July 1965: 137.

Argues that *Roar Lion Roar* is the work of a very penetrating, original writer. Yet the whole thing seems to have as much literary or human validity as a series of snappy, amateur character impersonations after a dinner party. Concludes that the electric hum of energy is here, but that does not make this literature.

"Counting the Tears." Rev. of *Roar Lion Roar and Other Stories. Times Literary Supplement* 5 Aug 1965: 673.

Explains that in *Roar Lion Roar* Faust shows he is a writer of spectacular skills. Notes that he also has a sharp, angry, impetuous disgust with the phoney attitudes of conventional America and is everywhere scoring and prodding about the effects it has on its victims.

Davis, L. J. "Tale of a Nice Cop." Rev. of *The File on Stanley Patton Buchta. Washington Post Book World* 2 Aug. 1970: 2.

Asserts that this novel begins promisingly and quickly descends to the level of a first-rate comic strip, which is where it stays. Describes the contents, and concludes that though Faust writes with vigor and clarity, he has only managed to produce caricatures and stereotypes. Good material goes begging, and all the important questions go unanswered.

Donoghue, Denis. "Tales of America." Rev. of *Roar Lion Roar and Other Stories. New Statesman* 2 July 1965: 19-20.

Calls *Roar Lion Roar* a remarkably fine collection of short stories documenting the lives of all-American desperation in which the flow of organic feeling is blocked off, and frustration issues as decadent poetry. Describes several of the stories.

Duhamel, P. Albert. "Unicorns and Angels." Rev. of *The Fair. New York Times Book Review* 12 Apr. 1964: 36.

Describes *The Fair* as ironic, fantastic, light of touch, and mysterious. Commends it for avoiding the T. H. White problem of tedious seeming realism in 600 pages of epic form. Details some of the contents.

Elliott, George P. "The New Books." Rev. of *Roar Lion Roar and Other Stories. Harper's* Apr. 1965: 114-16.

Describes *Roar Lion Roar* as a set of stories about aliens who have strayed into an outrageous world. Describes several of the stories and concludes that they are delightful, serious, and definitely worth listening to.

Enright, Elizabeth. "The Ordinary is Priceless." Rev. of *The Snowflake and the Star.*

Sees *The Snowflake and the Star* as a fairy tale in the Hans Anderson tradition, but which gives the impression of having been dashed off a little too quickly. Concludes that it has occasional flashes of wit and a lively quality.

"Fantasy on the River." Rev. of *The River Journey. New York Times Book Review* 11 Sept. 1949: 8.

Calls *The River Journey* a novel which draws a fine line between charm and confusion. Mostly describes plot and characters.

Frakes, J. R. "No Stranger to Fiction." Rev. of *Willy Remembers. Washington Post Book World* 5 Sept. 1971: 2.

Describes contents of the novel, and finds it essentially a pastiche of memories that is nutty, moving, and quite funny in its way.

Fremont-Smith, Eliot. "Shel Game." Rev. of *The Steagle. New York Times* 11 July 1966: 27.

Calls *The Steagle* a coalition of all the jokes, tricks, fantasies, and nostalgia clues that fly from Mr. Faust's typewriter, fine imagination, and not very critical memory. Concludes that despite its abundance, the contents of this book are not really what the reader came for.

Garmel, Marion Simon. "My Son, the Pole Vaulter." Rev. of *Willy Remembers. National Observer* 23 Aug. 1971: 19.

Describes *Willy Remembers* as a book full of verbal explosions and massive imagination. The novel is flawed because the author is still overly fond of playing with cliches and puns; however, he has the potential to be America's most skilled literary magician.

Gilman, Richard. "The Make Believe Ballroom." Rev. of *The Steagle. Chicago Tribune Book Week* 10 July 1966: 4, 15.

Calls Faust a voluptuary of space and time in *The Steagle*. Sees it as an artistic defeat because with almost total recall it covers the popular culture of the 30s and 40s, sentimental, undistinguished, and full of moral or psychological insights. Provides a detailed description of contents.

Gilman, Richard. "Short Circuits in the Plugged-in Generation." Rev. of *Roar Lion Roar and Other Stories*. *Chicago Tribune Book Week* 24 Jan. 1965: 6.

Complains that *Roar Lion Roar and Other Stories*, Faust's first book of short stories, is uneven, urban, and mostly about men. Describes several of the stories and their contents and style.

Gold, Herbert. "The Magnificent Bone-Misery of the City." Rev. of *The Year of the Hot Jock and Other Stories*. *New York Times Book Review* 14 July 1985: 13.

Argues that *The Year of the Hot Jock and Other Stories* is a book which offers neither revolution nor grand reconciliation. Claims that he does bring a partial but careful and accurate rendering of a time in history in which he has been looking for occasions for trust, bleakly. Describes several of the stories.

Gold, Ivan. "Life as News." Rev. of *Newsreel*. *New York Times Book Review* 13 Apr. 1980: 15, 32-33.

Recounts the main events of the plot of the novel he claims is trying to tell us that "history is senseless except as it reverberates through the mortal, limited, more or less crazed private party (namely, you and me); that events, however 'global,' ultimately take on the most secret of meanings as they sink into our individual sensibilities." Concludes that *Newsreel* is a good book to have in an election year.

"Groping About the City." Rev. of *Roar Lion Roar and Other Stories*. *National Observer* 5 Apr. 1965: 19.

Describes this collection of stories as focusing on the inhabitants of a depersonalized city, groping through its hurried, syncopative rhythms in search of a place to rest. Concludes that they are loud and free-wheeling, explosive and flamboyant.

Hicks, Granville. "A Lot of Living in a Few Words." Rev. of *Roar Lion Roar and Other Stories*. *Saturday Review* 23 Jan. 1965: 39.

Claims that Faust's great asset is his sense of human possibilities. Notes that his characters refuse to behave as the reader expects. New York, urban, and Jewish, they are constructed with great authority out of those vernaculars. Details several of the stories.

Hicks, Granville. "Strange Games and Sea Changes." Rev. of *The Steagle*. *Saturday Review* 16 July 1966: 25.

Calls *The Steagle* a brilliant study of a man whose life is deflected from its normal course by the threat of a stupendous catastrophe.

Jones, D. A. N. "Pow! Now." Rev. of *The File on Stanley Patton Buchta*. *New York Review of Books* 13 Aug. 1970: 26, 28-30.

Argues that *The File on Stanley Patton Buchta* dodges uneasily between subjective fantasy and objective reportage, between social comment and self-indulgence, between wiseacre knowingness and bewildered mystification. Provides an excellent account of the contents of the novel.

Kauffmann, Stanley. "The Electric Hum of Talent." Rev. of *Roar Lion Roar and Other Stories*. *New Republic* 30 June 1965: 22-23.

Describes Faust's primary gift in *Roar Lion Roar and Other Stories* as "seeing" his stories and dramatizing them with a delicacy that heightens but does not obtrusively contrive. Describes several individual stories. Concludes that his prose is a distilled, heightened, accelerated vernacular.

Kauffmann, Stanley. "Pop Pilgrim's Progress." Rev. of *The Steagle*. *New Republic* 16 July 1966: 26, 28-29.

Details the contents of *The Steagle* and concludes that Faust has an unusually sensitive antenna for his environment. Complains that the book is splotched with self-indulgence and a touch of arrogance which sometimes afflicts truly sensitive writers.

Kenner, Hugh. "Reviewer's Choice." Rev. of *Willy Remembers*. *Life* 10 Dec. 1971: 8.

Describes the mixed-up connections Willy makes as he reminisces about his experiences in the Spanish-American War, confusing names, places, and events. Concludes that these notions are "weirdly true in the world of myth."

Kroll, Steven. "More New York 'Awareness.'" Rev. of *Foreign Devils*. *Commonweal* 24 Aug. 1973: 459-60.

A review of *Foreign Devils* which first reviews all of Faust's previous novels and then claims that in this novel all the previous themes have been brought together and taken further. Reviews the main character, Sidney Benson, describes the contents of the novels, and concludes that like the others, this is a flawed novel. Asserts, however, that this is a novel well worth reading because of its insight into the American character, its humor, and it richness.

Lask, Thomas. "The Light and the Dark." Rev. of *The File on Stanley Patton Buchta*. *New York Times* 6 July 1970: 29.

Claims that *The File on Stanley Patton Buchta* is emotional, highly charged, and full of tomorrow's headlines. Describes Buchta, the cop hero, and the society he polices as fear-ridden, self-righteous, and willing to sweep under the rug its own doubts, fears, and evils. A generally positive review.

Lehmann-Haupt, Christopher. "On the Junkheaps of History." Rev. of *Foreign Devils*. *New York Times* 11 July 1973: 39.

Sees *Foreign Devils* as an audacious experiment in verbal games which in the long run fails, despite the fact that it is most interesting where it fails. Gives a detailed account of the book's contents.

Leonard, John. "Books of the Times." Rev. of *Newsreel*. *New York Times* 8 Apr. 1980: C8. Rpt. in *Books of the Times* June 1980: 248-49.

Discusses *Newsreel* as a novel with a hero who is an unravelled mass of nerve endings and attitudes. Claims that the novel brilliantly portrays the Jewish romance with American popular culture and its ending in schizophrenia. Concludes that it is a funny, sad, impossible novel.

Lingeman, Richard R. "The Comedian as Hero." Rev. of *A Star in the Family*. *New York Times* 3 July 1975: 2A.

Indicates that *A Star in the Family* is a savingly likeable book. It contains much that is trendy, funny, and full of gas. Ultimately, however, it contains cameo-like characters, gentle parody, lively speech, and some historical artificialities.

Lingeman, Richard R. "Nov Shmoz Ka Pop and All That." Rev. of *Willy Remembers*. *New York Times* 30 Aug 1971: 26.

Describes *Willy Remembers* as Faust's fourth and perhaps best book. Claims that despite all its high jinks, the book is finally morally weak because of its neutrality. Concludes that we are left without a sense of the meaning of life and an adequate denouement.

Ludwig, Jack. "Catching -Up on Making Out." Rev. of *The Steagle. New York Times Book Review* 17 July 1966: 4.

Describes the contents of the novel in detail and comments that the only thing that prevents the novel from being boring is its ambitious, funny, yet serious treatment of boredom in American culture. Concludes that at bottom, the book is compassionate, serious, comic, sadly accepting, and uses fantasy as a refuge.

Malin, Irving. Rev. of *The Steagle. Commonweal* 28 Oct. 1966: 114-15.

Describes the protagonist, the contents of the novel, the carefully chosen language, and the difficulties Faust has in making his characters completely realized. Concludes: "It is like many Hollywood creations, exciting, one-dimensional, and forgettable."

Mano, D. Keith. Rev. of *Foreign Devils. New York Times Book Review* 20 May 1973: 7.

Describes the plot of the novel, the central character, and the story-within-the-story structure. Commends Faust for his terrific ear and superior performance. Concludes: "Faust does things here that will not easily be done again. Or as well."

Millstein, Gilbert. "Pity the Poor Comic." Rev. of *A Star in the Family. New York Times Book Review* 30 Mar. 1975: 13.

Describes his knowledge of and interest in stand-up comics as the foundation for his reading of the novel in which he found "absolute accuracy, absolute fidelity to the milieu; a rendering of conversation without a false note; an exact estimate of who represents what on any level of show business; an impeccable story-line moving inexorably from bright beginning to dismal end; technical devices not new but used expertly; in short, a thoroughly professional performance." Concludes that he was disappointed because he "did not feel," and doesn't know why. Complains: "The reader could have pieced together the story himself from a year's issues of *Variety*."

"One More Jerusalem." Rev. of *Road of Ages. Nation* 20 Feb. 1935: 228-29.

Argues that *Road of Ages* is the work of a minor novelist whose talents are of a restricted but decent quality. Claims that along with a gift for fantasy and satire, he enchants, amuses, and provides delicate humor and lithe language.

Poore, Charles. "Whirlpools in the Mainstream of Morality." Rev. of *Roar Lion Roar and Other Stories. New York Times* 30 Jan 1965: 25.

Describes *Roar Lion Roar* in detail and commends it as a fine book of short stories. Concludes that as a true storyteller he doesn't reflect or question accepted values, but rather lends them great vitality by showing them in collision.

Prescott, Peter S. "Mixed-up Kid." Rev. of *Willy Remembers. Newsweek* 30 Aug. 1971: 79, 81.

Describes the contents of this farcical novel that maintains a delicate balance between vulgar satire and legitimate pathos. Concludes that but for all his pyrotechnics and spasmodic brilliance, Faust seems to have no clear idea of what we are to make of the book.

"The Questing Beast." Rev. of *The Steagle. Newsweek* 25 July 1966: 93-94.

Describes the contents of the novel, the fleeing and searching of the protagonist, and the theme of American malaise. Concludes that the novel "dances across that fine edge of hysteria where comedy can make its most cutting social comment."

Rev. of *Willy Remembers. New Republic* 11 Sept. 1971: 32.

Describes the contents of the novel (its 93-year-old hero has a confused mind and uses many puns, conundrums, and bits of barracks humor), and concludes that readers may be left wondering what the point is. Concludes that the story suffers from fast pace and too many events too sketchily covered.

Rhav, Philip. "New American Fiction." Rev. of *Roar Lion Roar and Other Stories. New York Review of Books* 8 Apr. 1965: 8-9.

Describes the stories in this collection favorably, but notes that some are too ingenious and anecdotal to make good fiction. Advises Faust to reduce his use of "city jargon" if he is not to be stranded in incomprehensibility.

Sale, Roger. "American Fiction in 1973." Rev. of *Foreign Devils. Massachusetts Review* 14.4 (1973): 835.

Finds this story of the Boxer Rebellion an attempt to rid the author of his own foreign devils—the devils in his head that give him writer's block and the devils outside himself, including a mother and an estranged wife. Concludes that it is "a perfectly pleasant read . . . but . . . totally unmarked with originality or distinction in the central conception, in the writing, in the Boxer story."

Schott, Webster. "'Boo,' said Googs Korngold." Rev. of *Roar Lion Roar and Other Stories. New York Times Book Review* 7 March 1965: 5.

Comments on the uncomfortable feeling one derives from Faust that he or she has read these stories before, perhaps under the name of O'Henry. Notes also Faust's ability to portray marginal Jews and Blacks, Puerto Ricans, actors, Gimbel demonstrators, the misunderstood messages of the big city, and all its comic forms.

Schott, Webster. "Wild Ride to Black Nostalgia." Rev. of *The Steagle. Life* 20 July 1966: 13.

Considers that *The Steagle* curves upward from black humor and black nostalgia to crashing thunderbolt-age fiction and ordered chaos. Concludes that Faust is as inventive as a fortune-teller, equipped with cultural recall, and runs on a talent so rare he can spend it as he chooses.

Sheppard, R. Z. "A Diamond in the Fluff." Rev. of *Willy Remembers. Time* 30 Aug. 1971: 54-55.

Argues that *Willy Remembers* is a Faustian novel that goes so fast and is so gratuitous that it seems as if he has loosed havoc upon his creations in order to cover up the compassion and sentiment that went into their making. Concludes that this is an amusing but amorphous novel.

Sheppard, R. Z. "Dreams of Glory." Rev. of *Foreign Devils. Time* 21 May 1973: 100.

Describes the story and protagonists, and concludes that Faust has always relied on cultural trivia to create atmosphere, but unlike *Roar Lion Roar* where the artifacts of popular culture possess his characters like real demons, here they are mere nostalgia.

Simon, Marion. "Even Off Stride, Irving Faust Can Deliver the Goods." Rev. of *The File on Stanley Patton Buchta. National Observer* 10 Aug 1970: 21.

Criticizes *The File on Stanley Patton Buchta* as a failure because of arbitrary authorial invention, but notes, nevertheless, that it has gold in it because of some unusually fine descriptions of what it is like to be trapped in an American riot zone. Concludes that Faust should hurry on to novel number three.

Simon, Marion. "A Sporting Name, But a Story of Lost Dreams and Failed Promises." Rev. of *The Steagle*. *National Observer* 1 Aug 1966: 19.

Decides that *The Steagle* is no great novel, but that Faust has a gift for making the incredibly sad sound deliciously funny. Provides a detailed summary of contents.

"The Wattage of Inertia." Rev. of *The File on Stanley Patton Buchta*. *Time* 6 July 1970: 74.

Describes the character of Stanley and the major events in his life. Suggests that Faust takes him to be typical urban American—rootless, tough, guiltlessly selfish, and easily moved by chance winds. Compares him with characters in other works by Faust, and concludes that Faust understands why people do what they do because he understands and respects their passions—or lack of them.

Interviews

Bruccoli, Matthew J. "Irvin Faust." *Conversations with Writers II*. Detroit: Clark/Gale, 1978. 46-72.

An extensive interview in which Faust talks of his activities in WWII, his education at CCNY, his career as a guidance counselor, his first published stories, his later novels, and his method of working. Much biographical information.

Biographical Sources

Boken, Julia B. "Irvin Faust." *Twentieth-Century American-Jewish Fiction Writers*. Ed. Daniel Walden. Detroit: Gale, 1984. Vol. 28 of *Dictionary of Literary Biography*. 94 vols. to date. 1978- . 51-58.

More than details of his life, this is a career biography, tracing the development of the author's canon, describing the contents and themes of his works, evaluating his reputation, and placing him in the larger context of American literary history. Includes lists of primary and secondary sources and illustrations.

Campenni, Frank. "Irvin Faust." *American Novelists Since World War II.* Eds. Jeffrey Helterman and Richard Layman. Detroit: Gale, 1978. Vol. 2 of *Dictionary of Literary Biography.* 94 vols. to date. 142-48.

More than details of his life, this is a career biography, tracing the development of the author's canon, describing the contents and themes of his works, evaluating his reputation, and placing him in the larger context of American literary history. Includes a list of primary sources and illustrations.

Cassill, R. V. "Irvin Faust." *Dictionary of Literary Biography Yearbook: 1980.* Eds. Karen L. Rood, Jean W. Ross, and Richard Ziegfeld. Detroit: Gale, 1981. 40-44.

An update to the article in Vol. 2 of *DLB* which concentrates on more recent developments in his career, and which provides analysis of *Newsreel* published in 1980.

Raymond Federman

1928 –

Primary Sources

Novels

Double or Nothing: A Real Fictitious Discourse. Chicago: Swallow, 1971, 1973; Athens: Ohio UP, 1971.

Smiles on Washington Square (A Love Story of Sorts). New York: Thunder's Mouth, 1985.

Take It Or Leave It: An Exaggerated Second-Hand Tale to Be Read Aloud Either Standing Or Sitting. New York: Fiction Collective, 1976; New York: Braziller, 1976.

To Whom It May Concern. Boulder: Fiction Collective, 1990.

The Twofold Vibration. Brighton: Harvester; Bloomington: Indiana UP, 1982.

The Voice in the Closet / La Voix dans le Cabinet De Debarras. Madison: Coda, 1979 (1979 ed. includes "Echos a Federman" by Maurice Roche); Barrytown: Station Hill, 1986.

Short Fiction in Anthologies

"The Captain and the Kids." *Assembling*. Ed. Richard Kostelanetz. New York: Assembling, 1970. n.p.

"Federman: Voices within Voices." *Performance in Postmodern Culture*. Eds. Michel Benamou and Charles Caramello. Madison: Coda, 1977. 159-98.

"Setting and Tripping." *Statements: New Fiction from the Fiction Collective*. Ed. Jonathan Baumbach. New York: Braziller, 1975. 86-91.

"The Voice in the Closet." *Statements 2: New Fiction*. Eds. Jonathan Baumbach and Peter Spielberg. New York: Fiction Collective, 1977. 95-105.

Short Fiction in Periodicals

"Buickspecial." *North American Review* 259.2 (1974): 29-34.

"Cyrano of the Regiment." *Partisan Review* 42.2 (1975): 215-24.

"False Evidence." *Kolokon* 1 (Sum. 1966): 34-40.

"From 'Moinous & Sucette (A Love Story of Sorts).'" *SubStance* 37-38 (1982): 7-27.

"An Impromptu Swim." *Out of Sight* 73 (Apr. 1974): pag. not available.

"Inside the Thing." *Oyez Review* 8 (Fall 1974): 88-91; *Cream City Review* 5 (1979): 90-94.

"The Man on the Bridge." *Mica* 1.1 (1960): 18-22.

"Moinous Dreams." *Polis* 4 (1983): 28-30.

"Moinous, Nam, and Dostoevsky." *Paris Review* 23.81 (1981): 118-31.

"On Jazz." *Partisan Review* 40.1 (1973): 65-73.

"Parsifal in Hamburg." *Chicago Review* 31 (Spr. 1980): 136-46.

"Premembrance." *Mississippi Review* 7.3 (1978): 100-13.

"'The Rigmarole of Contrariety' (from Moinous & Sucette—A Love Story of Sorts)." *StoryQuarterly* 15-16 (1982): 53-58.

"Vociferations and Further Vociferations." *Chicago Review* 26.4 (1975): 33-50.

"The Voice in the Closet." *TriQuarterly* 38 (1977): 168-73; *Paris Review* 20.74 (1978): 120-41.

"Voicelessness." *Chicago Review* 28 (Spr. 1977): 109-14.

Secondary Sources

Books

Kutnik, Jerzy. "Part II: Raymond Federman." *The Novel as Performance: The Fiction of Ronald Sukenick and Raymond Federman.* Crosscurrents/Modern Critiques. Third Series. Carbondale: Southern Illinois UP, 1986. 147-236.

Articles and Chapters

Bryant, Paula. "Extending the Fabulative Continuum: DeLillo, Mooney, and Federman." *Extrapolation* 30.2 (1989): 156-65.
Argues that the contemporary novelists such as De Lillo, Mooney, and Federman are rendering an implicit message of their own postmodernist legacy explicitly by questioning reality in surreal syntax. Examines *The Twofold Vibration* as a disjointed narrative set up to challenge our notions of time, space, and our relative place within their dimensions.

Caramello, Charles. "Flushing Out *The Voice in the Closet*." *SubStance* 20
    (1978): 101-13. Rpt. in *Silverless Mirrors: Book, Self and Postmodern
    American Fiction*. Tallahassee: UP of Florida, 1983. 131-42.

A major treatment of Federman's fiction that provides detailed and technical analysis of the experimental techniques and fictional questions
being asked by the texts. Provides a little biographical background on the
Holocaust experience lying behind some of the fiction. Primarily concerns itself with the revelation of meaning through the experimental
strategies Federman employs.

Cornis-Pop, Marcel. "Narrative (Dis)articulation and *The Voice in the
    Closet* Complex in Raymond Federman's Fictions." *Critique* 29.2
    (1988): 77-93.

Sees Federman warning that narration cannot fill the existential gap with
the undeniable presence of speech. Describes his narrative as illustrating
the essential paradox of all fiction in its encounter with something real,
while not being either the truth or its meaning. Develops the thesis that
Federman is asking whether the narrative act can ever recapture the living circumstantiality of the world or if it is condemned to remain a mere
simulacrum.

Dienstfrey, Harris. "The Choice of Inventions." *Fiction International* 2-3
    (1974): 147-50.

Argues that *Double or Nothing* does brings the whole issue of the last
two hundred years of standardized novel page format into question. Calls
the book comic, dazzling, inventive, elegantly written, and quite unconventional. Describes the narrative tracks, organization, characters, new
conventions, and content of the novel. Concludes that the point of the
novel is the anxiety of storytelling.

Dowling, David. "Raymond Federman's America: Take It or Leave It."
    Contemporary Literature 30.3 (1989); 348-69.

Argues that Federman's self-reflexive textual play enacts reverberations
which provide an archetype of American experience. Calls this a semiotic system. Discusses the interplay in Federman's work between
biography, history, voice and narrative, text and context. Asserts that
Federman's fiction responds to the wake of deconstruction and its dissemination into the social sciences generally, and discusses how novels
can escape the perpetual freeplay of difference and be political in the
manner of their great nineteenth-century precursors.

Eder, Doris L. "'Surfiction': Plunging into the Surface." *Boundary 2* 5.1 (1976): 153-65.

Outlines the theoretical position of Federman with regard to "surfiction" or "metafiction." Primarily a history of critical theory that places Federman in an important position among the theorists of experimental fiction. Also provides a critique of his book *Surfiction*.

Friedman, Melvin J. "Making the Best of Two Worlds: Raymond Federman, Beckett, and the University." *The American Writer and the University*. Ed. Ben Siegel. Newark: U of Delaware P, 1989. 136-45.

Comments that few individuals have combined the academy and the creative life more happily or successfully than Raymond Federman. Describes Federman's scholarly interest in Beckett who has become the cornerstone of his career as his "special subject" as well as the prime influence on his life. Explores this subject in depth, and concludes that, for Federman, the university is a place in which to study, think, experiment, question his own writing, and take refuge.

Hornung, Alfred. "Absent Presence: The Fictions of Raymond Federman and Ronald Sukenick." *Indian Journal of American Studies* 14.1 (1984): 17-31.

Points out some of the characteristics of Federman's and Sukenick's texts, their similarities and differences. Also provides an in-depth account of the theories of narratology subscribed to by each, and their particular uses of such terms as "surfiction" or "metafiction." Claims that the all-informing principle of the writing and reading process in each author seems to be that of the "absent presence" of negative affirmation of fiction and life. Concludes that the text is actually the present mirror of the absent actual thing.

Hornung, Alfred. "Recollection and Imagination in Postmodern Fiction." *Representation and Performance in Postmodern Fiction*. Ed. Maurice Couturier. Montpellier: Delta, 1983., 57-70.

Discusses the treatment of the themes of recollection and imagination and such postmodern fiction as that written by Pynchon, Doctorow, Coover, Barth, Vonnegut, Abish, and Federman. Reviews the significant philosophical and literary instances in the development of these twin themes, and traces the re-emergence of a recollective imagination which affects contemporary narrative practices. Discusses Federman's *The Voice in the Closet*, and Abish's *How German Is It*.

Karl, Frederick R. *American Fictions 1940/1980: A Comprehensive History and Critical Evaluation*. New York: Harper, 1983. 488-89.

In his assessment of the novels of the 70s, Karl discusses Federman's attempts at defining and writing surfiction, concluding that his old-fashioned or exhausted content rearranged typographically as voices, entrances, and departures is really a dead end.

Klinkowitz, Jerome. "How Fiction Survives the Seventies." *North American Review* 258.3 (1973): 69-73.

Describes Federman as representative of a group of writers who have truly disrupted the course of American fiction writing. Places him in historical context with several other seventies writers. Briefly mentions individual novels and their techniques.

Klinkowitz, Jerome. Introduction. *The Self-Apparent Word: Fiction as Language/Language as Fiction*. Carbondale: Southern Illinois UP, 1984. 1-6.

Provides a fairly detailed treatment of Federman's philosophy and experimental technique. Covers several of his works.

Klinkowitz, Jerome. "Literary Disruptions; or, What's Become of American Fiction?" *Partisan Review* 40.3 (1973): 433-44. Rpt. in revised form in *Surfiction: Fiction Now . . . and Tomorrow*. Ed. Raymond Federman. Chicago: Swallow, 1975. 2nd ed. 1981. 165-79.

Discusses how a group of new writers—Sukenick, Barthelme, Federman, and Kosinski—have cleared the way for renewed experimentation in the American novel. Discusses Federman's theory, technique, objectives, and novel *Double or Nothing* to show how his artistic representation focuses on the book itself as the real entity, not a second hand lie about the world.

Klinkowitz, Jerome. "Raymond Federman's Visual Fiction." *Visual Literature Criticism: A New Collection*. Ed. Richard Kostelanetz. Carbondale: Southern Illinois UP, 1979. 123-24.

Argues that Federman needs a visual form for his fiction to succeed, hence the photographed typescript of *Double or Nothing*. Notes that each page has its own form, and is done somewhat like a secretary's typewriter game with the words in the forms of Christmas trees, diagrams, etc. Claims that part of Federman's inventiveness is finding appropriate forms, including maps and mazes for the reader just when the story calls for them. Discusses a number of his novels.

Klinkowitz, Jerome. "Ronald Sukenick & Raymond Federman." *Literary Disruptions: The Making of a Post-Contemporary American Fiction.* Jerome Klinkowitz. Urbana: U of Illinois P, 1975. 2nd ed. 1980. 119-53.

Asserts that what unites these two writers is their distaste for literature that suspends disbelief and their search for a new form that can adequately handle the reality of twentieth-century life. A major chapter that discusses novels by both writers and explores their informing philosophy and content in great detail, along with their respective narrative methods.

McCaffery, Larry. "The Fiction Collective." *Contemporary Literature* 19.1 (1978): 108-10.

Describes *Take It or Leave It* in an article about the Fiction Collective, calling it audacious, ambitious, and energetic with its experimental techniques, metafictional journey into chaos, digressions, typographical games, politics, sex, values, current literary attitudes, ironic reversals, cancellations, anecdotes, and fabricated distortions.

McCaffery, Larry. "Raymond Federman and the Fiction of Self-Creation: A Critical Mosaic." *Par Rapport* 3-4 (1980-81): 31-44.

Provides a biographical sketch of Federman and a novel by novel synopsis of contents and technique. A useful though brief introduction.

McCaffery, Larry. "Literary Disruptions: Fiction in a Post-Contemporary Age." *Boundary 2* 4 (1976): 137-51.

An essay about the false prophecy of the sixties writers and critics concerning the death of the novel, combined with an appreciation of several experimental writers like Federman. A useful introduction to both Federman and writers like him.

Pearce, Richard. "Riding the Surf: Raymond Federman, Walter Abish, and Ronald Sukenick." *The Novel in Motion: An Approach to Modern Fiction.* Richard Pearce. Columbus: Ohio State UP, 1983. 118-30.

A major chapter discussing the influence of Robbe-Grillet upon Abish, Federman, and Sukenick.

Quartermain, Peter. "Trusting the Reader." *Chicago Review* 20 (1980): 65-74.

Describes the formation, publishing philosophy, and history of The Fiction Collective founded in 1974 under the moving force of Sukenick.

Describes the participation in this publishing group of both Federman and Sukenick. Provides general descriptions of most of the work published with some critical appraisal.

Russell, Charles. "Postmodernism and the Neo-Avant-garde." *Poets, Prophets, and Revolutionaries: The Literary Avant-garde from Rimbaud Through Postmodernism.* Charles Russell. New York: Oxford UP, 1985. 236-70.

Describes Federman as being fascinated by the willed permutations of identity, but less concerned with active creation of alternative present and future selves. Comments on the biographical and aesthetic claustrophobia of the texts and his bias toward autobiography. A major article on the subject of postmodernism with significant commentary on Federman.

Russell, Charles. "Subversion and Legitimation: The Avant-garde in Postmodern Culture." *Chicago Review* 23 (1982): 54-59.

In the context of a discussion of the *avant garde* writer as alienated from the dominant aesthetic, ethical, and spiritual values of modern culture, aesthetic activism, and the historical mission of the *avant garde* writer, Federman's work is discussed, along with that of several other writers.

Scholes, Robert. "Raymond Federman's *Double or Nothing* and J. M. G. LeClezio's *Book of Flights* (January 1972)." *Fabulation and Metafiction.* Robert Scholes. Urbana: U of Illinois P, 1979. 136-38.

A mock interview with a French professor questioning whether experimental fiction, a French innovation, can succeed in English. Finds Federman's novel French because it contains French passages, and because Federman has written books on Beckett. Compares fictional experimentation with scientific experimentation, and notes that scientists don't publish their failures. Complains that Federman's work, like Beckett's, consists of intentional boredom, but unlike Beckett, Federman is only a little funny. Concludes that Federman's typography does give us something to look forward to—blank spaces.

Tatham, Campbell. "Crap: Lie or Die." *Margins* [Milwaukee] Dec. 1974: 5-11, 57.

A piece of pseudo-criticism or rival fiction which in tone, language, format, typographical play, thematic invention, and general style, imitates and comments on that of Federman.

Tatham, Campbell. "Mythotherapy and Postmodern Fictions: Magic Is Afoot." *Performance in Postmodern Culture*. Eds. Michel Benamou and Charles Caramello. Madison: Coda, 1977. 137-57.

In this lengthy article on the use of myth and magic in American experimental fiction, Tatham discusses Federman as one of the chief gurus of the method. Argues that Federman sings, plays, dances, and gives us such reflections of ourselves as varied, split, split again, doubled, or nothing. Reproduces illustrative passages from Federman, and concludes that mythotherapy is finally a game to tap these innate skills, and that postmodern fictions provide the pieces of the game and the field on which it may be played.

Werner, Craig Hansen. "Everybody's Joyce: Donald Barthelme, Raymond Federman, William Melvin Kelley, William Burroughs." *Paradoxical Resolutions: American Fiction Since James Joyce*. Craig Hansen Werner. Urbana: U of Illinois P, 1982. 96-122.

Traces Federman's fictional antecedents to Samuel Beckett and the French New Novelists. A technical and detailed discussion concentrating primarily on *Double or Nothing*.

Wilczynski, Marek. "Surfiction as Theory and Practice of Fiction: The Novels of Raymond Federman." *Kwartalnik Neofilologiczny* 31.4 (1984): 427-40.

Discusses the tradition of self-reflexive, self-conscious fiction, and makes the point that the new autonomous reality of fiction is the reality of words and visual design. Notes how writers encounter the system of language together with the inventory of possible typographical variations and are thus entitled to do anything they please. Argues that the specific appellative function in *Double or Nothing* and *Take It or Leave It* is supposed to destroy the normal habits of the reader's perception forcing him or her to follow the chaos of forms, participate in visual disorder and accept its essential meaninglessness.

Wilde, Alan. "Irony in the Postmodern Age: Toward a Map of Suspension." *Boundary 2* 9.1 (1980): 15-20. Rpt. as "A Map of Suspensiveness" in *Horizons of Assent: Modernism, Postmodernism, and the Ironic Imagination*. Alan Wilde. Baltimore: Johns Hopkins UP, 1981. 136-41.

Discusses the views of Federman and Sukenick on the relationship between reality and the new fiction, and applies these views to their own fictional practices. Discusses Federman's *Take It or Leave It*.

Reviews

Bolling, Doug. Rev. of *The Twofold Vibration. American Book Review*
     Nov.-Dec. 1983: 7.

Considers Federman to be in the forefront of American experimental
writing in both its fictive and theoretical aspects. Claims that his work
reveals the strengths and the weaknesses of the movement and yet
remains both readable and challenging. Notes that *The Twofold Vibration*
is full of ironies, reflexivity, lucidity, horror, and digressions. Details the
contents of the book, and concludes that this novel builds solidly for both
theorist and reader.

Cagnon, Maurice. "Reviews." Rev. of *The Voice in the Closet. French
     Review* 54.2 (1980): 364-65.

Calls this novel a triptych because its outer panels are bilingual transcripts, one in French, one in English, of what is ostensibly the same
work. Describes the center panel as a grim deconstruction of Federman's
dual text authored by Maurice Roche.

Caramello, Charles. "Duplicities/Complicities: The Voice in the
     Closet/La Voix dans le Cabinet de Debarras." Rev. of *The Voice in
     the Closet. American Book Review* 1981: 10-12.

Argues that because of the disrupted narrative sequence, composed with
typographical configurations that allow the reader to reconstruct any
page in a number of different orders, Federman's novels imply that people, places, events are only a process of words, unattributable to an
ordinary reality. An erudite essay not only on this novel, but on the conventions of experimental fiction.

Chamberlain, Lori. Rev. of *The Twofold Vibration. Chicago Review* 34.1
     (1983): 117-23.

Describes the novel as following thematically in the wake of earlier
works, but this time circumscribing the unutterable story of the
Holocaust. Describes the futuristic contents of the novel, the characters,
and the experimental narrative techniques. Claims that the central question posed by the narrative has to do with causality, circularity, the
nature of destiny. Sees Federman asking the central questions of how one
escapes and how one avoids the closure imposed by a circle imposed by
even the ending of the novel.

Cornis-Pop, Marcel. "A Love Story of Sorts." Rev. of *Smiles on Washington Square. North American Review* 271.1 (1986): 67-69.

Describes the novel as a seemingly impossible narrative with formidable obstacles, which is more relaxed, less typographically oriented, and full' of the narrative irony of escaping the past. Claims that Federman employs a serious philosophical perspective emphasizing the conflict between narration and fictionality, authorial (or readerly) freedom to invent and test determinism, or between the inner possibilities and the constraints of a narrative form (genre).

D'Amico, Maria Vittoria. "Smiles, Hope, Desire, Desperation." Rev. of *Smiles on Washington Square (A Love Story of Sorts). American Book Review* Sept.-Oct. 1986: 22-23.

Describes the novel as experimental fiction that reverses familiar social roles and retells its central event over and over in slightly different light. Concentrates on the manner in which Federman drives back to the original drama of his stories, to the true dramatic origin of some wandering characters, the source of their restlessness—to the Holocaust. Concludes that witnessing the shattered dreams of the protagonist, the reader sees one more case of offended innocence, as in the great tradition of American literature: Bill Budd, the stammering sailor, or, Moinous, the outcast with the exotic accent, are both victims of the same chimeric dream.

Friedman, Melvin J. "Book Reviews." Rev. of *Smiles on Washington Square. International Fiction Review* 13.1 (1986): 47-48.

Describes the novel entirely in terms of its experimental style, novel-within-the-novel technique, characters, and self-reflexivity.

Kennedy, Dorothy Mintzlaff. "Recent Fictions." Rev. of *Double or Nothing. Michigan Quarterly Review* 13.1 (1974): 86.

Calls the novel a bold experiment in comic fiction, but claims that it suffers from the fact that as novel it first bounces through a writer's brain, then goes through drafts, and is not intrinsically interesting to a reader. Asserts that for the eye to simply decipher the typographical eccentricities is a chore whose accomplishment should richly reward the reader. But concludes that the writer Federman creates has not yet approached the point of polishing his novel for the reader's delight.

Lehman, David. Rev. of *The Twofold Vibration. Yale Review* 72.3 (1983): xii-xiii.

Describes the novel as a book that fails to deliver the goods it promises. Argues that hidden behind its relentlessly self-regarding prose, garrulous and coy by turns, is far too much perspiration and far too little inspiration. Concludes that there isn't much of a straight story to tell.

Lemon, Lee T. "Artist's Life." Rev. of *Double or Nothing. Prairie Schooner* 46.4 (1973): 365-66.

Describes the novel briefly in terms of its style, contents, and typography.

McCaffery, Larry. "New Rules of the Game." Rev. of *Take It or Leave It. Chicago Review* 29.1 (1977): 145-49.

Describes the novel as an adventure with new rules in which we see cancellation of one formal or genre expectation after another. Details contents and characters, and provides a good indication of the nature of the experimental innovations. Concludes that the book exudes enormous energy and a manic sense of pace.

Morton, Brian. "Room for a View." Rev. of *The Two-Fold Vibration. Times Literary Supplement* 3 Dec. 1982: 1344.

Calls *Two-Fold Vibration* a disturbing book, thin on plot, heavy on circumstantial development. Claims that, at its most vicious and sexual, it is reminiscent of a bad Charles Bukowski, but at its best it does rival Beckett. Concludes that this book is at the very least an entertaining and salutary journey through the darker and more troubled outlands of contemporary history and fiction.

Porush, David H. "Reviews." Rev. of *Take It or Leave It. Eureka Review* 2 (1977): 85-88.

Claims that Federman's *Take It Or Leave It* brings the intimacy and pleasure of the text and the complicity between narrator and reader to sensuous proportions. Concludes that from the first page of this novel the reader is set agog, disoriented, cajoled, bullied, seduced, buggered, bugged, and buggied about by a comedian-cum-philosopher who exhorts us to laugh as we ponder our wordly distress.

Rose, Mark. "The Time Is New Year's Eve, 1999." Rev. of *The Twofold Vibration. New York Times Book Review* 7 Nov. 1982: 12, 26.

Finds this novel a mildly *avant garde* cream puff with a science fiction flavor and more conventional and successful than his earlier novels. Comments that it appears to have been conceived as an illustration of

Federman's term "surfiction," a narrative concerned with the ambiguity between fiction and reality.

Rovit, Earl. Rev. of *Double or Nothing. Contemporary Literature* 15.4 (1974): 548.

Calls the novel a rare accomplishment full of typographical games, enormous inventiveness, ratiocination, fantasy, and serious statement about the nature of fiction.

Scholes, Robert. Rev. of *Double or Nothing. Saturday Review* 22 Jan. 1972: 67.

A book review of *Double or Nothing* done in the format of an interview demonstrating the style, philosophy, and thematic intent of the novel. Concludes that the book goes on too long, is somewhat deficient in variety, but nevertheless, fails brilliantly.

Sukenick, Ronald. "Refugee from the Holocaust." Rev. of *Double or Nothing. New York Times Book Review* 1 Oct. 1972: 40-41.

Calls the novel both a considerable achievement with its fine visual patterns, suppressions, and yet complains that it is perversely trivial at times.

Interviews

Abadi-Nagy, Zoltan. "An Interview with Raymond Federman." *Modern Fiction Studies* 34.2 (1988): 157-70.

In this interview Federman discusses: the term "surfiction," his beginnings, relationship to tradition, roots in the experimental tradition stemming from Sterne, the postmodern novel, the nature of reality, truth as subjective, literature as a means of improving the world, his madhouse metaphors, madness as a phenomenon, the implied reader, and anti-mimesis.

Federman, Raymond, and Ronald Sukenick. "The New Innovative Fiction." *Antaeus* 20 (1976): 138-49.

This dialogue between Federman and Sukenick that took place in 1974 over KPFA, a Pacifica radio station, covers Federman's typographical idiosyncrasies, his novel *Double or Nothing*, the concreteness of language, Sukenick's objections to this use of the visual page, the dynamics of the act of reading, their respective views on fiction as lying and fiction as truth telling, the loss of art as representation, the writer as part of his own fiction, the loss of plot and characterization, the use of anecdote in their places, the relationship between form and content, the question of meaning and illusion, the cultural lag between Europe and America, the American cultural inferiority complex, official morality and the contemporary novel, the review process for experimental novels, and the use of writing as part of the search for freedom and liberation.

McCaffery, Larry. "Excerpts from an Interview." *Perception.* Ed. Don Wellman. Toward a New Poetics 2. Cambridge, MA: O.ARS, 1982. 185-89.

This is a short essay incorporating Federman's creative and perceptual processes and literary philosophy replete with illustrative diagrams.

McCaffery, Larry. "An Interview with Raymond Federman." *Contemporary Literature* 24.3 (1983): 285-306. Rev. version rpt. in *Anything Can Happen: Interviews with Contemporary American Novelists.* Eds. Tom LeClair and Larry McCaffery. Urbana: U of Illinois P, 1983. 126-51.

In this interview Federman discusses: his family tragedy and background, his father's surrealist paintings, reverence for Trotsky, his re-creations of his father in his own life and fiction, dealing with future time in his fiction, his interest in Beckett, the original impulses behind the composition of *Double or Nothing,* his use of multi-voices, his sparse use of story in *Take It or Leave It,* coming to the typographical design of his pages, writers he admires, his theory of the use of colloquial language, Marquez's novels as models, Sukenick's friendship, Gass's influence, and his own latest work in progress.

Meyer, Charlotte. "An Interview with Raymond Federman." *Story-Quarterly* 15-16 (1983): 37-52.

In this interview Federman describes: the relationship of the modern novel to the experimental novel, the problem of self and character, the postmodern character, the problem of unreadability, the role of time and memory, the issue of realism for the contemporary writer, his own obsession with the Holocaust, various of his novels, his sense of laughter, his attitudes towards male-female relationships, and the whole issue of surfiction.

Zavarzadeh, Masud, Raymond Federman, and Joseph Hynes. "Tri(y)log." *Chicago Review* 28.2 (1977): 93-109

An interview with Masud Zavarzadah, Raymond Federman, and Joseph Hynes in which Federman discusses his attitudes towards Hawke's fiction, language, experimental literature, overwriting, style, European writers, morality, literary viewpoint, tradition, new fiction, form, gimmicks, British fiction, surfiction, playfulness, Joyce, Proust, Celine, Beckett, Barthelme, Coover, Bellow's false fiction, and paracriticism.

Biographical Sources

Everman, Welch D. "Raymond Federman." *Dictionary of Literary Biography Yearbook: 1980*. Eds. Karen L. Rood, Jean W. Ross, and Richard Ziegfeld. Detroit: Gale, 1981. 195-201.

More than details of his life, this is a career biography, tracing the development of the author's canon, describing the contents and themes of his works, evaluating his reputation, and placing him in the larger context of American literary history. Includes lists of primary and secondary sources and illustrations.

Dissertations

Schroeder, Michael LeRoy. "Rhetoric in New Fiction." Diss. Kent State U, 1986.

Winkelman, Aaron. "Authorial Presence in American Metafiction: The Novels of Coover, Federman, Sorrentino, and Sukenick." Diss. U of California, Los Angeles, 1986.

Edna Ferber

1885 – 1968

Primary Sources

Novels

American Beauty. New York: Grosset, 1931; New York: Avon, 1931; Garden City: Doubleday, 1931, 1935, 1961; London: Heinemann, 1931; Collection of British and American Authors. Tauschnitz ed. 5048. Leipzig: Tauschnitz, 1932; New York: The Literary Guild, 1938; Greenwich: Crest-Fawcett, 1974, 1977; Cleveland: Tower-World, 1946; Mattituck: Amereon, d. not available. Serialized in *Ladies' Home Journal* July 1931: 3-7, 102-04, 107-10, 112-13, 115, 117-20, 122; Aug. 1931: 8-9, 76-77, 79, 81, 83; Sept. 1931: 22-23, 105, 107-08, 111-12, 115-16, 119; Oct. 1931: 24-25, 127-28, 131-32, 135-36, 138, 140; Nov. 1931: 20-21, 85-86, 89-90, 92-94, 96.

Cimarron. Garden City: Doubleday, 1930, 1936, 1940, 1951, 1962; New York: Grosset, 1930; New York: Eds. for the Armed Services, 1930; New York: Book League of America, 1930; Garden City: International Collectors, 1930; Heinemann: London, 1930; New York: Literary Guild, 1938; New York: Madison Square-Grosset, 1942; New York: Triangle, 1943; Books of Distinction. New York: Grosset, 1943; Toronto: Blue Ribbon, 1943; New York: Penguin, 1946; New York: Globe, 1954; New York: Bantam, 1958; London: Pan, 1960; New York: Crest-Fawcett, 1976, 1979; Large Print ed.

Boston: Hall, 1981; Mattituck: Amereon, d. not available; Toronto: McClelland, d. not available. Serialized in *Woman's Home Companion* Nov. 1929: 7-11; Dec. 1929: 20-24; Jan. 1930: 9-13; Feb. 1930: 26-30; Mar. 1930: 32-36; Apr. 1930: 26-30; May 1930: 28-30.

Come and Get It. Garden City: Doubleday, 1935, 1936; New York: Grosset, 1935; London: Heinemann, 1935; New York: Literary Guild, 1938; Cleveland: World, 1948; Toronto: McClelland, 1948. Serialized in *Woman's Home Companion* Oct. 1934: 7-10; Nov. 1934: 9-13; Dec. 1934: 22; Jan. 1935: 21-25; Feb. 1935: 19-21; Mar. 1935: 27-28.

Dawn O'Hara, the Girl Who Laughed. New York: Grosset, 1911; New York: Stokes, 1911; London: Methuen, 1925; Cleveland: World, 1947.

Fanny Herself. Garden City: Doubleday, 1917, 1936; New York: Stokes, 1917; London: Methuen, 1923; New York: Literary Guild, 1938; Cleveland: Tower-World, 1948; Toronto: McClelland, 1948; The Modern Jewish Experience. New York: Arno, 1975. Serialized in *American Mercury* Apr. 1917: 9-14, 103-09; May 1917: 29-32, 108-115; June 1917: 40-43, 92-99; July 1917: 51-55+; Aug. 1917: 45-49+; Sept. 1917: 47-51+; Oct. 1917: 48-51+; Nov. 1917: 48-51+.

Giant. New York: Grosset, 1952, 1954; Garden City: Doubleday, 1952; Chicago: Sears Readers Club, 1952; London: Gollancz, 1952, 1957; London: Four Square-Landsborough, 1959; New York: Cardinal-Pocket, 1966; London: Coronet, 1971; New York: Crest-Fawcett, 1973; Bath: Chivers, 1974; Ulverscroft Large Print Series: Fiction. Leicester: Ulverscroft, 1976; The Collector's Library of the World's Best-Loved Books. Franklin Center: Franklin, 1979; Bath: New Portway-Chivers, 1980. Serialized in *Ladies' Home Journal* June 1952: 34-35, 60; July 1952: 32, 68, 70-71, 73-76, 78-80, 82-83; Aug. 1952: 38-39, 110-13, 115-16, 118-20, 122-24; Sept. 1952: 68-69, 74, 76-78, 80-84, 86-88, 90; Oct. 1952: 54-55, 78, 80, 85, 87, 91-96, 98-102, 104; Nov. 1952: 68-69, 72, 75-76, 78-80, 83, 85, 87-88.

The Girls. New York: Grosset, 1921; Garden City: Doubleday, 1921, 1936; Heinemann: London, 1922; New York: Literary Guild, 1938; Cleveland: World, 1948; Toronto: McClelland, 1948.

Great Son. Garden City: Doubleday, 1945; New York: Eds. for the Armed Services, 1945; Toronto: McClelland, 1945; London: Heinemann, 1945; New York: Forum-World, 1946; Melbourne: Oxford, 1946; New York: Penguin, 1947; New York: Tower-World, 1948; Toronto: Doubleday, 1960; New York: Avon, 1961; New York: Crest-Fawcett, 1974.

Half Portions. Garden City: Doubleday, 1920; Short Story Index Reprint Series. Freeport: Books for Libraries, 1970.

The Homely Heroine: A Contest Selection. Baker Published Manuscript Reading 30. Boston: Baker, 1926.

Ice Palace. Garden City: Doubleday, 1958; Book Club ed. Garden City: Doubleday, 1958; London: Gollancz, 1958; New York: Bantam, 1959; London: Four Square, 1960; New York: Macfadden, 1964; Greenwich: Crest-Fawcett, 1971; Bath: Chivers, 1977. Serialized in *Ladies' Home Journal* Apr. 1958: 62-63, 90-95, 98, 100, 102, 104-06; May 1958: 48-49, 70, 72-74, 76-78, 81-82, 84, 87; June 1958: 58-59, 75, 77-78, 80-82, 84-85, 87-91.

No Room at the Inn. Garden City: Doubleday, 1941, 1942; Toronto: McClelland, 1941.

Personality Plus: Some Experiences of Emma McChesney and Her Son, Jock. New York: Stokes, 1914; New York: Grosset, 1914; Toronto: Doubleday, 1914; Short Story Index Reprint Series. Freeport: Books for Libraries, 1971.

Roast Beef, Medium: The Business Adventures of Emma McChesney. New York: Grosset, 1913, 1915; New York: Stokes, 1913; Toronto: Doubleday, 1913; London: Methuen, 1920; Short Story Index Reprint Series. Freeport: Books for Libraries, 1971.

Saratoga Trunk. Garden City: Doubleday, 1941, 1951; New York: Grosset, 1941; Toronto: McClelland, 1941; London: Heinemann, 1942; Sydney: Angus, 1942; Cleveland: Forum-World, 1946; New York: Penguin, 1947; London: Landsborough, 1959; New York:

Bantam, 1960; New York: Macfadden, 1963; London: Baker, 1969; Greenwich: Crest-Fawcett, 1974, 1979; Mattituck: Amereon, 1979; Large Print ed. Boston: Hall, 1981.

Show Boat. Garden City: Doubleday, 1926, 1932, 1936, 1945, 1951; New York: Grosset, 1926, 1928, 1929; Garden City: International Collector, 1926; New York: Book League of America, 1926; London: Heinemann, 1926, 1932; Collection of British and American Authors. Tauchnitz ed. Leipzig: Tauchnitz, 1927; New York: Modern Library, 1935; Toronto: Macmillan, 1935; Story Library Series. London: Heinemann, 1937; New York: Literary Guild, 1938; New York: Pocket, 1939, 1943; Greenwich: Crest-Fawcett, 1954, 1971, 1977; London: Foursquare-Landsborough, 1959; New York: Cardinal-Pocket, 1962; London: Consul-World, 1964; London: Baker, 1970; London: Sphere, 1972; Large Print ed. Boston: Hall, 1981. Serialized in *Woman's Home Companion* Apr. 1926: 7-11; May 1926: 19-23; June 1926: 21-25; July 1926: 21-25; Aug. 1926: 26-29; Sept. 1926: 29-30.

So Big. Garden City: Doubleday, 1924, 1925, 1936, 1945, 1951, 1953, 1957, New York: Grosset, 1924, 1937; New York: Book League of America, 1924; Cleveland: World, 1924; New York: Eds. for the Armed Services, 1924; New York: Country Life, 1924; London: Heinemann, 1924, 1932, 1938; New York: Literary Guild, 1938; New York: World, 1947; New York: Avon, 1967; London: Baker, 1970; Greenwich: Crest-Fawcett, 1973, 1978; Franklin Center: Franklin, 1978; Large Print ed. Boston: Hall, 1981.

Collected Works

Buttered Side Down. New York: Stokes, 1912; New York: Grosset, 1914; London: Methuen, 1926; Garden City: Doubleday, 1941; Short Story Index Reprint Series. Freeport: Books for Libraries, 1971.

Contents: The Frog and the Puddle, The Man Who Came Back, What She Wore, A Bush League Hero, The Kitchen Side of the Door, One of the Old Girls, Maymeys from Cuba, The Leading Lady, That Home-Town Feeling, The Homely Heroine, Sun Dried, Where the Car Turns at 18th.

Cheerful by Request. Garden City: Doubleday, 1918, 1919; London: Methuen, 1919; New York: Grosset, 1925; Freeport: Books for Libraries, 1971.

Contents: Cheerful by Request, The Gay Old Dog, The Tough Guy, The Eldest, That's Marriage, The Woman Who Tried to Be Good, The Girl Who Went Right, The Hooker-up-the-Back, The Guiding Miss Gowd, Sophy-As-She-Might-Have-Been, The Three of Them, Shore Leave.

Emma McChesney & Co. New York: Grosset, 1915, 1917; New York: Stokes, 1915; Garden City: Doubleday, 1944; Freeport: Books for Libraries, 1971.

Contents: Broadway to Buenos Aires; Thanks to Miss Morrissey; A Closer Corporation; Blue Serge; "Hoops, My Dear!"; Sisters Under Their Skin; An Etude for Emma.

Five Complete Novels. New York: Avenel, 1981.

Contents: *So Big, Show Boat, Cimarron, Saratoga Trunk, Giant.*

Gigolo. Garden City: Doubleday, 1922, 1936; London: Heinemann, 1923; New York: Grosset, 1925; New York: Literary Guild, 1936, 1938; Short Story Index Reprint Series. Freeport: Books for Libraries, 1971.

Contents: The Afternoon of a Faun, Old Man Minick, Gigolo, Not a Day over Twenty-One, Home Girl, Ain't Nature Wonderful!, The Sudden Sixties, If I Should Ever Travel!

Mother Knows Best. New York: Grosset, 1927; Garden City: Doubleday, 1927, 1936; London: Heinemann, 1927; London: Readers' Library, 1929; New York: Literary Guild, 1938; Large Print ed. Freeport: Books for Libraries, 1954; Short Story Index Reprint Series. Freeport: Books for Libraries, 1970.

Contents: Mother Knows Best, Every Other Thursday, Classified, Holiday, Consider the Lilies, Our Very Best People, Perfectly Independent, Blue Blood.

Nobody's in Town. Garden City: Doubleday, 1938, 1939; Toronto: McClelland, 1938; London: Heinemann, 1938; New York: Grosset, 1939; New York: New Avon Library, 1944.

Contents: Nobody's in Town, Trees Die at the Top.

Old Man Minick. Garden City: Doubleday, 1924; London: Heinemann, 1924. Publ. with "Minick," a play based on the short story.

One Basket, Thirty-One Short Stories. New York: Simon, 1947; Chicago: Peoples Book Club, 1947; Garden City: Doubleday, 1947, 1957; New York: Bantam, 1958; New York: Bartell-Macfadden, 1964; New York: Manor, 1972; The Collected Stories of the World's Greatest Writers. Franklin Center: Franklin, 1982.

Contents: The Woman Who Tried to Be Good, The Gay Old Dog, That's Marriage, Farmer in the Dell, Un Morso Doo Pang, Long Distance, The Maternal Feminine, Old Man Minick, The Afternoon of a Faun, Old Lady Mandle, Gigolo, Home Girl, The Sudden Sixties, Classified, Holiday, Our Very Best People, Mother Knows Best, Every Other Thursday, Blue Blood, Hey! Taxi!, The Light Touch, They Brought Their Women, Glamour, Keep It Holy, Blue Glasses, Trees Die at the Top, Nobody's in Town, No Room at the Inn, You're Not the Type, Grandma Isn't Playing, The Barn Cuts off the View.

Show Boat, So Big, Cimarron: Three Living Novels of American Life. Garden City: Doubleday, 1924, 1958, 1962.

They Brought Their Women. New York: Grosset, 1933; Garden City: Doubleday, 1933, 1936, 1938; London: Heinemann, 1933; Hamburg: Albatross, 1934; New York: Literary Guild, 1938; New York: Avon, 1944; Short Story Index Reprint Series. Freeport: Books for Libraries, 1970.

Contents: Glamour, Fraulein, Meadow Lark, Hey! Taxi!, Wall Street-'28, They Brought Their Women, No Foolin', Keep It Holy.

Your Town. Cleveland: World, 1948; Books of Merit. Cleveland: World, 1948; Toronto: McClelland, 1948.

Contents: *Buttered Side Down*; *Cheerful, by Request*; and *Gigolo*. See above for list of stories in each of these collections.

Short Fiction in Anthologies

"The Afternoon of a Faun." *The Bedside Book of Famous American Stories*. Eds. Angus Burrell and Bennett Cerf. New York: Random, 1936, 1940. 881-96; *An Anthology of Famous American Stories*. Eds.

Angus Burrell and Bennett Cerf. New York: Modern Library, 1953, 1963. 835-50.

"The Eldest." *An American Family Album: Stories of American Family Life.* Ed. F. H. Spencer. New York: Harper, 1946. 141-61.

"The Fast." *A Golden Treasury of Jewish Literature.* Ed. Leo W. Schwarz. New York: Farrar, 1937; Philadelphia: Jewish Pub. Soc. of America, 1937. 57-68; *Treasures of the Kingdom: Stories of Faith, Hope and Love.* Ed. T. Everett Harre. New York: Rinehart, 1947. 181-92; *Tales of Our People: Great Stories of the Jew in America.* Ed. Jerry D. Lewis. New York: Geis, 1969. 17-29.

"Fraulein." *The Panorama of Modern Literature.* Garden City: Doubleday, 1934. 82-104; *A Lady's Pleasure: The Modern Woman's Treasury of Good Reading.* New York: Penn, 1946. 63-85.

"The Gay Old Dog." *The Best Short Stories of 1917.* Ed. Edward J. O'Brien. Boston: Small, 1918. 208-33; *My Story That I Like Best.* New York: International Magazine, 1924. 15-52; *This is Chicago, an Anthology.* Ed. Albert Halper. New York: Holt, 1952. 1-22.

"Grandma Isn't Playing." *Wave Me Goodbye: Stories of the Second World War.* Ed. Anne Boston. London: Virago, 1988. 98-115.

"His Mother's Son." *Americans All: Stories of American Life To-Day.* Ed. Benjamin A. Heydrick. New York: Harcourt, 1920, 1921; Freeport: Books for Libraries, 1971. 117-29.

"Home Girl." *Best American Short Stories of 1923.* Ed. Edward J. O'Brien. Boston: Small, 1924. 216-39.

"Molly Brandeis Takes Hold." *Feast of Leviathan.* Ed. Leo W. Schwarz. New York: Rinehart, 1956. 52-69.

"Mother Knows Best." *20 Best Short Stories in Ray Long's 20 Years as an Editor.* Ed. Ray Long. New York: Long, 1933. 323-47.

"No Room at the Inn." *This Is My Best*. Ed. Whit Burnett. New York: Dial, 1942; Garden City: Halcyon, 1944. 997-1004; *Jewish Short Stories*. Ed. Ludwig Lewisohn. New York: Behrman, 1945. 96-108; *"May Your Days Be Merry and Bright" and Other Christmas Stories by Women*. Ed. Susan Koppelman. Detroit: Wayne State UP, 1988. 156-64.

"Old Lady Mandle." *To Mother with Love*. Ed. Frederick Ungar. New York: Daye, 1951. 193-219.

"Old Man Minick." *Yisroel: The First Jewish Omnibus*. Ed. Joseph Leftwich. London: Heritage, 1933. 247-66; Rev. ed. London: Clarke, 1945. 198-213; Rev. ed. New York: Beechhurst, 1952. 198-213; Rev. ed. New York: Yoseloff, 1963, 146-61. (Clarke ed. titled *Yisroel: The Jewish Omnibus*); *Contemporary Short Stories*. Ed. Maurice Baudin. Indianapolis: Bobbs, 1954. 65-87; *"The Safe Deposit" and Other Stories about Grandparents, Old Lovers, and Crazy Old Men*. Ed. Kerry M. Olitzky. New York: Wiener, 1989. 175-203.

"One Hundred Per Cent." *War Stories*. Eds. Roy J. Holmes and A. Starbuck. New York: Crowell, 1919. 95-118.

"You've Got to Be Selfish." *The Stories Editors Buy and Why*. Ed. Jean Wick. N.p.: n.p., 1921. 169-92.

Short Fiction in Periodicals

"$16.50-Trimmed." *Delineator* June 1919: 15, 67.

"The Afternoon of a Faun." *Collier's* 12 Nov. 1921: 3-4, 16-17, 25-26; *Golden Book* Mar. 1930: 33-41.

"Ain't Nature Wonderful!" *Golden Book* Aug. 1926: 149-58.

"Catching up with Christmas." *American Magazine* Jan. 1913: 55-61.

"Chickens: Neither of the Poultry Yard nor the Menu Card." *American Magazine* Feb. 1912: 497-504.

"Classified." *Golden Book* Nov. 1931: 319-33.

"The Clinker." *Child Labor Bulletin* Nov. 1914: 7-11.

"The Dancing Girls." *Collier's* 11 Mar. 1920: 5-6, 52-57.

"Dictated But Not Read." *American Magazine* Apr. 1914: 29-34.

"The Eldest." *McClure's* June 1916: 14-18, 54-55.

"The Frog and the Puddle." *American Magazine* Mar. 1911: 676-81.

"Gay Old Dog." *Good Housekeeping* Feb. 1939: 28-29, 168, 170-79.

"Gigolo." *Woman's Home Companion* Nov. 1922: 7-8, 102+.

"The Girl Who Went Right." *Saturday Evening Post* 16 Aug. 1913: 3-4, 29-30.

"The Girls." *Woman's Home Companion* Aug. 1921: 7-12; Sept. 1921: 11-15; Oct. 1921: 21-23.

"His Mother's Son." *American Magazine* Mar. 1912: 555-62.

"The Homely Heroine." *Everybody's* Nov. 1910: 602-08.

"The Hooker-up-the-Back." *Saturday Evening Post* 24 May 1913: 5-7, 32-33.

"If I Should Ever Travel!" *Woman's Home Companion* Aug. 1922: 9-11, 94-95.

"In the Absence of the Agent." *American Magazine* Apr. 1913: 55-60.

"Knee Deep in Knickers." *American Magazine* Mar. 1913: 54-60.

"Lifeboat." *Scholastic* 1 Feb. 1943: 25-26, 32-34.

"Making Good with Mother." *American Magazine* Jan. 1914: 22-26.

"The Man Who Came Back." *American Magazine* Apr. 1911: 720-26.

"The Man Within Him." *American Magazine* June 1914: 19-25.

"The Maternal Feminine." *Golden Book* June 1927: 799-807.

"Maymeys from Cuba." *American Magazine* Oct. 1911: 705-11.

"Meadow Lark." *Senior Scholastic* 2 Feb. 1942: 25-26, 35-37; 9 Feb. 1942: 25-26, 35.

"Next Stop, Hoboken!" *Ladies' Home Journal* May 1919: 28, 78, 80-82.

"No Room at the Inn." *Collier's* 16 Dec. 1939: 13, 44-45.

"Not a Day over Twenty-One." *Collier's* 13 Aug. 1921: 3-4, 19-22, 24.

"Old Lady Mandle." *Collier's* 17 Jan. 1920: 5-6, 36, 38-41.

"Old Man Minick." *Woman's Home Companion* June 1922: 5-7, 104+.

"One of the Old Girls." *American Magazine* Sept. 1911: 552-58.

"Personality Plus: A McChesney Story." *American Magazine* Feb. 1914: 17-22.

"Pink Tights and Ginghams." *American Magazine* Apr. 1912: 681-88.

"Representing T. A. Buck." *American Magazine* Aug. 1911: 442-49.

"Roast Beef, Medium, Served Hot." *American Magazine* Dec. 1911: 157-64.

"The Self Starter: A Story of Emma & Jock McChesney." *American Magazine* Sept. 1914: 11-16.

"Selina." *Woman's Home Companion* Dec. 1923: 8-13; Jan. 1924: 16-21; Feb. 1924: 17-20; Mar. 1924: 17-19.

"Simply Skirts." *American Magazine* June 1912: 170-79.

"Sophy-As-She-Might-Have-Been." *Saturday Evening Post* 19 Sept. 1914: 10-12, 57-58.

"The Sudden Sixties." *Woman's Home Companion* Oct. 1922: 18-19, 114, 117.

"That Home-Town Feeling." *American Magazine* Jan. 1912: 371-76.

"Trees Die at the Top." *Cosmopolitan* Aug. 1956: 123-31.

"Underneath the High-Cut Vest." *American Magazine* Aug. 1912: 453-61.

"What She Wore." *American Magazine* July 1911: 314-20.

"The Woman Who Tried to Be Good." *Saturday Evening Post* 14 June 1913: 8-9, 48.

Secondary Sources

Books

Shaughnessy, Mary Rose. *Women and Success in American Society in the Works of Edna Ferber*. New York: Gordon, 1977.

Articles and Chapters

Barrymore, Ethel. "Why I Want to Play Emma McChesney." *American Magazine* Nov. 1915: 40-42.

Provides useful insights into Ferber's character by Barrymore, who greatly desired to create Emma on the stage.

Francis, Michelle. "The James Adams Floating Theatre: Edna Ferber's Showboat." *Carolina Comments* 28.5 (1980): 135-42.

Provides invaluable historical background on Ferber's discovery of the tradition of American show boats and the drama companies who lived and performed on them. Provides historical information about several specific showboats and Ferber's personal research on them.

Gray, James. "The Catastrophe of Competence." *On Second Thought*. James Gray. Minneapolis: U of Minnesota P, 1946. 154-64. Originally appeared in the *St. Paul Pioneer Press and Dispatch*.

Calls Ferber a gifted and thoughtful analyst of the human experience, which qualities she seldom reveals in her fiction. Describes the events of a Ferber novel as contrived. Finds her autobiography, *A Peculiar Treasure*, her richest and truest story. Praises her for her respect for her Jewish forbears, her dramatic flair, and her humor.

Hamblen, Abigail Ann. "Edna Ferber and the American Dream." *Journal of Popular Culture* 11.3 (1968): 404-9.

An admiring retrospective on Ferber's literary career and major works focusing on her persistent theme of the viability of the American Dream as the American story.

Heydrick, Benjamin A. "Edna Ferber." *American All: Stories of Life Today*. Ed. Benjamin A. Heydrick. New York: Harcourt, 1920; Short Story Index Reprint Series, 1971. 130-32.

Provides a brief sketch of her early life, education, beginnings, subsequent publications, and present work.

Horowitz, Steven P., and Miriam J. Landsman. "The Americanization of Edna: A Study of Ms. Ferber's Jewish American Identity." *Studies in American Jewish Literature* [Albany] 2 (1982): 69-80.

Argues that the work of people like Edna Ferber has been substantially ignored because the critical establishment is biased toward male, urban, Eastern Jewish authors. Details Ferber's background, writing, and lifestyle as an Americanized Jew. Discusses her views on anti-Semitism and on the oppression of women. Comments that her female characters are strong, self-determined, and perceptive in contrast to her male characters who are generally weak, romantic, and foolish. Sees her as a German Jew who had reverence for her Jewishness, but who was not raised to practice Jewish customs. Concludes with a portrait of Ferber as an American patriot.

Irwin, Betty J. "Character Names in Edna Ferber's Illinois Fiction." *Festschrift in Honor of Virgil J. Vogel*. Ed. Edward Callary. Papers of North Central Names Institute 5. DeKalb: Illinois Name Society, 1985. 23-45.

Provides an exhaustive gloss on the names used in Ferber's twenty-one short stories and three novels set in Illinois. Describes how Ferber uses names to show strength and weakness of character, irony, affection, personal identity, and theme.

Overton, Grant. "Edna Ferber." *Women Who Make Our Novels*. Grant Overton. New and Completely Rev. ed. New York: Dodd, 1928. 126-38.

A biographical and critical sketch of Ferber's life and career as a writer. Mentions all of the major novels briefly, dealing mostly with their content. Deals finally with Ferber's social commentary on New York City.

Overton, Grant. "The Social Critic in Edna Ferber." *Bookman* Oct. 1926: 138-43.

Provides a partly humorous, partly serious portrait of Ferber, highlighting her social attitudes. Also provides a detailed review of Ferber's social commentary in *Show Boat* and *So Big*. Admires the way Ferber reveals social attitudes in her novels without actually condemning anyone. Concludes that she has not yet found a subject worthy of her powers.

Parker, William R. "A Stranger's Story of Edna Ferber." *English Journal* June 1930: 447-49.

Reacts to an essay entitled "A Friend's Story." Believes that the story overstates Ferber's literary talents which he, by comparison, finds meager. Provides a series of reasons for her failure as a major talent.

Plante, Patricia R. "Mark Twain, Edna Ferber and the Mississippi." *Mark Twain Journal* 13.2 (1966): 8-10.

Notes the marked resemblances between Ferber's *Show Boat* and Twain's *Life on the Mississippi* and *Huckleberry Finn*. Sees her using the symbol of the river as God in nature, and Magnolia as a character who, like Huck Finn, is at once sustained and made to suffer by its rages, at once fulfilled by its beauty and made to fear its mystery and majesty. Catalogs the river's deific qualities in *Show Boat*, and provides a detailed comparison of Magnolia and Huck. Other comparisons include a variety of characters, situations, and themes. Concludes that "in spite of a common, profound awareness of evil, both Twain and Ferber cherished a belief in the native American myth of happiness and freedom on steamboats, where cub pilots were initiated to the mystery and danger, and on showboats, where audiences laughed and cried in the right places and believed everything—and where the River ruled as the native god."

Quinn, Arthur Hobson. "Booth Tarkington and the Later Romance." *American Fiction: An Historical and Critical Survey.* Arthur Hobson Quinn. New York: Appleton, 1936. 606-08.

Shows Ferber's influence on Booth Tarkington in writing romances of escape and the use of the romantic elements of the Midwest. Briefly discusses her short stories and several novels including *The Girls*, *Show Boat*, *So Big*, and *Come and Get It*. Concludes that her contribution to American Fiction remains the romance of the business woman, the romance of the theatre, and the romance of the Mid-Western city.

Stedman, Jane W. "Edna Ferber and Menus with Meaning." *Journal of American Culture* 2.3 (1979): 454-62.

Locates Ferber with Dickens in her consistent use of food as intrinsic to theme and characterization. Argues that "Food nourished and animated Edna Ferber's style and dominated her imagery. Finds her novels and short stories using tastes and menus as characterizing devices, even as tests of individual characters, and that, for her, food provided a standard of national and human values, as well as being a source of incident and theme, part of the plot. Claims that food is intrinsic to the regionalism of her novels and to their Americanism, based as it was on a Theodore Roosevelt combination of great excitement about life and great concern with conservation. Concludes that, for Ferber, appetite was good and greed was bad.

Stuckey, W. J. "Consolidation of the Tradition." *The Pulitzer Prize Novels: A Critical Backward Look.* W. J. Stuckey. Norman: U of Oklahoma P, 1966. 47-57.

A critical essay on *So Big* designating it a work of sentimental realism that provides a homily on rugged American individualism following a familiar daydream formula. Also comments on *A Peculiar Treasure* in which

Ferber induces her readers to believe in her daydreams. Calls her particular brand of realism the stuff of which movies and romances are made.

Uffen, Ellen Serlen. "Edna Ferber and the 'Theatricalization' of American Mythology." *Midwestern Miscellany* 8 (1980): 82-93.

Argues that the "enormous popularity of Edna Ferber's novels lay in her ability to create a consistent fictional universe based in popularly known and accepted American mythology; plucky, self-reliant boys and girls gain success and fame in colorful settings ranging from the old Wild West to the new wilds of Alaska." Claims that Ferber sees myth as a paradigmatic possibility and like children listening to fairy tales, we believe. Believes that Ferber's appeal lies in this response of her audience. Provides a biographical sketch of the young writer and her growing interest in the theatre. Suggests that her novels rely not on plot but on character, and that her figures are flat characters because they are mythic and therefore self-consciously theatrical; consequently, we hiss the villains, applaud the heroines, and weep over the plight of the wronged. Concludes that the theatrical milieu is not only a metaphor, but also a distancing device separating us from our own reality, while enabling us to enter Ferber's reality.

"The Way of a Novelist." *Literary Digest* 5 Dec. 1931: 14-15.

Recounts, with quotes from her novel and from New England newspapers, the furor created by Ferber's use of thinly disguised people and places in Brookfield, Connecticut in *American Beauty*.

Wernick, Robert. "The Queens of Fiction: Frances Parkinson Keyes, Taylor Caldwell and Edna Ferber Are the New York Yankees in the League of Best-Sellers." *Life* 6 Apr. 1959: 140-42.

Casts Ferber as belonging to a group of female American fiction writers who produce "old fashioned" and "decent" novels. Sees most of Ferber's women as "gracious homebodies" who rise to the occasion when heroes fail. Discusses Ferber's resentment of not being accorded first literary rank by reviewers, despite the fact that in her early years she was part of the group of writers who met at the Round Table of the Hotel Algonquin in New York. Reviews her childhood, early career, later life, and most of her major literary accomplishments.

White, William Allen. "Edna Ferber: In the Forefront of the Reporters of Her Age." *World Today* Aug. 1930: 221-25.

A tribute to Ferber for her skills as a journalist in her fiction writing.

Details the stages of her life and career with numerous anecdotes. Useful biographical information.

White, William Allen. "A Friend's Story of Edna Ferber." *English Journal* Feb. 1930: 101-06.

An admiring sketch of the content of Ferber's fiction and its connection with her personal life. Literary analysis remains at the general level.

Williams, Blanche Colton. "Edna Ferber." *Our Short Story Writers.* Modern American Writers. New York: Dodd, 1929. 146-59.

An admiring critical chapter arguing that the agenda radiating from Ferber's work is the joy and value of work. Explicates many of the novels and short stories from this perspective. Also provides some background and biographical information. A useful short overview of Ferber's life and works.

Reviews

Adams, Phoebe Lou. "At War with Texas." Rev. of *Giant. Atlantic Monthly* Oct. 1952: 100-01.

Describes the plot, and comments that while Ferber writes to entertain, which she never fails to do, she also pursues two themes in nearly all her novels: the corrosive effect of money and the evils of group prejudices. Quips that Texas makes a perfect subject for both.

"American Beauty." Rev. of *American Beauty. Times Literary Supplement* 5 Nov. 1931: 862.

Admires the genuine gusto of Ferber's *American Beauty* and its compelling story.

Barkham, John. "Where It's the Biggest and Bestest." Rev. of *Giant. New York Times Book Review* 28 Sept. 1952: 4-5.

In discussing the contents of the novel Barkham lauds the book for its wealth piled on wealth. Concludes that though the novel presents Texas larger and more chromatic than life, and though it is rather slick, Ferber writes with conviction and sincerity.

Blackman, Ruth Chapin. "Miss Ferber's Alaska." Rev. of *Ice Palace. Christian Science Monitor* 27 Mar. 1958: 7.

Sees this novel as stylized, full of contrived deaths and uncomplicated characters. Concludes, however, that it is also vivid, interesting, accurate, and concerned with values.

Bullock, Florence Haxton. "Edna Ferber Tells a Big-as-Life Story of Oil-and-Cattle Texas." Rev. of *Giant*. *New York Herald Tribune Book Review* 28 Sept. 1952: 1.

Calls *Giant* a novel full of ideas and based on a fascinating story of unchanging Texas life. Mostly an account of story and contents.

"Came, Didn't Get It." Rev. of *Giant*. *Time* 29 Sept. 1952: 94.

Describes the plot and characters, and labels the novel a blend of regionalism, super-slick storytelling, and full money's worth of good reading.

Canby, Henry Seidel. "Gusto vs Art." Rev. of *American Beauty*. *Saturday Review of Literature* 17 Oct. 1931: 201.

Asserts that Ferber's vigor and sense of tangible reality are unequalled, but that she fails to attain her objective, no matter how brilliantly she mops up the trenches as she goes. Argues that she fails to capture the spiritual realities of her American scene. Concludes that her gifts can be too easily vulgarized and that she should school herself to join the ranks of truly fine artists.

"Chronicle and Comment." Rev. of *Buttered Side Down*. *Bookman* May 1912: 225-27.

Claims that *Buttered Side Down* is a collection of short stories worthy of attention. Accuses Ferber of amusement and naivete in her baseball story, "A Bush League Hero," but admires the strong, sound philosophy of "The Man Who Came Back," and the genuine humor of all the pieces.

Colby, Nathalie Sedgwick. "Simultaneous Differences." Rev. of *Mother Knows Best*. *Saturday Review of Literature* 14 May 1927: 819-20.

Calls this is a book of small novels bound together. Describes several of them briefly.

Crawford, John W. "Edna Ferber's Show Boat on the Mississippi." Rev. of *Show Boat*. *Literary Digest International Book Review* Sept. 1926: 608-09.

Describes the contents of the book in detail. Details the background history, characters, individual scenes, quality of writing, imaginative powers, and energy. Calls this Ferber's best vehicle so far in the literal and figurative sense.

Davidson, Donald. "Edna Ferber." Rev. of *Show Boat. Nashville Tennessean* 22 Aug. 1926: Rpt. in Donald D. Davidson. *The Spyglass: Views and Reviews, 1924-1930.* Comp. and ed. John Tyree Fain. Nashville: Vanderbilt UP, 1963. 70-74.

Characterizes *Show Boat* and *So Big* as novels in which Ferber set out determinedly to find the romantic element in American life. Sees her in opposition to the *"Main Street"* school of American fiction led by Sinclair Lewis. Spends the balance of the article discussing *Show Boat* as depicting river life in a manner that nobody has touched since Mark Twain. Praises its panoramic dimensions and its dramatic qualities. Finds the ending incongruous, however, and its treatment of theatrical life in New York City ironic and satiric. Argues that unfortunately the book seems forever on the point of becoming serious and never does because it skirts the edge of tragedy and leaves the ingredients carefully mixed for a popular audience. Concludes that Ferber does not go as deep as male novelists of the period do, and therefore remains merely charming because she is neither "virile" nor willing to tackle the "innards" of things like her male counterparts.

Downey, Fairfax. "Ferber . . ." Rev. of *Saratoga Trunk. Saturday Review of Literature* 22 Nov. 1941: 18.

Praises the novel for its absorbing excitement, well-turned phrases, and tale-telling ability. Argues that while some incidents could have been better developed, the whole novel is good theater.

Edgett, Edwin Francs. "Edna Ferber and Her Incisive Art." Rev. of *Mother Knows Best. Boston Evening Transcript* 16 Apr. 1927: 4.

Comments on *Mother Knows Best* as a volume of short stories suggesting Ferber's wide command of literary form. Describes several of the stories individually and commends Ferber for her economy, vitality, powers of characterization, thematic emphasis, and gifts as a storyteller.

Edgett, Edwin Francis. "Edna Ferber Creates a Valiant Woman." Rev. of *So Big. Boston Evening Transcript* 23 Feb. 1924: 4.

Provides a plot summary and historical background for the novel.

Edgett, Edwin Francis. "Ferber Strikes a Dominant Note." Rev. of *Come and Get It. Boston Evening Transcript* 23 Feb. 1935: 1.

Provides an elaborate description of the contents along with commentary on the action, human interest, and American life. Details the defects of the story as a novel.

Edgett, Edwin Francis. "*Half Portions* from Edna Ferber." Rev. of *Half Portions. Boston Evening Transcript* 2 June 1920: 4.

Describes the contents of this collection of short stories, commenting that they penetrate deeply toward the heart of nature and human nature because they are thronged with flesh and blood men and women.

Edgett, Edwin Francis. "We Visit Oklahoma with Edna Ferber." Rev. of *Cimarron. Boston Evening Transcript* 29 Mar. 1930: 3.

Describes the contents of the novel and the history of the State of Oklahoma that it catalogs. Commends Ferber for her wise choice of historical subject matter since so few know anything about the history of the state. Also admires her large sweep and incredible command of detail. Concludes that this is a book crowded with human figures and action.

"Edna Ferber's Best." Rev. of *So Big. Bookman* Mar 1924: 68.

Commends *So Big* for its restraint, dramatic qualities, firm technique, sympathy, and intuition.

"Edna Ferber's Gigolo." Rev. of *Gigolo. Literary Digest International Book Review* Dec. 1922: 56-57.

Discusses *Gigolo* as a collection of eight short stories of varying degrees of merit, descending from skillful, appealing mixtures of humor and pathos and genuine homespun realism to the creakily contrived. Concludes that these are very human little stories of pungent and often delicate wit.

"Emma McChesney." Rev. of *Emma McChesney and Company. New York Times Book Review* 17 Oct. 1915: 390, 396.

Describes the contents of the book and suggests that by now, if it were not for Ferber's ingenuity, she and the reader would be tired of her heroine, Emma. Describes this book as warm, funny, human, and full of types and characters.

Feld, Rose. "A Rich, Lusty Story of a Family and a City." Rev. of *Great Son. New York Herald Tribune Weekly Book Review* 28 Jan. 1945: 3.

Hails *Great Son* as a fine achievement by a writer who creates character brilliantly and writes potently. Provides an excellent plot and character commentary.

Feld, Rose. "Saratoga and New Orleans—and Edna Ferber." Rev. of *Saratoga Trunk. New York Herald Tribune Books* 2 Nov. 1941: 5.

Describes *Saratoga Trunk* as a lusty, romantic, lively account of life among the wealthy in New Orleans. Concludes that she has taken meticulous care with background and characterization, finally producing a book with an unfailing dramatic quality.

"Ferber Fundamentals." Rev. of *Great Son. Time* 5 Feb. 1945: 94, 96, 98.

Briefly argues that this novel is less strongly plotted than previous works but nevertheless slickly written, "cinemadaptable," and American.

"Ferber's Texans." Rev. of *Giant. Newsweek* 29 Sept. 1952: 97-98.

Briefly reviews the plot, finding this novel far less effective than some of her earlier works. Comments on unjustified complaints from Texans about her characterizations.

Fergusson, Harvey. "A Pioneer Oklahoma Family." Rev. of *Cimarron. New York Herald Tribune Books* 23 Mar. 1930: 9.

Calls *Cimarron* soundly designed, uncompromisingly written, and entertaining. Faults it for its overload of facts, and for its ignoring the legendary values of the Western experience. Faults Ferber also on her lack of knowledge about life in a wild country. Concludes that the book insufficiently fuses its immense mass of material with emotion.

"Fiction." Rev. of *Cimarron. Bookman* July 1930: 440.

Argues that *Cimarron* is Edna Ferber at her best. Claims that her native vigor allows Ferber to avoid many narrative pitfalls, and yet she falls into other problems with her enthusiasm and humor. Concludes that, as far as she is from art, Ferber reaches very close to the heart of life. Describes the contents.

"Fiction." Rev. of *Show Boat. Spectator* 6 Nov. 1926: 824.

Calls *Show Boat* a richly packed, highly romantic, incident-filled, and colorful book. Claims that it has a genuine ring and is both touching and readable. Details the contents.

"Fiction." Rev. of *So Big. Outlook* 28 May 1924: 160-61.

Describes the theme of the novel as what it means to be alive with interest in life. Describes the elegant Dirk's lack of vital life force and the corresponding sense of adventure, hardship overcome, and wounds healed in the characters of Selma, Roelf, Paula, and General Goguet. Concludes that this book doesn't preach, it shows.

Field, Louise Maunsell. "From Gopher Prairie on to High Prairie." Rev. of *So Big. New York Times Book Review* 24 Feb. 1924: 9.

Provides a detailed plot and character summary. Describes the novel as a chronicle with a slight plot, but rich in feeling, variety, and contrast. Concludes that, at the crux of the book, is the question of values—which things are worth something and which things are not.

Field, Louise Maunsell. "Latest Works of Fiction." Rev. of *The Girls. New York Times* 30 Oct. 1921: 16.

Describes *The Girls* as a broad-minded and interesting narrative. Provides a detailed description of the contents.

Gale, Zona. "Edna Ferber's Roaring North Woods Tale." Rev. of *Come and Get It. New York Herald Tribune Books* 24 Feb. 1935: 3.

Describes *Come and Get It* as a lively account of the old Wisconsin lumber days and the grab for wealth. Argues that this is no tapestry of a past woven and many-colored, but the record of a past seen in hard sunlight, heard very near at hand, and without a moment's dull or still.

"Glimpses of Reality." Rev. of *Fanny Herself. Nation* 18 Oct. 1917: 431-32.

Describes *Fanny Herself* primarily in terms of its contents. Particularly notes her comments on the shaping factors in the Jewish experience and personality.

Gould, Gerald. "New Fiction." Rev. of *So Big. Saturday Review* [London] 12 Apr. 1924: 392.

Complains that the novel is thesis-bound and that its author lacks the genius to enable her open discussions of beauty to survive. Dismisses the moral formula that devotion to unworldly standards brings appreciation and exaltation in this world, and concludes that it would be wrong to "a charming novel" to pursue it too closely with speculation.

Gruening, Ernest. "Edna Ferber's Novel of Alaska's Dreams and Drama." Rev. of *Ice Palace. New York Herald Tribune Book Review* 30 Mar. 1958: 1.

Describes the setting, characters, plot, and furnishings of *Ice Palace*. Commends the book for its vivid and sympathetic understanding of Alaskan culture, politics, and people.

Hackett, Francis. Rev. of *The Girls. New Republic* 4 Jan. 1922: 158-59.

Comments that unlike many writers, such as Norris and Dreiser, Ferber does not strain at taking on Chicago as a theme for her novel, and the city permeates her book. Describes the story and characters, and notes that the flat, trite ending is a weakness, but that it has "an enormous command of detail and a fine observation, a real enthusiasm for theme."

Havinghurst, Walter. "Big A." Rev. of *Ice Palace. Saturday Review* 29 Mar. 1958: 26.

Calls *Ice Palace* a book in which Ferber sees people in large dimension, and whole galleries of them. Claims that, heightened and exaggerated, they match the seas and skies and mountains of the Alaskan setting. Mainly describes the story.

Hawthorne, Hildegarde. "Everyday Folk." Rev. of *Roast Beef, Medium. New York Times* 20 Apr. 1913: 232.

Argues that in this description of *Roast Beef, Medium*, Ferber has produced a brave, ordinary, and fun-loving book. Contains detailed plot summary.

"Igloo Reading." Rev. of *Ice Palace. Time* 31 Mar. 1958: 88.

Claims that Ferber at seventy is still not over the best-seller habit judging by this novel. Describes plot and characters, and concludes that Ferber generously shares with the reader all her new-found and often interesting Alaskan lore. Concludes that when she raises her voice it sounds as if she really cares.

Janeway, Elizabeth. "Strong Men Face to Face." Rev. of *Ice Palace. New York Times Book Review* 30 Mar. 1958: 4.

Complains that the plot of *Ice Palace* is absent-minded if not ramshackle, the form hybrid, the narrative bald, the effect labored, the characterization thin, and the local color merely amusing. Concludes that this is social history, not fiction.

Kittrell, William. "Land of the Boiling Gold." Rev. of *Giant. Saturday Review* 27 Sept. 1952: 15.

Begins by announcing that *Giant* should be on the lists of the Texas Folklore Society. Recounts the plot and labels the work a fable. Calls attention to Ferber's care with the facts and background material of Texas ranch life.

Kronenberger, Louis. "Salt and Gusto in New Tales of Edna Ferber." Rev. of *Mother Knows Best. New York Times* 17 Apr. 1927: 2.

Praises Ferber's smooth, bright, stylistic gusto and command of detail. Claims that the whole effect is a strange mixture of romance and realism. Concludes that in each of the stories she avoids sentimentality and produces characters alive enough to sustain them, but with insufficient depth to survive in a novel.

Kronenberger, Louis. "*Show Boat* Is High Romance: Edna Ferber Goes Barnstorming Down the Old Mississippi." Rev. of *Show Boat. New York Times Book Review* 22 Aug. 1926: 5.

Describes reading the book in a prevailing atmosphere of realism as a great relief. Sees the novel as a "spirited, full-breasted, tireless story, romantic because it is too alive to be what realists call 'real'; because it bears within itself a spirit of life which we seek rather than have; because it makes a period and mode of existence live again, not actually different from what they were, but more alluring than they could have been."

"Latest Works of Fiction." Rev. of *Cheerful By Request. New York Times Book Review* 22 Sept. 1918: 399, 408.

Calls these short stories outwardly simple and inwardly complex, utilizing one similar type of female character throughout. Claims that they picture accurately the life of the small town, domestic, lingerie saleswoman and a great mass of other workaday people. Concludes that there is much humor here, but even more tragedy and tears.

"Latest Works of Fiction." Rev. of *Fanny Herself. New York Times Book Review* 7 Oct. 1917: 380.

Considers the first part of the book human and real, the second rather lacking in interest. Primarily a character study of Fanny.

"Latest Works of Fiction." Rev. of *Gigolo. New York Times* 5 Nov. 1922: 10.

Details the contents of each of the stories, and concludes that Ferber knows her characters intimately and writes about them vividly and well.

"Latest Works of Fiction." Rev. of *Half Portions. New York Times* 9
  May 1920: 236.
Calls *Half Portions* a collection of short stories which are thoroughly
enjoyable and laughable from beginning to end. Notes that the undergirding philosophy suggests that all things good or evil should be viewed
with a great sense of humor.

Loveman, Amy. "Processional." Rev. of *They Brought Their Women.*
  Saturday Review of Literature 13 May 1933: 587.
Praises the novel for its keen and precise powers of observation, selection of significant detail, fidelity to fact, compactness, and humor.
Complains, however, that the stories lack originality of theme and psychological subtlety, that they skim the surface of life and avoid the
complex entanglements of human relationships. Dismisses the stories as
excellent magazine fiction for those with an idle hour.

MacBride, James. "Thirty-One by Ferber." Rev. of *One Basket: Thirty-
  One Short Stories. New York Times Book Review* 16 Feb. 1947: 3.
Describes *One Basket* as a selection of Ferber's best short stories which
will repay close reading. Considers each a vigorous example of a writer
at the top of her form. Claims that they exhibit a shrewd ear for dialogue,
a virtuoso lightness of phrasing, and a real understanding of the standard
problems Americans face.

Mann, Dorothea Lawrance. "*Fanny Herself*, A Successor to Edna
  Ferber's *Mrs. McChesney*." Rev. of *Fanny Herself. Boston Evening
  Transcript* 17 Nov. 1917: 7.
Describes the contents, style, and tone of the novel as a book full of sym-
pathy, humanity, sense, impulsiveness, and warmth. Discusses the theme
of anti-Semitism in the novel.

Marsh, Fred T. ""Edna Ferber's *Come and Get It*." Rev. of *Come and
  Get It. New York Times Book Review* 24 Feb. 1935: 6.
Primarily details the contents of the novel. Claims that her methods suggest the realistic social historian novelist at one end of the scale, and the
theater at the other end.

McCall, Lillian B. "Edna Ferber's America." Rev. of *One Basket:
  Thirty-One Short Stories. Commentary* Sept. 1957: 277-78, 280.
Condemns Ferber for her monotonous vocabulary, her stock characters,

her well-worn plots, her small-town suspiciousness, her distaste for the big-city rich, her general lack of depth, and, above all, her "didacticism" and moral arrogance.

McFee, William. "Life on the Mississippi—New Style." Rev. of *Show Boat*. *New Republic* 15 Sept. 1926: 101-02.

Argues that the pace is that of the short story, not the novel, and claims that its appeal lies in the subject matter of the Mississippi show boat culture.

"Miss Ferber's Vivid Tale of Oklahoma Settling." Rev. of *Cimarron*. *New York Times* 23 Mar. 1930: 4.

Calls *Cimarron* a book written with exuberance, gusto, and robust romanticism. Asserts, however, that those readers who like their novels unerring in their psychology will find Ferber quite unsatisfying. Argues that this is a book to be read for its vivid recreations and splendidly kaleidoscopic view of a young American city coming into existence. Concludes that it leaves an indelible picture.

"New Novels." Rev. of *So Big*. *Times Literary Supplement* 13 Mar. 1924: 158.

Describes *So Big* as a compressed allegory of the changed attitude of the American writer. Accuses Ferber of being more interested in describing a world in which women pull the strings than she is in crediting a character like Dirk with genuine qualities. Provides detailed description of the stylistic deficiencies of the work.

"New Yorker." Rev. of *Mother Knows Best*. *Times Literary Supplement* 9 June 1927: 406.

Describes *Mother Knows Best* in terms of content, and concludes that despite her sentimentality, there is a certain crispness and thematic impetus to the book.

"Other New Novels." Rev. of *Nobody's in Town*. *Times Literary Supplement* 5 Nov. 1938: 713.

Describes the contents of the two long stories which make up the volume *Nobody's in Town*. Calls them pleasant rather than vital reading, and comments that they are sustained by fairly well-worn themes.

Paterson, Isabel. "Troupers on the Mississippi." Rev. of *Show Boat*. *New York Herald Tribune Books* 22 Aug. 1926: 3.

Describes the contents of *Show Boat,* and commends Ferber for her keen ear, graphic colloquial phrases, local color, good research, unflagging storyline and interest, and skill in characterization. Concludes that Ferber has a genuine feeling for the joys and sorrows of her fellow beings, an infectious love of her work, and little understanding of what a novel really is.

Pearson, Edmund. "The Book Table." Rev. of *Show Boat. Outlook* 15 Sept. 1926: 90-91.

Describes the setting, characters, and contents of the novel, and goes on to complain that the panoramic nature of the thing does not allow close attention to construction or unity of plan, though it fits the subject.

Rascoe, Burton. "Among the New Books." Rev. of *Cimarron. Arts and Decoration* Sept. 1930: 71, 101.

Finds her works have more "gusto" than the works of most masculine writers. Seems particularly impressed with the uncanny accuracy of the language that is characteristic of the early settlers of Oklahoma, but also finds her greatest fault to be her "extreme readability."

Rice, Jennings. "Cross-Section of American Life." Rev. of *One Basket*: Thirty-One Short Stories. *New York Herald Tribune Weekly Book Review* 16 Feb. 1947: 7.

Describes these stories as dealing with a wide variety of experiences of American life in the last thirty years. Complains that they are compassionate, astringent, and compressed; they reveal her pride in America, and document the lives of selfish women, elderly people, simple lives imbued with pioneer spirit, backstage and cinema stories, home-front war stories, and World War I stories.

Rothman, N. L. "Love-Letter to Seattle." Rev. of *Great Son. Saturday Review of Literature* 27 Jan. 1945: 24.

Argues that *Great Son* reads like a slingshot job when it should have been a trilogy. Remarks that it is a wonder it is readable at all. Concludes that it has verve, enthusiasm, humor, and love of both people and America. Describes setting, characters, and story lines.

"Shorter Notices." Rev. of *They Brought Their Women. Nation* 28 June 1933: 734.

Sees the novel as a book which fails to penetrate life deeply. Finds her stories are like prose extensions of a popular song and therefore innocent of any individual characterization.

"Showing America." Rev. of *Show Boat. Saturday Review of Literature* 21 Aug. 1926: 49, 54.

Calls *Show Boat* Ferber's re-creation of local color writing that takes great efforts with characters and settings, and little in plot. Precedes this with a brief essay on the history of local color writing.

Smertenko, Johan J. "The New Books." Rev. of *American Beauty. Outlook* 11 Nov. 1931: 345.

Claims that this novel reveals Ferber's liquid felicity of style and genuine humor in her treatment of the American scene. Notes, however, that despite the fact that she has never really been given her due by critics, this book is weighted by its ambitiousness, attempt at historical significance, and false style. Concludes that the story is told with extraordinary skill, but in a style become stiff with the crinoline formalities of a past age.

Towne, Charles Hanson. "Edna Ferber Again Answers Her Critics." Rev. of *So Big. Literary Digest International Book Review* Apr. 1924: 344, 412.

Claims that *So Big* is notable in its restraint and passion because it is characterized by her energy, broad human sympathy, humor, compassion, comprehension, and force. Admires the story for being powerful and engrossing. Details the contents, and concludes that this is one of those cosmic books with a glowing theme which cannot be analyzed.

"Two New Types of Heroine." Rev. of *Roast Beef, Medium. Current Opinion* June 1913: 491.

Describes *Roast Beef, Medium* as a collection of magazine fiction containing both wit and social ethics, as well as philosophy.

Van Doren, Dorothy. "American Beauty Shoppe." Rev of *American Beauty. Nation* 28 Oct. 1931: 462-63.

Calls *American Beauty* a book which betrays the ambition of the writer to write about a great subject greatly. Notes that, unfortunately, she was not content to let New England tell its own story, but has to introduce romantic interest and pander to the great American reading public who will not mind a little vulgarity.

Van Doren, Dorothy. "A Pioneer Fairy Story." Rev. of *Cimarron. Nation* 23 Apr. 1930: 494.

Sees *Cimarron* as dashing, colorful, and full of gorgeous, colorful characters acting our their lives against an equally gorgeous backdrop.

Concludes that, unfortunately, her despairs are less convincing than her triumphs, hence it is not the great book it ought to be.

Vestal, Stanley. "Miss Ferber's Myth." Rev. of *Cimarron*. *Saturday Review of Literature* 22 Mar. 1930: 841.

Accuses Ferber of spending insufficient time in Oklahoma where the novel is set and of failing to provide sufficient notation of the human heart. Calls the novel excellent reporting, marvelous storytelling, and excellent fantasy.

Wallace, Margaret. "A Connecticut Pageant by Miss Ferber." Rev. of *American Beauty*. *New York Times Book Review* 18 Oct. 1931: 7.

Calls *American Beauty* yet another excursion into the annals of American history. Details the contents, and concludes that the novel finally lacks plot and a central character to give it force and unity. Considers that it falls below the level of her best work.

Wallace, Margaret. "Edna Ferber's *Saratoga Trunk* and Other New Fictions." Rev. of *Saratoga Trunk*. *New York Times Book Review* 2 Nov. 1941: 4.

Describes *Saratoga Trunk* as a flamboyant story with a setting to match, prose which is not always polished, and an irresistible energy. Concludes that the impression it leaves behind is nervous, dazzling, and colorful.

Walton, Edith H. "Edna Ferber's Volume of Short Stories." Rev. of *They Brought Their Women*. *New York Times Book Review* 14 May 1933: 7.

Describes *They Brought Their Women* as a collection of short stories lacking profound emotion. Alive and warm and observant, her stories skim the cream from the surface of modern life and preserve all its richness. But that is all they do. Depth, subtlety, and intensity are beyond Miss Ferber.

Walton, Edith. "Tales By Edna Ferber." Rev. of *Nobody's in Town*. *New York Times Book Review* 13 Feb. 1938: 7-8.

Describes *Nobody's in Town* as a book which neither surprises nor fails. Claims that both novelettes glitter with polish and make their points with clear, crisp pungency. Comments that while there is little depth here, there is little diminishment of artistry. Contains a detailed account of contents and characters.

"The Week's Reading." Rev. of *Cimarron*. *Outlook and Independent* 9 Apr. 1930: 588.

Claims that this novel, like *Show Boat,* is marred by what made it popular. Comments on its panoramic melodrama about settling Oklahoma; many incidents, particularly two striking scenes; atmosphere; and fine characterization. Concludes, however, that it is a crude picture, a chromo, a piece of lively illustration rather than a work of art.

Weeks, Edward. "Where Men Are Men." Rev. of *Ice Palace. Atlantic* May 1958: 77-78, 80.

Outlines the plot of predatory commercial interests in Alaska, and then argues that the process of overenlargement, which stems from her extravagant phrasing, causes the book to be less than believable. Concedes its sincerity and moral passion.

Winslow, Thyra Samter. "A Collection of Little Novels." Rev. of *Mother Knows Best. New York Herald Tribune Books* 24 Apr. 1927: 3-4.

Details the contents of *Mother Knows Best,* and complains that she has read every one of them before. Concludes, however, that on second reading the stories seemed even better than before.

Interviews

Hutchens, John K. "Edna Ferber." *New York Herald Tribune Book Review* 5 Oct. 1952: 2.

Contains the report of an interview and luncheon with Ferber on the occasion of the publication of *Giant.* Provides biographical and critical information.

Nichols, Lewis. "Talk with Edna Ferber." *New York Times Book Review* 5 Oct. 1952: 30.

Describes the sweep and emotional impact of *Giant.* Reports significant amounts of an interview with Ferber on the subject of this and other books.

Van Gelder, Robert. "An Interview with Edna Ferber." *New York Times Book Review* 4 Feb. 1945: 3. Rpt. in *Writers and Writing.* Robert Van Gelder. New York: Scribners, 1946. 360-65.

An interview presented in the third person covering such matters as dinner table political conversation, unfulfilled writing ambitions, the position of young writers, social inhibitions of the era she grew up in, typical choices of subject matter, early contracts, and assorted other matters.

Biographical Sources

Bromfield, Louis. "Edna Ferber." *Saturday Review* of Literature 15 June 1935: 10-12.

A tribute to and biographical portrait of Ferber written by a great admirer who believes she should have been an actress. Contains much eulogy and only a little useful biographical information.

Cerf, Bennett. "Trade Winds." *Saturday Review* of Literature 27 Jan. 1945: 20.

Comments on Ferber's relationship with her publisher and problems with foreign publishers.

Dickinson, Rogers. *Edna Ferber: A Biographical Sketch with a Bibliography*. Garden City: Doubleday, 1925.

A detailed personal account full of pity, anecdote, and minutiae rather than a chronological account of her life. Appended to the sketch is a complete bibliography of primary works up to 1925.

Ernst, Morris L. "My Friend Ferber." *The Best Is Yet . . .* Morris L. Ernst. New York: Harper, 1945. 181-84.

Commends Ferber for being a historian of the folkways of America, and for her ability to write of her country with love and loyalty. Generally a slight piece of admiring biography.

Ferber, Edna. *A Kind of Magic*. Garden City: Doubleday, 1963.

Ferber, Edna. *A Peculiar Treasure*. New York: Doubleday, 1939.

Ferber, Edna. "Some Important Fall Authors Speak for Themselves." *New York Herald Tribune Book Review* 12 Oct. 1952: 18.

Gilbert, Julie Goldsmith. *Ferber: A Biography*. Garden City: Doubleday, 1978.

Horowitz, Steven P., and Miriam J. Landsman. "Edna Ferber." *Twentieth-Century American-Jewish Fiction Writers*. Ed. Daniel Walden. Detroit: Gale, 1984. Vol. 28 of *Dictionary of Literary Biography*. 94 vols. to date. 1978- . 58-64.

More than details of her life, this is a career biography tracing the development of the author's canon, describing the contents and themes of her works, evaluating her reputation, and placing her in the larger context of American literary history. Includes lists of primary and secondary works and illustrations.

Hughes, Carol. "Edna Ferber's American Story." *Coronet* Sept. 1953: 136-40.

A general and brief tribute full of anecdotes, pieces of humor, biographical tidbits, and a reasonably well-sustained account of her rise to fame in both letters and the theater, her love of New York, and her sense of humor.

"The Literary Spotlight, IV: Edna Ferber." *Bookman* Jan. 1922: 434-39. Rpt. in *The Literary Spotlight*. Ed. John C. Farrar. New York: Doran, 1924. 135-45.

A tribute and biographical sketch of Ferber containing such information as her background, upbringing, early writing, early career as a journalist, struggle to get published, interest in the stage, domestic life, travels, and general interests.

Patrick, Arnold. "Getting Into Six Figures, V: Edna Ferber." *Bookman* Apr. 1925: 164-68.

A general review of Ferber's life and writing career.

Pattee, Fred Lewis. *The New American Literature 1890-1930*. New York: Century, 1930. 322-23.

Provides a brief biographical sketch of Ferber and her writing career.

Reed, Paula. "Edna Ferber." *American Novelists 1910-1945, Part I: Louis Adamic-Vardis Fisher*. Ed. James J. Martine. Detroit: Gale, 1981. Vol. 9 of *Dictionary of Literary Biography*. 94 vols. to date. 1978- . 306-13.

More than details of her life, this is a career biography tracing the development of the author's canon, describing the contents and themes of her works, evaluating her reputation, and placing her in the larger context of American literary history. Includes lists of primary and secondary sources and illustrations.

Uffen, Ellen Serlen. "Edna Ferber." *American Short Story Writers, 1910-1945, First Series*. Ed. Bobby Ellen Kimbel. Detroit: Gale, 1989. Vol. 86 of *Dictionary of Literary Biography*. 94 vols. to date. 1978- . 91-98.

More than details of her life, this is a career biography tracing the development of her short story canon, describing the contents and themes of her works, evaluating her reputation, and placing her in the larger context of American literary history. Includes a list of primary and secondary sources and illustrations.

White, William Allen. "Edna Ferber." *World's Work* June 1930: 36-38, 90.

An admiring biographical tribute that ranges across her novels and the various phases and periods of her writing career. Touches on her newspaper reporting career, her initial fame as a writer, and the major social events of her day that shaped her writing. Pays particular attention to Ferber's personality as discerned by White and other newspaper reporter colleagues who traveled to various political conventions and other events with her.

Bibliographies

Brenni, Vito J., and Betty Lee Spencer. "Edna Ferber: A Selected Bibliography." *Bulletin of Bibliography* 22.7 (1958): 152-56.

Dissertations

Lichtenstein, Diane Marilyn. "On Whose Native Ground? Nineteenth-Century Myths of American Womanhood and Jewish Women Writers." Diss. U of Pennsylvania, 1985.

Leslie Fiedler
1917 –

Primary Sources

Novels

Back to China. New York: Stein, 1965.

The Messengers Will Come No More. New York: Stein, 1974.

The Second Stone: A Love Story. New York: Stein, 1963; Toronto: McClelland, 1963; London: Heinemann, 1966.

Unfinished Business. New York: Stein, 1972.

Collected Works

The Last Jew in America. New York: Stein, 1966.
Contents: The Last Jew in America, The Last WASP in the World, The Last Spade in the West.

Nude Croquet. New York: Stein, 1969, 1974; London: Secker, 1970.
Contents: Nude Croquet, The Teeth, Let Nothing You Dismay, Dirty Ralphy, The Fear of Innocence, An Expense of Spirit, Nobody Ever Died from It, Pull Down Vanity!, The Stain, Bad Scene at Buffalo Jump, The

Girl in the Black Raincoat, The Dancing of Reb Hershl with the Withered Hand.

Pull Down Vanity, and Other Stories. Philadelphia: Lippincott, 1962; London: Secker, 1963.

Contents: The Teeth, The Fear of Innocence, An Expense of Spirit, Nobody Ever Died from It, Pull Down Vanity!, The Stain, Nude Croquet, The Dancing of Reb Hershl with the Withered Hand.

Short Fiction in Anthologies

"Dear Friends and Gentle Hearts." *Stories from Epoch: The First Fifty Issues (1947-1964).* Ed. Baxter Hathaway. Ithaca: Cornell UP, 1966. 276-81.

"The Last Jew in America." *A Fiedler Reader.* New York: Stein, 1977. 450-89.

"Nobody Ever Died from It." *A Fiedler Reader.* New York: Stein, 1977. 490-509.

"Nude Croquet." *Love Is the Theme.* Eds. Douglas Angus and Sylvia Angus. Greenwich: Fawcett, 1970. 161-203; *A Fiedler Reader.* New York: Stein, 1977. 403-49; *Great Esquire Fiction: The Finest Stories from the First Fifty Years.* Ed. L. Rust Hills. New York: Penguin, 1983. 95-126.

Short Fiction in Periodicals

"Bad Scene at Buffalo Jump." *Esquire* Mar. 1965: 100-01, 117-19.

"The Dancing of Reb Hershl with the Withered Hand." *Kenyon Review* 17.2 (1955): 193-207.

"Dirty Ralphy." *Commentary* Nov. 1947: 432-34.

"An Expense of Spirit." *Partisan Review* Jan. 1949: 7-24.

"Fear of Innocence." *Partisan Review* Aug. 1949: 775-821.

"The Girl in the Black Raincoat." *Partisan Review* 32.1 (1965): 35-41.

"Let Nothing You Dismay." *Commentary* Mar. 1948: 229-32.

"Nude Croquet." *Esquire* Sept. 1957: 134, 136-38, 140-48.

"Pull Down Vanity!" *Partisan Review* July 1954: 361-70, 435-64.

Secondary Sources

Books

Malin, Irving. *Jews and Americans*. Crosscurrents/Modern Critiques. Carbondale: Southern Illinois UP, 1965. passim.

Treats seven authors, including Fiedler, all of whom are Jews, all of whom deal with the Jew in America and who face their Jewishness. Discusses how they deal with the Jewish Experience—social, religious, and psychological—with the center of that experience being God. Devotes chapters to the ideas of exile, fathers and sons, time, head and heart, transcendence, irony, and fantasy, as well as the parable in the Jewish-American experience as demonstrated in their works.

Mark Royden Winchell. *Leslie Fiedler*. Twayne's United States Authors Series 492. Boston: Twayne, 1985.

Articles and Chapters

Bakker, J. "Leslie Fiedler: The Darkness and The Light in the Land of Affirmation." *Dutch Quarterly Review of Anglo-American Letters* 1 (1971): 3-14.

A major article which discusses the significance (for a European reader—[Bakker was Dutch]) of Fiedler's trilogy *Death and Love, Waiting for the End,* and *The Return of the Vanishing American*. A scholarly and erudite discussion which highlights much of the critical argument in Fiedler's critical work.

Bellman, Samuel I. "The American Artist as European Frontiersman: Leslie Fiedler's *The Second Stone*." *Critique* 6.3 (1963): 131-43.

Sees the novel as a droll tale filled with Baedeker details of Rome—"the minutiae of toilet functions, anatomical particulars of lovemaking, and Yiddish-English dialect sequences"—that is far more interesting as a fictional commentary on Fiedler and the Fiedler canon than as a story. Discusses the evidence of interest in Marxism and myth as themes, along with a tendency to autobiography. Also notes the theme of homosexual miscegenation, and Fiedler's endeavor to define a central American mythos of love "in which the lover is an outcast or orphan and the beloved a dark-skinned, primitive male," along with the theme of the rebel who eschews "the uninspiring materialism and paralyzing flatness of his own country to seek in Europe a seedground for his imagination."

Bellman, Samuel I. "Leslie A. Fiedler: Lazarus or Prophet?" *Congress Bi-Weekly* 21 Dec. 1964: 10-12.

Describes *The Second Stone* as a political, sexual satire characterized by tormented attitudes toward Judaism, endless political and literary references, and an obsessive bathroom fixture motif. Analyzes Fiedler's *angst* as that of the disappointed ex-Marxist of the 1930s, as the Jew who will not accept Christian hope, and as the *enfant terrible* of literary criticism who has seen too many literary movements fail. Characterizes him as a sort of secular modern-day descendent of the Hebrew prophets of old trying to awaken the consciences of the people to destroy false idols of the marketplace, tribe, cave, and theater. Claims that the novel has endless bathroom scenes, replete with genito-urinary details deliberately framed to startle the reader out of his arrested state of adolescence, out of his self-pride, and into a state of mind where he could begin to grasp Fiedler's canon of higher truths about today's society and the position of the Jew in it.

Bluefarb, Sam. "Pictures of the Anti-Stereotype: Leslie Fiedler's Triptych, *The Last Jew in America*." *CLA Journal* 18.3 (1975): 412-21.

A detailed and interpretive account of plot, character, and theme in the three novellas, along with a lengthy account of the many variations on the Jewish quest for identity in a WASP America. An excellent account of the theme and contents of the work.

Curran, Ronald. "'Fallen King' as scapegoat in Fiedler's 'Nude Croquet.'" *Notes on Contemporary Literature* 4.1 (1974): 8-13.

Interprets the ritual murder in this story in light of Frazer's Scapegoat

King. Sees Marvin as the conventional scapegoat, and asserts that killing him allows the group to symbolically kill aging and death and the "dignity of failure" he embodies. An elaborate exegesis focusing mainly on character expose. Sees croquet as an ironic metaphor for the false order of civilization. Concludes that this is "a blackly humorous tale of the savage and atavistic naivete of one East Coast Jewish branch of the American *nouveau riche*."

Davis, Robert Gorham. "Leslie Fiedler's Fictions." *Commentary* Jan. 1967: 73-77.

Argues that we must take Fiedler seriously as a writer since his four books of criticism are opposed by his four books of fiction that treat the same themes. Sees that the fiction, judged beside the criticism, is appalling, but not through want of talent. Claims that much of the material shows talent, wit, and eloquence, but the preoccupations of the criticism get exaggerated and misapplied in the fiction because all Fiedler's writing is obsessed by lies, duplicity, and false role-playing. Complains that once his fiction has unmasked the characters, nothing is left, unlike what happens after the unmasking in *Moby Dick, Huckleberry Finn*, and *The Scarlet Letter*. Provides an elaborate analysis of the genesis and effects of Fiedler's preoccupation with duplicity throughout many of his fictional and critical works, describing characters, themes, images, and arguments which exemplify the theme.

Dembo, L. S. "Dissent and Dissent: A Look at Fiedler and Trilling." *Contemporary American-Jewish Literature: Critical Essays*. Ed. Irving Malin. Bloomington: Indiana UP, 1973. 134-55.

Explains the finer points of Fiedler's *No, in Thunder* as opposed to the small metaphysical "no," and explains its implication in his work. Includes much biographical data, and discusses several essays, short stories, and novels. Details his attack on New Criticism, his attack on the anti-Semitism of Pound and Fitzgerald, his politics of myth criticism, his uncovering of stereotypes, and his disdain of the "establishment." The remainder of the article distinguishes Trilling from Fiedler.

Kostelanetz, Richard. "Leslie Fiedler." *Studies in the Twentieth Century* 13 (1965): 21-38.

Touts Fiedler as a writer who has forged an utterly singular cultural achievement, not just as critic and historian. Provides an overview of his fiction and insights into his cultural aesthetic, background, politics, and style.

Schulz, Max F. "Leslie A. Fiedler and the Hieroglyphs of Life."
  Twentieth Century Literature 14.1 (1968): 24-34. Rpt. in *Radical
  Sophistication: Studies in Contemporary Jewish/American Novelists.*
  Max F. Schulz. Athens: Ohio UP, 1969. 154-72.

Shows how, in Fiedler's novels, the disorder within society betrays the
primitive sexual energy of the essential man into neurotic dissonance.
Shows that when he attempts to honor his human birthright of creativity,
man finds himself frustrated into fulfilling his cultural heritage for self-
destruction. Sees the central irony of this as Fiedler's major subject in
the criticism and the fiction. Provides a detailed exegesis of *The Second
Stone, Back to China,* and various short pieces. Covers a wide range of
Fiedler themes and comments.

Reviews

Adams, Robert Martin. "Books." Rev. of *The Second Stone: A Love
  Story. Partisan Review* 30.1 (1963): 130-31.

Describes the contents of the novel, and condemns it as one of the messi-
est novels written by a man of obvious literary talent. Yet argues that, for
all its deficiencies, it is not a dead piece of work, even if it does transport
us into a world where practically every fresh and spontaneous sentiment
has been depraved by the self-pitying, loathsome, self-serving,
omnipresent ego. Concludes that there is a weird sort of vitality of an
interminable, bad dream.

Aldridge, John W. "Clem and His Campaign for Mrs. Stone." Rev. of
  The Second Stone: A Love Story. New York Times Book Review 14
  Apr. 1963: 5, 36. Rpt. as *"The Second Stone."* in *Time to Murder and
  Create: The Contemporary Novel in Crisis.* John W. Aldridge. New
  York: McKay, 1966. 225-29.

Condemns the novel about the sex life of the American intellectual as an
embarrassment of the kinds of cliches found in the novels Fiedler himself has criticized. Claims that what might have been a fine
free-wheeling sexual comedy is actually a second-hand protest against
taboos that manages to sound, in its thrilled insistence upon the nasty, as
if grandma with her poor old fluttering indignation were the principal
reader in view. Argues that the chief character, Clem, has a sadistic
hatred of women and sex, putting him into the tradition of male homosexual love that Fiedler has claimed to be the hidden theme of the
American novel from Cooper to Melville. Concludes that the book final-

ly reveals love between a man and woman to be a snare and a delusion, posting the real thing as reserved for us boys all alone together out there on that raft.

Alter, Robert. "Leslie Fiedler in the 25th Century." Rev. of *The Messengers Will Come No More. New York Times Book Review* 29 Sept. 1974: 5-6.

Argues that instead of being a delightful spoof of science fiction, playing exuberantly with contemporary vogues and movements in past and future settings, the novel deteriorates into a series of tediously sophomoric reversals of contemporary facts. Claims that the novel, then, proves to be a farrago of cliches, taken not only from science fiction but from sensationalist popular history and history of religion, which is somehow meant to be read as a statement of profound spiritual issues. Concludes that the ultimate difficulty with this novel is the heavily portentous vagueness at its core. Finally condemns the novel as trying to simulate novelty chiefly through the aggressiveness of bad taste.

Barrett, William. "Three That Misfired." Rev. of *Back to China. Atlantic Monthly* June 1965: 145-46.

Comments that Fiedler is a brilliant critic, but this doesn't make him a successful novelist. Describes the contents of the novel, but finds the passages of direct, incisive writing mixed with "tomfoolery" only hinting that he could write a good novel.

Bellman, Samuel I. "Baro Led a Barren Life." Rev. of *Back to China. Saturday Review* 1 May 1965: 40.

Claims that *Back to China* seems a slight work full of improbable characters and corny flashbacks. Yet argues that for all its shortcomings, it should not be written off because Fiedler does better on the short runs than on the longer pieces. Also argues that this book contains a number of themes of genuine importance, whatever the quality of the narrative itself. Concludes that this is a harrowing picture of academic futility and aridity by a challenging gadfly writer.

Bellman, Samuel I. "The Frontiers of Leslie Fiedler." Rev. of *Pull Down Vanity and Other Stories. Southwest Review* 68.1 (1963): 86-89.

Describes the content of the individual stories, calling them in part frontier yarns of territory disputes between bad bourgeois society and good artist. Notes that they are also about the removing of counterfeit face and the triumph of the artist. Concludes that in the final analysis, the stories are charmingly sincere and remarkably innocent attempts to portray Promethean heroes.

Bellman, Samuel I. "In Groups Within Groups." Rev. of *The Last Jew in America*. *Saturday Review* 30 July 1966: 31-32.

Accuses Fiedler of being inept, fantastic, literarily false, full of stereotypes, hysterical, and meaningless in these three tales. Says Fiedler's writing represents a series of "emotional fits." Describes this work as being full of suffering exiles, anachronistic Jews, an anti-Semitic Pulitzer poet, a Negro night club operator—all exiles in a town Bellman identifies as Missoula, Montana. Concludes that the work could do with less matter and more art.

Bellman, Samuel I. "Visions and Fixations." Rev. of *The Last Jew in America*. *Congress Bi-Weekly* 24 Oct. 1966: 17.

Sees Fiedler as a fiction writer of impressive power, praising especially three stories from his collection *Pull Down Vanity*. But also feels his novels overindulge his fondest fixations. Notes that the title story of this collection of three is well done, but that the other two are "tasteless and frenzied." Concludes that what he needs is "higher seriousness, more disciplined control of his materials," so he may begin living up to the promise in his rich and diversified talents.

Bemis, R. "Books In Brief." Rev. of *Back to China*. *National Review* 1 June 1965: 476.

Argues that in *Back To China*, Fiedler is so busy answering his own criticism of other novelists that the success of his hardworked parody will depend on his reader's knowledge of, and snappish contempt for, literature of the kind his novel inverts and mocks.

Bryden, Ronald. "My Son the Frontiersman: *Pull Down Vanity and Other Stories*." Rev. of *Pull Down Vanity and Other Stories*. *Spectator* 29 Mar. 1963: 396-97. Rpt. in *The Unfinished Hero and Other Essays*. Ronald Bryden. London: Faber, 1969. 239-42.

Provides a brief overview of Fiedler's academic stance, his childhood as urban Jewish liberal, and his tireless flailing of Eastern Seaboard liberal intellectuals. But, nevertheless, concludes that his own character gets in the way of his writing, fictional and critical. Complains that Fiedler has not succeeded in shaking the worst of "Eastern theoretic egg-headedness" from his style which remains tortuous and overwritten. Concludes with a brief critique of his short story "Nude Croquet."

Buitenhuis, Peter. "A Fury of Betrayals." Rev. of *Pull Down Vanity and Other Stories. New York Times Book Review* 6 May 1962: 4, 26.

Judges *Pull Down Vanity* as bearing the angry and definite stamp of their author. Admires the author and his social agendas concerning youth, alienation of the Jews and Blacks, and all others who face a hostile society.

"Casting a Stone." Rev. of *The Second Stone: A Love Story. Newsweek* 4 Mar. 1963: 86.

Raises the question as to whether the idiocies on the book jacket are ever an exact reflection of the book inside. Cites the blurb from the book jacket to show it does, and adds that Fiedler has great nerve to write *this* novel.

"Crazy Mythed-Up People." Rev. of *The Second Stone: A Love Story. Time* 8 Mar. 1963: 99.

Calls *The Second Stone* a brilliantly conceived novel with virtues which, nevertheless, does not succeed. Identifies the trouble as Fiedler's intention of dealing with men and women in their archetypal reality as dreamed of by writers rather than lived by people.

Croman, Charlotte. "Books." Rev. of *The Last Jew in America. Commonweal* 6 Jan. 1967: 378-80.

Calls *The Last Jew in America* a fictional projection of several chapters of literary criticism critiquing the contemporary scene. Notes that, unfortunately, the prose fails to shine, and finds that the whole production lacks imagination. Details the contents of the individual stories, and concludes that the collection does add another important contribution to the Judaization of American culture.

"Current and Various." Rev. of *Back to China. Time* 23 Apr. 1965: 109.

Describes the protagonist, Finkelstone, as a silly Schnook, whose pleasure is pain. Notes that he can find no sense of having done wrong, but he feels he must suffer as though he were guilty. Concludes that he is a travesty of all the middle-aged Jewish liberals who ever lived in fiction.

Daniels, Guy. "The Sorrows of Baro Finklestone." Rev. of *Back to China. New Republic* 22 May 1965: 25-27.

Describes *Back to China* as campus fiction, sluggish but broadbacked, written in dull classroom prose, and with facile sophistry.

Davenport, Guy. "Books in Brief." Rev. of *The Second Stone: A Love Story. National Review* 4 June 1963: 467.

Calls *The Second Stone* full of the dandruff of symbolism and therefore a delight to the term-paper hunting graduate student. Comments that the story opens with vomit, closes with drunk crowing, and is punctuated with rage and pointless conversation in between.

Davenport, Guy. "Over-told, Half-told, Well-told." Rev. of *Nude Croquet. National Review* 4 Nov. 1969: 1123-24.

Argues of *Nude Croquet* that somehow Fiedler has managed no style at all. Claims that his tone is a surly growl, while the pace of the stories is epileptic, raucous one minute, and stalled the next. Concludes that, like the novels, his stories are middens of slovenliness wrecked upon bombast.

Davenport, Guy. "Two Flops and a Winner." Rev. of *The Last Jew in America. National Review* 6 Sept. 1966: 893-94.

Comments on *The Last Jew in America* that it shouts and whacks about on the subject of nothing amidst much drinking and vomiting. Concludes that no author whose stock in trade is rich Connecticut people or Jews, WASPS, and Negroes in the Far West need feel his fame has been jeopardized.

Davis, Robert Gorham. "Reviews." Rev. of *The Second Stone: A Love Story. Hudson Review* 16.2 (1963): 284-85.

Argues that *The Second Stone* represents a satire in which the satirist has no position of his own. Claims that the reader finally feels trapped and is forced into a prolonged intimacy with Clem's body that suggests some of Burrough's obsessions.

"Fiction." Rev. of *The Second Stone: A Love Story. Books and Bookmen* June 1966: 39.

Describes *The Second Stone* as unconsoling, misplaced, a desert without an oasis, full of weird characters, and begging to be sniggered at.

Fremont-Smith, Eliot. "Ethnic Tales From Out West." Rev. of *The Last Jew in America. New York Times* 25 July 1966: 25.

Calls *The Last Jew in America* an outrageously funny, abrasive, erratically plotted, cliched, and ethnically hilarious book. Complains that the weaknesses of the book finally outweigh its hilarity, however, and leave us with a book that merely entertains.

Grant, Annette. "The Astronomer and the Boy." Rev. of *Nude Croquet.* *Nation* 22 Sept. 1969: 287-88.

Says *Nude Croquet* offers a panorama of the author's pet obsessions: Jewish identity wrung from exile and alienation, Gentile desire to assimilate and to discriminate against outsiders, white guilt over Indians and Negroes, the political failures of liberals in the 1930s, men's sexual revenge on women, fear of sterility, and various forms of male homosexual love.

Greenfeld, Josh. "Black, Blue, and White." Rev. of *The Last Jew in America. Chicago Tribune Book Week* 14 Aug. 1966: 5.

Calls Leslie Fiedler an imaginative and free-ranging fictional thinker full of wit, zest, and genuine comic invention. After touching briefly on several of the stories in *The Last Jew in America*, comments that for all the hipster language and eye-catching titles, Fiedler is not writing about the new Negro, the old Jew, or the dying WASP, but providing a loud wail of traditional romantic lament for the passage of sentiment, the death of innocence, and the end of pure love.

Hicks, Granville. "From Precocity, A New Sensibility." Rev. of *Pull Down Vanity and Other Stories. Saturday Review* 5 May 1962: 16.

Thinks *Pull Down Vanity* seems to be a collection of interesting stories not entirely successful. Describes the contents of individual stories, and concludes that the typical Fiedler hero seems to be a version of a man of his own sensibility, and that while this sensibility does somewhat characterize the age, beyond that it is not to be relied on.

Hicks, Granville. "Love's Savor Lost." Rev. of *The Second Stone: A Love Story. Saturday Review* 2 Mar. 1963: 22.

Finds *The Second Stone* weak in spots, yet still interesting. Provides an elaborate account of the contents and concludes that though Fiedler has a gift for fiction, his grip on the craft is uncertain. Claims that some of his comic scenes are really funny and some of his dramatic episodes are compelling, but that a good many of his characters never come to life.

"Hors D'Oeuvres." Rev. of *Pull Down Vanity and Other Stories. Times Literary Supplement* 1 Mar. 1963: 149.

Argues that when all is said and done in *Pull Down Vanity*, it is Fiedler's incidental virtues which stand out. Thinks his charting of the Jewish-Gentile relationship is subtle and intelligent, as is his report of the shifting political allegiances of American intellectuals.

Kostelanetz, Richard C. "The Critic's Fiction." Rev. of *Pull Down Vanity and Other Stories* and *The Second Stone: A Love Story. Midstream* 9.3 (1963): 93-97.

Discusses Fiedler's reputation and opinions, the unmasking of characters in his fiction, the peeling away of artifice, the range of characters, the failure of much of the fiction to match the author's intentions, satire and humor, the angry language in the fiction, and the range of his literary endeavors.

Kostelanetz, Richard. "Finklestone Carries On." Rev. of *Back To China. New York Times Book Review* 1 Aug 1965: 26-27.

Calls *Back To China* a book which is funny enough but finally mired in faint preposterousness. Notes, however, that the language has the typical ebullient Fiedler energy and that those descriptions which are not particularly gross are rich and imaginative. Concludes that its themes are modest: marriage as a sufferable agony, adultery, and ambivalent attitudes toward paternity.

Leonard, John. "Behind the Mask, A Hole in History." Rev. of *Nude Croquet. New York Times* 20 Aug. 1969: 45. Rpt. as "Leslie Fiedler's *Nude Croquet* in *This Pen for Hire*. John Leonard. Garden City: Doubleday, 1973. 61-63.

Calls *Nude Croquet* a collection of stories which adds to Fiedler's attempt to bring us the rich complexity of our literary heritage. Notes, however, that the stories here about left-wing politics and Jews in academia are not quite up to his novels.

Lerner, Laurence. "New Fiction." Rev. of *Pull Down Vanity and Other Stories. Listener* 28 Feb. 1963: 391.

Notes that *Pull Down Vanity* is full of seeming pornography and involved ironic structures as it describes the world of the urban American intellectual. Concludes that complexity ultimately robs these stories of shape.

Lid, Richard W. "Intellectual Fiction of L. A. Fiedler." Rev. of *Pull Down Vanity and Other Stories. San Francisco Chronicle* 24 June 1962: 32.

Believes *Pull Down Vanity* will confirm the prevailing opinion of Fiedler as a wild man. Claims that its premise is that casual, low thought of people, especially libido-ridden artists and pseudo-intellectuals, is inherently interesting and particularly significant. Concludes that this isn't true because the characters are merely novel for the short time it takes to stop and watch someone else's accident.

Malcolm, Donald. "Much Ado." Rev. of *The Second Stone: A Love Story. New Yorker* 17 Aug. 1963: 84, 86, 89, 90-91.

Calls *The Second Stone* charming, ticketed with literary significance labeled for the reviewers. Comments that many of the scenes are so heavy with significance they are permeated with a sense of their importance. Concludes that the satire is mean and obvious, while the discussions lack intelligence and interest. Remains generally unimpressed with the weight of Fiedler's agendas.

Malin, Irving. Rev. of *Pull Down Vanity and Other Stories. Chicago Jewish Forum* (Spr. 1963): 248.

Finds Fiedler at his best when confronting the problem of being a Jew in America, as he does in this collection of stories. Describes several stories, pointing out that Fiedler uses the physical deformities of his characters to symbolize the "high and low" vision of the Jews, and that he delights in deformity insofar as it enables him to accept their vanity, their deformity, their heritage.

Maloff, Saul. "The End of Life." Rev. of *The Last Jew in America. New York Times Book Review* 31 July 1966: 4.

Describes *The Last Jew in America* as a book which for all its raucous hijinks and working out of Fiedler's critical theories, nevertheless fades into gimmickry and anecdote. Claims that the pathos in the end becomes hysterical, and that the inept clowning reveals the author's uncertainties. Concludes that, wound up to breaking point, the scenes finally run down.

Mayne, Richard. "Out of the Ruck." Rev. of *The Second Stone: A Love Story. New Statesman* 18 Mar. 1966: 388-90.

Concludes that *The Second Stone* is clearly a young man's book with a wildly comic but authentic background. Describes themes, characters, and setting.

"The Nasty Story." Rev. of *Pull Down Vanity and Other Stories. Time* 11 May 1962: 93.

Claims that this is a modish collection of tales constituting a sort of kitsch fiction in which every character and experience is as nasty as possible. Concludes that they are masterpieces of fictional illness. Details several of the stories.

Nott, Kathleen. "Books and Writers." Rev. of *Pull Down Vanity and Other Stories. Encounter* June 1963: 81-82.

Considers the stories in this collection to be about writers, artists, layabouts and the spiritually displaced, anti-Semitism, and thirtyish leftism as well as drink and behavioristic sex with a background of the century's ideological worries as they hit writers.

Novick, Julius. "The Week in Fiction." Rev. of *Pull Down Vanity and Other Stories. New York Herald Tribune Books* 6 May 1962: 6.

Argues that this story collection deals with what it means to be a Jew, an intellectual, and an ex-Marxist in mid-century America. Claims that for the first few stories this self-pity is out of control, self-indulgent, and engulfing. Notes that subsequent stories are full of brilliant wise-guyisms and lively situations. Concludes that Fiedler is clearly capable of widely differing kinds of excellence.

Oates, Joyce Carol. "The Search For a Sense of Self." Rev. of *Nude Croquet. New York Herald Tribune Book World* 26 Oct 1969: 4.

Describes Fiedler's collection of short stories, *Nude Croquet,* as a book which shows concern for personality, faith, artistic ideals, and genuine companionable love. Concludes that when Fiedler is deeply committed to his subject, he is brilliant.

"Oh Wasp Where Is Thy Sting." Rev. of *The Second Stone: A Love Story. Times Literary Supplement* 24 Mar. 1966: 237.

Calls *The Second Stone* the novel which illustrates the central thesis of *Love and Death in the American Novel* because it illustrates the inability of the American novelist to portray maturely heterosexual relationships. Provides elaborate plot summary.

Phelps, Robert. "Wanted: More Passion at the Love Congress." Rev. of *The Second Stone: A Love Story. New York Herald Tribune Books* 14 Apr. 1963: 7.

Sees *The Second Stone* as conscientiously clever, and three books instead of one. Comments that its treatment of sexual love is rendered with complexity if not brilliance.

Poore, Charles. "Leslie Fiedler's Portrait of a Modern Picaro." Rev. of *Back to China. New York Times* 27 Apr. 1965: 35.

Calls *Back To China* absorbing and illuminating reading as a commentary on the times. Provides a detailed description of Baro, the central protagonist, and of the pictographic character of the pages themselves.

"Pratfall Power." Rev. of *Back to China. Newsweek* 10 May 1965: 125-26.

Describes the contents and characters, and concludes that Fiedler hasn't been able to make the narrative time-present and time-past a single, coherent tale. Calls even the best episodes only clever, not significant.

Price, Martin. "New Books in Review." Rev. of *The Second Stone: A Love Story. Yale Review* 52.4 (1963): 604-06.

Calls this a love story full of argument, snarl, and refutation. Notes that all the changes are rung on the problem of identity and on political ideology. Suggests that the novel insists on the physicality of love, the dark crypts below luminous churches, excrement as the mansion of love, comic routines, satire, and characters who belabor each other with noisy insults.

Richler, Mordecai. "Huckleberry Finklestone." Rev. of *Back to China. New York Herald Tribune Book Week* 16 May 1965: 5.

Calls *Back to China* a fiction charged with malicious invention, cynicism, dazzle, and humor. Says Fiedler plays clownishly on his Jewish harp and again attacks the WASP community. Describes major characters and some of the incidents.

Stade, George. "A Book by and a Talk with Leslie Fiedler." Rev. of *Freaks. New York Times Book Review* 5 Mar. 1978: 9, 37.

Discusses the characters and subject matter of the book as mytho-history. Sees it as the culmination of his earlier novels. Argues that Fiedler utilizes the characters of freaks as a metaphor for the fragile boundaries of sanity and identity we all cling to. Concludes that, unfortunately, this is not the great book Fiedler has seemed from time to time to have in him.

Sterne, Richard Clarke. "Pick of the Paperbacks." Rev. of *Nude Croquet. Saturday Review* 27 Dec. 1969: 34-35.

Considers *Nude Croquet* an uneven collection of stories reflecting a lively mind. Details the politics of Fiedler's career, and provides insight into the contents of the stories.

Taubman, Robert. "Farewell to Moonstone." Rev. of *Pull Down Vanity and Other Stories. New Statesman* 1 Mar. 1963: 311-12.

Calls Fiedler a student of the humiliation of Jews, Blacks, and homosexuals who goes in for perverse exaggeration. Claims that *Pull Down Vanity* is a collection of stories about Fiedler's acting out as anti-institutional heavy.

"Three-Card Trick." Rev. of *The Last Jew in America. Time* 19 Aug. 1966: 80.

Describes the novel in detail along with its treatment of Jews, Blacks, minorities, and dissidents and deviates. Also describes its style, humor, and politics.

Tucker, Martin. "Books." Rev. of *Back to China. Commonweal* 11 June 1965: 387-88.

Identifies the central theme as revenge and the style as undigested. Argues that there is no compelling structure in the novel, merely literariness and autobiography. Concludes that while the novel attempts a large view of society and is not afraid to reveal its author's feelings, Fiedler grasps for the heavens and stumbles.

"Virtuoso Trick." Rev. of *The Last Jew in America. Newsweek* 15 Aug. 1966: 89-90.

Describes the three novelettes in this collection as stories of outsiders brought together with Everybody Else by a ritual and a ceremonial event. Briefly describes the stories and the main character of each.

Yardley, Jonathan. "Recent, Notable Fiction." Rev. of *The Messenger Will Come No More. New Republic* 9 Nov. 1974: 42-44.

Denounces the book as a dull piece which is neither fiction nor polemic.

Interviews

DeMott, Benjamin. "A Book by and a Talk with Leslie Fiedler." *New York Times Book Review* 5 Mar. 1978: 9, 36.

Discusses his reactions to the 60s, his admiration of young people seeking vulgarity, his lack of a childhood during the depression, his novel *The Freaks*, his use of the sci-fi genre, a new work he is writing on popular literature, and his dislike of formalism.

Feinstein, Herbert. "Contemporary American Fiction: Harvey Swados and Leslie Fiedler." *Wisconsin Studies in Contemporary Literature* 2.1 (1961): 88-98.

Discusses the meaning of his book title borrowed from Melville, *No! In Thunder*; the relative importance of the novels of Henry Roth and Nathanael West from the thirties; the social conditions of the thirties and their impact on Roth, West, Farrell, and Dos Passos; the reasons for the large audience among non-Jews for Jewish fiction and interest in Jewish life in America; and the difference in appeal to readers of Uris and Philip Roth.

Green, Geoffrey. "Reestablishing Innocence: A Conversation with Leslie Fiedler." *Genre* 14.1 (1981): 133-49. Rpt. in *Novel vs. Fiction: The Contemporary Reformation.* Eds. Jackson I. Cope and Geoffrey Green. Norman: Pilgrim, 1981. 133-49.

In this interview Fiedler discusses: his work as critic and writer of fiction, the nature of fiction in the recent contemporary period, his values as a critic, his early works, what happens when writers use myth in secondary kinds of ways, his views on Lawrence, the subject of innocent reading and innocent writing, the influence of Freud, his views on Gaddis, and his general attitudes towards self-conscious writers and their works.

Kannan, Lakshmi. "The Contemporary Jewish-American Writer: A Conversation with Leslie A. Fiedler." *Indian Journal of American Studies* 5.1-2 (1975): 76-81.

Discusses the audience of contemporary minority writers, the issue of ethnic self-hatred, Jewish writers as spokesmen for America, the WASP middle-class glorification of Jews after Hitler, the Jewish sacramentalizing of the everyday, Jewish suffering, and the disappearance of any one school of criticism in American colleges.

Masilamoni, E. H. Leelavathi. "The Fiction of Jewish Americans: An Interview with Leslie Fiedler." *Southwest Review* 64.1 (1979): 44-59.

Discusses in this extensive interview: the Jewish and American sense of alienation, the attempt to regain Jewish identity, Jewish leadership in cultural life in America, issues of marginality, the Jew as writer in America, his mixed views on Bellow and Malamud, his praise of Cahan, the demise of the art novel, science fiction as a form of religious literature, comments on *The Freaks*, and the androgyne character in classical and contemporary literature.

Whalen, Patricia. "An Interview with Leslie Fiedler." *Northwest Review* 9.3 (1968): 67-73.

Discusses Fiedler's arrest on charges of possession of marijuana; the effects of his lectures in London and Amsterdam; the state of academic freedom in England; England as a dead literary scene; his views on American Indian culture; his wish to close racial, gender, and age gaps; and his views on crossing between worlds.

Biographical Sources

Gates, David. "Fiedler's Utopian Vision." *Newsweek* 9 Jan. 1984: 11.

A brief biographical sketch and tribute to Fiedler as of 1984.

Meras, Phyllis. "The Author." *Saturday Review* 30 July 1966: 32.

A brief biographical sketch, a view of his home life, and a report of conversation with Fiedler about his new book, *The Last Jew in America*.

Whitfield, Stephen J. "Leslie Fiedler." *Twentieth-Century American-Jewish Fiction Writers*. Ed. Daniel Walden. Detroit: Gale, 1984. Vol. 28 of *Dictionary of Literary Biography*. 94 vols. to date. 1978- . 64-69.

More than details of his life, this is a career biography tracing the development of the author's canon, describing the contents and themes of his works, evaluating his reputation, and placing him in the larger context of American literary history. Includes a list of primary sources and illustrations.

Dissertations

Woolf, M. P. "A Complex Fate: Jewish-American Experience in the Fiction of Leslie Fiedler, Edward Wallant, Chaim Potok and Jerome Charyn." Diss. U of Hull, 1981.

Waldo Frank

1889 – 1967

Primary Sources

Novels

The Bridegroom Cometh. London: Gollancz, 1938; New York: Doubleday, 1939.

Chalk Face. New York: Boni, 1924.

City Block. Darien: Frank, 1922; New York: Scribner, 1932.

The Dark Mother. New York: Boni, 1920; New York: AMS, d. not available.

The Death and Birth of David Markand; An American Story. New York: Scribner, 1934; Series in American Studies. New York: Johnson Reprint, 1971.

Holiday. New York: Boni, 1923.

The Invaders. New York: Duell, 1948.

Island in the Atlantic. New York: Duell, 1946; Westport: Greenwood, 1970.

Not Heaven; a Novel in the Form of Prelude, Variations, and Theme.
New York: Hermitage, 1953.

Rahab. New York: Boni, 1922.

Summer Never Ends, a Modern Love Story. New York: Duell, 1941.

The Unwelcome Man. Boston: Little, 1917; New York: Boni, 1923.

Short Fiction in Anthologies

"Bread Crumbs." *Creating the Short Story.* Ed. Henry Goodman. New
York: Harcourt, 1929. 457-75.

"The Fruit of Misadventure." *The Smart Set Anthology.* Eds. Burton
Rascoe and Groff Conklin. New York: Reynal, 1934. 353-77.

"John the Baptist." *The Best Short Stories of 1922.* Ed. Edward J.
O'Brien. Boston: Small, 1922. 132-50.

"Under the Dome." *The Best Short Stories of 1921.* Ed. Edward J.
O'Brien. Boston: Small, 1922. 130-41; *Yisroel, the First Jewish
Omnibus.* Ed. Joseph Leftwich. London: Heritage, 1933. 267-78; Rev.
ed. London: Clarke, 1945. 214-23; Rev. ed. New York: Beechhurst,
1952. 214-23; Rev. ed. New York: Yoseloff, 1963. 162-71. (Clarke
ed. titled *Yisroel: The Jewish Omnibus*); *The Jewish Caravan: Great
Stories of 25 Centuries.* Ed. Leo W. Schwarz. New York: Farrar,
1935; Philadelphia: Jewish Pub. Soc. of America, 1935. 613-21.

Short Fiction in Periodicals

"John the Baptist." *Dial* Sept. 1922: 312-28.

"A Place to Lay One's Head." *Esquire* Jan. 1935: 35, 99.

"Stepan and Natasha." *Esquire* June 1937: 80, 158.

"Under the Dome." *Dial* Oct. 1920: 329-40.

Secondary Sources

Books

Bittner, William. *The Novels of Waldo Frank*. Philadelphia: U of Pennsylvania P, 1958. Publication of his doctoral dissertation, U of Pennsylvania, 1955.

Carter, Paul J. *Waldo Frank*. Twayne's United States Authors Series 125. New York: Twayne, 1967.

Munson, Gorham Best. *Waldo Frank: A Study*. New York: Boni, 1923. Rpt. Norwood: Norwood, 1975; Folcroft: Folcroft, 1975; Philadelphia: R. West, 1977.

Perry, Robert L. *The Shared Vision of Waldo Frank and Hart Crane*. University of Nebraska Studies, ns 33. Lincoln: U of Nebraska P, 1966.

This four-chapter monograph develops in great detail the nature of Waldo Frank's influence on Hart Crane. It covers Frank's career, what body of ideas he represented, and which of those were important to him. In addition, it discusses what part Frank's ideas played in Crane's major work "The Bridge." A major work of biographical criticism.

Articles and Chapters

Baldwin, Charles C. "Waldo Frank." *The Men Who Make Our Novels*. Charles C. Baldwin. New York: Dodd, 1924. 174-79; Essay Index Reprint Series. Freeport: Books for Libraries, 1967. 174-79.

After a series of witticisms about Frank's treatment at the hands of less-than-impressed reviewers, Baldwin commends him for broadening our horizons, revivifying the language, and refusing to be comforted lest still other innocents be slaughtered in our fear of usurpers, in our terror of any change, and our worship of the rights of property.

Beach, Joseph Warren. "Expressionism: Waldo Frank." *Twentieth Century Novel*. Joseph Warren Beach. New York: Appleton, 1932. 495-500.

Calls Frank sympathetic in his insight into soul, capable of imaginative force, and more merciful than most stream-of-consciousness writers.

Provides a detailed analysis of Frank's use of stream-of-consciousness, and other expressionist techniques in *Rahab* and *Holiday*.

Bittner, William. "Waldo Frank as a Jewish Writer." *Chicago Jewish Forum* 15 (1957): 158-62.

Discusses how Frank describes not the assimilation of Jews into American materialism, but of America into a share of the covenant. An overview covering Frank's history, belief in American values, mystical awareness of Jewish inheritance in Judaism, stylistic technique, and accounts of various novels.

Bittner, William. "Waldo Frank as Novelist." *Literary Review* 1.4 (1958): 478-84.

Reviews Frank's early career as one of the literary radicals. Goes on to commend him as a cultural critic of acute perception, and one of the most promising young writers in the country. Discusses individual novels in order of publication.

Chapman, Arnold. "New Pioneers." *The Spanish American Reception of United States Fiction, 1920-1940*. Arnold Chapman. U of California Publications in Modern Philology 77. Berkeley: U of California P, 1966. 57-74.

A major chapter that sees Frank as singing a song of the American self. Primarily discusses the discovery of Frank as a novelist in Spanish America, and the translations of his works.

Cooley, John. "White Writers and the Harlem Renaissance." *The Harlem Renaissance: Revaluations*. Eds. Amritjit Singh, William S. Shiver, and Stanley Brodwin, eds. Critical Studies on Black Life and Culture 17. New York: Garland, 1989. 13-22.

Briefly describes Frank as a writer who found a vitality and earthly wholesomeness in the black homes and communities he visited, which he contrasted with the spiritual depravity of white civilization. Applauds his detached point of view in *Holiday*, arguing that it provides the necessary distance from the attitudes and actions of his black protagonists, a distance he believes rarely occurs for white writers.

Hatcher, Harlan. "Eroticism and the Psychological Novel." *Creating the Modern American Novel*. Harlan Hatcher. New York: Farrar, 1935. 173-79.

Describes Frank as a contemporary of Sherwood Anderson and details the literary climate of the era. Lists each of his novels in turn and categorizes him as a writer inspired by Jung, Adler, and Freud in the use of unconscious and libidinal impulses in his characters. Considers many of his books deficient in art and yet poetic in their way.

Heath, Robert L. "Kenneth Burke's Break with Formalism." *Quarterly Journal of Speech* 70.2 (1984): 132-43.

In this article primarily about the evolution of Burke's search for a new aesthetic, Heath describes the mutual influence and the ensuring correspondence between Frank and Burke. Places Frank in a broad historical and philosophical framework.

Helbling, Mark. "Jean Toomer and Waldo Frank: A Creative Friendship." *Phylon* 41.2 (1980): 167-78.

Describes the initial meeting and subsequent friendship and correspondence between Frank and Toomer. Develops the story of Frank's troubled association with Sherwood Anderson, and then discusses in depth the mutual commentary both men conduct on their own, each other's, and Anderson's work.

Hoffman, Frederick J. "Frank—Critic of Freudianism." *Freudianism and the Literary Mind.* Frederick J. Hoffman. Baton Rouge: Louisiana State UP, 1945. 256-76. 2nd ed. 1957. 250-63; New York: Grove, 1959. 250-63.

Develops the thesis that Waldo Frank's work is dominated by a restless search for organic wholeness. Discusses his view of the sterility of American culture because of its formlessness, imitativeness, and rootlessness. Discusses also Frank's faith in the power of art over science, and his contribution as an American critic. A major article which analyzes Frank's fictional espousal and ultimate critique of Freudianism.

Jocelyn, John. "Getting at Waldo Frank." *Sewanee Review* 40.4 (1932): 405-14.

Analyzes Frank's mode and characteristic uses of it throughout both critical essays and fiction. Describes him by turns as expressionistic, picaresque, poetic, lyrical, and obsessed with human betterment.

Karier, Clarence J. "Margaret Naumberg and Waldo Frank: Art in a Therapeutic Age." *Scientists of the Mind: Intellectual Founders of*

Modern Psychology. Clarence J. Karier. Urbana: U of Illinois P, 1986. 283-310.

Describes the era in which Frank emerges as a writer, his developing career, major works, life in Greenwich Village, and emergent political values. Mostly a discussion of modernism and Frank's role as a modernist writer.

Munson, Gorham. "Herald of the Twenties." *Forum* [Huston] 3.7 (1961): 4-14. Rpt. as "Waldo Frank—Herald of the Twenties" in *The Awakening Twenties: A Memoir-History of a Literary Period*. Gorham Munson. Baton Rouge: Louisiana State UP, 1985. 54-69.

Discusses the young writers of the 1920s, and then proceeds to detail Frank's life and contributions as critic and writer. Pays tribute to him primarily as an *avant-garde* courier for new aesthetic and intellectual values. Spends considerable time discussing the merits of Frank as the editor of *Seven Arts Reader*.

Nilsen, Helge. "Crane and Frank: Images of America." *Hart Crane Newsletter* 1.1 (1977): 36-42.

Discusses individual works of both Crane and Frank, who, Nilsen argues, shared the idea that the real America is a state of mind, a revelation in the eyes of the beholder.

Nilsen, Helge Norman. "The Status of Waldo Frank in American Letters." *American Studies in Scandinavia* 12.1-2 (1980): 27-32.

Comments that Frank is now a neglected figure in American letters with most of his books out of print. Argues that those parts of his work which remain significant and must not be neglected are his mystical and metaphysical approaches to American culture. Mostly describes Frank's unique image of America.

Rosenfeld, Paul. "Waldo Frank." *Men Seen: Twenty-Four Modern Authors*. New York: Dial, 1925. 89-109.

Considers Frank's literary gift vigorous, and argues that he should be considered among the inventors of English prose. A lengthy treatment of Frank's prose and individual novels.

West, Thomas Reed. "Waldo Frank, The Machine in Cultural Ferment." *Flesh of Steel: Literature and the Machine in American Culture*. Thomas Reed West. Nashville: Vanderbilt UP, 1967. 35-53.

Considers Frank's work to represent twentieth-century American literature at its most experimental: eager in artistic innovation and in the
assimilation of modern intellect. A biographical and literary critique of
Frank's influence on other writers, his view of American culture, and his
understanding of the theory of literature. Discusses his individual work
in passing.

Willingham, John R. "The Achievement of Waldo Frank." *Literary
Review* 1.4 (1958): 465-77.

Reviews the early promise of Franks's career and reputation. Traces his
style and the influences upon him. Delineates the cultural milieu out of
which he came, and which develops, without him. Calls him the most
Whitmanesque of the 1920s critics, and describes the major influence of
The Seven Arts on the careers of several other writers. Pays tribute to the
many intellectual movements which interested him, and finds reflected in
his writing, expressionism, naturalism, poetic realism, liberalism, communism, socialism and Marxism. An important tribute.

Reviews

Abel, Lionel. "Mr. Frank's Seriousness." Rev. of *Death and Birth of
David Markand. Nation* 7 Nov. 1934: 542-43.

Sees *Death and Birth of David Markand* as undramatic and, despite its
effective characterization, imprecise in its language. Provides a detailed
account of the contents of the novel.

Boynton, H. W. "Two Ways of Singing." Rev. of *Rahab. The
Independent and the Weekly Review* 25 Mar. 1922: 314-16.

Describes Frank as a virtuoso exceptional in his use of English, taxing to
the reader, and possibly self-conscious and artificial. Claims that there is
too much excitable straining for effect and not enough large creative
impulse.

Brooks, Van Wyck. "An American Oblomov." Rev. of *The Unwelcome
Man. Dial* 22 Mar 1917: 244-45.

Discusses *The Unwelcome Man* as a study of character types rather
unwelcome to American readers. Sees this as an interesting book rather
than an artistic one. Claims that the human material is not sufficiently
thrown into relief, and that sometimes we are too close to the central
character to be able to see him clearly.

Bullock, Florence Haxton. "New Novels of Trouble North and South."
Rev. of *Summer Never Ends*. *New York Herald Tribune Books* 24
Aug. 1941: 8.

Sees *Summer Never Ends* as a neatly conceived, smartly written idyll-in-
reserve. Describes the contents, and complains that the book leaves a
slight sediment of distaste in the mouth because the narrative pretends to
have an importance and a seriousness it fails to achieve. Concludes that
it is a disturbing, intensely interesting book.

Burke, Kenneth. "The Consequences of Idealism." Rev. of *Rahab* and
City Block. *Dial* Oct. 1922: 449-52.

Discusses both *Rahab* and *City Block*. Comments on the eager, pulsing
universe emerging from Frank's poetic aesthetics. Comments that, while
many passages are thick with beauty, the books finally lack that cold-carv-
ing, bloodless autopsy of the emotions which allows a Mallarme so near an
approach to perfection. Concludes that Frank has done a marvelous job in
fighting against the inhibitory baggage which American art has to lug.

Chapman, Emmanuel. "Books of the Day." Rev. of *The Bridegroom
Cometh*. *Commonweal* 19 May 1939: 107-08.

Claims that *The Bridegroom Cometh* presents a definitive advance over
his previous fiction. Argues that the characters live with more intense life,
the action goes deeper, the prose is more richly orchestrated, and the elements are fused into a more organic whole. Provides a detailed
description of contents, and decides this book has rich philosophical
implications.

Cowley, Malcolm. "Pilgrim's Progress." Rev. of *The Death and Birth of
David Markand*. *New Republic* 17 Oct. 1934: 279-80.

Provides a detailed account of the background, characters, and contents
of *The Death and Birth of David Markand*. Comments that Frank is a
proud writer still trying to fit new materials into an old structure.
Concludes that he is trying to make a working agreement between mysticism and reality, between Spinoza and Marx, between *Pilgrim's
Progress* and the proletariat, but that the two sides won't be reconciled.

Davidson, Donald. "Reviews." Rev. of *Death and Birth of David
Markand*. *American Review* Dec. 1934: 233-38.

Describes the novel in detail. Believes Frank should perhaps have written this piece in poetry, since he does poorly with actual reality. Claims

that as it stands, the novel invites too obviously the scrutiny that fictional argument must undergo, and the poetry of it gets neglected.

Douglas, A. Donald. "Waldo Frank—Poet." Rev. of *Chalk Face*. *Saturday Review of Literature* 1 Nov. 1924: 244.

Sees *Chalk Face* as a book by a man who is not a novelist, but who is a poet of phantasmal imitations and torment of spirit.

Fields, Eugene. "Current Books." Rev. of *Island in the Atlantic*. *Congress Weekly* 20 Dec. 1946: 13.

Comments that *Island in the Atlantic* is about the early days of New York from the Civil War to the beginning of World War I, but that, unfortunately, the book does not reach deep enough. Complains that, for all of its often brilliant writing, it has weak reflections and obvious symbolism. Concludes that Frank's gestures toward affirmation are vain, as he allows Jonathan's ship to sink to the bottom of the Atlantic.

Fuller, Edmund. "Crisis at 'Land's End.'" Rev. of *The Invaders*. *Saturday Review of Literature* 12 June 1948: 27.

Calls this a novel about the use of the atom bomb. Describes plot and characters, and dismisses the general effect as half-baked. Concludes that the novel is a hodge podge that fails its thesis, resulting in something that does not even add up to being a good borscht.

"Gibberish." Rev. of *Chalk Face*. *New York Times Book Review* 12 Oct. 1924: 16.

Calls *Chalk Face* a mystery story woven of Poe-like materials of the grotesque and the arabesque. Comments that the story is weird, phantasmagorical, symbolical, and profound.

Jack, Peter Monro. "*The Bridegroom Cometh* and Other Recent Works of Fiction." Rev. of *The Bridegroom Cometh*. *New York Times Book Review* 21 May 1939: 6.

Sees *The Bridegroom Cometh* as long enough to be wearisome in its symbolism, mysticism, and psychological contradictions, not to mention its lack of clarity. Suggests that perhaps it is no novel at all, but a research into the author's creative consciousness and philosophic feeling. Details the contents.

Jones, Bess. "Frank..." Rev. of *Summer Never Ends*. *Saturday Review of Literature* 13 Sept. 1941: 19.

Sees this novel as essentially adolescent in its subject matter. Describes plot and character, and concludes that immature characterization, wooden dialogue, ironic themes, and atrocious style mar this book.

Lasker, Bruno. "Doors Opened Southward." Rev. of *Holiday*. *Survey* 1 Nov. 1923: 190-91.

Calls this novel capable of penetrating right to the heart of race relations issues in the South, and doing so with striking artistic effect. A cogent critical essay dealing with style, characterization, plot, description, and sociology.

"Latest Fiction." Rev. of *Rahab*. *New York Times Book Review* 23 Apr. 1922: 14, 16.

Considers Frank influenced by ultra modern theories of writing in *Rahab* because clear, continuous narrative has been replaced by kaleidoscopic events. Notes that, in addition, the prose does not tell a story as much as it lays bare a soul. Complains that Frank is not a fully mature thinker, although he does have a sharp visual sense and feeling for spiritual strife. Calls his style bizarre, freakish, and straining after effects.

"Latest Works of Fiction." Rev. of *The Dark Mother*. *New York Times Book Review* 21 Nov. 1920: 22.

Suggests that *The Dark Mother* is propaganda masquerading in the guise of a novel. Calls this kind of dangerous sophistry insidious, especially when coming from an eloquent writer who is the unconscious victim of unsound thinking. Details the contents of the book. Praises Frank for his powers of characterization and galaxy of types. Criticizes the talky chapters and Frank's mannered artifices in sentences ending in a string of dots.

"Latest Works of Fiction." Rev. of *Holiday*. *New York Times Book Review* 16 Dec. 1923: 6.

Calls *Holiday* an unoriginal story written in a perverse prose poem in which Nazareth, a perverse southern town, is critiqued throughout the story of a young white woman luring a Negro to his death.

Lee, Lawrence. "Good Man." Rev. of *The Invaders*. *New York Times Book Review* 23 May 1948: 5, 31.

Discusses the importance of Frank's recent themes, and then describes *The Invaders* in terms of plot, generating circumstance, characters, and settings. Concludes that, though the concept of the novel is admirable, its moral methods are never quite clear.

"Latest Works of Fiction." Rev. of *The Unwelcome Man. New York Times Book Review* 11 Mar. 1917: 89.

Calls this a novel related in minutely detailed analysis of mental and emotional states. Claims that the people are almost never allowed to speak for themselves. Concludes that some of the best scenes are of great natural beauty. Details contents.

Lee, Lawrence. "Materialism and the American Ideal." Rev. of *Island in the Atlantic. New York Times Book Review* 8 Sept. 1946: 4.

Considers *Island in the Atlantic* a warning about the spiritual foundations of America and their conditions now. Describes the setting and contents of the novel and its ponderous symbolism. Concludes that, though this book is admirably researched, it fails to quite come to life. Wonders if Frank himself has lost his faith in America and come upon nihilism.

Littell, Robert. "Waldo Frank." Rev. of *Holiday* and *City Block. New Republic* 26 Sept. 1923: 12, 14.

Claims that *City Block* is a book in which Frank has produced synthetic rather than genuine springs of life. Shows how many of its stories sound repetitive and the material half congealed. Commends Frank for his sincerity, and comments that it is not enough to portray the mainspring of the watch without including all its little cogs and wheels as well.

Marsh, Fred T. "A Quest of a Modern American Ulysses." Rev. of *The Death and Birth of David Markand. New York Herald Tribune Books* 7 Oct. 1934: 5.

Considers *The Death and Birth of David Markand* a prodigious, generational chronicle. Comments that faults of taste and style are lost in the vastness of the project and its overwhelming power, passion, purpose, and insight. Details the contents of the novel, and describes its hero at length.

McLaughlin, Richard. Rev. of *Island in the Atlantic. Commonweal* 4 Oct. 1946: 600-01.

Calls *Island in the Atlantic* a book searching for an audience in a sick world. Describes Frank as a mystic, much beleaguered and living through angry times. Views him as a modern Bunyan who loves mankind.

"A Modern Odyssey." Rev. of *The Death and Birth of David Markand. New York Times Book Review* 21 Oct. 1934: 7, 19.

Claims that *The Death and Birth of David Markand* is of dubious intellectual clarity, lacking objectivity and failing to fully develop its theme
in any satisfactory way because much of the character motivation is
unaccountable. Concludes that the book bears little relation to life.

Mumford, Lewis. "Rahab." Rev. of *Rahab. New Republic* 16 Aug. 1922:
    339-40.

Considers the materials in this novel as stale as David's adultery; nevertheless, the smell of spring pervades Frank's treatment. Believes he does
not succeed in working out all the complexities of his novel, and that
many passages seem murky and incomplete. Concludes, however, that
when he succeeds he succeeds magnificently.

Nerber, John. "Ultimate Verities." Rev. of *Not Heaven, a Novel in the
    Form of Prelude, Variations, and Themes. New York Times Book
    Review* 24 May 1953: 25.

Sees *Not Heaven* as a group of short stories forming a thematic development of an increasingly complex spiritual crisis and its final, triumphant
resolution. Insists these are beautifully written and totally absorbing stories.

Pitts, Rebecca. "The Trimmed Lamp." Rev. of *The Bridegroom Cometh.
    New Republic* 21 June 1939: 193.

Describes *The Bridegroom Cometh* as extraordinarily rich in its portrait
of America from 1914-1924. Calls this a wise book written out of a deep
sense of urgency, and a cry of life written in an authentic manner despite
problems of rhythm, pace, and phrasing.

Redman, Ben Ray. "The Guilty Generation." Rev. of *Island in the
    Atlantic. Saturday Review of Literature* 21 Sept. 1946: 18.

Identifies the novel's central metaphysical concerns as fundamentals and
universals. Calls the style difficult, and concludes that the appeal will
definitely not be to facile readers.

Redman, Ben Ray. "Progress of an Innocent." Rev. of *The Bridegroom
    Cometh. Saturday Review of Literature* 20 May 1939: 6.

Claims that realism and a kind of mysticism inform this novel as surely
as they inform Dostoyevsky's *The Idiot.* Argues, however, that as the
increasing frequency of acute observation and sound psychology yield to
mystical yearnings and vague raptures, the sure writing grows torrid with

the swelling and involvement of the thought. Concludes that it is, never-theless, a vastly interesting book.

Rolo, Charles J. "A-bomb on America." Rev. of *The Invaders. Atlantic Monthly* June 1948: 114, 116.

Asserts that *The Invaders* has serious blemishes. Complains that the writ-ing is flecked with sententiousness with parts of it demonstrating a droll pomposity. Calls its whole *mise en scene* awkwardly contrived. Concludes, however, that the destructive climax manages an awesome intensity. Details contents and theme. Insists this book is a serious and worthwhile read.

Rosenberg, Harold. "Continent in the Sky." Rev. of *Island in the Atlantic. Commentary* Dec. 1946: 595-96.

Comments that *Island in the Atlantic* is a novel about rediscovering America. Asks the question, "What fullness of life has been created?" Traces American life from the start of industrial building. Claims that Frank finds Americans discontented to the point of despair and violence. Sees it as a savage attack on America's immediate past, and labels its mood as one of unfulfilled yearning. A lengthy essay on the central char-acters of the novel and its stylistic effects.

Rosenfeld, Paul. "The Novels of Waldo Frank." Rev. of *The Dark Mother. Dial* Jan. 1921: 95-105.

A general approach to Frank's novels claiming the immense narrative power of Frank is still intimate rather than revealed. Calls it tangled, une-ducated, and unchanneled. Also discusses his expressionistic methods in the portrayal of the "dark mother" in his novels.

Rosenfeld, Paul. "Waldo Frank's Dream." Rev. of *The Bridegroom Cometh. Nation* 20 May 1939: 590.

Sees *The Bridegroom Cometh* as his most objective, mature, and interest-ing book so far. Comments that Frank is often gifted, vigorous, and immensely thoughtful. Concludes that the vision to be inward and com-prehensive. Details the contents.

Ross, Mary. "Emotional Patterns." Rev. of *The Bridegroom Cometh. New York Herald Tribune Books* 21 May 1939: 5.

Argues that *The Bridegroom Cometh* is not a novel of ideas in the intel-lectual sense. Refuses to see it as a novel of propaganda, though it is about characters who have ideas and who live by dogmas. Concludes that it is, instead, an ambitious novel which attempts to trace the story of a young girl who learns truth is not to be feared.

Ross, Mary. "Three New York Generations." Rev. of *Island in the Atlantic. New York Herald Tribune Weekly Book Review* 15 Sept. 1946: 6.

Describes the novel in detail, and lauds it as a book on a grand scale, rich in events, people, atmosphere, and immediacy. Concludes that this is an honest, thoughtful, and carefully researched book.

Rothman, N. L. "A Novel of Ideas." Rev. of *The Death and Birth of David Markand. Saturday Review of Literature* 10 Nov. 1934: 277.

Calls Frank a social philosopher and *The Death and Birth of David Markand* a portrait of pre-war America that attempts to reveal all the seeds of disorder. Sees it as a vigorous and ambitious book whose structural weaknesses defeat its purposes. Considers the materials ill-handled and distorted by the very fire of his vision. He is also seen to be lacking as a historian.

Strauss, Harold. "Waldo Frank's Modern Love Story." Rev. of *Summer Never Ends. New York Times Book Review* 24 Aug. 1941: 4, 21.

Suggests that *Summer Never Ends* is a modern love story written with intensity and emotion. Notes that, unfortunately, Frank has hoisted himself, intellectual armor and all, upon the charge of idealism and ridden off to crusade against cynics, materialists, and positivists. Concludes that he also has a difficult time disentangling love from lust, and that, finally, the whole thing reads like a stifled scream.

Toomer, Jean. "Waldo Frank's Holiday." Rev. of *Holiday. Dial* Oct. 1923: 383-86.

Discusses *Holiday* from the perspective of Frank's attitudes towards race, human repression, Southern history, and white attitudes towards Negroes. Mostly a laudatory review which also reveals breaks in the texture of the novel, problems with the dialogue, and problems of clarity. Concludes that this, however, does not impair the solid, tight structural and artistic finish of the novel.

Van de Water, Frederic F. "Books and So Forth." Rev. of *Holiday. New York Tribune* 19 Aug. 1923: 19.

Comments quite unsympathetically that *Holiday* possesses a power and vigor incompletely harnessed. Complains about Frank's misuse of verbs and adjectives, the distorted subjects and predicates, and sloppy workmanship. Argues sarcastically that the book is either lazily written or representative of an artistic insurrection. Concludes finally that for all its incomprehensibility, it appears to be a "jolly disquisition" on the Negro problem with sadism and masochism thrown in for good measure, along with the statutory lynching and attempted rape.

Webster, Harvey Curtis. "Frank's Fine Novel." Rev. of *Not Heaven, a Novel in the Form of Prelude, Variations, and Theme. New Republic* 29 June 1953: 21-22.

Calls *Not Heaven* as good a book as there is on the human condition since the end of WWII. Suggests that perhaps it is one of the best works of fiction in this century. Comments mainly on the profound prophecy of disaster contained in the book.

Weiss, Carol H. "Variations." Rev. of *Not Heaven, a Novel in the Form of Prelude, Variations and Theme. Commonweal* 3 July 1953: 327-28.

Describes *Not Heaven* as more like a collection of stories than a novel. Notes that its episodes are emotionally powerful, and that its author has a predilection for the eccentric. Concludes that Frank evidently regards religion as an externalization since none of the characters turns to religion for understanding.

Young, Stark. Rev. of *The Dark Mother. New Republic* 29 Dec. 1920: 150.

Claims that *The Dark Mother* takes nature as its theme, ultimately assuming the character of Demeter, the ancient mother of Greek poetry, as life darkens to a kind of Freudian Black Mammy. Calls this a courageous but willful book—sincere but not important. Concludes that it lacks power and reality for all that it introduces us to the idea that there are vast areas of our life literature is yet to address.

Biographical Sources

Adams, Mildred. "Waldo Frank: Sage and Simpleton." *Review* (Spr. 1974): 53-59.

Describes Frank as a literate and valuable New Yorker of great mental energy who has been a journalist, editor, and commentator on North American values. Describes his works, politics, background, personal qualities, experiences in South America and Spain, his numerous love affairs, his trip to Cuba with Hart Crane, and visits to Russia, Bolivia, Peru, Chile, and Venezuela. Also comments on his involvement during the McCarthy years and the publication of *Memoirs.*

Brooks, Van Wyck. *An Autobiography.* New York: Dutton, 1965. 274-83.

Mostly a historical and biographical account of Frank's European background, sojourn in France, and subsequent discovery of his own Americanness. Discusses several of his novels.

Duke, David C. "Waldo Frank: Egoism, Activism, and the Dream of American Unity." *Distant Obligations: Modern American Writers and Foreign Causes.* New York: Oxford UP, 1983. 198-227.

Comments on Frank's life and literary reputation in the U.S. and South America. Describes his privileged childhood in a cultivated, intellectual home, his early reading, academic career, life as a reporter, writing experience in Paris, life in Greenwich Village, marriage, trips to Latin America, politics, sojourn in Spain, return to Latin America in 1942, experiences in Argentina, neglect in America, his egoism, and commitment to political visions.

Toman, Susan F. "Rediscovering Waldo Frank." *Americas* May 1973: 17-24.

Describes his long South American lecture tour, and his influence on Latin American writers for whom he became a major prophet. Primarily a pictorial essay on Frank combining biographical commentary, literary critique, and reminiscence.

Trachtenberg, Alan, ed. *Memoirs of Waldo Frank.* Amherst: U of Massachusetts P, 1973.

Dissertations

Cook, Stephan Harvey. ""No Place for Paragraphs": The Correspondence Between Hart Crane and Waldo Frank." Diss. Marquette U, 1978.

Gordon, Nicholas Karl. "Jewish and American: A Critical Study of the Fiction of Abraham Cahan, Anzia Yezierska, Waldo Frank, and Ludwig Lewisohn." Diss. Stanford U, 1968.

Kloucek, Jerome W. "Waldo Frank: The Ground of His Mind and Art." Diss. Northwestern U, 1958.

Miller, Peter Douglas. "The Rediscovery of Waldo Frank." Diss. U of California, Irvine, 1977.

Sacks, Claire. "The *Seven Arts* Critics: A Study of Cultural Nationalism in America, 1910-1930." Diss. U of Wisconsin, 1955.

Bruce Jay Friedman

1930 –

Primary Sources

Novels

About Harry Towns. New York: Knopf, 1974; New York: Bantam, 1974, 1976; London: Cape, 1975; New York: Atlantic, 1990.

The Current Climate. New York: Atlantic, 1989.

The Dick. New York: Knopf, 1970; London: Cape, 1971: New York: Bantam, 1972; Harmondsworth: Penguin, 1973.

A Mother's Kisses. New York: Simon, 1964; London: Cape, 1965; Harmondsworth: Penguin, 1968; New York: Pocket [Cited in PBIP, 1969]; New York: Fine, 1985.

Stern. New York: Simon, 1962, 1966; New York: Signet-NAL, 1963; London: Deutsch, 1963; New York: Clarion-Simon [Cited in PBIP, 1969]; New York: Pocket, 1970; Arbor House Library of Contemporary Americana. New York: Arbor, 1983; New York: Atlantic, 1990.

Tokyo Woes. New York: Fine, 1985; New York: Penguin, 1986; London: Abacus, 1986.

Collected Works

Black Angels. New York: Simon, 1966; London: Cape, 1967; New York: Pocket, 1968.

Contents: Black Angels, The Punch, The Investor, The Operator, Brazzaville Teen-Ager, A Change of Plan, The Interview, Show Biz Connections, The Enemy, The Death Table, The Night Boxing Ended, The Neighbors, The Hero, Let Me See Faces, The Mission, The Humiliation.

Far from the City of Class, and Other Stories. New York: Frommer, 1963; A Pocket Book ed. Richmond Hill: Simon, 1968.

Contents: For Your Viewing Entertainment; Far from the City of Class; When You're Excused You're Excused; The Trip; A Foot in the Door; The Subversive; The Little Ball; Mr. Prinzo's Breakthrough; The Good Time; The Man They Threw Out of Jets; Wonderful Golden Rule Days; The Holiday Celebrators; Yes, We have No Ritchard; The Big Six; The Canning of Mother Dean; 23 Pat O'Brien Movies.

Let's Hear It for a Beautiful Guy. New York: Carroll, 1984, 1985; New York: Fine, 1984.

Contents: The Candide of Copiers, The Tax Man, Detroit Abe, King of the Bloodies, The Scientist, The Adventurer, An Ironic Yetta Montana, The War Criminal, Marching Through Delaware, Living Together, Business Is Business, The Mourner, The Pledges, A Different Ball Game, The Best We Have, The Car Lover, Our Lady of the Lockers, Let's Hear It for a Beautiful Guy.

Stern and A Mother's Kisses. New York: Simon, 1966.

Short Fiction in Anthologies

"The Big Six." *Jewish-American Literature: An Anthology*. Ed. Abraham Chapman. New York: Mentor-NAL, 1974. 109-17.

"Black Angels." *Black Humor*. Ed. Bruce Jay Friedman. New York: Bantam, 1965, 1969; London: Transworld, 1965. 17-22; *Great Esquire Fiction: The Finest Stories from the First Fifty Years*. Ed. L. Rust Hills. New York: Penguin, 1983. 304-09.

"The Blind Side." *All Our Secrets Are the Same: New Fiction from Esquire*. Ed. Gordon Lish. New York: Norton, 1976. 37-42.

"The Enemy." *Stories from the Transatlantic Review*. Ed. Joseph F. McCrindle. New York: Holt, 1970; London: Gollancz, 1970. 202-09; Harmondsworth: Penguin, 1974. 280-89.

"The Man They Threw Out of Jets." *New Sounds in American Fiction*. Ed. Gordon Lish. Menlo Park: Cummings, 1969. 31-40.

"The Punch." *The Discovery of Fiction*. Ed. Thomas E. Saunders. Glenview: Scott, 1967. 587-95.

"When You're Excused You're Excused." *How We Live: Contemporary Life in Contemporary Fiction*. Eds. Penny C. Hills and L. Rust Hills. New York: Macmillan, 1968. 660-69.

Short Fiction in Periodicals

"The Adventurer." *Playboy* Dec. 1981: 175, 284, 286, 288.

"The Antelope Cage." *Playboy* May 1974: 130-32, 170, 172-74, 178, 180, 182, 184.

"Black Angels." *Esquire* Dec. 1964: 133, 276, 278.

"The Blind Side." *Esquire* Jan. 1974: 98-102, 138.

"Brazzaville Teen-Ager." *Esquire* July 1965: 78, 108.

"The Car Lover." *Esquire* June 1968: 120, 138, 144.

"A Change of Plan." *Esquire* Jan. 1966: 96-97, 111-12.

"Detroit Abe." *Esquire* Mar. 1983: 234-39.

"A Different Ball Game." *Esquire* Dec. 1969: 229, 231, 282.

"The Enemy." *Transatlantic Review* 13 (1962): 41-49.

"Far from the City of Class." *Mademoiselle* Apr. 1961: 142-43, 176-82.

"A Foot in the Door." *Playboy* Oct. 1960: 79, 82, 118, 120-21.

"High, Wide, and Handsome." *Esquire* Oct. 1971: 126-27, 170, 172, 174.

"The Interview." *Esquire* July 1964: 62-81.

"The Investor." *Playboy* Feb. 1962: 84-86, 98.

"An Ironic Yetta Montana." *Rolling Stone* 10 Dec. 1981: 31-32, 108.

"Just Back from the Coast." *Harper's* Mar. 1970: 68-70.

"The Killer in the TV Set." *Playboy* Aug. 1961: 59, 68, 104-05.

"Lady." *Esquire* Jan. 1973: 98-101, 153-54, 157.

"Living Together." *Esquire* Dec. 1981: 118-20, 123.

"The Man They Threw Out of Jets." *Antioch Review* 15.3 (1955): 375-84.

"The Mission." *Saturday Evening Post* 7 Mar. 1964: 46-47, 50-51.

"The Partners." *Esquire* Aug. 1969: 72-74.

"Pitched Out." *Esquire* July 1988: 62-68.

"The Pledges." *Esquire* Sept. 1967: 133, 156.

"The Punch." *Esquire* Feb. 1965: 117-19.

"The Scientist." *Esquire* Apr. 1967: 105, 107.

"The Trip." *Commentary* June 1957: 548-52.

"23 Pat O'Brien Movies." *Playboy* Dec. 1960: 81-82, 148.

"Wonderful Golden Rule Days." *New Yorker* 31 Oct. 1953: 108-12.

Secondary Sources

Books

Schulz, Max F. *Bruce Jay Friedman.* Twayne's United States Authors Series 219. New York: Twayne, 1974.

Articles and Chapters

Algren, Nelson. "The Radical Innocent." *Nation* 21 Sept. 1964: 142-43.
Claims that *Stern* is a book about unJewishness, and that Friedman has nothing of the cleverness of Bellow and Roth. Comments that Friedman embodies not tradition but the disorder of the great city. Insists *Stern* has nothing to do with the fall of *The Rise of David Levinsky* and everything to do with the fall of Jack Ruby. Provides a very brief gloss on all the novels. Concludes that Friedman is a compulsive writer whose innocence ultimately makes his flaws of greater value than the perfections of skilled mechanics.

Bellman, Samuel I. "Two More Jewish Storytellers." *Congress Bi-Weekly* 30 Dec. 1963: 12, 17-18.

Argues that the Jewish novel and short story have become excessively familiar genres, often due to the ignoble or trivial position the central figure very frequently occupies in a fictional world dominated by the emotions of humiliation and self-pity. Claims that *Stern* fits into this description all too neatly. Describes *Stern* and *Far from the City of Class* in this light. Concludes that Friedman is "capable of giving us poignant insights into the things that really matter in life."

Berman, Ronald. "*A Mother's Kisses.*" *Survey of Contemporary Literature.* Ed. Frank N. Magill. Rev. ed. 12 vols. Englewood Cliffs: Salem, 1977. 8: 5111-13.

A standard reference article that discusses *A Mother's Kisses* in terms of principal characters, themes, symbolism, contents, style, social commentary, and impact.

"The Black Humorists." *Time* 12 Feb. 1965: 94.

An article describing the work of several black humorists (Purdy, Barth, Heller, Donleavy, etc.). Briefly describes the story line and theme of *Stern*, which makes racial prejudice appallingly funny.

Friedman, Melvin J. "The Schlemiel: Jew and Non-Jew." *Studies in the Literary Imagination* 9.1 (1976): 139-53.

This article contains a brief mention of several Friedman characters, developing the idea that they are all variations on the model of the *schlemiel*.

Gallo, Louis. "Bruce Jay Friedman." *Critical Survey of Short Fiction.* Ed. Frank N. Magill. 8 vols. Englewood Cliffs: Salem, 1981. 4: 1423-28.

A standard reference article covering principal short fiction, other literary forms, influence, story, biography, analysis of *Far from the City of Class and Other Stories.*

Goldman, Albert. "Boy-Man Schlemiel: Jewish Humor." *Commonweal* 29 Sept. 1967: 605-8. Rpt. in an expanded version as "Boy-Man Schlemiel: The Jewish Element in American Humor." in *Explorations: An Annual on Jewish Themes.* Ed. Murray Mindlin. Chicago: Quadrangle, 1968. 3-17.

Discusses Jewish humor, particularly the use of the *schlemiel*, suggesting its use is standard in the novels of Friedman. Useful for background, but does not discuss his novels.

Greenfeld, Josh. "Bruce Jay Friedman is Hanging by His Thumbs." *New York Times Magazine* 14 Jan. 1968: 30-32, 34, 36, 38, 41-42.

A general article on Friedman's life and works, prompted by performance at the New Theater, New York, of his play, *Scuba Duba.* Contains a photographic essay on Friedman.

Guttmann, Allen. "The Black Humorists." *The Jewish Writer in America: Assimilation and the Crisis of Identity.* Allen Guttmann. New York: Oxford UP, 1971. 76-79.

Classes Friedman as a black humorist, and lists his thematic concerns as anti-Semitism, Oedipal conflicts, and adultery. Finds his terminal bravado tedious.

Janoff, Bruce. "Black Humor: Beyond Satire." *Ohio Review* 14.1 (1972): 5-20.

In an article which provides history and definition of the post-war phenomenon of black humor, Janoff identifies the style and effects of Friedman's black humor in several of the novels and stories.

Klein, Marcus. "Further Notes on the Dereliction of Culture: Edward Lewis Wallant and Bruce Jay Friedman." *Contemporary American-Jewish Literature: Critical Essays.* Ed. Irving Malin. Bloomington: UP of Indiana, 1973. 229-47.

Sees both authors as lacking the imaginative will to create imposing fictions, but having the ability to create the shapes of a unitary common knowledge about the age. Provides a detailed description of the contents and tone of the Friedman novel as it reveals the surfaces and emotional substratum of contemporary big city life through its very cliches.

Lewis, Stuart. "Myth and Ritual in the Short Fiction of Bruce Jay Friedman." *Studies in Short Fiction* 10.4 (1973): 415-16.

Claims that Friedman writes stories juxtaposing the world-of-nature myths with our modern technological society through a veiled use of myths associated with vegetation rites. Notes that the result of the juxtaposition is a realization of how we have become alienated from our affinity with the cycle of nature. Concentrates mainly on the short stories in *Black Angels*.

Lewis, Stuart A. "Rootlessness and Alienation in the Novels of Bruce Jay Friedman." *College Language Association Journal* 18.3 (1975): 422-33.

Describes Friedman's novels as quintessentially rootless, the stories of a humorous and pathetic modern existence. Describes a variety of ways in which each of the major protagonists is physically, spiritually, and emotionally rootless and alienated.

Mesher, David R. "Three Men on the Moon: Friedman, Updike, Bellow, and Apollo Eleven." *Research Studies* 47.1 (1979): 67-75.

Discusses the uses of the Apollo Eleven mission in the first part of *About Harry Towns*. Suggests that Friedman rejects the mission with the implication that, if Towns believes in it, there must be something wrong, reflecting problems not only in Harry himself, but in the society about Towns as well.

Peden, William. "A Mad World, My Masters." *The American Short Story: Continuity and Change, 1940-1975*. 2nd ed. Boston: Houghton, 1975. 104-05.

Describes *Far From the City of Class* and *Black Angels* as representative of black humor prevalent in the 1960s. Sees them both exploring the fictional possibilities of the grotesque, the bizarre, the fantastic, and the sick. Comments that, but for the darkly comic, theirs is a literature of juxtaposition, the perverse, and the outrageous. Concludes that Friedman's contribution is to lighten much of this humor and to create a more relaxed style and stripped, economical narrative structure.

Pinsker, Sanford. "*The Dick*." *Survey of Contemporary Literature*. Ed. Frank N. Magill. Rev. ed. 12 vols. Englewood Cliffs: Salem, 1977. 3: 1943-45.

A standard reference account of *The Dick* that covers principal characters, background, settings, themes, style, and impact.

Pinsker, Sanford. "The Graying of Black Humor." *Studies in The Twentieth Century* 9 (Spr. 1972): 15-33. Rpt. in *Between Two Worlds: The American Novel in the 1960s*. Sanford Pinsker. New York: Whitston, 1980. 11-27.

Argues that we find black humor in its purest kind in the novels of Friedman. Provides a detailed exegesis of *Stern* as an urban complaint novel fraught with black humor typically revolving around cuckoldry. Describes the psychodynamics of black humor shrinking to momism in *A Mother's Kisses* where Pinsker claims that all too often black humor "becomes a blank check issued to the unbridled imagination." Accuses both novels of superficiality and refusing to face up to the enigmatic. Argues that the device of black humor forces the novelist from the outrageous to the zany with steady escalation until it exhausts him. Concludes that, at times, it even becomes desperate and shrill as in *The Dick*.

Pinsker, Sanford. "*Stern*." *Survey of Contemporary Literature*. Ed. Frank N. Magill. Rev. ed. 12 vols. Englewood Cliffs: Salem, 1977. 11: 7227-29.

A standard reference article covering background, influences, plot, character, themes, and style in *Stern*.

Schulz, Max F. "The Aesthetics of Anxiety; and, the Conformist Heroes of Bruce Jay Friedman and Charles Wright." *Black Humor Fiction of the Sixties: A Pluralistic Definition of Man and His World.* Max F. Schulz. Athens: Ohio UP, 1973. 91-123.

Elaborately paints in the anxiety and disorder of post-war America, tracing his theme in great detail into all of Friedman's fiction. Demonstrates how the emphasis remains on the distinctive fictional strategies Friedman uses to convey this world view.

Schulz, Max F. "Wallant and Friedman: The Glory and the Agony of Love." *Critique* 10.3 (1968): 31-47. Rpt. as "Edward Lewis Wallant and Bruce Jay Friedman: The Glory and the Agony of Life." *Radical Sophistication: Studies in Contemporary Jewish/American Novelists.* Max F. Schulz. Athens: Ohio UP, 1969. 173-97.

Describes the theme of Friedman's novels as the betrayal of love, bewilderment, skepticism, black humor, all conveyed through the prose of outrageous banter, mystery, sexual wonder, and the unspoken horror of family antagonisms. Describes the progress of the novels as swirls and eddies rather than plot development. Commends the novels for their rich texture of surface detail.

Skerrett, Joseph Taylor, Jr. "Dostoievsky, Nathanael West, and Some Contemporary American Fiction." *University of Dayton Review* 4.1 (1967): 23-35.

In the context of a broad discussion of black humor in contemporary fiction, Skerrett provides a brief discussion of *Stern.*

Trachtenberg, Stanley. "The Humiliated Hero: Bruce Jay Friedman's *Stern.*" *Critique* 7.3 (1965): 91-93.

Calls *Stern* abrasive rather than comic, peopled with a self-generated victim rather than the usual anti-hero. "Stern, like Kafka's Joseph K has been on trial in which his guilt is determined by his very insistence on his innocence. Until he begins to question the meaning of both, laughs Friedman bitterly, he will continue to be the self-created victim, responding to experience rather than initiating it, fearfully clutching tighter than he intends to the elusive promise of life."

Vandyke, Patricia. "Choosing One's Side with Care: The Liberating Repartee." *Perspectives on Contemporary Literature* 1.1 (1975): 105-17.

Begins with a detailed discussion of repartee in minority short fiction, and the tendentious joke in particular. Rests its thesis on the Freudian theory of the defensive and aggressive comedy involving an aggressive teller, a victim, and a sympathetic listener. Then provides a detailed treatment of Friedman's short story "Kessler" from this perspective.

Wisse, Ruth R. "The American Dreamer." *The Schlemiel As Modern Hero*. Chicago: U of Chicago P, 1971 [Paperback ed. 1980]. 87-91.

Discusses *Stern* as a novel in which there is a deliberate increase between the *schlemiel's* point of view and that of the novel. Also discusses the reductionist nature of the satire and Friedman's desire to criticize and deflate the protagonist-*schlemiel*.

Reviews

Ackroyd, Peter. "Nothing to Say." Rev. of *About Harry Towns*. *Spectator* 15 Feb. 1975: 183-84.

Describes *About Harry Towns* as specializing in a sour and deadpan American prose untouched by human hand. Implies that it is autobiographical, full of irony, and yet a cut above the usual urban complaint novel. Concludes that the book and its style become a very effective description of the toneless way in which Americans conduct their affairs and the bland way in which they conduct each other.

Amis, Martin. "Tour de Farce." Rev. of *About Harry Towns*. *New Statesman* 21 Feb. 1975: 250.

Calls Friedman refreshingly unpretentious and yet rather unskilled in *About Harry Towns*. Claims that the novel is only a discursive, anecdotal evocation of the urban male menopause.

Bell, Pearl K. "A Surfeit of Sex." Rev. of *About Harry Towns*. *New Leader* 13 May 1974: 19-20.

Calls the style of the novel feeble, flaccid, and boneless, a dead giveaway of Friedman's desperate lack of belief in his limp enterprise. Details the contents of the novel, and concludes that if this is the best Friedman can do with his portrait of American male infantilism in the hedonistic present, it is not worth trying. And it is not worth reading.

Bellman, Samuel I. "New York! New York!" Rev. of *The Dick*. *Congress Bi-Weekly* 25 Dec. 1970: 32-33.

Commends the novel for being well-crafted and Friedman for having an ear for the big city speech and life. But condemns it for repeating old material and attitudes.

Bellman, Samuel I. "Old Pro." Rev. of *Black Angels. Congress Bi-Weekly* 8 May 1967: 19.

Argues that, at the bottom of Friedman's fiction, his view of man owes much to the Hebrew Bible, the news and entertainment media, camp culture, and pop psych. Briefly describes the content of each of the stories, and concludes that, while Friedman provides no easy answers, he always suggests larger realms of possibility.

Bellman, Samuel I. "Reviews." Rev. of *Far from the City of Class and Other Stories. Studies in Short Fiction* 1.2 (1964): 167-69.

A review of *Far From the City of Class* in which he calls the stories upbeat, moral sensibility tales full of weird, ironic satire, absurd humor, and brilliantly insipid dialogue. Sees also grotesque blends of necromancy, diabolism, and corporate power-structure politics. Provides a very brief gloss on the contents of the main stories.

Black, Susan. "The High Wires Got Crossed." Rev. of *Far from the City of Class and Other Stories. New York Herald Tribune Book Review* 10 Nov. 1963: 21.

Describes several of the stories, and concludes that Friedman likes to have fun with such treacherous subjects as paraplegics and lovemaking on the eve of Yom Kippur. Concludes that, whatever Mr. Friedman's assumptions in his stories, sex is remarkably unpleasant because his obsession with groins, buttocks, breasts, underwear, and earbiting renders the book a distasteful bore.

Boroff, David. "The Grotesque Hilarity of the Commonplace." Rev. of *Far from the City of Class and Other Stories. New York Times Book Review* 6 Oct. 1963: 38.

Suggests that this collection of stories may help to consolidate Friedman's reputation but will do little to advance it. Claims that the stories, mostly published previously, antedate *Stern*, and that their technique serves ultimately to cheapen an otherwise impressive talent.

Broyard, Anatole. "Black Humor More Black Than Humorous." Rev. of *The Dick. New York Times Book Review* 16 Aug. 1970: 4, 29.

Comments that *The Dick* is covered with a coat of humor hiding its multitude of sins. Calls the writing deadpan, flat, and clumsy. Complains that, unfortunately, Friedman has just one bag of *shticks*, and the book is a bargain basement of symbolisms. Concludes that, if the book gives anything to boast about at all, it is that Friedman is twenty years ahead of his time.

Broyard, Anatole. "Books of the Times." Rev. of *Let's Hear It for a Beautiful Guy*. *New York Times* 29 Aug. 1984: C21.

Comments that *Let's Hear It for a Beautiful Guy* is a collection of stories exploiting the tensions and incongruities of a culture taking itself too seriously. Suggests that this is Friedman in his manic phase, sputtering with invention as he was in *Stern*. Details the contents of several of the eighteen stories, and spends most of his time on the romance of failure.

Chester, Alfred. "Submitting, Not Rising, to the Heroic Gesture." Rev. of *Stern*. *New York Herald Tribune Book Review* 23 Sept. 1962: 8.

Calls this a novel about an elaborately oversensitized Jew who sees anti-Semitism in every Gentile gesture. Commends Stern as a marvelously comic character who typifies the cringing, cowardly dreamer. Complains that the secondary characters exist through tricky surface characteristics endlessly repeated.

Cook, Bruce. "In Harry's Nightmare, A Playboy Fantasy Sours." Rev. of *About Harry Towns*. *National Observer* 29 June 1974: 19.

Claims that *About Harry Towns* is confessional in tone, precise, analytical, detailed, unpleasant to read, scary, and tough. Describes Harry Towns's character.

Crain, Jane Larkin. "Books in Brief." Rev. of *About Harry Towns*. *Saturday Review* 1 June 1974: 26.

Briefly describes the story, and asserts that the attitudes and assumptions about success, marriage, family, and the Bourgeois American Dream embodied in the novel are by this time shopworn and hackneyed. Concludes that Harry is a singularly distasteful and unengrossing character, and wonders what Friedman expects readers to find of importance.

Davenport, Guy. "Good People in Trouble." Rev. of *The Dick*. *National Review* 20 Oct. 1970: 1115.

Sees Friedman as determined to understand middle-class life through the character of the policeman in *The Dick*. Considers the novel delightfully Brechtian and full of irony. Sees it exploding many fond liberal stereotypes and, like good satire, ends by catching the audience along with the villain in its snare.

Davies, Russell. "Monster of Our Times." Rev. of *About Harry Towns*. *Times Literary Supplement* 14 Feb. 1975: 156.

Argues that in *About Harry Towns* perplexing figures appear as adolescent failures whom we know down to their last pimple, hemorrhoid, or balloon-breasted fantasy, but who actually do not regard themselves as worth knowing about. Complains that they show up as more than mere objectifications of authorial self-loathing transmuted into humor to make it look a little more like self-mockery. Concludes that the impulse behind them is more therapeutic than literary.

De Feo, Ronald. "Too Little, Too Soon." Rev. of *About Harry Towns*. *National Review* 16 Aug. 1974: 938.

Calls *About Harry Towns* another Friedman disappointment. Claims that it is really a collection of six disconnected chapters focusing on Harry Towns, a forever restless, mildly depressed screenwriter. Argues that there is none of the intensity and concern of earlier novels, particularly *Stern*. Concludes that Friedman is too distant from his creation and writes efficient prose, nothing more.

Donoghue, Denis. "Ghosts and Others." Rev. of *The Dick*. *New York Review of Books* 5 Nov. 1970: 23-24.

Describes *The Dick* as a book written with American verve, fast drive, and lots of humor. Concludes that, unfortunately, the book is all margin and no text because it has no subject or content.

Edwards, Thomas R. "A Facile Cop-and-Bull Story." Rev. of *The Dick*. *Life* 28 Aug. 1970: 10.

Argues that *The Dick* is about White America's domestic anxieties—racial tension in suburbia, the psychopathology of the local police, sex after thirty, drugs, and teenagers. Concludes, however, that the book is finally a cop out because, even as an experienced novelist, Friedman cannot resist old novelistic habits and temptations.

Frakes, James R. "Two Novels." Rev. of *About Harry Towns*. *New York Times Book Review* 23 June 1974: 32.

Calls the character Harry Towns a swinging compendium of vulnerabilities, rudderless, and separated from his wife. Complains that, though it is a book of brilliant episodes, there is little development. Concludes that Friedman solves nothing for his well-meaning protagonist.

Frankel, Haskel. "Oedipus Schmoedipus." Rev. of *A Mother's Kisses*. *New York Times Book Review* 16 Aug. 1964: 5.

Calls *A Mother's Kisses*, like other Friedman novels, a world ordained by Freud and populated by the Keystone Cops. Describes characters and plot in detail.

Frankel, Haskel. Rev. of *The Dick*. *Saturday Review* 19 Sept. 1970: 46.

Argues that, while Friedman's first two novels were interesting, the characters in *The Dick* come through not as participants in a black comedy but as inventions, each with *shtick* attached. Complains that there is something outlandish about everyone; they are characters not in a novel, but in search of one. Concludes that *The Dick* is composed of quirky types, inventive incidents, well-written scenes, but nothing that adds up to a meaningful whole.

Fremont-Smith, Eliot. "How Job Got an Ulcer." Rev. of *Stern*. *Village Voice* 4 Oct. 1983: 53.

Calls *Stern* an odyssey of a *schlemiel* who tries everything—including laughing at himself—and, despite all, ends up bravely persevering. Calls the book funny but also cruel and sadistic. Concludes that it is the black humor story of a long and artful procrastination which confounds us because it is scary, morally obsessed, and heroic.

Fremont-Smith, Eliot. "Treading Water." Rev. of *Black Angels*. *New York Times* 10 Oct. 1966: 39.

Argues that *Black Angels*, Friedman's second collection of stories, trips the black comedy fantastic. Praises these sixteen stories for being neat, poignant, and arrestingly bizarre. Yet concludes that it is a series of instantly clever and very peripheral ideas—what the short story seems more and more to be used for these days.

Friedman, Melvin J. "Recent Fiction." Rev. of *About Harry Towns*. *New Republic* 27 July-3 Aug. 1974: 28.

Suggests that *About Harry Towns* is full of fantasy, reality, and the incongruous, and contains less Jewish content than the previous novels. Admires the remarkable consistency of the work and its mature verbal rhythms.

Fuller, Richard. "Angst Goes East." Rev. of *Tokyo Woes*. *New York Times Book Review* 19 May 1985: 21.

Calls *Tokyo Woes* an urban *angst* and black comedy. Claims that it feels like a Steve Martin comedy routine. Details some of the zanier contents.

Gilman, Richard. "Oedipus, Shmedipus, Mama Loves You!" Rev. of *A Mother's Kisses*. *New York Herald Tribune Book Week* 23 Aug. 1964: 5, 8-9.

Describes *A Mother's Kisses* as much less imagined than *Stern*, and accuses it of failing to transform its materials from personal history into fiction.

Goodheart, Eugene. "An Uncertain Smile." Rev. of *Stern*. *Saturday Review* 13 Oct. 1962: 38.

Comments that *Stern* is an interesting novel, but argues that Friedman's attitude and manner immediately arouse expectation of continuous wit and wildness, both in fantasy and expression. Concludes that, despite some extraordinary situations, the execution is strangely timid and thin. Describes the central character and the plot.

Gray, Paul. "Cassette Guys." Rev. of *Tokyo Woes*. *Time* 22 Apr. 1985: 70, 75.

Describes this novel as a kind of goofy, dumb parody that sounds like lonely guy bar talk that could be given a miss since it is sure to appear in video on MTV.

Haworth, David. "Dirty Dick." Rev. of *The Dick*. *New Statesman* 19 Mar. 1971: 397.

Comments that *The Dick* is black comedy about life in an East Coast homicide bureau. Complains that taste is absent, the cops are monsters obsessed by guns and perversion, and the whole thing is genuinely comic.

Hentoff, Nat. "Anxiety and Paranoia." Rev. of *Stern*. *Commonweal* 7 Dec. 1962: 294-95.

Describes the contents of *Stern,* and comments that in his first novel Friedman has distilled the central preoccupation with psychopathology which dominates the decade for Jew and non-Jew alike. Describes his handling of detail as achingly realistic, and his description of fragmented self-delusion as masterful. Concludes that Friedman offers neither solution nor catharsis at the end of the novel, but observes that he does take off the bandages so we can see the wounds.

Hochman, Baruch. "End As a Man: The Ordeal of Citizen Stern." Rev. of *Stern*. *Judaism* 12.2 (1963): 237-42.

Puzzles over the success of *Stern* since it seems to have been little more than a pretentious, occasionally brilliant caricature of the contemporary

Jew as he is in relation to himself and the world. Details the paranoid breakdown of the protagonist in considerable detail.

Hughes, Riley. "Always Enter Laughing." Rev. of *Far from the City of Class and Other Stories. Saturday Review* 14 Dec. 1963: 46.

Suggests that this book is full of whoops of scornful laughter, inanities, anxieties, pretensions, and blasting therapeutic logic. Claims that most of the sixteen stories are parables of logical inversion. Describes the contents of several.

Hyman, Stanley Edgar. "An Exceptional First Novel." Rev. of *Stern. New Leader* 1 Oct. 1962: 22-23. Rpt. in *Standards: A Chronicle of Books of Our Time.* Stanley Edgar Hyman. New York: Horizon, 1966. 98-102.

Calls *Stern* an uproarious, exceptional first novel. Details the events of the story and the fact that for Stern Jewishness has no national, religious, or cultural content, only a shameful inherited inferiority and guilt first learned from his father. Comments on misfires in style, the problematic ending, and the fiercely honest demeanor of the book.

Hyman, Stanley Edgar. "Joseph and His Mother." Rev. of *A Mother's Kisses. New Leader* 17 Aug. 1964: 18-19.

Calls *A Mother's Kisses* a book which centers on the savage caricature of the dominating mother, Meg. Argues that Friedman produces an authentic child's world in which all adults are engaged in a conspiracy against the child. Yet claims that with this sort of realism goes the wildest fantasy and exaggeration. Calls his imagination garish and violent. Concludes that the book fails in its length, total organization, and relevance when compared to *Stern.*

"John and Bruce." Rev. of *Black Angels. Newsweek* 26 Sept. 1966: 116-116B.

Describes the book as nervous, jargonized tales of hard-up lotharios and weird urban *dybbuks* living out the urban-suburban marriage-go-round. Calls the tales rawly ironic, sometimes humorous and nostalgic, usually with large doses of black humor thrown in.

Kakutani, Michiko. "Mike on the Ginza." Rev. of *Tokyo Woes. New York Times* 27 Apr. 1985: 13.

Calls *Tokyo Woes* a comic novel which, while it is extremely diverting, is also lacking in depth and compassion. Considers it outrageous, flip, full of infectious language, and lacking in anger and tenderness.

Kauffmann, Stanley. "Frightened Writer." Rev. of *Black Angels*. *New Republic* 8 Oct. 1966: 20, 37.

Accuses Friedman of using writing as *juju* to control, appease, or amuse the pressing uglinesses of everyday life. Calls *Black Angels* a collection of stories of limited scale. Suggests that the successes among them are small bizarre offerings to forces that threaten us all. Considers that the stories serve to mollify or perhaps entertain and thus serve the author and us. Also discusses anti-Semitism, style, critical reception, and verbal effects in his novels.

Kennedy, William. "Mr. Friedman Offers a World of Funny Fantasy in *Black Angels*." Rev. of *Black Angels*. *National Observer* 24 Oct. 1966: 23.

Comments that *Black Angels* is funny, weighted with significance, stylistically pure, wacky, hip, and full of meaning used as an afterthought to humor.

Larner, Jeremy. "Compulsion to Toughness." Rev. of *Stern*. *Nation* 1 Dec. 1962: 380-81.

Sees *Stern* as less a novel than a record of a particular kind of mentality. Calls it essentially poetic, accumulating its effects with a steady impact.

Lieber, Joel. Rev. of *Far from the City of Class and Other Stories*. *Hadassah Magazine* Nov. 1963: 18-19.

Calls this a richly entertaining collection of short stories, heavily stylized, and still containing the same grotesque, surrealistic qualities as *Stern*. Sees fantasy as a major element in these sixteen stories where the characters inhabit a phantom world and are goaded by nightmarish desires. Concludes that Friedman must decide whether he is writing fables, fantasies, or just short stories.

Macaulay, Robie. "Cartoons and Arabesques." Rev. of *Black Angels*. *New York Herald Tribune Book Week* 25 Sept. 1966: 4.

Comments that *Black Angels* shows Friedman's tendency to reach out for a nifty, neatly packaged, entirely forgettable plot. Calls these stories full of cartoon cleverness, ultimately diminishing the more serious pieces.

"Megomania." Rev. of *A Mother's Kisses*. *Time* 4 Sept. 1964: 107, E7.

Describes the novel in detail and Meg as a blowup of a caricature Yiddishe Moma. Sees this as a funnier book than *Stern*, somewhat less organized and smaller in scope, but still vigorous and unsettling. Concludes, nevertheless, that few novels can claim as much.

Mitchell, Adrian. "Style and Dreams." Rev. of *Stern*. *Spectator* 21 June 1963: 815.

Calls *Stern* a book in which the author takes an irony that starts cold and rises to a branding heat. Describes it as a slow probing of the terror of anti-Semitism done with great cunning.

Moberg, Verne. "Tormented Hero." Rev. of *A Mother's Kisses*. *Harper's* Oct. 1964: 135.

Complains that the son's passivity and the mother's vulgarity in this hopeless psychological snarl gradually wear on the reader's nerves. Yet notes that the evocation of stereotypes is a refreshing stimulant. Concludes that this is a provocative cross between modern myth and reality, tempting the reader to wonder where stereotypes leave off and actual people begin.

Morse, J. Mitchell. "Where is Everybody?" Rev. of *Black Angels*. *Hudson Review* 19.4 (1966-7): 677-78.

In a composite review of sixteen contemporary novels, Morse finds that most of them deal with Yahoos, not Houyhnhnms. Argues that in Friedman's *Black Angels* he sees a "cynical pro . . . slick, slick, slick." Concludes that Friedman achieves his aims, but that he doesn't aim high.

Newfield, Jack. "Sprints into Lunacy." Rev. of *Black Angels*. *New Leader* 24 Oct. 1966: 23-24.

Argues that some stories are labored one-line jokes, mere premature ejaculations that give no satisfaction because the writer lacked patience to let them ripen inside his brain. Makes an exception of three stories which are brilliant. Concludes that, though one may accuse Friedman of being too self-indulgent, too narrow in vision, or too bereft of humanism, he is a stylist, and he makes the reader laugh.

Newlove, Donald. Rev. of *About Harry Towns*. *Village Voice Literary Supplement* 6 June 1974: 33.

Argues that the six periods of Harry Town's life which are the substance of *About Harry Towns* are done with wit, insight, and skill. Claims that his writing has a lovely ingenious surface and, in the end, a list of vacuities. Concludes that, after 180 pages of marvelous writing, it is finally not enough. Details the life of the major character.

Peden, William. "Recent Fiction." Rev. of *Let's Hear it for a Wonderful Guy*. *Western Humanities Review* 39.3 (1985): 269.

Comments that this collection is fun to read if not taken too seriously or too many at a time. Claims that there is a manic quality about many of the stories and sometimes a perverse sense of humor—never obtrusive but always there.

"Red Hot Mama." Rev. of *A Mother's Kisses*. *Newsweek* 17 Aug. 1964: 85-86.

Calls this a moving first novel told in wild, grotesque fashion. Details the plot, and concludes that this book abounds with brilliant scenes and enough comic characters to populate a dozen novels. Claims that Friedman explores the real meaning of the national cult of mother love with a furious single-mindedness. Concludes, unfortunately, that there is no framework of sufficient scope and coherency to contain the turbulence Friedman unleashes with regard to the mother character.

Ribalow, Harold U. "Mama: Alive and Kicking." Rev. of *A Mother's Kisses*. *Congress Bi-Weekly* 26 Oct. 1964: 20.

Calls *A Mother's Kisses* a major American novel about Jewish family relationships. Claims that it has patches of humor that make one laugh out loud and much to say about the uncertainties and neuroses of Jewish-Gentile conflicts. Describes the contents fully.

Saal, Rollene W. "Pick of the Paperbacks." Rev. of *A Mother's Kisses*. *Saturday Review* 31 Jan. 1970: 36.

A general overview of Friedman's humor and previous books written to announce the upcoming production of his play, *Steambath*. Includes some biographical detail.

Sale, Roger. "Reviews." Rev. of *A Mother's Kisses*. *Hudson Review* 17.4 (1964-65): 615-16.

Describes *A Mother's Kisses* as a book which deals in some types, but which is much more than simple jokes and tears. Criticizes the language which is often splendidly flamboyant.

Schott, Webster. "Shockers and Gutbusters." Rev. of *Black Angels*. *New York Times Book Review* 2 Oct. 1966: 4-5.

Describes the contents of *Black Angels*, and then comments on instances of black humor; glittering, brilliant invention; the full range of his prose; and the particular style of absurdity that Friedman offers.

Segal, David. "Only Funny." Rev. of *A Mother's Kisses*. *Commonweal* 20 Nov. 1964: 302-04.

Calls *A Mother's Kisses* a book which is only funny, not brilliant. Complains that there is no movement in the plot, that the two main characters remain frozen in relation to one another, and that the rest is all rhetoric and cartoon. Considers the father dim to the point of nonexistence and the sexual pantomime without a final explosion.

Sheppard, R. Z. "Cop-Out." Rev. of *The Dick. Time* 7 Sept. 1970: 63.

Describes *The Dick* as a book written in mimicry of detective story dialogue, journalism clichés, police blotter prose, and a series of burlesque sketches. Complains that the book becomes an embarrassment when Friedman tries to stick existential purpose into his low comedy hero. Concludes that any second banana would have told him it wouldn't *shtick.*

Sorrentino, Gilbert. "Shooting Blanks." Rev. of *The Dick. Nation* 23 Nov. 1970: 536-37.

Calls *The Dick* another example of Friedman's black humor steeped in the bathos of its tattered symbolism. Complains that it has a deliberately clanking conventional plot; a typically non-existent story-line; thick, dead language; and dubious satirical power.

Stern, Daniel. "An Anguish Worn with a Difference." Rev. of *The Dick. Washington Post Book World* 13 Sept. 1970: 4. Rpt. in *New York Times Book Review* 27 Sept. 1970: 11.

Calls Friedman the man of the age of anxiety. Suggests that *The Dick* deals with the horrors and seductions of violence that surface in modern life. Details the contents of the book, and commends it to readers for its uniqueness and burlesque black humor.

Stern, Daniel. "Mamma Knows Best." Rev. of *A Mother's Kisses. Saturday Review* 15 Aug. 1964: 41-42.

Calls *A Mother's Kisses* a worthy successor to *Stern*. Sees it as a hilarious, mordant account. Describes the plot, and concludes that the book is suffused with a disturbed sexuality. Sees the author's real victory as one of style because the style is the subject, the characters' lives, and their language. Considers Friedman a poet of the wild and secret life.

"Suburban Diaspora." Rev. of *Stern. Time* 21 Dec. 1962: 81, 84.

Calls *Stern* strange and touching for a first novel. Details the character of Stern, his habits, environs, and dilemmas. Considers it a Jewish *schlemiel* story.

Taubman, Robert. "Look at Me." Rev. of *A Mother's Kisses*. *New Statesman* 11 June 1965: 927.

Calls *A Mother's Kisses* a book in which the reader struggles with the idea of being progressively alienated and disoriented. Argues that, in Joseph's world, seen with deadpan vision, he understands little and the reader less. Describes several of the characters as impeccable successes.

"That Mother." Rev. of *A Mother's Kisses*. *Times Literary Supplement* 17 June 1965: 489.

Calls *A Mother's Kisses* charming, original, and genuinely comic. Notes that the jokes are pungent, the sentimentality kept under keen control, and the mother balanced by a keen-eyed, quite believable son who has punch of his own and is supported by a diversely comic supporting cast.

Thompson, Toby. "Oh Dad, Poor Dad." Rev. of *About Harry Towns*. *Washington Post Book World* 16 June 1974: 2.

Argues that what Bruce Jay Friedman has accomplished in *About Harry Towns* is to have created a character straight out of a fiction writer's dreams: unique, haunting, and completely memorable. Claims that each of the stories stands on its own and complements the other brilliantly. Concludes that the book is simultaneously a novel, short fiction, and essay.

Todd, Richard. "Getting Real." Rev. of *About Harry Towns*. *Atlantic* May 1974: 128.

In a review of several of what he calls "minor works," Todd briefly describes Towns's situation. Finds Friedman's spare method working in some episodes, but complains that, in the end, you're asked to invest more in Towns' agonies than he seems to himself.

Tucker, Martin. "Black Angels." Rev. of *Black Angels*. *Commonweal* 9 Dec. 1966: 297.

Describes the contents of the stories in *Black Angels*, and comments that they are all about escaping the gilded trap of the ghetto only to enter the rootlessness of the city. Praises Friedman for capturing their resiliency and illogical zest by painting a universe both painful and entertaining.

Van Vactor, Anita. "Minor Burghers." Rev. of *The Dick*. *Listener* 25 Mar. 1971: 389.

Describes *The Dick* as a book about the working out of an identity crisis in middle America's suburbia. Notes that Friedman's smugness is offensive and makes the book, despite its initial liveliness of invention, finally inert. Concludes that his too obvious delight in his own talents as mime and ventriloquist prevent him from recognizing how this gift implicates him along with his puppets in the situation he so glibly mocks.

Wakefield, Dan. "Life in the New Middle Ages." Rev. of *The Current Climate*. *Washington Post Book World* 26 Nov. 1989: 3, 8.

Recalls his reactions to the humor in Friedman's earlier novels. Describes *The Current Climate*, finding it less playful than pathetic in its account of the aging writer, Harry Towns, until Friedman reverses the reader back in time to the 1950s, in a kind of novella within the novel, when Harry was beginning as a writer, which he finds witty and charming. Concludes that Towns, like Friedman, "shows in the end the amazing resilience, inventiveness, hope and good humor that enable writers to survive."

Walsh, George. "A Real Swinging Mother." Rev. of *A Mother's Kisses*. *Cosmopolitan* Oct. 1964: 31-32.

Argues that *A Mother's Kisses* is about the tortured thrashings of maternal love and is surely the funniest book published this year. Praises his mastery of character and idiom. Details the contents, and describes key episodes in detail.

Weales, Gerald. "Reviews." Rev. of *Stern*. *Kenyon Review* 25.1 (1963): 186-87.

Describes *Stern* as a clever book in which the author's cleverness finally becomes a liability. Describes the theme of Jewishness running through the book, and argues that it finally fails to distinguish whether the grotesqueness is in the world or in Stern's mind.

Winegarten, Renee. "A Sick Joke." Rev. of *Stern*. *Jewish Observer and Middle East Review* 19 July 1963: 23.

Finds this a far-fetched American novel whose only virtue is its brevity. Sees it as a mix of crude anti-Semitism, Jewish masochism, and adolescent sexual illusion. Concludes that it is thoroughly nasty in its attitudes and in its view of life and of people.

Wolff, Geoffrey. "Walking Wounded." Rev. of *The Dick*. *Newsweek* 17 Aug. 1970: 90-91.

The Dick is funny, deadpan, full of freaks and grotesques, superbly crafted, a sourcebook of the contemporary vernacular, and full of gags.

However, the best this book deserves is a mixed notice. It does not repeat the triumph of his first novel.

Interviews

Stahl, Jerry. "Conversation with Bruce Jay Friedman." *Transatlantic Review* 60 (1977): 55-59.

Friedman discusses his writing, particularly *Stern*, commenting on his characters, his use of language, how much of himself is in his characters, his regret that he changed the ending of *Stern* to make it more positive to satisfy his editors, and the subjects he wants to write about.

Biographical Sources

Avery, Evelyn. "Bruce Jay Friedman." *Twentieth-Century American-Jewish Fiction Writers*. Ed. Daniel Walden. Detroit: Gale, 1984. Vol. 28 of *Dictionary of Literary Biography*. 94 vols. to date. 1978- . 69-74.

More than details of his life, this is a career biography, tracing the development of the author's canon, describing the contents and themes of his works, evaluating his reputation, and placing him in the larger context of American literary history. Includes lists of primary and secondary sources and illustrations.

Rood, Karen. "Bruce Jay Friedman." *American Novelists Since World War II*. Eds. Jeffrey Helterman and Richard Layman. Detroit: Gale, 1978. Vol. 2 of *Dictionary of Literary Biography*. 94 vols. to date. 1978- . 157-62.

More than details of his life, this is a career biography, tracing the development of the author's canon, describing the contents and themes of his works, evaluating his reputation, and placing him in the larger context of American literary history. Includes a list of primary sources and illustrations.

Taylor, John. "The Funny Guy's Book of Life." *New York* 9 Oct. 1989: 46-50.

Tells several anecdotes concerning Friedman's comeback, describes his past works, provides a significant group photograph of Friedman, and details the contents of *About Harry Towns*. Discusses his invisibility during the 1980's, and provides several comments from Friedman on the matter. Provides biographical information, and describes his publishing history in some detail.

Daniel Fuchs

1909 –

Primary Sources

Novels

Homage to Blenholt. New York: Vanguard, 1936; London: Constable, 1936; New York: Medallion-Berkley, 1965; Proletarian Literature Series. Detroit: Omnigraphics, 1990.

Low Company. New York: Vanguard, 1937; New York: Medallion-Berkley, 1965.

Neptune Beach. London: Constable, 1937; Cheaper ed. London: Constable, 1938.

Summer in Williamsburg. New York: Vanguard, 1934; London: Constable, 1935; New York: Medallion-Berkley, 1965; New York: Carroll, 1983.

West of the Rockies. New York: Knopf, 1971; New York: Popular, 1971; London: Secker, 1971; St. Albans: Panther, 1975.

Collected Works

The Apathetic Bookie Joint. New York: Methuen, 1979; London: Secker, 1980.

Contents: The Apathetic Bookie Joint; Love in Brooklyn; A Clean, Quiet House; Okay, Mr. Pappendass, Okay; The Hosiery Shop; The Sun Goes Down; Loew's King, the Chinks, and a Ride Home; There's Always Honolulu; The First Smell of Spring and Brooklyn; The Amazing Mystery at Storick, Dorschi, Pflaumer, Inc.; People on a Planet; The Man from Mars; The Morose Policeman; Kinds of Laughter; The Language of Love; A Hollywood Diary; Man in the Middle of the Ocean; Ecossaise, Berceuse, Polonaise; The Golden West; Triplicate; The Earthquake of 1971; Ivanov's "The Adventures of a Fakir"; The Williamsburg Bridge Plaza; Twilight in Southern California.

Three Novels by Daniel Fuchs. New York: Basic, 1961. Published as *The Williamsburg Trilogy.* New York: Equinox-Avon, 1972.

Contents: *Summer in Williamsburg, Homage to Blenholt, and Low Company.*

The Williamsburg Trilogy: Summer in Williamsburg, Homage to Blenholt and Low Company. New York: Equinox-Avon, 1972. Published as *Three Novels by Daniel Fuchs.* New York: Basic, 1961.

Short Fiction in Anthologies

"A Clean, Quiet House." *55 Short Stories from the New Yorker.* New York: Simon, 1942. 348-55.

"The Golden West." *Stories.* New York: Farrar, 1956. 238-61; *A Book of Stories.* London: Gollancz, 1957; *Short Stories from the New Yorker: 1950-1960.* New York: Simon, 1960. 19-39.

"Love in Brooklyn." *Short Stories from the New Yorker.* New York: Simon, 1940. 392-401.

"Man in the Middle of the Ocean." *Stories.* New York: Farrar, 1956. 197-217; *A Book of Stories.* London: Gollancz, 1957. Pag. not available.

"Twilight in Southern California." *Stories*. New York: Farrar, 1956. 218-37; *A Book of Stories*. London: Gollancz, 1957. Pag. not available; *Jewish-American Stories*. Ed. Irving Howe. New York: Mentor-NAL, 1977. 252-69.

Short Fiction in Periodicals

"All or Nothing." *Collier's* 14 Oct. 1939: 12-13, 26-29.

"All the Tricks." *Collier's* 14 Sept. 1940: 9-10, 31-32, 36.

"Amazing Mystery at Storick, Dorschi, Pflaumer, Inc." *Scribner's* Feb. 1938: 19-24, 96-98; *Scholastic* 1 Apr. 1939: 33-37, 46.

"A Clean, Quiet House." *New Yorker* 30 May 1942: 14-18.

"Crazy Over Pigeons." *Collier's* 29 Apr. 1939: 20-21, 64-66.

"Daring Young Man." *Collier's* 24 Aug. 1940: 22, 42-44, 46.

"Ecossaise, Berceuse, Polonaise." *New Yorker* 1 Aug. 1953: 17-22.

"Fabulous Rubio." *Collier's* 4 Jan. 1941: 12-14, 38.

"Fortune and Men's Eyes." *Saturday Evening Post* 10 Dec. 1938: 12-13, 74-75, 77-78.

"Golden West." *New Yorker* 10 July 1954: 21-30.

"If a Man Answers, Hang Up." *Collier's* 22 Apr. 1939: 68.

"Ivanov's 'The Adventures of a Fakir.'" *Commentary* June 1975: 60-64.

"The Language of Love." *New Yorker* 14 Dec. 1940: 16-20.

"Last Fall." *Saturday Evening Post* 5 Mar. 1938: 16-17, 94, 96-98.

"Life Sentence." *Collier's* 19 Nov. 1938: 57-64.

"Loew's Kings, the Chink's and a Ride Home." *New Yorker* 5 Apr. 1941: 66-70.

"Lucky Loser." *Collier's* 15 Oct. 1938: 22.

"Man in the Middle of the Ocean." *New Yorker* 11 July 1953: 22-30.

"Matter of Pride." *Collier's* 22 Oct. 1938: 19.

"Mink Coat Each Morning." *Collier's* 27 Jan. 1940: 17, 42, 44-45.

"Not to the Swift." *Collier's* 13 May 1939: 20-21, 34-36, 41.

"Okay, Mr. Pappendass, Okay." *Southern Review* [Baltimore] 7.4 (1942): 824-35.

"The Politician." *New Republic* 11 Oct. 1939: 267-69.

"Pug in an Opera Hat." *Collier's* 23 Mar. 1940: 16-17, 25-30.

"Racing Is a Business." *Collier's* 5 Oct. 1940: 20-21, 54-55.

"Strange Things Happen in Brooklyn." *Collier's* 1 Feb. 1941: 14, 41.

"Such a Nice Spring Day." *Collier's* 23 Apr. 1938: 12.

"The Sun Goes Down." *New Yorker* 14 Sept. 1940: 24-25.

"There's Always Honolulu." *New Yorker* 10 Aug. 1940: 14-16.

"Toilers of the Screen." *Collier's* 8 July 1939: 20-21, 44-45.

"Twilight in Southern California." *New Yorker* 3 Oct. 1953: 26-34.

"A Village by the Sea." *Dimensions in American Judaism* 3 (Sum. 1969): 25-27.

"The Woman in Buffalo." *Esquire* Apr. 1939: 50-51, 155.

Secondary Sources

Books

Miller, Gabriel. *Daniel Fuchs.* Twayne's United States Authors Series 333. Boston: Twayne, 1979.

Articles and Chapters

Allen, Walter. "Two Neglected American Novelists." *London Magazine* May 1962: 77-84. Rpt. as "The Thirties: American" in *The Modern Novel in Britain and the United States.* Walter Allen. New York: Dutton, 1964. 175-78; *Tradition and Dream: The English and American Novel from the Twenties to Our Time.* Walter Allen. London: Phoenix, 1964. London: Hogarth, 1986. 175-78.

Describes Fuchs's novels as warm, humorous, ironic, sentimental at times, and even self-mocking. Admires his third novel, *Low Company,* the most because of its ability to show the underside of violence which conditions the lives of his characters. Provides excellent overviews of the contents of all of Fuchs's novels. Highlights the particularly fine comic passages and incidents, underscoring Fuchs's skill as a comic writer and as a charitable observer of life.

Beaver, Harold. "In the Dark." *The Great American Masquerade.* New York: Barnes; London: Visson, 1985. 214-28.

Sees Fuchs's novels reflecting a myriad of separate, inturned, lonely consciousnesses who portray the sadness of lost hope, lost opportunities, lost beauty, lost youth, lost illusions, and lost love. Sees Fuchs's characters as trapped between insecurity at home and isolation at work—all stalled in their good intentions. Goes on to describe Fuchs's career in the Hollywood studios and his ultimate vision of California as a "Golden West bleak with matrimonial and professional failure."

Eisinger, Chester E. "Character and Self in Fiction on the Left." *Proletarian Writers of the Thirties.* Ed. David Madden. Crosscurrents/Modern Critiques. Carbondale: Southern Illinois UP, 1968. 158-83.

Spends most of the essay defining the issue of the identity of the self in terms of the alienationist, Marxist milieu of the thirties as reflected in the novels of writers like Fuchs, Halper, and Levin. Only briefly mentions Fuchs, but gives a helpful, interpretive context for viewing his novels.

Greenspan, Ezra. "Starting Out in the Thirties." *The Schlemiel Comes to America*. Metuchen: Scarecrow, 1983. 59-79.

Discusses Fuchs in the context of the 1930s. Regards him as a writer who inherited a longstanding Jewish sympathy for the Left and social reform, and who became a vigorous proponent of proletarian aesthetics. Sees him also as apolitical and loathe to mix politics and literature. Yet notes that he did respond to mass desperation as a deeply disillusioned dreamer watching the failure of the American Dream. Concludes that what differentiated Fuchs from the mainstream was not his themes per se but his peculiar individuality in art and temperament. A major chapter dealing with *Summer in Williamsburg, Homage to Blenholt, Low Company*, and *West of the Rockies*.

Guttmann, Allen. "How Some of Us Made It: Meyer Levin and Daniel Fuchs." *The Jewish Writer in America: Assimilation and the Crisis of Identity*. Allen Guttmann. New York: Oxford UP, 1971. 44-48.

Discusses Fuchs's Williamsburg trilogy, but finds it more a tryptich. Notes that each novel has a hero, but minor characters continually usurp attention, resulting in comedy. Sees Fuchs as the first Jewish-American writer to "take apart the world of Sholom Aleichem's Kasrilevka and to reconstruct it on the sidewalks of New York." Sees the major theme of the novels as "the gap between old and new customs and the strain of Americanization."

Harap, Louis. "Daniel Fuchs." *Creative Awakening: The Jewish Presence in Twentieth-Century American Literature, 1900-1940s*. Contributions in Ethnic Studies 17. New York: Greenwood, 1987. 107-12

Calls his recognized Williamsburg novels naturalistic, depicting the "depressing, frustrating, deprived lives of the characters . . . unsparingly." Describes each of the novels, their protagonists, themes, and ideas.

Howe, Irving. "The American Jewish Novelists." *World of Our Fathers*. New York: Harcourt, 1976. 585-97.

Discusses *Summer in Williamsburg* and *Homage to Blenholt*, finding them obsessed with "escape and trap," and dominated by a sense of place, which "grasps a man's life and breaks him to its limits." Considers *Homage to Blenholt* his best work, showing "a gift for exuberant comedy, a sweetly mocking play with Jewish daydreams."

Howe, Irving. "Daniel Fuchs: Escape from Williamsburg, The Fate of Talent in America." *Commentary* 6 July 1948: 29-34.

Reviews the pain of Fuchs's adolescence in dreary Williamsburg, the poorest of all the Jewish slum neighborhoods. Describes how he was influenced by the proletarian novels of the thirties and forties. Reviews all of the novels in turn, commenting on the possible biographical origins of tone, character, and incident. Comments on Fuchs's depiction of women as the this-worldly sex who chain men to the earth. Shows how his novels are disturbed by a barely hidden undercurrent of antipathy towards women who seem to him personifications of the earth force, the champions of the reality principle, and binders of men to the sort of life that ends with a cigarette and a window. Concludes that the final feeling of a Fuchs's novel is one of entrapment and oppression because "Fuchs reduced all of Jewish life to a slum." Laments Fuchs' final lapse into silence.

Howe, Irving. "Daniel Fuchs' Williamsburg Trilogy: A Cigarette and a Window." *Proletarian Writers of the Thirties*. Ed. David Madden. Crosscurrents/Modern Critiques. Carbondale: Southern Illinois UP, 1968. 96-105.

A tribute to and literary historical appraisal of the seminal works of Fuchs in the 1930s. Comments that the books are a little adolescent, dominated by a sense of place, naturalistic in philosophical disposition, redolent with pictures of the trapped youth of Williamsburg, and imbued with humor and irony. Reviews the contents of all the novels, and comments specifically on the structure, style, and effects of each. Concludes that Fuchs's are some of the most winning fictions about Jewish-American life and, despite a narrow scope, achieve pure tone.

Michelson, Paul. "Communal Values in the Fiction of Daniel Fuchs." *Studies in American Jewish Literature* [University Park, PA] 5 (1986): 69-79.

Stresses that in the "Williamsburg Trilogy" it is the theme of communal breakdown, deteriorating communal bonds, and the disappearance of brotherhood, charity, and kindness that Fuchs believed sustained these bonds. Treats each of the novels in turn and concludes that Fuchs finally suggests that virtue actually produces happiness and that the values of his ancestors still provide communal value wherever people practice friendship and love.

Miller, Gabriel. "The Gangster as Existential Hero." *Screening the Novel: Rediscovered American Fiction in Film*. Gabriel Miller. New York: Ungar, 1980. 143-66.

Describes how Fuchs adapted his novel *Low Company* for use as the script of the 1947 movie, *The Gangster*. Goes on to describe the life and works of Fuchs with substantial commentary on individual works.

Miller, Gabriel. "Williamsburg in Wonderland: Daniel Fuchs' 'Triplicate.'" *Studies in American Jewish Literature* [Kent State] 7.1 (1988): 80-89.

Discusses *Triplicate* as a book in which he displays his ability to capture the essence of a moment and place that distinguishes his novella as his most significant fiction since the thirties and the centerpiece of *The Apathetic Bookie Joint*. Sees it as a story of spiritual death and human isolation done this time in a fresh, multiple perspective.

Shaw, Irwin. "Irwin Shaw on Daniel Fuchs' *Homage to Blenholt*." *Rediscoveries: Informed Essays in Which Well-Known Novelists Rediscover Neglected Works of Fiction by One of Their Favorite Authors.* Ed. David Madden. New York: Crown, 1971. 67-74.

Provides a detailed plot summary of the novel replete with reports of key incidents and full character summaries. Argues that this novel is one of the ancestors of the whole school of Jewish-American fiction that portrays the domineering woman, the henpecked husband, the husband-hunting sister, and the bookish, rebellious son. Concludes that Fuchs sowed the seeds that writers like Roth reaped.

Sherman, Bernard. "Jewishness in *Summer in Williamsburg*." *The Invention of the Jew: Jewish-American Education Novels (1916-1964)*. Bernard Sherman. New York: Yoseloff, 1969. 102-07, passim.

Calls Fuchs a painterly novelist with a sharp eye for the cinematic effects of life. Provides a detailed account of Fuchs's New York novels, style, perspective, and nostalgia.

Updike, John. "Phantom Life." *New Yorker* 23 Oct. 1971: 176-79. Rpt. in *Picked-Up Pieces*. John Updike. New York: Knopf, 1975. 444-48.

Describes the prose as glimmering diffidence, the story as tersely sketched, and the effect of the whole as dreamlike, or movie-like. An excellent reader-response account of the main effects of the novel.

Yudkin, Leon I. "The Immigrant Experience in America." *Jewish Writing and Identity in the Twentieth Century*. Leon I. Yudkin. London: Helm, 1982. 27-44.

Discusses the Jewish immigration to America as the most remarkable demographic event in Jewish history and shows its impact on America as it emerged as a great world power. Also sees the Jewish writers Cahan, Lewisohn, Hecht, Fuchs, Michael Gold, and Henry Roth as expanding the range of an exotic consciousness in America but also showing the "Jew on the outside trying to get in (in various ways), or perhaps coming to terms with his outsider status." Discusses the major works of each of these writers and how these works demonstrate the struggles, the conflicts, and the costs of their Jewish protagonists to become assimilated into American life.

Reviews

Alpert, Hollis. "The Southside Story." Rev. of *Three Novels by Daniel Fuchs. Saturday Review* 23 Sept. 1961: 17-18.

Describes how, after writing the best three novels of the decade, Fuchs met with indifferent responses from the reading public and turned to writing short stories for the *New Yorker*. Briefly reviews the novels, and concludes that with the opinion that Fuchs was a more important novelist than Farrell with his gift for the comic, for dialogue, and for realism. Sees the trilogy as an American classic.

Beaver, Harold. "The Down Syndrome." Rev. of *The Apathetic Bookie Joint. Times Literary Supplement* 18 Apr. 1980: 431-32.

A review of *The Apathetic Bookie Joint* which identifies its tone as similar to that of an S. J. Perelman and a Nathanael West, with its peculiar blend of irony and humor. Describes the idiom as one of self-confidence undermined by riddling self-scrutiny and self-exposure. Calls the novel a comic classic, and hails Fuchs as the Jewish laureate.

Bell, Pearl K. "Hollywood's Siren Song." Rev. of *West of the Rockies. New Leader* 17 May 1971: 5-6.

Describes the novel as inflexibly limited in focus because it deals with personalities rather than the texture and tone of Hollywood itself. Claims that none of the characters seems worthy of attention from Fuchs's genius. Hopes perhaps one day Fuchs will write seriously about Hollywood the way he did about Brooklyn.

Blow, Simon. "Quick Eye." Rev. of *The Apathetic Bookie Joint. New Statesman* 11 Apr. 1980: 558.

Calls this a collection of short stories with an open-ended, easy-going out-look that does not disturb. Notes that the earliest stories date back to the thirties. Complains, though, that the neat removal from reality of the situations described and infused with native humor leaves the reader cold.

Davies, R. R. "West Country." Rev. of *West of the Rockies*. *New Statesman* 8 Oct. 1971: 483-84.

Argues that this novel is about a fading, half-hysterical filmstar. Claims that it is not a great novel, and that much of it is curiously hushed and introverted. Notes that the style and subject matter have much in common with Nathanael West.

Davis, Robert Gorham. "The Rat Race on the Brooklyn Track." Rev. of *Three Novels by Daniel Fuchs*. *New York Times Book Review* 10 Sept. 1961: 5, 22.

Describes the contents of the three novels (*Summer in Williamsburg*, *Homage to Blenholt*, and *Low Company*), and concludes that, except for the movies and radio programs they name, these novels are not in the least dated. Claims that they deal with bad housing, widespread dishonesty, and racketeering in a remarkably fresh manner. Finds Fuch's work has much in common with Algren, Farrell, and Bellow.

"Death of Youth." Rev. of *Homage to Blenholt*. *Times Literary Supplement* 1 Aug 1936: 631.

Calls this novel a slum comedy of the sad sort designed to make angels weep. Describes the contents, and concludes that, though the reader will see the author's point, he might feel that so fatuous, so wrong-headed, and so self-centered a person is in need of awakening, and that such an awakening will more likely be the birth than the death of real living.

Elman, Richard. "Dr. Fuchs' Hollywood Brother." Rev. of *The Apathetic Bookie Joint*. *Nation* 26 Jan. 1980: 87-88.

Condemns the stories as bearing the deformations of their martyrdom: pandering to types, a tic of colloquial language asserting itself rather too heavily at times, like paprika in a cream sauce, and far too many colorful characters with odd streetwise things to say.

Elman, Richard. "A Survivor's Hollywood Fable." Rev. of *West of the Rockies*. *New York Times Book Review* 13 June 1971: 7, 10.

Calls this novel a self-righteous, nostalgic survivor's fable about a marriage of convenience between two characters on the ropes. Provides a scathing commentary on the Hollywood scene and Fuchs's inability to leave it alone as a theme.

Evanier, David. "Feeding the Lake." Rev. of *The Apathetic Bookie Joint.* *National Review* 2 May 1980: 541-42.

Comments on the book as a collection of short stories giving common people stature without coloring or distorting their reality. Notes that, like many other writers of non-Tolstoyan stature, trickles of wonderful writers like Fuchs and Jean Rhys nevertheless feed the lake.

Farrell, James T. "Soda Parlor in Brooklyn." Rev. of *Low Company.* *Nation* 27 Feb. 1937: 244.

Details the setting, characters, and contents of the novel. Comments that Fuchs views life as a spectacle, and regards his characters with sympathy. Claims that the novel is constructed like a drama with considerable dependence on dialogue and a fairly strict effort to maintain objectivity. Concludes that Fuchs' novels have great value as social documentation rich with the poetry of the streets.

Goodheart, Eugene. "Brooklyn Is a Special Place." Rev. of *Three Novels by Daniel Fuchs. Midstream* 8.1 (1962): 105-08. Rpt. as *Three Novels by Daniel Fuchs"* in *Pieces of Resistance.* Eugene Goodheart. Cambridge: Cambridge UP, 1987. 125-29.

Sees the Williamsburg section of Brooklyn of today much like what it was in the thirties when Fuchs wrote these three novels. Describes each novel, describing the protagonists' conflicts and frustrations in their efforts to free themselves from the hopelessness of life in the ghetto. Also discusses Fuchs' preface in which he rationalizes his reasons for "selling out" and going Hollywood, which disinherited him from his world.

Greenberg, Martin. "Books." Rev. of *Three Novels by Daniel Fuchs.* *Partisan Review* 29.1 (1962): 151-52, 154, 156, 158.

Finds *Summer in Williamsburg* a book with no plot and a crowded series of scenes through which a young observer wends his way. Claims that Fuchs loses detachment in his personal argument with intellectuals and culture in general. Also discusses *Homage to Blenholt* as being about "some dopes who nurse illusions," and finds *Low Company* full of brilliant portraits.

Halper, Albert. "Child of Sorrow." Rev. of *Low Company*. *New Republic* 24 Feb. 1937: 89-90.

Briefly describes the plot, noting it does not do justice to the novel. Notes that Fuchs is a master of dialogue; his characters live, struggle, breathe, and squirm in frenzy. Considers him not a comic writer, but a writer with a burden who is consumed by hate, and finally appears as a child of sorrow.

"Hangups on the Set." Rev. of *West of the Rockies*. *Times Literary Supplement* 15 Oct. 1971: 1290.

Calls this a novel about Hollywood, though the people and events it deals with are far removed from the stardust image. Claims that Fuchs develops the notion of dependence and muted anguish with considerable skill, relying not only on what he tells us, but on what he deliberately omits to convey: the pressures and decidedly unglamorous aspects of stardom on Hollywood's terms.

Howe, Irving. "A Gathering of Good Works." Rev. of *West of the Rockies*. *Harper's* 24 July 1971: 88-89.

Comments on his shock that so talented and so young a novelist should "have begun to write at a good distance beyond the familiar margins of hope or even despair, and then so quickly have found himself at home in the scarred territories of resignation." Wonders about some sediment of racial experience, some pressure of remembered Jewish woe and weariness. Discusses the trilogy of novels, and provides a gloss on *West of the Rockies* as a fable of human composition. Commends the integrity of the book, and argues that Fuchs's negative vision limits his range as a novelist.

Howe, Irving. "Last Exit to LA." Rev. of *The Apathetic Bookie Joint*. *New York Review of Books* 6 Dec. 1979: 10-11.

Comments that Fuchs is a pure novelist because he has "no designs on his readers. No large thoughts, no postcards to deaf intellectuals, no theories about the future of the novel, not even grudges against relatives." Discusses his career, his work in Hollywood, and his formative years in Brooklyn, which have given him the sense of place as it grips a man's life and breaks him to its limits. Finds the stories in this collection have lost the sweetness of voice and comic playfulness of his novels. Characterizes the stories as possessing an irresistible honesty.

Hyman, Stanley Edgar. "In the Jungles of Brooklyn." Rev. of *Three Novels by Daniel Fuchs*. *New Leader* 11 Dec. 1961: 8-9. Rpt. in

Standards: A Chronicle of Books of Our Time. Stanley Edgar Hyman. New York: Horizon, 1966. 43-47.

Reviews the contents of the Williamsburg Trilogy, and locates Fuchs in the tradition of Nathanael West and Henry Roth—the tradition of symbolists and fantasists. Claims that, at his best, Fuchs is bold, imaginative, garish, grotesque, and funny. Describes the contents, characters, politics, setting, Jewish life, and milieu.

Jonas, Gerald. "Browsing." Rev. of *The Apathetic Bookie Joint. Present Tense* 7.3 (1980): 61.

Points out the startling parallels between Fuchs's and Fitzgerald's careers. Sees this collection of short stories as full of supercharged stories, excellent dialogue, and autobiographical essays. Yet is finally disappointed by the constant emphasis on the depths of despair that fail to encompass their human mystery.

Kauffman, Stanley N. "The Collapse Yet to Come." Rev. of *West of the Rockies. New Republic* 15 May 1971: 29-30.

Argues that *West of the Rockies* is pretty much on the level of all Fuchs's earlier fiction. Notes that it does appear he is trying to write himself out of superficiality and into seriousness. Concludes that Fuchs has a humane gift, but not sufficient range and skill to properly characterize his two main protagonists.

Kazin, Alfred. Rev. of *Low Company. New York Herald Tribune Books* 14 Feb. 1937: 8, 10.

Calls *Low Company* a terse, clever book that avoids using Jewishness as a backdrop for the well-worn theme of Jewish trials and tribulations. Commends Fuchs for his characterizations and sense of humor. Yet notes that this novel lacks the passion that poorer novelists in this genre have in abundance, apparently the price for his delicacy and modulation. Concludes that several scenes are too brittle because their weight has been too carefully distributed.

Malin, Irving. "Surviving Twilight." Rev. of *The Apathetic Bookie Joint. Congress Monthly* Sept.-Oct. 1980: 19.

Denies that Fuchs offers a merely fatalistic view of life, and praises him for having created such vivid and compelling characters. Argues that, though Fuchs would not like to be considered a religious comedian like Kafka, he belongs in the world of the early masters. Concludes: "He makes us laugh and cry at the same time; he urges us, moreover, not to give up but to survive cruel and funny onslaughts. He is, therefore, an important, sympathetic, and serious writer whose stories will be read even after the 'twilight' arrives."

Mangione, Jerre. "Chiefly in Praise of Four New Novels." Rev. of *Homage to Blenholt. New Republic* 1 Apr. 1936: 229-30.

Sees Fuchs' second novel as switching from the naturalistic approach to a racy, caricaturing manner, appealing strongly to the sense of humor. Claims that he is similar to other satirists, but has a manner of his own. Describes the contents, and concludes that Fuchs could develop into an outstanding satirist.

Mangione, Jerre. "Ghetto Summer." Rev. of *Summer in Williamsburg. New Republic* 28 Nov. 1934: 80.

Finds this first novel a realistic picture of life in Williamsburg, a Jewish quarter of Brooklyn; however, the total impression is one of sordidness and stagnation. Claims that suicide is the only escape. Describes the contents and characters who are like those in Zola's novels. Concludes that the book would have had more of the drive of naturalistic novels without Fuchs's cynicism.

Marsh, Fred T. "Delicatessen and Dreams in Brooklyn." *Rev. of Homage to Blenholt. New York Herald Tribune Books* 23 Feb. 1936: 6.

Claims that *Homage to Blenholt* is a book grounded in irony and pity. Sees it as a gentle satire on the romantic spirit, but with an eye to the incongruous and the grotesque. Describes contents and characters in detail. Concludes that this is a book which would probably not move people to do anything, but would enlarge their hearts.

Merkin, Daphne. Rev. of *The Apathetic Bookie Joint. New Leader* 31 Dec. 1979: 13.

Finds this collection of stories exemplifies Fuchs's different styles of writing: pre-Hollywood and post-Hollywood. Describes the style, characters, and contents of many of the stories.

Moss, Howard. "The Novels of Daniel Fuchs." Rev. of *Three Novels by Daniel Fuchs. New Yorker* 11 Nov. 1961: 231-32, 234, 236-38, 241-42.

Provides a detailed account of the newly re-issued Williamsburg Trilogy. Sees the works as rhapsodic, full of felt description pungent with Jewish idiom, but lacking in its use and embodiment of the quality of daydream. Comments on the economic squalor and sense of hopelessness in the works. Offers substantial glosses on each of the novels. Concludes that his works will survive the obscurity of other novels of the thirties.

Quennell, Peter. "New Novels." Rev. of *Homage to Blenholt. New Statesman and Nation* 8 Aug. 1936: 194.

Calls *Homage to Blenholt* a knockabout comedy of Jewish-American life that has the pathos of the Chaplinesque. Notes that all the characters in the crowded tenement the story centers on are excitable Jews who rush through the narrative revealing the smallness and humor of their lives. Provides a detailed description of the contents.

Richler, Mordecai. "In the Beginning, Williamsburg." Rev. of *The Apathetic Bookie Joint. New York Times Book Review* 11 Nov. 1979: 9, 18, 20.

Thinks Fuchs will always occupy an honored place in the pantheon of Jewish writers for making the work of the next generation possible. Sees his work as charged with uncommon vitality, and a rare sense of character and place. Finally, sees this collection of short stories as fitfully mapping Fuchs's own odyssey from Williamsburg to affluent Beverly Hills. Comments that the Williamsburg stories are more laconic and poignant while the others feel thin, lacking the rich material of the Williamsburg era. Concludes that they are of interest only because they were written by the same author who put other Jewish-American writers in his debt with the Williamsburg Trilogy.

Strauss, Harold. "*Low Company* and Other Recent Works of Fiction." Rev. of *Low Company. New York Times Book Review* 28 Feb. 1937: 6.

Describes *Low Company* as harshly realistic, yet tinged with beauty. Claims that unlike Farrell, who hates humanity, Fuchs has deep compassion for all his characters, and a Dostoyevskian capacity to pity and forgive the unamiable, futile, and evil characters who people his world.

Thompson, John. "Words." Rev. of *West of the Rockies. Commentary* Oct. 1971: 109-110.

A review of *West of the Rockies* which claims that while it may take others through words into a vision of the realities of the old Palm Springs and old Hollywood, the ancient scandals, and gossip, and glamor, and squalor, for this reviewer they were words and phrases, just lingo, and they are gone, they have split, they are no longer there.

"A Trilogy Grows in Brooklyn." Rev. of *Three Novels by Daniel Fuchs*. *Time* 1 Sept. 1961: 64-65.

Reviews the plot of each novel, and concludes that they look less like notable achievements than noteworthy beginnings.

Wallace, Margaret. "Tenement Lives." Rev. of *Summer in Williamsburg*. *New York Times Book Review* 18 Nov. 1934: 6.

Describes the novel as a book impossible not to be moved by, but flawed by its self-consciousness, naivete, and lack of central moral vision. Praises the competent, incisive style and excellent dialogue.

Young, Stanley. "*Homage to Blenholt* and Other Works of Fiction." Rev. of *Homage to Blenholt*. *New York Times Book Review* 23 Feb. 1936: 6.

Details the contents of the novel, and says that Fuchs's strokes are too expressionistic, his burlesques distortions, and his clowning insufficient. Concludes that, despite the lack of order, the book demonstrates a strong talent.

Biographical Sources

Fuchs, Daniel. "Strictly Movie." *Commentary* Sept. 1989: 38-46.

Fuchs describes his writing career, and his "rediscovery" as a novelist, his life in Hollywood, his experiences as a screen writer, and his ideas on what makes a good story.

Golden, Daniel. "Daniel Fuchs." *American Novelists, 1910-1945, Part II: F. Scott Fitzgerald-O. E. Rolvaag*. Ed. James J. Martine. Detroit: Gale, 1981. Vol 9 of *Dictionary of Literary Biography*. 94 vols. to date. 1978- . 35-38.

More than details of his life, this is a career biography, tracing the development of the author's canon, describing the contents and themes of his works, evaluating his reputation, and placing him in the larger context of American literary history. Includes lists of primary and secondary sources and illustrations.

Miller, Gabriel. "Daniel Fuchs." *Twentieth-Century American-Jewish Fiction Writers*. Ed. Daniel Walden. Detroit: Gale, 1984. Vol. 28 of *Dictionary of Literary Biography*. 94 vols. to date. 1978- . 74-83.

More than details of his life, this is a career biography, tracing the devel-

opment of the author's canon, describing the contents and themes of his works, evaluating his reputation, and placing him in the larger context of American literary history. Includes lists of primary and secondary sources and illustrations. A useful introduction.

Dissertations

Krafchick, Marcelline. "World Without Heroes: The Brooklyn Novels of Daniel Fuchs." Diss. U of California, Davis, 1985.

Michelson, Paul Frederick. "Daniel Fuchs: Chronicler of Williamsburg." Diss. Washington State U, 1981.

Miller, Gabriel. "A Butterfly in the Subway: The Fiction of Daniel Fuchs." Diss. Brown U, 1975.

Nye-Applebaum, Mika. "Restructuring the Beginning: Three Writers in the 1930s: The Novels of Michael Gold, Henry Roth, and Daniel Fuchs." Diss. State U of New York at Buffalo, 1980.

Herbert Gold

1924 –

Primary Sources

Novels

Birth of a Hero. New York: Viking, 1951.

Family: A Novel in the Form of a Memoir. New York: Arbor, 1981; New York: Pinnacle, 1983; London: Severn, 1983.

Fathers: A Novel in the Form of a Memoir. New York: Random, 1967; London: Secker, 1967; Greenwich: Fawcett, 1968; London: Corgi, 1968; Berkeley: Creative Arts, 1980; New York: Arbor, 1983.

A Girl of Forty. New York: Fine, 1986; New York: Dell, 1987.

The Great American Jackpot. New York: Random, 1969, 1970; New York: Ace, 1969; London: Weidenfeld, 1971.

He/She. New York: Arbor, 1980; London: Severn, 1982.

The Man Who Was Not with It. Boston: Little, 1956; New York: Avon, 1956; New York, Random, 1956, 1965; London: Secker, 1965; New York: Bard-Avon, 1969, 1974; Chapel Hill: Algonquin, 1987; Publ. as *The Wild Life,* New York: Permabooks, 1957.

Mister White Eyes. New York: Arbor, 1984; London: Severn, 1985.

The Optimist. Boston: Little, 1959; New York: Pocket, 1965.

The Prospect before Us. Cleveland: World, 1954; New York: Universal, 1964. Publ. as *Room Clerk*. New York: Signet-NAL, 1955.

Salt. New York: Dial, 1963; New York: Random, 1963, 1968; New York: Pocket, 1964; London: Secker, 1964; New York: Avon, 1971; Reading for Men. Garden City: Doubleday, 1963. Doubleday ed. publ. with *Cockatrice* by Wolf Mankowitz.

Slave Trade. New York: Arbor, 1979.

Swiftie, the Magician. New York: McGraw, 1974; London: Hutchinson, 1974.

Therefore Be Bold. New York: Dial, 1960; New York: Lancer, 1962; London: Deutsch, 1962; London: Mayflower, 1964.

True Love. New York: Arbor, 1982; London: Severn, 1984; New York: Grove, 1986.

Waiting for Cordelia. New York: Arbor, 1977; New York: Avon, 1978, 1984; London: Hutchinson, 1978.

Collected Works

Fifteen by Three Eds. R. V. Cassill, Herbert Gold and James B. Hall. New York: New Directions, 1957. Includes five stories by each editor/author.
Contents: The Heart of the Artichoke, Susanna at the Beach, A Celebration for Joe, Aristotle and the Hired Thugs, The Burglars and the Boy.

Love & Like. New York: Dial, 1960; Cleveland: World, 1961; London: Deutsch, 1961.

Contents: The Heart of the Artichoke, Susanna at the Beach, A Celebration for Joe, The Burglars and the Boy, Encounter in Haiti, Ti-Moune, Paris and Cleveland Are Voyages, Aristotle and the Hired Thugs, The Panic Button, Sello, What's Become of Your Creature, Love and Like, A Tale of Two Husbands, Jim the Man.

Lovers & Cohorts: Twenty-Seven Stories. New York: Fine, 1986.

Contents: Ti-Moune; Susanna at the Beach; What's Become of Your Creature?; Paris and Cleveland are Voyages; Love and Like; From Proust to Dada; Young Man, Old Days; A Death on the East Side; A Selfish Story; A Haitian Gentleman; Max and the Pacemaker; Waiting for the Forty-One Union; Winter of '73; A Dark Norwegian Person; San Francisco Petal; Blind, Blind Date; Child of Embassy; A Karmic Lover; Bart and Helene at Annie and Fred's; Christmas in Dakar; Paternity; Contingency Planning; A Ninety-Six-Year-Old Big Sister; Annique; The Smallest Part; Cohorts; Stages.

The Magic Will: Stories and Essays of a Decade. New York: Random, 1971. Contains both fiction and essays.

Stories of Misbegotten Love. Capra Back-to-Back Series 4. Santa Barbara: Capra, 1985; Publ. with *Angel on My Shoulder* by Don Asher.

Contents: His Wife & Her Husband, Stages, San Francisco Petal, A Dark Norwegian Person, Bart and Helene at Annie and Fred's.

Short Fiction in Anthologies

"Aristotle and the Hired Thugs." *Breakthrough: A Treasury of Contemporary American-Jewish Literature.* Eds. Irving Malin and Irwin Stark. New York: McGraw, 1964. 95-103.

"Dance of the Divorced." *How We Live: Contemporary Life in Contemporary Fiction.* Eds. Penney Chapin Hills and L. Rust Hills. New York: Macmillan, 1968. 339-46.

"Death in Miami Beach." *The Single Voice: An Anthology of Contemporary Fiction.* Ed. Jerome Charyn. New York: Collier, 1969. 427-44.

"A Death on the East Side." *The Best American Short Stories, 1972*. Ed. Martha Foley. Boston: Houghton, 1972. 48-74; *Prize Stories 1972: The O. Henry Awards*. Ed. William Abrahams. Garden City: Doubleday, 1972. 235-64. *Writer's Choice*. Ed. L. Rust Hills. New York: McKay, 1974. 195-221.

"Encounter in Haiti." *Prize Stories 1957: The O. Henry Awards*. Eds. Paul Engle and Hansford Martin. Garden City: Doubleday, 1957. 37-47; *The Midstream Reader*. Ed. Shlomo Katz. New York: Yoseloff, 1960. 362-72.

"Girl Getting Educated at Noon on Sunday." *Love is the Theme*. Eds. Douglas Angus and Sylvia Angus. Greenwich: Fawcett, 1970. 79-91.

"The Heart of the Artichoke." *Stories of Modern America*. Eds. Herbert Gold and David L. Stevenson. New York: St. Martin's, 1961. 14-44; *American Short Stories Since 1945*. Ed. John Hollander. New York: Harper, 1968. 119-54; *Jewish-American Stories*. Ed. Irving Howe. New York: NAL, 1977. 270-300.

"Jim the Man." *The Human Commitment: An Anthology of Contemporary Short Fiction*. Ed. Don Gold. Philadelphia: Chilton, 1967.

"Love and Like." *The Best American Short Stories, 1959*. Eds. Martha Foley and David Burnett. Boston: Houghton, 1959. 137-71; *Fiction of the Fifties: A Decade of American Writing*. Ed. Herbert Gold. Garden City: Doubleday, 1959. 205-42; Garden City: Dolphin-Doubleday, 1959. 205-42; *Prize Stories 1960: The O. Henry Awards*. Eds. Paul Engle and Hansford Martin. Garden City: Doubleday, 1960. 146-82; *The Process of Fiction: Contemporary Stories and Criticism*. Ed. Barbara McKenzie. New York: Harcourt, 1969. 171-202.

"Nicholas in Exile." *The American Judaism Reader: Essays, Fiction and Poetry from the Pages of American Judaism*. Ed. Paul Kresh. New York: Abelard, 1967. 162-71.

"Susanna at the Beach." *Modern Short Stories: The Fiction of Experience*. Eds. M. X. Lesser and John N. Morris. New York:

McGraw, 1962. 242-49; *The Shape of Fiction: Stories for Comparison.* Ed. Alan Casty. Boston: Heath, 1967. 294-300.

"The Witch." *Prize Stories 1954: The O. Henry Awards.* Eds. Paul Engle and Hansford Martin. Garden City: Doubleday, 1954. 133-41; *The Process of Fiction: Contemporary Stories and Criticism.* Ed. Barbara McKenzie. New York: Harcourt, 1969. 153-67.

Short Fiction in Periodicals

"96-Year-Old Big Sister." *Mademoiselle* Oct. 1981: 52-53, 57, 88.

"All Married Women Are Bad, Yes?" *Playboy* Nov. 1955: 25, 36, 38, 40, 56.

"The Ancient Company." *Playboy* Nov. 1966: 99-100, 102, 210, 212-14, 216.

"Aristotle and the Hired Thugs." *Commentary* July 1957: 36-41.

"Barbara Girl." *Playboy* Nov. 1962: 75-76, 128, 132, 135-36, 144-46, 148, 150-54, 156-61.

"Caroline, Campe." *Vogue* May 1959: 136-37, 171-73, 175-76.

"Caruso the Truck Driver." *Saturday Evening Post* 4 Apr. 1964: 56-58.

"A Celebration for Joe." *Antioch Review* 14.3 (1954): 284-92.

"Christmas in Dakkar." *Moment* Mar. 1983: F13-F15.

"City of Light '65." *Playboy* Oct. 1965: 84-86, 92, 215-18.

"Cohorts." *Midstream* June-July 1980: 26-28.

"Contingency Planning." *Midstream* Aug.-Sept. 1975: 56-58.

"Dance of the Divorced." *Saturday Evening Post* 23 May 1964: 68-73.

"Death in Miami." *Noble Savage* 3 (1961): 105-21.

"A Death on the East Side." *Esquire* May 1971: 140, 160, 162, 164, 166, 168, 170, 172, 174.

"Detroit Sons." *Atlantic* Feb. 1970: 66-67, 70.

"The Devil's Age." *Antioch Review* 16.1 (1956): 104-14.

"Do Nice Artistic Girls?" *Playboy* Aug. 1957: 27-28, 44, 67.

"Down the Ladder Awhile." *Evergreen Review* Feb. 1966: 29-32.

"The Elsewhere People." *Harper's Bazaar* Dec. 1969: 182-83.

"Encounter in Haiti." *Midstream* 2.1 (1956): 61-69.

The 44 Year Old Boy Disc-Jockey and the Sincere Type Songstress. *Playboy* Feb. 1957: 47-48, 64, 66, 68.

"The Game of Hide and Seek." *Playboy* July 1965: 97, 118-19, 121.

"Girl Getting Educated at Noon on Sunday." *Playboy* June 1968: 80-82, 84, 90.

"A Haitian Gentleman." *Hudson Review* 18.1 (1965): 54-66.

"The Happy Hipster." *Playboy* Aug. 1964: 81-82, 146-47.

"The Heart of the Artichoke." *Hudson Review* 4.3 (1951): 335-65.

"How Adele Deployed Mama." *Collier's* 11 Dec. 1953: 72-75.

"I Want a Sunday Kind of Love." *Hudson Review* 14.3 (1961): 396-407.

"The Incredible Adventures of Dino." *Playboy* July 1959: 71, 76, 80-82.

"Jackpot." *Playboy* June 1964: 71-72, 74, 138-42, 144, 147-49.

"The Little Treasury of WASP Folklore." *Transatlantic Review* 32 (1969): 63-71.

"Love and Like." *Hudson Review* 11.3 (1958): 329-62.

"Love Potion Number Last." *Ladies' Home Journal* Nov. 1968: 72.

"Love, the Healer." *Playboy* Jan. 1956: 41, 50, 66-67, 69.

"The Man Who Gave Up Pleasure." *Harper's* Apr. 1959: 53-60.

"Marriage, Food, Money, Childen, Ice-Skating." *Playboy* Apr. 1966: 127, 162, 164-69.

"Max and the Pacemaker." *Paris Review* 15.60 (1974): 160-70.

"Meester Boris." *Midstream* Jan. 1975: 32-41.

"My Father and His Gangsters." *Playboy* June 1966: 95, 106, 186-88.

"My Father, His Father and Ben." *Playboy* Aug. 1966: 97, 100, 140, 142-43.

"The Not Nice Guy." *Playboy* May 1957: 47-48, 70-71.

"O Manahatta, Mother of Waters." *Playboy* Mar. 1962: 58-60, 74, 128-29, 131-34.

"One Sunday Morning at the Russian Bath." *Hudson Review* 15.1 (1962): 15-37.

"The Only Pure Love." *Playboy* Aug. 1963: 103-04, 105-06.

"Panic Button." *Vogue* 15 Feb. 1953: 94-95.

"Paris and Cleveland Are Voyages." *Hudson Review* 10.1 (1957): 66-85.

"Peacock Dreams." *Playboy* June 1967: 137, 170-71.

"The Psychodynamist." *Playboy* Mar. 1956: 47-48, 54.

"Reality for This Lad." *Playboy* Aug. 1961: 38-40, 42, 97-98, 100-03.

"The Right Kind of Pride." *Playboy* Oct. 1956: 21-22, 26, 36.

"Room at the Inn." *Playboy* Dec. 1988: 118-20, 217-18.

"Running Man." *Playboy* Nov. 1964: 136-38, 148.

"San Francisco Petal." *Playboy* Nov. 1973: 134, 251-52, 254.

"The Sender of Letters." *Playboy* Aug. 1959: 33-34, 86-92.

"A Selfish Story." *Harper's* May 1967: 88-92, 96-97.

"Sleepers, Awake!" *Playboy* Sept. 1958: 56-58, 62, 82; *Pocket Playboy* 1 (1973): 119-33.

"The Smallest Part." *Atlantic* Aug. 1973: 67-71.

"The Song of the Four-Colored Sell." *Playboy* Mar. 1963: 62-64, 138-45.

"Stages." *TriQuarterly* 47 (1980): 224-37.

"A Steady, High-Type Fellow." *Playboy* July 1955: 23-24, 30-31.

"Susanna at the Beach." *Atlantic* May 1954: 48-51.

"The Sweet Sinner and Traveling." *Playboy* Feb. 1961: 53-54, 114-15.

"A Tale of Two Husbands." *Hudson Review* 12.4 (1959-60): 523-36.

"That Sweet Sinner and Traveling I." *Playboy* Feb. 1961: 53-54, 114-15.

"Trouble in Makeoutsville." *Playboy* May 1960: 30-32, 62, 103-06.

"An Unevenness of Blessings." *Playboy* Sept. 1965: 112-13, 138, 212-16.

"The Urban Cowboy and the Stranger." *Atlantic* May 1980: 76-79.

"A Very Good Sidewalk Story." *Playboy* Oct. 1959: 59-60, 88, 107-08.

"Weird Show." *Playboy* Apr. 1958: 16-18, 62, 64.

"The Western White House Did Not Fall." *Esquire* Apr. 1975: 120-21, 142, 144, 147.

"What's Become of Your Creature?" *Playboy* Apr. 1959: 21-22, 32, 40, 58, 84-88.

"Widening Flaw." *American Mercury* Apr. 1952: 58-66.

"Winter of '73." *Playboy* July 1974: 101, 163-64.

"The Witch." *Yale Review* 42.4 (1953): 537-46.

Secondary Sources

Articles and Chapters

Allen, Walter. "War and Post War: American." *The Modern Novel in Britain and the United States.* Walter Allen. New York: Dutton, 1964. 328-30.

A brief assessment of *Therefore Be Bold* that details its contents, and concludes that it is a novel rooted in the field in which the notion of possibility has its being.

Clarke, Gordon W. *"Fathers." Survey of Contemporary Literature.* Ed. Frank N. Magill. Rev. ed. 12 vols. Englewood Cliffs: Salem, 1977. 4: 2492-94.

A standard reference article discussing principal characters, historical background, themes, style, contents, and impact.

Gehle, Quentin. *"The Great American Jackpot." Survey of Contemporary Literature.* Ed. Frank N. Magill. Rev. ed. 12 vols. Englewood Cliffs: Salem, 1977. 5: 3095-97.

A standard reference article covering background, influence, style, theme, and plot in *The Great American Jackpot.*

Gold, Herbert. "The Mystery of Personality in the Novel." *The Living Novel: A Symposium.* Ed. Granville Hicks. New York: Macmillan, 1957. 92-105.

An address in which Gold discusses how personality is created in the novel, what critical standards apply, his methods, his novelist's credo, other writers, and the writer as an authorized signifier of mystery.

Gollin, Rita K. "Understanding Fathers in American Jewish Fiction." *Centennial Review* 18.3 (1974): 273-87.

Argues against the prevailing critical opinion that the primacy of the Jewish father is diminished in much American Jewish fiction. Sees *Fathers* paying tribute to the continued importance of the Jewish father.

Hassan, Ihab H. "Encounter with Possibility: Three Novels by Gold, Cheever, and Donleavy." *Radical Innocence: Studies in the Contemporary American Novel.* Ihab H. Hassan. Princeton: Princeton UP, 1961. 180-202.

Provides a brief overview of Gold's novelistic career, and gives a detailed appraisal of *The Optimist*, commending its openness to life's possibilities. Notes, however, that in the final analysis, the style tries to give hope and humor to dramatic material weighted down by genuine desperation. Fears the novel remains "a self-created metaphor of hope, and an ironic act of dissection." Calls the hero a severely diminished man who still wants more of everything. Sees metaphor and action suffering from the disunity of age, and illusion and reality impossible in a common perspective. Concludes that irony, which endeavors to reconcile opposites, also assumes that things at bottom are irreconcilable.

Hicks, Granville. "Generations of the Fifties: Malamud, Gold, and Updike." *The Creative Present: Notes on Contemporary American Fiction.* Eds. Nona Balakian and Charles Simmons. Garden City: Doubleday, 1963. 217-37.

Views Gold's early work, such as *Birth of a Hero,* as disciplined and mature but conventional. Sees the later work as a total departure in style, if not in theme. Comments generally on several of the novels, and asserts that Gold has the ability to write about the theme of self-discovery and make particularly fine use of the vernacular. Describes Gold as prolific but unself-critical, and praises him for daring to believe men can be better than they are.

Johnson, Clarence O. "Herbert Gold." *Critical Survey of Short Fiction.* Ed. Frank N. Magill. 8 vols. Englewood Cliffs: Salem, 1981. 4: 1501-05.

A standard reference article on principal short fiction, influence, story, biography, and analysis of *Love and Like.*

Karlen, Arno. "The MacGregor Syndrome and Other Literary Losses." *Georgia Review* 37.2 (1983): 285-304.

Sees *Swiftie the Magician* as having been ignored because it wounded cherished illusions. Claims that Swiftie Dixon becomes Gold's emblem of the age, a female mountebank who lures with beauty and style during an era of faddish self-congratulation. Calls her a queen of the transvestite culture who, ironically, appalls the narrator whose own career as a shoddy filmmaker using "nubile chicklets" along the way is equally shallow and disgusting. Sees Gold as the master of the cinematic quick cut, the pitiless ear for banality, and the verbal twist. Concludes that he is also shrewd about the politics of desertion. Claims that reviewers were wrong to have ignored a book that projected such an accurate view of the age.

Krupp, Kathleen McCoy. "Psychological Tripling in 'The Witch.'" *The Process of Fiction.* Ed. Barbara McKenzie. New York: Harcourt, 1969. 161-67.

Provides a detailed analysis and interpretation of "The Witch." Argues that the strong emotional impact of the story derives from an unusual

congruence of two worlds: the domestic comedy of a perpetually quarreling couple and the bizarre element of the witch as a device to set off
conflict. Claims that, in this story, rich, evocative language has created a
brilliant metaphor for the madness and horror submerged in the human
mind—for the darkness that sometimes rises to the surface, spilling over
into daylight, straining and destroying what it touches.

Moore, Harry T. "The Fiction of Herbert Gold." *Contemporary
American Novelists.* Ed. Harry T. Moore. Crosscurrents/Modern
Critiques. Carbondale: Southern Illinois UP, 1964. 170-81.

This lengthy chapter provides the best single and systematic treatment of
all of Gold's works. Characterizes Gold as a writer with a fine sense of
humor, an ironist, an anti-sentimentalist, and a notable stylist with considerable potential, despite harsh treatment by reviewers.

Roth, Philip. "Writing American Fiction." *Commentary* Mar. 1961: 223-33.

Sees Gold as one of the most productive and respected novelists of the
contemporary period. Yet notes that he is a writer whose own life is in
competition with his fiction. Claims that many of the novels list all of the
cities Gold has lived in or visited while working on that book. Concludes
that Gold is at his best when he is expressing delight, and suggests that
his prose tends otherwise to be extravagant and confessional, with far too
many appendices about his own divorces or private life.

Seiden, Melvin. "Characters and Ideas: The Modern Novel." *Nation* 25
Apr. 1959: 387-92.

Calls *The Optimist* a "curiously flat performance" and a thoroughly conventional novel. Complains about the overly assertive euphoria besetting
the novel, Gold's doctrine of joy—aliveness—that is never allowed to
become incarnate, the baroque style, and the characters' lack of resonance.
Concludes that Gold need not have restrained his freewheeling prose quite
so much as to completely tie his hands behind his back. Contrasts this
novel with the much better one, *The Man Who Was Not With It.*

Serlen, Ellen. "The American Dream: From F. Scott Fitzgerald to
Herbert Gold." *Midamerica* 4 (1977): 122-37.

Argues that Gold's heroes pick up where Fitzgerald's left off—they
show the American Dream altered, embellished, and the worse for wear.
Claims that Gold's heroes, who now "inhabit a more complicated, post-
Depression America weaned on the myths of Hollywood, and

swaggering with possibility, are content with only one dream. A gained desire to them merely serves as progenitor to another dream, and so on, Sisyphus-like." A major treatment of the theme of the failed American Dream in Gold's novels.

Sherman, Bernard. "Therefore Be Bold." *The Invention of the Jew: Jewish-American Education Novels (1916-1964).* Bernard Sherman. New York: Yoseloff, 1969. 211-14.

Claims that *Therefore Be Bold* is a book with more than a touch of the derivative, some humor, and much braggadocio and sneering of adolescent mannerisms. Suggests, however, that the final effect is to dignify adolescence.

Smith, Larry. "Herbert Gold—Belief and Craft." *Ohioana Quarterly* 21 (1978): 148-56.

A critical eulogy of Gold's contributions to American literature praising him for his "brilliant short story collections and solid novels." Sees Gold as conventional and traditional in form "favoring the energetic and self-revealing style of colloquial first person narratives. His chief experimentation is with content and style. A practitioner of both journalism and fiction, Gold sees a thin line separating their material and treatment." Praises Gold for his style and classic and compelling story-telling art. Offers qualitative comments on several of the major works, and concludes that Gold is a modern myth maker "who both penetrates and deepens the mystery of existence."

Stevenson, David L. "Styron and the Fiction of the Fifties." *Critique* 3.3 (1960): 47-58.

Discusses briefly some of Gold's novels along with those of his contemporaries whose novels are "not metaphysically hopped-up, but genuinely concerned with the ultimate and the unconditional."

"Therefore Be Bold." *Survey of Contemporary Literature.* Ed. Frank N. Magill. Rev. ed. 12 vols. Englewood Cliffs: Salem, 1977. 11: 7523-25.

A standard reference article covering background, influence, plot, character, themes, and style in *Therefore Be Bold.*

Weinberg, Helen. "Minor American Novelists in the Activist Mode." *The New Novel in America: The Kafkan Mode in Contemporary Fiction.* Helen Weinberg. Ithaca: Cornell UP, 1970. 165-85.

Sees Gold as writing ironic, affirmative novels in the activist mode. Provides a brief critique of *The Optimist* and *Salt.*

Wohlgelernter, Maurice. "Fathers—Artichokes, Choosers, Carpenters—And All Their Sons." *Tradition: A Journal of Orthodox Thought* 9.3 (1967): 125-40.

An account of *Fathers* treated in the context of several other American and Jewish-American novels about fathers and sons. Mostly a summary of the contents of the novel.

Reviews

Abeel, Erica. "Psycho-Dynamists and Others." Rev. of *A Girl of Forty. New York Times Book Review* 10 Aug. 1986: 11.

Gives a plot summary. Observes that Gold's language, "ambiguous, hackneyed, or simply lost to meaning," undermines an otherwise compelling satire.

Adams, Robert Martin. "The Short Stories of Herbert Gold." Rev. of *Love and Like. Hudson Review* 13.2 (1960): 303-07.

Argues that Gold has an unerring sense of pace, a fine ear for idiom, very little self-pity, a talent for hitting crucial issues, and a natural ability to tell stories. Concludes that these qualities characterize the stories in this collection. Describes several of the stories.

Adler, Renata. "Salt Into Old Scars." Rev. of *Salt. New Yorker* 22 June 1963: 104, 106, 109-111. Rpt. in *Toward a Radical Middle: Fourteen Pieces of Reporting and Criticism.* Renata Adler. New York: Random, 1970. 31-37.

Complains that the novel is a clichéd satire full of worn, familiar targets—"cynical Madison Avenue, opportunistic Wall Street, sterile suburbia, impersonal New York—set up once again and duly re-assassinated." Provides a detailed account of the contents of the book, its symbolic patterns, and its structural devices, along with appraisal of the style of humor, tone, and language.

Alter, Robert. "Manhattan Merry-Go-Round Set to a Wry Tune." Rev. of *Salt. New York Herald Tribune Books* 21 Apr. 1963: 5.

Argues that *Salt* brilliantly realizes the possibilities for comedy in the condition of dehumanized loneliness that we now automatically associate with life in the metropolis. Calls this a triptych of quietly desperate Manhattan figures, and demonstrates how, when it moves from narration to declaration, dramatic dialogue to rhetoric, it loses its power to convince, despite passages of great imagination and power.

"The American Game of Happy Families." Rev. of *Fathers. Times Literary Supplement* 21 Dec. 1967: 1233.

Describes *Fathers* as a cliché of the Jewish, American, and male experience, but also sees it as a brilliant comic portrait of Sam Gold in the novel. Concludes that, otherwise, this is a story of the Middle West, the power center of the U.S.

Andrews, Peter. "The New Wild West." Rev. of *True Love. New York Times Book Review* 12 Dec. 1982: 14.

Labels Gold as the most reliable cataloguer of exotic California. Describes the contents and characters of the novel, and likens its anthropological contributions to those of Margaret Mead.

"Bad Dream." Rev. of *The Great American Jackpot. Times Literary Supplement* 21 May 1971: 600.

Calls this novel another sourly sardonic, bemused, and near-desperate victim of a consumer society, suffering unbearable withdrawal pains as a result of having woken up from the American Dream. Concludes that the book is a veritable jungle of verbal and emotional mixed connections.

Balliett, Whitney. "The Burning Bush." Rev. of *The Optimist. New Yorker* 13 June 1959: 129-30.

Calls this a book in which Gold shoots from the hip, and writes nimble sentences. Complains that his theme is hackneyed and passed from the muckrakers into the soaps long ago—beware the ambitious American whose aggressiveness and intensity destroy both himself and those about him. Concludes that Gold is capable of some rather good writing in the fashionable semi-poetic, documentary manner.

Barrett, William. "Bohemian Wrecks." Rev. of *Salt. Atlantic* June 1963: 132.

Calls *Salt* brilliant, witty, mournful, and rather well-worn as a story. Admits that Gold does prod life into it through his unrelenting verbal brilliance, but, when the razzle dazzle dies down, the whole thing is a bit forlorn.

Bellman, Samuel I. "Tales of Woe." Rev. of *Fathers. Congress Bi-Weekly* 6 Nov. 1967: 22.

Lumps the novel together with several like it, and complains that they all show the devastation of humane, viable Jewish family life. Details the contents of the novel.

Bergonzi, Bernard. "'Eat! Eat!'." Rev. of *Fathers. New York Review of Books* 1 June 1967: 30-31.

Claims that *Fathers* is written in a collusive idiom where the reader's assent is solicited for every judgment on life the author cares to make. Worries that the reader may feel inclined to love Sam Gold only in the sense that he loves all God's creatures, and to admire to whatever extent any self-made tycoon.

Borklund, Elmer. "A New Fictional Hero." Rev. of *Love and Like. Commentary* Aug 1960: 176-77.

Describes this collection of fourteen stories as having an effect so joyless one wonders if Gold still believes in heroes. Sees the later stories as almost obsessive in their concern with painful probing, largely without joy or satisfaction, and lonely, ambitious Platonists reduced to brutal egotism.

Boroff, David. "The Spice without the Savor." Rev. of *Salt. Saturday Review* 20 Apr. 1963: 45-46.

Provides a synopsis of the novel. Sees Gold, a major young talent, describing New York City as the Holy City of Existentialism. Argues that, while older writers dealt with the loss of values by the generation they wrote about, Gold talks about a generation who never had any. Describes Gold's characters as "automatons of pleasure, slaves of the transient itch, picturesque anti heroes in expensive clothing." Concludes, nevertheless, that Gold has misspent his creative vitality in this novel.

Brickner, Richard P. "Too Uncritical to be the Critic." Rev. of *Swiftie the Magician. New York Times Book Review* 15 Sept. 1974: 44.

Provides an account of the characters and events of the novel along with an argument that the point-of-view character is too poorly developed for the kinds of lines he has to deliver. Sees the novel as careless and glib. Decides that, for a ninth novel, it is not promising—it reads like literary hack work.

Broyard, Anatole. "Books of the Times." Rev. of *He/She. New York Times* 6 June 1980: C23.

Argues that *He/She* is reminiscent of the closing lines of Sylvia Plath's poem "The Applicant": "My boy, it's your last resort/ Will you marry it, marry it, marry it?" Provides a detailed account of plot and characters. Concludes that this is one of the faces the broken hearted wear in our time.

Broyard, Anatole. "Gold, Simenon, Latham." Rev. of *Waiting for Cordelia. New York Times Book Review* 22 May 1977: 14.

Reviews Gold's treatment at the hands of the critics, and wonders why he has not been held more accountable to his craft. Accuses him of doing *shtick* instead of character development, and of not being ambitious or pretentious enough. Concludes that, because head triumphs over the imagination, Gold causes the book to read like a relentless talkathon.

Buckler, Robert. "Anguished Americans." Rev. of *Swiftie the Magician. Listener* 11 Sept. 1975: 350.

Calls this novel a sixties retrospective partly remembered through a hangover. Deems this a tale about much more than showbiz.

Cassidy, Thomas E. "Familiar Search." Rev. of *The Optimist. Commonweal* 21 May 1959: 236-37.

Describes the hero of *The Optimist* as a confused, valueless hero whose sexual gymnastics become wearisome, and his depiction as a hard rock sergeant, oversensitive Jew, and closet poet rather cliché. Concludes that Gold makes no moral or intellectual growth; consequently the novel never really gets going.

Charyn, Jerome. "A Homage to His Women." Rev. of *Family: A Novel in the Form of a Memoir. New York Times Book Review* 13 Dec. 1981: 12, 42.

Praises the memoir for its intimacy of detail and the characters for their vulnerability. Commends the book mostly for the homage it pays to the women in Gold's life. Lists the names of the female characters briefly, and contrasts them with the much less important male characters in the novel.

"Coketown Fringe, U.S.A." Rev. of *The Man Who Was Not with It. Times Literary Supplement* 4 Mar. 1965: 161.

Calls the world of this novel a garish carnival, showing a microcosm of the American sham, distortion, and illusion. Concludes that, thematically, the novel has obvious parallels with Bellow's *The Victim*, though it is far more uneven.

Corwin, Phillip. "In Zany *Jackpot* Everybody Seeks, But Nobody
   Finds." Rev. of *The Great American Jackpot*. *National Observer* 2
   Mar. 1970: 21.

Argues that *The Great American Jackpot* is a semi-serious sociological
spoof, a humorous mind-blower of a novel peopled with zany, wacky,
but occasionally dull misfits: the speedfreaks, the petty criminals, the
bookies, the fuzz, militant revolutionaries all brought together into one
disharmonious jackpot. Concludes that at the center is America and the
question of what happened to the American Dream, a question for which
Gold finds no simple answer.

Cunningham, Valentine. "Happy Ever-Aftering." Rev. of *Swiftie the
   Magician*. *Times Literary Supplement* 13 June 1975: 643.

Regards this novel as a slapstick attempt to monumentalize the style of
the sixties—a period of bubble reputations and hollow flamboyance when
the panache of pose mattered most in the Kennedy-Carnaby Camelot.

Curzon, Daniel. "The Heterosexual Underbelly of the City by the Bay."
   Rev. of *Dreaming*. *Los Angeles Times Book Review* 17 Apr. 1988: 2.

Argues that *Dreaming* will win few points with feminists and Chinese,
and it is not until two-thirds through the novel that the story picks up.
Worries that those who stay with it that long will be rewarded by a book
moving through its unsentimental world examining some eighties people
with rather large warts.

Davis, Robert Gorham. "Heart of the Artichoke." Rev. of *Fathers*. *New
   Leader* 22 May 1967: 7-9.

An appreciative description of *Fathers* describing Gold as having found
the fictional self he now interposes between us and the father's life
described in the novel. Details plot, characters, particularly admired
scenes, and style.

Davis, Robert Gorham. "A Tour in Vaudeville on the Stage of Life." Rev.
   of *Therefore Be Bold*. *New York Times Book Review* 9 Oct. 1960: 4.

Sees this as a tender, witty novel functioning like a metaphysical poem to
adolescence. Claims, however, that despite Gold's artfulness, occasionally his wit falsifies while his period authenticity lapses. Details contents.

Delbanco, Nicholas. "Hutch Tries to Get His, and Does." Rev. of
   Dreaming. *New York Times Book Review* 27 Mar. 1988: 9.

Notes that *Dreaming* recycles some themes and characters from his previous fiction. Calls the storyline simple, and describes the bulk of the book as dealing with Hutch's attempt to realize his dreams. Suggests that the San Francisco in which he tries to do it conjures up Yoknaptawha or a Paris of "Comedie Humaine."

"The Devil Made the Town." Rev. of *Salt. Times Literary Supplement* 13 Feb. 1964: 121.

Argues that in *Salt* Gold tells us that the world he depicted in *Manhattan Transfer* with its various chronic depletions is worse than ever. Calls the style tense, verbose, and brilliantly useful to demonstrate Dan's and Mr. Goldman's ambivalence toward New York. Concludes that, basically, it is a story about the urban narcissus.

Donoghue, Douglas. "Connections." Rev. of *The Man Who Was Not With It. New Statesman* 26 Feb. 1965: 328.

Describes the contents of the novel. Concludes that it is not quite the real thing, and lacks the integrity of his earlier works.

Engle, Paul. "To Control the Energetic Heart." Rev. of *Love and Like. Saturday Review* 2 Apr. 1960: 20.

Calls *Love and Like* an admirable collection of short stories written with shrewd wit and a disenchanted pity for all human creatures. Notes that the prose is supple and expressive, while the impact of the stories themselves is uneven. Concludes, nevertheless, that it is writers like Gold who are managing to keep the grace and force of the American short story.

Engle, Paul. "A Young American Asking For More." Rev. of *The Optimist. Chicago Sunday Tribune Magazine of Books* 10 May 1959: 18.

Describes *The Optimist* as being about Burr Fuller who wants desperately to enter law, politics, and marriage as an optimist. Details the contents of the story.

F., F. J. "The New Books." Rev. of *Prospects Before Us. San Francisco Chronicle This World Magazine* 21 Mar. 1954: 22.

Calls this novel a fine piece of realism, although it almost stalls out by its own failures on a couple of occasions. Argues that despite the fact that much of it manages to look pretty bleak, even the presence of one worthwhile character is a rarity in a novel these days.

"Fiction." Rev. of *Stories of Misbegotten Love. Kirkus Reviews* 15 Aug.
    1985: 807-08.

Briefly describes the five stories with "their numbing evenness of voice
and subject," and comments that the only thing "misbegotten" about
these "distasteful stories is their re-publication."

"Fiction Originals." Rev. of *Stories of Misbegotten Love. Publishers
    Weekly* 30 Aug. 1985: 418.

Briefly notes that the stories "center around the vicissitudes of modern
relationships." Claims that the men spin their wheels in self-analysis, and
that the women regularly jilt them.

Foster, Richard. "Reviews." Rev. of *Therefore Be Bold. Hudson Review*
    14.1 (1961): 146-48.

Sees *Therefore Be Bold* as essentially an entertainment, a humorous
yielding to rose-hazed nostalgia—an extemporized, anecdotal ramble
which, alas, is more often exhausting than refreshing and diverting.

Freeman, Gillian. "Fathers and So On." Rev. of *Fathers. New Statesman*
    2 June 1967: 768.

Calls *Fathers* an autobiographical novel, written in flat, diffident style.
Notes its concern with the Jewish father-son relationship, and views
Gold's treatment of it as perfunctory. Briefly describes the characters.

Fremont-Smith, Eliot. "Generations." Rev. of *Fathers. New York Times* 5
    Apr. 1967: 45.

Comments that *Fathers* is about the irretrievable loss of childhood, the
strength of life, and the power of memories. Calls this novel the stuff of
ritual, myth, art, imagination, and nostalgia. Details the contents.

Gardner, Peter. "Books in Brief." Rev. of *Waiting for Cordelia. Saturday
    Review* 23 July 1977: 42.

Sees *Waiting for Cordelia* as a zany, engaging, and irritating story.
Comments that Gold is a master of the freak portrait gallery, an acute
observer of comedy and the pathos of pretense, as well as a skilled word-
smith. Concludes, however, that the book never really answers the larger
question about love, and ends up merely dazzling.

Garis, Robert. "Varieties of the Will." Rev. of *Fathers. Hudson Review*
    20.2 (1967): 329-30.

A brief review of Gold's autobiographical novel, *Fathers*, that attempts to "bridge by faith the 'abyss' of incommunicability between parental and filial love," but which finally encourages "our disbelief in the father he hoped to honor."

Gentry, Curt. "Politics Enters the Picture in Gold's Fourth Novel." Rev. of *The Optimist*. *San Francisco Chronicle* 24 May 1959: 26.

Calls *The Optimist* a failure because of its shopworn methods, and because its characters and situations rarely become more than stereotypes. Notes that the craftsmanship is effective, and some of the passages perceptive. Concludes, however, that none of this is enough to make the novel worthy of Gold's talent.

Goldman, Albert. "Most Happy Fellow." Rev. of *Salt*. *New Republic* 8 June 1963: 23-24, 26.

Calls Gold a highly successful young writer because he is a master of the going thing. Sees his stories and novels as zeroed in on a new generation who suffer early sorrow, make an early marriage, father children at an early age, and then—surrounded by the symbols of middle-class domesticity—find their hearts festooned with unrealized adolescence. Provides a detailed account of contents and characters in *Salt* from this perspective.

Gordon, David J. "Trust and Treachery: Some Recent Novels." Rev. of *Fathers*. *Yale Review* 57.1 (1967): 106-07.

Reviews *Fathers* as a novel forwarding the theme of trust between the generations. Sees the novel as dividing itself equally between the topics of fatherhood and sonhood. Praises the piece for its flexibility of tone. Criticizes it for its depiction of women and verbal slapstick. Questions Gold's sincerity in some incidents, and condemns the portrait of the father, Sam Gold, as ultimately facile and idealized.

Greenfeld, Josh. "A Search for Love." Rev. of *Fathers*. *New York Times Book Review* 19 Mar. 1967: 1, 57.

Describes the contents of the novel in detail, compares its contents with that of Hutchins, and concludes that this is a splendid book.

Gresham, William Lindsay. "Traveling with Carnies." Rev. of *The Man Who Was Not With It*. *New York Times Book Review* 19 Feb. 1956: 5.

Argues that *Fathers* contains a jumble of themes which Gold ties into a unity of sorts with an undeniable impact. Details the contents.

Halio, Jay. "The Way It Is and Was." Rev. of *Fathers. Southern Review [Baton Rouge]* 6.1 (1970): 256-57.

Describes the plot, characters, setting, style, and tone. Concludes that this is fictionalized autobiography.

Hamill, Pete. "Veteran Journalist Running from Love." Rev. of *Mister White Eyes. New York Times Book Review* 11 Nov. 1984: 15.

Deals exclusively with how well Gold has depicted the character of the journalist in a novelistic treatment. Claims that *Mister White Eyes* confronts directly the problem of the veteran journalist—of always seeing himself in the third person. Ranks this book with other books featuring journalists as protagonists such as *The Sun Also Rises* and *Miss Lonelyhearts*. Concludes that this is a solid and honorable novel.

Hicks, Granville. "Amour, Amour, Amour." Rev. of *Therefore Be Bold. Saturday Review* 1 Oct. 1960: 15. Rpt. as *"Therefore Be Bold"* in *Literary Horizons: A Quarter Century of American Fiction.* Granville Hicks with Jack Alan Robbins. New York: New York UP, 1970. 164-67.

Identifies Gold's major theme of love and self-discovery as each other's prerequisites. Notes that this novel continues the study of love, and scrutinizes adolescents from suburban Cleveland. Calls it a book written in praise of human possibilities. Concludes that the style is original and powerful, the conversations brilliant.

Hicks, Granville. "Each Generation Had Its Own Dream." Rev. of *Fathers. Saturday Review* 25 Mar. 1967: 25-26. Rpt. as *"Fathers"* in *Literary Horizons: A Quarter Century of American Fiction.* Granville Hicks with Jack Alan Robbins. New York: New York UP, 1970. 167-70.

An account primarily of the contents of the novel, and some personal impressions of Gold gained at a surprise meeting with him at Saratoga Springs. Praises the book for its sensitive portrayal of the generation gap between the original immigrants and their children. Calls Gold's vision affirmative and enlightening.

Hicks, Granville. *"The Man Who Was Not with It* and Other Novels by Herbert Gold." Rev. of *The Man Who Was Not with It.* New Leader 20 Feb. 1956: 16-17. Rpt. as "The Man Who Was Not with It" in *Literary Horizons: A Quarter Century of American Fiction.* Granville Hicks with Jack Alan Robbins. New York: New York UP, 1970. 156-60.

Views Gold as being Balzacian in spirit because of the importance he attaches to personhood even for seemingly insignificant people. Argues that, from this perspective, Gold deals with themes of selfhood and relationships in this novel as well as in *Birth of a Hero* and *The Hero Before Us*. Gives fairly elaborate plot summaries and character analyses for all three novels.

Hicks, Granville. "Report on Herbert Gold." Rev. of *The Optimist*. *Saturday Review* 25 Apr. 1959: 12. Rpt. As *"The Optimist"* in *Literary Horizons: A Quarter Century of American Fiction*. Granville Hicks with Jack Alan Robbins. New York: New York UP, 1970. 161-64.

Finds himself puzzled and disappointed with this novel, whose achievement has fallen short of Gold's real talent. Provides a detailed plot summary, and complains that Burr, the central character, is elusive. Notes that the failure of Burr's marriage tells us nothing about him, and concludes that this novel shows the failure of a first-rate novelist.

Hicks, Granville. "Three New Novels about Negroes Which Transcend the Old Formulas." Rev. of *The Prospect Before Us*. *New Leader* 1 Mar. 1954: 21-22. Rpt. in revised form as *"The Prospect Before Us"* in *Literary Horizons: A Quarter Century of American Fiction*. Granville Hicks with Jack Alan Robbins. New York: New York UP, 1970. 153-55.

Reviews the plot, and praises Gold's mastery of colloquial style, seemingly artless and perfect dialogue, and creation of "an original and moving novel."

Hjortsberg, William. "A Bank Robber from Berkeley." Rev. of *The Great American Jackpot*. *New York Times Book Review* 25 Jan. 1970: 40.

Argues that this novel, Gold's eighth, fails because it is both pretentious and dishonest. Describes the contents, setting, characters, point of view, and style. Condemns the book because it tries to be too many things at once, falling into an unfortunate hip style that fails.

Hungerford, Edward B. "Girl Chasing by Empty Males in an Empty Society." Rev. of *Salt*. *Chicago Sunday Tribune Magazine of Books* 5 May 1963: 7.

Claims that *Salt* celebrates the withdrawal from fiction of the hero, and that the first and last parts of the book are written in a fairly orthodox style while the middle portions resemble a beat style—taut but with barely relevant intrusions. Concludes that readers in search of vicarious knowledge of life as it is lived by the unattached in metropolitan circles will like the book.

Hyman, Stanley Edgar. "Herbert Gold's Glitter." Rev. of *Salt. New Leader* 13 May 1963: 8-9.

Describes *Salt* as funny, touching, full of wonderful scenes, savagely satiric, and occasionally uproarious. But claims that beneath all this verbal coruscation and glitter, beneath the sexual frankness and topical freshness, is old-fashioned naturalism. Concludes that, at best, this is a readable book that is not quite an insult to the intelligence. Describes the contents thoroughly.

Johnson, Nora. "Two Westerns." Rev. of *Slave Trade. New York Times Book Review* 22 Apr. 1979: 15, 33.

Describes the novel in detail, and then condemns it. Argues that there is nothing funny to cause the faintest smile in this book that reads like a sewer and is full of characters who are either psychotic or alienated. Concludes by asking why a novelist of Gold's stature has written this book.

Jones, D. A. N. "Live Argument." Rev. of *The Great American Jackpot. New York Review of Books* 21 May 1970: 36-37.

Calls *The Great American Jackpot* a long novel about young Californians which fails to be sprightly or surprising. Concludes that it is mostly about play acting rather than sincerity.

Junker, Howard. "Poe vs. Artichokes." Rev. of *Fathers. Newsweek* 27 Mar. 1967: 104, 106.

Calls *Fathers* something that is not even a novel from an author who never really quite pulls off the big one. Finds himself bemused by the quaint normalcy of these father-son scenes that never really explore their human consequences. Concludes that Gold lacks the intensity and capacity for metaphor Malamud has.

Kaiser, Robert G. "Climbing Out of Love." Rev. of *He/She. Washington Post Book World* 15 June 1980: 5.

Praises Gold for being a master of time-capsule fiction which discusses what happens to marriage in the time of female awakenings. Sees Gold as a gifted reporter whose characters' dilemmas are rooted in precise cultural moments. Notes that, although the characters are universal, Gold gives them no names. Sees He as a male chauvinist and his wife as a woman of the 1970s fallen out of love with the institution of marriage and her husband. Concludes, "This is a document of our time and a lovely piece of writing."

Kelly, James. "Fat Harry's Defiance." Rev. of *The Prospect Before Us.* *New York Times Book Review* 14 Feb. 1954: 5, 25.

Sees this novel as less well constructed than previous novels. Notes that the scenes are often strung together necklace style, while the characters seem to have labels stuck to them. Complains, "it is a cerebral performance with a tangle of long, long thoughts, most of them entertainingly presented in colorful runaway language." Attributes to Gold a high fidelity ear and eye, and concludes that the candid conviction and jocular low humor of small encounters drawn from the author's own diary as hotel night manager provide the right enveloping action.

King, Francis. "Neato." Rev. of *Waiting for Cordelia. Spectator* 12 Aug. 1978: 20-21.

Sees the novel as a "clever, expert, cynical creation but one that suggests that the author has succumbed to the imaginative equivalent of hardening arteries, fibrillation and general debility." Claims that, even though Gold has successfully given a picture of modern San Franciso, created pathetic and grotesque characters, and displayed "an amusingly 'scummy' wit," with the disparate elements showing a "hectic vigor," nothing holds them together, or coordinates their movement.

Knuepfel, George. Rev. of *Mr. White Eyes. San Francisco Review of Books* (Spr. 1985): 12.

Argues that the omniscient third person point of view does not work to the story's advantage. Notes that there are lapses of wrong, awkward, and prosaic language and improbable conversations. Claims that events in the story lose power because nothing is related in relief. Concludes with the fear that not too many readers would have remained long enough with the book to hear it.

Korn, Eric. "A Prof Among Pros." Rev. of *Waiting for Cordelia. Times Literary Supplement* 11 Aug. 1978: 905.

Calls *Waiting for Cordelia* a golden oldie plot set in melancholy, permissive San Francisco. Notes that the style veers between Bay Area Baroque and Playboy Pretentious. Calls the action episodic, and the structure non-existent. Concludes that the story is intermittent, intelligent, and entertaining.

Kriegel, Leonard. "The Wondering Jew." Rev. of *Fathers. Nation* 3 July 1967: 23-24.

Finds Gold at his best in this novel, treading "dangerously sentimental territory," but notes that "only in fleeting instances does the novel succumb to sentiment." Concludes that Gold uses the myth of the Jew as wanderer, molding it to his own purposes.

Lamport, Felicia. Rev. of *The Magic Will: Stories and Essays of a Decade. Saturday Review* 12 June 1971: 32.

Argues that, at its best, the collection is poignant, evocative, ironic, lyric, and witty, but that at its worst, it is turgid, self-enunciatory, righteous, pretentious, and slipshod. Cautions, however, that "exasperation should not entirely blot out appreciation of Mr. Gold's considerable talent. Careless flaws and self-indulgent foibles may threaten him with tenure as dean of the promising young writers, but the promise remains."

Lassell, Michael J. "To Find the Truth, To Find the Self." Rev. of *Mister White Eyes. Los Angeles Times Book Review* 14 Oct. 1984: 3.

Calls this an insightful book full of the details of a variety of worlds and the minutiae of human existence. Complains, however, that the prose alone is not sufficient to carry the interest because "the novel vacillates between inventive literary devices of contemporary fiction and the conventions of pulp." Concludes that the characters seem poorly motivated, and that the ending comes not as a catharsis, but as a sudden gush, tangential and inaccessible.

Levenson, Michael. "Humble Pies." Rev. of *Swiftie the Magician. Harper's* Nov. 1974: 110, 112.

Sees the novel as a satiric chronicle of the Sixties in which Gold shares the defects of the things he is assailing. Claims that "writing about the superficial and the frivolous, he writes superficially and frivolously." Believes "the targets Gold knocks over [Orange County, the jet set, aging rock stars] were already so moldy and tottering they would have fallen over on their own." Sees the novel as a picaresque that moves not from place to place, but from fashion to fashion. Claims that Gold has a journalist's temperament, and sees the book as unrelievedly topical. Concludes that he makes little attempt to understand the phenomena, content to reproduce them, making the book more a sociological than a literary specimen.

Levine, Paul. "Reviews." Rev. of *Fathers. Hudson Review* 20.2 (1967): 347-48.

Describes *Fathers* as a sensitive, affectionate portrait, virtually unadorned by verbal self-indulgence. Claims that though it lacks the pungency of a Bellow novel, it remains an affecting fictive memoir.

Levine, Paul. "Reviews." Rev. of *Salt. Hudson Review* 16.3 (1963): 458.

Says *Salt* is a western of the *Playboy* world written in sweet, sardonic, sour style. Claims that, unfortunately, Gold wants to be hip with the hipsters and moral with the moralists. Concludes, finally, that the book is irritating and unconvincing: Hugh Hefner would have loved it.

Lindroth, James R. "Book Reviews." Rev. of *Fathers. America* 15 Apr. 1967: 565-66.

Describes *Fathers* as standard Franklinesque autobiography—a record of initiation and education. Details the rites of passage of the account and its unifying theme of the American Dream. Concludes that nostalgia is the novel's main mood.

"Lost Magic." Rev. of *Fathers. Time* 31 Mar. 1967: 96, 98.

Calls *Fathers* a nostalgic memoir of the 1930s with a strong sense of the absurd and frequent cynical insights. Describes the plot and central characters. Concludes that, even if similar stories have been told, they have not been told with Gold's particular skill.

Luria, Jack. "Books." Rev. of *Fathers. Jewish Frontier* July-Aug. 1967: 25-26.

Claims that, while Gold is as talented as Bellow, Malamud, or Roth, he is too involved with the materials of his experience, and cannot yet write about them with objectivity. Claims that what he does give in *Fathers* is an honest and impassioned report of life felt and observed by a sensitive man. Concludes that there are no dull patches in his work and that he avoids the strained objectivity of Hemingway and his school, functioning as a soliloquist.

Maddocks, Melvin. "Oh Dad, Dear Dad, Sons Will Mellow." Rev. of *Fathers. Christian Science Monitor* 23 Mar. 1967: 11.

Calls the story of *Fathers* an old one told gracefully but without passion or nostalgia.

Mahon, Derek. "Song of Mirrors." Rev. of *The Great American Jackpot. Listener* 4 Mar. 1971: 280.

Argues that *The Great American Jackpot* is about a hero bored with the planet. Calls it a very funny book with some great descriptive writing: Haight-Ashbury, a folk-rock open air concert, and a freestyle Berkeley sociology seminar where even "the fuzz" call themselves social workers and talk about linguistics.

Malin, Irving. Rev. of *The Great American Jackpot*. *Commonweal* 10 July 1970: 349-50.

Primarily details the contents of *The Great American Jackpot*. Concludes that Gold is a gifted writer once he escapes from nostalgia, and that he is at his best when he is fresh, jumpy, and metaphysically biting.

McDonnell, Thomas P. "Solid Gold." Rev. of *Fathers*. *Critic* June-July 1967: 88-89.

Claims that *Fathers* is a novel saved by the grace and sinew of Gold's mature style from lapsing into cliché and mere banality. Sees it as a richly layered book.

McMurtry, Larry. "Marital Problems." Rev. of *He/She*. *New York Times Book Review* 25 May 1980: 10, 21.

Sees this as a story about the tenacity of relationships, and praises its sharp focus. Concludes, however, that Gold's usual light comedic touch is missing from this overly serious book about marital failure.

Mellors, John. "Roman Road." Rev. of *Waiting for Cordelia*. *Listener* 7 Sept. 1978: 318-19.

Briefly recounts the plot, and finds "too much 'wet soul' in this ramblingly episodic book."

Merkin, Daphne. "Lost Souls." Rev. of *He/She*. *New Leader* 28 July 1980: 16.

Sees *He/She* as a stark, wistful novel about domestic terror and marital break-up, all told from an almost myopically male perspective. Claims that it discloses the ache of maleness in an exacting, claustrophobic, and intense novel in which two people come to understand each other without being sure they truly want to.

Mitgang, Herbert. "Books of the Times." Rev. of *A Girl of Forty*. *New York Times* 23 July 1986: C18.

Claims that in *A Girl of Forty*, Gold has created a California Holly Golightly and more. Notes that it contains accurate dialogue and scenes as well as brilliant portraits of many of Gold's generation. Concludes that this novel has a heartbeat all its own. Details the contents of several of the stories.

Monaghan, Charles. "In *Fathers* Herbert Gold Constructs a Work of Exorcism Rather Than a Novel." Rev. of *Fathers*. *National Observer* 27 Mar. 1967: 19.

Complains that *Fathers* displays little of the novelist's necessary removal from his subject matter, and feels more like an exorcism than a novel. Thinks that, finally, it fails as art because Sam is romanticized out of all proportion. Admires the prose for being bare and supple, and worthy of a man for whom literature is not only business, but serious business. Concludes that, unfortunately, verbal economy is not enough.

Moore, Harry T. "Experience Accumulates." Rev. of *Love and Like*. *New York Times Book Review* 27 Mar. 1960: 5.

Notes that *Love and Like* contains fourteen of his stories which will no doubt strengthen Gold's reputation. Describes many of them, and concludes that this is more than just another collection of stories.

Moore, Harry T. "Skimming the Surface." Rev. of *The Optimist*. *New York Times Book Review* 26 Apr. 1959: 40.

Complains that *The Optimist* fails to sound new depths in its chosen subject matter, and thus fails in spite of its brilliant capturing of surfaces. Adds that its themes are often overworked.

Morris, Robert K. "We Don't Know What We Want." Rev. of *The Magic Will: Stories and Essays of a Decade*. *Nation* 8 Nov. 1971: 475-76.

Calls *The Magic Will* a collection of stories and essays representing related islands of experience from Gold's personal odyssey of adolescence to manhood. Notes that it is a collection showing his obvious distaste for the values of middle America, and ranges from self-adulation to self-condemnation. Calls him a Sancho Panza of humanistic values.

Pesetsky, Bette. "Lovers & Cohorts." Rev. of *Lovers &Cohorts*. *Los Angeles Times Book Review* 4 May 1986: 3.

Argues that marriage gets short shrift in many of the stories in *Lovers &Cohorts*. Admits they are written in lucid style, colloquial wit, and often with slick use of devices like quips, discourse, reminiscences, proverbs, and jokes. Concludes that there is technical proficiency here, but that passion cannot be supplied by mere craftsmanship.

Phelps, Robert. "Mr. Gold Paints a Portrait." Rev. of *The Optimist*. *New York Herald Tribune Book Review* 26 Apr. 1959: 8.

Calls *The Optimist* a collection of short stories representing a decade's backlog of articles, sketches, and reviews. Commends the collection for its sense of adventure, swift nimble prose, and ability to shoot from the hip.

Pickrel, Paul. "And Finally, Some Men." Rev. of *Salt. Harper's* June 1963: 108.

Calls *Salt* a character study depicting two young men on the prowl in New York who hang onto the world of youth too long. Describes the shabby funny contrivances to which they stoop to prolong their uncommitted lifestyles.

Pinsker, Sanford. "Jewish Fathers and Sons: A New View." Rev. of *Fathers. Reconstructionist* 1 Dec. 1967: 22-23.

Believes that the prevailing view of the Jewish Father in American Fiction as the stern, unloving, Freudian disciplinarian and representative of Jewish orthodoxy is broken in Gold's novel.

Poore, Charles. "Books of the Times." Rev. of *Salt. New York Times* 20 Apr. 1963: 25.

Calls *Salt* a book which reflects the loss of daring in the *avant garde* novel and its replacement by a general nihilism. Notes that the only saving grace of this novel is Gold's satirizing his characters and not justifying their furiously aimless existences. Hopes that Gold will pick more promising shouters for his next novel and concludes that not even television will find much savor in *Salt*.

Poore, Charles. "Books of the Times." Rev. of *Therefore Be Bold. New York Times* 4 Oct. 1960: 41.

Thinks that *Therefore Be Bold* is written with a fine reminiscent gusto. Deems Gold a gifted storyteller whose scenes come alive. Calls this fiction functioning as a branch of history. Identifies this as fresh writing with swift insights that combine the tragic and the absurd. Details the contents and the characters.

Price, Martin. "New Books in Review." Rev. of *The Optimist. Yale Review* 68.4 (1959): 601.

Claims that in *The Optimist* Gold has familiar themes, some of them imaginatively treated by social scientists and other novelists, but treated by Gold with a nagging insistence. Complains that the characters lack depth and substance, and are too often presented as symbolic vignettes or bundles of symptoms. Concludes that, although there is intelligence in this book, it settles for clever packaging.

Rechy, John. "A Brazen Hilarity of Modern Heresies." Rev. of *True Love. Los Angeles Times Book Review* 5 Dec. 1982: 1.

Calls *True Love* a superbly written, defiantly hilarious, and insidiously entertaining novel which will draw anger.

Rosenblatt, Rebecca W. Rev. of *The Great American Jackpot. Saturday Review* 7 Mar. 1970: 36.

Describes the novel as a satire with a pasteboard backdrop and a good story. Notes that there are countless good one-liners here, and yet complains that the reader feels cheated because the material is unoriginal and out of date. Concludes that perhaps this should be a movie called "Post-Graduate."

Sale, Roger. "Fooling Around, and Serious Business." Rev. of *Swiftie the Magician. Hudson Review* 27.4 (1974-75): 628-29.

Briefly discusses *Swiftie the Magician* along with the works of several other contemporary writers. Sees Gold's novel as "an honorable holding action" in a career that hasn't gone anywhere for several years. Concludes that Gold "isn't interested enough in his uninteresting hero to work out his relation to hero and scene carefully."

Schickel, Richard. Rev. of *The Great American Jackpot. Harper's* Feb. 1970: 121-22.

Points out that during his career Gold has touched many fictional bases thematically speaking, but that in *The Great American Jackpot* he has unfortunately produced a thin, predictable, and utterly lacking story minus all surprise and suspense. Calls it a smug, cold, compassionless, nearly unreadable book.

Schott, Webster. "A Luxurious Storyteller, A Concerned Human Being." Rev. of *The Magic Will. New York Times Book Review* 4 July 1971: 6.

Claims that this collection of twenty-one short stories and essays (the result of ten years of work) shows Gold's "personal approximations" of our collective magic will as a nation. Notes that he reveals himself as a superior writer working in a conventional and attractive tradition. Concludes that, while he does not find himself deeply attracted to the mysteries of form and letters for their own sake, he does have much to tell us about the conditions of our times.

Schott, Webster. "Moving Chronicle of Life with Father." Rev. of
   Fathers. Life 7 Apr. 1967: 17.

Argues that this is a well-written and beautiful book telling the classic
story of the "hungry-eyed Jewish immigrant instinctively seizing from
the novelties of raw private enterprise and a card game in a steam bath."
Claims that this novel "escapes sentimentality and takes the heart."

Sherman, Bernard. "Books." Rev. of *Fathers. Chicago Jewish Forum*
   26.1 (1967): 54-56.

Suggests that Gold's is a real and beloved father rather than the usual
portrait familiar to readers of American Jewish fiction—the orthodox,
embittered, and ineffectual father. Concludes, "It is Sam Gold, the father
who makes this novel worth reading."

Sklar, Judith. Rev. of *Fathers. Commonweal* 28 July 1967: 474.

Calls this story fake, unsettling, and too easy, despite its warm and sympathetic treatment of the subject. Claims that because Gold flinches and shirks
the insights he should have come to, the novel loses its hard edge, and that
the interaction which should have happened between father and son actually
fizzles out. Argues that, next to his father, Gold seems dull. Somewhere in
Fathers a novel exists, but Gold has somehow failed to find it.

Solotaroff, Theodore. "The Old Wave." Rev. of *Fathers. New York
   Herald Tribune Book Week* 9 Apr.1967: 5, 12. Rpt. as "Remember
   Those Tissues They Wrapped the Fruit In . . .?" in *The Red Hot
   Vacuum, and Other Pieces on the Writing of the Sixties.* Theodore
   Solotaroff. New York: Atheneum, 1970. 237-41.

An essay on *Fathers* tracing the earlier published short stories incorporated into the novel, and observing that the novel is uneven in tone and
style as a result. Complains that there is also a lack of developing power
in the book created by weak form. Concludes that "the pangs and ela-
tions of the Jewish slant have become as predictable as those of the
Southern writers of a decade ago."

Southern, Terry. "New Trends, Old Hats." Rev. of *Therefore Be Bold.*
   Nation 19 Nov. 1960: 381-82.

Claims that *Therefore Be Bold* is a novel about the joys and tribulations
of adolescence, and will not disappoint readers because of its lack of professionalism and its catering to popular taste.

Spector, Robert Donald. "Herbert Gold: His Gift, His Problem." Rev. of *Therefore Be Bold. New York Herald Tribune Book Review* 16 Oct. 1960: 11.

Calls the book a scratching pad for a series of wisecracks that fizzle and never leave the ground. Claims that the revelations art should provide are not there. Yet notes, despite all this, that Gold is a craftsman who does know how adolescents feel, and talk, and act. Concludes, "He appreciates the melange of nobility and absurdity, selfishness and idealism that confuses their wisdom and illuminates their ignorance."

Stein, Benjamin. "After Camelot, It Was All Downhill." Rev. of *Swiftie the Magician. Wall Street Journal* 26 Sept. 1974: 14.

Claims that *Swiftie, the Magician* brilliantly conveys the sense of anguish and hate which grip the heart of the rejected lover. Notes that Gold also knows how to duplicate ecstacy and happiness in print to mesh perfectly with the feelings the readers know as ecstacy and happiness in life. Concludes that his dialogue is excellent, and that the whole novel has a kind of 3-D quality.

Stern, Daniel. "New Fiction." Rev. of *Fathers. Hadassah Magazine* Mar. 1967: 23.

Argues that the first half of the book deals with the Americanization of Sam, while the latter half deals with the author's childhood, youth, and finally, and most touchingly, the disintegration of his marriage. Considers it a warm and human book.

Stevenson, David L. "Fumblers at Life." Rev. of *Salt. New York Times Book Review* 28 Apr. 1963: 5.

Calls the novel a "brilliant and corrosively comic fantasia on men and women caught alive in our time who avoid the prime questions of life on earth and constantly mistake the body's clamoring for love." Sees the characters as fumblers at life and the ending of novel as startling and emotionally moving.

Stevenson, David L. "Heart of the Matter." Rev. of *Love and Like. New Leader* 6 June 1960: 25-27.

Calls the publication of this story collection a significant literary event comparable to the appearance of Hemingway's *Men Without Women*, and Steinbeck's *The Long Valley*. Admires several of the stories for their refusal to arouse false pathos and their ability to evoke genuine feelings deeper than the story itself would suggest. Concludes that his fiction has power to add measurably to our non-clinical awareness of the nature of the human condition.

Stuttaford, Genevieve. "Forecasts." Rev. of *A Girl of Forty*. *Publishers Weekly* 6 June 1986: 57.

A brief review that sees this as "*the* definitive California novel," a "cautionary tale of real power and truth."

Swados, Harvey. "A New Kind of Hero." Rev. of *Birth of a Hero*. *Nation* 6 Oct. 1951: 283-84.

Sees the novel as an exercise in producing an ironic antihero of the suburbs whose heroics are merely the antics of a bored suburban generation of commuters and adulterers. Concludes that Gold writes with benevolent wit, radical perception, and intellectual vigor.

"Talents in Miniature." Rev. of *Love and Like*. *Times Literary Supplement* 10 Mar. 1961: 149.

Briefly discusses this collection of short stories, and comments that the stories dealing with the theme that "sexual love betrays" are pseudo-profound. Concludes that the two or three stories about Jewish family relationships are "quite excellent."

Taubman, Robert. "Place and Planetarium." Rev. of *Salt*. *New Statesman* 31 Jan. 1964: 177.

Argues that *Salt* ultimately disappoints because it lacks perspective and leads nowhere. Complains that it has no heights and a few near depths. Concludes, however, that it is a genuinely warm and euphoric novel full of ideas.

Taylor, David. "American Dreaming." Rev. of *The Man Who Was Not With It* and *Dreaming*. *American Book Review* Nov.-Dec. 1988: 9.

Describes *The Man Who Was Not With It* and *Dreaming* mostly in terms of their contents. Comments on the darkening of Gold's vision, his treatment of the American Dream, and his characters' capacity for growth.

Thomas, Ross. "The Thrill of the Chase." Rev. of *Slave Trade*. *Washington Post Book World* 3 June 1979: 1, 4.

Recounts the plot of this "suspense" novel, and observes that the style, "a kind of San Francisco flip, is relentless and ultimately wearying" as is the "hero's continuous maundering over his lost wife, lost youth, lost chances, and lost toe."

Tilden, David. "How a Man Finds Himself." Rev. of *Birth of a Hero*. *New York Herald Tribune Book Review* 9 Sept. 1951: 6.

Claims that *Birth of a Hero* is the first novel in which Gold manages to animate both the commonplace and the bizarre persons of his story. Details character and plot.

Toynbee, Philip. "Fathers and Sons." Rev. of *Fathers*. *New Republic* 17 June 1967: 21-22.

Calls *Fathers* semi-autobiographical, concerned with father-son relationships, and full of violent color, ribaldry, wit, and excess. Concludes, however, that the novel has a curiously seductive quality despite its corniness and folksiness.

Tyler, Anne. "Herbert Gold, Two Bags, $20, and California. What?" Rev. of *Waiting for Cordelia*. *National Observer* 6 June 1977: 19.

Calls Gold an ambidextrous writer who keeps his readers guessing which side of him will produce his next novel. Notes that *Waiting for Cordelia*, is a snazzy book, but that its particularity shuts the reader out. Declares she will wait for Lily Tomlin starring in the screen version, and hopes that next time Gold writes from his non-Californian self.

Van Ghent, Dorothy. "New Books in Review." Rev. of *The Man Who Was Not with It*. *Yale Review* 45.4 (1956): 632-33.

Claims that this novel belongs to the tradition of the picaresque which Gold has fitted with the existentialist idea of the tragedy of engagement as figuration of destiny. Suggests that he talks of the awful risk of adult faith between men. Suggests, also, that the ancient myth and fairy tale behind the story is beautifully incarnated here. Complains about the obscurity of much of the carnival language.

Vansittart, Peter. "The Last Bohemian." Rev. of *Salt*. *Spectator* 31 Jan. 1964: 151-52.

Argues that this *Salt* is that which has lost its savor. Says that "if fiction is ultimately to be written by computers, the way is not unprepared. Supply the evidence: joking relationships, indiscriminate sex, too much booze, and receive an efficient, electronic plot with glittering intimations of period, though none of history, hanging in moral and political vacuum and perhaps reconciling the average sensual reader to civilization's alleged failures of nerve." Concludes that Gold is employing unusual talent too cautiously in mapping such well-travelled territory as that of divorce-seeking, analysis-ridden Manhattan careerists.

Wain, John. "An Adolescence in Slow Motion." Rev. of *Therefore Be Bold. New Republic* 24 Oct. 1960: 19-21.

Calls *Therefore Be Bold* a book which one reads absent-mindedly. Complains that it is overcharged with verbal technique, and delights one with its mannered pre-Hemingwayesque sentences and reliance on Dylan Thomas and James Joyce.

Washburn, Martin. "The Fantasy of the Sixties." Rev. of *Swiftie the Magician. Village Voice* 21 Nov. 1974: 47-48.

Calls *Swiftie the Magician* a subtle and surprising look at the sixties which fathoms their aftermath. Claims that Gold's characters use language like a code which they can no longer crack, but which they can still employ to brilliant advantage. Sees this novel as like a minor masterpiece which sums up the *zeitgeist* of a period. Concludes that Gold's book is a talisman of the vacuum the seventies must build on.

Waugh, Oberon. "Oberon Waugh on Gold in California." Rev. of *The Great American Jackpot. Spectator* 6 Mar. 1971: 319.

Describes *The Great American Jackpot* as having a story of sorts, some satire, much that is fantastic and improbable, and much that is cliché. Claims that the book would improve with a drastic cutting of large blocks of chapters at a time. Also criticizes Gold's assessment of White/Black racial politics.

West, Anthony. "The World of Shadow." Rev. of *The Man Who Was Not With It. New Yorker* 10 Mar. 1956: 146, 149.

Hails this novel as a work of promise that is mechanically a great advance over Gold's previous two books. Sees the establishment of character and setting as rapid and authoritative, and the creation of tension effective. Provides a detailed account of the contents, and concludes that this novel heralds great things to come from Gold.

Wetzel, Donald. "Stories That Range from Good to Excellent." Rev. of *Love and Like. New York Herald Tribune Book Review* 27 Mar. 1960: 8.

Calls this a collection of all but one of Gold's best stories. Claims that though they differ widely in theme and treatment, there is no mistaking their authorship. Judges the voice to be sometimes raw or wild, but always rich, vigorous, genuine, and almost never dull.

Wolff, Geoffrey. "Nitty-Gritty." Rev. of *The Great American Jackpot*. *Newsweek* 26 Jan. 1970: 80.

Argues that, though this novel contains singularly perishable materials, it is still marvelously funny. Suggests that Gold seems to be saying that the props are rotten and the times are very bad, but there are people graced with imagination and energy to work themselves out of binds. Details the plot, and concludes that what Gold is doing is cutting away some of the fat of American culture to get at the muscle. Notes that there are splendid comic interludes here, even if they will only be short lived for a year or two.

Wolitzer, Hilma. "First Together, Then Apart." Rev. of *Lovers & Cohorts*. *New York Times Book Review* 20 Apr. 1986: 11.

Describes *Lovers & Cohorts* as a collection of twenty-seven stories about the pain of love's dissolution. Details the contents of several stories, and concludes that Gold is a fine craftsman with much insight into the currents that draw us together and pull us apart.

Worthy, Judith. "On Carnivals and Motor-Racing." Rev. of *The Man Who Was Not with It*. *Books and Bookmen* Mar. 1966: 46.

Suggests that this novel is about the closely knit community of the itinerant carnival where the life, the language, and the morality are a world apart. Claims that even Gold's most minor characters have dimension, and even though this is not his most memorable book, it is still impressive.

Zeitlin, Naomi. "Fathers and Sons." Rev. of *Fathers*. *World Jewry* Sep.-Oct. 1967: 30.

A brief comparison of *Fathers*, Potok's *The Chosen*, and Cohen's *The Carpenter Years*.

Interviews

Burnson, Patrick. "P. W. Interviews Herbert Gold." *Publishers Weekly* 1 Aug. 1986: 60-61.

Provides a detailed description of the contents of *A Girl of Forty*. Calls it

Gold's first genuinely feminist novel. Calls Gold a methodical practitioner who crafts each of his novels with a finely honed sense of tonal
accuracy and an acute ear for the vernacular.

Hofheins, Roger, and Dan Tooker. "Herbert Gold." *Transatlantic Review*
    49 (1974): 110-19.
Gold discusses various aspects of his writing, including his methods, his
ideas on creativity, his problem with writer's block, writers who have
influenced him, his style, his reactions to reviews of his works, the shaping of his work for an audience, his avoidance of symbols, why he
doesn't publish his poetry, and his journalism.

Kiener, Robert. "An Exclusive Interview with Herbert Gold." *Writer's
    Digest* Sept. 1972: 29-31, 62.
Gold discusses how the boundaries between previously separate genres
such as fiction and journalism are beginning to be broken down by contemporary writers. He also describes the act of writing at the typewriter as akin
to sculpting with words because words have weight and texture. Comments
on the values of teaching writing in the classroom, and then lists his favorite
writers, his schedule, his habits as a writer, and his methods of revision.

Newquist, Roy. "Herbert Gold." *Counterpoint.* Roy Newquist. Chicago:
    Rand, 1964. 280-88.
A general introductory commentary on Gold which discusses several of
the novels individually. Provides some interview material in which Gold
discusses: Kerouac, Mailer, his study of philosophy, his early work in
Paris, the later novels, his views on contemporary writing, and the outsider status of the writer in America.

Thorpe, Stephen J. "Interview: Herbert Gold." *California Quarterly* 5
    (1973): 65-76.
In this interview Gold discusses: his childhood habit of making up stories
in order to master life, writing to an audience as an act of communion, his
college writing career, his early novels, his trips (Europe, Russia, Haiti,
Paris), the influence of other writers on his writing (Henry James,
Raymond Quenaeu, Flaubert, Balzac, and others), his experience in the
army, and his coming to terms with death and mortality.

Biographical Sources

Gold, Herbert. *My Last Two Thousand Years*. New York: Random, 1972.

Jensen, George. "Herbert Gold." *American Novelists Since World War II*. Eds. Jeffrey Helterman and Richard Layman. Detroit: Gale, 1978. Vol 2. of *Dictionary of Literary Biography*. 94 vols. to date. 1978- . 196-202.

More than details of his life, this is a career biography, tracing the development of the author's canon, describing the contents and themes of his works, evaluating his reputation, and placing him in the larger context of American literary history. Includes lists of primary and secondary sources and illustrations.

Landon, Brooks. "Herbert Gold." *Dictionary of Literary Biography Yearbook: 1981*. Eds. Karen L. Rood, Jean W. Ross, and Richard Ziegfeld. Detroit: Gale, 1982. 70-75.

An update to the article in Vol. 2 of *DLB*, concentrating on more recent developments in his career and discussing his new works, published since 1979, particularly *He/She*.

Poppy, John. "The Author." *Saturday Review* 20 Apr. 1963: 46.

Describes Gold's attitudes toward his works, his enjoyment of life through strictly controlling it, and his places of residence and their impact on his work. Also discusses the importance he feels for the novel form, which he feels sensitizes us again, if it is good.

Dissertations

Barmor, Yitzhak. "The Father Figure in Jewish-American Literature." Diss. Kent State U, 1988.

Kuhn, Howard F. "A Critical Analysis of the Novels of Herbert Gold." Diss. U of Oregon, 1970.

Michael Gold

1893 – 1967

Primary Sources

Novels

Jews Without Money. New York: Liveright, 1930; New York: Carroll, 1984.

Collected Works

120 Million. New York: International, 1929; London: Modern Books, 1929; Short Story Index Reprint Series. Freeport: Books for Libraries, 1971.
Contents: Proletarian Sketches, Proletarian Chants and Recitations.

The Damned Agitator, and Other Stories. Chicago: Daily Worker, 1926; Little Red Library 7. Chicago: Daily Worker, n.d.
Contents: The Damned Agitator, Free, The Coal Breaker.

Short Fiction in Anthologies

"Blood Money." *Theme and Variation in the Short Story.* Eds. John De Lancey Ferguson, Harold A. Blaine and Wilson R. Dumble. New York: Cordon, 1938; Short Story Index Reprint Series. Freeport: Books for Libraries, 1972. 502-14.

"Damned Agitator." *Mike Gold: A Literary Anthology*. Ed. Michael Folsom. New York: International, 1972. 24-32.

"God Is Love." *Mike Gold: A Literary Anthology*. Ed. Michael Folsom. New York: International, 1972. 33-43.

"Love on a Garbage Dump." *The Mike Gold Reader*. New York: International, 1954: 37-44; *Mike Gold: A Literary Anthology*. Ed. Michael Folsom. New York: International, 1972. 177-85.

"My Mother." *The Jewish Caravan: Great Stories of Twenty-Five Centuries*. Ed. Leo W. Schwarz. New York: Farrar, 1935. 624-37.

"The Password to Thought—to Culture." *Mike Gold: A Literary Anthology*. Ed. Michael Folsom. New York: International, 1972. 100-10.

"The Saint of the Umbrella Store." *A Golden Treasury of Jewish Literature*. Ed. Leo W. Schwarz. New York: Farrar, 1937; Philadelphia: Jewish Pub. Soc. of America, 1937. 20-28.

"Two Mexicos." *Mike Gold: A Literary Anthology*. Ed. Michael Folsom. New York: International, 1972. 49-61.

Short Fiction in Periodicals

"Reb Samuel." *American Mercury* Feb. 1930: 176-80.

Secondary Sources

Articles and Chapters

Aaron, Daniel. "The Cult of the Proletarian." *Writers on the Left: Episodes in American Literary Communism*. Daniel Aaron. New York: Harcourt, 1961. 205-11.
Locates Gold historically and ideologically among proletarian thinkers who expected the machine age to usher in a dawning proletarian culture

making great works of art out of its social realities. Outlines Gold's objectives for Proletarian Realism.

Aaron, Daniel. "Go Left, Young Writers." *Writers on the Left: Episodes in American Literary Communism*. Daniel Aaron. New York: Harcourt, 1961. 161-98.

Argues that Gold, more than any writer of the Left, fussed over and admonished the uncommitted liberal artist to become politically committed. Suggests that his main message was not to become the cultured hired hands of the *nouveaux riche*. Describes Gold's work for *The New Masses* and within the communist movement.

Avery, Evelyn Gross. "In Limbo: Immigrant Children and the American Dream." *Melus* 8.4 (1981): 25-31.

Discusses the generational conflicts, cultural clashes, and family strife central to *Jews Without Money*. For Gold, there is no reconciling of these differences. Michael does assume responsibility for his crippled father and ineffective mother destroyed by a society that rejects them and directs his bitterness toward America, the new Babylon, turning to communism and political revolution.

Chametzky, Jules. "Immigrant Fiction as Cultural Mediation." *Yiddish* 5.4 (1984): 14-21.

Discusses first the concept of mediation from a Marxist perspective, and argues that consciousness and its products are integral and constitutive elements of "reality," not mere reflections of some other more basic, primary reality. Notes that American immigrant culture produced such various forms and modes in profusion that it is valuable to see its function as mediator and creator of culture. Discusses *Yekl* and *Jews Without Money* from this perspective.

Chametzky, Jules. "Notes on the Assimilation of the American Jewish Writer: Abraham Cahan to Saul Bellow." *Jahrbuch fur Amerikastudien* 9 (1964): 172-80.

Claims that American Jewry has had three distinct phases of acculturation and adjustment beginning with the familiar traumas of the early immigrants, proceeding to the stage of aggressive-defensiveness, and culminating in the 1950s with a secure sense of Americanism following a growth in the idea of American tolerance. Illustrates this three-generation process with reference to Cahan, Michael Gold, Odets, and Bellow.

Cowley, Malcolm. "The Michael Golden Legend." *Think Back on Us: A Contemporary Chronicle of the 1930s by Malcolm Cowley.* Ed. Henry Dan Piper. Carbondale: Southern Illinois UP; London: Feffer, 1967. 189-96. Originally published in Klaus Mann's *Decision*, July 1941.

Reviews Gold's political opinions as expressed in a series of articles in proletarian journals. Claims that the purpose of the articles was to cover the excesses of communism, and, at the same time, decry the so-called capitalist writers of the 1930s—to present a new myth for proletarian writers of the period to use at a time when communism had appeared to fail. The remainder of the article is a critique of the flaws in Gold's arguments and an analysis of what had caused the so-called capitalist writers to lose all interest in the writers of the Left. Decrys Gold's claims about a renewal of literary interest in the Left on the part of American writers.

Farber, Frances. "Yiddish Voices in American Jewish Fiction." *Yiddish* 5.4 (1984): 22-41.

A major article which discusses how Roth, Angoff, Gold, and Bellow reconstruct the experiences of Yiddish-speaking Jews in America and evoke the tensions and conflicts, brought from the *shtetl* in the lives of these immigrants and their children. Describes each author's highly individualized style, employing specific techniques in representing the language of the Jew and in creating what Alfred Kazin has called "the classic bitterness of Jewish dialogue."

Fiedler, Leslie A. *The Jew in the American Novel.* Leslie Fiedler. Herzl Institute Pamphlets 10. New York: Herzl, 1959. 30-32; A Seven Star Book 5. 2nd ed. New York: Herzl, 1966. 30-32; Rpt. in *The Collected Essays of Leslie Fiedler.* 2 vols. New York: Stein, 1971. 2: 89-91; *To the Gentiles.* New York: Stein, 1972. 89-91.

Sees Gold as one of the radical writers of the thirties. Discusses briefly his Jewish local color, Jewish nationalism, proletarian views, and special conception of Judaism as Messianic, prophetic, and fanatically religious.

Folsom, Michael Brewster. "The Education of Michael Gold." *Proletarian Writers of the Thirties.* Ed. David Madden. Crosscurrents/Modern Critiques. Carbondale: Southern Illinois UP, 1980. 222-51.

Begins his article with the statement that after *Jews Without Money*, Gold's literary endeavors are negligible. A major chapter of critical biography focusing on Gold's upbringing, influence, literary career, and legacy.

Folsom, Michael Brewster. "Introduction: The Pariah of American Letters." *Mike Gold: A Literary Anthology.* Ed. Michael Brewster Folsom. New York: International, 1972. 7-20.

Gives biographical information and surveys his journalism, his literary work, his communism, and his political activism. Comments that Gold died perhaps the most detested writer in our history. Reveals how Gold himself collaborated in gathering this collection until his death in 1967.

Gitenstein, R. Barbara. "Reznikoff's *By the Waters of Manhattan* and Gold's *Jews Without Money.*" *Yiddish* 5.4 (1984): 42-48.

Argues that, in these two autobiographical novels, it is more than financial poverty signalled by the Wall Street collapse that is being depicted, it is the poverty of the recent immigrant to the country, the poverty of the Jewish urban resident during the early years of the twentieth century.

Gorchov, Robert. "Michael Gold's *Jews Without Money.*" *Jewish Spectator* 49 (Fall 1984): 41-45.

Provides a brief biography of Gold, details his writing career, highlights incidents about his childhood from the book, and concludes that, in this book, Gold presented a picture of the Jews of the East Side as they really were, not as people might like to see them.

Greenbaum, Leonard. "The Hound & Horn Archive." *Yale University Library Gazette* 39.3 (1965): 137-46.

An account of *The Hound & Horn* little magazine with brief references to Gold's participation within its pages.

Guttmann, Allen. "Jews and Proletarians." *The Jewish Writer in America: Assimilation and the Crisis of Identity.* Allen Guttmann. New York: Oxford UP, 1971. 140-42.

Commends *Jews Without Money* as a book which communicates much of the spirit of the ghetto. Unlike other novelists of the ghetto, Gold emphasizes the pimps, gamblers, peanut politicians, pugilists, prostitutes, and longshoremen. Details the contents of the book, and claims that, because it was such a commercial success, a generation of younger writers took Gold for their model.

Harap, Louis. *Creative Awakening: The Jewish Presence in Twentieth-Century American Literature, 1900-1940s.* Contributions in Ethnic Studies 17. New York: Greenwood: 1987.

In a discussion of proletarian literature of the 30s, for which Gold was the central advocate, Harap discusses Gold's famous review of Wilder's *The Bridge of San Luis Rey*, which, according to Edmund Wilson, "marks definitely the eruption of Marxist issues out of literary circles of the radicals into the field of general criticism." Discusses *Jews Without Money*, his only novel, as not conforming to the typical formula for the proletarian novel, but "its unmistakably rebellious and class-conscious viewpoint attaches it to this genre." Briefly describes the novel and its proletarian elements.

Hatcher, Harlan. "The Proletarian Novel." *Creating the Modern American Novel*. Harlan Hatcher. New York: Farrar, 1935. 262-74.

Provides a brief reference to *Jews Without Money* and its depiction of the East Side ghetto in the context of a detailed discussion of the proletarian novel of the thirties.

Klein, Marcus. "Itzok Granich and Michael Gold." *Foreigners: The Making of American Literature 1900-1940*. Marcus Klein. Chicago: U of Chicago P, 1981. 231-48.

A detailed critical biography of Gold and his contribution to the proletarian traditions of the American novel.

Klein, Marcus. "The Roots of Radicals: Experiences in the Thirties." *Proletarian Writers of the Thirties*. Ed. David Madden. Crosscurrents/Modern Critiques. Carbondale: Southern Illinois UP, 1968. 134-57.

A general description of radical writing in the 1930s which provides a definitive perspective on Gold's life, ideology, and writings.

Payne, Kenneth William. "Naturalism and the Proletarians: The Case of Michael Gold." *Anglo American Studies* 3.1 (1983): 21-37.

Discusses the role naturalism played as the only available model for the young proletarian writers of the twenties and thirties, including Michael Gold. Provides a major treatment of the influence of naturalism in his writings.

Reilly, John M. "Two Novels of Working Class Consciousness." *Midwest Quarterly* 14.2 (1973): 183-93.

Discusses *Jews Without Money* as a novel providing a legitimate picture of the American working class and a sense of Jewish ethnic culture. Considers, however, that above all, the novel tells of the creation of a proletariat "without the resources of tradition—a spiritual sustenance for life—and lacking the skills or social connections to enter the American economy (an indeed enduring deliberate exclusion because they are Jewish), they have become 'free' laborers who are candidates for the modern working class."

Riche, James. "Revisionism and The Radical Literature of the 1930s in the USA." *Literature & Ideology* 7 (1970): 1-14.

Briefly discusses Gold's contribution, through the pages of *The New Masses*, to the spirit and ideology of the proletarian literature of the 1930s.

Rideout, Walter B. "Class War." *The Radical Novel in the United States, 1900-1954*. Walter B. Rideout. Cambridge: Harvard UP, 1956. 135-64.

A major treatment of Left Wing politics in the U.S.A during the 1920s and 1930s that provides the best context in which to view the works of Gold. Treats *Jews Without Money* more specifically in the context of the economic and spiritual crisis of 1930, a year in which intellectuals felt increasingly the need of choosing sides. Notes that, at this point, literary radicals could point to the achievements of an established writer like Gold who seemed to be one of theirs.

Sherman, Bernard. "The Marxist Education Novel." *The Invention of the Jews: Jewish-American Education Novels (1916-1964)*. Bernard Sherman. New York: Yoseloff, 1969. 74-82.

Describes Gold's novels as typical Marxist education novels highlighting class struggle within human relationships. Also contains biographical and historical background.

Sisk, John P. "The Devil and American Epic." *Hudson Review* 40.1 (1987): 31-47.

Discusses Michael Gold briefly in the context of a major discussion of the epic impulse in American literature, even when that impulse disguises itself as the anti-epic.

Tuerk, Richard. "*Jews Without Money* as a Work of Art." *Studies in American Jewish Literature* [Kent State] 7.1 (1988): 67-79.

Reviews critical opinion on *Jews Without Money* and argues that while it is more than a series of vivid, episodic, factual but rough-hewn sketches of East Side life, it is indeed the product of much revision and comes

closer to fiction than fact. Examines the actual novel by comparing it
with the earlier published versions. Concludes that while the novel is not
often faithful to Gold's life, it does contain an imaginative reworking of
episodes that contribute to the overall effect of the book. Concludes that
in the last analysis it is not a series of rough-hewn memoirs but a carefully worked, unified piece of art.

Tuerk, Richard. "Michael Gold on Walt Whitman." *Walt Whitman
    Quarterly Review* 3.4 (1986): 16-23.

A detailed article on the extent to which Whitman was the literary precursor of Gold, and influenced both his life and his writing.

Tuerk, Richard. "Recreating American Literary Tradition: Michael Gold
    on Emerson and Thoreau." *Markham Review* 15 (1985-86): 6-9.

Details the influence of both Emerson and Thoreau on the life and writings of Gold.

White, William. "Michael Gold." *New York Times Book Review* 13 Feb.
    1966: 47.

A letter to the editor commenting on the missing last dozen lines from
the Avon edition of *Jews Without Money*, and the manuscripts in the
Feinberg Collection in Detroit, which also show a variation from the
printed version of the novel.

Wilson, Edmund. "The Literary Class War." *New Republic* 4 May 1932:
    319-23. Rpt.in *The Shores of Light: A Literary Chronicle of the Twenties
    and Thirties*. Edmund Wilson. New York: Farrar, 1952. 534-39.

An account of the effects and consequences of Gold's attack on the works
of Thornton Wilder as representative of bourgeois interests, devoid of concentration on the plight of the working class during the Depression years.
Concludes: "There is no question that the Gold-Wilder case marks definitely the eruption of the Marxist issues out of the literary circles of the radicals
into the field of general criticism. Concludes that it has now become plain
that the economic crisis is to be accompanied by a literary one."

Yudkin, Leon I. "The Immigrant Experience in America." *Jewish
    Writing and Identity in the Twentieth Century*. Leon I. Yudkin.
    London: Helm, 1982. 27-44.

Discusses the Jewish immigration to America as the most remarkable
demographic event in Jewish history and shows its impact on America as

it emerged as a great world power. Also sees the Jewish writers Cahan, Lewisohn, Hecht, Fuchs, Michael Gold, and Henry Roth as expanding the range of an exotic consciousness in America, but also showing the "Jew on the outside trying to get in (in various ways), or perhaps coming to terms with his outsider status." Discusses the major works of each of these writers and how they demonstrate the struggles, the conflicts, and the costs of their Jewish protagonists to become assimilated into American life.

Reviews

Brody, Alter. "The Jew in Effigy." Rev. of *Jews Without Money. Nation* 9 Apr. 1930: 428-29.

Sees this novel as a book that peddles Jewish picturesqueness to Gentiles.

Burton, Rasco. "Among the New Books." Rev. of *Jews Without Money. Arts and Decoration* Apr. 1930: 110.

Briefly details the contents of the book.

Calverton, V. F. "Proletarian Fiction." Rev. of *120 Million. Nation* 5 June 1929: 675.

Call this novel a genuine piece of proletarian fiction, despite its crude style, cheapness, and melodrama. Concludes, however, that Gold does escape much of the sentimentality that usually weakens the force and beauty of radical literature.

Erlich, Leonard. "Extremities of Behavior." Rev. of *Jews Without Money. Saturday Review of Literature* 19 Apr. 1930: 944.

Claims that Gold sets down his childhood with no small amount of bitterness and violence. Comments that it lacks shadow and light, but is full of authenticity and power instead of poetry.

Feld, Rose C. "Boyhood on the Old East Side." Rev. of *Jews Without Money. New York Times Book Review* 23 Mar. 1930: 11.

Calls *Jews Without Money* uneven, and accuses the author of occasionally offensive taste. But claims that none of this spoils the overwhelming power of the book as a whole. Concludes that it has the deep picture of a Rembrandt painting and the high challenge of a Whitman poem. Details the contents.

Folsom, Michael Brewster. "Book of Poverty." Rev. of *Jews Without Money*. *Nation* 28 Feb. 1966: 242-45.

Deplores the expurgation by Avon and an earlier paperback publisher of the final paragraphs of the book where Gold recounts his awakening to the workers' revolution. Calls the book "a simple work, and an artless one—if literary art consists in the self-conscious achievement of 'style' and in the strenuous formal reordering of experience by the imagination." Guesses the book is 85% autobiographical, but not about Gold. Concludes that it is what Gold said it is: a truthful book of poverty. Concludes that it is a simple book, rich in clarity, force, truth and art.

Grenier, Judson A. "Book Reviews." Rev. of *Mike Gold: A Literary Anthology*. *Journalism Quarterly* 50.2 (1973): 375-76.

Provides a brief account of Gold's life and contribution to proletarian literature. Describes the volume, its contents, and their arrangement.

Klein, A. M. "A Curse on Columbus." Rev. of *Jews Without Money*. *Canadian Jewish Chronicle* 18 Apr. 1930. Rpt. in A. M. Klein. *Literary Essays and Reviews*. Eds. Usher Caplan and M. W. Steinberg. Collected Works of A. M. Klein. Toronto: U of Toronto P, 1987. 225-26.

Describes *A Curse on Columbus* as a book written by a Jew intimate with New York City. However, wonders why he seems to know more about the social condition of being Jewish than the ethnic condition and Judaica itself. Notes the poetic vigor of the Yiddishisms in the book and the splendidly portrayed characters. Concludes that no one with discrimination can read this book and thereafter continue to mouth capitalistic cliches.

Levy, Melvin P. "Michael Gold." Rev. of *Jews Without Money*. *New Republic* 26 Mar. 1930: 160-61.

Discusses the sincerity and power of Gold to move readers through his compelling writing power. Details his unsuccessful efforts to make this novel fulfill a revolutionary purpose: as a communist, he wants to write about the proletariat, but his people are only poor. Concludes that he is a writer of historical importance because he embodies in his work the conflicts typical of our time.

Lhamon, W. T., Jr. "In History's Ashcan." Rev. of *Mike Gold: A Literary Anthology*. *New Republic* 27 May 1972: 27-29.

Provides a critical biographical history of Gold's contributions to American literature. Gives a brief history of his life, his career and his proletarian values as a writer. Concludes that Folsom's editing of Gold makes for no jolly occasion, but argues that it is a corrective book, useful for showing how truly difficult it has been to live in the spurious melting pot.

Salzman, Jack. "Not M. Gorky But Still Mike Gold." Rev. of *Mike Gold: A Literary Anthology. Nation* 10 July 1972: 22-24.

A brief review of *Mike Gold: A Literary Anthology*, which places the volume in a politico-historical context. Places discussion of the novel also in the context of the Edmund Wilson MLA debate of 1968, in which he takes the MLA to task for sponsoring the publication of definitive texts of classic American authors while omitting the contributions of the proletarian writers of the 1930s.

Bibliographical Sources

Aaron, Daniel. "Expatriates and Radicals." *Writers on the Left: Episodes in American Literary Communism*. Daniel Aaron. New York: Harcourt, 1961. 84-90.

A biographical portrait of Mike Gold including his early life on the East Side, his young adult years as a Bohemian anarchist artist, his association with the Provincetown Playhouse as a playwright, his brief stay at Harvard, the trip to Mexico in 1917, his contributions to *The Liberator* in 1921, his assumption of the proletarian image, and his writings to that effect. Concludes with his vision of New York City five hundred years from now, a vision including those of Ruskin, Bellamy, Whitman, and Fourier.

Angoff, Charles. "Mike Gold: Leader of Proletarian Culture." *The Tone of the Twenties, and Other Essays*. Charles Angoff. New York: Barnes; London: Yoseloff, 1966. 182-88. Originally published in New York University *Arts and Sciences* (Wint. 1964-65).

An anecdotal account of Angoff's acquaintanceship with Mike Gold. Details his leadership of the proletarian culture, the author's impressions of him, and the genesis of some of the material that went into *Jews Without Money*. Of most interest is a near verbatim report of a conversation on the topic of communism that took place between Gold and Mencken. A subsequent conversation records Gold's asking Angoff about Mencken's alleged anti-Semitism.

Folsom, Michael Brewster. "Michael Gold." *American Novelists, 1910-1945, Part II: F. Scott Fitzgerald-O. E. Rolvaag*. Ed. James J.

Martine. Detroit: Gale, 1981. Vol. 9 of *Dictionary of Literary Biography.* 94 vols. to date. 1978- . 72-74.

More than details of his life, this is a career biography, tracing the development of the author's canon, describing the contents and themes of his works, evaluating his reputation, and placing him in the larger context of American literary history. Includes lists of primary and secondary sources and illustrations.

Levenberg, Diane. "Three Jewish Writers and the Spirit of the Thirties: Michael Gold, Anzia Yezierska, and Henry Roth." *Book Forum* 6.2 (1982): 233-44.

A brief, critical biographical account of Gold's life and work.

Sillen, Samuel. Introduction. *The Mike Gold Reader from the Writings of Michael Gold.* Ed. Samuel Sillen. New York: International, 1954. 7-13.

An excellent biographical introduction to Mike Gold, his era, and his politics.

Tuerk, Richard. "Michael Gold (Irwin Granich)." *Twentieth-Century American-Jewish Fiction Writers.* ed. Daniel Walden. Detroit: Gale, 1984. Vol. 28 of *Dictionary of Literary Biography.* 94 vols. to date. 1978- . 83-87.

More than details of his life, this is a career biography, tracing the development of the author's canon, describing the contents and themes of his works, evaluating his reputation, and placing him in the larger context of American literary history. Includes lists of primary and secondary sources and illustrations.

Dissertations

Brogna, John Joseph. "Michael Gold: Critic and Playwright." Diss. U of Georgia, 1982.

Gartner, Carol Blicker. "A New Mirror for America: The Fiction of the Immigrant of the Ghetto, 1890-1930." Diss. New York U, 1970.

Hertz, Howard Lee. "Writer and Revolutionary: The Life and Works of Michael Gold, Father of Proletarian Literature in the United States." Diss. U of Texas at Austin, 1974.

Laufer, Pearl David. "Between Two Worlds: The Fiction of Anzia Yezierska." Diss. U of Maryland, 1981.

Also discusses *Jews Without Money.*

Naficy, Azar. "The Literary Wars of Mike Gold, A Study in the Background and Development of Mike Gold's Literary Ideas, 1920-1941." Diss. U of Oklahoma, 1979.

Nye-Applebaum, Mika. "Restructuring the Beginning. Three Writers in the 1930s: The Novels of Michael Gold, Henry Roth and Daniel Fuchs." Diss. State U of New York at Buffalo, 1980.

William Goldman
1931 –

Primary Sources

Novels

Boys and Girls Together. New York: Atheneum, 1964; New York: Bantam, 1965, 1977; London: Joseph, 1965; London: Corgi, 1966; London: Transworld, 1978, 1988; New York: Warner, 1984, 1988.

Brothers: A Sequel to Marathon Man. London: Grafton, 1986, 1988; Book Club ed. New York: Warner, 1987; New York: Warner, 1988.

The Colour of Light. New York: Warner, 1984, 1985; London: Granada, 1984; London: Panther, 1985.

Control. New York: Delacorte, 1982; London: Hodder, 1982, 1983; New York: Dell, 1983.

Edged Weapons. London: Granada, 1985; London: Grafton, 1987. Publ. in U.S. as *Heat.*

Father's Day. New York: Harcourt, 1971; New York: Bantam, 1971; London: Joseph, 1971; London: Corgi, 1973.

Heat. New York: Warner, 1985, 1988. Publ. in England as *Edged Weapons.*

Magic. New York: Delacorte, 1976; London: Macmillan, 1976; New York: Dell, 1977; London: Pan, 1978.

Marathon Man. New York: Delacorte, 1974; Geneva: Heron-Editon, 1974; New York: Dell, 1975, 1976; London: Macmillan, 1975; London: Pan, 1976; Mattituck: Amereon, d. not available.

No Way to Treat a Lady. New York: Harcourt, 1964, 1968; A Fawcett Gold Medal Book. New York: Fawcett, 1964; London: Mueller, 1964; London: Coronet, 1968; London: Hodder, 1968.

The Princess Bride: S. Morgenstern's Classic Tale of True Love and High Adventure. The 'Good Parts' Version, Abridged. New York: Harcourt, 1973; New York: Ballantine, 1974, 1975, 1977, 1987; New York: Del Rey-Ballantine, 1974; London: Macmillan, 1975; London: Pan, 1976; London: Severn House, 1988; N.p.: Futura, 1988.

The Silent Gondoliers. New York: Del Rey-Ballantine, 1983, 1985. Publ. under pseudonym of S. Morgenstern.

Soldier in the Rain. New York: Atheneum, 1960; London: Eyre, 1960; New York, Bantam, 1965, 1966, 1970; London: New English Library, 1965.

A Start in Life. London: Fortune, 1947.

The Temple of Gold. New York: Knopf, 1957; Toronto: McClelland, 1957; New York: Bantam, 1958, 1968; London: Corgi-Transworld, 1961; Laurel Leaf Library. New York: Dell, 1976.

A Tent of Blue. London: Grey Walls, 1946.

The Thing of It Is . . . . New York: Harcourt, 1967; London: Joseph, 1967; New York: Bantam, 1968; London: Corgi, 1969.

Tinsel. New York: Delacorte, 1979; London: Macmillan, 1979; New York: Dell, 1980; London: Pan, 1980.

Your Turn to Curtsy, My Turn to Bow. Garden City: Doubleday, 1958; New York: Bantam, 1960.

Short Fiction in Anthologies

"A Blighted Romance." *'. . . In England and in English': A Collection of Modern Stories by Jewish Writers.* Ed. William Goldman. London: Art & Educ. Pub., 1947. 43-52.

"Da Vinci." *New World Writing 17.* Philadelphia: Lippincott, 1960. 205-21.

"The Ice Cream Eat." *Stories from the Transatlantic Review.* Ed. Joseph F. McCrindle. New York: Holt, 1970; London: Gollancz, 1970. 290-98; Harmondsworth: Penguin, 1974. 397-407.

"A Youthful Idyll." *'. . . In England and in English': A Collection of Modern Stories by Jewish Writers.* Ed. William Goldman. London: Art & Educ. Pub., 1947. 139-63.

Short Fiction in Periodicals

"The Ice Cream Eat." *Transatlantic Review* 2 (1958): 108-17.

"Life Class." *Fortnightly* Aug. 1952: 123-27.

"The Simple Pleasures of the Rich." *Transatlantic Review* 50 (1974): 62-69.

"Something Blue." *Rogue* Apr. 1958: 13-83.

"Till the Right Girls Come Along." *Transatlantic Review* 8 (1961): 50-61.

Secondary Sources

Books

Andersen, Richard. *William Goldman.* Twayne's United States Authors
Series 326. Boston: Twayne, 1979.

Articles and Chapters

Dunson, Douglas. "William Goldman." *Beacham's Popular Fiction of
America.* Ed. Walter Beacham. 4 vols. Washington: Beacham, 1986.
2: 534-41.

A standard reference article covering social concerns, themes, characters,
techniques, literary precedents,and adaptations in *Marathon Man, The
Temple of Gold* and *Tinsel.*

Schroth, Raymond A. "The Temple of Goldman." *America* 9 Sept. 1967:
250.

Comments snidely that in *Boys and Girls Together* the sexual episodes
may recur like the clatter of workmen drilling open a sidewalk, but that
these are only stammering moments in the fruitless dialogue between
human beings trying to grow up. Calls *The Temple of Gold* a novel in
which love is equally poorly described—this time in Gunga Din fashion.
Concludes that Goldman never seems to guess the isolation and unreality
of his characters, though there is some evidence he grows to hate them.

Reviews

Adams, Phoebe. "Two Musketeers." Rev. of *Soldier in the Rain. Atlantic*
Aug. 1960: 97-98.

Describes the methods and contents of the novel. Concludes that
Goldman fails at straight sentiment and plausibility, but that the lapses
are too few to spoil the book.

Bensen, D. R. "Golden Quest." Rev. of *The Temple of Gold. Saturday
Review* 19 Oct. 1957: 21.

Calls *The Temple of Gold* an entertaining account of the beat generation
growing up in a midwestern college town. Details the story, and concludes that its message is simply that you have to finally rid yourself of

everything about your childhood—all influences, good and bad, before you are free to be your own person.

Block, Lawrence. "Mobsters and Superagents." Rev. of *Heat. Washington Post Book World* 16 June 1985: 8.

Describes *Heat* as the story of Nick Escalante, a sort of civilian of fortune, master of edged weapons, and the most dangerous man alive inside of twenty feet. Calls the violence here genuine, more emotionally satisfying, and finally more disturbing. Complains that some plot elements strain credulity, along with an ending which some may find unsatisfying. Concludes that this is an author incapable of writing an awkward sentence.

"Bookstack." Rev. of *The Thing of It Is... Books and Bookmen* Jan. 1968: 29.

Argues that *The Thing of It Is...* is clear-cut in its style, and full of stark realities. Notes that from one page to the next the reader is right in the thick of it, watching two people batter their way to mutual annihilation. Describes the contents and characters briefly.

Cameron, Julia. "Hollywood Up Front." Rev. of *Tinsel. Washington Post Book World* 19 Aug. 1979: 12.

Considers this novel junk, but comments that a taste for Goldman is like a taste for junk food, beginning in adolescence and lingering into adulthood. Discusses his breast motif at some length, and briefly describes the story line.

Clemons, Walter. "A Father, a Mother in Trouble." Rev. of *Father's Day. New York Times* 25 Jan. 1971: 41.

Considers *Father's Day* thoroughly professional in its execution, fast-moving, and yet still a failure. Finds it sticky in its portrayal of father-daughter games, and comments that much is abrasive and done in showbiz dialogue. Provides a detailed account of the contents.

Clemons, Walter. "Fleshing Out Fantasyland." Rev. of *Tinsel. Newsweek* 13 Aug. 1979: 73.

Calls *Tinsel* a satisfying book with a good nuts-and-bolts supply of corroborating narrative detail. Applauds Goldman's three interesting women for not seeming to be pasted together out of old gossip columns. Considers their careers to be independently plausible and the effect of the whole to be nasty, hard-edged entertainment.

Cromie, Robert. "Lively and Amusing Army Tale." Rev. of *Soldier in the Rain*. *Chicago Sunday Tribune Magazine of Books* 7 Aug. 1960: 5.

Comments that *Soldier in the Rain* swings along and makes refreshing reading. Calls it a delightfully amusing book with poignant and tender moments whose effect is heightened by their unexpectedness. Discusses characters and content briefly.

Dempsey, David. "In Search of a 'Handle.'" Rev. of *The Temple of Gold*. *New York Times Book Review* 17 Nov. 1957: 54.

Comments that the central symbol of this story, the temple of gold, sits too heavily on an unassuming and rollicking story. Complains that Goldman never probes very deeply into his characters, and that the book is reeled off at a fast clip, though there are moments of tenderness and real humor. Concludes, however, that the effect of the whole is facile, leaving no echoes.

Dobyns, Stephen. "Ma's Perfect Killer." Rev. of *Brothers*. *New York Times Book Review* 15 Feb. 1987: 18.

Argues that readers looking for a realistic spy novel like those of John Le Carre, or something fanciful and exciting like *Marathon Man*, will be disappointed in *Brothers* because it is implausible, poorly plotted, sadistic, and awash with gratuitous violence.

Drawbell, James. "On the G.A.N." Rev. of *Boys and Girls Together*. *Books and Bookmen* Mar. 1965: 24.

Calls this novel formidable in size, readable, bursting with life, vulgar, raucus, tender, frustrating, and heartbreaking.

Epstein, Joseph. "The Army's Grotesquery." Rev. of *Soldier in the Rain*. *New Leader* 28 Nov. 1960: 17.

Calls this a novel whose author laughs at the preposterousness of a non-combat army in America. Notes Goldman's ability to imbue life with flatness, fantasy, and a sort of Robinson Crusoe atmosphere.

Evans, William R. Rev. of *Marathon Man*. *Best Sellers* 1 Nov. 1974: 335.

Calls the style of *Marathon Man* crisp and straightforward. Considers Goldman a master of swift action, mysterious goings-on, and exciting adventure stories. Concludes that its serious implications involve the reader in issues of hatred, war, destruction, and why they go on decade after decade.

French, Warren. "Season of Promise: Spring Fiction 1967." Rev. of *The Thing of It Is....* Missouri Literary Frontier Series 2. Columbia: Missouri UP, 1968. 26-32.

Calls Goldman cynical, discusses his earlier work, and describes *The Thing of It Is...* as a book focusing on the American inability to cope with success and marriage in disintegration. Details plot and characters, and concludes that Goldman's novels are particularly timely with the conditions of affluence.

Fuller, Edmund. "A Gothic Put-On and a Rising Tycoon." Rev. of *The Princess Bride. Wall Street Journal* 30 Oct. 1973: 18.

Comments that *The Princess Bride* illustrates the magnetic power of a good, old-fashioned, fun-type story. Details the contents, and concludes that this is an irresistibly funny book, booby-trapped for the literal-minded. Considers it a lovely, loving parody of an immense and ancient genre, the gothic romance.

Galloway, David D. "The Light Fantastic." Rev. of *Boys and Girls Together. Spectator* 12 Mar. 1965: 334.

Notes that *Boys and Girls Together* is compiled rather than composed. Calls it a polymorphous novel spinning together with inexhaustible inventiveness and unflagging vitality. Considers the language of these stories dazzling and versatile, placing Goldman with Bellow, Updike, and Malamud.

Goran, Lester. "The Old Gang, Up to All the Old Things." Rev. of *Boys and Girls Together. Chicago Sunday Tribune Magazine of Books* 2 Aug. 1964: 1.

Sees *Boys and Girls Together* as a book where conversations go on forever, geography is vague to invisible, ideas are simple, and life seems meaningless. Concludes that Goldman must have read *The Old Bunch*.

Hill, William B. Rev. of *Father's Day. Best Sellers* 15 Mar. 1971: 535-36.

Argues that, though Goldman might be bewildering, he is not dull because he races swiftly through narrative and dialogue in the novel, leaving the effective impression of a sad, pathetic figure of a lost man bound in an acerbic marriage to a stupid, cruel woman.

Hunter, Evan. "How to Change the Past." Rev. of *Control. New York Times Book Review* 25 Apr. 1982: 13.

Describes the novel as a book you have to read twice to figure out what is going on. Notes that the pacing is swift and sure, the dialogue crackling and humorous, and Goldman's sense of background impeccable. Concludes, however, that it is a shame Goldman did not play this entertaining novel more honestly.

Kaveny, Roz. "Box of Tricks." Rev. of *Brothers. Books and Bookmen* Nov. 1986: 32.

Suggests that *Brothers* is another novel just like *Marathon Man* which works just like a box of the same tricks. Notes that Goldman proceeds wittily with all the tricks and cliches of the popular storyteller while pointing in the other direction and laughing. Considers the work to have human value partly because Goldman is a sentimentalist, and partly because he observes the real emotion of the barfight or academic domesticity.

Knickerbocker, Conrad. "Playing the Game." Rev. of *Boys and Girls Together. New York Times Book Review* 26 July 1964: 24.

Argues that, with the publication of *Boys and Girls Together*, Goldman makes his bid for the Wouk, Uris, Stone pinnacle. Concludes, however, that this particular novel extends the Californization of the novel form. Quips that it works in aerosol fashion: two ounces worth of material pressurized with harmless gas-producing foam, noise, and yawns.

Lehmann-Haupt, Christopher. "Books of the Times." Rev. of *Magic. New York Times* 5 Nov. 1976: C21.

Describes how *Magic* begins with excerpts from a journal kept by a ventriloquist's dummy—a schizoid personality. Complains that it is a book that leaves one without an aftertaste, except for trickiness, and finally has little to say.

Lehmann-Haupt, Christopher. Rev. of *Tinsel. New York Times* 24 July 1979: C9. Rpt. in *Books of the Times* July 1979: 347-48.

Calls *Tinsel* poor stuff based on the story of Marilyn Monroe's suicide. Suggests that it appeals to movie-makers and the baser instincts of most readers. Finds no significant message, unless one considers it news that life for the weak in Hollywood is solitary, nasty, and brutish.

Lehmann-Haupt, Christopher. "Books of the Times." Rev. of *Brothers. New York Times* 5 Feb. 1987: C24.

Complains that it is impossible to figure out what is going on in the novel because it fails to puzzle constructively, and then seeks to keep us amused with gimmicks so wilfully inventive one refuses to respond to them.

Lochle, Dick. Rev. of *Brothers*. *Los Angeles Times Book Review* 17 May 1987: 6.

Calls *Brothers* a sneaky, depraved, heart-rending, maddening, manipulative tale. Suggests that this book is destined not as great literature, but as a sequel movie script. Describes contents.

Lownsbrough, John. "Hollywood and Whine." Rev. of *Tinsel*. *MacLean's* 20 Aug. 1979: 39-40.

Calls *Tinsel* notably Hollywood in its packaging and content. Comments that there is the usual assortment of studs and bimbos, burned out cases, people with money, and people without money. Considers this book to be as scintillating as back issues of *People*.

Lynch, John A. "A Rampage." Rev. of *The Temple of Gold*. *Commonweal* 29 Nov. 1957: 238-39.

The Temple of Gold is a tasteless but credible book up to the death of Zock Crowe, at which point the author begins to take liberties even with the realities of life. Yet concludes that the novel is without intellectual involvement and reflection. There is no character, no plot, and nothing to actually hold our attention.

Lyons, Gene. "Four Novels." Rev. of *Marathon Man*. *New York Times Book Review* 27 Oct. 1974: 50-51.

Describes the contents of the novel as childishly mawkish in style, full of improbabilities, all strung together in cinematic layout. Complains that the socially redeeming value of the book occurs in scenes recited by a graduate student historian while pumping bullets into a dying fascist and commenting we should have been giving pain back all along—a not very clever piece of hard-eyed bathos.

Mamet, David. "Las Vegas, Love It or Leave It." Rev. of *Heat*. *New York Times Book Review* 19 May 1985: 15.

Argues that *Heat* is made of stuff that is ultimately satisfying, and all written in the galloping style of Count Vronsky's steeple-chase. Sees Goldman as the master storyteller who makes us all want to live in the same world as the protagonist—where friendly hookers, honorable gangsters, wealthy benefactors, sneering toughs whose faces will be shoved in the dirt, and interesting friends will be true to us until death.

McAleer, John. "A Feuding 'Family,' and Other Tales of Domestic Life." Rev. of *Brothers. Chicago Tribune Books* 15 Feb. 1987: 6.

Considers *Brothers* a scintillating patchwork that takes us on an astonishing journey. Describes the contents of the novel, and compares it to *Marathon Man.*

McMurtry, Larry. "Three Novels." Rev. of *Tinsel. New York Times Book Review* 26 Aug. 1979: 14.

Complains that this novel never really gets past the stereotypes on which Goldman flops down as if they were warm sand without admitting to himself or the reader they are tinsel. Further argues that this is both glib and dull, offering information, not dimension, and despite that fact that some of the dialogue is bright and readable, it does not cover the cracks.

Mehren, Elizabeth. "Fuller's Brush with the Lint of Life." Rev. of *The Color of Light. Los Angeles Times Book Review* 20 May 1984: 10.

Calls *The Color of Light* actually leaden, and notes that where it should shine it shuffles. Details the plot with derision and fine detail.

Mitgang, Herbert. "Bugles and Belles." Rev. of *Soldier in the Rain. New York Times Book Review* 17 July 1960: 26.

Complains that Goldman fails to draw a poignant character in the novel. Notes that it moves briskly, but aimlessly, especially in its humorous parts. Suggests that, to its credit, the novel does accurately capture the talk and the ways of young people.

Morgan, Al. "Soldiers, Tears, Laughter." Rev. of *Soldier in the Rain. New York Herald Tribune Book Review* 17 July 1960: 5.

Calls *Soldier in the Rain* a minor miracle for its genuinely funny, touching account of barracks life. Disdains the easy surface, shallow, slick, and professional humor on the subject, but applauds this as a full measure of rich reading pleasure running the gamut from belly laughs to tear-jerking. Concludes that this is a marvelous book.

Poore, Charles. "An Ironic Chronicle of the Enlisted Elite." Rev. of *Soldier in the Rain. San Francisco Chronicle* 26 July 1960: 27.

Calls *Soldier in the Rain* an ironic chronicle of the enlisted elite on a Southern army post. Comments on the wonderfully funny scenes, much larcenous and licentious mischief, and some tragic scenes.

Poore, Charles. "Six Characters in Search of a Manhattan Destiny." Rev. of *Boys and Girls Together. New York Times* 21 July 1964: 31.

Argues that this is not exactly a nursery tale, but rather a long, conglomerate novel about growing up in America between the thirties and sixties. Comments on the massive segments of biography and autobiography. Concludes that there is a kind of grudging enthusiasm here that makes the book readable. Considers this evidence of the mongrelization of the American novel.

Quammen, David. "Living to Find 'Material.'" Rev. of *The Color of Light. New York Times Book Review* 15 Apr. 1984: 18.

A sarcastic romp through the plot of the novel pointing out bathos, implausibilities of plot, and the break-neck speed with which the novel was written.

Scott, Paul. "New Novels." Rev. of *Soldier in the Rain. New Statesman* 26 Nov. 1960: 850.

Calls *Soldiers in the Rain* a likeable book, and proceeds to list its contents, setting, conflicts, characters, and concerns. Concludes that it reaffirms belief in the spirit of man with its funny, lyrical, hardheaded, warmhearted, and sane spirit.

"A Smile—And Women." Rev. of *Soldier in the Rain. Newsweek* 18 July 1960: 91.

Describes the contents of the novel, and concludes that it is a slight piece— "really frail and 4-F" (on a scale of A to F, where A is for gorgeous).

Warner, Edward F. Rev. of *Magic. Best Sellers* Dec. 1976: 278-79.

Describes *Magic* as a fascinating novel about a man's mind driven to its inevitable end. Suggests that aside from the fragmented approach at the beginning, the novel reads easily. Concludes that this along with the intriguing plot, no doubt spell a bestseller.

Wheeler, Elizabeth. "Goldman: When the Cheater Wins." Rev. of *Control. Los Angeles Times Book Review* 6 June 1982: 10.

Calls *Control* a novel which is all plot. Complains that, though there are many people hanging around, there are no real characters. Also notes that besides these demerits, the plot is "tricky-wicky." Considers this a weaseling novel, hence its great success.

Wickenden, Dan. "A Novel Whose Hero Is, Well, Novel." Rev. of *The Temple of Gold*. *New York Herald Tribune Book Review* 3 Nov. 1957: 9.

Considers *The Temple of Gold* a considerable achievement because the author has worked out his own adroit way of conveying a novel across a considerable amount of time. Notes that the narrator's idiom is fresh and vigorous, and his characters wholly alive and engrossing in their actions. Calls this a notably clever and readable first novel.

Wood, Michael. "Novel Visions." Rev. of *Tinsel*. *American Film* Sept. 1979: 68-69.

Describes *Tinsel* as the world of Hollywood engulfed in myth and ultimately distorted. Gives a very detailed account of contents, and concludes that this is not so much a story as it is a bright idea surrounded by halfhearted attempts to create character all written in slack prose.

Woodrell, Daniel. "'Marathon Man': Part Two." Rev. of *Brothers*. *Washington Post Book World* 15 Feb. 1987: 5.

Considers *Brothers* the sequel to *Marathon Man*, and calls it highly skilled storytelling with much violence and many strong-arm tactics. Describes it as fast-paced, mayhem-filled, frequently clever, and occasionally funny. Concludes that it is an old scenario with quirky new wrinkles guaranteeing a rocking good ride.

Interviews

Frankel, Haskel. "Professors to Ping Pong Players." *Saturday Review* 25 July 1964: 22-23.

In this account of an interview with Goldman on the eve of the publication of his novel *Boys and Girls Together*, Goldman describes his writing career, and Haskel gives his impression of the author and his wife.

Steinberg, Sybil S. "PW Interviews William Goldman." *Publishers Weekly* 18 Mar. 1983: 26-27.

In this interview Goldman discusses: his previous novels, screen-play writing career, his play "The Season," and his methods of writing.

Biographical Sources

Goldman, William. "Dark Room, Bright Light, Typewriter." *New York Herald Tribune Book Review* 14 Aug. 1960: 2.

An autobiographical account of Goldman's becoming a writer, his writing habits, and personal interests.

Klemesrud, Judy. "Behind the Best Sellers: William Goldman." *New York Times Book Review* 16 Sept. 1979: 42.

A biographical sketch of Goldman interspersed with the interviewer's impressions of him. Covers Goldman's interest in screen writing, past publications, family life, views on the reviewers of his novels, and the novels themselves.

Stone, Botham. "William Goldman." *American Screen Writers, Second Series*. Ed. Randall Clark. Detroit: Gale, 1986. Vol. 44 of *Dictionary of Literary Biography*. 94 vols. to date. 1978- . 145-51.

Primarily a discussion of Goldman's screenwriting career which provides useful information about his stories, many of which have been made into films.

Dissertations

Andersen, Richard Arnold. "The Fiction of Reality and Fantasy in William Goldman." Diss. New York U, 1977.

Albert Halper

1904 –

Primary Sources

Novels

Atlantic Avenue. New York: Dell, 1956.

Chicago Side-Show. New York: Modern Editions, 1932.

The Chute. New York: Viking, 1937; Toronto: Macmillan, 1937; London: Cassell, 1938; New York: AMS [Cited in BIP].

The Foundry. New York: Viking, 1934; Toronto: Macmillan, 1934; London: Cassell, 1934; Novels of Distinction. New York: Grosset, 1939; New York: AMS [Cited in BIP].

The Fourth Horseman of Miami Beach. New York: Norton, 1966.

The Golden Watch. New York: Holt, 1953; Toronto: Clarke, 1953.

Good-Bye, Union Square; A Writer's Memoir of the Thirties. Chicago: Quadrangle, 1970.

The Little People." New York: Harper, 1942; The Labor Movement in Fiction and Non-Fiction. New York: AMS, 1976.

On the Shore; Young Writer Remembering Chicago. New York: Viking, 1934; Toronto: Macmillan, 1934.

Only an Inch from Glory. New York: Harper, 1943; Toronto: Musson, 1943; London: Cassell, 1945.

Sons of the Fathers. New York: Harper, 1940; Toronto: Musson, 1940; London: Cassell, 1941.

Union Square. New York: Viking, 1933; New York: Literary Guild, 1933; London: Cassell, 1933; New York: Belmont, 1962; Proletarian Literature Series. Detroit: Omnigraphics, 1990.

Short Fiction in Anthologies

"Brothers over a Grave." *The Jewish Caravan: Great Stories of Twenty-Five Centuries.* Ed. Leo W. Schwarz. New York: Farrar, 1935; Philadelphia: Jewish Pub. Soc. of America, 1935. 650-53.

"Going to Market." *Best Short Stories, 1933.* Ed. Edward J. O'Brien. Boston: Houghton, 1933. 161-69.

"A Herring for My Uncle." *A Golden Treasury of Jewish Literature.* Ed. Leo W. Schwarz. Philadelphia: The Jewish Pub. Soc. of America, 1937. 3-11.

"A Morning with the Doc." *New Masses: An Anthology of the Realist Thirties.* Ed. Joseph North. New York: International, 1969. 84-91.

"My Aunt Daisy." *Woollcott's Second Reader.* Ed. Alexander Woollcott. New York: Viking, 1937. 595-615; *This Is Chicago.* Ed. Albert Halper. New York: Holt, 1952. 243-59; *Great Jewish Short Stories.* Ed. Saul Bellow. New York: Laurel-Dell, 1963. 290-307.

"My Mother's Love Story." *These Your Children*. Ed. Harold U. Ribalow. New York: Beechhurst, 1952. 126-41.

"The Penny-Divers." *When I Was a Child*. Ed. Edward C. Wagenknecht. New York: Dutton, 1946. 367-81.

"The Poet." *The Best Short Stories, 1937*. Ed. Edward J. O'Brien. Boston: Houghton, 1937. 95-104.

"Prelude." *The Best Short Stories, 1939*. Ed. Edward J. O'Brien. Boston: Houghton, 1939. 94-108; *Point of Departure*. Ed. Robert Gold. New York: Dell, 1967; New York: Laurel Leaf-Dell, 1981. 67-79; *Twenty Grand Short Stories*. Ed. Ernestine Taggard. New York: Bantam, 1947, 1968; New York: Pathfinder-Bantam, 1963. 146-56.

"Scab!" *Proletarian Literature in the United States: An Anthology*. Ed. Granville Hicks. New York: International, 1935. 84-91.

"Warm Matzos." *Feast of Leviathan*. Ed. Leo W. Schwarz. New York: Rinehart, 1956. 28-45.

"White Laughter." *The American Caravan; A Yearbook of American Literature*. New York: Macaulay, 1927. 358-66.

Short Fiction in Periodicals

"The Adventurer." *Old Line* [U of Maryland] Apr. 1943: 17-18, 30.

"The Battle of the Boiled Hams." *Saturday Evening Post* 23 Sept. 1944: 18, 56, 59, 61, 63.

"The Big Order." *Clay, A Literary Notebook* 1 (Wint. 1931-32): 32-36.

"The Big Slide." *Commentary* Dec. 1951: 558-63.

"Brothers over a Grave." *Menorah Journal* Apr. 1929: 365-67.

"The Call of the Soil." *Collier's* 1 Apr. 1944: 70-71, 73.

"Chicago Mail Clerks." *Debunker* Feb. 1929: 3-11.

"Crime Wave." *New Masses* 8 June 1943: 18-21.

"Dentist." *Commentary* Nov. 1959: 421-28.

"The Doctor." *Pagany, A Native Quarterly* 3.4 (1933): 66-69.

"Doctor Winton." *Atlantic* Dec. 1935: 703-11.

"Ernie and the Barber's Daughter." *Parade* 1 (Spr. 1936): 7-8, 39-40.

"A Farewell to the Rising Son." *Pagany, A Native Quarterly* 2.2 (1931):
    1-21; 2.3 (1931): 94-118; 2.4 (1931): 115-31.

"Farm Hand." *New Republic* 6 Apr. 1932: 208-10.

"Fate, or Destiny, or Something." *Collier's* 10 July 1943: 14, 61-62.

"Feud in the Rotunda." *American Mercury* Mar. 1933: 305-12;
    Scholastic 6 Apr. 1935: 4-6.

"Five Men and a Woman." *The Bermondsey Book, A Quarterly Review
    of Life and Literature* 6 (June-July-Aug. 1929): 100-08.

"From Down South." *Pagany, A Native Quarterly* 1.3 (1930): 34-39.

"Going to Market." *Harper's* Oct. 1932: 592-97.

"The Goose Dinner." *The Midland* July-Aug. 1929: 177-83.

"A Guy Like Dostoevski." *Friday Magazine* 15 Mar. 1940: 9, 17, 21.

"Hot Night in Rockford." *Esquire* Aug. 1934: 66-67, 117.

"Hot Night on the West Side." *Menorah Journal* Nov. 1929: 186-89.

"Looking for a Job." *The Left, A Quarterly Review of Radical and Experimental Art* 1 (Sum.-Aut. 1931): 64-65.

"Memorial." *Menorah Journal* May 1930: 460-65.

"Milly." *Redbook* May 1935: 42-45, 109.

"Miss Leland Lived in an Old Brownstone House." *Woman's Day* Apr. 1948: 36-37, 107-11.

"Model Wanted." *Esquire* Jan. 1936: 41, 182B.

"Money." *Yale Review* 38.3 (1949): 520-29.

"A Morning with the Doc." *New Masses* 15 May 1934: 14-16.

"My Aunt Daisy." *American Mercury* Dec. 1932: 486-96.

"My Brother's Confirmation." *Direction* June 1938: 17-22.

"My Cousin Louie." *Collier's* 29 Apr. 1944: 20, 64, 66-67.

"My Father's Broad Shoulders." *New Yorker* 6 Sept. 1947: 44, 46-50.

"My Mother's Love Story." *Story* Mar.-Apr. 1946: 23-32.

"My Mother's Uncle from Lithuania." *The Sunday Review of the Brooklyn Daily Eagle* 10 Dec. 1933: 10-13.

"Old-Timer." *Woman's Day* Nov. 1946: 40-41, 78-80, 83-86.

"The Oldest Brother." *Prairie Schooner* 5.2 (1931): 168-71.

"On the Shore." *Dial* Mar. 1929: 225-28.

"Over the Bridge in the Bronx." *Harper's* Feb. 1933: 319-26.

"Payday on the Night Shift." *Nativity: An American Quarterly* 1 (Spr. 1931): 27-30.

"The Penny-Divers." *North American Review* May 1933: 395-405.

"The Photograph." *New Yorker* 14 Aug. 1948: 54-59.

"Play, Tutti, Play." *American Magazine* Dec. 1945: 36-37, 136-40.

"The Poet." *Virginia Quarterly Review* 12.2 (1936): 248-59.

"Prelude; A Story for These Times." *Harper's* Aug. 1938: 302-08; *Scholastic* 18 Feb. 1939: 27-29, 32.

"The Prophet of Lake Street." *Collier's* 11 Mar. 1944: 13, 61-62, 64.

"The Race." *Midland* 16.4 (1930): 169-74.

"Relatives." *Menorah Journal* June 1929: 557-60.

"The Return." *Menorah Journal* Apr. 1930: 364-68.

"Road Home." *American Magazine* Aug. 1945: 22-23, 87-88, 91, 93.

"Scab!" *American Mercury* June 1934: 232-37.

"A Small Matter." *Scholastic* 6 Apr. 1949: 23-24, 36-38; *Scholastic* 25 Mar. 1953: 20, 23, 26-27, 29.

"A Small West Side Family." *Trend* 1 (Sept.-Oct.-Nov. 1932): 87-89.

"The Soldier Who Wanted to See Whitman." *Prairie Schooner* 22.1 (1948): 82-91; *Scholastic* 10 Mar. 1954: 21-22, 28-29.

"Song Writer in the Family." *Yale Review* 33.2 (1943): 258-67; *Scholastic* 5 Mar. 1945: 21-22, 28-30; *Scholastic* 9 Nov. 1949: 19-21, 29.

"They Do the Same in England." *Partisan Review* July-Aug. 1935: 29-36.

"Two Sisters." *Pagany, A Native Quarterly* 1.4 (1930): 78-82.

"Winter Evening." *American Mercury* Sept. 1933: 25-31.

Secondary Sources

Books

Hart, John E. *Albert Halper.* Twayne's United States Authors Series. Boston: Twayne, 1980.

Articles and Chapters

Champney, Freeman. "Albert Halper and His Little People." *Antioch Review* 2.4 (1942): 628-34.

Begins with the proposition that Halper has received the critical brush off from the literary establishment, and subsequently sets out to correct the record. Suggests that, while Halper's prose is not elegant, and that he has introduced no innovations in the novel form, he has found a technique and a structural plan. Thinks his relation to his people and his time has been relaxed, and he has managed to make it through the turbulent eighties sticking to his own agenda—the documenting of the main flow of American life. Considers his depictions of the plant, the shop, and the works a major achievement because they give the feel of what life means to most urban Americans. Discusses each of the novels in turn.

Eisinger, Chester E. "Character and Self in Fiction on the Left." *Proletarian Writers of the Thirties*. Ed. David Madden. Crosscurrents/Modern Critiques. Carbondale: Southern Illinois UP, 1968. 162-65.

Sees Halper as a writer who, while dealing with group identity, has no ideological commitment. Describes Halper's efforts to document the effects of capitalism on the worker, but complains of his essential lack of creative talent. Details the contents of each of the books, and concludes that, while he does well with the external social contexts of the novels, he has trouble tracing the characters' inner psychological workings.

Hart, John E. "Albert Halper's World of the Thirties." *Twentieth Century Literature* 9.4 (1964): 185-95.

Claims that Halper is concerned with the struggle of people, not the struggle of classes. Notes that the novels are wonderful social and historical commentaries on the thirties written with wit and sensitive insight. Also sees them as interesting for their stylistic techniques and symbolic portrayals of thought and feeling and the relationships of people as they make their way through a jungle of machines and economic dilemmas. A major article dealing with each of the novels and highlighting both style and theme in the Halper novel.

Klein, Marcus. "The Roots of the Radicals: Experience in the Thirties." *Proletarian Writers of the Thirties*. Ed. David Madden. Crosscurrents/Modern Critiques. Carbondale: Southern Illinois UP, 1968. 134-57.

Discusses, very briefly, Halper's *Union Square* as a novel which focuses on the nature and purposes of proletarian arts and the proletarian artist. Lauds Halper for his representative sociology in the novel and for his intensity.

Luccock, Halford E. "The Voice of Labor." *American Mirror—Social Ethical and Religious Aspects of American Literature 1930-1940*. Halford E. Luccock. New York: Macmillan, 1941. 160-62.

A brief appreciation which calls Halper one of the most skillful portrayers of labor, who writes from a varied experience of all kinds of labor. Discusses *Union Square* and *The Chute* as accurate sociologies of the failure of capitalism and as good, detailed descriptions of the workplace.

Sherman, Bernard. "On the Shore and The Golden Watch." *The Invention of the Jew: Jewish-American Education Novels (1916-1964)*. Bernard Sherman. New York: Yoseloff, 1969. 204-05, passim.

Lists Halper's novels, and comments on their nostalgia and Jewish cultural material.

Weber, Brom. "Some American Jewish Novelists." *Chicago Jewish Forum* 4.2 (1946): 177-84.

Calls Halper a writer impelled by great sympathy and love for the desperation with which the great mass of humankind live their lives. Suggests that his primary concern is with character. Observes that their sufferings are real and that the general mood is one of pathos. Complains that he has relied too much on his compassion to carry the novels along, and has been mistakenly labeled a proletarian novelist even though he has portrayed the social surfaces of American life with much accuracy.

Reviews

Algren, Nelson. "Record of a Sure Hand." Rev. of *The Golden Watch*. *Saturday Review* 7 Mar. 1953: 27-28.

Describes Halper's humor in *The Golden Watch*, his innocence, unpretentiousness, and unaffected warmth.

Appel, Benjamin. "Albert Halper's New Approach." Rev. of *Only an Inch from Glory*. *Saturday Review of Literature* 9 Oct. 1943: 18.

A review essay on *Only an Inch from Glory* which describes Halper as a generous, Dickensian kind of writer whose works are always socially significant, and always welded together with a simple but powerful unity. Considers that, in this novel, Halper confines himself to four characters only and substitutes, instead of the physical base, an emotional base for the novel. Details the main characters and the circumstances of the plot, while praising the book for its achievement of genuine pathos and useful social commentary.

Barry, Griffin. "The Other War." Rev. of *Sons of the Fathers*. *New Republic* 27 Jan. 1941: 123-24.

Describes *Sons of the Fathers* as an anti-war story dealing with the impact of events in 1917 on an immigrant Jewish-American family. No literary commentary.

Bessie, Alvah C. "Men and the Machine." Rev. of *The Foundry*. *Saturday Review of Literature* 8 Sept. 1934: 96.

Calls *The Foundry* a book reflective of the attitudes and methods of Sherwood Anderson, who was able to depersonalize personal experience into universal archetypes. Details the contents and complains about the wooden characterizations that lack vitality. Concludes that because of these and other deficiencies, the novel remains amorphous, lumbering clumsily through chapters in which nothing happens.

Burnham, James. "Proletarian Grand Hotel." Rev. of *The Foundry*. *Nation* 12 Sept. 1934: 306.

Lists the faults of *The Foundry* as lack of organic form, psychological penetration, sustained style, philosophic depth, and a real conception of the novel as form. Comments on the earthy breeziness, vigor, and accurate observation of the foundry milieu.

Chamberlain, John. "Union Square On and Off the Soap Box." Rev. of *Union Square*. *New York Times Book Review* 5 Mar. 1933: 6.

Calls *Union Square* an exciting and ironic novel about the welter of life around Union Square. Describes the class war set up in the novel, and the characters and events comprising it. Likens its structure to Dos Passos's novels, and applauds the book for coming splendidly alive.

"Cops and Robbers." Rev. of *The Chicago Crime Book*. *Times Literary Supplement* 2 Jan. 1969: 4.

Considers how in *The Chicago Crime Book* Halper seems unaware of the picture he is drawing of both crime and Chicago. Details the contents of the novel, and concludes that this is a book for the uncritical, but, that as a picture of Chicago crime, it is not very successful. Suggests that in this aspect, as in others, Chicago is "the hog butcher" rather than the dedicated artist.

Farrell, James T. "Saul Bergman's Sons." Rev. of *Sons of the Fathers*. *Saturday Review of Literature* 2 Nov. 1940: 12.

Calls this a political novel advancing the thesis of American isolationism, and drawing the picture of an American family under the strain of war. Concludes that this is a sentimental Americanism and an equally sentimental isolationism.

Feld, Rose. "New York Quartet." Rev. of *Only An Inch From Glory*. *New York Times Book Review* 10 Oct. 1943: 4.

Calls *Only An Inch From Glory* a book with swift-moving narrative and crisp dialogue which catches not only the tempo of the world the characters move in, but their own individual differences. Commends Halper for several of the characters, and points out the weaknesses of others.

"Fiction." Rev. of *The Fourth Horseman of Miami Beach. New Yorker* 1 Oct. 1966: 223.

Briefly discusses the characters and the contents of the novel, and concludes that Halper shows extraordinarily realistic and convincing writing, but that his characters lack spirit. Complains that they are empty, pathetic, and dulled with calculation.

Gregory, Horace. "When Village Bohemia Moved to Union Square." Rev. of *Union Square. New York Herald Tribune Books* 5 Mar. 1933: 7.

Describes the contents of *Union Square,* and comments on Halper's warm promise of rich vitality, remarkable gift for storytelling, and clever characterization.

Hansen, Harry. "Memoirs of Life in a Jewish Family, and a Boy Growing Up." Rev. of *The Golden Watch. New York Herald Tribune Book Review* 15 Mar. 1953: 4.

Complains that *The Golden Watch* reads like a series of detached stories about the same characters, which it actually was originally. Notes that the best episodes portray the storyteller as an observant but not precocious lad taking part in experiences common to boys everywhere. Concludes that the past in these stories is touched with warmth and friendliness.

Kazin, Alfred. "Life in the 'Golden Rule Mail-Order House.'" Rev. of *The Chute. New York Herald Tribune Books* 31 Oct. 1937: 1.

Calls *The Chute* a novel which feels a little empty, though it is fundamentally true. Notes that Halper has the gift for depicting life in the mass, and more he talks their language and shares their bad jokes. Describes the story in detail, and concludes that this is a portrait of the Sussmans full of delightful touches.

Kronenberger, Louis. "Albert Halper's Vivid New Novel." Rev. of *The Foundry. New York Times Book Review* 9 Sept. 1934: 6.

Argues that this novel is far too earnest to make much of an impact on the reader. Declares there is too much absorption in the concrete and in social philosophy. Concludes that though he does a wonderful job of animating the place, and though the book has tenderness and humanity, it lacks depth and breadth.

Kronenberger, Louis. "Mail-Order Movie." Rev. of *The Chute. Nation* 6 Nov. 1937: 511-12.

Comments on Halper's surface similarity to Dickens and his rapid character-izing power. Commends him for his sense of life, visual integration of scenes, dramatic manner, and fine suspense. Notes that he has also tackled the task of showing kids developing class-consciousness, but the whole tone is a little too vivacious and his characters without any surprising turns of mind. Concludes that this book contains a great deal of warm-heartedness.

Leighton, G. R. "Brought to Life." Rev. of *Union Square. Saturday Review of Literature* 4 Mar. 1933: 465.

Comments that Halper successfully brings to life a section of a great city. Describes the characters, some of whom are dull, but dull in their way and not the author's.

Lewis, Sinclair. "Blowing Loud Bugles for Edward Halper." Rev. of *The Foundry. New York Herald Tribune Books* 9 Sept. 1934: 1.

Declares *The Foundry* as very soundly written. Sees it as earthy, solid, human, and decidedly significant. Suggests that it is also humorous and dramatic. Details the characters, plot, and general impact.

"Men and Machines: Endless Round of the Foundry's Din." Rev. of *The Foundry. Newsweek* 8 Sept. 1934: 40.

A brief review of *The Foundry* detailing the contents of the book and criticizing it for its strained rhetorical flourishes and its sheer length. Asserts, however, that the book is still a brilliant feat of reportage.

Moore, Harry Thornton. "Zola Americana." Rev. of *The Chute. New Republic* 1 Dec. 1937: 111.

Primarily describes the contents of the book, and comments on the insight into potential human goodness the author provides.

Ross, Sam. "Pop Ran the Grocery." Rev. of *The Golden Watch. New York Times Book Review* 1 Mar. 1953: 5.

Describes *The Golden Watch* as something not quite a novel in the real sense, but rather a series of portraits, all of which could stand by them-selves. Concludes that the book is warm, touching, and rewarding.

Rothman, N. L. "Albert Halper's Industrial Novel." Rev. of *The Chute. Saturday Review of Literature* 6 Nov. 1937: 6.

Describes *The Chute* as easy and artless, full of a pulsing, rhythmic qual-ity, simple but severe in diction. Gives a good account of the contents.

Rothman, N. L. "Halper . . ." Rev. of *The Little People. Saturday Review of Literature* 17 Oct. 1942: 15-16.

Discusses the novel's treatment of department store life, and praises Halper's sure ear for the half-inarticulate talk of the little people, "choked with cliches and repressed passions."

Rugoff, Milton. "Draft, War, and a Family." Rev. of *Sons of the Fathers. New York Herald Tribune Books* 17 Nov. 1940: 4.

Comments that, while *Sons of the Fathers* centers around the plight of a middle-class family faced by conscription and the World War, it offers very uncanny parallels for the present times. Calls it an old story, but one told with convincing detail and color. Suggests that this is a painfully rich novel with meanings for the immediate future.

Rutenber, Ralph D., Jr. "Foundrymen and Bosses." Rev. of *The Foundry. New Republic* 19 Sept. 1934: 165-66.

Details the contents of the novel, and admires the realism, detail, dialogue, internal development of the characters, eye for the dramatic, and general narrative excellence of the piece.

Schneider, Isidor. "Rain in Union Square." Rev. of *Union Square. Nation* 26 Apr. 1933: 478-79.

Comments that *Union Square* is unusually gloomy in setting and outcome for the characters. Shows how Halper produces character types rather than characters for whom the author has some love. Suggests that the focus of the novel is sex, and that all the couples are presented as drearily and messily working out domestic disharmonies. Concludes, however, that this is the work of a talented writer even though technique is not enough.

Sherman, Bernard A. "Books." Rev. of *The Fourth Horseman of Miami Beach. Chicago Jewish Forum* 25.4 (1967): 307-08.

Likens Halper to naturalistic writers like Drieser, and describes the contents of the novel. Accuses Halper of being incapable of crafting a smooth, light piece and of writing humor.

Strauss, Harold. "At Sutton & Co." Rev. of *The Little People. New York Times Book Review* 11 Oct. 1942: 7.

Calls *The Little People* the first novel Halper has written without anger, and claims that it is by far his best. Details characters and situations. Concludes that the book is marred by switching point of view, but this time Halper's work is not marred by an oppressive thesis and accompanying documentation.

Strauss, Harold. "Mr. Halper Writes of Mail Order Workers." Rev. of *The Chute. New York Times Book Review* 7 Nov. 1937: 7.

Calls *The Chute* a book by an author convinced that man is a passive thing acted upon rather than acting. Suggests that, though the work is sincere, it is a book full of naive perplexity and awe in the face of the industrial age. Provides a detailed plot summary.

Strauss, Harold. "What Happened to a 'Little Man' in the Last War." Rev. of *Sons of the Fathers. New York Times Book Review* 20 Oct. 1940: 5.

Describes *Sons of the Fathers* as a novel loaded with controversial dynamite, sincerely written, and redolent with homely detail. Notes that the picture Halper paints is warm, intimate, and accurate. Concludes, however, that the novel lacks urgency for the modern reader because of Halper's simplistic treatment of the war itself. Suggests that this renders the novel more like a tract.

Biographical Sources

"Albert Halper." *Wilson Bulletin for Librarians* Apr. 1935: 402, 404.

A general description of Halper's life and works. Provides a thumbnail sketch of the contents of his books. A useful brief introduction.

"Albert Halper." *Scholastic* 18 Feb. 1939: 28.

A brief biographical sketch listing his novels to date and providing a comment on the theme of *Prelude*, "Look out, here comes Fascism!"

Halper, Albert. *Good-bye, Union Square: A Writer's Memoir of the Thirties.* Chicago: Quadrangle, 1970.

Halper deals with his friends and acquaintances, his aloofness from the politics of the day, the literary milieu, and his "solitary, very satisfactory life."

Halper, Albert. "Thoughts on Being Twayned." *American Scholar* 51.1 (1981-1982): 105-14.

Reminisces about his writing career on the occasion of receiving the volume about him in the Twayne United States Authors Series.

Halper, Albert. "Under Forty: A Symposium on American Literature and the Younger Generation of American Jews." *Contemporary Jewish Record* Feb. 1944: 23-25.

In response to an invitation to discuss the relationship of his Jewish heritage to his writing, Halper considers himself different from his Christian colleagues because of the impact of the Holocaust and the deaths of millions of Jews on his consciousness. But he sees this as only one symptom of a betrayal of the world—of the Negroes, of labor, of the poor—by free enterprise. He feels that all writers need to produce works that mean something to their times because not only Jews but the human race will be "forced to dig its own grave if it is not awakened from its somnambulism."

Hart, John E. "Albert Halper." *American Novelists, 1910-1945, Part II: F. Scott Fitzgerald-O. E. Rolvaag.* Ed. James J. Martine. Detroit: Gale, 1981. Vol. 9 of *Dictionary of Literary Biography.* 94 vols. to date. 1978- . 91-96.

More than details of his life, this is a career biography, tracing the development of the author's canon, describing the contents and themes of his works, evaluating his reputation, and placing him in the larger context of American literary history. Includes lists of primary and secondary sources and illustrations.

Mark Harris

1922 –

Primary Sources

Novels

Bang the Drum Slowly by Henry Wiggen; Certain of His Enthusiasms Restrained by Mark Harris. New York: Borzoi-Knopf, 1956, 1960; Lincoln: U of Nebraska P, 1956, 1983; Toronto: McClelland, 1956; Garden City: Doubleday, 1962; New York: Dell, 1973, 1974; Cutchogue: Buccaneer, 1981.

The Goy. New York: Dial, 1970; New York: Bantam, 1973.

It Looked Like for Ever. New York: McGraw, 1979, 1984; Lincoln: Bison-U of Nebraska P, 1989.

Killing Everybody. New York: Dial, 1973; Sag Harbor: Second Chance, 1987.

Lying in Bed. New York: McGraw, 1985.

Something about a Soldier. New York: Macmillan, 1957; London: Deutsch, 1958; London: Hamilton, 1961; New York: Ballantine, 1976; Lincoln: Bison-U of Nebraska P, 1985.

The Southpaw, by Henry W. Wiggen; Punctuation Freely Inserted and Spelling Greatly Improved by Mark Harris. Indianapolis: Bobbs, 1953; Toronto: McClelland, 1953; Garden City: Permabooks, 1954; Indianapolis: Charter-Bobbs, 1962; Cutchogue: Buccaneer, 1982; Lincoln: Bison-U of Nebraska P, 1984.

Speed New York: Fine, 1990.

A Ticket for a Seamstich. New York: Knopf, 1957; Toronto: McClelland, 1957; Lincoln: U of Nebraska P, 1984; Lincoln: Bison-U of Nebraska P, 1985.

Trumpet to the World. New York: Reynal, 1946; Toronto: McClelland, 1946; Lincoln: Landmark-U of Nebraska P, 1989.

Wake Up, Stupid. New York: Knopf, 1959, 1962; Toronto: McClelland, 1959; London: Deutsch, 1960; London: Consul-World, 1963; New York: McGraw, 1984.

Collected Works

Short Work of It: Selected Writing by Mark Harris. Ed. Mark Harris. Pittsburgh: U of Pittsburgh P, 1979; London: Feffer, 1979.
Contents: At Prayerbook Cross, Touching Idamae Low

Henry Wiggen's Books. New York: Avon, 1977.
Contents: *The Southpaw, Bang the Drum Slowly, A Ticket for a Seamstitch.*

Short Fiction in Anthologies

"The Self-Made Brain Surgeon." *The Best American Short Stories, 1961.* Eds. Martha Foley and David Burnett. Boston: Houghton, 1961. 152-67; *How We Live: Contemporary Life in Contemporary Fiction.* Eds. Penny C. Hills and L. Rust Hills. New York: Macmillan, 1968. 441-53.

Short Fiction in Periodicals

"At Prayerbook Cross." *Cimarron Review* 6 (1968): 6-10, 12-13.

"Carmelita's Education for Living." *Esquire* Oct. 1957: 84-85.

"Conversation on Southern Honshu." *North Dakota Quarterly* 27.3 (1959): 62-65.

"From the Desk of the Troublesome Editor." *Virginia Quarterly Review* 65.3 (1989): 418-39.

"Henry Wiggen's Last Pitch." *Esquire* 24 Apr. 1979: 70-72, 75, 77-80, 84-86.

"Iron Fist of Oligarchy." *Virginia Quarterly Review* 36.1 (1960): 78-96.

"La Lumiere." *Denver Quarterly* 18.3 (1983): 38-57.

"The Self-Made Brain Surgeon." *Noble Savage* 1 (Mar. 1960): 140-58.

"Titwillow." *Michigan Quarterly Review* 25.3 (1986): 511-24.

"Touching Idamae Low." *Esquire* 25 Apr. 1978: 61-67.

Secondary Sources

Books

Norman Lavers. *Mark Harris*. Twayne's United States Authors Series 304. Boston: Twayne, 1978.

Articles and Chapters

Bachner, Saul. "Baseball as Literature: *Bang the Drum Slowly*." *English Record* 25.2 (1974): 83-86.
Describes *Bang the Drum Slowly* as an interesting tale which takes the reader through a complete season with the Mammoths' baseball team. Considers the characterization first-rate and the tale engrossing. Concludes that this is pennant-winning reading, and that English teachers would do well to consider it.

Cochran, Robert. "Bang the Drum Differently: The Southpaw Slants of Henry Wiggen." *Modern Fiction Studies* 33.1 (1987): 151-59.

Comments on the spate of baseball novels in the 1980s in American literature. Describes several of these novels in order of appearance, and asserts that *Bang the Drum Slowly* is much more than a mere sequel to *The Southpaw*. Considers Harris's main achievement in this book as the voicing of a fundamental faith in the common sense and strong independence of the common man. Provides a formalist exegesis of the novel.

Guttman, Allen. "Literature, Sociology, and 'Our National Game.'" *Prospects: Annual Journal of American Cultural Studies* 1 (1975): 119-36.

Sees baseball as an expression of the American spirit, particularly in the 1950s. Considers its chief appeal the ability of baseball to evoke rural nostalgia, the technological impetus, and the presence of folk heroes. Examines Shaw's *Voices of a Summer Day* and Mark Harris's *Bang the Drum Slowly* in which pastoral elements interact with the *Realitatsprinzip*. A detailed exegesis of the symbolic meaning of baseball in these and other novels.

Harris, Mark. "Bring Back That Old Sandlot Novel." *New York Times Book Review*. 16 Oct. 1988: 44-45.

Discusses the baseball novel, suggesting that the genre derives from such traditions as the stories of success (Horatio Alger) and the American vernacular (*Huckleberry Finn*), but not until Malamud's *The Natural* and his own *The Southpaw* have they been considered serious, adult fiction. Discusses a number of baseball novels important to the development of the genre. Concludes by describing the contemporary baseball novel, noting that "the national game is played now in the image of reality, money, sex, egomania, told in the fully expressive range of the English language denied and suppressed by the creator of Baseball Joe and the heirs to the Alger tradition."

Higgs, Robert J. "A Country Boy from the City." *Laurel and Thorn: The Athlete in American Literature*. Lexington: UP of Kentucky, 1981. 132-38.

Briefly discusses *The Southpaw, Bang the Drum Slowly*, and *A Ticket for a Seamstitch* as romances and baseball stories offering a counter-thrust to twentieth-century nihilism.

Ladenson, Joyce Ruddel. "Feminist Reflections on *Bang the Drum Slowly*." *American Examiner* 3.3 (1974): 22-24.

Provides a detailed feminist critique of the female stereotypes and caricatures in *Bang the Drum Slowly* and the femaleless sanctity of the male world of sports, sentimentalized male friendships, and general denigration of the world of women.

Lavers, Norman. "Mark Harris." *Critical Survey of Long Fiction.* Ed. Frank N. Magill. 9 vols. Englewood Cliffs: Salem, 1981. 4: 1277-85.

A critical essay that covers Harris's birthplace, principal long fiction, achievements, biography, a general analysis of his fifteen books, and a list of publications exclusive of the long fiction.

Oriard, Michael. "Youth and Age in American Sports Fiction." *Dreaming of Heroes: American Sports Fiction, 1868-1980.* Chicago: Nelson-Hall, 1982. 138-53.

Calls *The Southpaw* Harris' *Adventures of Huckleberry Finn,* a novel explicitly concerned with youth, initiation, and the possibilities of maturation in the modern world. Discusses the indefinite quality of contemporary maturity as reflected in the novel by the examples of aging and the mid-life crisis.

Schafer, William J. "Mark Harris: Versions of (American) Pastoral." *Critique* 19.1 (1977): 28-48.

Discusses the history of Harris's novels, commenting that he has worked virtually alone in his own individual territory all during the fifties and sixties without a critical audience and has been grouped in with Jewish American writers. Says that he might be passed over as a quirky offshoot of vernacular Americana like Twain and Lardner, but that he has indeed worked his own individual territory in the intricate maze in the heart of America, and has written some of the finest comic fiction during those decades. Claims that what he has done while exploring the collision of young experience with a hard world, the pluralist and conformist patterns of American life, is write versions of the American *pastorale.* Deals with *The Southpaw, Bang the Drum Slowly, A Ticket for a Seamstitch, Trumpet to the World,* and *Something about a Soldier.*

"Something About a Soldier." *Survey of Contemporary Literature.* Ed. Frank N. Magill. Rev. ed. 12 vols. Englewood Cliffs: Salem, 1977. 11: 7098-100.

A standard reference article covering background, influences, plot, character, theme, and style in *Something About a Soldier.*

Umphlett, Willy Lee. "The Neo-Romantic Encounter." *The Sporting Myth and the American Experience: Studies in Contemporary Fiction.* Lewisburg: Bucknell UP, 1975. 139-45.

Discusses Bruce Pearson of *Bang the Drum Slowly* as an innocent type who, unlike other sporting figures, has little actual status. Describes his relationship with Henry Wiggen, who takes him under his wing.

Reviews

Brooks, John. "A Ward Case of Innocence." Rev. of *Something About a Soldier. New York Times Book Review* 27 Oct. 1957: 5, 42.

Argues that *Something About a Soldier* is virtually unclassifiable as a World War II novel. Calls it a sort of amiable nightmare in which some of the magic prevents the worst from happening. Suggests, however, that though it falls short of complete effectiveness, its style is sometimes arch, its point of view sentimental, its characterization deft, and its passages of wild humor delightful.

Bush, Kent. "Baseball—It's a Man's Game, and Democratic." Rev. of *The Southpaw. Christian Science Monitor* 9 July 1953: 11.

Reviews a series of notable American baseball novels, and locates *The Southpaw* as one of them. Briefly describes its world of masculine ritual, initiation rites, men's talk, feminine influence, and baseball knowledge.

Charyn, Jerome. "Languishing for Mariolena." Rev. of *Lying in Bed. New York Times Book Review* 17 June 1984: 23.

Describes *Lying in Bed* as a series of letters between an impotent novelist-professor and Lee Youngdahl, a character from an earlier Harris work, *Wake Up, Stupid.* Claims it has all the illnesses of the epistolary novel. Concludes that despite this, it is mostly a funny, squawky story about the telling of stories, written in a long playful epistle to readers and writers.

Cromie, Robert. "Readable Novel in Lardner Tradition Tells Southpaw's Jump to Big Leagues." Rev. of *The Southpaw. Chicago Sunday Tribune Magazine of Books* 3 May 1953: 6.

Calls *The Southpaw* more than a merely funny book. Considers it a readable, fine thing by a competent craftsman with a fine ear for dialogue. Describes the contents briefly.

Daley, Robert. "Henry was a Southpaw." Rev. of *Bang the Drum Slowly*. *New York Times Book Review* 18 Mar. 1956: 5.

Considers *Bang the Drum Slowly* to be a percussive dirge for Bruce Pearson. Claims that when it sticks to its character and the baseball background, it makes wonderful reading. Concludes that though it is awfully funny in parts, the pennant race is a persistent intrusion that keeps this from being a first-rate novel.

Dennis, Patrick. "Problems of Private Epp." Rev. of *Something About a Soldier*. *New York Herald Tribune Book Review* 15 Dec. 1957: 4.

Argues that *Something About a Soldier* is wise, witty, and well-written, but ought to have been a better novel, or something else altogether. Condemns all the elderly and irritating literary affectations. Concludes that, despite the fact the book is very much about love, war, communism, boys, girls, and men, it is mostly about laughter.

"Echoing Ring." Rev. of *Bang the Drum Slowly*. *Time* 19 Mar. 1956: 110, 112.

Suggests that *Bang the Drum Slowly* is reminiscent of Ring Lardner. Describes the character and life of Bruce Pearson, the left-handed catcher, and complains of the banality of the book. Does consider that Harris has mastered the offbeat scene, and that even if all his characters are no more than one-dimensional, it is a dimension Harris has measured with heart, eye, and ear.

Feiffer, Jules. "Nixon and the Fat Lady." Rev. of *Mark the Glove Boy*. *Commentary* May 1964: 86-88.

Calls *Mark the Glove Boy* a book in which Harris, by neutralizing himself as the author, succeeds in neutralizing his subject matter. Argues that there is nothing new to learn here about Nixon, or about Mark the glove boy. Considers the rest of the story taken up with the writing of the article, the disappointment of Harris's friends, and a beside-the-point whammy on Nixon.

Fitzgerald, Edward J. "Jeu de Spring." Rev. of *The Southpaw*. *Saturday Review* 11 Apr. 1953: 58.

Considers *The Southpaw* a serious novel using the folklore and mythology of baseball to illuminate some pleasant and unpleasant aspects of contemporary American character. Concludes that this is a long and penetrating look at American movies and morals, all the while telling an absorbing and exciting action story.

German, William. "Harris and the Mighty Wiggen Had a Bad Season." Rev. of *A Ticket for a Seamstitch*. *San Francisco Chronicle* 17 Feb. 1957: 22.

Describes *A Ticket for a Seamstitch* in detail along with its central character, Henry Wiggen. Comments primarily on its failure to meet the standards of *The Southpaw*. Concludes that, fortunately, Harris still has a fine adult approach to baseball and a number of healthy swings. Sees its humor as spoiled only occasionally by Damon Runyan tipping the bat.

German, William. "A Nobody Up at Bat in the Vulgar, Wonderful Big League." Rev. of *Bang the Drum Slowly*. *San Francisco Chronicle This World Magazine* 25 Mar. 1956: 24.

Calls *Bang the Drum Slowly* a new book by an important new author, although a sequel to *Southpaw*. Describes the central character.

Gottlieb, Gerald. "This Professor Is in a Class by Himself." Rev. of *Wake Up, Stupid*. *New York Herald Tribune Book Review* 19 July 1959: 4.

Calls *Wake Up, Stupid* a funny, warm novel. Considers Harris a marvel and a delight, and predicts that if he goes on writing like this, he will be numbered among the great American humorists like Lardner and Nathanael West. Provides a full account of characters and plot.

Gottlieb, Robin. "Here's That Southpaw Again." Rev. of *A Ticket for a Seamstitch*. *New York Herald Tribune Book Review* 17 Feb. 1957: 8.

Considers *A Ticket for a Seamstitch* a satisfying, rib-tickling, little tale, but lacking in the richness and fullness of the previous novel.

Gray, Paul. "Dies Irae." Rev. of *Killing Everybody*. *Time* 11 June 1973: 100.

Argues that *Killing Everybody* is a comedy bordering on moral outrage. Notes an undertone of finely controlled anger. Is disappointed in a novelist who sets himself up as a lecturer instructing foolish readers and characters alike. Concludes, however, that this is a fortunate fall from lofty disgust, and that Harris has captured the pathology of the present age without gloating over it.

Groberg, Nancy. "An Embittered Race Novel." Rev. of *Trumpet to the World*. *Saturday Review of Literature* 20 Apr. 1946: 13-14.

Shows how *Trumpet to the World* is done without the bitterness, emotionalism, and loss of perspective which mar so many of the books that attempt to deal with the plight of the American Negro. Concludes that this is clear-headed, sincere, beautifully written, and timely.

Hall, Donald. "Henry Wiggen at Liberty." Rev. of *It Looked Like For Ever*. *New York Times Book Review* 30 Sept. 1979: 13, 18.

Calls *It Looked Like For Ever* a baseball novel about a left-handed pitcher. Argues that there is considerable variety of place and action, and a compelling background of action against which the characters play out their moral dramas. Concludes that the language is influenced by Ring Lardner, with Mark Twain as a reasonable grandfather, and Damon Runyan as a disreputable uncle.

Hicks, Granville. "A Fine New Novel by Mark Harris and Collected Stories of J. F. Power." Rev. of *Bang the Drum Slowly*. *New Leader* 26 Mar. 1956: 22-23.

Describes *The Southpaw* primarily in terms of its contents and its relationship with *Bang the Drum Slowly*. Concludes that, in both books, Harris demonstrates the heroic potential of our species as it attempts to reclaim a large part of our reusable past.

Hicks, Granville. "Harris's *Ticket for a Seamstitch* and Gill's *The Day the Money Stopped*." Rev. of *Ticket for a Seamstitch*. *New Leader* 25 Feb. 1957: 23.

Relates *Ticket for a Seamstitch* to earlier novels with the same hero, *Bang the Drum Slowly* and *The Southpaw*. Admires the shrewd and amusing writing about baseball, while commenting that there is a little more of it than necessary.

Hicks, Granville. "Portrait of a Non-Conformist." Rev. of *Wake Up, Stupid*. *Saturday Review* 18 July 1959: 13.

Calls Harris engaging, and a writer of incorruptible high spirits. Describes the contents, style, and methods of *Wake Up, Stupid*. Traces the autobiographical elements of the novel, and complains of some extraneous material, lack of discipline, loose ends, offset to some degree by wonderful comic passages and originality.

"Hilarity Everywhere." Rev. of *Wake Up, Stupid*. *Times Literary Supplement* 10 June 1960: 374.

Calls *Wake Up, Stupid* brash, smart, surrealistic, and occasionally very funny. Comments that it is written in the form of letters, and indulges in all kinds of typographical pranks. Concludes that Harris is a witty and knowing "bloke."

Hogan, William. "An Experimental Novel of a Disorganized Hero." Rev. of *Wake Up, Stupid. San Francisco Chronicle* 19 July 1959: 19.

Calls *Wake Up, Stupid* a frankly experimental novel written in the form of a series of letters, jottings, and occasional enclosures. Suggests, however, that the reader is more conscious of Harris' juggling act than he is of the characters being juggled. Concludes that this is razzle-dazzle entertainment for the alert college crowd.

Hogan, William. "Mark Harris' Soldier at War with the U.S." Rev. of *Something About a Soldier. San Francisco Chronicle* 22 Oct. 1957: 23.

Believes that *Something About a Soldier* asks the question of whether the Army is unfit for Private Epstein. Mostly details contents, and provides a character analysis of Jacob Epstein.

Kupferberg, Herbert. "Trials and Triumphs of a Rookie Pitcher." Rev. of *The Southpaw. New York Herald Tribune Book Review* 12 Apr. 1953: 18.

Considers *The Southpaw* primarily a baseball novel written in a fairly straight-forward fashion, moving with logical enough progression. Concludes that, underneath all of this, the story is really about a left-hander in a right-handed world.

Maddocks, Melvin. "A Problem of Definition." Rev. of *Wake Up, Stupid. Christian Science Monitor* 23 July 1959: 11.

Notes that *Wake Up, Stupid* is occasionally smug, savingly satirical, amusing, and new. Describes some of the characters and events, and the thematic thrust of the stories.

Malcolm, Donald. "The Pitcher in the Rye." Rev. of *A Ticket for a Seamstitch. New Republic* 18 Feb. 1957: 17-18.

Considers the story of *A Ticket for a Seamstitch* to be slight, but divertingly told. Complains of occasional lapses into Runyonese, but concedes that the author's ear is generally good and his eye for character even better. Concludes that Harris is a comic artist of considerable skill whose subject, baseball, just happens to be a national sport.

Marcus, Steven. "Experimental Writing." Rev. of *Something About a Soldier. Commentary* Mar. 1958: 269-71.

Considers *Something About a Soldier* as too self-conscious, too coy, and too vaguely abstract. Calls this a thorough-going experiment in form and style, character, and conception. Describes the contents of the novel in detail, and then criticizes the prose, mythical characterizations, use of the popular culture, and its missed chance to provide a concrete sense of the army.

Millstein, Gilbert. "Wiggen on the Mound." Rev. of *A Ticket for a Seamstitch*. *New York Times Book Review* 17 Feb. 1957: 7.

Claims *A Ticket for a Seamstitch* is good, real, funny, and doesn't try for the size of *The Southpaw* or *Bang the Drum Slowly*. Describes several scenes and the main character.

Nordell, Roderick. "Airy Fantasies...Punctured Balloons." Rev. of *The Goy*. *Christian Science Monitor* 15 Oct. 1970: 13.

Argues that *The Goy* is done with fine institutional and personal detail. Sees it as a wryly amusing book, not a gloomy one. Notes that the myth-like characters always come down to earth, and that the Goy emerges as a man who daily capitulates to his own temptations.

Ozick, Cynthia. "Jews and Gentiles." Rev. of *The Goy*. *Commentary* June 1971: 104, 106-08.

Sees *The Goy* as an enterprise which makes large claims for itself and lays large claims on our attention and our inquiries. Shows how it represents a conversion from being baseball to being Fickelstein. Labels the book as an attack on goy culture and its liberal humanism. Develops this thesis through careful analysis of the novel and its meanings.

Saal, Hubert. "Green Punk." Rev. of *A Ticket for a Seamstitch*. *Saturday Review* 16 Feb. 1957: 17.

Argues that *A Ticket for a Seamstitch* is not as good a work as his first two because it fails to treat issues of any magnitude or complication. Concludes that it is all frosting without any cake. Describes the contents briefly.

Sisk, John P. "College Humor." Rev. of *Wake Up, Stupid*. *Commonweal* 28 Aug. 1959: 452-53.

Calls this a serious but genuinely funny book. Details the contents at some length, and concludes that it is as amusing as Mary McCarthy's *The Groves of Academe*.

Sisk, John P. "One Man's Trial." Rev. of *Something About a Soldier*. *Commonweal* 22 Nov. 1957: 214-15.

Describes *Something About a Soldier* as being about a trial by fire of the innocent as it traces a seventeen-year-old debating champion's passage into a mid-WWII army, redtape, communism, complexity, malevolence, love, and death. Concludes that this book is an enjoyable performance full of humor, sympathy, relish in language, and affectionate irony.

Sokolov, Raymond A. "A Tacky World from Top to Bottom." Rev. of *Killing Everybody*. *New York Times Book Review* 1 July 1973: 23.

Considers *Killing Everybody* to be based on entirely improbable situations that make its dreams actual probabilities. But notes that they come true in a glancing style normally reserved for flashes of wishful thinking. Concludes that Harris has centered his tightly structured modern myth in a massage parlor, the current symbol of meager dreams automatically fulfilled. Describes contents.

Sullivan, Richard. "For 'Hammock' Reading." Rev. of *Wake Up, Stupid*. *Chicago Sunday Tribune Magazine of Books* 19 July 1959: 4.

Describes *Wake Up, Stupid* as a fine book loaded with japery. Notes, however, that, close to the end, it breaks a little, and that sometimes the satire veers into irresponsibility. Concludes that, despite this, the book remains joyous and honorable.

Sylvester, Harry. "Touching All Bases." Rev. of *The Southpaw*. *New York Times Book Review* 12 Apr. 1953: 5.

Calls *The Southpaw* a serious novel about baseball and a distinguished and unusual one at that. Describes the particular cultural view of baseball revealed by the book and its main character, Henry Wiggen.

Weales, Gerald. "Journal-Maker Among the Jews." Rev. of *The Goy*. *Midstream* Dec. 1970: 71-74.

Calls *The Goy* a mixed achievement because of its preoccupation with old themes, its convoluted narrative method, and its frequently boring patches. Provides a detailed account of the plot, and concludes that ultimately the ambiguities of the book fail to bring it artistic richness. Identifies the real weakness of the book as the character of Westrum, who is merely a type.

West, Ray B., Jr. "Arts and Letters." Rev. of *Bang the Drum Slowly*. *Sewanee Review* 65.3 (1957): 502-03.

Argues that *Bang the Drum Slowly* deals almost exclusively with baseball players, but that it is really a book about something more. Notes that Harris's style, comical in its exaggeration, does create a pathetic situation in the events surrounding Pearson, and a quality of compassion. Concludes that, though skilfully done, this is a slight book.

Wilson, Robert. "Banging the Drum for Mark Harris." Rev. of *It Looked Like Forever* and *A Short Work of It*. *Washington Post Book World* 20 Jan. 1980: 8, 10.

Describes contents and style of *It Looked Like Forever* and *A Short Work of It*. Claims that it is written in "Henry Wiggen" manner, the comic colloquial tradition of Mark Twain and Ring Lardner. Calls the weaknesses of the novel those of its point-of-view character. Describes *A Short Work of It* as a collection of Harris's journalism and essays, plus a couple of short stories. Mostly describes the contents of the pieces.

Yardley, Jonathan. "Dr. Westrum's Search for Identity." Rev. of *The Goy*. *New York Times Book Review* 18 Oct. 1970: 50-51.

Claims that *The Goy* reveals just how Mark Harris can't shuck Mark Harris. Describes the contents, likens it to the fiction of Updike, and praises the book for its prose style and minor triumphs.

Interviews

Enck, John. "Mark Harris: An Interview." *Wisconsin Studies in Contemporary Literature* 6.1 (1965): 15-26.

In this interview, Harris discusses writing and teaching, structuring novels, beginning to write, the symbolic function in the novel, the natural evolution of characters, mistrust of writer's jargon, naming reality in the novel, breaking the pattern of one's own sentences and paragraphs, mistrust of criticism, comic techniques, the comic as an integral element, use of vernacular speech for comic effects, the sentimentality of *Bang the Drum Slowly*, the baseball novels, death, fiction as problem solving, interest in autobiography, methods of writing, and the writer in the university.

Horvath, Brooke K., and William J. Palmer. "Three On: An Interview with David Carkeet, Mark Harris, and W. P. Kinsella." *Modern Fiction Studies* 33.1 (1987): 183-94.

In this interview Harris responds to the accusation that contemporary literature is full of cliches, rhetorical overkill, and sports metaphors. He discusses: his childhood love of baseball, his ability to draw on this in his literature, his research into the matter, his problematic epigraph in *Bang the Drum Slowly*, sports as literary subject matter, why so many writers write about baseball, Henry Wiggen, his character, the comic voice in his novels, and the larger issues sports evoke in his novels.

Biographical Sources

Bannow, Steve. "Mark Harris." *American Novelists Since World War II*. Eds. Jeffrey Helterman and Richard Layman. Detroit: Gale, 1978. Vol. 2 of *Dictionary of Literary Biography*. 94 vols. to date. 1978- . 215-22.

More than details of his life, this is a career biography, tracing the development of the author's canon, describing the contents and themes of his works, evaluating his reputation, and placing him in the larger context of American literary history. Includes lists of primary and secondary sources and illustrations.

Harris, Mark. *Best Father Ever Invented: The Autobiography of Mark Harris*. New York: Dial, 1976.

Harris, Mark. *Twentyone Twice: A Journal*. Boston: Little, 1966.

Lavers, Norman. "Mark Harris." *Dictionary of Literary Biography Yearbook: 1980*. Eds. Karen L. Rood, Jean W. Ross, and Richard Ziegfeld. Detroit: Gale, 1981. 46-53.

An update to the article in Vol. 2 of *DLB*, concentrating on more recent developments in his career and providing analysis of works published since 1977. Includes an interview with Harris about his career and works.

Sheff, David. "Mark Harris Finally Exorcises an Eerie Writer's Block Called Saul Bellow." *People Weekly* 13 Apr. 1981: 107-08, 110, 112.

Dissertations

Lass, Terry Russell. "Discoveries of Mark Harris and Henry Wiggen." Diss. U of Missouri—Columbia, 1986.

Ben Hecht
1893(?) – 1964

Primary Sources

Novels

The Bewitched Tailor. New York: Viking, 1941.

Count Bruga. New York: Putnam, 1921; New York: Boni, 1926;
Liveright Fiction Reprints. New York: Liveright, 1931; Abridged ed.
Chicago: Royce, 1944.

Cutie: A Warm Mama. Chicago: Hechtshaw, 1924, 1925; New York:
Boar's Head, 1952.

Erik Dorn. New York: Putnam, 1921; New York: Modern Library,
1921?; New York: Boni, 1924; Chicago in Fiction. Chicago: U of
Chicago P, 1963.

Fantazius Mallare, a Mysterious Oath. Chicago: Covici, 1922;
Supernatural and Occult Fiction. New York: Arno, 1976; New York:
Ayer, 1976; New York: Harcourt, 1978.

The Florentine Dagger; A Novel for Amateur Detectives. New York:
Boni, 1923; Cleveland, World, 1923; London: Heinemann, 1924,
1934; London: Harrap, 1930; New York: Tower-World, 1942.

Gargoyles. New York: Boni, 1922; New York: Liveright, 1928.

Humpty Dumpty. New York: Boni, 1924, 1925.

I Hate Actors! New York: Crown, 1944; Toronto: Ambassador, 1944; New York: Bartholomew, 1946. Serialized in *Collier's* 4 Mar. 1944: 11-13, 30, 32, 35, 38, 41, 43-45; 11 Mar 1944: 19, 27-28, 30, 32, 34, 36-37, 39-42, 44-46; 18 Mar. 1944: 22-23, 35, 37-38, 40, 42, 44, 46, 48-49, 51-52, 55; 25 Mar 1944: 20, 30, 32, 34, 37-38, 41-42, 45-46, 49-50.

In the Midst of Death. London: Mayflower-Dell, 1964.

A Jew in Love. New York: Covici, 1931; New York: Grosset, 1932; London: Fortune, 1934; New York: Triangle, 1938; New York: Blue Ribbon, 1938; Toronto: McClelland, 1938; Garden City: Sun Dial, 1942.

The Kingdom of Evil: A Continuation of the Journal of Fantazius Mallare. Chicago: Covici, 1924, 1926; Supernatural and Occult Fiction. New York: Arno, 1976; New York: Harvest-Harcourt, 1978.

Miracle in the Rain. New York: Knopf, 1943; Toronto: Ryerson, 1943; Sydney: Huston, 1945, 1946.

The Sensualists. New York: Messner, 1959; London: Blond, 1960; Toronto: Copp, 1960; London: Four Square, 1961; Four Square Books. London: New English Library, 1964; New York: Dell, 1964; London: New English Library, 1969.

Collected Works

Actor's Blood. New York: Covici, 1936; Toronto: McLeod, 1936.
Contents: Actor's Blood, In the Midst of Death, The Mystery of the Fabulous Laundryman, Crime without Passion, Snowfall in Childhood, The Ghost of the San Mareno Hotel, The Boy Pirate, The Widow Cagle's Trousers.

A Book of Miracles. New York: Viking, 1939; Toronto: Macmillan, 1939; London: Nicholson, 1940; Garden City: Sun Dial, 1941.

Contents: A Lost Soul, The Little Candle, The Missing Idol, Death of Eleazer, Remember Thy Creator, The Heavenly Choir, The Adventures of Professor Emmett.

Broken Necks, and Other Stories. Girard: Haldeman, 1924.

Contents: Broken Necks, Decay, The Bomb Thrower, Dog Eat Dog, Fragments.

Broken Necks; Containing More "1001 Afternoons." Chicago: Covici, 1926.

Contents: Broken Necks, The Philosopher's Benefit, Decay, Mishkin's Idealist, The Bomb Thrower, A Nigger Who Was Hanged, Dog Eat Dog, The Imposter, Fragments, Melancholia Preceding Seduction, Life, My Last Park Bench, Depths, Rendezvous, Gratitude, The New Skyscraper, Nocturne, The Psychological Phantom, Black Umbrellas, The Wrong "Front," The Yellow Goat, Lenin and Wilson Talk, The Movie Maniac, Caricature, The Policewoman's Daughter, Shanghaied, Jazz, The Man with One Wife, Infatuation, The Unlovely Sin.

The Champion from Far Away. New York: Covici, 1931.

Contents: The Champion from Far Away, A Wistful Blackguard, The Bull That Won, Baby Milly and the Pharaoh, The Rival Dummy, The Shadow, Lindro the Great, An American Kangaroo, The Quarrel, The Ax, The Masquerade, The Terrified Doctor, The Lost Soul.

The Collected Stories of Ben Hecht. New York: Crown, 1945; New York: Grosset, 1945; Toronto: Ambassador, 1950; London: Hammond, 1950.

Contents: Concerning a Woman of Sin, Miracle of the Fifteen Murderers, Remember Thy Creator, The Mystery of the Fabulous Laundryman, The Adventures of Professor Emmett, Cafe Sinister, The Champion from Far Away, Death of Eleazer, The Pink Hussar, The Shadow, God Is Good to a Jew, The Wistful Blackguard, Spectre of the Rose, The Bull That Won, Actor's Blood, Crime Without Passion, The Rival Dummy, In the Midst of Death, The Axe, The Lost Soul, The Heavenly Choir.

Concerning a Woman of Sin, and Other Stories. New York: Avon, 1947; New York: Eds. for the Armed Services, 1943; London: Mayflower-Dell, 1964.

Contents: Concerning a Woman of Sin, Cafe Sinister, The Pink Hussar, Specter of the Rose, The Ax, The Lost Soul, Crime Without Passion,The Rival Dummy.

Eleven Selected Great Stories. New York: Avon, 1943.

Contents: Crime Without Passion, The Champion from Far Away, The Ghost of the San Mareno Hotel, The Wistful Blackguard, The Bull That Won, The Shadow, In the Midst of Death, The Mystery of the Fabulous Laundryman, Lindro the Great, Actor's Blood, The Widow Cagle's Trousers.

Infatuation, and Other Stories of Love's Misfits. Little Blue Book 1166. Girard: Haldeman, 1927.

Contents: Infatuation, Caricature, Shanghaied, Fanny, The Auctioneer's Wife.

Jazz, and Other Stories of Young Love. Little Blue Book 1165. Girard: Haldeman, 1927.

Contents: Jazz, The Devil Slayer, Exhibit A, Ten Cent Wedding Rings, Where the "Blues" Sound, The Little Fop, Don Quixote and His Last Windmill.

The Policewoman's Love-Hungry Daughter and Other Stories of Chicago Life. Little Blue Book 1163. Girard: Haldeman, 1927.

Contents: The Policewoman's Love-Hungry Daughter, The Monster, The Movie Maniac, The Soul of Sing Lee, The Great Traveler.

The Sinister Sex and Other Stories of Marriage. Little Blue Book 1167. Girard: Haldeman, 1927.

Contents: The Sinister Sex, Happiness, Fifteen Minutes, The Man Hunt, Grass Figures.

Tales of Chicago Streets. Little Blue Book 698. Girard: Haldeman, 1924.

Contents: Life, Depths, Gratitude, Nocturne, Black Umbrellas, The Yellow Goat.

A Treasury of Ben Hecht: Collected Stories and Other Writings. New York: Crown, 1959.

Contents: Some Slightly Crazy People, Snowfall in Childhood, The

Little Candle, Mystery of the Fabulous Laundryman, The Bull That Won, Broken Necks, Fanny, Nocturne, Decay, Sergt. Kuzick and the Reporter, The Champion from Far Away, Miracle of the Fifteen Murderers, Specter of the Rose, Crime without Passion, The Rival Dummy, The Adventures of Professor Emmett, Cafe Sinister, The Pink Hussar, The Wistful Blackguard, Actor's Blood.

The Unlovely Sin and Other Stories. Little Blue Book 1164. Girard: Haldeman, 1927.

Contents: The Unlovely Sin, The Man with One Wife, A Humoresque in Ham, Ill-Humoresque, The Man With a Question, Fog Patterns.

Short Fiction in Anthologies

"Baby Milly and the Pharoah." *A Golden Treasury of Jewish Literature.* Ed. Leo W. Schwarz. New York: Farrar, 1937; Philadelphia: Jewish Pub. Soc. of America, 1937. 376-89.

"God Is Good to a Jew." *Jewish Short Stories*. Ed. Ludwig Lewisohn. New York: Behrman, 1945. 109-41; *These Your Children*. Ed. Harold U. Ribalow. New York: Beechhurst, 1952. 103-25.

"A Humoresque in Ham." *The Smart Set Anthology*. Eds. Burton Rascoe and Groff Conklin. New York: Reynal, 1934. 378-91.

"Life." *The Best Short Stories of 1915*. Ed. Edward J. O'Brien. Boston: Small, 1916. 80-83.

"The Little Candle." *The Questing Spirit*. Eds. H. E. Luccock and Frances Brentano. New York: Coward, 1947. 229-50.

"The Lost Soul." *75 Short Masterpieces: Stories from the World's Literature*. Ed. Roger B. Goodman. New York: Bantam, 1961, 1977. 134-38.

"The Pig." *Theme and Variation in the Short Story*. Eds. John De Lancey Ferguson, Harold A. Blaine and Wilson R. Dumble. New York: Cordon, 1938; Short Story Index Reprint Series. Freeport: Books for Libraries, 1972. 377-81.

"Snowfall in Childhood." *A World of Great Stories*. Eds. Hiram Haydn and John Cournos. New York: Crown, 1947. 95-102; *Point of Departure*. Ed. Robert S. Gold. New York: Dell, 1967; New York: Laurel Leaf-Dell, 1981. 154-64.

Short Fiction in Periodicals

"Actor's Blood." *Saturday Evening Post* 20 Feb. 1932: 3-5, 76-78, 81.

"Baby Milly and the Pharoah." *Saturday Evening Post* 12 July 1930: 6-7, 97-98, 101-02, 105-06, 109.

"A Caballero of the Law." *Saturday Evening Post* 6 May 1933: 5-7, 34, 37; *Saturday Evening Post* Sept. 1977: 34-36, 94, 96-97.

"Cafe Sinister." *Collier's* 21 Aug. 1943: 11-12, 66-70, 72.

"The Champion from Far Away." *Saturday Evening Post* 9 Aug. 1930: 3, 9, 40, 43, 46.

"Cinderella from Cedar Rapids." *Collier's* 3 Nov. 1951: 18-19, 47-49.

"Concerning a Woman of Sin." *Collier's* 11 Mar. 1927: 24, 26-28, 30.

"Doughboy's Dream." *Collier's* 27 Feb. 1943: 11-13.

"God Is Good to a Jew." *Collier's* 31 July 1943: 14, 68, 70, 72-73.

"Lucky Handkerchief." *Good Housekeeping* Nov. 1945: 22-23, 214-25.

"Miracle in the Rain." *Saturday Evening Post* 3 Apr. 1943: 9-11, 70, 73, 75, 77-78; *Saturday Evening Post* Jan.-Feb. 1984: 48-51, 80; Mar. 1984: 68, 70, 72; Apr. 1984: 34-36.

"Miracle of the Fifteen Murderers." *Collier's* 16 Jan. 1943: 11-12, 22, 24, 26.

"No Room for Vice." *Playboy* Jan. 1959: 51-52, 54.

"The Pink Hussar." *Collier's* 25 Sept. 1943: 12-13, 30, 32, 35-38, 40.

"The Sentimentalist." *American Mercury* Oct. 1924: 213-16.

"Sic Transit." *Esquire* Dec. 1954: 87.

"Snowfall in Childhood." *Esquire* Nov. 1934: 40-41, 122.

"Some Slightly Crazy People." *Saturday Evening Post* 28 Mar. 1959: 26-27, 48-50, 52.

"Swindler's Luck." *Saturday Evening Post* 12 Jan. 1952: 18-19, 51, 54, 56, 58.

"The Tired Horse." *Esquire* Sept. 1954: 42-43.

"Vagabondia." *Scholastic* 30 Mar. 1935: 9, 30.

Secondary Sources

Books

Fetherling, Doug. *The Five Lives of Ben Hecht.* Toronto: Lester, 1977.

Articles and Chapters

Algren, Nelson. "A Thousand and One Afternoons in Nada." *Erik Dorn. Chicago in Fiction.* Chicago: U of Chicago P, 1963. vii-xvii.
Describes Erik Dorn as a man who seems, to himself, to be a perfect translation of his country and his day: one who has lived since boyhood in a changeless vacuum waiting for something to happen, a contract to overtake him, or reality to seize him. Concludes that, finally, nothing has happened at all.

Farrell, James T. "The Mind of Ben Hecht." *Literary Essays, 1954-1974.* Ed. Jack Alan Robbins. Literary Criticism Series. Port Washington: Kennikat, 1976. 70-76.

Discusses Hecht's mistrust of ideas and inordinate trust in language. Describes Hecht's ideas and autobiography as being banal. Briefly discusses the impact on him of several of Hecht's works and in particular *1001 Afternoons in Chicago.* Accuses the books of lacking sympathy, and points out Hecht's affinities with Mencken. Concludes that, seen now, Hecht appears a man of talent, of easy prejudices, and without values.

Felheim, Marvin. "Tom Sawyer Grows Up: Ben Hecht As A Writer." *Journal of Popular Culture* 9.4 (1976): 908-15.

Describes Hecht as a Wildean romantic with an excessively literary imagination. Provides primarily a history of Hecht's period and his participation in it. Discusses individual novels from the perspective of their biographical contents, and develops the thesis that Hecht was in fact a boyish Tom Sawyer all his life.

Fiedler, Leslie A. "Genesis: The American-Jewish Novel Through the Twenties." *Midstream* 4.3 (1958): 21-33. Rpt. in *The Jew in the American Novel.* Leslie Fiedler. Herzl Institute Pamphlets 10. New York: Herzl, 1959; A Seven Star Book 5. 2nd ed. New York: Herzl, 1966. 20-24; "The Jew in the American Novel." *The Collected Essays of Leslie Fiedler.* 2 vols. New York: Stein, 1971. 2: 79-84; *To the Gentiles.* New York: Stein, 1971. 79-84.

Describes the main business of the marginal writers among American Jews in the 1920s to be the assertion that it is possible to establish an image of the Jew satisfying to both Jew and Gentile. Claims that the writing of an American-Jewish novel is essentially an act of assimilation, and that this effort by writers of the 1920s fails to impress mainstream American readers for whom the images of the overgrown boy scout and hangdog lover projected by Hemingway's Cohn are the images that prevail in the imagination. Discusses Hecht's *A Jew in Love* as "a work of inspired self-hatred: a portrait of the Jewish author as his own worst (Jewish) enemy." Concludes that the novel is a "self-criticism of the Jewish intellectual that cuts much deeper than personal satire and which is marred by an imprecision of language and an uncertainty of tone that ends in incoherence."

Fincke, Gary. "Polarity in Ben Hecht's Winkelbergs." *Critique* 15.2 (1973): 103-09.

An in-depth treatment of the sociological and thematic significance of the different Winkelberg characters of *Humpty Dumpty.* Discusses his polarized view of life and his cynicism.

Hansen, Harry. "Ben Hecht: Pagliacci of the Fire Escape." *Midwest Portraits: A Book of Memories and Friendships.* New York: Harcourt, 1923. 305-57.

A major biographical and critical treatment of Hecht which covers the following topics: critical opinions of him, anecdotes from Hecht about his own life, a chronological sketch of the main events in his life, major influences, his views on his career as a writer, his days as a reporter, commentary on each of the major works, public reception of each of the works, legends that have become attached to his name, and forecasts of his future in American letters.

Harap, Louis. *Creative Awakening: The Jewish Presence in Twentieth-Century American Literature, 1900-1940s.* Contributions in Ethnic Studies 17. New York: Greenwood, 1987.

In the context of discussing Jewish anti-Semitism, Harap describes the contents and characteristics of *A Jew in Love*, finding the story "profoundly self-hating and anti-Semitic." Considers Hecht both confused and anti-Semitic like his protagonist, although he may not be aware of it. Notes that even in his autobiography twenty-five years later, he shows no evidence that he was aware of his novel's anti-Semitic character.

Hatcher, Harlan H. "The 'Young Generation'." *Creating the Modern American Novel.* Harlan H. Hatcher. New York: Farrar, 1935. 84-85.

Briefly describes Hecht's novels from *Erik Dorn* (1921) to *A Jew in Love* (1931). Adds that his style of short, declarative sentences, often clever, brilliant, and gay, reflect the sentences of the jazz age that "sound its shallower cadence."

Karsner, David. "Ben Hecht." *Sixteen Authors to One: Intimate Sketches of Leading American Story Tellers.* David Karsner. New York: Copeland, 1928. 235-45.

Locates Hecht as one of the Chicago school of writers, admires his verbal pyrotechnics, describes his career as a journalist, discusses *Erik Dorn* as his most revealing book, discusses the impact and contents of several of the other books, and concludes that Ben Hecht was a man of cool, cynical intelligence.

McDonnell, Thomas P. "From Ben Hecht to Pasternak." *Catholic World* Apr. 1959: 39-43.

Dismisses Hecht as an intellectual lightweight and a gimmicky writer, and then goes on to compare him unfavorably with Pasternak.

Mersand, Joseph. "Ben Hecht: The Re-Discovery of the Artist."
    *Traditions in American Literature: A Study of Jewish Characters and
    Authors*. Joseph Mersand. New York: Modern Chapbooks, 1939. Port
    Washington: Kennikat, 1968. 112-17.

Characterizes Hecht as a typical Jewish man of letters to the core, details the
Jewish characters portrayed in his works, and concludes that Hecht speaks
for the common people in giving them heroes willing to die for them. Sees
him as dedicated to the elevation of mankind and as a member "of that noble
fraternity of artistic legislators of mankind, the spiritual descendants of
Prometheus, bringing to their era the torch of enlightenment and truth."

Michaud, Regis. "Ulysses' Companions: Robert McAlmon, Ben Hecht,
    William Carlos Williams." *The American Novel Today: A Social and
    Psychological Study*. Regis Michaud. Boston: Little, 1928. 257-83.

A brief sketch of Hecht identifying him as a writer whose cynicism veils
sadness and moral confusion. Primarily discusses *Erik Dorn* and *Humpty
Dumpty*.

Newquist, Roy. "Ben Hecht." *Counterpoint*. Roy Newquist. Chicago:
    Rand, 1964. 346-53.

A good, introductory chapter to Hecht's life and works comprised mostly
of interview material. Contains much first person anecdote and biographical detail about Hecht.

Ravitz, Abe C. "Assault with Deadly Typewriter: The Hecht-Bodenheim
    Vendetta." *Cabellian* 4 (1972): 104-11.

Provides a detailed, definitive account of the relationship between Hecht
and Maxwell Bodenheim, an alter ego for Hecht. Describes how Hecht
fabricated literary capital out of the materials of Max Bodenheim's life,
thus making a legend out of him. Describes the outbreak of the vendetta
between the two which took place in 1926 after which Bodenheim paints
equally unflattering pictures of Hecht in his own work.

Ravitz, Abe C. "Ballyhoo, Gargoyles, & Firecrackers: Ben Hecht's
    Aesthetic Calliope." *Journal of Popular Culture* 1.1 (1967): 37-51.
    Rpt. in *A Question of Quality: Popularity and Value in Modern
    Creative Writing*. Ed. Louis Filler. Bowling Green: Bowling Green U
    Popular P, 1976. 229-43.

Represents the Hecht the literary establishment saw as a literary show-
man who represented the antidote to the "boobeoisie." Unveils a revised

picture of him as much more than a hatchet-wielding, pedestrian journalist, and describes each of the major works. Details the Hecht-Bodenheim relationship, and concludes with Vachel Lindsay's assessment of Hecht's prose as a "Kallyope."

Sherman, Stuart P. "Ben Hecht and the Supermen." *Critical Wood Cuts.* New York: Scribner's, 1926. 63-72.

Provides a brief biographical portrait of Hecht, plus an account of his opinions, effects on others, and major works.

Wain, John. "The Case of Ben Hecht." *New Republic* 28 Sept. 1959: 16-18. Rpt. as "Ben Hecht" in *The Critic as Artist: Essays on Books 1920-1970.* Ed. Gilbert A. Harrison. New York: Liveright, 1972. 343-50.

A general overview of Hecht's personality, life, and works on the occasion of the publication of *A Treasury of Ben Hecht.* Sees him as a man of the 1890s uncomfortable with the era into which he was born. Calls him the Runyon of the New York streets and spiritually akin to the *poets maudits* of the age. Provides an in-depth look at his prose, tone, and subject matter in several works.

White, Ray Lewis. "Sherwood Anderson, Ben Hecht, and *Erik Dorn.*" *American Literature* 49.2 (1977): 238-41.

Discusses the long hostility and literary quarrel between Hecht and Anderson, and suggests that our best clues to it lie in the story contained in *Erik Dorn.*

Yudkin, Leon I. "The Immigrant Experience in America." *Jewish Writing and Identity in the Twentieth Century.* Leon I. Yudkin. London: Helm, 1982. 27-44.

Discusses the Jewish immigration to America as the most remarkable demographic event in Jewish history and shows its impact on America as it emerged as a great world power. Also sees the Jewish writers Cahan, Lewisohn, Hecht, Fuchs, Michael Gold, and Henry Roth as expanding the range of an exotic consciousness in America but also showing the "Jew on the outside trying to get in (in various ways), or perhaps coming to terms with his outsider status." Discusses the major works of each of these writers and how these works demonstrate the struggles, the conflicts, and the costs of their Jewish protagonists to become assimilated into American life.

Reviews

Bell, Lisle. Rev. of *I Hate Actors. New York Herald Tribune Book Week*
      10 Sept. 1944: 6.

Describes *I Hate Actors* as hectic and resourceful in plot. Mostly details
the contents of the novel.

"Ben Hecht's Sketches." Rev. of *Broken Necks. New York Times Book
      Review* 5 Dec. 1926: 30.

Claims that *Broken Necks* chiefly explores the author's own vehement
and many-sided ego. Adds that Hecht is essentially a hurt romantic and
that this book contains much early material characterized by unevenness,
shakiness, and faulty technique. Mentions several pieces by title.

"Ben Hecht's Stories." Rev. of *The Champion From Far Away. New
      York Times Book Review* 6 Sept. 1931: 6.

Describes the stories in *The Champion From Far Away* as sure and brilliant in their colorful settings and characters, their use of any form, and
their general inventiveness. Details the contents of the collection.

Colum, Mary M. "Literature and Journalism." Rev. of *Erik Dorn.
      Freeman* 30 Nov. 1921: 282.

Calls *Erik Dorn* first class journalism which is brilliant, vivid, interesting, and brimful of opinions and ideas. Complains of Hecht's liberties
with grammar and usage, and concludes with Mencken that this book is a
"gaudy and fantastic panorama, in which the movement is almost acrobatic and the colour is that of a kaleidoscope."

Crawford, John W. "Ben Hecht Recovers His Literary Balance." Rev. of
      Count Bruga. New York Times Book Review 16 May 1926: 7.

Describes *Count Bruga* as a virtuoso display of verbal skills and mordant
contempt for human nature with an undercurrent of wistfulness and
amusement underneath all the sardonic humor and satire. Concludes that
the whole effect is one of brilliance.

Davenport, Basil. "Acts of God." Rev. of *A Book of Miracles. Saturday
      Review of Literature* 17 June 1939: 14.

Describes the contents of *A Book of Miracles* as ranging from Heaven to
Hollywood. Criticizes the collection of stories as satire because they seriously fall short of the standards of Anatole France and Voltaire.

Dell, Floyd. "New Styles and Old." Rev. of *Gargoyles. The Bookman* Nov. 1922: 347.

Considers Hecht "gifted with a faculty of improvisation, [and] wild guesswork, which leads him to tease the reader with fantastic inventions which seem to have come into his head only at the time of writing them down." Concludes that "this disorderly imaginativeness spoils the effect of his more sober motive-analysis."

Du Bois, William. "Death Among the Actors." Rev. of *I Hate Actors. New York Times Book Review* 27 Aug. 1944: 13.

Describes *I Hate Actors* as giving a funny and refreshingly off-center glimpse of the cinema capital. Claims that, as a "whodunit," the novel is jerry-built and that in those occasional moments when the fun lags, the reader wonders what he is doing reading the book at all.

F., J. W. "Reviews." Rev. of *Gargoyles. Double Dealer* Nov. 1922: 249-51.

Calls *Gargoyles* a "study of contorted souls, twisted grotesquely out of shape by the current taboos and prohibitions and indeed by current affirmations and ideals."

Fadiman, Clifton. "Mr. Hecht Passes a Few Miracles." Rev. of *A Book of Miracles. New Yorker* 17 June 1939: 89-90.

Comments on the new-found gift of reverence and glee in *A Book of Miracles*, which ranges from allegory to farce and satire. Contains considerable detail on individual stories.

Farrell, James T. "That Brilliant Man Ben Hecht." Rev. of *Actor's Blood. New York Herald Tribune Books* 9 Feb. 1936: 2.

Claims that *Actor's Blood* reveals a writer unparalleled in the last two decades of American letters. Considers his gift brilliant in dramatic metaphor and in the ability to capture the color and surface of an American city. Describes the title story and touches upon several others.

"Fun From Hollywood." Rev. of *A Book of Miracles. Time* 19 June 1939: 78.

Calls *A Book of Miracles* a collection of present-day fairy tales, sharp, satirical, and imaginative, and written in a Mencken-like tone.

Goldberg, Isaac. "The Depths of Realism." Rev. of *Erik Dorn. Boston Evening Transcript* 19 Oct. 1921: 6.

Calls *Erik Dorn* a book with faults and weaknesses outweighed by its virtues. Adds that the book has a surfeit of cleverness, simple candor, kaleidoscopic range, and impressive style. Details contents and places the book in historical context.

Hackett, Francis. Rev. of *Erik Dorn*. *New Republic* 31 Aug. 1921: 24-25.

Argues that Erik Dorn is not a rounded character, but one who comes over as hard, repellent, small, and cold. Comments that the novel is reasonably well-sustained for a first work, but fails to achieve separation of self from the major character; thus, egoism flows everywhere conveying mere sterility. Conludes that the cynical formula is altogether too arid and the stridency too tiresome.

Kauffmann, Stanley. "After the Altar, the Alternations." Rev. of *The Sensualists*. *Saturday Review* 4 Apr. 1959: 22.

Complains that this is a novel by a novelist twenty years out of practice. Finds the characters devoid of reality, the story old hat, and the whole thing laced with facile Freud. Concludes that the novel seems to be a sort of seminar of modern eroticism.

Kronenberger, Louis. "One of the Sophisticates." Rev. of *Count Bruga*. *Saturday Review of Literature* 12 June 1926: 854.

Calls *Count Bruga* a preposterous and amusing caricature. Describes the book as keen and good, vivid and versatile, as well as remarkably entertaining.

"Latest Works of Fiction." Rev. of *Erik Dorn*. *New York Times Book Review* 9 Oct. 1921: 12, 18.

Calls *Erik Dorn* a curious, fantastic, chaotic novel full of strange verbal madness and rich descriptive passages. Concludes that it is a striking literary production which promises even better things from Hecht when he gets himself in hand.

"Latest Works of Fiction." Rev. of *The Florentine Dagger*. *New York Times Book Review* 16 Sept. 1923: 24.

Calls the tempo of *The Florentine Dagger* rather breathless, and its content imaginative and striking. Contains a detailed plot summary for the thriller.

"Latest Works of Fiction." Rev. of *Gargoyles*. *New York Times Book Review* 1 Oct. 1922: 22.

Describes *Gargoyles* as a sour book in which Hecht portrays Americans on the eve of WWI as hideous, despicable, hopeless, and about to find out just how foul human nature really is.

Lewisohn, Ludwig. "Kaleidoscope." Rev. of *Erik Dorn*. *Nation* 19 Oct. 1921: 453.

Comments that *Erik Dorn* is disorderly, but not without form. Describes the style as telegraphic Meredithianistic, rendering in the end only its own vain torment. Concludes that Hecht must use his talent more carefully and cease to bombinate.

Marsh, Fred T. "Ben Hecht's Stories." Rev. of *Actor's Blood*. *New York Times Book Review* 9 Feb. 1936: 7, 20.

Calls *Actor's Blood* rough, gaudy, precise, easy to read, and equally divided between laughs and suspense. Describes individual stories and their characters.

Marsh, Fred T. "Miracles by Hecht." Rev. of *A Book of Miracles*. *New York Times Book Review* 18 June 1939: 7.

Calls this a bold, contrived, swashbuckling, modacious diatribe, full of magic, miracle and allegory. Adds its bluster and absurdity might have been muted a little. Details the contents of each story.

"Mr. Hecht's Mockery." Rev. of *A Jew in Love*. *New York Times Book Review* 25 Jan. 1931: 8.

Claims that *A Jew in Love* demonstrates Hecht's sustained pirouetting over the great emptiness of life as he conceives it. Adds that it is full of verbal epithet and biting sarcasm through which Hecht reclaims his lordship over the anarchistic void. Calls the book all shade and no light, finally becoming a vexation to the spirit.

"Playboy's Defeat." Rev. of *Humpty Dumpty*. *New York Times Book Review* 16 Nov. 1924: 8, 14.

Claims *Humpty Dumpty* turns into an extended editorial with a superficial glitter of metaphor and simile on contemporary life, rather than an integrated illusion. Provides a detailed account of the successes and failures of characterization, background, plot, and general effects.

Rascoe, Burton. "An American Epithetician." Rev. of *Erik Dorn*. *Bookman* Oct. 1921: 164-66.

Mockingly compares Hecht with Huysmans, and provides a brief account of his mental qualities and satiric, sardonic insights. Regrets that *Erik Dorn* will probably not be received on its considerable artistic merits. Provides a closely written account of the aesthetic harmony of the work, and concludes that, although the work is not sustained throughout, it has an unusual acuteness of vision.

Rascoe, Burton. "Mr. Hecht's *Gargoyles*." Rev. of *Gargoyles*. *New York Tribune* 24 Sept. 1922: 7.

Calls *Gargoyles* a book which shows Hecht to be more talented, intelligent, experienced, and assured than any other post-war writer. Adds that he also lacks discipline and restraint and that his writing is often careless and impatient. Describes the contents of the novel in great detail.

Redman, Ben Ray. "The Theory and Practice of Ben Hecht." Rev. of *The Collected Stories of Ben Hecht*. *Saturday Review of Literature* 23 June 1945: 15.

Discusses *The Collected Stories of Ben Hecht* as a series in which there are no dull characters or scenes, no lack of wit and verbal feathers, much pseudo-subtlety, and much stripping away. Concludes that the flourish and swagger mask Hecht's sensitivity and tenderness.

Rexroth, Kenneth. "Not All the Wind Came Off the Lake." Rev. of *Erik Dorn*. *New York Herald Tribune Book Review* 5 Apr. 1964: 5, 15.

Describes *Erik Dorn* as full of real Chicago moonshine, one hundred percent pure corn, and two hundred proof. Claims that the sentimentalism, loving self-regard, and frisky imagination are positive virtues in this *roman a clef*.

Rosenberg, Harold. "Man as Anti-Semite." Rev. of *A Guide for the Bedeviled. Discovering the Present: Three Decades in Art, Culture, and Politics*. Harold Rosenberg. Chicago: U of Chicago P, 1973. 241-45. Rpt. from *Contemporary Jewish Record* 1 (1944).

Discusses Hecht's literary caricatures and attacks on the character of the anti-Semite. Criticizes his idea that the anti-Semite is merely a stupid, backward person with a killer instinct, and that the Jew is a psychological type whose violent Great God becomes his alter ego. Concludes that Hecht offers no strategy for dealing with anti-Semitism because he is too easily satisfied by "beating the German *Golem* with a Nietzschean bladder" and kicking the man in the shins for being what he is.

Salomon, Louis B. "From Another World." Rev. of *A Book of Miracles*. *Nation* 24 June 1939: 733-34.

Considers *A Book of Miracles* to be versatile, sentimental, biting, tender, funny, and refreshing.

Seldes, Gilbert. "Arriviste and Aristocrat." Rev. of *Erik Dorn*. *Dial* Nov. 1921: 597-600.

A severe denunciation of the book in which Seldes accuses Hecht of lack of imagination, cynicism, manipulation, stupid games, mockery, wilful artlessness, and verbal excess.

Seldes, Gilbert. "First Inversions." Rev. of *Gargoyles*. *Dial* Jan. 1923: 100-02.

Finds this novel sterile, full of little lives, and likely to produce very little that is alive. Concludes that, regrettably, the expression of Hecht's hatred of hypocrisy does not distinguish itself in this fiction.

Sherman, Beatrice. "Soldier from Heaven." Rev. of *Miracle in the Rain*. *New York Times Book Review* 17 Oct. 1943: 4.

Asserts that this novel contains good, warm, and fine things told with a tender and disarming style. Calls it a Cinderella story with the prince in khaki.

"Slot Machine; Peephole." Rev. of *Actor's Blood*. *Time* 17 Feb. 1936: 69-70.

A description of *Actor's Blood* which calls it full of hocum and verbiage, lavish in wit, and stuffed with greasepaint dramatics.

Soskin, William. "Hecht's Newest Miracles." Rev. of *A Book of Miracles*. *New York Herald Tribune Books* 18 June 1939: 5.

Argues that *A Book of Miracles* is many-faceted, shiny, versatile, and brilliant as a collection of short stories. Finds Hecht's miracles brightly illuminated, performed in clouds of sensationally colored and scented smoke and steam, explosive, exciting—superb entertainment.

Van Doren, Mark. "Gargoyles." Rev. of *Gargoyles*. *Literary Review* 28 Oct. 1922: 143.

Calls Hecht an incurably vulgar writer who is also afflicted with an unpardonable pedantry. Adds that, at the expense of clarity, humor, and interesting truth, Hecht has become obsessed with science. Concludes that this book lacks frankness, strength, and animal spirits.

Biographical Sources

Baldwin, Charles C. "Ben Hecht." *The Men Who Make Our Novels*.
Charles C. Baldwin. Rev. ed. New York: Dodd, 1924; Essay Index
Reprint Series. Freeport: Books for Libraries, 1967. 219-26.
Locates Hecht historically as stemming from Sherwood Anderson,
Masters, William Marion Reedy, and Ed Howe of Atchison, Kansas.
Sees him as a scourge who goes about his business with a fine air of
detachment and the ability to instantly dramatize our transgressions.
Provides a biographical portrait borrowed from Harry Hansen's *Midwest
Portraits*, discusses his reading preferences, his provinciality, and the
probability that Hecht will ultimately turn to drama.

Bernheim, Mark. "Ben Hecht." *Twentieth-Century American-Jewish
Fiction Writers*. Ed. Daniel Walden. Detroit: Gale, 1984. Vol. 28 of
Dictionary of Literary Biography. 94 vols. to date. 1978- . 92-101.
More than details of his life, this is a career biography, tracing the devel-
opment of the author's canon, describing the contents and themes of his
works, evaluating his reputation, and placing him in the larger context of
American literary history. Includes lists of primary and secondary
sources and illustrations.

Hecht, Ben. *A Child of the Century*. New York: Simon, 1954.

Hecht, Ben. *Gaily, Gaily*. New York: Doubleday, 1963; London: Elek,
1964.

Nizer, Louis. "Ben Hecht." *Between You and Me*. Louis Nizer. New
York: Beechhurst, 1948. 122-26.
Discusses Hecht's gifts as a conversationalist, repeats several of his
favorite anecdotes, and concludes that Hecht's future reputation may
well rest on his heroism and his "wielding an unconquerable pen against
the callousness and cruelty of the human race."

MacAdams, William. *Ben Hecht: The Man Behind the Legend*. New
York: Scribner's, 1990.

Sandler, Gilbert. "Ben Hecht and H. L. Mencken: Exit Laughing."
Menckeniana 65 (1978): 12-16.

Contains a series of biographical anecdotes about Hecht, his political views, and his writing. Compares and contrasts his personality and views with Mencken's.

Schmuhl, Robert. "Ben Hecht." *American Short Story Writers, 1910-1945, First Series.* Ed. Bobby Ellen Kimbel. Detroit: Gale, 1989. Vol. 86 of *Dictionary of Literary Biography.* 94 vols. to date. 1978- . 130-38.

A career biography tracing the development of Hecht's short story canon, describing the contents and themes of his works, evaluating his reputation, and placing him in the larger context of American literary history. Includes a list of primary and secondary sources and illustrations.

Walden, Daniel. "Ben Hecht." *American Novelists, 1910-1945, Part II: F. Scott Fitzgerald- O. E. Rolvaag.* Ed. James J. Martine. Detroit: Gale, 1981. Vol. 9 of *Dictionary of Literary Biography.* 94 vols. to date. 1978- . 96-100.

More than details of his life, this is a career biography, tracing the development of the author's novelistic canon, describing the contents and themes of his works, evaluating his reputation, and placing him in the larger context of American literary history. Includes a list of primary and secondary sources and illustrations.

Dissertations

Fincke, Gary William. "The Fiction of Ben Hecht: A Study in Polarity." Diss. Kent State U, 1974.

Roberts, Ronald Marc. "The Novels of Ben Hecht." Diss. Baylor U, 1970.

Sims, Norman Howard. "The Chicago Style of Journalism." Diss. U of Illinois at Urbana-Champaign, 1979.

Laura Z. Hobson
1900 – 1986

Primary Sources

Novels

The Celebrity. New York: Simon, 1951; London: Cresset, 1953; New York: Avon [Cited in PBIP, 1969]. Serialized in *Woman's Home Companion* July 1951: 26-27, 49-50, 53, 58-59, 62, 64, 67-70, 72-73; Aug. 1951: 36-37, 107, 109-10, 112, 116, 133-38, 140; Sept. 1951: 40, 123-28, 147-57, 160.

Consenting Adult. Garden City: Doubleday, 1975; London: Heinemann, 1975; New York: Warner, 1975, 1976.

First Papers. New York: Random, 1964; London: Heinemann, 1965.

Gentleman's Agreement. New York: Simon, 1947; New York: Eds. for the Armed Services, 1947; Melbourne: Musson, 1947; New York: Grosset, 1948; London: Cassell, 1948; New York: Avon, 1968; Marietta: Larlin, 1979; Thorndike: Thorndike, 1982; New York: Arbor, 1983.

The Other Father. New York: Simon, 1950; Chicago: Sears Readers Club, 1950; London: Cassell, 1950; New York: Avon [Cited in PBIP, 1969].

Over and Above. Garden City: Doubleday, 1979.

The Tenth Month. New York: Simon, 1971; London: Heinemann, 1971; New York: Dell, 1972; London: Pan, 1973.

The Trespassers. New York: Simon, 1943; Toronto: Musson, 1943, 1945; London: Gollancz, 1944; Cleveland: Forum-World, 1945; Sydney: Dymock, 1945; New York: Avon [Cited in PBIP, 1969].

Untold Millions. New York: Harper, 1982; Large Print ed. Boston: Hall, 1982.

Short Fiction in Periodicals

"Aggressive Dame." *Good Housekeeping* Mar. 1952: 52-53, 173-74, 176-78, 180-82.

"Custody." *Ladies' Home Journal* Sept. 1970: 88-89, 122-27, 129-30.

"The Girl I Left." *Woman's Home Companion* Jan. 1944: 18-19, 86-93.

"Lost Girl." *McCall's* Jan. 1973: 121-28.

"The Lovely Duckling." *Woman's Home Companion* Dec. 1956: 48-49, 68-70, 72, 74-79.

"Play Something Simple." *Collier's* 28 Dec. 1935: 14-15, 44-45.

"The Reward." *Good Housekeeping* Oct. 1953: 49-51, 202-53.

"Single, Age Twenty-Five." *Good Housekeeping* June 1966: 87-89, 192, 194-96, 198, 200, 202, 210, 212, 214, 216, 218, 220-24, 227-28, 230-33.

"The Tenth Month." *Redbook* Dec. 1970: 139-61.

"The Unfaithful." *Good Housekeeping* Sept. 1955: 50-53, 158-93.

"The Wrong Job." *Collier's* 29 Feb. 1936: 10-11, 40, 42.

Secondary Sources

Articles and Chapters

Hirsch, Shula. "Laura Z. Hobson." *Popular World Fiction 1900-Present.* Eds. Walton Beacham and Suzanne Niemeyer. 4 vols. Washington: Beacham, 1987. 2: 736-42.

A standard reference work entry on Hobson which discusses: her publishing history, critical reception, honors, popularity, selected titles, character, techniques, social concerns, themes, and literary precedents. Covers *Gentleman's Agreement, First Papers,* and *Consenting Adult.*

Reviews

Barnes, Julian. "Mother's Pride." Rev. of *Consenting Adult. Times Literary Supplement* 5 Sept. 1975: 998.

Considers *Consenting Adult* a book about gay men that indulges in all the same overblown banalities of romantic fiction that apply to heterosexual love. Concludes that a propagandist novel like this can hardly be expected to succeed at this point in time, and that Hobson would have been wise to realize it.

Bates, Gladys Graham. "Modern Mixture." Rev. of *The Trespassers. Saturday Review of Literature* 18 Sept. 1943: 18.

Calls the novel strange, intense, embattled, and sharply individualized. Finds breadth, depth, entertainment value, slick dialogue, and smart magazine type detail in the novel. Concludes: "It has something to say and says it with sincerity and vigor."

"The Bookshelf." Rev. of *The Other Father. Christian Science Monitor* 10 June 1950: 8.

Provides a brief plot summary, and complains that the author is writing with her tongue in cheek when she admires her characters, or has failed to make her own position clear. Concludes that she has "sacrificed much of the dramatic potentiality and moral validity of her book" in the process.

Boroff, David. "High Society, Lower East Side." Rev. of *First Papers. Saturday Review* 27 Feb. 1965: 32-33.

Complains that *First Papers,* while it has considerable charms, ultimately distresses us, because of its mixture of the sentimental and the authentic, its bad editing, and its use of the chronicle format.

Bullock, Florence Haxton. "Laura Hobson's New Novel." Rev. of *The Other Father*. *New York Herald Tribune Book Review* 14 May 1950: 4.

Asserts that *The Other Father* searches deeply into the relationship between parent and child, particularly that between a father and his daughters. Concludes that Hobson has been very effective in providing a study of this middle-aged man's emotional makeup. Provides a plot summary and description of the characters.

Bullock, Florence Haxton. "Publicity—It's Wonderful!" Rev. of *The Celebrity*. *New York Herald Tribune Book Review* 21 Oct. 1951: 8.

Shows how *The Celebrity* deals readably with its subject and functions like a textbook in techniques of celebrity building. Describes the plot and characters.

Bullock, Florence Haxton. "Themes Deftly Intermingled." Rev. of *The Trespassers*. *New York Herald Tribune Weekly Book Review* 19 Sept. 1943: 6.

Claims that Hobson uses tremulous *vox humana* in this "vigorously contemporary novel," and carrying her story with a high hand, sustaining its suspense, and failing to mediate complicated detail. Adds that because she imparts more meaning and more significant character making in the novel, "she has invaded Nancy Hales's and Clare Boothe's field, 'the women' and, in one respect at least, beaten both at their game" because she is a novelist of "large ideas."

Burt, Struthers. "The Poison in Our Body Politic." Rev. of *Gentleman's Agreement*. *Saturday Review of Literature* 1 Mar. 1947: 14.

Views the central protagonist of the novel as "prejudice" in small town America. Calls it a thesis novel which falls into the category of a tract at times. Yet argues that Hobson skillfully avoids many of the pitfalls her righteous passion might have led her into. Sees the story as exciting and original.

Curley, Thomas. "Careworn Crusader." Rev. of *First Papers*. *New York Times Book Review* 1 Nov. 1964: 28.

Briefly recounts plot and character, and then goes on to complain of the switching of narrative viewpoint in the novel and the sheer number of incidents. Argues that the tragic too often becomes sentimental or quixotic. Concludes: "It is as if God Himself were not a capitalist—but a purblind doomster, made in the image of Thomas Hardy."

Denuel, Eleanor P. "Fiction." Rev. of *Untold Millions. Best Sellers* Apr. 1982: 7.

Depicts the novel as the story of the growth of two immature adults who pay a terrible price for maturity. Calls it "a multi-dimensional word portrait of one child helping another, one who learns a great deal from the experience and one who is left behind." Claims that, while the book imparts the flavor of the twenties, it is not a period piece.

Du Bois, William. "Schuyler Green's Metamorphosis." Rev. of *Gentleman's Agreement. New York Times Book Review* 2 Mar. 1947: 5, 36.

Calls the novel a grade A tract cleverly camouflaged as a novel. Praises its brilliance and dispatch, taut description and honesty—despite the fact that the plot is "thimble rigged." Provides a brief plot summary.

Duberman, Martin. "Gentlemen's Agreement." Rev. of *Consenting Adult. New York Times Book Review* 6 July 1975: 5-6.

Describes the contents of this novel concerned with male homosexuality. Claims that much of the novel's success in reaching us hinges on its complex characters and the decision to tell the story from the parents' point of view. Commends the novel for its sociological information, and says little by way of literary comments.

Fadiman, Edwin Jr. Rev. of *The Tenth Month. Saturday Review* 16 Jan. 1971: 34, 62.

Calls the novel a "woman's book, a story whose immediate appeal is to women," and which is also much more. Recounts the plot, and comments that it is a celebration of calculated decency, warmth, and maturity in a time of spiritual cold and spiteful childishness. Praises the competent writing, the spicy aphorisms, the wit, the "rattling good story," and the fact that the novel has something to say.

Farber, Marjorie. "Refugees' Dilemma." Rev. of *The Trespassers. New York Times Book Review* 19 Sept. 1943: 5.

Outlines the plot, then complains that the first half of the book has been written in an emotional vacuum with all the warmth and directness of feeling being devoted to the refugee problem. Believes this unevenness is reflected in the style. Sees this novel depicting honest anger at America's treatment of refugees.

"Fathers and Daughters." Rev. of *The Other Father. Time* 29 May 1950: 92.

A review of *The Other Father* which claims that, while Hobson lacks a first-class novelist's art in creating full-sized characters, the book still has a strong appeal because of its father-daughter-other theme "and for its between-the-lines message: everybody can live a wiser family life."

Fremont-Smith, Eliot. "The Cute Non-Conformist." Rev. of *First Papers. Hadassah Magazine* Dec. 1964: 15.

Argues that *First Papers* is a politically liberal ladies book and a safe one; its politics are the politics of sentiment, its causes, its outrages, and fever encased in comfy nostalgia. Political engagement is thus vicarious, and can be experienced by simple agreement with verities of liberty and moderation from a sitting position. Considers it not a bad book, but finds the emotions it engenders fraudulent. Concludes that she has taken a fiery old socialist and made him acceptable, endearing, and lovable. Describes the story in detail.

Griffiths, Joan. "A Limited Device." Rev. of *Gentleman's Agreement. Nation* 3 May 1947: 521.

Provides a thorough character analysis of the protagonist, and a full description of the theme of anti-Semitism developed in the work.

Havighurst, Walter. "No School for Parents." Rev. of *The Other Father. Saturday Review of Literature* 27 May 1950: 17.

Pronounces *The Other Father* painful and veracious, full of pity and understanding, and based on Freudian concepts. Contains mostly plot summary.

Huston, McCready. "Domestic Novel of Tears and Laughter." Rev. of *First Papers. San Francisco Chronicle This World Magazine* 8 Nov. 1964: 32.

Describes *First Papers* as an insight into a Russian-Jewish family in suburban downtown New York fifty years ago, written in untiring episodal style with fast-paced prose and plotting, and with an eye to screen adaptation. Applauds the historical realism of its descriptions.

Johnson, Nora. "Money Problems." Rev. of *Untold Millions. New York Times Book Review* 28 Mar. 1982: 14, 29.

Provides a brief recounting of the financial exploitation of the heroine and the role of money in the novel.

Kent, Cerrulia. "Books." Rev. of *Consenting Adult. Saturday Review* 9 Aug. 1975: 42.

A review of *Consenting Adult* which sees it attacking middle American bigotry against homosexuality. Provides a plot summary and a brief interpretation of the character's motivations.

Lamport, Felicia. "Two Square Pegs Who Really Fit." Rev. of *First Papers. New York Herald Tribune Book Week* 8 Nov. 1964: 5.

Describes *First Papers* as a leisurely, warm-hearted novel telling the story of immigrant parents and their American-born children in the period leading up to WWI. Provides a detailed description of contents.

Lee, Charles. "The Father of a Family." Rev. of *The Other Father. New York Times Book Review* 14 May 1950: 5.

A review of *The Other Father* which briefly outlines the plot and claims that there is more to this novel than psychoanalytical melodrama. Concludes that it raises the right questions about fatherhood, and deserves the attention of intelligent readers.

M., L. Rev. of *Untold Millions. West Coast Review of Books* May 1985: 35.

Expresses disappointment with the novel because, despite its lively characters and Hobson's flawless ear for dialogue, the story is insipid, the conclusion is pat and predictable, and the story is lacking in interest. Concludes that Hobson's exquisite style alone isn't quite worth the book's price.

Mankiewicz, Don M. "Fame Is a Crowded Room." Rev. of *The Celebrity. New York Times Book Review* 21 Oct. 1951: 4.

Claims that this is her best novel. Provides a brief plot summary, and asserts that the book is told with meticulous calm and careful understatement, which makes it possible for it to tread close to caricature without losing touch with reality. Concludes, however, that while mostly compelling and appealing, the one flaw in the novel is that it "offers satisfying support to those who hold that there is as valid Americana to be found on Madison Avenue as on Main Street."

Monhemius, Johanna. "Fiction." Rev. of *The Tenth Month. Books and Bookmen* Mar. 1971: 47-48.

Argues that this is a poignantly told story with a generosity of feeling, but that the overall impression is of a personal account of pregnancy about which is woven an extremely intriguing plot. Concludes that there is an improbability in the story, but concedes that emotions are well portrayed.

Nelson, Elizabeth. Rev. of *The Tenth Month. America* 10 Apr. 1971: 388-89.
Considers the novel frustrating to male readers because it is totally permeated by female perspectives, but argues that it should not be relegated
to the limbo of "women's fiction." Concludes that it is characterized by
idealization, sentiment, and domestic bliss.

"Notable." Rev. of *The Tenth Month. Time* 29 Mar. 1971: 90.
Describes the implausible heroine of this novel that "pretends to take on
the problem of the unwed mother." Concludes that Hobson's answer to
the question of whether Dori finds happiness as an unwed mother is just
too untrue to be good.

"Notables." Rev. of *The Tenth Month. New Republic* 6 Feb. 1971: 34.
Recounts the plot, and calls the book "an extremely slick, genteel soap
opera, in novel form."

Parker, James Reid. Rev. of *Gentleman's Agreement. Survey Graphic*
     May 1947: 312-13.
Describes the plot and contents of *Gentleman's Agreement* as serviceable,
entertaining, worthy of a movie, and not as tastelessly written as some
might suppose. Concludes that it is propaganda of the most artful kind.

"PW Forecasts, Fiction." Rev. of *Over and Above. Publishers Weekly* 2
     July 1979: 95.
Complains that the theme of the novel is written so large it overwhelms
characterization that might otherwise have brought it to life. Concludes
that, while to some the novel may read as a propaganda tract for Israel
and against international terrorism, "to others . . . including those who
are engaged in the generational tug-of-war between mother and daughter,
it will strike a responsive chord."

Smith, Harrison. "Decay of Honesty." Rev. of *The Celebrity. Saturday
     Review of Literature* 13 Oct. 1951: 20.
A review of *The Celebrity* which claims for the novel passionate honesty, satirical and humorous thrusts, and "a brightly packaged lesson on
the decay of manners and honesty in the modern world."

Stout, Rex. "A Jew for Two Months—What He Learned." Rev. of
     Gentleman's Agreement. New York Herald Tribune Book Review 9
     Mar. 1947: 5.

Calls *Gentleman's Agreement* a propaganda novel about types of people suffering from and acting out anti-Semitic ideologies, which, while not a strong story, is a strong statement. Calls it a tough, acute, and comprehensive portrait.

Trainin, Barbara. Rev. of *Over and Above. Hadassah Magazine* Nov. 1979: 23.

A review of *Over and Above* which recounts the key thematic tensions in the book, and accuses the author of not bringing potentially interesting characters to life. Complains that the dialogue is too intellectualized, and that Jewish identity is more a response to anti-Semitism than a self-motivating entity. Praises the character of Amy Light as a memorable addition to the pantheon of American-Jewish fictional creations.

Trilling, Diana. "Americans Without Distinction." Rev. of *Gentleman's Agreement. Commentary* Mar. 1947: 290-92.

Calls this a novel about anti-Semitism which makes a strong appeal to Gentiles to bring the Jewish issue full into the light and fight it. Complains that the book is full of liberal cliches, and concludes that, despite its commendable purpose, it is a poor, dull, non-dimensional thesis novel without atmosphere.

V., J. "Among the New Books." Rev. of *The Other Father. San Francisco Chronicle This World Magazine* 16 July 1950: 20.

Claims that in *The Other Father* Hobson leaves the reader unsatisfied. Says that although she still writes very well, her intention is unclear. The dark, latent forces which supposedly exist in Andrew are never realized and implication is less clear than direct statement would have been. Details the contents.

Interviews

Newquist, Roy. "Laura Z. Hobson." *Conversations.* Roy Newquist. Chicago: Rand, 1967. 144-53.

An interview in which Hobson discusses: her early life ambition to become a writer, first novels and contracts, what makes a good novel, motion picture versions of the novels, *First Papers*, her autobiography, her obligations to the readers, dealing with writer's block, the literary status of our time, and advice to younger writers.

Steinberg, Sybil S. "PW Interviews Laura Z. Hobson." *Publishers Weekly* 2 Sept. 1983: 82-83.

In this interview Laura Z. Hobson discusses: her appearance at 83 years of age, her hectic love affairs, her major themes, her biography, her early feminism, her publishing and career history, plus details about her own family and present lifestyle.

Biographical Sources

Gitenstein, R. Barbara. "Laura Z. Hobson." *Twentieth-Century American-Jewish Fiction Writers*. Ed. Daniel Walden. Detroit: Gale, 1984. Vol. 28 of *Dictionary of Literary Biography*. 94 vols. to date. 1978- . 107-10.

More than details of her life, this is a career biography, tracing the developments of the author's canon, describing the contents and themes of her works, evaluating her reputation, and placing her in the larger context of American literary history. Includes a list of primary and secondary sources and illustrations.

Hobson, Laura Z. *Laura Z: A Life*. New York: Arbor, 1983.

Tells the story of her journey to success from advertising copy writer to best-selling novelist, her ups and downs, friendships, betrayals, the influence of her family, the social and political scene of the 1920s to 1940s, her feminism, and her financial dealings and rewards.

Fannie Hurst

1889 – 1968

Primary Sources

Novels

3 A. M. New York: American Assn. for Social Security, n.d.

Anitra's Dance. New York: Collier, 1934; New York: Harper, 1934; London: Cape, 1934, 1936; New York: Burt, 1935; New York: Pyramid, 1974.

Anywoman. New York: Harper, 1950; London: Cape, 1950.

Appassionata. New York: Knopf, 1926; New York: Collier, 1926; London: Cape, 1926, 1931; New York: Grosset, 1928; London: Florin-Cape, 1936; London: Baker, 1970.

Back Street. Broadway ed. New York: Collier, 1930; New York: Grosset, 1931; New York: Cosmopolitan, 1931; New York: Burt, 1931; London: Cape, 1931; London: Florin-Cape, 1934; New York: Grosset, 1941; New York: Permabooks, 1961; London: Hamilton, 1961; London: Baker, 1970; New York: Pyramid, 1974.

Family! Garden City: Doubleday, 1960; New York: Permabook-Pocket, 1962; New York: Pyramid, 1975.

Five and Ten. New York: Harper, 1929; New York: Collier, 1929; London: Cape, 1929, 1934; New York: Burt, 1931.

Fool—Be Still. New York: Doubleday, 1964; New York: Pocket, 1965; London: Hale, 1966.

Get Ready the Wreaths. Little Blue Book 1037. Girard: Haldeman, n.d.

God Must Be Sad. New York: Doubleday, 1961; New York: Pyramid, 1975.

Great Laughter. New York: Collier, 1936; London: Harper, 1936; Garden City: Triangle-Blue Ribbon, 1937; London: Cape, 1937.

Hallelujah. New York: Harper, 1944; Cleveland: Forum-World, 1945.

The Hands of Veronica. New York: Harper, 1947; London: Cape, 1947; Cleveland: Forum-World, 1948; Toronto: McClelland, 1948.

"Ice Water Pl——!" Little Blue Book 1039. Girard: Haldeman, n.d.

Imitation of Life. New York: Harper, 1933; Cleveland: World, 1933; New York: Broadway-Collier, 1933; New York: Burt, 1933; Cleveland: Tower-World, 1943; New York: Permabooks, 1959; New York: Pyramid, 1974.

Lonely Parade. New York: Harper, 1942; London: Cape, 1942; New York: Grosset, 1943; New York: Pyramid, 1975.

Lummox. New York: Harper, 1923; New York: Broadway-Collier, 1923; New York: Burt, 1923, 1929; London: Cape, 1924, 1934; London: Readers Library, 1931; London: Florin-Cape, 1932; London: Baker, 1970.

The Man with One Head. London: Cape, 1953.

Mannequin. New York: Knopf, 1926; New York: Grosset, 1926, 1928.

Once upon a Time. N.p.: n.p., 1935.

A President Is Born. New York: Harper, 1928; London: Cape, 1928, 1934.

Star-Dust; The Story of an American Girl. New York: Harper, 1921; New York: Burt, 1921; New York: Broadway-Collier, 1921.

T. B. Little Blue Book 1038. Girard: Haldeman, 1916.

Collected Works

8 Long Short Stories from "We Are Ten." New York: Avon, 1944.
Contents: Carrousel; Soiled Dove; Elaine, Daughter of Elaine; God Made Little Apples; Hattie Turner Versus Hattie Turner; Nothing Ever Happens; The Laugh Was on Harry; Home, James.

Every Soul Hath Its Song. New York: Harper, 1916.
Contents: Sea Gullibles, Rolling Stock, Hochenheimer of Cincinnati, In Memoriam, The Nth Commandment, T. B., Summer Resources, Sob Sister, The Name and the Game.

Gaslight Sonatas. New York: Harper, 1918; London: Hodder, 1918.
Contents: Bitter-Sweet; Sieve of Fulfilment; Ice Water, Pl——!; Hers Not to Reason Why; Golden Fleece; Nightshade; Get Ready the Wreaths.

Humoresque: A Laugh on Life with a Tear Behind It. New York: Burt, 1910, 1920; New York: Harper, 1918, 1919; Cleveland: World, 1919; New York: Collier-Harper, 1920; New York: Smith, 1934; Cleveland: Forum-World, 1946; Little Blue Book 1062. Girard: Haldeman, n.d.
Contents: Humoresque, Oats for the Woman, A Petal on the Current, White Goods, "Heads," A Boob Spelled Backward, Even As You and I, The Wrong Pew.

Just Around the Corner; Romance en Casserole. New York: Harper, 1914.
Contents: Power and Horse-Power, Other People's Shoes, The Other Cheek, Marked Down, Breakers Ahead, The Good Provider, Superman, The Paradise Trail, The Squall.

Procession. New York: Harper, 1929; New York: Collier, 1929; London: Cape, 1929; New York: Burt, 1931.

Contents: The Left Hand of God, The Third Husband, The Young Prince, The Hossie-Fressie, Give This Little Girl a Hand.

Song of Life. New York: Knopf, 1927; London: Cape, 1927, 1931.

Contents: Song of Life, Madagascar Ho!, The Gold in Fish, White Apes, Here Comes the Bride, The Brinkerhoff Brothers, Forty-Five, Wrath, Who Are You?

The Vertical City. New York: Harper, 1922; New York: Collier, 1922.

Contents: She Walks in Beauty, Back Pay, The Vertical City, The Smudge, Guilty, Roulette.

We Are Ten. New York: Harper, 1937; Short Story Index Reprint Series. Freeport: Books for Libraries, 1971.

Contents: Carrousel; Soiled Dove; Elaine, Daughter of Elaine; God Made Little Apples; Hattie Turner Versus Hattie Turner; Candy Butcher; Dolly and the Colleagues; Nothing Ever Happens; The Laugh Was on Harry; Home, James.

Short Fiction in Anthologies

"Bitter-Sweet." *Americans All: Stories of American Life of To-day.* Ed. Benjamin A. Heydrick. New York: Harcourt, 1921; Freeport: Books for Libraries, 1971. 135-65.

"Get Ready the Wreaths." *The Best Short Stories of 1917.* Ed. Edward J. O'Brien. Boston: Small, 1918. 326-60.

"Guilty." *20 Best Short Stories in Ray Long's Years as an Editor.* New York: Long, 1933. 73-102.

"Home, James." *A Lady's Pleasure: The Modern Woman's Treasury of Good Reading.* New York: Penn, 1946. 188-98.

"Humoresque." *My Favorite Story.* Ed. Ray Long. New York: [International Magazine], 1928. 5-55.

"Ice Water, Pl——!" *The Best Short Stories of 1916*. Ed. Edward J. O'Brien. Boston: Small, 1917. 181-211.

"The Nth Commandment." *"May Your Days Be Merry and Bright" and Other Christmas Stories by Women*. Ed. Susan Koppelman. Detroit: Wayne State UP, 1988. 126-55.

"Oats for the Woman." *Between Mothers and Daughters: Stories Across a Generation*. Ed. Susan Koppelman. Old Westbury: Feminist, 1985. 83-112.

"Seven Candles." *Best American Short Stories of 1923*. Ed. Edward J. O'Brien. Boston: Small, 1924. 277-306.

"She Walks in Beauty." *Creating the Short Story*. Ed. Henry Goodman. New York: Harcourt, 1929. 375-418.

"T. B." *The Best Short Stories of 1915*. Ed. Edward J. O'Brien. Boston: Small, 1916. 84-117.

Short Fiction in Periodicals

"Candy Butcher." *Pictorial Review* Sept. 1936: 16-19, 41-42, 44.

"Ice Water, Pl——!" *Collier's* 21 Oct. 1916: 5-7, 32, 34-35, 38, 40.

"Mamma and Her First National Bank." *Saturday Evening Post* 18 Mar. 1939: 16-17, 98, 100-01.

"Mamma and Papa." *Saturday Evening Post* 19 Nov. 1938: 10-11, 44, 46, 48-49, 52.

"The Name Is Mary." *American Magazine* Jan. 1947: 52-54, 56, 58, 61-62, 64, 66, 68, 70-72, 74-76, 78-80, 82-83.

"One in Three Thousand." *Pictorial Review* Oct. 1932: 8-9, 61-64.

"Play That Thing." *Pictorial Review* Mar. 1939: 7-9, 32, 34-37, 40-41.

"Rosemary for Remembrance." *Good Housekeeping* Aug. 1940: 28-29, 129-33.

"Spangle That Could Be a Tear." *Bookman* Dec. 1923: 373-77.

"Sugar House." *Pictorial Review* Nov. 1932: 8-11+; Dec. 1932, 16-17+; Jan. 1933: 18-19+; Feb. 1933: 20-21+; Mar. 1933: 20-21+; Apr. 1933: 22+.

"Sunday Afternoon." *Woman's Home Companion* July 1940: 16-17, 32, 34, 37, 40, 44+.

"The Vertical City." *Golden Book* Feb. 1929: 66-74.

"What Does Miss Firper Think About?" *Good Housekeeping* Jan. 1942: 30-31, 78-82.

"White Apes." *Forum and Century* Mar.-Apr. 1924: 459-78.

"Who Is Sylvia?" *Good Housekeeping* July 1942: 20-21, 151-56.

Secondary Sources

Articles and Chapters

Burke, Virginia M. "Zora Neale Hurston and Fannie Hurst as They Saw Each Other." *College Language Association Journal* 20.4 (1977): 435-47.

A detailed account of the first meeting and subsequent relationship between Hurston and Hurst. Concentrates primarily on how these two viewed each other and each other's work. Of particular focus is the exaggerated manner in which each saw the other's wealth or poverty, early childhood homes, upbringing, and education.

Collins, Joseph. "Gallantry and Our Women Writers." *Taking the Literary Pulse: Psychological Studies of Life and Letters.* Joseph Collins. New York: Doran, 1924. 122-26.

Contains a brief tribute to the gallantry of women writers like Fannie Hurst. Also contains a series of character portraits of Hurst's most memorable characters, and praises Hurst for her disgusting but truthful depiction of New Yorkers of the day.

DaGue, Elizabeth. "Images of Work, Glimpses of Professionalism in Selected Nineteenth- and Twentieth-Century Novels." *Frontiers: A Journal of Women Studies* 5.1 (1980): 50-55.

Discusses Hurst's heroine, Bea Pullman, as a portrait of a type of working woman who, despite business success, neither begins nor ends her career with commitment to her profession. Claims that underneath the executive facade is a lonely woman longing for a husband and home, two things which she ultimately loses because her talents lie in matters of business and not in matters of the heart. Shows how she ends her life as a magnificent legend to her grandchildren, and interprets the author to be asking the question, "who can love a legend?"

Farrar, John C. "The Literary Spotlight XXVI: Fannie Hurst." *Bookman* Jan. 1924: 552-56. Rpt. in *The Literary Spotlight*. Ed. John C. Farrar. New York: Doran, 1924. 268-76.

Discusses Hurst's early short story "Sob Sister," her idiosyncracies as a writer, her ponderously awkward style, her marvelous knowledge of human nature, her feeling for the subtle values of words, and the stunning force of her brief phrases. Calls Hurst a genius with a sure attack, regardless of the medium she is writing in. Contains much biographical material and eulogy.

Grimshaw, Myrtle Lecky. "Fannie Hurst: Celebrated Author." *Distinguished American Jews*. Ed. Philip Henry Lotz. Creative Personalities 6. New York: Association, 1945. 48-55.

An admiring biographical portrait of Hurst which discusses her early life, her apprenticeship as an author, her early success, the content of her books, and their style.

Harrison, Austin. "Sign-Posts of Fiction." *Contemporary Review* July 1925: 82-89.

Depicts Hurst in the same light as social reform novelists like Dickens and Gissing. In *Lummox* she adds not only ideas concerning women and social reform, but also psychology and a modern analytical method of writing. Calls the writing brilliant, febrile, sensational and written entirely from a woman's standpoint, hence brutal and swift in its social commentary. States that, by ignoring her public in a way Dickens and Gissing never did, Hurst commands the reader to follow her. Concludes that in this novel we sense a new force—that of an educated and creative woman.

Koppelman, Susan. "The Educations of Fannie Hurst." *Women's Studies International Forum* 10.5 (1987): 503-16.

A major resource document which provides a synopsis of her life, her contributions as a professional writer, a listing of all the fields her life and work might make a contribution to, her writing process, the contradictory images of her generated by critical opinion, her formal and informal education, and her contribution to women's studies, Jewish studies, and family studies.

Lawrence, Margaret. "Go-Getters." *The School of Femininity*. Margaret Lawrence. New York: Stokes, 1936. 183-209.

Discusses the changing codes of American womanhood after WWI, identifying Fannie Hurst as a new type of American woman opening up new topics for discussion. Characterizes her as a go-getting woman who likes to write about underdogs and women, a writer who has shrewdly estimated the intermixture of sadism in the human response to a sad story. Sees her work as interpreting the racial passion of women as it functions in the sifting and blending of races in the new world.

Lichtenstein, Diane. "Fannie Hurst and Her Nineteenth-Century Predecessors." *Studies in American Jewish Literature* [Kent State] 7.1 (1988): 26-39.

Discusses the ambivalence and complexity that afflicted Hurst and several of her 19th-century predecessors in the matter of being Jewish, American, and female. Traces a similar ambivalence in Rebekah Gumpert Hyneman and Emma Wold who preceded her.

Loggins, Vernon. "Fannie Hurst." *I Hear America . . . Literature in the United States Since 1900*. Vernon Loggins. New York: Crowell, 1937. 344-48.

Briefly describes the kind of audience which found Hurst appealing, her methods of writing, her background, and her work.

Maurice, Arthur Bartlett. "The History of Their Books: V. Fannie Hurst." *Bookman* May 1929: 258-60.

Discusses briefly *Five and Ten*, Hurst's excursions into department store life, her traveling steerage, and toiling as a scrubwoman in order to enter into the lives of her characters. Hints at the influence of Balzac upon Hurst, her style, her publishing history, and her personal life.

Overton, Grant. "Fannie Hurst." *The Women Who Make Our Novels.* Grant Overton. Rev. ed. New York: Dodd, 1928. 180-86.

Begins with a brief comparison of Ferber and Hurst, then discusses Hurst's life, her early writing career, her short stories, and her novels. Contains a listing of her primary works of fiction.

Salpeter, Harry. "Fannie Hurst: Sob-Sister of American Fiction." *Bookman* Aug. 1931: 612-15.

An article which discusses Hurst's appeal or non-appeal to certain kinds of women readers, her self-consciousness as a woman novelist, and her sensitivity to the classes and types of women depicted in her novels. Concludes with a description of her popular image and a recounting of her biography.

Uffen, Ellen Serlen. "The Novels of Fannie Hurst: Notes Toward a Definition of Popular Fiction." *Journal of American Culture* 1 (1978): 574-83.

Begins with a working definition of what constitutes popular fiction, the role of the audience in its creation, and the assertion that Fannie Hurst was extremely influential in creating the popular novel as we know it today. Proceeds to a detailed and erudite discussion of the actual novels and their popular fiction formula.

Williams, Blanche Colton. "Fannie Hurst." *Our Short Story Writers.* Blanche Colton Williams. New York: Dodd, 1929. 237-55.

A good general introduction to Hurst's life, work, public reception, attitudes towards women, education, and specific novels.

Reviews

"Anitra's Dance." Rev. of *Anitra's Dance. Times Literary Supplement* 17 May 1934: 358.

States that *Anitra's Dance* has abundance, rhythm, sensuous detail, pace, exuberance, and a general air of romantic opulence which the reader is unable to escape. Concludes that there are a few garish passages, but generally Hurst carries the reader along through sheer force of storytelling.

Balakian, Nona. "'Miss Hurst's Streamlined Healer.'" Rev. of *The Hands of Veronica. New York Times Book Review* 26 Jan. 1947: 16.

Describes *The Hands of Veronica* as a book about the crisis of faith in our day whose author is more than a little confused on the subject. Adds that, by deifying science, she would seem to be encouraging a new brand of atomic-age superstition.

Bennett, Isadora. "Fiction." Rev. of *Five and Ten. Bookman* Dec. 1929: 450-51.

Calls this novel a penetrating, vigorous, contemporary portrait of a pitifully rich man which contains her usual deep perception and genuine ability to invest relationships with significance and poignance. Concludes that its central characterization is distinctive, and its telling forthright.

"The Bookshelf." Rev. of *A President is Born. Woman's Journal* 28 Mar. 1925: 30.

Praises the novel for its strikingly unusual form, well individualized characters, details of the rural Midwest, some nervous repetition of words, and a strong pulling interest.

Broun, Heywood. "It Seems to Me." Rev. of *Lummox. New York World* 30 Oct. 1923: 1.

Describes *Lummox* as a thrilling book although somewhat crude. Calls Hurst thumpingly direct in her sentences, and commends her gift for vehement similes. Concludes that, by dint of trying (often without subtlety), she hits her mark. Details the contents.

Bullock, Florence Haxton. "Deceptive Girl." Rev. of *Anywoman. New York Herald Tribune Book Review* 16 Apr. 1950: 10.

States *Anywoman* reveals Hurst's prodigally generous creative powers, her corresponding lack of fastidiousness as an artist, and her want of selectiveness, restraint, and balance. Concludes that devotees who respond to Hurst's largess will enjoy this book, the more discerning will be disappointed.

"Business Woman." Rev of *Imitation of Life. New York Times Book Review* 5 Feb. 1933: 7, 14.

Argues that this book bares the stamp of a novelist who wants to be widely read. Claims that the description of a spiritual vacuum Hurst attempts here is one of the most difficult things to write about, and that she certainly fails. Concludes that too many themes are picked up and dropped in the course of the novel.

Canby, Henry Seidel. "How to Make a President." Rev. of *A President Is Born. Saturday Review of Literature* 28 Jan. 1928: 545-47.

Claims that this novel intends to present the Schuyler family as essential America. Describes the contents of the novel and comments on its reading of American history. Expresses skepticism of Hurst's account and journalistic tendencies. Admires the honesty of the book and criticizes its prose style.

"Career Woman." Rev. of *Lonely Parade. Newsweek* 26 Jan. 1942: 54.

A review of *Lonely Parade* which argues that the book falls short of the author's best storytelling efforts. Concludes that the novel is plotless, and presents mostly a lush series of overpainted pictures.

Conrad, George. "A Bewildered Healer." Rev. of *The Hands of Veronica. New York Herald Tribune Weekly Book Review* 9 Feb. 1947: 16.

A detailed description of the contents of the novel. No literary commentary.

Davenport, Basil. "Descent to Tragedy." Rev. of *Back Street. Saturday Review of Literature* 31 Jan. 1931: 565.

Describes the novel as a book written in bad style, imprecise diction, and awkward sentences. Commends it for its triumphant avoidance of thinness, its richness, warmth, and intimacy.

Douglas, Donald. "Fanny Hurst Relates a Girl's Pilgrimage." Rev. of *Appassionata. Literary Digest International Book Review* Feb. 1926: 191, 194.

Calls *Appassionata* a woman's novel that explores every nook and cranny of its heroine's mind. Claims it to be an achievement of extraordinary, corroborative detail.

Dupee, Frederick. Rev. of *Back Street. Bookman* Feb. 1931: 636.

Describes the novel as unrealistic, yet fraught with all the trappings of Balzac and Zola popularized.

Eaton, Walter Prichard. "A President Is Born." Rev. of *A President is Born. Mentor* Apr. 1928: 49.

Says the novel contains pictures and emotions from *Main Street* which Lewis ignored. Calls the novel a thing of living warmth and passionate life.

"Fannie Hurst Portrays a New York 'Lummox.'" Rev. of *Lummox. New York Times Book Review* 14 Oct. 1923: 5.

Claims that the novel fails to be a great story, but succeeds as the etching of a notable character in verbal mezzotint of several types of New York people. Concludes that it tinges the commonplace with beauty, and touches the deepest wells of human emotion.

"Fannie Hurst Writes of Squalor and Luxury." Rev. of *Mannequin. New York Times Book Review* 8 Aug. 1926: 6.

Provides a detailed plot summary of the novel, and comments that her technique is not quite the equal of her imagination here.

"Fannie Hurst's Stories." Rev. of *Song of Life. New York Times Book Review* 3 Apr. 1927: 7, 10.

Argues that *Song of Life* leaves Hurst's literary reputation as a popular writer about where it was before. Provides a severe stylistic drubbing, and concludes that there is a poverty of resource in her work which all the clamor from her sheet-iron thunder cannot conceal.

Farrar, John. "Epic of Maternity." Rev. of *Lummox. New York Tribune* 14 Oct. 1923: 24.

Calls *Lummox* an annoying, offensive, and puzzling novel. Describes its style as naturalistic yet emanating a rather Greek sense of the structure of life. Considers the theme superbly executed in a vivid staccato style.

"Fiction." Rev. of *Appassionata. Spectator* 17 Apr. 1926: 730.

Argues that *Appassionata* should have more properly been called *Morbidezza* because of its focus on an hysterical girl swinging between an unhealthy attitude towards religion and an unbalanced interest in love and marriage. Concludes that it is most definitely bad fiction which, from Miss Hurst, is a tragedy. Decides that it is kindest to leave this book unopened.

Field, Louise Maunsell. "In This Month's Fiction Library." Rev. of *Mannequin. Literary Digest International Book Review* Sept. 1926: 645.

Calls *Mannequin* a book written in jerky style with paragraphs made of verbless sentences, a relentless panorama of tenements, and sudden appearances of new characters. Concludes that, if this is announced as the winner of a new prize, one's heart goes out to the judges.

"Gaslight Sonatas." Rev. of *Gaslight Sonatas. New York Times Book Review* 28 Apr. 1918: 193.

Considers this a collection of stories with humor, humanity and lack of sentimentality. Finds the characters are portrayed with the inimitable touch of the artist.

Graham, Gladys. "Here Are Ladies." Rev. of *Procession. Saturday Review of Literature* 6 Apr. 1929: 853.

Calls *Procession* a collection of short stories in which all sorts of people go marching by. Details the contents of a few of the stories.

Graham, Gladys Chandler. "Modified Steinism." Rev. of *Mannequin. Saturday Review of Literature* 7 Aug. 1926: 22.

Thinks *Mannequin* is plotted out of melodrama and sentimental ballad. Views it as a triumph of word painting and striking imagery: One gets the feel of multitudinous objects that brush through the pages of flesh, of silk, of grimy denim, of damask, of velvets, etc. Concludes that Hurst seems to have adopted some of the bizarre style of Gertrude Stein in this work, which finally becomes irritating and incomprehensible. Describes the contents.

"Great-Grandmother." Rev. of *Great Laughter. Times Literary Supplement* 17 Apr. 1937: 291.

Calls *Great Laughter* an immensely long book which follows in detail the careers of an amazing number of people. Calls it essentially a woman's book because of its perspective, and commends Hurst as a competent, efficient author who even when she dislikes her characters cannot make them other than living.

"Gregrannie." Rev. of *Great Laughter. Time* 19 Oct. 1936: 91-92.

Discusses the novel as focusing mainly on the portrait of Gregrannie. Praises it for its vigor and for its original portrait of the grandmother.

"Hallelujah, Another Hurst." Rev. of *Hallelujah. Newsweek* 17 Jan. 1944: 88.

A negative review of one of the biennial novels produced by Hurst. Calls it morbid, uninhibited, and unreal. Describes it containing some of the weirdest phony characters ever assembled and some of the strangest plot situations.

Kennedy, P. C. "New Novels." Rev. of *Appassionata*. *New Statesman* 22 May 1926: 142.

Describes *Appassionata* as frankly emotional, violent in style, and somewhat hysterical. Claims that the story is conceived with considerable insight but that talent has gone awry here.

Kronenberger, Louis. "Fannie Hurst's Portrait of a Genius." Rev. of *Anitra's Dance*. *New York Times Book Review* 25 Mar. 1934: 9.

Calls this a classic anecdote about a young girl whom Hurst manages to bring to life. Describes it as a large scale and ambitious book.

"Latest Works of Fiction." Rev. of *Humoresque*. *New York Times Book Review* 6 Apr. 1919: 174, 178.

Describes this book of short stories as capable of bringing swift tears on the heels of laughter. Complains that the stories are too rhythmic and too Hurst-like in their metaphorical flights.

"Latest Works of Fiction." Rev. of *Star-Dust*. *New York Times Book Review* 10 Apr. 1921: 18-19.

Calls *Star-Dust* a thoughtful and sincere first novel. Provides a detailed plot summary, and concludes that the book contains some admirable pictures of American life even though the author is yet to gain artistic skill.

"Latest Works of Fiction." Rev. of *The Vertical City*. *New York Times Book Review* 30 Apr. 1922: 14.

Describes the volume as containing six fugitive pieces presumably gleaned from the magazines. Considers the style morbid, journalistic, aimed at the working class reader, and possessed of an uncanny flair for the right word. Sees her worst vice as sentimentality, her worst fault, cheapness. Concludes nastily that she writes only for women, and is likely to leave the male reader floundering helplessly as to whether the next page will introduce the latest brand of cold cream or some clandestine feminine habit.

Littell, Robert. "Five Novels." Rev. of *Appassionata*. *New Republic* 3 Feb. 1926: 302.

Briefly describes the story, and then concentrates on Hurst's style, which he finds both fascinating and annoying. Wonders if her magnificent, inexhaustible, maddening, helter-skelter, unfastidious talent were tamed like a wild horse, it would lose in fascination what it gained in discipline.

Littell, Robert. "Rich and Strange." Rev. of *Lummox*. *New Republic* 19 Dec. 1923: 99-100.

Calls *Lummox* overwhelmingly prodigal with both language and feeling. Claims that, superficially, the novel is a series of sparks, shocks, and fireworks, naked realistic detail, and simple unrestrained emotion by an author who has a big heart and great tenderness for her characters.

"Longing Hearts." Rev. of *Lonely Parade*. *Times Literary Supplement* 10 Oct. 1942: 497.

Calls *Lonely Parade* exuberant, flowery, theatrical, and rather wordy. Claims that Hurst is never at a loss and never in doubt. Says she is an overpoweringly lush writer, but also manifests supreme gusto, shrewdness, sympathy, and robust comic observation. Concludes that these are qualities which reconcile the otherwise grudging reader to the lavishness and general hyperbole of her style.

Mann, Dorothea Lawrance. "Another Milestone for Fannie Hurst." Rev. of *Lummox*. *Boston Evening Transcript Book Section* 27 Oct. 1923: 5.

Describes the plot and characters, and argues that Hurst cannot easily be placed in any literary category. Sees *Lummox* as a big and elemental novel that moves in large rhythms, and does not get itself written with ease.

Mann, Dorothea Lawrance. "Fannie Hurst and Her." Rev. of *Appassionata*. *Boston Evening Transcript Book Section* 6 Feb. 1926: 4.

Considers minds to be the stuff of Hurst's novel. Traces the history of the reclusive Laura Reagan, and explores her narcissism, devotion to the beautiful self, and subsequent hysterical paralysis. Comments on the breathless, intensely subjective, and compellingly rhythmic language she has developed here.

Mann, Dorothea Lawrance. "Fannie Hurst Views the Five and Ten." Rev. of *Five and Ten*. *Boston Evening Transcript Book Section* 14 Sept. 1929: 2.

Calls this a book written with great simplicity of style and immediacy. Details the story of a rich man who makes his fortune from American chain stores. Commends Hurst for her development as a writer, and for the steady flow of novels produced for such a large audience.

Mann, Dorothea Lawrance. "A President Is Born to the Nation." Rev. of
  A President Is Born. Boston Evening Transcript Book Section 7 Jan.
  1928: 2.

Describes the novel as a book in which America's Puritan heritage and
its subsequent development are discussed. Details the contents.

Mann, Dorothea Lawrance. "The Prize-Conquering Fannie Hurst." Rev. of
  Mannequin. Boston Evening Transcript Book Section 7 Aug. 1926: 2.

Commends Hurst for the size of her prize winnings as a writer, and for
her interest in character. Provides an elaborate description of the contents.

Mann, Dorothea Lawrance. "The Schuyler Tradition." Rev. of *A
  President Is Born. New York Herald Tribune Books* 8 Jan. 1928: 7.

Claims that *A President Is Born* shows the real quality of Hurst's imagination because it is a book which explores heredity, opportunity, and
social conditioning in its examination of what goes into the making of a
president. Provides an outline of the story. Concludes that this is Hurst at
her best, with emotion leashed and breadth of canvas to work with.

Mann, Dorothea Lawrance. "Success . . . in Fannie Hurst's Own Style."
  Rev. of *Imitation of Life. Boston Evening Transcript Book Section* 4
  Feb. 1933: 2.

Discusses the novel in terms of its contents and contribution to fiction
about city women.

Mann, Dorothea Lawrance. "A Teller of Tales." Rev. of *Every Soul Has
  Its Song. Boston Evening Transcript Book Section* 6 Jan. 1917: 9.

Commends this novel for its warm humanity, authentic city voices, ability to listen to Americans, vitally accurate scenes, powerful description,
and moving story. Describes plot and chief characters.

Mann, Dorothea Lawrance. "Through Back Street with Fannie Hurst."
  Rev. of *Back Street. Boston Evening Transcript Book Section* 17 Jan.
  1931: 3.

States that this novel has been created out of the molten metal of life
itself. Commends the book for its passion, power of characterization,
challenge, and prose style. Provides an elaborate plot summary.

"Miss Hurst's Stories." Rev. of *Every Soul Hath Its Song. New York
  Times Book Review* 12 Nov. 1916: 483-84.

Describes *Every Soul Hath Its Song* as a collection of stories with a keen feeling for the relative values of life rendered in a remarkable, realistic mode. Details contents of several of the stories, and concludes that the reader leaves the book with an abiding sense of its truth and conformity to real life, and a conviction of the dignity and value of human emotion in whatever station or through whatever medium it may be expressed.

"The New Books." Rev. of *Five and Ten. Saturday Review of Literature* 28 Dec. 1929: 608.

Asserts that *Five and Ten* is told with unbridled intensity, limitless energy, rococo passages, impressive narrative, and long-winded stretches of pretentious exposition. Concludes that it still manages to come out on top, remain a readable novel, and qualify as good popular psychology.

"New Novels." Rev. of *Appassionata. Times Literary Supplement* 25 Mar. 1926: 234.

Calls *Appassionata* distressingly burdened with background history, and complains that this outpouring has neither form nor sublimity. Concludes that except for the character of the nun, Mother Agatha, it is life at the level of the sub-human.

"New Novels." Rev. of *Back Street. Times Literary Supplement* 19 Mar. 1931: 225.

Sees *Back Street* as a book lacking concision, the bane of most American writing. Provides a brief plot summary.

"No. 22." Rev. of *Hallelujah. Time* 31 Jan. 1944: 100, 103-04.

Describes her writing history, publications, civic service, and politics, her apartment and ideas about possessions. Also reviews the novel, describes the plot and characters, and concludes that, without specific descriptions she manages to make the superheated atmosphere quiver with a heavy, middle-aged eroticism.

Osborn, E. W. "A Few Lines Touching On Fiction of Mid-October." Rev. of *Lummox. New York World* 14 Oct. 1923: 8.

Calls *Lummox* Hurst's crowning creation because it is a book brim full of Manhattan stories, mind poems, and mental descents to Avernus gathered into a whole. Concludes that, despite the multitude of things with which this volume is concerned, there is no confusion of incident or of tongues.

Parker, Dorothy. "Re-Enter Miss Hurst, Followed by Mr. Tarkington."
    Rev. of *A President Is Born*. *New Yorker* 28 Jan. 1928: Rpt. in *The
    Portable Dorothy Parker*. Rev. & Enlarged ed. New York: Viking,
    1973. 483-86.

A sarcastic treatment of *A President Is Born* which concludes, "I can
find in *A President Is Born* no character or any thought to touch or excite
me. . . . I am awfully sorry, but it is to me a pretty dull book."

Parsons, Alice Beal. "Faith and Things." Rev. of *Five and Ten*. *Nation* 2
    Oct. 1929: 358.

Describes the contents of Five and Ten, and commends the novel for
being an idea bursting with interesting characters.

"A President is Born." Rev. of *A President Is Born*. *Times Literary
    Supplement* 17 May 1928: 376.

Argues that in *A President Is Born* Hurst achieves remarkable power in
her generational chronicle. Adds there is excessive earnestness and a
marked lack of humor in the work, which does not spoil the whole effect.

Pritchett, V. S. "New Novels." Rev. of *Great Laughter*. *New Statesman
    and Nation* 10 Apr. 1937: 596.

Claims that *Great Laughter* is a vast, efficient character factory. Details the
contents, and concludes that this is an ungainly, impressive book of gossip.

Proteus. "New Novels." Rev. of *Back Street*. *New Statesman and Nation*
    28 Feb. 1931: 26, 28.

Argues that *Back Street* is a book that tries to blurt out its story in one
breath. Describes plot and characters. Concludes that the latter half of the
book is quite terrible at moments, because Hurst's feverish monotone
makes her difficult to read.

Robbins, Frances Lamont. Rev. of *Back Street*. *Outlook and Independent*
    28 Jan. 1931: 148.

Calls Hurst "the most expert sob-sister among our novelists," and faults
the novel for its vulgarity. Describes the story, and concludes that
Hurst's faults are defects of taste. Cautions the squeamish to avoid reading the last fifteen pages, in which "success is gold-plated and wears too
many diamonds, and tragedy wails too loud and long."

Robbins, Frances Lamont. "When the President Was Young." Rev. of *A President Is Born. Outlook* 18 Jan. 1928: 116, 118.

Details the characters and contents. Comments that this is a commonplace but good story that causes the reader to believe it. Adds that the effect of her biographical narrative is good, but her use of English is atrocious and a cause of anger from a writer with so much intellect and high talent. Concludes that this is an absorbing and readable book that gives an unprejudiced and significant picture of American life.

Ross, Mary. "At 'Twenty-One East'." Rev. of *Lonely Parade. New York Herald Tribune Books* 11 Jan. 1942: 2.

States that *Lonely Parade* discusses once again the theme of essential human aloneness. Mostly describes plot and characters through which this theme is developed. No literary comment.

Ross, Mary. "Fannie Hurst Chronicler of the Inarticulate." Rev. of *Great Laughter. New York Herald Tribune Books* 18 Oct. 1936: 4.

Describes the contents of *Great Laughter* and applauds Hurst for her great cast of varied characters, her ability to articulate their feelings, and her evocation of the historical period. Describes much of the plot.

Ross, Mary. "From a Waffle Shop to a World Wide Business." Rev. of *Imitation of Life. New York Herald Tribune Books* 5 Feb. 1933: 4.

Describes *Imitation of Life* in terms of characters, story, plot, and scenes. States that it moves absorbingly through a gamut of two women's lives with a quick, sure sympathy and becomes a story of the triumph of the black women more than the white.

Rothman, N. L. "Hurst . . ." Rev. of *Lonely Parade. Saturday Review of Literature* 31 Jan. 1942: 5.

Argues that *Lonely Parade* has a new capacity for social irony as solid as it is unexpected. Concludes that, though the book is rich in what are called the furnishings of the novel, its real interest this time is in the three lonely female characters at its heart, from whom she maintains a remarkable distance and objectivity.

S., E. "New Novels." Rev. of *Five and Ten. New Statesman* 28 Dec. 1929: 394.

Claims that *Five and Ten* falls neatly and comfortably into the readable class of novels. Asserts that Hurst preaches the edifying doctrine that wealth does not bring happiness, and has painted a brilliant background and produced her characters with cleverness. Details the plot.

Slesinger, Tess. "The President's Father's Son." Rev. of *A President Is Born. New York Evening Post* 14 Jan. 1928: 13.

Describes the plot and contents of *A President Is Born.* Complains that, this time, Hurst has really gone sentimental with what amounts to an American pastoral complete with pastoral romance.

"Some Political Romancing." Rev. of *A President Is Born. New York Times Book Review* 8 Jan. 1928: 5.

Claims that *A President Is Born* is another example of the persistence with which the Middle West enforces itself upon our literary awareness. Sees one outstanding merit of this book to be that it steers clear of the tedium of the Mid-West versus cosmopolitan New York thesis. Details the elaborate history of this farming family and the rise of one of its members to the Presidency.

Stevens, George. "Wagging Furiously." Rev. of *Anitra's Dance. Saturday Review of Literature* 7 Apr. 1934: 614.

Claims that *Anitra's Dance* might easily be taken for a sordid melodrama when it is in fact a humorous parody. Sees many strengths in style and plot. Calls the end rather macabre, and complains that the most attractive character is killed off merely to let Bruno finish his symphony.

"Stories by Fannie Hurst." Rev. of *Procession. New York Times Book Review* 27 Jan. 1929: 8, 16.

In discussing *Procession* complains that all that could be said has already been said of previous work, because Miss Hurst has small regard for the judgments of her reviewers. Complains that she makes a style of the raw material of style. Details the contents of several of the stories, and concludes that the stories are graphic, read swiftly, and make good use of physical detail.

Stuart, Henry Longan. "Matter Wins Over Form in *Appassionata*." Rev. of *Appassionata. New York Times Book Review* 24 Jan 1926: 5.

Details the contents of the novel, its moral passion, and its realism while deploring the actual prose. Claims that Hurst is trying to depict a very subtle and intense personality in totally trivial terms and consequently fails.

Sullivan, Richard. "Virgie Knows Best." Rev. of *Family!*. *New York Times Book Review* 16 Oct. 1960: 43.

A review of *Family!* which outlines characters and plot, claims that the book is exclamatory and contrived, and concludes that its choppy phrases, heart-string plucking, and feminized world cause the novel to fail because of flatness.

Taylor, Coley. "Fannie Can Do Better." Rev. of *Five and Ten*. *Survey* 1 Nov. 1929: 166, 168.

Describes the novel briefly, and criticizes it as an exceedingly dull tract full of types instead of people, all done in the fashion of an awkward chromo.

Towne, Charles Hanson. "Fannie Hurst's Saga of the Poor." Rev. of *Lummox*. *Literary Digest International Book Review* Oct. 1923: 42-43.

An admiring biographical and critical appraisal of the novel and its central character, Bertha. Describes style, background, and literary strengths of the piece in great detail. Concludes that this is a book by a woman with vision, comprehension, and genius, because it is dramatic, pathetic at times, and eminently re-readable.

Tunstall, Caroline. "A Novel by Miss Hurst." Rev. of *Family!*. *New York Herald Tribune Lively Arts and Book Section* 25 Dec. 1960: 31.

Sees *Family!* as an odd book with half a dozen characters whose development is given inexplicable space. While Claudia's story reaches a climax, the rest are left hanging. Concludes that it has a style which is pleasant, chatty, and uninspired.

Van Doren, Carl. "Born *and* Made." Rev. of *A President Is Born*. *Nation* 21 Mar. 1928: 323-24.

Complains bitterly that Hurst should ask some editor to check her proofs before rushing into publication. Claims that she has power, writes with a clear head and a swelling heart, and an unfortunately thick and opaque style.

Wallace, Margaret. "An American Panorama by Fannie Hurst." Rev. of *Back Street*. *New York Times Book Review* 18 Jan. 1931: 9.

Sees *Back Street* as notable for its concrete detail, vividly drawn characters, and faithful rendering of social background. Also considers it notable for its lack of profundity, depth, and validity. Calls this a work of photography rather than portraiture, and objects that the melodramatic conclusion is in keeping with its plot.

Wallace, Margaret. "Fannie Hurst Portrays the Newly Rich." Rev. of
    Five and Ten. *New York Times Book Review* 8 Sept. 1929: 7.

Argues that *Five and Ten* will never be ranked as one of Hurst's best
books, but might be remembered as the one in which she displays to the
full some of her peculiar talents. Objects that ultimately the book is
unconvincing as an argument, and unilluminating as a contribution to
sociology, but that it has the enormous advantage over other and more
cogent discussions by being successfully entertaining.

Wallace, Margaret. "Four Generations." Rev. of *Great Laughter*. *New
    York Times Book Review* 18 Oct. 1936: 7.

Claims that this novel contains Hurst's best-known characters and situations, and is certainly her most ambitious work. Yet argues that, almost by
virtue of these very traits, she misses the mark because the end result is
neither convincing as a family portrait, nor philosophically illuminating.

Walton, Edith H. "Fannie Hurst's Stories." Rev. of *We Are Ten*. *New
    York Times Book Review* 26 Sept. 1937: 27.

Sees this as an uneven performance with some of the stories being irredeemably bad. Objects to their perfunctory and mechanical air,
transparency, triteness, and carelessness.

Walton, Edith H. "Perfect Pollyanna." Rev. of *Hallelujah*. *New York
    Times Book Review* 9 Jan. 1944: 5.

Sees *Hallelujah* as a novel full of preposterous moments and a few
episodes which actually come to life. Concludes that it is ultimately a
theatrical and unappetizing botch.

Watson, Wilbur. "Mr. Wrong." Rev. of *Anywoman*. *New York Times
    Book Review* 30 Apr.1950: 32.

Describes the novel as having a wealth of absorbing detail, vivid impressions of city life, and a fine story.

Winslow, Thyra Samter. "Nine Excellent Stories." Rev. of *Song of Life*.
    New York Herald Tribune Books 13 Mar. 1927: 5.

Describes *Song of Life* primarily in terms of its panoply of characters.
Complains of Hurst's word tricks, use of trick sounds, and other irritating verbal habits. Details the contents of many of the stories.

Winsten, Archer. "Keeping Up with the Novelists." Rev. of *Imitation of Life. Bookman* Feb. 1933: 197-98.

Complains that *Imitation of Life* is another sloppy, verbless mess of sentimental hokum, strange vitality, and honest rhetorical observation. Calls it another rags-to-riches success story with less than usual emotional wallop. Admits that, although the ending is trite and predictable, all those who think with their hearts will find food for thought here.

Interviews

Sabine, Lillian. "That Elusive Something." *Independent Woman* Mar. 1934: 70.

An interview summarizing Hurst's views on women today and what she thinks makes women interesting and appealing. Mostly interview material not found elsewhere.

Biographical Sources

Currier, Susan. "Fannie Hurst." *American Short Story Writers, 1910-1945, First Series.* Ed. Bobby Allen Kimbel. Detroit: Gale, 1989. Vol. 86 of *Dictionary of Literary Biography.* 94 vols. to date. 1978- . 151-58.

More than details of her life, this is a career biography, tracing the development of the author's canon, describing the contents and themes of her works, evaluating her reputation, and placing her in the larger context of American literary history. Includes lists of primary and secondary sources and illustrations.

"Fannie and Annie." *New Yorker* 22 Jan. 1944: 16-17.

Basically discusses her attitudes toward the outdoors and describes her exercise program for herself and her dogs.

"Fannie Hurst—By Herself." *Mentor* Apr. 1928: 50-51.

Describes her birth, childhood, parents, schooling, early publication efforts, college years, and her hopes for ultimate success.

Heydrick, Benjamin A. "Fannie Hurst." *American All: Stories of American Life To-Day.* Ed. Benjamin A. Heydrick. New York: Harcourt, 1920. 166-69; Short Story Index Reprint Series. Freeport: Books for Libraries, 1971. 166-69.

Provides a thumbnail sketch of Hurst's early life, education, the beginning of her writing career, and subsequent stories.

Hurst, Fannie. *Anatomy of Me*. Garden City: Doubleday, 1958; London: Cape, 1959; New York: Arno, 1980.

Hurst, Fannie. "The Author and His Home Environment: Where and How I Write My Two-Thousand Dollar Short Stories." *Arts & Decoration* June 1923: 9, 55, 62.

Hurst, Fannie. "I Come Across: The Autobiography of a Girl Who Left a Comfortable Middle-Western Home to Struggle for Success in New York." *American Magazine* Mar. 1919: 38-39, 126, 128-30.

Describes her writing and publishing efforts and rejections beginning at age fourteen and continuing to graduation from college; includes publication of her stories in the college magazine of which she was the editor. Then describes Hurst going to New York City to write and publish, and the encouragement she received from Robert H. Davis.

Hurston, Zora Neale. "Fannie Hurst by Her Ex-Amanuensis." *Saturday Review of Literature* 9 Oct. 1937: 15-16. Rpt. in *Saturday Review Gallery*. Ed. John Haverstick. New York: Simon, 1959. 220-24.

Describes her appearance, her talents, her background, her efforts at writing and publication, her love of beauty, travels, and the little girl elements in her approach to life.

Irwin, Inez Haynes. "Literary Portraits: Three." *Bookman* June 1921: 335.

Characterizes Hurst through the symbolic colors, sounds, and objects found in her works. Considers the characterization she has created of the author to be contradictory.

Kilmer, Joyce. "'Chocolate Fudge' in the Magazines: Fannie Hurst." *Literature in the Making By Some of Its Makers*. Ed. Joyce Kilmer. New York: Harper, 1917. 241-50.

A brief biography and appreciation of Hurst which contains Hurst's responses to a variety of questions such as the corrupting influence of the commercial magazine editors upon American fiction writers. Brief but interesting.

Mayes, Herbert R. "Trade Winds." *Saturday Review* 23 Mar. 1968: 19.

A reminiscence at her death that characterizes her work as not of much consequence, though her popularity as an author was enormous. Concludes: "Her stature as a storyteller was high; as a writer, low. She will be remembered for reruns of movies made of her books."

"Powerhouse." *New Yorker* 31 Jan. 1959: 22.

Recounts a visit with Hurst, describing her "extraordinary apartment," her penchant for lilies, her autobiography, her walks, her writing habits, and her TV program.

Shuler, Marjorie. "Fannie Hurst Advises a Plan." *Christian Science Monitor Weekly Magazine Section* 7 Aug. 1935: 10, 13.

Discusses Hurst's typical daily walking route, her apartment and pets, her work habits, her opinions on what the great human need is, and her opinions on women.

Wilentz, Gay. "White Patron and Black Artist: The Correspondence of Fannie Hurst and Zora Neale Hurston." *Library Chronicle of the University of Texas* 35 (1986): 20-43.

A detailed account of Hurst's life, works, and reputation during her day. Discusses her political activism, her manuscript collection, her ambivalence about being Jewish, her involvement in the Harlem Renaissance, and her meeting with and patronage of Zora Neale Hurston. Also contains a detailed portrait of Hurston's background, and comments on the correspondence between the two.

"You Hear Her Heartbeat." Rev. of *Anatomy of Me. Newsweek* 6 Oct. 1958: 94-95.

Reviews her autobiography, and includes incidents from her life and writing career. Also reports on an interview with Hurst.

Dissertations

Brandimarte, Cynthia Ann. "Fannie Hurst and Her Fiction: Prescriptions for America's Working Women." Diss. U of Texas at Austin, 1980.

Lichtenstein, Diane Marilyn. "On Whose Native Ground? Nineteenth-Century Myths of American Womanhood and Jewish Women Writers." Diss. U of Pennsylvania, 1985.

Erica Jong
1942 –

Primary Sources

Novels

Any Woman's Blues. New York: Harper, 1990; London: Chatto, 1990.

Fanny: Being the True History of the Adventures of Fanny Hackabout-Jones. New York: NAL, 1980, 1981; London: Granada, 1980; Scarborough, Ont.: Signet-NAL of Canada, 1981; London: Panther, 1981.

Fear of Flying. New York: Holt, 1973; New York: Signet-NAL, 1973, 1974; New York: Plume-NAL, 1973, 1975; London: Secker, 1974; London: Panther, 1976.

How to Save Your Own Life. New York: Holt, 1977; New York: NAL, 1977, 1978; London: Secker, 1977; London: Panther, 1978.

Parachutes & Kisses. New York: NAL, 1984, 1985; London: Granada, 1984; London: Panther, 1985.

Serenissima: A Novel of Venice. Boston: Houghton, 1987; New York: Dell, 1988.

Short Fiction in Periodicals

"From the Country of Regrets." *Paris Review* 14.56 (1973): 98-107.

"The Madman." *Ms.* Oct. 1973: 60+.

"The Rolls-Royce Love Affair." *Playboy* Jan. 1977: 115, 140, 192, 194.

"Take a Lover." *Vogue* Apr. 1977: 164-65.

Secondary Sources

Articles and Chapters

Avery, Evelyn Gross. "Tradition and Independence in Jewish Feminist
    Novels." *MELUS* 7.4 (1980): 49-55.

Addresses the issue of non-traditional heroines in the Jewish American
novel, and in particular Isadora Wing of *Fear of Flying*. Describes
Isadora's uncertain voyage toward self-acceptance and self-sufficiency
which ends in divorce and confusion. Compares this character with the
heroines of *Falling* by Susan Fromberg Schaeffer, and *Long Division* by
Ann Roiphe.

Baumli, Francis. "Erica Jong Revisited (or) No Wonder We Men Had
    Trouble Understanding Feminism." *University of Dayton Review* 17.3
    (1985-86): 91-95.

An anecdotal account of a male attempt to come to terms with feminism
by a male feminist, which concerns itself with evaluating Jong's
misandry. Includes a male reader's defense against the way Jong's fiction reduces men to sex objects and sex to sadism.

Bennetts, Leslie. "Forever Jong." *Vanity Fair* Feb. 1990: 64-76.

Discusses Jong's fame as a celebrity, her latest novel *Serenissima* and
her accurate pulse-taking of contemporary culture. Describes her heroines in general terms and her lifestyle. Comments at length on her
sizeable ego and details the contents of *Any Woman's Blues*. Contains
miscellaneous pieces of biographical information.

Betsky-Zweig, S. "The Female Flight." *Dutch Quarterly Review of Anglo-American Letters* 6 (1976): 247-56.

An essay on *Fear of Flying* which argues that this is a very conventional comic novel both in subject matter and in technique. Provides detailed discussion on Jong's humor and the comedy of sex in the novel. Discusses psychoanalysis, the mother-daughter relationship, and anti-Semitism as themes, with the central metaphor as fear of flying.

Broner, E. M. "The Dirty Ladies: Earthy Writings of Contemporary American Women—Paley, Jong, Schor and Lerman." *Regionalism and the Female Imagination* 4.3 (1979): 34-43.

Provides a general discussion of earthy language and female psyche in the writings of several women, including Jong in *Fear of Flying*. Discusses Isadora Wing's obsessions with such language and its psychological function for her.

Burstein, Janet. "Jewish-American Women's Literature: The Long Quarrel with God." *Studies in American Jewish Literature* [Kent State] 8.1 (1989): 9-25.

In this general article Burstein argues that while some Jewish women writers cast Jewish tradition as an adversary, others see it as a source of nurturance, some ignore it, and still others tell of a search for substitute commitments. Nonetheless, all seem to engage in a one-sided quarrel with God. Discusses briefly Jong, Kaufman, Shulman, Greenberg, Olsen, Rosen, Paley, Yezierska, and Broner.

Butler, Robert J. "The Woman Writer as American Picaro: Open Journeying in Erica Jong's *Fear of Flying*." *Centennial Review* 31.3 (1987): 308-29.

Comments on the uses of journeying in Old World exploration and New World psychological journeying. Notes the journeying motif in American literature is mostly a male tradition, while female experience is traditionally depicted as enclosure. Sees *Fear of Flying* as the most complete celebration of open motion in recent women's fiction and as a novel in the main tradition of American picaresque fiction because it so strongly endorses both its heroine's suspicion of anything which would fix her in time and place, and her quest for a life of 'flying' into new forms of open space which liberate the self. Concludes that, no longer flying on borrowed wings, she can move toward the same protean world which has liberated Natty Bumpo, Huck Finn, Ishmael, and scores of other picaresque heroes.

Chabot, C. Barry. *"Fear of Flying." Survey of Contemporary Literature.* Ed. Frank N. Magill. Rev. ed. 12 vols. Englewood Cliffs: Salem, 1977. 4: 2520-23.

A standard reference article on *Fear of Flying* covering principal characters, style, themes, social commentary, and impact. Discusses also the autobiographical elements of the work.

Clark John R. "An Humble Predacity upon the *Corpus* of Erica Jong." *Maledicta: The International Journal of Verbal Aggression* 1 (1977): 211-13.

Contrasts Sterne's ability to button up one cause of vexation!—and unbutton to another with Jong's fantasizing in *Fear of Flying* about zipless sex, insisting that logically we can safely assert that that which is zipped must be unzipped. Concludes that we cannot anymore have zipless debaucheries than the eighteenth century could have buttonless pleasure.

Cohen, Sarah Blacher. "The Jewish Literary Comediennes." *Comic Relief: Humor in Contemporary American Literature.* Ed. Sarah Blacher Cohen. Urbana: U of Illinois P, 1978. 172-86.

A major article which begins by describing codes of femininity in traditional Jewish communities throughout history, and provides a description of how women have been depicted in Jewish folk literature. Then proceeds to describe how they are currently being depicted in contemporary Jewish American fiction. Describes Isadora Wing of *Fear of Flying* as wide-ranging and complex in her humorous observations. Notes that the prime objects of her raillery are creativity-destroying English professors, psychiatrists, demented suitors, adulterous Arabs, and her family. Concludes that Isadora's laughter at herself is not the laughter of a self-hater, but that of a woman who likes herself for her ready wit.

Diamond, Arlyn. "Flying from Work." *Frontiers: Journal of Women Studies* 2.3 (1975): 18-23.

Argues that *Fear of Flying* portrays erotic fantasies which must be suspect in a culture where women's natural sex drives have been manipulated and channeled, where in our youth we dreamt we were Prom queens in our Maidenform bras, and in our maturity we can buy an extraordinary collection of sex fantasies written by a sexually liberated woman to help her less sophisticated and more frustrated sisters. Claims that this book exhibits a spurious and marketable concern with the subject of liberation, but presents instead crippled fantasies and no mention of serious work for the liberated woman.

Dillon, Millicent. "Literature and the New Bawd." *Nation* 22 Feb 1975: 219-21.

Discusses the stereotypical, now anachronistic, bawd of earlier fiction, and suggests that her modern replacement is Isadora Wing of *Fear of Flying*.

Diot, Rolande. "Sexus, Nexus and Taboos versus Female Humor, the Case of Erica Jong." *Revue Francaise d'etudes Americaines* 30 (1986): 491-99.

Argues essentially that for all the comic invention in her several novels, Jong is not Miller, the comic humorist, nor is she Rabelais or Joyce. Comments that her downfall is the sexual inequality of humor because of the metaphorical connection between sex, power, humor, and impotence. For a woman like Jong, he concludes, there are too many taboos hedging the female literary comedienne.

Ferguson, Mary Anne. "The Female Novel of Development and the Myth of Psyche." *Denver Quarterly* 17.4 (1983): 58-74. Rpt. in *The Voyage In: Fictions of Female Development*. Eds. Elizabeth Abel, Marianne Hirsch, and Elizabeth Langland. Hanover: UP of New England, 1983. 228-43.

Describes the archetypal pattern of the male novel of development, and suggests that the female pattern involves: 1) circular rather than spiral motion, 2) home as a proving ground, 3) rites of passage occurring in the realm of relationships, 4) rebellion bringing ridicule, not integrity, and 5) the whole development being viewed as inferior. Claims only recently have there been novels which show successful development in the world at large. Uses the pattern of the psyche myth to delineate the pattern of several novels, including *Fanny*. In this paradigm, both male and female questors rejoin society and help cure its ills.

Francke, Linda. "Mother Confessor." *Newsweek* 16 Dec. 1974: 65-66.

Describes the aftermath of the publication of *Fear of Flying* on Jong's personal life—phone calls from women day and night, obscene mail from men, the impact on her husband, her fame, and her ability to work on her next novel.

Friedman, Edward H. "Girltalk: Narrative Discourse in the Feminine Picaresque Novel and Erica Jong's *Fanny*." *Whimsy II: Western Humor and Irony Membership Serial Yearbook: Metaphors be with You: Humor and Metaphor*. Eds. Don L. F. Nilsen and Alleen Pace

Nilsen. Proc. of the 1983 WHIM Conference. Tempe: English Dept., Arizona State U, 1983. 55-57.

Applies characteristics of the picaresque form to *Fanny*, finding particularly significant the form of expression, which makes process inseparable from product. Also observes that the novel offers an impressive balance of picaresque consciousness with social consciousness; her text occupies the middle ground between its literary precedents and modern women's liberation, in an ironic looking backward and pointing forward. Concludes, however, that the novel finds no social solution: both Fanny and Jong find that peaceful coexistence between the sexes remains a dream of the future.

Giusto-Davis, Joann. "'I'm Not a Witch,' Says Jong, Awaiting Next Book." *Publishers Weekly* 11 Sept. 1981: 50.

Discusses *Witches,* a nonfiction work Jong wrote after doing extensive research on the subject for her novel *Fanny*.

Gribble, James. "Literature and Truth." *Literary Education: A Revaluation.* James Gribble. Cambridge: Cambridge UP, 1983. 7-14, 22, 45.

Uses *Fear of Flying* to discuss and illustrate the way in which literature attempts to approximate truth. Points out that Isadora (and Jong) suggest that the failure of literature to get at the truth is that language necessarily falsifies experience. Objects to this by pointing out that she says "How can I know what I think unless I see what I write?" Finally suggests that Isadora strikes an attitude of ruthless honesty which is self-engrossed rather than self-exploratory. Concludes that this desire to see herself as plumbing the depths of her thoughts, her experience, through her writing reflects a contemporary admiration for such qualities as honesty and sincerity in life as well as literature.

Harder, Kelsie B. "The Masculine Imperative: Naming by Gael Greene and Erica Jong." *Literary Onomastics Studies* 11 (1984): 147-63.

Discusses *Fear of Flying* as a novel filled with the freedom of language usage resulting from the revolution of the sixties and taking advantage of the right to describe sexual encounters that are hardly more than light sparring matches. Shows how she also uses eighteenth- and nineteenth-century naming characteristics to allow her greater breadth in the novel. Comments mainly on *Fanny*.

Harder, Kelsie B. "Onomastic Centrality." *Literary Onomastics Studies* 7 (1980): 33-54.

Discusses uses of names in literature by using *How to Save Your Own Life* as an example of using names as metaphor. Concludes that, in this work, names as metaphor appear too often to form a structural outline, for they do not contribute to the central metaphor of Isadora Duncan, but Jong has "pushed—'shoved' would be better—the boundaries of name-metaphor beyond the ordinary in writing style."

Horton, Susan R. "Desire and Depression in Women's Fiction: The Problematics and the Economics of Desire." *Modern Fiction Studies* 4.2 (1978): 181-95.

Discusses the prevalence of two kinds of melancholy in woman-written fiction—that born of powerlessness, and that born of sadness over the issue of impulse and its ambiguous nature. Claims Isadora Wing of *Fear of Flying* fame is accused of the former.

Johnson, Diane. "Should Novels Have a Message? Joan Didion, Bertha Harris, and Erica Jong." *Terrorists and Novelists*. Diane Johnson. New York: Knopf, 1982. 124-33.

Calls *How to Save Your Life* a failure as a serious didactic work, and the reading equivalent of an inert substance. Concedes there are some interesting things about the book because it has the value of recording the ramblings of the deserted friend who has taken to the tape recorder and submitted the unedited transcript, we can abandon it without hurting her feelings or damaging our own self-regard. Concludes that Jong presents women as insecure, banal, and demanding.

Jong, Erica. "Jong Triumphant." *Vogue* Aug. 1980: 228-30, 279-80.

Jong discusses her new novel, *Fanny*, explaining why she chose an eighteenth- century setting and the historical novel form—echoing *Fanny Hill, Tom Jones*, Pope, and Swift. Notes that she sees many similarities between that era and our own. Says women still suffer from sex—but oh, how differently! Includes an excerpt from the novel.

Jong, Erica. "Writing A First Novel." *Twentieth Century Literature* 20.4 (1974): 262-69.

Assigned to speak about writing a first novel, Jong first discusses the meaninglessness of this reviewer's category, and then describes her efforts to find a model or pattern into which she could write her life experience, her initial efforts at writing a novel, her writing poetry, and finally her writing of *Fear of Flying*.

Jong, Erica. "Ziplash: A Sexual Libertine Recants." *Ms.* May 1989: 49.

Jong discusses her famous phrase from *Fear of Flying*, "the zipless fuck," insisting that she never advocated it, only chronicled it, and that she refuses to defend it. Goes on to talk about society's experimentation with sexual freedom, and concludes that a careful rereading of her novel will show that "free love was never so very free at all."

Karl, Frederick. *American Fictions 1940/1980: A Comprehensive History and Critical Evaluation.* New York: Harper, 1983. 431-33.

Describes *Fear of Flying* as set in a psychoanalytic frame of reference and presenting the dichotomy between the free life and the secure life. Sees Isadora as the prototype of the urban Jewish "with-it" young woman, close to thirty, deracinated, and, as a mother-wounded young woman, as self-seeking as any of Roth's young men. Ultimately sees this novel, and male novels like it, as evidence of middle-class literary indulgence. Concludes that Isadora remains infantile.

Klinkowitz, Jerome. "Ideology or Art: Women Novelists in the 1970s." *North American Review* 260.2 (1975): 88-90.

Accuses *Fear of Flying* of belonging to the fields of sociology and books like *Sexual Politics* and *The Female Eunuch*. Compares Jong's treatment of sexuality with that of Roth in *Portnoy's Complaint*, and suggests that, after a certain amount of refreshing candor, comes flatness and boredom.

Lohrey, Amanda. "The Liberated Heroine: New Varieties of Defeat?" *Meanjin* 38 (1979): 294-304.

An essay on an emerging genre of biographical novels of a single, heroic, female self, among which the critic includes *How to Save Your Own Life*. Sees Jong as the feminine counterpart of Mailer. Sees sexuality used in ways opposite to those described in *Sexual Politics*. Concludes that Isadora Wing becomes the female Byronic lover.

"The Loves of Isadora." *Time* 3 Feb. 1975: 69-70.

Describes the success of *Fear of Flying*, and gives biographical details about Jong, her feminism, and selected reactions of critics and feminists.

Mickelson, Anne Z. "Erica Jong: Flying or Grounded?" *Reaching Out: Sensitivity and Order in Recent American Fiction by Women.* Anne Z. Mickelson. Metuchen: Scarecrow, 1979. 35-48.

Calls *Fear of Flying* a ritual baptism in the celebration of the female body. Sees it also as a novel which unfolds the story of a dying marriage and a woman's odyssey to love. Also sees it discussing how to fuse together the physical and intellectual parts of being a woman. The remainder of the article discusses a series of topics including detail and observation, the issue of marriage for the modern heroine, *How to Save Your Own Life* as a sequel, humor, naming, male and female friendship, and the sexual vocabulary.

Mitchell, Sally. "Erica Jong." *Beacham's Popular Fiction of America.* Ed. Walter Beacham. Washington: Beacham, 1986. 706-12.

A standard reference article covering publishing history, critical reception, honors, popularity, social concerns, themes, characters, techniques, literary precedents, and related titles in *Fear of Flying* and *Fanny*.

Nitzsche, Jane Chance. "'Isadora Icarus': The Mythic Unity of Erica Jong's *Fear of Flying.*" *Rice University Studies* 64.1 (1978): 89-100.

Sees the unity of the novel coming from its undergirding mythology based on the stories of Daedalus and Icarus. Notes that flying as a theme begins and ends the novel, and that the myth of the labyrinth is also used. Provides a detailed and erudite explication of this thesis.

Pearson, Carol, and Katherine Pope. "All for Love." *The Female Hero in American and British Literature.* New York: Bowker, 1981. 33-38, 126-28, 160-76, 184-86, 192-94.

Describes the disproportionate needing and wanting in traditional female-male relationships, and applies this to a detailed formalistic exegesis of *Fear of Flying* and *How to Save Your Own Life.* Asserts that this argument hinges mainly on the assumption of male supremacy in romantic attachments.

Peer, Elizabeth. "Sex and the Woman Writer." *Newsweek* 5 May 1975: 70-74, 76-77.

Discusses the new novels by women writers that are stirring to wrench the image of women from male hands: The new women writers insist on speaking for themselves, and many of them are using the novel less as art than as documentation in an outpouring of books packed with rage, pain, irony, humor, and deep-focus pictures of the way women live now. Claims the new vein of feminine candor ranges through the entire experience of American women, encompassing almost every variety of sensibility and style. Discusses Jong and *Fear of Flying* and the contributions she is making to this new definition of women by women. Concludes that Jong and the other women novelists have "stripped off the pretty masks that women traditionally wear, exposing them as vulgar, lecherous and greedy, frightened and flawed—in short, as bewilderingly human. Also includes a separate section on Jong and the relationship of her work to her life and ideas.

Reardon, Joan. *"Fear of Flying*: Developing the Feminist Novel." *International Journal of Women's Studies* 1.3 (1978): 306-320.

Notes that, read against the background of the *bildungsroman, Fear of Flying* traces the fictional journey of Isadora Wing from youth to maturity, from fantasy to reality, from archetypal child to "housewife as artist." Claims that the novel also shows the coming of age of the author and that Jong adopts and explores the potentialities of a distinctively female idiom through her use of private metaphors of sexual experience. Concludes that the novel is a compelling statement on growing up female in America.

Suleiman, Susan Rubin. "(Re)writing the Body: The Politics and Poetics of Female Eroticism." *The Female Body in Western Culture*. Ed. Susan Rubin Suleiman. Cambridge: Harvard UP, 1986. 7-29.

Uses *Fear of Flying* and Rita Mae Brown's *Rubyfruit Jungle* to illustrate the contemporary attempt, by women, to rewrite and rethink the female body and female sexuality, because they correspond to the first wave of the American women's movement. Argues that the heroines of both books are trying to define themselves sexually and are aware of the contradictions. Notes that Jong's use of obscene language (the first by an American woman fiction writer) was a self-conscious reversal of stereotypes, and in some sense a parody of the language of the tough-guy narrator/heroes of Henry Miller or Norman Mailer. Finds the book significant for its usurpation of four-letter words to talk about a woman's sexual desires and fantasies.

Toth, Emily. "Dorothy Parker, Erica Jong, and New Feminist Humor." *Regionalism and the Female Imagination* 3.2-3 (1977): 70-85.

Discusses the female writer's experience as defined in all of Jong's works.

Reviews

Ackroyd, Peter. "Born Twee." Rev. of *How to Save Your Own Life. Spectator* 7 May 1977: 24.

Shows how this novel continues the story of Isadora Wing, and argues that it fails for the same reasons it failed before—pervasive self-adulation, detailed descriptions of luxuriant sex, puppet-like characters, luxuriant prose, and gaping holes in which one has to guess what is going on.

Aiken, Joan. "Erica Jong's Carnival of Venice." Rev. of *Serenissima: A Novel of Venice. Washington Post Book World* 19 Apr. 1987: 4-5.

Describes *Serenissima* as wild, complicated action. Complains that the dialogue problems are not solved; neither is the problem of plausibility. Describes the characters and some of the action.

"Altitude Sickness." Rev. of *Fear of Flying. Times Literary Supplement* 26 July 1974: 813.

Describes *Fear of Flying* as a book in which the creator might not quite be aware of the failure of her protagonist at being cute, appealing, sophisticated, or bold. Identifies a note of despair in her prattle, and condemns her ultimately female attitudes towards men because they have been more winningly expressed in Erica Jong's poems than in this stodgy novel.

Bell, Pearl K. "Women on Women." Rev. of *Fear of Flying. New Leader* 9 Dec. 1974: 3-4.

Calls *Fear of Flying* a shrill, flamboyant, picaresque work that, underneath all its sexual trapeze work and feminist grievances, is really a daughter of *Marjorie Morningstar*. Calls the book narcissistic, prolix, and flabby. Concludes that this book would set feminism back fifty years if it weren't so ludicrous.

Binding, Paul. "Italy!" Rev. of *Serenissima: A Novel of Venice. Listener* 24 Sept. 1987: 30.

Accuses *Serenissima* of being drivel of a quite breathtaking kind. Describes plot and characters, and wonders what the Italians might think of Jong's negative assessment of Italy and Italians.

Blythe, Ronald. "In Cahoots or in the Dirt." Rev. of *Fear of Flying. Listener* 2 May 1974: 576.

Praises the novel for its merriment and intelligence, and for its treatment of men, Germans, and Americans abroad.

Broyard, Anatole. "Books of the Times." Rev. of *Fanny: Being the True History of The Adventures of Fanny Hackabout-Jones. New York Times* 28 Aug. 1980: C17.

Calls *Fanny* a period picaresque which builds into an impressive performance. Suggests that for all Jong's ingenuity and elan, it is only a
performance, for it is held down by the habits of the eighteenth-century
novel—inert moralizing, relentless archness, and picaresque construction.

Burgess, Anthony. "Jong in Triumph." Rev. of *Fanny: Being the True
    History of the Adventures of Fanny Hackabout-Jones. Saturday
    Review* Aug. 1980: 54-5.

Praises Jong for her truthfulness, describes her uses of the eighteenth-century picaresque tradition, and lauds the stylistic distinction of the novel.

Clemons, Walter. "Beware of the Man." Rev. of *Fear of Flying.
    Newsweek* 12 Nov. 1973: 114.

A review of *Fear of Flying* which provides a brief plot summary plus a
character study, and then lauds the book as gutsy, too cute, funny,
bawdy, energetic, full of wisecracks, and generous with talent.

Coates, Joseph. "An Artist Spray-Painted with Thick, Purple Prose."
    Rev. of *Any Woman's Blues. Chicago Sunday Tribune Magazine of
    Books* 7 Jan. 1990: 7.

Claims *Any Woman's Blues* is a remarkably good book fighting to free
itself from the pretentious gabble it is written in. Yet concludes that it is not
a good novel. Describes the central character, her voice, and predicaments.

Cooke, Judy. "You Name It." Rev. of *Fanny: Being the True History of
    the Adventures of Fanny Hackabout-Jones. New Statesman* 24 Oct.
    1980: 24-25.

Argues that in *Fanny,* the theme repels and the length appalls. Complains
that the prose style races through the consciousness like wet cotton wool,
while the plot is a mock epic that lacks bite, demonstrates cold sex, and
hygenic, illustrated Kinsey. Claims feminists will be appalled at the
book's degradation of women and critique of the women's movement.
Provides a detailed description of the contents.

Coyne, Patricia S. "Women's Lit." Rev. of *Fear of Flying. National
    Review* 24 May 1974: 604.

Commends the snappy, highly readable, and amusing prose. Considers
Jong in the forefront of liberated women writers for her attitude, style,
and choice of subject matter.

Crain, Jane Larkin. "Feminist Fiction." Rev. of *Fear of Flying*. *Commentary* Dec. 1974: 58-62.

Discusses contemporary feminist fiction, finding the characters one-dimensional shapes more appropriate to figures in an allegory, or a burlesque, than a novel. Notes that these novels deal primarily with marriages, supposedly created and perpetuated by men for their own comfort and convenience, in which the women are trapped, unfulfilled, and victimized. Yet claims Jong shows no men receiving a trace of either comfort or convenience. Concludes that these writers, who obviously share the spirit of the Women's Liberation Movement, have a demeaning vision of their sex (a male writer would do so nowadays at peril of life) that reeks of the hatred of women. Discusses *Fear of Flying* in this context.

Cunningham, Valentine. "Back to Shiftwork." Rev. of *Serenissima: A Novel of Venice*. *Times Literary Supplement* 18 Sept. 1987: 1025.

Summarizes the plot, describes the setting, and observes that this is a novel full of masks, actors, costumes, and performances. Praises the novelist for her use of doubling, command of words, and her "whippy trans-historical shuttle" which both amuses and dazzles.

DeMott, Benjamin. "The Fruits of Sin." Rev. of *Any Woman's Blues*. *New York Times Book Review*. 28 Jan. 1990: 13.

Details the contents of the story and complains that literary self-indulgence has spoiled it, creating something now hysterical, now sanctimonious, but seldom entertaining. Concludes that, as a whole, the book feels leaden.

DeMott, Benjamin. "Isadora and Adrian, John and Mimi." Rev. of *Fear of Flying*. *Atlantic Monthly* Dec. 1973: 125-26.

Describes *Fear of Flying* as a book with a chill. Provides a detailed description of the contents, and concludes that its primary cultural interest lies in its relationships between lovers.

Dunn, Douglas. "Selected Books." Rev. of *How to Save Your Own Life*. *London Magazine* Aug.-Sept. 1977: 119-20.

Finds this novel unintentionally convincing, lyrical, and orgiastic by turns, but usually generously humane.

Durrant, Digby. "Surviving." Rev. of *Fear of Flying*. *London Magazine* Aug.-Sept. 1974: 145-46.

Calls *Fear of Flying* a bracing gallop that one may not exactly enjoy, but which will be invigorating. Provides a hilarious plot summary, and concludes that it is an easy read with depression and remorseless wisecracks every so often giving way to pieces of committed, serious writing, including a very funny description of the American Army base in Heidelberg.

Dworkin, Susan. "In Which the Author Hides Under the Skirts of an 18th-century Wench Thereby Indulging Herself and Us." Rev. of *Fanny: Being the True History of the Adventures of Fanny Hackabout-Jones. Ms.* Nov. 1980: 45.

Describes the style, character, mode, plot, language, and tone of the novel as well as its feminist ideology. Claims the whole thing, written in eighteenth-century style as it is, is likely to put anyone off. Concludes that what is finally appealing is the wise self-mockery of the author herself.

Dyer, Richard. "." Rev. of *Serenissima: A Novel of Venice. Boston Globe* 16 Apr. 1987: 81.

Describes *Serenissima* as the fantasy of a limited talent trying hopelessly to imagine what it would be like to serve as a muse to genius. Describes Jessica Pruitt's story in considerable detail. Comments on the sex scenes and the historical research in the novel.

"Fiction." Rev. of *How to Save Your Own Life. New Yorker* 4 Apr. 1977: 140-41.

A brief account of the contents and style of a novel that has many insouciant things to say about love, marriage, sexual experimentation, and middle-class guilt. Claims its main defect is a cloying, tough-sweet winsomeness of the kind one usually associates with child actors.

FitzGerald, Karen. "What Do the '60s and '70s Say to the '80s?" Rev. of *Fear of Flying. Ms.* July 1986: 56, 84-86.

Describes the exploits of Isadora Wing as material firmly rooted in the 1970s when the shock value of such bravado was premium. Sees it is now more enjoyable as history than as literature, since many of its concerns have ceased to be real issues.

Friedman, Alan. "Erica Jong Circa 1750." Rev. of *Fanny: Being the True History of the Adventures of Fanny Hackabout-Jones. New York Times Book Review* 17 Aug. 1980: 1, 20.

A review of *Fanny* which hails its author as a prodigy and the novel as both literary and pornographic. Provides a brief chronicle of events, and concludes that the book's feminism is problematic, but that its language is exceptionally beautiful.

Fuller, Edmund. "Isadora Wing: Incitement to Celibacy." Rev. of *How to Save Your Own Life. Wall Street Journal* 14 Mar. 1977: 16.

Claims that *How to Save Your Own Life* is plagued between a natural earthiness and licentiousness, and the mistaking of openness and lack of pretense for a desire to titillate. Concludes that this is merely an erotic love story whose characters are all the wrecks of sex washed up on the shores of the sexual revolution.

Haskell, Molly. "A Novel by Erica Jong." Rev. of *Fear of Flying. Village Voice Literary Supplement* 22 Nov. 1973: 27.

Describes the contents of this novel as raunchy and comical. Identifies its basic flaw as the insistence that Isadora Wing is insecure when, in fact, it is hard to believe she is afraid of anything. Concludes that this is an exhilarating fuel-burner, a blaze of one-woman energy and sexual plenty. Summarizes, *Fear of Flying* as a vehicle for exceeding the limits on the open road.

Helgesen, Sally. "Instant Tradition: Jong's Free-Form History." Rev. of *Fanny: Being the True History of the Adventures of Fanny Hackabout-Jones. Harper's* Jan. 1981: 81-82.

Argues that *Fanny* is ultimately a false, vulgar, implausible, self-conscious book which finally subverts its own purposes. Sees Fanny, gushing onward with each variation on the numerical possibilities of sex, as a heroine of pornographic literature. Claims that her anger is as old as Eve's, and, though her swinger's attitude is new, concludes that it is finally a book which resorts to cheap tricks and anachronistic shallowness.

Jackson, Marni. "Crash Landing." Rev. of *Any Woman's Blues. Maclean's* 19 Feb. 1990: 55.

Calls *Any Woman's Blues* a book written in confessional style and at least partially about the perils and power of addiction. Describes its effect as compelling, confused, and straining for a moral clarity that is beyond its grasp. Concludes that it is as if Jong had invited her guests to a vegetarian banquet and passed by with trolleys of broiled steaks.

Jacoby, Susan. "The Bawdy Bard." Rev. of *Serenissima: A Novel of Venice. Chicago Tribune Books* 5 Apr. 1987: 7.

A review of *Serenissima* describing it as an historical fantasy novel imbedded within a twentieth-century *roman a clef*. Accuses Jong of being tedious at times, and concludes that it is no work of genius.

James, Clive. "Fannikin's Cunnikin." Rev. of *Fanny: Being the True History of the Adventures of Fanny Hackabout-Jones. New York Review of Books* 6 Nov. 1980: 25.

Claims that *Fanny* is a book which uses pornography to preach a feminist message—a peculiarly modern confusion of motives. Suggests that it is meant to be an edifying joke, but fails because, finally, the sheer disproportion of the enterprise—its utter inability to compress, allude, or elude—is hard to forgive.

James, Darlene. "Lazy, Hazy, Summer Fare." Rev. of *Serenissima: A Novel of Venice. Macleans* 20 July 1987: 50-51.

Calls the novel a book that draws on the author's crazy quilt of identities—poet, crafter of outrageous erotic fantasies, serious literary scholar, and jet setter. Details the contents.

Johnson, Diane. "Hard Hit Women." Rev. of *How to Save Your Own Life. New York Times Book Review* 28 Apr. 1977: 6, 8.

Provides a review of *How to Save Your Own Life*, calling it a mostly autobiographical work. Contains a brief plot summary.

Kapp, Isa. "And Erica." Rev. of *How to Save Your Own Life. Washington Post Book World* 20 Mar. 1977: H1, H4.

Argues that *How to Save Your Own Life* features the author in the starring role of a crusader reminding women of their rights. Complains that the book floats upon a zeppelin of compliments, fan mail, baleful allusions to hostile reviews, past and future, and even reassurance from a writer who resembles Henry Miller that these last are only life-shrinkers. Concludes that there is energy, jauntiness, and chutzpah here.

Keating, Peter. "Erica, or Little by Little." Rev. of *How to Save Your Own Life. Times Literary Supplement* 6 May 1977: 545.

Sees *How to Save Your Own Life* primarily as evidence of Jong's sense of the ridiculous. Provides a fine review of the contents of the novel.

Kemp, Peter. "Moll Flounders." Rev. of *Fanny: Being the True History of the Adventures of Fanny Hackabout-Jones. Listener* 30 Oct. 1980: 588-89.

Argues that *Fanny* is somewhat of a travesty as a mock eighteenth-century novel. Finds its 500 pages swollen with the fruits of too little scholarship and full of female indictments of everything from rationalism on, while hymning the joys of sisterhood. Concludes that, only in its length, does this approximate an eighteenth-century novel.

Kendall, Elaine. Rev. of *Parachutes and Kisses. Los Angeles Times Book Review* 11 Nov. 1984: 3.

Describes *Parachutes and Kisses* as a sequel to *Fear of Flying* in which Isadora Wing, who has subsequently prospered mightily, is continuing on in her irrepressible and pedantic way. Remarks that, when the author is able to turn her mind to non-sexual matters, the book can be quite entertaining and affecting.

Klein, Julia M. "Books and the Arts." Rev. of *Fanny: Being the True History of the Adventures of Fanny Hackabout-Jones. New Republic* 20 Sept. 1980: 38-40.

A review of *Fanny* which concentrates on the structure, style, and conventions of the eighteenth-century novel reflected in it. Sees it as a better book than *Fear of Flying* or *How to Save Your Own Life*. Sees more of a reconciliation between previously incompatible roles of artist, mother, and wife in *Fanny*.

Kuehl, Linda. Rev. of *How to Save Your Own Life. Saturday Review* 30 Apr. 1977: 27.

Claims that this novel is not a *roman a clef*, and asserts that the heroine's adventures are too weighted down with solipsistic ruminations to be picaresque, and too unknowing to develop into a *bildungsroman*. Claims that Jong is too canny and full of life to settle for this whistle in the dark. Concludes with the hope she will regain distance and write her next novel with less concern about how people see her.

Laurel, Hya. "Jong's Latest Novel Centers on a Venetian Love Triangle." Rev. of *Serenissima: A Novel of Venice. Atlanta Journal and Constitution* 26 Nov. 1987: F38.

A review of *Serenissima* which provides plot summary and a description of character. Calls the novel a high adventure but pretty heavy stuff also.

Lehmann-Haupt, Christopher. "Books of the Times." Rev. of *How to Save Your Own Life. New York Times* 11 Mar. 1977: C25.

Finds *How to Save Your Own Life* a work of sheer profusion, finally causing the reader's mind to wander. Claims that it is hard not to read this novel as Jong's own autobiography. Sees much of it as a pastiche of Whitman and Lawrence, Henry Miller and Karl Hummer. Concludes that it finally overlaps the narrower issues of women's liberation, and comes down a splash on the side of life, freedom, and other such vagaries of passion.

Lehmann-Haupt, Christopher. "Nuances of Women's Liberation." Rev. of *Fear of Flying. New York Times* 6 Nov. 1973: 35.

Complains that *Fear of Flying* contains all the nuances of contemporary feminism, and holds together for a while before eventually falling apart. Concludes that after much sexual mayhem, boredom sets in, and we start to squirm. "Four hundred pages?—No thanks."

Leonard, John. "Isadora Wing Flies Again." Rev. of *How to Save Your Own Life. New York Times Book Review* 20 Mar. 1977: 2.

Criticizes Jong for protesting too much and too unnecessarily. States: "If Jong wants to write a book about how bad it feels to be an unhappily married celebrity, and to put everyone into it, and to tell us how she cured herself of fragmentation by finding a lover who was also a friend, she's entitled." Yet goes on to express skepticism about the autobiographical elements of the novel, and to complain that, finally, "the prose bogs down alarmingly."

Malone, Michael. "The True Adventures of Shylock's Daughter." Rev. of *Serenissima: A Novel of Venice. New York Times Book Review* 19 Apr. 1987: 12.

Provides a witty summary of the contents of the book, and lauds Jong for being able to write Rabelaisan, witty, buoyant prose, and an historical novel capable of honoring the tradition with affectionate parody while at the same time creating its own full fictional reality.

Mano, D. Keith. "The Authoress as Aphid." Rev. of *How to Save Your Own Life. National Review* 29 Apr. 1977: 498-99.

A self-consciously masculine pan of the novel mostly on account of its feminism. Calls Jong a sideshow geek, and concludes that as far as literature is concerned, Erica Jong still fears flying.

Martin, Judith. "The Pleasure of Her Company." Rev. of *Fanny: Being the True History of the Adventures of Fanny Hackabout-Jones. Washington Post Book World* 17 Aug. 1980: 4.

A witty review of *Fanny* written in imitation of the same eighteenth-century style of the novel itself. Provides mainly an introduction to the character of Fanny.

Maslin, Janet. "Isadora and Erica." Rev. of *How to Save Your Own Life. Newsweek* 28 Mar. 1977: 82-83.

Calls the novel a semi-confessional sequel to *Fear of Flying*. Describes the plot, and concludes that Jong has always been her best and only object of contemplation. States that her prose is chatty and engaging, full of disarming details and very witty. Complains that the self-indulgence, solipsism, crankiness, and spite of Jong's new book can be perversely amusing, but that underlying everything is an irritating disingenuousness. Concludes that Jong is a real performer, but this time out she is too unbecomingly petty to be entertaining.

Mellors, John. "Learning to Fly." Rev. of *How to Save Your own Life. Listener* 12 May 1977: 634-35.

Asserts that Jong has a delicious sense of humor, a greedy appetite for experience, and a romantic attitude to love that combines to make *How to Save Your Own Life* neither inflexibly feminist nor waywardly titillating.

Meyer, Ellen Hope. "The Aesthetics of 'Dear Diary.'" Rev. of *Fear of Flying. Nation* 12 Jan. 1974: 55-56.

Sees *Fear of Flying* as marvelously entertaining, but ultimately solipsistic and belonging to a lesser category called "dear diary." Concludes that this novel falls somewhere between educated Jet-set talk and well-written true confessions.

Mitgang, Herbert. "Books of the Times." Rev. of *Parachutes and Kisses. New York Times* 10 Oct. 1984: C23.

Argues that, while God is in her feminist's heaven, all's not right with Miss Wing's earthly Connecticut dream. Suggests that now she is forty years old, she lives in suburbia, and seeks after men who enjoy her poetry. Concludes that, when she is not taking herself seriously, Miss Wing is a marvelously comic Central Park West character. Details contents.

Morrow, Lance. "Oral History." Rev. of *How to Save Your Own Life*. *Time* 14 Mar. 1977: 74-5.

Calls the novel a breathlessly up-to-date confessional bulletin. Describes the variety of styles in the book, and condemns it for its vulgarity. Also complains that it has been extravagantly overpraised.

Novak, Ralph. "Picks & Pans: Pages." Rev. of *Any Woman's Blues*. *People Weekly* 5 Mar. 1990: 26.

Calls *Any Woman's Blues* full of babble-brained sentences and a sex-crazed artist obsessed with penises. Complains that the book is so filled with phallic symbols that if they were laid end to end—which they are—they would stretch from here to Timbuktu. Discusses the miscellaneous contents of the book, and concludes that, finally, the book only generates questions.

Prose, Francine. "A Wing Without a Prayer." Rev. of *Any Woman's Blues*. *Savvy Woman* Feb. 1990: 27, 95.

Describes the novel as a book that begins with a bang and proceeds from there to sexual gymnastics and a large dollop of literary gamesmanship. Suggests that while Jong is mostly harmless, sometimes her cure is worse than the disease. Labels the serious issues in the book as addiction, female masochism, and the desperate need for male approval, and betrayal.

Pyrah, Gill. "Erica Tries a Parachute." Rev. of *Parachutes and Kisses*. *Times* 2 Nov. 1984: 11.

Describes Jong's appearance, her relationship to her character Isadora, her feminism, and the changes in the feminist movement in the 1980s, her latest novel that she describes as "the search for the grandfather," her impatience with critics who see only the sexual frolics and "leave aside other themes," and concludes that the novel is "a millstone, and one grinding very little substance exceedingly small." Also describes her style as tediously self-indulgent, interminable, navel-gazing, and immature.

Raban, Jonathan. "Lullabies for a Sleeping Giant: New Fiction." Rev. of *Fear of Flying*. *Encounter* July 1974: 76.

Describes *Fear of Flying* as a particular kind of liberated bawdy which falls short of the mark set by its historical male analogues. Concludes with a summary of Jong's effect on her reviewers in England.

Reuben, Elaine. Rev. of *Fear of Flying. New Republic* 2 Feb. 1974: 27.

Complains that *Fear of Flying* has an unconvincing solution to unconvincing problems because Jong doesn't dramatize or connect the problems of this class of women represented by Isadora Wing to any reality outside her consciousness. Argues that it is primarily a surfeit of parody full of literary games, because nowhere does Jong suggest "liberation" might have more to do with women caring about each other, in their lives and in their work, than caring or not caring about men.

Rifkind, Donna. "Masochists in Love." Rev. of *Any Woman's Blues. Wall Street Journal* 30 Jan. 1990: A16.

Sarcastically describes *Any Woman's Blues* as a novel that clanks along with its repellent, promiscuous content and an overabundance of self-help cliches. Objects most to the titillating drinks, sex, and drugs.

Rogers, Pat. "Blood, Milk and Tears." Rev. of *Fanny: Being the True History of the Adventures of Fanny Hackabout-Jones. Times Literary Supplement* 24 Oct. 1980: 1190.

Reviews the contents and style of *Fanny*, adding that the language and factual background are convincingly presented, while the novel itself has considerable substance.

Rubin, Merle. "Diving into Shallows of Narcissism." Rev. of *Parachutes and Kisses. Christian Science Monitor* 24 Oct. 1984: 21-22.

Asserts that in *Parachutes and Kisses* Jong actually thinks she invented the sexual revolution. Accuses her fictional alter ego, Isadora Wing, of being insufficiently altered, the book of being excessively sincere, and her love of her subject frothy narcissism. Claims that Jong is clearly her own favorite subject, and that to call her a shaper or mirror of the times is to give her entirely too much credit.

Sage, Lorna. "Up, Up and Away." Rev. of *Fear of Flying. New Review* May 1974: 90-92.

A review of *Fear of Flying* primarily detailing the contents of the novel and concludes: "though she (Isadora) is rather like those early aviators, with an incongruous collection of feathers and rockets strapped to their backs, uncertain whether to follow nature or art . . . . her story still has lots of joins and the glue isn't even dry when at the end she returns to confront her deserted husband with her newly acquired self and waits to see what he is going to do about it."

See, Carolyn. "Where There's a Will, There's a Way for Jessica." Rev.
  of *Serenissima: A Novel of Venice. Los Angeles Times* 18 May 1987:
  sec. 5-: 2.

Describes the contents of the novel, and makes no literary assessments.

Shapiro, Laura. "Isadora's Complaint." Rev. of *Parachutes and Kisses.*
  Newsweek 5 Nov. 1984: 88, 90.

Calls this book one more example of Jong still having a fine time writing
novels about sex. Sees this latest novel as bulging with literary references that beg us to take the book seriously, but, in fact, have all the
breathy, portentous mannerisms of a cover story in *Cosmopolitan.*
Snidely remarks that Isadora Wing, the voluptuary, has an orgasmic
capacity that deserves a write-up in the *New England Journal of
Medicine.* Concludes, however, that Jong will very likely be forgiven for
pretensions—by men, if not by women, of letters.

Stanley, Alessandra. "Too Blue." Rev. of *Any Woman's Blues. Time* 5
  Feb. 1990: 67-68.

Calls *Any Woman's Blues* a book about a sexually obsessed alter ego
looking for love in all the wrong places. Complains that Jong takes her
boorish self-deluded heroine far too seriously and expects the reader to
do the same. Concludes that there is too much careless repetition and that
the book prompts the reader to say, ultimately, "Oh, shut up!"

Stein, Benjamin. "The Painful Acquisition of Self-Esteem." Rev. of *Fear
  of Flying. Wall Street Journal* 8 May 1974: 20.

Calls *Fear of Flying* a confused story which offers the female answer to
Portnoy's Complaint. Sees it as profoundly irritating and difficult to read.
Claims that its gutter vulgarity adds nothing to the book although the book
does become a latter-day "Ulysses" with a female Bloom stumbling, groping, and surviving—a hopeful symbol for confused people of either sex.

Stokes, Terry. "In Freud's Old Backyard." Rev. of *Fear of Flying. New
  York Times Book Review* 11 Nov. 1973: 40-41.

Describes the novel in considerable detail, calling it an energetic and
well-conceived first novel whose energy and bawdiness are spoiled by
the whining that gets in the way. Comments that, though there is great
humor in the book, the male figures are either lifeless or fall guys.
Concludes that Isadora herself is either condescending or self-conscious.

Strouse, Jean. "Fanny Gets Even." Rev. of *Fanny: Being the True History of the Adventures of Fanny Hackabout-Jones. Newsweek* 8 Sept. 1980: 76-77.

Calls *Fanny* a feminist *bildungsroman* about a beauteous and bookish character through whom the world of female experience can be described from a female point of view. Argues that the book leaves one alternately impressed by Jong's knowledge of piracy, slaving, and witchcraft, and entertained by Fanny's exploits. Concludes that, nevertheless, this is a narcissistic *tour de force* which is very clever but not much more.

Theroux, Paul. "Hapless Organ." Rev. of *Fear of Flying. New Statesman* 19 Apr. 1974: 554.

Finds Jong's witless heroine "looming like a mammoth pudenda, as roomy as the Carlsbad Caverns," and concludes that this "crappy novel" misuses "vulgarity to the point where it becomes purely foolish . . . devaluing imagination in every line." Concludes that, funded by a grant from the National Endowment for the Arts, this is justification for us to refuse paying taxes this year.

Tovey, Roberta. Rev. of *How to Save Your Own Life. New Republic* 19 Mar. 1977: 34-35.

Calls this a novel cold with self-satisfaction and complacency. Argues that feminists will find it hard to be more outraged than bored by an ending that endorses the power of the male. Concludes that, ultimately, it is a boring book.

Treglown, Jeremy. "Zippy." Rev. of *How to Save Your Own Life. New Statesman* 6 May 1977: 612-13.

Calls this novel a fresh and exciting sequel to *Fear of Flying*. Describes the contents as torrid, and details the zanier episodes.

Updike, John. "Jong Love." Rev of *Fear of Flying. New Yorker* 17 Dec. 1973: 149-50, 153. Rpt. in *Picked-Up Pieces*. John Updike. New York: Knopf, 1975. 411-15.

Calls the novel lovable and delicious, describing its contents in detail and lauding it for its language, inventiveness, fearlessness, and freshness. Concludes: "Mrs. Jong has arrived non-stop at the point of being a literary personality; may she now travel on toward Canterbury."

Widmer, Eleanor Rackow. "Poppa Freud, Dr. Yussel, and the Great American Novelist." Rev. of *Fear of Flying. Arts in Society* 12.1 (1975): 122-26.

Sees the novel as "a 'fun' analysis which is forbidden on the couch, where, if you make a joke, your doctor will insist that you analyze it." Claims that the "soundings of her sexual exploits, like the proverbial pebble dropped into a pool, are intended for widening her observations until the entire surface quivers." Concludes that her larger generalizations deal with the tenuousness of human relationships and the fragility of the creative, bourgeois psyche, despite its riches, its advantages, its cadre of specialists, including analysts, who minister to its needs.

Wood, Michael. "Flirting with Disintegration." Rev. of *Fear of Flying. New York Review of Books* 21 Mar. 1974: 19-20.

Argues that the book does not have enough pace and intelligence, frequently lapses into self-indulgence, and flogs too many feminist dead horses.

Interviews

Balderston, Jean Carol Jennings, and Mary Kathryn Stillwell. "Craft Interview with Erica Jong." *New York Quarterly* 16 (1974): 23-48.

An extensive interview with Jong which covers her creative processes, the writing of *Fear of Flying*, the finding of a poet's voice, authenticity, the problem of being a woman, the biographical element in her work, the lack of an extensive tradition of women's writing to tie into, women's knowledge as a lesser category, condescension toward women in the reviewing process, her early imitating of the male writers, her reading habits, her Jewish sense of self and living in Germany, the unimportance of locale, a room of her own, attitudes towards drugs, teaching creative writing, publishing as a poet, the nature of poetry, confessional poetry and the subject matter fallacy, and the writer's *zeitgeist*.

Broyard, Anatole. "Women and Men and Art." *New York Times Book Review* 27 Dec. 1981: 23.

A brief interview in which Jong discusses: the problem of the male reviewer of female fiction, female versus male gutter wisdom in fiction, and the world of art for the woman writer.

Gardner, Janet. "Interview with Erica Jong." *Feminist Art Journal* 3.3 (1974): 3-4.

Discusses the gender conflicts which harp on the superiority of phallic power as manifested by atypical men like Mailer and Roth, and exempts the majority of male writers from this accusation. Discusses also the struggle of the woman as artist, her experience in analysis, the future of erotic literature for women, the failure of the female audience to accept sexuality, and the primacy of sexless writers like Woolf, McCullers, and Welty. Discusses female responses to her own work, the label of "confessional literature" as a male put down of female writers, her life in Germany, the actual writing of *Fear of Flying*, and her reactions to the work of Anais Nin.

Kern, John L. "Erica: Being the True History of the Adventures of Isadora Wing, Fanny Hackabout-Jones, and Erica Jong." *Writer's Digest* June 1981: 20-25.

A profile of Erica Jong's literary career, relationship to the women's movement, problems with the critics, personal life, work habits, experience in therapy, opinions about breaking into a male-dominated writer's world, attitudes toward public response to the books, and the research process in the novels.

Martin, Wendy. "Erica Jong." *Women Writers Talking*. Ed. Janet Todd. New York: Holmes, 1983. 21-32.

An interview of Jong discussing authors who have influenced her, her genre preferences as a writer, the writing processes of both novel writing and poetry, the readership and its influence, the normal work day, living in Manhattan, the influence of a baby, reactions to accusations of merely being popular, dealing with fears and insecurities, the concerns of women writers and readers in the 1980s, and the concerns of women as mothers and career women at the end of the century.

McNeese, Gretchen. "Erica Jong." *Playboy* Sept. 1975: 61-78, 202-3.

This interview begins with a useful sketch of Jong's life and career and proceeds to discuss: important changes between the sexes, sexual politics, the social implications of traditional roles for women and men, male responses to liberated women, politics, male and female responses to divorce and various forms of rejection, women who support men, attitudes toward orgasm and other topics related to male and female sexuality. Does not discuss her writing.

Showalter, Elaine, and Carol Smith. "An Interview with Erica Jong." *Columbia Forum* 4 (Wint. 1975): 12-17.

An interview with Jong about the composition of *Fear of Flying*. Covers such topics as significant changes made during the writing of the first draft, the meaning of the last part of the novel, motherhood as a form of defeat, work and independence, the origins of the title, flying as metaphor, the alternate endings, the humor, the influence of *Portnoy's Complaint*, the use of epigraphs, the effects on her life of writing a best-seller, her working patterns after the success of this novel, reactions to the reviewers, her favorite writers, the future of her feminist writing, wished-for changes for women novelists, her adherence to Jungian psychology, and her use of analysis.

Biographical Sources

Barr, Pat. "Poet Without Prejudice." *Nova* Apr. 1974: 84.

Discusses Jong's development and contributions as a female writer, noting that her work transcends the narrow definitions of the so-called sex war, and speaks to all, men and women, who love, lose, know solitude, touch joy, fear death, and have the courage to look clearly at these things. Also reprints several of her poems.

Champlin, Charles. "Erica Jong, Still Flying Fearlessly." *Los Angeles Times* 16 May 1987: sec. 6: 1, 3.

This article discusses: her publicity tour for *Serenissima*, the possibility of filming *Fear of Flying*, her travels, her views on Shakespeare, the present situation for women writers, and her view of herself as a writer.

Crookston, Peter. "A Life in the Day of Erica Jong." *Sunday Times Magazine* 29 May 1983: 54.

Describes her writing day and relationships with her household staff and mentor.

Hopkins, Ellen. "Literary Lights: Erica Jong."*Harper's Bazaar* Aug. 1989: 73, 80.

Briefly describes Jong's career—her difficulties getting accepted, her financial success, and critical acceptance. Also describes her ability to finally accept her appearance, her feelings about being in her forties and knowing herself, and her ability to pursue her goals as a writer without succumbing to offers to do screenplays, lectures, or talk shows.

Krupp, Charla. "Erica Jong's Solution to the Man Shortage." *Glamour* Oct. 1983: 83, 319.

Briefly describes Jong's literary output, and traces her changing views about male-female relationships, particularly her belief that a relationship between equals is possible.

Laughridge, Jamie. "Erica Jong: The Survivor." *Harper's Bazaar* Aug. 1984: 197, 249.

Discusses Jong's divorce from Fast, her views on divorce, and her use of divorce and its aftermath in her new novel, *Parachutes & Kisses*.

Rosen, Richard. "Heirs to Maxwell Perkins." *Horizon* Apr. 1981: 50-53.

Includes Jong's own statement of her relationship with her editors Aaron Asher and Elaine Koster.

Toomey, Philippa. "From Rhyming Couplets to Sex, Satire and Success." *Times* 18 May 1977: 13.

An article based on an interview with Jong in which she talked about her life, her writing, and her views on critics. Says she is a poet who happens to write novels.

Toth, Emily. "Erica Jong." *Twentieth-Century American-Jewish Fiction Writers*. Ed. Daniel Walden. Detroit: Gale, 1984. Vol. 28 of *Dictionary of Literary Biography*. 94 vols. to date. 1978-. 111-16.

More than details of her life, this is a career biography, tracing the development of the author's canon, describing the contents and themes of her works, evaluating her reputation, and placing her in the larger context of American literary history. Includes a list of primary and secondary sources and illustrations.

Dissertations

Coker, Judith Briggs. "Sexuality in Discourse: Feminine Models in Recent Fiction by American Women." Diss. U of Oklahoma, 1986.

Steve Katz

1935 –

Primary Sources

Novels

The Exagggerations [sic] of Peter Prince. The New American Fiction Series 1. New York: Holt, 1968.

Florry of Washington Heights. Los Angeles: Sun & Moon, 1987; London: Serpent's Tail, 1988.

The Lestriad. Lecce: Milella, 1962; Flint: Bamberger, 1987.

Moving Parts. New York: Fiction Collective, 1977.

Posh. An Evergreen Black Cat Book. New York: Grove, 1971. Publ. under the pseudonym of Stephanie Gatos.

Saw. New York: Borzoi-Knopf, 1972; Berkeley: Small Press, 1972.

Wier & Pouce. The New American Fiction Series. Washington: Sun & Moon, 1984.

Collected Works

Creamy and Delicious; Eat My Words (in Other Words). New York: Random, 1970.

Contents: Satisfying Stories; Mythologies: Faust, Diana, Plastic Man, Hermes, Wonder Woman; In Our Thyme; Kelly; Mythologies: Thomas, Nasser, Goliath, Crane, Oedipus; Nino; Mythologies: Nancy & Sluggo, Gandhi, Dickens, Mandrake, Achilles; Haiku; Mythologies: Sampson, Poseidon, Danae, Apollo, Homer; Blossoms.

43 Fictions. New American Fiction Series 20. Los Angeles: Sun & Moon, 1991.

Contents: To be published June 1991.

Stolen Stories. New York: Fiction Collective, 1984.

Contents: The Perfect Life, Friendship, One on One, Mongolian Whiskey, Two Seaside Yarns, Two Essays, Smooth, Three Essays, Death of the Band, Bumpkin, Made of Wax, On Self Knowledge, The Stolen Stories.

Short Fiction in Anthologies

"Death of the Band." *Statements: New Fiction from the Fiction Collective*. Ed. Jonathan Baumbach. New York: Venture-Braziller, 1975. 119-32.

"Keeper." *Contemporary American Fiction*. Ed. Douglas Messerli. Washington: Sun & Moon, 1983. 285-315.

"Two Seaside Yarns." *Statements 2: New Fiction*. Eds. Jonathan Baumbach and Peter Spielberg. New York: Fiction Collective, 1977. 145-48.

Short Fiction in Periodicals

"Home-Cooked Meal for the Astronaut." *New American Review* 11 (1971): 144-60.

"Leroy." *Iowa Review* 4.1 (1970): 52-63.

"The Lestriad." *Chicago Review* 17.4 (1965): 5-45.

"On Hidden Blessings." *TriQuarterly* 35.1 (1976): 12-13.

"On the Difference Between the 60's and 70's." *TriQuarterly* 35.1 (1976): 13-14.

"Some Exaggerations of Peter Prince." *Chicago Review* 18.3/4 (1966): 111-41.

"The Sweet Salento, with Edmond Kulik, and Peter Stern Among the Woptimists." *Paris Review* 11.42 (1968): 139-56.

Secondary Sources

Articles and Chapters

Cornis-Pop, Marcel. "Inside a Stratified Whale: Melville's Textual Semiotics and the Postmodern Novel." *Semiotics 1985*. Ed. John N. Deely. Lanham: UP of America, 1986. 286-301.

Discusses Katz very briefly in a discussion about the continuities of experimental narrative technique between *Moby Dick* and postmodern fiction.

Cowley, Julian. "A Disintegrating Song: The Fiction of Steve Katz." *Critique* 27.3 (1986): 131-43.

Describes the key strategy of Katz's fiction as the playing of the equivalence of words as printed phenomena against their differentiated value as semantic units within our epistemological frameworks. An erudite and useful description both of *The Exagggerations of Peter Prince* and the technique of Katz's fictional universe generally.

Frankel, Haskel. "On the Fringe." *Saturday Review* 7 Sept. 1968: 34.

Not a review but an account of his discussion with Katz about the publication of *The Exagggerations of Peter Prince*. Describes the typographical experiments and their effects on the reader. Calls this a "Baedeker to Katz's typographical fiesta."

Glicksberg, Charles I. "Experimental Fiction: Innovation Versus Form."
   Centennial Review 18.2 (1974): 127-50.

In the context of a discussion of the experimental novel, which he sees as
becoming an experiment in language and intermingling with the essay,
philosophy and sociology in theme and narrative technique, Glicksberg
discusses the experimental techniques used by Katz in *The Exagggeration
of Peter Prince.* Concludes that the "verbal pyrotechnics are not enough
to save [it] from failure. The parts . . . do not cohere to form a meaningful,
aesthetically satisfying whole, but he ignores such 'artificial' standards."

Grant, J. Kerry. "Fiction and the Facts of Life: Steve Katz's *Moving
   Parts.*" *Critique* 24.4 (1983): 206-14.

A major philosophical essay on *Moving Parts* describing the experimental premises and methods on which the novel is based. Compares Katz's
techniques with those of several other experimental writers.

Gregory, Sinda J., and Larry McCaffery. "Steve Katz." *Dictionary of
   Literary Biography Yearbook: 1983.* Eds. Mary Bruccoli and Jean W.
   Ross. Detroit: Gale, 1984. 271-79.

Describes Katz's career and works in detail. Hails him as a writer whose
particular artistry rests with the force of his speculative powers to invent
codes for and contexts of experience unlike any we know, transforming
familiar ideas and a familiar world into strange, often funny, and highly
implausible ones.

Kawin, Bruce F. "The Mind of the Text." *The Mind of the Novel:
   Reflexive Fiction and the Ineffable.* Bruce F. Kawin. Princeton:
   Princeton UP, 1982. 246-51.

Claims that *The Exagggerations of Peter Prince* uses many of Sterne's
devices such as textual foregrounding, crossed out pages, parallel sub-
texts, announcements that certain vital transitions were not interesting
enough to write down, as well as having certain characters discuss the
novel in progress.

Klinkowitz, Jerome. "How Fiction Survives the Seventies." *North
   American Review* 258.3 (1973): 72.

Claims that Steve Katz experiments in this novel with fresh structural
devices to storytelling by using the device of a seducer who is actually a
sphere. Describes the central characters and some of the experimental
narrative method.

Klinkowitz, Jerome. Introduction. *The Self-Apparent Word: Form as Language/Language as Form*. Jerome Klinkowitz. Carbondale: Southern Illinois UP, 1984. 9-14.

Provides a fairly detailed treatment of Katz's experimental techniques in a variety of works.

Klinkowitz, Jerome. *The Life of Fiction*. Urbana: U of Illinois P, 1977. 104-15.

Begins with a biographical sketch of Katz. Proceeds with a piece about Katz done in experimental fashion in mimicry of his own style. Intersperses Katz's taped recorded material with commentary that functions like a rival fiction.

Klinkowitz, Jerome. Prologue. *Literary Disruptions: The Making of a Post-Contemporary American Fiction*. Urbana: U of Illinois P, 1975; 2nd ed. 1980. 18-20.

Calls *The Exagggerations of Peter Prince* a book that speaks to the humor moving from story to non-story in the heartbreaking impossibility of narrative. Concludes that, fortunately, Katz has more to write about than the impossibility of his own inability to write. But claims that, beyond a few bare facts, this story is untellable.

McCaffery, Larry. "The Fiction Collective." *Contemporary Literature* 19.1 (1978): 99-115.

Describes the publishing purposes of the Fiction Collective, its history, and its members. Primarily an historical essay describing a larger number of works published by the Collective, including those of Steve Katz.

McCaffery, Larry. "The Fiction Collective, 1974-1978: An Innovative Alternative." *Chicago Review* 30.1 (1978): 107-26.

Provides a justification for the formation of the Fiction Collective and its publication policy. Provides a series of letters from writers connected with it, suggesting the history of its evolution and its founding participants. Includes a letter from Steve Katz giving his thoughts that this collective is not a school of fiction, nor should it establish a new range of taste. Rather, he concludes, it should be an alternative outlet for work that would have a difficult time being accepted by other presses. Describes the difficulties of his own work, *Moving Parts*, and wishes the collective luck.

McCaffery, Larry. "Form, Formula, and Fantasy: Generative Approaches in Contemporary Fiction." *Bridges to Fantasy*. Eds. Eric Rabkin, Robert Scholes, and George Slusser. Carbondale: Southern Illinois UP, 1982. 30-32.

Claims that Katz explores the transformational possibilities of myth, and seeks to disrupt the myth's universality, fixated order, and immobilizing power by introducing new and disruptive elements into the system.

Reviews

Alexander, Michael. "A Bit of a Put-On, *Peter Prince* Is. . .Uh. . .Refreshing." Rev. of *The Exagggerations of Peter Prince. National Observer* 7 Oct. 1968: 23.

Considers *The Exagggerations of Peter Prince* gotten up in a hokey pop-arty volume, and appearing to be terribly experimental beneath its layers of simultaneous action, interjections, and carefully crossed out pages. Calls this a funny and refreshing book, that is if you are turned off on old-fashioned, four-square, characters-and-plot sorts of novels.

Baumbach, Jonathan. Rev. of *Creamy and Delicious: Eat My Words (in Other Words). Saturday Review* 10 Oct. 1970: 34.

Calls *Creamy and Delicious* a far-out, abrasively funny series of punning and self-mocking short fictions. Concludes that these stories share much common ground with Borges, Burroughs, Barthleme, and Coover.

Blackburn, Sara. "Book Marks." Rev. of *The Exagggerations of Peter Prince. Nation* 23 Sept. 1968: 286.

Argues that, while Katz might be a good writer, it is hard to tell from the *The Exagggerations of Peter Prince* which is an exceedingly vacant novel with intentionally comic strip characters. Concludes that it is all too carefully zany.

Brickner, Richard P. "Romeo and Juliet of Upper Manhattan." Rev. of *Florry of Washington Heights. New York Times Book Review* 19 July 1987: 6.

Describes *Florry of Washington Heights* as innovative, even though this novel he considers a throwback—a talented, stylistically accomplished, conventional example from a genre whose grandfather is Studs Lonigan. Argues that, in this novel, Katz has written beautifully of a neighborhood and a period, but, being such a traditional novel, he has written with less effect than he might have done.

Cassill, R. V. "Shards, Ligatures and Lumps." Rev. of *The Exagggerations of Peter Prince. New York Times Book Review* 8 Sept. 1968: 4.

Calls *The Exagggerations of Peter Prince* a book which has scrambled all the conventions prevailing among both novelists and typesetters. Describes these scrambled conventions in detail.

"Fiction Forecasts." Rev. of *Creamy and Delicious: Eat My Words (in Other Words). Publishers Weekly* 4 May 1970: 59.

Argues that much of *Creamy and Delicious* is devoted to mythologies, half-humorous, half-horrifying, and occasionally political about everyone from Homer to Mandrake, to Wonder Woman. Claims that, on the whole, the stories lack development, no matter how much you like experimental fiction. Concludes that it is hard to get over the ill-conceived shifts, false drama, and abrupt endings of these tales.

"Fiction Forecasts." Rev. of *Saw. Publishers Weekly* 17 July 1972: 113.

Describes *Saw* as told from the perspective of a sphere and covering such subjects as sex, violence, rallies, and poverty. Finally devolves into random anecdotes.

Halliday, Bob. "Meetings by Chance." Rev. of *Wier and Pouce. Washington Post Book World* 7 Apr. 1985: 9.

Argues that *Weir and Pouce* is not a whimsical exercise in word play, but a work of power and imagination. Shows how it is made of a dozen interlocking tales which have the aura of dream and are astonishingly imaginative. Concludes that the book is vastly readable in spite of its complexity, and full of emotional wallop.

Levin, Martin. "New & Novel." Rev. of *Saw. New York Times Book Review* 1 Oct. 1972: 42.

Considers *Saw* full of loose-jointed episodes and witty fantasy. Describes plot briefly.

McHale, Brian. "Unmaking the Well-Made Short Story/ Making Up the Novel." Rev. of *Stolen Stories. American Book Review* Nov.-Dec. 1985: 17-18.

Argues that Katz has brought in wrecking tools, dismantled the traditional short story, and left behind something just as satisfying and much harder to describe. Describes the contents of several stories and their experimental methods.

Mobilio, Albert. "Brief Encounters." Rev. of *Weir and Pouce*. *Village Voice Literary Supplement* Apr. 1985: 3.

Describes the fictional methods, style, contents, and effects of *Weir and Pouce*. Concludes that this book is a tribute to pure invention and imagination in literature.

Pjerrou, Mary. "1985 Answer to *War and Peace*." Rev. of *Weir and Pouce*. *Los Angeles Times Book Review* 6 Jan. 1985: 4.

Argues that *Weir and Pouce* is so full of tricks it seems post, post, post Joycean. Finds it perversely defeats our interest in old-fashioned humanity, and winds us into a maze of dissatisfactions, grotesqueries, and other horrors. Concludes that this book is claustrophobic and unreadable, but still quite interesting.

Plate, Thomas Gordon. "Tell Us a Story." Rev. of *The Exagggerations of Peter Prince*. *Newsweek* 9 Sept. 1968: 89, 92.

Describes *The Exagggerations of Peter Prince* as a prophetic work which tries to be an anti-book. Calls this the non-novel of non-novels. Describes the unconventional typography of the text and its experimental methods.

Press, D. Paul. "Reviews." Rev. of *Moving Parts*. *Studies in Short Fiction* 16.1 (1979): 82-83.

Argues that *Moving Parts* fluctuates between hard-core fantasy and untampered chronicle, skipping completely over the middle ground of selective-detail realism. A small but compact critical essay detailing contents.

Pritchard, William H. "Reviews." Rev. of *The Exagggerations of Peter Prince*. *Kenyon Review* 30.5 (1968): 685-86.

Calls *The Exagggerations of Peter Prince* remarkable. Describes its visual and other effects on the reader and some of its experimental techniques.

Quammen, David. "Of Cannibals, Paid Vacations and Talking Dogs." Rev. of *Stolen Stories*. *New York Times Book Review* 9 Sept. 1984: 9.

Claims that *Stolen Stories* ventures out beyond the conventions of style into bare, disembodied monologues, and other flashes of relaxed wit. Argues that some are even accessible and perhaps thereby dull. Details several of the pieces.

Salmonson, Jessica Amanda. "Three Magic Realists." Rev. of *Stolen Stories*. *Fantasy Review* Feb. 1986: 24-25.

Comments that *Stolen Stories* portrays characters who satirize American customs and sexual mores as though we are exotics. Concludes that, on the surface, the theme represents adolescent men's obsessions, but on close examination such themes become psychologically complex, sparkling, and imaginative.

Stephens, Michael. Rev. of *Moving Parts*. *American Book Review* Dec.-Jan. 1978-79: 5.

Discusses *Moving Parts* within the context of Katz's earlier works, dealing with content, experimental style, characters, and general effects. Concludes that, like Rimbaud, Katz was formed of "ice and polar night—hurt, hurting, loved, loving, a contentious knight of Hope out to do battle with the toothless electronic Dragon of Commerce."

Wallenstein, Barry. "On the Edge of Chaos." Rev. of *The Exagggerations of Peter Prince*. *Catholic World* Sept. 1968: 281-82.

Calls this a novel with a hippy ambiance that delights in photos, concrete poetry, different type sizes, marginalia, and other such experimental techniques.

Interviews

McCaffery, Larry. "An Interview with Steve Katz." *Anything Can Happen: Interviews with Contemporary American Novelists*. Eds. Tom LeClair and Larry McCaffery. Urbana: U of Illinois P, 1983. 219-34.

Katz discusses: his reasons for writing, his innovative forms, publishing history, poetry writing, search for identity, stylistic methods, similarities to Sukenick, other influences, experimental methods, the Fiction Collective, experiments in other media, his pornography novel, and his definition of art.

Dissertations

Karfiol, Judith. "New American Fiction and the Aesthetics of Camus and Robbe-Grillet." Diss. U of Southern California, 1978.

Robert Kotlowitz
1924 –

Primary Sources

Novels

The Boardwalk. New York: Borozi-Knopf, 1977.

Sea Changes. San Francisco: North Point, 1986.

Somewhere Else. New York: Charterhouse, 1972; London: Gollancz, 1973; New York: Dell, 1974.

Secondary Sources

Articles and Chapters

Berger, Alan L. "Judaism as a Secular Value System." *Crisis and Covenant: The Holocaust in American Jewish Fiction.* SUNY Series in Modern Jewish Literature and Culture. Albany: New York State UP, 1985. 144-49.

Describes Kotlowitz's upbringing and attitudes toward Jewish identity. Discusses *The Boardwalk* as a portrayal of the conflict between covenant history in terms of the struggle for the allegiance of fourteen-year-old Teddy Lewin. Describes it as a critique of American Jewry on the eve of the Holocaust laying bare the religious and social rifts.

Kotlowitz, Robert. "The Astonishing Life of a Jewish Novel." *Congress Bi-Weekly* 26 Oct. 1973: 15-18.

Contains the text of Kotlowitz's acceptance remarks for the 1972 Edward Lewis Wallant Memorial Book Award for his novel *Somewhere Else*.

Kotlowitz, Robert. "The Making of a Jewish Novel." *Jewish Digest* May 1974: 41-45.

Traces his own "peculiar post" in an attempt to find the appropriate subject matter for a Jewish novel. Repeats much of the material in his essay "On Being A Jewish Writer."

Kotlowitz, Robert. "On Being a Jewish Writer." *Jewish Heritage* 15.3 (1973): 15-17.

A major personal essay on the subject of being a Jew and a writer in America. Mostly personal anecdote.

Reviews

Aberbach, David. Rev. of *Somewhere Else*. *European Judaism* 9 (1974-75): 43-45.

Argues that *Somewhere Else*, though sincere and genuinely engrossing, seems to lack the overall texture of realism that other Jewish writers in the United States achieve so well. Describes the story as about alienation with the narrative and characterization being both terse and fascinating. Provides a lengthy description of contents, and concludes that, despite its tragic end, the novel is a full-blooded affirmation of the beauty inherent in human relationships.

Bell, Pearl K. "Sad in Greenwich Village, Glad in Atlantic City." Rev. of *The Boardwalk*. *New York Times Book Review* 9 Jan. 1977: 8.

Calls *The Boardwalk* a deeply affectionate celebration of the ordinariness of adolescence. Provides an elaborate plot summary of Teddy Lewin's doings in the novel.

Bell, Pearl K. "Understanding the Past." Rev. of *Somewhere Else*. *New Leader* 13 Nov. 1972: 14-15.

Describes *Somewhere Else* as a unique and beautifully authentic re-creation of a Jewish life in the small Polish town of Lomza in the nineteenth and twentieth centuries. Claims that Kotlowitz attempts a loving and sharply attentive verisimilitude free from the distorting blur of synthetic nostalgia.

Garmel, Marion Simon. "In *Somewhere Else*, One Dreamer Dreams of Another." Rev. of *Somewhere Else*. *National Observer* 18 Nov. 1972: 29.

States that Robert Kotlowitz is a fine dreamer. Considers *Somewhere Else* pieced together from tales told over the dinner table, snatched from key-holes, overheard at a cousin's wedding. Concludes, that with this first novel, it would appear that Kotlowitz is a major talent. Details the contents.

Goldreich, Gloria. "Fiction for Summer Reading." Rev. of *Somewhere Else*. *Hadassah Magazine* June 1973: 21.

Considers *Somewhere Else* a stunning new novel which captures the life of the *shetl* and the essence of cosmopolitan London as it concerns itself with the genesis of modern Jewish life. Concludes that this book re-creates the life that vanished with precision of detail, tenderness of nuance, and rare insight into how it was lived.

Hendin, Josephine. "New Characters: Caring, Needing, Dreaming, Abusing." Rev. of *Somewhere Else*. *New York Times Book Review* 5 Nov. 1972: 4.

Calls *Somewhere Else* a first novel of tense, dry brilliance remarkable for the immensity of its scope and the individual power of its characters. Details the plot and characters, and comments on the merciless realism of the book. Considers this a bitter, beautiful, and unsentimental book.

Lask, Thomas. "The Choice of the Way." Rev. of *Somewhere Else*. *New York Times* 18 Nov. 1972: 35.

Describes *Somewhere Else* mostly in terms of its contents. Concludes that the world of the *shetl* is convincingly portrayed, especially its sights, smells, and physical aspects. But believes the desire to portray the *shetl* unsentimentally emphasizes its repellent aspects and downplays the sweetness of its religious life. Claims that behind its genre trappings this is a thesis novel, but considers it still a work of art.

Lingeman, Richard R. "Holding on at the Beach." Rev. of *The Boardwalk*. *New York Times* 9 Mar. 1977: 25C.

Calls *The Boardwalk* a flawlessly conceived and shaped novel full of life's resonances about classic family events and rites of passage. Provides a brief plot summary.

Maloff, Saul. Rev. of *The Boardwalk. New Republic* 15 Jan. 1977: 31-32.

Argues that *The Boardwalk* stands directly and unabashedly in what is now the antique tradition of the Jewish family novel. Describes the central characters, the time, and the setting in Atlantic City. Claims that this book is poised uneasily between memoir and fiction, yet completely domesticates the imagination, creating massive problems for the writer who comes in its wake, lest reality can be dislodged from the terms in which it has been set in this novel.

Merkin, Daphne. "Looking Back." Rev. of *The Boardwalk. Commentary* July 1977: 63-65.

Describes the contents of *Somewhere Else* and then turns to *The Boardwalk*. Calls the latter a consistently intelligent and attentive novel done in a plaintive, subdued mood. Locates its most serious flaw in its use of a teenage protagonist. Concedes that the novel is an effective and moving rendition of the process of coming to terms with the burden of mature consciousness, and is, ultimately, an admirable book.

Murray, Michele. "Old Wine in a Bright New Bottle." Rev. of *Somewhere Else. Washington Post Book World* 12 Nov. 1972: 4, 10.

Argues that *Somewhere Else* makes fresh and palatable the now familiar tale of the Jewish life of Poland and the young man from the provinces in search of experience. Considers it the story of the break-up of the *shetl* life and the impact of modern ideas. Claims that Kotlowitz does it better than Singer does in *The Manor*. Praises the narrative, the characterization, the picaresque qualities of the book, and its strongly intelligent treatment of the whole subject.

Oberbeck, S. K. "Out of the Ghetto." Rev. of *Somewhere Else. Newsweek* 13 Nov. 1972: 108.

Describes *Out of the Ghetto* as a mini-saga and a quietly swirling social history with loads of ethnic nuance pertaining to the Jewish ghetto as a European world crumbles into conflict.

Pinsker, Sanford. "New Fiction/ Old Orders." Rev. of *The Boardwalk* and *Somewhere Else. Jewish Spectator* 42.3 (1977): 29-30.

Describes *The Boardwalk* and *Somewhere Else* as sharply realistic pictures of East European Jewry, which both accumulate weight of detail of ordinary things, and seem rather Victorian in mode. Provides a detailed description of the contents of both books.

"Plain Living." Rev. of *Somewhere Else. Times Literary Supplement* 21 Dec. 1973: 1557.

Describes *Somewhere Else* as about ingrowing Jewishness as both warmth and prison. Finds Kotlowitz a luminous writer who manages his canvas expertly, but whose double-edged piety spills over to infect the book itself, which thus becomes splendid and stifling. Details the story, and describes Mendel, the main character.

Ribalow, Harold U. "Unsentimental Journey." Rev. of *The Boardwalk. Congress Monthly* Feb. 1977: 19-20.

States that *The Boardwalk* is better than most Jewish adolescent novels because Kotlowitz writes with loving care, artistic detail, and sentimentality. Details the contents, and concludes that this is a quiet, disciplined slice of Jewish-American social history.

Rubin, Merle. "Fiction Roundup: New Novels by Kotlowitz, Gray, and Moore." Rev. of *Sea Changes. Christian Science Monitor* 28 Nov. 1986: 34.

Sees *Sea Changes* as about dislocation, rites of passage into a violent adult world, and metamorphosis. Argues that much of the setting is described with convincing fidelity to atmosphere and detail.

Spaulding, Martha. "Short Reviews." Rev. of *The Boardwalk. Atlantic Monthly* Feb. 1977: 96-97.

Comments that *The Boardwalk* is an artful recreation of the tinny pomp of Atlantic City and its lazy assault on the senses. Briefly describes contents.

Stern, David. "Odyssey of a Jew." Rev. of *Somewhere Else. Commentary* Jan. 1973: 102-03.

Calls the story of *Somewhere Else* commonplace, but sees that through his aesthetic distance and rare mastery of the novelist's craft, Kotlowitz transforms the commonplace into a novel uncommon for its elegance and honesty. Calls the re-creation of the Lomza *shetl* remarkable. Details the plot and characters.

Straub, Peter. "One More for the Road." Rev. of *Somewhere Else. New Statesman* 23 Nov. 1973: 782.

Argues that *Somewhere Else* is a Kerouac-type novel, seeming random, unfocused, and overly long. States that it could have been a deft, telling novel about its hero's inability to engage deeply with life and with others, but its theme is too slender to carry off the writer's tendency to doze off into the interior thoughts of every minor and incidental character. Concludes that it is a flat book.

Temple, Joanne. "Choosing the Chosen People." Rev. of *Somewhere Else*. *Village Voice* 24 May 1973: 24-25.

Describes *Somewhere Else* in terms of its contents, and then places it in a context of Jewish thought and politics. Provides both a description of contents and a commentary of socio-political attitudes. Commends both the quiet lustre of the style, and the ethnic humanism of the book.

Yardley, Jonathan. "The Americanization of Manfred Vogel." Rev. of *Sea Changes*. *Washington Post Book World* 30 Nov. 1986: 3.

Sees *Sea Changes* as about the Americanization of Manfred Vogel, and as a tale told with sympathy, compassion, and a wonderfully observant eye for the nuances of pre-war adolescent life, for the topography, both physical and social, of a Baltimore long since disappeared. Discusses characters, themes, and geography of the novel, and concludes that it is a small world with everything in it just about right.

Interviews

Bosworth, Patricia. "PW Interviews Robert Kotlowitz." *Publishers Weekly* 18 Dec. 1972: 8-9.

A mixture of first-person statements by Kotlowitz, and questions by Bosworth. Kotlowitz comments on the scope and power of his *Somewhere Else*, his early life, the incentive for his writing about himself, and the creative process which possesses him.

Ribalow, Harold U. "A Conversation with Robert Kotlowitz." Harold U. Ribalow. *The Tie That Binds: Conversations with Jewish Writers*. San Diego: Barnes, 1980. 95-109; London: Tantivy, 1980. 95-109.

In this interview Kotlowitz discusses: his writing career; his background as a Polish Jew; the biographical element of *Somewhere Else;* Charles Angoff's novels; David Miller; his depiction of powerful women; his ties to Baltimore, Zionism, Israel, and Jewishness; his personal reading; and his job as a television programmer.

Alan Lelchuk

1938 –

Primary Sources

Novels

American Mischief. New York: Farrar, 1973; London: Cape, 1973; New York: Signet-NAL, 1974; London: Quartet, 1975; New York: McGraw, 1990.

Brooklyn Boy. New York: McGraw, 1990.

Miriam at Thirty-Four. New York: Farrar, 1974; New York: Signet-NAL, 1975; London: Cape, 1975; New York: McGraw, 1990.

Miriam in Her Forties: The Further Adventures of Miriam. New York: Houghton, 1985; New York: McGraw, 1990.

On Home Ground. San Diego: Gulliver-Harcourt, 1987.

Shrinking: The Beginning of My Own Ending. An Atlantic Monthly Press Book. Boston: Little, 1978; New York: NAL, 1979.

Short Fiction in Periodicals

"Cambridge Talk." *Modern Occasions* 1 (Fall 1970): pag. not available.

"The Doctor's Holiday." *Atlantic* Mar. 1981: 73-82.

"Of Our Time." *New American Review* 4 (1968): 215-64.

"Sundays." *Transatlantic Review* 21 (1966): 141-53.

"Winter Image." *Transatlantic Review* 32 (1969): 114-29.

Secondary Sources

Articles and Chapters

Barasch, Frances K. "Faculty Images in Recent American Fiction."
   College Literature 10.1 (1983): 28-37.

Describes American professors depicted in contemporary fiction as over-
sexed, white, male neurotics who are probably Jewish. Deals with a
whole series of these novels, and then provides some careful critical
insights into *Shrinking* as one of this genre.

Hindus, Milton. "The Case of *American Mischief. Midstream* Sept. 1973:
   65-71.

Defends his colleague, Lelchuk, against the generally negative reviews
he received for his novel, *American Mischief*, by pointing out that he is
not his characters from the novel, although he has superficial similarities
with both Kovell and Pincus. But he is mature, sane, and has a sense of
humor. Hindus then reviews the reviews written about this novel that
have appeared in over a dozen sources, and concludes that Lelchuk has
aspired to "art" not "official art," and has produced a tour de force that
"shows significant promise for the future of literature in America."

Roth, Philip. "Alan Lelchuk." *Esquire* Oct. 1972: 133, 198. Rpt. as
   "Imagining the Erotic: Three Introductions. 1. Alan Lelchuk" in
   Reading Myself and Others. Philip Roth. New York: Farrar, 1975.
   195-200.

A lengthy exposition of the contents of the book, its cultural roots, style,
and effects.

Reviews

Ackroyd, Peter. "Natural Wonder." Rev. of *Miriam at Thirty-Four*. *Spectator* 7 June 1975: 692.

Describes *Miriam at Thirty-Four* as a cliche story of the American divorcee ceased to be interesting. Claims that everything has gone in indiscriminately, and that sheer content usurps the claims of style. Complains that there is also something embarrassingly coy about the frankness over sex and the ease with which people are supposed to relate.

Altbach, Philip G. "Faculty Wives." Rev. of *Miriam at Thirty-Four*. *Progressive* Apr. 1975: 43-44.

Discusses Lelchuk's *Miriam at Thirty-Four* and Laurie's *The War Between the Tates* as good examples of a rash of academic novels that have appeared in recent years, raising questions about whether all professors are maladjusted, all female graduate students bent on seducing male professors, and whether all professors ever do is jump in and out of bed. Concludes that, while these novels paint a distorted picture of campus life and are not good books, they are good reading and contain enough truth about campus life to be worthwhile.

Bell, Pearl K. "The Porn Is Green." Rev. of *American Mischief*. *New Leader* 22 Jan. 1973: 15-16.

Comments that *American Mischief* is neither brilliant nor original, merely spuriously topical. Claims that updating the events of 1968 to 1972 merely increases rather than updates the literal credibility of the narrative. Considers the political fantasies merely window dressing for a different intent—nasty, brutish pornography. Calls this a gleefully personal and infantile vision which mocks and degrades establishment intellectuals, and claims it is an attempt to even the score with the intellectual elite Lelchuk so bitterly resents and envies.

Blackburn, Sara. "The Loves in Her Life." Rev. of *Miriam at Thirty-Four*. *New York Times Book Review* 17 Nov. 1974: 50.

Describes the liberated female protagonist and her sexual experiences that lead ultimately to a profound punishment and humiliation. Objects to Lelchuk's depending on the readers' "recognition of up-to-the-minute cultural and political trappings instead of developing character or plot," the punishment the character gets despite Lelchuk's assurance that she has a right to her own sexuality, and, finally, to his sensationalizing and trivializing the character and culture he is trying to illuminate.

Broyard, Anatole. "Betting Your Life on You." Rev. of *Miriam at Thirty-Four. New York Times* 13 Nov. 1974: 41.

Calls *Miriam at Thirty-Four* a drastic and original portrait of a woman running for her life—from what she was to what she might be. Details the contents, and agrees that, had this book of female liberation-to-pursue-self been written by a woman, it would have been hailed as a feminist novel and highly praised.

Caplan, Brina. "Rigged Systems, Special Pleas." Rev. of *Shrinking. Nation* 1 July 1978: 22-23.

Sees *Shrinking* as a book containing over 500 pages of special pleading to be let alone by critics. Claims it borrows public figures for self-conscious demonstrations of power, and that, behind it all, the modern novel is being discussed along with its critics. Concludes that characters do not matter in themselves, and that the energy of *Shrinking* is devoted to gimmickry.

Chernaik, Judith. "American Fiction - II." Rev. of *Miriam at Thirty-Four. London Magazine* Oct./Nov. 1975: 117-18.

Describes the plot and characters of *Miriam at Thirty-Four*, and concludes that it is all plausible enough, but none of it has much reality beyond the surface fidelity to facts—street names, radio stations, phonographic records, reflections on life, and other topical matters.

Clemons, Walter. "Murdering Mailer." Rev. of *American Mischief. Newsweek* 12 Feb. 1973: 90.

Calls *American Mischief* a 138-page sexual confession that is more fun to hear about than to read. Complains the Mailer murder is implausible, the up-to-the-minute dating has an opportunistic look, and a ramshackle confusion of purpose sinks the novel's final section. Concludes that Lelchuk seems to have no higher mischief in mind than to make a splash and a bundle.

Cook, Bruce. "Books." Rev. of *American Mischief. Commonweal* 13 Apr. 1973: 142-43.

Sees *American Mischief* as breathtakingly bad, and a kind of sustained power fantasy in which violence and sexuality are presented purely as modes of dominance. Notes most of the women to whom we are introduced are mere shadows, fantasy figures without personality, reality, or individuation. Concludes that this book is so totally crude in its sexual chauvinism it would probably convert William F. Buckley to the cause of women's liberation.

Crain, Jane Larkin. "New Books." Rev. of *Miriam at Thirty-Four.*
   Saturday Review World 16 Nov. 1974: 26.

Describes the contents of *Miriam at Thirty-Four* and notes that
Lelchuk's fantasies notwithstanding, "it is unlikely that this novel will
provoke much outrage; a lot of it is, in fact, 'dirty,' but it is rather ridiculous for him to intimate that sex scenes could raise eyebrows—let alone
inspire puritanical fury—in 1974."

Crinklaw, Don. "Seventies Mischief." Rev. of *American Mischief.*
   National Review 13 Apr. 1973: 427-28.

Calls *American Mischief* a noisy, overlong, lurching, and fitfully interesting book. Details the contents and concludes that Pincus eludes Lelchuk
as a character because he doesn't understand anarchists much better than
the rest of us do and really doesn't like him.

Davis, L. J. "Academic Mischief." Rev. of *Shrinking: The Beginning of
   My Own Ending. Washington Post Book World* 4 June 1978: E5.

Describes *Shrinking* as an academic novel which is probably as good as
that form gets. Admires Lelchuk's ambition, and lists many of the situations, obsessions, and characters. Sees some of the stylistic devices as
dated and quaint.

DeMott, Benjamin. "The Significant Self." Rev. of *Miriam at Thirty-
   Four. Atlantic Monthly* Oct. 1974: 104-06.

Describes *Miriam at Thirty-Four* in great detail in this review essay.
Comments that dignifying the central protagonist's challenge to orthodoxy probably won't enable the author to escape censure in *Ms,* whether
for reducing the women's movement to a gesture on behalf of sexual
licence, or for failing to condemn a context of adaptation to norms of
familial and social participation. Considers this a clear headed and serious book about serious things. A lengthy and useful essay.

Epstein, Joseph. "General Ideas and Great Conceit." Rev. of *American
   Mischief. Washington Post Book World* 11 Feb. 1973: 3, 8-9.

Begins by discussing some of the reactions to the novel by those, such as
Philip Roth, who want to praise it in spite of its faults, and by Mailer,
who wanted the scene describing his humiliating death expunged.
Describes its subject as "the wild scrambling of values—sexual, political, ethical, social—that occurred in the mid 1960s. Also describes the
two major characters, the weak organization, and its supposed "wittily

pornographic style." Asserts that it is as "botched a piece of literature as has come along in some while," and that "if the novel really does die, it will be the novelists who have killed it off" as Lelchuk has killed this one by "choosing the flashy over the serious, by inept craft, and by a narrow vision both of the novel's possibilities and of life itself."

Frank, Sheldon. "Behind the Ballyhoo, a Downhill Slide." Rev. of *American Mischief. National Observer* 10 Feb. 1973: 25.

Notes that *American Mischief* is much touted as a brilliant first novel, but questions how much of that is true. Describes its first third as superb, but then demonstrates a steady downhill slide interrupted by occasional pages of genuine power as Lelchuk moves from what he really knows to merely showing off. Complains it finally trails off into apocalyptic blather. Describes each of these sections of the novel, and concludes that, when Lelchuk leaves safe ground, his prose becomes forced and his characters become puppets.

Fremont-Smith, Eliot. "A Trashing Bore." Rev. of *American Mischief. Saturday Review* 17 Feb. 1973: 75-77.

Details the pre-publishing hooplah that preceded the appearance of *American Mischief* in very disgruntled fashion. Comments that the book has genuine literary and intellectual quality but that there are chinks in Lelchuk's sparkling armor. Sees chunks of it as unreadable despite its brilliance. Describes the plot and characters and criticizes the amount of sex and violence needed to flesh it all out. Concludes, finally, that the book is mostly a publishing phenomenon.

Hochswender, William J. "The Life of a Boy of Summer." Rev. of *On Home Ground. Los Angeles Times Book Review* 27 Mar. 1988: 8.

Sees *On Home Ground* as a short, sweet novel for young adults, full of misty nostalgia nicely captured in a series of illustrations. Briefly describes contents.

Jacobson, Mark. "Children's Books." Rev. of *On Home Ground. New York Times Book Review* 14 Feb. 1988: 25.

Argues that *On Home Ground* was written for children, and exudes postwar Brooklyn in a fable-like manner. Calls the prose clear-visioned, and notes it raises contemporary questions for its young readers, therefore achieving a success far beyond an exercise in baseball and nostalgia.

Kazin, Alfred. Rev. of *American Mischief. New York Times Book Review*
11 Feb. 1973: 2-3.

Finds the first 164 pages, written as sexual memoir by a college dean,
"spicier than anything Timothy Leary could have brought back from the
spiritworld," but boring. The second part, however, about the student
activist, Lenny Pincus, who has been brought up on novels, is lively and
provocative because the author loves him even if he doesn't know what
to do with him. Considers this novel ultimately to be not about the conflict between fiction and reality, but about fiction and fame, about the
"love-hate toward 'established' writers."

Kreiger, Barbara. "The Jewish Literary Hero: Political Transformation in
America." Rev. of *American Mischief. Response* 7.2 (1973): 131-38.

Describes the particular view of history, the politics, and the characters
in *American Mischief.* Details the biographical background of the central
character, Pincus, and his complex relationship with his father. Considers
the book a forceful portrayal of violence and sex which will be offensive
to some, but argues this is not a particularly Jewish novel because the
characters break the Jewish tradition. Concludes, however, that we are
witnessing a revolution in Jewish thinking and literature.

Lehmann-Haupt, Christopher. "An All-American Fizzle." Rev. of
American Mischief. New York Times 24 Jan. 1973: 39.

Calls *American Mischief* a comic nightmare, or a black comedy. Claims
that Lelchuk may never have worked out a clear relationship to his subject, and that the book is finally about everything and nothing at all.
Details the contents with some sarcasm, and concludes that the only
incentive in this book is to find out what it is all about—not much rec-
ommendation at all.

Leonard, John. "Books of the Times." Rev. of *Shrinking: The Beginning
of My Own Ending. New York Times* 8 May 1978: C16.

Describes the contents and characters in *Shrinking,* and complains that
this is another novel about novels full of a twitching and facetious "I"
and the seethings of the subconscious. Finds a great deal of tedium,
much extreme subjectivity, and a general careening from a comedy of literary manners to a seriousness so earnest, nervous and defensive you
want to give Lelchuk a calming lollipop. Concludes that this novel is too
clever and too feverish.

Mahon, Derek. "Mr. Alabama." Rev. of *American Mischief. Listener* 21 June 1973: 840.

Describes *American Mischief* in terms of content and characters. Considers Lenny a good portrait, if not a nice character. Calls the book an interesting and frequently pretentious extravaganza based on a very particular kind of American university.

Mudrick, Marvin. "Reviews." Rev. of *American Mischief. Hudson Review* 26.3 (1973): 548-49.

Describes *American Mischief* as a book teeming with irony, ambiguity, paradox, and bad writing. Concludes that it aspires to be the thinking man's *Johnathan Livingstone Seagull,* but turns into another kiddie book of monsters.

"Notes On Current Books: Fiction." Rev. of *American Mischief. Virginia Quarterly Review* 49.2 (1973): lvi.

Argues that *American Mischief* is licentious, and quickly loses its piquancy due to stale, exploited material and messages that no longer apply. Claims that prolixity plagues the author and wearies the reader.

O'Malley, Michael. "Books." Rev. of *American Mischief. Critic* May-June 1973: 65-67.

Complains that this novel is a bedlam, an outcry, an unleashed storm unashamedly Dostoevskyan in character, pitch, and purpose. Details the plot and characters, and concludes that this is a literary event of the first importance because Lelchuk is adept, cool, crystalline in intensity, and always powerful.

Pochoda, Elizabeth Turner. "The Oldest Story Ever Told." Rev. of *Miriam at Thirty-Four. Ms.* Apr. 1975: 118, 20.

Calls Lelchuk the up-and-coming chronicler of our cultural fancies. Describes contents and concludes that the style is lumpy, the background information delivered in parentheses near people's names, and the sexual language "soiled" like "the cue lines in someone's jerk-off book." Finally accuses Lelchuk of expending a great deal of energy in this portrait of a woman without ever establishing fictional roots which will allow his ideas to take hold.

"The Portable Sin." Rev. of *American Mischief. Times Literary Supplement* 1 June 1973: 605.

Argues that *American Mischief* is a noisy, engaged, and stimulating novel centering on the psychopathology of student protest and revolutionary millennialism.

Pritchard, William H. "Telling Stories."Rev. of *Shrinking: The Beginning of My Own Ending. Hudson Review* 31.3 (1978): 518-19.

Describes the story briefly and compares the protagonist, Lionel, a novelist and literature professor, to Lelchuk. Suggests that the novel is about the consequences of confusing literature with life: "you go to pieces, but with some memorable times along the way." Finds the novel full of "emotional overkill" along with "intelligence, passion, and clarity of seeing."

Sale, Roger. "American Fiction in 1973." Rev. of *American Mischief. Massachusetts Review* 14.4 (1973): 835-36.

Calls Lelchuk as mindless, gaudy, and violent as the current experimental mode, and driven by a simple, brutal energy.

Sale, Roger. "A Dirty Dean and a Brazen Head." Rev. of *American Mischief. New York Review of Books* 8 Feb. 1973: 21.

Compares the novel to the State Farm Insurance ad depicting life in a small American town, finding both merely fantasies despite the attempts of the ad agency and the novelist to make their depictions seem real. Describes the story in detail and faults it for trying to "confront us with the moral dilemma when in fact he is giving us only a crude political choice" and for having "no life of its own, only to repulse or excite or frighten its readers."

Schickel, Richard. "Tailing Mailer and Other Literary Mischief." Rev. of *American Mischief. World* 13 Feb. 1973: 49-50.

Comments on the scandalous notoriety that *American Mischief* achieved before its publication. Discusses the scandal at the center of the novel, its style, relationship to living people, and thematic concerns. Concludes that Lelchuk's talent is miniscule for all his straining to produce a major work. Accuses him of having a bad ear that betrays his breeding.

Shem, Samuel. "Setting Her Sights on Herself." Rev. of *Miriam in Her Forties. New York Times Book Review* 3 Nov. 1985: 15.

Sees *Miriam in Her Forties* as a convergent close-up study of three months in the life of Miriam Sheinman. Suggests that this is a dense, fine-grained, and trenchant slide show of modern life. Concludes that Lelchuk is a writer of intelligence, sexual sensibility, and drive.

Sheppard, R. Z. "Heckzapoppin." Rev. of *American Mischief. Time* 26
  Feb. 1973: 94.

Argues that *American Mischief* is the novel in which Norman Mailer is
shot to death and in which the author seems to want to satirize the visceral and cultural preoccupations of liberal intellectuals in the 1960s.
Claims that, lacking an authentic bite, it winds up proving only that
Lelchuk is one of the fastest lips in the East.

Sissman, L. E. "Most Distressful Nations." Rev. of *American Mischief.*
  New Yorker 7 Apr. 1973: 147-50.

Calls Lelchuk an anointed novelist. Provides an elaborate account of the
zany episodes and contents of *American Mischief*. Doubts, however, that
Lelchuk has a serious purpose since so many of his narrators take such
pleasure in shocking the reader. Notes also the book is awash in little
nagging inaccuracies that undermine the narrative. Concludes that
Lelchuk is not untalented, but he has not been served well by his pro-
posers, seconders, and editors.

Spitz, Robert Stephen. "Books in Brief." Rev. of *Shrinking: The
  Beginning of My Own Ending. Saturday Review* 24 June 1978: 35.

Calls *Shrinking* a discordant study of one man's madness orchestrated by
greed and desire. Argues that, written in the form of a spiritual purge, the
book is a self-analytic discourse on the endurance of man, the capitaliza-
tion of society, middle age, and the death of literature.

Stade, George. "The Realities of Fiction and the Fiction of Reality." Rev.
  of *American Mischief. Harper's* May 1973: 94-95.

Comments that *American Mischief* is not a book restrained by any
recipes of prescriptive realism. Calls the book 500 pages of unremitting
explicitness and tendentious detail, but for all the recipes of realism it
reads like pure fantasy. Details the contents and concludes that it is precisely the uncanny world of multiple realities represented in the work of
modernist writers that protects us from being conned or bullied by the
fantasies of reality-instructors such as in Lelchuk.

Tanner, Tony. "Not Politics, But Sex." Rev. of *American Mischief.*
  London Magazine Oct.-Nov. 1973: 146-48.

Claims that *American Mischief* is enormously ambitious, but collapses
into a fudge of contemporaneity, thereby sacrificing the novel form.

Taylor, Joan. "Title Page." Rev. of *Miriam in Her Forties. Los Angeles Times Book Review* 12 Jan. 1986: 4.

Briefly describes the contents of the novel, and comments that Lelchuk gives Miriam a voice that is too polemical and self-absorbed. Concludes that she ends up being a mouthpiece for a contemporary woman who gets lost somewhere along the way.

Towers, Robert. "Nervous Breakdown." Rev. of *Shrinking: The Beginning of My Own Ending. New York Times Book Review* 21 May 1978: 11.

Describes *Shrinking* as ultimately preposterous, and not at all funny. Details the plot, and explains the theme as the incompatibility of extreme sexual experience and calm domestic love. Complains that Roth's wit and comic dimensions are missing from this account. Concludes that the writing is often slapdash, and the dialogue banal and absurd.

Meyer Levin
1905 – 1981

Primary Sources

Novels

The Architect. New York: Simon, 1981.

Citizens. New York: Viking, 1940; Toronto: Macmillan, 1940, 1960; Garden City: Sun Dial, 1941; Toronto: Blue Ribbon, 1941; New York: AMS, 1974.

Compulsion. New York: Simon, 1956; London: Muller, 1957; New York: Cardinal-Pocket, 1958; London: Corgi-Transworld, 1959; New York: NAL, 1968; Toronto: Signet-NAL of Canada, 1968; New York: Pocket, 1973; New York: Arbor, 1984.

Eva. New York: Simon, 1959; London: Muller, 1959; New York: Cardinal-Pocket, 1960; London: Corgi-Transworld, 1961; London: Corgi, 1971, 1976; A Jewish Legacy Book. New York: Behrman, 1979.

The Fanatic. New York: Simon, 1963; New York: Pocket, 1965.

Frankie and Johnnie, A Love Story. New York: Day, 1930. Rev. ed. publ. as *The Young Lovers.* New York: Signet-NAL, 1952.

Gore and Igor: An Extravaganza. New York: Simon, 1968; London: Allen, 1968; New York: NAL [Cited in PBIP, 1969].

The Harvest. New York: Simon, 1978; New York: Bantam, 1979.

My Father's House. New York: Viking, 1947; Toronto: Macmillan, 1947; New York: Ace [Cited in PBIP, 1969].

The New Bridge. New York: Covici, 1933; London: Gollancz, 1933; Cheaper ed. London: Gollancz, 1942.

The Obssession. New York: Simon, 1973.

The Old Bunch. New York: Simon, 1937, 1958; New York: Viking, 1937; Toronto: Macmillan, 1937; New York: Citadel, 1942, 1945; New York: Macfadden, 1962; New York: Giant-Avon, 1970; Secaucus: Citadel, 1985; New York: Stuart, 1985.

Reporter. New York: Day, 1929.

The Settlers. New York: Simon, 1972; London: Allen, 1972; New York: Pocket, 1972; London: Sphere, 1975; New York: Bantam, 1978, 1987.

The Spell of Time: A Tale of Love in Jerusalem. New York: Praeger, 1974.

The Stronghold. New York: Simon, 1965; London: Allen, 1965; London: Mayflower, 1967.

Yehuda. New York: Cape, 1931; Chicago: Ballou, 1931.

The Young Lovers. New York: Signet-NAL, 1952. Rev. ed. of *Frankie and Johnnie.* New York: Day, 1930.

Short Fiction in Anthologies

"After All I Did for Israel." *These Your Children.* Ed. Harold U. Ribalow. New York: Beechhurst, 1952. 377-89; *Yisroel: The First Jewish Omnibus.* Ed. Joseph Leftwich. New York: Yoseloff, 1963. 202-09. *Tales of Our People—Great Stories of the Jew in America.* Ed. Jerry D. Lewis. New York: Geis, 1969. 211-20.

"Chicago, America." *The American Judaism Reader: Essays, Fiction and Poetry from the Pages of American Judaism.* Ed. Paul Kresh. New York: Abelard, 1967. 128-39.

"The Dance." *Feast of Leviathan.* Ed. Leo W. Schwarz. New York: Rinehart, 1956. 88-103.

"Egypt, 1937." *A Golden Treasury of Jewish Literature.* Ed. Leo W. Schwarz. New York: Farrar, 1937; Philadelphia: Jewish Pub. Soc. of America, 1937. 31-38.

"Flappers and Jellybeans." *This is Chicago, An Anthology.* Ed. Albert Halper. New York: Holt, 1952. 116-29.

"Israel and the Enemy." *The Jewish Caravan: Great Stories of Twenty-Five Centuries.* Ed. Leo W. Schwarz. New York: Farrar, 1935; Philadelphia: Jewish Pub. Soc. of America, 1935. 377-80.

"Maurie Finds His Medium." *This Land, These People.* Ed. Harold U. Ribalow. New York: Beechhurst, 1950. 178-89.

"The Old Bunch." *The Rise of American Jewish Literature.* Ed. Charles Angoff. New York: Simon, 1970. 319-63.

"The Water-Spirit." *A Treasury of Jewish Sea Stories.* Ed. Samuel Sobel. New York: David, 1965; *Jewish Sea Stories.* Ed. Samuel Sobel. Middle Village: David, 1985. 110-15.

Short Fiction in Periodicals

"After All I Did for Israel." *Commentary* July 1947: 57-62.

"Big Winner." *Collier's* 16 Nov. 1940: 20.

"The Commune." *Menorah Journal* Mar. 1931: 297-304.

"Dr. Fabian's One Man Show." *Esquire* July 1954: 38, 104-05.

"The Gift of Mr. Rubius." *Esquire* Jan. 1956: 64, 66, 68.

"Glamor Girl in Your Home." *Collier's* 13 Jan. 1940: 22, 36-37.

"His Clever Wife." *Esquire* Feb. 1958: 81-82.

"Home to Mother." *Collier's* 18 Mar. 1939: 15, 61-62.

"How Satan Defeated Rabbi Israel in His Struggle Against the False
    Messiah." *Menorah Journal* Apr. 1932: 21-25.

"Idea Man." *Collier's* 28 Sept. 1940: 10-11, 27-28, 30.

"If We'd Only Met Ten Years Ago." *Collier's* 6 Sept. 1941: 20, 42.

"Love Made Simple." *Collier's* 21 May 1938: 18, 70, 72.

"A Love Note." *Collier's* 16 Oct. 1937: 19, 32-33; *Scholastic* 23 Apr.
    1938: 3-4, 33, 35.

"The Married Man." *Accent* 1.1 (1940): 32-36.

"Maurie Finds His Medium." *Menorah Journal* Aug. 1928: 175-81.

"Night Work." *Collier's* 3 Aug. 1940: 16.

"No Excuse for Ace." *Collier's* 12 Apr. 1941: 25, 91-93.

"O Jerusalem!" *Jewish Frontier* Oct. 1967: 18-22.

"Plenty of Experience." *Collier's* 6 July 1940: 12.

"A Private Argument." *Collier's* 8 Feb. 1941: 16.

"Reb Feivel Read the Holy Books." *Menorah Journal* Feb. 1930: 129-35.

"A Seder." *Menorah Journal* Apr. 1924: 139-46.

"To Fire the Wife." *Collier's* 13 Dec. 1941: 15, 47-50.

Secondary Sources

Books

Rubin, Steven J. *Meyer Levin.* Twayne's United States Authors Series 406. Boston: Twayne, 1982.

Articles and Chapters

Bellman, Samuel I. "The Literary Creativity of Meyer Levin." *Jewish Book Annual* 33 (1975): 111-16.

An appreciation of Levin asserting that he will remain an important Jewish writer because he is a latter-day Jewish prophet, a literary artist, and a reporter commissioned to publish the truth. Details the five character types found in his novels: the camera eye; the still, small voice; the fanatic; the bumbler; and the seeker.

Dafni, Rinna. "A Talk with 'Eva'." *New York Times Book Review* 23 Aug. 1959: 4, 18.

Reports an interview with Ida Lev, whose story of survival is told in *Eva* in which she describes how she met Levin and told him her story in spite of a language barrier.

Darby, William. "If You Stop and Think About It, It Scares You." *Necessary American Fictions: Popular Literature of the 1950s*. William Darby. Bowling Green: Bowling Green U Popular P, 1987. 279-87.

Describes the Leopold-Loeb case on which *Compulsion* is based. Details the plot, themes, and characters in considerable detail.

Eisinger, Chester E. "Character and Self in Fiction on the Left." *Proletarian Writers of the Thirties*. Ed. David Madden. CrossCurrents/Modern Critiques. Carbondale: Southern Illinois UP, 1968. 167-70.

Describes both *Citizens* and *The Old Bunch* as proletarian and collectivist novels primarily concerned with the issue of Jewish identity. Also describes the political and social agendas of both novels, and concludes that, despite Levin's marked disabilities as a novelist, they do not stem from his ideological Marxism.

Field, Leslie. "Meyer Levin's *The Old Bunch*: Children of the Immigrants." *Yiddish* 6.4 (1987): 73-86.

Describes the book as achieving for second and third generation Jews what James T. Farrell had done in *Studs Lonigan* for the Irish Catholics on the South Side. Calls it a landmark book, and measures it against the works of Cahan, Ozick, Henry and Philip Roth, Bellow, Malamud, and Potok. Calls the novel stark, realistic, sincere, and often nakedly naturalistic. Provides an in-depth look at the point-of-view, settings, and voices in the novel.

Fife, Stephen. "Meyer Levin's *Obsession*." *New Republic* 2 Aug. 1982: 26-30.

Recounts the history of the novel *Obsession* and its subsequent passage from the French translation where he found it to the American stage. The article is largely an account of lawsuits, bitternesses, accusations of plagiarism, and the replacement of Levin and his original script. Very detailed and possibly the definitive account of the whole affair.

Filler, Louis. "Meyer Levin's *Compulsion*." *A Question of Quality: Popularity and Value in Modern Creative Writing*. Ed. Louis Filler. Bowling Green: Bowling Green U Popular P, 1976. 148-59.

Traces the treatment Levin received from critics during his day, as well as the historical circumstances behind the publication of *Compulsion* based on the Leopold-Loeb case.

Frankel, Haskel. "The Facts Behind the Fiction." *Saturday Review* 6
   Nov. 1965: 31.

A brief account of the contents of the novel and of Levin's life.

Gendel, Evelyn. "The Successful Novelist and the Committed Jew."
   Jewish Digest July 1966: 77-80.

Calls Levin a writer for whom life and art have never been divided.
Profiles his life and writing career, politics, individual novels, and causes. A tribute written on the occasion of his sixtieth birthday.

Glicksberg, Charles I. "When Is a Novel Anti-Semitic?" *Congress
   Weekly* 1 Nov. 1954: 11-13.

Discusses *The Old Bunch* and his autobiography, *In Search*, as well as
works by Budd Schulberg and Jerome Weidman to support his thesis that
the writer, Jew or non-Jew, must present the truth he/she sees, no matter
how unpleasant to some, so long as they present it with completeness
and integrity. To do this, they must show the complex network of environmental forces and social conditions that influence the human soul and
shape it in a given way for good or evil.

Guttmann, Allen. "How Some of Us Made It: Meyer Levin and Daniel
   Fuchs." *The Jewish Writer in America: Assimilation and the Crisis of
   Identity*. Allen Guttmann. New York: Oxford UP, 1971. 37-44.

Describes the historical background of Levin's literary career and the
general theme of assimilation and problematic Jewish identity evident in
his novels. Contains a detailed discussion of *The Old Bunch* and some of
his earlier works.

Harap, Louis. *Creative Awakening: The Jewish Presence in Twentieth-
   Century American Literature, 1900-1940s*. Contributions in Ethnic
   Studies 17. New York: Greenwood, 1987. 118-20, 159-60.

Agrees with Levin that *The Old Bunch* is a sociological novel, and finds
that it makes no pretense at high art. Sees it as a Jewish counterpart to
Farrell's *Studs Lonigan*'s Irish side at Chicago. Lists Cahan, Lewisohn,
and Mike Gold as influencing Levin's work, and describes the contents
of *The Old Bunch* in detail, assessing it as one of the memorable novels
of the 30s. Also briefly discusses *Citizens*, which he considers a proletarian novel.

Klein, Marcus. "The Roots of Radicals: Experience in the Thirties." *Proletarian Writers of the Thirties*. Ed. David Madden. Carbondale: Southern Illinois UP, 1968. 155-57.

Describes the contents and style of *The Old Bunch*, and likens it to works by Dos Passos. Comments on its multiple stories, Jewish immigrant material, and the intersection of its characters with American history.

Levin, Meyer. "Objection & Reproof." *New York Times Book Review* 23 Apr. 1933: 17.

A letter to the editor objecting to a review of his novel, *The New Bridge*. Calls the review supercilious, snooty, and basically incompetent. Comments that the reviewer has a "Hitlerite mind" when he objects to the two villains in the novel being given Anglo-Saxon names and to giving the Jewish immigrants nobility.

Liptzin, Sol. "Impact of Israel." *The Jew in American Literature*. New York: Bloch, 1966. 218-221.

Discusses the impact of Israel on the attitudes of Jews to their own heritage and their sense of self. Discusses *The Old Bunch* as a novel which presents a cross section of Jewish life from 1921-1937, and demonstrates how Jews felt about these matters before Israel was established. Claims that by 1950, Levin presents a different sense of heritage in his novels and finds himself equally at home in Israel or Chicago.

Ribalow, Harold U. "A Note on Meyer Levin." *Chicago Jewish Forum* 9 (Fall 1950): 9-11.

Comments that, even though Levin adds little new material, his perceptions are important and he speaks to more than just a Jewish audience. Mostly describes the contents of his autobiography, *In Search*.

Ribalow, Harold U. "Zion in Contemporary Fiction." *Mid-Century: An Anthology of Jewish Life and Culture in Our Time*. Ed. Harold U. Ribalow. New York: Beechhurst, 1955. 570-91.

Discusses the thesis that to the student of Jewish-American literature Zionist aspirations were treated lightly, if at all, because Zionism as such did not exist, so far as the majority of America's Jews were concerned until the Hitler era and, for many, not until the exciting political and military events which lead to the establishment of the State of Israel. Writers of the caliber of Ludwig Lewisohn and Meyer Levin did write about Zionism in the context of other political ideas and in doing so cut themselves off from the mainstream of Jewish-American literature. Traces the theme with particular reference to Levin and Lewisohn.

Rubin, Steven J. "Ethnic Autobiography: A Comparative Approach." *Journal of Ethnic Studies* 9.1 (1981): 75-79.

This article discusses ethnic autobiography as a genre embracing cultural and personal self-assertion, and briefly discusses several of Levin's novels as examples of this thesis.

Sherman, Bernard. "*The Old Bunch* as a Naturalist Novel." *The Invention of the Jew: Jewish-American Education Novels 1916-1964.* Bernard Sherman. New York: Yoseloff, 1969. 92-99, passim.

Calls *The Old Bunch* a naturalistic novel comparable to *Studs Lonigan* and concerned with an attempt to justify Levin's own relationship to his past, Jewish life in America, and the conflict of generations.

Varon, Benno Weiser. "The Haunting of Meyer Levin." *Midstream* Aug.-Sept. 1976: 7-23.

A major essay describing Levin's career, his major works, his politics, his treatment at the hands of the literary establishment, the contents of his individual novels, Varon's personal experiences with Levin, as well as comparisons between Levin and other writers, and the harm done him by the supporters of *Partisan Review* and *New York Review of Books*.

Weber, Brom. "Some American Jewish Novelists." *Chicago Jewish Forum* 4 (Spr. 1946): 178-79.

Sees Levin as a writer whose work, like that of West, satirizes and condemns trends and individuals for whom he has no imagination. Argues that, unlike West, Levin does have a capacity for feeling, even though the cumulative effect of his work is social history not quite transformed into life.

Reviews

Alpert, Carl. "Dusting Off the Bookshelf, XV - *Yehuda*, by Meyer Levin: A Reappraisal." Rev. of *Yehuda*. *Congress Weekly* 5 Feb. 1951: 12-13.

Calls this the first novel of its genre—an American novel on Jewish Palestine. Describes some of the characters, the basic situation of the story, and the person and incidents it was based upon, and views the novel in the perspective of Levin's autobiography, *In Search*. Suggests the need for American and Israeli Jews to have more works that can interpret the two communities to each other.

Barkham, John. "Masquerade on the Road to Survival." Rev. of *Eva*. *New York Times Book Review* 23 Aug. 1959: 4, 12.

Calls *Eva* a book that should have moved him but failed to do so because the events of Eva's life are too distant. Comments on the limitations of the first-person narrative and the improbabilities of the ending.

Bauke, Joseph P. "A Day of Judgments." Rev. of *The Stronghold*. *Saturday Review* 6 Nov. 1965: 33.

Argues that the strengths of *The Stronghold* lie in its fusion of fast-paced plot combined with the quest for moral values. Also claims it to be a masterpiece of storytelling.

Bell, Pearl K. "Meyer Levin's Obsessions." Rev. of *The Harvest*. *Commentary* June 1978: 66-68.

Mostly an account of Levin's life; Zionism; earlier works; and trip to Cambridge, Massachusetts, to address the Harvard-Radcliffe Zionist Alliance on the issue of Israel. Sees him as heavily indebted to Dos Passos, Singer, Mann, and Asch because of his proclivity for family sagas.

Bellman, Samuel Irving. "The New Bunch." Rev. of *Gore and Igor: An Extravaganza*. *Saturday Review* 24 Feb. 1968: 44-45.

Calls *Gore and Igor* full of slapdash bombast and smut interspersed with interesting battle scenes and readable, respectable prose. Suggests that perhaps this is Levin's literary contribution to pop art, and that perhaps he has really conveyed a painful message to his friends and readers.

Bellman, Samuel Irving. "Obsession with Justice." Rev. of *The Fanatic*. *Congress Bi-Weekly* 9 Mar. 1964: 13-14.

Describes the novel as unusually gripping and filled with majestic seriousness, mesmeric suspensefulness, and sheer competence. Contains a detailed summary of its contents.

Ben-Asher, Naomi. "Books." Rev. of *The Stronghold*. *Jewish Frontier* Mar. 1966: 22-24.

Considers the book economically structured, psychologically developed, and focused on significant issues. Comments on its concern with the meaning of the Holocaust, the nature of Jewish identity, and the Christian church as a chief source of anti-Semitism. Provides an excellent recounting of the plot.

Boroff, David. "Demons of Anger." Rev. of *The Fanatic. American Judaism* (Spr. 1964): 18, 61-62.

Argues that Levin has been undervalued. Considers *The Old Bunch* a minor masterpiece, and *Compulsion* a magnificent documentary novel. Describes Levin's long, drawn-out quarrel with Broadway over the script of *The Diary of Anne Frank*. Sees the latest novel, *The Fanatic*, as dogged, humorless, triumphant, unrelenting, written with stunning authority, and a little disingenuous.

Boroff, David. "Injustice Collector." Rev. of *The Fanatic. New York Times Book Review* 26 Jan. 1964: 5.

Sees the novel as an endlessly tormented saga, part fiction, part philosophic dialogue. Calls it dogged, unrelenting, humorless, and stunning in the authority with which it conjures up a nightmare world. Also sees it as Levin's vendetta against Broadway producers and the father of Anne Frank. Concludes that the book does have raw power and the hypnotic grip of its obsessed hero, Maury.

Broyard, Anatole. "Building a Novel." Rev. of *The Architect. New York Times* 19 Dec. 1981: 20.

Describes this as a novel built on a major theme based as it is on the life of Frank Lloyd Wright. Criticizes his unsatisfying sentimentality, treatment of women characters as angels, and his general lack of passion.

Buckmaster, Henrietta. "Maintaining a Standard Under Stress." Rev. of *Eva. Christian Science Monitor* 3 Sept. 1959: 7.

Sees *Eva* as a novel about ordinary people caught up in extraordinary circumstances. Primarily describes story and characters.

Bullock, Florence Haxton. "Some of the New Novels." Rev. of *My Father's House. New York Herald Tribune Weekly Book Review* 7 Sept. 1947: 8, 10.

Describes *My Father's House* as having a fairy tale atmosphere of breathless unreality. Sees most of the characters as super-humanly kind, while the commune resembles a girl scout camp on a practice trip. Argues that when Levin introduces extraneous material, it finally becomes interesting and convincing, and that the book is an immensely valuable mine of information about modern Israel.

Chassler, Philip I. "More Confession Than Expose." Rev. of *The Obsession. Midstream* Apr. 1975: 70-72.

Describes *The Obsession* as the account of Levin's enormous difficulties encountered with publishers, playwrights, lawyers and editors, producers, and agents when attempting to stage his play *Anne Frank: The Diary of a Young Girl.*

Cosgrave, Mary Silva. "The Outlook Tower." Rev. of *The Spell of Time: A Tale of Love in Jerusalem. Horn Book* Feb. 1975: 77.

Calls the novel a spellbinding story that combines a highly suspenseful blend of legendary Hasidic mysticism with modern science.

Davis, Robert Gorham. "Land of Community and Achievement." Rev. of *My Father's House. New York Times Book Review* 31 Aug. 1947: 6.

Describes the novel as a book illuminating atavistic nationalism, all inside the mind of a boy Holocaust victim. Claims that its appeal comes not from its psychiatry, which is lacking, but from its charm and meaning.

Ehrlich, Leonard. "The Nation Israel." Rev. of *Yehuda. Saturday Review of Literature* 6 June 1931: 880.

Describes *Yehuda* as the story of a commune in modern Israel and a discussion of the sociology, history, and politics of the whole venture. Applauds its remarkable insight into the stresses and strains of working relationships within groups, their triumphs and their deep failings. Concludes that this is a fine, eloquent, groping, pathetic story of a little settlement on the rim of the wilderness.

Fadiman, Clifton. "Take Your Choice." Rev. of *Citizens. New Yorker* 30 Mar. 1940: 65-66.

Sees *Citizens* as a story about the Chicago steel riots of Memorial Day 1937 which is not written to expose but to interpret the knotty social, racial, and political factors that make possible such violence. Concludes that it is far too long and too talkative, but that its meaningful and arresting content is handled with intellectual consciousness.

Farrell, James T. "Between Two Wars." Rev. of *The Old Bunch. Saturday Review of Literature* 13 Mar. 1937: 5.

Calls *The Old Bunch* a novel of panoramic sweep and serious themes. Complains that Levin seeks to overleap the limitations of his method and theme through organization and structure, hence allowing his efforts to become mechanical and obvious. Notes that he touches upon the sources and methods of several generations of American novelists such as Dreiser, Hemingway, Lewis, Cahan, Dos Passos, and Fitzgerald. Concludes that this is one of the most serious and ambitious novels yet produced by the current generation of American novelists.

Farrell, James T. "Realistic Fiction and Meyer Levin." Rev. of *Citizens. Saturday Review of Literature* 30 Mar. 1940: 11.

Describes *Citizens* as not just social history but realistic fiction whose style derives from Steinbeck and Dos Passos. Points out his ability to see detail with a reportorial eye, and criticizes his vague treatment of politics and his many dull discussions.

Feld, Rose. "Guilty with Mitigating Circumstances." Rev. of *Compulsion. New York Herald Tribune Book Review* 28 Oct. 1956: 5.

Recounts the story of the Leopold-Loeb murder trial and the subsequent account of it in this novelistic documentary. Notes that Levin describes the scenes of legal and intellectual battle in the crowded courtroom with craft and wit. Concludes that this is a brilliant re-creation of the high suspense of this tragic story.

Feld, Rose. "Meyer Levin's Story of a Brave Girl." Rev. of *Eva. New York Herald Tribune Book Review* 30 Aug. 1959: 10.

Calls *Eva* a tragic and moving story of a young, female, Auschwitz victim told as a survivor tale. Notes that, even if this novel fails as a novel, it has its importance as a dark reminder of a recent page of history.

Fisch, Harold. "High Adventure and Spiritual Quest." Rev. of *The Settlers. Midstream* Jan. 1973: 72-73.

Sees the strength of *The Settlers* not to be in its display of the grand march of history, but in the gritty and deeply experienced account it gives of the conditions in which the earlier settlements and kibbutzim were established.

Fox, G. George. "Tales of a Jewish Mystic." Rev. of *The Golden Mountain. Christian Century* 7 Dec. 1932: 1515-16.

Places this work in the recent trend of novelistic interest in Chassidism. Calls the forty tales in the collection weird, foreign, powerfully interesting, moral, and splendidly written.

Frankel, Haskel. "A Rage for Right." Rev. of *The Fanatic. Saturday Review* 22 Feb. 1964: 59.

Describes the content of the novel, and comments that this is not Levin's strongest book, despite its strong plot. Claims that the novel pays for its size with a loss of pace and subtlety. Concludes that, in spite of these shortcomings, this is a big book in every sense of the word.

Fuchs, Daniel. "The Life of Meyer Levin." Rev. of *The Architect. New York Times Book Review* 3 Jan. 1982: 9, 21.

Describes his first California meeting with Levin and his family, and then gives a biographical sketch of his life. Says little about the novel.

Gardner, Erle Stanley. "Killers for Kicks." Rev. of *Compulsion. New York Times Book Review* 8 Oct. 1956: 7.

Describes the criminal events of the Leopold-Loeb case lying behind the content of this novel, and cites Levin's contribution to our understanding of it in his meticulous search for causes. Calls this an important book written in highly readable style despite its shortcomings.

Goodman, Paul. "The Crime of Our Century." Rev. of *Compulsion. Midstream* 3.3 (1957): 86-92.

Describes *Compulsion* which documents the events of the Leopold-Loeb murder case. Argues that the novel is fairly good in terms of its medical, journalistic, and legal material, but claims that it does not compare with Dreiser's work, *An American Tragedy*. A complex essay which ranges back and forth between both works discussing each in detail. Concludes that these two adolescents have not actually committed the crime of the century but merely anticipated juvenile delinquency by a decade.

Greenfield, Jerome. "Books." Rev. of *Gore and Igor: An Extravaganza. Jewish Frontier* Apr. 1969: 29-31.

Describes the novel as a book reflecting Levin's sensitivity to the subtle variations and changes in modern life—the impact of contemporary events on language, personal attitudes, values, and events. Sees this as a satiric commentary using exaggeration, burlesques, caricatures, and impossible situational juxtapositions.

Greenfield, Jerome. Rev. of *The Harvest. Jewish Frontier* June-July 1978: 23-24.

Asserts that *The Harvest* deals with Jewish history from the late 1920s to the formation of Israel. Suggests that it is Levin's *War and Peace* written in the service of Zionism. Notes its rich design and its references to the major issues of contemporary consciousness and history which result in Levin's exploring new fictional possibilities. Concludes that, for these reasons, it constitutes a major achievement in the cast canon of Levin's writings.

Guidry, Frederick H. "Punishment, Reward . . . and Justice." Rev. of *The Fanatic. Christian Science Monitor* 7 Feb. 1964: 11.

Claims that in *The Fanatic*, Levin transcends ethnic bounds in his discussion of the kind of justice this protagonist seeks. Provides an excellent account of the contents of the novel. Asserts that Levin's intense concentration on Maury's spiritual odyssey overwhelms the other points of view, failing to illuminate other characters. Concludes that, nevertheless, this is a work of fascinating intricacy and challengingly serious purpose.

Hicks, Granville. "A Family Bound for Jaffa." Rev. of *The Settlers. New York Times Book Review* 23 Apr. 1972: 30, 32.

Calls *The Settlers* a sort of Israeli Swiss Family Robinson. Sees it as Levin's most ambitious and best book despite his throwing in Hebrew words and giving too much reportorial detail. Decides Levin gives the air of one who knows his history of the early settlement of Israel.

Hill, William B. "Methods of Madness." Rev. of *The Fanatic. America* 25 Apr. 1964: 576.

Describes *The Fanatic* as thorough and accurate, slight of plot, and interesting in its depiction of a man's search for personal and literary integrity. Calls the story too full and undisciplined.

Hutchens, John K. "Screwball Tale." Rev. of *Gore and Igor: An Extravaganza. New York Herald Tribune Book World* 7 Apr. 1968: 12.

Argues that in *Gore and Igor* Levin both does and doesn't succeed. Notes that he has a bit of satirical fun, knows nothing about libidos, wishes he had not laid it on so thick, and criticizes him for trying to keep up with his auctorial juniors who cannot keep their characters out of bed for more than three pages, especially when they are better at it than he is.

"In Common Despair." Rev. of *The New Bridges. New York Times Book
    Review* 2 Apr. 1933: 6-7.

Complains that *The New Bridges* is about dull, common minds and contains too many transcripts of the workings of those minds. Asserts that
once the novelty of his subject's speech has worn off, it becomes a lifeless
book. Remarks that Levin's talent might be put to better use. Describes
the contents.

"Inside Story." Rev. of *The Fanatic. Newsweek* 27 Jan. 1964: 80-81.

Calls *The Fanatic* a more autobiographical than an actual novel, and
labels it a long, tedious whine, dulling the senses of the sensitive reader
as it argues a personal vendetta about Levin's play on *The Diary of Anne
Frank*. Gives a major plot summary.

"Jews in Chicago." Rev. of *The Old Bunch. Time* 15 Mar. 1937: 92, 94-95.

Describes the contents of the novel, and likens its characters to those of
the *Studs Lonigan* ilk. Regards this as not so much a chronicle as a chron-
ically cheap piece of realism. Yet notes that these characters think, speak,
and act with complete naturalness—so long as they are in Chicago.
Concludes that this is an impressive job, but that it is too self-consciously
Jewish, too uneven, too exhausting to be rated in the first rank.

Karp, David. "In Search of a Motive." Rev. of *Compulsion. Saturday
    Review* 27 Oct. 1956: 16.

Sees *Compulsion* as an attempt to provide the missing murder motive in
the famous Leopold-Loeb case. Complains that Levin's personal intrusion into the story is a serious problem. Concludes that, though fiction
and fact flow easily together, ultimately Levin's conclusions sound like
do-it-yourself psychology.

Kauffmann, Stanley. "Season in Hell." Rev. of *The Fanatic. New York
    Review of Books* 20 Feb. 1964: 5-6.

Describes the novel as going on too long, somewhat artless, and clumsily
spurious. Claims that Levin writes poorly, verges on the sententious, yet
remains very sincere.

Kazin, Alfred. "Before, During, After the Boom in Chicago." Rev. of
    The Old Bunch. New York Herald Tribune Books 14 Mar. 1937: 5.

Comments on the veracity of the novel and its social milieu. Likens *The
Old Bunch* to James T. Farrell's work, and calls it symbolic realism, pre-

dicting that though this might not be a great novel, it is a true social picture of a generation of Chicago Jewish neighborhood kids and what they do and don't make of the aspirations of their immigrant parents.

Kupferberg, Herbert. "The Pioneers, the Fighters, and the Struggle for Israel." Rev. of *The Settlers. National Observer* 3 June 1972: 21.

Describes how this novel provides a chronicle of the brave exploits of those first settlers in Israel whose lives have been overshadowed by the heroic military exploits of subsequent generations of settlers.

Laski, Marghanita. "To Live in a Time of Death." Rev. of *Eva. Saturday Review* 29 Aug. 1959: 13-14.

Describes how *Eva* is told in the doubtful mode of the first-person with the author adopting the persona of a woman. Comments that Levin is somewhat successful with this. Also wonders how non-Jews respond to this Holocaust material, and commends Levin for creating a living central character. Questions the happy ending, and sees the whole thing as propaganda rather than literature.

Lechlitner, Ruth. "Fiction." Rev. of *Yehuda. Bookman* Apr. 1931: 196-97.

Demonstrates that in *Yehuda*, the life of a farm-commune under the new Zionist movement in Palestine is presented in an absorbingly vivid and consistent way.

Lingeman, Richard R. "With a Castable Cast." Rev. of *Gore & Igor: An Extravaganza. New York Times Book Review* 18 Feb. 1968: 46.

Calls *Gore and Igor* a directable movie script, though it is hardly the quality of satire of a *Catch 22*. Concludes that it is a book of horny gaiety, extravagances, and literary digs.

Markfield, Wallace. "A Woe-Sayer Switches to Comedy." Rev. of *Gore and Igor: An Extravaganza. Life* 16 Feb. 1968: 6.

Calls this novel funny, zippy, zany farce—an irreverent kibitzing of Israel from a tough, old, Zionist shooter. Describes the contents of the novel.

Marshall, Margaret. "Notes by the Way." Rev. of *Citizens. Nation* 20 Apr. 1940: 515.

Describes *Citizens* as Levin giving genuine shape to the historical events behind the novel. Sees it as an absorbing book with the interest and power of good reporting, not fiction. Complains that the character of Dr.

Wilner does not satisfy the demand for understanding that it creates, and yet concludes that the book is excellently written.

Moore, Harry. "Ah, Paranoia!" Rev. of *The Obsession. New Republic* 2 Feb. 1974: 21.

Recounts the difficulties and rejections Levin encounters in bringing *The Diary of Anne Frank* to the American stage, and calls Levin's response to all of this "obsessional." Calls it one of the most exciting and hard-punching tracts of its kind since Zola's *J'accuse* of 1898.

Moore, Harry Thornton. "Anatomy of Chicago." Rev. of *The Old Bunch. New Republic* 7 Apr. 1937: 273-74.

Describes the characters and setting of the novel, and finds the prose hard-driving, colloquial, cinematic, and full of sharp characterizations. Complains of the lack of psychological depth. Concludes that, on the whole, this is a fine, brawling, lusty novel of the world's fourth largest city.

"Murder & the Supermen." Rev. of *Compulsion. Time* 12 Nov. 1956: 130.

Describes the Leopold-Loeb case on which the novel is based, and comments that, though Levin claims he is following the tradition of Dostoevsky, he is actually closer to the tradition of Kinsey and Hearst. Concludes snidely that this reconstruction has all the hypnotic fascination of a name tag on a slab in the city morgue.

Navasky, Victor S. "The Ordeal of Meyer Levin." Rev. of *The Obsession. New York Times Book Review* 3 Feb. 1974: 5-6.

Recounts the background details of the plot, and finally values the novel for what it can tell (not whether Levin is a paranoiac) but its account of the tensions within the Jewish community of the free-lancing business, the relationships of literateurs and lawyers, and the impact of McCarthyism on America.

"Pop War." Rev. of *Gore and Igor: An Extravaganza. Time* 23 Feb. 1968: 98.

Sees *Gore and Igor* as a fast-moving action novel with everything jerky and smaller than human. Complains that love, sex, and poetry demand some viewpoint from the author, and Levin supplies none.

Purdy, Theodore Jr. "Youth in Love." Rev. of *Frankie and Johnnie. Saturday Review of Literature* 26 Apr. 1930: 992.

Calls this novel a brutal and frank assessment of the realistic constraints on young love in an urban setting. Further describes it as a bleak and uncomfortably fleshy tale unleavened by pity or tenderness and presented against a background of cruel veracity.

Rabinowitz, Dorothy. "Books in Brief." Rev. of *The Obsession. Saturday Review/World* 23 Feb. 1974: 28.

Discusses the novel as a recording of the details of Levin's twenty-year obsession with *The Diary of Anne Frank*, his long quarrel with its stage treatment, and the severely damaged reputation that proceeded from the quarreling. Also discusses his objections to the play which was divested of its strongly Jewish character. Concludes that the reader catches a view of the world as Mr. Levin sees it and has felt with an almost unnatural immediacy the shock of his shock, the force of his anger.

Rahv, Philip. "American Jews in Chicago." Rev. of *The Old Bunch. Nation* 3 Apr. 1937: 384-85.

Calls *The Old Bunch* an ambitious literary and social documenting of defeat and frustration in the Dreiser, Farrell, Dos Passos fashion. Argues, however, that this does not really make up for its lack of tension because the narrative is monotonous and the characters not distinctive enough.

"Red Sea Beachniks." Rev. of *Gore and Igor: An Extravaganza. Times Literary Supplement* 6 June 1968: 569.

Describes the characters as gladiating their way through a veritable world series of funny-symbolic contests and ultimately joining forces, pooling talents, and making common cause in Jerusalem by serenading the triumph of the Five Days War. Notes that beneath the hilarity, the political implications are a bit sour, and one wonders just how aware of them Levin is. Concludes that this is rather a leaden extravaganza which would have been a joy at half the length.

Reichert, Victor E. "Good and Evil." Rev. of *The Fanatic. National Jewish Monthly* Apr. 1964: 6, 9.

Calls *The Fanatic* a novel about good and evil which does not let the reader grope too much in the dark. Describes it as full of genuinely bitter, heartfelt commentary on and concerned with religious and ethical matters. Admires its prevailing mood of gratitude for the gift of life. Discusses the theological and moral issues from within a Jewish context.

Ribalow, Harold U. "Books." Rev. of *The Fanatic. Chicago Jewish Forum* 23 (Sum. 1964): 339-40.

Describes Levin as a novelist with a cause who conveys a sense of urgency, functions as a Jewish moralist, and writes in the service of social causes. Sees *The Fanatic* as his best work to date. Provides a detailed plot summary, and concludes that this book is one great, long cry for justice.

Ribalow, Harold U. "Levin's Spell." Rev. of *The Spell of Time. Congress Bi-Weekly* 27 Dec. 1974: 19.

Calls Levin a versatile and prolific novelist. Briefly outlines the contents of *The Spell of Time*, and concludes that, though it is a slight book, it remains in the mind.

Ribalow, Harold U. "Obsessed with the Problem of Justice." Rev. of *The Fanatic. Reconstructionist* 2 Oct. 1964: 29-30.

Claims that *The Fanatic* is written in the tradition of realistic fiction, and, as thus, is readable and persuasive. Sees the characters as well-defined and the book as an ambitious survey of more than a decade of Jewish life. Concludes that Levin conveys his passion despite the awkward technique he employs, retaining the reader's attention throughout.

Ribalow, Harold U. "'The Pure Essence of Murder.'" Rev. of *Compulsion. Congress Weekly* 10 Dec. 1956: 14.

Describes *Compulsion*, based on the Leopold-Loeb murder case, as a documentary account of the case, brilliantly handled on a sophisticated psychological level and superbly told. Considers it emotional, moving, and full of sharp insights into human behavior.

Rugoff, Milton. "They Picket Forever." Rev. of *Citizens. New York Herald Tribune Books* 24 Mar. 1940: 4.

Calls *Citizens* written lavishly well with the expertness of a social scientist and the power to bring full-bodied, rudely impressive characters to life with an indispensable quota of human compassion. Concludes that this is a richly laden novel with a compelling theme.

"Sagas of Survival." Rev. of *Eva. Time* 24 Aug. 1959: 78.

Calls *Eva* an attempt to follow up on the Anne Frank story. Concludes, however, that while *The Diary of Anne Frank* is an authentic human account, *Eva*, though powerful, is the product of the present-day and already a historical fiction.

Schott, Webster. "Meyer Levin: A Novel and a Talk." Rev. of *The Harvest. New York Times Book Review* 19 Feb. 1978: 14, 33.

Describes the novel as a continuation of *The Settlers*, continuing Levin's account of the founding of Israel. Finds the novel fails as fiction, but passes any reasonable test as education. Concludes that it captures the divergent but complementary Jewish yearnings, world events, compassion, and barbarism that coalesced in the birth of Israel.

Segal, David I. Rev. of *The Fanatic. New York Herald Tribune Book Week* 2 Feb. 1964: 8.

Describes the novel as a bore for the same reason that "serious" TV plays are boring—situation, character, and style do not develop from any inner necessity but are manipulated to produce a preconceived thesis. Claims that the focus of the novel is narrowed down to only a kind of conspiracy against truth. Concludes that the style is a welter of self-pity, rhetorical phrases, and inflated writing.

Shapiro, Charles. "The Crime of Our Age." Rev. of *Compulsion. Nation* 1 Dec. 1956: 482-84.

Describes the Leopold-Leob murder case and the other background material out of which *Compulsion* is built. Calls the novel slapped together, but still a strong indictment of our ignorance, our malice, and our inhumanity. Concludes, however, that the book fails on several counts: the first half is spotty and awkward, the pseudo-documentary methods have drawbacks, the book abounds with annoying kindergarten popularization, and it has an air of sophomoric wisdom to go along with its crudities.

Shubow, Joseph S. "Books." Rev. of *The Fanatic. American Zionist* May 1964: 10.

Claims that *The Fanatic* demonstrates the political integrity of its author. Sees Levin as a true defender and honest champion of Zionism, Israel, and martyrdom.

Sokolov, Raymond A. "Mass Lubricity." Rev. of *Gore and Igor: An Extravaganza. Newsweek* 12 Feb. 1968: 101-02.

Describes *Gore and Igor* in terms of its lurid, zany content. Views it as a picaresque romp. Comments that actually, the book is too silly to be sexy, but represents new-wave soft porn aimed at the family trade.

Springer, Ann. "The Dispossessed." Rev. of *Citizens. Boston Evening Transcript* 30 Mar. 1940: 1.

Considers Levin the Steinbeck of Illinois, and commends the novel for its drawing to the attention of Americans their shameful double dispossession. Details the contents.

Strauss, Harold. "A Novel of Youth in Chicago." Rev. of *The Old Bunch. New York Times Book Review* 28 Mar. 1937: 6.

Describes *The Old Bunch* as a landmark development in the realistic novel. Argues that Levin does for the Chicago Jews what James Farrell did for the Chicago Irish. Concludes that, though this book is plotless, each incident makes exciting, memorable, and brilliant reading.

Strauss, Harold. "A Strike Novel on Broad Lines." Rev. of *Citizens. New York Times Book Review* 31 Mar. 1940: 2.

Sees *Citizens* as notable for its fresh approach to an industrial theme by striking the fetters of photographic realism from the strike novel. Concludes that, rather than being a call to arms for one side or the other, it is an attempt to understand the moral issues involved in class struggle.

Trilling, Lionel. "Modern Palestine in Fiction." Rev. of *Yehuda. Nation* 24 June 1931: 684.

Complains that *Yehuda*, the commune story, is exaggerated, while the ideological content is very necessary. Concedes, however, that the characters' group behaviors can be and are appropriately portrayed in this commune setting.

Trilling, Lionel. "The Promise of Realism." Rev. of *Frankie and Johnnie. Menorah Journal* May 1930. Rpt. in *Speaking of Literature and Society*. Ed. Diana Trilling. *The Works of Lionel Trilling*. New York: Harcourt, 1980. 27-33.

Briefly discusses *Frankie and Johnnie,* calling it a respectable piece of work written in the old tradition of realism but without the inherent faith in America embodied in that tradition.

Weintroub, Benjamin. "Books." Rev. of *The Stronghold. Chicago Jewish Forum* 23 (Wint. 1965-66): 171.

Calls *The Stronghold* provocative and exciting. Details the plot, and concludes that this is a masterful adventure story solidly substantiated by the author's bitter Jewish yesteryears.

Werner, Alfred. "The Face of Palestine." Rev. of *If I Forget Thee. New York Times Book Review* 7 Dec. 1947: 48.

Claims that *If I Forget Thee*'s heroes are chiefly refugees, illogically arrived in the Holy Land after WWII. Remarks that the photographs accompanying this tale would have delighted a Steiglitz.

Wincelberg, Anita M. "Crime and Expiation." Rev. of *Compulsion. New Leader* 8 Apr. 1957: 23-24.

Describes *Compulsion* as a tribute to Levin's skill in dramatizing the Leopold-Leob case. Claims that it leaves us with a very clear picture of Judd Steiner, and provides a skillful and utterly readable dissection of the two boys' minds, largely from their own point of view. Concludes that Levin successfully uses the psychoanalytic technique in the novel. Reviews the circumstances of the case in its own day and now.

Woodburn, John. "Even as the Foxes." Rev. of *My Father's House. Saturday Review of Literature* 30 Aug. 1947: 19, 27.

Describes the novel in detail, and concludes that Levin has written the novel pretty straight, resisting the temptation to editorialize. Admires him for cutting a clear path through the complex political and racial situation to tell a warm, simple, lovingly written, and insistently touching story.

"Young Morons." Rev. of *Frankie and Johnnie. New York Times Book Review* 1 June 1930: 9.

Argues that *Frankie and Johnnie* reflects arduous research into contemporary idiom, manners, and morals of Chicago's poor. Considers Levin's job workmanlike and the finished narrative as bearing every semblance of credibility. But complains that the theme is of little substance and Levin refuses to give his characters one shred of sympathy. Concludes that the book is finally thin and repetitious.

"A Zionist Colony." Rev. of *Yehuda. New York Times Book Review* 22 Mar. 1931: 21.

Sees *Yehuda* as chiefly remarkable for the information it conveys about the first fruits of the Zionist movement, and suggests that those not interested in Zionism will find it unsatisfying. Complains that what Levin gains in accuracy, he loses in dramatic significance.

Interviews

Morton, Frederic. "Meyer Levin: A Novel and a Talk." *New York Times Book Review* 19 Feb. 1978: 14, 32-33.

In this article Levin discusses: his presence on the American literary scene, his development as a writer, the influence on him and the differences from him of other Jewish writers—the early writers like Cahan and Lewisohn, the thirties and forties self-hating, be an American, be a success writers, and the contemporary writers like Bellow and Roth who honor their Judaism, but are totally detached from the living Jewish community. He also discusses his literary career and current plans.

Ribalow, Harold U. "A Conversation with Meyer Levin." *Midstream* Jan. 1978: 39-43. Rpt. in *The Tie That Binds: Conversations with Jewish Writers*. Harold U. Ribalow. San Diego: Barnes; London: Tantivy, 1980. 63-75.

Levin discusses: the situation of the Jewish writer; his books *The Old Bunch* and *In Search*; Kazin's disappointment over his work; trying to publish *The Obsession*; his experience publishing *The Fanatic, The Spell of Time,* and *Compulsion*; his methods of historical research; his relationship to Israel; and his feelings after a lifetime in the novel writing business.

Biographical Sources

Bernstein, Mashey M. "Meyer Levin." *Twentieth-Century American-Jewish Fiction Writers*. Ed. Daniel Walden. Detroit: Gale, 1984. Vol. 28 of *Dictionary of Literary Biography*. 94 vols. to date. 1978- . 136-41.

More than just details of his life, this is a career biography, tracing the development of the author's canon, describing the contents and themes of his works, evaluating his reputation, and placing him in the larger context of American literary history. Includes lists of primary and secondary sources and illustrations.

Fuchs, Daniel. "Meyer Levin." *Dictionary of Literary Biography Yearbook: 1981*. Eds. Karen L. Rood, Jean W. Ross, and Richard Ziegfeld. Detroit: Gale, 1982. 99-102.

An account of Levin's career written in 1981 following his death. In a brief tribute Mailer calls *The Old Bunch* the best novel about Jews in America.

Levin, Meyer. *In Search, An Autobiography.* New York: Horizon; Paris: Author's, 1950; London: Constellation, 1951; New York: Paperback, 1961; New York: Pocket, 1973.

Levin, Meyer. "The Writer and the Jewish Community: Case History of a 'Culture-Maker.'" *Commentary* June 1947: 526-30.

Describes his role as a Jewish-American culture-maker and his development as a writer.

Miller, Alyce Sands. "Meyer Levin." *American Novelists, 1910-1945, Part II: F. Scott Fitzgerald-O. E. Rolvaag.* Ed. James J. Martine. Detroit: Gale, 1981. Vol. 9 of *Dictionary of Literary Biography.* 94 vols. to date. 1978- . 161-69.

More than details of his life, this is a career biography, tracing the development of the author's canon, describing the contents and themes of his works, evaluating his reputation, and placing him the larger context of American literary history. Includes lists of primary and secondary sources and illustrations.

Dissertations

Bossin, Gary. "The Literary Achievement of Meyer Levin." Diss. Kent State U, 1980.

Greenberg, Abraham Herbert. "The Ethnocentric Attitudes of Some Jewish American Writers: Educational Implications." Diss. Yeshiva U, 1956.

Ludwig Lewisohn
1882 – 1955

Primary Sources

Novels

An Altar in the Fields. New York: Harper, 1934; Toronto: Musson, 1934; London: Hamilton, 1934.

Anniversary. New York: Farrar, 1948; Toronto: Clarke, 1948; Toronto: Smithers, 1948; Westport: Greenwood, 1972.

Breathe upon These. Indianapolis: Bobbs, 1944; Toronto: McClelland, 1944.

The Broken Snare. New York: Dodge, 1908; London: Paul, 1908.

The Case of Mr. Crump. Paris: Titus, 1926, 1931; New York: Henderson, 1930; New York: Farrar, 1947, 1965; London: Bodley Head, 1948; Masters of Modern Literature. New York: Noonday, 1965; London: Lane, 1979; Penguin Modern Classics. Harmondsworth: Penguin, 1985. Also publ. as *The Tyranny of Sex: The Case of Mr. Crump.*

The Defeated. London: Butterworth, 1927. Subsequent eds. publ. as *The Island Within.*

Don Juan. New York: Boni, 1923.

For Ever Wilt Thou Love. New York: Dial, 1939; Toronto: McClelland, 1939; New York: Signet-NAL, 1949.

The Golden Vase. New York: Harper, 1931.

Holy Land. New York: Harper, 1926.

In a Summer Season. New York: Farrar, 1955; Toronto: Ambassador, 1955.

The Island Within. New York: Harper, 1928; New York: Modern Library, 1940; Toronto: Macmillan, 1940; The JPS Library of American Jewish Fiction. Philadelphia: Jewish Pub. Soc. of America, 1968; The Modern Jewish Experience. New York: Arno, 1975; New York: Ayer, 1979; A Jewish Legacy Book. New York: Behrman, 1979. Publ. as *The Defeated.* London: Butterworth, 1927.

The Last Days of Shylock. New York: Harper, 1931; London: Butterworth, 1931; Cheaper ed. New York: Harper, 1932; New York: Behrman, 1939.

Renegade. New York: Dial, 1942; Philadelphia: Jewish Pub. Soc. of America, 1942; Toronto: Longmans, 1942.

Roman Summer. New York: Harper, 1927; London: Butterworth, 1929.

The Romantic. Paris: Titus, 1931.

Stephen Escott. New York: Harper, 1930; Cheaper ed. New York: Harper, 1934. Publ. as *The Memories of Stephen Escott.* London: Butterworth, 1930. Cheaper ed. 1935; *The Vehement Flame: The Story of Stephen Escott.* New York: Farrar, 1948; Toronto: Clarke, 1948.

This People. New York: Harper, 1933.

Trumpet of Jubilee. New York: Harper, 1937; Toronto: Musson, 1937.

The Tyranny of Sex: The Case of Mr. Crump. New York: Penguin, 1947; New York: Sun Dial, 1948; London: Sphere, 1969. Same as *The Case of Mr. Crump.*

Collected Works

The Golden Vase; Roman Summer: Two Novels. The Albatross Modern Continental Library. Hamburg: Albatross, 1932.

Short Fiction in Anthologies

"Holy Land." *Yisroel: The First Jewish Omnibus.* Ed. Joseph Leftwich. London: Heritage, 1933. 216-24; Rev. ed. London: Clarke, 1945. 173-79; Rev. ed. New York: Beechhurst, 1952. 173-79; Rev. ed. New York: Yoseloff, 1963. 139-45. (Clarke ed. titled *Yisroel: The Jewish Omnibus*); *A Golden Treasury of Jewish Literature.* Ed. Leo W. Schwarz. New York: Farrar, 1937; Philadelphia: Jewish Pub. Soc. of America, 1937. 69-76.

"The Romantic." *The Jewish Caravan: Great Stories of Twenty-Five Centuries.* Ed. Leo W. Schwarz. New York: Farrar, 1935; Philadelphia: Jewish Pub. Soc. of America, 1935. 539-64.

"The Story Ashland Told at Dinner." *The Smart Set Anthology.* Eds. Burton Rascoe and Groff Conklin. New York: Reynal, 1934. 344-51.

Short Fiction in Periodicals

"The Endless Test." *Esquire* June 1947: 88-89, 229-30.

"Holy Land." *Harper's* Oct. 1925: 523-27.

Secondary Sources

Books

Gillis, Adolph. *Ludwig Lewisohn: The Artist and His Message.* New York: Duffield, 1933.

Lainoff, Seymour. *Ludwig Lewisohn*. Twayne's United States Authors
  Series 435. Boston: Twayne, 1982.

Articles and Chapters

Analyticus [James Waterman Wise]. "Ludwig Lewisohn." *Jews Are Like
  That!* New York: Brentano's, 1928. 109-26.

Describes many of Lewisohn's writings as autobiographical and proceeding forth not out of egocentrism, but out of the conviction that he
has discovered certain vital truths. Proceeds to illustrate this thesis with
reference to several of the pieces, and adds steady doses of biographical
information. Comments are poorly organized, general, and admiring with
much recounting of plot.

Angoff, Charles. "From a Jewish Writer's Notebook." *Congress Weekly*
  8 Dec. 1958: 15.

Briefly assesses Lewisohn's contributions to Jewish-American culture.
Notes that Lewisohn wanted to be known most for his fiction, but considers that his major contribution has been to help in the return of Jewish
intellectuals back to their Jewishness. Concludes that his failure as a novelist was that he had no youthful Jewish experience, which gives a writer
"an understanding of the heart." Claims that his Jewishness came at middle age and was intellectual, resulting in essays and editorials, but
considers his best novels largely non-Jewish.

Bates, Ernest Sutherland. "Lewisohn into Crump." *American Mercury*
  Apr. 1934: 441-50.

Discusses the banning by the post office of *The Case of Mr. Crump*, its
subsequent appearance on the literary scene, and the subsequent annoy-
ance of the readership that it was not salacious at all. Recounts the plot
of the novel, and declares that reader interest lies mainly in the central
female character, who becomes purely detestable to the reader, and the
central male character, (thinly disguised as Lewisohn himself) who
becomes the embodiment of all virtue. Accuses Lewisohn of being one
of the very rare American writers to write from pure hatred and malice.
Describes his life and publishing career in detail.

Bragman, Louis J. "The Case of Ludwig Lewisohn: A Contribution to
  the Psychology of Creative Genius." *American Journal of Psychiatry*
  11.2 (1931): 319-31.

A rather detailed but simplistic psychology of the writer based on biographical material from the novels. Recounts much of his life, and places an early developmental psychology at the base of the account. Concludes that, as a creative genius, he was never able to detach himself from his intimate problems—problems which determined the course of his creative career.

Bridges, Horace James. "Up Stream: Mr. Ludwig Lewisohn Versus America." *Standard* July 1923: 14-23. Rpt. in *The God of Fundamentalism and Other Studies*. Horace James Bridges. Chicago: Covici, 1925. 269-96.

Decries the thesis of Lewisohn's *Upstream* that America has failed him in every but one respect. Provides a detailed account of the contents of the book, systematically refuting each of the author's complaints about America. Concludes that this is an admirably written treatise which ultimately reflects a hypersensitive and somewhat unfortunately compacted spirit.

Cargill, Oscar. "The Freudians." *Intellectual America: Ideas on the March*. Oscar Cargill. New York: Macmillan, 1941. 727-35.

Provides a biography and publishing history of Lewisohn, but concludes that his fiction writing abilities do not "warrant full discussion of his novels."

Chyet, Stanley F. Introduction. *The Island Within*. Philadelphia: Jewish Pub. Soc. of America, 1968. ix-xvi.

Recounts much of Lewisohn's background, his sense of himself as an exile, the griefs of his personal and publishing life, his late attachment to Jewishness, some of the flaws of the book, and its dissonances.

Chyet, Stanley F. "Lewisohn and Crevecoeur." *Chicago Jewish Forum* 22.2 (1963-1964): 130-36.

Describes the nativist bigotry which prevailed during *fin de siecle* American letters and which nearly destroyed Lewisohn. Recounts his encounter with the writings of Crevecoeur whose *Letters to An American Farmer* he was later to reprint and write an introductory essay for. Provides a detailed account of Lewisohn's appreciation of Crevecoeur and which of his values impressed him the most.

Dreiser, Theodore. "To Ludwig Lewisohn." *Letters of Theodore Dreiser: A Selection*. Ed. Robert H. Elias. 3 vols. Philadelphia: U of Pennsylvania P, 1959. 2: 451-53.

Responds to Lewisohn's request for a "helping hand" with his new novel, *The Case of Mr. Crump*. Suggests that Lewisohn is too close to the actual events (his failed marriage) on which the story is based to approach them with the clear, uncolored, unemotional viewpoint which any writer must have when fictionizing that which lies nearest his heart.

Fiedler, Leslie A. "Genesis: The American-Jewish Novel Through the Thirties." *Midstream* 4.3 (1958): 21-33. Rpt. in *The Jew in the American Novel*. Leslie Fiedler. Herzl Institute Pamphlets 10. New York: Herzl, 1959; A Seven Star Book 5. 2nd ed. New York: Herzl, 1966. 20-24; *The Collected Essays of Leslie Fiedler*. 2 vols. New York: Stein, 1971. 2: 79-84; *To the Gentiles*. New York: Stein, 1971. 79-84.

Describes the main business of the marginal writers of American Jews in the 1920s to be the assertion that it is possible to establish an image of the Jew satisfying to both Jew and Gentile. Claims that the writing of a Jewish-American novel is essentially an act of assimilation, and this effort by writers of the twenties fails to impress mainstream American readers for whom the images of the overgrown boy scout and hangdog lover, projected by Hemingway's Cohn are the images that prevail in the imagination. Discusses *Don Juan and The Island Within*, comparing and contrasting his handling of the erotic theme with Hecht's and concluding that the only subject Lewisohn responds to fervently in his fiction is his own sex life desperately projected as typical. Concludes that he has exhausted the erotic-assimilationist novel and that, after *The Island Within*, Jewish-American novelists have known a direction they cannot go.

Gertel, Elliot B. "Visions of the American Jewish Messiah." *Judaism* 31.2 (1982): 153-65.

Reviews Lewisohn's life and writing career, and attributes to him the distinction of having written the first messianic novel produced by a Jew in American literature, *Trumpet of Jubilee* (1937). Draws attention to Lewisohn's return to Judaism, the number of born-again Jews among his fictional creations, his treatment of the ironies of Jewish self-hatred and blindness to the permanence of anti-Semitism, and the evils of pseudo-messianism like socialism and fascism. Provides a lengthy exegesis of *Trumpet of Jubilee* as a messianic novel which, if not exactly of first literary quality, nevertheless deals with important spiritual issues.

Glicksberg, Charles I. "Ludwig Lewisohn: Critic and Novelist." *Congress Weekly* 15 June 1953: 9-11.

Calls Lewisohn luminous in style and rich in substance. Describes many of his works of literature and criticism in turn, including the autobiography. Places Lewisohn in a sociological, historical, and intellectual context, and attempts to evaluate his total influence and effects on the literary scene of his day.

Harap, Louis. *Creative Awakening: The Jewish Presence in Twentieth-Century American Literature, 1900-1940s.* Contributions in Ethnic Studies 17. New York: Greenwood, 1987. 55-59.

Notes that Lewisohn was not only the first Jewish intellectual to achieve national literary and cultural influence, but also an early literary advocate of Zionism. Gives brief biographical information, and describes his writing career, the development of his anti-assimilationist leanings, and his novel *The Island Within,* noting its autobiographical elements. Also quotes a number of his statements against assimilation and his assertion that "the Jewish problem is the decisive one of Western civilization. By its solution this world of the West will stand or fall, choose life or death."

Hoffman, Frederick J. "Further Interpretations." *Freudianism and the Literary Mind.* Frederick J. Hoffman. Baton Rouge: Louisiana State UP, 1945. 288-95; 2nd ed. 1957. 281-86.

Discusses *The Case of Mr. Crump* as one of the ugliest books in modern literature. Mostly a polemic against the values espoused in the book. Also discusses several of his other works.

Kazin, Alfred. "Liberals and New Humanists." *On Native Grounds: An Interpretation of Modern American Prose Literature.* Alfred Kazin. Harcourt, 1942, Rpt. 1963. 273-80.

Asserts that few critics in America have had so moving an ideal of the critic's function or kept to it so stubbornly. Accuses Lewisohn of refusing with messianic confidence and perfect gravity ever to look beyond his own ideas and sentimentality. Objects to his idea that the Nordic protestant masses had no consciences, and faults him for knowing no European languages first-hand. Treats him as part of the history of liberal criticism.

Levy, Felix A. "Ludwig Lewisohn, 1882-1955." *Jewish Book Annual* 14 (1956-1957): 46-55.

A brief sketch of Lewisohn's life and works written as a commemorative piece just after his death.

Mann, Thomas. Preface. *The Case of Mr. Crump* New York: Farrar, 1965.

Describes the novel as astutely composed fiction utilizing all the methods of modern technique, a cool tone, and a serene silence. Considers the book's indifference and voluntary renunciation of mere aesthetic distinction, and then notes that this is a horrifying depiction of marriage as an inferno.

Melnick, Ralph. "Oedipus in Charleston: Ludwig Lewisohn's Search for the Muse." *Studies in American Jewish Literature* [Albany] 3 (1983): 68-84.

An amplified version of the previous piece including passages from Lewisohn's journals. A useful overview of his early years and first publications with particular emphasis on his relationship to women.

Mezvinsky, Norton. "The Jewish Thought of Ludwig Lewisohn." *Chicago Jewish Forum* 16.2 (1957-1958): 77-82.

Calls Lewisohn an amazing intellectual for his work as literary critic, novelist, essayist, lecturer, translator, and professor of literature. Mostly provides anecdotal material about his contribution to a Jewish sense of identity. Asserts that, while he is not an original thinker, his contributions have been considerable.

Nilsen, Helge Normann. "Jewish Nationalism: A Reading of Ludwig Lewisohn's *The Island Within*." *American Studies in Scandinavia* 15.2 (1983): 59-68.

Describes *The Island Within* as an attack on all forms of anti-Semitism in America. Sees the novel as Lewisohn's attempt to establish an ethnic awareness and sense of identity which does not depend on religious heritage. Comments that it also indicates Jews can never become wholly integrated into the larger society. Provides an excellent account of the contents of the novel.

Samuel, Maurice. "In Tribute to Ludwig Lewisohn." *Congress Weekly* 16 Jan. 1956: 5-7.

An essay praising Lewisohn for his mental and spiritual energy and his influence on a generation of Jewish thinkers. Also describes his slow coming to his Jewish identity, his merits as a writer and prose stylist, and as a man. Contains valuable biographical material.

Samuel, Maurice. "Ludwig Lewisohn—Apostle to the Jews." *Congress Weekly* 15 June 1953: 7-9.

Mostly an admiring essay setting Lewisohn in historical, social, and intellectual context. Honors Lewisohn mostly as a thinker and an apostle of hope. Also provides some brief assessments of his literary achievements and his views as a Zionist.

Sherman, Bernard. "The Boy in the Sun and The Island Within." *The Invention of the Jew: Jewish-American Education Novels (1916-1964).* Bernard Sherman. New York: Yoseloff, 1969. 65-67, passim.

Describes the contents and literary qualities of the two novels.

Singer, David F. "Ludwig Lewisohn: A Paradigm of American-Jewish Return." *Judaism* 14.3 (1965): 319-29.

Discusses Lewisohn's return to his Jewish roots in spite of his contributions to American intellectual life. Suggests that Lewisohn saw that Christianity had failed to provide a peaceful and secure life, largely because of the infusion of Pauline philosophy into Jesus' teachings. Further suggests that he found his own solution for such failure in a new synthesis of Hellenism and Hebraism, of science and conduct, of nature and spirit.

Singer, David. "Ludwig Lewisohn: The Making of an Anti-Communist." *American Quarterly* 23.5 (1971): 738-48.

Traces the development of Lewisohn's liberalism, his views on Europe and America during the Depression years, his growing anti-Communism and increasing conservatism in contrast to other leftleaning, liberal intellectuals of his day, and his fiction which extolls the virtues of American civilization and the evils of Communism.

Sollors, Werner. "Region, Ethnic Group, and American Writers: From 'Non-Southern' and 'Non-Ethnic' to Ludwig Lewisohn; or the Ethics of Wholesome Provincialism." *Prospects* 9 (1984): 441-62.

Discusses the mixture of German, Southern, and Jewish characteristics in Lewisohn's work, and his use of the themes of ethnic identity in his novels.

Steinhauer, H. "Ludwig Lewisohn." *Canadian Forum* Feb. 1931: 178, 80-81.

Describes Lewisohn's career as a professor of German, his writings on aesthetics, fictional prose style, treatment of the Jewish question and relations between the sexes in his work, his politics, and his career as a Jewish-American writer.

Weber, Brom. "Some American Jewish novelists." *Chicago Jewish Forum* 4 (Spr. 1946): 180-81.

Sees Lewisohn's novels as the consistent expression of an extreme individualism so intense and courageous, and impelled by liberal idealism inspiring in its rarity. Considers him a vigorous polemicist rather than a novelist, and claims that his works suffer from unrealized characters and the general feeling they have had their strings pulled. Concludes that, ultimately, his illumination of bourgeois morality goes hand in hand with Sherwood Anderson's and that his rediscovery of the Jewish heritage is similar to the rediscovery of Emerson's, Whitman's, and Melville's legacy to American culture.

Wise, James Waterman. "Ludwig Lewisohn: An Introduction." *A Jew Speaks: An Anthology from Ludwig Lewisohn*. Ed. James Waterman Wise. New York: Harper, 1931. ix-xxiv.

Provides an introduction to Lewisohn's writing career, life, politics, and psychology. A useful beginning place though dated.

Yudkin, Leon I. "The Immigrant Experience in America." *Jewish Writing and Identity in the Twentieth Century*. Leon I. Yudkin. London: Helm, 1982. 27-44.

Discusses the Jewish immigration to America as the most remarkable demographic event in Jewish history and shows its impact on America as it emerged as a great world power. Also sees the Jewish writers Cahan, Lewisohn, Hecht, Fuchs, Michael Gold, and Henry Roth as expanding the range of an exotic consciousness in America, but also showing the "Jew on the outside trying to get in (in various ways), or perhaps coming to terms with his outsider status." Discusses the major works of each of these writers and how these works demonstrate the struggles, the conflicts, and the costs of their Jewish protagonists to become assimilated into American life.

Reviews

Ascherson, Neal. "Ill Mated." Rev. of *The Case of Mr. Crump*. *New Statesman* 20 Apr. 1979: 560-61.

Calls *The Case of Mr. Crump* an ugly Victorian gag turned upside-down. Describes the vicious portraits of women and the autobiographical quality.

Baldanza, Frank. "Revenants." Rev. of *The Case of Mr. Crump*.

Southern Review 5.1 (1969): 251-52.

Discusses the novel as a book whose author remains a ghost. Traces Lewisohn's marriage failure as reported in the novel. Comments on the malice, and the naturalistic passages adhering like barnacles to the surface of the narrative. Considers also the fatalism, sexual and economic determinism, the evolutionary ameliorism, and the plug for original sin.

Britten, Florence Haxton. "Saner and More Humane Ideas." Rev. of *The Last Days of Shylock. New York Herald Tribune Books* 11 Jan. 1931: 3.

Considers this novel a prose narrative of psychological adventure that provides a compassionate answer to man's search for joy. Describes the contents in considerable detail and claims that the writing is exquisitely beautiful. Complains in conclusion that Lewisohn is not at his best in this retrospective view of the Jewish people.

Brody, Alter. "Are Artists People?" Rev. of *Roman Summer. Nation* 8 June 1927: 646.

Dismisses *Roman Summer* as a tedious account of an artist's attempt to discover the possibility for producing art in middle America versus Rome. Provides a detailed plot summary.

Brophy, Brigid. "Poor Herbert." Rev. of *The Case of Mr. Crump. Listener* 14 Mar. 1968: 346.

Calls *The Case of Mr. Crump* a curiosity of literature, though, in fact, literature it is not. Describes the story in detail, and complains of the disguised first-person observer point of view, and the sometimes mannered prose style.

Bullock, Florence Haxton. "Battle for Integrity." Rev. of *Anniversary. New York Herald Tribune Weekly Book Review* 25 Jan. 1948: 9.

Calls *Anniversary* an impassioned plea for the first-rateness of the individual, for the development of the will it takes to achieve freedom of spirit. Describes the contents of the story, and concludes that this is a brilliant Jeremiad against our increasingly cheerful acceptance as a people of the second-rate.

Bullock, Florence Haxton. "Powerful and Very Bitter Book." Rev. of *The Case of Mr. Crump. New York Herald Tribune Weekly Book Review* 6 Apr. 1947: 2.

Considers the novel an unsparing account of a terrible marriage to a venomous and vindictive wife. Traces the history of the parallels between Lewisohn's own marriage and that of his protagonist. Describes the divorce proceedings of the Lewisohn marriage and his ex-wife's lawsuit.

Burrows, Miles. "Mismatched." Rev. of *The Case of Mr. Crump. New Statesman* 15 Mar. 1968: 349.

Calls this a novel about the entrapment of a young musician by a monstrously manipulative woman who assumes almost mythical proportions. Notes that it shares much in common with Faustus, dealing with personal disintegration, and the development and wounding of the artist.

Canby, Henry Seidel. "Novel or Pamphlet?" Rev. of *Don Juan. Nation* 5 Dec. 1923: 649-50.

Discusses *Don Juan* by detailing the contents of the novel and talking about the divorce issue which lies at its heart. Criticizes the author for stacking the deck by choice of character and situation, and therefore of failing to convince the reader.

Clark, Harry Hayden. "Fiction." Rev. of *Stephen Escott. Bookman* Apr.-May 1930: 209-10.

States that *Stephen Escott* is a dramatic and artistic externalization of problems of sex and marriage in relation to modern economic life, the modern individualistic woman, winds of radical doctrine, and inherited ambitions. Provides a detailed description of the contents, and concludes that the ultimate conviction of the book is that abiding peace is the result of control in the interest of human needs.

Collins, Joseph. "Certain Novels, Pleasant and Unpleasant." Rev. of *Don Juan. Literary Digest International Book Review* Dec. 1923: 42-43. Rpt. in revised form as "Unpleasant Novels." *Taking the Literary Pulse: Psychological Studies of Life and Letters.* Joseph Collins. New York: Doran, 1924. 161-64.

Argues that *Don Juan* is about the corruption of Bolshevism and one Bolshevist in particular, Lucien Curtis, who is really a German masquerading as an American. Details the plot exhaustively, focusing on its unpleasantness.

Cooper, Frederic Tabor. "Shylock Redrawn." Rev. of *The Last Days of Shylock. Saturday Review of Literature* 7 Feb. 1931: 579-80.

Describes the novel in detail, calling it a well-documented, scholarly volume set in sixteenth century Venice and brimming with anecdote and incident straight out of ancient records. Sees it as a grim mosaic of a century of fanatical oppression, a solid and haunting piece unrelieved by any saving piece of humor. Notes that Shakespeare's Shylock is a tragic grotesque, a symbolic figure of revenge, greed, and rancor while this Shylock is different.

Cowley, Malcolm. "Freud in Fiction." Rev. of *Trumpet of Jubilee. New Republic* 19 May 1937: 51.

Calls *Trumpet of Jubilee* a fine novel describing the torture and degradation of the Jews under Hitler. Sees this as an overpowering mystical tract in favor of mystical Jewish nationalism. Provides an excellent account of the contents and style of the novel.

"The Creative Eros." Rev. of *The Golden Vase. New York Times Book Review* 11 Oct. 1931: 7.

Sees *The Golden Vase* as driven by its author's favorite themes—racial identity, tradition, eros in relation to creativity—but this time employed to rather limited effect. Notes, however, that there is much sound commentary on the state of literature and culture in America and Europe, and a shrewd appraisal of the effects of war on individuals and classes.

Daniels, Jonathan. "Marriage in America." Rev. of *Stephen Escott. Saturday Review of Literature* 15 Mar. 1930: 821.

Sees this novel as an impassioned treatise on marriage in America, and comments that the only real character in the novel is the author. Considers all the women to be figures potent for tragedy and the war of the sexes. Concludes despite that, that the novel is packed with discussion and philosophy, and that the central story of Paul Glover is magnificent drama, moving, exiting, and full of artistic truth.

Davis, Robert Gorham. "A Marriage That Was Made in Hell." Rev. of *The Case of Mr. Crump. New York Times Book Review* 30 Mar. 1947: 4, 39.

Notes that *The Case of Mr. Crump* records Lewisohn's divorce experience. Details its inception, the author's intentions for the book, its publishing history, and publishing debut in the United States after being banned for many years.

De Voto, Bernard. "Jewry in America." Rev. of *The Island Within.*

Saturday Review of Literature 5 May 1928: 840.

Discusses the novel as a book in which the epic intentions have eclipsed some literary considerations. Considers the portrayal of gentile and Jewish worlds tragic, brilliant, and vivacious.

Edman, Irwin. "Odyssey." Rev. of *The Island Within. Menorah Journal* 14.5 (1928): 508-11.

Describes the novel as spiritually eloquent, precise, and of large canvas. Applauds it as a social document with great convincing power and passionate preachment. Provides a full account of its contents.

"Genteel Traditions." Rev. of *Roman Summer. New York Times Book Review* 1 May 1927: 17, 19.

Considers *Roman Summer* a book in which the characters achieve a sort of laboratory life as embodiments of critical tenets or foils for so many opinions or beliefs. States that these characters fail to come to life, and that the author would have us believe he is representing true greatness come to grief through a complex of unconquerable forces.

Hauser, Marianne. "Freedom Discovered." Rev. of *Renegade. New York Times Book Review* 22 Feb. 1942: 7.

Claims that *Renegade* recreates the eighteenth century in France with remarkable authenticity, while commenting that, at the center of the novel, stands a French Jew pretending he is a Gentile. Considers much in this book to be dubious from a literary standpoint, yet admires Lewisohn's superb talent as a storyteller which makes this book rank well above the average good novel.

Hellman, Geoffrey T. "Personal Problems." Rev. of *Stephen Escott. New Republic* 23 Apr. 1930: 278.

Describes the plot and contents of *Stephen Escott* and complains that it is too much a piece of these. Considers Lewisohn's morbid sensitiveness that the conclusions he reaches are as prejudiced as those of his most biased characters. Concludes that the style is often awkward and self-conscious.

Hicks, Granville. "A Daniel for Shylock." Rev. of *The Last Days of Shylock. Nation* 18 Feb. 1931: 187-88.

Calls this a moving book written with great dignity and much somber beauty. Shows how the character of Shylock is fundamentally antipathetic to the virtues of the Renaissance, but asserts that the book, as a whole, is concerned with moral choices and rights.

Hicks, Granville. "Jews Without Judaism." Rev. of *This People. Nation* 12 Apr. 1933: 415-16.

Describes *This People* as containing five stories, each dealing with Jews who have tried to escape from their racial heritage. Considers this an interesting social document and an impressive and accurate reflection of life.

"A Homily on Marriage." Rev. of *Stephen Escott. New York Times Book Review* 9 Mar. 1930: 8.

Considers *Stephen Escott* to have been written glibly, but in a clear style. Comments that it may have value as an essay on sex but considers the Freudian treatment of character heavy-handed. Concludes that, as a novel, it is a complete failure as was *Roman Summer*. Claims that one can put it to one side and hope for another *Island Within*.

"A Jewish Family." Rev. of *The Island Within. New York Times Book Review* 11 Mar. 1928: 7.

Argues that *The Island Within* is welded together of flesh and blood feeling, movement, and ideas. Comments that there is clarity and compression in this story of heritage and the Jewish family. Details the story and characters.

Jones, E. B. C. "New Novels." Rev. of *An Altar in the Fields. New Statesman & Nation* 19 May 1934: 768-69.

Considers *An Altar in the Fields* to be about the modernity of the central protagonists of the novel and their modern dilemma. Details contents, and concludes that the book fails to convince us that the seeds of failure lie within Dick and Rose. Claims that the error is in the choice of subject matter.

Kazin, Alfred. "A World of Moral Splendor." Rev. of *Trumpet of Jubilee. New York Herald Tribune Books* 2 May 1937: 2.

Argues that *Trumpet of Jubilee* is a call for ancient values. Sees in it a new confession of faith, an address to a hostile world, and a grand moral statement. Describes the contents of the book, discusses aspects of Lewisohn's life and previous work, and concludes by calling the book uneven because of its surliness with regard to the Arab characterizations, even though they are intermingled with beautiful poetry.

King, Francis. "Semi-Fiction." Rev. of *The Case of Mr. Crump*.
   Spectator 31 Mar. 1979: 26-27.

Considers this a book written to nail woman and wife as a monstrous
jailer, and to exculpate himself. Comments that Lewisohn has both an
extraordinary ferocity and pathos as well as some major stylistic inadequacies. Concludes that the book feels stripped naked and terribly
immediate in its portrayal of a monstrous marriage and wife.

Kronenberger, Louis. "A Lewisohn Parable." Rev. of *An Altar in the
   Fields*. *New York Times Book Review* 25 Feb. 1934: 9, 15.

Calls *An Altar in the Fields* the work of a writer with strong, uncompromising opinions. Comments, however, that as a story representing people
and events, it has grave weaknesses. Concludes that he brings us conso-
lation in extremes, but no cure.

Krutch, Joseph Wood. "Significant Ugliness." Rev. of *The Case of Mr.
   Crump*. *Nation* 9 Feb. 1927: 149-50.

Discusses *The Case of Mr. Crump* as a hideously powerful story about the
unequal conflict between the creative artist and the vulgar entanglements
of his disordered life. Reviews the contents of the novel, and concentrates
on describing the sluttishness and malignant characteristics of Mrs.
Crump. Concludes: "Perhaps Mr. Lewisohn is the only man alive capable
of writing such a book, and capable at the same time of maintaining that
the world which it describes is something more than sound and fury.

"Latest Works of Fiction." Rev. of *Don Juan*. *New York Times Book
   Review* 21 Oct. 1923: 9.

Claims that *Don Juan* is a book which treats the problem of marriage and
personal freedom with considerable insight. Asserts that the story drives
home because it deals not with the exotic and the abnormal but with
plain people, and considers the telling to be excellently done.

Levy, M. P. "The Island Within." Rev. of *The Island Within*. *New
   Republic* 16 May 1928: 398-99.

Describes the two parts of the novel, its characters, its setting, and its
epic proportions. Considers its style beautiful and the whole production
old-fashioned and morally informed.

Mandel, Siegfried. "The War Between Men and Women." Rev. of *In a
   Summer Season*. *New York Times Book Review* 12 June 1955: 14.

Argues that *In a Summer Season* Lewisohn pushes his characters to the edge of despair, but does not entirely succeed in making the reader care whether or not they topple over. Concludes that, by implication, he sees an end to the ceaseless battle between the sexes if relations were more firmly set on compatibility, children, and religion.

Marsh, Fred T. "Mr. Lewisohn's Prophetic Novel." Rev. of *Trumpet of Jubilee. New York Times Book Review* 25 Apr. 1937: 2.

Calls *Trumpet of Jubilee* half Jeremiad and half jubilee. Notes that it sings and thunders in Lewisohn's biblical prose. Concludes that it is a book of meanings, metaphysics, prophecies, laments, and intellectual enlightenment.

Mencken, H. L. "Portrait of a Lady." Rev. of *The Case of Mr. Crump. American Mercury* Mar. 1927: 379-80.

Describes *The Case of Mr. Crump* as a full-length study of an absurd marriage followed by a detailed and merciless study of Mrs. Crump's soul, especially in its more revolting outward manifestations. Considers Lewisohn has achieved a portrait of indelible reality and poignancy.

"A Modern Fable." Rev. of *The Romantic. New York Times Book Review* 23 Aug. 1931: 6.

Claims that *The Romantic* is a book which asserts that the Jewish people must seek some mystic reintegration with their own past. Calls the book beautifully written, smooth, flowing, and ultimately without depth. Concludes that it does not move as good psychological writing or dramatic writing should.

"Mr. Lewisohn's Stories." Rev. of *This People. New York Times Book Review* 19 Mar. 1933: 18.

Comments that *This People* shows its author as Zionist, artist, and preacher. Suggests that this makes the novel rather dogged and thesis-ridden. Concludes, however, that the stories are interesting and written with poetic ardor.

Rascoe, Burton. "Comforting, Like a Lullaby." Rev. of *An Altar in the Fields. Nation* 18 Apr. 1934: 450-51.

Calls *An Altar in the Fields* an agreeable, old-fashioned novel crafted with words that function with avuncular eighteenth- century grace and self-assurance. Concludes that, for all its charm, so easy and gentle is the formula few will obey it or even take it seriously.

"Repulsive but Human." Rev. of *The Case of Mr. Crump. Times Literary Supplement* 30 May 1968: 545.

Considers the novel overpraised in the 1920s. Describes the contents in considerable detail, its banning in the U.S., and its subsequent publication in Paris.

Ribalow, Harold. "Ludwig Lewisohn's *The Island Within.*" Rev. of *The Island Within. Jewish Heritage* 5 (Fall 1963): 44-48.

Describes the historical period in which the book was written, and construes the central theme as the conflict between the Jewish world in America and the outer world of the nation. Details the contents of the novel, and commends it to all young Jews seeking a sense of identity.

Rich, Amy C. "Books and Writers." Rev. of *The Broken Snare. Arena* Nov. 1908: 481-82.

Considers *The Broken Snare* a strong and well-written study of one phase of the marriage problem. Details the story and characters. Concludes that this novel will be one of the talked of novels of the season with its vigorous and unconventional treatment of the subject.

Robbins, Frances Lamont. "Prophet and Propagandist." Rev. of *The Last Days of Shylock. Outlook* 14 Jan. 1931: 67.

Calls the novel another chapter in Lewisohn's ongoing elegiac history of his race. Considers him a prophet for a people who use parable in biblical fashion and who possess a considerable narrative gift and richness of style. Describes contents briefly.

Robbins, Frances Lamont. "Speaking of Books." Rev. of *The Island Within. Outlook* 4 July 1928: 394-95.

Calls *The Island Within* an admirable novel from a philosopher, poet, and moralist who writes pure and stirring prose. Suggests that this novel is another chronicle of the wandering Jew who moves from Gentile marriage, fatherhood, and professional life to a mission to suffering Jews in the Balkans. Concludes that it is characterized by a fine sense of the picturesque and brilliant historical narrative.

Robbins, Frances Lamont. "The Wisest Word." Rev. of *Stephen Escott. Outlook* 19 Mar. 1930: 465-66.

Calls *Stephen Escott* evidence of Lewisohn's humane, idealistic spirit.

Details plot and characters, commends the book for its truth, and concludes that it is full of structural faults.

Rosenfeld, Isaac. "'It Is Hard to Be a Jew.'" Rev. of *Breathe Upon These*. *New Republic* 10 Apr. 1944: 509.

Calls *Breathe Upon These* a book which angrily indicts the Allies and Great Britain for hypocrisy toward the Jews. Considers the novel poorly written, a failure, and altogether too polite for such a cry for help on such a momentous matter. Concludes that, ultimately, Lewisohn's courage fails him.

Rothman, Nathan L. "A Novel—and a Prophecy." Rev. of *Trumpet of Jubilee*. *Saturday Review of Literature* 1 May 1937: 7.

Argues that this novel suffers badly because of the presence of irreconcilable elements within it. Calls the prose style beautifully articulate, yet fails to stop the book turning from novelette into an amorphous and confused document. Concludes that the ideas touch on every ill we have in the world and yet fail to cohere with the element of prophecy.

Sherman, Beatrice. "Ludwig Lewisohn's Tale of Love." Rev. of *For Ever Wilt Thou Love*. *New York Times Book Review* 12 Mar 1939: 7.

Calls *For Ever Wilt Thou Love* a tender, compassionate love story written in a poetic, fervid style providing a fascinating commentary on modern love and marriage.

"Shylock's Last Days." Rev. of *The Last Days of Shylock*. *New York Times Book Review* 11 Jan. 1931: 9.

Argues that *The Last Days of Shylock* contains both good work and bad. Notes that it is written in stilted and artificial prose, and pictures Shylock as a good Zionist. Concludes that, unfortunately, Shakespeare's comic edges and flashes of insight into the character are gone, but there is still more of merit than expected.

Smertenko, Johan. "Jew and Gentile in America." Rev. of *The Island Within*. *Nation* 18 Apr. 1928: 452.

Sees this as a great popular novel as well as a *piece à thèse*. Commends it for its passion and command of situation.

Sykes, Gerald. "Fiction." Rev. of *The Last Days of Shylock*. *Bookman* Mar. 1931: 81.

Describes *The Last Days of Shylock* as a book learnedly and capably written, but without imagination. Sees it as an exploitation of persecution and a piece of professional Judaizing that sensitive Jew and Gentile alike will find unpleasant.

Trilling, Lionel. "Flawed Instruments." Rev. of *Stephen Escott. Speaking of Literature and Society.* Lionel Trilling. New York: Harcourt, 1980. 21-26. Rpt. from *Menorah Journal* Apr. 1930.

Considers this novel a flawed work, nice in conception, but full of stereotypes, and poor style. Claims that the novel is conceived as an instrument of moral instruction and that this alone perverts his art. Concludes that we have need of idealism about Jews and Judaism, but that if this idealism is not based on sound reality, it inflates the vanity of the ignorant and turns the knowing away with smiles.

Untermeyer, Louis. "No Hiding Place." Rev. of *An Altar in the Fields. Saturday Review of Literature* 21 Apr. 1934: 645.

Finds this a problem novel because it asks such profoundly unanswerable questions about loss of hope for postwar generations. Details plot and characters. Concludes that, unfortunately, the plot fails and earnestness prevails over eloquence. Also notes that the ending is falsely happy, and the characters shadowy and unreal.

Van Doren, Dorothy. "Fable and Prophecy." Rev. of *Trumpet of Jubilee. Nation* 19 June 1937: 708-09.

Sees *Trumpet of Jubilee* as dramatizing the struggle of man in the Western world today against fascism. Describes the setting in Germany of the 1930s, and the development of the plot and the characters. Concludes that, though Lewisohn uses too many adjectives, his style is for the most part pure and penetrating.

Witherspoon, Frances. "Eloquent Refugees." Rev. of *Breathe Upon These. New York Times Book Review* 19 Mar. 1944: 20,22.

Says *Breathe Upon These* contains the thesis that we have become inured to the martyrdom of a great people, the Jews. Argues, however, that it is not the thesis that is questionable but the method of the novel. Claims that the lengthy narrative of oppression finally gets mislaid somewhere in the book and Lewisohn fails to maximize his climax. Concludes that the central characters do finally emerge as vital, distinguished people, despite being narrative devices.

Biographical Sources

Avery, Evelyn. "Ludwig Lewisohn." *American Novelists, 1910-1945, Part II: F. Scott Fitzgerald-O. E. Rolvaag.* Ed. James J. Martine. Detroit: Gale, 1981. Vol. 9 of *Dictionary of Literary Biography.* 94 vols. to date. 1978- . 185-90.

More than details of his life, this is a career biography, tracing the development of the author's canon, describing the contents and themes of his works, evaluating his reputation, and placing him in the larger context of American literary history. Includes lists of primary and secondary sources and illustrations.

Chyet, Stanley F. "Ludwig Lewisohn: The Years of Becoming." *American Jewish Archives* 11.2 (1959): 125-47.

A detailed historical account of Lewisohn's early years as immigrant, American, Southerner and Christian. Also covers his college education, and early career.

Chyet, Stanley F. "Ludwig Lewisohn in Charleston (1892-1903)." *American Jewish Historical Quarterly* 54.3 (1964-1965): 296-322.

A detailed historical account of the birth, family, neighborhood, growing-up experiences, education, formation, attitudes toward being American, politics of Jewishness, Jewish sense of identity, and the young manhood of Lewisohn, with particular regard to the issue of being Jewish in Charleston at this period of time.

De Casseres, Benjamin. "Portraits en Brochette." *Bookman* July 1931: 488-89.

A very brief biographical sketch of Lewisohn's life.

Glicksberg, Charles I. "Ludwig Lewisohn." *American Literary Criticism, 1900-1950.* Charles I. Glicksberg. New York: Hendricks, 1951. 198-201.

Provides a brief biography of Lewisohn's life and career.

Guttmann, Allen. "The Forgotten Achievement of Ludwig Lewisohn." *The Jewish Writer in America: Assimilation and the Crisis of Identity.* Allen Guttmann. New York: Oxford UP, 1971. 100-08.

A useful introductory essay on Lewisohn's life, works, themes, style, and contribution to Jewish-American literature. Excellent biographical material.

Hindus, Milton. "Ludwig Lewisohn: From Assimilation to Zionism." *Jewish Frontier* 31.1 (1964): 22-30.

A detailed biographical account of Lewisohn's life and writing career.

Lewisohn, James. "My Father, Ludwig Lewisohn: A Personal Reminiscence." *Midstream* Nov. 1966: 48-50.

Shows impressions of Lewisohn written by his son ten years after his death. Comments on his writing habits, his teaching, and his Jewishness.

Lewisohn, Ludwig. "Ludwig Lewisohn." *Nation* 21 Nov. 1923: 583-84.

Agrees with a friend who has called him a radical about life and a classicist about literature, so long as he can define his terms. Explains his approach to criticism, writing, and teaching.

Lewisohn, Ludwig. *Mid-Channel: An American Chronicle*. New York: Harper; London: Butterworth, 1929; New York: Blue Ribbon, 1931; Modern Jewish Experience Series. New York: Arno, 1975.

Lewisohn, Ludwig. *Upstream: An American Chronicle*. New York: Boni; London: Richards, 1923; The Modern Library of the World's Best Books. New York: Mod. Lib., 1926; St. Clair Shores: Scholarly, 1977.

"Ludwig Lewisohn: In Memoriam." *American Jewish Archives* Nov. 1965: 109-13.

A brief and admiring account of Lewisohn's life and work. Concludes that his was a life of triumphant self-mastery which had significant impact on two generations of Americans.

Melnick, Ralph. "Ludwig Lewisohn." *Twentieth-Century American-Jewish Fiction Writers*. Ed. Daniel Walden. Detroit: Gale, 1984. Vol. 28 of *Dictionary of Literary Biography*. 94 vols. to date. 1978- . 141-54.

More than details of his life, this is a career biography tracing the development of the author's canon, describing the contents and themes of his works, evaluating his reputation, and placing him in the larger context of American literary history. Includes lists of primary and secondary sources, and illustrations.

Melnick, Ralph. "Ludwig Lewisohn: The Early Charleston Years." *Studies in the American Jewish Experience II*. Eds. Jacob R. Marcus and Abraham J. Peels. Cincinnati: American Jewish Archives, 1984. 105-26.

A perspective on Lewisohn's social status and personal history while growing up in Charleston. Provides a perspective on the social history of Charleston itself, which sheds further light on Lewisohn. Incorporates several anecdotes not found in other biographical pieces.

Ross, Jean W. "Ludwig Lewisohn." *American Writers in Paris, 1920-1939*. Ed. Karen L. Rood. Detroit: Gale, 1980. Vol. 4 of *Dictionary of Literary Biography*. 94 vols. to date. 1978- . 248-50.

Provides brief information about Lewisohn's early career, marriages, and publishing history of *The Case of Mr. Crump*.

Spiro, Saul S. *The Jew As Man of Letters: Being Some Notes on Ludwig Lewisohn*. Burlington: Vermont Zionist Youth, Masada, 1935. 3-16.

An admiring portrait of Lewisohn at fifty-two. Contains some biographical elements and much definition of him as Jew and role model for the young.

Dissertations

Gartner, Carol Blicker. "A New Mirror for America: The Fiction of the Immigrant Ghetto, 1890-1930." Diss. New York U, 1970.

Gordon, Nicholas Karl. "Jewish and American: A Critical Study of the Fiction of Abraham Cahan, Anzia Yezierska, Waldo Frank and Ludwig Lewisohn." Diss. Stanford U, 1968.

Greenberg, Abraham Herbert. "The Ethnocentric Attitudes of Some Jewish American Writers: Educational Implications." Diss. Yeshiva U, 1956.

Leonard Michaels

1933 –

Primary Sources

Novels

The Men's Club. New York: Farrar, 1981; London: Cape, 1981; New York: Avon, 1982; London: Triad, 1983.

Shuffle. New York: Farrar, 1990.

Collected Works

Going Places. New York: Farrar, 1969; New York: NAL, 1969, 1973; New York: Dell, 1970; London: Panther, 1970; London: Weidenfeld, 1970.

Contents: Manikin, City Boy, Crossbones, Sticks and Stones, The Deal, Intimations, Making Changes, Mildred, Fingers and Toes, Isaac, A Green Thought, Finn, Going Places.

I Would Have Saved Them If I Could. New York: Farrar, 1975; New York: Bantam, 1977.

Contents: Murderers; Eating Out; Getting Lucky; Story Teller, Liars, and Bores; In the Fifties; Reflections of a Wild Kid; Downers; Trotsky's Garden; Annabella's Hat; I Would Have Saved Them If I Could; Hello Jack; Some Laughed; The Captain.

Short Fiction in Anthologies

"City Boy." *The Single Voice: An Anthology of Contemporary Fiction.*
Ed. Jerome Charyn. New York: Collier, 1969. 287-97; *Stories from
the Sixties.* Ed. Stanley Elkin. Garden City: Doubleday, 1971. 137-48.

"Getting Lucky." *Many Windows: 22 Stories from American Review.* Ed.
Ted Solotaroff. New York: Harper, 1982. 280-83.

"Making Changes." *Stories from the Transatlantic Review.* Ed. Joseph F.
McCrindle. New York: Holt, 1970; London: Gollancz, 1970. 35-41;
Harmondsworth: Penguin, 1974. 57-65.

"Manikin." *Superfiction, or The American Story Transformed.* Ed. Joe
David Bellamy. New York: Vintage, 1975. 129-36.

"Murderers." *Matters of Life and Death; New American Stories.* Ed.
Tobias Wolff. Green Harbor: Wampeter, 1983. 132-35; *American
Short Story Masterpieces.* Eds. Raymond Carver and Tom Jenks. New
York: Delacorte, 1987. 289-92.

Short Fiction in Periodicals

"The Captain." *Partisan Review* 39.3 (1972): 319-35.

"City Boy." *Paris Review* 10.39 (1966): 40-50.

"Crossbones." *New American Review* 3 (1968): 141-43.

"The Deal." *Massachusetts Review* 7.1 (1966): 61-70.

"Fingers and Toes." *Paris Review* 11.42 (1968): 12-24.

"Going Places." *Transatlantic Review* 23 (1966): 109-14.

"Getting Lucky." *New American Review* 10 (1970): 99-102.

"Hello Jack." *Partisan Review* 42.1 (1975): 30-34.

"Isaac." *Partisan Review* 36.1 (1969): 80-82.

"Jealousy." *Paris Review* 28.100 (1986): 250-52; *Harper's* Mar. 1987: 36-37.

"Making Changes." *Transatlantic Review* 26 (1967): 84-91.

"Manikin." *Massachusetts Review* 9.1 (1968): 33-38.

"Men's Club." *Esquire* Dec. 1978: 54-60, 62, 65-66.

"Robinson Crusoe Liebowitz." *Esquire* Mar. 1970: 140-41, 158.

"The Statue of John Wayne." *Antaeus* 52 (1984): 54-59.

"Storytellers, Liars, and Bores." *New American Review* 13 (1971): 57-66.

"The Sound of Hirsch." *Playboy* Sept. 1962: 81-82, 84, 207.

"Three Short Stories: 'Pretty Women,' 'Imagine a Man,' 'You.'" *American Review.* 26 (1977): 284-85.

"Toiler." *Partisan Review* 51.4 (1984-85): 540-51.

"The Words for Penis." *TriQuarterly* 35.1 (1976): 30-31.

Secondary Sources

Articles and Chapters

DeCurtis, Anthony. "Self Under Siege: The Stories of Leonard Michaels." *Critique* 21.2 (1979): 101-11.

Suggests that in his two story collections, *Going Places* and *I Would Have Saved Them If I Could,* Michaels depicts the contemporary struggle to shape a sensibility that is sufficiently intelligent, flexible, detached, and controlled to negotiate the contemporary world. Calls his positive characters witty, smart individuals for whom thinking is an active, energetic process culminating in actions in the world. Shows how, by isolating the pitfall of being entrapped by mind to the point of emotional paralysis, of seeking in the mind for solutions that only action can bring, Michaels has defined a psychological drama central to contemporary American fiction.

Klinkowitz, Jerome. "Experimental Realism." *The Self-Apparent Word: Form as Language/Language as Form.* Carbondale: Southern Illinois UP, 1984. 124-26.

Describes the tendency of experimental fiction to be antihierarchical and in avoidance of values which exist outside the work. Quotes from Michaels and several others in making this point.

Michaels, Leonard. "The Making of a Writer: 'Anything Might Influence Me.'" *New York Times Book Review* 9 Aug. 1981: 3.

Discusses his wife's dreams, the weather, music, pain, politics, and other matters that influence his writing. Mostly a biographical monologue of anecdotes about his views of himself as a writer and his sources of inspiration.

Neilson, Keith. *"I Would Have Saved Them If I Could." Survey of Contemporary Literature.* Ed. Frank N. Magill. Rev. ed. 12 vols. Englewood Cliffs: Salem, 1977. 6: 3593-96.

Details background, influences, character, style, plot, and themes.

Peden, William. "A Mad World, My Masters." *The American Short Story: Continuity and Change, 1940-1975.* 2nd. ed. Boston: Houghton, 1975. 110-12.

Discusses *Going Places* as a work of black humor full of striking contrasts, reversals, kaleidoscopic glimpses of life in Sin city, and a curious, manic collage of surreal, comic, and tragi-comic scenes done in vivid color and vague grayness.

Queenan, Joe. "Character Assassins." *American Spectator* Dec. 1988: 14-16.

Comments on Michaels' contempt for white collar types and the absence of an entire technocracy in American society. Sees his stories populated by weirdos because he thinks American life is dull. Lists several of his character types.

Stevick, Philip. "Naive Narration: Classic to Post Modern." *Modern Fiction Studies* 23.4 (1977-78): 531-42. Rpt. in edited form in *Alternative Pleasures: Postrealist Fiction and the Tradition.* Philip Stevick. Urbana: U of Illinois P, 1981. 77-93.

Discusses the entire complex subject of naive narration in the works of the great modern masters, and out of this lengthy context turns to postmodernist naive narration and the work of Michaels, who represents a transitional figure for him. Talks specifically about Michael's use of a young, more naive narrator and the technical problems that arise when the author's more mature vision must be projected through such a viewpoint character. Describes his use of prose, collage, voice, visual devices, and psychological insight.

Reviews

Baldeschwiler, Eileen. "Reviews." Rev. of *Going Places. Studies in Short Fiction* 8.4 (1971): 643-44.

Argues that *Going Places* is commercial, smart talking, stylized, designed to sell, and titillating. Insists, however, it also has something solid to offer. Suggests that the major theme of the collection is how each of us fashions our own destructions. Michaels knows all there is to know about symbolism, time schemes, point of view, stream of consciousness, and seventeenth-century style wit. Concludes that the real question is whether these faults are merely stylistic or whether they betray a shallow and vulgar mind.

Bazerman, Charles. "Danger, Fear and Self-Revulsion." Rev. of *I Would Have Saved Them If I Could. Nation* 15 Nov. 1975: 502-04.

Reveals, in this collection, the confused, scarred self behind the mask of fashionable attitudes. Finds he no longer needs to rely on the bizarre to gain effects, hence the weightier emotional effects of the stories. Concludes that, though his world is not attractive, these stories are denser than they seem at first glance.

"Books." Rev. of *The Men's Club. Time* 27 Apr. 1981: 74.

Calls Michaels a short story writer who occupies a place somewhere between Philip Roth and Donald Bartheleme in the periodic table of

American prose writers. Comments that *The Men's Club* is not so much a burlesque as a carefully paced intellectual strip tease. Concludes that male armor is dropped to show emotional paralysis.

Corn, Alfred. "Reader's Guide." Rev. of *The Men's Club. Yale Review* 70.4 (1981): xiv, xvii-xviii.

Suggests that *The Men's Club* will verify the bleakest of female surmises about male psychology. Suggests also that others will be surprised to discover how much American men fret over their wives. Labels most of the men stock characters from movieland, and describes Michaels' style as including a broad spectrum of effects and tones, including the neat and funny.

Donoghue, Denis. "Couples." Rev. of *Going Places. New York Review of Books* 10 July 1969: 17-18.

Complains that this collection of stories is violent, hard driving in terms of language, uneven, possibly gothic, and sometimes excessive. Describes several stories in detail.

Edwards, Thomas R. Rev. of *I Would Have Saved Them If I Could. New York Times Book Review* 3 Aug. 1975: 1-2.

Gives a short publishing history for Michaels, and provides a description of several of the stories in *I Would Have Saved Them If I Could.* Pays particular attention to "In the Fifties." Provides much literary commentary and plot summary.

Evanier, David. "A Man's World." Rev. of *The Men's Club. National Review* 18 Sept. 1981: 1088-89.

Describes the contents of *The Men's Club* and its particularly piercing dialogue. Suggests that, while not a masterpiece, this is a significant novel full of relentlessly dark and brilliant strength. Compares the effect of the whole piece with that of *The Iceman Cometh.*

Finkle, David. "Fiction Briefs." Rev. of *The Men's Club. Saturday Review* Apr. 1981: 73.

Argues that this novel lacks elan and vigorous strokes, but is still worth reading because it cuts deeply and because its humor, sentiment, and brutality bubble forth constantly in its attempt to make sense of women.

Fremont-Smith, Eliot. "Reciprocating Motion." Rev. of *The Men's Club. Village Voice* 8 Apr. 1981: 33, 39.

Describes the contents of *The Men's Club* calling it a relentless, subtlely psychological send-up of "women's lib fiction" and a prime example of storm-smasher social comedy. Concludes that it is really about women as described by the men of the club.

Gilbert, Elliot L. "Reviews." Rev. of *Going Places*. *Kenyon Review* 31.3 (1969): 422-25.

Calls *Going Places* a long short story with remarkable stylistic density. Details several of the thirteen stories, and describes Michaels' virtuoso style which ranges from cinematic jump cuts, to complex flashbacks, and other experimental techniques. Identifies the theme as each person's search for their own fate. Calls this a brilliant first book.

Goodwin, Stephen. "Talk Around the Clock." Rev. of *The Men's Club*. *Washington Post Book World* 26 Apr. 1981: 4-5.

Comments that *The Men's Club* is too much like ordinary life, always reverting back to its base nature, and resisting perfection as intransigently and successfully as Caliban resists Prospero. Concludes that these artlessly-told pilgrim tales are full of guile, and reflect conditions rather than personalities; passions here are figurative, not felt. Concludes that we get the meaning, but we miss the experience.

Gross, Barry. "Fiction." Rev. of *Going Places*. *Saturday Review* 2 Aug. 1969: 27.

Complains that *Going Places* vividly conveys life like a bad dream or a sickening taste in the mouth. Sees the prose, like the subject matter, as jittery and jarring. Complains that the rhythms seem to be unpredictable most of the time and that the reader needs to make extraordinary efforts to get into Mr. Michaels's wavelength. Concludes that it is not enough to tell readers that life is absurd—readers want to know how it got that way.

Halio, Jay L., Jr. "Fantasy and Fiction." Rev. of *Going Places*. *Southern Review* 7.2 (1971): 637-38.

Argues that as an art Michaels's work reveals a strong grappling with the medium of language, as well as the expression of ideas, feelings, and attitudes.

Halio, Jay L., Jr. "Violence and After." Rev. of *I Would Have Saved Them If I Could*. *Southern Review* 15.3 (1979): 704-05.

Suggests that *I Would Have Saved Them If I Could* is a splendid successor to *Going Places*, capturing the absurdities of cosmopolitan life and wielding declarative sentences with style which cuts right to the heart of sensation, emotion, or image.

Hamlin, William C. "On the Brink." Rev. of *Going Places*. *New York Times Book Review* 25 May 1969: 49.

Calls Michaels a writer of considerable awareness and humor. Finds the commonplace set alongside the unexpected and the horrifying as aftermaths of passion. Compares his style and range in a discussion of Purdy, O'Connor, Malamud, and Salinger.

Harper, Howard M. Jr. "American Fiction." Rev. of *Going Places*. *Contemporary Literature* 12.2 (1971): 215-16.

Notes that *Going Places*, a collection of 13 stories, is Michaels's first book and reveals an impressive talent. Comments that his pessimistic view of the possibilities of human life are neither original nor unique, but that they are presented with exceptional force and validity, depth and vitality. Complains that, unfortunately, too many of his scenes dissolve into a general green sickness of random sexuality, violence, and death.

Heller, Amanda. "Short Reviews." Rev. of *I Would Have Saved Them If I Could*. *Atlantic* Oct. 1975: 108.

Considers some of the effects in *I Would Have Saved Them If I Could* flashy and manic. Argues that Michaels pays homage to Borges, and has produced a puzzling, unsettling, intense, powerful collection of stories.

Howard, Maureen. "Seize the Day." Rev. of *Going Places*. *Partisan Review* 37.1 (1970): 134-35.

Calls *Going Places* a remarkable first novel with a strong sense of style. Notes that the stories range from fables, to realism, to Jewish idiom pieces, to nightmare accounts. Concludes that the least successful are the most experimental.

Howe, Irving. "Vectors." Rev. of *I Would Have Saved Them If I Could*. *New York Review of Books* 13 Nov. 1975: 42.

Calls *I Would Have Saved Them If I Could* a collection of stories that make one wish Michaels had never heard of alienation, sentiment of being, and nihilism, so that his fragile talent might have flourished in comparative innocence. Complains that these are stories crusted with the junk of fashionable culture, full of Bellowian swagger without Bellow's rich complication, and ripe with Rothian sexual assertiveness, without Roth's sense of fun. Concludes that this is a confusion of vectors for the reader.

Korn, Eric. "Agony Column." Rev. of *I Would Have Saved Them If I Could. Times Literary Supplement* 25 Feb. 1977: 201.

Considers *I Would Have Saved Them If I Could* a collection of stories containing distinctive style, diction going straight to the self-pitying core, a manner at once cocky and irritating, and certain that the agonies of middle-class New York Jews are somehow exemplary for the suffering world, all of which seems to give the author the right to answer his own rhetorical questions before anyone else can get a word in edgeways. Concludes that the view is always sidelong, and that a sly knowingness invades the whole collection.

Kramer, Hilton. "Lonely Rituals." Rev. of *I Would Have Saved Them If I Could. Commentary* Dec. 1975: 79-80.

Describes *I Would Have Saved Them If I Could* as the antic, self-conscious, self-doubting, self-mocking, male offspring of the Jewish middle-class. Notes that the whole thing speaks in brief muffled screams. Concludes that this is an exquisitely made object, but miniature in size.

Kubal, David. "Fiction Chronicle." Rev. of *The Men's Club. Hudson Review* 34.3 (1981): 460-61.

Calls this a novella with no whimpers, only feral roars. Complains that it is a tedious book in which a series of typical Californian types swap tales of sexual misadventures through a long, tedious night. Sees it as a book of desperation that functions more as a jeering shrug than as art in its effort to point out some grave moral disorders in our male culture.

Lehmann-Haupt, Christopher. "Rescuing Art from the Horror." Rev. of *I Would Have Saved Them If I Could. New York Times* 30 July 1975: 31.

Considers *I Would Have Saved Them If I Could*, a collection of thirteen short stories, many of which stand alone as exceptionally crafted. Comments that they are all written in a nervous, graphic style as if the author could not bear to dwell on the details. Reads much like a Kafkaesque dream. Details several stories, and concludes that Michaels does finally rescue art from horror.

Lehmann-Haupt, Christopher. "Short Stories—To Be Taken as Prescribed." Rev. of *Going Places. New York Times* 14 Apr. 1969: 43.

Calls *Going Places* a violent, hostile, absurd world in which people lovingly grope for each other, yet can only touch one another by inflicting
damage. Suggests that here Michaels's fictional technique propels coherent language and familiar situations to the boundaries of realism, and
then crashes out into surrealist dream territory.

Leonard, John. "Books of the Times." Rev. of *The Men's Club*. *New
    York Times* 7 Apr. 1981: C13. Rpt. in *Books of the Times* June 1981:
    278-80.

Describes the comic elements, plot, and contents of the novel. Describes
the men as perplexed about their gluttony, lost in their work, short on
meaning, and looking to women to supply it, while women are looking
elsewhere, stealing somebody else's dessert. Concludes that the reader
laughs and gags, but that this is still an excellent book.

Lieberman, Laurence. "Words into Skin." Rev. of *Going Places*. *Atlantic*
    Apr. 1969: 131-32.

Considers *Going Places*, a first collection which fuses agonized settings
with the plights of the characters. Notes that it is full of emblematic stage
sets and street dialogue. Comments that some stories are wacky sexual
fantasies, while others have the density and compression of a lyric.
Enumerates the gimmicky dialogues, quirky personalities, and mutila-
tions of sound and sentence, and concludes that the story becomes frayed
at the seams and overextended.

Mahon, Derek. "More Dancing Than Writing." Rev. of *Going Places*.
    Listener 26 Mar. 1970: 424.

Finds *Going Places* written with the great vigor and grace of poetry.
Notes that the work is unbelievable and mind-blowing and so is the
humor. Concludes that, though he may be somewhat limited as yet, his
talent is big enough to expand.

Morse, J. Mitchell. "Reviews." Rev. of *Going Places*. *Hudson Review*
    22.2 (1969): 327.

Considers this collection of stories less assured, less mature, and even for
all their newer techniques, less bold than when Rabelais, Joyce, and
other writers first used these techniques. Claims that Michaels reminds
him of Chagall. Concludes that, though Michaels plays with language,
few writers of his generation can even work with it.

Mount, Ferdinand. "Books and Writers." Rev. of *I Would Have Saved Them If I Could. Encounter* June 1977: 52.

Calls this a collection of Jewish New York fragments, some of them one paragraph long and others full short stories. Comments on the suffering, callousness, and horrors so often dealt with in a shrug or laconic gesture.

Oates, Joyce Carol. "Please Tell Me Its Just a Story." Rev. of *Going Places. Chicago Tribune Book World* 30 Mar. 1969: 6.

Comments that *Going Places* suffers because it cannot take itself seriously. Suggests that these stories seem archly effective when viewed separately; gathered into one slim volume their formula and the comic skeleton of their being becomes too prominent. Notes that while the influence of Malamud is obvious, so is that of Barthleme and Roth. Concludes that if Michaels is going to create fiction in proportion to his obvious intelligence, his own whimsical anecdotal style needs something harder behind it, something less arbitrary and less cartoon-like.

Phillips, Robert. "Books." Rev. of *I Would Have Saved Them If I Could. Commonweal* 7 Nov. 1975: 538-39.

Calls these stories less admirable than their critical reception has indicated. Comments that they contain tricky sexual fantasies, constipated dialogue, gimmicky characters, perversions, little drama, too much exposition, too few rounded characters, and too many anecdotes all strung together. Notes that mothers come off badly in almost every story. Judges there are also extraordinary strengths that may become more apparent in other work.

Prescott, Peter S. "Rogue Males." Rev. of *The Men's Club. Newsweek* 27 Apr. 1981: 96. Rpt. as "After Marriage," in *Never in Doubt: Critical Essays on American Books, 1972-1985.* Peter S. Prescott. New York: Arbor, 1986. 149-50.

Calls the stories these men tell moving and adroitly wrought. Suggests that the novella's frame may be coarse and the men unmemorable, but concludes that the book deserves to be read for the brief tales it tells. Concludes that the whole thing has a feminist cast that is far more appealing than most novels written by angry women today.

Reid, David. "Jolly Good Fellows." Rev. of *The Men's Club. Threepenny Review* 2.2 (1981): 8.

Describes *The Men's Club* as a satire on California culture. Describes the contents in detail, and concludes that these characters have been produced by a master phenomenologist of dread and desire, taking some of their shape from Dostoevsky, Chekhov, Chaucer, Kafka, Kierkegaard, Hegel, and Nietzsche.

Robins, Corrine. Rev. of *The Men's Club. American Book Review* Mar.-Apr. 1982: 8.

Calls *The Men's Club* Michaels's version of a Walpurgis Night in the Freudian male herd reborn in a group of California men. Michaels is trying to reach the raw edge of being human in order to examine the emotions on which human beings turn. Gives a full description of both characters and plot. Shows how each of the characters is tortured by the tragedy and impossibility of oneness in the little more than momentary exchange, while women become the butts of their blame and the silent sufferers.

Rumens, Carol. "Off the Leash." Rev. of *The Men's Club. Times Literary Supplement* 16 Oct. 1981: 1219.

Complains that *The Men's Club* has surprisingly little to add to that lacklustre debate on sexual politics because it corroborates traditional views on the male and the female. Shows how Michaels writes a choppy, muscle-flexing prose intending perhaps to express an ironical stance towards the Maileresque style of literary tough-talking. Concludes that, having accustomed oneself to nouns lopped off their articles and full stops like kicks in the shins, one must admit that such a style has immediacy and modulates easily into dialogue.

Scammell, William. "With and Without Women." Rev. of *The Men's Club. London Magazine* Oct. 1981: 98-99.

Describes the characters, contents, plot, and technique of *The Men's Club*.

Segal, Lore. "Captivating Horrors." Rev. of *Going Places. New Republic* 19 July 1969: 31-33.

Calls *Going Places* a satisfactorily written book that delivers much pain and very little obvious compassion. Provides a very detailed account of the stories in the collection, and concludes that the bleak and hideous are balanced by the hilarious, beautiful, and pleasurable.

Steiner, Joan E. "Books." Rev. of *Going Places. Michigan Quarterly Review* 9.4 (1970): 287-88.

Describes Michaels' first collection of thirteen stories impressive in their depth and range. Notes that they are predominantly Jewish in their orientation, and ultimately transcend their sphere to comment on the human condition in general and modern disorder in particular. Describes the style in detail, and concludes that Michaels is a major talent.

Taylor, Stephan. "Books." Rev. of *Going Places. Village Voice* 19 Feb. 1970: 6, 28.

Comments that the mood of these stories is predominantly comic and that their rhythms are those of laughter. Notes that it is a rich prose full of metaphor, laced with crazy juxtapositions and abrupt translations. Comments that the comic routine takes place on a tightrope and is suffused with urban despair. Describes the contents of several of the stories.

Thompson, John. "Clubland." Rev. of *The Men's Club. New York Review of Books* 16 July 1981: 41-42.

Calls *The Men's Club* a very clever conception by a very talented writer which fails as a story. Comments that as an allegory it is as dull as propaganda, and so enigmatic the reader must decipher what it has to say about the war of the sexes. Concludes that the characters and the story are tedious.

Towers, Robert. "Men Talking About Women." Rev. of *The Men's Club. New York Times Book Review* 12 Apr. 1981: 1, 28-29.

Calls the stories in *The Men's Club* hip and urban Jewish in sensibility. Notes that they are full of casual violence, nerve-scraping New York encounters, and trivialized or debased sex. Places the book as late modernist in its fragmented and plot-refusing structures and excessively literary in its expression. Concludes that its appeal will no doubt be its topicality. Provides a very detailed account of the contents.

Tyler, Anne. "Men Will Be Boys." Rev. of *The Men's Club. New Republic* 2 May 1981: 31-32.

Suggests that *The Men's Club* is more a short story writer's idea of a novel—a mistaken idea of a novel written in an oversimplified tone. Complains that while it features a large cast of characters, it reveals no new layers as the story progresses. Considers even its considerable virtues to be a short story's virtues—stunning efficiency, speedy flashes of description, and a breathtaking singleness of purpose. Details the contents, and concludes that it would be interesting to compare men's and women's reactions to this book.

Woiwode, Larry. "Out of the Fifties." Rev. of *I Would Have Saved Them If I Could. Partisan Review* 44.1 (1977): 125-30.

Details several of the stories in this collection, and comments on their fascination with violence, suicide, and death. Considers them denser, more mature, and more complex than his earlier work. Concludes that on the whole this is a carefully-constructed statement of our times, movingly developed throughout each of its sections, interlocking, and precise, and morally courageous.

Wolcott, James. "Books." Rev. of *The Men's Club. Esquire* May 1981: 19.

Calls *The Men's Club* a pop allegory, and sees a talky little novella which functions as a prose homage to Kafka. Sees this as Kafakesque slapstick, much deadpan comedy, slightly askew lyricism, and show-off coarseness. Considers its style lacking clarity and compactness. Complains that the spilling, sprawling secrets of these Berkeley clubbies soon leave the book awash in chatter and confusion. Concludes that, brief as the book is, it is still a long-winded wheeze.

Zweig, Paul. "Delicate Intentions." Rev. of *I Would Have Saved Them If I Could. Harper's Magazine* Sept. 1975: 68-69.

Describes the book as a hot collection of short stories in which prose is wielded like a weapon: part bludgeon. Notes that, with insane precision Michaels drops stink bombs in this urban madhouse where love is a hand job on the subway and community a surreal orgy on Sutton Place. Concludes that culture becomes a photographer's view of the Holocaust and that all of this is executed in excruciatingly precise, almost sculptural prose. Provides a detailed account of the contents.

Biographical Sources

Michaels, Leonard. "In the Fifties: Growing Up." *Partisan Review* 41.2 (1974): 197-202.

In an attempt to characterize the fifties, Michaels describes his experiences as a college student and teaching assistant in Michigan and California, working at odd jobs in Boston and other places, using drugs, drinking, his friends and acquaintances, his meeting some celebrities, and his participating in demonstrations.

Interviews

Benedict, Helen. "A Talk with Leonard Michaels." *New York Times Book Review* 12 Apr. 1981: 30-32. Rpt. in *Portraits in Print: A*

Collection of Profiles and the Stories Behind Them. Helen Benedict. New York: Columbia UP, 1991. 115-25.

Discusses in this interview *The Men's Club,* his own mid-life crisis, his views on art, his interest in themes of the failure of love, friendship, communication, and hope. Also reviews his writing style, personal life, personal reading, education, teaching career at Berkeley, and current work.

Robert Nathan

1894 – 1985

Primary Sources

Novels

Autumn. New York: McBride, 1921, 1923, 1935.

The Bishop's Wife. Indianapolis: Bobbs, 1928; Novels of Distinction. New York: Grosset, 1928; London: Gollancz, 1928; New York: Literary Guild, 1938; New York: Eds. for the Armed Services, 1938.

But Gently Day. New York: Knopf, 1943, 1945; Toronto: Ryerson, 1943.

The Color of Evening. New York: Knopf, 1960; Toronto: McClelland, 1960; London: Allen, 1960; New York: Popular [Cited in PBIP, 1970].

The Concert. New York: House of Books, 1940.

The Devil with Love. New York: Knopf, 1963; Toronto: Random, 1963; London: Allen, 1963.

The Elixir. New York: Knopf, 1971; Large Print ed. Boston: Hall, 1971.

The Enchanted Voyage. New York: Knopf, 1936, 1941, 1966, 1968; New York: Popular, 1936; London: Constable, 1937; New York: Eds. for the Armed Services, 1945; Westport: Greenwood, 1986; South Yarmouth: Curley, 1989.

The Fair. New York: Knopf, 1964; Toronto: Random, 1964.

The Fiddler in Barly. New York: McBride, 1926; London: Heinemann, 1927.

Heaven and Hell and the Megus Factor. New York: Delacorte, 1975; Large Print ed. Boston: Hall, 1975; Large Print ed. London: Prior, 1976.

The Innocent Eve. New York: Knopf, 1951; Toronto: McClelland, 1951.

Jonah; Son of Amittai. New York: McBride, 1925; London: Heinemann, 1925. Publ. as *Jonah or the Withering Vine.* New York: Knopf, 1934.

Journey of Tapiola. New York: Knopf, 1938, 1944; Toronto: Ryerson, 1938; London: Constable, 1938.

Long After Summer. New York: Knopf, 1948, 1966; Toronto: McClelland, 1948; London: Low, 1949; New York: Laurel Leaf-Dell, 1974.

The Mallot Diaries. New York: Knopf, 1965.

The Married Look. New York: Knopf, 1950; Toronto: McClelland, 1950. Publ. as *His Wife's Young Face.* London: Staples, 1951.

The Married Man. New York: Knopf, 1962; Toronto: Random, 1962.

MIA. New York: Knopf, 1970; New York: Avon, 1970; London: Allen, 1970.

Mr. Whittle and the Morning Star. New York: Knopf, 1947; New York: Ryerson, 1947; London: Low, 1947.

One More Spring. New York: Knopf, 1933; New York: Grosset, 1933; New York: Watts, 1933; Toronto: Cassell, 1933; Stamford: Overbrook, 1935; Bestseller Library. New York: American Mercury,

1940; New York: Eds. for the Armed Services, 1945; New York: Bantam, 1945; New York: Keith Jennison-Watts, 1966; New York: Popular, n.d.

The Orchid. Indianapolis: Bobbs, 1931; London: Mathews, 1932.

Peter Kindred. New York: Duffield, 1920.

Portrait of Jennie. New York: Keith Jennison-Watts, 1939; New York: Knopf, 1940, 1945, 1964; Toronto: Ryerson, 1940; London: Heinemann, 1940; New York: Eds. for the Armed Services, 1945; Cleveland: Forum-World, 1946; New York: Penguin, 1947; London: Low, 1949; New York: Eagle-Popular, 1962; New York: Laurel-Dell, 1967, 1977; New Haven: Tandem, 1969; New York: Popular, 1969; Cutchogue: Buccaneer, 1976; Greenport: Harmony, 1981. Serialized in *Redbook* Oct. 1939: 16-19, 87-97; Nov. 1939: 32-35, 98-106; Dec. 1939: 58-62, 74-82.

The Puppet Master. New York: McBride, 1923, 1925; London: Lane, 1924.

The Rancho of the Little Loves. New York: Knopf, 1956.

The River Journey. New York: Knopf, 1949; Toronto: McClelland, 1949. Serialized in *Woman's Home Companion* Apr. 1949: 18-19, 146-51, 172-83; May 1949: 28-29, 42, 44, 47-48, 50, 53-54, 56, 59.

Road of Ages. New York: Knopf, 1935; London: Constable, 1935; Darby: Darby, 1986.

The Sea-Gull Cry. New York: Knopf, 1942, 1959; Toronto: Ryerson, 1942; New York: Popular, n.d. Serialized in *Redbook* May 1942: 14-17, 63-66, 68; June 1942: 18-21, 78-86; July 1942: 26-29, 59-60, 62, 64.

Sir Henry. New York: Knopf, 1955; London: Barker, 1956; San Bernardino: Borgo, 1979.

So Love Returns. New York: Knopf, 1958; Toronto: McClelland, 1958; New York: Pyramid, 1959; London: Allen, 1959. Serialized in *Saturday Evening Post* 13 Sept. 1958: 25, 87-91, 94-97; 20 Sept. 1958: 33, 100, 102-04, 106; 27 Sept. 1958: 39, 60, 63-64, 70-71, 73, 76.

A Star in the Wind. New York: Knopf, 1962; London: Allen, 1962; New York: Popular, 1963.

Stonecliff. New York: Knopf, 1967; New York: Popular, 1967.

The Summer Meadows. New York: Delacorte, 1973; New York: Dell, 1974.

Tapiola's Brave Regiment. New York: Knopf, 1941; Toronto: Ryerson, 1941.

There Is Another Heaven. Indianapolis: Bobbs, 1929; Toronto: McClelland, 1929.

They Went on Together. New York: Knopf, 1941; Toronto: Ryerson, 1941; London: Heinemann, 1941. Publ. in *McCall's* Mar. 1941: 4, 6-7, 9, 96-101, 103-04, 110, 114-23.

Train in the Meadow. New York: Knopf, 1953; Toronto: McClelland, 1953.

The Wilderness Stone. New York: Knopf, 1961; Toronto: McClelland, 1961; London: Allen, 1961.

Winter in April. New York: Knopf, 1938, 1967; Toronto: Ryerson, 1938; London: Constable, 1938; New York: Popular [Cited in PBIP, 1970]. Serialized in *Redbook* Oct. 1937: 15-19, 90-100; Nov. 1937: 30-33, 70, 73-74, 76-80; Dec. 1937: 60-62, 65-66, 68, 71.

The Woodcutter's House. Indianapolis: Bobbs, 1927; London: Mathews, 1932.

Collected Works

The Adventures of Tapiola. New York: Knopf, 1950, 1952; Toronto: McClelland, 1952.

Contents: *Journey of Tapiola, Tapiola's Brave Regiment.*

The Barly Fields: A Collection of Five Novels. New York: Knopf, 1938, 1942, 1946, 1967; New York: Literary Guild of America, 1938; Toronto: Ryerson, 1939, 1941; London: Constable, 1939, 1941; Mattituck: Amereon, d. not available.

Contents: *The Fiddler in Barly, The Woodcutter's House, The Bishop's Wife, The Orchid, There Is Another Heaven.*

Nathan 3. London: Staples, 1952.

Contents: *The Sea-Gull Cry, The Innocent Eve, The River Journey.*

Short Fiction in Anthologies

"Children in Heaven." *Designed for Reading: An Anthology Drawn from the Saturday Evening Review of Literature, 1924-1934.* Ed. Henry S. Canby. New York: Macmillan, 1934. 453-62.

"A Death in the Stadium." *Editor's Choice.* Ed. Alfred Dashiell. New York: Putnam, 1934. 155-58.

"Home to Truro." *Vogue's Fireside Book.* London: Hammond, 1944. 20-23.

"Pannickin." *The New Yorker Scrapbook.* Garden City: Doubleday, 1931. 121-28.

"A Parable of Peace and War." *Feast of Leviathan.* Ed. Leo W. Schwarz. New York: Rinehart, 1956. 75-83.

"Portrait of Jennie." *Six Novels of the Supernatural.* Ed. E. C. Wagenknecht. Viking Portable Library. New York: Viking, 1944. Pag. not available; *Modern Mystery and Adventure Novels.* Ed. Jay E. Greene. New York: Globe, 1951. 3-129; *Stories to Remember.* Eds. Thomas B. Costain and John Beecroft. New York: Doubleday, 1956; New York: Popular, 1956. 230-96.

"The Testing of Jonah." *The Ways of God and Men: Great Stories from the Bible in World Literature.* Ed. Ruth Selden. New York: Daye, 1950. 197-212.

Short Fiction in Periodicals

"Apres Moi, le Deluge." *Harvard Monthly* Mar. 1915: 171-73.

"Atauism: A Tale of Passions in the Rough." *Smart Set: A Magazine of Cleverness* Sept. 1916: 197-202. Publ. under pseudonym of John Florance.

"Children in Heaven." *Saturday Review of Literature* 16 Nov. 1929: 396-97.

"A Death in the Stadium." *Scribner's* Sept. 1927: 367-68.

"Dr. Stokes' Statue." *New Yorker* 11 Feb. 1933: 16-17.

"The High Hat." *New Yorker* 26 Mar. 1938: 17-18.

"Journey of Tapiola." *Atlantic* May 1938: 595-614.

"The Pair of Pants." *Scribner's* Feb. 1930: 216-18.

"Sacred and Profane." *Harvard Monthly* Mar. 1914: 30-32.

"To Come Unto Me." *Woman's Home Companion* Dec. 1946: 37.

"The Tragedy of Octave Moll." *Reviewer* Dec. 1921: 115-21.

Secondary Sources

Books

Bromfield, Louis. *The Work of Robert Nathan.* Indianapolis: Bobbs-Merrill, n.d..

Gives an admiring anecdotal account of Nathan's life and work, with a bibliography.

Sandelin, Clarence K. *Robert Nathan.* Twayne's United States Authors Series 147. New York: Twayne, 1968.

Articles and Chapters

Baldwin, Charles C. "Robert Nathan." *The Men Who Make Our Novels.* Rev. ed. New York: Dodd, 1924; Essay Index Reprint Series. Freeport: Books for Libraries, 1967. 394-99.

Describes very briefly several of Nathan's novels, their tone, style, and contents.

Benet, Stephen Vincent. "The World of Robert Nathan." *The Barly Fields: A Collection of Five Novels by Robert Nathan.* New York: Knopf, 1938. v-xii.

Discusses Nathan, his life, career, and five major novels.

Dorian, Edith McEwen. "While a Little Dog Dances—Robert Nathan: Novelist of Simplicity." *Sewanee Review* 41.1 (1933): 129-40.

Provides the most complete description of Nathan's life and works. Stresses the simplicity and life-affirming nature of Nathan's works. Identifies the prevailing conviction that where disillusion appears it is tempered by the conviction that love and beauty lie close at hand, that man may yet work out his salvation. Concludes that, while profundity is perhaps beyond Nathan, wisdom is not.

Fay, Eliot G. "Borrowings from Anatole France by Willa Cather and Robert Nathan." *Modern Language Notes* May 1941: 377.

Describes Nathan's use of the image of the dressmaker's model in *Anatole France 1844-1896* in his novel *Winter in April.*

Indick, Ben. "Portrait of Nathan." *Exploring Fantasy Worlds: Essays on Fantastic Literature.* Ed. Darrell Schweitzer. San Bernardino: Borgo, 1985. 89-97.

Surveys Nathan's prodigious literary output. Discusses the themes of his novels, noting the similarities in style and substance. Finds love at the heart of all his works, and explores this in several novels. Also discusses his use of fantasy and semi-fantasy as favorite devices. Provides a useful overview of a long career, including a checklist of his published works by the editor.

Laurence, Dan H. "Robert Nathan: Master of Fantasy." *Yale University Library Gazette* 37.1 (1962): 1-7.

Considers Nathan foremost among authors who has managed to steer a course between all the nihilistic exigencies of modern literature. Calls him prolific, poetic, witty, urbane, warm-humored, humane, and full of fantasy. Describes his particular gift for fantasy as satiric and ironic in manner, and his gift for epitomizing character, his acrid Hebrew heritage, and his ability to unmask human foibles. Concludes, above all, that fantasy in Nathan's work unmasks truth, giving the impression not of fact, but its essence.

Loggins, Vernon. "Cap and Bells: Robert Nathan." *I Hear America . . . Literature in the United States Since 1900*. Vernon Loggins. New York: Crowell, 1937. 303-06.

Considers Nathan's fantasies as gentle and warm as a medieval saint's tale. Reviews Nathan's life and career. Describes most of the major novels, and concludes that Nathan's aesthetic is finally less important than his rabbinical heritage.

Magarick, Pat. "The Sane and Gentle Novels of Robert Nathan." *American Book Collector* 23.4 (1973): 15-17.

An admiring overview of Nathan's contribution of peace, sanity, and hope to the American novel. Contains some anecdotes, much praise, a brief review of his publishing career, brief notes on several works and characters, and random commentary on style and satire.

Mersand, Joseph. "Robert Nathan: Master of Style and Mood." *Traditions in American Literature: A Study of Jewish Characters and Authors*. Joseph Mersand. New York: Modern Chapbooks, 1939; Essay and General Literature Index Reprint Series. Port Washington: Kennikat, 1968. 93-111.

Provides a full chapter description of Nathan's life, works, and literary style. Details his identification with Jewish political interests and his religious heritage. Also identifies his style as that of the prose-poet.

Poulton, Jane W. "*The Elixir*." *Survey of Contemporary Literature*. Ed. Frank N. Magill. Rev. ed. 12 vols. Englewood Cliffs: Salem, 1977. 4: 2191-92.

A standard reference article discussing the genre, principal characters, style, themes, content, and impact.

Rao, J. Srihari. "The Quest For Innocence in Robert Nathan's Novels." *Indian Journal of American Studies* 7.2 (1977): 54-62.

Claims that Nathan introduced a dissident note in the 1920s because his fiction ran counter to the naturalistic vein of prevailing taste. Shows how, by comparison, his works sought not guilt but innocence, not social indictment but affirmation. Describes the themes of his early novels as concerning God, religion, and death. Suggests that finally, disillusioned with God, he turns persistently to the theme of innocence as an alternate view of life, thereby eschewing realistic modes and techniques, adopting instead the pastoral, the fable, and the satirical fantasy. Concludes that the quest for innocence may be regarded as one of the vital themes in Nathan's novels.

Tapley, Roberts. "Robert Nathan: Poet and Ironist." *Bookman* Oct. 1932: 607-14.

Calls Nathan a neglected master of the realistic novel. Provides a detailed critique of *Peter Kindred*, and then shows how after this novel Nathan veers away from realistic writing and into fantasy—hence signalling his dissent from modernism. Calls *Jonah* his best novel, and commends Nathan for his rare combination of intellectual hardness and emotional tenderness. Concludes that his whole universe is alive with poetic qualities, engaging meanings, reverence, and exaltation.

Weaver, John D. "Robert Nathan: A Personal View of a Magician at 80—and His Wife the Former Movie Star." *Publishers Weekly* 8 Oct. 1973: 57-59.

Describes in a warmly anecdotal article, Nathan's career, recent publications and life at 80. Describes also his marriage to Anna Lee, his writing schedule, and present pursuits.

Reviews

Bates, Ernest Sutherland. "Jews into Exile." Rev. of *Road of Ages. New Republic* 20 Feb. 1935: 52.

Finds *Road of Ages* enriched by strikingly diversified and realistic individual portraits blending into a mass picture, the whole presented with the author's habitual beauty of style with the wonted undertones of pathos, irony, and humor. Considers its sweep epic and its style grandiosely allegorical. Concludes that, unfortunately, Nathan's philosophy lags behind his style, making him seem indifferent toward the cultural values of the future.

Benet, Laura. "Satire Delicate and Bitter." Rev. of *There is Another Heaven. Nation* 27 Nov. 1929: 634.

Argues that in *There is Another Heaven* the satire is delicately masked under the fantastic and simple narration. Concludes that Nathan is too clever for this faithless and perverse modern generation, and forsees him probably being misunderstood.

Benet, Rosemary Carr. "Philosophic Dog." Rev. of *The Journey of Tapiola. Saturday Review of Literature* 29 Oct. 1938: 7.

Calls this a *roman a clef* written with delicate humor, wisdom, and gentle satire. Describes the contents.

Benet, Stephen Vincent. "Mr. Nathan's Meek Inherit a Lovely Earth." Rev. of *The Enchanted Voyage. New York Herald Tribune Books* 30 Aug. 1936: 3.

Describes *The Enchanted Voyage* in considerable detail. Calls it a comedy of the humble and the gentle built around a kind of realism true to the thoughts and dreams of a thousand screen-fed people. Comments on the inimitable combination of irony and tenderness, subtlety and concision. Concludes that because of Nathan's deep knowledge of the heart and his faithfulness to all the engaging humors of moral nature he has transmuted everyday life into a fable.

Benet, Stephen Vincent. "Unransomed Saints." Rev. of *There Is Another Heaven. Saturday Review of Literature* 28 Sept. 1929: 179.

Calls this a charming, satirical, wise, and deceptively lucid book, perhaps his best, and entirely original. Provides a plot summary, and concludes Nathan to be a scrupulous literary talent of full stature.

Berkman, Sylvia. "Flawed Fulfillment." Rev. of *The Train in the Meadow. New York Times Book Review* 16 Aug. 1953: 5.

Calls *The Train in the Meadow* a mild, little parable turned with a practiced hand.

"The Bishop's Wife and Other New Works of Fiction." Rev. of *The Bishop's Wife. New York Times Book Review* 16 Sept. 1928: 6.

Describes *The Bishop's Wife* as tender, subtle, gentle, ironic, and unpretentious. Claims that, above all, it weaves realism and fantasy together in magical fashion, while reserving its most beautiful writing for Juliet.

Brandi, Linda. "Solace and Sea Witches." Rev. of *So Love Returns.* *Saturday Review* 11 Oct. 1958: 36.

Describes the book as a gentle story of a loss of love and its eventual return. Gives a full plot summary, and commends it for its charm.

Brickell, Herschel. "Across the Jordan." Rev. of *There Is Another Heaven. New York Herald Tribune Books* 29 Sept. 1929: 4.

Describes *There Is Another Heaven* as written in Nathan's usual poetic prose style, richly full of emotional echoes and admirably suited to the evocation of moods or the creation of atmospheres. Concludes that it is written with painstaking care and much delightful humor. Describes the plot and characters briefly.

Brickell, Herschel. "A Home in the Park." Rev. of *One More Spring.* *Saturday Review of Literature* 4 Feb. 1933: 414.

Argues that *One More Spring* blends fable and satire with perfect skill. Finds brooding tenderness, mixed with irony, melancholy, humor, and poetry. Concludes that this author's charm consists of his brilliant prose and refusal to give up belief in magic. Details contents.

Brickell, Herschel. "Robert Nathan as Satirist." Rev. of *The Bishop's Wife. New York Herald Tribune Books* 16 Sept. 1928: 4.

Describes *The Bishop's Wife* as satire upon the existing state of civilization in the United States in which the story matters less than its telling. Concludes that this is a rare and lovely book which will be read and reread with delight.

Brown, Catherine Meredith. "Mortarboard Jeremiah." Rev. of *Mr. Whittle and the Morning Star. Saturday Review of Literature* 22 Mar. 1947: 28.

Commends Nathan for his realistic characters, his ability to evoke atmosphere, his sense of humor, his poetic prose, and the merging of the mundane with the mystic.

Bullock, Florence Haxton. "Borderline Between Reality and Fantasy." Rev. of *The Married Look. New York Herald Tribune Book Review* 20 Aug. 1950: 7.

Considers this one of Nathan's shorter, smaller, yet wholly characteristic efforts—a pretty piece cut out of the fabric of his life's work as a novelist. Concludes that this is a half portion but a tempting little dish.

Chamberlain, John. "Gentle Satire in *One More Spring*." Rev. of *One More Spring*. *New York Times Book Review* 5 Feb. 1933: 7.

Describes *One More Spring* as a novel full of rueful irony, playfulness, and sadness, even melancholy, by the gentlest of writers. Concludes that this depression novel does not gloss reality, yet trades in miracles. Believes him to be a writer worth cherishing.

Chubb, Thomas Caldecot. "Book Reviews." Rev. of *The Enchanted Voyage*. *North American Review* 242.2 (1936-37): 441-41.

Describes the contents of the novel and asserts that it is a brave fantasy wherein perplexed souls seek a sort of happiness and concludes that it will be read, enjoyed, quickly forgotten.

Codman, Florence. "One More Jersualem." Rev. of *Road of Ages*. *Nation* 20 Feb. 1935: 228-29.

Argues that this novel is the work of a minor novelist with talents of a restricted but decent quality. Notes Nathan's gift for fantasy and satire, with which he enchants, amuses, provides delicate humor, and lithe language.

Cox, Thomas A. "Satirical Fantasy at Its Very Best." Rev. of *The Devil with Love*. *San Francisco Chronicle This World Magazine* 21 Apr. 1963: 26.

Describes the novel in terms of plot and incident. Calls Nathan's manner calm and the genre satirical fantasy. Commends the book as good reading for those days the world's ills makes one feel a little unwell.

Crowther, Florence. "Fantasy on the River." Rev. of *The River Journey*. *New York Times Book Review* 11 Sept. 1949: 8.

Calls this a novel drawing a fine line between charm and confusion. Mostly describes plot and characters.

Dangerfield, George. "Nathan . . ." Rev. of *The Sea-Gull Cry*. *Saturday Review of Literature* 11 July 1942: 12.

Describes the contents of *The Sea-Gull Cry*, and comments that this is a story which sheds its mature and tragic meanings, emerging as something wide-eyed and childlike. Admires Nathan's ability to evoke place and describe character.

Davenport, Basil. "Ironic Melancholy." Rev. of *The Orchid. Saturday Review of Literature* 2 May 1931: 794.

Comments that *The Orchid* contains delicate, sustained satire from a mind that can see the ridiculous for what it is. Notes also the gentle melancholy, irony, and dignity. Describes a little of the plot.

Douglas, Donald. "Survey of the Latest Books." Rev. of *The Puppet Master. New York Tribune* 28 Oct. 1923: 23.

Calls this novel a masterpiece of beautiful, limpid prose, twilight melancholy, and elfin humor. However, also notes that this manner soon results in the failure of true art. Details contents and concludes that the characterization, prose, and style are remarkable.

Duhamel, P. Albert. "Unicorns and Angels." Rev. of *The Fair. New York Times Book Review* 12 Apr. 1964: 36.

Describes *The Fair* as ironic, fantastic, light of touch, and mysterious. Commends it for avoiding the T. H. White problem of tedious seeming-realism in a 600-page epic form. Details some of the contents.

Eaton, Evelyn. "Fiction Notes." Rev. of *The Innocent Eve. Saturday Review of Literature* 9 June 1951: 44.

Describes the contents of *The Innocent Eve*, and comments that the book is readable, magical, complex, and full of the dreams and hopes, tosses and turns of assorted humane preoccupations, despairs, and disapprovals. Concludes that it is also notably witty.

Espey, John J. "Enchantment of First Love." Rev. of *Long After Summer. New York Herald Tribune Weekly Book Review* 26 Sept. 1948: 3.

Comments that *Long After Summer* creates a sunswept, rainswept world of weather and seasons done with deftness and gravity, in which the characters walk gravely, inspecting one another with quiet wonder and slow gestures of sympathy and tenderness. Concludes that Nathan's affection more than makes up for the loss of immediacy in the story.

Feld, Rose. "A Fine Fantasy by Robert Nathan." Rev. of *Portrait of Jennie. New York Times Book Review* 7 Jan. 1940: 7.

Sees *Portrait of Jenny* as a brilliant and delicate exploration of the planes of timelessness. Notes that it contains profound and delicate portraiture.

Feld, Rose. "A Highly Romantic Tale." Rev. of *The Wilderness Stone. New York Herald Tribune Lively Arts and Book Review* 11 June 1961: 25.

Calls this a novella in which Nathan takes a backward look at the world gone by. Sees it as a criticism of a present-day life and its preoccupation with status and security.

Feld, Rose. "Robert Nathan's Tale of Exile." Rev. of *The Sea-Gull Cry. New York Times Book Review* 5 July 1942: 7.

Describes *The Seagull Cry* in terms of plot and character. Concludes that the tenderness, humor, and pathos give the book a glittering radiance.

Follett, Wilson. "A 'Skilled Meringue.'" Rev. of *Long After Summer. New York Times Book Review* 3 Oct. 1948: 23.

Considers *Long After Summer* a novel which got so committed to operating as a mental clinic, all it can do is reel on through the Age of Psychiatry and out the other side. Calls Nathan a romancer whose spun sugar effects are no less in evidence here than in previous works. Concludes that it is not a novel with much to do with the lower realities.

Frank, Grace. "Rich Bouquet." Rev. of *The Bishop's Wife. Saturday Review of Literature* 29 Sept. 1928: 163.

Describes *The Bishop's Wife* as guilelessly written in delicately patterned filaments. Notes that it has beauty, charm, wit, and wisdom. Describes the contents in detail.

Fuller, Edmund. "Denizens of Nathanland." Rev. of *The Color of Evening. New York Times Book Review* 10 Apr. 1960: 42.

Calls *The Color of Evening* another hot cross bun from Nathan's pastry shop, baked with the same ingredients as other saleable confections. Concludes that the whole thing is pervaded by a sugary aura from the sentimental story to the cover.

Fuller, Edmund. "Mysterious Comforter." Rev. of *So Love Returns. New York Times Book Review* 14 Dec. 1958: 17.

Thinks *So Love Returns* is a book written with polish, wit, and experience. Yet notes that it is too sentimental and soothing, and oversimplifies the happy side of the affirmative vision of life. Concludes that this book has undeniable charm, but that it is a brief and fragile story pushed at times with too transparent a technique.

Gilman, Dorothy Foster. "Robert Nathan's Satirical and Dramatic Novel Dealing with Life in a Clergyman's Household." Rev. of *The Bishop's Wife. Boston Evening Transcript* 13 Oct. 1928: sec. 3: 3.

Describes the novel's plot, characters, ambience, style, and feeling. Calls it a gentle satire beautifully written and humorous. Gives a detailed plot summary.

Jackson, Joseph Henry. "A Satirical Fantasy on the Life of Man." Rev. of *Sir Henry. San Francisco Chronicle* 28 Jan. 1955: 17.

Considers *Sir Henry* a fantastically delicious comic tale of the knight errant. Calls it a charming fable of the troubles of all mankind. Describes the contents, and concludes that Nathan's gift is disguising his moral behind a gentle, merely comic tale up to the moment of final irony.

Jones, Howard Mumford. "Nathan . . ." Rev. of *They Went on Together. Saturday Review of Literature* 19 Apr. 1941: 6, 12.

Describes the book as a distinctively Nathanesque novel in style and form. Calls it a contribution to the literature praising the little man. Details the contents, and concludes that, though Nathan's lyric method has certain limitations and that his formula is rather transparent, both work very well. Concludes that though the theme is of epic proportions, Nathan only succeeds in moving us to pity rather than pity and terror.

Jones, Howard Mumford. "No News in Nathan but Much to Learn of Human Nature." Rev. of *Journey of Tapiola. Boston Evening Transcript Book Review* 29 Oct. 1938: 1.

Claims this novel is not about the animals it depicts, but about people, philosophy, and life itself. Concludes that, though not a great and important book, it is charming, sensitive, and worthwhile.

Kelly, James. "The Unknightly Knight." Rev. of *Sir Henry. New York Times Book Review* 16 Jan. 1955: 5.

Describes *Sir Henry* as a rather fantastic, comic, medieval romance.

Kennebeck, Edwin. "An Easy Fantasy." Rev. of *So Love Returns. Commonweal* 24 Oct. 1958: 106-07.

Sees *So Love Returns* as charming, witty, pleasant, decorated with sentimental philosophical observations, and excellently crafted.

Kohn, Walter F. "Jonah the Jew." Rev. of *Jonah*. *Saturday Review of Literature* 28 Mar. 1925: 627.

Considers *Jonah* a book full of melancholy, mellowness, and sentimental sympathy. Describes the contents of the story and its biblical parallels. Criticizes Nathan's handling of a larger canvas, his shifts in point of view and all too conscious irony. Concludes, however, that this book is rich with Nathan's uniquely opulent Jewish impressions, overtones, rhythms, and nuances.

Kronenberger, Louis. "Concerning Jonah." Rev. of *Jonah*. *New York Times Book Review* 15 Feb. 1925: 8-9.

Calls *Jonah* an Old Testament story of Jonah's desire to be a prophet. Describes contents and style. Concludes that Nathan goes just a little far in his delineations of God and God's conversations.

Kronenberger, Louis. "One More Nathan." Rev. of *The Barly Fields*. *New Republic* 13 July 1938: 286.

Describes the world depicted in *The Barly Fields* as foolish, loveable, and haphazard, but reduced to whimsical order and values. Considers Nathan's gifts to be measure, balance, and grace. Concludes that his mind is insufficiently critical and his imagination less visionary than whimsical.

"Latest Works of Fiction." Rev. of *Autumn*. *New York Times Book Review* 11 Dec. 1921: 10.

Considers *Autumn* a fine piece of writing belonging to no particular school. Notes that the book is delicate and memorable mostly for its tone rather than for its characters and story. Concludes that we are never carried away in a stream of actions but rather bathed in mood and tone.

"Latest Works of Fiction." Rev. of *Peter Kindred*. *New York Times Book Review* 25 Jan. 1920: 50.

Asserts that *Peter Kindred* requires reader persistence. Thinks it is obviously a first novel, opening with a long, drawn-out account of Peter's school days at Exeter where he makes no friends and wins no sympathy from the reader. Concludes that overall, Nathan shows small sense of drama and even less of light and shade.

Lee, Charles. "Hard-Put Knight." Rev. of *Sir Henry*. *Saturday Review* 5 Feb. 1955: 16, 32.

Considers *Sir Henry* a riddling little book certain to delight lovers of fantasy. Calls it moonlight and meringue done in April scents. Describes the story and characters, and concludes that Nathan is surely a sorcerer.

Lerner, Edna. "Excursion in Time." Rev. of *But Gently Day*. *Saturday Review of Literature* 11 Sept. 1943: 11.

Claims that *But Gently Day* shows a continuing interest in love and time which absorbed Nathan in earlier novels. Describes the contents of the novel, and concludes that "Mr. Nathan's excursion in time has the unpretentious charm which his readers have come to love. If it never achieves the magic and suggestiveness of that great sortie into the past—Henry James's 'Sense of the Past'—it manages also to avoid the sentimentalism of John L. Balderstein's 'Berkeley Square.'"

Levine, Yehuda. "A Star for the Alienated." Rev. of *A Star in the Wind*. *Congress Bi-Weekly* 14 May 1962: 23-24.

Describes the contents of the book, and sees it hinging on an alienated young Jew's quest for identity. Calls Nathan a master of satiric fantasy. Comments on the number of "Hollywood" elements present in the volume, and concludes that this book is missing insight and conviction.

Levy, Melvin P. "American Precieuses." Rev. of *The Woodcutter's House*. *New Republic* 11 Jan. 1928: 228.

Commends *The Woodcutter's House* as delightfully sweet and tender, full of magic and melancholy love.

Mallett, Isabelle. "Professor and God." Rev. of *Mr. Whittle and the Morning Star*. *New York Times Book Review* 23 Mar. 1947: 5, 39.

Describes *Mr. Whittle and the Morning Star* as a satiric fantasy. Provides a good description of contents.

Mann, D. L. "Jonah Through Modern Eyes." Rev. of *Jonah*. *Boston Evening Transcript* 18 Mar. 1925: sec. 3: 3.

Calls *Jonah* a remarkable book. Details the contents and commends the treatment of the biblical account and its amusing rendering.

Mann, D. L. *"The Puppet Master*: A Fantastic Story of an Artist in His Shop." Rev. of *The Puppet Master. Boston Evening Transcript* 24 Oct. 1923: sec. 3: 4.

Calls *The Puppet Master* delicate, fragrant, beautifully written, exquisite in touch, wisdom, and magic. Concludes that this is one of the most idyllic stories of the season, containing much beauty and truth.

Marsh, Fred T. "Mr. Nathan's Fantasy of Jews in Exile." Rev. of *Road of Ages. New York Times Book Review* 3 Feb. 1935: 6.

Argues that *Road of Ages* demonstrates Nathan's mastery of American prose and ability to open up new vistas. Describes the contents of the book.

Maxwell, William. "Love out of Season." Rev. of *Winter in April. Saturday Review of Literature* 8 Jan. 1938: 5.

Describes *Winter in April* as thematically unlike any of Nathan's previous books despite its clearly having been authored by Nathan. Concludes that it is a slender story told with simplicity of form, in the first person, but that it seems to lack emotional content.

Maxwell, William. "Wishing Game." Rev. of *Portrait of Jennie. Saturday Review of Literature* 6 Jan. 1940: 5-6.

Describes the contents of *Portrait of Jennie* as resembling a daydream which is charming but very minor in the larger scheme of things. Concludes that Nathan's work is a blend of humor, warmth, tenderness, and imagination.

Millar, Neil. "A Gentle, Subtle Time-Bomb Silently Exploding." Rev. of *Mia. Christian Science Monitor* 27 June 1970: 9.

Considers this short novel an allegory, but also a serious ghost story, a sad little joke about the trickery of time, a satire, a melancholy but not hopeless meditation, a love story-parable, and an ethereal shaggy-dog story. Concludes that whatever it is, it is fragile, beautifully told, and gentle.

Morris, Lloyd. "Men, Women, Puppets, and the Comic Spirit." Rev. of *The Puppet Master. New York Times Book Review* 28 Oct. 1923: 7.

Calls *The Puppet Master* a vision of pure comedy reflecting Nathan's great love of his fellow men. Applauds his tone and style. Describes the contents of the novel. Concludes that Nathan comes close to Barrie in his exquisite gift of fantasy.

"Mr. Nathan's Fable." Rev. of *The Orchid. New York Times Book Review* 22 Mar. 1931: 6.

Describes the contents of *The Orchid* as being built upon the stuff of a thousand realist novels but invested with the sublime, the gently ridiculous, and the lightly satirical. Comments on the lack of lyrical and melancholy passages in it, concluding that it does not quite reach Nathan's former efforts.

"New Books in Brief Review." Rev. of *The Woodcutter's House. Independent* 24 Dec. 1927: 637.

Comments that, with a novel like *The Woodcutter's House,* Nathan has almost created a genre of his own. Concludes that his work is sensitive, ironic, fantastic, and wistful.

"New Novels." Rev. of *Road of Ages. Times Literary Supplement* 11 July 1935: 446.

Claims that *Road of Ages* is written with Nathan's general sense of fantasy and delicate style which invests restrained poetic sentiment with a fancy born of the stress of nationalism in the modern world. Concludes that it is a deeply felt story, written in a very graceful fashion.

Nichols, Lewis. "Christmas in Las Vegas." Rev. of *The Rancho of the Little Loves. New York Times Book Review* 21 Oct. 1956: 5.

Describes *The Rancho of the Little Loves* entirely in terms of its contents, except to say that Mr. Nathan's saints in this fairy tale are so human they would come to dinner in their shirt sleeves.

Noyes, Charles E. "A Rip Van Winkle Town." Rev. of *The Fiddler in Barly. Saturday Review of Literature* 27 Nov. 1926: 335.

Describes this novel as delicate, restrained, careful, and precise. Notes its level of fine urbanity and subdued humor. Details the plot and contents.

Oser, Maureen. "Ice Age Rock 'n' Roll." Rev. of *The Mallot Diaries. Saturday Review* 11 Sept. 1965: 43.

Considers *The Mallot Diaries* full of fantasy about a tribe of aborigines. Concludes that, despite the moralizing and many fine passages of writing in between, this is not good social criticism.

Parke, Andrea. "Ruth and Clementine." Rev. of *The Married Look. New York Times Book Review* 20 Aug. 1950: 20.

Describes *The Married Look* as urbane, wise, tenuously plotted, and rich in mood and atmosphere. Concludes, however, that the climax is regrettably mechanical despite the charms of the writer.

Paterson, Isabel. "Life in a Tool Shed in Central Park, 1932." Rev. of *One More Spring*. *New York Herald Tribune Books* 5 Feb. 1933: 5.
Calls *One More Spring* a delightful, subtle, simple, original, and heartfelt book. Mostly describes the plot and characters.

Paterson, Isabel. "Most Delightful Book of the Year." Rev. of *Journey of Tapiola*. *New York Herald Tribune Books* 30 Oct., 1938: 4.
Describes the contents of the novel and commends it for its charm, compactness, and capacity to delight.

Paulding, Gouverneur. "After the First Rapture." Rev. of *The Married Look*. *Saturday Review of Literature* 14 Oct. 1950: 16.
Describes *The Married Look* in detail and praises it for its cool, quiet precision, customary thoughtfulness, and compassion.

Peterson, Virgilia. "Alfred Sneeden's Pact with Lucifer." Rev. of *The Devil with Love*. *New York Times Book Review* 28 Apr. 1963: 44.
Describes *The Devil with Love* as a mocking and tender fable haunting and possessing with its theme of the antiphony between absurdity and dignity the music of the heart. Concludes that this is a graceful and delicate book in both form and taste.

Peterson, Virgilia. "Eternal Lovers." Rev. of *The Wilderness-Stone*. *New York Times Book Review* 23 Apr. 1961: 34.
Describes the contents of Nathan's *The Wilderness Stone*, and calls it a valedictory to America and to the friends of Nathan's youth. Asks young readers to suspend their disbelief, and promises older readers the opportunity to rediscover their youth. Sees a new depth in this novel.

Peterson, Virgilia. "A Moonstruck Knight, a Tender Parable of Man's Folly." Rev. of *Sir Henry*. *New York Herald Tribune Book Review* 23 Jan. 1955: 4.
Claims that *Sir Henry* shows Nathan to have one of the most modulated and tender voices of our day. Argues that, though the novel lacks vibrancy and variety and seems too delicate and guarded, who else can write

such limpid language and induce a smile at both folly and fate. Describes the story.

Peterson, Virgilia. "Mr. Nathan's Lyric Tale of Painter, Pupil and Maiden." Rev. of *The Color of Evening. New York Herald Tribune Book Review* 10 Apr. 1960: 4.

Claims that this novel is less immediately fresh and more of an echo of his best work than it is his best work itself. Notes, though, his special signature is still evident here and that his cadence is not large, but limpid. Briefly describes the main character.

Peterson, Virgilia. "With the People of the Bear." Rev. of *The Mallot Diaries. New York Times Book Review* 22 Aug. 1965: 4-5.

Claims that in *The Mallot Diaries* Nathan raises the question of who, what, and why we are. Calls it a story of a modern encounter with a remote past done in a modest, oblique and lightly funny manner.

"A Philosophical Fable." Rev. of *The Woodcutter's House. New York Times Book Review* 16 Oct. 1927: 8.

Describes Nathan as a law unto himself with his creation of *The Woodcutter's House* and its bestiary-like qualities. Concludes that it is, however, too slight and fantastic a creation to win many readers in this noisy age.

Pippett, Aileen. "Infernal Visitants." Rev. of *The Devil with Love. Saturday Review* 24 Aug. 1963: 49.

Details the contents of the novel, and concludes that the tale is artfully constructed with great simplicity, gentle melancholy, sweetness, and feather-soft touches.

Rascoe, Burton. "Robert Nathan's New Fantasy Charms Us." Rev. of *Road of Ages. New York Herald Tribune Books* 3 Feb. 1935: 1.

Sees *Road of Ages* as a book we all should read for comfort, pleasure, reassurance, and charity. Claims that he throws a cloak of charity over our political indolence, and as a talented poet, musician, and novelist, takes up refuge in a benignant irony against the unpleasantness in the world.

Redman, Ben Ray. "Only a Rose." Rev. of *The Color of Evening. Saturday Review* 9 July 1960: 21.

Calls this novel a pleasing culmination of Nathan's lovely, lyrical prose and succession of meditative characters. Describes the content of this story of the life of Max Loeb, a painter in his sixties.

"Shaggy Dragon Story." Rev. of *Sir Henry*. *Time* 17 Jan. 1955: 94.

Describes *Sir Henry* as a whimsical, fantastic, satirical, slaphappy tale, full of suburban bliss. Describes Nathan as a descendent of James Branch Cabell with his light touch, gentle spoofing, and satirical fantasy.

Sherman, Beatrice. "Tapiola Marches On." Rev. of *Tapiola's Brave Regiment*. *New York Times Book Review* 9 Nov. 1941: 22.

Describes *Tapiola's Brave Regiment* as simple in style, poetic and "pawky." Concludes that, in essence, it is a charming fantasy transparently veiling a mildly caustic comment on the world today.

Sherman, Beatrice. "A Terrier's Odyssey." Rev. of *Journey of Tapiola*. *New York Times Book Review* 30 Oct. 1938: 7.

Calls *Journey of Tapiola* a gentle, gossamer-thin, graceful, beautifully told tale.

Smith, Bradford. "Temporal Paradox." Rev. of *Long After Summer*. *Saturday Review of Literature* 25 Sept. 1948: 11.

Describes the plot and characters of the novel and comments that this is another of Nathan's porcelain miniatures done with quiet perfection, tenuousness of plot, and sure evocation of atmosphere. This is a clear rendering of nature and a quietly appealing story.

Stallings, Laurence. "The First Reader." Rev. of *Jonah*. *New York World* 8 Feb. 1925: 1M.

Considers Nathan rich in originality, fantasy, charm, and good- natured satire. Calls *Jonah* an account of that recalcitrant prophet's sin and subsequent retribution. Concludes that Nathan preserves the simplicity of the Old Testament story, while adding his own gentle spoofing.

Strunsky, Robert. "Sailing Through the Land on Rollers." Rev. of *The Enchanted Voyage*. *Saturday Review of Literature* 5 Sept. 1936: 7.

Calls Nathan the nation's most successful dealer in fantasy. Claims he handles it with great discretion, pathos, melancholy, precision, and poetry. Concludes that unfortunately the story comes weakly to an end. Details the plot and characters.

Sugrue, Thomas. "Luminous Tale for Today." Rev. of *Mr. Whittle and the Morning Star. New York Herald Tribune Weekly Book Review* 23 Mar. 1947: 7.

Describes the contents of the novel and concludes that it is off target as a fantasy, and as a story, lacks resolution. Concludes that only its prose has the pure, sure Nathan touch, its smoothness being as dependable as running water.

Tapley, Roberts. Rev. of *One More Spring. Bookman* Feb. 1933: 194-95.

Notes that Nathan's subtle disdain of eccentricity "teeters constantly on the verge of banality but never quite tumbles in." Discusses the characters of Elizabeth Cheney, the prostitute protagonist, Mr. Sheridan, the wealthy banker, and Mr. Otkar, a down-and-outer, to show that Nathan's favorite characters are notable for "the modesty of their hopes," caring only for simple things, like one more spring, and getting their desires and no more. Concludes that even when showing Mr. Otkar killing and roasting a pigeon in the park to ease his hunger, Nathan's "sense of a fine, warm, and delicate feeling expressed and meaning magnificently conveyed" keeps the reader from being distressed.

"*There is Another Heaven* and Other Recent Fiction." Rev. of *There is Another Heaven. New York Times Book Review* 6 Oct. 1929: 6.

Calls *There is Another Heaven* lucid satire undertaken in a mood of quiet renunciation. Notes that this is art purged of art with its delicate, perfected sentences. Considers it a book which tells us life is all that we have for certain, thus we must make what we can out of it.

Tompkins, Lucy. "A New Novel by Robert Nathan." Rev. of *The Enchanted Voyage. New York Times Book Review* 30 Aug. 1936: 6.

Describes *The Enchanted Voyage* in considerable detail. Concludes that this is not one of Nathan's finest books despite its clear, exquisite prose, gentle melancholy, pure joy and irony.

Tourtellot, Arthur Bernon. "The Contrasts of Winter and Spring in Life." Rev. of *Winter in April. Boston Evening Transcript* 29 Jan. 1938: sec. 3: 2.

Calls *Winter in April* a refreshing substance because it is an admirable refutation of the popular myth that age does not and cannot understand youth. Considers Nathan a profoundly sensible observer and judge of the human beings writing novels today. Details the contents.

"The Trek of the Hebrews Along the Road of Ages." Rev. of *Road of Ages*. *Boston Evening Transcript* 2 Feb. 1935: sec. 3: 2.

Calls *Road of Ages* a book employing a large canvas, working with considerable subtlety, handling complex characterization, and avoiding obvious pitfalls. Describes contents in detail.

"Voyage: Sensitive Story of Man Who Went to Sea Ashore." Rev. of *The Enchanted Voyage*. *News-Week* 29 Aug. 1936: 26.

Considers this latest work reminiscent of *One More Spring*, though lacking most of the satire and poignant tenderness which distinguished its 1933 predecessor. Calls it one of the most delightful books of the year.

Walton, Edith H. "American Fable." Rev. of *But Gently Day*. *New York Times Book Review* 5 Sept. 1943: 6, 11.

Considers *But Gently Day* a suave, tender fantasy which reminds one of *Berkeley Square*. Concludes that it is written in Nathan's typical lucid, clean cut, incisive, colloquial style.

Waugh, Auberon. "New Novels." Rev. of *Mia*. *Spectator* 19 Dec. 1970: 810-11.

Calls *Mia* a delightful novel, unpretentious and economical. Describes background, plot, and characters.

Weeks, Edward. "The Atlantic Bookshelf." Rev. of *They Went on Together*. *Atlantic* May 1941: N. pag.

Finds Nathan at his best in this story of helpless civilian evacuees at the beginning of World War II. Details the contents of the story, which Nathan describes as neither a wishing well, nor a pit of desolation.

Weeks, Edward. "Delight in Each Other." Rev. of *Long After Summer*. *Atlantic* Nov. 1948: 106.

Describes *Long After Summer* as taciturn in speech, full of descriptive beauty and sensuous feeling for spring and summer.

Weeks, Edward. "A Houseboat on the Styx." Rev. of *River Journey*. *Atlantic* Oct. 1949: 76.

Admires the novel for its simple, exquisite sentences, the effortless lucidity of Housmanlike lyricism, and a touch of the heart. Details the contents.

Weeks, Edward. "Memory of Love." Rev. of *The Married Look. Atlantic* Sept. 1950: 74.

Considers this love story as nearest to *Portrait of Jennie* than anything he has written. Describes the contents of the story, and notes that Nathan is the master of the double meaning.

Weeks, Edward. ""The People of the Bear"." Rev. of *The Mallot Diaries. Atlantic* Sept. 1965: 145.

Claims *The Mallot Diaries* to be composed of primitive and sophisticated fantasy, besides being quite charming.

Weeks, Edward. "Satire in a Minor Key." Rev. of *Mr. Whittle and the Morning Star. Atlantic* Apr. 1947: 144, 146.

Describes the story, and compliments Nathan on his rare combination of farsightedness and tender-mindedness. Claims he has a good balance of satire and sentiment, but that the staging is too apparent, the cues too pat, the discovery of the lovers too well-timed, and God's voice too much like that of Gabriel Heatter's.

Weeks, Edward. "Traveling Together." Rev. of *The Train in the Meadow. Atlantic* Oct. 1953: 80.

Describes the contents of the novel, and wishes he could say more in praise of this new book, which does not measure up to *A Portrait of Jennie* or *Road of Ages*.

"Whimsical Fantasy." Rev. of *The Fiddler in Barly. New York Times Book Review* 12 Dec. 1926: 38.

Calls the novel a whimsical book touched with fantasy and sprightly humor. Comments that sadly its characters are outlined rather than clearly lined. Notes that it is chaotic in form, sketchy in substance, and discursive to the last degree. Concludes that this book will fill a pleasant hour or two and leave a cheerful aftereffect.

Wickenden, Dan. "Miracle at Las Vegas: A Saint Drops in for a Visit." Rev. of *The Rancho of the Little Loves. New York Herald Tribune Book Review* 11 Nov. 1956: 6.

Calls this a fresh and original novel, a little book of miracles. Details the contents.

Woodburn, John. "Buying Memories on the Missouri." Rev. of *The River Journey. Saturday Review of Literature* 17 Sept. 1949: 13-14.

Describes *The River Journey* as satirical, rueful, and acidulous. Details the contents briefly and concludes that this is pure Nathan, smooth, unpretentious, dove-colored writing, the satire gentle, and the fantasy controlled. Claims that it has a valentine quality with the prose a little too sweetly strained.

Woods, Katherine. "Mr. Nathan's *They Went On Together.*" Rev. of *They Went On Together. New York Times Book Review* 13 Apr. 1941: 7.

Describes the plot of *They Went On Together*, and commends the book for the reality of its twin depictions of childhood and war. Concludes that here love and philosophy are fused.

Wyman, Elizabeth Heywood. "In This Month's Fiction Library." Rev. of *Jonah. Literary Digest International Book Review* May 1925: 428.

Calls *Jonah* a poetic rendering of the biblical narrative that shows the author's irony, satirical sense, and compassion for the frailties of such a character. Concludes that this is the book of an artist of understanding.

Young, Stanley. "A New Novel by Robert Nathan." Rev. of *Winter in April. New York Times Book Review* 9 Jan. 1938: 6.

Cites *Winter in April* as another example of Nathan going against the tide. Notes that the prose is sometimes simple and a little pale from distillation and that much gentle irony and questioning commentary can be found unobtrusively threaded through the tender pattern of the story. Concludes that near the end the plot becomes a little strained, and the characterization a little shadowy—a minor pair of lapses in an otherwise delightful book.

Interviews

Breit, Harvey. "A Talk with Robert Nathan." *New York Times Book Review* 7 May 1950: 14. Rpt. as "Robert Nathan" in *The Writer Observed.* Harvey Breit. Cleveland: World, 1956. 119-21.

Provides an account of his meeting with Nathan, their conversation about literature in general and Nathan's own works in particular. Details also Nathan's career.

Roberts, Francis. "Robert Nathan: Master of Fantasy and Fable." *Prairie Schooner* 40.4 (1966): 348-61.

Describes Nathan's manner and physical build, and his major works and career. Nathan discusses the background to his first published novel, his early attempts at poetry, his methods of composition, his compulsion to write fantasy, his scriptwriting, his opinions of other up-and-coming writers, and his views on the progression of literary history.

Van Gelder, Robert. "An Interview with Mr. Robert Nathan." *Writers and Writing*. Robert van Gelder. New York: Scribners, 1946. 173-76.

Comments on his philosophy of the writer's relationship with a book, Wolfean naturalism, contemporary nihilism, poetry and narrative, work habits, and belief in his own work.

Biographical Sources

Coppersmith, Jay Don. "Robert Nathan." *American Novelists, 1910-1945, Part II: F. Scott Fitzgerald-O. E. Rolvaag*. Ed. James J. Martine. Detroit: Gale, 1981. Vol. 9 of *Dictionary of Literary Biography*. 94 vols. to date. 1978- . 233-38.

More than details of his life, this is a career biography tracing the development of the author's canon, describing the contents and themes of his works, evaluating his reputation, and placing him in the larger context of American literary history. Includes lists of primary and secondary sources and illustrations.

Meyers, Julia R. "Robert Nathan." *Supernatural Fiction Writers: Fantasy and Horror*. Ed. Everett F. Bleiler. 2 vols. New York: Scribners, 1985. 2:813-19.

Provides a very comprehensive account of Nathan's life, education, writing career, and specific novels with brief descriptions of contents, style, and literary assessments, along with a bibliography of titles.

Redman, Ben Ray. "Expert in Depressions: A Portrait of Robert Nathan." *Saturday Review of Literature* 13 Oct. 1934: 206.

Provides a literary historical backdrop for Nathan's entry onto the literary scene in the 1920s. Notes his Jewish background, personality traits, poetry, education, illustrious ancestry, politics as a young man, and his dilemma as Jew and artist. Mainly a retrospective on the occasion of his fortieth year.

Bibliographies

Laurence, Dan H. *Robert Nathan: A Bibliography*. New Haven: Yale U Library, 1960.

Lists primary sources only—books, contributions to books, periodical publications, translations of his works, musical contributions, and lyrics.

Schweitzer, Darrell. "A Robert Nathan Checklist." *Exploring Fantasy Worlds: Essays on Fantastic Literature*. Ed. Darrell Schweitzer. San Bernardino: Borgo, 1985. 94-96.

A list of novels, nonfiction, poetry, plays, and uncollected shorter works with no publishing information except publication dates.

Dissertations

Einstadter, Marcel. "The Concept of Time in Rabbinic Thought and Romantic Literature." Diss. Fordham U, 1976.

Simpson, Herbert M. "Mencken and Nathan." Diss. U of Maryland, 1965.

Trachtenberg, Stanley. "Robert Nathan's Fiction." Diss. New York U, 1963.

Jay Neugeboren
1938 –

Primary Sources

Novels

Before My Life Began. New York: Simon, 1985.

Big Man. Boston: Houghton, 1966; Cambridge: Riverside, 1966; Belmont: Belmont [Cited in PBIP, Nov. 1970].

Listen, Ruben Fontanez. Boston: Houghton, 1968; London: Gollancz, 1968; Harmondsworth: Penguin, 1972.

An Orphan's Tale. New York: Holt, 1976.

Poli: A Mexican Boy in Early Texas. San Antonio: Corona, 1989.

Sam's Legacy. New York: Holt, 1974.

The Stolen Jew. New York: Holt, 1981; New York: Pinnacle, 1983.

Collected Works

Corky's Brother and Other Stories. New York: Farrar, 1969; London: Gollancz, 1970.

Contents: Luther, Joe, The Application, The Zodiacs, Finkel, A Family Trip, Ebbets Field, The Campaign of Hector Rodriguez, Something Is Rotten in the Borough of Brooklyn, The Child, Elijah, The Pass, Corky's Brother.

Short Fiction in Anthologies

"The Application." *The Best American Short Stories, 1965*. Ed. Martha Foley. Boston: Houghton, 1965; New York: Ballantine, 1965. 251-58.

"Ebbets Field." *Prize Stories 1968: The O. Henry Awards*. Ed. William Abrahams. Garden City: Doubleday, 1968. 195-210.

"Luther." *The Single Voice: An Anthology of Contemporary Fiction*. Ed. Jerome Charyn. New York: Collier, 1969. 473-90.

"The Zodiacs." *Stories from the Transatlantic Review*. Ed. Joseph F. McCrindle. New York: Holt, 1970; London: Gollancz, 1970. 120-30; Harmondsworth: Penguin, 1974. 172-85.

Short Fiction in Periodicals

"The 7th Room." *Forthcoming: Jewish Imaginative Writing* 5 (1984): 41-46.

"The Application." *Transatlantic Review* 17 (1964): 52-57.

"Before the Camp." *Congress Monthly* Apr. 1982: 14-15.

"Bonus Baby." *John O'Hara Journal* 3 (Fall-Wint. 1980): 10-21.

"Cold Storage." *Massachusetts Review* 26.1 (1985): 63-80.

"Connorsville, Virginia." *Transatlantic Review* 31 (1969): 11-23.

"Corky's Brother." *Transatlantic Review* 25 (1967): 5-37.

"Don't Worry about the Kids." *Georgia Review* 41.1 (1987): 121-39.

"Ebbets Field." *Transatlantic Review* 24 (1967): 64-76.

"A Family Trip." *Transatlantic Review* 32 (1969): 25-30.

"Finkel." *Esquire* Oct. 1969: 128, 209-13.

"His Violin Story." *Atlantic* Nov. 1978: 48-50.

"The Imported Man." *Midstream* Feb. 1982: 17-21.

"Jonathan." *TriQuarterly* 50 (1981): 155-69.

"Kehilla." *Present Tense* 6.2 (1979): 39-43.

"Leaving Brooklyn." *Literary Review* 25.1 (1981): 21-34.

"Luther." *Commentary* Jan. 1966: 42-48.

"Minor Sixths, Diminished Sevenths." *GQ: Gentlemens Quarterly* 60.6 (1990): 129, 132, 136, 229.

"Monkeys and Cowboys." *Present Tense* 3.4 (1976): 39-44.

"My Son, the Freedom Rider." *Colorado Quarterly* 13.1 (1964): 71-76.

"Noah's Song." *Present Tense* 7.2 (1980): 42-48.

"An Orphan's Tale." *Moment* 1.10 (1976): 53-59.

"The Pass." *Mademoiselle* Oct. 1969: 164-65, 208.

"The Place-Kicking Specialist." *Transatlantic Review* 50 (1974): 111-25.

"Poppa's Books." *Atlantic* July 1980: 59-63.

"Reflections at Thirty." *New American Review* 5 (1969): 216- 34.

"Something Is Rotten in the Borough of Brooklyn." *Ararat* 8 (1967): 27-34.

"The St. Dominick's Game." *Atlantic* Dec. 1979: 54-62.

"Stairs." *Present Tense* 13.1 (1985): 31-35.

"Star of David." *TriQuarterly* 45 (1979): 5-15.

"Stolen Jew." *National Jewish Monthly* Sept. 1978: 48-50, 52, 54, 57.

"Visiting Hour." *Shenandoah* 31 (1980): 23-29.

"The Zodiacs." *Transatlantic Review* 20 (1966): 84-95.

Secondary Sources

Articles and Chapters

Candelaria, Cordelia. "A Decade of Ethnic Fiction by Jay Neugeboren." *MELUS* 5.4 (1978): 71-82.
Provides a novel-by-novel synopsis of contents, plot, and character.

Dong, Stella. "Story Behind the Book: How a Persistent Author Turned 19 Short Stories into a Complete Novel." *Publishers Weekly* 27 Mar. 1981: 29.
Describes the publication history of *The Stolen Jew*. Claims that after Neugeboren submitted it 16 times as a novel, the original reviewer at Holt accepted the book as a collection of short stories.

Moran, Charles. "Parentheses." *Massachusetts Review* 11.3 (1970): 613-16.
Calls *Parentheses* the record of a struggle to write fiction in contemporary America. Provides an account of the biographical materials contained within the book, and concludes that this book finally excites us because Neugeboren's search is our struggle to find a life pattern workable in today's America.

Oriard, Michael. "The Nonathlete and the Sexual Ideal." *Dreaming of Heroes: American Sports Fiction, 1868-1980*. Chicago: Nelson-Hall, 1982. 200-02.

In a discussion of the nonathlete and the sexual ideal in America, Oriard uses the example of Izzy Cohen in "Something is Rotten in the Borough of Brooklyn" from *Corky's Brother* as an alienated outsider, who defines himself by the athletic stereotype but lacks the athletic ability to participate. Describes Izzy and his relationships with characters and events of the story.

Solomon, Eric. "Counter-Ethnicity and the Jewish-Black Baseball Novel: The Case of Jerome Charyn and Jay Neugeboren." *Modern Fiction Studies* 33.1 (1987): 49-63.

This major article provides a brief look at the sociology of baseball, a glance at the history of the baseball novel as genre, and a detailed examination of two novels by Neugeboren and Charyn that twist the genre into a postmodern, parodic, anti-realist form.

Umphlett, Wiley Lee. "Epilogue: Some Recent Trends and Variations." *The Sporting Myth and the American Experience: Studies in Contemporary Fiction.* Lewisburg: Bucknell UP, 1975. 171-73.

Describes the character of Mack Davis in *Big Man* as an ironic and symbolic representation of the sporting myth. Argues that Davis, having been exploited by the system of college sports and gambling, finds his only sense of integrity and identification in the schoolyard pick-up game.

Reviews

Balitas, Vincent D. "The Many Faces of Bigotry." Rev. of *The Stolen Jew. America* 22 Aug. 1981: 76-77.

Considers this the author's best novel because of its tight construction, excellent tapestry of characters, broad range, sharply presented themes, and special magic. Concludes that this is a major novel.

Bell, Pearl K. Rev. of *An Orphan's Tale. New York Times Book Review* 15 Aug., 1976: 12, 14.

Claims that this is the story of a pilgrimage back to an orthodox Jewish mode of ethical identity. Describes the contents of the book. Comments that Neugeboren has come a long way from the sententious, political radicalism he was preaching six years ago in *Parentheses*. Finally finds him to be far more powerful and complex than Ozick despite the fact that his characters are not completely realized.

Cheuse, Alan. Rev. of *Before My Life Began*. *Los Angeles Times Book Review* 6 Oct. 1985: 14.

Argues that this book fails to solve its own design problems and remains broken backed. Claims that ambition has played hopscotch and hob with potentially marvelous material.

Cole, Diane. "Wandering Jews." Rev. of *The Stolen Jew*. *Present Tense* 9.3 (1982): 60-61.

Argues that *The Stolen Jew* is about the theme of guilt that binds brother to brother. Provides an excellent account of the contents of the novel and its chief dramatic situations. Concludes that this is a work of great moral seriousness but with several flaws—the constant psychobabble, poorly dramatized scenes, insufficient information about Jewish ritual, and non-integrated digressions. Concludes, however, that this is a highly inventive and powerful novel, full of energy and insight.

Conner, John W. "Book Marks." Rev. of *Corky's Brother*. *English Journal* Mar. 1970: 436-37.

Calls this an excellent collection of twelve short stories and a novella describing adolescence in the urban ghetto. Comments on its bitter-sweet humor, expert storytelling, dramatic irony, and never-failing assertion that life is always hard, unreasonable, and funny.

Dienstag, Eleanor. "West Side Story." Rev. of *Listen Ruben Fontanez*. *New York Times Book Review* 28 Apr. 1968: 42.

Argues that *Listen Ruben Fontanez* is self-consciously written as a West Side story. Describes the character of Fontanez and his cohorts, the setting, and the story. Concludes that unfortunately, it is the hero and narrator of the book, Meyers himself, who hangs like a block of cement around the neck of the novel and ultimately drags it to its death.

Drabelle, Dennis. "Books to Beat the Dog Days." Rev. of *Before My Life Began*. *Washington Post Book World* 4 Aug. 1985: 6.

Comments that *Before My Life Began* opens promisingly and proceeds with impassioned earnestness. Claims that its intensity and earnestness mesh perfectly, while the prose is charged and the narrative terse. Details the contents briefly.

Elkin, Lillian. "'God Created the World Because He Loved Stories.'" Rev. of *The Stolen Jew. Congress Monthly* May 1982: 20.

Commends *The Stolen Jew* because of its lively manner, mood of mystery, and method of writing a novel within an interior novel. Details the contents, and concludes that this is a skillful and sometimes humorous novel.

"A Few Make a Stab at 'Telling It Like It Is.'" Rev. of *Listen Ruben Fontanez. National Observer* 22 Apr. 1968: 19.

Finds *Listen Ruben Fontanez* full of the language of urban Jewish city life. Sees it as about the encounter between Jew and Puerto Rican in one of the darker corners of New York. Claims that the characters are brought convincingly to life and conclude the novel by waving, jerking, and shouting like so many puppets.

Goldleaf, Steven. "A Jew Without Portfolio." Rev. of *The Stolen Jew. Partisan Review* 50.3 (1983): 454-56.

Calls *The Stolen Jew* a rarity which can be read as a love story, a historical novel, a metafiction, a psychological study, an espionage tale, or a ghost story. Concludes that the author's craft in interweaving his genre is such that he extracts the genre's strength while discarding its foibles.

Gornick, Vivian. "Inside an Outsider." Rev. of *The Stolen Jew. New York Times Book Review* 5 July 1981: 6-7, 16-17.

Argues that *The Stolen Jew* is written in the tradition of urban American savvy trained on Jewishness, which was pioneered by Bellow and Roth. Explains the experimental techniques and plot of the story, and in so doing claims Jewishness as a dominant experience of the collective American psyche, one capable of achieving metaphoric dimension. Concludes that, unfortunately, this material now fails to yield up a sense of immediacy because it is without daily content, and not one of his characters has a single, arresting thing to say.

Greenfeld, Josh. "Black, Blue, and White." Rev. of *Big Man. Chicago Tribune Book Week* 14 Aug. 1966: 15.

Big Man is ostensibly about a six-foot, six-inch basketball star caught in the scandals of 1951. It is the basketball version of Malamud's *The Natural*. It is really about the paralyzing debilitating effects of "embottled" self-pity.

Hamlin, William C. Rev. of *Corky's Brother*. *Saturday Review* 18 Oct. 1969: 40.

Notes that *Corky's Brother* is about growing up in Brooklyn, making the settings a fast-moving, kaleidoscope light show serving as the background to the slow process of maturity and the sad awareness accompanying the passing of childhood. Claims that there is a little forcing and an occasional lapse, and some need for further polish, but most of the dialogue and characters ring true. Concludes that this is a solid book.

Hoffman, Eva. "A Double Life." Rev. of *Before My Life Began*. *New York Times* 3 Aug. 1985: 13.

Sees *Before My Life Began* as a novel of large ambition which nevertheless deals in the stale familiarity of growing up Jewish. Describes this as an odd melange, a tired tableaux of truisms, which make it too difficult to decipher the novel's perspective. Provides a very detailed description of the contents.

Jonas, Gerald. "Browsing." Rev. of *Sam's Legacy*. *Present Tense* 2.3 (1975): 80.

Describes the setting—a decaying Brooklyn neighborhood—and the plot, and praises Neugeboren's knack for making the bizarre seem believable, even endearing. Concludes that, despite the author's obvious control of his material, much remains obscure in the novel.

Jonas, Gerald. "Browsing." Rev. of *Before My Life Began*. *Present Tense* 13.1 (1985): 63.

Describes the contents of the novel, and commends it for its authentic descriptions and ability to build tension. Concludes that the characters flow and only occasionally does the author show his hand.

Kellman, Steven G. "A Jewish Tale." Rev. of *The Stolen Jew*. *Midstream* Feb. 1983: 61-62.

Calls *The Stolen Jew* a mature book of earned wisdom. Describes the contents of the earlier novels, and relates this novel to them. Concludes that this is an ambitious bid for sooth, an abundant song of experience growing out of a sexagenarian life and the ripeness of Jewish-American history.

Krim, Seymour. "Idealist on the Lam." Rev. of *Before My Life Began*. *New York Times Book Review* 11 Aug. 1985: 10.

Calls *Before My Life Began* Neugeboren's sixth and most successful novel, noting he has broken away from ethnic realism and seems sick to death of the sounds of Jewish naturalism. Details the plot.

Kroll, Steven. "Something Is Rotten in Brooklyn." Rev. of *Corky's Brother. New York Times Book Review* 19 Oct. 1969: 53.

Describes the contents of the novel, and concludes that Neugeboren is talented enough to become a very good writer.

Lardner, Rex. "Star for Sale." Rev. of *Big Man. New York Times Book Review* 14 Aug. 1966: 6.

Calls *Big Man* a lively fictional account of the adventures of a point-spread expert five years after he was caught and expelled from college. Concludes that this is a moving novel whose style and point of view are similar to *The Hundred Dollar Misunderstanding*.

Lask, Thomas. "A World of Their Own." Rev. of *Listen Ruben Fontanez. New York Times* 19 Mar. 1968: 45.

Argues that *Listen Ruben Fontanez* is ambitious in theme and structure, its focus wider, and its incidents, more varied than *Big Man*. Claims, however, that its construction is not as neat. Details the contents, and concludes that the text is there for those who can read. Considers it a dividend in a rewarding work combining understanding and compassion, a shrewd concrete eye for detail, and a literary ability of impressive order.

Leonard, John. "Books of the Times." Rev. of *The Stolen Jew. New York Times* 4 June 1981: C21. Rpt. in *Books of the Times* Aug. 1981: 379-80.

Describes *The Stolen Jew* as an indoors book, written inside an apartment house, or on a bus, or in the cabin of an airplane. Notes that there is no season, place, or weather. Details the contents, and concludes that this is no-thrills fiction—the deeper we go, the smaller we get, the more fearful we become.

Leviant, Curt. "A Brooklyn Boyhood." Rev. of *Corky's Brother. Hadassah Magazine* May 1970: 21.

Calls *Corky's Brother* another in a genre called "Brooklyn fiction," and describes, story by story, each of the characters, stories, and situations invoked in the book. Calls Neugeboren a realist with a straightforward narrative manner who relies on accurate dialogue, story development, and characterization.

Lieber, Joel. "Monkeys Who See, Speak and Hear Evil." Rev. of *Listen Ruben Fontanez*. *Saturday Review* 23 Mar. 1968: 42.

Considers *Listen Ruben Fontanez* a short, weird, original creation whose New York setting is rendered with considerable authenticity because of the author's ear and eye for poignant detail. But notes that under the graphic surface, at once actual and surreal, lurk allegory and symbolism galore. Concludes that this is a disturbing and yet challenging work readably rendered.

Moran, Charles. "Reviews." Rev. of *Corky's Brother*. *Studies in Short Fiction* 8.4 (1971): 644-46.

Argues that, though the fiction in this collection of short stories is conventional, almost old-fashioned, it is storytelling at its very best. Describes individual pieces, laments that there are some subjects Neugeboren cannot write about, yet commends the title story of *Corky's Brother*, and praises his ability to write about big city life.

Morgan, Edwin. "Brooklyn Boys." Rev. of *Corky's Brother*. *Listener* 30 July 1970: 157.

Calls *Corky's Brother* sympathetic and freshly observed. Suggests that the portraits these stories create are half-fantastic but full of insight and menace, none of which is carried forward into tragedy. Describes much of the setting and several of the characters.

O'Hara, J. D. "A Little Flatbush Goes a Long Way." Rev. of *Sam's Legacy*. *New York Times Book Review* 28 Apr. 1974: 6-7.

Calls *Sam's Legacy* a detailed and realistic story which expands realism in several ways with researched and authentic details. Yet concludes that this is not enough despite the complex web of symbolism: a little Flatbush goes a long way.

Pequigney, Joseph. "Books." Rev. of *Listen Ruben Fontanez*. *Partisan Review* 36.1 (1969): 148-49.

Describes *Listen Ruben Fontanez* as a realistic work which places the action against the swarming variegated life of an American metropolis. Notes that the heart of the narrative lies in the unfolding relationship between a Jewish teacher in his mid-sixties and a Puerto Rican pupil in his mid-teens. Complains that the theme is too facilely imposed on the harsh fictional environment and appears out of key with the sordidness, violence, prejudice, exploitation, and rigidities that loom so large in this tough, knowing depiction of city existence.

Reich, Tova. "Sons and Brothers." Rev. of *The Stolen Jew. New Republic* 16 Sept. 1981: 38-40.

Describes the familiar landmarks of the Jewish novel in *The Stolen Jew,* and provides a generous account of the contents of the novel and its narrative organization. Concludes that the book has a strong, propulsive force that keeps it aloft, and what it lacks in particulars it makes up for in passion.

Reynolds, Stanley. "Cosy Souls." Rev. of *Corky's Brother. New Statesman* 14 Aug. 1970: 185.

Calls this a collection of stories combining youthful glow and hardheaded realism. Notes that many of the characters are already familiar to the reader, and concludes that this collection should be particularly valuable to those still capable of recalling their own youth.

Sherman, Carl. "A Casualty of Jewish America." Rev. of *An Orphan's Tale. Midstream* Oct. 1977: 74-76.

Describes the central character of *An Orphan's Tale* and his central predicament. Calls this a book with a deceptive aura of simplicity and artlessness. Sees the book's chief virtue as its illumination of the complex patterns embedded in ordinary experience. Concludes that it offers a picture of Jewish-American life that is not entirely attractive because it recognizes that American Jews have been and still are slumlords as well as savants.

Stein, Norman. "Novels." Rev. of *Listen Ruben Fontanez. Washington Post Book World* 7 Apr. 1968: 13.

Considers *Listen Ruben Fontanez* as succeeding largely insofar as it affirms and explains middle-class terror. Describes the central character and the novel's thesis about alienation.

Stevens, Shane. "One Small Miracle." Rev. of *Corky's Brother. Washington Post Book World* 8 Feb. 1970: 13.

Calls *Corky's Brother* an uneven short story collection in which the good get lost among the bad, and the miraculous disappear entirely. Describes several of the stories.

Stubbs, Jean. "Boy's World." Rev. of *Corky's Brother*. *Books and Bookmen* Dec. 1970: 44.

Claims that Neugeboren's world teems with vitality and progesses at a fast pace. Applauds his perspicacity and ebullient humor, violence tempered with gentleness, and passionate loyalties. Describes contents and concludes that the wonderful/terrible magnetism of Jewish life is reflected in *Corky's Brother*.

Wakefield, Dan. Rev. of *Listen Ruben Fontanez*. *Commonweal* 7 June 1968: 365-66.

Details the events of the novel, and concludes that Neugeboren has captured the complexity of Meyer's character and the sociology of his situation.

Wolff, Geoffrey. "Neighborhood Myths." Rev. of *Corky's Brother*. *Newsweek* 13 Oct. 1969: 118-20.

Calls *Corky's Brother* a collection of stories exploring Brooklyn and its rich mix of blacks, Jews, Italians, and Puerto Ricans, all conveyed through Corky's brother and the American baseball myth in the spirit of the 1950s. Suggests that it is a delicately wrought evocation of a young man's first brush with mortality, and exudes the sense of a fable dreamt. Concludes that it is a fine novella.

Interviews

Abel, Robert. "Jay Neugeboren's Second Life: An Interview." *Literary Review* 25.1 (1981): 5-20.

In this interview Neugeboren discusses: his earlier novels, his experience in therapy and in visiting his brother in various mental institutions, *The Stolen Jew*, the biographical elements of the novel, its characters, the theme of suicide in the book, his attitudes toward the Holocaust and his Russian roots, issues of Jewish history, women in the Bible, theories of personal tragedy and love, attitudes toward Stalinism, the bureaucratization of everyday life, and the madness of history.

Biographical Sources

Candelaria, Cordelia. "Jay Neugeboren." *Twentieth-Century American-Jewish Fiction Writers*. Ed. Daniel Walden. Detroit: Gale, 1984. Vol. 28 of *Dictionary of Literary Biography*. 94 vols. to date. 1978- . 181-88.

More than details of his life, this is a career biography, tracing the devel-

opment of the author's canon, describing the contents and themes of his works, evaluating his reputation, and placing him in the larger context of American literary history. Includes lists of primary and secondary sources and illustrations.

Willis, Michael A. "From Kerouac to Koch." *Columbia College Today* (Wint.-Spr. 1971): 46-51.

Primarily identifies Neugeboren as a student of Columbia. Briefly describes his life, his writing career, and his political involvement.

Hugh Nissenson

1933 –

Primary Sources

Novels

My Own Ground. New York: Farrar, 1976; London: Secker, 1976; New York: Avon, 1977; New York: Perennial, 1987.

The Tree of Life. New York: Harper, 1985; New York: Perennial, 1986; Large Print ed. South Yarmouth: Curley, 1986.

Collected Works

The Elephant and My Jewish Problem: Selected Stories and Journals. New York: Harper, 1988.
Contents: The Blessing, The Groom on Zlota Street, The Well, The Law, The Prisoner, Charity, A Pile of Stones, Going Up, The Throne of Good, The Crazy Old Man, Forcing the End, In the Reign of Peace, Lamentations.

In the Reign of Peace. New York: Farrar, 1972; London: Secker, 1972; N.p.: Curtis [Cited in PBIP, 1974].
Contents: The Throne of Good, The Crazy Old Man, Charity, Grace, In the Reign of Peace, Forcing the End, Going Up, Lamentations.

A Pile of Stones, Short Stories. New York: Scribner, 1965.
Contents: The Groom on Zlota Street, The Prisoner, The Blessing, The Well, The American, The Law, A Pile of Stones.

Short Fiction in Anthologies

"The American." *The American Judaism Reader: Essays, Fiction and Poetry from the Pages of American Judaism.* Ed. Paul Kresh. New York: Abelard, 1967. 140-47.

"The Crazy Old Man." *Jewish-American Literature: An Anthology.* Ed. Abraham Chapman. New York: Mentor-NAL, 1974. 129-36; *"The Safe Deposit" and Other Stories about Grandparents, Old Lovers, and Crazy Old Men.* Ed. Kerry M. Olitzky. New York: Wiener, 1989. 117-28.

"The Law." *My Name Aloud: Jewish Stories by Jewish Writers.* Ed. Harold U. Ribalow. South Brunswick: Yoseloff, 1969. 315-33; *Adolescence in Literature.* Ed. Thomas West Gregory. New York: Longman, 1978. 340-55.

"The Well." *The Shape of Fiction.* Eds. Leo Hamalian and Karl Frederick. New York: McGraw, 1967. 422-40; *Publisher's Choice: Ten Short Story Discoveries.* New York: Scribner, 1967: 228-51.

Short Fiction in Periodicals

"The Blessing." *Harper's* Nov. 1959: 64-68.

"Charity." *Esquire* Apr. 1970: 140-41.

"The Crazy Old Man." *Esquire* Aug. 1968: 96-97, 110.

"Going Up." *Midstream* Nov. 1970: 41-49.

"Grace, Grace, Grace, Grace." *Esquire* June 1970: 192-96.

"The Groom on Zlota Street." *Commentary* Dec. 1959: 497-505.

"In the Reign of Peace." *Harper's* July 1969: 63-65.

"In the Valley." *Harper's* Oct. 1963: 78-83.

"In the Wilderness: A Report from Israel." *Keeping Posted* Nov. 1972: 19-23.

"Lamentations." *New Yorker* 19 Sept. 1970: 32-34.

"The Law." *Commentary* Nov. 1960: 423-34.

"The Mission." *Playboy* Dec. 1964: 207-08, 242-44, 247-49.

"On Jaffa Road." *Midstream* May 1969: 23-25.

"A Pile of Stones." *Esquire* May 1964: 92, 168-69.

"The Sentence." *University of Kansas City Review* Dec. 1959: 107-14.

"The Well." *Harper's* Jan. 1961: 84-93.

Secondary Sources

Articles and Chapters

Alter, Robert. "Sentimentalizing the Jews." *Commentary* Sept. 1965: 71-75. Rpt. in *After the Tradition*. Robert Alter. New York: Dutton, 1969. 35-45.

Alter denies the validity of the concept of a renaissance in Jewish-American literature and in the related mythological concept of Jewishness and Jews themselves. Claims that such writers are really more American than Jewish in the first place, emerging somehow as the imaginary creatures non-Jews would claim them to be, rather than as they are.

Aronson, Steven M. L. "Frontier Obsession: Realizing History Through Tomahawks, Blunderbusses, Buckskins, Powder Horns, Drums, and a Hudson's Bay Coat." *House and Garden* Nov. 1985: 70, 76, 80, 84.

Describes Nissenson's historical novel *The Tree of Life* as an exercise in absolute realism, historical pointillism, and total immersion in time and place. Describes in great detail the artifacts that Nissenson surrounded himself with in order to absorb the atmosphere of the nineteenth-century frontiersman.

Berger, Alan L. "Judaism as a Religious Value System." *Crisis and Covenant: The Holocaust in American Jewish Fiction.* Ed. Sarah Blacher Cohen. SUNY Series in Modern Jewish Literature and Culture. Albany: New York State UP, 1985. 59-65.

Claims that Nissenson's Holocaust fiction is concerned with examining the relationship between the covenantal God and the historical situation of his people. Notes that, like Ozick's, Nissenson's Holocaust writing reflects a religious affirmation of covenant and a secular view in which the covenant is severely impaired because of the ravages of history. Sees Nissenson as a genuinely religious writer. Discusses *A Pile of Stones* as an exploration of covenant faith in its pre-Holocaust dimensions. Also discusses "The Prisoner" and "The Law."

Berger, Alan L. "Pre-Holocaust America: Jewish Existence and Covenant Diminishment." *Crisis and Covenant: The Holocaust in American Jewish Fiction.* Ed. Sarah Blacher Cohen. SUNY Series in Modern Jewish Literature and Culture. Albany: New York State UP, 1985. 137-44.

Discusses mainly *My Own Ground* as a first novel departing from the Jewish covenantal hope of earlier characters in the short fiction. Claims that, although depicting pre-Holocaust Judaism, the novel underscores the Holocaust—problematic of Jews who appear overwhelmed by their historical burden of portraying a tradition whose divine covenantal partner appears striking by His absence.

Berkove, Lawrence I. "American *Midrashim*: Hugh Nissenson's Stories." *Critique* 20.1 (1978): 75-82.

Suggests that Nissenson's stories are really *midrashim* or revelatory commentaries in fiction on religious texts. Concludes that in a *Pile of Stones* the author's unifying concern is the problem of belief. Concludes that doubt, despair, secularism, ignorance, and indifference are represented as internal, fifth column adversaries of external persecution—all pressing on the Jew. Describes each story and how it fits into this paradigm.

Rosenfeld, Alvin H. "Israel and the Idea of Redemption in the Fiction of Hugh Nissenson." *Midstream* Apr. 1980: 54-56.

Calls Nissenson one of the few writers to respond to the challenge of Israel reborn. Comments that "his subjects center in problems of cultural and religious disconnection and, as a consequence, the difficulties of living without redemptive possibilities. How meaning is to be discovered in such a world, one broken into fragments and always shadowed by violence and death, is the question behind just about everything he has published to date." Concludes that the issue is framed in *Notes From the Frontier*, his memoir of *kibbutz* life.

Wisse, Ruth R. "American Jewish Writing, Act II." *Commentary* June 1976: 40-45.

Notes that in his fiction Nissenson imposes his moral design upon his characters. Discusses his novel *My Own Ground*, describing the main characters, the plot, and the events of the story. Asserts that the book "suggests the collective unconscious of American Jewry, the repressed trauma of its passage from the old world to the new," yet is beholden to Women's Lib ideas. Concludes that the "'centrally Jewish' writer is still under the influence of an American culture which is much more powerful than his own."

Reviews

Abrahamson, Irving. "Capturing the 'Breath and Spirit' of the Jews." Rev. of *The Elephant and My Jewish Problem: Selected Stories and Journals, 1957-1987. Chicago Tribune Books* 11 Dec. 1988: 8.

Considers this collection of stories and journal excerpts deceptively simple. Argues that in his fiction, Nissenson probes the meaning of history beyond history. Comments also on his parallels, ironies, ambiguities, ear for Jewish voices, and grasp of Jewish history.

Bailey, Paul. "Desirable Dreads." Rev. of *My Own Ground. Times Literary Supplement* 23 July 1976: 905.

Claims that this book makes an amiable read, but that for all the fantasizing its characters indulge in, it never really takes off. Concludes that there is a fatal air of contrivance about it.

Bell, Pearl K. "Idylls of the Tribe." Rev. of *My Own Ground. New Leader* 12 Apr. 1976: 19.

Describes the contents of the novel, and commends Nissenson for his unwavering command of time and place, "the redolent immediacy of the streets and the houses, the red coals steaming in the pressing irons, the herring and the black bread." Concludes that the question this novel asks is if time will redeem such human suffering.

Bellman, Samuel Irving. "Low-Keyed but Powerful Tales." Rev. of *In the Reign of Peace. Congress Bi-Weekly* 30 June 1972: 24-25.

Describes *In the Reign of Peace* as a brilliant collection of fictions, and commends the writer for the powerful emotional effects he created in such low-keyed ways.

Bergonzi, Bernard. "Mixed Company." Rev. of *A Pile of Stones. New York Review of Books* 3 June 1965: 20.

Calls *A Pile of Stones* a rather slender collection of short stories examining Jewish experience in the twentieth century. Concludes that it is brooding and precisely written, if a little chilly.

Beyers, Coralie. "Reviews." Rev. of *The Tree of Life. Western American Literature* 21.3 (1986): 238-39.

Calls *The Tree of Life* a brief, original novel about the Ohio Valley during the 1811-1812 years of its development. Describes its contents, and commends Nissenson for his inventive use of graphic editorial comment and bold reinforcing images consistent with the intent and flow of the novel.

Cheuse, Alan. "News from Cafe and Kibbutz." Rev. of *The Elephant and My Jewish Problem: Selected Stories and Journals, 1957-1987. New York Times Book Review* 11 Dec. 1988: 15.

Calls this an intriguing collection of tales that adds up to a century of suffering, a meditation on evil, and an occasional redemption. Advises the reader to read the tales together to understand the motif important to the hearts and minds of concerned Jewish Americans.

Cole, Diane. "Books." Rev. of *The Tree of Life. Present Tense* 13.1 (1985): 57-59.

Reviews current critical opinion on Nissenson, his previous books, and his Jewishness. Then proceeds to describe this novel as a dramatization between Hebraic and pagan elements—one of the great dramas of the Western soul. Notes the central image, the tree of life, as the image shared by Jews and Christians, and manifest in numerous other cultures. Quotes Nissenson's account of his own loss of faith while covering the Eichmann trial in Jerusalem for *Commentary*. Summarizes by pointing out that Nissenson believes deeply in illuminating both the horror and the beauty of the human heart, and in cultivating in his imagination, the tree of life that bears knowledge, truth, and art.

Cunningham, Valentine. "Penetration." Rev. of *My Own Ground*. *New Statesman* 16 July 1976: 87.

Calls *My Own Ground* bulky, gratifying, and sturdily rooted in the specifics of Jewish life on the Lower East Side in 1912. Describes the contents, and comments that this is really only a small caboose on the train of the Jewish novel.

Daiker, Donald A. "Reviews." Rev. of *In the Reign of Peace*. *Studies in Short Fiction* 10.3 (1973): 291-92.

Argues that the central opposition in the stories collected in *In The Reign of Peace* concerns the opposition between heaven and heart. Describes the contents of most of the individual stories, and comments that Nissenson's stories place him firmly in the tradition of twentieth-century American realism begun by Sherwood Anderson. Claims that Nissenson sometimes writes in the tradition of Hemingway—stark and unsentimental. Concludes that few American writers have been capable of crafting short fiction as clear, forceful, and aesthetically satisfying as Nissenson's.

Doig, Ivan. "A Settler's Ohio, Day by Day." Rev. of *The Tree of Life*. *New York Times Book Review* 27 Oct. 1985: 14.

Comments that *The Tree of Life* is written in the form of a settler's diary—the most democratic form of literature. Claims that it is diligently detailed, that conversations occur in paraphrase, and, as in most diaries, that life is held at a peculiar angle. Concludes that the craft of diary construction is problematic but interestingly handled here.

Feron, James. "Holding the Line." Rev. of *Notes from the Frontier*. *New York Times Book Review* 28 Apr. 1968: 16, 18.

Describes this novel as supposedly the story of the Arab-Israeli Six-Day War, but which falls between the categories of fiction and nonfiction. Comments that the characters are real enough, but ultimately do not involve our emotions. Regards this as a primer on *kibbutz* life.

Fisch, Harold. "High Adventure and Spiritual Quest." Rev. of *In the Reign of Peace. Midstream* Jan. 1973: 71-72.

Describes *In the Reign of Peace* as a gifted collection of short stories of uneven merit, yet well constructed and written with crispness and economy. Sees the endings as too contrived and the allegorical construction too patent. Credits Nissenson for his particular interest in the cultural apartheid which exists in Israeli society between the religious and secular communities, a theme Nissenson argues, few Israeli authors have discovered.

Fremont-Smith, Eliot. "Ohio Death Trip." Rev. of *The Tree of Life. Village Voice* 22 Oct. 1985: 45.

Calls this a fine, taut, deceptively simple, funny, boisterous novel full of running invention. Discusses characters and contents, concluding that its weaknesses include lack of resolution for the central issue of faith and occasional archaisms. Concludes that its strengths include its ruse of authenticity and suspense as tight as a ringbolt.

Gray, Paul. "In Search of Immortality." Rev. of *The Tree of Life. Time* 21 Oct. 1985: 87.

Claims that this book represents the extended range beyond the usual Jewish themes of Nissenson. Notes that it is written with unbearable intensity—dream, and nightmare. Provides a very detailed account of the contents.

Kauffmann, Stanley. "Two Novels." Rev. of *My Own Ground. New York Times Book Review* 4 Apr. 1976: 6-7.

Describes *My Own Ground* as attempting to re-create life on the Lower East Side in 1912. Provides considerable detail on plot, characters, and descriptions. Notes that the true action is evil and chaos in the New Paradise. Complains of the limitations of first person narrative and the consequent flatness in the characterization, as well as strains between the material and the form. Considers Hannah the most grievous shortcoming, because instead of being plunged into her fires, we get statements and reportage. Prefers Nissenson's short stories to his novels.

Kendall, Elaine. Rev. of *The Tree of Life. Los Angeles Times Book Review* 3 Nov. 1985: 14.

Describes this as a small novel that works like a laser beam with its inhabitantism, artifacts, dwellings, customs, and behavior. Considers its power out of all proportion to its modest length.

Koningsberger, Hans. "Seven People of the Book." Rev. of *A Pile of Stones. New York Times Book Review* 11 July 1965: 38.

Argues that this work is a coherent whole, while its characters, for all their blunders and misfortunes, invoke our admiration rather than our pity. Details the characters and stories in the collection.

Lask, Thomas. "What Is Most and What Is Said." Rev. of *In the Reign of Peace. New York Times* 18 Mar. 1972: 29.

Claims that this collection demonstrates the gift of evocation and tone. Considers "the frame around the stories [to be] firm and four square." Concludes that the settings are solid and easy to imagine in these superbly crafted tales.

LeClair, Tom. "The Complexities of the Simple Life." Rev. of *The Tree of Life. Washington Post Book World* 3 Nov. 1985: 5.

Considers *The Tree of Life* celebratory of backwoods lucidity, sensory knowledge, wit, neighborly charity, and courage. Claims that Nissenson's theme from the beginning is transaction—perceptually and physically trading with the world rather than imposing sentimental and often self-destructive ideas. Describes form, plot, and characters.

Lehmann-Haupt, Christopher. "Books of the Times." Rev. of *The Tree of Life. New York Times* 14 Oct. 1985: C20.

Sees this novel as an extraordinary *tour de force* of realism, a puzzle to be solved, and a book that affects us at the level of our deepest fantasies and their intersection with history. Commends its rich texture and its ability to plant deep seeds in our minds.

Lehmann-Haupt, Christopher. "World of Our Nightmares." Rev. of *My Own Ground. New York Times* 30 Mar. 1976: 29.

Calls this a book dense in symbol and full of narrative as dream. Notes that Nissenson has trouble catching the reader's interest before the reader catches onto the symbolism. Sees the faults in the book to be more than made up for by the eloquent message that neither the promise of heaven nor of paradise below can provide meaning to life. Concludes that we must stand on our own ground.

Lester, Margot. "The Price of Redemption." Rev. of *My Own Ground. Jewish Quarterly* (Aut. 1976): 48, 50.

Argues that this first novel explores the possible irrelevance of the Torah in the post-Holocaust, post-State of Israel era. Suggests even that another revelation is necessary. Describes the protagonist and the contents. Concludes that in the final pages of this pain-filled novel, "the ache of the waiting for that time, [when God will wipe the tears from the faces of the sufferers], the desolation before that time, are both implicit in those last quiet moments."

Leviant, Curt. "Briefly Recommended." Rev. of *In the Reign of Peace.* *Hadassah Magazine* June 1972: 24.

Commends Nissenson for skillfully evoking the atmosphere of various corners of Israel, for his discussions of moral confrontation—religion versus free-thinking, old and young, violent and nonviolent, nationalistic and humane. Concludes that Nissenson's stories reveal imagination and fine delineation of mood.

Lustig, Arnost. "Through the Valley of the Shadow." Rev. of *The Elephant and My Jewish Problem: Selected Stories and Journals, 1957-1987. Washington Post Book World* 8 Jan 1989: 11.

Calls the author of this collection of stories a man who is perhaps an existentialist, a realist, a naturalist, a surrealist, or some combination of all three, who also happens to be a profound writer able to lead us to dizzying heights and frightening depths. Claims that it tells us how this planet looked to Jews from the beginning of the century and how the Jews have looked to the unbending anti-Semites. Judges the stories to be by turns excellent, breathtaking, and unforgettable.

Malin, Irving. Rev. of *A Pile of Stones. Chicago Jewish Forum* 113 (Fall 1965): 57-58.

Comments that seven stories in *A Pile of Stones* all explore the meaning of exile: what causes it, what transcends it, and whether it is inescapable. Argues that this text is interested in metaphysical estrangement and the spiritual encounters of the heart. Describes each of the stories briefly, and concludes that Nissenson is a shocking talent.

Malin, Irving. "Faith and Fiction." Rev. of *My Own Ground. Present Tense* 4.3 (1977): 67-68.

Describes the novel in terms of plot, characters, and basic tensions. Calls the novel impressive, vividly rendered, clearly under the shadow of death, and strangely positive.

Malin, Irving. "The Other Dimension." Rev. of *In the Reign of Peace.*
Reconstructionist 20 Oct. 1972: 29-30.

Calls the stories in *In the Reign of Peace* parables of another dimension
testifying to the numinous of non-orthodox Jewish belief. Details the
contents of most of the stories and, summarizes the basic theme of the
collection to be "evil as the throne of good."

Mano, D. Keith. "The Genuine Article." Rev. of *My Own Ground.*
National Review 9 July 1976: 737-38.

Calls this a slender museum full of elemental themes, objects, events,
processes. Considers that their authenticity will stand guaranteed for less
researchable matters: passion, spirit, and human worth. Concludes that
the hero is more utensil than hero, and complains that the tense, impartial
narrative clanks.

Ozick, Cynthia. "Christians Call it Grace, Zen Buddhists Satori, Jews
Kavanna." Rev. of *In the Reign of Peace. New York Times Book
Review* 19 Mar. 1972: 4, 22.

Considers the stories in *In the Reign of Peace* lucidly conceived, uncommon in scope, theological in imagination, and determined to sink into
Godhead itself. Notes that each story is a *midrash*, a revelatory commentary. Observes the almost Hebraic language and the setting of six of the
tales in the Biblical and rabbinic texts. It would seem the author believes
contemporary America cannot contain the themes of Judaism.

Prescott, Peter S. "In the Cold Fire." Rev. of *In the Reign of Peace.*
Newsweek 10 Apr. 1972: 90, 92.

Calls this collection a very cool set of eight stories, spare, economical to
a fault—perhaps even technically perfect. But the intention seems scant,
the story skates past us, and we must grasp for the anchor of irony.

Schoffman, Stuart. "Philosophically Jewish." Rev. of *The Elephant and
My Jewish Problem: Selected Stories and Journals, 1957-1987. Los
Angeles Times Book Review* 15 Jan. 1989: 1, 6.

Calls this collection an elegant retrospective of previously published
works that constitute variations on a theme: the parlous and paradoxical
nature of Jewish existence. Describes the contents of individual stories
and quotes passages from several.

Shaw, Peter. Rev. of *My Own Ground*. *New Republic* 10 Apr. 1976: 29-30.

Describes Jake Brody of *My Own Ground*, and details how Nissenson uses the character to launch an assault on the immigrant myth with his many accounts of sexual and workplace atrocities on Lower East Side immigrant life.

Sheppard, R. Z. "Well-Chosen People." Rev. of *A Pile of Stones*. *New York Herald Tribune Book Week* 13 June 1965: 14.

Calls this a collection of stories about Jewishness, the burden of faith, and its transfiguration from the Warsaw Ghetto of the early 1900s to Israel, the Promised Land, and America.

Stern, Daniel. "Hatred of Man and Silence of God." Rev. of *A Pile of Stones*. *Saturday Review* 3 July 1965: 29.

Describes *A Pile of Stones* as a carefully organized collection of well-wrought stories about the journey of a whole generation from belief to alienation. Comments that they evoke, with fine understatement, a way of life in which being Jewish was a rich and accepted mode of living among men and for God.

Interviews

Baker, John F. "PW Interviews Hugh Nissenson." *Publishers Weekly* 1 Nov. 1985: 67-68.

Describes Nissenson's support system of family and friends; his education at Swarthmore in the early fifties; his literary career; his childhood; his research for *The Tree of Life*; his working methods, research techniques and reactions to the early reviews of his latest novel.

Cole, Diane. "A Conversation With Hugh Nissenson." *National Jewish Monthly* Sept. 1977: 8-16.

In this reported conversation Nissenson describes himself as a classic religious personality, a frequent visitor to Israel, an American who grew up in New York City, a reader of Russian nineteenth-century novelists, a student of world mythologies, and a creator of characters essentially mystics and seekers. Describes his father the storyteller, his fascination with the sound of the spoken word, covering the Eichmann trial in Jerusalem, his respect for the teachings of Martin Buber and Gershom Scholem, and his own atheism.

Kurzweil, Arthur. "An Atheist and His Demonic God: An Interview with Hugh Nissenson." *Response* 11 (Wint. 1978-79): 17-23.

In this interview Nissenson discusses: his religious position and subsequent use of religious metaphor in his works, his militant atheism, how people experience a sense of the numinous, his childhood experience with Biblical stories, his use of the short story and the novel for spiritual biography, his personal mystical experiences, his experiences in Israel, fascination with mythologies of redemption, Israel as a redemptive polity, the meaning of the Holocaust, his encounter with Martin Buber, covering the Eichmann trial, and the demonic aspect of God.

Ribalow, Harold U. "A Conversation with Hugh Nissenson." *The Tie That Binds: Conversations with Jewish Writers*. Harold U. Ribalow. San Diego: Barnes; London: Tantivy, 1980. 139-63.

In this interview Nissenson discusses: how he earns his living, his view on the Bible, individual works, the *kibbutz* he lived on in 1965, his commitment to American language, his relationship with Israel, anecdotes of his experiences in Israel, his attachment to Zionism, his emotional relationship to the Holocaust, his childhood, and his opinions on several other Jewish-American authors.

Biographical Sources

Goldman, Liela H. "Hugh Nissenson." *Twentieth-Century American-Jewish Fiction Writers*. Ed. Daniel Walden. Detroit: Gale, 1984. Vol. 28 of *Dictionary of Literary Biography*. 94 vols. to date. 1978- . 189-95.

More than details of his life, this is a career biography, tracing the development of the author's canon, describing the themes and contents of his works, evaluating his reputation, and placing him in the larger context of American literary history. Includes lists of primary and secondary sources and illustrations.

Tillie Olsen

1913 –

Primary Sources

Novels

Yonnondio: From the Thirties. New York: Delacorte, 1974; New York: Laurel-Dell, 1975, 1983; London: Faber, 1975; London: Virago, 1980; Magnolia: Smith, 1984; New York: Delta-Dell, 1989.

Collected Works

Tell Me a Riddle. Keystone Short Stories. Philadelphia: Lippincott, 1961; New York: Delacorte 1961, 1979; New York: Delta-Dell, 1961; London: Faber, 1961, 1964; New York: Laurel-Dell, 1976, 1981; Virago Modern Classics. London: Virago, 1980; Magnolia: Smith, 1984; New York: Dell, 1989.

Contents: I Stand Here Ironing; Hey Sailor, What Ship?; O Yes; Tell Me a Riddle.

Tell Me a Riddle and Yonnondio. London: Virago, 1990.

Short Fiction in Anthologies

"Help Her to Believe." *Stanford Short Stories, 1956*. Eds. Wallace Stegner and Richard Scowcroft. Stanford: Stanford UP, 1956. 34-42. Renamed "I Stand Here Ironing" in other collections.

"Hey Sailor, What Ship?" *New Campus Writing No. 2.* Ed. Nowland Miller. New York: Putnam, 1957. 199-213; *Stanford Short Stories*. Eds. Wallace Stegner and Richard Scowcroft. Stanford: Stanford UP, 1957. 1-21; *Twenty Years of Stanford Short Stories*. Eds. Wallace Stegner and Richard Scowcroft. Stanford: Stanford UP, 1966. 295-313.

"I Stand Here Ironing." *The Best American Short Stories, 1957*. Ed. Martha Foley. Boston: Houghton, 1957. 264-71; *The Woman Who Lost Her Names: Selected Writings of American Jewish Women*. Ed. Julia Wolf Mazow. San Francisco: Harper, 1980. 29-37; *The Norton Book of American Short Stories*. Ed. Peter S. Prescott. New York: Norton, 1988. 441-48. *Women in Literature: Life Stages Through Stories, Poems, and Plays*. Ed. Sandra Eagleton. Englewood Cliffs: Prentice, 1987. 202-07. Originally titled "Help Her to Believe."

"O Yes." *The Norton Introduction to Fiction*. Ed. Jerome Beaty. 2nd ed. New York: Norton, 1981. 180-91.

"Requa I." *The Best American Short Stories, 1971*. Eds. Martha Foley and David Burnett. Boston: Houghton, 1971. 237-65.

"The Strike." *Years of Protest: A Collection of American Writings of the 1930s*. Ed. Jack Salzman. New York: Pegasus, 1967. 138-44.

"Tell Me a Riddle." *Stanford Short Stories, 1960*. Eds. Wallace Stegner and Richard Scowcroft. Stanford: Stanford UP, 1960. 82-122; *New World Writing 16*. Ed. Stewart Richardson. Philadelphia: Lippincott, 1960. 11-57; *Fifty Best American Short Stories, 1915-1965*. Ed. Martha Foley. Boston: Houghton, 1965. 656-90; *First-Prize Stories from the O. Henry Memorial Awards*. Ed. Harry Hansen. Garden City: Doubleday, 1966. 616-45; *12 from the Sixties*. Ed. Richard Kostelanetz. New York: Dell, 1967. 194-229; *Contemporary American Short Stories*. Eds. Douglas Angus and Sylvia Angus. Greenwich: Fawcett, 1967. 380-414; *Stories from the Sixties*. Ed. Stanley Elkin. Garden City: Doubleday, 1971. 313-56; *Images of Women in Literature*. Ed. Mary Anne Ferguson. Boston: Houghton, 1973. 331-57; *Jewish-American Stories*. Ed. Irving Howe. New York: Mentor-NAL, 1977. 82-117; New York: Ballantine, 1983. 475-518.

Short Fiction in Periodicals

"Baptism." *Prairie Schooner* 31.1 (1957): 70-80.

"Help Her to Believe." *Pacific Spectator* 10.1 (1956): 55-63.

"I Stand Here Ironing." *Short Story International* Feb. 1983: 155-63.

"The Iron Throat." *Partisan Review* 1.2 (1934): 3-9. Publ. as Tillie Lerner.

"Requa." *Iowa Review* 1.3 (1970): 54-74.

"The Strike." *Partisan Review* 1.4 (1934): 3-9. Publ. as Tillie Lerner.

"Thousand Dollar Vagrant." *New Republic* 29 Aug. 1934: 67-69. Publ. as Tillie Lerner.

Secondary Sources

Books

Martin, Abigail. *Tillie Olsen*. Western Writers Series 65. Boise: Boise State U, 1984.

Orr, Elaine Neil. *Tillie Olsen and a Feminist Spiritual Vision*. Jackson: U P of Mississippi, 1987.

Articles and Chapters

Bauer, Helen Pike. "'A Child of Anxious, Not Proud, Love': Mother and Daughter in Tillie Olsen's 'I Stand Here Ironing.'" *Mother Puzzles: Daughters and Mothers in Contemporary American Literature*. Ed. Mickey Pearlman. Contributions in Women's Studies 110. Westport: Greenwood, 1989. 35-39.

Describes the mother-daughter relationship in "I Stand Here Ironing."
Sees Emily as reflecting in her complex and fragile state her mother's
lifelong economic precariousness. Notes that she also embodies her
mother's strength, impulse towards life, and harmony.

Bernikow, Louise. *Among Women.* New York: Harmony, 1980;
     Colophon-Harper, 1981. 264-65.

Uses Olsen's story "O Yes" to illustrate her view that the differences
between black and white people are not given, not chemical or theological, but can be changed. In the story a black and a white girl experience
the erosion of their friendship between them as they reach adolescence.

Bevilacqua, Winifred Farrant. "Women Writers and Society in 1930s
     America: Tillie Olsen, Mendel LeSuer, and Josephine Herbst." *Tillie
     Olsen Week: The Writer and Society* Mar. 21-26, 1893: 1-9. A sympo-
     sium sponsored by St. Ambrose College and Marycrest College,
     Davenport IA; Augustana College, Rock Island, IL; Scott Community
     College, Bettendorf, IA; Black Hawk College, Moline, IL.

Describes the general characteristics of radical women writers in the
1930s, Tillie Olsen among them. Discusses her treatment of the
Depression, poverty, family life, working class differences, and social
issues.

Burkom, Selma and Margaret Williams. "De-Riddling Tillie Olsen's
     Writings." *San Jose Studies* 2.1 (1976): 65-83.

Describes Olsen's lecture on Virginia Woolf, her background and early
life, her political views and activities, early poetry, early fiction, marriage, the emergence of *Tell Me A Riddle, Yonnondio,* and the later
essays.

Burstein, Janet. "Jewish-American Women's Literature: The Long
     Quarrel with God." *Studies in American Jewish Literature* [Kent
     State] 8.1 (1989): 9-25.

Burstein argues that while some Jewish women writers cast Jewish tradi-
tion as an adversary, others see it as a source of nurturance, some ignore
it, and still others tell of a search for substitute commitments.
Nonetheless, all seem to engage in a one-sided quarrel with God.
Discusses briefly Jong, Kaufman, Shulman, Greenberg, Olsen, Rosen,
Paley, Yezierska, and Broner.

Casper, Leonard. "Tillie Olsen." *Popular World Fiction 1900-Present.* Eds. Walton Beacham and Suzanne Niemeyer. 4 vols. Washington: Beacham, 1987. 3: 1149-54

A standard reference work entry on Olsen which describes her publishing history, critical reception, honors, popularity, and selected titles. Also discusses the themes, social concerns, techniques, and literary precedents of the works. Includes *Yonnondio: From the Thirties* and *Tell Me a Riddle.*

Clayton, John. "Grace Paley and Tillie Olsen: Radical Jewish Humanists." *Response* 14 (Spr. 1984): 37-52.

Describes the essence of both women's work as that of the Jewish immigrant socialist tradition. Explores the Jewish identity of both writers as reflected in their works. Discusses character, tone, idiom, language, socialist philosophy, the perspectives of the poor, and Jewishness itself in various texts. Suggests also the ways in which they diverge.

Culver, Sara. "Extending the Boundaries of the Ego: Eva in *Tell Me A Riddle.*" *Midwestern Miscellany* 10 (1982): 38-48.

Describes the fictional portraits of frustrated women artists in the Olsen canon. Builds on the theme expounded in Susan Griffin's *Pornography and Silence* when she discusses the artificially imposed split demanded by society between nature and culture. Describes Eva as the archetypal example of this: the original creatrix and law-giver for humankind becomes a drudge whose words are unheeded and whose wisdom is despised.

Cunneen, Sally. "Tillie Olsen: Storyteller of Working America." *Christian Century* 21 May 1980: 570-74.

Tries to answer the question of the source of power in Olsen's work. Pays tribute to the subtle blend of the realistic dialogue, evocative interior monologues, snatches of song, lyric quality, and subtle shifting from outside to inside the characters. Details the contents of most of the works.

DeShazer, Mary. "In the Wind of the Singing: The Language of Tillie Olsen's 'Tell Me a Riddle.'" *Tillie Olsen Week: The Writer and Society* Mar. 21-26, 1983: 20-32. A symposium sponsored by St. Ambrose College and Marycrest College, Davenport IA; Augustana College, Rock Island, IL; Scott Community College, Bettendorf, IA; Black Hawk College, Moline, IL.

Discusses Olsen's preoccupation with the paradoxical motifs of silence and speech, forced suppressions and jubilant expressions of the diverse languages which comprise the "mother tongue." Shows her celebration of chants, croons, keens, serenades, and other forms of eloquence.

Duncan, Erika. "The Hungry Jewish Mother." *The Lost Tradition: Mothers and Daughters in Literature*. Eds. Cathy N. Davidson and E. M. Broner. New York: Ungar, 1980. 231-41.

Argues the thesis that the underside of the nag and the *Yenta* of Jewish fiction who devours the soul with every cup of chicken soup she gives, is a woman who is asked, almost from birth, to give a nurturance she never receives. Claims she is starved for actual food which she must turn over to others, and also for the stuff of self, soul, love, and song. Explicates Eva as just such a character.

Frye, Joanne S. "'I Stand Here Ironing': Motherhood as Experience and Metaphor." *Studies in Short Fiction* 18.3 (1981): 287-92.

Suggests that motherhood as a literary experience has hardly existed at all—except through sons in the painful process of separation from the mother, and through the eyes of husbands. Claims that this story is unique because it fuses motherhood as metaphor and experience, which is stripped of romantic distortion and reinfused with the power of genuine metaphorical insight into the problems of selfhood in the modern world.

Gelfant, Blanche H. "After Long Silence: Tillie Olsen's 'Requa.'." *Studies in American Fiction* 12.1 (1984): 61-69.

Argues that *Requa* is a still-to-be-finished story that develops the theme of human continuity in ways seemingly subversive. Shows that its form is discontinuous, as though to challenge its theme, and that the text is broken visibly into fragments separated from each other by conspicuous blank spaces and gaps the eye must jump over.

Graulich, Melody. "Violence Against Women: Power Dynamics in Literature of the Western Family." *The Women's West*. Eds. Susan Armitage and Elizabeth Jameson. Norman: U of Oklahoma P, 1987. 111-25.

Discusses the issue of wife abuse, and examines its manifestations in four works of Western American literature, including *Yonnondio*. Points out that The Blaska boys, like many of the sons in these works, suffer from what Talcott Parsons has called 'compulsive masculinity,' characterized by aggression toward women who 'are to blame.' Concludes that these books demonstrate that violence is circular because of society's devalued view of women and because the implicit support of male domination causes violence, and because men learn to further devalue women through watching them being beaten.

Jacobs, N. M. "Olsen's 'O Yes': Alva's Vision as Childbirth Account." *Notes on Contemporary Literature* 16.1 (1986): 7-8.

Accounts for the imagery in Alva's dream vision of herself as an abandoned teenager pregnant with her first child and who sees the clinic as a hellish "convey line."

Jacobs, Naomi. "Earth, Air, Fire and Water in *Tell Me A Riddle*." *Studies in Short Fiction* 23.4 (1986): 401-06.

Describes the story's true plot as a profound spiritual rebirth, a plot presented not through action but through imagery based on the four pre-scientific elements: earth, air, fire, and water.

Johnson, Sally H. "Silence and Song: The Structure and Imagery of Tillie Olsen's 'Tell Me a Riddle.'" *Tillie Olsen Week: The Writer and Society* Mar. 21-26, 1983: 33-45. A symposium sponsored by St. Ambrose College and Marycrest College, Davenport IA; Augustana College, Rock Island, IL; Scott Community College, Bettendorf, IA; Black Hawk College, Moline, IL.

Calls this a carefully structured story in which a pattern of auditory images (silence, song, ear, music) reinforces the central theme of grief. Discusses also the related rhythms of ambiguity that give such power to the work.

Kamel, Rose Yalow. "Riddles and Silences: Tillie Olsen's Autobiographical Fiction." *Aggravating the Conscience: Jewish-American Literary Mothers in the Promised Land*. Rose Yalow Kamel. American University Studies: Ser. 4, English Language and Literature 64. New York: Lang, 1988. 81-114.

Describes Olsen's "Silences" as a lament for the waste of creative potential in working-class women's lives, mourning her own sparse literary output and that of other women. Provides a lengthy and useful chapter on Olsen's life, themes, works, social class affiliations, and much critical commentary on individual works.

Kaplan, Cora. Introduction. *Tell Me a Riddle*. London: Virago, 1980.

Claims that Olsen's fiction speaks on behalf of the unnumbered, voiceless working men and women whose needs and aspirations went unfulfilled because of a war, a depression, and poverty. Describes

Olsen's life as mother, wife, and writer. Discusses recurring themes of class, color, sex and silence.

Kaplan, Cora. Introduction. *Yonnondio: From the Thirties.* London: Virago, 1980. N. pag.

Provides a general introduction which locates *Yonnondio* historically, and describes its inception and ultimate completion, character, setting, plot, themes, and style, the theme of silence, and the subject of women's oppression, as well as other works by Olsen.

Kirschner, Linda Heinlein. "I Stand Here Ironing." *English Journal* Jan. 1976: 58-59.

Discusses Olsen's use of "I Stand Here Ironing" with high school English students as they analyze the impact of circumstances on Emily and the chances for her overcoming the psychological implications of her condition.

Lester, Elenore. "The Riddle of Tillie Olsen." *Midstream* Jan. 1975: 75-79.

Reviews Olsen's work, her place in relation to other feminists, her life, and some notes on *Tell Me A Riddle.*

Lyons, Bonnie. "Tillie Olsen: The Writer as a Jewish Woman." *Studies in American Jewish Literature* [University Park, PA] 5 (1986): 89-102.

Argues that what is most deeply Jewish in Olsen is the secular messianic utopianism she inherited from her immigrant parents. Her political and social ideology directly reflect the radical Jewish background in which she grew up. However, it is her experience as a woman that is much more central and is especially noticeable in her patterns of imagery in which she repeatedly emphasizes the human body, mother-child relationships—all aspects of human experience strongly identified with the female. Concludes that Olsen has created uncanny, bittersweet harmonies by interweaving dirge and song by vividly depicting the sheltering of or preying upon vulnerabilities, starving hungers, and the blighting of potentials.

Malpezzi, Frances M. "Sisters in Protest: Rebecca Harding Davis and Tillie Olsen." *Re: Artes Liberales* 12.2 (1986): 1-9.

Compares and contrasts *Life in the Iron Mills* and *Yonnondio* as accounts of the lives of working class women. A useful insight into Olsen.

McAlpin, Sara. "Mothers in Tillie Olsen's Stories." *Tillie Olsen Week: The Writer and Society* Mar. 21-26, 1983: 46-58. A symposium sponsored by St. Ambrose College and Marycrest College, Davenport IA; Augustana College, Rock Island, IL; Scott Community College, Bettendorf, IA; Black Hawk College, Moline, IL.

Describes the extraordinary skill, empathy, and insight motherhood brings to the writer and the writer's subsequent depictions of motherhood in this particular instance. Tracks the depictions of motherhood throughout the writings.

McCormack, Kathleen. "Song as Transcendence in the Works of Tillie Olsen. *Tillie Olsen Week: The Writer and Society* Mar. 21-26, 1983: 59-69. A symposium sponsored by St. Ambrose College and Marycrest College, Davenport IA; Augustana College, Rock Island, IL; Scott Community College, Bettendorf, IA; Black Hawk College, Moline, IL.

Argues that song functions as a structural principle of her works. Traces Olsen's development of this principle to reveal her over-arching theme of the transcendent worth of each human being.

McElhiney, Annette Bennington. "Alternative Responses to Life in Tillie Olsen's Work." *Frontiers: Journal of Women Studies* 2.1 (1977): 76-91.

Explores the questions about self and life, and when there is time to sift and weigh its meaning in the life of a working woman as revealed in Olsen's work.

Meese, Elizabeth A. "Deconstructing the Sexual Politic: Virginia Woolf and Tillie Olsen." *Crossing the Double-Cross: The Practice of Feminist Criticism.* Elizabeth A. Meese. Chapel Hill: U of North Carolina P, 1986. 89-113.

Discusses Woolf and Olsen as women who provide a feminist reading of society and who usually have their feminism apprehended by the reader as theme emerging from text. This reading deals with deconstruction and reconstruction as strategies within the text which enable the two women to demythologize the sexual politic.

Mintz, Jacqueline A. "The Myth of the Jewish Mother in Three Jewish, American, Female Writers." *Centennial Review* 22.3 (1978): 346-55.

Provides a brief social history of the transition of breadwinning Jewish wives from Eastern Europe and their transition and disinheritance in America through the first two generations. Discusses Eva in this social transition and Olsen's radical revision of the stock figure of the Jewish Mother through this character.

Neilson, Keith. *Yonnondio. Survey of Contemporary Literature.* Ed. Frank N. Magill. Rev. ed. 12 vols. Englewood Cliffs: Salem, 1977. 12: 8479-82.

Covers, in a standard reference article, the background, influences, style, theme, plot, and character in *Yonnondio*.

Niehus, Edward L., and Teresa Jackson. "Polar Stars, Pyramids, and 'Tell Me a Riddle.'" *American Notes & Queries* Jan.-Feb. 1986: 77-83.

Tracks down the reference to Thuban (the pole star), Egyptian tombs, and astronomy made by Eva as she is dying. Suggests that all this concerns the mystery of death and illuminates Eva's attitude toward it.

Nilsen, Helge N. "Tillie Olsen's 'Tell Me a Riddle': The Political Theme." *Etudes Anglaises* 37.2 (1984): 163-69.

Claims that "Tell Me a Riddle" is a story offering a strongly felt ideological and social vision. Describes the idealism in terms of its political content. Explicates the plot, characters, and themes.

Nunnally, Tiina, and Fran Hopenwasser Petersen. "Mothers and Daughters in Recent North American Literature." *Edda* 1 (1980): 23-31.

Argues that girls focus on the pattern of powerless motherhood in patriarchal society by experiencing it directly through their mothers, thus leading to a double bind as they try to free themselves of these norms. Claims that daughters fear becoming like the mothers (matrophobia) and at the same time desperately seek their mother's approval. Suggests, therefore, that due to a multiplicity of causes, mothers in nuclear families make it difficult for their daughters to complete the process of differentiation. This is traced briefly in *Tell Me A Riddle*.

O'Connor, William Van. "The Short Stories of Tillie Olsen." *Studies in Short Fiction* 1.1 (1963): 21-25.

Provides mostly a plot summary of several of the stories. Compares Olsen to Wilder and Hardy. Claims that she is at her best in *Tell Me A Riddle* and that she belongs among eminent short story writers.

Park-Fuller, Linda, and Tillie Olsen. "Understanding What We Know: *Yonnondio: From the Thirties.*" *Literature in Performance* 4.1 (1983):

65-74.

Describes in detail the performance of the stage version of *Yonnondio*. The article answers three questions: 1) what specific textual knowledge was gained through production; 2) how did that knowledge evolve through the production process; and 3) how effective was the reporting process in clarifying what was learned through the performance.

Pearson, Carol, and Katherine Pope. *The Female Hero in American and British Literature*. New York: Bowker, 1981. 44-45.

Describes *Tell Me A Riddle* as a story in which the female protagonist manifests great anger at her husband and children. Discusses the themes of guilt, control, anger, and love in *Yonnondio* and *Tell Me A Riddle*.

Peden, William. *The American Short Story: Continuity and Change, 1940-1975*. 2nd ed. Boston: Houghton, 1975. 64-65.

Briefly describes the common themes of Olsen's stories—"the dilemmas of existence, the hopes, the consolations, disappointments, and tragedies of day-to-day living and dying" and her unblinkingly confronting "the universal problem of the artist"—that of suggesting the meaning that underlies the appearance, of embodying the ultimate reality that exists beyond the actions and thoughts of her characters. Also briefly describes "I Stand Here Ironing," "Hey Sailor, What Ship" and "Tell Me a Riddle."

Rhodes, Carolyn. "'Beedo' in Olsen's *Yonnondio*: Charles E. Bedaux." *American Notes & Queries* Oct. 1976: 23-25.

Describes the Bedaux system for efficiency designed by Charles E. Bedaux, in which work was measured in units called B's per hour. Discusses the horror of this system in Chapter 8 as the reader sees the killing pace felt by Jim Holbrook, and a heart attack revealed through the surreal descriptions of hellish conditions, and through the harsh, grating rhythms of her prose.

Rohrberger, Mary. "Tillie Olsen." *Critical Survey of Short Fiction*. Ed. Frank N. Magill. 7 vols. Englewood Cliffs: Salem, 1981. 5: 2020-24.

Provides a brief formalistic overview of *Tell Me a Riddle*, commenting on biography and influence.

Rose, Ellen Cronan. "Limning: or Why Tillie Writes." *Hollins Critic* 13.2 (1976): 1-9, 11, 13.

Gives a patronizing portrait of Olsen, her life, and work.

Rosenfelt, Deborah. "From the Thirties: Tillie Olsen and the Radical Tradition." *Feminist Studies* 7.3 (1981): 370-406.

Focuses on Tillie Olsen's experience as a woman, a writer, and an activist of the Old Left of the 1930s.

Shanahan, Thomazina. "Tillie Olsen: In Mutuality." *Heliotrope* May-June 1977: 1-5.

Tells, in anecdotes, her encounter with Olsen and the effect Olsen has had on other women writers and feminists. Provides a very general overview of Olsen's work.

Shulman, Alix Kates. "Overcoming Silences: Teaching Writing for Women." *Harvard Educational Review* 49.4 (1979): 527-33.

Traces the history of Olsen's writing career and her various publications, with particular emphasis on her essay, "Silences."

Staub, Michael. "The Struggle for 'Selfness' through Speech in Olsen's *Yonnondio: From the Thirties*." *Studies in American Fiction* 16.2 (1988): 131-39.

Calls *Yonnondio* a highly compressed catalog of sounds and silences from start to finish. Articulates the social class aspect of the text and story and, comments that from the perspective of the book, to be denied an audience that cares to listen to women—particularly poor women—is to descend into madness. Notes that speech and selflessness are related by the presentation of a "reverse case": Maxie's speechlessness results in identity confusion.

Stimpson, Catherine R. "Tillie Olsen: Witness as Servant." *Polit: A Journal for Literature and Politics* 1 (1977): 1-12.

Comments that Tillie Olsen, like Marge Piercy, works towards a synthesis of racial, feminist, and political concerns in her radical analyses. Notes that she describes poor women as the double proletariat while reserving a rich and special role for motherhood and the domestic life. Describes the contents of *Yonnondio*, and comments at length on its theme of aspiration.

"Tell Me a Riddle." *Survey of Contemporary Literature*. Ed. Frank N. Magill. Rev. ed. 12 vols. Englewood Cliffs: Salem, 1977. 11: 7424-25.

Covers, in a standard reference article, background, influences, theme, plot, character, and style.

Turan, Kenneth. "Breaking Silence." *New West* 28 Aug. 1978: 56-57, 59
A general treatment of Olsen's life, career, and thematic treatment of silence and female silencing. Provides a brief overview of each of her works and an excerpt from a variety of interviews.

Vincent, Sally. "Tillie, Not So Unsung." *Observer* 5 Oct. 1980: 34.
Provides an anecdotal account of Tillie Olsen, captured by a British reviewer on Olsen's trip to England. Contains a few snatches of Olsen's commentary on her writing career.

Walkiewicz, E. P. "1957-1968: Toward Diversity of Form." *The American Short Story, 1945-1980: A Critical History*. Ed. Gordon Weaver. Boston: Twayne, 1983. 46-47.
Discusses the themes with which Olsen is concerned in her fiction: familial relationships, isolation, and regret. Notes her small fictional output, but finds each of the stories in *Tell Me a Riddle* a masterpiece. Briefly describes each story, and concludes that Olsen portrays the torment of a generation by capturing the private agonies of her characters.

Reviews

Ackroyd, Peter. "The Living Image." Rev. of *Yonnondio: From the Thirties*. *Spectator* 14 Dec. 1974: 767-68.
Describes *Yonnondio* as a beautifully achieved and remarkably innocent, unsentimental portrait of the 1930s. Calls it a romantic novel dependent less on the conventional plot than on patterns of interwoven images, dialogue, and language.

Atwood, Margaret. "Obstacle Course." Rev. of *Silences*. *New York Times Book Review* 30 July 1978: 1, 27.
Describes the voice of *Silences* as unique and the subject matter as the obstacle course run by a mother who also writes. Calls its construction a patchwork quilt which is stylistically breathless and perfectly attuned.

Avant, John Alfred. Rev. of *Yonnondio: From the Thirties*. *New Republic* 30 Mar. 1974: 28-29.
Details the contents of the novel, locates the reference to Whitman found in the title, describes the fragmented writing process involved in its final

completion, and concludes that the work, though flawed, is extraordinary.

Baro, Gene. "Stories That Live." Rev. of *Tell Me a Riddle*. *New York Herald Tribune Books* 17 Dec. 1961: 8.

Briefly admires Olsen and *Tell Me a Riddle*, concluding that these stories are too deeply experienced and pondered because they are the product of a fine, discriminating intelligence.

Boucher, Sandy. "Tillie Olsen: The Weight of Things Unsaid." Rev. of *Tell Me a Riddle* and *Yonnondio: From the Thirties*. *Ms.* Sept. 1974: 26, 28-30.

Describes the contents of the collection. Gives an account of Olsen herself reading passages from it to an audience gathered at the Panjandrum Press in San Francisco. Reports much of the autobiographical information given by Olsen, and provides background and some explication of both her books.

Bryant, J. A. "Arts and Letters." Rev. of *Tell Me a Riddle*. *Sewanee Review* 71.1 (1963): 116-17.

Describes *Tell Me a Riddle* as an incredibly well-wrought first collection of stories. Briefly treats most of the stories.

Buford, Bill. "Leave of Absence." Rev. of *Yonnondio: From the Thirties*, *Tell Me a Riddle*, *Silences*. *New Statesman* 31 Oct. 1980: 23-24.

Describes Olsen's background with the radical left and the contents of *Yonnondio*. Discusses the recent appearance of *Silences*, a collection of essays centering around the kinds of silences that dominate a writer's life. Calls this a silence, not of conception but of production. Describes the contents of *Tell Me a Riddle*.

Chevigny, Bell Gale. Rev. of *Yonnondio: From the Thirties*. *Village Voice* 23 May 1974: 38-39.

Recounts Olsen's early life, and discusses the contents of *Yonnondio*.

Coles, Robert. "Reconsideration." Rev. of *Tell Me a Riddle*. *New Republic* 6 Dec. 1975: 29-30. Rpt. as "Tillie Olsen: The Iron and the Riddle." *That Red Wheelbarrow: Selected Literary Essays*. Robert Coles. Iowa City: U of Iowa P, 1988. 122-27.

Relates Olsen to the long tradition of women finding themselves in a predicament when it comes to a literary career. Reviews the contents of *Tell Me A Riddle*, and commends the stories for their language and structure.

Dillon, David. "Art and Daily Life in Conflict." Rev. of *Silences*. *Southwest Review* 64.1 (1979): 105-07.

Describes *Silences* as a book about the relationships between literature and circumstances, as well as a commentary on the mysterious workings of the creative imagination.

"Dressed To Kill." Rev. of *Tell Me a Riddle. The Times Literary Supplement* 6 Feb. 1964: 101.

Calls *Tell Me a Riddle* an emotionally exhausting book: severe, insistent, and death distorted. Calls Olsen's poetical intensity indicative that the old, relaxed ways of telling a story are all used up.

Elman, Richard M. "The Many Forms Which Loss Can Take." Rev. of *Tell Me a Riddle. Commonweal* 8 Dec 1961: 295-96.

Commends *Tell Me a Riddle* as authentic memoir which never succumbs to mere naturalism. Claims that Olsen's prose reads like lyric poetry because of its tremendous compression. Argues that each story is a perfectly realized work of art. Concludes that her suffering is made extraordinarily vivid and historic.

Fisher, Elizabeth. "The Passion of Tillie Olsen." Rev. of *Tell Me a Riddle. Nation* 10 Apr. 1972: 472-73.

Provides a reader response to *Tell Me a Riddle* commenting on the politics, feminism, history, and biography out of which the piece is fashioned. Comments also on the contents of the other stories in the volume.

Gelfant, Blanche. "Chronicles and Chroniclers." Rev. of *Yonnondio: From the Thirties. Massachusetts Review* 16.1 (1975): 139-41.

Describes a little of Olsen's background, the composition of *Yonnondio*, and the subject matter it covers.

Gottlieb, Annie. "A Writer's Sounds and Silences." Rev. of *Yonnondio: From the Thirties. New York Times Book Review* 31 Mar. 1974: 5.

Provides a brief history of the writing of the book, its social background, and a description of its contents. Argues that the most fully drawn characters are the women.

Howe, Irving. "Stories: New, Old, and Sometimes Good." Rev. of *Tell Me a Riddle. New Republic* 13 Nov. 1961: 22.

Praises the stories, and describes the title story, finding it written with steady hardness of tone, clinging to one perception—the perception of loss and forgetting.

McNeil, Helen. "Speaking for the Speechless." Rev. of *Silences, Yonnondio: From the Thirties,* and *Tell Me A Riddle. Times Literary Supplement* 14 Nov. 1980: 1294.

Provides the background of Tillie Olsen's life along with a brief explanation of the contents of *Silences, Yonnondio,* and *Tell Me A Riddle.*

Oates, Joyce Carol. Rev. of *Silences. New Republic* 29 July 1978: 32-34.

Calls *Tell Me A Riddle* relentless, supremely beautiful in its nuances, and perfect in details. Talks of Olsen's life and other works. Concludes that *Silences* is full of unanswered questions, inconsistent feminist homiletics, and poor editing.

Peters, Joan. "The Lament for Lost Art." Rev. of *Silences. Nation* 23 Sept. 1978: 281-82.

Describes *Silences* as a book of stories and essays which explore the relationships of circumstance, class, color, sex and the times into which one is born, to the act of producing literature. Calls it literarily powerful and politically weak.

"Radicals and Working Stiffs." Rev. of *Tell Me a Riddle. Time* 27 Oct. 1961: 101.

Calls this a book well worth waiting for. Notes that the stories are written with compassionate knowledge of radical working immigrants and working stiffs who fought the big industrial battles of the early part of the century.

Salzman, Jack. "Fragments of Time Lost." Rev. of *Yonnondio: From the Thirties. Washington Post Book World* 7 Apr. 1974: 1.

Describes *Yonnondio* as an extraordinary achievement written with great compassion and outstanding characterization. Describes its major elements, its inception and completion.

Stimpson, Catharine R. "Three Women Work it Out." Rev. of *Yononndio: From the Thirties. Nation* 30 Nov. 1974: 565-566.

Describes *Yononndio* as a recovered text. Details its contents and period. Comments on Olsen's politics of anger, her compelling gift for the lyrical, and her sensitivity towards victims.

Wiegand, William. "Tormented Alienation Dramas." Rev. of *Tell Me a Riddle. New Leader* 5 Feb. 1962: 29-30.

Calls Olsen's stories notable for their astonishing technical range, great intensity, and raw, jagged expressiveness. Decides that, thematically, the stories are about alienation. Describes several stories in turn.

Interviews

Mills, Kay. "Surviving Is Not Enough: A Conversation with Tillie Olsen." *Los Angeles Times* 26 Apr. 1981: 3.

Describes her outrage against the untruths told about life and how they are incorporated into her stories, the situation of women, her books, her writing, the long years when she couldn't write, and the possibility of literature in this country.

Park-Fuller, Linda. "An Interview With Tillie Olsen." *Literature in Performance* 4.1 (1983): 75-77.

Discusses her feelings about seeing *Yonnondio* in performance, the effects created by narrative chorus and chorus leader, and the manner in which representative issues of economic, sexual, and social inequality were represented.

See, Lisa. "PW Interviews Tillie Olsen." *Publishers Weekly* 23 Nov. 1984: 76, 79.

Provides a general overview of Olsen's reputation, life, works, theory of literature, and attitudes toward the institution of motherhood.

Yalom, Marilyn. "Tillie Olsen." *Women Writers of the West Coast: Speaking of Their Lives and Careers.* Ed. Marilyn Yalom. Santa Barbara: Capra, 1983. 57-66.

Gives a lengthy conversation with Olsen in which she discusses her early life, political activism, and life as a mother and writer. Also discusses her attitude toward class, gender, and race. Provides much useful insight into her narrative strategies and her point of view.

Biographical Sources

Barr, Marleen. "Tillie Olsen." *Twentieth-Century American-Jewish Fiction Writers.* Ed. Daniel Walden. Detroit: Gale, 1984. Vol. 28 of *Dictionary of Literary Biography.* 94 vols. to date. 1978- . 196-203.

More than details of her life, this is a career biography, tracing the development of the author's canon, describing the contents and the themes of her works, evaluating her reputation, and placing her in the larger context of American literary history. Includes lists of primary and secondary sources and illustrations.

Duncan, Erika. "Coming of Age in the Thirties: A Portrait of Tillie Olsen." *Book Forum* 6.2 (1982): 207-22. Rpt. as "Tillie Olsen" in *Unless Soul Clap Its Hands: Portraits and Passages.* Erika Duncan. New York: Schocken, 1984. 31-57.

Provides a major, critical biographical account of Olsen's life and works.

Olsen, Tillie. "Silences: When Writers Don't Write." *Harper's* Oct. 1965: 153-61. Special Supplement: "The Writer's Life, Part I.".

Asserts that, through examples chosen from literary history and her own experiences, Olsen discusses the persistent influences that keep a writer from writing, and the toll these forced silences exact. Provides useful insights into Olsen's own writing career.

Rhodes, Carolyn, and Ernest Rhodes. "Tillie Olsen." *Dictionary of Literary Biography Yearbook: 1980.* Eds. Karen L. Rood, Jean W. Ross, and Richard Ziegfeld. Detroit: Gale, 1981. 290-97.

More than details of her life, this is a career biography, tracing the development of the author's canon, describing the contents and themes of her works, evaluating her reputation, and placing her in the larger context of American literary history. Includes a list of primary sources and illustrations.

Schwartz, Helen J. "Tillie Olsen." *American Women Writers.* Eds. Lina Mainiero and Langdon Lynne Faust. 3 vols. New York: Ungar, 1981. 3: 303-05.

Outlines Olsen's life, politics, books, and current teaching. Deals with *Tell Me a Riddle, Yonnondio,* and "Silences."

Van Horn, Christina. "Writer Tillie Olsen: Upbeat on Woman's Future." *Boston Sunday Globe* 31 May 1981: A6.

Describes Olsen's self-confessed need at the point of old age to talk into existence all the lost women's lives and failed potential. Discusses her writings about the silencing of women. Quotes extensively from Olsen's interview material.

Dissertations

Blustein, Bryna D. "Beyond the Stereotype: A Study of Representative Short Stories of Selected Contemporary Jewish American Female Writers." Diss. Saint Louis U, 1986.

Coiner, Constance. "'Pessimism of the Mind, Optimism of the Will': Literature of Resistance." Diss. U of California, Los Angeles, 1987.

Faulkner, Mara. "Blight, Fruit, and Possibility in the Writing of Tillie Olsen." Diss. U of Minnesota, 1988.

Jones, Nancy Baker. "On Solid Ground: The Emergence of the Self-Created Woman in Contemporary American Literature." Diss. U of Texas at Austin, 1986.

Orr, Miriam Elaine Neil. "Tillie Olsen's Vision: A Different Way of Keeping Faith." Diss. Emory U, 1985.

Park-Fuller, Linda Marguerite. "Tillie Olsen: A Phenomenological Study of Consciousness with Implications for Performance." Diss. U of Texas at Austin, 1980.

Samuelson, Joan Wood. "Patterns of Survival: Four American Women Writers and the Proletarian Novel." Diss. Ohio State U, 1982.

Swigart, Margaret Jane Bugas. "The Mother in Modern Literature." Diss. State U of New York at Buffalo, 1986.

Yoder, Linda Kathryn. "Memory as Art: The Life Review in Contemporary American Fiction." Diss. West Virginia U, 1983.

Cynthia Ozick

1928 –

Primary Sources

Novels

The Cannibal Galaxy. New York: Knopf, 1983; New York: Obelisk-Dutton, 1984; Harmondsworth: King-Penguin, 1984; London: Secker, 1984.

The Messiah of Stockholm. New York: Knopf, 1987; London: Deutsch, 1987; New York: Vintage, 1988.

The Shawl. New York: Borzoi-Knopf, 1989; London: Cape, 1991.

Trust. New York: NAL, 1966; London: MacGibbon, 1966; New York: Pocket, 1977; New York: Obelisk-Dutton, 1983.

Collected Works

Bloodshed and Three Novellas. New York: Knopf, 1976; London: Secker, 1976; New York: Plume-NAL, 1977; New York: Obelisk-Dutton, 1983.
Contents: A Mercenary, Bloodshed, An Education, Usurpation-(Other Peoples' Stories).

Levitation: Five Fictions. New York: Knopf, 1982; London: Secker, 1982; New York: Obelisk-Dutton, 1983; Harmondsworth: King-Penguin, 1986.

Contents: Levitation, Puttermesser, Shots, From a Refugee's Notebook, Puttermesser and Xanthippe.

The Pagan Rabbi, and Other Stories. New York: Borzoi-Knopf, 1971; London: Secker, 1972; New York: Schocken, 1976; New York: Obelisk-Dutton, 1983.
Contents: The Pagan Rabbi; Envy, or Yiddish in America; The Suitcase; The Dock-Witch; The Doctor's Wife; The Butterfly and the Traffic Light; Virility.

The Shawl. New York: Vintage, 1990.
Contents: The Shawl, Rosa.

Short Fiction in Anthologies

"Bloodshed." *All Our Secrets Are the Same: New Fiction from Esquire*. Ed. Gordon Lish. New York: Norton, 1976. 73-77.

"The Dock-Witch." *The Best American Short Stories, 1972*. Ed. Martha Foley. Boston: Houghton, 1972. 256-89.

"Envy; Or Yiddish in America." *Jewish-American Stories*. Ed. Irving Howe. New York: Mentor-NAL, 1977. 129-77.

"Levitation." *The Norton Book of American Short Stories*. Ed. Peter S. Prescott. New York: Norton, 1988. 554-66.

"The Pagan Rabbi." *My Name Aloud: Jewish Stories by Jewish Writers*. Ed. Harold U. Ribalow. South Brunswick: Yoseloff, 1969. 334-61; *Black Water: The Book of Fantastic Literature*. Ed. Alberto Manguel. New York: Potter, 1983. 675-703.

"The Shawl." *The Best American Short Stories, 1981*. Eds. Hortense Calisher and Shannon Ravenel. Boston: Houghton, 1981; Harmondsworth: Penguin, 1982. 271-75; *The Bread Loaf Anthology of Contemporary American Short Stories*. Eds. Robert Pack and Jay Parini. Hanover: UP of New England, 1987. 247-52.

"Usurpation: Other People's Stories." *All Our Secrets Are the Same: New Fiction from Esquire.* Ed. Gordon Lish. New York: Norton, 1976. 11-22.

Short Fiction in Periodicals

"At Fumicaro." *New Yorker* 6 Aug. 1984: 32-38, 41-42, 44-47, 50-58.

"Bloodshed." *Esquire* 1 Jan. 1976: 100-01, 130-31, 134, 138.

"The Doctor's Wife." *Midstream* Feb. 1971: 53-71.

"An Education." *Esquire* Apr. 1972: 98-102, 176.

"Envy; Or, Yiddish in America." *Commentary* Nov. 1969: 33-53.

"Laughter of Akiva." *New Yorker* 10 Nov. 1980: 50-60, 63-64, 67-68, 71-72, 75-76, 79, 82, 85-86, 88, 91-92, 94, 99-100, 102, 107-08, 110, 115-16, 118, 123-26, 131-32, 134-38, 140-41, 144, 146-66, 168-73.

"Levitation." *Partisan Review* 46.3 (1979): 391-405.

"The Mercenary." *New American Review* 23 (1975): 1-37.

"The Pagan Rabbi." *Hudson Review* 19.3 (1966): 425-54.

"Puttermesser: Her Work History, Her Ancestry, Her Afterlife." *New Yorker* 9 May 1977: 38-44.

"Rosa." *New Yorker* 21 Mar. 1983: 38-48, 51-52, 56-59, 61-62, 65-66, 71.

"Sewing Harems." *TriQuarterly* 40 (1977): 237-44.

"The Shawl." *New Yorker* 26 May 1980: 33-34.

"Usurpation." *Esquire* May 1974: 124-28, 158, 162, 164, 167-68, 173-75.

Secondary Sources

Books

Bloom, Harold, ed. *Cynthia Ozick*. Modern Critical Views. New York: Chelsea, 1986.

Lowin, Joseph. *Cynthia Ozick*. Twayne's United States Authors Series 545. Boston: Twayne, 1988.

Pinsker, Sanford. *The Uncompromising Fictions of Cynthia Ozick*. Literary Frontiers Edition 29. Columbia: U of Missouri P, 1987.

Articles and Chapters

Alexander, Edward. "The Holocaust in American Jewish Fiction: A Slow Awakening." *The Resonance of Dust: Essays on Holocaust Literature and Jewish Fate*. Edward Alexander. Columbus: Ohio State UP, 1979. 121-46.
Provides a description of Ozick's "America: Toward Yavneh" lecture essay in which she makes it clear that American Jews, for the most part, remain in their corner of Exile because they love to be flattered for having those very trials that are so easily claimed by people without power or responsibility. Describes also their devotion to "Mankind," their pacific character, their widespread, indiscriminate philanthropy. Concludes that Ozick's call for Jewish-American culture to assume, alongside Israeli culture, responsibility for the reconstruction of Jewish life has already stirred a response in younger writers.

Baumgarten, Murray. "Language Rules." *City Scriptures: Modern Jewish Writing*. Cambridge: Harvard UP, 1982. 129-35.
Discusses Ozick's exploration of the possibilities of Jewish identity in the modern world focussed on the topic of exile. Sees her as seeking a way to recover traditional Jewish culture and make it a vital presence in American Jewish life. Notes that her vision is based on powerful insights into the historical situation, for she knows that, like rabbinic Judaism, Yiddish culture emerged from the Jewish talent for making a home even with the homelessness of exile.

Berger, Alan L. "Judaism as a Religious Value System." *Crisis and Covenant: The Holocaust in American Jewish Fiction.* Ed. Sarah Blacher Cohen. SUNY Series in Modern Jewish Literature and Culture. Albany: New York State UP, 1985. 49-59.

Argues that Ozick's redemptive literature expresses two types of response to the Holocaust: 1) the singularity of the survivor as a covenental witness, and 2) the post-Holocaust Jewish identity treated by merging Holocaustal and feminist concerns stressing character portraits of Holocaust survivors. Discusses *Bloodshed, The Shawl,* and "Levitation." Concludes that Ozick offers a tough-minded and uncompromising portrayal of Judaism in which confronting the Holocaust becomes the litmus test of Jewish authenticity.

Berger, Alan L. "Judaism as a Secular Value System." *Crisis and Covenant: The Holocaust in American Jewish Fiction.* Ed. Sarah Blacher Cohen. SUNY Series in Modern Jewish Literature and Culture. Albany: New York State UP, 1985. 120-37.

A major chapter on Ozick that provides a close analysis of values, style, structure, and narrative strategies in "Rosa" and *The Cannibal Galaxy,* works that represent a shift from her earlier focus on the religious efficacy of survivors' testimony. Berger claims that these later works explore the trauma of survival, elevate the role of women, and, in the novel, emphasize the necessity of the midrashic method for authentic, post-Holocaust Jewish existence.

Bloom, Harold. "Introduction." *Cynthia Ozick.* Ed. Harold Bloom. Modern Critical Views. New York: Chelsea, 1986. 1-7.

In this brief introduction Ozick is presented as an author whose precursor is Bernard Malamud and whose commitment to covenant, Jewish history, and theology is indisputable. Also locates some of Ozick's thematic concerns in Anglo tradition as well as within a Jewish tradition. Also discusses her major critical essays such as those collected in *Art and Ardor.*

Burstein, Janet Handler. "Cynthia Ozick and the Transgressions of Art." *American Literature* 59.1 (1987): 85-101.

Argues that Ozick asks with Hawthorne and others whether art impedes the making of moral choices. Claims that she brings a unique perspective on the moral and religious conflict implicit in Jewish aestheticism. Discusses *Cannibal Galaxy* and several of the short stories. Sees in these an indictment of the artist for succumbing to idolatry and an indictment of Jewish-American culture for its failure to reconstruct covenant Judaism. Provides stylistic and thematic critique of individual pieces.

Cohen, Sarah Blacher. "The Fiction Writer as Essayist: Ozick's *Metaphor & Memory.*" *Judaism* July 1990: 276-81.

Discusses the relationship between Ozick's literature and her essays.

Cohen, Sarah Blacher. "The Jewish Literary Comediennes." *Comic Relief: Humor in Contemporary American Literature.* Ed. Sarah Blacher Cohen. Urbana: U of Illinois P, 1978. 172-86.

A major article that describes codes of femininity in traditional Jewish communities throughout history, provides a description of how women have been depicted in Jewish folk literature, and describes how they are currently being depicted in contemporary Jewish American fiction.

Cole, Diane. "I Want to Do Jewish Dreaming." *Present Tense* 9.4 (1982): 54-57.

Provides a general profile of Ozick and her work. Comments that when the chroniclers of our literary age catch up to what has been going on, some of her stories will be reckoned among the best written in our time.

Criswell, Jeanne Sallade. "Cynthia Ozick and Grace Paley: Diverse Visions in Jewish and Women's Literature. *Since Flannery O'Connor: Essays on the Contemporary American Short Story.* Eds. Loren Logsdon and Charles W. Mayer. Essays in Literature. Macomb: Western Illinois U, 1987. 93-100.

Recounts the story of "Usurpation," and uses it to support the argument that Ozick cannot simply be dismissed as a regional writer whose particular region, gender, and religious differences tell us all about her fiction. Sees the central issue of this story as a sophisticated discussion on the nature of story and storytelling itself. Concludes that, for all that she can be classified as a woman and a Jew, such classifications are only loose guidelines to the literature.

Epstein, Joseph. "Cynthia Ozick, Jewish Writer." *Commentary* Mar. 1984: 64-69. Rpt. as "Miss Ozick Regrets" in *Plausible Prejudices: Essays on American Writing.* Joseph Epstein. New York: Norton, 1985. 221-37.

An overview of Ozick's life and work describing her early devotion to James and the religion of Art, her first as yet unpublished novel, her fifteen year apprenticeship, her coming to consciousness as a Jew, her style and primary thematic concerns. Concludes that she is brilliant, quirky, outrageous, and profound, despite her shortcomings as a writer.

Fisch, Harold. "Introducing Cynthia Ozick." *Response* 8.2 (1974): 27-34.

Describes the three phases of Jewish-American literature, and places Ozick in the most recent phase which deals even more intensely with the issues of Jewish identity. Describes her life, her principal fiction, and its style and thematic intent.

Fisch, Harold. "Myth and Antimyth." *A Remembered Future: A Study in Literary Mythology*. Harold Fisch. Bloomington: Indiana UP, 1984. 157-58.

Discusses the rich comic effect achieved by setting the archetypes against the trivializing background of the life of a great modern city. Discusses the Golem legend as a Faustian archetype, other myths dealing in salvation, and the dialectical interplay of myths of nature and of history.

Fishman, Sylvia Barack. "Imagining Ourselves: Cynthia Ozick's *The Messiah of Stockholm*." *Studies in American Jewish Literature* [Kent State] 9.1 (1990): 84-92.

Argues that *The Messiah of Stockholm* brings to Ozick's concern about artistic idolatry a vivid, intense, poetic apotheosis. Further suggests that it explores a subject of crucial interest to contemporary Jews even though it is not set among the urban, intellectual Jews of the American Northeast. Notes that Ozick is worrying about the Americanization of the Jewish-American mind and its beginning to do without history and the loss this represents.

Gertel, Elliot B. "Cynthia Ozick and the 'Jewish' Short Story." *Midstream* Dec. 1983: 43-47.

Argues that the issue of whether or not there is such a thing as the Jewish short story within the context of a discussion of Ozick's self-identification as a Jewish writer. Concludes that we finally cannot turn to Ozick for help with such a definition. Calls her writing exquisite, describing several of the works in detail.

Gitenstein, R. Barbara. "The Temptation of Apollo and the Loss of Yiddish in Cynthia Ozick's Fiction." *Studies in American Jewish Literature* [Albany] 3 (1983): 194-201.

Claims that at the heart of Ozick's fiction lies her unconscious and yet passionate desire for a distinctive Jewish foundation—a passion so strong that, as an artist and an intellectual, she must create it from some rationalized foundation for her creative output.

Goodheart, Eugene. "Cynthia Ozick's *Trust*." *Critique* 9.2 (1967): 99-102. Rpt. as *"Trust"* in *Cynthia Ozick*. Ed. Harold Bloom. Modern Critical Views. New York: Chelsea, 1986. 11-14.

Confesses to not having enjoyed *Trust*, and wonders why Ozick's language is always askew. Guesses she would rather present the arduous struggle for discovery rather than the facile shock of recognition. Has trouble understanding the plot, and criticizes the massive accumulation of detail, the constant nuancing of every situation which obfuscates the fable. Claims that the heroine speaks as if she has the taste of ash in her mouth. Suggests that, though the novel shows symptoms of power and talent, one wants to mitigate its harshness of judgment. Concludes that, finally, there is not enough accommodation between language and feeling.

Greenstein, Michael. "The Muse and the Messiah: Cynthia Ozick's Aesthetics." *Studies in American Jewish Literature* [Kent State] 8.1 (1989): 50-65.

Argues that Ozick's aesthetic has been informed by her program for a new Yiddish in which a Jewish-American writer should steep him or herself in Jewish subject matter, and her second belief, more recently abandoned, concerning the "aniconic second commandment forbidding the creation of graven images." Examines the revised aesthetics of *The Cannibal Galaxy* as a critique of the education system. Discusses its point of view emphasizing themes of perception and sight and subtle intertextual strategies making Ozick simultaneously faithful to a Jewish spirit as well as a postmodernist one. Concludes that implied in this aesthetic is an infinity of heretical hermeneutics fiercely anti-aesthetic and combating the false Messiahs of closure and representation in a dialectical covenant that embraces *midrash, aggadah,* and *pilpul*—those interpretive, imaginative, and didactic poles of a multidimensional, self-conscious humanism.

Harap, Louis. "The Religious Art of Cynthia Ozick." *Judaism* 33.3 (1984): 353-63.

Describes the return to religion of several new Jewish writers, including Ozick. Traces this passage from *Trust*, her first novel, forward into the more recent works. Discusses her commitment to a Judaism bereft of a belief in God. Discusses the fine particulars of what Ozick does and does not accept as religious obligation, and describes the element of religious fantasy in her works. Also, discusses her perceptions of the gender of God. Provides excellent insight into specific works.

Kauvar, Elaine M. "American Jewish Writers and the Breakup of Old Faiths." *Contemporary Literature* 30.3 (1989): 452-61.

Discusses and illustrates the opposing views of whether Jewish writers should seek their artistic sustenance from their ethnic tradition or from the surrounding culture. Asserts that Ozick in her critical essays and fiction shows "the importance of Jewish identity and warns of the obscurity and failure that result from denying cultural roots." Also discusses Pinsker's *The Uncompromising Fictions of Cynthia Ozick* and Bloom's *Cynthia Ozick*, a collection of essays, and finds the former "offers little insight into Ozick's ideas or her fiction," while the latter "provides future critics with glimpses into the complexities of Ozick's fiction."

Kauvar, Elaine M. "Cynthia Ozick's Book of Creation: *Puttermesser and Xanthippe*." *Contemporary Literature* 26.1 (1985): 40-54. Rpt. as "Ozick's Book of Creation" in *Cynthia Ozick*. Ed. Harold Bloom. Modern Critical Views. New York: Chelsea, 1986. 145-157.

Calls the book a complex, witty, and moving depiction of consuming intellectual passion, burgeoning self-discovery, and the veneration of artistic perfection. Traces the evolution of the characters from Ozick's earlier fiction, the sources of ideas originating in Jewish folklore, and the themes of conquest of self and the redemption of the past, the values of tradition, and the struggles against veneration.

Knopp, Josephine Z. "The Jewish Stories of Cynthia Ozick." *Studies in American Jewish Literature* [University Park, PA] 1.1 (1975): 31-38. Rpt. as "Ozick's Jewish Stories" in *Cynthia Ozick*. Ed. Harold Bloom. Modern Critical Views. New York: Chelsea, 1986. 21-29.

Comments that Jewishness and Judaism are seen here as central concerns. Notes that all her work is shaped by a sense of Jewish history and the contemporary precariousness of Jewish life. Traces the major themes and works in the Ozick canon.

Kremer, S. Lillian. "The Dybbuk of All the Lost Dead: Cynthia Ozick's Holocaust Fiction." *Witness Through the Imagination: Jewish*

American Holocaust Literature. S. Lillian Kremer. Detroit: Wayne State UP, 1989. 218-78.

Argues that Ozick, deeply knowledgeable in Jewish religious sources, language, and history, treats the Holocaust as the orienting event of the century. Claims that, though she prefers not to write about the Holocaust directly, the subject enters her work "unbidden," "unsummoned." Finds Holocaust allusion, experience, and thought manifest in much of Ozick's fiction, and claims that it would be unthinkable for a writer as deeply moved by Jewish history as Ozick is to create fiction that is Holocaust free. Discusses all her work to date.

Lowin, Joseph. "Cynthia Ozick, Rewriting Herself: The Road from 'The Shawl' to 'Rosa.'" *Since Flannery O'Connor: Essays on the Contemporary American Short Story*. Eds. Loren Logsdon and Charles W. Mayer. Essays in Literature. Macomb: Western Illinois U, 1987. 101-12.

Argues that *Usurpation* is a good example of critical arguments that writing is not only based on reality, but also on previous writing, thus constituting rewriting as much as anything else. Likens Ozick to the French symbolist poets, who write not of the thing but of the effects of the thing. Explicates both "The Shawl" and "Rosa."

Martin, Margot L. "The Theme of Survival in Cynthia Ozick's "The Shawl."

Discusses the theme of personal and Jewish survival and the lengths to which a person will go to persevere and endure in "The Shawl," by concentrating on the symbolism and imagery associated with the three main characters. Discusses the characters and events of the story that inform this interpretation.

McCloskey, Mark. *"The Messiah of Stockholm."* Magill's Literary Annual: 1988. Ed. Frank N. Magill. 2 vols. Englewood Cliffs: Salem, 1988. 2: 549-52.

A standard reference article covering author, publisher, setting, locale, and principal characters in *The Messiah of Stockholm*. Describes plot, theme, and characters in detail. Concludes that this book focuses on the mysterious nature of fiction itself to produce a luminous dramatized essay on the "literariness" of the characters.

Mort, Jo-Ann. "Cynthia Ozick and the Future of American Jewish Literature." *Jewish Frontier* Jan. 1985: 20-21, 26.

Argues that Ozick challenges the myth of the writer as a lonely, urban animal. Notes that she opts for orthodoxy, deliberately excludes non-orthodox Jews, while disdaining universalism or secularism as buying into the American culture. Concludes that, in the process, she challenges all aspects of Jewishness including her own orthodoxy, but left out of this picture is the unbelieving Jew.

Ottenberg, Eve. "The Rich Visions of Cynthia Ozick." *New York Times Magazine* 10 Apr. 1983: 46-47, 62-68.

A generalized article discussing her life, awards, critical acclaim, works, and political views.

Pifer, Ellen. "Cynthia Ozick: Invention and Orthodoxy." *Contemporary American Women Writers: Narrative Strategies.* Eds. Catherine Rainwater and William J. Scheick. Lexington: UP of Kentucky, 1985. 89-109.

Places Ozick in a postmodernist or antirealist tradition—a tradition which deals in sophisticated, self-conscious narrative techniques. Claims that Ozick roots herself in a vision of the moral and spiritual truths of the Old Testament and Mosaic Law. Sees, in addition, that the fiction irradiates the quotidian landscape while elements of the fantastic cast a symbolic light on local characters and conditions. Discusses "Puttermesser": her work history, her ancestry, her afterlife and the subsequent novella *Puttermesser and Xanthippe*.

Pinsker, Sanford. "Jewish-American Literature's Lost-and-Found Department: How Philip Roth and Cynthia Ozick Reimagine Their Significant Dead." *Modern Fiction Studies* 35.2 (1989): 223-35.

Comments on Ozick's participation in illusions, phantasmagoria, transfigurations, and religious forces both spiteful and lifegiving. Sees her, as well as Roth, reimagining her significant dead with the result that the lost and found department of American literature rediscovers and honors those writers who survive in new, experimental combinations.

Rainwater, Catherine, and William J. Scheick. "'Some Godlike Grammar': An Introduction to the Writings of Hazzard, Ozick, and Redmon." *Texas Studies in Literature and Language* 25.2 (1983): 181-211. Rpt. as "The Unsurprise of Surprise" in *Cynthia Ozick*. Ed. Harold Bloom. Modern Critical Views. New York: Chelsea, 1986. 69-78.

Argues that, at the deepest philosophical levels, these three writers contemplate the "welling together" of impressions and experiences in a flow of time that sweeps humans along toward apparently predestined ends. Suggests that, caught up in this ebb and flow, the characters of these three contemporary authors find only tentative meaning and design in an indefinite, incomplete past. Concludes that each author seeks some "god-like grammar" in narrative technique to describe the unreconcilable chaos of human existence.

Rose, Elisabeth. "Cynthia Ozick's Liturgical Postmodernism: *The Messiah of Stockholm.*" *Studies in American Jewish Literature* [Kent State] 9.1 (1990): 93-107.

Argues that in *The Messiah of Stockholm* Ozick counters counter-traditionalism and subverts the meaning of subversiveness, our modern literary norm. Suggests that Ozick uses in this experimental novel traditional Jewish elements: the overt references to mysticism, the constant allusions to Diaspora, the oppressive odor of burning, the sympathetic view of the orphan Lar's misguided idolatrous worship, thereby turning postmodernism into a public religious service of a monotheistic god rather than the literary muses. Concludes that in its high-pitched striving, its meaning-saturation, and its zestful word play, the novel infuses its corona with piety becoming a Jewish mystical symbol.

Rosenberg, Ruth. "Covenanted to the Law: Cynthia Ozick." *MELUS* 9.3 (1982): 39-44. Rpt. as "Covenanted to the Law." in *Cynthia Ozick.* Ed. Harold Bloom. Modern Critical Views. New York: Chelsea, 1986. 57-61.

Records Ozick's statements on fiction given at the Weizman Institute in Rehevot and her praise of Bellow, Gershom, Scholem, and Singer. Provides a gloss on the theory of fiction espoused in "Usurpation," and makes numerous references to Harold Bloom's valuation of the piece.

Rosenberg, Ruth. "Cynthia Ozick." *Critical Survey of Short Fiction.* Ed. Frank N. Magill. 8 vols. Englewood Cliffs: Salem, 1981. 5: 2035-39.

A standard reference article discussing Ozick's birthplace, principal short fiction, other literary forms, influences, story characteristics, and biography.

Rovit, Earl. "The Two Languages of Cynthia Ozick." *Studies in American Jewish Literature* [Kent State] 8.1 (1989): 34-49.

States that Ozick's work presents considerable difficulties to her readers because the density, allusiveness, intellectual concern, and ambiguities characterizing her work all tend to give it a weight and importance that outweigh the rather modest amount of writing. Notes that the two languages she employs are the didactic essay voice and the multilayered tale voice, deliberately skewed and elusive in meaning.

Scrafford, Barbara. "Nature's Silent Scream: A Commentary on Cynthia Ozick's 'The Shawl.' *Critique* 31.1 (1989): 11-15.

Describes Ozick's technique in "The Shawl" as her exclusive focus on Rosa, while Rosa focuses only on Magda, and Magda focuses only on the shawl. Discusses the absence of extraneous description, scene-setting, or narration by showing how all that is left gives the story final shape and ironic contrasts. Concludes that this story is about how the massacred six million fade into the shadows as the author hones in on Rosa to show us what it is like to be a mother in the time of the hunted.

Sokoloff, Naomi B. "Interpretation: Cynthia Ozick's *Cannibal Galaxy*." *Prooftexts* 6.3 (1986): 239-57.

Sees *Cannibal Galaxy* as a satiric look at Jewish education because the novel features an elusive, uncommunicative child character, who, by dint of her enigmatic qualities, serves mainly to show how the rest of the world responds to her. Suggests that she is instrumental in Ozick's satire, alerting the reader to the assumptions and norms of her environment and magnifying the attitudes of those around her.

Strandberg, Victor. "The Art of Cynthia Ozick." *Texas Studies in Literature and Language* 25.2 (1983): 266-312. Rpt. in *Cynthia Ozick*. Ed. Harold Bloom. Modern Critical Views. New York: Chelsea, 1986. 79-120.

A major article which deals with each of the works chronologically and does not have a particular thesis. Its purpose is to provide a major gloss on Ozick's works, themes, theories of art, and artistry. The most thorough single article on Ozick.

Uffen, Ellen Serlen. "*The Messiah of Stockholm*." *Yiddish* 7.1 (1987): 106-11.

Describes *The Messiah of Stockholm* as an exploration of existence in the post-Holocaust world. Provides a good plot summary, and unravels several of the literary-historical allusions in the novel.

Weiner, Deborah Heiligman. "Cynthia Ozick, Pagan vs Jew (1966-1976)." *Studies in American Jewish Literature* [Albany] 3 (1983): 179-93.

Describes Ozick's view of America as glorifying pagan modes of life, thereby undermining Jewish life and values in America. Hence, her ugly pictures of modernity. Comments that she finds nature reflects the pull of paganism. Traces this theme throughout much of the fiction.

Wisse, Ruth R. "American Jewish Writing, Act II." *Commentary* June 1976: 40-45. Rpt. as "Ozick as American Jewish Writer" in *Cynthia Ozick*. Ed. Harold Bloom. Modern Critical Views. New York: Chelsea, 1986. 35-45.

Sees Ozick as the self-styled spokesperson and most audacious writer of the second movement in Jewish American literature which involves a turning back to roots. Comments that Ozick's work foretells the emergence of a new kind of literature as part of this general cultural renaissance—a liturgical literature of alienation. Concludes that it is an attempt to draw directly from Jewish sources.

Zatlin, Linda. "Cynthia Ozick's *Levitations: Five Fictions*." *Studies in American Jewish Literature* [Albany] 4 (1985): 121-23.

Describes Ozick's use of the past and the present in her works. Details the contents of the stories, identifies some of the major themes, and comments in particular on her interest in creation, the way her characters wrestle with their Judaism, her indebtedness to Yiddish writers, her talent for creating mystical occurrences, and her awareness of the issues concerning Jewish womanhood.

Reviews

Allen, Bruce. "MacArthur Award Winners Produce Two of Season's Best." Rev. of *The Cannibal Galaxy*. *Christian Science Monitor* 4 Nov. 1983: B4.

Argues that Ozick's *The Cannibal Galaxy* contains a virtuoso display of her talent and ranks as one of the finest books of the year.

Alter, Robert. "Defenders of the Faith." Rev. of *The Messiah of Stockholm*. *Commentary* July 1987: 52-55.

Discusses *The Messiah of Stockholm* by describing its plot and characters, relating it to *Don Quixote* by its tradition. Calls it Ozick's most admirable work technically but finally feels it lacking because it is too cerebral. Half-heartedly admires its stylistic razzle-dazzle, the high order of inventiveness, the violent extravagance of the metaphors, and the novel's notable ability to render sensations. Concludes, however, that it tries to substitute rhetorical depth for experiential depth.

Alvarez, A. "Flushed with Ideas." Rev. of *Levitation: Five Fictions. New York Review of Books* 13 May 1982: 22-23. Rpt. as "Flushed with Ideas: *Levitation*" in *Cynthia Ozick.* Ed. Harold Bloom. Modern Critical Views. New York: Chelsea, 1986. 53-56.

Calls Ozick a stylist in the best sense for her language, wit, apprehension of reality, and curious, crooked flights of imagination. Calls her writing intricate, immaculate, poetic, and precise. Claims that there are colloquial and allusive changes of pace and tone, and that her subtle passionate ironies and nagging self-pity build gradually and logically to a climax.

Alvarez, A. "Games People Play." Rev. of *The Cannibal Galaxy. New York Review of Books* 10 Nov. 1983: 27-28. Rpt. as "On *The Cannibal Galaxy*" in *Cynthia Ozick.* Ed. Harold Bloom. Modern Critical Views. New York: Chelsea, 1986. 133-35.

Calls *The Cannibal Galaxy* a parable of intellectual yearning and delusion. Claims that it discusses the burden of European inheritance dumped down among the bright, brash certitudes of the Jewish middle-classes in middle America. Provides a detailed description of contents.

Apple, Max. "Wresting Life from the Void." Rev. of *The Cannibal Galaxy. New Leader* 12 Dec. 1983: 14-15. Rpt. in *Cynthia Ozick.* Ed. Harold Bloom. Modern Critical Views. New York: Chelsea, 1986. 137-39.

Suggests that *The Cannibal Galaxy* moves with great subtlety through the various meanings of empty and desolate, the cosmic, social and personal meanings. Sees that for Ozick the void is the world and also the main character. Concludes that this is a book fearlessly looking at the central mysteries of creation.

Bailey, Paul. "Desirable Dreads." Rev. of *Bloodshed and Three Novellas. Times Literary Supplement* 23 July 1976: 905.

Calls *Bloodshed* a book of stories representing puzzles about puzzles leaving one satisfyingly bewildered. Outlines each of the plots.

Batchelor, John Calvin. "Three Novels: Obsession and the Nature of Writing." Rev. of *The Messiah of Stockholm. Washington Post Book World* 8 Mar. 1987: 1, 8.

Calls *The Messiah of Stockholm* a magical species of slapstick comedy
which transforms itself into the most stone-written of tragedies. Sees this
as a tumbling fox chase set in Stockholm, and dealing with revenge, illusion, ambition, and foolishness. Concludes that the prose is deft and the
writer a first-rate intelligence.

Baumbach, Elinor. "Girl in a Gilded Cage." Rev. of *Trust*. *Saturday
    Review* 9 July 1966: 34.

Comments that *Trust*, Ozick's Jamesian novel, is direct, inventive, playful, and full of wisdom. Provides a detailed account of the contents of the
story, its themes, and characters. Concludes that Ozick is a competent,
committed, serious writer who has written a brilliant first novel.

Baumgaertner, Jill. "Books." Rev. of *The Shawl*. *Christian Century* 7
    Mar., 1990: 258-59.

Considers Ozick's fiction consumate in moral vision and artistry. Details
the story and contents of "The Shawl," and calls its style rich in character,
irony, poetry, theology, philosophy, narrative, paradox, and contradictions.

Baumgaertner, Jill. "Pedagogues and Their Mysteries." Rev. of *The
    Cannibal Galaxy*. *Cresset* Sept. 1984: 24-26.

Considers *Cannibal Galaxy* a book every teacher and school administra-
tor striving for excellence should read and ponder because it is the story
of educating middle America. Details the contents of the book.

Bell, Pearl K. "Idylls of the Tribe." Rev. of *Bloodshed and Three
    Novellas*. *New Leader* 12 Apr. 1976: 18-19.

Discusses *Bloodshed* as amazingly inventive and ethically cumbrous.
Comments that for all of its capricious ingenuity and austere self-dis-
trust, the novella is too schematic and its moral conundrums too stubborn
to come to life. Describes her attitudes toward American Jews and their
responses to the Holocaust as obsessive, and concludes that the rhetorical
shape of her conviction has become too sententious and literary.

Bernays, Anne. "A Stolen Life." Rev. of *The Shawl*. *Washington Post
    Book World* 5 Nov. 1989: 7.

Calls Ozick the Mozart of fiction writers, whose surfaces dazzle and
whose depths are full of surprises. Argues that this story distills the horror of the Holocaust in perfectly controlled language. Recounts contents
and characters.

Blake, Patricia. "A New Triumph for Idiosyncracy." Rev. of *The Cannibal Galaxy*. *Time* 5 Sept. 1983: 64.

Sees the book as brilliantly harnessing the steeds of myth and mysticism in the Jewish tradition, and as centering on Europe as the cannibal galaxy which devours smaller galaxies. Commends Ozick for the dense erudition from Jewish sources which characterizes her work, and for focussing on the theme of Jewish heritage albeit idiosyncratically. Includes a brief biographical sketch.

Blakeston, Oswell. "Fiction." Rev. of *The Pagan Rabbi and Other Stories*. *Books and Bookmen* Aug. 1972: 70-71.

Describes the central dilemma of several of the stories in this collection, and comments that each draws its strength from contemporary Jewish backgrounds. Comments briefly on her use of archetype and legend, concluding that because Ozick does not make one know in new ways, the reader can put her down at any time.

Bloom, Alice. "Why the Novel (Still) Matters." Rev. of *The Shawl* 43.1 (1990): 156-58.

Reviews the contents of "The Shawl" at length, showing how Rosa, a Holocaust survivor views life as a result of her camp experiences. Friends and relatives try to help her put the past behind her, but for Rosa, "before [the camps] is a dream. After is a joke. Only during stays. And to call it a life is a lie."

Bloom, Harold. "The Book of the Father." Rev. of *The Messiah of Stockholm*. *New York Times Book Review* 22 Mar. 1987: 1, 36.

Claims that *The Messiah of Stockholm* is full of Polish Jews obsessed by their origins. Sees Ozick's vision of these people and her art as infused with her anxiety about idolatry. Details the contents of the book thoroughly.

"Books."Rev. of *Trust*. *Time* 12 Aug. 1966: 80.

Calls Ozick an intense mouse, who, after six and half years, has brought forth an elephant of a book. Labels her perspective Tolstoyan, and her dialogue a constant delight. Suggests that, at times, her prose gains a Jamesian sonority. Concludes that she imparts an impression of power and control, and promises larger worlds still waiting to be born.

Brookner, Anita. "Things Past and Things Passed On." Rev. of *The Messiah of Stockholm*. *Spectator* 16 Jan. 1988: 29-30.

Calls *The Messiah of Stockholm* a less-than-perfect book by a remarkable writer who owes much to Philip Roth. Many of the stories are described in detail.

Brown, Rosellen. Rev. of *Bloodshed and Three Novellas*. *New Republic* 5 June 1976: 30-31.

Calls Ozick a scholar and a reveller in language whose work develops along the tensions strung between rationalist/holy thinker on the one hand, and tale-maker/invoker of magic and miracle on the other hand. Details the contents of the volume, providing accompanying literary commentary.

Cassill, R. V. "A Very Dissimilar Trio." Rev. of *The Pagan Rabbi and Other Stories*. *Washington Post Book World* 6 June 1971: 5.

Calls this a collection of long, dense stories full of stunning images, precise dialogue, and exotic comic characters. Concludes that they are tangled, mysterious, and strange.

Clapp, Susannah. "Game Patties." Rev. of *Bloodshed and Three Novellas*. *New Statesman* 23 July 1976: 121.

Describes this collection as containing four combative stories that twist themselves around possible objections, tricking expectations, warily accommodating both persecution and defense. Describes the thematic materials in "Usurpation," and the stylistic techniques of the other three pieces.

Clute, John. "Reviewing from the Edge." Rev. of *The Messiah of Stockholm*. *Times Literary Supplement* 13-19 Nov. 1987: 1249.

Calls the novel a book about the spiritual orphaning of the modern world. Sees the underlying vision of the novel as remorseless, the prose intense with a dreamlike acuity, the pace gay, and the whole effect one of bumptious exuberance.

Cohen, Arthur A. Rev. of *The Pagan Rabbi and Other Stories*. *Commonweal* 3 Sept. 1971: 461-63.

Comments that, in these stories, Ozick breaks up familiar experiences, such as escape fantasy and transmogrifying the flesh, and reconstructs them in surprising ways. Suggests that, unlike the genteel mood of most short stories, Ozick brings a Jewish vision, a distraught series of characters, and an avoidance of mere sociology. Concludes that, though many of the stories end in bleakness and obduracy, there is also a prevailing sense of mutual compassion and reconciliation.

Cohen, Arthur A. "New Truths and Revelations." Rev. of *The Pagan Rabbi and Other Stories*. *Congress Bi-Weekly* 17 Sept. 1971: 22-23.

Calls the book a cubist masterpiece. Claims that Ozick breaks up familiar experiences, reconstructing them in such surprising ways that common passions—the wish to escape and transmogrify the flesh, the exaltation of fantasy into a lifesaving reality, the overlapping estrangement of Jew and Gentile—transcend toward new truths.

Crain, Jane Larkin. "New Books." Rev. of *Bloodshed and Three Novellas*. *Saturday Review* 17 Apr. 1976: 32.

Calls this book a difficult but commanding performance by a first-rate storyteller, executed with a lot more dazzle and sense than one has come to expect from contemporary writers of fiction. Concludes that she is a masterworker, original, idiosyncratic, compelling.

Cunningham, Valentine. "Even Unto Nantwich." Rev. of *The Pagan Rabbi and Other Stories*. *Listener* 22 June 1972: 841.

Calls the stories in *The Pagan Rabbi* a rich delicatessen of style in which Ozick reveals language as her true theme. Approves of the straining for mythic proportion, her resurrection of old literary themes, and her liberation of virile Jewish-American versions from the old Gentile graveclothes.

Edelman, Lily. "Good Reads from Jewish America." Rev. of *The Pagan Rabbi and Other Stories*. *National Jewish Monthly* July-Aug. 1971: 40-41.

States that these stories reveal dazzling versatility, a haunting range of encounters by Jew and man with his own raw humanness, his doubt and despair, his envy and greed, his lust and love, his compassion and lack of generosity, his non-comprehension and understanding.

Eder, Richard. "The Principal Import As a Porsche." Rev. of *The Cannibal Galaxy*. *Los Angeles Times Book Review* 18 Sept. 1983: 1, 7.

Calls this a book of wit beyond which lies flinty metaphysical poetry. Details the contents of the individual stories.

Edwards, Thomas R. "The Short View." Rev. of *Bloodshed and Three Novellas*. *New York Review of Books* 1 Apr. 1976: 34, 36-37. Rpt. as "*Bloodshed*." in *Cynthia Ozick*. Ed. Harold Bloom. Modern Critical Views. New York: Chelsea, 1986. 31-33.

Claims that *Bloodshed* tells of Ozick's fondness for the novella. Notes her fiction as episodic, anecdotal, informal, and anxious, religiously speaking. Details the contents of all four stories.

Ehrenfeld, Temma. "In Short." Rev. of *The Cannibal Galaxy*. *Ms*. Dec. 1983: 38-39.

Claims that this is a book salted with rages and capable of curdling one's stomach with excitement. The language has all the shimmer of a fire-eating act. But the unhappiness of the story is almost unbearable.

Enright D. J. "Visions and Revisions." Rev. of *The Messiah of Stockholm*. *New York Review of Books* 28 May 1987: 18-19.

Describes the book as an intriguing mystery we admire for its intrinsic interest and lively intellectuality. Argues that the end of the book fails; hence, the whole thing ceases to be great literature. A detailed critical essay that describes content.

Epstein, Leslie. "Stories and Something Else." Rev. of *Levitation: Five Fictions*. *New York Times Book Review* 14 Feb. 1982: 11, 25. Rpt. in *Cynthia Ozick*. Ed. Harold Bloom. Modern Critical Views. New York: Chelsea, 1986. 47-51.

Calls each of the pieces in *Levitation* dazzling, beautiful, and original. Details the contents of the stories, and identifies her major themes.

Fein, Richard J. "A Double World." Rev. of *The Pagan Rabbi and Other Stories*. *Judaism* 20.4 (1971): 507-09.

Calls *The Pagan Rabbi* an impressive volume of stories dealing with the theme of the Diaspora Jew. Details the contents of the stories.

Finkelstein, Norman. "From Drohobycz to Stockholm." Rev. of *The Messiah of Stockholm*. *Salmagundi* 76-77 (1988): 243-49.

Discusses *The Messiah of Stockholm*, comparing Ozick's style and themes to those of Bruno Schulz for whom she has had a well-publicized admiration. Contains valuable interpretive commentary on the contents of the work.

Garrett, George. "Arts and Letters." Rev. of *Bloodshed and Three Novellas*. *Sewanee Review* 85.1 (1977): 108.

Claims that Ozick is clever, exciting, poetic, forceful, a narrative virtuoso, and always entertaining and funny. Discusses several of her stories and books.

Geringer, Laura. "Fiction." Rev. of *Levitation: Five Fictions. Saturday Review* 8 Jan. 1981: 66.

Argues that in *Levitation* Ozick writes with precision, irony, and luminous intelligence. Suggests that her view is universal, but occupies a unique niche. Concludes that it can only be compared to itself. Calls this a worthy sequel to her earlier books.

Giddins, Gary. "Brief Encounters." Rev. of *Levitation: Five Fictions. Village Voice* 16 Feb. 1982: 54.

Sees *Levitation* as finely textured, buoyant, full of finesse, hilarity, hyperbole, and invention. Concludes that her diction is as rich as her fantastic plots.

Glassgold, Peter. "Between Athens and Jerusalem." Rev. of *The Pagan Rabbi and Other Stories. New Leader* 14 June 1971: 24.

Describes Ozick's early works and their respective receptions by critics. Goes through *The Pagan Rabbi* story by story commenting on style, cultural polarities, themes, characters, and general effects. Concludes that she promises to become a writer of considerable power.

Goldreich, Gloria. "Good Stories about Jews." Rev. of *The Pagan Rabbi and Other Stories. Hadassah Magazine* Oct. 1971: 24.

Finds these stories haunting and brilliant. Describes Ozick as more than competent in any sphere because of her prose, a rare reading experience.

Gorra, Michael. "Laughter and Bloodshed." Rev. of *The Cannibal Galaxy. Hudson Review* 37.1 (1984): 151-52.

States that Ozick's prose startles with its beauty. Describes the contents of the novel.

Gray, Paul. "Alien Tongue." Rev. of *Bloodshed and Three Novellas. Time* 12 Apr. 1976: 95-96.

Describes the contents of *Bloodshed* without making any critical comments.

Grumbach, Doris. "Feats of Intellect and Prestidigitation." Rev. of *Levitation: Five Fictions. Washington Post Book World* 28 Feb. 1982: 3, 11.

Argues that *Levitation* is stunning in force and originality. Comments that this is an important voice in American literature whose intelligence pervades all she writes. Describes Ozick's earlier work. Calls her a writer of uncommon magical gifts. Details some of the stories.

Halperin, Irving. "Rosa's Story." Rev. of *The Shawl. Commonweal* 15 Dec. 1989: 711-12.

Considers "Rosa" and "The Shawl" two organic pieces of one whole since Rosa is the main character in both, and echoes of the Holocaust reverberate through both pieces. Calls them a stunning tour de force of redemptive possibility and splendid literary art.

Harris, Robert R. "The Complex Magic of Cynthia Ozick." Rev. of *Levitation: Five Fictions. Saturday Review* Feb. 1982: 58-59.

Calls Ozick an incredibly self-conscious writer who steadily shuns overindulgence and has produced a rich body of work deeply rooted in folklore. Sees the works as weighty and consequential, shimmering with intelligence, glorying in language and puzzle. Comments that she equates the magic in her stories with the magical process of writing fiction.

Hegi, Ursula. "A Frail, Connecting Thread." Rev. of *The Shawl. Los Angeles Times Book Review* 8 Oct. 1989: 2.

Calls "The Shawl" devastating and exquisite. Describes the psychological makeup of the protagonist, and concludes that this is a brilliant, moving, and chilling story conveying a terror so immense that it renders the characters speechless and the readers powerless.

Heller, Amanda. "Short Reviews." Rev. of *Bloodshed and Three Novellas. Atlantic* May 1976: 108.

Praises the multihued characters of *Bloodshed* as natural, supernatural, stolid, and self-possessed. Concludes that her humor is wry, quirky, intelligent, edgy, eccentric, and beautiful.

Horn, Carole. "Oy!" Rev. of *Bloodshed and Three Novellas. Washington Post Book World* 13 Mar. 1977: E5.

Comments that *Bloodshed* is about lust. Sees it is a flawed, unwieldy, highly unusual book—ludicrously funny, sage, serious, and totally original.

J., L. "Too Much Gossamer in the Web?" Rev. of *Trust. Christian Science Monitor* 1 Sept. 1966: 11.

Discusses *Trust* as a first novel whose sentences are too long, time span too long, faces too long, and prose too Jamesian. Concludes that finally, the reader is left with an overwhelming sense of tedium.

Kakutani, Michiko. "Books of the Times." Rev. of *The Cannibal Galaxy*. *New York Times* 29 Aug. 1983: 14.

Describes the themes of her work, her prose style, and her Jewishness while reviewing *The Cannibal Galaxy*. Calls the book wilfully recondite, focused on metaphysics at the expense of language, narrative, and character, and dense with ideas and philosophic speculation.

Kakutani, Michiko. "Idol Worshipers." Rev. of *The Messiah of Stockholm*. *New York Times* 28 Feb. 1987: 18.

Claims that *The Messiah of Stockholm* is full of deep suspicion about the creative process. Suggests that it is a game of mirrors and deceptions full of moral highs and seriousness. Notes that beneath is a narrative of hijinks. Claims that this fiction both delights and instructs. Concludes that it is all a precisely observed naturalistic tableau of figures in a Chagall painting.

Kaplan, Johanna. "A Lust for God's Earthly Forms." Rev. of *The Pagan Rabbi and Other Stories*. *New York Times Book Review* 13 June 1971: 7, 14. Rpt. as "*The Pagan Rabbi and Other Stories*." *Cynthia Ozick*. Ed. Harold Bloom. Modern Critical Views. New York: Chelsea, 1986. 15-17.

Comments that when we enter Ozick's narrative instantaneously we are right in the center of a mind, in the swirl of a world. Notes that place is brilliantly evoked and that we are engaged with her in a search for an answer to the question of what is holy. Calls Ozick a narrative hypnotist with an extraordinary range including intense lyricism, brilliant inventiveness, jokes, lists, letters, poems, parodies, and satires. Concludes that her work awakens and restores.

Lanchester, John. "Ozick's No." Rev. of *The Messiah of Stockholm*. *London Review of Books* 4 Feb. 1988: 17.

Describes *The Messiah of Stockholm* in a very useful essay on Ozick's Jewish orthodoxy, aesthetics, and critical essays. Details the plot and contents of the book, comparing it to Roth's *The Ghost Writer*. Comments on its style, restraint, aesthetics, content, and effects.

Lasdun, James. "Books & Writers." Rev. of *The Cannibal Galaxy*. *Encounter* May 1984: 64.

Calls Ozick more ambitious than Weldon, and her subject matter much more complex with its heavy gloss of intellectuality.

Lask, Thomas. "A Disciple of the Master." Rev. of *Trust*. *New York Times* 9 July 1966: 25.

Calls *Trust* a long, lapidary, Jamesian work, and a first novel. Comments that Ozick's prose is full of periphrastic utterances, half-completed words, and parentheses which are nets thrown over her most elusive thoughts. Concludes that neither the skeleton of the novel, nor the characters are firm enough to fill the bright, verbal outergarment. Finds *Trust* is not so much a failure as a rueful disappointment.

Lask, Thomas. "Rough Stones On Road to Glory." Rev. of *The Pagan Rabbi and Other Stories*. *New York Times* 5 July 1971: 17.

Claims that *The Pagan Rabbi* works out of a European tradition employing a broad canvas, an abundance of characters, and a variety of incidents. Comments that Ozick's imagination runs toward the artistic and the supernatural. Notes also that she treats her art with an uncontemporary seriousness, and brings to it that order, stability, and balance so obviously lacking in the life she is mirroring.

Lehman, David. "Art Against Art's Sake." Rev. of *The Messiah of Stockholm*. *Partisan Review* 54.3 (1987): 481-85.

Describes *The Messiah of Stockholm* as concentrating largely on Ozick's views of art for art's sake. Provides a paraphrase of the contents of the novel, designates it as psychological drama working by Jamesian indirection and nuance. Suggests that the reliability of the narrative is constantly in doubt. Concludes that she explores in all its complexity the interplay between writing as a species of artistic invention and writing as sacred covenant.

Lehman, David. "Tracking Down a False Messiah." Rev. of *The Messiah of Stockholm*. *Newsweek* 16 Mar 1987: 74.

Comments that *The Messiah of Stockholm* uses literary artifice and illusion for a paradoxical purpose—to warn us against literature and illusion. Yet notes that this book doesn't just chart fanciful flights of its madmen and impostors, it also charges their desperate cries with meaning.

Leonard, John. "Books of the Times." Rev. of *Bloodshed and Three Novellas*. *New York Times* 7 May 1976: C16.

Suggests that *Bloodshed* reveals Ozick as an artist, a Talmudic expert, and a mind salesman of images, likenesses, stories, births of telling, narratives, suspenses, turning points, palaces, foam of sea, mermen, and the demonic. Concludes that this book establishes her as one of our best writers.

Malcolm, Janet. "Graven Images." Rev. of *The Messiah of Stockholm*. *New Yorker* 8 June 1987: 102-04.

Provides a detailed exegesis of Ozick's short story, "Rosa." Describes the literary strategy of the story to be that of the master ironists, Nabokov and Singer: registering the crime of the Germans through the evocation of the beauty, pleasure, and culture the Jews of Europe were confidently, carelessly enjoying on the eve of the catastrophe. Details also Ozick's view of literature and strategies.

Malin, Irving. "Faith and Fiction." Rev. of *Bloodshed and Three Novellas*. *Present Tense* 4.3 (1977): 67-68.

Describes Ozick as erudite, concerned with Jewish identity, able to flavor her work with Yiddish and references to Jewish law, the writer of gripping tales, and the inventor of convoluted tales. Briefly describes the stories in *Levitation*.

Mallon, Thomas. "The Holocaust and the 'Stewpot'." Rev. of *The Messiah of Stockholm*. *Wall Street Journal* 10 Apr. 1987: 21.

Describes *The Messiah of Stockholm* as brilliant, quirky, difficult, gorgeous, Kafkaesque, and wholly admirable.

Manguel, Alberto. "Paternity Suite." Rev. of *The Messiah of Stockholm*. *Village Voice* 21 Apr. 1987: 45.

Describes *The Messiah of Stockholm* as evidence of Ozick's split between self-as-writer and self-as-orthodox Jew. Contains mostly a reported conversation with Ozick in which she describes this split.

Mars-Jones, Adam. "Fantastic Flushes." Rev. of *Levitation*. *Times Literary Supplement* 23 Apr. 1982: 456.

Describes *Levitation* as a book full of passionate learning and phrasing. Considers Ozick's specialties to be prose poetry, intellectual slapstick, meticulous detail, wild rhetorical fantasy, and a running battle between realism and a rhetoric that undercuts appearances. Concludes, however, that although this rocket takes off, it makes a vivid, exhilarating flight and comes clattering down as a scorched stick among the trees.

Mellors, John. "Airs of Reality." Rev. of *Levitation: Five Fictions.*
Listener 15 Apr. 1982: 23-24.

Calls *Levitation* a collection of stories in which Ozick makes the magic
seem real, although he points out that she does use an excess of invention
to make her point. Notes that her style is sometimes too wry and dry,
though one should be grateful enough to enjoy the exotic products of a
fertile imagination.

Mesher, David R. "Reviews." Rev. of *Bloodshed and Three Novellas.*
Studies in Short Fiction 13.4 (1976): 521-22.

Calls *Bloodshed* captivating, excellent stories. Notes, though the Preface
denies it, the central plot device of the story is Chekovian. Sees all her
stories as heavy pockets to be emptied by the reader. Discusses the content of each piece.

Montrose, David. "Wise Child." Rev. of *The Cannibal Galaxy. Times
Literary Supplement* 20 Jan. 1984: 71.

Calls *The Cannibal Galaxy* a polemic rather than an entertainment.
Claims that it has too many extraneous episodes. Yet, notes also that
these shortcomings make the novel no less interesting, merely a work
whose energy might have been more efficiently focused.

Moynahan, Julian. "A Writer With a Lot on Her Mind." Rev. of *Bloodshed
and Three Novellas. New York Times Book Review* 11 Apr. 1976: 8.

Argues that uppermost in Ozick's mind are issues concerning the conflict
of cultures taking place in the hearts and minds of Jews living just one
generation from the Holocaust. Discusses her questions on how a Jew
can write effectively without violating the second commandment.
Describes the contents of *Bloodshed* and the other three novellas.

Penner, Jonathan. "The Prime of Mr. Joseph Brill." Rev. of *The
Cannibal Galaxy. Washington Post Book World* 25 Sept. 1983: 5.

Claims that *The Cannibal Galaxy* is full of vivid people and gorgeous
writing coupled with an austere plot. Suggests that it is also a radical critique of pedagogy. Details the plot and characters.

Pinsker, Sanford. "Jewish Tradition and the Individual Talent." Rev. of
Art and Ardor. Georgia Review 37.3 (1983): 676-80. Rpt. in *Cynthia
Ozick.* Ed. Harold Bloom. Modern Critical Views. New York:
Chelsea, 1986. 121-25.

Claims that Ozick shares much of the restless energy, the taste for polemics, and the sheer brilliance that characterized earlier New York Jewish intellectuals, but with this crucial difference—she is out to discover what it is like to *think* as a Jew. Briefly reviews the contents of her book of essays *Art and Ardor*. Useful for insights into her fiction.

Pinsker, Sanford. "Reviews." Rev. of *Levitation: Five Fictions*. *Studies in Short Fiction* 19.2 (1982): 177-78.

Sees *Levitation* as more imaginative than her earlier stories, written in a stronger voice, and full of rich possibilities for American storytelling. Describes the contents of the five pieces, and concludes that the result of this collection is that it puts many of Ozick's essays on Judaica to an imaginative test. Notes that, if the measure of a great storyteller is that nobody else could tell this story, then Ozick is a great storyteller. Concludes that we read her fiction with equal measures of familiar recognition and unending surprise.

Pinsker, Sanford. "A Serious Writer, A Subtle Voice." Rev. of *The Pagan Rabbi and Other Stories*. *Reconstructionist* 19 Nov. 1971: 17-18.

Commends *The Pagan Rabbi* for its craftsmanship and seriousness. Sees Ozick as successor to the renaissance in Jewish American literature and as one unusually conversant with Jewish culture. Calls the volume a triumph of tone, balancing the comic with the poignant but managing to divide our sympathies among a wide range of responses to Yiddish literature itself.

Pinsker, Sanford. "A Taste of Utopia, Hobgoblins and Revolution." Rev. of *Levitation: Five Fictions*. *Congress Monthly* June 1982: 14-15.

Discusses *Levitation* as a volume which has transmogrifying possibilities and which unleashes powerful religious complexities. Praises Ozick's intellect as big enough to encompass both poles, with a moral vision capable of moral sympathy, symbolic transference, and terrifying honesty.

Prescott, Peter S. "Looking for Life." Rev. of *The Pagan Rabbi and Other Stories*. *Newsweek* 10 May 1971: 114.

Suggests that the stories in *The Pagan Rabbi* are among the best seven stories written by Americans in recent years. Notes that these are stories informed by a sense of play and fun, as well as a sense of how frustrating life can be. Sees many as to do with the horror of actually getting what you have asked for, while others have to do with living fraudulently. Concludes that these stories will be with us for a long time.

Prescott, Peter S. "Quick-Change Artist." Rev. of *Levitation: Five Fictions. Newsweek* 15 Feb. 1982: 85. Rpt. as "Fraudulent Lives" in *Never in Doubt: Critical Essays on American Books, 1972-1985.* Peter S. Prescott. New York: Arbor, 1986. 148-49.

Comments that, while Ozick's story output is small, some of them will be considered among the best of our time. Finds her stories energetic, witty, playful, and invigorated with the intrusion of the more irrational aspects of Judaic tradition. Briefly describes the stories in the collection, and notes, in conclusion, that while her previous stories dealt with men, these are about women.

Prescott, Peter S. "Stories Within Stories." Rev. of *Bloodshed and Three Novellas. Newsweek* 12 Apr. 1976: 107-08. Rpt. as "Fraudulent Lives" in *Never in Doubt: Critical Essays on American Books, 1972-1985.* Peter S. Prescott. New York: Arbor, 1986. 146-48.

Calls the stories often flawed but full of driving energy and intense art. Notes that sometimes what Ozick writes is so compressed it is not quite coherent, as in *Usurpation.* Concludes that her stories are severe, sensuous, witty, and judgmental.

Prescott, Peter S. "Vision and Design." Rev. of *The Cannibal Galaxy. Newsweek* 12 Sept. 1983: 76, 78-79.

Comments that *Cannibal Galaxy* is extremely well-written and displays intelligence, design, and energy. Describes characters and plot.

Prose, Francine. "Idolatry in Miami." Rev. of *The Shawl. New York Times Book Review* 10 Sept. 1989: 1, 39.

Calls the experience of reading *The Shawl* puzzling. Finds the collection resonant and weighty. Details the contents of "Rosa" in particular. Concludes that history has repeatedly proved to have a dark imagination and that there are lives, even in sunny Florida, that put paranoia to shame.

Redmon, Anne. "Vision and Risk: New Fiction by Oates and Ozick." Rev. of *The Messiah of Stockholm. Michigan Quarterly Review* 27.1 (1988): 208-13.

Describes *The Messiah of Stockholm* as a book in which the writer faces a purely existential terror. Provides a summary of plot and characters, and argues that, while the Christian writer must make images, the Jewish writer must record images.

Rosenfeld, Alvin H. "The Education of Joseph Brill." Rev. of *The Cannibal Galaxy*. *Midstream* Feb. 1984: 58-59.

Calls *Cannibal Galaxy* a vividly drawn satire on intellectual pretentiousness, (mis)education, and some of the more wayward strains of Jewish hope and ambition. Comments that the dramatic action may seem lacking and the book too narrowly restricted in theme. Identifies the major theme as the challenge to Jewish primacy by the ideals of alien and antithetical cultures.

Rovit, Earl. "The Bloodletting." Rev. of *Levitation: Five Fictions*. *Nation* 20 Feb. 1982: 207-08.

Calls *Levitation* fully successful because Ozick extends and diversifies her range and seems to have reached her prime. Suggests that she is still experimenting with different moods and muscles, and that the work shows some unevenness. Concludes, nevertheless, that she is talented, crafty, ironic, civilized, and very good at going straight for the jugular. Finds the driving passion of her art is performance, despite the philosophical and intellectual mugging.

Schechner, Mark. "Other People's Stories." Rev. of *Bloodshed and Three Novellas*. *Moment* Apr. 1976: 74, 77.

Discusses *Bloodshed*, calling Ozick a seventeenth-century writer because of her metaphysics. Describes the amphibious characters, and details the contents of individual stories.

Sheppard, R. Z. "Cabalarama." Rev. of *Levitation: Five Fictions*. *Time* 15 Feb. 1982: 74.

Claims that this work presents Ozick in the role of a woman wonder-rabbi spreading paradox and fantasy. Complains that Ozick tries too hard, and that fantasy requires a lighter touch than is found here. Argues that she is more successful when she builds on realism. Describes several of the stories, and concludes that one cannot fail to be impressed with this collection despite the fact that it has more to do with willful invention than with imagination. Condemns her magic, which too often arrives at commentary, and her hectoring, which takes the place of persuasion.

Simpson, Mona. "Cynthia Ozick's Brilliant Fable of a Search for God." Rev. of *The Messiah of Stockholm*. *Chicago Tribune Books* 1 Mar. 1987: 7.

Describes Ozick as one of the finest living writers, and commends *The Messiah of Stockholm* as classic, fibular, brilliantly written, resonant, and intellectually muscled. Concludes that this is a sharp, hilarious, rueful, beautiful tale. Describes the contents.

Stevenson, David L. "Daughter's Reprieve." Rev. of *Trust. New York Times Book Review* 17 July 1966: 29. Rpt. in *Cynthia Ozick*. Ed. Harold Bloom. Modern Critical Views. New York: Chelsea, 1986. 9-10.

Calls *Trust* a first novel and an extraordinary literary entity contained and produced by a rich creative imagination. Describes the contents of the novel thoroughly, and concludes that this book is the product of a highly perceptive intelligence produced from the deepest recesses of self-knowledge.

Theroux, Paul. "Miseries & Splendours of the Short Story." Rev. of *The Pagan Rabbi and Other Stories. Encounter* Sept. 1972: 69-75. Rpt. as "On *The Pagan Rabbi*. Ed. Harold Bloom. Modern Critical Views. New York: Chelsea, 1986. 19-20.

Relates the plot of the story, and commends Ozick for creating characters that would not be at ease in the company of people who appear in the work of Malamud, Bellow, Roth, and company. Examines each story in the collection very briefly. Concludes that she is a vigorous, sly, skilled, and impressive writer who deserves a wide audience.

Thorpe, Douglas. "Books." Rev. of *The Cannibal Galaxy. Christian Century* 21-28 Mar. 1984: 315-16.

Describes the contents of *The Cannibal Galaxy*, considering it superbly narrated if rather dark, and commends it for its rich ore.

Trapido, Barbara. "Champagne." Rev. of *Levitation: Five Fictions. Spectator* 27 Mar. 1982: 25.

Describes the work as edgy, brilliant, fantastical, and poignantly lyric. Describes the contents of several of the stories.

Tucker, Martin. "Well of Sensibility." Rev. of *Trust. New Republic* 13 Aug 1966: 31,33.

Calls *Trust* a long, leisurely, literary novel hearkening back to Henry James and E. M. Forster. Suggests that she attempts much with style uppermost in her mind. Concludes that it is a book demonstrating a great sense of fun and much acute social observation, although sometimes the cleverness and style become obtrusive.

Tyler, Anne. "The Mission." Rev. of *The Messiah of Stockholm. New Republic* 6 Apr. 1987: 39-41.

Argues that *The Messiah of Stockholm* reveals Ozick's cousinship to Singer. Notes that Golems, dryads, and dock witches scamper across the pages, and that the Jewishness of her characters is central to her storytelling. But claims that her prose lacks Singer's simplicity and directness. Comments that physical descriptions seem oddly lacking, and that she has a backhanded approach to narrative. Concludes, however, that this volume does intrigue, entertain, and weave a richly imagined tale.

Wandor, Michelene. "Necessity's Daughter." Rev. of *The Messiah of Stockholm. New Statesman* 8 Jan. 1988: 32.

Notes that this novel is set in a winter twilight land of Sweden. Considers that Ozick has woven a dense, elliptical series of tapestries around shifts in subjectivity, cleverly leading the reader right to the point. Provides a detailed plot summary.

Weinberg, Helen. "Held in Trust." Rev. of *Trust. Congress Bi-Weekly* 20 Mar. 1967: 17-18.

Sees *Trust* as a novel embodying a young woman's search for value and meaning, especially as they are proposed by three men. Commends the work for its fine irony and moral seriousness, details its contents, and criticizes it for its excessive play with words.

Wiesel, Elie. "Ozick Asks Whether There Can Be Life After Auschwitz." Rev. of *The Shawl. Chicago Tribune Books* 17 Sept. 1989: 6.

Describes this as a book about the women who described the Holocaust. Calls the writing dense, sad, vivid, and highly condensed. Recounts the contents.

White, Edmund. "Images of a Mind Thinking." Rev. of *The Cannibal Galaxy. New York Times Book Review* 11 Sept. 1983: 3, 46. Rpt. in *Cynthia Ozick.* Ed. Harold Bloom. Modern Critical Views. New York: Chelsea, 1986. 127-31.

States that in *Cannibal Galaxy* idolatry is Ozick's great theme. Describes Joseph Brill in detail, and critiques the middle-American high school as idolatrous. Notes that this is beautiful prose never allowed to sing arias. Finds everything relative. Identifies a Gogolian zest for details that never actually sink a sentence, but rather spurt out of it her vivid rendering of an inspired but cracked dream.

Wimsatt, Margaret. "Metaphors & Monotheism." Rev. of *The Cannibal Galaxy. Commonweal* 4 May 1984: 286. Rpt. in *Cynthia Ozick.* Ed. Harold Bloom. Modern Critical Views. New York: Chelsea, 1986. 141-43.

Calls *The Cannibal Galaxy* a novel which hangs together well, reads learnedly, and concentrates on the relationship between words and art. Details character and plot.

Zaslowsky, Dyan. "Fiction." Rev. of *Levitations: Five Fictions. Hadassah Magazine* Apr. 1982: 26-27.

Describes *Levitations* as a weird combination of science fiction and Jewish *angst.* Details the contents of the volume and concludes that until there is comprehension, there is the clean space of Ozick's language to swirl one's thoughts through.

Interviews

Kaganoff, Penny. "PW Interviews Cynthia Ozick." *Publishers Weekly* 27 Mar. 1987: 33-34.

Provides an overview of Ozick's teenage years, her early discipleship with James, her lifestyle, her theories of fiction, her own fiction, and her identification as feminist and Jew.

Kauvar, Elaine M. "An Interview with Cynthia Ozick." *Contemporary Literature* 26.4 (1985): 375-401.

In this lengthy interview Ozick discusses: Eco's *The Name of the Rose,* Judaism as a major philosophy, her audience, the critics' responses, reactions to being labelled a Jewish writer, the primacy of aural/oral culture, the female literary predicament, her feminism, her early years as a Jewish child in *cheder,* her vision of the Torah as a source of feminism, her objections to Freud's theories, present writing projects, definitions of the novel, views on Bellow, the idolatry of the imagination, the photographic quality of her images, her character, her Herzogian love of letter writing, writing and magic, mysticism and religion.

Rainwater, Catherine, and William J. Scheick. "An Interview with Cynthia Ozick (Sum. 1982)." *Texas Studies in Literature and Language* 25.2 (1983): 255-65.

Describes her literary influences, her beliefs, the publishing history of several of the works, the process of writing, voice, the novella as form,

Judaism, writing in English, her admirations for other writers, her definition of the function of a good critic.

Teicholz, Tom. "The Art of Fiction XCV: Cynthia Ozick." *Paris Review* 102 (1987): 154-90. Rpt. in *Writers at Work: The Paris Review Interviews, Eighth Series.* Ed. George Plimpton. New York: Viking. *Women Writers at Work: The Paris Review Interviews.* Ed. George Plimpton. New York: Viking, 1989. 291-317.

In this interview Ozick discusses her working habits, her compulsive mail answering, her correspondence with Lionel Trilling, her own education, her first novel, graduate school, her Jewishness, her relation to history, views on biography, the outrage over the publication of "Envy," her perception that she is not read, the Holocaust characters in her stories, the sacrifices of a writer's life, and her life as a reader.

Biographical sources

Cole, Diane. "Cynthia Ozick." *Twentieth-Century American-Jewish Fiction Writers.* Ed. Daniel Walden. Detroit: Gale, 1984. Vol 28 of *Dictionary of Literary Biography.* 94 vols. to date. 1978- . 213-25.

More than details of her life, this is a career biography, tracing the development of the author's canon, describing the themes and contents of her works, evaluating her reputation, and placing her in the larger context of American literary history. Includes lists of primary and secondary sources and illustrations.

Currier, Susan. "Cynthia Ozick." *Dictionary of Literary Biography Yearbook: 1982.* Ed. Richard Ziegfeld. Detroit: Gale, 1983. 325-33.

More than details of her life, this is a career biography, tracing the development of the author's canon, describing the contents and themes of her works, evaluating her reputation, and placing her in the larger context of American literary history. Includes lists of primary and secondary sources and illustrations.

Bibliographies

Chenoweth, Mary J. "Bibliographical Essay:: Cynthia Ozick." *Studies in American Jewish Literature* [Kent State] 6 (1987): 147-63.

Currier, Susan, and Daniel J. Cahill. "A Bibliography of Writings by Cynthia Ozick." *Texas Studies in Literature and Language* 25.2

(1983): 313-21. Rpt. in revised form in *Contemporary American Women Writers: Narrative Strategies*. Eds. Catherine Rainwater and William J. Scheick. Lexington: UP of Kentucky, 1985. 109-16.

Dissertations

Blustein, Bryna Lee Datz. "Beyond the Stereotype: A Study of Representative Short Stories of Selected Contemporary Jewish American Female Writers." Diss. Saint Louis U, 1986.

Ehrlich, Reva. "A Study of Jewish Literary Identity in Contemporary Writers in America: A Curriculum." Diss. St. Johns U, 1985.

Kielsky, Vera Emuna. *Inevitable Exiles: Cynthia Ozick's View of the Precariousness of Jewish Existence in a Gentile World*. Diss. Arizona State U, 1985. Twentieth Century American Jewish Writers 2. New York: Lang, 1989.

Liron, Naomi. "Cynthia Ozick, the Self-Subverting Artist." Diss. U of California, Berkeley. 1987.

Grace Paley

1922 –

Primary Sources

Collected Works

Enormous Changes at the Last Minute. New York: Farrar, 1960, 1974; New York: Dell, 1975; London: Deutsch, 1975; Virago Modern Classics. London: Virago, 1979.

Contents: Wants; Debts; Distance; Faith in the Afternoon; Gloomy Tune; Living; Come on, Ye Sons of Art; Faith in a Tree; Samuel; The Burdened Man; Enormous Changes at the Last Minute; Politics; Northeast Playground; The Little Girl; A Conversation with My Father; The Immigrant Story; The Long-Distance Runner.

Later the Same Day. New York: Farrar, 1985; London: Virago, 1985; Penguin Contemporary American Fiction Series. New York: Penguin, 1986; Harmondsworth: King-Penguin, 1987.

Contents: Love; Dreamer in a Dead Language; In the Garden; Somewhere Else; Lavinia: An Old Story; Friends; At That Time, or The History of a Joke; Anxiety; In This Country, But in Another Language, My Aunt Refuses to Marry the Men Everyone Wants Her To; Mother; Ruthy and Edie; A Man Told Me the Story of His Life; The Story Hearer; This Is a Story about My Friend George, the Toy Inventor; Zagrowsky Tells; The Expensive Moment; Listening.

The Little Disturbances of Man. Garden City: Doubleday, 1959; New
   York: Meridian, 1960; London: Weidenfeld, 1960; New York:
   Viking, 1968; New York: Bantam, 1969; London: Deutsch, 1969;
   New York: Plume-NAL, 1973; Virago Modern Classics. London:
   Virago, 1980; The Penguin Contemporary American Fiction Series.
   New York: Penguin, 1985.

Contents: Goodbye and Good Luck; A Woman, Young and Old; The
Pale Pink Roast; The Loudest Voice; The Contest; An Interest in Life;
An Irrevocable Diameter; Two Short Sad Stories from a Long and
Happy Life: The Used-Boy Raisers [and] A Subject of Childhood; In
Time Which Made a Monkey of Us All; The Floating Truth.

Short Fiction in Anthologies

"A Conversation with My Father." *The Norton Introduction to Fiction.*
   Ed. Jerome Beaty. 2nd ed. New York: Norton, 1981. 497-501.

"Dreamer in a Dead Language." *Full Measure: Modern Short Stories on
   Aging.* Ed. Dorothy Sennett. St. Paul: Gray Wolf, 1988. 127-46; *"The
   Safe Deposit" and Other Stories about Grandparents, Old Lovers, and
   Crazy Old Men.* Ed. Kerry M. Olitzky. New York: Wiener, 1989. 129-52.

"Faith: In a Tree." *Many Windows: 22 Stories from American Review.*
   Ed. Ted Solotaroff. New York: Harper, 1982. 144-59.

"Friends." *The Best American Short Stories, 1980.* Eds. Stanley Elkin
   and Shannon Ravenel. Boston: Houghton, 1980; Harmondsworth:
   Penguin, 1981. 250-61.

"Goodbye and Good Luck." *Great Jewish Short Stories.* Ed. Saul
   Bellow. New York: Laurel-Dell, 1963. 392-402; *My Name Aloud:
   Jewish Stories by Jewish Writers.* Ed. Harold U. Ribalow. South
   Brunswick: Yoseloff, 1969. 362-71; *Accent: An Anthology 1940-60.*
   Eds. Daniel Curley, George Scouffas and Charles Shattuck. Urbana:
   U of Illinois P, 1973. 189-97.

"In Time Which Made a Monkey of Us All." *The Single Voice: An
   Anthology of Contemporary Fiction.* Ed. Jerome Charyn. New York:
   Collier, 1969. 159-75.

"An Interest in Life." *The World of Modern Fiction: American.* Ed. Steven Marcus. 2 vols. New York: Simon, 1966. 1: 512-25; *Great American Love Stories.* Ed. Lucy Rosenthal. Boston: Little, 1988: 642-56.

"The Long-Distance Runner." *All Our Secrets Are the Same: New Fiction from Esquire.* Ed. Gordon Lish. New York: Norton, 1976. 85-89; *The Woman Who Lost Her Names: Selected Writings of American Jewish Women.* Ed. Julia Wolf Mazow. San Francisco: Harper, 1980. 81-96; *Major American Short Stories.* Ed. A. Walton Litz. Revised ed. New York: Oxford UP, 1980. 764-77; *Great Esquire Fiction: The Finest Stories from the First Fifty Years.* Ed. L. Rust Hills. New York: Penguin, 1983. 387-402.

"The Loudest Voice." *Breakthrough: A Treasury of Contemporary American-Jewish Literature.* Eds. Irving Malin and Irwin Stark. New York: McGraw, 1964. 136-41; *Tales of Our people: Great Stories of the Jew in America.* Ed. Jerry D. Lewis. New York: Geis, 1969. 245-51; *Jewish-American Stories.* Ed. Irving Howe. New York: Mentor-NAL, 1977. 465-70; *Women in Literature: Life Stages Through Stories, Poems, and Plays.* Ed. Sandra Eagleton. Englewood Cliffs: Prentice, 1987. 42-46; *"May Your Days Be Merry and Bright" and Other Christmas Stories by Women.* Ed. Susan Koppelman. Detroit: Wayne State UP, 1988. 222-29.

"A Subject of Childhood." *New Sounds in American Fiction.* Ed. Gordon Lish. Meno Park: Cummings, 1969. 129-36; *The Norton Book of American Short Stories.* Ed. Peter S. Prescott. New York: Norton, 1988. 506-12.

"Two Short Sad Stories from a Long and Happy Life." *How We Live: Contemporary Life in Contemporary Fiction.* Eds. Penney Chapin Hills and L. Rust Hills. New York: Macmillan, 1968. 349-59.

"The Used-Boy Raisers." *Women in a Changing World.* Ed. Uta West. New York: McGraw, 1975. 88-94; *American Short Story Masterpieces.* Eds. Raymond Carver and Tom Jenks. New York: Delacorte, 1987. 335-39.

Short Fiction in Periodicals

"Dreamer in a Dead Language." *American Review* 26 (1977): 391-411.

"Distance." *Atlantic* Dec. 1967: 111-15.

"Enormous Changes at the Last Minute." *Atlantic* May 1972: 70-75.

"The Expensive Moment." *Short Story International* June 1988: 145-56.

"Faith: In a Tree." *New American Review* 1 (1967): 51-67.

"Friends." *New Yorker* 18 June 1979: 32-38.

"In the Garden." *Fiction* 4.2 (1976): 8-9.

"Lavinia." *Delta* May 1982: 41-45.

"The Little Girl." *Paris Review* 14.57 (1974): 194-200.

"The Long-Distance Runner." *Esquire* Mar. 1974: 102-04, 108, 182, 184.

"Love." *New Yorker* 8 Oct. 1979: 37.

"Mom." *Esquire* Dec. 1975: 85-86.

"Somewhere Else." *New Yorker* 23 Oct. 1978: 34-37.

"The Story Hearer." *Mother Jones* Dec. 1982: 32-36.

"Tagrowsky Tells." *Short Story International* Feb. 1987: 140-56.

"Telling." *Mother Jones* May 1985: 34-37, 39-42.

"This Is a Story about My Friend George, the Toy Inventor." *Transatlantic Review* 58-59 (1977): 5-6.

"Two Stories from Five Boroughs: I. "Samuel," II. "The Burdened Man"." *Esquire* Mar. 1968: 88-89, 151.

"Two Stories: I. "Debts," II. "Wants"." *Atlantic* May 1971: 66-67.

"Unknown Parts of Far, Imaginable Places." *Mother Jones* Dec. 1983: 12-17.

Secondary Sources

Books

Isaacs, Neil D. *Grace Paley: A Study of the Short Fiction.* Twayne's Studies in Short Fiction 13. Boston: Twayne, 1990.

Taylor, Jacqueline. *Grace Paley: Illuminating the Dark Lives.* Austin: U of Texas P, 1990.

Articles and Chapters

Aarons, Victoria. "Talking Lives: Storytelling and Renewal in Grace Paley's Short Fiction." *Studies in American Jewish Literature* [Kent State] 9.1 (1990): 20-35.

Argues that for Paley's characters, telling stories of their own lives and the lives of their families and friends becomes a sort of moral obligation. Framing communities and forming individual identities, storytelling for Paley's characters is both obligatory and restorative, a conviction heard in their individual and collective voices. Claims that her characters, consequently, are not autonomous; they are rarely separately defined from communities and from their connections and obligations from others. Suggests, in fact, that it is precisely when such a disconnection occurs that we witness their greatest source of shame and personal failure. Concludes that ultimately, these characters are defined through their discourse and interaction with others—through fervent, reverential talk.

Baba, Minako. "Faith Darwin as Writer-Heroine: A Study of Grace Paley's Short Stories." *Studies in American Jewish Literature* [Kent State] 7.1 (1988): 40-54.

Analyzes Faith's career as woman and writer over a period of three decades and evaluates the achievement of Paley's artistic vision in what amounts to a "sociology of metafiction," that rare combination of humanistic concerns and novelistic attention. Traces the evolution of Faith's character through each of the fictions and concludes that such an examination in psychological, sociological, and aesthetic terms shows a shift from domesticity to larger family, to neighborhood and society as a whole.

Barthelme, Donald, William Gass, Grace Paley, and Walker Percy. "A Symposium on Fiction." *Shenandoah* 27.2 (1976): 3-31.

This is a symposium in which Paley participates with Barthleme, Gass, and Percy. Contains valuable commentary from Paley on a variety of topics such as narrative strategy, language, audience, humor, and the writing process.

Baumgarten, Murray. "City Premises." *City Scriptures: Modern Jewish Writing*. Cambridge: Harvard UP, 1982. 149-51.

Calls Paley's writings an intimate series of portraits taking the sweep of urban life as a backdrop and then focusing on the relationship between intellectuals and power in the modern era. Claims that sexuality as revolution is also frequently discussed with the way women cope with the results (mostly children) its subsequent theme.

Blake, Harry. "Grace Paley: A Plea for English Writing." *Delta* 14 (1982): 73-80.

Designates the modern period as the downfall of realism, and postmodernism the period in which syntax has become enthroned as the crux of thought and thought process. Suggests that postmodernism is the most interesting of the literary movements arising in America in the postwar period and is the context in which Grace Paley can be read. Calls her a fundamental writer within the American crisis in the conception of a new form of writing fiction outside the cliches of plain American thought.

Broner, E. M. "The Dirty Ladies: Earthy Writings of Contemporary American Women—Paley, Jong, Schor and Lerman." *Regionalism and the Female Imagination* 4.3 (1979): 34-43.

Calls writing a dirty and cleansing humorous business. Traces the uses of the word "cunt" in various of these writers to discover its new reinvested meanings, the ways in which it has been rescued from pejorative status in such writings. Also describes "dirty writing" as an attempt to dethrone male power through laughter. Describes Paley's characters as more human than those of the other writers. Comments: "Her characters hope that men will not leave them, that if they do, welfare will heed them, that the men will return to be seduced once more. The laughter is a response to exclusion from solemn ceremony. Their writing is a kind of holy cursing. Paley's women look for the right kind of language for that original sexual battle."

Bruce, Melissa. "*Enormous Changes at the Last Minute*: A Subversive Songbook." *Delta* 14 (1982): 97-113.

Describes the various modes of discourse in Paley's fiction primarily as discursive narratives. Considers this book full of the language of suppression and explosion. Sees it as generally an abortive act, for it is language as subversion in the form of political or narrative song which, for Paley, is the most important mode of discourse.

Burstein, Janet. "Jewish-American Women's Literature: The Long Quarrel with God." *Studies in American Jewish Literature* [Kent State] 8.1 (1989): 9-25.

In this general article Burstein argues that while some Jewish women writers cast Jewish tradition as an adversary, others see it as a source of nurturance, some ignore, it, and still others tell of a search for substitute commitments. Nonetheless, all seem to engage in a quarrel with God. Discusses briefly Jong, Kaufman, Shulman, Greenberg, Olsen, Rosen, Paley, Yezierska, and Broner.

Clayton, John. "Grace Paley and Tillie Olsen: Radical Jewish Humanists." *Response: A Contemporary Jewish Review* 14 (Spr. 1984): 37-52.

Describes Paley and Olsen as sharing a vision and an expression of that vision deriving largely from the Jewish immigrant socialist tradition. Quotes Clayton's definition of the Jewish Diaspora tradition to which he and they belong as characterized by 1) intense identification with suffering people, including Jews, 2) critical detachment from ordinary institutions and culturally held truths, 3) longing for an ordinary life which could be called holy. Concludes that this heritage serves as a major source of values in Paley's work. Discusses several of the stories by way of illustration.

Coppula, Kathleen A. "Not for Literary Reasons: The Fiction of Grace Paley." *Mid-American Review* 7.1 (1986): 63-72.

Describes the early stories as more traditional and full of loud, quirky voices. Suggests that possibility becomes more important in her second collection of stories as they incorporate more of Paley's personal and political philosophies. Concludes that, while other contemporary writers address the inadequacies of language and communication in their fiction, Paley asserts her belief in the power of language to make important changes in our lives.

Cousineau, Diane. "The Desires of Women, the Presence of Men." *Delta* 14 (1982): 55-66.

Contends that in Paley's fiction the consciousness of difference is central to the question of feminine desire. Suggests that woman's sensitivity to the line of partition separating the two sexes is intensified by the experience of division that is inscribed within her own body. Discusses several of the stories from this perspective.

Crawford, John W. "Archetypal Patterns in Grace Paley's 'Runner.'" *Notes on Contemporary Literature* 11.4 (1981): 10-12.

Describes running to escape in this story as an inherent archetypal motif depicting the ego's attempt to reduce excessive stimuli and survive. Suggests that like Rabbit in *Rabbit Run* or the Red Cross Knight in *The Faerie Queene*, Paley's heroine returns to the grave of her past to be renewed only to discover herself in Hades and a new guide awaiting her. Concludes that her running returns her after the appropriate epiphany.

Criswell, Jeanne Sallade. "Cynthia Ozick and Grace Paley: Diverse Visions in Jewish and Women's Literature." *Since Flannery O'Connor: Essays on the Contemporary American Short Story.* Eds. Loren Logsdon and Charles W. Mayer. Essays In Literature. Macomb: Western Illinois U, 1987. 93-100.

Describes briefly the similarities between Ozick's and Paley's backgrounds and experiences, and then demonstrates through an explication of several stories that "the visions which drive their stories remain far apart." Notes that they both "encompass in their art divergent views of their art," but that they "approach the traditional theme of Jewish identity and the question of assimilation from nearly antithetical perspectives." Concludes that classifying them as Jewish women writers implies a closer similarity than can be justified by their works and that such classification can be "considered only loose guides to the literature."

DeKoven, Marianne. "Mrs. Hegel-Schtein's Tears." *Partisan Review* 48.2 (1981): 217-23.

Describes how in the stories of Paley the impulse to create form coheres with the impulse to tell a story about everyday life. Describes some of the stories from this perspective. Concludes that she uses innovative form as much as she uses innovative activism to remake the new, endlessly dreary, and shameful moral-political world we inhabit.

Gelfant, Blanche. "Grace Paley: Fragments for a Portrait in Collage." *New England Review* 3 (Wint. 1980): 276-93. Rpt. in *Women Writing in America: Voices in Collage.* Hanover: UP of New England, 1984. 11-29.

Provides much useful anecdotal material about Gelfant's meetings with Paley. Discusses the central protagonist, Faith; numerous of the characters in individual stories; stylistic concerns; humor; cynicism; hope; dissolution; attachments; endings; continuities; and all their opposition which comprise the fiction.

Hulley, Kathleen. "Grace Paley's Resistant Form." *Delta* 14 (1982): 3-18.

A major article which attempts to comprehend the direction of Paley's formal strategies. Asserts that Paley's isomorphic repetition of patterns of resistance is a strategy of dissemination which accounts for both her stylistic achievement and her subject matter.

Humy, Nicholas Peter. "A Different Responsibility: Form and Technique in G. Paley's 'A Conversation with Father.'" *Delta* 14 (1982): 87-95.

Elucidates the meaning of the story and its narrative strategies through an examination of the views on storytelling held by the father in the story and those emerging from the story itself.

Iannone, Carol. "A Dissent on Grace Paley." *Commentary* Aug. 1985: 54-58.

An account of Paley's childhood, origins, political activism, and reports from her trip to Russia to visit political dissidents. Concludes with a short treatment of the fiction which presents it as grim, fateful writing not expressive of optimism. Supports this argument with references to her depictions of Jewish history, male/female relationships, and the plight of women. Expresses disappointment over her denunciations of men.

Kamel, Rose Yallow. "To Aggravate the Conscience: Grace Paley's Loud Voice." *Journal of Ethnic Studies* 11.3 (1983): 29-49. Rpt. in rev. form as "Aggravating the Conscience: Grace Paley's Loud Voice" in *Aggravating the Conscience: Jewish-American Literary Mothers in the Promised Land.* Rose Yalow Kamel. American University Studies: Ser. 4, English Language and Literature 64. New York: Lang, 1988. 115-49.

Calls Paley's pastoral paradises "the small grassy places in city play-grounds." Notes the "expansive maternal eroticism whereby the city-scape seems an extension of her narrators' bodies [and] suggests a kinship with pagan fertility goddesses—quite a feat, considering that firmly located in the Judaic tradition, a daughter of immigrants, Paley is 'the child of puritans who is only halfway here.'" Comments that her language is an amalgam of both ethnic and woman centered with invert-ed syntax, Yiddishisms, and New York slang echoing Irish, Italian, Black and Hispanic rhythms of speech. Concludes that her images are clearly sensual and celebrate femaleness.

Klinkowitz, Jerome. "Grace Paley: The Sociology of Metafiction." *Delta* 14 (1982): 81-85. Rpt. in *Literary Subversions: New American Fiction and the Practice of Criticism.* Ed. Jerome Klinkowitz. Crosscurrents/Modern Critiques. Third Series. Carbondale: Southern Illinois UP, 1985. 70-76.

Discusses the self-reflective author discussing the art of her own fiction in the stories and claims that, despite this metafictional trait, she holds fast to several older, sociological concerns. Suggests that for Grace Paley, metafiction—fiction which explores the conditions of its own making—is a peculiarly social matter, filled with the stuff of realism other metafictionists have discarded.

Klinkowitz, Jerome. "Ideology as an Art: Women Novelists in the 1970s." *North American Review* 260.2 (1975): 88-90.

Discusses *Enormous Changes at the Last Minute* as a unified collection of tales about apartment house dwellers on the fringe who speak unique lan-guages and engage in more artistic self-reflection than real-life moralizing.

Lavers, Norman. "Grace Paley." *Critical Survey of Short Fiction.* Ed. Frank N. Magill. 8 vols. Englewood Cliffs: Salem, 1981. 5: 2040-44.

A standard reference article discussing her birthplace, principal short fic-tion, other literary forms, story characteristics, biography, and an analysis of *The Little Disturbances of Man.*

Lyons, Bonnie. "Grace Paley's Jewish Miniatures." *Studies in American Jewish Literature* [Kent State] 8.1 (1989): 26-33.

Explores Paley's Jewishness and her use of Jewish material. Notes that her voice is obviously influenced by Yiddish, that *Yiddishkeit* is the source of her values, and that many of her stories are grounded in

American Jewish experience. Explicates some of her stories, including those in *The Little Disturbances of Man* and *Enormous Changes at the Last Minute*, in support of her thesis.

Malin, Irving. "The Verve of Grace Paley." *Genesis West* 1.5 (1963): 73-78.

Describes her themes as malevolent time, the joyous Jewish substantiality of the world, and the body's lust for warmth and liveliness. Comments that in each of the stories we whirl from violence, to lust, to sadness, and to joy. Discusses several of the stories, and concludes with a treatment of her choice of narrators and language.

Mandel, Dena. "Keeping up with Faith: Grace Paley's Sturdy American Jewess." *Studies in American Jewish Literature* [Albany] 3 (1983): 85-98.

Calls Faith a sturdy American Jewess who is a persistent optimist and an emblem of hope in a hopeless world. Notes that she has willfully chosen her crusty life and is sustained by a rosy, secular creed. Discusses several of the stories from this perspective. Sees that it is Faith who reduces tragedy to no more than the little disturbances of man, and who has the courage to envision the possibility of enormous changes at the last minute.

Meier, Joyce. "The Subversion of the Father in the Tales of Grace Paley." *Delta* 14 (1982): 115-27.

Describes Paley as responding with special intensity to the Father-artist aesthetic, which relegates female creativity to an ancillary position. Notes that in this aesthetic, the women serve as either foils or foes to the male artist's genius. Claims that Paley subverts this father in her fiction where everyone is imagined into life except the father. Concludes that most of her women characters are almost archetypes of subversion.

Mickelson, Anne Z. "Grace Paley." *Reaching Out: Sensitivity and Order in Recent American Fiction by Women*. Anne Z. Mickelson. Metuchen: Scarecrow, 1979. 221-34.

A detailed treatment of characters and humor in *The Little Disturbances of Mankind* and *Enormous Changes at the Last Minute*. Covers dialect; character types; sense of humor; reflections of motherhood; absence of fathers; female bonds; sex; loss of family; bawdy, transient lovers; and economic survival as major themes of the stories.

Morley, Hilda. "Some Notes on Grace Paley While Reading Dante: The Voice of Others." *Delta* 14 (1982): 67-71.

Describes language, voice, and narrative technique in Paley's works and how they compare to some of the last cantos of the *Inferno* and *Purgatorio*.

Neff, D. S. "'Extraordinary Means': Healers and Healing in 'A Conversation with My Father'." *Literature and Medicine* 2 (1983): 118-124.

Argues that in this story the writer, a daughter of a physician, seeks to establish a new dialectal balance between medical and literary efforts to cope with mortality. Notes that she fabricates a metafiction simultaneously reinforcing and undermining the aesthetic integrity of fictional remedies for death's sting, forcing art to wrestle with its artifice as it investigates the ethical complexities of healing.

Park, Clara Claiborne. "Faith, Grace, and Love." *Hudson Review* 38.3 (1985): 481-88.

Describes Paley's fiction as beggaring critical review and reducing the critic to pointing out. Discusses style, language, voice, and narrative technique. Provides considerable commentary on Faith, and the thematic and moral implications of the fiction. Concludes that the stories are heirlooms of our moment, beautiful, permanently made things.

Peden, William. "Oh, These Jews—These Jews! Their Feelings, Their Hearts!" *The American Short Story: Continuity and Change, 1940-1975*. 2nd. ed. Boston: Houghton, 1975. 125-27.

Comments on *The Little Disturbances of Man* and *Enormous Changes at the Last Minute* as simply, powerfully, and seemingly artlessly written stories about first and second generation Jewish-Americans fighting their way up and occasionally down from the tenements of New York, falling apart or pulling themselves together. Describes her characters coming to life with one brush stroke and their emergence through nervous, staccato dialogue.

Queenan, Joe. "Character Assassins." *American Spectator* Dec. 1988: 14-16.

Comments on Paley's contempt for white collar types and the absence of an entire technocracy in American society. Sees her stories populated by weirdos because she thinks American life is dull. Lists several of her character types.

Reeves, Bruce D. *"Enormous Changes at the Last Minute." Survey of Contemporary Literature.* Ed. Frank N. Magill. Rev. ed. 12 vols. Englewood Cliffs: Salem, 1977. 4: 2282-85.

A standard reference article discussing settings, characters, themes, tone, style, individual stories, and the impact of the volume.

Robinson, James C. "1969-1980: Experiment and Tradition." *The American Short Story, 1945-1980: A Critical History.* Ed. Gordon Weaver. Boston: Twayne, 1983. 103-04.

A general article discussing Paley's terse style, experimental surfaces, humor, tensions, word play, atmosphere, use of time, sense of losses, and use of first-person narrator.

Schleifer, Ronald. "Grace Paley: Chaste Compactness." *Contemporary American Women Writers: Narrative Strategies.* Eds. Catherine Rainwater and William J. Scheick. Lexington: UP of Kentucky, 1985. 30-49.

Argues that at her best Paley achieves the chaste, short, compact spaciousness of short stories in which authority does not come from deathbed pronouncements and summings up, but can best be figured in terms of deathbeds, listening, and calling forth voices. Elucidates several of the stories by applying Kristeva's feminist theory to them. Includes a bibliography of her writings and interviews to 1985.

Sorkin, Adam. "'What Are We, Animals?': Grace Paley's World of Talk and Laughter." *Studies in American Jewish Literature* [Albany] 2 (1982): 144-54.

Calls the fiction vivid moments of contemporary local color and regional sensibility. Focuses on the predominant concerns of Paley's art, and analyzes the meaning and affect of her short story "In Time Which Made a Monkey Out of Us All."

Suarez-Lafuente, Maria. "The Contemporary Disruption in Grace Paley's Narrative." *Cross-Cultural Studies: American, Canadian and European Literatures: 1945-1985.* Ed. Mirko Jurak. Ljubljana: Eng. Dept., Filozofska Fakulteta, Edvard Kardelj U, 1988. 171-76.

Considers Paley's stories reflective of the terminal disease of contemporary life with its characters living in an erratic present and staring forward to the hopeless mess of old age. Comments that the world of these stories is one peopled by women, where men are only a necessary evil; women are plagued by desertions, and the male is marked simultaneously as a breeder and prison warden of female freedom. A major treatment of family and gender roles in her novels and of the unifying persona, Faith.

Wilde, Alan. "Grace Paley's World-Inventing Words." *Middle Grounds: Studies in Contemporary American Fiction*. Philadelphia: U of Pennsylvania P, 1987. 173-87.

A generalized but erudite article discussing Paley's feminist strategies as a writer and her determination to provide the illumination of what isn't known, the lighting up of what is under a rock, or what has been hidden.

Wisse, Ruth R. "The American Dreamer." *The Schlemiel as a Modern Hero*. Chicago: U of Chicago P, 1971; Paperback ed., 1980. 82-85.

Uses Paley's "Goodbye and Good Luck," one of the few stories with a female schlemiel, Aunt Rosie, to show the power of the monologue for humor, and to show the social status of the speaker. Fat Aunt Rosie, who is considered pitiable by her married sisters, uses the form to mock her supposed pitiable condition to her little niece Lillie, who sympathizes with her aunt's position, not her mother's.

Reviews

Ackroyd, Peter. "Light Relief." Rev. of *Enormous Changes at the Last Minute*. *Spectator* 22 Feb. 1975: 214-15.

Describes Paley as a writer for whom everything depends on the tone of voice. Calls the prose naive and willfully direct, never mawkish, and always attuned to the ethnic aspects of American experience. Concludes that the various Irish, Jewish, Puerto Rican, and Negro voices are well and living from moment to moment, because everyone, real or invented, deserves the open destiny of life.

Annan, Gabriele. "Father and Daughter." Rev. of *Enormous Changes at the Last Minute*. *Times Literary Supplement* 14 Feb. 1975: 157.

Suggests that *Enormous Changes at the Last Minute* establishes character and relationship through conversation and interior monologue. Calls this a funny, authentic, witty, punchy collection of stories exploring the themes of the transitoriness of life, the sorrow of old age, the fear of death, and the irreplaceability of love.

Baumbach, Jonathan. "Life-Size." Rev. of *Enormous Changes at the Last Minute. Partisan Review* 42.2 (1975): 303-06.

Sees this as a volume about lost and found love, about divorce, death, ongoing life—the most risky and important themes—in a style in which words count for much, sometimes for almost all. Comments that her stories resist the intrusion of critical language. Describes the voice of Paley's fiction as quirky, tough, wise-ass, vulnerable, bruised into wisdom by the knocks of experience, and describes the contents of individual stories.

Bendow, Burton. "Voices in the Metropolis." Rev. of *Enormous Changes at the Last Minute. Nation* 11 May 1974: 597-98.

Describes her as a butterfly in winter whose self-appointed task it is to dispel gloom. Argues that as a born comedienne, Paley writes resolutely airy or ruefully sincere stories whose endings often seem tacked on. Notes that many end with a thoughtful question or a wistful affirmation. Claims that all her stories refuse to look tragedy in the face. Commends her for the faultlessly correct local anthropology and speech, and details the contents of the individual stories in *Enormous Changes at the Last Minute*.

Blake, Patricia. "Little Disturbances of Woman." Rev. of *Later the Same Day. Time* 15 Apr. 1985: 98.

Calls *Later the Same Day* Paley's third volume about the same kinds of heroines—all of whom have aged little, and all of whom are still leavened by the author's lively, erotic imagination and her invincible ironies. Suggests that her writing ministers to the walking wounded of the 1960s and identifies more nostalgic couplings than in the previous volumes. Concludes that, fortunately for Paley, the little disturbances of women have a way of adding up to a major work.

Broner, E. M. "Grace and Faith." Rev. of *Later the Same Day. Women's Review of Books* Sept. 1985: 7-8.

Sees *Later the Same Day* as a book in which the characters, like family now, sit around the kitchen table and tell their stories. Comments that it is the children, as with the Passover story, who are the subjects and heirs of the tales. And it is children and grandchildren to whom the book is dedicated. Concludes that Paley's book is one of talking, clarifying, consoling, praising, and ultimately gracing. Details several of the stories and characters.

Clemons, Walter. "The Twists of Life." Rev. of *Enormous Changes at the Last Minute. Newsweek* 11 Mar. 1974: 78.

Calls *Enormous Changes at the Last Minute* quieter and more reflectively personal than previous work. Details the contents of some of the stories.

Crain, Jane Larkin. "'Ordinary' Lives." Rev. of *Enormous Changes at the Last Minute. Commentary* July 1974: 92-93.

Describes the narrative voice of *Enormous Changes at the Last Minute* as cryptic and highly stylized, and the people as primarily lower-class immigrant or second generation "ethnic" New York. Comments that relationships seem sketched in a tone of mutual mystification because people's lives are lived in almost surreal psychic isolation and a passivity bordering on despair. Notes the ever present threat of emotional violence and the characters constantly laboring under limited horizons. Concludes that Paley's sense of herself as a friend to the friendless is endlessly reiterated in these pages.

Davidon, Ann Morrissett. "Women Writing." Rev. of *The Little Disturbances of Man. Nation* 10 Sept. 1973: 213-15.

Describes the novel as full of tough-kid humor, but hiding a sympathetic heart, incongruous malapropisms, ethnic material, lurching and unexpected vivid language, gentle irony, and women narrators.

DeKoven, Marianne. "Later and Elsewhere." Rev. of *Later the Same Day. Partisan Review* 53.2 (1986): 315-17.

Calls *Later the Same Day* a collection of stories in which Paley is formally innovative but outside recognizably *avant-garde* or experimental traditions. Shows she is leftist, feminist, but not polemical. Notes that she avoids both the nineteenth-century realist forms of the earnestly, coherently political and the post modernist absurd-grotesque of the satirically, anarchical political. Concludes that each story is the next installment of the last: same characters, same world, though older, evolved from the 1950s-1960s.

Drummond, Mary Jane. "Life Is Too Short." Rev. of *The Little Disturbances of Man. Times Educational Supplement* 4 July 1980: 18.

Suggests that *The Little Disturbances of Man* indicates a certain contempt on Paley's part for the short story. Identifies a dozen or so voices throughout, and all completely different. Yet claims that all face the sapping question of "What is man that woman lays down to adore him?" Suggests that mostly Paley wisecracks around the no-man's land between the sexes. Sees all that's necessary for survival, male or female, an interest in life, good, bad, or peculiar. Concludes that Paley is a great survivor.

Feinstein, Elaine. "Getting Through." Rev. of *Enormous Changes at the Last Minute. New Statesman* 14 Feb. 1975: 216.

Briefly describes Paley's fiction as full of jokes, horrors, humor, unfulfilled lives, human pain, and optimism.

Friebert, Stuart. "Kinswomen." Rev. of *Leaning Forward. Field: Contemporary Poetry and Poetics* 34 (Spr. 1986): 93-102.

Discusses Paley's collection of poetry, but also provides useful insight into her fiction.

Gelfant, Blanche. "Chronicles and Chroniclers." Rev. of *Enormous Changes at the Last Minute. Massachusetts Review* 16.1 (1975): 141-43.

Calls Paley nervous, smart, funny, and triumphant over the forces of silence. Discusses several of the stories in *The Little Disturbances of Man* and *Enormous Changes at the Last Minute*. Calls the stories breezy chronicles of time passing in the old universal ways—with vicissitudes, dire events, and tragedy. Notes the infinite possibilities for change.

Gold, Ivan. "On Having Grace Paley Once More Among Us." Rev. of *The Little Disturbances of Man. Commonweal* 25 Oct. 1968: 111-12.

Describes the stories of *The Little Disturbances of Man* as quirky, anguished, funny, loving, deep, and antic glimpses into the hearts and lives of children, mothers, lovers, spouses divorced and abandoned, aging and the old in a prose as resilient and unpredictable as one imagines the fate of her characters to be at any story's end, no matter how often one has read it.

Gornick, Vivian. Rev. of *Enormous Changes at the Last Minute. Village Voice* 14 Mar. 1974: 25, 28.

Praises Paley highly because her characters illustrate the endless surprises that afflict human life and lead the reader safely onto the shores of emotional survival New York style. Cites Paley's idea that she can't write a simple plot story because it takes all hope away, and that everyone, real or invented, deserves the open destiny of life. Finds Paley has captured the idiom of New York street life better than any other writer. Also notes that the sense of hungry aliveness at the center of the pedestrian stillness of ongoing life is one of Paley's great achievements.

Harris, Lis. "New Yorkers That Sound Like New Yorkers." Rev. of
    Enormous Changes at the Last Minute. New York Times Book Review
    17 Mar. 1974: 3.

Considers *Enormous Changes at the Last Minute* a droll collection of fifteen stories about dyed-in-the-wool New Yorkers, lonely people, junkies,
unwed mothers, losers of all sorts, and the lady downstairs who is often
drunk. Comments that all her ethnics sound authentic as does the rendition of the complexities of love between parents and children, or the
cutting edge of sexual combat. Criticizes some of the fishy, pat endings
and the general unevenness of the collection.

Harris, Robert R. "Pacifists with Their Dukes Up." Rev. of *Later the
    Same Day. New York Times Book Review* 14 Apr. 1985: 7.

Provides a small history and list of works along with general comments
of approbation on *Later the Same Day*. Calls the work honest, guileless,
illuminating, cruelly ironic, feminist, and quirky. Details the contents of
several of the stories.

Healy, Robert C. "Enter A New Storyteller." Rev. of *The Little
    Disturbances of Man. New York Herald Tribune Book Review* 26 Apr.
    1959: 8.

Describes *The Little Disturbances of Man* as small in compass, limited in
range, hilariously poignant, and very impressive in its articulation of the
lives of the women portrayed.

Hicks, Granville. "Some Stopped Short and Sold." Rev. of *The Little
    Disturbances of Man. Saturday Review* 27 Apr. 1968: 29.

Briefly describes the contents of several of the stories in the collection,
and notes that Miss Paley's great gift is for making something remarkable out of the commonplace.

Hollinghurst, Alan. "Heroic Integrity." *New Statesman* 14 Mar. 1980: 402.

Comments that the stories in *The Little Disturbances of Man* give no
background or substantiation. Claims that they pitch the reader into the
midst of rapid or complicated personal developments to do with love,
families, women—young and old—all narrated in hilarious New York,
Jewish idiom alternately grotesque and laconic.

Jacobs, Rita D. "Fiction." Rev. of *Later the Same Day. World Literature
    Today* 60.2 (1986): 310-11.

Describes *Later the Same Day* as done with sharp characterization, narrative skill, and deft details. Notes that each of the seventeen stories leaves the reader with a sense of wonder at the varieties and complementaries of human motivation and action, a poignant sense of the effects of change and loss which permeate the stories. Concludes that this is a vision of a world flawed, yet filled with moments of extraordinary tenderness and insight.

Kakutani, Michiko. "Books of the Times." Rev. of *Later the Same Day*. *New York Times Book Review* 10 Apr. 1985: C20.

Describes *Later the Same Day* as sad, funny, and elliptical, while the moral center of the stories is loyalty to one's family, friends, and social ideals. Describes several of the characters and individual stories. Concludes that Paley's storytelling is a necessary and redemptive act.

Kapp, Isa. "City People in Tight Places." Rev. of *The Little Disturbances of Man*. *Commentary* Oct. 1959: 356-58.

Describes the settings, situations, characters, tone, humor, and world view expressed in *The Little Disturbances of Man*. Details several of the stories, and concludes that Paley has done well by the general language of literary love in the Western world by shifting it a few inches away from the romantic darkness of the gynecological light toward the agitation of the mind, the limbs, and the funny bone.

Kapp, Isa. "Husbands and Heroines." Rev. of *Enormous Changes at the Last Minute*. *New Leader* 24 June 1974: 17-18.

Provides a description of Faith as gabby, gregarious, urban, witty, tough, and modestly bawdy. Calls Paley a writer with a strong sense of fraternity with her own gender who pays eloquent tribute to her community. Details individual stories, and concludes that it is the tangential and hinted parts of life she does so well with.

LaSalle, Peter. "Hearing Whispers of Poetry." Rev. of *Later the Same Day*. *Commonweal* 21 June 1985: 376-77.

Describes Paley as having a "primal instinct" for the short story which emerges in her magical yet simple style. Describes her favorite protagonists as women who have been through the wilds of marriages and children, left-wing activism, and New York City's vanishing neighborhood life. Comments that she renders everyday speech with a perfect pitch capturing human feeling and empathy, humor and irony.

Lask, Thomas. "Three But Not of a Kind." Rev. of *The Little Disturbances of Man. New York Times* 23 Mar. 1968: 29.

Comments on her imagination, toughness, humor, and use of words. Notes that she "kites them, skitters them, schoons them along the frozen surface of our minds."

Lehmann-Haupt, Christopher. "Changes Not For the Better." Rev. of *Enormous Changes at the Last Minute. New York Times* 28 Feb. 1974: 35.

Compares this collection of stories unfavorably with her earlier *The Little Disturbances of Man,* finding her stories getting closer to autobiography as if she no longer had the strength or will to transmute life into art. Considers this new collection as growing out of the activist Sixties, not the quieter Fifties when socially-conscious writers projected passions into well-crafted stories.

Lyons, Bonnie. "Reviews." Rev. of *Later the Same Day. Studies in Short Fiction* 22.4 (1985): 484-85.

Calls the seventeen stories in *Later the Same Day* not all uniformly successful. Argues that some seem to be sketches or mere ideas for stories. Claims that the best center on Faith (Paley's alter ego) and her friends. Notes a major theme to be the celebration of friendship among these women which is at least as powerful, if not more so, than a marriage vow.

MacManus, Patricia. "Laughter from Tears." Rev. of *The Little Disturbances of Man. New York Times Book Review* 19 Apr. 1959: 28-29.

Sees this first of Paley's published collections of short stories possessing an all too infrequent literary virtue—the comic vision. Describes the characters in several of the stories as revealed through the wry devices that man contrives.

Mars-Jones, Adam. "From Red-Diaper Baby to Mother of the Planet." Rev. of *Later the Same Day. Times Literary Supplement* 22 Nov. 1985: 1311.

Discusses the "skinniness" of the stories in the collection, their feminism, nightmarish yoking of cant and cuteness, oddly divided sensibility, political views, and the conflicting claims of her feminism and old radicalism. Details the contents of several of the stories.

McMurtry, Larry. "New Life in a Dying Art." Rev. of *Enormous Changes at the Last Minute. Washington Post* 25 Feb. 1974: B4.

Calls this a funny, lean, sad, modest, energetic, and acute collection of stories whose qualities are more or less free floating. Notes that Paley writes with humor and warmth, wisdom and unfailing compassion. Claims that she does the vulnerability of childhood particularly well. Concludes that the Faith stories are clearly the best because here the writing is natural, pliant, and unforced.

Mellors, John. "Americans and Others." Rev. of *Enormous Changes at the Last Minute. Listener* 22 May 1975: 685-86.

Calls *Enormous Changes at the Last Minute* equally irritating and admirable. Considers Paley often self-consciously gossipy, chatty, and full of cliché conversational phrases marring the writing. Sees this as a shame because at her best she is vigorous, vivacious, and highly individual.

Merriam, Eve. "In Praise of Grace." Rev. of *Later the Same Day. Ms.* Apr. 1985: 13-14.

Calls *Later the Same Day* an uneven compilation, but still entirely satisfying because of the completely authentic voice which never cheats or becomes trendy. Describes Paley's political activism and her depiction of women who are social beings with loving concerns.

Murray, Michele. Rev. of *Enormous Changes at the Last Minute. New Republic* 16 Mar. 1974: 27.

Argues that, beneath their jauntiness, Paley's stories sag into consistent failure as evidenced by the life of Faith. Notes that death and old age are leitmotifs of this collection, even when young people are featured. Concludes that most of the stories are quick sketches, blackouts, or comic monologues spoken in a theater bereft of audience by a voice increasingly desperate for coherence.

Muth, Dayis. "Paley's Delicate Stories Ring with Voices from the Bronx." Rev. of *Later the Same Day. Christian Science Monitor* 7 May 1985: 25, 27.

Calls these stories delicate, gourmet, polished, light, funny, agile, and incredibly phonetic. Notes that she mostly describes the little places of New York City and bewildered, good, earnest people trying to cope with today's oversized era.

Novak, William. "The Uses of Fiction: To Reveal and to Heal." Rev. of
   Enormous Changes at the Last Minute. America 8 June 1974: 459-60.

Describes this collection as containing a remarkably wide range of character, insistent realism, lack of conventional sense of action, reliance on
language to produce reality, emphasis on telling, unique language, and
exposing the inherent limitations of her own technique. Concludes that
there is also the hint of a moral imperative.

Peden, William. "Arts and Letters." Rev. of *Enormous Changes at the
   Last Minute. Sewanee Review* 82.4 (1974): 721-23.

Describes the seventeen stories that make up *Enormous Changes at the
Last Minute* as unique and wonderful in style and content. Describes
moments in individual stories.

Phillips, Robert. Rev. of *Enormous Changes at the Last Minute.
   Commonweal* 1 Nov. 1974: 116-17.

Argues that many of the stories in this collection are made of slighter
stuff and have somehow not been transformed into stories. Notes that
also missing is the vivid characterization of the earlier stories. Concludes
that the book will not do much to strengthen her reputation, but admits it
does contain three outstanding stories.

Rabinowitz, Dorothy. "Books in Brief." Rev. of *Enormous Changes at
   the Last Minute. Saturday Review/World* 23 Mar. 1974: 44-45.

Finds this collection, except for a couple of stories, inferior to her earlier
collection, *The Little Disturbance of Man*, largely because of politicized
themes and situations. Notes that, instead of storymaking, she offers a
sort of sociological shorthand and offers additional proof that progressive politics is a downright heavy burden on the art of fiction.

See, Carolyn. Rev. of *Later the Same Day. Los Angeles Times Book
   Review* 19 May 1985: 2, 10.

Calls this work a tense, artful intelligent book that presents seventeen
complete and discrete worlds containing the private deaths and lifelong
attachments of anxious women who ultimately discover that relationships with friends and children finally count for more than relationships
with men.

Shulman, Alix Kates. "The Children's Hour." Rev. of *Later the Same
   Day. Village Voice Literary Supplement* June 1985: 9-10.

A nostalgic reminiscence of the reviewer's coming to political consciousness through Paley, her experience of the first volume, and recognition of the Greenwich Village characters of *Later the Same Day*. Contains some literary commentary on individual stories.

Sternhell, Carol. "Remember Dat?" Rev. of *Later the Same Day*. *Nation* 15 June 1985: 739-41.

Suggests that this is a book that registers its author's ability to notice passion in the familiar, quirkiness in the quotidian, that essential core that stares out at us and listens to voices on park benches. Calls her work a Jewish Greek chorus of witnesses and survivors. Details the contents of several of the stories.

"The Syntax of Surprise." Rev. of *The Little Disturbances of Man*. *Time* 3 May 1968: 86.

Suggests that *The Little Disturbances of Man* is animated at the source by its language, supple, colloquial and framed in the syntax of surprise. Shows how, through this medium, Paley builds personality and salty descriptive surfaces for her otherwise callow characters. Concludes that spunky, compassionate, and abandoned, these women characters saddled with poverty and children evoke the mysteries of life and loneliness.

Taliaferro, Frances. "Lox, Lettuce and Love." Rev. of *Later the Same Day*. *Washington Post Book World* 28 Apr. 1985: 3, 13.

Calls *Later the Same Day* a cause for rejoicing. Comments that again, the New York tenement and city block are her microcosm, her ideology that of a practical feminist, and love and friendship, modified by time, the interchange subjects. Notes that a vocabulary of critical pomposity simply will not describe these stories because her lens zooms from the intermediate, to the mediate, and then to the universal. Concludes that the stories move in short, straight lines from one emotion to another. Claims that they deserve to be read as poetry and song.

Towers, Robert. "Moveable Types." Rev. of *Later the Same Day*. *New York Review of Books* 15 Aug. 1985: 27-28.

Says that not one of these stories contains a whiff of the academic. Praises her idiosyncratic style, verbal surprises, and oblique humor. Details the contents of several stories, while identifying several of her themes.

Tyler, Anne. "Mothers in the City." Rev. of *Later the Same Day*. *New Republic* 29 Apr. 1985: 38-39.

A treatment of *Later the Same Day* which appraises Paley's characters, settings, politics, narrative methods, and moral concerns. Concludes that all of the stories are ideologically, spiritually, and on puritanical principle against despair.

Walshe, Robert. "Paley's Planet." Rev. of *Later the Same Day*. *London Review of Books* 17 Apr. 1986: 17.

Claims that in *Later the Same Day* Paley leaves out infinitely more than she puts in. Calls Paley a risk-taker, a miniaturist, a humorous satirist, and a close-up artist. Notes that her themes are womanhood, motherhood, youth, old age, desertion, and the failure of heterosexual love.

Winegarten, Renee. "Paley's Comet." Rev. of *Enormous Changes at the Last Minute*. *Midstream* Dec. 1974: 65-67.

Recounts the emergence of Paley's first work and its remarkable critical reception. Speculates about the fifteen year gap between the first and second publication, and draws the conclusion that what is said about the contemporary female's freedom is a delusion.

Wood, Michael. "Flirting with Disintegration." Rev. of *Enormous Changes at the Last Minute*. *New York Review of Books* 21 Mar. 1974: 21-22.

Discusses Paley's style, language, and capturing of the New York idiom and situation. Finds her language sometimes in danger of falling off the highwire. Observes that her humor and jokes in her stories are an expression of her hope, a personal, human cancellation of life's mournful lack of a sense of humor.

Interviews

Batt, Noelle, and Marcienne Rocard. "An Interview with Grace Paley." *Caliban* 25 (1988): 119-37.

In this lengthy interview Paley discusses her preference for the short story form, writing poetry, writing her first story, her creation of voice first, her daily writing routines, talking out loud as a method of composition, revision processes, humor writing as a way of understanding the world, new ethnic speakers in literature, music and inflection in language, assimilation through language, Jewishness, New York, women's issues, her relationship to her characters, her relationship to faith, and her relation to her time.

Burns, Alan, and Charles Sugnet. "Grace Paley." *The Imagination on Trial: British and American Writers Discuss Their Working Methods.* Alan Burns and Charles Sugnet. London: Allison, 1981. 120-32.

Begins with an outline of Paley's life and works. Describes her subject matter as domestic, her female protagonists as feisty, and her political leanings feminist, conservationist, and anti-war. Describes her themes as female friendship, the Holocaust and its aftermath, children, love, and family. Describes her working habits, explains why her stories do not contain accounts of her radical politics, how hard it is to be a woman writer, and her views on the short story.

Friedler, Maya. "An Interview with Grace Paley." *Story Quarterly* 13 (1981): 32-39.

An interview in which Paley discusses family, political activism, writing, people, relationships, women's oppression, her opposition to plot, women's voices, influences, her method of composition, periodic silences, the women's peace movement, attitude toward despair, and the arms race.

Hulley, Kathleen. "Interview with Grace Paley." *Delta* 14 (1982): 19-40.

In this interview Paley describes: her favorite themes as generational relations; the lives of women generally; the coming together of language and voice in the lives of her women characters; the search for the story teller; the writer's experience of grace; her reading and writing as a child; her writing process; her politics; her central protagonist, Faith; her association with children; the surrealistic imagery; her poetry; her views on language; the women's movement; men in relationship to women; men as social victims; the lack of guilt in the stories; her views on nuclear arms; her visits to China, Chile, Russia, and Vietnam; her feminism; her views on plot; and her work in progress.

Lidoff, Joan. "Clearing Her Throat: An Interview with Grace Paley." *Shenandoah* 32.3 (1981): 3-26.

A composite record of conversations, readings, and lectures given by Paley at University of Texas at Austin in April of 1981. Discusses her view of storytelling, her family, her Yiddish inheritance, poetry writing, first publishing success, the character of Faith, feminist views, the sex scenes, narrative technique, and her friendship with Tillie Olsen.

Marchant, Peter, and Earl Ingersoll, eds. "A Conversation with Grace Paley." *Massachusetts Review* 26.4 (1985): 606-14.

Discusses her poetry, love of the short story, creation of voices, writing habits, life as a mother, other writers, politics, comic view, mentors and teachers, and her views on women.

Michaels, Leonard. "Conversation with Grace Paley." *Threepenny Review* 3 (1980): 4-6.

A report of a conversation between Paley and an audience gathered at the Berkeley Writer's Conference in 1980. She discusses her unpublished pages, views on storytelling, impetus for beginning to write, her favorite "ordinary" subject matter, her teaching, the relationship between dialogue and descriptive paragraph, her use of ideas, responses to her work, avoiding the abstract, the relationship between lyricism and self love, her own reading tastes, and autobiography as storytelling.

Perry, Ruth. "Grace Paley." *Women Writers Talking.* Ed. Janet Todd. New York: Holmes, 1983. 34-56.

In this interview Paley discusses: the lack of anger in the stories, her anti-war politics, subsequent arrests, the lack of hierarchy in women's politics, methods of writing, inspiration for new stories, getting started in the fifties, individual stories, biographical reminiscences, love for Robinson Jeffers and Auden, her responses to Jong, her friendship with Tillie Olsen, and her fascination with the whole actual round of women's lives.

Satz, Martha. "Looking at Disparities: An Interview with Grace Paley." *Southwest Review* 72.4 (1987): 478-89.

Discusses Paley's views on listening, early life, socialist politics, family background, trying to re-imagine her mother, her relationship with her father, experiences in the New York City school system, attitudes toward the Holocaust, views on Judaism and women, and the recording of female experience in fiction.

Shapiro, Harriet. "Grace Paley: 'Art Is on the Side of the Underdog.'" *Ms.* May 1974: 43-45.

An account of an interview giving mostly general biographical information on Paley with her ideas on her favorite themes and her methods of writing.

Silesky, Barry Robin Hemley, and Sharon Solwitz. "Grace Paley: A Conversation." *Another Chicago Magazine* 14 (1985): 100-114.

In this interview Paley discusses: her political activism, humor, present political activities, the contemporary state of feminism, her anti-militarism, her childhood upbringing, graduate school writing programs, the expansion of small press literary activity, her own writing processes, her teaching, and her attachment to family.

Smith, Wendy. "PW Interviews Grace Paley." *Publishers Weekly* 5 Apr. 1985: 71-72.

Calls her work strikingly individualistic. Describes her apartment, her life and background along with several of the short stories.

Taylor, Jacqueline. "Interview: Grace Paley on Storytelling and Story Hearing." *Literature in Performance: A Journal of Literary and Performing Art* 7.2 (1987): 46-58.

Paley discusses her language, beginning in poetry, finding the voices for the stories, listening to her own fiction, teaching methods, doing readings, literature as public performance, her own performances, the film of *Enormous Changes at the Last Minute*, her coming to know women, her humor, and her Jewish background.

Biographical Sources

Cevoli, Cathy. "These Four Women Could Save Your Life." *Mademoiselle* Jan. 1983: 104-07.

Describes Paley's politics, life, and works. Focuses mostly on her anti-war, anti-nuclear stance.

Davis, Hope Hale. "A Memoir: On Writers and Politics." *New Leader* 14 Dec. 1981: 22-24.

A brief description of Paley's political activism.

Figes, Eva. "With Grace in the Bronx." *Observer* 23 July 1978: 24.

Briefly talks about her life and background, her political activism, her writing, and her reputation.

Midwood, Barton. "Short Visits With Five Writers and One Friend." *Esquire* Nov. 1970: 150-53.

Provides a little historical background on Paley, her personal and political situation, teaching career, influences, published books, and family life.

Sorkin, Adam J. "Grace Paley." *Twentieth-Century American-Jewish Fiction Writers*. Ed. Daniel Walden. Detroit: Gale, 1984. Vol. 28 of *Dictionary of Literary Biography*. 94 vols. to date. 1978- 225-31.

More than details of her life, this is a career biography, tracing the development of the author's canon, describing the contents and themes of her works, evaluating her reputation, and placing her in the larger context of American literary history. Includes lists of primary and secondary sources and illustrations.

Bibliographies

Hulley, Kathleen. "Bibliography on Grace Paley." *Delta* 14 (1982): 147-50.

Dissertations

Blustein, Bryna Lee Datz. "Beyond the Stereotype: A Study of Representative Short Stories of Selected Contemporary Jewish American Female Writers." Diss. Saint Louis U, 1986.

Jones, Nancy Baker. "On Solid Ground: The Emergence of the Self-Created Woman in Contemporary American Literature." Diss. The U of Texas at Austin, 1986.

Shinn, Thelma J. Wardrop. "A Study of Women Characters in Contemporary American Fiction, 1940-1970." Diss. Purdue U, 1972.

Swigart, Margaret Jane Bugas. "The Mother in Modern Literature." Diss. State U of New York at Buffalo, 1986.

Chaim Potok

1929 –

Primary Sources

Novels

The Book of Lights. New York: Knopf, 1981; Large Print ed. Thorndike: Thorndike, 1982; New York: Crest-Fawcett, 1982; London: Heinemann, 1982; Harmondsworth: Penguin, 1983.

The Chosen. New York: Simon, 1967; Greenwich: Crest-Fawcett, 1967, 1970, 1978, 1982; New York: Fawcett World, 1976; London: Heinemann, 1977; New York: Fawcett Crest-Ballantine, 1982, 1987; Greenwich: Fawcett, 1986; Harmondsworth: Penguin [cited in BBIP, 1988].

Davita's Harp. New York: Knopf, 1985; Large Print ed. Boston: Hall, 1985; New York: Fawcett Crest, 1986; New York: Ballantine, 1986.

The Gift of Asher Lev. New York: Knopf, 1990; London: Heinemann, 1990.

In the Beginning. New York: Knopf, 1975; Book Club ed. New York: Borzoi-Knopf, 1975; Greenwich: Fawcett, 1975; Greenwich: Crest-Fawcett, 1976, 1986; London: Heinemann, 1976; Harmondsworth: Penguin, 1977.

My Name Is Asher Lev. New York: Borzoi-Knopf, 1972; Book Club ed. New York: Knopf, 1972; Greenwich: Crest-Fawcett, 1972, 1984; London: Heinemann, 1972; Harmondsworth: Penguin, 1974; Greenwich: Fawcett Crest-Ballantine, 1983.

The Promise. New York: Borzoi-Knopf, 1969; New York: Crest-Fawcett, 1969; Book Club ed. New York: Knopf, 1969; Large Print ed. Buffalo: Associated Reprinting, 1969; Greenwich: Fawcett, 1970, 1978; London: Heinemann, 1970; Harmondsworth: Penguin, 1971; Greenwich: Crest-Fawcett, 1976, 1985.

Short Fiction in Periodicals

"The Cats of 37 Alfasi Street." *American Judaism* 16 (Fall 1966): 12-13, 25-26, 28-29; *World Over* 27 Oct. 1967: 12-13+.

"The Dark Place Inside." *Dimensions* 2 (Fall 1967): 35-39.

"The Gifts of Andrea." *Seventeen* Oct. 1982: 152-53, 168, 171.

"A Tale of Two Soldiers." *Ladies' Home Journal* Dec. 1981: 16, 18-19.

Secondary Sources

Books

Abramson, Edward A. *Chaim Potok.* Twayne's United States Authors Series 503. Boston: Twayne, 1986.

Articles and Chapters

Barnett, Dan. "Chaim Potok." *Critical Survey of Long Fiction.* Ed. Frank N. Magill. 9 vols. Englewood Cliffs: Salem, 1983. Supplement: 313-21.

A standard reference article on Potok covering his origins, principal long fiction, other literary forms, achievements, and biography. Gives a brief analysis of each major work.

Benjamin, J. C. "The Novels of Chaim Potok." *Jewish Quarterly* 29.1 (1981): 19-21.

Provides a general overview of Potok's novels, their major themes and preoccupations, the characters, and the Jewish issues they raise. Provides a brief formalist critique, along with stylistic commentary, of several of the novels.

Bluefarb, Sam. "The Head, The Heart and the Conflict of Generations in Chaim Potok's *The Chosen.*" *College Language Assocation Journal* 14.4 (1971): 402-09.

Describes the conflict in Potok's novels as generational, temperamental, between head and heart, the opposition between a petrified fanaticism and a human tolerance, and finally the split between two visions of God and man's relationship to him.

Campbell, Patty. "The Young Adult Perplex." *Wilson Library Bulletin* June 1985: 688-89.

An essay comparing *Cranes at Dusk* and *Davita's Harp* in terms of themes, parallel structures, cultural dilemmas, and storytelling techniques.

Cheever, Leonard A. "Rectangles of Frozen Memory: Potok's *In the Beginning.*" *Publications of the Arkansas Philological Association* 4 (1978): 8-12.

Discusses the meaning of the event in which David Lurie ponders a photograph which he conceives as a "rectangle of frozen memory." Discusses why David refuses to accept as final the framing limitations of the photograph. Claims that his intellectual and spiritual development can best be understood in terms of attempts to reconcile this "frozen rectangle" and others in his life with the dynamic living truth. Argues that metaphors of framing permeate the whole novel.

Cheuse, Alan. "His Name is Chaim Potok." *Present Tense* 11.2 (1984): 53-56.

Describes the core-to-core cultural conflict at the heart of each of Potok's novels and Potok's relation to his own Jewish community. Covers several novels concluding with a discussion of *Davita's Harp.*

Del Fattore, Joan. "Women as Scholars in Chaim Potok's Novels." *Studies in American Jewish Literature* [Albany] 4 (1985): 52-61.

Describes all five of Potok's novels as centered around the theme of scholarship for both males and females, although only male scholars have been featured in previous critical commentary. Focuses on the women scholars, their scholarship, family conflicts, emotional traumas, the reactions of their sons, and their lack of commitment to traditional forms of Jewish religious scholarship.

Dembo, L. S. "Asher Lev: The Mariolatry of a Hasid." *The Monological Jew: A Literary Study*. Madison: Wisconsin UP, 1988. 112-16.

Describes the nature of Asher Lev's artistic formalism and its relation to the fusion of Christological martyr models and female nudes. Details Asher's conflict between this formalist aesthetic and the values of traditional Judaism.

Field, Leslie. "Chaim Potok and the Critics: Sampler from a Consistent Spectrum." *Studies in American Jewish Literature* [Albany] 4 (1985): 3-12.

A major bibliographical essay providing an excellent summary of the full spectrum of critical opinion on Potok.

Gilmore, Michael. "Communications: *The Promise*: Michael Gilmore Replies." *Midstream* Mar. 1970: 66-67.

Gilmore replies to Douglas Greener's objections to his review of *The Promise*.

Grebstein, Sheldon. "The Phenomenon of the Really Jewish Best-Seller: Potok's *The Chosen*." *Studies in American Jewish Literature* [University Park, PA] 1.1 (1975): 23-31.

Asks why a book like this with its gray tone, lack of sex and violence, lack of gripping action, and romantic cast can end up on the bestseller list. Sees this novel as part of a movement of interest in American-Jewish literature, and uniquely American at the same time. Claims that it contains nostalgia, generational conflict, religious issues, an unmitigated tone of sincerity, and male protagonists who represent a provocative combination of force and weakness, intelligence and stupidity. Adds that its binary oppositions are also appealingly structured. Concludes that it teaches good lessons and provides lucid formulations of important issues and dilemmas.

Greener, Douglas L. "Communications: *The Promise*." *Midstream* Mar. 1970: 66.

Objects to Michael Gilmore's review of *The Promise* (*Midstream* Jan. 1970), suspicioning that Gilmore "judges all books by his own yardstick of how they stack up to the activist youth revolt," rather than recognizing that Potok is neither ignoring nor stressing the Jewish passion for social reform (it is just not appropriate in the framework of this story) as much as he is stressing Jewish values. Gilmore replies that it is Potok himself who goes outside the framework of the story in order to pass judgment on the sixties.

Guttmann, Allen. "The Postwar Revival of Peoplehood." *The Jewish Writer in America: Assimilation and the Crisis of Identity*. Allen Guttmann. New York: Oxford UP, 1971. 120-28.

Discusses Wouk, Cohen, and Potok as writers who have dramatized the commitment to peoplehood. Discusses *The Chosen* and *The Promise*, reviewing the basic plots and pointing out that not since Cahan's *The Rise of David Levinsky* has a writer taken seriously the details of religious observance and the theological controversies among traditional Jews.

Kremer, S. Lillian. "Dedalus in Brooklyn: Influences of *A Portrait of the Artist as a Young Man* on *My Name is Asher Lev*." *Studies in American Jewish Literature* [Albany] 4 (1985): 26-38.

Asserts that Potok's experiments with interior monologue, stream-of-consciousness techniques, and epiphany, in addition to his fusion of socio-religious dynamic with individual character clearly reveal the substantive Joycean influence.

Kremer, S. Lillian. "Eternal Light: The Holocaust and the Revival of Judaism and Jewish Civilization in the Fiction of Chaim Potok." *Witness Through the Imagination: Jewish American Holocaust Literature*. S. Lillian Kremer. Detroit: Wayne State UP, 1989. 300-23.

A major chapter on Potok arguing that along with Bellow, Malamud, Ozick, Cohen, and Singer, Potok rejects alienation in favor of the affirmative position of Jewish idealism in the face of evil and suffering. Points out that Jewish history, including repeated outbreaks of anti-Semitism and its 1939-1945 genocidal manifestation, resonates through Potok's fiction. Concludes like these other writers, that Potok sees Jewish history refracted through the ocean of blood that is the Holocaust.

Lauter, Evelyn. "Chaim Potok Talks About Hasidism and U. S. Jewry." *National Jewish Monthly* June 1968: 20, 24.

Reports a discussion with Potok on Hasidism, its origins 200 years ago, its survival in America after the Holocaust in Europe, its function in Judaism today, and how his novel, *The Chosen*, dramatizes the impingement of the world on this Jewish tradition.

Leeper, Faye. "What Is in the Name?" *English Journal* Jan. 1970: 63-64.

Discusses the reaction of high school juniors to *The Chosen*, concentrating on the various meanings of the word "chosen" from the title. Concludes that this novel lends itself well to the study of problems of importance to young adults.

Lipskar, Mendel. "My Name is Not Asher Lev." *Jewish Affairs* May 1977: 31-32.

Complains that South African Jews on the occasion of Potok's visit were unnecessarily mesmerized. What follows is a general discussion of several of the novels for the beginning reader of Potok.

Margolies, Edward. "Chaim Potok's *Book of Lights* and the Jewish American Novel." *Yiddish* 6.4 (1987): 93-98.

Begins with a discussion of what the Jewish-American novel is and is not. Criticizes Potok for his lackluster prose, lack of imaginative skill and lyricism; dubs him a popular novelist; comments on Gershon Loran's mysticism and the difficulty of portraying it in a novel. Concludes that Potok presents an America which has been good to Jews and, therefore, poses the greatest threat to them.

Marovitz, Sanford E. "*The Book of Lights*: Jewish Mysticism in the Shadow of the Bomb." *Studies in American Jewish Literature* [Albany] 4 (1985): 62-83.

Sees profound moral guilt as the unifying factor in this novel which is structured around the contrasts between dehumanized science, man against good, human pride against divine mystery, destruction against creation, and hate against love. Claims that it is also a novel which brings together many different kinds of light imagery, and makes use of kabbalistic theosophy and language as it explores the complex moral implications of the bomb. Sees this as Potok's most immediately and universally relevant novel.

Marovitz, Sanford E. "Freedom, Faith, and Fanaticism: Cultural Conflict in the Novels of Chaim Potok." *Studies in American Jewish Literature* [Albany] 5 (1986): 129-40.

Argues that young Reuven's quest for a meaningful life on the order of his father's anticipates the central theme of all but the last of the other five novels Potok has published thus far, though the manner in which he learns his lesson does not typify the relation of father to son in all of them. Even in *The Chosen* that bond is represented in a completely different manner through the portraits of the Hasidic Reb Saunders and his son Danny, whose relationship is characterized by silence.

Merkin, Daphne. "Why Potok is Popular." *Commentary* Feb. 1976: 73-75.

Discusses *In the Beginning* as a book with no clearly discernible main theme, stylistic panache or metaphysical clarity. Puzzles over why no one complains about Potok's bad writing, closed worlds, and an approach which forgoes dealing with the larger issues of humanity. Comments that when he is reviewed, proper critical judgment is suspended as is always the case in religious works or ethnic theater. Concludes that finally Potok is insular and unskilled, even if he has a certain appeal as a storyteller.

Pinsker, Sanford. "The Crucifixion of Chaim Potok/The Excommunication of Asher Lev: Art and the Hasidic World." *Studies in American Jewish Literature* [Albany] 4 (1985): 39-51.

Accuses Potok of turning the melodramatic sagas of the ultra orthodox into a thriving cottage industry. Concedes that he is a good read, and notes that despite his telegraphing his narrative strategies ahead of time, he does get his facts right. Goes on to detail the actual Lubavitcher Hasidim used as models, and numerous details of Hasidic life and practice correctly represented in the book. Concludes that in this novel Potok really superimposes the *kunstlerroman* structure over Lubavitcher life, resulting in something resembling "A Portrait of the Artist as a Young Hasidic Man."

Regenbaum, Shelly. "Art, Gender, and the Jewish Tradition in Yezierska's *Red Ribbon on a White Horse* and Potok's *My Name is Asher Lev*." *Studies in American Jewish Literature* [Kent State] 7.1 (1988): 55-66.

Compares the similar predicaments of the two Jewish artists in Yezierska and Potok's books. Traces the familial and cultural conflicts suffered by the two protagonists and the issues of Jewish orthodoxy surrounding each. Concludes by commenting on the different fates of the two as Asher's ancestor appears to empower him and Anzia's ancestor appears to punish her.

Ruddle, Lee Petrie. *The Chosen. Survey of Contemporary Literature.* Ed.
     Frank N. Magill. Rev. ed. 12 vols. Englewood Cliffs: Salem, 1977. 2:
     1254-56.

Describes the main character of the novel, the milieu, themes, conflicts,
historical insights, and stylistic habits. A brief reference article.

Schiff, Ellen. "To Be Young, Gifted and Oppressed: The Plight of the
     Ethnic Artist." *MELUS* 6.1 (1979): 73-80.

Calls *My Name Is Asher Lev* a novel which demonstrates that an ethnic
society is no more tolerant than any other of a member who marches to a
different drummer. Concludes that, indeed, the ethnic nonconformist is
shown to provoke special harshness from his already insecure people
who view his differences as baffling and somehow threatening.

Sgan, Arnold D. "The *Chosen, The Promise,* and *My Name Is Asher
     Lev.*" *English Journal* Mar. 1977: 63-64.

Finds Potok's three novels excellent works with which to help adolescents
explore themselves, their dreams, and their promises of reality. Insists that
the books are emotionally and intellectually powerful, that they deal with
adult or real themes of importance, and that they are brilliantly written.

Soll, Will. "Chaim Potok's *Book of Lights*: Reappropriating Kabbalah in
     the Nuclear Age." *Religion and Literature* 21.1 (1989): 111-35.

Notes that in *The Book of Lights* Potok has filled his novel with a great
deal of scholarly discussion of Jewish mysticism and its twentieth-century relevance. Dicusses the Kabbalistic vocabulary, imagery, and
depictions of terror, brokenness, and promise. Describes the speculative
frame of reference the Kabbalah creates to depict the relation of God to
the world, and proceeds to discuss Potok's use of this framework and its
imagery in the novel.

Sutherland, Sam III. "Asher Lev's Visions of His Mythic Ancestor." *Re:
     Artes Liberales* 3.2 (1977): 51-54.

Explicates the identity and mythic function of the traveling ancestor of
My Name is Asher Lev. Claims that as the novel develops, Asher devel-
ops his own version of the myth as he develops his art and his identity.
Concludes that the novel becomes a long session in demythology.

Timmerman, John H. "A Way of Seeing: Chaim Potok and Tradition."
     Christian Century 16 May 1984: 515-18.

Discusses in detail the cultural conflicts with the Jewish tradition that Potok is writing about, and applies this thesis to *My Name is Asher Lev.*

True, Warren R. "Potok and Joyce: The Artist and His Culture." *Studies in American Jewish Literature* [Albany] 2 (1982): 181-90.

Begins with Evelyn Waugh's influence on Potok and that of other modern writers in using the novel to depict cultural breakdown and conflict. Draws the parallels between Stephen Daedelus and Asher Lev.

Uffen, Ellen Serlen. "*My Name is Asher Lev*: Chaim Potok's Portrait of the Young Hasid as Artist." *Studies in American Jewish Literature* [Albany] 2 (1982): 174-180.

Considers this a book about a hero establishing a self beyond the definition set by Jewish identity. Suggests that only by an act of exorcism can he grow up. Details the contents of the book, and underscores the relationship between this novel and Joyce's *Portrait of The Artist as a Young Man.*

Walden, Daniel. "Chaim Potok, *Zwischenmench* ('Between-Person') Adrift in the Cultures." *Studies in American Jewish Literature* [Albany] 4 (1985): 19-25.

Describes the cultural dilemma of the growing Potok and how this is reflected in the core-to-core cultural confrontations of all his heroes. Discusses Potok's deliberate use of the novel, after reading Evelyn Waugh, to depict the breakup of things historical and cultural. Provides a summary of contents for each of the novels.

Wisse, Ruth R. "Jewish Dreams." *Commentary* Mar. 1982: 47-48.

Discusses how Jewish tradition has long been fascinated with the theme of rebellion against tradition and how autobiographies of the eighteenth and nineteenth centuries reflect this. Concludes that Potok's works suggest that this theme is not yet exhausted.

Wohlgelernter, Maurice. "Fathers—Artichokes, Choosers, Carpenters—And All Their Sons." *Tradition* 9.3 (1967): 125-40.

A general article on the subject of fathers and sons in American Jewish fiction. Discusses *The Chosen* in detail.

Young, Bruce. "Chaim Potok." *Beacham's Popular Fiction of America.* Ed. Walter Beacham. Washington: Beacham, 1986. 1118-30.

A standard reference article detailing Potok's publishing history, critical reception, the characters, contents, techniques, social concerns, literary precedents, and adaptations of *The Chosen, My Name Is Asher Lev, The Book of Lights,* and *Davita's Harp.*"

Yudkin, Leon I. "From the Periphery to the Centre in America." *Jewish Writing and Identity in the Twentieth Century.* Leon I. Yudkin. London: Helm, 1982. 112-28.

Shows how the immigrant Jews have moved from the periphery of American life to its center and discusses the works of several major novelists—Trilling, Bellow, Malamud, Mailer, Potok—as demonstrations of that movement. Sees Potok as the only one of these writers who attempts to present an understanding of Judaism from different points of view. Describes the protagonists of *The Chosen* and *The Promise,* who represent the liberal and conservative aspects of Judaism, and discusses how they resolve the conflicts within their culture and themselves. Concludes that this is not the greatest Jewish writing, but it does suggest a synthesis of worlds and has brought an awareness of Jewish issues to a contemporary audience by restating a perenniel conflict illuminated in earlier literture.

Zlotnick, Joan. "The Chosen Borough: Chaim Potok's Brooklyn." *Studies in American Jewish Literature* [Albany] 4 (1985): 13-18.

An account of Potok's early life in Brooklyn among the Lubavitcher Hasidim, and the reflection of these conflicts and experiences in the novels.

Reviews

Aspler, Tony. "Pogroms and Megrims." Rev. of *In the Beginning. Listener* 8 Apr. 1976: 454.

Comments that this novel is marred by lengthy passages of esoteric biblical exegesis and history. Notes that, otherwise, the novel proceeds like a stately fugue in its complex interplay of characters and naturalistic motifs, repetition of ideas, and images.

"Back to the Fold." Rev. of *The Promise. Times Literary Supplement* 5 Mar. 1970: 241.

Describes the novel as beautifully narrated *shmalz,* self-torment, or turgidity. Considers Potok's descriptions of Judaism to be enthralling.

Bandler, Michael J. "A Sequel to *The Chosen*." Rev. of *The Promise*. *Christian Science Monitor* 16 Dec. 1969: 13.

Describes *The Promise* as more complex, more pressing, and less beautiful than its predecessor. Notes that what is missing is joy and warmth.

Barson, Anthony. "The Artist As a Novel." Rev. of *My Name Is Asher Lev*. *Christian Science Monitor* 14 June 1972: 11.

Calls Potok a failure because of the dull, ponderous, humorless account of the rise of Asher Lev. Suggests that those wishing some sort of empathy with a real painter try the "Letters of Vincent Van Gogh."

"Books." Rev. of *Davita's Harp*. *Time* 25 Mar. 1985: 78-80.

Complains that *Davita's Harp* is a book that suggests a worthier sequel. Describes the story in detail.

Clark, Gilbert, and Enid Zimmerman. "A Great Author Writes About a Great Artist." Rev. of *My Name Is Asher Lev*. *School Arts* Jan. 1983: 22-23.

Argues that *My Name Is Asher Lev* compellingly traces Lev's life and artistic development. Commends the book to all who work with or teach young people.

Cook, Bruce. "Allegorical Tale Painfully Told, But Impressive." Rev. of *The Chosen*. *National Observer* 8 May 1967: 23.

Considers *The Chosen* the book of wisdom every good man carries within him. Claims that it is specifically about how Jews can immerse themselves in American experience without sacrificing their Jewishness. Sees the language as impossibly stiff and notes that the historical background of Hasidism is dropped before the reader in a great lump. Concludes that it lacks polish, flow, and grace—but is ultimately impressive and worth a long night's reading.

Cowan, Paul. "The Faiths of Her Childhood." Rev. of *Davita's Harp*. *New York Times Book Review* 31 Mar. 1985: 12-13.

Calls *Davita's Harp* Potok's bravest book, but not his best. Details the characters, the world they inhabit, and their dilemmas of identity. Sees it as full of the horrors of the twentieth century, while still portraying people willing to nurture one another in the worst of times. Details the contents.

Dame, Enid. "Bellow & Potok: The Saving Force." Rev of *In the Beginning. Congress Monthly* Apr. 1976: 20-22.

Compares and contrasts David Lurie of *In the Beginning* with Charlie Citrine of *Humboldt's Gift*. Suggests that both books explore the problem of the creative person in a society distrusting of him and his message. Provides a detailed plot summary of both novels and the social conflicts each hero experiences.

Davenport, Guy. "Collision with the Outside World." Rev. of *My Name Is Asher Lev. New York Times Book Review* 16 Apr. 1972: 5, 18.

Argues that this novel takes the themes of the coming of the Hasidim to Brooklyn and turns them into a finely articulated tragic novel. Details the contents, and suggests that Potok's novels are deceptively plain with their lack of ostentation and self-conscious rhetoric. Concludes that the voice is honest and guileless, and above all, compassionate.

Edelman, Lily. "A Jewish Book: What Is It?" Rev. of *The Promise. National Jewish Monthly* Jan. 1970: 47-48.

Complains of the never-ending creation of Jewish books, and that most of these books contain hack exercises in self-exploitation. *The Promise* picks over the rich ore of the earlier novels and, because of Potok's lackluster pen, turns out to be of little interest. Asserts that he fails to bring to life or transform the streets and persons and confrontations he knows so well with the result that much is a distorted and unintentionally counterfeit vision of Jewishness and Jewish concern. Edelman finds *The Promise* a stilted, sentimental walk through exotica devoid of insight, inspiration, or even, of promise.

Elkin, Lillian. "Books." Rev. of *The Promise. Jewish Frontier* Mar. 1970: 25-26.

Describes *The Promise* as a book which cannot fulfill all the expectations set up by the previous novel. Sees the story as weaker and less interesting, the characters as less awesome, and the situation as less appealing. Considers the painful yielding of Rav Kalman as magnificently conceived. Concludes that while Potok does not possess the certainty of craft and brilliant techniques of Bellow and Malamud, he does possess the passion of the search and the enviable ring of authenticity.

Elson, Brigid. "Jewish Life." Rev. of *The Book of Lights. Queen's Quarterly* 90.1 (1983): 219-21.

Calls this book a poetic narrative of some of the formative years of protagonist Gershon Loran. Notes that the power of the book lies in its
narrative techniques, imagery, and themes. Complains that Arthur
Leiden and Loran are not quite three-dimensional. Concludes that while
this is not a masterwork, Potok is a major talent.

Firestone, Bea. "Choose *The Chosen*." Rev. of *The Chosen*. *United
Synagogue Review Quarterly* 21 (July 1968): 16-17.

Describes the book as beautifully written, intelligent, and free from questionable adult material. Details the plot.

Frank, Mike. "Portrait of the Artist." Rev. of *My Name Is Asher Lev*.
American Zionist Sept. 1972: 40-42.

Calls Potok a writer whose reach exceeds his grasp, yet who has enviable
skills as a storyteller and local colorist. Claims that he creates sympathetic, if
not always convincing, characters who maintain a reasonable amount of tension in the story. Deals with several of the novels, noting that *My Name Is
Asher Lev*, narrated in a self-indulgent and myopic fashion, contains a fundamentally flawed plot. Comments that Asher is "so damned good that the
reader wishes he would do just one stupid, mean, or irresponsible thing."

Freedman, Richard. "A Warm Glow in a Cruel, Cold World." Rev. of
The Promise. *Washington Post Book World* 14 Sept. 1969: 3.

Suggests that *The Promise* suffers from a slight case of "sequelitis," yet
sees both novels as leagues ahead of the facile *haimish Yiddishkeit* of
Fiddler on the Roof. Concludes that while overall there is a glow of
humane erudition and compassion suggesting Potok would be an ideal
rabbi, perhaps he is too nice to be a great writer.

Fremont-Smith, Eliot. "Sons and Fathers." Rev. of *The Chosen*. *New
York Times* 24 Apr. 1967: 31.

Finds the softball game that begins the novel the dramatic high point,
with the characters and story later sacrificed to theme. Reviews the major
plot conflicts and concludes that it is an interesting but awkward novel
because of its heavy emphasis on theme."

Fuller, Edmund. "*The Chosen*, Rare, Reverent Novel." Rev. of *The
Chosen*. *Wall Street Journal* 15 May 1967: 18.

Calls *The Chosen* a novel of exceptional beauty and freshness at a time
when hedonism, vulgarity, brutality, cynicism, and corruption are com-

monplace themes. Suggests that this book is about reverence, responsibility, holiness, learning, tradition, and the pain of defending these things against the world. Commends Potok for his delicate sense of balance and briefly describes the contents.

Fuller, Edmund. "Potok's Spirit-Nourishing Tale." Rev. of *My Name is Asher Lev. Wall Street Journal* 25 Apr. 1972: 28.

Discusses the contents of *My Name Is Asher Lev* and considers its genius to be the evocation of a community of commitment and belief. Concludes that this book is profound in its vision of humanity. Describes plot and characters.

Gilmore, Michael T. "A Fading Promise." Rev. of *The Promise. Midstream* Jan. 1970: 76, 78-79.

Details the contents of the book. Criticizes Potok for the predictability of his two male characters, Danny and Reuven, who can always be counted on to act sadly, mildly, quietly, thoughtfully, or solemnly—never with rage or passion. Complains that to imagine such characters surviving the sixties is to tax the reader too much. Concludes that what Potok has written about is a world that thankfully is no more, or perhaps never was.

Goldreich, Gloria. "Disraeli, Doctors and Hasidim in New Novels." Rev. of *My Name Is Asher Lev. Hadassah Magazine* Sept. 1972: 21-22.

Briefly reviews the plot and discusses the theme which, similar to his earlier novels, is the conflict between the Hasidic community and the pursuit of personal interests. Claims that he uses the same simplistic and sometimes simple style, and that his novelistic skill falls somewhat short of the challenge of his material.

Goldreich, Gloria. Rev. of *Davita's Harp. Hadassah Magazine* Mar. 1985: 45.

Argues that only in later chapters does Potok explore the girl's confrontation with her new womanhood and David Dinn's awareness of his sexuality. Suggests that Potok has inadvertently written two stories, one of Ilana Chandal caught up in her parents' ideological drama, and the other is the story of Davita Dinn struggling to understand her Judaism and her people. Concludes that the music of the door harp symbolizing the divergent tales and traditions of the world unites the two stories—a melodic and forgivable deception.

Goldreich, Gloria. "Striking Roots in the New World." Rev. of *In the Beginning. Hadassah Magazine* Feb. 1976: 21.

Describes the contents of the book, and adds that the world of *In the Beginning* is a European world, as well as an American one. Sees its obsessions to be Jewish obsessions and complains that the culture conflict never reaches the level of intermarriage and changing names. Yet notes that the recreation of the world where boys dream of the European forests their fathers and mothers had known, and live in the shadow of their parents' fears and memories is one of Potok's gifts to readers who seek to walk softly backward into their history.

Gottlieb, Freema. "Traumatic Experience." Rev. of *The Promise. Books and Bookmen* Apr. 1970: 38.

Calls the novel a book about how to teach people to regard the tradition critically and with love. Also sees it as a commentary on postwar Judaism.

Greenfeld, Josh. "A Universal Parable Grows in Brooklyn." Rev. of *The Chosen. Life* 21 Apr. 1967: 8, 12.

Claims that this book renders the parochial as a pure blessing, the mark of a true novelist. Notes that the story is stroked along with the thematic overtones of a parable and contains considerable significance for Jewry and non-Jewry alike. Concludes that this is a wise and fine novel.

Grusd, Edward E. "A Novel Worth Reading." Rev. of *The Chosen. National Jewish Monthly* Sept. 1967: 72-73.

A highly complimentary and uncritical assessment of the novel. Concludes that, besides the beauty of the writing and superb mastery of the materials, *The Chosen* is a pleasure to read because it is not filled with Jewish self-hate and anti-Semitism, to say nothing of monotonous clinical descriptions of sex and violence.

Haltrecht, Monty. "In the Shadow of Giants." Rev. of *The Book of Lights. Times Literary Supplement* 28 May 1982: 594.

Describes the plot and contents of *The Book of Lights*. Concludes that Potok has chosen a difficult and exalted theme, but that the development of the hero is not sufficiently related to the experiences he undergoes during his quest; nor are the changes themselves made vivid or interesting. Concludes that for all the emphasis on light, this proves to be a rather glum Odyssey.

Hicks, Granville. "Good Fathers and Good Sons." Rev. of *The Chosen*. *Saturday Review* 29 Apr. 1967: 25-26.

States that one of the most important literary phenomena of recent years is the number of novels written by and about Jews. Comments that this author manages to make his good Jewish boys, as well as Judaism, interesting and to keep his central conflicts accurately presented. Concludes that the result is a fine, moving, and gratifying book.

Hochman, Baruch. "The Jewish Vogue." Rev. of *The Chosen*. *Commentary* Sept. 1967: 107-08.

Calls *The Chosen* a novel written in psychological optative, a wish fulfillment fairy tale concluding with the familiar, sugary projection of desiderated relationships. Calls it not an altogether convincing justification of the ways of fathers with their sons.

Irwin, Michael. "A Full-time Condition." Rev. of *In the Beginning*. *Times Literary Supplement* 9 Apr. 1976: 413.

Argues that in *In the Beginning* the author has miscalculated. Suggests that his patterning is too careful, too insistent. It lacks spontaneity and makes being Jewish look like an exhaustingly full-time condition imposing a conversational style that moves only between the gnomic and the wry. Worse, the hero is insufficiently interesting.

Isaac, Dan. "The Search for the Spiritual Father." Rev. of *The Chosen*. *Dimensions* 2 (Fall 1967): 58-62.

Describes the style as wooden and simple. Complains that it all hinges on the search for one's spiritual father and one's true tribal allegiance. Adds that baseball becomes the perfect symbol of the conflict between Judaism and the American enlightenment.

Kaplan, Johanna. "Two Ways of Life." Rev. of *The Book of Lights*. *New York Times Book Review* 11 Oct. 1981: 14-15.

Describes the novel as a depiction of the melancholy, baffling inner journey of Gershon Loran for whom the fathers have so blasted the planet there is no place left to inherit. Considers the novel full of controversy and enigma, seriousness, and passion.

Kellman, Martin. "Book Reviews." Rev. of *The Chosen*. *Conservative Judaism* 22.1 (1967): 79-81.

Claims that the central conflict of this book constricts the characters fatally, so as to reduce them to allegorical abstractions devoid of life, algebraic symbols that stand for something but not themselves. Says the dialogue is hollow and the symbolic machinery creaks. Adds that this is not to deny the virtues of the book as creative sociology. Concludes that for all its artless, contrived superficiality, the book does inform the Midwesterner, and even brings a nostalgic sigh or *ktechtz* to past and present denizens of its milieu.

Kellman, Steven G. "Light Reading." Rev. of *The Book of Lights*. *Midstream* Aug.-Sept. 1983: 58-59.

Discusses *The Book of Lights* as an epistle to the gentiles and as a warning to Jews in process of assimilation. Claims that we are eased into the book because it deals with typically twentieth- century tensions. Complains that Potok is unsubtle in his manipulation of symbols, drawn to sententious comments, and always deadpan.

Lask, Thomas. "The Heir and His Heritage." Rev. of *My Name Is Asher Lev*. *New York Times* 21 Apr. 1972: 37.

Discusses the theme—the isolation of the artist from society—played out in the world of Hasidism. Describes the major characters, and concludes that it would have been a greater accomplishment if it weren't for Potok's primer style.

Lehmann-Haupt, Christopher. "New Promises, Familiar Story." Rev. of *In the Beginning*. *New York Times* 3 Dec. 1975: 43.

Argues that through the series of incidents David Lurie encounters, Potok explores the nature of evil in human affairs and how Jews ought to respond. However, many of these things are random. Claims that what it all really boils down to is a series of conflicts between orthodox and modern approaches to scripture. Concludes that beneath all the surface complexities it is the same old Potok story all over again.

Leviant, Curt. "The Hasid as American Hero." Rev. of *The Chosen*. *Midstream* Nov. 1967: 76-78, 80.

Calls the writing of *The Chosen* pseudo-literary, ridicules the obvious symbolism, and accuses Potok of being more scholar than imaginative writer. Complains the prose is flat and cliché-ridden, and the dialogue and exposition lacking.

Leviant, Curt. Rev. of *The Promise*. *Saturday Review* 20 Sept. 1969: 37-38.

Describes *The Promise* as a book burdened with the same protagonist and the same unvital prose as its predecessors. Complains about the monochrome, mono-rhythmed rhetoric which gives dubious unity to the novel; then about the purposeless running literary allusion from Joyce, with the fancy epigraphs from Pascal, Kafka, Joyce, the Midrash, and the Rebbe of Kotzk. Crowning all this is an irritating Hemingway style. Concludes that in this book one looks in vain for a touch of poetry, the imaginative slant, or extra-dimensional quality that makes reading a delight.

Maddocks, Melvin. "A Genius Grows in Brooklyn." Rev. of *My Name Is Asher Lev*. *Life* 14 Apr. 1972: 20.

Argues that this novel reads like a manuscript found under a cornerstone of Brooklyn's oldest subway and then translated. Claims that Potok is a cross between neo-innocence and early Hemingway. Concludes that Potok finally persuades the emancipated reader that a real live civil war rages in the heart of the community and that the individual is torn between being God's man and himself.

Merling, Bernard. "Overshooting the Target." *Jewish Life* Mar.-Apr. 1970: 56-59.

Calls *The Promise* a tableau of ideas whose major characters have been mightily influenced by ideologies they were born into—and their interrelationships. Sees it as a sharply polemical work touching the entire Jewish community. Discusses the contents, and concludes with a detailed argument concerning whether or not Orthodoxy has become ossified or reached an impasse.

Merling, Bernard. "Too Good to Be True." Rev. of *The Chosen*. *Jewish Life* Jan.-Feb. 1968: 63-66.

Describes *The Chosen* as a beautiful story which, unfortunately, is too good to be true. Comments that it is neither as ideal, nor as fanatic as Potok portrays it to be. Wants to know where the confused and ignorant irreligious Jews are who also people this world. Complains that orthodox Judaism is always presented as something to break away from and that the beauty of the Torah's way of life never really shines through.

Milch, Robert J. Rev. of *My Name Is Asher Lev*. *Saturday Review* 15 Apr. 1972: 65-66.

Describes the deluge of Jewish writing in the last several decades, and distinguishes Potok as a writer for whom Judaism is a living, complex force, not a simple matter of garbled, nostalgic recall. Sees this novel as superior to the rest because the auctorial voice is not nearly so prominent. Calls the style heartfelt and straightforward.

"More Chicken Soup." Rev. of *The Chosen. Time* 21 Apr. 1967: 107, 110.

Describes *The Chosen* as a book about the way things were not rather than the way they were, and more's the pity. Provides a very thorough plot summary.

Murray, James G. Rev. of *The Promise. America* 4 Oct. 1969: 274.

Sees the novel as interesting, but fraught with artistic difficulties because the quality of philosophical interior meditation mitigates against firm character development. Calls the plot wooden and the characters silly, but concedes that the issues raised, historical background, and social commentary are excellent.

Nissenson, Hugh. "The Jews Have Long Since Embarked." Rev. of *The Promise. New York Times Book Review* 14 Sept. 1969: 5, 21.

Describes *The Promise* as a brilliantly conceived book in which the psychiatrically ill Gordon child becomes the *doppelganger* character for Danny and Reuven's hostility and ambivalence toward their own fathers, and the parallel conflicts each is experiencing with Judaism. Suggests that all the males in the novel put themselves on the line and take enormous risks in order to realize human development. Faults Potok for his craftsmanship and frequent reluctance to dramatize.

Nissenson, Hugh. "My Name is David Lurie." Rev. of *In the Beginning. New York Times Book Review* 19 Oct. 1975: 36, 38.

Describes *In the Beginning* as an intelligent *bildungsroman* about the issues of the book of Genesis. Comments that the book's structure is a technical accomplishment with well-handled flashbacks and much intensity. Concludes that the mythic elements are superbly manipulated, while the sexual elements are handled too reticently.

Nissenson, Hugh. "The Spark and the Shell." Rev. of *The Chosen. New York Times Book Review* 7 May 1967: 4-5, 34.

Calls the style of *The Chosen* rough and unpolished, although this is transcended by the configuration of events which make up this story. Suggests that what really fascinates and transcends the book is the essence of God's silence and the beautifully contrapuntal relationship between the two boys.

Pfeffer, Susan Beth. "Chaim Potok's Flawed Sequel." Rev. of *The Promise. Congress Bi-Weekly* 21 Nov. 1969: 21-22.

Finds this novel inferior to *The Chosen*, largely because the first-person point of view results in the story being more about Reuven than Danny, who is actually the more interesting character. Suggests that Potok also has difficulty with women, with his style, and with his interruptions to identify the use of Hebrew and Yiddish phrases. Concludes that had Potok developed both stories separately and equally, he would have written a fascinating novel instead of leaving his readers unsatisfied.

Pinsker, Sanford. "Portrait of the Hasid as Artist." Rev. of *My Name Is Asher Lev. Jewish Spectator* Nov. 1972: 29-30.

Recounts the plot and its Oedipal conflicts with conspicuously absent or sternly authoritarian Hasidic fathers and neurotic and saintly Hasidic mothers.

R., D. H. Rev. of *Davita's Harp. West Coast Review of Books* May 1985: 34.

Describes the story, and concludes that if there is incongruity, it is part of the charm and grace of Potok's weaving. His story emerges as a whole and most impressive tapestry.

Rabinowitz, Dorothy. "Sequels." Rev. of *The Promise. Commentary* May 1970: 106, 108.

Finds Potok a yarn spinner who knows what a plot is. Claims that his problem is his sensibility represented in his language, which is Jewish-American genteel and academic to the bone. Complains of a special form of intrusive, genteel, educational psychologizing, along with a heavily explicit rendering of every thought of every character who has one.

Ratner, Rochelle. "Variations on a Theme." Rev. of *Davita's Harp. Midstream* Mar. 1986: 60-61.

Criticizes the plot for being simplistic, and argues that this is Potok's sixth try at the same book. A lengthy essay covering all main aspects of the novel. Concludes that the conflicts are not developed far enough.

Reed, J. D. "Illuminations." Rev. of *The Book of Lights. Time* 19 Oct. 1981: 102.

Argues that *The Book of Lights* is written in excessively plain prose, but neither the cast nor the text is simple. Comments that Potok knows that personal illuminations, like those of physics, are transitory, and must be discovered again and again, generation after generation. Concludes ironically, that it is the sense of impermanence that grants the novel its sense of durability and makes it, literally, a book of lights.

Reed, Susan. "The Melody of *Davita's Harp* May Be New, But Author Chaim Potok's Judaic Themes Are Familiar." Rev. of *Davita's Harp*. *People Weekly* 6 May 1985: 81-82, 84.

Explains the source of the title of the novel (a door harp bought by the Potoks in Vermont), briefly describes the plot, and points out his popularity among non-Jewish readers. Deals mostly with Potok's life, his writing, his success, and his reception by Jews.

Ridley, Clifford A. "In Its Sequel, Chaim Potok Surpasses *The Chosen*." Rev. of *The Promise*. *National Observer* 29 Sept. 1969: 31.

Comments that *The Promise* manifests humanity and compassion. Sees the narrative as more complex than *The Chosen*, with a richer thematic structure and more detailed evocation of character. Describes the plot.

Ridley, Clifford A. "Novelist Chaim Potok: A Writer Who Happens to Be a Rabbi." Rev. of *My Name Is Asher Lev*. *National Observer* 20 May 1972: 23.

Considers *My Name Is Asher Lev* a Jewish novel in subject, if not in implications. Describes an interview with Potok, and describes also his previous novels.

Ridley, Clifford A. "Potok and Singer: The Link is the Past." Rev. of *In the Beginning*. *National Observer* 29 Nov. 1975: 23.

Compares Singer and Potok as writers through their love of the past. *In the Beginning* and *Passion* are both treated and compared in terms of settings, tone, characters—but mostly in terms of their treatments of the Jewish past.

Rosenbaum, Stanley N. "Books." Rev. of *The Book of Lights*. *Christian Century* 17 Feb. 1982: 184-85.

Criticizes the author's obsessive light symbolism in the book, but admires its bravery of style. Considers that ultimately the book fails rhetorically despite Potok's skill. Concludes that whatever one may think of it as philosophy, as a novel it fails to come off.

Schachter, Stanley J. "Books." Rev of *The Chosen. Reconstructionist* 7
    July 1967: 28-29.

Describes *The Chosen* as anti-sick, anti-vulgar, and dealing with the ideological battle within Jewish life, and the Jewish scholar as hero.

Schmidt, Sandra. "Passage to Manhood: Sight Becomes Insight." Rev. of
    The Chosen. Christian Science Monitor 20 July 1967: 5.

Claims that the intense life of this book resists explanation, and commends it for its lack of *schmaltz*. Describes the contents in detail.

Shapiro, Karl. "The Necessary People." Rev. of *The Chosen. World
    Journal Tribune Book Week* 23 Apr. 1967: 4, 12.

Views *The Chosen* as a deeply considered exegesis of modern Judaism.
Sees the plot as strong and graceful, though slight. Concludes that the
theme—the world must replace its Jews—is the message of this novel.

Sherman, Bernard A. "Books." Rev. of *The Chosen. Chicago Jewish
    Forum* 26.3 (1968): 215-16.

Calls *The Chosen* an old-fashioned novel of quiet relationships narrated
in straightforward fashion. Claims that its dilemma is how to present theology and history in a novel, and how to keep the secondary figures from
becoming stock characters. Concludes this to be a consistently humane
treatment of a serious, unhackneyed theme.

Silver, Marc. "Potok's Women." Rev. of *Davita's Harp. Jewish Monthly*
    Mar. 1985: 32, 34.

Argues that in the end neither Davita nor her mother are as clearly characterized as their male counterparts. Suggests that this is little more than
a drag version of Potok's previous sagas.

Stampfer, Judah. "The Tension of Piety." Rev. of *The Chosen. Judaism*
    16.4 (1967): 494-98.

Describes the contents of the novel in terms of the tensions which exist
within the society of the pious. Concludes that the book is at its strongest
as a rendition of yeshiva life with its sober wrestling with decency and
fanaticism.

Stark, Irwin. "Fathers and Sons." Rev. of *The Promise. Hadassah
    Magazine* Oct. 1969: 25-26.

Describes *The Promise* as one more Potok exploration of the father-son relationship so central to Judaism. Sees the conflict, complication, climax, and resolution as irresistible and old-fashioned. Considers the whole thing glibly arrived at, full of characters who are prototypes rather than people.

Stern, David. "Two Worlds." Rev. of *My Name is Asher Lev.* *Commentary* Oct. 1972: 102, 104.

Complains that in *My Name is Asher Lev* the heroes move from the religious to the secular under the spell of an aimless, even gratuitous inevitability. Claims that Potok has been unsuccessful in depicting the double life and its pain. Concludes that as a novelist Potok lacks imaginative richness and narrative strength.

Stiller, Nikki. "Art Is and Affliction." Rev. of *The Gift of Asher Lev.* *New York Times Book Review* 13 May 1990: 29.

Comments on the central conflicts in *The Gift of Asher Lev*, and complains that the book offers simplistic answers. Concludes that for all the distance Asher Lev has come, he might as well have stayed in Brooklyn's Eastern Parkway.

Toynbee, Philip. "Fathers and Sons." Rev. of *The Chosen.* *New Republic* 17 June 1967: 21-22.

Notes the intellectual disposition of all the characters in *The Chosen*, and considers Potok as operating on the border of sentimentality. Considers much of the writing feeble although he paints with impressionistic skill. Concludes that, despite these shortcomings, this is a fascinating book.

"Trying to be Jewish." Rev. of *The Chosen.* *Times Literary Supplement* 31 Aug. 1967: 777.

Considers *The Chosen* to be a distinct addition to the literature of Jewish self-exploration. Details the contents briefly.

Wiesel, Elie. "A Shtetl Grows in Brooklyn." Rev. of *The Chosen.* *Hadassah Magazine* Apr. 1967: 13.

Describes the survival of the Eastern European *shtetl* in Brooklyn and its depiction in *The Chosen*. Claims that the book's power is its purity and immunity from vulgarity.

Wohlgelernter, Maurice. "Between Promise and Fulfillment." Rev. of
   The Promise. American Zionist Dec. 1969: 40-42.

Reviews the plot and theme of the novel, finding them too similar to *The Chosen*. Also finds a lack of awareness of the central aspect of Hasidic life and life in general—a sense of humor, and a misalliance of theme and style. Concludes that the work is more journalism than literature, and not good journalism at that.

Zancanella, Don. Rev. of *Davita's Harp. English Journal* Nov. 1985: 92.

Sees the novel as difficult for young readers, richly complex psychologically, written in slow but powerful style, and very honest in its discussion of the traumas of growing up in a family with the personal dimensions of political and religious conviction.

Zeitlin, Naomi. "Fathers and Sons." Rev. of *The Chosen. World Jewry*
   Sept.-Oct. 1967: 30.

A brief comparison of the novel to Cohen's *The Carpenter Years* and Gold's *Fathers*.

Zucker, David Jeremy. "Chaim Potok: Always the Same." Rev. of
   Davita's Harp. Jewish Spectator 50 (Sum. 1985): 53-54.

A review of *Davita's Harp* which accuses Potok of using old plots and formulas, resulting in a book that is vintage Potok, but finally unconvincing. Recounts the plot and characters.

Interviews

Abrams, Alan. "When Cultures Collide." *Detroit Jewish News* 22 June
   1984: 13, 41, 54-55.

An interview with Potok in which he discusses the film version of *The Chosen*, the chances of *My Name is Asher Lev* being filmed, writing film scripts, living in Jerusalem, working for the Jewish Publication Society, the autobiographical aspects of the books, core-to-core culture conflict, the writing of *Davita's Harp*, work to date on his Jerusalem novel, his intentions in writing about the Holocaust, the influence of Joyce, the translations of his books, and his personal reading tastes.

Forbes, Cheryl. "Judaism Under the Secular Umbrella: An Interview
   with Chaim Potok." *Christianity Today* 8 Sept. 1978: 14-17, 20-21.

In this interview Potok discusses: the theology in his novels, definitions of Jewishness, his own beliefs, the relationship between Judaism and the evangelical Christian church, his aesthetic values, mysticism, Jewish origins in ancient Sumeria, the history of Jewish persecution, secular humanism, his commitments as a teacher, Bible criticism, the Arab-Israeli conflict, anti-semitism, the Jewish view of the historical Jesus, and his exit from Jewish fundamentalism.

Kauvar, Elaine M. "An Interview with Chaim Potok." *Contemporary Literature* 27.3 (1986): 291-317.

An interview in which Potok discusses: his relationship with his audience; the importance of meaning; definitions of the novel; Freud; the experience of reading Joyce, Mann, and Waugh; a possible sequel to *Davita's Harp*; the structural similarity of all the novels; central metaphors; painting and aesthetics; early life; Picasso; the modern artist; Roth and Zuckerman; the Jewish writer; Jewish assimilation; Harold Bloom and Kabbalah; isolation and silence; the dark side; using a female protagonist; feminism and orthodox Judaism; reading Dos Passos; his own Judaism; Oriental culture; and present-day considerations.

Kremer, S. Lillian. "A Conversation with Chaim Potok." *Dictionary of Literary Biography Yearbook: 1984.* Ed. Jean W. Ross. Detroit: Gale, 1985. 83-85.

In this brief interview Potok discusses his writing methods, difficulties, wish list of topics, interest in music and painting, father's reaction to his writing career, method of character construction, debt to Evelyn Waugh and others, and reactions to the critics.

Kremer, S. Lillian. "An Interview with Chaim Potok, July 21, 1981." *Studies in American Jewish Literature* [Albany] 4 (1985): 84-99.

In this interview Potok discusses: his Hebraic learning, the fusion of Jewish theological seminary with Western liberal traditions, his sparse treatment of women, the potential use of Arab-Israeli conflict in his novels, New Criticism, Hasidic response to his novels, his experience as an army chaplain, the writing of *Wandering*, autobiographical elements of the characters, his treatment of the Holocaust, the optimism of his characters, his first female protagonist, the maturing of his craftsmanship in later novels, his affinity with other Jewish writers, and his Anglo-European literary forbearers.

Lindsay, Elaine. "Chaim Potok: Interview." *Literature in North Queensland* 6.3 (1978): 68-70.

Potok discusses in this essay why he writes, how much of his work is based on personal experience, the conflicts within the Jewish situation, the conflict between moral and aesthetic blindness, the lack of Jewish artistic tradition, the Jew as artist, and the price of being a writer.

Morgan, Doug. "When Culture Confronts Faith: An Interview with Chaim Potok." *College People* Oct. 1983: 8-13.

An interview in which Potok defines core-to-core culture conflict; illustrates this with examples from his novels, references to the Kabbalah in *The Book of Lights,* apocalyptic literature, and this novel. Discusses also his sense of history as a Jew, his work for the Jewish Publication Society of America and its translation of the Hebrew Bible, his feelings about the making of the movie *The Chosen,* his belief in Sabbath observance, and the difficulty of religious groups to maintain identity and tolerance of others at the same time.

Ribalow, Harold U. "A Conversation with Chaim Potok." *The Tie That Binds: Conversations with Jewish Writers.* Harold U. Ribalow. San Diego: Barnes, 1980. 111-37.

In this interview Potok discusses: his surprise about becoming a bestseller writer, the place of the imagination in Jewish life, reading Alan Sillitoe, his fan mail, the effects of his books on non-Jews, the richness and wealth at the heart of paganism, Freudian theory, Western secular humanism, early life as student and beginning writer, reading Evelyn Waugh, his definition of a Jewish-American writer, his life in Israel, his respect for Israeli writers, his career as an editor, firsthand experience of the Hasidim, how the novels are planned, Judaism and the crucifixion, anti-Semitism, the underlying symbolic structure of *The Chosen,* problems in characterizing several of the protagonists, illegal yeshivas in Russia, his own experiments with painting, the process of revision and stripping down the prose, seeing the Pieta for the first time, Biblical criticism, his views on Ozick, and finally, his attitudes toward his own success.

Shelton, Ken. "Writer on the Roof." *BYU Today* Apr. 1983: 9-11.

A general appreciation of Potok's values, and a description of the core-to-core conflict within Judaism at the heart of his novels. Contains reportage from a campus presentation given by Potok.

Speers, W. "Chaim Potok: He Quietly Built a Reputation; Now He Is
Going Public." *Philadelphia Inquirer* 11 Apr. 1983: 1C, 4C.

An interview touching on Potok's painting, background, doubts, and
writing methods.

Biographical Sources

Bannon, Barbara A. "Authors & Editors." *Publishers Weekly* 3 Apr.
1967: 25. Rpt. in *The Author Speaks: Selected PW Interviews, 1967-
1976.* New York: Bowker, 1977. 127-28.

Provides a general biographical overview of Potok's life and work.

Kremer, S. Lillian. "Chaim Potok." *Twentieth-Century American-Jewish
Fiction Writers.* Ed. Daniel Walden. Detroit: Gale, 1984. Vol. 28 of
Dictionary of Literary Biography. 94 vols. to date. 1978- . 232-43.

More than details of his life, this is a career biography, tracing the development of the author's canon, describing the themes and contents of his
works, evaluating his reputation, and placing him in the larger context of
American literary history. Includes lists of primary and secondary
sources and illustrations.

Potok, Chaim. "Culture Confrontation in Urban America: A Writer's
Beginnings." *Literature and the American Urban Experience: Essays
on the City and Literature.* Eds. Michael C. Jaye and Ann Chalmers
Watts. New Brunswick: Rutgers UP, 1981. 161-67. Papers presented
at the Conference on Literature and the Urban Experience. Rutgers U,
Apr. 1980.

Potok discusses growing up in the Bronx of the 30s and 40s and the
impact on his writing.

Potok, Chaim. "The First Eighteen Years." *Studies in American Jewish
Literature* [Albany] 4 (1985): 100-106.

Potok describes his current concerns and the first eighteen years of his
creative life by reviewing what he hoped to achieve in each of the novels. Describes this as a turning point in his career as a writer.

Bibliographies

Fagerheim, Cynthia. "Chaim Potok: A Bibliographic Essay." *Studies in
American Jewish Literature* [Albany] 4 (1985): 107-20.

Dissertations

Clarke, Loretta Marie. "A Critical Approach to Four Novels of Adolescence." Diss. The U of Iowa, 1970.

Gregory, Thomas West. "Friendships Between Adolescent Males in Selected American Novels from 1945 to 1970." Diss. The U of Iowa, 1972.

Woolf, M. P. "A Complex Fate: Jewish-American Experience in the Fiction of Leslie Fiedler, Edward Wallant, Chaim Potok and Jerome Charyn." Diss. U of Hull, 1981.

Isaac Rosenfeld
1918 – 1956

Primary Sources

Novels

Passage from Home. New York: Dial, 1946; London: Secker, 1947;
Cleveland: Meridian-World, 1961; Masterworks of Modern Jewish
Writing Series. New York: Wiener, 1988.

Collected Works

Alpha and Omega: Stories. New York: Viking, 1966; Toronto:
Macmillan, 1966; London: MacGibbon, 1966.

Contents: The Hand That Fed Me; My Landlady; Joe the Janitor; The
Colony; The New Egypt; The Misfortunes of the Flapjacks; The
Brigadier; The Railroad; The Party; The Fireman, His Story; Three
Parables and a Dissertation; Alpha and Omega; An Experiment with
Tropical Fish; George; Coney Island Revisited; Wolfie; King Solomon.

Preserving the Hunger: An Issac Rosenfeld Reader. Ed. Mark Shechner.
Detroit: Wayne State UP, 1988.

Contents: Coney Island Revisited, George, The Hand That Fed Me, King
Solomon, The Misfortunes of the Flapjacks, The Party, The Railroad,
Red Wolf, Wolfie, The World of the Ceiling.

Short Fiction in Anthologies

"The Boys." *The Midstream Reader.* Ed. Shlomo Katz. New York: Yoseloff, 1960. 398-422.

"The Brigadier." *The Realm of Fiction: 65 Short Stories.* Ed. James B. Hall. New York: McGraw, 1965; 2nd. ed. 1970; 3rd. ed. 1977. 466-72.

"The Hand That Fed Me." *Modern Jewish Stories.* Ed. Gerda Charles. London: Faber, 1963. 180-95; Englewood Cliffs: Prentice, 1965. 223-43; *Jewish-American Literature: An Anthology.* Ed. Abraham Chapman. New York: Mentor-NAL, 1974. 84-98.

"King Solomon." *Stories of Modern America.* Eds. Herbert Gold and David Stevenson. New York: St. Martin's, 1961. 369-83; *Great Jewish Short Stories.* Ed. Saul Bellow. New York: Laurel-Dell, 1963. 351-67; *Jewish-American Stories.* Ed. Irving Howe. New York: Mentor-NAL, 1977. 67-81.

Short Fiction in Periodicals

"Bazaar of the Senses." *Commentary* Feb. 1946: 36-42.

"The Boys." *Midstream* 4.2 (1958): 41-60.

"George." *Partisan Review* 19.4 (1952): 410-19.

"The Hand That Fed Me." *Partisan Review* 11.1 (1944): 22-36.

"A Jewish Family." Trans. from Yiddish by Philipp Veit. *Prooftexts* 2.2 (1982): 145.

"King Solomon." *Harper's* July 1956: 55-62.

"The Knife." Trans. from Yiddish by Philipp Veit. *Prooftexts* 2.2 (1982): 135-42.

"The Misfortunes of the Flapjacks." *Harper's* June 1947: 556-61.

"My Landlady." *New Republic* 8 Dec. 1941: 803-06.

"The Party." *Kenyon Review* 9.4 (1947): 572-607.

"A Philosophical Approach to Life." Trans. from Yiddish by Philipp Veit. *Prooftexts* 2.2 (1982): 142-43.

"The Railroad." *Kenyon Review* 9.2 (1947): 235-47.

"Red Wolf." *Epoch* 1.3 (1948): 17-27.

"A Tailor." Trans. from Yiddish by Philipp Veit. *Prooftexts* 2.2 (1982): 143-45.

"The World of the Ceiling." *Midstream* 2.1 (1956): 34-38.

Secondary Sources

Articles and Chapters

Baumgarten, Murray. "City Premises." *City Scriptures: Modern Jewish Writing*. Cambridge: Harvard UP, 1982. 144-46.

Argues that in *Passage From Home*, Rosenfeld deals with Jewishness as a sense of homelessness and sadness from which both assurance and violence has forever vanished. Concludes that it is the elegiac ambivalence that structures the novel and echoes its pathos.

Bilik, Dorothy Seidman. "Backgrounds: Literary and Nonliterary." *Immigrant-Survivors: Post Holocaust Consciousness In Recent American Fiction*. Dorothy Seidman Bilik. Middletown: Wesleyan UP, 1981. 11-35.

Reviews the Jewish immigration to America up to the end of World War II. Discusses Cahan's *The Rise of David Levinsky* and Roth's *Call It Sleep*. Reissued in 1960, these two novels have created renewed interest in the Jewish American immigrant past and a post-Holocaust awareness.

Discusses these novels in detail, relating the experiences of their protagonists to the social realities of Jews in American society. Also discusses Rosenfeld's *Passage from Home* as an example of Jewish writers, such as Bellow and Schwartz, who show Jewish writing moving from adolescence to maturity but with their protagonists alienated both from their own Jewish roots and from the dominant culture.

Goldman, Liela. "Source for Saul Bellow's *Mr. Sammler's Planet.*" *American Notes and Queries* Mar.-Apr. 1982: 117-19.

Finds in Rosenfeld's short story "King Solomon" the source for Bellow's Mr. Sammler. In the story Solomon is not a sage but another human being facing the same problems as others, with the problems becoming more pronounced as he ages. Bellow "synthesizes Rosenfeld's idea of Solomon, the discontent, irascible individual, impotent with age, stripped of his royalty" with the biblical presentation of the aged Solomon perceived in his traditional role as the septuagenarian commentator of society who looks back upon his life in an attempt to assess its meaning.

Greenspan, Ezra. "Breaking Away in the Forties." *The Schlemiel Comes to America.* Metuchen: Scarecrow, 1983. 122-37, passim.

Calls Rosenfeld one of three promising young writers of the forties (Schwartz and Bellow were the others) who broke with Jewish orthodoxy, pursued idealism, and cultivated inwardness with unceasing, uncompromising devotion. Details his life, philosophy, fiction, friends, lifestyle, and death. Discusses several of the stories very briefly.

Guttmann, Allen. "Fathers and Sons: Henry Roth and Isaac Rosenfeld." *The Jewish Writer in America: Assimilation and the Crisis of Identity.* Allen Guttmann. New York: Oxford UP, 1971. 55-57.

Compares *Passage from Home* to *Call It Sleep* in scope and quality. Describes the contents of the novel, and compares its protagonist with Stephen Daedelus.

Harap, Louis. "A Literature of Alienation: Schwartz and Rosenfeld." *In the Mainstream: The Jewish Presence in Twentieth-Century Literature, 1950s-1980s.* Louis Harap. Contributions in Ethnic Studies 19. New York: Greenwood, 1987. 91-97.

Sees Rosenfeld as typically Jewish, intellectual, modernist, and Trotskyist. Describes his Kafka-like sensibility, details of his life, views on religion, comparison with Schwartz, *Passage from Home*, Oedipal problems, Jewish upbringing, and general sense of alienation. Discusses several of his stories.

Kostelanetz, Richard C. "The Talent of Isaac Rosenfeld." *Chicago Jewish Forum* (Wint. 1963/64): 145-48.

Provides a brief overview of Rosenfeld's life and literary output. Also critiques the contents of *Passage From Home* as curiously undistinguished in style, technique, and characterization. Objects to several sentimental passages, commends his ideas, approves of the essays, and enjoys his portraits of Ghandi. Concludes that Isaac Rosenfeld was not a major critic either of literature or of his time.

Lyons, Bonnie. "Isaac Rosenfeld's Fiction: A Reappraisal." *Studies in American Jewish Literature* [University Park, PA] 1.1 (1975): 3-9.

Argues that what remains of Rosenfeld's career is more the criticism than the fiction, more the man than the writer. Blames Rosenfeld's friends for the personal legend surpassing the reputation of the writing, and commends several of his pieces. Uses the criticism to provide insight into his own writing. A valuable reassessment of Rosenfeld the writer—a man with moral vision, intellectual precision, formal poise, and breadth.

Malin, Irving. *Jews and Americans*. Crosscurrents/Modern Critiques. Carbondale: Southern Illinois UP, 1965. passim.

Treats seven Jewish authors, including Rosenfeld, who deal with the Jew in America and face their own Jewishness. Discusses how they deal with the Jewish social, religious, and psychological experience. Devotes chapters to the ideas of exile, fathers and sons, time, head and heart, transcendence, irony, and fantasy and parable in the Jewish-American experience as demonstrated in their works.

Shechner, Mark. "From Isaac Rosenfeld's Journals." *Partisan Review* 47.1 (1980): 9-28.

An introduction to excerpts from Rosenfeld's journals of the 1950s which discusses his early promise as a fiction writer, his association with *Partisan Review*, the influence of Wilhelm Reich's theories on the sexual basis of life, and his unsuccessful struggles to become the novelist he wanted to be. The excerpts from the journals published here are different from those in the *Salmagundi* article.

Shechner, Mark. "Introduction to 'Yiddish Fables'." *Prooftexts* 2.2 (1982): 131-34.

A remarkable essay that functions as introduction, critical appraisal, and obituary for Isaac Rosenfeld. Describes his association with the *Partisan Review* crowd, his major works, untimely death, reputation in the afterglow of the era, and his vivid and magnetic personality. Provides a detailed critical introduction to his three *Yiddish Fables* published in 1959.

Shechner, Mark. Introduction. *Passage from Home*. New York: Wiener, 1988. Rpt. as "Isaac Rosenfeld's *Passage*" in *The Conversion of the Jews and Other Essays*. New Directions in American Studies. London: Macmillan, 1990. 17-30.

Describes the content, style, tone, characters, and plot of *Passage from Home*. Also comments on its depiction of Jewish family life in extremis and this novel in relation to many other novels in the same vein.

Shechner, Mark. "Isaac Rosenfeld's World." *Partisan Review* 43.4 (1976): 524-43.

Argues that Rosenfeld's career was a small one, and that its importance stands apart from the weight of its achievements. Claims he offers a fierce lucidity that belongs to distillations and miniatures, while his career is emblematic, standing for larger historical designs. Notes that his history took place under the shadow of an extraordinary history, one that included the betrayal of the Russian Revolution, the failures and eventual collapse of the American left, the rise and defeat of Hitler, and the massive embourgoisement of Jews in America. Concludes that he became the sort of Jew and writer that his age demanded.

Shechner, Mark. "The Journals of Isaac Rosenfeld: Introduction." *Salmagundi* 47-48 (1980): 30-47.

This introduction precedes excerpts from Rosenfeld's journals. Focuses primarily on his psychological and philosophical ideas. This same introduction was later used as the beginning pages of Shechner's introduction to Rosenfeld's *Preserving the Hunger* (see below). The excerpts from the journals published here are different from those in the *Partisan Review* article.

Shechner, Mark. "Preserving the Hunger: Isaac Rosenfeld." *After the Revolution: Studies in the Contemporary Jewish American Imagination*. Mark Shechner. Bloomington: Indiana UP, 1987. 102-20. Rpt. in shorter version as Introduction. *Preserving the Hunger: An Isaac Rosenfeld Reader*. Ed. Mark Shechner. Detroit: Wayne State UP, 1988. 21-37.

Describes the intensely painful intellectualism of Rosenfeld, and his attempts to reconcile hedonism, responsibility, fierce conscience, and pleasure while avoiding moral laxity. Describes his attempts at secular grace called gratified desire that could only resolve itself in shame and humiliation—the bedrock of consciousness. A detailed portrait of both the man and his moral/intellectual philosophy.

Sherman, Bernard. "Isaac Rosenfeld." *The Invention of the Jew: Jewish-American Education Novels (1916-1964)*. Bernard Sherman. New York: Yoseloff, 1969. 115-25.

A detailed chapter of biographical criticism on Rosenfeld that also contains a detailed critical treatment of *Passage from Home*.

Solotaroff, Theodore. "Isaac Rosenfeld: The Human Use of Literature." *Commentary* May 1962: 395-404. Rpt. as "The Spirit of Isaac Rosenfeld" in *The Red Hot Vacuum and Other Pieces on the Writing of the Sixties*. Theodore Solotaroff. New York: Atheneum, 1970. 3-21; *Jewish-American Literature: An Anthology of Fiction, Poetry, Autobiography, and Criticism*. Ed. Abraham Chapman. New York: Mentor-NAL, 1974. 638-53; and in expanded form as Introduction. *An Age of Enormity: Life and Writing in the Forties and Fifties*. Ed. Theodore Solotaroff. Cleveland: World, 1962. 15-40.

A major essay describing Rosenfeld as a Greenwich Village seer, academic bohemian, or quintessential Jewish American intellectual. Deals with each of these mystical personas, and begins to correct the picture through a close examination of his thought and literary works. Develops the thesis that Rosenfeld did not believe in T. S. Eliot's influential notion of literature as an escape from personality. Asserts that writing, for Rosenfeld, was a test, a way of putting his reactions and his values through the fire of honesty and clarity.

Wisse, Ruth R. "The American Dreamer." *The Schlemiel as a Modern Hero*. Chicago: U of Chicago P, 1971; Paperback ed., 1980. 82-85.

Discusses the story "The Hand That Fed Me," finding that through the epistolary dialogue, the protagonist voices his despair and makes him aware of his willingness to risk disappointment. In effect, "the process of laying bare his sickness, uncover[s] his commitment to health."

Reviews

Atlas, James. "Golden Boy." Rev. of *Passage from Home* and
  *Preserving the Hunger: An Isaac Rosenfeld Reader. New York Review
  of Books* 29 June 1989: 42-46.

Almost a memoir of Rosenfeld's life and writing career that depicts him
as a golden boy who in his final years turned gloomy, solitary, and died
alone. Discusses the new edition of *Passage from Home,* and describes
its contents, feelings, contribution, and history. Concentrates primarily
on its autobiographical elements.

Dennison, George. "Artist in His Skin." Rev. of *Alpha and Omega.*
  Commentary Nov. 1966: 102-04.

Provides a biographical sketch of Rosenfeld's life, his commitment to
thought, and his mastery of the short story form. Describes *Alpha and
Omega* as a collection of stories in which perhaps only four are successful. Discusses them in turn, and identifies the major thematic issues that
arise in each.

Farber, Marjorie. "Journey into Life." Rev. of *Passage from Home. New
  Republic* 3 June 1946: 809-10.

Comments that, until some future novelist works out a better technique
for drawing more closely our love-hate relationships, *Passage from
Home* must stand as a backward advance—from the Proustian present
toward our psychological past.

Fields, Harold. "Story Without Climax." Rev. of *Passage from Home.*
  Saturday Review of Literature 11 May 1946: 14-15.

Briefly describes *Passage from Home,* and commends its undismissable
story and concerns. Suggests that, as a novel, it lacks a sense of continuity and proceeds pedestrian-like in an atmosphere of unrelatedness
running between detailed episodes and labored delvings into philosophy.
Yet concludes that, even as it fails to provide a climax, it touches upon
important problems.

Howe, Irving. "Of Fathers and Sons." Rev. of *Passage from Home.*
  Commentary Aug. 1946: 190-92.

Calls Rosenfeld a writer of self-perception and talent who in *Passage
from Home* skirts some of the pitfalls of Jewish family fiction and succumbs to others. Suggests that it is neither sentimental reminiscence nor

neurotic retribution, because it explores the ambiguous zones between surface and essence. A lengthy critical essay dealing with character, style, contents, setting, and tone.

Leviant, Curt. "In the Shade of the Kafka Tree." Rev. of *Alpha and Omega. Congress Bi-Weekly* 24 Oct. 1966: 17-18.

Considers the tales in *Alpha and Omega* explorations of the mind and consciousness of such diverse characters as a native leader, a janitor, a general, a railroad man, a fireman, a thinking whore, a WPA writer, and a returnee to Coney Island. Considers them Talmudic, close, precise, and incisive like those of Kafka, even though they are not overtly about Jews. Concludes by praising the virtuosity of Rosenfeld's imagination and the depths of his probing even though, at times, the stories fail to touch the heart.

Rifkind, Donna. "Hunger Artist." Rev. of *Preserving the Hunger: An Isaac Rosenfeld Reader* and *Passage from Home.* New Criterion Nov. 1988: 75-77.

Discusses Rosenfeld's mind and ideas as revealed in his essays and stories collected in the *Reader*, and details briefly the contents of *Passage from Home.* Concludes that it was not his published writings that were his great work, but his personality itself, which was cut off at thirty-eight, leaving him "a kind of minor tragic hero in the history of American intellectual life."

Sullivan, Richard. "Growing Up." Rev. of *Passage from Home. New York Times Book Review* 12 May 1946: 5.

Argues that *Passage from Home* analyses events more than human beings. Notes that there is little narrative compulsion and precise, full, illuminating but slow exposition of the how and why of things and what they signify. Calls the prose warm, neat, and entirely readable. Comments, however, that there is a peculiar insufficiency to the novel because all it results in is a faintly melancholic bewilderment devoid of resolution. Complains further that it is all done in a minor and disappointing tone.

Sundel, Alfred. "In Diogenes' Bathtub." Rev. of *An Age of Enormity: Life and Writing in the Forties and Fifties. New Leader* 3 Sept. 1962: 21-22.

Provides a memoir replete with anecdotal stories as preface to a discussion of the literary qualities and contents of *An Age of Enormity.* Believes Rosenfeld's fiction to be the result of writing with his left hand for meal tickets. Concludes with an explanation of Rosenfeld's rationalism and his humanity.

Trilling, Diana. "Fiction in Review." Rev. of *Passage from Home*. *Nation* 18 May 1946: 606-08.

Calls *Passage from Home* a novel of profound universal meanings. Claims that Rosenfeld's is a fiction writing gift of high order. Remarks that, as a first novel, it has faults, but considers these shortcomings only a minor consequence compared to its major accomplishment—the taking of life at such a high moral pitch.

Biographical Sources

Bell, Daniel. "Isaac Rosenfeld: An Appreciation." *New Leader* 30 July 1956: 21.

A brief essay paying tribute to Rosenfeld's life and writing. Contains useful biographical information which mentions his humor, prankishness, and engaging manner.

Bellow, Saul. Foreword. *An Age of Enormity: Life and Writing in the Forties and Fifties*. By Isaac Rosenfeld. Ed. Theodore Solotaroff. Cleveland: World, 1962. 11-14. Rpt. in *Preserving the Hunger: An Isaac Rosenfeld Reader*. Ed. Mark Shechner. Detroit: Wayne State UP, 1988. 13-16.

An important biographical sketch, tribute, and critical appraisal of Rosenfeld by his close friend, Saul Bellow. An insightful understanding of what Rosenfeld was like, his origins, idiosyncracies, achievements, and talent. Describes the cultural milieu in which he became trapped.

Bellow, Saul. "Isaac Rosenfeld." *Partisan Review* 23.4 (1956): 565-67.

Contains the now famous account of Bellow's personal acquaintanceship with Rosenfeld. Bellow discusses Isaac the man; their experience at the Tuley Debating Club; his room in his father's house near the University of Chicago; his life in Madison, Wisconsin; their sojourn on the West Seventies in New York; his disguise under absurdity; and his triumph in enlarging his own capacities to love.

Kazin, Alfred. "Midtown and the Village." *Harper's* Jan. 1971: 82-89. Rpt. in revised form in *New York Jew*. Alfred Kazin. New York: Knopf, 1978. 35-68.

A memoir about Kazin's personal acquaintance with Rosenfeld through Rosenfeld's wife, Vasiliki, Kazin's secretary. Describes the close association of Rosenfeld and Bellow, their professional expectations of themselves, their intellectual insurrections in New York, and their respective world views at this early stage. A brief but essential biographical sketch of Rosenfeld's early years.

Lyons, Bonnie. "Isaac Rosenfeld." *Twentieth-Century American-Jewish Fiction Writers.* Ed. Daniel Walden. Detroit: Gale, 1984. Vol. 28 of *Dictionary of Literary Biography* 94 vols. to date. 1978- . 252-56.

More than details of his life, this is a career biography, tracing the development of the author's canon, describing the contents and themes of his works, evaluating his reputation, and placing him in the larger context of American literary history. Includes lists of primary and secondary sources and illustrations.

Phillips, William. "Four Portraits." *Partisan Review* 50.4 (1983): 546-47.

Describes his own association with Rosenfeld, his physical appearance, character, and career. Also describes briefly Rosenfeld's favorite topics of conversation, eccentricities, translation abilities, politics, and Reichianism.

Rosenfeld, Isaac. "Under Forty: A Symposium on American Literature and the Younger Generation of American Jews." *Contemporary Jewish Record* Feb. 1944: 34-36.

In response to an invitation to discuss the relationship of his Jewish heritage to his writing, Rosenfeld responds that Jewish writers are aware of their minority status, which creates not only traumas, fears of violence, and defenses against aggression but a feeling that they will be required to account, not for their art, but for their Jewishness. Discusses the advantages to the Jewish writer of being an outsider alienated from the dominant culture: they can observe much hidden from the native eye, they are open to more influences than any other class, they are centrally exposed to all movements in art and thought, many retain a sense of an earlier community, they have experienced directly the insecurity that is a fundamental theme of modern literature, and out of their sufferings may come inevitable moral discoveries that may save the world.

Henry Roth
1906 –

Primary Sources

Novels

Call It Sleep. New York: Ballou, 1934; An Avon Library Book. New York: Avon, 1934, 1968; Paterson: Pageant, 1960; London: Joseph, 1963; New York: Bard-Avon, 1964, 1974, 1976; New York: Cooper Square, 1965, 1970, 1976; Penguin Modern Classics. Harmondsworth: Penguin, 1976, 1983.

Collected Works

Shifting Landscape: A Composite, 1925-1987. Philadelphia: Jewish Pub. Soc. of America, 1987.

Contents: Impressions of a Plumber, If We Had Bacon, Broker, Somebody Always Grabs the Purple, Many Mansions, The Prisoners, At Times in Flight: A Parable, The Dun Dakotas, The Surveyor, Final Dwarf.

Short Fiction in Anthologies

"Heder." *A Golden Treasury of Jewish Literature.* Ed. Leo W. Schwarz. New York: Farrar, 1937; Philadelphia: Jewish Pub. Soc. of America, 1937. 38-44.

"The Surveyor." *The Best American Short Stories, 1967.* Eds. Martha Foley and David Burnett. Boston: Houghton, 1967; New York: Ballantine, 1967. 239-55; *My Name Aloud: Jewish Stories by Jewish Writers.* Ed. Harold U. Ribalow. South Brunswick: Yoseloff, 1969. 408-23; *Jewish-American Stories.* Ed. Irving Howe. New York: Mentor-NAL, 1977. 51-66.

Short Fiction in Periodicals

"At Times in Flight." *Commentary* July 1959: 51-54.

"Broker." *New Yorker* 18 Nov. 1939: 45-48.

"The Dun Dakotas." *Commentary* Aug. 1960: 107-09.

"Family Jacobs." *Transatlantic Review* 27 (1967): 75-81.

"Final Dwarf." *Atlantic* July 1969: 57-61.

"If We Had Bacon." *Signatures: Work in Progress* 1.2 (1936): 139-58.

"Petey and Yotsee and Mario." *New Yorker* 14 July 1956: 70-74.

"Somebody Always Grabs the Purple." *New Yorker* 23 Mar. 1940: 69-70.

"The Surveyor." *New Yorker* 6 Aug. 1966: 22-30.

Secondary Sources

Books

Lyons, Bonnie. *Henry Roth: The Man and His Work.* New York: Cooper, 1977.

Articles and Chapters

Adams, Stephen J. "The Noisiest Novel Ever Written: The Soundscape of Henry Roth's *Call It Sleep.*" *Twentieth Century Literature* 35.1 (1989): 43-64.

Argues that *Call It Sleep* offers many lessons in the verbal evocation of "soundscape." Sees this text as both auditory and visual. Claims that the text evokes David's soundscape on three levels of awareness: on one level it records sound simply as part of the child's general perception, on the second level David reacts to sounds with a wide range of emotions, and on the third level he acts as interpreter as well.

Allen, Walter. Afterword. *Call It Sleep.* New York: Equinox-Avon, 1964. 442-47.

Recounts the history of his first encounter with *Call It Sleep*, its initial reception, and its rediscovery by such people as Alfred Kazin and Leslie Fiedler. Describes the book not as a proletarian novel, but as a psychological novel focusing on the emotional patterns of immigrant life through an examination of David Schearl's life.

Allen, Walter. "American Spokesman." *The Urgent West: The American Dream and Modern Man.* Walter Allen. New York: Dutton, 1969. 97-104.

Along with books by Cather, Farrell, and James, Allen discusses *Call It Sleep* as examples of novels that show the extraordinary complexity of the American relationship with Europe. Suggests that this novel shows us sharply the degradation and the reduction in human dignity, that was often the immigrant's lot when he transplanted himself from an environment with a traditional culture to one with almost none at all.

Allen, Walter. "Two Neglected American Novelists." *London Magazine* ns 2.2 (1962): 77-84. Rpt. as "The Thirties: American" in *The Modern Novel in Britain and the United States.* Walter Allen. New York: Dutton, 1964. 172-75; *Tradition and Dream: The English and American Novel from the Twenties to Our Time.* London: Phoenix, 1964. Hogarth, 1986. 172-75.

Details the publishing history of *Call It Sleep* and its subsequent reception, neglect, and rediscovery. Describes the family circumstances and plot of the novel, its basis in Freudian concepts, the rawness of the slum life depicted, its unique plunge into the mind of a child, Roth's artistry with the flight and with speech.

Altenbernd, Lynn. "An American Messiah: Myth in Henry Roth's *Call It Sleep*." *Modern Fiction Studies* 35.4 (1989): 673-87.

Suggests that the religious theme developed in *Call It Sleep* depicts the birth and childhood of a New World Messiah whose story conflates elements of the Jewish and the Christian traditions. Considers it a version of the birth-of-a-hero myth dealt with by Otto Rank and Joseph Campbell in *The Myth of the Birth of a Hero* (1909) and *The Hero with a Thousand Faces* (1949). A major treatment of the events of the novel in relation to these paradigms as well as the Freudian family drama paradigm.

Baumgarten, Murray. "An Urban Phenomenon." *City Scriptures: Modern Jewish Writing*. Murray Baumgarten. Cambridge: Harvard UP, 1982. 5-10, 33-37, 145-46.

Discusses Roth's *Call It Sleep* to illustrate his idea that the city provides a setting for exploring the ambiguities of Jewish experience, and also becomes the bridge for moving from tradition to modernity and from communal to personal identity. Shows how David Schearl's crossing from Brownsville to Manhattan is a rite of passage where he can "confront his past and raise it to a new level of consciousness." Finds that the ultimate secret of the process is linguistic, with Yiddish, Hebrew, and English all playing a role, and that the power of the novel "derives from the religious force with which David Schearl pursues the immigrant's desire to find a place for himself."

Bellman, Samuel I. "Sleep, Pride, and Fantasy: Birth Traumas and Socio-Biologic Adaptation in the American-Jewish Novel." *Costerus* 8 (1973): 1-12.

Argues that the basic substance of the American Jewish novel has been stressed too heavily. Describes the immigrant's dilemmas, the cross-cultural conflicts, and the high cost of material success. Describes *Call It Sleep* as one of a series of "child as scapegoat" novels with enormous narrative power and Joycean touches. Sees the central protagonist as a mother-oriented Oedipus without many benefits, constantly threatened by his father.

Bilik, Dorothy Seidman. "Backgrounds: Literary and Nonliterary." *Immigrant-Survivors: Post Holocaust Consciousness In Recent*

American Fiction. Dorothy Seidman Bilik. Middletown: Wesleyan UP, 1981. 11-35.

Reviews the Jewish immigration to America up to the end of World War II. Discusses Cahan's *The Rise of David Levinsky* and Roth's *Call It Sleep*. Reissued in 1960, these two novels have created renewed interest in the Jewish American immigrant past and a post-Holocaust awareness. Discusses these novels in detail, relating the experiences of their protagonists to the social realities of Jews in American society. Also discusses Rosenfeld's *Passage from Home* as an example of Jewish writers, such as Bellow and Schwartz, who show Jewish writing moving from adolescence to maturity but with their protagonists alientated both from their own Jewish roots and from the dominant culture.

Dembo, L. S. "David Schearl in the Polyphonic World." *The Monological Jew: A Literary Study*. L. S. Dembo. Madison: Wisconsin UP, 1988. 76-83.

Argues that in *Call It Sleep*, David Schearl is a hypersensitive child, driven by fear and feelings of guilt to obtain knowledge, secular and divine. Concludes that, while the ways he follows are Jewish ones, they do not lead to Jewish conclusions, and one of God's names is never revealed to him.

Diamant, Naomi. "Linguistic Universes in Henry Roth's *Call It Sleep*." *Contemporary Literature* 27.3 (1986): 336-55.

Discusses the many levels language functions on in the novel from territory defining behaviors, use of Yiddish, and contrasting uses of colloquial English. Suggests that the novel is structured around a series of concentric circles determined by linguistic criteria. Concludes that these linguistic universes, however, raise issues of far greater complexity because language in this novel is both a technical resource and thematic material of some importance.

Dickstein, Morris. "Call It An Awakening." *New York Times Book Review* 29 Nov. 1987: 1, 33, 35-36.

Discusses receiving a complete collection of all Roth's writings, letters, and other materials subsequent to *Call It Sleep* from Roth's Italian translator Mario Materassi. Describes briefly Roth's nervous breakdown at the end of the 1930s, and his agonizing conflict with writer's block. Also covers some of the later years with mention of his fascination with Israel and return to Judaism.

Epstein, Gary. "Auto-Obituary: The Death of the Artist in Henry Roth's
  Call It Sleep." *Studies in American Jewish Literature* [University
  Park, PA] 5.1 (1979): 37-45.

Claims that the quest of an eight-year-old boy for transcendence from a
horrible world is so attractive it has caused repeated misreadings of the
novel that perceive him to have achieved that quest out of a desire for
redemption. Argues that, in fact, it is nothing at all like a mystical experience, only one more of a series of delusions and disappointments his
own artist's yearning for beauty has thrust upon him. Concludes that perhaps the event heralds death, and teaches that there is no longer any
motive for attempting to transcend the depravity of the world.

Farber, Frances. "Yiddish Voices in American Jewish Fiction." *Yiddish*
  5.4 (1984): 22-41.

A major article which discusses how Roth, Angoff, Gold, and Bellow
reconstruct the experiences of Yiddish-speaking Jews in America and
evoke the tensions and conflicts brought from the *shtetl* in the lives of
these immigrants and their children. Describes each author's highly individualized style, employing specific techniques in representing the
language of the Jew and in creating what Alfred Kazin has called "the
classic bitterness of Jewish dialogue."

Farr, Cecilia K. "Roth's *Call It Sleep.*" *Explicator* 46.2 (1988): 49-51.

Argues that, while on the surface this novel vividly portrays the strains
of immigrant life, on the symbolic level it typifies the Jews' relationship
with their often vengeful God.

Fein, Richard J. "Fear, Fatherhood and Desire in *Call It Sleep.*" *Yiddish*
  5.4 (1984): 49-54.

Considers *Call It Sleep* the classic portrayal of the Americanized son
who pits himself against the unyielding immigrant father. Concludes that
the novel is haunted by the problem of how the child can become reconciled with the powerful father and the unrelenting harsh forces he comes
to represent in the child's mind.

Fein, Richard J. "The Novelist and His Character: Henry Roth and David
  Schearl." *Studies in American Jewish Literature* [University Park,
  PA] 5.1 (1979): 46-50.

Traces the connection between David Schearl's fascination with power
and control and Roth himself whose long silence has been broken only by

a few minor pieces since *Call It Sleep*. Develops the thesis around Roth's own perceptions of the inadequacy of art in the face of modern realities as the clues to David's motivations and major events in the novel.

Ferguson, James. "Symbolic Patterns in *Call It Sleep*." *Twentieth Century Literature* 14.4 (1969): 211-20.

Sees the novel not so much as proletarian fiction but as the story of the development of a religious sensibility. Concludes that its implications are far more profoundly theological and metaphysical than they are social. Sees the patterns the novel records as those which show growth from estrangement and alienation toward reconciliation, from the limiting and self-defeating desire for stasis toward a full acceptance of the dynamic and paradoxical nature of human experience.

Fiedler, Leslie A. "Henry Roth's Neglected Masterpiece." *Commentary* Aug. 1960: 102-07. Rpt. in *The Collected Essays of Leslie Fiedler*. Leslie Fiedler. 2 vols. New York: Stein, 1971. 2: 271-79; *A Fiedler Reader*. Leslie Fiedler. New York: Stein, 1977. 211-19.

Describes the initial publication of *Call It Sleep* and its reception, the literary climate of the time, other authors prominent on the literary scene, the social ideas of the novel, Roth's childhood biographical material in the novel, and its important theme of redemption. A major interpretive essay which was highly significant in the re-valuation of the novel.

Field, Leslie. "Henry Roth's Use of Torah and Haftorah in *Call It Sleep*." *Studies in American Jewish Literature* [University Park, PA] 5.1 (1979): 22-27.

Argues that one of the structural keys to understanding *Call It Sleep* is the reference to the Torah and Haftorah in the cheder passages. Shows how the Torah selection, coming as it does from one of the five books of Moses, always takes precedence over the Haftorah, which acts as a comparative and prophetic commentary on the Torah portion. Sees the Jethro chapter of Exodus as central to "Coal" and maybe the most important section of all five books since it is about decentralizing authority followed by a revelation. Points out that the Haftorah records a revelation that comes to Isaiah in his early manhood. Applies this to David's subsequent actions.

Freedman, William. "Henry Roth and the Redemptive Imagination." *The Thirties: Fiction, Poetry, Drama*. Ed. Warren French. Deland: Edwards, 1967. 107-14.

Suggests that *Call It Sleep* offers us no patentable answer to the sufferings of David Schearl and his family, but that it does bring us into contact with them as identifiable human beings. Describes the characters, style, and psychological issues explored in the novel. Concludes that, by defying the dark and seeking in it the means of release, David comes to grips with the light found in the midst of darkness.

Freedman, William. "Mystical Initiation and Experience in *Call It Sleep*." *Studies in American Jewish Literature* [University Park, PA] 5.1 (1979): 27-37.

Argues that the theme of redemption undergirds this heavily symbolic psychological novel. Sees the book as focussing on an immigrant Jewish boy who, impelled by a threatening environment and threatened psychic existence, and guided by a symbolic vision that is at once mythic and personal, embarks on a quest for redemption, salvation, and the blazing light of God.

Geismar, Maxwell. "A Critical Introduction." *Call It Sleep*. New York: Pageant, 1960. xxxvi-xlv.

Rejoices in the occasion of the reprinting of *Call It Sleep*. Locates it in the devalued tradition of American Realism and more particularly the era of the 1920s and 1930s. Celebrates the absorbing narrative of the book, its evocation of an old-world Jewish family and structure, and its new world assimilation and conflict. Highlights language, character, plot, and individual episodes within the novel.

Girgus, Sam B. "A Portrait of the Artist as a Young Luther: Henry Roth." *The New Covenant: Jewish Writers and the American Idea*. Sam B. Girgus. Chapel Hill: U of North Carolina P, 1984. 95-107.

A detailed account of Jewish migration from the *shtetl* to the New York ghettoes culminating in the thesis that *Call It Sleep* constitutes a major step toward establishing the tradition of the New Covenant between Jewish writers and intellectuals and the American idea. Suggests that it functions as a paradigmatic Jewish novel of initiation of a boy whose imagination, brilliance, and sensitivity make him an archetype for the Jewish hero of thought. Points out that the story of the youth's rebirth on the streets of New York takes the American frontier narrative myth of regeneration and moves it to the hostile urban environment. Concludes that, moreover, the novel moves inexorably toward a conclusion that rearticulates the rhetoric of the myth of America.

Greenspan, Ezra. *The Schlemiel Comes to America.* Metuchen: Scarecrow, 1983. 43-56, passim.

Provides a useful, interpretive essay on *Call It Sleep* as well as an introductory essay on Roth's early life, talent, subsequent avoidance of writing, and politics.

Harap, Louis. *Creative Awakening: The Jewish Presence in Twentieth-Century American Literature, 1900-1940s. Contributions in Ethnic Studies* 17. New York: Greenwood, 1987. 112-18.

Gives a brief overview of Roth's life, writing, career, Communist Party involvement, and the reasons for his failure to write any novels following *Call It Sleep.* Describes this novel in detail, discussing its symbolism, the use of Yiddish and English, its structure, and its authenticity in depicting Jewish life on the Lower East Side. Also points out why it is not a proletarian novel, showing that it goes beyond merely depicting working-class life, and instead penetrates deeply into the psychology of the child protagonist. Yet, it also "has a universality derived from deep explorations of the particular in which general human problems are illuminated."

Harris, Lis. "In the Shadow of the Golden Mountains." *New Yorker* 27 June 1988: 84-92.

Traces the history of Roth's reputation, the reprinting of *Call It Sleep,* and the recent publication of *Shifting Landscapes,* a collection of stories, essays, letters, and journal entries. Provides a lengthy critical essay on *Sleep* covering setting, characters, influences, psychological awareness, Jewish cultural background, style, and impact. A major essay that attempts to recall a lost masterpiece.

Howard, Jane. "The Belated Success of Henry Roth." *Life* 8 Jan. 1965: 75-76.

Describes Roth's wincing acceptance of the rediscovery and republication of his novel and his life since 1935.

Howe, Irving. "Strangers." *Yale Review* 66.4 (1977): 481-500.

Useful background account of growing up Jewish in New York City in the 1920s. Good background material which briefly mentions Roth.

Inge, M. Thomas. "The Ethnic Experience and Aesthetics in Literature: Malamud's *The Assistant* and Roth's *Call It Sleep.*" *Journal of Ethnic Studies* 1.4 (1974): 45-50.

Argues that what makes this novel great is Israel and the return to Judaism.

Kleederman, Frances F. "The Interior Monologue in *Call It Sleep*." *Studies in American Jewish Literature* [University Park, PA] 5.1 (1979): 2-11.

Argues that Roth creates the illusion of arresting and recording the jumble of images which flow through young David Schearl's mind so that the reader is caught up in the mental experience of a child. Claims that he does this by carefully arranging words in such a way as to suggest the issue of consciousness.

Kleederman, Francis F. "Yiddish Language and Culture in *Call It Sleep*." *Studies in American Jewish Literature* [University Park, PA] 1 (Wint. 1975): 10-20.

Argues that *Call It Sleep* reveals a people in social and linguistic transition. Describes how Roth's use of language reveals this moment in Jewish-American social history.

Knowles, A. Sidney, Jr. "*Call It Sleep*." *Survey of Contemporary Literature*. Ed. Frank N. Magill. Rev. ed. 12 vols. Englewood Cliffs: Salem, 1977. 2: 1045-49.

A standard reference article on *Call It Sleep* listing principal characters, and discussing publishing history and contents, and outlining themes and characters.

Knowles, A. Sidney, Jr. "The Fiction of Henry Roth." *Modern Fiction Studies* 11.4 (1965-66): 393-404.

Provides a publication history of the novel, discusses its rediscovery, and locates it within the tradition of urban naturalism and the *bildungsroman*. Sees it also as a Freudian novel and as a powerful evocation of childhood.

Ledbetter, Kenneth. "Henry Roth's *Call It Sleep*: The Revival of a Proletarian Novel." *Twentieth Century Literature* 12.3 (1966): 123-30.

Sees *Call It Sleep* as the most authentic and compelling expression the American proletariat has ever received. A major article that demonstrates this thesis by examining the period in which it is set, Roth's communism, and the text itself.

Lesser, Wayne. "A Narrative's Revolutionary Energy: The Example of Henry Roth's *Call It Sleep*." *Criticism* 23.2 (1981): 155-76.

Argues that relations among literary, linguistic, and cultural values as they are embodied in texts suggest the source of literature's revolutionary potential. Explores this thesis through an analysis of *Call It Sleep*. A major article, tracing the process of cultural identification functioning within the narrative's struggle among its deconstructive and productive impulses.

Levenberg, Diane. "Three Jewish Writers and the Spirit of the Thirties: Michael Gold, Anzia Yezierska, and Henry Roth." *Book Forum* 6.2 (1982): 233-44.

Describes the writing of *Call It Sleep*, its structure, characters, and symbolism. Also includes biographical information about Roth and his attempts at and plans for writing another novel.

Levin, Meyer. "A Personal Appreciation." *Call It Sleep*. New York: Pageant, 1960. xlvi-li.

In this introduction to the novel, Levin restates his initial opinion of the quality of *Call It Sleep* recounting its contents, intensity, and ideas. Outlines its psychological aspects, marvelling at its ability to increase human understanding through its pure art.

Lyons, Bonnie. "After *Call It Sleep*." *American Literature* 45.4 (1974): 610-12.

Describes what happened to Roth after *Call It Sleep* was published.

Lyons, Bonnie. "'Broker': An Overlooked Story by Henry Roth." *Studies in Short Fiction* 10.1 (1973): 97-98.

Calls this a well-written and engaging story capturing the essence of the ethnic experience of a black truck driver in New York City. Argues that, full of wry humor, the protagonist sees the absurdity of life and delights ruefully in its craziness. Provides a full account of the contents of the story.

Lyons, Bonnie. "Roth's *Call It Sleep*." *Explicator* Oct. 1974: 10.

A brief note on onomatopoeic sounds in *Call It Sleep*, the word *zwank* in particular.

Lyons, Bonnie. "The Symbolic Structure of Henry Roth's *Call It Sleep*." *Contemporary Literature* 13.2 (1972): 186-203.

Outlines the theme of redemption underlying the whole book, developed through an intricate pattern of symbols such as the cellar, picture, coal, and rail motifs, each of which correspond to the four parts or books within the novel.

Mooney, Theresa R. "The Explicable 'It' of Henry Roth's *Call It Sleep*." *Studies in American Jewish Literature* [University Park, PA] 5.1 (1979): 11-18.

Discusses the literal and figurative uses of sleep in Roth's novel as a clue to the "It" in the title. Concludes that "it" is the sleep in which rampant imagination overbalances all voluntary faculties and which David must shake off during the redemptive experience of electric shock.

Nelson, Kenneth M. "A Religious Metaphor." *Reconstructionist* 26 Nov. 1965: 7-16.

Describes the novel as a religious testament. Argues that, for the Jew, in the metaphor of the little, lost boy, the world has become unreliable and untrue. Describes all the major events of the plot as developing a sense of shame in the child and a subsequent sense of the necessity of purification—emblematic of the historic Jewish quest for the humanization of man.

Nilsen, Helge Normann. "The Protagonist in Henry Roth's *Call It Sleep*." *Trondheim Workingpapers* (1982): 1-21. Rpt. as "A Study of the Protagonist in Henry Roth's *Call It Sleep*." *Dutch Quarterly Review of Anglo-American Letters* 13 (1983): 28-41.

Calls the novel visionary prose capable of probing considerable emotional and psychic depths. Argues that it is not a tragic work, but moves toward affirmation and integration. Concludes that, as in Poe and Hawthorne, a tortured psyche inhabits a polarized world in which symbolic extremes include both serenity and nightmares.

Pinsker, Sanford. "Henry Roth - In Galut." *Midstream* May 1980: 57-60.

Deals primarily with *Call It Sleep* and Roth's subsequent withdrawal from the literary scene. Also talks of his tentative efforts to re-enter the scene and the results of Pinsker's personal interview with him in his trailer park in New Mexico. An historically important account.

Pinsker, Sanford. "The Re-Awakening of Henry Roth's *Call It Sleep*." *Jewish Social Studies* 28.3 (1966): 148-58.

Provides the best account of the details surrounding the initial reception and ultimate re-issuing of the novel, along with commentary on current critical interest in the novel. Discusses David as the central protagonist and several of the significant events and characters in the novel.

Place, Ethan. "Henry Roth's Freudian Messiah." *Modernist Studies: Literature and Culture* 2.3 (1977): 37-43.

Outlines the classic Oedipal pattern of David's attachment to his mother. Suggests that actually the novel represents some sort of compendium of Freudian concepts circulating in the intellectual atmosphere of America in the 1930s. A major psychoanalytic treatment of the text.

Redding, Mary Edrich. "Call It Myth: Henry Roth and *The Golden Bough*." *Centennial Review* 18.2 (1974): 180-95.

Argues that a close examination of the recurring patterns and symbols in the novel reveals an extensive system of pagan and folk myths. Insists that this is not to deny the presence of Hebraic myth; in fact, the dramatic impact of the novel is itself a product of the tension between both sets of myths. Sees the Schearles as not only the holy family, but a pagan family; and at the end of the novel, biblical symbols yield to their revolutionary symbolic counterparts, as the ideological soap-box orator supplants the Hebrew prophet. Claims that the key to these symbols is *The Golden Bough* with its information about the symbols surrounding the corn-spirit and other agricultural myths.

Ribalow, Harold U. "Henry Roth and His Novel *Call It Sleep*." *Wisconsin Studies in Contemporary Literature* 3.3 (1962): 5-14.

Traces the psychology of Henry Roth, and provides a formalistic treatment of the novel focusing on the "crack-ups" of many American writers like Roth. Contains material from letters between Ribalow and Roth plus general critical observations about the novel.

Ribalow, Harold U. "The History of Henry Roth and *Call It Sleep*." *Call It Sleep*. New York: Pageant, 1960. xi-xxxv.

This introduction to the reprint edition of *Call It Sleep* delineates the location, historical background, childhood, education, and formation of Henry Roth, author. Describes the initial reviewers' reactions to its publication and its eventual disappearance from literary history. Shows the historical interest in the novel, its reappearance, critical reception, and some information about the author. An important and informative essay on the book, its history, and its author.

Rideout, Walter B. "Art Is a Class Weapon." *The Radical Novel in the United States 1900-1954: Some Interrelations of Literature and Society*. Walter B. Rideout. Cambridge: Harvard UP, 1956. 163-224.

Contains general critical and interpretive observations on *Call It Sleep* as a proletarian protest novel.

Salzman, Jack. "A Note on Roth and *Call It Sleep*." *Midstream* Jan. 1977: 55-56.

Reviews the publishing history of *Call It Sleep*, and its rediscovery. Notes also some additional literary activities and publications by Roth.

Samet, Tom. "Henry Roth's Bull Story: Guilt and Betrayal in *Call It Sleep*." *Studies in the Novel* 7.4 (1975): 569-83.

Describes the movement from terror and alienation to tranquility and reconciliation outlined by many previous critics, and argues for the remainder of the article that David's moments of illumination are essentially bogus—images of betrayal rather than of salvation. Concludes that David's final action can only be towards sleep, a numbed withdrawal.

Saperstein, Jeffrey. "Roth's *Call it Sleep*." *Explicator* 46.1 (1987): 47-48.

Tries to decide whether the crucial question raised by the novel is will David Schearl emerge from his recessive shell, or will he remain forever a disoriented foreigner? Argues that the answer lies in the last paragraph.

Seed, David. "The Drama of Maturation: Henry Roth's *Call It Sleep*." *Etudes Anglaises* 32.1 (1979): 46-55.

Comments that, since it avoids propagandism and a naturalistic assemblage of local details, this novel is more concerned with the maturation of the protagonist, David Schearl. Sees it as the starting point of his journey away from dependence on his mother and towards adulthood.

Sheres, Ita. "Exile and Redemption in Henry Roth's *Call It Sleep*." *Markham Review* 6 (1977): 72-77.

Analyzes symbolically the mystical motif of initial darkness and sin as it is found in "The Cellar"; the prophetic motif of purification for the purposes of communication with God as expressed in "The Coal"; and man's exile in the Lurianic redemption as it is described in "The Rail." Asserts that, though it cannot be proved, Roth understood Lurianic mysticism, and is clearly interested in both private and communal redemption.

Sherman, Bernard. "*Call It Sleep* as a Depression Novel." *The Invention of the Jews: Jewish-American Education Novels (1916-1964).* Bernard Sherman. New York: Yoseloff, 1969. 82-92, passim.

Describes *Call It Sleep* as a book showing a vile world full of oppressive sexuality and which functions somewhat as an underground classic. Provides a biographical and historical account of the novel as well as some explication of the text.

Sokoloff, Naomi. "Discoveries of Reading: Stories of Childhood by Bialik, Shahar, and Roth." *Hebrew Annual Review* 9 (1985): 321-42.

In this major essay on stories from childhood, Sokoloff discusses Roth's *Call It Sleep*, Bialik's *Aftergrowth*, and Shahar's "First Lesson." Compares and contrasts the works and discusses the discovery of reading and tradition in each of these texts as pivotal in their child protagonists' attitudes toward language and religion. Also discusses the artistic implications of this concept.

Walden, Daniel. "Henry Roth's *Call It Sleep*: Ethnicity, 'The Sign,' and the Power." *Modern Fiction Studies* 25.2 (1979): 268-72.

Discusses some biographical details of Roth's life and their relevance to the novel. Suggests that, on a more basic level, this novel is not just autobiographical, but is about the varieties and persistence of ethnicity in the age of energy.

Walden, Daniel. "'Sleep' at the Switch: The Net Effect in *Call It Sleep*." *Studies in American Jewish Literature* [University Park, PA] 5.1 (1979): 18-21.

Argues that the prevailing belief that Anglo-Saxon civilization was the dye with which God would stamp the peoples of the earth is what causes David to experience the island of his own ethnicity in a sea of nationalized Christianity, hence turning to technology for security and energy.

Walden, Daniel. "Urbanism, Technology and the Ghetto in the Novels of Abraham Cahan, Henry Roth, and Saul Bellow." *American Jewish History* 73.3 (1984): 296-306.

Discusses the socio-historical role of the urban ghetto as portrayed in the works of Cahan, Roth, and Bellow. Provides an account of the problems of the "New Immigrant" in the Americanization process, the ghetto conditions in the 1920s, industrialism, electricity, energy, power, and disillusionment as depicted in *Call it Sleep*.

Wirth-Nesher, Hana. "The Modern Jewish Novel and the City: Franz
    Kafka, Henry Roth, and Amos Oz." *Modern Fiction Studies* 24.1
    (1978): 91-109.

Discusses the extent to which the city becomes a central metaphor in these
novels. Says of *Call It Sleep* that its protagonists never lose a sense of urban
alienation. Concludes that Roth uses the child as representative of immigrant status in the novel, but that it is the city that gives the novel its energy.

Yudkin, Leon I. "The Immigrant Experience in America." *Jewish
    Writing and Identity in the Twentieth Century.* Leon I. Yudkin.
    London: Helm, 1982. 27-44.

Discusses the Jewish immigration to America as the most remarkable
demographic event in Jewish history and shows its impact on America as
it emerged as a great world power. Also sees the Jewish writers Cahan,
Lewisohn, Hecht, Fuchs, Michael Gold, and Henry Roth as expanding
the range of an exotic consciousness in America but also showing the
"Jew on the outside trying to get in (in various ways), or perhaps coming
to terms with his outsider status." Discusses the major works of each of
these writers and how these works demonstrate the struggles, the conflicts, and the costs of their Jewish protagonists to become assimilated
into American life.

Reviews

Alter, Robert. "Awakenings." Rev. of *Shifting Landscape* and *Call It
    Sleep. New Republic* 25 Jan. 1988: 33-37.

Describes *Shifting Landscape* as a collection of his short pieces published between 1925-1987. Briefly describes the contents of both books.
Claims that the pieces exhibit flickerings of enormous talent, but hardly
any of them transcend the slightness of a fictional sketch or exercise.
Covers many aspects of Roth's life, writing, personal psychology, and
failed writing career.

Boynton, H. W. "The Story of a Ghetto Childhood." Rev. of *Call It
    Sleep. New York Times Book Review* 17 Feb. 1935: 7.

Claims that *Call It Sleep* is a novel one approaches without much hope.
Suggests thats the outline behind the story is thin despite the rich, polyglot existence of the Lower East Side threaded through it and the
fascinating buildup to David's mystical trial by fire.

Bradbury, Malcolm. "New Novels." Rev. of *Call It Sleep. Punch* 30 Oct. 1963: 647-48.

Calls this novel a long, underestimated work of considerable distinction. Details the early modernist style, contents, and characters. Also describes the Jewish immigrant culture portrayed in the book and the Yiddish language it employs. Considers the life of this book to have been drawn with a delicate responsiveness and an accurate rendering of dialects.

Cohen, Peter. "Journey into Life." Rev. of *Call It Sleep. Spectator* 25 Oct. 1963: 538.

Describes *Call It Sleep* in detail, and praises its penetration to the heart of New York life in the slums like no other book has done. Claims that this is not the usual dribble about the cruel lives of the underprivileged, but is actually a book of great beauty.

"East-Side Story." Rev. of *Call It Sleep. Times Literary Supplement* 25 Oct. 1963: 847.

Describes *Call It Sleep* as powerful, political, Joycean, and competently plotted. Provides a very detailed account of the contents and requisite biographical details about Roth's life which make a good introduction to the novel.

Fleischer, Leonard. "Have You Read?" Rev. of *Call It Sleep. Jewish Heritage* (Spr. 1963): 19-21.

Describes the 1960 reprinting of *Call It Sleep*, and hails it as a novel of major importance. Outlines the publication history of the book, its earlier reception, and its story. Also updates the biographical information on Roth.

Frankel, Haskel. "Awake at Last." Rev. of *Call It Sleep. Saturday Review* 21 Nov. 1964: 29.

Calls *Call It Sleep* one of the finest novels in twentieth-century American fiction. Details the contents of the novel, the publishing history, and Roth's subsequent life. Hails its republication, and reports on Roth's stunned puzzlement about it.

Howe, Irving. "Life Never Let Up." Rev. of *Call It Sleep. New York Times Book Review* 25 Oct. 1964: 1, 60.

Describes the publishing history and initial, critical reception of *Call It Sleep*. Provides a detailed description of its contents, admires the strength of the writing, the powerful urban vignettes, the mythic qualities of the story, the monumental character of Aunt Bertha, and the accuracy of the speech.

Jacobson, Dan. "Jew Light." Rev. of *Call It Sleep*. *New Statesman* 11 Oct. 1963: 495.

Describes the contents of the novel, the theme, the symbolism, and the views of Fiedler and Walter Allen. Finds the book's greatest strength is not its religious or transfigurational aspects, but its realism despite the grimy and disgusting picture of reality it portrays. Concludes that it is a singular and impressive achievement.

Levin, Meyer. "Dusting Off the Bookshelf." Rev. of *Call It Sleep*. *Congress Weekly* 18 Dec. 1950: 12-13.

Provides a detailed history of the original reception of *Call It Sleep*; his own early, high opinions of it; and its contents. Concludes that the book is a fully realized work of art regardless of its status as a first novel. Admires it from a sociological as well as from a psychological point of view.

Ribalow, Harold U. Rev. of *Call It Sleep*. *Chicago Jewish Forum* (Fall 1961): 50.

Describes the history of *Call It Sleep* as remarkable, and its republication as laudable. Comments on the story, redemption themes, symbolism, recreation of an era, and the extraordinary replication on the page of Yiddish English.

Rifkind, Donna. "Call It Irresponsible." Rev. of *Shifting Landscape: A Composite, 1925-1987*. *New Criterion* Feb. 1988: 75-76.

Calls *Shifting Landscape* a book full of protests by Roth that Marxism or communism fell like a shunt across his career. Notes that it comprises Roth's total output since *Call It Sleep*, and that it contains half a dozen complete short stories and published and unpublished interviews and political commentaries. Considers Materassi's idea to publish *Shifting Landscape* irresponsible and insulting.

Syrkin, Marie. "Revival of a Classic." Rev. of *Call It Sleep*. *Midstream* 7.1 (1961): 89-93.

Reviews the initial critical response to *Call It Sleep*, her own heralding of Roth as a major talent, and the subsequent disappearance of Roth from the literary scene. Describes the contents of the book, and gives a retrospective critical essay that focuses on the theme of redemption and the subsequent narrative and symbolic structure of the novel.

Wilson, S. J. "Awaking to Bigger Nightmares." Rev. of *Call It Sleep*. *New York Herald Tribune Book Week* 20 Dec. 1964: 10.

Describes the contents of the novel, and concludes that it is a plot-your-own-ending novel full of poetry, relentless fury, and unfleshed, and unresolved characters. Concludes that the reader must have the practiced eye and forgiving heart of a fine editor.

Interviews

Bronsen, David. "A Conversation with Henry Roth." *Partisan Review* 36.2 (1969): 265-80.

A first-person biographical account of his birth in Galicia in 1906, his childhood and early career as a writer, his subsequent withdrawal, his return to Judaism, and his attachment to Israel. Extremely detailed and pertinent to the study of his novel. Details many of the parallels between his own traumas and those of his fictional persona.

Freedman, William. "A Conversation with Henry Roth." *Literary Review* 18.2 (1975): 149-57.

Reports on Roth's shying away from the public eye, his work history since 1935, love of Israel, current writing project, the cause of his subsequent lifelong writer's block, key episodes in the novel, his indebtedness to Freud, and his return to Brownsville to review the scene of his childhood.

Freedman, William. "Henry Roth in Jerusalem: An Interview." *Literary Review* 23.1 (1979): 5-23.

In this lengthy interview Roth discusses: his first and subsequent visits to Israel, the impressions he formed, and his sense of rediscovering his Jewishness and of now belonging to some collectivity greater than himself. Calls his novel mystical and messianic, describes his writer's block. Talks about the Depression, his brief encounter with Communism, his search for a home, his new book, the failure of diaspora Judaism for him, his conviction that the urge toward the artistic and the transcendent is part of instinctual human nature, and his hopes for the triumph of the Israeli state.

Friedman, John S. "On Being Blocked & Other Literary Matters: An Interview." *Commentary* Aug. 1977: 27-38.

In this interview Roth discusses: the writing of *Call It Sleep*, his parents, life in New York, anti-Semitism, his early childhood attachment to his mother, Eda Lou Walton's early encouragement and his subsequent

flight from her ten years later, graduating from CCNY, the influence of
Synge on the language of the novel, other literary influences, life in
Greenwich Village, contact with other writers of his generation, his communism, being investigated by Hoover, going to Yaddo in 1938, starting
a family, working as a precision grinder for Keystone, moving to Maine,
working as a psychiatric attendant, the impact of Stalin's death, and his
attachment to the state of Israel.

Kaganoff, Penny. "PW Interviews Henry Roth." *Publishers Weekly* 27
    Nov. 1987: 67-68.

An account of the re-publication of *Call It Sleep*. Details Roth's responses to this event, his life since 1935, his opinions on Judaism, and his
rediscovery of his Jewishness through interest in Israel. Contains also
comments by Roth on writers, writing, his lifelong writer's block, and
his current living arrangements.

Lyons, Bonnie. "An Interview with Henry Roth." *Shenandoah* 25.1
    (1973): 48-71.

In this interview Roth discusses: his family relationships as a child, the
biographical parts of the novel, Eda Lou Walton, his politics in the
1930s, his marriage to Muriel, his methods of construction in the novel,
the influence of Freud and Joyce, sources in mythology, the apocalyptic
vision at the heart of the novel, his Jewishness, his mysticism, the beginning of the writer's block, and his present feelings about his relationship
with his father.

Lyons, Bonnie. "Interview with Henry Roth, March, 1977." *Studies in
    American Jewish Literature* [University Park, PA] 5.1 (1979): 50-58.

In this interview Roth discusses: his writer's block, subsequent jobs and
lifestyle, early life and communist politics, preoccupation with mathe-
matics, the influence of Eliot and Eda Lou Walton, response to other
Jewish novelists, the Yiddish point of view, Jewish American literature,
views on Israel, current work, and ideological commitments.

Biographical Sources

Lyons, Bonnie. "Henry Roth." *Twentieth-Century American-Jewish
    Fiction Writers*. Ed. Daniel Walden. Detroit: Gale, 1984. Vol. 28 of
    Dictionary of Literary Biography. 94 vols. to date. 1978- . 257-64.

More than details of his life, this is a career biography, tracing the devel-

opment of the author's canon, describing the contents and themes of his works, evaluating his reputation, and placing him in the larger context of American literary history. Includes lists of primary and secondary sources and illustrations.

Bibliographies

Greenstone, Maryann D. "The Ghetto Revisited: *Call It Sleep* by Henry Roth." *Studies in Bibliography and Booklore* 9 (Spr. 1970): 96-100.

Young, Debra B. "Henry Roth: A Bibliographical Survey." *Studies in American Jewish Literature* 5.1 (1979): 62-71.

Reviews the research and criticism on Roth, and suggests further areas needing study, particularly his stories. Suggests that this may need to wait until they are collected.

Dissertations

Barmor, Yitzhak. "The Father Figure in Jewish-American Literature." Diss. Kent State U, 1988.

Davis, Cheryl Sue. "A Rhetorical Study of Selected Proletarian Novels of the 1930s: Vehicles for Protest and Engines for Change." Diss. U of Utah, 1976.

Kleederman, Frances Farber. "A Study of Language in Henry Roth's *Call It Sleep*: Bilingual Markers of a Culture in Transition." Diss. New York U, 1974.

Laufer, Pearl David. "Between Two Worlds: The Fiction of Anzia Yezierska." Diss. U of Maryland, 1981.

Lyons, Bonnie Kaplan. "Henry Roth: A Critical Study." Diss. Tulane U, 1973.

Nye-Applebaum, Mika. "Restructuring the Beginning: Three Writers in the 30s: The Novels of Michael Gold, Henry Roth, and Daniel Fuchs." Diss. State U of New York at Buffalo, 1980.

Sheres, Ita G. "Prophetic and Mystical Manifestations of Exile and Redemption in the Novels of Henry Roth, Bernard Malamud, and Saul Bellow." Diss. U of Wisconsin, 1972.

Tewarie, Bhoendradatt. "A Comparative Study of Ethnicity in the Novels of Saul Bellow and V. S. Naipaul." Diss. Pennsylvania State U, 1983.

Maurice Samuel

1895 – 1972

Primary Sources

Novels

Beyond Woman. New York: Coward, 1934.

The Devil That Failed. New York: Knopf, 1952; London: Gollancz, 1953.

The Outsider. New York: Duffield, 1921; London: Constable, 1922; Boston: Stratford, 1929.

The Second Crucifixion. New York: Knopf, 1960; London: Gollancz, 1961.

Web of Lucifer: A Novel of the Borgia Fury. New York: Borzoi-Knopf, 1947; London: Hale, 1948.

Whatever Gods. New York: Duffield, 1923.

Short Fiction in Periodicals

"Curly Commits Murder." *American Mercury* Apr. 1936: 464-75; *Fiction Parade and Golden Book Magazine* May 1936: 92-101.

"A Good Place to Eat." *Coronet* Dec. 1936: pag. not available.

"A Reasonable Success." *Forum* July 1935: 54-63; *Fiction Parade and Golden Book Magazine* Nov. 1935: 43-58.

"Unspoken Message." *North American Review* 244.1 (1937): 90-109.

Secondary Sources

Articles and Chapters

Levin, Leonard. "Maurice Samuel: An Appreciation." *Conservative Judaism* 31.1-2 (1976-77): 3-15.

Calls Samuel a man who bridged both worlds of Jewish concern in his day: solidarity with Israel and the quest for roots in the recent Yiddish-speaking past. Notes that Samuel, fated to be one of the least understood Jews of his day, was primarily a Renaissance man of broadly ranging interests, who, for fulfillment, had to participate fully in both the Jewish and general culture of his time, and who could deal fully with the problems of either, except in the context of the other. Claims that, in the general culture, Samuel was especially interested in a cluster of problems raised by modern liberal thinkers, while in literature, he was interested in the modern masters. Argues that these experiences were the principal determinants of his orientation to the world, and that they strongly colored his perception of Judaism, while his response to them was in turn determined by his primary Jewish identity. A major essay tracing the roots of the intellectual influences on Samuel's thinking and writing.

Ozick, Cynthia. Foreword. *The Worlds of Maurice Samuel: Selected Writings*. Ed. Milton Hindus. Philadelphia: Jewish Publ. Soc. of America, 1977. xv-xx;. Rpt. as "Remembering Maurice Samuel" in *Art and Ardor*. Cynthia Ozick. New York: Knopf, 1983. 210-16.

A reminiscence that pictures a lecture hall in New York where Samuel and Erwin Goodenough appeared as discussants and lecturers, and influenced Ozick permanently through their love of Jewish history. A detailed, firsthand account of Samuel's stature, style, presence, and comments. An erudite account of him in the context of Jewish identity and history issues.

Sanders, Ronald. "Maurice Samuel: An Appreciation." *Midstream* 19.2 (1973): 43-64.

Sanders describes his own early academic encounter with Samuel the debunker in the pages of *The Jewish Daily Forward*. Then describes his gradual attempt to learn classical Yiddish through reading Samuel's novels. A lengthy reminiscence covering both Sanders's growth as a self-conscious Jewish scholar, and the role Samuel played in that growth. A major essay providing much formalistic analysis of the majority of the works.

Reviews

Chubb, Thomas Caldecot. "Borgia Lieutenant." Rev. of *Web of Lucifer*. *New York Times Book Review* 23 Feb. 1947: 5.

Calls this a historical and psychological novel written in cloak-and-dagger style with an excellent historical atmosphere. Details plot and characters.

Fuller, Edmund. "Marcella of Rome." Rev. of *The Second Crucifixion*. *New York Times Book Review* 18 Sept. 1960: 4-5.

Describes this as a drama of decadent Rome developed through an unusual narrative device of hearing the heroine imploring Samuel to tell her story. Details the contents.

Goldin, Grace. "Jews and Christians." Rev. of *The Second Crucifixion*. *Jewish Frontier* Jan. 1961: 26-29.

Calls *The Second Crucifixion* a passionate spectacular book which succeeds because of the variety of points of view about history which are expressed at a time when Christianity's history was still fluid and each character still is able to speak for himself. Describes many of the big, spectacular scenes. Claims that, Samuel is honest, convincing, passionate, and partisan, and deserves to be heard by Christian and Jew alike. Concludes that, if he had written in the first century of this era, he would have added an anonymous, prophetic book to Apocryphal literature.

Heston, Charlton. "Anti-Semitism in Second Century Rome." Rev. of *The Second Crucifixion. Chicago Sunday Tribune Magazine of Books* 2 Oct. 1960: 2.

Describes *The Second Crucifixion* as exploring the Rome of Hadrian's reign at the beginning of the second century. Claims that its characters are melodramatic and stereotypical, and the history more-or-less accurate. Sees the end of the story as knotted, jerked tight, and cut off abruptly. Argues that its theme is the dark seeds of anti-Semitism born in the schismatic contentions of small, struggling Christian sects. Argues that it is a book written out of passionate conviction.

Hindle, W. H. "Pioneers in a 'Promised' Land." Rev. of *Harvest in the Desert. Saturday Review of Literature* 19 Aug. 1944: 20-22.

Designates *Harvest in the Desert* as a story about Zionism, Jewish colonization, and the Diaspora. Claims that the story is told sympathetically and with passion. Considers the intrusion of polemics into the human interest stories intrusive to the reader, but inevitable. Discusses Samuel's politics and the complex picture of all the issues as they are developed by the book.

Lee, Charles. "Whoops! A Ton." Rev. of *The Devil That Failed. Saturday Review* 22 Nov. 1952: 19-20.

Calls *The Devil That Failed* an imagination tickler that teases the mind. Finds it a refreshingly intellectual tale of adventure, almost all of whose curious action takes place in one room. Describes the contents, and concludes that there is both cleverness and weight here.

Lehrman, Hal. "A Plea for Humility and Quality." Rev. of *Level Sunlight. New York Times Book Review* 29 Nov. 1953: 18.

Considers this a book by a distinguished writer whose knowledge of Zionism is buttressed by superb prose and the occasional rueful chuckle. Approves of Samuel's assessment of the need for Israeli Jews to understand American Jewry, and concludes that it makes a major contribution to both worlds.

Lowenthal, Marvin. "The Jews and Their Palestine." Rev. of *Harvest in the Desert. New York Herald Tribune Weekly Book Week* 2 July 1944: 4.

Describes *Harvest in the Desert* in detail, and notes that it is dramatic in its implications for the future of Israel. Commends the book for both its historical account of the birth of Israel and its sound analysis.

Lowenthal, Marvin. "Wide Range in Narrow Room." Rev. of *Prince of the Ghetto. New York Herald Tribune Book Review* 19 Dec. 1948: 4.

Describes *The Prince of the Ghetto* as a fictional account of the life of the Yiddish writer, Peretz. Provides a background to the Yiddish literary forefathers of Peretz and an account of the contents of the book.

McGrory, Mary. "Concerning Ideas and Morality." Rev. of *Prince of the Ghetto. New York Times Book Review* 17 Oct. 1948: 43.

Finds this book full of tales of Peretz, a vital moral force among Polish Jews. Claims that these tales show Peretz's love of ancient traditions, his fancy, his gnomic wisdom, his association with fabled animals and tales of the supernatural, and his affection for Chasidism.

Montor, Martha Neumark. "Anti-Semitism Traced from Its Start." Rev. of *The Second Crucifixion. American Zionist* Oct.-Nov. 1960: 9.

Calls *The Second Crucifixion* a carefully crafted historical novel in which research and composition achieve a rare blend. Claims that, however many ages unfold, the characterizations ring of truth.

Nerber, John. "A Dwarf's Revenge." Rev. of *The Devil That Failed. New York Times Book Review* 28 Dec. 1952: 13.

Calls this a cunning, improbable retelling of the Gulliver opus which is nearly successful, but not quite. Concludes that it is only half convincing because Samuel tried too hard to make it credible by paying heed to the master's satire too carefully.

Petuchowski, Jakob J. "Men and Ideas in Conflict." Rev. of *The Second Crucifixion. Congress Bi-Weekly* 2 Jan. 1961: 37-38.

Calls this a gripping tale of love, spiritual and physical, of courage and pathos that brings into focus the entire epoch of the early Christian Church, spelling the death knell for Judeo-Christianity.

R., M. J. "A Tale of Hate Triumphant—And Other New Books." Rev. of *The Second Crucifixion. San Francisco Chronicle This World Magazine* 11 Sept. 1960: 29.

Describes the novel as a Sholem Asch-like novel of love and hate fought by two men for an almost incredibly valorous woman. Claims that it is a skillfully interwoven story of early Christian history, philosophy, and theology. Recounts the story, and comments that although Samuel's humor is regrettably missing, his descriptive word magic is much in evidence in many scenes.

Rubenstein, Richard L. "Historic Conflict." Rev. of *The Second Crucifixion. Midstream* 12.2 (1961): 100-04.

Argues that this book explores the historical factors of the terminal explosion of the conflict in Nazi Germany while perusing its real concern—modern anti-Semitism. Describes the contents of the book in detail while commenting on the success or lack of certain fictional choices. Probes deeply into the validity of Samuel's interpretations of Jewish and Christian history.

Searles, P. J. "Dramatic Novel of Cesare Borgia's Time." Rev. of *Web of Lucifer. New York Herald Tribune Weekly Book Review* 2 Mar. 1947: 5.

Argues that *Web of Lucifer* is a swashbuckling, cloak-and-dagger melodrama about fifteenth-century Italy compounded of battles, duels, intrigues, assassinations, and debaucheries. Notes that Samuel's knowledge of the times is prodigious, and his insight into the human mind commendable.

Spector, Robert Donald. "A Novel of Religious Tensions in the Rome of Hadrian." Rev. of *The Second Crucifixion. New York Herald Tribune Book Review* 18 Sept. 1960: 8.

Calls this an honest appraisal of the religious situation in Hadrian's Rome which sacrifices literary quality for history. Suggests that characterization is ancillary to the theme of anti-Semitism, and that its real subject is the schismatic nature of Jewish theology after the crucifixion of Christ. Concludes that this book lacks dramatic tension because the theological controversy becomes all-absorbing to the author.

Tyler, Parker. "Arts and Letters." Rev. of *Web of Lucifer. Sewanee Review* 55.2 (1947): 338-39.

Argues that *Web of Lucifer* is constructed in equal parts of Borgian passion, Machiavellian morality, and what traditionally passed for human decency. Describes characters and plot.

Wallace, Margaret. "A Novel That Is Freighted with Ideas." Rev. of *Beyond Woman. New York Times Book Review* 30 Sept. 1934: 7.

Calls this a simple story and perhaps overly long book whose very length presents an embarrassment of riches. Notes that it has more ideas than it can contain, and hangs together on the central thread of life's depths and complexities. Details the plot and contents.

Biographical Sources

Alter, Robert. "Maurice Samuel & Jewish Letters." *Commentary* Mar. 1964: 50-54.

Calls Samuel a one-man educational movement in American Jewish life. Provides a complete overview of Samuel's life, writing, teaching, public performances, cultural background, and contribution. A major tribute with valuable summary information of books as well as Samuel's life.

Goldberg, B. Z. "Recollections of Maurice Samuel." Trans. Yuri Prizel. *Yiddish* 2.2-3 (1976): 58-61.

Commends Samuel for the important role he has played in the cultural life of Jewish America, and labels him a pioneer. Describes Samuel's life, some of his books and their impact, his skill as a translator, his speaking ability, and his other media performances.

Montor, Henry. "Maurice Samuel Gets an Award." *Congress Weekly* 28 Apr. 1944: 13-15.

Celebrates Samuel having been granted the Ainsfield Award for the best interracial book of the year by the *Saturday Review of Literature*, and laments that he has not been summarily rewarded by the Jewish people whom he has served for twenty-five years. Provides a thumbnail sketch of Samuel's life and achievements.

"A Tribute to Maurice Samuel." *Reconstructionist* 17 Mar. 1967: 5-6.

Provides a thumbnail sketch of Samuel's life and contribution to Jewish intellectual life in America. Mostly praises him for receiving the Jewish Heritage Award for Excellence.

Van Doren, Mark. "Maurice Samuel: An Appreciation." *United Synagogue Review Quarterly* 25 (Fall 1972): 14-15.

A warm, admiring portrait and reminiscence of Samuel and Van Doren's personal acquaintance with him. Calls Samuel a poet, storyteller, theologian, moralist, raconteur, and commentator, who loved the Bible in a deep, rich, and personal way.

Van Doren, Mark. "Maurice Samuel: A Remembrance." *Conservative Judaism* 26.4 (1972): 13.

An endearing account of Van Doren's first encounter with Maurice Samuel at a summer session of The Eternal Light Program. Comments that no man was more at home in the Bible than Samuel because he was one of its characters, and concludes that no man enjoyed being a Jew more than he did.

Susan Fromberg Schaeffer

1941 –

Primary Sources

Novels

Alphabet for the Lost Years. San Francisco: Gallimaufry, 1976.

Anya. New York: Macmillan, 1974; London: Cassell, 1975, 1976; New York: Avon, 1976; New York: Bard-Avon, 1980, 1986; London: Pavanne, 1986.

Buffalo Afternoon. New York: Knopf, 1989.

The Dragons of North Chittendon. A Little Simon Book. New York: Simon, 1986.

Falling. New York: Macmillan, 1973; New York: Signet-NAL, 1974; New York: Bard-Avon, 1982.

The Four Hoods and Great Dog. New York: St. Martin's, 1988.

The Injured Party. New York: St. Martin's, 1986, 1988; London: Hamilton, 1986, 1987.

Love. New York: Dutton, 1981; Norfolk: Paperback, 1982; New York: Pocket, 1982.

The Madness of a Seduced Woman. New York: Dutton, 1983; Toronto: Bantam, 1984; London: Hamilton, 1984; London: Pan, 1985.

Mainland. New York: Simon, 1985; Book Club ed. New York: Simon, 1985; London: Hamilton, 1985; Toronto: Bantam, 1986; London: Pavanne, 1986; London: Pan-Pavanne, 1987.

Time in Its Flight. New York: Doubleday, 1978; New York: Pocket, 1979.

Collected Works

The Queen of Egypt. New York: Dutton, 1980.
Contents: Advice, Antiques, Destinies, The Exact Nature of Plot, His Daughter's House, The Queen of Egypt, The Priest Next Door, The Taxi, Why the Castle, The Yglesias of Ignatius Livingstone Island.

Short Fiction in Anthologies

"Bluebeard's Second Wife." *Great American Love Stories*. Ed. Lucy Rosenthal. Boston: Little, 1988. 566-78.

"The Exact Nature of Plot." *Prize Stories 1978: The O. Henry Awards*. Ed. William Abrahams. New York: Doubleday, 1978. 292-300.

Short Fiction in Periodicals

"The Exact Nature of Plot." *Little Magazine* 10.3-4 (1976): 5-12.

"In the Hospital and Elsewhere." *Prairie Schooner* 55.4 (1981-82): 42-63.

"The Taxi." *TriQuarterly* 35.1 (1976): 55-57.

"Virginia: Or, A Single Girl." *Prairie Schooner* 57.3 (1983): 3-40.

"Why the Castle." *Story Quarterly* 9 (1979): 58-64.

Secondary Sources

Articles and Chapters

Avery, Evelyn Gross. "Tradition and Independence in Jewish Feminist Novels." *MELUS* 7.4 (1980): 49-55.

Discusses *Falling* as a novel in which the heroine eventually acknowledges her Judaism, comprehends her predicament, and seeks a positive solution. Categorizes the novel as one in which a third generation Jewish female self-hater becomes terrified of living, blames her inadequacies on family and heritage, and finally finds some kind of peace and integration.

Berger, Alan L. "Holocaust Survivors and Children in *Anya* and *Mr. Sammler's Planet.*" *Modern Language Studies* 16.1 (1986): 81-87.

Examines the topic of survival literature and the psycho-social meaning of survivor parenting in *Anya*. Argues that Anya's task takes the form of her obsessive concern for Ninka and for her grandchildren, while simultaneously revealing the ambiguity of post-Holocaust Jewish existence.

Berger, Alan L. "Judaism as a Secular Value System." *Crisis and Covenant: The Holocaust in American Jewish Fiction.* SUNY Series in Modern Jewish Literature and Culture. Ed. Sarah Blacher Cohen. Albany: New York State UP, 1985. 110-20.

Describes Schaeffer as a third-generation American Jewess of Russian origin. Describes each of her major works and *Anya* in particular. Sees the story as redolent with theological issues concerning post-Holocaust Jewish identity and religion: the image of God, the purpose of closeness, the meaning of suffering, the complexity of Jewish-Christian relationships, and the Holocaust's continuing impact on survivors and their children.

Bilik, Dorothy Seidman. "Schaeffer's Romantic Survivor." *Immigrant-Survivors: Post-Holocaust Consciousness in Recent Jewish American Fiction.* Dorothy Seidman Bilik. Middletown: Wesleyan UP, 1981. 101-11.

Calls *Anya* unique among American immigrant-survivor novels in that the author was not born until 1941, and because the major action takes place in Eastern Europe before, during, and after the war. In addition, *Anya* is the only new immigrant novel discussed in the book that is told in the first-person by the survivor. Calls the survivor-narrator a remarkable but broken woman whose testimony reveals the mental, emotional, and physical scars of her devastating experience.

Gottschalk, Katherine K. "Paralyzed in the Present: Susan Fromberg Schaeffer's Mothers, or Daughters." *Mother Puzzles: Daughters and Mothers in Contemporary American Literature*. Ed. Mickey Pearlman. Contributions in Women's Studies 110. Westport: Greenwood, 1989. 1941-57

Discusses all of Schaeffer's novels in terms of their depiction of women writers who must work out a connection between their past, the present, and thus the future and suffer paralysis when they cannot. Systematically treats each novel and concludes that it might be difficult for each of these women, with their visions of continuity, to claim the present and future, rejoin their families, and go on without the guidance of the male outsider.

Mintz, Jacqueline A. "The Myth of the Jewish Mother in Three Jewish, American, Female Writers." *Centennial Review* 22.3 (1978): 346-55.

Provides a brief social history of the transition of breadwinning Jewish wives from Eastern Europe and their transition and disinheritance in America through the first two generations. Describes the plot of *Anya* and discusses the perversion of motherhood that Anya, saved from extermination and resettled in America, smothers her daughter with until she loses her daughter's love. Notes that Schaeffer retraces historically and psychologically the stages contributing to the psyche of the American Jewish mother today.

Pearlman, Mickey. "Susan Fromberg Schaeffer: The Power of Memory, Family, and Space." *American Women Writing Fiction: Memory, Identity, Family, Space*. Ed. Mickey Pearlman. Lexington: UP of Kentucky, 1989. 136-52.

Describes Schaeffer's metier as the family saga of the nineteenth century British ilk. Provides a glimpse at the style and thematic elements of her novels as a group, then focuses on an in-depth description of *The Injured Party*. Explores this and other novels from the perspective of the role played by each protagonist in terms of memory, the colonizing of personal space for therapeutic reasons, and the relation of these two to the influence and presence of family. Suggests that the idea of enclosed personal space is linked constantly to the work of memory, which in turn is related to issues of family.

Schaeffer, Susan Fromberg. "Artists on Art: The Unreality of Realism." *Critical Inquiry* 6.4 (1980): 727-37.

Based on critical reactions to her own poetry and fiction, Schaeffer discusses the relationship between fiction and reality. Useful for its insight into her works and ideas.

Reviews

Ballantyne, Sheila. "Dinner in the Crypt." Rev. of *The Injured Party*. *New York Times Book Review* 16 Nov. 1986: 15-16.

Claims that *The Injured Party* suffers from its near-exclusive focus on one woman's midlife obsession. Complains that this novel aspires to be, but lacks the slowly built and fully-fleshed fictional grounding that is necessary for their successful transmission. Concludes that the scope of her other concerns eclipses careful attention to the original development of the characters from whom these ideas must spring. Details the plot and contents.

Baveystock, Fred. "Out and Back." Rev. of *Buffalo Afternoon*. *Times Literary Supplement* 24 Nov. 1989: 1313.

Calls *Buffalo Afternoon* an ambitious Vietnam novel suffering from the author's conflicting desire to make her tale both universal and particular. Provides an extensive description of its contents.

Bell, Pearl K. "From Brooklyn and the Bronx." Rev. of *Falling*. *New Leader* 6 Aug. 1973: 15-16.

Details the contents of *Falling* and hails it as a superb first novel which takes risks most young authors would not even consider taking. Suggests that even while focusing on material which has been done to death— Brooklyn Jewish life, graduate school, attempted suicide, psychoanalysis, and scrabbling in the family dirt for the Holy Grail of self—Schaeffer has managed to establish an original claim to these materials.

Bell, Pearl K. "Suffering and Survival." Rev. of *Anya*. *New Leader* 14 Oct. 1974: 16-17.

Calls *Anya* an audacious account of a holocaust survivor. Describes the plot and characters. Concludes that because the author became so submerged in memory, surrendering her own inventive energy to the appalling facts of the story, her book is marred by morally admirable but novelistically tedious effort to relate every detail. Concludes that the power of selection and emphasis has been sacrificed to sentimentality rather than wisdom.

Benet, Mary Kathleen. "To Do with Blood." Rev. of *The Madness of a Seduced Woman*. *Times Literary Supplement* 23 Mar. 1984: 311.

Complains that the elements of this story are lurid, the technique all too easy, the tone dispassionate and cool. Suggests that the writer finds the theme of the genesis of passion and its limitations more compelling than passion itself. Concludes that this is a book whose superiority lies not in its originality, truth, and style, but in its superior pretensions.

Bernstein, Victor H. "Book Reviews." Rev. of *Anya*. *Hadassah Magazine* Jan. 1975: 22.

Comments that because it is based on actual events, the novel transforms the story into an epic that inspires rather than depresses.

Booth, Wayne C. "Elizabeth's Fight for a Life of Her Own." Rev. of *Falling*. *New York Times Book Review* 20 May 1973: 56-57.

Gives the novel high praise and describes the journey it outlines as convincing and often very funny. Sees the males as pitiful and hilarious, and the resolution full of compassion. Concludes that Schaeffer is one of the finest new talents to come along in a while.

Brandmark, Wendy. "Autopsy." Rev. of *The Injured Party*. *New Statesman* 5 Dec. 1986: 29-30.

Briefly reviews the plot and notes that the heart of this novel is a confrontation with mortality, an "extraordinary mental journey in the everyday." Finds that everything that is said, thought, or which occurs in the story is commented on or reflected on at length, so that this novel, unlike her earlier ones, doesn't pull us into the complex emotional lives of her characters. Considers this not so much a novel as an exquisitely written testimony, a critical analysis of a breakdown.

Brockway, James. "The Trickery of Art." Rev. of *Anya*. *Books and Bookmen* Aug. 1976: 49-50.

Details the contents of the novel and comments on the effectiveness of the style.

Brown, Rosellen. "Perpetual Emotion." Rev. of *The Madness of a Seduced Woman*. *New York Times Book Review* 22 May 1983: 14, 33.

Calls this a part of the endlessly compelling literature of obsessive love. Notes that unfortunately, the ideas in the novel never get beyond redundant descriptions of inescapable biology. Yet even so her best moments are visual images which reverberate through repetition in a dark panorama of excess. Suggests that it is an earnest exploration of mind versus body, and family history versus personal freedom. Concludes that it is an absorbing, wonderfully inventive psychological tale of a woman imagined as we would never dare, or want, to be.

Cargas, Harry James. Rev. of *Anya. America* 26 Oct. 1974: 237-38.
Considers the descriptions in this novel magnificent, the material overpowering, and the writing beautiful.

Dickstein, Lore. "Trouble, Trouble." Rev. of *Love. New York Times Book Review* 11 Jan. 1981: 10, 30.
Describes *Love* as a typical though better than usual immigrant novel which at times is unremittingly bleak and at others full of folk humor. Notes that there is little love in the story and that much of it unfolds like a taped interview. Concludes, however, that the series of short sketches it contains are a stunning finale to an otherwise unimaginative novel.

Epps, Garrett. "The Writer in Her Own Backyard." Rev. of *The Queen of Egypt: Short Fiction. Washington Post Book World* 3 Feb. 1980: 12.
Describes this work as full of dreams, tales, and reflections. Considers the origins and prevalence of Schaeffer's dream symbolism and details the contents of several of the stories.

Gies, Judith. "Books in Short." Rev. of *The Queen of Egypt: Short Fiction. Ms.* Feb. 1980: 39-40.
Describes the novel as subtle, poetic, occasionally strained, and sometimes irritating. Suggests, however, that most of the stories combine imagination and craft with memorable results. Concludes that the use of the grotesque is often mitigated by a sense of the absurd and that although uneven, the collection is worth reading for Schaeffer's rare and eclectic imagination.

Howard, Richard. "Telling Time." Rev. of *Falling. Partisan Review* 40.3 (1973): 510-12.
Calls *Falling* funny, deprecatory, wry, unassuming, yet stylistically sophisticated. Describes the narrative methods by which the heroine can be perceived to have come gradually into her own powers. Comments on how the author uses telling the time and the forgiveness of losing time in order to develop her character.

Johnson, Greg. "Jane Eyre in Montpelier." Rev. of *The Madness of a Seduced Woman. Southwest Review* 69.1 (1984): 93-96.

Argues that *The Madness of a Seduced Woman* harks back to the nineteenth century modes of realistic storytelling, mammoth inclusiveness, and unashamed melodrama. Likens the heroine to Jane Eyre and continues to develop the analogy through plot and style parallels. Concludes that the author is skillful, felicitous, and abundant. Calls this a respectable and compelling addition to the literature of passion.

Jonas, Gerald. "Browsing." Rev. of *Anya. Present Tense* 2.1 (1974): 80.

Calls *Anya* a magnificent novel which recreates the world of well-to-do Russian Jews in Vilna, Poland, before WW II. Details the contents of the novel and provides a sketch of the main character.

Jordan, Ruth. "Classical Epic of Polish Jewry." Rev. of *Anya. Jewish Observer and Middle East Review* 2 Apr. 1976: 13.

Calls this a gripping book with the enduring quality of a classical epic. Details the contents of the novel and the character of Anya.

Karp, Lila. Rev. of *Falling. Ms.* Aug. 1973: 34.

Describes *Falling* as it traces Elizabeth's life from the arrival of her Russian grandparents to her own adult dilemmas. Suggests that it is a story about self-hate, self-blame, and mental paralysis.

Korelitz, Jean Hanff. "Living with Strangers." Rev. of *The Injured Party. Times Literary Supplement* 12 Dec. 1986: 1409.

Calls the novel a book of heavy-handed symbolism, often ponderous and hampered by not only the unlikelihood of its central device, but its more than generous helping of melodrama.

McDonald, Cynthia. "Family Epic." Rev. of *Time in Its Flight. Washington Post Book World* 18 June 1978: E5.

Calls *Time in Its Flight* a novel about time from a fine storyteller who excels at the family saga. Suggests that though much of the ambition in this novel is realized, it takes on too much, but that even as a flawed book it is well worth reading. Describes the contents and the style.

Mellors, John. "Anya's War." Rev. of *Anya. Listener* 25 Mar. 1976: 378.

Commends this novel for its authentic achievement of voice that gives it the air of a memoir. Describes the contents of the story and concludes that no other book has recorded so much bewilderment and pain in its account of civilians trapped in the dangers and degradation of total war.

Mintz, Alan. "Mothers and Daughters." Rev. of *Anya. Commentary* Mar. 1975: 88-90.

Describes *Anya* as a very strong novel which illuminates a neglected and troubling aspect of the Holocaust—its effects on non-Jews. Details the mother-daughter relationship and concludes that this book is a serious probing of the complexity of the human emotional response to evil.

Muske, Carol. "Death Did Them Part: The Beauty in Bedlam." Rev. of *The Madness of a Seduced Woman. Los Angeles Times Book Review* 24 July 1963: 6.

Regrets that this novel was not properly edited and that the author tried too hard to establish the protagonist as a case study for feminism. Complains that there is too much heavy-handed symbolism, and that the heroine is finally buried alive in style.

Nichols, Kathleen L. Rev. of *The Queen of Egypt. Midwest Quarterly* 23.4 (1982): 450-52.

Describes reading this novel as wandering through a strange world of familiar but eccentric types whose detached angles of vision render their lives so remote and eventless that the reader hardly knows what to make of their pointless journeys toward destiny. Concludes that there is too much building on the Freudian roots of childhood and, finally, too much emotional distance.

Novack, William. "Jewish History Larger Than Life." Rev. of *Anya. New York Times Book Review* 20 Oct. 1974: 36.

Sees *Anya* as representing a new kind of maturity in Jewish-American fiction because it looks at history straight in the eye, engaging it with a stubborn fierceness. Calls it a triumph of realism in art. Details the contents of the novel and commends it for its achievement with dialogue and supporting cast of brilliant metaphors.

Nowik, Nan. "A Winter's Tale." Rev. of *The Injured Party. Belles Lettres* Mar.-Apr. 1987: 8.

Calls this a dark comedy written in effective language, a richly textured narrative, gorgeous descriptions, and recurring dream states. Details the plot and concludes that this brooding novel just might find an audience.

Parrinder, Patrick. "Shedding One's Sickness." Rev. of *The Injured Party. London Review of Books* 20 Nov. 1986: 13.

Comments that Schaeffer is an ingenious writer in *The Injured Party*, which is written in a religious and romantic, idealistic mode. Calls this a touching myth of emotional foundering and regeneration, but which is unfortunately interspersed with scenes worthy of TV commercials about such things as West Country Cottages or the Cornish Pastry industry.

Proffitt, Nicholas. "Pete Bravado's War and Peace." Rev. of *Buffalo Afternoon. New York Times Book Review* 21 May 1989: 7.

Describes the contents of *Buffalo Afternoon*, a Vietnam War novel told by a woman from a man's point of view. Calls this a remarkable job of reporting because it squeezes the whole Vietnam story into one epic narrative. Provides detailed accounts of individual characters and scenes, and concludes that she has told the veteran's story well and is a trustworthy writer.

Ratner, Rochelle. Rev. of *The Queen of Egypt: Short Fiction. American Book Review* Jan.-Feb. 1981: 10-11.

Describes *The Queen of Egypt* as an interesting probe into the uselessness of extreme wealth and extreme beauty in a twentieth century Brooklyn family who pretends to be living in nineteenth century England. Comments, however, that the second half of the book is nothing but superficial farce. Finds Schaeffer capable of sensitivity and depth but notes that her ultimate concern is with the trivial.

Reuben, Elaine. "Novel of Power." Rev. of *Anya. New Republic* 18 Jan. 1975: 30-31.

Calls *Anya* a survivor narrative told by a character with an elegiac voice and the kind of reality that makes a reader believe it to be a first-hand account. Considers it unobtrusively crafted and an achievement of power and importance.

Ribalow, Harold U. "Holocaust Survivor." Rev. of *Anya. Congress Bi-Weekly* 6 Dec. 1974: 20.

Calls Schaeffer a natural novelist, who in *Anya*, has taken a massive subject and tamed it down and thrust the entire era back into our minds. Concludes that *Anya* is a remarkable achievement.

Richie, Mary. "Tough Times, True Grit." Rev. of *Anya. Washington Post Book World* 17 Nov. 1974: 3.

Comments that *Anya* is about the creation of the world of darkness, and of laughter stopped forever in the open throat. Suggests that this world of provincial prewar Poland might have been as irretrievably lost as that of *Beowulf.* Describes both the story and literary style.

Schott, Webster. "Happy Family." Rev. of *Time in Its Flight. New York Times Book Review* 13 Aug. 1978: 34.

Details the contents of *Time in Its Flight* and calls it a poor intellectual companion, capriciously organized and confusing without purpose. Suggests that her characters are incidental to their environment and that the whole thing is panorama and chatter.

Schwartz, Lynne Sharon. "Books in Brief." Rev. of *Time in Its Flight. Saturday Review* 24 June 1978: 35.

Describes *Time in Its Flight* as formidable in scope and length, and teeming with imagination, ideas, and anecdotes. Notes that unfortunately, she patronizes her characters, renders them too cute or quirky and sometimes plunges the reader into tedium. Concludes that overall the work is too lax and comprehensive to sustain excitement.

See, Carolyn. "One Woman's View of an 'Adulterous Affair.'" Rev. of *Mainland. Los Angeles Times* 20 Aug. 1985: 8.

Mainland is described almost solely in terms of its contents and the particular plot and tonal differences that occur when a woman writes the story of the adulterous affair from a very different perspective than the male writer traditionally has done.

Sheppard, R. Z. "Strong Sister." Rev. of *Falling. Time* 18 June 1973: 84, 87.

Suggests that *Falling* for all its efforts is really a case study of a middle-class Jewish girl all the way from broken engagement to suicide attempt, analysis, and literature teaching. Concludes that the author handles this with great credibility and tact, but that the book still remains somewhat of a cliche.

Skow, John. "So Well Remembered." Rev. of *Anya. Time* 14 Oct. 1974: 88, 90.

Calls *Anya* a book in which one remembers the overwhelming impression of brooding wartime Poland, but complains that the novel focuses on an actual life remembered rather than of events and characters tailored and fitted to the pattern of the story.

Spacks, Patricia Meyer. "Necessities of Memory." Rev. of *Time in Its Flight*. *Hudson Review* 31.4 (1978-79): 669-71.

Argues that *Time in Its Flight* broadcasts the novel as an act of historical reconstruction and does so with dubious results. Notes that this fiction celebrates the female, and that its center is Edna Dickenson. Concludes that finally the novel, for all its tedious accumulation of detail and pseudo-fact, does possess undeniable power derived partly from its relentless accumulation, which envelopes us in the created and remembered world of our ancestors.

Thurman, Judith. "Unchanged by Suffering?" Rev. of *Anya*. *Ms*. Mar. 1975: 46-47.

Argues that in *Anya* the Holocaust itself is never allowed to upstage the characters. Notes that the reality of this book is solid, tangible, and able to bear the full weight of one's trust. Describes the setting, narrative methods, characters and inner dynamics of the book. Concludes that there is no attempt to make the Holocaust a metaphor either.

Ward, Elizabeth. "Susan Fromberg Schaeffer's American Gothic." Rev. of *The Madness of a Seduced Woman*. *Washington Post Book World* 12 June 1983: 5.

Calls *The Madness of a Seduced Woman* a romantic, nineteenth century blockbuster replete with some explicit scenes. Suggests that though it is too long, the heroine babbles on, the language feels pedestrian, and it is not great literature, only an uncannily gripping story. Suggests that one is quietly forced to ponder again the old conundrum of love. Raises the question of who is to define the wavering lines between love and obsession, fruitful commitment, and destructive dependence.

White, Edmund. "Two Views on Love in Vermont." Rev. of *The Madness of a Seduced Woman*. *Nation* 9-16 July 1983: 57-58.

Finds this novel a patient accretion of detail offered as a kind of trial psychiatry, as well as an inside look at the central character. Concludes that she re-examines all the cliches about romantic love and provides the reader with a deeper, more powerful vision.

Wickenden, Dorothy. "Book Briefs." Rev. of *Love*. *Saturday Review* Jan. 1981: 70, 72.

Calls *Love* part novel, and part folktale, and part generational saga. Complains that it contains much sentimentality and flatulent imagery.

Interviews

Pearlman, Mickey. *"Belles Lettres* Interview." *Belles Lettres* May-June 1988: 9.

An account of Schaeffer's house, her workplace, habits, previous novels, issues of female depression and isolation, the lives of her fictional women, reviewing women's fiction, biographical information, and comments on several of her novels.

Ribalow, Harold U. "A Conversation with Susan Fromberg Schaeffer." *The Tie That Binds.* Harold U. Ribalow. San Diego: Barnes; London: Tantivy, 1980. 77-92. Rpt. from *Pioneer Woman.*

In this interview Fromberg discusses writing her first novel, methods of composition, her family ties, poetry, *Falling, Anya,* being Jewish, the Holocaust, Israel, suffering, synagogues, her husband's career, feelings about reviewers, and her work-in-progress.

Steinberg, Sybil S. "PW Interviews Susan Fromberg Schaeffer." *Publishers Weekly* 8 Apr. 1983: 60-61.

An interview in which Schaeffer discusses the broad range of her life, teaching, family, publishing, views of fiction writing, and Jewishness.

Biographical Sources

Kress, Susan. "Susan Fromberg Schaeffer." *Twentieth-Century American-Jewish Fiction Writers.* Ed. Daniel Walden. Detroit: Gale, 1984. Vol. 28 of *Dictionary of Literary Biography.* 94 vols. to date. 1978- . 276-80.

More than details of her life, this is a career biography, tracing the development of the author's canon, describing the contents and themes of her works, evaluating her reputation, and placing her in the larger context of American literary history. Includes lists of primary and secondary sources and illustrations.

Dissertations

Heinemann, Marlene Eve. "Women Prose Writers of the Nazi Holocaust." Diss. Indiana U, 1981.

Budd Schulberg

1914 –

Primary Sources

Novels

The Disenchanted. New York: Random, 1950; London: Bodley Head, 1951; London: Lane, 1951; Sydney: Invincible, 1951; New York: Grosset, 1952; Harmondsworth: Penguin, 1960, 1975; London: New English Library, 1969; New York: Bantam [Cited in PBIP, 1969]; New York: Viking, 1975; London: Allison, 1983; New York: Primus-Fine, 1987.

Everything That Moves. Garden City: Doubleday, 1980; New York: Pinnacle, 1981; London: Robson, 1981.

The Harder They Fall. New York: Random, 1947; London: Lane, 1947; New York: Grosset, 1948; Sydney: Invincible, 1948; London: Bodley Head, 1948; London: Viking-World, 1957; London: Transworld, 1962; London: Corgi-Transworld, 1967; New York: NAL [Cited in PBIP, 1969]; London: Sphere, 1971; London: White Lion, 1975.

Sanctuary V. New York: NAL-World, 1969; London: Allen, 1970; London: Signet-NAL, 1971.

Swan Watch. New York: Delacorte, 1975; London: Robson, 1975.

Waterfront. New York: Random, 1955; London: Bodley Head, 1956; London: Lane, 1956; Corgi Modern Reading. London: Corgi, 1966; New York: Popular Library [Cited in PBIP, 1969]; London: White Lion, 1974; Cambridge: Bentley, 1979; The Library of Contemporary Americana. New York: Godine, 1983; Primus Library of Contemporary Americana. New York: Fine, 1987. Publ. as *On the Waterfront.* London: Corgi-Transworld, 1959; London: Corgi, 1964; London: Sphere, 1971; London: Allison, 1988.

What Makes Sammy Run? New York: Random, 1941; Garden City: Sun Dial, 1941, 1943; Toronto: Macmillan, 1941; London: Jarrolds, 1941; Toronto: Blue Ribbon, 1942; New York: Bantam, 1945, 1964; New York: Modern Library, 1952; London: Corgi-Transworld, 1958; London: Bodley Head, 1961; Modern Classic ed. New York: Bantam, 1968; A Fawcett Gold Medal Book. Greenwich: Fawcett, 1970; London: Sphere, 1971; New York: Penguin, 1978, 1981; Cambridge: Bentley, 1979; Anniversary ed. New York: Random, 1990.

Collected Works

Love, Action, Laughter and Other Sad Tales. New York: Random, 1989.

Contents: Say Good Night to Owl; The Real Viennese Schmaltz; Senor Discretion Himself; Passport to Nowhere; The Funny Part Is . . .; The Howling Dogs of Taxco; Letter to MacFadden; Hollywood Versus Chris Samuels, Age Nine; The Docks of New York; A Second Father; The Reluctant Pilgrim; Counterintelligence in Mexico City; The Barracudas; The Pettibone Plan: A Fable; Mother of Them All; Love, Action, Laughter.

Senor Discretion Himself and Other Sad Stories. New York: Random, 1990.

Contents: Not available.

Some Faces in the Crowd. London: Bodley Head, 1954, 1964; London: Lane, 1954; London: Panther-Hamilton, 1959.

Contents: Your Arkansas Traveller, A Short Digest of a Long Novel, A Table at Ciro's, Memory in White, The Breaking Point, My Christmas Carol, The One He Called Winnie, Crowd Pleaser, The Typical Gesture of Colonel Duggan, Our White Deer.

Some Faces in the Crowd. New York: Random, 1953; New York: Giant-Bantam, 1954.

Contents: Your Arkansas Traveler; A Short Digest of a Long Novel; A Table at Ciro's; Memory in White; The Breaking Point; The Face of Hollywood; A Foxhole in Washington; The Pride of Tony Colucci; A Note on the Literary Life; My Christmas Carol; Ensign Weasel; The Dare; The One He Called Winnie; Enough; Crowd Pleaser; The Legend That Walks Like a Man; The Typical Gesture of Colonel Duggan; Meal Ticket; Third Nightcap, with Historical Footnotes; Our White Deer.

Short Fiction in Anthologies

"All the Town's Talking." *This Week's Short-Short Stories*. Ed. Stewart Beach. New York: Random, 1953. 146-52.

"My Christmas Carol." *An Anthology of Famous American Stories*. Eds. Angus Burrell and Bennett Cerf. New York: Modern Library, 1953, 1963. 1289-96.

"Passport to Nowhere." *These Your Children*. Ed. Harold U. Ribalow. New York: Beechhurst, 1952. 254-90.

"The Real Viennese Schmalz." *The Best American Short Stories, 1942*. Ed. Martha Foley. Boston: Houghton, 1942. 259-68.

"The Road to Recovery." *New Stories for Men*. Ed. Charles Grayson. New York: Doubleday, 1941; Garden City: Garden, 1943. 417-28.

"Somebody Has to Be Nobody." *Post Stories of 1941*. New York: Random, 1941. 297-311.

"Spotlight." *Famous Short Stories I*. Ed. Kurt Singer. Minneapolis: Denison, 1968. 157-61.

Short Fiction in Periodicals

"The Barracudas." *Playboy* Dec. 1957: 23-24, 34, 50, 79-81; *Short Story International* Dec. 1985: 89-105.

"The Bell of Tarchova." *Saturday Evening Post* 24 Oct. 1942: 12-13, 53, 56-57, 59-60.

"The Breaking Point." *Esquire* Dec. 1948: 78, 215-18.

"Calling Major Adam's Car." *Collier's* 25 June 1938: 22.

"The Celebrity." *Illustrated London News* Christmas Number. 18 Nov. 1954: 17-18, 35.

"The Dare." *Esquire* May 1949: 38-39, 97-98, 100-01.

"The Downfall of Innocence." *Esquire* July 1943: 69.

"Eddie Buys a Car." *Collier's* 7 Jan 1939: 24-25, 42-44.

"Formula Fighter." *Saturday Evening Post* 21 Mar. 1953: 26, 138-40, 142-44.

"A Foxhole in Washington." *New Yorker* 22 Apr. 1944: 28-29.

"A Free Man." *Esquire* Aug. 1953: 32.

"The Funny Part Is, She's Happy." *Collier's* 12 Nov. 1949: 22-23, 34, 36-38.

"Hollywood Doctor." *Collier's* 6 Aug. 1938: 9-10, 32-33.

"Hollywood Ghost." *Collier's* 11 June 1938: 14-15, 57-58, 60-61.

"Hollywood vs. Chris Samuels, Age Nine." *Esquire* Dec. 1953: 109, 242-43.

"I'll Take Care of It." *Collier's* 19 Feb. 1938: 20-21, 49-50.

"Kiss and Forget." *McCall's* Nov. 1953: 40-41, 84, 90, 92-93.

"A Latin from Killarney." *Playboy* Jan. 1968: 115, 204-06.

"The Legend That Walks Like a Man." *Esquire* Aug. 1950: 41, 99-100.

"Love, Action, Laughter." *Collier's* 15 Jan. 1938: 16-17, 54-56.

"Memory in White." *Collier's* 26 Sept. 1942: 20, 52-53, 56.

"Murder on the Water Front." *Collier's* 1 Oct. 1954: 82-89.

"Passport to Nowhere." *Story* May 1938: 57-77.

"The Real Viennese Schmalz." *Esquire* Sept. 1941: 68, 102-03.

"Say Good Night to Owl." *Redbook* Aug. 1965: 62-63, 127-31.

"A Second Father." *Playboy* Feb. 1957: 16-18, 26, 30, 36, 38, 46, 54, 58.

"Senor Discretion Himself. *Playboy* Jan. 1966: 140-42, 240-44, 246; *Short Story International* June 1985: 106-29.

"Somebody Has to Be Nobody." *Saturday Evening Post* 18 Oct. 1941: 12-13, 51, 53-54.

"The Stars Repeat." *Collier's* 23 Dec. 1939: 19.

"Third Nightcap, with Historical Footnotes." *New Yorker* 23 May 1942: 50.

"The Time Is Always." *Saturday Evening Post* 9 Jan. 1943: 22-23, 55-56.

"The Typical Gesture." *Good Housekeeping* Oct. 1946: 22-23, 206-12, 218-23.

Secondary Sources

Articles and Chapters

Burgess, Anthony. "The Disenchanted." *Ninety-Nine Novels: The Best in English Since 1939.* Anthony Burgess. London: Allison, 1984. 50.

Describes Schulberg's life, the publication of the *The Disenchanted,* the nature of Fitzgerald's last years in Hollywood, and the parallels in the book with Fitzgerald's life. Commends the book for the way it delineates the torments of a writer in decline and the fundamental nobility of artistic dedication.

Eisinger, Chester. "Budd Schulberg: The Popular Voice of the Old Liberalism." *Fiction of the Forties.* Chester Eisinger. Chicago: U of Chicago P, 1967. 102-06.

Discusses *The Disenchanted* as a story about the failure of commitment in old-fashioned liberalism. Sees Schulberg as a child of the 30s who never outgrew his childhood, becoming an upper middle-class Marxist and radical bourgeois. Regards him as the literary chronicler of the American entertainment world who writes of radio, television, and boxing. Discusses the contents of several of his novels from this perspective. Concludes that what causes Schulberg's fiction to fail is a thoughtless and habitual loyalty to unexamined liberal precepts as instruments for analysis of American society.

Farr, Finis. "In a Workmanlike Manner." *National Review* 11 Apr. 1959: 656-58.

Discusses mainly Fitzgerald, and calls *The Disenchanted* masterly and even eerie in its accuracy.

Glicksberg, Charles I. "When Is a Novel Anti-Semitic?" *Congress Weekly* 1 Nov. 1954: 11-13.

Discusses *What Makes Sammy Run?* and other works by Jerome Weidman and Meyer Levin to develop his thesis that writers, Jew or non-Jew, must present the truth they see, no matter how unpleasant to some, so long as they present it with completeness and integrity. Insists that to do this, they must show the complex network of environmental forces and social conditions that influence the human soul and shape it in a given way for good or evil.

Harap, Louis. *Creative Awakening: The Jewish Presence in Twentieth-Century American Literature, 1900-1940s. Contributions in Ethnic Studies* 17. New York: Greenwood, 1987. 161-62.

Briefly discusses the misconception of some readers that *What Makes Sammy Run?* is Schulberg's story of Jewish self-hatred. Counters that instead Sammy is following the path that promised success to anyone in the first half of this century. Notes that Schulberg throughout the novel, as in his physical description of Sammy, deliberately tries to depart from the stereotypical Jew to make him an American, not a Jew.

Patterson, Alice Conger. "Budd Schulberg." *Popular World Fiction 1900-Present.* Eds. Walton Beacham and Suzanne Niemeyer. 4 vols. Washington: Beacham, 1987. 4: 1343-52.

A standard reference article discussing Schulberg's publishing history, critical reception, honors, and popularity. Discusses the social concerns, themes, character, techniques, literary precedents, related titles, and adaptations of *What Makes Sammy Run?*

Sherman, Bernard. *"I Can Get It for You Wholesale* and *What Makes Sammy Run?" The Invention of the Jew: Jewish-American Education Novels (1916-1964).* Bernard Sherman. New York: Yoseloff, 1969. 176-78.

Provides a brief account of the contents, Jewish themes, and style of the two novels. Also deals with weaknesses in both works.

Spatz, Jonas. "Some Versions of the American Myth." *Hollywood in Fiction.* Jonas Spatz. The Hague: Mouton, 1969. 67-72, 78-80, 89-94.

Comments that throughout this book there are numerous mentions of each of Schulberg's Hollywood novels, primarily *The Disenchanted*, and assessments of their accuracy in depicting the American myth of success. A key literary-historical assessment of Schulberg.

Thomas, Phil. "50th Anniversary: Sammy Still Running." *Daily Herald* [Provo, Utah] 26 Mar. 1990: B6.

An AP article that reports Schulberg's remembrances of the publication history of *What Makes Sammy Run?*—it has sold over 2 million copies, has almost always been in print, and is now re-issued in a new hardback edition Random House calls the *"Fiftieth Anniversary Edition."* Describes also Schulberg's background, his work as a screenwriter-son of a Paramount Studio CEO, the reaction of readers to his novel, and the loss of his welcome in Hollywood for a time by the bigwigs. Schulberg notes that in addition to writing a broadway musical based on the novel, he is working on a screenplay of it that is to be produced this year.

Wells, Walter. "Tycoon Sammy." *Tycoons and Locusts.* Walter Wells. Crosscurrents/Modern Critiques. Carbondale: Southern Illinois UP, 1973. 86-102.

Provides an extensive critical treatment of *What Makes Sammy Run?*. Describes the novel as fiction and the chief character, Sammy, as one of American fiction's most memorable caricatures.

Widmer, Kingsley. "The Hollywood Image." *Coastlines* 5.1 (1961): 17-27.

Discusses the image of Hollywood in the so-called Hollywood novels. Makes several pertinent references to Schulberg's Hollywood novels along the way.

Winchell, Mark Royden. "Fantasy Seen: Hollywood Fiction Since West." *Los Angeles in Fiction: A Collection of Original Essays.* Ed. David Fine. Albuquerque: U of New Mexico P, 1984. 147-68.

In this major treatment of Hollywood fiction since Nathanael West, Schulberg's *What Make Sammy Run?* is described as a cynic's version of the decline of Hollywood. Discusses his and Fitzgerald's knowledge of each other, and compares and contrasts their respective depictions of Hollywood.

Reviews

Adams, J. Donald. "Speaking of Books." Rev. of *The Disenchanted. New York Times Book Review* 19 Nov. 1950: 2.

Calls *The Disenchanted* a book whose success will rest not on its own power and skill, but on its subject—F. Scott Fitzgerald. Claims that even though this novel has not completely fulfilled its intention, Fitzgerald does successfully emerge as a tormented character. Concludes, however, that this book too often relies on reportage and not the techniques of the art novel.

Alpert, Hollis. "Golden Boy of Letters Badly Tarnished." Rev. of *The Disenchanted. Saturday Review of Literature* 28 Oct. 1950: 11.

Describes *The Disenchanted* as a novel about the crack up of F. Scott Fitzgerald. Sees the scenes as sharply authentic, although the book is disjointed and dreamlike, and the subject is of too large a magnitude for Mr. Schulberg.

Bernikow, Louise. "Books." Rev. of *What Makes Sammy Run?*
Cosmopolitan Jan. 1990: 24.

Calls *What Makes Sammy Run?* one of the most insightful Hollywood
novels ever written. Describes the contents, and concludes that the power
of Schulberg's storytelling is certain to touch a new generation of readers
who may not know that all cliches about the type Sammy Glick represents have their origins in this wonderful book.

Boatwright, Taliaferro. "Heels and Stuffed Shirts." Rev. of *Some Faces in
the Crowd*. *New York Herald Tribune Book Review* 7 June 1953: 12.

Describes *Some Faces in the Crowd* as dealing with a broken assortment
of Hollywood caliphs, broken-down prizefighters, literary luminaries,
tinpot military brass, and just everyday stuffed shirts. Describes several
of the stories.

"The Bottom of the Glass." Rev. of *The Disenchanted*. *Time* 13 Nov.
1950: 106.

Summarizes the plot, and says of its basis in the life of F. Scott Fitzgerald,
that "at least 50%, and maybe more, of the book is true." Says the book
originally aimed at tragedy, but actually slipped to tense melodrama.

Breit, Harvey. "In and Out of Books." Rev. of *Waterfront*. *New York
Times Book Review* 7 Aug. 1955: 8.

Describes a little of *Waterfront*, the movie written by Schulberg, and
comments on the novel soon to be published.

Burg, Victor. "Dream People Happening to Events." Rev. of *Sanctuary
V*. *Christian Science Monitor* 5 Mar. 1970: 9.

Describes the contents and philosophical issues of *Sanctuary V*.
Questions the adequacy of placing two-thirds of the tale in a nightmarish
adult asylum since this setting has now become such a contrivance in the
modern novel.

Burnett, W. R. "Docker's Dilemma." Rev. of *Waterfront*. *Saturday
Review* 24 Sept. 1955: 17.

Describes the excessive reportage and difficulties of style; notes that
Schulberg is never quite at home with his leading character. Concludes
that the novel goes by fits and starts even though it is more honest than
the movie.

Cain, James M. "A Tarnished Hero of the Jazz Age." Rev. of *The Disenchanted*. *New York Times Book Review* 29 Oct. 1950: 1.

Calls *The Disenchanted* a book which successfully fuses its disparate material into a living, breathing portrait so vivid you forget who sat for it. Details the contents thoroughly. Concludes that this is a classic anecdote.

Cargas, Harry J. Rev. of *Sanctuary V. America* 4 Apr. 1970: 374.

Criticizes *Sanctuary V* as having been written for the movies. Describes the scenes as vivid, the characters as violent, and the writing as unexceptional. Suggests that there are major defects in characterization and the level of intercultural understanding manifest in the text.

Chapin, Ruth. "Tarnished Tinsel." Rev. of *The Disenchanted*. *Christian Science Monitor* 7 Dec. 1950: 28.

Describes *The Disenchanted* as a book which captures the full essence of the Fitzgerald decades. Details the plot and contents.

Connolly, Cyril. "Scott Fitzgerald: I." Rev. of *The Disenchanted*. *Previous Convictions*. Cyril Connolly. New York: Harper, 1963. 299-301. Rpt. from *Sunday Times*.

Describes the contents of *The Disenchanted* and Schulberg's sensitive reporting of the Fitzgerald decline. Finds the first ten chapters admirable, before his gift for macabre clowning runs away with him, and the book fails.

Cook, Bruce. "Shock of Recognition." Rev. of *The Disenchanted*. *Washington Post Book World* 2 Mar. 1975: 1, 4.

Describes his second reading of the republished *The Disenchanted*. Establishes the context of Fitzgerald's life and times and subsequent scholarship and biography on his achievements. Details some of the parallels between Fitzgerald's actual life and the novel. Calls *The Disenchanted* a fine, honest, solid novel with marvelously flowing dialogue, but slightly poorer narrative prose. Concludes that it is respectful of its subject.

Davis, Robert Gorham. "In the End, the Cost Must Be Paid." Rev. of *Some Faces in the Crowd*. *New York Times Book Review* 17 May 1953: 4-5.

Describes *Some Faces in the Crowd* as a generous collection. Notes Schulberg's having been influenced by popular fiction formulas, as well as by Hemingway, Lardner, and Fitzgerald. Considers the chief virtue of these stories to be their dramatic presentation and clarity.

Downing, Francis. "So They Tell Me: The Disenchantment of Scott Fitzgerald." Rev. of *The Disenchanted. Commonweal* 10 Nov. 1950: 117-18.

Calls *The Disenchanted* a synthetic part of a revival of interest in the Jazz Age. Argues that it is foolish to consider Fitzgerald "disenchanted" because, after all, he was a Puritan in Babylon. Comments very little on the novel.

Engel, Paul. "The Joyride That Couldn't Last Forever." Rev. of *The Disenchanted. Chicago Sunday Tribune Magazine of Books* 5 Nov. 1950: 3.

Describes the contents of *The Disenchanted*, and comments that, while the author produced some of the most significant fiction during the 1920s, this book shows him as magnificent even in his disintegration. Describes the contents of the book, and comments on some of its shortcomings.

Farrell, Paul V. "Books." Rev. of *The Disenchanted. Commonweal* 10 Nov. 1950: 124.

Calls *The Disenchanted* a fictionalized biography of F. Scott Fitzgerald written in a flashy, erratic style, and juxtaposed with scenes of great power and vividness.

Ferguson, Otis. "The Incredible City." Rev. of *What Makes Sammy Run? New Republic* 31 Mar. 1941: 442-43.

Describes *What Makes Sammy Run?* as a better than usual portrait of the grossness of Hollywood life. Suggests that Schulberg approaches the scene with understanding and grim tolerance. Provides an extensive account of characters and contents. Concludes, however, that his book is not good reading because of too much contrivance and slickness.

Fiedler, Leslie A. "A Murder Story." Rev. of *The Disenchanted. New Leader* 18 Dec. 1950: 19-20.

Considers *The Disenchanted* basically an inept book, failing to achieve its focus and presenting us with a dull, priggish Marxist for a central protagonist. Also condemns Schulberg for his treatment of Fitzgerald in the novel.

Freedman, Morris. "New England and Hollywood." Rev. of *Some Faces in the Crowd. Commentary* Oct. 1953: 389-90, 392.

Claims that *Some Faces in the Crowd* is Schulberg's antipathetic account of Hollywood, an account marked by adolescent malice, narrowness of concentration, and the assumption of a pose he knows will get admiration.

Considers that much of what he writes has a fierce, pitiless lack of understanding and involvement, as well as a certain amount of self-identification.
Sees Schulberg as another Jewish writer whose work has skimmed the
shores of genuine literary achievement. Concludes that, unfortunately,
Schulberg lacks a sense of a genuine artistic tradition, and that he has substituted one idol for another, Hollywood for Hollywood rebellion.

Gibbs, Wolcott. "The Mantle of Wakeman." Rev. of *The Harder They
Fall. New Yorker* 16 Aug. 1947: 76-78.

Describes *The Harder They Fall* in detail, and then critiques it as being
fatally handicapped by Schulberg's romantic and indignant outlook on life,
not to mention a sort of rosy embarrassment about the English language.

Godfrey, Eleanor. Rev. of *What Makes Sammy Run? Canadian Forum*
May 1941: 60.

Considers that *What Makes Sammy Run?* has many of the stigmata of a
first novel, but on the whole, this is a readable, thoughtful, and planned
story. Regards the language as too functional, seldom leaving a memorable mark in the mind of the reader.

Greenfeld, Josh. "Justo Was Conned from the Start." Rev. of *Sanctuary
V. New York Times Book Review* 25 Jan. 1970: 40.

Describes the subject matter, plot, and characters in *Sanctuary V.*
Comments that this story employs his old formula, implores with his old
liberalism, and writes a story that is at least half thriller and half tract.
Describes the result as downright disappointing.

Greenya, John. "A Bit Hokey." Rev. of *Sanctuary V. New Republic* 7
Mar. 1970: 29-30.

Calls *Sanctuary V* a novel written by a writer motivated by profit. Details
the contents of the book, and concludes that the final effect is "hokey"
and self-consciously patriotic.

Hartung, Philip T. Rev. of *What Makes Sammy Run? Commonweal* 6
June 1941: 163.

Calls *What Makes Sammy Run?* a novel to end all novels about heels in
Hollywood. Sees it as a crude, shocking account of Hollywood in 1941,
and a truthful one despite its being banned.

Hogan, William. "Schulberg Takes on *Waterfront* as a Novel." Rev. of
Waterfront. San Francisco Chronicle 9 Sept. 1955: 17.

Describes the contents of *Waterfront* and comments on the fine maritime smell Schulberg gets into his prose. Unfortunately, his earlier work is better novelistically. This novel smacks too much of a gimmick, transposed as it is from the movie script.

Horn, John. "Brilliant Saga of the Ring." Rev. of *The Harder They Fall*. *New York Times Book Review* 10 Aug. 1947: 3.

Suggests that *The Harder They Fall* is clearly influenced by Hemingway, Fitzgerald, and Weidman. Details plot and characters. Predicts the novel will be a sensation, based as it is on an inversion of the typical American success story.

Jackson, Joseph Henry. "Schulberg's New Novel: A Tragedy of the Twenties Meeting the Fifties." Rev. of *The Disenchanted*. *San Francisco Chronicle This World Magazine* 29 Oct. 1950: 16, 22.

Claims that *The Disenchanted* is fuller and richer than his previous work. It is also one of his most sad and tragic novels. Details the plot and characters, and concludes that Schulberg is unsparing with his readers. He magically evokes the 1920s with his fictionalized portrait of F. Scott Fitzgerald and the Hollywood scenes.

Jones, Ernest. "Defeat of an Artist." Rev. of *The Disenchanted*. *Nation* 25 Nov. 1950: 487-88.

Details the contents of *The Disenchanted*, and hails it as a serious study of the American artist who, after early success, exists for a space as a kind of Peter Pan. Identifies the book's thesis as nothing fails like success. Denies this is a successful novel with its "fugitive generalizations" and its general fictional unsoundness. Claims that it is one of those novels eagerly read for information, not for aesthetic reasons. Complains that the main characters are obscured in a cloud of explanations, labels, and deft verbalizations.

Kazin, Alfred. "Compassion Without Approval." Rev. of *The Disenchanted*. *New Yorker* 4 Nov. 1950: 154-57.

Describes the myth of Fitzgerald that lies behind this novel. Details its contents, its style, its milieu, and its major characters. Suggests the problem with this book to be that Schulberg pities Fitzgerald, and never really approves of him with a creative understanding and acceptance.

Kelly, James. "In a Harbor of Greed and Violence." Rev. of *Waterfront*. *New York Times Book Review* 11 Sept. 1955: 5.

Calls *Waterfront* the best of Schulberg, whether one thinks of it as journalism or as intensely personalized, white hot fiction with all the menace, suspense, narrative flow, fresh characterization, and social message anyone could reasonably expect in a novel. Considers this a full-fledged performance by a gifted American writer.

Kelly, James. "World of Big-Wheels." Rev. of *Some Faces in the Crowd. Saturday Review* 16 May 1953: 14-15.

Calls Schulberg's collection of short stories *Some Faces in the Crowd* the work of a sound journalist and full of verisimilitude. Suggests, however, that the collection also reveals the range of subjects, the depth of his perception, his point of view, style, and paucities. Concludes ultimately, that Schulberg's eye and ear fail in this collection.

King, Francis. "Unholy Union." Rev. of *Everything That Moves. Spectator* 12 Sept. 1981: 21-22.

Claims that *Everything That Moves* reads as if Schulberg were summarizing a script to some money men either too illiterate or too busy to assimilate it from the page. Suggests that, depite the fact there is little psychological subtlety in the characterization, it does hold the reader's attention. Concludes that it should make a good film.

Kresh, Paul. "Fiction." Rev. of *Sanctuary V. Saturday Review* 14 Feb. 1970: 44.

Calls *Sanctuary V* a shocking, Cuban-type microcosm with its own pecking order where the resourceful can make out. Calls the characters colorful types, and remarks that the storytelling is expert. Concludes that, unfortunately, Schulberg does not seem to know his own strength or the pungency of his own prose.

Lazarus, H. P. "Sammy Glick." Rev. of *What Makes Sammy Run? Nation* 19 Apr. 1941: 477.

Calls *What Makes Sammy Run?* uneven, badly written, poorly developed, full of paltry patois, and stuffed with small-story sophistication and typewriter chatter. Notes, however, that this is a first novel and improves considerably. Still objects to the niggardliness of expressed emotion, the careful indifference, the special argot of understatement and the determined bathos of the characters before the probity of their feelings.

Lescaze, Lee. "Gordon Gekko's Grandfather." Rev. of *What Makes Sammy Run? Wall Street Journal* 19 Dec. 1989: A12.

Describes the staying power of *Sammy* at the time of its 1989 republication, noting that Sammy Glick has become the emblem for a type we all have known. Commends Schulberg's accomplishment in a first novel and his knowledge of Hollywood. Discusses the tone, themes, and his use of language. Concludes by objecting to Schulberg's recent assertion that today many Americans consider Sammy a role model.

Levitas, Gloria. "All About Heels." Rev. of *Some Faces in the Crowd. New Leader* 8 June 1953: 23-24.

Comments that *Some Faces in the Crowd* continues Schulberg's interest in the American phenomenon of the heel. Describes several of the stories in the collection, and concludes that many of them are compelling and fascinating. Suggests that, beneath the deceptively facile flow of words, lies horror and anguish, all brought out with his careful delineation of character and background as well as sense of drama.

Lockridge, Richard. "Two New Novels: England Today, America in the 1920s." Rev. of *The Disenchanted. New York Herald Tribune Book Review* 29 Oct. 1950: 1, 26.

Describes characters, plot, and contents of *The Disenchanted*. Complains that the motivations of the central character, Halliday, remain mysterious. Sees the major virtue of the book to be that it is believable and interesting.

Marsh, Fred T. "Here Is An All-American Heel!" Rev. of *What Makes Sammy Run? New York Herald Tribune Books* 30 Mar. 1941: 2.

Describes *What Makes Sammy Run?* in detail. Suggests that this book is not well written, but concedes that Sammy does deserve a mention as a unique American rogue.

Mitchell, Kendall. "Hollywood Heart." Rev. of *Love, Action, Laughter and Other Sad Tales* and *What Makes Sammy Run? Chicago Tribune Books* 7 Jan. 1990: 5.

Describes the repercussions among Hollywood moguls in 1941 when *What Makes Sammy Run?* was first published, and notes that the novel is being republished to coincide with the release of a film version in 1989. Describes several of the stories in *Love, Action, Laughter and Other Sad Tales*, several of which also deal with Hollywood, but finds them predictable with "a few nice touches and moments of insight."

Molloy, Robert. "Continuation of *Waterfront* Formless, But Still Powerful." Rev. of *Waterfront. Chicago Sunday Tribune Magazine of Books* 18 Sept. 1955: 3.

Criticizes the false relationship between characters, celebrates the power inherent in the material, and comments that the climax does not have the full power and horror it should. Concludes that possibly more reworking and a stronger editorial hand would have helped.

Nossiter, Bernard D. "Unsuccessful Reverse." Rev. of *Waterfront. Nation* 1 Oct. 1955: 288.

Argues that *Waterfront* lamely tells us that most Americans don't live in railroad flats. Calls the characters outsized screen characters, and not always believable. Considers that, with his reporter's eye, Schulberg gives the reader the sense of being outside the pale. Concludes that the ending is tacked on and bewildering.

Ostermann, Robert. "To Schulberg, His First Novel in 15 Years Is No 'Comeback'." Rev. of *Sanctuary V. National Observer* 19 Jan. 1970: 23.

Argues that *Sanctuary V* renews the conclusion that Schulberg is an old-fashioned moralist who hopes his work will make a positive difference in the way people live. Suggests that this accounts for the astonishing and crude force of his fictional characters, the dramas developing around them, and their successful sales. Describes the contents of the novel.

"Other Books." Rev. of *Some Faces in the Crowd. Newsweek* 18 May 1953: 119.

Describes the contents of *Some Faces in the Crowd*.

Pfaff, William. "On the Docks." Rev. of *Waterfront. Commonweal* 28 Oct. 1955: 100-01.

Describes the book *Waterfront* as the story of the movie. Notes that it is not his best book, but that it is a good and solid one. Considers the two chief characters superbly explored.

Reynolds, Stanley. "Summer Miscellany." Rev. of *The Disenchanted. Punch* 17 Aug. 1983: 53.

Regards *The Disenchanted* to be illustrating the clash of the Twenties and Thirties politics, the Hollywood of the decade, and a re-creation of Scott and Zelda Fitzgerald. Calls this fascinating stuff for the movie studios.

Rugoff, Milton. "Budd Schulberg Goes to the Docks Again." Rev. of *Waterfront. New York Herald Tribune Book Review* 11 Sept. 1955: 4.

Describes the novel in detail, and commends it as a record of social conditions fostering few illusions about the lives of longshoremen.

Schickel, Richard. "Books in Brief." Rev. of *Sanctuary V. Harper's* Nov. 1969: 136.

Sees *Sanctuary V* as containing ideas which are neither as interesting nor as novel as Schulberg thinks. Describes its first-person locations as fake, simple, and tiresome. Concludes that this is a very gassy book, as vulgar in action as it is in thought and expression.

Schulberg, Budd. "*Waterfront*—'More Than a 90-Minute Movie'." Rev. of *Waterfront. New York Times Book Review* 26 Apr. 1987: 1, 38.

In this brief essay Schulberg describes in first-person the process of his research on the waterfront in preparation for his novel *Waterfront*. Also discusses the aesthetics of the novel and its translation into a screenplay *On the Waterfront*.

Shea, Robert J. "Victim of a Revolution." Rev. of *Sanctuary V. Washington Post Book World* 18 Jan. 1970: 7.

Calls *Sanctuary V* an intelligent, humanistic examination of Cuban-style revolution, as well as a vivid portrayal of deterioration in captivity. Concludes, however, that the novel fails to come up to the quality of earlier works.

Trilling, Diana. "Fiction in Review." Rev. of *The Harder They Fall. Nation* 6 Sept. 1947: 236-37.

Describes *The Harder They Fall* as about the world of boxing which is uncomfortably thin in the realm of moral imagination and lacking in narrative power. Calls this book more fervent than wise.

Tunney, Gene. "Carneravorous Fight Racketeers." Rev. of *The Harder They Fall. Saturday Review of Literature* 9 Aug. 1947: 9-10.

Calls the book witty, brilliant at times, cynical, and full of pathos. Details the contents of the novel, and concludes that it is the best book on fighting since Shaws' "Cashel Byron's Profession."

Van Gelder, Robert. "*What Makes Sammy Run?* and Other New Works of Fiction." Rev. of *What Makes Sammy Run? New York Times Book Review* 30 Mar. 1941: 6.

Describes *What Makes Sammy Run?* as a brilliantly effective first novel based on the theme of "you can't eat your brothers and have them too." Praises it for its hopeful mood, clever dialogue, swift pace, and excellent characterization. Describes contents.

Walker, Stanley. "A Brutal Novel of the Prize Ring." Rev. of *The Harder They Fall. New York Herald Tribune Weekly Book Review* 17 Aug. 1947: 3.

Argues that *The Harder They Fall* is brutal, and the truest and most detailed account of a prize fight in our literature. Notes that, at bottom, it is a novel of high morality. Considers the final result an acute, unsparing, piece of reporting. Concludes that there has been no comparable picture of the sleazy side of this business.

Watts, Richard. "Manly Art." Rev. of *The Harder They Fall. New Republic* 11 Aug 1947: 27-28.

Describes *The Harder They Fall* in detail, and commends its potentially sticky characters for never being described sentimentally or farcically. More comments on the subject of prizefighting than on the book itself.

Weeks, Edward. "The Boxing Fraternity." Rev. of *The Harder They Fall. Atlantic* Sept. 1947: 120.

Describes the contents of *The Harder They Fall*, and argues that not since Hemingway's "Fifty Grand" has there been a story so idiomatic, so physically cruel, and so underscored with the disgust of the corrupted.

Weeks, Edward. "The Novelist Who Couldn't Stand Success." Rev. of *The Disenchanted. Atlantic* Nov. 1950: 90.

Sees *The Disenchanted* as a story of F. Scott Fitzgerald and the whole Hollywood side of American life. Commends Schulberg for his ferocious knowledge of Hollywood, his satirical portraits, and his moral passion. Concludes, however, that it is ultimately a dreary story with a hero too far gone to ever be interesting.

"What Makes Justo Fall?" Rev. of *Sanctuary V. Time* 11 May 1970: 108.

Calls *Sanctuary V* a bold attempt to evade the thoughts of an aging revolutionary. Considers Schulberg well-equipped to blueprint the attitudes and agonies of a man who once had high hopes for revolutionary reform, but whose reach embarrassingly exceeds his grasp in dealing with

Moreno's inner conflicts. Notes that what the book lacks is not philosophy or knowledge, but a cohesive narrative skill.

"Work for a Godly Man?" Rev. of *Waterfront. Newsweek* 12 Sept. 1955: 108-09.

Describes *The Waterfront* as a religious novel with serious defects of glibness and inability to portray inner conflict. Details the contents of the novel.

Interviews

Breit, Harvey. "Talk With Mr. Schulberg." *New York Times Book Review* 5 Nov. 1950: 28. Rpt. in *The Writer Observed*. Harvey Breit. Cleveland: World, 1956. 139-41.

A report of an interview with Schulberg that outlines his early life, education, career as a writer, and latest work, *The Disenchanted*. Comments on the likeness of the central character to F. Scott Fitzgerald and the effects of Hollywood on writers like Faulkner.

Georgakas, Dan. "The Screen Playwright as Author: An Interview with Budd Schulberg." *Cineaste* 11.4 (1982): 6-15, 39.

Schulberg discusses his attitude towards directors and producers, his anecdotes about them, his research for *On the Waterfront*, his view of filmmaking in *Moving Pictures*, his dubious reputation as a serious writer, the lack of social status of screenwriters, the overvaluation of directors, views on the movie *Raging Bull*, his scripting of *The Harder They Fall*, his Jewishness, the success of Jews in Hollywood, Jerry Lewis, Charlie Chaplin, communism in Hollywood, politics of the 1970s, Cuba, the Polish Solidarity movement, and the political issues involved in *Naming Names*.

Gross, Ken. "Budd Schulberg." *People Weekly* 18 Dec. 1989: 93-97.

A report of an interview with Schulberg in which he discusses the screenplay for *What Make Sammy Run?*, Sammy Glick his anti-hero, anecdotes about his school days, his writing about the Hollywood experience, his naming friends who were Communist Party members, his marriages, and his views of life at sixty.

Van Gelder, Robert. "An Interview With Budd Schulberg." *New York Times Book Review* 10 Aug. 1941: 2, 21. Rpt. in *Writers and Writing*. Robert Van Gelder. New York: Scribner's, 1946. 197-200.

This report of an interview with Schulberg contains information about his early life, writing career, physical appearance, personality, and opinions on Hollywood.

Biographical Sources

Cerf, Bennett. "Trade Winds." *Saturday Review of Literature* 14 Oct. 1950: 4, 6.

Describes his meeting with Schulberg, his self-effacing personality, and his subsequent successes. Contains amusing anecdotes about Schulberg and the prediction that *The Disenchanted* will be a major success.

Knopp, Josephine Zadovsky. "Budd Schulberg." *Twentieth-Century American-Jewish Fiction Writers*. Ed. Daniel Walden. Detroit: Gale, 1984. Vol. 28 of *Dictionary of Literary Biography* 94 vols. to date. 1978- . 280-84.

More than details of his life, this is a career biography, tracing the development of the author's canon, describing the contents and themes of his works, evaluating his reputation, and placing him in the larger context of American literary history. Includes lists of primary and secondary sources, and illustrations.

Richler, Mordecai. "The Famous Sammy G." *Gentlemen's Quarterly* Feb. 1990: 115-18.

Reviews the reactions to *What Makes Sammy Run?* at its first publication, its fifty-year staying power, and the reactions of Jews who considered it anti-Semitic. Describes the character of Sammy Glick, citing passages from the novel to show how Sammy worked. Concludes that Damon Runyon's assessment of the book as the quintessential novel about the all-American heel still fits.

Dissertations

Bonora, Diane Christine. "The Hollywood Novel of the 1930's and 1940's." Diss. State U of New York at Buffalo, 1983.

Lokke, Virgil L. "The Literary Image of Hollywood." Diss. State U of Iowa, 1955.

Delmore Schwartz
1913 – 1966

Primary Sources

Collected Works

In Dreams Begin Responsibilities. Norfolk: New Directions, 1938.
Contents: In Dreams Begin Responsibilities, with essays and poetry.

In Dreams Begin Responsibilities and Other Stories. New York: New Directions, 1978; London: Secker, 1978.
Contents: In Dreams Begin Responsibilities, America! America!, The World Is a Wedding, New Year's Eve, The Commencement Day Address, The Track Meet, The Child Is the Meaning of This Life, Screeno.

Successful Love, and Other Stories. New York: Corinth, 1961; Toronto: McLeod, 1961; New York: Persea, 1985, 1990.
Contents: Successful Love, Tales from the Vienna Woods, The Fabulous Twenty-Dollar Bill, The Track Meet, An American Fairy Tale, The Gift, A Colossal Fortune, The Hartford Innocents.

The World Is a Wedding. Norfolk: New Directions, 1948; London: Lehmann, 1949.
Contents: The World Is a Wedding, New Year's Eve, A Bitter Farce, America! America!, The Statues, The Child Is the Meaning of This Life, In Dreams Begin Responsibilities.

Short Fiction in Anthologies

"America! America!" *Jewish-American Stories*. Ed. Irving Howe. New York: Mentor-NAL, 1977. 195-216.

"A Bitter Farce." *This Land, These People*. Ed. Harold U. Ribalow. New York: Beechhurst, 1950. 256-72.

"In Dreams Begin Responsibilities." *Spearhead: 10 Years' Experimental Writing in America*. New York: New Directions, 1947. 571-78; *The Short Story and the Reader*. Ed. Robert Stanton. New York: Holt, 1960. 336-42; *Modern Short Stories: The Fiction of Experience*. Eds. M. X. Lesser and John N. Morris. New York: McGraw, 1962. 453-60; *The Expanded Moment: A Short Story Anthology*. Ed. Robert Gordon. Boston: Heath, 1963. 159-65; *The Rite of Becoming: Stories and Studies of Adolescence*. Eds. Arthur Waldhorn and Hilda Waldhorn. Cleveland: World, 1966. 229-35; *Short Stories: Classic, Modern, Contemporary*. Eds. Marcus Klein and Robert Pack. Boston: Little, 1967. 478-85; *Introduction to Literature: Stories*. Eds. Lynn Altenbernd and Leslie L. Lewis. 2nd ed. Toronto: Macmillan, 1969. 468-72; *Jewish-American Literature: An Anthology*. Ed. Abraham Chapman. New York: Mentor-NAL, 1974. 55-62; *Jewish-American Stories*. Ed. Irving Howe. New York: Mentor-NAL, 1977. 186-94; *Contemporary American Short Stories*. Eds. Douglas Angus and Sylvia Angus. Greenwich: Premier-Fawcett, 1967. 222-29; New York: Ballantine, 1983. 275-84.

Short Fiction in Periodicals

"An American Fairy Tale." *Commentary* Nov. 1958: 420-24.

"The Fabulous Twenty-Dollar Bill." *Kenyon Review* 14.3 (1952): 378-405.

"The Gift." *Partisan Review* 26.3 (1959): 453-60.

"New Year's Eve." *Partisan Review* 12.3 (1945): 327-44.

"Successful Love." *Playboy* June 1955: 13-14, 16, 32, 36-38, 47, 50-51.

"Tales from the Vienna Woods." *Partisan Review* 20.3 (1953): 267-81.

"Track Meet." *New Yorker* 28 Feb. 1959: 28-34.

Secondary Sources

Books

McDougall, Richard. *Delmore Schwartz*. Twayne's United States Authors Series 243. New York: Twayne, 1974.

Articles and Chapters

Brans, Jo. "The Passion for Plato in Delmore Schwartz." *Centennial Review* 30.4 (1986): 507-28.

Discusses Schwartz's use of Plato's cave image and philosophy in his poetry and two of his short stories. Sees in "The World Is a Wedding" a Platonic republic, a "circle of human beings united by need and love." Argues that "In Dreams Begin Responsibilities" takes place within Plato's cave, or a cave within a dream. Discusses in detail how the events of the story reflect the cave image with its shadows and lights.

Cantor, Jay. "On Giving Birth to One's Own Mother." *TriQuarterly* 75 (1989): 78-91.

Discusses the usability of the "hysterics" personality in art and of the melancholic artist. In this context, Cantor explicates "In Dreams Begin Responsibilities," focusing on the metaphor of a film for the depressives untransformed. Commends it as decisively brilliant. Claims that it teaches us that if one does not acknowledge and overcome one's angry fascination with one's internalized parents, then one will unconsciously project them outward onto every one he or she encounters.

Dickstein, Morris. "Cold War Blues: Notes on the Culture of the Fifties." *Partisan Review* 41.1 (1974): 30-53.

A general article on the American Writers of the 1950s, including Delmore Schwartz. Provides an overview of his life and work.

Dike, Donald A., and David H. Zucker. Preface. *Selected Essays of Delmore Schwartz*. Eds. Donald A. Dike and David H. Zucker. Chicago: U of Chicago P, 1970. vii-xiv.

A general overview of Schwartz's life, writings, and final collapse.

Fiedler, Leslie A. "Master of Dreams." *Partisan Review* 34.3 (1967): 339-56.

A general article on the Biblical Joseph archetype in Jewish literature which touches on Delmore Schwartz.

Flint, Robert W. "The Stories of Delmore Schwartz." *Commentary* Apr. 1962: 336-39.

Calls Schwartz's short stories among the best things anywhere at the time—unique acts of discovery and celebration. Shows that they depict New York Jewry with an integrity and wholeness unmatched elsewhere before the Diaspora of the 1940s.

Goldman, Mark. "Reflections in a Mirror: On two Stories by Delmore Schwartz." *Studies in American Jewish Literature* [Albany] 2 (1982): 86-97.

A major treatment of Schwartz's stories detailing the contents of most of them and providing ongoing critical commentary. A major article whose primary thesis is the theme of the irrecoverable past in Schwartz's short stories.

Greenspan, Ezra. "Breaking Away in the Forties." *The Schlemiel Comes to America*. Ezra Greenspan. Metuchen: Scarecrow, 1983. 100-12, passim.

Describes the author's early life, temperament, and personality, several of his works, his lifestyle, characters, themes, and death.

Haffenden, John. "Delmore Schwartz: The American Auden." *Journal of American Studies* 14.1 (1980): 149-56.

An account of his early years, literary successes, personal failures, along with some critical commentary on the short stories. Describes him as a religious writer with antic and mythopoetic tendencies, and claims he possessed a lucent vision of social and moral estrangement as well as spiritual transcendence.

Halio, Jay L. "Fiction and the Malaise of Our Time." *Southern Review* 17.3 (1981): 622-30.

Argues in the brief section on Schwartz that his stories not only show what the form was capable of, but invoke a strong sense of their times, and demonstrate in fiction a sensibility as powerful as that in his poetry.

Harap, Louis. "A Literature of Alienation: Schwartz and Rosenfeld." *In the Mainstream: The Jewish Presence in Twentieth-Century American Literature 1950s-1980s*. Louis Harap. Contributions in Ethnic Studies 19. New York: Greenwood, 1987. 81-91.

Discusses Schwartz's writings by locating him as the standard bearer of a new post-1930s era mentality compounded of political disillusionment and an existentialist modernism heightened by the tensions of the second-generation Jew teetering on the margins of the semi-accultured worlds of his Jewish family and the native American cultural milieu. Useful both biographically and critically. Discusses much of his fiction and poetry.

Howe, Irving. "Delmore Schwart: An Appreciation." *Celebrations and Attacks: Thirty Years of Literary and Cultural Commentary*. Irving Howe. New York: Horizon, 1979. 183-88.

An appreciation written after Schwartz's death in which Howe discusses primarily his short stories, their style, their themes, their impact on readers, and their lasting contributions to American literature.

Karl, Frederick R. *American Fictions 1940/1980: A Comprehensive History and Critical Evaluation*. New York: Harper, 1983. 159-60.

Argues that in "In Dreams Begin Responsibilities" Schwartz uses techniques of realism, fabulism, visions, fantasies, and ethnic awareness that come to shadow an entire genre. An examination of the metafictional elements in Schwartz's short fiction.

Kazin, Alfred. "Delmore Schwartz, 1913-1966." *World Journal Tribune Book Week* 9 Oct. 1966: 1, 17-18.

Briefly describes his last visit with Schwartz in his squalid Greenwich Village room, discusses the bitterness and sadness of his failed life, and evaluates some of his major works. Considers "In Dreams Begin Responsibilities" a masterpiece and his greatest work. Also feels that his collection of short stories, *The World Is a Wedding*, is superior to his work of poetry, *Genesis*, and discusses the importance of the stories which are based on parody.

Kloss, Robert J. "An Ancient and Famous Capital: Delmore Schwartz's Dream." *Psychoanalytic Review* 65.3 (1978): 475-90.

An elaborate explication of the poetry and fiction through the application of current psychoanalytic dream theory.

Lehman, David. "Delmore, Delmore: A Mournful Cheer." *Parnassus: Poetry in Review* 7.2 (1979): 215-30.

A major article which discusses the Atlas biography, Schwartz's poetry, and his short stories. An excellent introduction to the writer.

Lyons, Bonnie. "Delmore Schwartz and the Whole Truth." *Studies in Short Fiction* 14.3 (1977): 259-64. A revision of a paper presented at the Northeast Modern Language Association meeting, Spring 1977.

A detailed reassessment of Schwartz's life and literary contribution to American letters. Concludes that his stories do not seem dated and do not remain of interest merely as social documents. Concentrates mainly on his first collection of short stories—*The World is a Wedding*.

Malin, Irving. *Jews and Americans*. Crosscurrents/Modern Critiques. Carbondale: Southern Illinois UP, 1965. passim.

Treats seven Jewish authors, including Schwartz, who deal with the Jew in America, and their own Jewishness. Discusses how they deal with the Jewish experience—social, religious, psychological—with the center of that experience being God. Devotes chapters to the ideas of exile, fathers and sons, time, head and heart, transcendence, irony, fantasy, and parable in the Jewish-American experience as demonstrated in their works.

New, Elisa. "Reconsidering Delmore Schwartz." *Prooftexts* 5.3 (1985): 245-62.

Argues that Schwartz's work is more interesting for its failures than for its successes. Views him in an overall treatment of American literature and the Jewish writer. An analytical essay on Schwartz as a literary and social phenomenon. Deals with letters, notebooks, poetry, and prose.

Novak, Michael Paul. "The Dream as Film: Delmore Schwartz's 'In Dreams Begin Responsibilities.'" *Kansas Quarterly* 9.2 (1977): 87-91.

An exegesis of the short story that illuminates Schwartz's use of the technical device of film as a metaphor for dreaming. Discusses how he matches the language to the medium of the silent movie, and how the use of film moves from being merely clever to being the key to the story's success.

Politzer, Heinz. "The Two Worlds of Delmore Schwartz: Lucifer in Brooklyn." Trans. Martin Greenberg. *Commentary* Dec. 1950: 561-68.

Describes the two worlds Schwartz lived in as that of his Brooklyn home, about which he wrote so much, and that of his education, an abstract universe of intelligence where he developed his consciousness. Goes on to describe the conflict between these two worlds in his writings.

Pollet, Elizabeth. Introduction. *Portrait of Delmore: Journals and Notes of Delmore Schwartz, 1939-1959*. Ed. Elizabeth Pollet. New York: Farrar, 1986. v-xvi.

Describes Pollet's reactions upon hearing of the death of Schwartz and her subsequent life's work of sifting through and transcribing 2100 sheets of journal entries and notes, very little of it legible. Describes the scope of these writings by Schwartz and the mental life of the man who wrote them. Comments on the lopsidedness of the picture they leave the reader and the inadequacy of language to render a life. Describes her marriage to Schwartz, the process of their mutual psychiatric therapy, his gradual breakdown through drugs and alcohol, and the eventual collapse of the marriage. Documents his early life, origins, education, intellectual bents, metaphysical views and works, and then lays a general background for the beginning of his journal at age twenty-six, his death, the textual difficulties with both journal entries and the surprising amount of poetry they contain.

Rahv, Philip. "Delmore Schwartz: The Paradox of Precocity." *New York Review of Books* 20 May 1971: 19-22. Rpt. in *Essays on Literature and Politics, 1932-1972*. Philip Rahv. Boston: Houghton, 1978. 85-92.

A preface to Schwartz's essays and reviews, which provides a series of arguments as to how he was undervalued and overvalued as a writer. Contains much biographical anecdote and attempts to re-evaluate him as a postwar American writer. Provides commentary on his critical essays of value to the student of his fiction since it contains his critical philosophy of fiction.

Rosenberg, Ruth. "Delmore Schwartz." *Critical Survey of Short Fiction*. Ed. Frank N. Magill. 8 vols. Englewood Cliffs: Salem, 1981. 6: 2203-08.

A standard reference article covering principal short fiction, influence, biography, analysis, and bibliography.

Saposnik, Irving S. "Delmore Schwartz's America." *Studies in Short Fiction* 19.2 (1982): 151-55.

Argues that the one constant in all Schwartz's work was his obsession, and finally paranoia, about being unable to cast off his Jewish identity and unable to find himself at home in America. He always saw himself as different from peers, family, and friends. Examines several of the short stories from this perspective.

Seif, Morton. "Fallen David and Goliath America: The Battle Report of Delmore Schwartz." *Jewish Social Studies* 13 (1951): 311-20.

A socio-historical report of the defeat of Schwartz by both internal and external forces. Accounts for influences from literature, history, and philosophy. A major essay that ranges across a large amount of source materials and discusses many of his writings.

Simpson, Louis. "The Ghost of Delmore Schwartz." *New York Times Magazine* 7 Dec.: 38, 40-43, 48, 52, 56.

Shows that Bellow's Humboldt in *Humboldt's Gift* is based on Schwartz's life and work.

Waldhorn, Arthur, and Hilda Waldhorn. "'In Dreams Begin Responsibilities': More About This Story." *The Rite of Becoming: Stories and Studies of Adolescence*. Eds. Arthur Waldhorn and Hilda Waldhorn. New York: World, 1966. 235-38.

Provides a Freudian analysis of Schwartz's short story, "The Road of Psychoanalytic Therapy."

Zolotow, Maurice. "'I Brake for Delmore Schwartz': Portrait of the Artist as a Young Liar." *Michigan Quarterly Review* 25.1 (1986): 1-22.

A major treatment of the poetry with implications for those interested in Schwartz's life and fiction. Argues that Schwartz was significant, overrated, irritating in the extreme, more ill than most supposed, and definitely not a genuine truth-seeking artist. Contains anecdote not recorded elsewhere.

Reviews

Ableman, Paul. "Second-Generation Apprentice." Rev. of *In Dreams Begin Responsibilities and Other Stories* and *Delmore Schwartz: The Life of an American Poet* by James Atlas. *Spectator* 6 Jan. 1979: 17-18.

Claims that Schwartz never really mastered, or even displayed much instinct for English prose. Feels his early admirers mistook originality for genius. Argues that his enduring contribution to literature was his poetry. Also includes a review of Atlas's biography of Schwartz and some biographical details.

Atlas, James. "Reconsideration." Rev. of *The World Is a Wedding. New Republic* 1 Nov. 1975: 36-39.

Comments on *The World Is a Wedding.* Argues that his work should have been given precedence in the commentary over and above his short and tragic life and sordid death. Recounts just what it was about each of these works that prompted early and generous praise.

B., V. Rev. of *The World Is a Wedding. San Francisco Chronicle* 3 Oct. 1948: 16.

Claims that Schwartz, whose stature as a poet is considerable, has exploited the medium of the long short story with striking success in *The World Is a Wedding.* Notes that he has written an account of conversations, ideas, and actions of a young group of intellectuals—a group so closely knit it is almost a cabal—that is moving, entertaining, and eventually symbolic of all human relationships in this century.

Bogan, Louise. "Young Modern." Rev. of *In Dreams Begin Responsibilities. Nation* 25 Mar. 1939: 353-54.

Sees *In Dreams Begin Responsibilities* as a young man's early work showing all the influences he has absorbed and writers he admires. Describes the variety of genres in the book and their contents. Concludes that he discovers how much simplicity and directness are needed to continue writing, seeing, and feeling.

Boroff, David. "The Theme is Innocence." Rev. of *Successful Love and Other Stories. New York Times Book Review* 10 Dec. 1961: 5.

Calls *Successful Love and Other Stories* a collection exploring the theme of innocence in a variety of ways. Describes several of the stories, and concludes that Schwartz found the right idiom for his stories and is indisputably a genuine man of letters.

Bryant, J. A., Jr. "Arts and Letters." Rev. of *Successful Love and Other Stories. Sewanee Review* 71.1 (1963): 118-19.

Describes the contents, style, and cultural commentary contained in *Successful Love and Other Stories.* These stories are elaborate mathematical propositions designed to permit the manipulation of a few primary values with a multitude of relevant factors. Schwartz is no Swift, but he has the power to seriously disturb us.

Casper, Leonard. "Reviews." Rev. of *In Dreams Begin Responsibilities and Other Stories*. *Studies in Short Fiction* 16.4 (1979): 365.

Calls the stories in *In Dreams Begin Responsibilities* a fearsomely comic collection reflecting a half-acceptance of man's imperfections, which however, subvert the true sense of community. Notes that the characters speak like would-be lovers; but time and again they turn out to be loners and losers. Suggests that the tensions of such stories portray not only immigrants trying to reconcile both unity and diversity, but also the author's task of combining intimacy and objectivity.

Farrelly, John. "City People." Rev. of *The World Is a Wedding*. *New Republic* 2 Aug. 1948: 26-27.

Describes *The World Is a Wedding* as a group of seven stories dealing with middle-class life in American cities which read like milieu studies. Claims that they exist halfway between traditional fiction and philosophical dialogue. Comments on the lack of imagery and visual sense in the stories. Commends Schwartz as a writer of great promise.

Fitts, Dudley. "Balanced Instrument." Rev. of *In Dreams Begin Responsibilities and Other Stories*. *Saturday Review of Literature* 29 Apr. 1939: 29.

Claims that this is primarily an important, new book of poetry prefaced by the title story. Notes that the story and lyrics are perfectly proportioned, becoming a controlled instrument that transforms what might have been adolescent nostalgia into a universal longing and pity.

"Golden Satire." Rev. of *Successful Love and Other Stories*. *Newsweek* 4 Dec. 1961: 90.

Calls *Successful Love and Other Stories* unusually appealing because it shows Schwartz's fine talent for vigorous, colloquial prose; ironic comedy; tender sketches; vitality; and downright good nature.

Greenberg, Martin. "The Artist and the Family." Rev. of *The World Is a Wedding*. *Commentary* Nov. 1948: 486-87.

Argues that *The World Is a Wedding* is written in severely commonplace style which is ironically employed, thus allowing the author to disavow the life he describes, and to affirm his relationship to it. Concludes that bare and brilliant poetry is found in this volume of stories.

Hall, Theodore. "Delmore Schwartz." Rev. of *In Dreams Begin Responsibilities and Other Stories. International Fiction Review* 7.1 (1980): 70-71.

Calls Schwartz a great commentator on the Jewish-American experience in his short stories. Details the contents of several of these stories and elucidates theme and technique along the way.

Hay, John. "Books." Rev. of *The World is a Wedding. Commonweal* 17 Sept. 1948: 551.

Describes Schwartz's style as spare and formal, and his subject matter as that of Jewish middle-class family life in mid-century New York City.

Howe, Irving. "Arts and Letters." Rev. of *The World Is a Wedding. Sewanee Review* 57.1 (1949): 146-49.

A general commentary on Schwartz which discusses several of his works. Concentrates primarily on the short stories in *The World Is a Wedding.*

Howe, Irving. "Delmore Schwartz—A Personal Appreciation." Rev. of *Successful Love and Other Stories. New Republic* 19 Mar. 1962: 25-27.

Literally an appreciation of Schwartz which includes Howe's recollections, some background history, much commentary on the quality of Schwartz's literary gifts and work, his life and his early death. Comments also on the particular dilemma of immigrant Jewish family life and the issue of the gifted son.

Jones, Ernest. "Fiction of a Poet." Rev. of *The World Is a Wedding. Nation* 11 Sept 1948: 294-95.

Considers *The World Is a Wedding* as a piece of poetry rather than as a chronicle. Argues that there is too much flat narrative, emblematic platitude, and dependence on knowledge of things Jewish. Yet the content seems completely lived and comprehendable even though presented in the sparest prose. Concludes that here the Jew is presented as Everyman at the center of the profound disorders of life.

Kapp, Isa. "Familial Relations." Rev. of *The World Is a Wedding. Kenyon Review* 11.4 (1949): 162-63.

Finds in the stories in this collection and in others of Schwartz's works impasses of communication between the characters. Describes some of the stories, and concludes that no one has approximated as shatteringly as Schwartz the chronic repressed hysteria of certain kinds of familial relations.

Lehmann-Haupt, Christopher. "Books of the Times." Rev. of *Letters of Delmore Schwartz. New York Times* 21 Dec. 1984: C36.

Letters of Delmore Schwartz reveals Schwartz to be a poet, critic, writer, professor, editor, failed husband, aging lover, baseball addict, cat lover, military historian, compulsive movie goer, student of literature, and superb literary politician. Concludes that we are not so aware of the clown and madman as we are of the articulate writer.

Mayhew, Alice Ellen. "Daisy Miller-Land." Rev. of *Successful Love and Other Stories. Commonweal* 26 Jan. 1962: 469-70.

Describes *Successful Love* as a set of stories exploring the relationships between dream and reality, good and evil, existentialism and conscience. Concludes that they are urbanely experimental and surrealistic, not to mention sincere and marvelously well-written.

Meyers, Jeffrey. "Downhill All the Way." Rev. of *The Letters of Delmore Schwartz. Virginia Quarterly Review* 62.2 (1986): 348-55.

Provides a critical appraisal of *The Letters of Delmore Schwartz* which argues that it is far too monumental for his rather slight literary achievement. A critical appraisal covering both his fiction and poetry.

Morrison, Blake. "All for Love." Rev. of *In Dreams Begin Responsibilities and Other Stories. New Statesman* 8 Dec. 1978: 793-94.

Claims that this book should focus us on the best talents Schwartz has to offer, but notes that too often the myth of a great talent wasted crops up into consciousness. Describes several of the stories and the autobiography.

"No Cavalry in Sight." Rev. of *Successful Love and Other Stories. Time* 22 Dec. 1961: 55.

Calls *Successful Love* another of the rainy, unpromisingly gray kinds of stories that find their way into the quarterlies because of their disgust with anything approaching the dramatic and a belief that the cavalry rarely does charge into anyone's life. Briefly describes the stories in the collection.

Phillips, Robert. "The Short Story—Four Collections." Rev. of *In Dreams Begin Responsibilities and Other Stories. Commonweal* 15 Sept. 1978: 599-60.

Comments primarily on the wisdom of Atlas's inclusion of stories for *In Dreams Begin Responsibilities and Other Stories.* Describes the contents of each of the stories.

Popkin, Henry. "Verbal Nets for Evasive Answers." Rev. of *Successful Love and Other Stories. Saturday Review* 2 Dec 1961: 25.

Argues that *Successful Love and Other Stories* is often written like verbal nets for meaning, some proving more effective than others. Suggests that though similar to the previous stories, these stories show more detachment and a somewhat larger range of experience. Concludes that the lapses are few enough to make us grateful he still cultivates his garden.

Ribalow, Harold U. "Jews in Short Stories." Rev. of *The World Is a Wedding. Congress Weekly* 10 Jan. 1949: 16.

Comments on *The World Is a Wedding* that Schwartz has written primarily about unhappy, maladjusted, tortured Jews; therefore, the stories have little narrative interest. Concludes that they seem like overextended essays, but are nevertheless readable and penetrating. Describes several of the stories.

Spector, Robert Donald. "A Poet's First Stories." Rev. of *Successful Love and Other Stories. New York Herald Tribune Books* 21 Jan. 1962: 4.

Argues that in this collection Schwartz indulges his poetic fancy, allows implausibilities in the narrative action and characters, and perceptively exaggerates American mores. Describes several of the stories.

"Stories Through Plate Glass." Rev. of *The World Is a Wedding. Time* 9 Aug. 1948: 86.

Predicts that with the publication of this collection of stories Schwartz should take his place among a dozen or so of the most accomplished young U.S. writers. Accuses the stories of a coyness that occasionally flaws the prose which is otherwise like a sheet of glass. Concludes that he will suffer no disgrace in being compared to Chekov or Stendahl.

Towers, Robert. "The Delmore File." Rev. of *In Dreams Begin Responsibilities and Other Stories* and *Delmore Schwartz: The Life of an American Poet* by James Atlas. *New York Review of Books* 23 Mar. 1978: 15-18.

In addition to a lengthy discussion of Atlas's biography of Schwartz,

Towers spends most of his time discussing Howe's foreword to this collection. Objects to Howe's conclusion that Schwartz's style is an "anti-rhetoric" with the "sing-song, slightly pompous intonation of Jewish immigrants educated in night schools, the self-conscious affectionate mockery of that speech by American-born sons, [and] its abstraction into the jargon of city intellectuals." Feels instead that this language could just as well be from Macon, Georgia, and that his style is Schwartz's "obeisance to the demands of T. E. Hulme and T. S. Eliot for 'classical' restraint as opposed to romantic wallowing." Concludes that with this collection of stories and Atlas's biography, "the file on the case of Delmore Schwartz is probably as complete as it needs to be."

Warner, Eric. "Schwartz's Moment." Rev. of *In Dreams Begin Responsibilities and Other Stories* and *Delmore Schwartz: The Life of an American Poet* by James Atlas. *Listener* 8 Feb. 1979: 233.

Discusses Schwartz's life and his dream of being the chronicler of the Jewish exodus from Europe. Finds that the stories contain a thinly-disguised portrait of Schwartz himself. Calls the title story "a stunningly inventive piece," but prefers "America! America!"

Biographical Sources

Atlas, James. "Unsentimental Education." *Atlantic* June 1983: 79-92.

An account of his research on the life of Schwartz for Atlas's biography of the writer. Particularly useful accounts of interviews with friends of Schwartz.

Atlas, James. *Delmore Schwartz: The Life of an American Poet.* New York: Farrar, 1977.

Auden, W. H. "Letter to Delmore Schwartz." *Antaeus* 23 (1976): 193-97.

Contains the script of a letter from Auden to Schwartz in which Auden discusses views on Rousseau and St. Augustine that had previously been expressed by Schwartz.

Barrett, William. "Delmore: A Thirties Friendship and Beyond." *Commentary* Sept. 1974: 41-54. Rpt. in modified form as "The Destruction of a Poet" in *The Truants: Adventures Among the Intellectuals*. William Barrett. Garden City: Anchor-Doubleday, 1982. 209-40.

A tribute containing an account of Barrett's friendship with Schwartz in the 1930s.

Bawer, Bruce. *The Middle Generation: The Lives and Poetry of Delmore Schwartz, Randall Jarrell, John Berryman, and Robert Lowell.* Hamden: Archon-Shoestring, 1986.

Carruth, Hayden. "Delmore, 1913-1966." *Texas Quarterly* 10.2 (1967): 43-47. Rpt. in *Working Papers: Selected Essays and Reviews by Hayden Carruth.* Ed. Judith Weissman. Athens: U of Georgia P, 1982. 131-37.

An account of Carruth's memories of the anguished final years of Schwartz's life.

Fraser, Russell. "Delmore Schwartz and the Death of the Poet." *Michigan Quarterly Review* 18.4 (1979): 592-605.

An account of the life, works, and tragic death of Schwartz. Deals with the short stories briefly amid mostly biographical discussion.

Goldman, Mark I. "Delmore Schwartz." *Twentieth-Century American-Jewish Fiction Writers.* Ed. Daniel Walden. Detroit: Gale, 1984. Vol. 28 of *Dictionary of Literary Biography.* 94 vols. to date. 1978- . 285-91.

More than details of his life, this is a career biography, tracing the development of the author's canon, describing the content and themes of his works, evaluating his reputation, and placing him in the larger context of American literary history. Includes lists of primary and secondary sources and illustrations.

Hook, Sidney. "Imaginary Enemies, Real Terror." Rev. of *Delmore Schwartz: The Life of an American Poet. American Scholar* 47 (1978): 406-12.

Essentially an anecdotal account of Hook's experiences with Schwartz as a student at NYU. Discusses his career and personal decline, accounting for it as latent insanity, but also pointing out that his early success went to his head and left him terrified lest he could not live up to expectations in his subsequent work.

Hook, Sidney. "The Radical Comedians: Inside *Partisan Review.*" *American Scholar* 54.1 (1984-85): 45-61.

An account of those associated with the *Partisan Review,* including Schwartz.

Kazin, Alfred. "Words." *New York Jew*. New York: Knopf, 1978. 23-26.

Contains interesting Schwartz anecdotes from *Partisan Review* days. Primarily biographical.

Levin, Harry. "Delmore Schwartz's Gift." *Canto: A Review of the Arts* (1978). Rpt. in *Memories of the Moderns*. Harry Levin. New York: New Directions, 1980. 156-65.

A biographical, anecdotal memoir of his associations with Schwartz and Schwartz's literary career.

Ludwig, Jack. "Icarus Grounded." Rev. of *Delmore Schwartz: The Life of an American Poet. Partisan Review* 1979: 636-43.

Provides an overview of Schwartz's life by detailing the contents of James Atlas' *Delmore Schwartz: The Life of An American Poet*.

MacDonald, Dwight. "Delmore Schwartz, 1913-1966." *Selected Essays of Delmore Schwartz*. Eds. Donald A. Dike and David H. Zucker. Chicago: U of Chicago P, 1970. xv-xxi.

Details MacDonald's first impressions upon receiving for publication *In Dreams Begin Responsibilities*. Contains subsequent anecdotal material on his association with Schwartz.

Schwartz, Delmore. "Under Forty: A Symposium on American Literature and the Younger Generation of American Jews." *Contemporary Jewish Record* Feb. 1944: 12-14.

In response to an invitation to discuss the relationship of his Jewish heritage to his writing, Schwartz comments that being born of immigrant parents is a special kind of experience. He discusses its impact on language and speech development, growing up in New York isolated from non-Jewish contacts and direct contact with anti-Semitism, Jewish schooling in contrast with public schools—all of which resulted in a kind of ignorance of the larger world. This ignorance and growing recognition of reality shaped him as an author in which his writing has been an attempt to understand his experiences. Concludes that his Jewishness has been an ever-growing good and can be "nothing but a fruitful and inexhaustible inheritance."

Shechner, Mark. "More on Delmore." Rev. of *Portrait of Delmore: Journals and Notes of Delmore Schwartz: 1939-1959*, ed. Elizabeth Pollet. *Partisan Review* 54.3 (1987): 497-502. Rpt. as "A Portrait of

Delmore" in *The Conversion of the Jews and Other Essays*. Mark Shechner. New Directions in American Studies. London: Macmillan, 1990. 85-90.

A rather unflattering essay that describes the recently published *Portrait of Delmore Schwartz: Journals and Essays* as bristling pathograms of resentment and outrage. Accuses Pollett, the estranged second wife, and critic Robert Phillips of "toiling in the ruins of Schwartz's career in the hopes, it seems, of making a museum of all that shattered masonry." Dismisses the volume as a trial to read that no one will pick up casually. "There have got to be better forms of homage than these 648 pages of undigested journal." Provides biographical details extracted from the journals.

Simpson, Eileen. *Poets in Their Youth: A Memoir*. New York: Random, 1982.

Spears, Monroe K. "Last Words of a Student of Joy." Rev. of *Portrait of Delmore: Journals and Notes of Delmore Schwartz, 1939-1959*, ed. Elizabeth Pollet. *The Washington Post Book World* 28 Sept. 1986: 3, 13.

Finds the biography casually and minimally edited and a mishmash of hasty and incomplete diary entries. Discusses how the promise of the author's greatness was never really fulfilled, and attempts to answer the question of why he failed so badly.

Bibliographies

Labuz, Ronald. "Delmore Schwartz: A Bibliographical Checklist." *American Book Collector* July-Aug. 1983: 42-50.

Dissertations

Choguill, Francine Olman. "Delmore Schwartz: The Moral Responsibility of the Writer." Diss. Syracuse U, 1968.

Hall, Theodore Dana. "A Student of the Morning Light: A Study of the Cultural and Salvational Vision of Delmore Schwartz." Diss. Syracuse U, 1976.

Irwin Shaw

1913 – 1984

Primary Sources

Novels

Acceptable Losses. New York: Arbor, 1982; New York: Avon, 1983; London: New English Library, 1983; Large Print ed. Leicester: Charnwood, 1984; Large Print ed. Guilford: Ulverscroft [Cited in BBIP, 1988].

Beggarman, Thief. New York: Delacorte, 1977; London: Weidenfeld, 1977; New York: Dell, 1978; London: Open Market-New English Library, 1978; London: New English Library, 1979, 1982.

Bread Upon the Waters. New York: Delacorte, 1981; London: Weidenfeld, 1981; Franklin Center: Franklin, 1981; Charnwood Library Series. Large Print ed. Leicester: Charnwood, 1982; London: New English Library, 1982; New York: Dell, 1982; Large Print ed. Guilford: Ulverscroft [Cited in BBIP, 1988].

Evening in Byzantium. New York: Delacorte, 1973; London: Weidenfeld, 1973; New York: Dell, 1974; London: New English Library, 1975.

Lucy Crown. New York: Random, 1956; London: Cape, 1956; New York: Signet-NAL, 1957; London: Pan, 1960; New York: Dell, 1971; London: New English Library, 1977; London: Severn, 1978.

Nightwork. New York: Delacorte, 1975; London: Weidenfeld, 1975; Large Print ed. Boston: Hall, 1976; New York: Dell, 1976, 1983; London: Pan, 1976, 1980; Large Print ed. London: Prior, 1976; [Sevenoaks]: New English Library, 1986.

Rich Man, Poor Man. New York: Delacorte, 1970; London: Weidenfeld, 1970; New York: Dell, 1971, 1976; London: New English Library, 1976.

The Top of the Hill. New York: Delacorte, 1979; London: Weidenfeld, 1979; New York: Dell, 1980; London: New English Library, 1980.

The Troubled Air. New York: Random, 1951; Chicago: Sears Readers Club, 1951; London: Cape, 1951; Four Square Books. London: Landsborough, 1958; London: Consul-World, 1965; London: New English Library, 1978; London: Inner Circle, 1985; New York: Dell, 1987.

Two Weeks in Another Town. New York: Random, 1960; London: Cape, 1960, 1979; London: Reprint Society, 1961; London: Pan, 1962; New York: Dell, 1971; London: New English Library, 1977.

Voices of a Summer Day. A Delacorte Press Book. New York: Dial, 1965; London: Weidenfeld, 1965; London: New English Library, 1977; New York: Dell, 1978; London: Severn, 1982; Large Print ed. Bath: Lythway-Chivers, 1984.

The Young Lions. New York: Random, 1948; New York: Modern Library, 1948, 1958, 1982; New York: Signet-NAL, 1948, 1950, 1958, 1971; London: Cape, 1949, 1980; London: Pan, 1957; New York: Dell, 1976, 1982; Franklin Center: Franklin, 1979; Sevenoaks: New English Library, 1985.

Collected Works

Act of Faith, and Other Stories. New York: Random, 1946; Short Story Index Reprint Series. Freeport: Books for Libraries, 1971; New York: Arno, 1980.

Contents: Preach on the Dusty Roads, Faith at Sea, Gunners' Passage, Walking Wounded, Hamlets of the World, Retreat, Part in a Play, The Priest, Night in Algiers, Medal from Jerusalem, The Veterans Reflect, Act of Faith.

God Was Here But He Left Early. New York: Arbor, 1972; New York: Dell, 1975, 1981; London: Pan, 1977; New York: Priam-Arbor, 1983.

Contents: God Was Here But He Left Early, Where All Things Wise and Fair Descend, Whispers in Bedlam, The Mannichon Solution, Small Saturday.

Irwin Shaw, Four Complete Novels. New York: Avenel, 1981.

Contents: *Rich Man, Poor Man; Beggarman, Thief; Nightwork; Evening in Byzantium.*

Love on a Dark Street, and Other Stories. New York: Delacorte, 1965; London: Cape, 1965; New York: Dell, 1966, 1981; Harmondsworth: Penguin, 1970; London: New English Library, 1978.

Contents: The Man Who Married a French Wife; The Inhabitants of Venus; Noises in the City; A Year to Learn the Language; Love on a Dark Street; Once, in Aleppo; Circle of Light; Wistful, Delicately Gay; Tune Every Heart and Every Voice; Goldilocks at Graveside.

Mixed Company: Collected Short Stories. New York: Random, 1950; London: Cape, 1952; London: Pan, 1961; London: New English Library, 1977.

Contents: The Girls in Their Summer Dresses; The Eighty-Yard Run; Act of Faith; Main Currents of American Thought; Strawberry Ice Cream Soda, Material Witness; Sailor off the Bremen; The Climate of Insomnia; God on Friday Night; Triumph of Justice; The City Was in Total Darkness; The Monument; Return to Kansas City; The Lament of Madam Rechevsky; Night, Birth and Opinion; It Happened in Rochester; Borough of Cemeteries; The Passion of Lance Corporal Hawkins; Welcome to the City; Widows' Meeting; Gunners' Passage; Mixed Doubles; Little Henry Irving; Hamlets of the World; The Indian in Depth of Night; Weep in Years to Come; The Priest; Medal from Jerusalem; Lemkau, Pogran & Blaufox; The Man with One Arm; Walking Wounded; The Dry Rock; Faith at Sea; Search through the Streets of the City; Night in Algiers; Preach on the Dusty Roads; The Green Nude.

Retreat, and Other Stories. London: New English Library, 1970, 1985.

Contents: Retreat, Part in a Play, The Veterans Reflect, The House of Pain, Pattern of Love, I Stand by Dempsey, Stop Pushing Rocky, The Deputy Sheriff, The Greek General, Residents of Other Cities.

Sailor off the Bremen, and Other Stories. New York: Random, 1939; London: Cape, 1940.

Contents: Sailor off the Bremen; I Stand by Dempsey; The Girls in Their Summer Dresses; Return to Kansas City; The Deputy Sheriff; Second Mortgage; March, March on Down the Field; Walk Along the Charles River; No Jury Would Convict; Santa Claus; The Monument; The Greek General; My Green Flower; Strawberry Ice Cream Soda; The Boss; Little Henry Irving; Stop Pushing, Rocky; Residents of Other Cities; Weep in Years to Come; Borough of Cemeteries.

Selected Short Stories. New York: Modern Library, 1961.

Contents: The Eighty-Yard Run; Main Currents of American Thought; The Girls in Their Summer Dresses; Sailor off the Bremen; Welcome to the City; Weep in Years to Come; Search Through the Streets of the City; Night, Birth and Opinion; The City Was in Total Darkness; Hamlets of the World; Walking Wounded; Gunners' Passage; Medal from Jerusalem; Act of Faith; Age of Reason; Mixed Doubles; The Climate of Insomnia; The Green Nude; Tip on a Dead Jockey; In the French Style; Voyage Out, Voyage Home; The Sunny Banks of the River Lethe; Then We Were Three.

Short Stories. New York: Random House, 1966.

Contents: Sailor off the Bremen; I Stand by Dempsey; The Girls in Their Summer Dresses; Return to Kansas City; The Deputy Sheriff; Second Mortgage; March, March on Down the Field; Walk Along the Charles River; No Jury Would Convict; Santa Claus; The Monument; The Greek General; My Green Flower; Strawberry Ice Cream Soda; The Boss; Little Henry Irving; Stop Pushing, Rocky; Residents of Other Cities; Weep in Years to Come; Borough of Cemeteries; The Eighty-Yard Run; Main Currents of American Thought; Welcome to the City; Search

Through the Streets of the City; Night, Birth and Opinion; The City Was in Total Darkness; Hamlets of the World; Walking Wounded; Gunners' Passage; Medal from Jerusalem; Act of Faith; Age of Reason; Mixed Doubles; The Climate of Insomnia; The Green Nude; Tip on a Dead Jockey; In the French Style; Voyage Out, Voyage Home; The Sunny Banks of the River Lethe; Then We Were Three; A Wicked Story; Peter Two; The Kiss at Croton Falls; The Wedding of a Friend; God on Friday Night; Free Conscience, Void of Offence; Material Witness; The House of Pain; Triumph of Justice; Select Clientele; The Indian in Depth of Night; It Happened in Rochester; The Dry Rock; Prize for Promise; Lemkau, Pogran and Blaufox; Dinner in a Good Restaurant; The Lament of Madam Rechevsky; Pattern of Love; Preach on the Dusty Roads; Faith at Sea; Retreat; Part in a Play; The Priest; Night in Algiers; The Veterans Reflect; The Passion of Lance Corporal Hawkins; Widows' Meeting; The Man with One Arm.

Short Stories, Five Decades. New York: Delacorte, 1978, 1984; London: Cape, 1978; New York: Laurel-Dell, 1983; London: Pan [Cited in BBIP, 1988].

Contents: The Eighty-Yard Run; Borough of Cemeteries; Main Currents of American Thought; Second Mortgage; Sailor off the Bremen; Strawberry Ice Cream Soda; Welcome to the City; The Girls in Their Summer Dresses; Search Through the Streets of the City; The Monument; I Stand by Dempsey; God on Friday Night; Return to Kansas City; Triumph of Justice; No Jury Would Convict; The Lament of Madame Rechevsky; The Deputy Sheriff; Stop Pushing, Rocky; "March, March on Down the Field"; Free Conscience, Void of Offence; Weep in Years to Come; The City Was in Total Darkness; Night, Birth and Opinion; Preach on the Dusty Roads; Hamlets of the World; Medal from Jerusalem; Walking Wounded; Night in Algiers; Gunners' Passage; Retreat; Act of Faith; The Man with One Arm; The Passion of Lance Corporal Hawkins; The Dry Rock; Noises in the City; The Indian in Depth of Night; Material Witness; Little Henry Irving; The House of Pain; A Year to Learn the Language; The Greek General; The Green Nude; The Climate of Insomnia; Goldilocks at Graveside; Mixed Doubles; A Wicked Story; Age of Reason; Peter Two; The Sunny Banks of the River Lethe; The Man Who Married a French Wife; Voyage Out, Voyage Home; Tip on a Dead Jockey; The Inhabitants of Venus; In the French Style; Then We Were Three; God Was Here But He Left Early; Love on a Dark Street; Small Saturday; Pattern of Love; Whispers in Bedlam; Where All Things Wise and Fair Descend; Full Many a Flower; Circle of Light.

Tip on a Dead Jockey. New York: Random, 1957; London: Cape, 1957; London: Pan, 1959, 1977; London: Consul-World, 1964; London: Mayflower, 1970.

Contents: Tip on a Dead Jockey; A Wicked Story; In the French Style; Peter Two; Age of Reason; The Kiss at Croton Falls; Then We Were Three; The Sunny Banks of the River Lethe; The Wedding of a Friend; Voyage Out, Voyage Home.

Welcome to the City, and Other Stories. New York: Random, 1942; New York: Avon, 1946.

Contents: The City Was in Total Darkness; Main Currents of American Thought; God on Friday Night; The Eighty-Yard Run; Welcome to the City; Free Conscience, Void of Offence; Material Witness; The House of Pain; Triumph of Justice; Night, Birth and Opinion; Search Through the Streets of the City; Select Clientele; The Indian in Depth of Night; It Happened in Rochester; The Dry Rock; Prize for Promise; Lemkau, Pogran and Blaufox; Dinner in a Good Restaurant; The Lament of Madam Rechevsky; Pattern of Love.

Whispers in Bedlam: Three Novellas. London: Weidenfeld, 1972.

Contents: *Whispers in Bedlam, Small Saturday, The Mannichon Solution.*

Short Fiction in Anthologies

"Act of Faith." *Modern Jewish Stories.* Ed. Gerda Charles. London: Faber, 1963. 90-107; Englewood Cliffs: Prentice, 1965. 99-120; *A World of Great Stories.* Eds. Hiram Collins Haydn and John Cournos. New York: Crown, 1947. 128-41; *55 Short Stories from the New Yorker.* New York: Simon, 1949. 64-79; *This Land, These People.* Ed. Harold U. Ribalow. New York: Beechhurst, 1950. 283-302; *An Anthology of Famous American Stories.* Eds. Angus Burrell and Bennett Cerf. New York: Modern Library, 1953, 1963. 1274-88; *Fifty Modern Stories.* Ed. Thomas Blair. New York: Harper, 1960. 441-54; *Two and Twenty: A Collection of Short Stories.* Ed. Ralph Singleton. New York: St. Martin's, 1962. 310-28; *Points of View: An Anthology of Short Stories.* Eds. James Moffett and Kenneth R. McElheny. New York: NAL, 1966. 366-82; *Tales of Our People—Great Stories of the Jew in America.* Ed. Jerry D. Lewis. New York: Geis, 1969. 107-22; *The Secret Sharer and Other Great Stories.* Eds. Abraham Lass and Norma Tassman. New York: Mentor-NAL, 1969. 243-61.

"The Dry Dock." *Masters and Masterpieces of the Short Story.* Ed. Joshua McClennen. New York: Holt, 1957. 72-76.

"The Eighty-Yard Run." *New Stories for Men.* Ed. Charles Grayson. New York: Doubleday, 1941; Garden City: Garden, 1943. 431-44; *Short Story Masterpieces.* Eds. Robert Warren and Albert Erskine. New York: Dell, 1954. 424-39; *Great Esquire Fiction: The Finest Stories from the First Fifty Years.* Ed. L. Rust Hills. New York: Penguin, 1983. 49-62; *The Norton Book of American Short Stories.* Ed. Peter S. Prescott. New York: Norton, 1988. 448-60.

"The Girls in Their Summer Dresses." *Short Stories from the New Yorker, 1925-1940.* New York: Simon, 1940. 3-8; *Understanding Fiction.* Eds. Cleanth Brooks and Robert P. Warren. 2nd ed. New York: Appleton, 1959. 84-88; *The Scope of Fiction.* Eds. Cleanth Brooks and Robert P. Warren. New York: Appleton, 1960. 58-62; *American Short Stories.* Eds. Eugene Current-Garcia and Walton Patrick. Rev. ed. New York: Scott, 1964. 612-17. *Fifty Great American Short Stories.* Ed. Milton Crane. New York: Bantam, 1965. 449-54; *The Shape of Fiction.* Eds. Leo Hamalian and Frederick Karl. New York: McGraw, 1967. 126-31; *Studies in the Short Story.* Ed. Adrian Jaffe. 3rd ed. New York: Holt, 1968. 149-53; *Images of Women in Literature.* Ed. Mary Anne Ferguson. Boston: Houghton, 1973. 235-39.

"God on Friday Night." *The Seas of God.* Ed. Whit Burnett. Philadelphia: Lippincott, 1944. 257-62.

"Gunners' Passage." *200 Years of Great American Short Stories.* Ed. Martha Foley. Boston: Houghton, 1975. 760-74.

"The Kiss at Croton Falls." *Fiction: Form and Experience.* Ed. William M. Jones. Lexington: Heath, 1969. 135-40.

"Love on a Dark Street." *The Best American Short Stories, 1962.* Eds. Martha Foley and David Burnett. Boston: Houghton, 1962. 378-99.

"Main Currents of American Thought." *Short Stories from the New Yorker, 1925-1940.* New York: Simon, 1940. 275-84; *Fifty Great*

Short Stories. Ed. Milton Crane. New York: Bantam, 1952. Pag. not available; *Perception and Pleasure: Stories for Analysis.* Ed. Fred Marcus. Boston: Heath, 1967. 26-33.

"Noises in the City." *The Best American Short Stories, 1963.* Eds. Martha Foley and David Burnett. Boston: Houghton, 1963. 315-26.

"The Passion of Lance Corporal Hawkins." *Reading Modern Diction: 30 Stories with Study Aids.* Ed. Winifred Lynskey. New York: Scribner, 1952. 446-56; *Reading Modern Fiction: 31 Stories with Critical Aids.* Ed. Winifred Lynskey. 4th ed. New York: Scribner, 1968. 451-61.

"Sailor off the Bremen." *Short Stories from the New Yorker, 1925-1940.* New York: Simon, 1940. 350-58.

"Search Through the Streets of the City." *The Best American Short Stories, 1942.* Ed. Martha Foley. Boston: Houghton, 1942. 269-78; *Fifty Best American Short Stories, 1915-1965.* Ed. Martha Foley. Boston: Houghton, 1965. 278-85.

"Strawberry Ice Cream Soda." *Twenty Grand Short Stories.* Ed. Ernestine Taggard. New York: Bantam, 1947, 1968. 188-98; New York: Pathfinder-Bantam, 1963; 188-98.

"Then We Were Three." *Identity: Stories for This Generation.* Ed. Katherine Hondius. Chicago: Scott, 1966. 234-61.

"The Veterans Reflect." *Accent Anthology: Selections from Accent, A Quarterly of New Literature.* Eds. Kerker Quinn and Charles Shattuck. New York: Harcourt, 1946. 293-306.

"Walking Wounded." *First Prize Stories 1919-1954 from the O. Henry Memorial Awards.* Garden City: Doubleday, 1954. 381-95; *First Prize Stories 1919-1966 from the O. Henry Memorial Awards.* Garden City: Doubleday, 1966. 381-95.

Short Fiction in Periodicals

"Act of Faith." *New Yorker* 2 Feb. 1946: 24-30, 32.

"Age of Reason." *New Yorker* 25 May 1946: 20-24.

"Circle of Light." *Esquire* Oct. 1958: 226-27, 230, 232, 236, 238, 240, 244-51.

"The City Was in Total Darkness." *New Yorker* 30 Aug. 1941: 13-19.

"Climate of Insomnia." *New Yorker* 2 Apr. 1949: 28-36.

"The Convert." *Esquire* Sept. 1947: 42-43, 143-51.

"The Dry Dock." *New Yorker* 31 May 1941: 14-18.

"Eighty-Yard Run." *Playboy* May 1955: 6-8, 10, 32, 40; *Esquire* Oct. 1973: 292-95, 488, 491-92.

"Faith at Sea." *New Yorker* 15 May 1943: 17-22.

"Free Conscience, Void of Offence." *New Yorker* 27 July 1940: 14-17.

"Full Many a Flower." *Playboy* Jan. 1978: 170-71, 174, 217-20; *Short Story International* Oct. 1980: 139-56.

"Girls in Their Summer Dresses." *New Yorker* 4 Feb. 1939: 15-17.

"God on Friday Night." *Story* Jan.-Feb. 1939: 92-95.

"God Was Here But He Left Early." *Esquire* July 1968: 94-95, 119, 122, 124-26.

"Goldilocks at Graveside." *Esquire* July 1964: 32-34, 99-100, 102-03.

"The Greek General." *Collier's* 15 Oct. 1938: 36, 53-54.

"Gunners' Passage." *New Yorker* 22 July 1944: 21-28, 30.

"Hamlets of the World." *New Yorker* 9 Jan. 1943: 22-26, 28-29.

"The House of Pain." *Esquire* Nov. 1940: 95, 189-91.

"In the French Style." *New Yorker* 17 Jan. 1953: 25-31.

"The Inhabitants of Venus." *Saturday Evening Post* 26 Jan. 1963: 44-51; *Short Story International* June 1986: 132-56.

"Instrument of Salvation." *New Yorker* 24 Apr. 1954: 28-33.

"It Happened in Rochester." *Esquire* Dec. 1939: 128, 280-81, 284.

"Kiss at Croton Falls." *Collier's* 11 May 1956: 50, 54-55.

"Love on a Dark Street." *Esquire* Mar. 1961: 130-36, 138-40, 142-43.

"Main Currents of American Thought." New Yorker 5 Aug. 1939: 15-19.

"The Man Who Married a French Wife." *Mademoiselle* June 1962: 98-99, 120-26; *Short Story International* Aug. 1987: 137-56.

"The Mannichon Solution." *Playboy* Dec. 1967: 110-14, 116, 122, 282-84, 286, 288.

"Material Witness." *New Yorker* 1 Feb. 1941: 12-14.

"Medal from Jerusalem." *Collier's* 13 Apr. 1946: 11-12, 36-37, 40, 42.

"Mixed Doubles." *New Yorker* 9 Aug. 1947: 19-23; *Short Story International* Aug. 1983: 156-66.

"The Monument." *Esquire* June 1939: 40, 132, 134.

"Night in Algiers." *New Yorker* 25 Sept. 1943: 19-20.

"Night, Birth, and Opinion." *Harper's* May 1941: 578-82.

"Noises in the City." *Playboy* June 1962: 85, 108-12.

"Once, in Aleppo." *Playboy* Dec. 1964: 113-16, 174, 271-76, 279-80, 282, 284-86.

"Part in a Play." *Collier's* 7 July 1945: 14-15, 61-62.

"The Passion of Lance Corporal Hawkins." *New Yorker* 29 Mar. 1947: 31-36.

"Peter Two." *New Yorker* 19 Apr. 1952: 29-32.

"Preach on the Dusty Roads." *New Yorker* 22 Aug. 1942: 13-16.

"The Priest." *New Yorker* 7 Apr. 1945: 20-24.

"Residents of Other Cities." *Esquire* July 1939: 32-33, 155.

"Retreat." *Collier's* 27 Jan. 1945: 26, 56.

"Sailor off the Bremen." *New Yorker* 25 Feb. 1939: 15-18.

"Search Through the Streets of the City." *New Yorker* 2 Aug. 1941: 13-16.

"Second Mortgage." *New Republic* 3 Nov. 1937: 367-68.

"Select Clientele." *New Yorker* 17 Aug. 1940: 15-18.

"The Single Brute." *Esquire* Oct. 1947: 64-65, 147-48, 150, 152, 154.

"Stop Pushing." *Collier's* 10 Dec. 1938: 27, 41.

"Strawberry Ice Cream Soda." *Scholastic* 22 Jan. 1940: 27-30.

"The Sunny Banks of the River Lethe." *New Yorker* 7 Feb. 1953: 29-35.

"Then We Were Three." *McCall's* Aug. 1955: 26-27, 79-80, 82-84, 86-87; *Short Story International* Feb. 1985: 126-59.

"Thomas in Elysium." *Playboy* Jan. 1970: 92-96, 100, 241-51.

"Tip on a Dead Jockey." *New Yorker* 6 Mar. 1954: 28-36, 38-41, 44-46, 48-50, 53-54, 56-59.

"Tittle Fading Back." *Esquire* Jan. 1965: 31-34, 119-22.

"Triumph of Justice." *Esquire* Dec. 1940: 99, 270-73; *Scholastic* 16 Feb. 1948: 21, 24, 27-28, 31.

"Tune Every Heart and Every Voice." *Playboy* Jan. 1962: 56-57, 119-21.

"Veterans Reflect." *Accent* 3.2 (1943): 67-76.

"Viola Player." *Yale Review* 29.1 (1939): 90-96.

"Voice of Conscience." *Collier's* 16 July 1938: 16, 24.

"Voyage Out, Voyage Home." *New Yorker* 12 Feb. 1955: 34-40, 43-44, 46-49, 51-55.

"Walking Wounded." *New Yorker* 13 May 1944: 30-36, 39, 40-42.

"Welcome to the City." *New Yorker* 17 Jan. 1942: 17-21.

"Where All Things Wise and Fair Descend." *Playboy* Feb. 1967: 70-72, 74, 171-73; *Short Story International* Feb. 1989: 111-28.

"Whispers in Bedlam." *Playboy* Feb. 1969: 75-78, 80, 86, 206-10, 212-16, 218-21; *Short Story International* June 1990: 105-56.

"A Wicked Story." *New Yorker* 28 Mar. 1953: 31-35.

"Widows' Meeting." *New Yorker* 19 Apr. 1947: 31-36, 38-40.

"Wistful, Delicately Gay." *Cosmopolitan* Oct. 1954: 50-60.

"A Year to Learn the Language." *Redbook* Nov. 1961: 44-47, 110-19.

Secondary Sources

Books

Giles, James R. *Irwin Shaw*. Twayne's United States Authors Series 443. Boston: Twayne, 1983.

Articles and Chapters

Aldridge, John W. "Mailer, Burns, and Shaw." *After the Lost Generation: Critical Studies of the Writers of Two Wars*. John W. Aldridge. New York: McGraw, 1951. 133-56.

Discusses Shaw's *The Young Lions* as a book which seems to have been written to reductive *New Yorker* formulas with its neat, bloodless prose, stopwatch climaxes, slick formulas, prefabrication, contrivance, and pulled punches. Details the contents of the novel.

Berke, Jacqueline. "Further Observations on "A Shaw Story and Brooks and Warren"." *CEA Critic* Nov. 1970: 28-29.

Agrees with Baird and Grajeda (*CEA Critic*, Feb. 1966) that Brooks and Warren misinterpret or ignore basic human nature in their explication of Shaw's "The Girls in Their Summer Dresses" in their book, *Understanding Fiction*. Suggests that the theme of this story is much deeper than merely the recognition and bitter acceptance of a failed marriage.

Bryant, Jerry H. "The Last of the Social Protest Writers." *Arizona Quarterly* 19.4 (1963): 315-25.

Describes *The Young Lions* as a social protest novel against the army as stand-in for corporate America.

Eisinger, Chester. "Irwin Shaw: The Popular Ideas of the Old Liberalism." *Fiction of the Forties*. Chester Eisinger. Chicago: U of Chicago P, 1967. 106-13.

Describes Shaw's work, then argues that he suffers from an inability to free himself from the 1930s and from the idols of respectability and success. Asserts that these forces have seriously disrupted the integrity of his work. Claims that his books read like tracts for the aspirin age written by an author who is a vigorous and implacable hater.

Evans, Bergen. "Irwin Shaw." *English Journal* Nov. 1951: 485-91.

Describes Shaw's writing career, his pacifism, his depiction of warfare, and his career as a playwright. Mostly a book-by-book report of the contents of the novels.

Fiedler, Leslie A. "Irwin Shaw: Adultery, The Last Politics." *Commentary* July 1956: 71-74.

Begins with a discussion about Shaw's dis-ease with critics, condemns him for lapsing into sentimentality, cites his lapses into "liberaloid cliches" and courting of large publication contracts. Concludes with extremely negative comments on each of his novels.

Fiedler, Leslie A. *The Jew in the American Novel.* Herzl Institute Pamphlets 10. New York: Herzl, 1959. 48-50; A Second Star Book 5. 2nd ed. New York: Stein, 1966. 48-50. Rpt. in *The Collected Essays of Leslie Fiedler.* 2 vols. New York: Stein, 1971. 2: 104-06; *To the Gentiles.* New York: Stein, 1971. 104-06.

Sees Shaw as a writer who depicts anti-Semitism, writes anti-war protest literature, and produces cliches of the Jew as combat hero. Claims that Shaw's work fulfills the ideal proposed to himself by the bureaucratized, intellectual dreaming of what he would do if released by Hollywood or the TV network.

Foley, Martha. "War Fiction—A Mirror for Americans." *Survey Graphic* Dec. 1948: 499-501, 516.

Provides a general treatment of recent American war novels, including *The Young Lions*, about which she comments briefly .

Giles, James R. "Irwin Shaw's Original Prologue to *The Young Lions.*" *Resources for American Literary Study* 11.1 (1982): 115-19.

The report of an interview with Shaw during July of 1980. Covers Shaw's attitudes towards his own novels, his career as a writer, and the central vision underlying his work.

Harap, Louis. *Creative Awakening: The Jewish Presence in Twentieth-Century American Literature, 1900-1940s. Contributions in Ethnic Studies* 17. New York: Greenwood, 1987. 142-43.

In a chapter on the novels of WWII depicting Jews, Harap discusses *The Young Lions*, finding it commercial and melodramatic. Describes the contents of the story with its center the encounters of Ackerman, the protagonist, with anti-Semitism. Concludes that the vicious string of fights stretches both credibility and probability and is "a commercial rather than an artistic approach to the novel's problems."

Heilman, Robert B. "Comment." *Modern Short Stories: A Critical Anthology.* Ed. Robert B. Heilman. New York: Harcourt, 1950. 172-73.

Explicates "Sailor off the Breman," describing the story line, the suspense, the meaning of the conflict, the point of view, the bestial imagery, the motives of the protagonist, and the theme that violence is the source of violence.

Higgs, Robert J. "Dionysus." *Laurel & Thorn: The Athlete in American Literature.* Robert J. Higgs. Lexington: Kentucky UP, 1981. 102-07.

Briefly discusses the character of Victor Herres in *The Troubled Air* as an example of the embattled American artistic sensibility at the hands of Herres.

Jaffe, Adrian H., and Virgil Scott. "Point of View." *Studies in the Short Story.* Adrian H. Jaffe and Virgil Scott. 2nd ed. New York: Holt, 1960. 87-88.

Discusses the point of view used in "The Dry Rock" and its application to theme and style. Uses this to illustrate the crucial role the objective point of view plays in modern fiction.

Kazin, Alfred. "The Mindless Young Militants: The Hero-Victims of the American War Novels." *Commentary* Dec. 1948: 495-501.

This wide-ranging article of the literary war hero comments in depth on Shaw's *The Young Lions*, which like many other novels, focuses not on the war itself, but America's social problems as reflected by the army. Sees *The Young Lions* as a book about what the army did to a nice, sensitive, bookish young man named Private Noah Ackerman at the hands of his violently anti-Semitic company in Florida.

Milic, Louis T. "Naming in Shaw's *The Young Lions.*" *Style* 23.1 (1989): 113-23.

Comments that in works like this, produced as a mini-series, a profusion of characters and exotic locales are standard features. Claims that in *The Young Lions* the names of many of the characters, in their origins and their associations, constitute an effort to create a structural framework for this apparently loose-jointed work.

Mitgang, Herbert. "Irwin Shaw, Extolled for Short Stories, Dies." *New York Times* 17 May 1984: A1, B19.

Reviews Shaw's writing career, his literary achievements, his contributions to younger writers, and his financial success from his writing. Also includes comments from his son and others about him, as well as biographical information.

Moorhead, Michael. "Hemingway's 'The Short Happy Life of Francis Macomber' and Shaw's 'The Deputy Sheriff.'" *Explicator* 44.2 (1986): 42-43.

Shows that Shaw purposefully named his deputy Macomber after Hemingway's character to enrich and elevate his work. Calls both losers, but at the end considers Shaw's is a bigger loser because he continues to live with his empty, dreary life and his dull wife. Concludes that Shaw's story does not deserve its total obscurity and is an excellent example of the literary practice of influence.

Morris, Willie. "Irwin Shaw's Quiet Craft: Friendship & the Bridge of Writing." *Washington Post* 18 May 1984: B1-B2.

An appreciation written by a friend who admired Shaw and his work. Finds in him an introspection and sadness that his hearty exterior belied. Senses Shaw worried about his place in American literature, and concludes that he needn't have done so because he wrote words that have become embedded in the irony and consciousness of our years, helping us to understand much in ourselves.

Oriard, Michael. "Youth and Age in Sports Fiction." *Dreaming of Heroes: American Sports Fiction, 1868-1980.* Michael Oriard. Chicago: Nelson-Hall, 1982. 155-57, 227-29.

Comments that in Shaw's fiction about sports, he frequently uses former athletic heroes in decline or a youth-addicted, success-oriented, hero-worshipping America. Comments specifically on "The Eighty-Yard Run."

Orvis, Mary Burchard. "Building the Structure." *The Art of Writing Fiction*. New York: Prentice, 1948. 70-73.

A brief examination of "The Girls in Their Summer Dresses" as a perfect example of the one-scene *New Yorker* short fiction. Discusses characters and setting.

Otten, Robert M. "Irwin Shaw." *Popular World Fiction 1900-Present*. Eds. Walton Beacham and Suzanne Niemeyer. 4 vols. Washington: Beacham, 1987. 4: 1361-72.

A standard reference article on Irwin Shaw covering his publication history, critical reception, honors, popularity, and actual novels. Describes each novel's social concerns, theme, character, techniques, literary precedents, related titles, and adaptations.

Peden, William. *The American Short Story: Continuity and Change, 1940-1975*. Ed. William Peden. 2nd ed. Boston: Houghton, 1975. 152-53.

Briefly describes Shaw's war stories, which Peden considers his best work, and concludes that while Shaw is a first-class journalist and a skillful fiction writer, his stories seem overcontrived and overmanipulated, faults that have become worse in his more recent works.

Petty, Chapel Louise. "Irwin Shaw." *Critical Survey of Short Fiction*. Ed. Frank N. Magill. 8 vols. Englewood Cliffs: Salem, 1981. 6: 2221-25.

A standard reference article covering principal short fiction, other literary forms, influence, story characteristics, biography, and critical analysis.

Prigozy, Ruth. "The Liberal Novelist in the McCarthy Era." *Twentieth Century Literature* 21.3 (1975): 253-64.

Provides a definition of the "political novel," and goes on to discuss several novels of the McCarthy era, including Shaw's *The Troubled Air*, which looks at McCarthyism in the broadcasting industry and the State Department.

Smith, Elliott L., and Andrew W. Hart. "By Way of Discussion." *The Short Story: A Contemporary Looking Glass*. Eds. Elliott L. Smith and Andrew W. Hart. New York: Random, 1981. 57-59.

Gives a detailed analysis of structural elements, meaning, character, style, and effects in Shaw's "The Dry Rock."

Startt, William. "Irwin Shaw: An Extended Talent." *Midwest Quarterly*
    2.4 (1961): 325-37.

Calls the Irwin Shaw of today a writer who is no longer the idealistic
writer of earlier times. Argues that Shaw is essentially a dramatist and
short story writer whose talent, however admirable, thins out and
becomes flat when applied to the longer and more integrated genre of the
novel. Traces this throughout the "big" novels.

Stegner, Wallace Richard Showcraft, and Boris Ilyin. "Analysis." *The
    Writer's Art*. Boston: Heath, 1950. 197-200.

Provides an analytical treatment of meaning, structure, style, characters,
themes, and significance in "The Eighty-Yard Run." Sees Christian
Darling as epitomizing the adolescent values of the 1920s rise and fall.
Notes that time is the main character in the story, and concludes that
through it, Shaw magnifies the failure of Christian Darling into the failure of the American Jazz Age.

"*Two Weeks in Another Town*." *Survey of Contemporary Literature*. Ed.
    Frank N. Magill. Rev. ed. 12 vols. Englewood Cliffs: Salem, 1977.
    12: 7851-54.

A standard reference article covering background, influences, theme,
style, plot, and character in *Two Weeks in Another Town*.

Umphlett, Wiley L. *The Sporting Myth and the American Experience:
    Studies in Contemporary Fiction*. Lewisburg: Bucknell UP, 1975.
    123-29, 150-51.

Discusses mostly the character of Christian Darling of "The Eighty-Yard
Run" as a character exemplifying what can happen after a fall from innocence.

Wetzsteon, Ross. "Irwin Shaw: The Conflict Between Big Bucks and
    Good Books." *Saturday Review* Aug. 1981: 12, 14, 16-17.

Describes the process by which Irwin Shaw has come to represent big
bucks and bad books. Comments that his latest novel, *Bread Upon the
Waters*, with its unadorned moral severity casts an arc of light back over
his entire work that once seemed vague and unclear and now seems brilliantly illuminated. Provides a detailed critical appraisal of the novel.

Yardley, Jonathan. "Popular in the Best Way." *Washington Post* 21 May
    1984: D1, D8.

Celebrates Shaw, who died the previous week, as an accomplished middle-brow writer like O'Hara, Marquand, Rawlings, DuMaurier writing for readers of some education and taste who expected their entertainment to be literate and intelligent as well as entertaining.

Reviews

"A $400,000 Novel." Rev. of *Lucy Crown. Newsweek* 2 Apr. 1956: 91, 93-94.

Discusses *Lucy Crown* from point of view of plot, character, and setting.

Ackroyd, Peter. "Watery Grave." Rev. of *Beggarman, Thief. Spectator* 3 Dec. 1977: 32.

Argues that the momentum in *Beggarman, Thief* comes from some deep depression. Notes that the elements at work here are crassly conventional ones that usually haunt mediocre fiction. Claims that Shaw drags his reader through redundant adjectives and adverbs, stopping here and there for a cliche and finally leaves us with the feeling that the significant events all happened a long time ago.

Adams, Phoebe. Rev. of *Tip on a Dead Jockey and Other Stories. Atlantic* Aug. 1957: 86.

Characterizes the ten stories in *Tip on a Dead Jockey and Other Stories* as neat, reserved in style, unusually amusing, and well-balanced.

Adams, Phoebe. "Reader's Choice." Rev. of *Two Weeks in Another Town. Atlantic* Feb. 1960: 116.

Calls *Two Weeks in Another Town* old-fashioned and fairly ordinary artistically. Concludes that, as a treatise on the limits of personal and social responsibility, Shaw is not impressive despite the rather artfully told story.

"Afternoon of a Fan." Rev. of *Voices of a Summer Day. Newsweek* 1 Mar. 1965: 88.

Deals with *Voices of a Summer Day* mostly in terms of an extended character sketch of Federov, Shaw's latest alter ego. Does not see the book as first division stuff.

Angoff, Charles. "Irwin Shaw's Journalistic Skill." Rev. of *The Troubled Air. Congress Weekly* 31 Dec. 1951: 14-15.

Calls *The Troubled Air* another serious moral and political novel which makes exciting and rewarding reading. Claims that, artistically, Shaw is lacking for a variety of reasons including the failure of some of the key characters to appear to be more than props for the thesis. Suggests that, perhaps, there are just too many editorials strung together in the name of the novel, rather than stirring portrayals of people. Concludes that, though an artistic failure, this novel has considerable documentary value.

Black, Susan M. "Of Youths and Elephants." Rev. of *Two Weeks in Another Town*. *New Republic* 22 Feb. 1960: 18.

Calls *Two Weeks in Another Town* a book full of deftly created minor characters and a generous amount of things to say. Comments on the sparkling dialogue, good plotting, and entertainment value. Complains, however, that it is all too slick and loudly organized beyond that. Concludes that Shaw is a contemplative and thoughtful writer despite having missed his larger goals.

Boroff, David. "The Past was Poor But Beautiful." Rev. of *Voices of a Summer Day*. *Saturday Review* 6 Mar. 1965: 28.

Argues that *Voices of a Summer Day*, which seems promising at first, is really only an exercise in nostalgia and a series of loosely strung vignettes unified by the author's penchant for sorting out his people into humane and heartless, good and bad. Suggests that, at best, Shaw is a fastidious writer with a keen eye. Concludes that this book is a cluster of jottings without a vision of the present.

Boyd, William. "Holding up the Wedding." Rev. of *Bread Upon the Waters*. *Times Literary Supplement* 3 July 1981: 878.

Calls *Bread Upon the Waters* a book afflicted with a moral point of view, a modestly stoical idea of how to cope with the world, and a terribly boring central consciousness through whom all events are mediated.

Brandel, Marc. "Three Men in the War." Rev. of *The Young Lions*. *New York Times Book Review* 3 Oct. 1948: 5.

Calls *The Young Lions* an immensely interesting first novel which, if it has a fault, reads too much like a collection of short stories. Outlines the plot and characters, complains of the contrived ending, and commends the book for its true emotional force.

"Broadway Blinkers." Rev. of *The Young Lions*. *Time* 11 Oct. 1948: 114, 116.

Calls Shaw's work too smooth and clever in the past. Sees this ambitious new novel as depressing evidence of how hard it is for a writer to slough off the habits of youth. Claims that *The Young Lions* disintegrates into crumbling unintegrated sketches and Broadway devices, characters, and settings.

Brookner, Anita. "Urged Downwards." Rev. of *Beggarman, Thief. Times Literary Supplement* 25 Nov. 1977: 1373.

Calls *Beggarman, Thief* a novel Shaw ought to be ashamed of with its sadly computerized production. Claims that his characters never know anything deeper than the sudden urge or itch for drink, sex, money, or trouble.

Buffington, Robert. "Speak, Mnemosyne." Rev. of *Short Stories: Five Decades. Sewanee Review* 88.3 (1980): 424-25.

Provides a retrospective on Shaw's previous works that sees him reflecting the Depression and the ominous signs of war. Comments on his literary forebears, general style, weaknesses, and strengths. Focuses mainly on his short story "An Act of Faith."

Butcher, Fanny. "Fortnight of Assorted Adventures in Rome." Rev. of *Two Weeks in Another Town. Chicago Sunday Tribune Magazine of Books* 31 Jan. 1960: 3.

Argues that *Two Weeks in Another Town* reveals Shaw's undeniable genius for recording conversation and probing into human motives. Suggests that the plot reads like naughty entertainment, full of the kind of sugariness, pseudo-profundity, and false violence that usually gets called "interesting." Concludes that Shaw can do much better.

Cassal, Gould. "Snapshots from Brooklyn Bridge." Rev. of *Sailor off the Bremen and Other Stories. Saturday Review of Literature* 2 Sept. 1939: 14-15.

Describes *Sailor off the Bremen* as a collection of short stories sharing the characteristics of melodrama, Broadway formulas, excellent realistic detail, wry sympathy, playwriting more than novelistic prose, and lack of sincere social criticism.

Cassill, R. V. "Horatio Alger Repolished." Rev. of *Rich Man, Poor Man. Chicago Tribune Book World* 27 Sept. 1970: 5.

Describes *Rich Man, Poor Man* as a novel built on a Horatio Alger formula for American success with abrupt shifts into realism. Details the contents of the novel, and concludes that Shaw stakes his reputation on the borderland where serious art and commercial sentimentalities blur comfortably. Concludes that, regardless of many defects, the milieus and situations he renders are done masterfully.

Chapin, Ruth. "A Crucial Problem." Rev. of *The Troubled Air. Christian Science Monitor* 7 July 1951: 9.

Calls *The Troubled Air* gripping, relevant, and basically flawed. Criticizes the book for its lack of vital integration of the brilliant, single scenes, and for inadequate dialogue. Commends it for its integrity of purpose.

Condini, N. E. "Made in Hollywood." Rev. of *The Top of the Hill. National Review* 18 Apr. 1980: 484.

Argues that *The Top of the Hill* shows Shaw revealing his hand at a new psychological fad, probing the relationship between high risk sports and the fear of death. Concludes that it gives the impression of watching a TV movie.

Cook, Bruce. "'No Country for Old Men.'" Rev. of *Evening in Byzantium. Washington Post Book World* 22 Apr. 1973: 9.

Distinguishes between writing aptitude (talent) and ability, and claims that Shaw, in *Evening in Byzantium,* has achieved a triumph of ability over aptitude. Describes the story, praises his characterization, and concludes that, unlike many of Shaw's earlier works, there is no slickness or glibness.

Cooper, Arthur. "Grand Larceny." Rev. of *Nightwork. Newsweek* 3 Nov. 1975: 92.

Calls *Nightwork* a great, fun, enormously likeable, first-rate piece of entertainment. Notes that its plot is improbable, the settings fast-changing and glamorous, the hero irresistible.

Cosgrave, Mary. Rev. of *Bread Upon the Waters. Horn Book Magazine* Dec. 1981: 692-93.

Calls *Bread Upon the Waters* a superbly written, spellbinding story of a New York family. Considers it a book reflecting well the author's deeply felt views on the uses and abuses of wealth and power, and the quality of ethical and ethnic values in contemporary society.

Cosgrave, Patrick. "Three Lapses." Rev. of *Rich Man, Poor Man. Spectator* 31 Oct. 1970: 525.

Describes the novel in detail, and concludes that Shaw shouts when he should be more subtle.

Cromie, Robert. "The Next Man you Meet." Rev. of *Love on a Dark Street and Other Stories. Saturday Review* 2 Oct. 1965: 59-60.

Considers this a book of short stories of marked quality. Describes several of them, and complains that some have contrived endings. Considers Shaw a fine observer with a fine ear, and claims that his work gives the impression of inevitability. Confesses he has a storyteller's gift.

Danielson, Richard E. Rev. of *Act of Faith and Other Stories. Atlantic* Nov. 1946: 172.

Describes *Act of Faith* as masterful, involved in the impact of war on human lives. Calls them dramatic, sure, and full of the perspective of an artist, soldier, observer, and spokesman. Considers these brilliant pictures of the background of war.

Davis, Robert Gorham. "Agony, Doubt and Dignity." Rev. of *Mixed Company: Collected Stories. New York Times* 15 Oct. 1950: 4, 45.

Describes *Mixed Company* as including thirty stories from Shaw's earlier collections of short stories, plus seven new pieces. Details the whole collection as cumulatively impressive, full of representative types and many important shared emotions of the era they portray. Comments that these stories draw strength from history as well as from art.

Davis, Robert Gorham. "Stories of the Dusty Roads of War." Rev. of *Act of Faith and Other Stories. New York Times Book Review* 25 Aug. 1946: 5.

Considers *Act of Faith* to be deeply moral and historically relevant. Describes each of the stories in turn, and concludes there to be a meagerness of political ideas because Shaw still thinks in terms of the anti-fascist slogans of 1936.

Davis, Robert Gorham. "When the Finger Points." Rev. of *The Troubled Air. New York Times Book Review* 10 June 1951: 8, 30.

Calls *The Troubled Air* a topical and brilliantly fascinating popular novel with a weak and unpolitical conclusion. Details the contents.

Dever, Joe. Rev. of *The Troubled Air. Commonweal* 13 July 1951: 339-40.

Describes the protagonist of the novel, the plot, and the issue of civil rights violation it raises. Commends Shaw for his x-ray insight and for making exciting drama out of preaching, despite the fact that his contrivances may be a little bothersome to some readers.

"An Element of Unreason." Rev. of *Tip on a Dead Jockey and Other Stories. Times Literary Supplement* 22 Nov. 1957: 701.

Calls *Tip on a Dead Jockey* a collection of thoroughly excellent and entertaining stories reflecting a humane and often humorous attitude to life. Considers these stories as contemplating missed opportunity and sometimes the sad nature of the world.

Emerson, Sally. "Recent Fiction." Rev. of *Acceptable Losses. Illustrated London News* Apr. 1983: 63.

Calls *Acceptable Losses* sensitive and searching with clear prose, a cunning plot, and an effectively gathering sense of gloom.

Esty, William. "Immense, Vulnerable Niceness." Rev. of *Tip on a Dead Jockey and Other Stories. Commonweal* 6 Sept. 1957: 572-73.

Accuses Shaw of having produced warmed-over, diluted, Hemingway malaise in *Tip on a Dead Jockey*. Complains that Shaw's tired content and characterization suggest that he is just racing the engine of a stalled vehicle. Considers his slickness as offered with the certain, insinuating plausibility of a ready-made daydream.

Feldman, Anita. "Books." Rev. of *Voices of a Summer Day. Commonweal* 23 Apr. 1965: 169-71.

Describes *Voices of a Summer Day* as moving in memory rather than in sensation or in passion. Considers it a loose series of associations and reveries framed by an afternoon whose events constitute a series of small epiphanies and pregnantly typical encounters. Concludes that the cool style can embody a comic or a stoic vision, but when it attempts to evoke commitment of humanity as meaning imposed upon a concrete situation, it becomes only a convention or a mannerism, and an inappropriate one at that.

Ferguson, Otis. "Reading for Pleasure." Rev. of *Welcome to the City and Other Stories. New Republic* 2 Feb. 1942: 157.

Calls *Welcome to the City* a book which may be momentous or casual, but always in motion. Comments that on a scale of one hundred for informative-readable, it gets a passing sixty.

Ferguson, Otis. "Runs Batted In." Rev. of *Sailor off the Bremen and Other Stories. New Republic* 13 Sept. 1939: 166-67.

Calls *Sailor off the Bremen* a tightly finished, "sketch from life" genre piece. Agrees the dialogue is good, but not brilliant. Sees Shaw as being an overrated playwright whose successes nevertheless have eased things for him in publisher's row.

Frakes, James R. "On the Riviera with Irwin Shaw." Rev. of *Evening in Byzantium. New York Times Book Review* 1 Apr. 1973: 6-7.

Considers *Evening in Byzantium* written by a truly professional writer who knows his way around many worlds. Claims that every action is convincingly motivated, the exposition is dramatized, the dialogue is unfailingly realistic, and the center of consciousness is both sensitive and consistent. Concludes with a comment that the intricate character sketch of the central protagonists gets a little too stereotyped.

Frank, Sheldon. "Shaw: Why Is It That Our Middle Brow Writers Are So Damned Serious?" Rev. of *Nightwork. National Observer* 6 Dec. 1975: 21.

Considers *Nightwork* a semi-pleasant surprise, but complains that, unfortunately, Shaw's heavy hand weighs down what may have been an enjoyable, cynical tale. Claims that this is slick melodrama posing as serious fiction. Concedes Shaw's undeniable gift for comedy in the latter sections of this novel, and concludes that he should develop it instead of trying to be so "damned serious."

Friedman, Bruce Jay. "Irwin Shaw's Stories." Rev. of *Short Stories: Five Decades. Esquire* 5 Dec. 1978: 99-100.

Compares Shaw's characters with those of Hemingway in his *Short Stories: Five Decades.* Commends his artless and matter-of-fact technique, his celebration of a world of tough, little guys against the big guys. Concludes that Shaw's stories move, inform, and entertain.

Gilman, Richard. "Sad and Sterile." Rev. of *Two Weeks in Another Town. Commonweal* 18 Mar. 1960: 680-81.

Calls Shaw's a sterile, absolutely immobile talent, and accuses him of being false, immature, melancholic, philosophically arrested, superficial, full of talk, unable to render speech properly, and providing an entertaining ape-like vision of love.

Gladstone, J. F. "Novel's Anti-Hero Looks Back in Languor." Rev. of *Voices of a Summer Day. Christian Science Monitor* 4 Mar. 1965: 4.

Sees *Voices of a Summer Day* as a description of the 1930-1970 era of American social history. Describes the book as written with distinguished ease and a broad canvas, but with a neatness which detracts and a Hemingwayesque style to the narrative which lacks Hemingway's depth.

Glazer, Nathan. "A Masque of Innocence." Rev. of *The Troubled Air*. *Commentary* July 1951: 92-94.

Considers *The Troubled Air* a presentation of a political position in the peculiar political setting of the 1950s, the great decade of the unveiling of one's record on Communism. Details the story of a radio station manager and his five employees accused of Communism. Contains a detailed critique of Shaw's views on Communism and that of the prevailing times.

Goldknopf, David. "Topic Number One." Rev. of *The Troubled Air*. *New Republic* 2 July 1951: 21.

Calls *The Troubled Air* a story about a very serious issue, but claims that it is often difficult to take the story seriously: the characters suffer from a mechanistic behaviorism and other kinds of anemia. Claims that the writing is too lathered up with a lot of wisecracking drivel studded with shrewd observation and provocative insights. Concludes that Shaw is a clever and insightful writer whose skills are not equal to those insights.

Goodman, Mark. "Homeward Bound." Rev. of *Nightwork*. *Time* 29 Dec. 1975: 65.

Calls *Nightwork* high entertainment, and describes the plot.

Greenwood, Gillian. Rev. of *Short Stories. Five Decades. Books and Bookmen* Mar. 1979: 57.

Praises the contents of *Short Stories: Five Decades*, for fluidity of style, expansiveness, emphasis, humor, a keen eye for hypocrisy, and abundance of entertainment.

Harris, Eric. "Reviews." Rev. of *Acceptable Losses. Books and Bookmen* Mar. 1983: 34.

Considers *Acceptable Losses* a somber and easy-paced story of one man's confrontation with death done in the style of probing psychological self-analysis. Concludes that it is a far cry from the light-hearted *Nightwork* or the simple morality of *Bread Upon the Waters*. Briefly summarizes plot.

Harsent, David. "Tiny Tears." Rev. of *Night Work*. *New Statesman* 24 Oct. 1975: 519.

Calls *Night Work* an easy and enjoyable read and a good-tempered novel. Describes the plot and central character.

Hogan, William. "Irwin Shaw Observes the Ungentle People." Rev. of *Lucy Crown*. *San Francisco Chronicle* 30 Mar. 1956: 17.

Calls *Lucy Crown* a woman's novel written by one of America's most polished writers. Notes that parts of it have buoyancy, grace and awareness, but complains that Shaw has milked this vignette of upper middle-class society to a point where we can almost hear the organ music in the background. Concludes that it is too slick and commercial, and that there is too much film flashback and many unpleasant scenes.

Hogan, William. "Irwin Shaw and Other Short Story Writers." Rev. of *Tip on a Dead Jockey and Other Stories*. *San Francisco Chronicle* 3 July 1957: 21.

Describes the contents of *Tip on a Dead Jockey* as diamond-hard, precision-tooled, and efficient.

Hogan, William. "Two Wild Weeks on the Hollywood Tiber." Rev. of *Two Weeks in Another Town*. *San Francisco Chronicle* 29 Jan. 1960: 25.

Describes the novel as shadowy rather than substantial, and permeated with a mood of slick virtuosity. Comments on Rome as a movie colony full of tortured beautiful people from the international set who fraternize with others who belong to a decadent social fringe and second-chop royalty. Concludes that Shaw is tired and bored with his craft.

Hunter, Evan. "Limitless Bounty." Rev. of *Bread Upon the Waters*. *New York Times Book Review* 23 Aug. 1981: 14-15.

Describes the plot and characters of *Bread Upon the Waters*, its themes of limitless bounty, culture, family dynamics, overindulgence, and the uses and abuses of power in big government. Calls the prose clean and spare, and the novel generally thoughtful and professional.

Jackson, Joseph Henry. "Bookman's Notebook." Rev. of *Act of Faith and Other Stories*. *San Francisco Chronicle* 24 Sept. 1946: 14.

Claims that *Act of Faith*, Shaw's new collection of stories, reveals him as one of the living masters of the short story. Describes several of the stories, and comments on the crusading mentality which infuses each.

Jackson, Joseph Henry. "The Man in the Middle." Rev. of *The Troubled Air. San Francisco Chronicle* 11 June 1951: 20.

Argues that in *The Troubled Air*, Shaw takes as his subject Communism and treats it in such a way that we are forced to distinguish between who is a Communist and who is a vague idealist, as well as between base and unsubstantiated accusations of Communism. Concludes that Shaw has the ability to put his finger unerringly on one of our tender spots and arouse the readers' emotions. Comments that this is both a pure and a topical novel.

Jackson, Joseph Henry. "Today's Young Lions." Rev. of *The Young Lions. San Francisco Chronicle* 12 Oct. 1948: 18.

Provides an overview of the contents of *The Young Lions* and, in particular, a profile of its three major protagonists. Calls Shaw's ability great, his message eloquent, his viewpoint right, and his emotional sympathy informed and appropriate.

Kalem, Theodore. "Passage into Fidelity, Courage, Decision." Rev. of *The Young Lions. Christian Science Monitor* 30 Sept. 1948: 11.

Calls *The Young Lions* a remarkable first novel, and provides a detailed account of its contents and, in particular, the moral transformation of Michael Whiteacre.

Kanfer, Stefan. "Secular Grace." Rev. of *Short Stories: Five Decades. Time* 6 Nov. 1978: 114.

Thinks this collection contains 63 polished works that tend to self-mockery turned up to full volume. Considers the stories dated and speaking exclusively in the past tense. Concludes that, because of them, Shaw's claims for redemption can be written in the future definite.

Kappler, Frank. "A Fast-Ball Artist Throws a Change-up." Rev. of *Voices of a Summer Day. Life* 12 Mar. 1965: 10, 16.

Describes *Voices of a Summer Day* as a quiet reflection on four decades of life. Calls this novel a welcome change of pace and a beauty.

Kauffmann, Stanley. "Herzog, Schmerzog." Rev. of *Voices of a Summer Day. New York Herald Tribune Book Review* 7 Mar. 1965: 12, 14.

Claims that this novel portrays the Sacco and Vanzetti trials to the Kennedy murder, abstracting and examining our society's attitudes toward sex, politics, idealism, and Jewish assimilation. Judges Shaw's master to be obviously Hemingway. Details the plot, and concludes that this book is ultimately not a good read.

Kaufmann, James. "When the Nature of the Call is Death." Rev. of *Acceptable Losses. Los Angeles Times Book Review* 9 Jan. 1983: 1.

Calls *Acceptable Losses* a philosophical novel whose reach exceeds its grasp. Considers Damon too culturally upscale. Concludes, however, that Shaw is still a fine storyteller.

Kelly, James. "Domestic Deception." Rev. of *Lucy Crown. Saturday Review* 31 Mar. 1956: 13.

Describes *Lucy Crown* as a remarkably apt comment on modern high-style marriage, complete with rudderless child and the freedom for neuroses. Also concedes that, for others, it is a loosely linked chain of domestic confrontations proving mostly that life is morose and laden with doom. Calls the prose clever and craftsmanlike.

Kupferberg, Herbert. "Probing Story of Love and Art in Rome." Rev. of *Two Weeks in Another Town. New York Herald Tribune Book Review* 31 Jan. 1960: 5.

Describes the novel solely in terms of plot, characters, and furnishings. Concludes that it is a dramatic, penetrating story about modern life.

Lardner, John. "Total Plot." Rev. of *The Young Lions. New Yorker* 2 Oct. 1948: 94-99.

Describes *The Young Lions* as a book demonstrating the difficulty of finding a frame in which to clearly and sharply make comments about WWII. Sees the book closer in literary merit to Mailer's *The Naked and the Dead* than most other war novels. Criticizes it for a jumbo "get it all in" approach using what might be called total plot.

La Salle, Peter. "Asking for Criticism, They Want Only Praise." Rev. of *Short Stories. Five Decades. America* 13 Jan. 1979: 16.

Describes the contents of *Short Stories: Five Decades* as quietly moving, plotted, and definitely literary. Expresses pleasure at the availability of the collection and its quality.

"Last Summer's Dresses." Rev. of *Tip on a Dead Jockey and Other Stories. Time* 8 July 1957: 74.

Claims that this collection will not set the world on fire, but that it is readable and exciting. Describes several of the stories, and concludes that they are blander, just as accomplished, but less impassioned than his earlier work.

Leggett, John. ".". Rev. of *Rich Man, Poor Man. Saturday Review* 17 Oct. 1970: 34-36.

Claims that *Rich Man, Poor Man* does not redeem Shaw's reputation as a writer of sprawling social concepts; oversimplified characters; glib, showy prose; and superficially contrived stories. Comments that Shaw is not one of our great writers. Describes the contents. Notes that Shaw has a master's hand, but not a master's heart.

Lehmann-Haupt, Christopher. "As Beautiful as Roses." Rev. of *Beggarman, Thief. New York Times* 17 Oct. 1977: 29.

Considers *Beggarman, Thief* a confusing novel because not many readers figure out it is a sequel to the printed version of *Rich Man, Poor Man.* Describes this sequel as more enjoyable than the prior work. Concludes that, though money and how to make it are the chief concerns here, surprisingly this does not make for a repellent fiction.

Lehmann-Haupt, Christopher. "Books of the Times." Rev. of *The Top of the Hill. New York Times* 30 Oct. 1979: C8.

Details the story of *The Top of the Hill,* and comments on Shaw's skill in social commentary, characterization, plotting, and dramatization. Considers this good entertainment.

Lehmann-Haupt, Christopher. "Books of the Times." Rev. of *Acceptable Losses. New York Times* 28 Sept. 1982: C20.

Describes *Acceptable Losses* as a meditation on the imminence of death and the effects of its sudden looming. Considers this a cleverly plotted and absorbing work of realism which seems to want to rise above this and be judged by higher standards. Considers that, unfortunately, the death symbols collapse into specificity, and, by the end, they have leaked out most of their significance.

Lehmann-Haupt, Christopher. "Fantasy for Our Greedy Time." Rev. of *Nightwork. New York Times* 18 Sept. 1975: 39.

Describes *Nightwork* as either the first post-Watergate novel or a personal confession. Calls it a cleverly plotted novel that excites one's sense of greed while offering mindless enjoyment. Details the contents.

Lehmann-Haupt, Christopher. "Moral: The Rich Have More Money Than the Poor." Rev. of *Rich Man, Poor Man. New York Times* 28 Sept. 1970: 39.

Argues that *Rich Man, Poor Man* is bad, bad—especially when it looks as if he is going to pull it off. Claims that apparently the 1960s bewilder Shaw. Details Shaw's earlier achievements and the contents of this novel, and concludes that the old fighter is on his back.

Lyons, Gene. "Four Novels." Rev. of *Beggarman, Thief. New York Times Book Review* 23 Oct. 1977: 15, 36.

Explains *Beggarman, Thief* as a sequel to *Rich Man, Poor Man.* Describes the contents, and dismisses the book as television material.

Malcolm, Donald. "Sex in the Suburbs." Rev. of *Lucy Crown. New Republic* 23 Apr. 1956: 18.

Describes *Lucy Crown* in detail, and argues that the massive amount of retaliation Shaw heaps on his characters for one summer's moral mistakes borders on the excessive. Complains that the flashback technique does not work and that the metamorphosis of the characters is too violent.

Maloney, John J. "The Foibles and Follies of a Generation." Rev. of *Mixed Company: Collected Stories. New York Herald Tribune Book Review* 22 Oct. 1950: 6.

Argues that *Mixed Company* incisively depicts foibles and follies of Americans because rather than creating his own world, Shaw recreates our world. Groups the stories by theme and type, and concludes that in this collection of thirty-seven stories, some are undistinguished while many are genuinely fine.

Match, Richard. "Epic Portrait of Men at Their Best and Worst." Rev. of *The Young Lions. New York Herald Tribune Weekly Book Review* 3 Oct. 1948: 3.

Describes *The Young Lions* in detail, giving high praise for a searing and successful story of war that should stand alongside *The Naked and the Dead.* Calls it less intestinal and mature than *The Naked and The Dead,* and commends it for its lavish imagination and action.

"Medium Rare." Rev. of *Welcome to the City and Other Stories. Time* 16 Feb. 1942: 92.

Briefly describes several of the stories in this collection. Comments that Shaw's material is fresh and handled with understanding, but claims that he lays it on too thick or too pat. Also suggests that he is more naturally a playwright than a storyteller.

Meissner, Purdie. "Hypnotic Novel of Marriage." Rev. of *Lucy Crown*. *Chicago Sunday Tribune Magazine of Books* 8 Apr. 1956: 3.

Describes *Lucy Crown* as a novel of marriage with hypnotic powers compelling the reader to the last page. Argues that the book is not always pleasant, but that it is provocative. Concludes that Shaw deserves a greater female protagonist given his talents, but, despite her shortcomings, he has been superbly successful.

"Middle of the Journey." Rev. of *Two Weeks in Another Town*. *Time* 1 Feb. 1960: 82.

Describes the novel in detail, concluding that his characters aren't large enough to carry the emotions forced on them.

Naipaul, V. S. "New Novels." Rev. of *Two Weeks in Another Town*. *New Statesman* 6 Feb. 1960: 195.

Considers *Two Weeks in Another Town* a competent piece of magazine fiction that need not be discussed with seriousness. Argues that there is little to bewilder here, and that the familiar mixture of sex, psychology, and pseudo-profundity are familiar. Describes contents, and concludes that standards for American machine fiction are so high that counterfeits such as this resemble the real more and more.

Nordell, Roderick. "Twin Portraits of Paris." Rev. of *Paris! Paris!*. *The Christian Science Monitor* 13 Apr. 1977: 23.

Commends the descriptive passages in *Paris! Paris!* as arialike and effective in their accumulation. Details plot and characters.

Osborn, John Jay, Jr. "Too Good to Be True." Rev. of *Acceptable Losses*. *New York Times Book Review* 3 Oct. 1982: 13, 19.

Claims that *Acceptable Losses* combines the suspense of a thriller with the intimacy of a character study. Considers it served up in a fast-paced narrative of broad appeal. Complains, however, that the book ends up being a kind of Rubik's Cube, more plastic puzzle than novel. Concludes that this could have been a great short story if a crafty editor had deleted all the extraneous.

"Paper Doll." Rev. of *Lucy Crown. Time* 2 Apr. 1956: 112.

Calls *Lucy Crown* a suspenseful novel with little literary claim. Describes the plot and characters. Concludes that this novel adds up to a massive debit account with reality and unearned emotion.

Peden, William. "Best of Irwin Shaw." Rev. of *Mixed Company: Collected Stories. Saturday Review of Literature* 18 Nov. 1950: 27-28.

Discusses *Mixed Company*, Shaw's collected stories, by making brief complimentary comments on most of them. Commends Shaw for his ability to render American mores authentically and to provide Dickensian caricatures and burlesques. Concludes that he communicates experience with a narrative simplicity and sincerity which redeems even a frequently far-fetched, sentimental, or one-sided situation.

Peden, William. "These Heroes Have Had It." Rev. of *Tip on a Dead Jockey and Other Stories. New York Times Book Review* 7 July 1957: 4.

Describes the typical hero of the stories in *Tip on A Dead Jockey* as recognizably *weltschmerzig*, melancholy, and "had it." Concludes that Shaw's extreme competence manages to turn this unpromising material into something more than highly effective journalism.

Perkins, Bill. "The Novel of the Year? Not So, But Shaw's Latest Moves Along." Rev. of *Rich Man, Poor Man. National Observer* 19 Oct. 1970: 21.

Explains that *Rich Man, Poor Man* is an epic novel showing the sweeping panorama of postwar USA, including sex, violence, big business, wheeling and dealing, glimpses of Hollywood life, and a kind of irresistible storytelling pull. Considers the style inventive, the story engrossing, the characters less than real and fully rounded. Complains that it lacks a unifying, coherent vision, and thus remains only a story.

Phillips, Robert. "Books." Rev. of *God Was Here But He Left Early. Commonweal* 30 Mar. 1973: 92-93.

Argues that Shaw fails to break new ground with this set of short stories. Describes the contents of the stories, makes stylistic comparisons, and concludes that nearly all of the male protagonists are Faust figures.

Pickrel, Paul. Rev. of *The Troubled Air. Yale Review* 60.4 (1951): 768.

Considers this the best American novel about Communism yet written.

Claims that it has not flinched or turned aside and marks a real advance in Shaw's powers. Applauds the lack of tender-hearted editorializing; consequently we get genuinely dramatic action culminating in revelations that come very close to those regions where life is lived at it most intense moments.

Poore, Charles. "Irwin Shaw's Portrait of a Rebellious Generation." Rev. of *Voices of a Summer Day. New York Times* 9 Mar. 1965: 33.

Considers *Voices of a Summer Day* full of hollowness in some places, and hip, hop slapdash in others. Comments that old bigotries appear in new disguises and are still detestable. Details the contents.

R., D. H. "Fiction." Rev. of *Acceptable Losses. West Coast Review of Books* Nov. 1982: 32.

Considers this an extraordinarily suspenseful novel that mesmerizes, jolting us into a re-evaluation of the qualities of existence rigidly and unreasonably sustained.

Raymond, John. "New Novels." Rev. of *Lucy Crown. New Statesman and Nation* 16 June 1956: 710.

Calls *Lucy Crown* a brilliant failure. Notes that the settings are realistic, the feeling and tone impeccable, and that the dialogue tingles like a highball. But concludes that the central situation is unreal and that the climax staggeringly improbable. Describes contents.

Ribalow, Harold U. "Irwin Shaw's Fiction." Rev. of *Mixed Company: Collected Stories. Congress Weekly* 18 Dec. 1950: 13-14.

Describes *Mixed Company* after a brief recap of Shaw's career and characteristic works. Praises him for the substantial amount of Jewish work to his credit and for his fine war novels. Describes the short stories contained in this collection, and concludes that Shaw is still a young writer of much promise.

Ridley, Clifford A. "The Modern Short Story: Sometimes Obscured by Methods and Mechanics." Rev. of *Love on a Dark Street and Other Stories. National Observer* 18 Oct. 1965: 25.

Argues that Mr. Shaw in *Love on a Dark Street* tells stories pure and simple. Notes that they are concerned with the process of discovery and cause and effect in relationships. Sees each story as constructed with perfect orientation, recognition, flashback, insight, and denouement. Yet concludes that too often we see the strings being manipulated.

Ridley, Clifford A. "The Scene Is Authentic, the People Less So at Shaw's Fictional Cannes." Rev. of *Evening in Byzantium. National Observer* 5 May 1973: 23.

Calls *Evening in Byzantium* a fat, middlebrow narrative in the hands of a proven storyteller. Thinks Shaw's generosity, tenderness, compassion, lucid introspection, and persuasive nobility of forgiveness are just too much. Complains that the book begins briskly and then dithers along in clumsy exposition and dreary flashback. Concludes that, for that matter, there is little real human sensibility or plot.

Rogers, W. G. "Rudolph, Tom and Gretchen." Rev. of *Rich Man, Poor Man. New York Times Book Review* 4 Oct. 1970: 46.

Describes the plot and characters of the novel, and concludes that it is an exciting book written with vigor and drive.

Rogow, Lee. "The Folks to Fight With." Rev. of *The Young Lions. Saturday Review of Literature* 2 Oct. 1948: 12-13.

Calls *The Young Lions* a rich, skillful, superbly readable first novel. Details the contents of the novel, and goes on to discuss how "actorish" and thin many of the characters seem compared to those in most modernist works. Concludes, however, that this is a book with stature, wit, and a dramatic sense of scene-making.

Rolo, Charles J. "One Fateful Summer." Rev. of *Lucy Crown. New York Times Book Review* 1 Apr. 1956: 4.

Comments that *Lucy Crown* belongs to a growing body of novels about marital dissolution. Sees the book as fresh and continuously absorbing, sharply charged, and painfully moving. Details plot and characters.

Rolo, Charles J. "Reader's Choice." Rev. of *The Young Lions. Atlantic* Nov. 1948: 106-08.

Reviews the plot of the story, discusses the picture of the war portrayed, and describes characters and basic story line. Also discusses the American WWII novel, noting its differences from those of WWI, finding that today's novelists are more politically minded, closer to the realities of war, and more determined to show its horrors to civilians.

Rolo, Charles. "Reader's Choice." Rev. of *The Troubled Air*. *Atlantic* July 1951: 86-87.

Describes *The Troubled Air* as ably written, skillfully plotted, charged with tension, and strong on surprise. Discusses the politics of the novel, and details its story line.

Roosevelt, Karyl. "Two Stories Simply for Reading." Rev. of *Nightwork*. *New York Times Book Review* 7 Sept. 1975: 41.

Calls *Nightwork* a novel combining the best and worst Shaw is capable of. Describes plot and characters in detail.

Rosenfeld, Isaac. "Left-Wing Middle-Brow." Rev. of *Act of Faith and Other Stories*. *Commentary* Nov. 1946: 491-94.

Describes *Act of Faith* in the words of Faulkner describing Popeye's face, "it has the depthless, vicious quality of stomped tin." Complains that what is so vulgar and horrible about such work is that it is directed so as not to offend the middlebrow readers, and written so clearly and distinctly that all may grasp the message. Calls Shaw hard-hitting but lacking Hemingway's clear rhythms, and accuses him of combining stilted simplicity of style with pseudo-sophistication. Concludes that his faith in America is all too fluent and shows no appetite for struggle.

Rugoff, Milton. "A Carson McCullers Omnibus—A New Irwin Shaw Novel." Rev. of *The Troubled Air*. *New York Herald Tribune Book Review* 10 June 1951: 1, 14.

Describes the moral climate and characters of *The Troubled Air*. Calls this novel Shaw at his typical best, seizing passionately a vital social issue and presenting it with a firm grasp not only of the intellectual and moral values, but of the many kinds of human beings it involves. Concludes that if at times it seems too smart and well-machined, these faults are not difficult to overlook in so mature a novel on so urgent a theme.

Rugoff, Milton. "Irwin Shaw Tells a Story of Chance, Shame and Ruin." Rev. of *Lucy Crown*. *New York Herald Tribune Book Review* 1 Apr. 1956: 4.

Calls *Lucy Crown* a book about the wages of sin in the matter of adultery. Sees it as a painful story of human frailty done with well-managed scenes etched with acid shame and grief. Contains a detailed plot summary.

Ruhm, Herbert. "In Our Time." Rev. of *Short Stories. Five Decades*. *National Review* 16 Feb. 1979: 246-47.

Comments on the interest many of Shaw's stories generated during the wartime effort and on how modern readers may find the war stories in particular less than interesting now. Finds *Short Stories: Five Decades* an uneven collection with some major weaknesses. Predicts, however, that Shaw will finally occupy a place in our literature, perhaps like that of Jewett or Mary E. Wilkins Freeman.

Saal, Hubert. "Disenchanted Men." Rev. of *Tip on a Dead Jockey and Other Stories. Saturday Review* 3 Aug. 1957: 12-13.

Considers that Shaw's place in American letters rests on his short stories. Describes *Tip on a Dead Jockey*, Shaw's collection of short stories. Commends him for his storytelling, concern with political issues, and sense of life's tragic possibilities. Describes the individual characters and plots.

Schumach, Murray. "Life Seemed to Imitate Old Movie Scenes." Rev. of *Two Weeks In Another Town. New York Times Book Review* 31 Jan. 1960: 4.

Describes the story and characters in *Two Weeks In Another Town*. No literary comments except for the observation that the stuff of the novel is what high action movie dramas are made of.

Shirley, Sylvia. "Ten Stories of the Post-War World." Rev. of *Tip on a Dead Jockey and Other Stories. New York Herald Tribune Book Review* 7 July 1957: 5.

Suggests that this collection of stories attests to Shaw's technical virtuosity. Notes that he manages to crystalize a moment just before change, to sharply clarify experience, and to provide revelation, disappointment, wonder, ache, or even wisdom.

Stepanchev, Stephen. "Shaw's Political Novel." Rev. of *The Troubled Air. Nation* 23 June 1951: 592-93.

Describes the contents of *The Troubled Air* and its expose of the impact of McCarthyism in the broadcasting industry. Concludes that, as a political novel, *The Troubled Air* falls between its political agendas and oversimplifying the human element.

Stewart, John L. "Five New Novels." Rev. of *The Young Lions. Sewanee Review* 57 (1949): 309-312.

Argues that *The Young Lions* has moments of fine precision, intensity, and feeling, yet notes Shaw's preference for ideas over art which makes his novel immense. Accuses him of caring little about the organic unity of his work, indulging in sensationalism, and often sacrificing the vitality that comes from the synthesis of rich and diverse experience into meaningful propositions about life.

Stong, Phil. "Irwin Shaw's Wartime Stories." Rev. of *Act of Faith and Other Stories. Saturday Review of Literature* 21 Sept. 1946: 33.

Sees *Act of Faith* as stories of war and military adventures of the peace told in clean, economical, and skillful fashion. But notes that the plots are plots of mood and emotion which deal in such mild climaxes the reader is left unsatisfied. Details several of the stories.

Sullivan, Richard. "Practiced Craftsmanship in 10 Irwin Shaw Stories." Rev. of *Tip on a Dead Jockey and Other Stories. Chicago Sunday Tribune Magazine of Books* 7 July 1957: 2.

Describes *Tip on a Dead Jockey* as containing ten short stories—all examples of sheer, practiced craftsmanship and good storytelling. Notes, however, that people often seem to be viewed and presented, not so much as individuals, but as objects of commiseration. Finds their ordeals sentimentalized and their warm compassion negative.

"Surrogate Shaw." Rev. of *Voices of a Summer Day. Time* 5 Mar. 1965: 106, 108.

Extols the early Shaw, writer of short stories as good as those of Fitzgerald and Hemingway, but feels that Shaw disappeared and that a surrogate Shaw has written his novels. Describes the plot of *Voice of a Summer Day* and concludes that this novel lacks "the inner eye's witness," a quality his writing once had.

Trilling, Diana. "Fiction in Review." Rev. of *The Young Lions. Nation* 9 Oct. 1948: 409-10.

Suggests that *The Young Lions* is not an arresting literary performance by any standards, but that it is more interesting than either his plays or his much admired short stories. Describes the contents of the novel and its war on fascism.

Trilling, Diana. "Wishful Writing." Rev. of *Act of Faith and Other Stories. Nation* 28 Sept. 1946: 358, 360.

Calls Shaw a member of that school of writing called "liberalistic over-simplification." Sees the twelve stories in *Act of Faith* as making distinctions about good and evil against a wartime backdrop with far too much facility. Describes the contents of several short stories. Concludes that, ultimately, his pieces fall short of the literary stature claimed for them.

Trilling, Lionel. "Some Are Gentle, Some Are Not." Rev. of *The Troubled Air. Saturday Review of Literature* 9 June 1951: 8-9.

Argues that Shaw's best medium is the short story. Notes that *The Troubled Air* is cast in a more exigent mold, because it is a large unit in which the observation and sentiment are unchecked in their tendency to the easy, happy demonstration of the obvious. Objects to the factitious conclusion of hope and new resolve and the fact that ideology in this novel transcends the literary elements.

Van Gelder, Robert. "The Dark City." Rev. of *Welcome to the City and Other Stories. New York Times Book Review* 1 Feb. 1942: 6-7.

Suggests that these stories were mostly written after the attack on Poland and before the attack on Pearl Harbor—hence most of these characters are forlorn, unliked, and the whole thing smacks of Saroyanesque writing. Shows how the rest of the people are undone by vanity and callousness, some few by generosity. Calls Shaw's dialogue smart, tough, and funny, but claims even his brilliance barely illuminates these characters.

Van Gelder, Robert. "The Short Stories of Irwin Shaw." Rev. of *Sailor off the Bremen and Other Stories. New York Times Book Review* 27 Aug. 1939: 6.

Argues that *Sailor off the Bremen* is a collection of stories which establishes Shaw as a dialogue specialist. Notes that Shaw is most at ease when he is writing of City College smarties, taxi drivers, hooligans, and fighting wives. Concludes it to be the essence of bar room and bath house wit.

Vincent, Lucy. Rev. of *Whispers in Bedlam. Books and Bookmen* Jan. 1973: 86.

Calls this a book full of distillation, clean style, and amusement. Details the contents of the most notable stories.

Wagner, Geoffrey. "A Love Convention." Rev. of *Lucy Crown. Commonweal* 13 Apr. 1956: 56-57.

Comments on *Lucy Crown* that there are no happy marriages in it, just hopeless triangles. Considers it really just magazine fiction which tricks us into taking it seriously. Concludes that, compared to the treatment Lawrence would have given the subject matter, this is a vulgar and meretricious performance.

Walker, Gerald. "Who Won the Ball Game?" Rev. of *Voices of a Summer Day*. *New York Times Book Review* 28 Feb. 1965: 44-45.

Claims that *Voices of a Summer Day*, unlike his previous novels with their wooden dialogue, smooth prose, and playable but forgettable scenes, fails in a different way. Concludes that, because Shaw cannot make the scheme of flashbacks work, what the hero sees and feels does not yield a Proustian lode.

West, Anthony. "Death of the Spirit." Rev. of *The Troubled Air*. *New Yorker* 16 June 1951: 109-111.

Calls *The Troubled Air* a topical, political novel about Communism and free speech. Describes the contents in detail, and argues that the author seems afraid his character will not be up to snuff and thus weights the story with emotional irrelevancies. Provides a critique of both stories and characters.

Willingham, John R. "Technique Above Comment." Rev. of *Lucy Crown*. *Nation* 16 June 1956: 516.

Calls *Lucy Crown* a novel full of parlor psychology and women's literary melodrama. States that, unfortunately, one is left with the conviction that, despite often brilliant parts, there just isn't any structural or thematic justification for *Lucy Crown*.

Wilson, David. "The Slippery Slope." Rev. of *Nightwork*. *Times Literary Supplement* 7 Nov. 1975: 1325.

States that in *Nightwork* the idea of the American Innocent rubs shoulders with the notion that survival depends on being one step ahead of the next man's dirty tricks. Concludes that, unfortunately, the situations and people in this novel are unbelievably stereotyped.

Woodburn, John. "Men at War." Rev. of *The Young Lions*. *New Republic* 18 Oct. 1948: 23.

Calls Shaw a fine short story writer and talented playwright, both talents which have managed to mar his novel *The Young Lions*. Considers the book long, panoramic, ambitious, and often capable of great feeling.

Concludes, however, that characters and plot are contrived and the ending more of a collision depending on coincidence than it is a denouement.

Yardley, Jonathan. "The Professional Pen." Rev. of *Short Stories. Five Decades.. Washington Post Book World* 5 Nov. 1978: G3.

Notes that the stories in *Short Stories* are arranged chronologically and reveal Shaw's development as a writer and the history of those who influenced him. Admires the war stories in particular, and praises the whole collection for its wide range of subjects, styles, characters, and interests. Calls Shaw workmanlike.

Interviews

Aurthur, Robert Alan. "Irwin Shaw Would Have Licked Hemingway, Easy." *Esquire* Oct. 1975: 28, 54, 58.

A rather flippant, amusingly reported interview with Shaw which provides a biographical sketch and a list of published fiction.

Chester, Lewis. "Scotch and Philosophy on the Rocks During a Night Watch with a Literary Lion." *Times* 1 Nov. 1975: 12.

Report of an interview with Shaw in a London bar on the publication of *Night Watch*. Discusses the book, his politics and social ideas, his reasons for writing best sellers, and his future plans.

Harsent, David. "Irwin Shaw in Conversation." *New Review* [London] 2.22 (1976): 52-56.

An interview with Shaw in which he discusses the effects of money and fame, *The Young Lions*, his likeness to Hemingway, his relationship with Hemingway, his views on Mailer, his experiences during the war, the process of filming his books, his short stories, writing for the *New Yorker*, editorial pressure, the researching of his books, his personal reading, and his attitudes towards commercial success.

Morris, Willie, and Lucas Matthiessen. "Irwin Shaw: The Art of Fiction IV, *continued.*" *Paris Review* 75 (1979): 248-62. Rpt. in *Writers at Work: The Paris Review Interviews*. 5th Series. Ed. George Plimpton. New York: Viking, 1981. 158-70.

An interview covering Shaw's life, work, and critical reputation in great detail. This updates an earlier interview published in 1953.

Newquist, Roy. "Irwin Shaw." *Counterpoint*. Roy Newquist. Chicago: Rand, 1964. 543-51.

An interview with Shaw in which he discusses his plays, novels, films, and personal politics. Also covers his remarks on war and *The Young Lions*, literary criticism in America, and contemporary movie making.

Phillips, John, and George Plimpton. "The Art of Fiction IV: Irwin Shaw." *Paris Review* 4 (1953): 27-49. Rpt. in *Writers at Work: The Paris Review Interviews*. Ed. George Plimpton. 5th Series. New York: Viking, 1981. 137-58.

An interview with Shaw in which he discusses his personal history, individual works, attitudes toward commercial writing, *The Young Lions*, which of his characters he knew and which are inventions, his political agenda, literary critics, the effects of failure and success, writing for the movies, Hollywood, his attitudes toward killing in wartime, his social critique throughout his works, writing for the theater, short stories, and work methods.

Biographical Sources

Alsterlund, B. "Irwin Shaw." *Wilson Library Bulletin* Mar. 1940: 494.

A useful one page sketch detailing the life and career of Shaw.

Barnes, Bart. "Irwin Shaw, 71, Prolific American Writer, Dies." *Washington Post* 17 May 1984: B12.

A lengthy obituary reviewing Shaw's writing career, citing his own summary of events spanning five decades from the end of World War I to Vietnam. Notes his accomplishments.

Mitgang, Herbert. "Irwin Shaw, Near 70, Adds It Up and Feels 'Right.'" *New York Times* 17 Feb. 1983: C21.

Describes Shaw's writing career, major events in his life, the changing views of life represented in his work, and his writing objectives. Also quotes his objections to being called a "master of the popular novel."

Ross, Walter W. "Irwin Shaw." *Dictionary of Literary Biography Yearbook: 1984*. Ed. Jean W. Ross. Detroit: Gale, 1985. 194-99.

An account of Shaw's career written following his death in 1984. Describes some of his major works, reviews the critical reaction to his work, and concludes that he was one of America's best storytellers who traded his integrity as a writer for big money. Includes tributes from a number of writers and critics.

Salter, James. "Winter of the Lion." *Esquire* July 1989: 69-76.

In this literary memoir Salter discusses his first encounter with Shaw, their dinner conversation, their joint literary agent (Max Wilkinson), the friendship they shared, other writers they both knew, trips to Europe, and a host of personal anecdotes.

Shnayerson, Michael. *Irwin Shaw: A Biography*. New York: Putnam, 1989.

"To the Memory of Irwin Shaw." *Soviet Literature* Oct. 1984: 168-70. Rpt. from *Izvestia* 1 July 1984.

Recaps Shaw's career, and provides a memoir on the occasion of his death. Contains anecdotal biographical material.

Alix Kates Shulman
1932 –

Primary Sources

Novels

Burning Questions. New York: Knopf, 1978; New York: Bantam, 1979; London: Deutsch, 1979; London: Fontana, 1980; New York: Thunder's Mouth, 1990.

In Every Woman's Life. New York: Knopf, 1987; New York: Ballantine, 1988.

Memoirs of an Ex-Prom Queen. Book Club ed. New York: Knopf, 1972; New York: Literary Guild, 1972; New York: Bantam, 1973; London: Hart-Davis, 1973; Toronto: Bantam, 1976; Chicago: Cassandra, 1985.

On the Stroll. New York: Knopf, 1981; London: Virago, 1983; Chicago: Cassandra-Academy, 1987.

Short Fiction in Anthologies

"A Story of a Girl and Her Dog." *Rediscovery; 300 Years of Stories by and about Women.* Ed. Betzy Dinesen. New York: Avon, 1982. Pag. not available.

Short Fiction in Periodicals

"Meditation on a Bird." *Ms.* Feb. 1973: 50-53, 114-15.

"Money Can't Buy a Home." *Redbook* June 1985: 66, 68-70, 72, 75-76, 156.

"Weather Report." *Redbook* Aug. 1973: 73-74.

Secondary Sources

Articles and Chapters

Bolch, Judith. *"Memoirs of an Ex-Prom Queen."* *Survey of Contemporary Literature.* Ed. Frank N. Magill. Revised. 12 vols. Englewood Cliffs: Salem, 1977. 7: 4910-12.

A standard reference article describing characters, plot, themes, and style of *Memoirs of an Ex-Prom Queen.*

Burstein, Janet. "Jewish-American Women's Literature: The Long Quarrel with God." *Studies in American Jewish Literature* [Kent State] 8.1 (1989): 9-25.

Burstein argues that while some Jewish women writers cast Jewish tradition as an adversary, others see it as a source of nurturance, some ignore it, and still others tell of a search for substitute commitments. Concludes, nonetheless, that all seem to engage in a one-sided quarrel with God. Discusses briefly Jong, Shulman, Greenberg, Olsen, Rosen, Paley, Yezierska, and Broner.

Horton, Susan R. "Desire and Depression in Women's Fiction: The Problematics and the Economics of Desire." *Modern Fiction Studies* 24.2 (1978): 181-95.

Provides a study of Mrs. Franklin Raybel in *Memoirs of an Ex-Prom Queen* in terms of her melancholy and depression.

Masinton, Martha, and Charles G. Masinton. "Second-Class Citizenship: The Status of Women in Contemporary American Fiction." *What Manner of Woman: Essays on English and American Life and Literature.* Ed. Marlene Springer. New York: New York UP, 1971. 309-10.

Describes the contents of *Memoirs of an Ex-Prom Queen* as a neo-feminist *bildungsroman* rather wrenched into shape by the novelist's need to demonstrate oppression of women. Argues that Sasha never emerges as a fully developed character, and that the entire novel continues to show the heroine victimized by men.

Schwartz, Lynne Sharon. "How Foolish I Was: How Mellow I've Become." *Ms*. Mar. 1978: 40-41.

Calls *Burning Questions* a novel ingeniously cast as an autobiography of a militant feminist done as a *bildungsroman*. Considers Shulman at her best when describing the passion of the young days of the movement. Notes that the second half of the book is vastly more exciting and written with much more conviction.

Shulman, Alix Kates. "Living Our Life." *Between Women: Biographers, Novelists, Critics, Teachers and Artists Write about Their Work on Women*. Eds. Carol Ascher, Louise DeSalvo, and Sara Ruddick. Boston: Beacon, 1984. 1-13.

Shulman describes her writing processes and her relationship to Emma Goldman, the subject of many of her own early writings. Discusses the themes they share in common, her original discovery of Goldman's writings, and her own subsequent political and literary choices. An acknowledgement of Goldman's influence on Shulman's work.

Reviews

Bell, Pearl K. "Her Life as a Rebel." Rev. of *Burning Questions*. *New York Times Book Review* 26 Mar. 1978: 12.

Wonders if the women's movement will survive its novelists. Complains that Shulman spares her rebel girl not one of the currently fashionable lib-rad-fem simplicities and platitudes about politics and history, men and women. Claims that it is tempting to read the book as a hilarious caricature and sly mockery of the feminist movement, but finds, alas, Mrs. Shulman's earnest conviction entirely unambiguous. Claims that, all unwitting, Shulman has produced a heroine so irredeemably self-absorbed, simple-minded, resentful, and credulous that she reinforces those myths she set out to demolish. Concludes that, if women can survive this novel, we are stronger than we know.

Bender, Marilyn. "The Girl Who Couldn't Say No." Rev. of *Memoirs of an Ex-Prom Queen*. *New York Times Book Review* 23 Apr. 1972: 34, 36.

Calls Sasha Davis a female cousin of Alexander Portnoy, germinated in the same peat moss of second-generation Jewish intellectual, flailing against bourgeois constraints and succumbing to sexual conflict. Considers this an angry little book with no lyrical or imaginative peaks. Provides a detailed account of the contents.

Benet, Mary Kathleen. "Ho Down." Rev. of *On the Stroll. Times Literary Supplement* 1 July 1983: 696.
Discusses *On the Stroll* as a heavily researched book about the lore of the New York theater district. Details plot and characters. Calls Shulman an intelligent and competant writer who twists her story into a knot of tension to keep us reading. Considers the tone disspassionate, didactic, and crackling with snap judgments, wry humor, and cartoonish minor characters.

Blackburn, Sara. Rev. of *Memoirs of an Ex-Prom Queen. Washington Post Book World* 14 May 1972: 13.
Praises the novel for its intentions to give a straight autobiographical portrait of the oppressive aspects of growing up white, middle-class and female in America. Enjoys its enlightened and self-flagellating humor. Is disappointed Sasha shows no concern for women outside her class, thus appearing shallow and selfish. Concludes, finally, that the book is isolationist, with Shulman displaying insufficient social conscience beyond her heroine's own struggle.

Broyard, Anatole. "Her Finite Variety." Rev. of *Burning Questions. New York Times* 18 Mar. 1978: 21.
Calls *Burning Questions* a revolutionary novel in which Shulman proves women can write as clumsily as men. Details the plot, and analyses the character of Zane at some length.

Cantwell, Mary. "Street People." Rev. of *On the Stroll. New York Times Book Review* 27 Sept. 1981: 12.
Declares that *On the Stroll* is not an exploration of feminism. Notes that Shulman is on new ground here. Details the characters and situations evoked in the book as a treatment of New York street people.

Emerson, Sally. "Recent Fiction." Rev. of *On the Stroll. Illustrated London News* Aug. 1983: 54.
Calls *On the Stroll* surprisingly fresh, warm, and understanding. Describes contents, and discusses narrative strategy.

Fremont-Smith, Eliot. "The Good, the Bad, and the Strange." Rev. of *Burning Questions. Village Voice* 3 Apr. 1978: 69.

Complains about the confusion of expectations the form of the novel presents. Details Zane's story, and concludes that this novel is a losing game for a male reader.

Geringer, Laura. "Books." Rev. of *On the Stroll. Saturday Review* Sept. 1981: 60-61.

Argues that *On the Stroll* tells about the Hell's Kitchen of New York from the points of view of three pilgrims in the Port Authority bus tunnel. Notes that without a fem-lib agenda on which to hang her plot, Shulman seems to be at a loss, and one wonders what the book is about. Concludes that there are isolated moments of poignancy, but one cannot tell who is gaming and who is for real.

Helgesen, Sally. "Seven Ages of Woman." Rev. of *Memoirs of an Ex-Prom Queen. Village Voice* 21 Sept. 1972: 32.

Complains that *Memoirs of an Ex-Prom Queen* is told in a flat narrative style and loses much of its humor and interest. Claims, however, that it is wonderful when read simply as a memoir because there is no attempt to fix blame, no bitterness, and no straining after solutions. Notes that she also reveals many of the real women's issues glossed over by political feminists, doing so in a simple and straightforward manner.

"In Brief." Rev. of *Memoirs of an Ex-Prom Queen. New Republic* 13 May 1972: 29.

Briefly delineates plot and comments that *Memoirs of an Ex-Prom Queen* is sprinkled with astute observations about society's sometimes subtle manipulation of children as it prescribes their sexual roles. It is also spiced with humor and irony as Sasha seeks to fulfill her role and herself.

Jefferson, Margo. "Rebel Woman." Rev. of *Burning Questions. Newsweek* 3 Apr. 1978: 83.

Argues that *Burning Questions* offers us a chronicle of its heroine's passage from personal iconoclasm to radical feminism in an attempt to show the individual in relation to historical events. Comments that it is based on the lives of Emma Goldman, Elizabeth Gurley, and Angela Davis. Concludes that, unfortunately, the heroine fails as a character, and we end up mistrusting the teller and the tale.

Karpf, Anne. "Feminist Fiction." Rev. of *Burning Questions. Books and Bookmen* Aug. 1979: 52-53.

Describes this book as showing that the women's movement has come of age, moving beyond didacticism to produce its own real literature. Argues that this rousing and funny novel manages to leaven with humor its feminist issues without fudging them. Commends the good writing, criticizes some of the narrative devices, and describes the book's two basic flaws—self-pitying whining and self-conscious stylishness.

L., S. "Fiction." Rev. of *On the Stroll. West Coast Review of Books* Feb. 1982: 34.

Calls *On the Stroll* a contemporary fable of New York City street life rich in fairy tale imagery, deft handling of narration, and stereotypical characters. Concludes that by using offbeat material, the author has brought home many essential truths.

Lichtenstein, Grace. "Wives and Lovers, Husbands and Paramours." Rev. of *In Every Woman's Life.... Washington Post Book World* 31 May 1987: 7.

Claims that *In Every Woman's Life* takes the humor of *Heartburn* and the fluent prose of *Rough Strife*, but that its strength lies in the character of Rosemary. Describes the contents of the book in detail, and asserts that here Shulman has summed up her case for marriage based neither on real passion nor intimacy, nor even true love, but on convenience. Concludes, even more provocatively, that she ends the book with some lines of poetry in praise of babies written by Gertrude Stein, who never had any.

Lipsius, Frank. Rev. of *Memoirs of an Ex-Prom Queen. Books and Bookmen* Aug. 1973: 77-78.

Calls this book a chronicle of the aging of the American woman who came of age in the 1950s. Criticizes the *mea culpa* confessions, the strident tone of renunciation, and her envy of younger women who escaped the exaggerated hang-ups which plague her in this book. Complains of the book's feminist politics and lack of literary quality.

Mahon, Derek. "Pantsing." Rev. of *Memoirs of an Ex-Prom Queen. Listener* 26 Apr. 1973: 560.

Calls *Memoirs of an Ex-Prom Queen* a bitter denunciation of society's standardization of woman. Sees it as a witty, compelling book, if a little episodic because it proceeds through a series of flashbacks. Comments on the abortion scene, and warns the squeamish against reading it.

Marcus, Greil. "Undercover." Rev. of *Burning Questions. Rolling Stone* 1 June 1978: 63-64.

Claims that *Burning Questions* announces itself as a political autobiography of a thirty-seven year old radical feminist. Calls this close to the perfect New York feminist fantasy. Concludes that the writing rings with political passion and humor derived from her instinct for satire. Details the contents.

Marsh, Pamela. "The Decline of Man's Superiority." Rev. of *Memoirs of an Ex-Prom Queen. Christian Science Monitor* 4 May 1972: B7.

Argues that this novel, supposedly about what women think, is a dreary thing. Wonders how the first generation of women's libbers would react to her sexual content, and having the central protagonist end up a neurotic housewife.

Moyer, Linda Lancione. "Two Bites of the Upper Crust." Rev. of *In Every Woman's Life. Christianity and Crisis* 28 Sept. 1987: 317-19.

Describes *In Every Woman's Life* as depicting professional people who are intellectual and financially at ease. Details the plot and comments on the dominant female characters. Discusses the manner in which the book stages the major feminist struggles, its dialogue, treatment of marriage, and insight without surprise or depth.

Naughton, John. "Lessons from Mayo." Rev. of *Burning Questions. Listener* 9 Aug. 1979: 190-91.

Claims that *Burning Questions* is an excellent novel, a soft-spoken celebration of the power of the women's movement, an explication of the paradoxical resilience inherent in its anarchic, diffused structure, and a reminder that it was long overdue.

O'Connell, Shaun. "Arts in Review." Rev. of *Memoirs of an Ex-Prom Queen. Massachusetts Review* 14.1 (1973): 193.

A generally snide and random piece that excoriates Shulman for her views on the efforts of 1950s American writers to erect a myth of male machismo for themselves. Criticizes this novel as Chinese theater *agitprop* in which the oppressive landowners are men and the peasants women.

Prescott, Peter S. "The Beauty Part." Rev. of *Memoirs of an Ex-Prom Queen. Newsweek* 1 May 1972: 118.

Calls *Memoirs of an Ex-Prom Queen* a sad, witty story excellently conceived and executed, into which is read the entire roster of feminist complaint. Deems this one of the better books on this subject.

Rosenthal, Lucy. Rev. of *Memoirs of an Ex-Prom Queen. Saturday Review* 20 May 1972: 76-77.

Calls *Memoirs of an Ex-Prom Queen* a remarkable breakthrough novel innovative in its rendering of the feminine experience and in its perfect marriage of thesis to art. Considers this the first important novel to emerge from the Women's Liberation Movement.

Shah, Diane K. "An Outspoken Fictional Manifesto Catalogs Everylibber's Complaint." Rev. of *Memoirs of an Ex-Prom Queen. National Observer* 20 May 1972: 23.

Suggests that *Memoirs of an Ex-Prom Queen* is about a female Alexander Portnoy which becomes a case history of every libber's complaints, but more than that, it catalogues sexism in society's protective attitude toward females. Notes that there is a wry humor, a refreshing turn of phrase, and a chord struck for every woman from happy housewives to radical feminists. Details the contents.

"Short Reviews." Rev. of *Burning Questions. Atlantic* May 1978: 94.

Asserts that this novel presents a radical feminist intended to be seen as a strong and articulate woman, affectionate, intellectual, humorous, and tempered in the movement.

Slung, Michele. "Fables of Forty-Second Street." Rev. of *On the Stroll. Washington Post Book World* 1 Nov. 1981: 8.

Calls *On the Stroll* an absorbing novel beaming compassion into the dark places behind the neon of 42nd Street. Notes that it is far removed from the luxuries of middle-class self-examination that dominated Shulman's previous books. Sees it as full of fairy tale and gritty realism, familiarity with street jargon and pimp's cant. Comments that she sometimes achieves an almost Dickensian sense of society's underside.

Spacks, Patricia Meyer. "Fiction Chronicle." Rev. of *Memoirs of an Ex-Prom Queen. Hudson Review* 25.3 (1972): 498.

Thinks *Memoirs of an Ex-Prom Queen* annoying in the superficiality of its prose, its self-satisfied air, and its relentless record of trivia. Suggests that commitment to an imagined consciousness backfires here because only the character's self-love is revealed.

Turin, Michele. Rev. of *Burning Questions*. *Best Sellers* July 1978: 109.

Argues that *Burning Questions* deals with feminist awareness from a well-written and intelligent perspective. Complains about many tedious political references and much hollow pontification. Concludes that this is a forceful and articulate appraisal of one woman's transformation.

Tyler, Anne. "After the Prom." Rev. of *Burning Questions*. *Washington Post Book World* 26 Mar. 1978: G3.

Calls *Burning Questions* a satisfyingly believable book which deserves to be read. Details plot and characters. Considers the character of Zane in some depth.

Walkowitz, Judith R. "Surviving on the Street: Oddball Alliances and Conventional Fantasies." Rev. of *On the Stroll*. *Ms.* Jan. 1982: 41-42.

Calls *On the Stroll* a triumph of feminist realism, dramatically interweaving the story of three people struggling to survive in Times Square. Commends Shulman for her characters, originality, insight, and refusal to sentimentalize or generalize from these characters.

Whitman, Alden. "Not a Prom Queen." Rev. of *Burning Questions*. *Nation* 15 Apr. 1978: 440-42.

Calls *Burning Questions* a book that tackles contemporary issues in a serious manner. Considers it a feminist, social realist novel that ends on a note of qualified optimism. Concludes that this is an important, credible, and mature book.

Yglesias, Helen. "News from the Sisterhood." Rev. of *Burning Questions*. *Harper's* Aug. 1978: 87.

Describes *Burning Questions* as an openly political novel which fails its stunning subject—a woman's passionate commitment to political activism.

Interviews

Mok, Michael. "Story Behind the Book." *Publishers Weekly* 5 June
    1972: 123.

An interview in which Shulman discusses how she learned to take herself seriously, what it meant to shut out the family, her early successes,
the readers' reactions to *Memoirs of an Ex-Prom Queen*, the financial
arrangements of the paperback contract, and the proposed movie version
of the novel.

Tess Slesinger

1905 – 1945

Primary Sources

Novels

The Unpossessed. New York: Simon, 1934; Toronto: Musson, 1934; London: Barker, 1935; New York: Avon, 1966; New York: Bard-Avon [Cited in PBIP, 1969]; Novels of the Thirties Series. Old Westbury: Feminist, 1984.

Collected Works

On Being Told That Her Second Husband Has Taken His First Lover, and Other Stories. Chicago: Quadrangle, 1971, 1974; New York: Time, 1974. Publ. as *Time: The Present; A Book of Short Stories*. New York: Simon, 1935.

Contents: On Being Told That Her Second Husband Has Taken His First Lover, After the Party, The Times So Unsettled Are, Mother to Dinner, Relax Is All, Jobs in the Sky, White on Black, The Mouse-Trap, Missis Flinders, The Friedmans' Annie, The Answer on the Magnolia Tree, A Life in the Day of a Writer.

Time: The Present; A Book of Short Stories. New York: Simon, 1935; Toronto: Musson, 1935; London: Barker, 1935; Publ. as *On Being Told That Her Second Husband Has Taken His First Lover, and Other Stories*. Chicago: Quadrangle, 1971, 1974; New York: Time, 1974.

Contents: On Being Told That Her Second Husband Has Taken His First Lover, After the Party, The Times So Unsettled Are, Mother to Dinner, Relax Is All, Jobs in the Sky, White on Black, The Mouse-Trap, Missis Flinders, The Friedmans' Annie, The Answer on the Magnolia Tree.

Short Fiction in Anthologies

"A Life in the Day of a Writer." *50 Best American Short Stories, 1915-1939*. Ed. Edward J. O'Brien. New York: Literary Guild, 1939. 655-68; *Fifty Best American Short Stories, 1915-1965*. Ed. Martha Foley. Boston: Houghton, 1965. 154-64.

"Mr. Palmer's Party." *Short Stories from the New Yorker, 1925-1940*. New York: Simon, 1940. 415-19.

"Mother to Dinner." *Between Mothers and Daughters: Stories Across a Generation*. Ed. Susan Koppelman. Old Westbury: Feminist, 1985. 141-60.

"The Mouse-Trap." *Writing Red: An Anthology of American Women Writers, 1930-1940*. Eds. Charlotte Nekola and Paula Rabinowitz. New York: Feminist, 1987. 106-26.

"White on Black." *The Norton Book of American Short Stories*. Ed. Peter S. Prescott. New York: Norton, 1988. 412-20.

Short Fiction in Periodicals

"For Better, for Worse." *Delineator* Jan. 1936: 18-19.

"The Friedmans' Annie." *Menorah Journal* Mar. 1931: 242-60.

"A Hollywood Gallery." *Michigan Quarterly Review* 18.3 (1979): 439-54.

"Jobs in the Sky." *Scribner's* Mar. 1935: 136-43.

"Mother to Dinner." *Menorah Journal* Mar. 1930: 221-34.

"Relax Is All." *Forum* Aug. 1933: 97-103.

"White on Black." *American Mercury* Dec. 1930: 470-76; *American Mercury* Dec. 1947: 722-30.

Secondary Sources

Articles and Chapters

Eisinger, Chester E. "Character and Self in Fiction on the Left." *Proletarian Writers of the Thirties*. Ed. David Madden. Crosscurrents/Modern Critiques. Carbondale: Southern Illinois UP, 1968. 158-83.

Discusses a number of novelists writing in the thirties and forties in a Marxian vein. Describes the protagonists in Slesinger's *The Unpossessed* in detail, showing how they face a problem with identity, having lost their belief in God and finding nothing to replace it. Marxist ideology plays little role in the novel except that in the background "looms the committed Party member who derives moral assurance, strength of purpose, and self-identity from a life of directed action."

Sharistanian, Janet. "Tess Slesinger's Hollywood Sketches." *Michigan Quarterly Review* 18.3 (1979): 429-38.

A broadly ranging overview of Slesinger's life and work, providing a very useful introduction to the writer. Also provides insightful comments about the unpublished manuscript materials for the unfinished novel and short stories.

Trilling, Lionel. "Young in the Thirties." *Commentary* May 1966: 43-51. Rpt. as Afterword in *The Unpossessed*. New York: Avon, 1966; and as "A Novel of the Thirties" in *The Last Decade: Essays and Reviews 1965-1975*. Ed. Diana Trilling. New York: Harcourt, 1979. 3-24.

Calls Slesinger a born novelist with vivacity, wit, and delicate powers of social observation. Sees *The Unpossessed* as not only a literary enterprise, but as a personal act whose accuracy is amazing. After commending the novel for its importance now and then, Trilling ends with personal anecdotes and a discussion of their young lives together as Jewish intellectuals. Concludes that it is definitely a female novel and lacks substantiality in the way female-authored novels often do.

Reviews

Adams, J. Donald. "*The Unpossessed* and Other Recent Works of
  Fiction." Rev. of *The Unpossessed. New York Times Book Review* 20
  May 1934: 6.

Considers this a good first novel. Notes that Slesinger has been a shrewd
observer of some parts of the scene, and yet has still produced a partial picture of the New York intellectual crowd. Concludes that, though the book
is too shut within the walls of the city, nevertheless, it is clever and wise.

Adams, Robert M. "Restorations." Rev. of *The Unpossessed. New York
  Review of Books* 20 Oct. 1966: 31-32.

Argues that what the critics found objectionable at its 1934 publication—
loose structure—can be excused today as an expressive device. Reviews
the plot of this satiric study of New York's radical intelligentsia, and
finds its technical deficiencies not due to a formula, but perhaps an
explanation of why Slesinger wrote no additional novels.

Angoff, Charles. "Little Tombstones." Rev. of *Time: The Present.
  Nation* 19 June 1935: 716-17.

Comments that this story collection reveals a thin but real talent. Calls
Slesinger's sympathies wider than Dorothy Parker's or Ernest
Hemingway's, but lacking their skill. Notes that she has a good eye for
the tombstones of life, is boisterously sensitive, and relatively unenlight-
ened in her discussions.

Benet, William Rose. "Observation of the Human Spectacle." Rev. of
  Time: The Present. Saturday Review of Literature 25 May 1935: 5.

Observes that Slesinger manifests an acute curiosity as to what is going
on in people's minds. Finds *Time: The Present* commendable for its
range and breadth of human sympathy, remarkable phrasing, and convincing transcripts of life. Details the contents.

Bromwich, David. "Character Revealed." Rev. of *On Being Told That
  Her Second Husband Has Taken His First Lover and Other Stories.
  Commentary* Nov. 1971: 100, 102.

Describes the characters in these stories as living in a world without generosity and redemptive signs. Comments that each goes through the
persistent ugliness of each day with their private neuroses and their small
monotonous failures. Calls Slesinger a writer who has learned the mod-

ernist tricks without being overwhelmed by them. Concludes that she is a serious and fully formed writer whose stories are also fully achieved.

Burnett, Whit. "The People of the Present: Clever, Sad, Tragic, Comic." Rev. of *Time: The Present. New York Herald Tribune Books* 26 May 1935: 7.

Describes *Time: The Present* as a collection of stories written with an ease that belies the hidden energy in them. Considers Slesinger's mind complex, delightful in its associative processes, and that phrases are woven back and forth until their last tint of richness emerges. Concludes that her observations spring naturally from an insatiable memory for unimportant details.

Butcher, Fanny. "Tess Slesinger Shows Gifts in *The Unpossessed*." Rev. of *The Unpossesed. Chicago Daily Tribune* 28 July 1934: 12.

Describes *The Unpossessed* as earnest, mercurial, and definitely not the greatest contribution to American literature. Suggests that it is a series of short stories, some brilliant, some episodic, many depicting the integration or disintegration of character. A generally snide and scathing review.

Caldwell, Gail. Rev. of *The Unpossessed. Boston Review* Feb. 1985: 23.

Discusses Lionel Trilling's original review of this novel, and gives historical context for it. Details the plot, and comments on how Slesinger treats her women characters, radicalized intellectuals, leftist politics, and the era she depicts.

Cantwell, Robert. "Outlook Book Choice of the Month." Rev. of *The Unpossessed. New Outlook* June 1934: 53, 57, 64.

Argues that *The Unpossessed* deals brilliantly with one segment of the chaos of the Depression years in the publishing industry. Details the characters and contents. Accuses Slesinger of being careless with minor characters, using stock phrases, and identifying subjects rather than providing understanding. Concludes that, nevertheless, the book fluctuates between being good and being brilliant.

Chamberlain, John. "Books of the Times." Rev. of *The Unpossessed. New York Times* 9 May 1934: 17.

Calls *The Unpossessed* the best novel about New York yet because of its ferocious drive, wild and unfaltering rhythm, quality of wit lightly blended with malice and understanding, a complete grasp of most characters concerned in the plot, the effective ending, and a contemporaneity that is remarkable. After detailing the contents of the stories, concludes that Slesinger is a psychic adept at plumbing feeling and motivation.

Coates, Robert M. "—and Other Stories." Rev. of *Time: The Present. New Republic* 24 July 1935: 312.

Finds these stories largely employ a stream of consciousness method not always successful. Describes individual stories and characters.

Davenport, Guy. "Novels in Braille." Rev. of *On Being Told That Her Second Husband Has Taken His First Lover and Other Stories. National Review* 18 May 1971: 539.

Comments that, originally published under the title, *Time: The Present,* these reprinted 1930s stories are as vivid as when they were written. Claims that Slesinger has wit and intelligence with a style to match and demonstrates that the age of Hemingway and Fitzgerald had a writer with the excellence of these two giants without their obsessions.

Gannett, Lewis. "Books and Things." Rev. of *The Unpossessed. New York Herald Tribune* 10 May 1934: 25.

Calls *The Unpossessed* a bitty-witty novel done with a fine satirical sense and a keen mind, if not sheer genius. Details the contents.

Gottlieb, Annie. "A Woman Writer Before Women Writers." Rev. of *On Being Told That Her Second Husband Has Taken His First Lover and Other Stories. New York Times Book Review* 13 Oct. 1974: 31, 34.

On the occasion of the republication of Slesinger's *On Being Told That Her Second Husband Has Taken His First Lover,* Gottlieb commends Slesinger for her shrewd observations on social class behavior, on female terror at the expectations of marriage in the 1930s, her self-confessed androgyny as a writer, and her insightful involvement in revealing the female mind and heart.

Gregory, Horace. "These Neurotic Young Folks." Rev. of *The Unpossessed. New York Herald Tribune Books* 13 May 1934: 2.

Describes *The Unpossessed* as a novel about the dilemmas of the young and liberated intellectuals of the 1930s. Calls the novel insightful and skilfully phrased. Details its characters and conflicts, and concludes that there is enough truth in Slesinger's portrait to make reading the book a remarkable experience. Remarks that she paints a bitter picture of her generation with a skill of a Dorothy Parker.

Jefferson, Margo. "Hellbent for Nowhere." Rev. of *The Unpossessed*. *Village Voice Literary Supplement* Nov. 1984: 7.

Calls *The Unpossessed* a jarring, exhilarating mix of dated wisecracks, brilliant insights, perfect moments, and exasperating mannerisms. Considers Slessinger's real *cri de coeur* in the novel to be against self-imposed sterility, whether of thought, action, or body. Describes the contents.

Jones, E. B. C. "Short Stories." Rev. of *Time: The Present*. *New Statesman and Nation* 12 Oct. 1935: 496, 498.

Argues that this collection is comprised of extreme cleverness, fluency, and precision. Calls it an intensely feminine book about bleakness, heartlessness, and unemployment, all combined with an agreeable feeling of settling down for a conversation with an intimate, disillusioned, gossipy, malicious, and often witty friend.

Kempton, Murray. "From the Depths of the Thirties." Rev. of *The Unpossessed*. *New Republic* 5 Nov. 1966: 25-28.

Argues that "To read Miss Slesinger is to remember how strident the 1930s were, and how repetitively and rudely they make their effects. She gathers barren men and women in a living room and sets them in motion." Describes her childhood and upbringing as a Jewish intellectual, her life in Hollywood, Trilling's "kindly patronizing assessments" of her, and her subsequent career. Concludes that she failed as an artist because her true complaint about being a woman in her kind of world could not be expressed with the means of discourse available to her. Argues that she felt cheated of a promise by feminism that failed to provide her with equality of intimacy with men. Concludes that her wounds speak to us more forcefully than her teachings and stories redolent with the lonely impulse to talk to someone.

Langer Elinor. "With One Symphony to Her Credit." Rev. of *On Being Told That Her Second Husband Has Taken His First Lover and Other Stories*. *Nation* 24 May 1975: 631-32, 634.

Details the contents of most of the stories, admiring all but one. Claims that they reveal a meticulous style and a cold-eyed radicalism.

Matthews, T. S. "Rackety Jackets." Rev. of *The Unpossessed*. *New Republic* 23 May 1934: 52.

Calls this an extraordinary first novel whose subject is neither fresh nor savory, but whipped into a lively semblance. Concludes that she is plausible, if not profound, and that, even if her intentions are not purely satirical, the effects are.

"New Novels." Rev. of *Time: The Present*. *Times Literary Supplement* 19 Sept. 1935: 578.

Describes *Time: The Present* as a collection of eleven tales of striking quality, poignant, neat, and remarkable for their sheer vividness, vitality, and changing scenes. Calls her character portrayal penetrating, precise, witty, and acid, yet still compassionate.

Nuhn, Ferner. "The Lost Generation and the New Morality." Rev. of *The Unpossessed*. *Nation* 23 May 1934: 597-98.

Describes *The Unpossessed* as a book whose colors are decidely mordant, and whose world is full of young New York intellectuals whose social protest remains mostly confined to cocktail party conversation. Commends the writer for her verbal brilliance, her ridicule, and her power. Calls it a brilliant, cutting first novel.

Prescott, Peter S. "Striking Gold." Rev. of *On Being Told That Her Second Husband Has Taken His First Lover and Other Stories*. *Newsweek* 3 May 1971: 104, 106.

Comments that *On Being Told That Her Second Husband Has Taken His First Lover* is written in the idiom of their time and, for the most part, is set in New York City. Notes that many of the stories are bright, witty, and nervous pieces, while others are satirical *tour de forces* and interior monologues. Concludes that she deserves a place at the front of the second rank of American writers.

Rahv, Philip. "Storm over the Intellectuals." Rev. of *The Unpossessed*. *New Masses* 29 May 1934: 26-27.

Describes the characters in *The Unpossessed*, and calls Slesinger a highly conscious literary technician who has put to good use a variety of methods which only the best of modern writers have used effectively. Notes, however, that her writing suffers from a lack of economy, while too often her ideas and perceptions are dissolved in the flow of verbal excitement.

Ricks, Christopher. "Convulsive Throes." Rev. of *On Being Told That Her Second Husband Has Taken His First Lover and Other Stories*. *New York Review of Books* 22 July 1971: 12-13.

Argues that these stories demonstrate a keen sense of the American plight and of what it is to be stretched on the rack of a too-easy chair. Concludes that, moreover, they despise despair.

Stafford, Jean. "A Golden Writer Rediscovered." Rev. of *On Being Told That Her Second Husband Has Taken His First Lover and Other Stories. Washington Post Book World* 2 May 1971: 6.

Suggests that this collection of stories is as full of materials about contemporary today as when it was first published, despite the fact that all the stories are set in the thirties. Describes the contents of several of them, and concludes with a lament that this golden writer died in 1945 when she was only thirty-nine.

Stevens, George. "Afraid to Grow Up." Rev. of *The Unpossessed. Saturday Review of Literature* 19 May 1934: 701.

Calls *The Unpossessed* a series of short stories written acutely and stylishly. Provides an account of the types of characters, style, and characteristic themes in the collection.

Walton, Edith H. "The Satirical Stories of Tess Slesinger." Rev. of *Time: The Present. New York Times Book Review* 26 May 1935: 7.

Calls *Time: The Present* a witty, satirical collection in the Dorothy Parker tradition. Details the contents of each story, and then complains that there is more glitter than feeling, more contemporaneity than depth in the stories, despite a frequent tenderness.

Weales, Gerald. "Small Servings of Pathos." Rev. of *On Being told that Her Second Husband Has Taken His First Lover and Other Stories. Commonweal* 9 July 1971: 360-62.

In this discussion of *On Being Told That Her Second Husband Has Taken His First Lover and Other Stories* Weales describes Slesinger's publishing history, discusses *The Unpossessed*, and defends Slesinger against the kind of comment that would hail the republication of her stories as the first whisper of a potential roar that died. Discusses the fate of her reputation during her lifetime, and defends her as a writer of talent with a merciless eye for social satire.

Biographical Sources

Biagi, Shirley. "Forgive Me for Dying." *Antioch Review* 35.2-3 (1977): 224-36.

A memoir and history of Slesinger which discusses her early death at thirty-nine; her association with Clifton Fadiman, Max Eastman, Dorothy Parker, Lionel Trilling, and Irvin Thalberg; her diary writing; her marriage to Solow and subsequent divorce; several of her short stories; her novel; her immediate critical reputation; the sojourn in Hollywood; her second marriage to Frank Davis; writing Hollywood motion picture scripts; and experiences at the hands of Hollywood Red-baiters. Concludes that Slesinger was an important intellectual chronicler of the leftist thought and woman of the first half of the twentieth century.

"Tess Slesinger." *Wilson Bulletin for Librarians* Nov. 1934: 170.

A brief listing of her works with even briefer biographical comments. Does contain one first-person anecdote about her early life.

Susan Sontag

1933 –

Primary Sources

Novels

The Benefactor. New York: Farrar, 1963, 1978, 1987; London: Eyre, 1964; New York: Bard-Avon, 1970; New York: Delta-Dell, 1978; London: Writers and Readers, 1983.

Death Kit. New York: Farrar, 1967, 1986; New York: Signet-NAL, 1968; London: Secker, 1968; Middlesex: Penguin, 1970; Harmondsworth: Penguin, 1970; New York: Delta-Dell, 1978.

Collected Works

I, etcetera. New York: Farrar, 1978, 1988; New York: Vintage, 1979; London: Gollancz, 1979; New York: Anchor, 1991.

Contents: Project for a Trip to China, Debriefing, American Spirits, The Dummy, Old Complaints Revisited, Baby, Doctor Jekyll, Unguided Tour.

Short Fiction in Anthologies

"Debriefing." *A Susan Sontag Reader*. New York: Farrar, 1982; New York: Vintage, 1983; Harmondsworth: Penguin, 1983. 287-301.

"Description (of a Description)." *Facing Texts: Encounters Between Contemporary Writers and Critics.* Ed. Heide Ziegler. Durham: Duke UP, 1988. 140-43.

"The Dummy." *The Uncommon Reader.* Ed. Alice S. Morris. New York: Avon, 1965. 327-35.

"Project for a Trip to China." *A Susan Sontag Reader.* New York: Farrar, 1982; New York: Vintage, 1983; Harmondsworth: Penguin, 1983. 267-86.

"Unguided Tour." *A Susan Sontag Reader.* New York: Farrar, 1982; New York: Vintage, 1983; Harmondsworth: Penguin, 1983. 371-81.

Short Fiction in Periodicals

"Baby." *Playboy* Feb. 1974: 74-76, 120, 204-08, 210-12.

"Description (of a Description)." *Antaeus* 53 (1984): 111-14; *Harper's* Jan. 1985: 32-34.

"Doctor Jekyll." *Partisan Review* 41.4 (1974): 539-52, 586-603.

"The Letter Scene." *New Yorker* 18 Aug. 1986: 24-32.

"Man with a Pain." *Harper's* Apr. 1964: 72-75.

"Project for a Trip to China." *Atlantic* Apr. 1973: 69-77.

"Unguided Tour." *New Yorker* 31 Oct. 1977: 40-45.

"The Way We Live Now." *New Yorker* 24 Nov. 1986: 42-51.

"The Will and the Way." *Partisan Review* 32.3 (1965): 373-96.

Secondary Sources

Books

Sayres, Sohnya. *Susan Sontag: The Elegiac Modernist*. New York: Routledge, 1990.

Articles and Chapters

Bassoff, Bruce. "Private Revolution: Sontag's *The Benefactor*." *enclitic* 3.2 (1979): 59-73.

Describes *The Benefactor* as being a novel full of embedded stories that complicate, reinforce, and contradict the main narrative—itself generated by dreams and punctuated by a fairy tale. Regards all incidents—dreams, memories, fantasies, and real events—in the same light. Describes each of the stories, the major characters, and the style of the narration. Begins to analyze the dynamics of the text with her reconstruction of the myth of the autogenists—the self-sufficient male deity Autogenes.

Bruss, Elizabeth W. "Susan Sontag." *Beautiful Theories: The Spectacles of Discourse in Contemporary Criticism*. Elizabeth W. Bruss. Baltimore: Johns Hopkins UP, 1982. 203-80.

A major treatment of Sontag's criticism, essays, short stories, and film that tries to account for the apparent disparity between her views as a critic and her own creative works. Unparaphraseable and perhaps the best single introduction to her career as a whole. More of a monograph than a chapter.

Geltman, Max. "Susan Sontag: Mistress of the Via Negativa." *Ideas* 4 (1973): 49-59.

A patronizing if not hostile article characterizing Sontag as beautiful, irrational, trendy, and unreadable. Describes *The Benefactor* as an unreadable, instantaneous disaster and *Death Kit* as unprintable. Labels Sontag's references to little-read non-British and American writers as "name-dropping" in order to provide the necessary ring of profundity. Accuses her of having a high regard for her own opinions and of being a master of planned obfuscation. Notes that when she seems to be most wise, chances are she is being most silly. The remainder of the article proceeds with patronizing references to the critic by her first name and graduate advisor-like nit-picking at many of the assertions expressed in the essays. The overall effect of this essay is to reduce Sontag to a precocious, beautiful, imbecile darling of the *avant-garde* literary community. Concludes that she probably arrived at these errors by too early a marriage and pregnancy. Concludes that "When still too young she wanted too much."

Hardwick, Elizabeth. Introduction. *A Susan Sontag Reader*. Susan Sontag. New York: Farrar, 1982; Vintage-Random; Harmondsworth: Penguin, 1983. ix-xv.

This introduction provides a general overview of Sontag's critical ideas, devotion to form, wide-ranging reading, cultural interests, fascination with epistemology, and her angular and devious fiction. Concludes that only the serious can offer us that rare, warm, bright-hearted felicity.

Heilbrun, Carolyn G. "Speaking of Susan Sontag." *New York Times Book Review* 27 Aug. 1967: 2, 30.

A brilliantly written account of Sontag's public image and private self, including an in-depth review of *Death Kit*.

Howard, Richard. "A Description of 'Description (of a Description).'" *Facing Texts: Encounters Between Contemporary Writers and Critics*. Ed. Heide Ziegler. Durham: Duke UP, 1988. 144-50.

Discusses Sontag's use of the story within the story, or play within the play, and the mirroring of writing by itself. Sees her title, "Description (of a Description)" as "invoking the geometrical sense: the tracing or traversing of a course, as the description of an arc or a circle; and, of course, the ingenious parallel to deconstruction —the de - scription of a description, the conversion of (any possible) function to WRITING."

Karl, Frederick R. *American Fictions 1940/1980: A Comprehensive History and Critical Evaluation*. New York: Harper, 1983. 402-05.

Calls Sontag a minimalist. Describes each of her works in turn, and assigns phases and lines of development to them. An excellent introduction to her work.

Kher, P. R. "Susan Sontag's Aesthetic: A Moral Point of View." *Osmania Journal of English Studies* 15 (1979): 55-64.

Contains a presentation of Sontag's moral philosophy and literary aesthetic. Describes this amalgam as an aesthetic of "inclusion" based on formalist theory and an acute awareness of the "camp" as style and aesthetic phenomenon. Demonstrates how she denies that the form-content problem cannot be resolved by the theory of organic unity. Considers art versus morality a pseudo-problem. It is the same consciousness which is nourished by aesthetic experiences that finds expression in moral action. Also discusses Sontag's doctrine of the curative and mystical powers of silence and her views on the social uses of pornography. Concludes that her aesthetic urges us to see more, learn more, and to feel more.

Koch, Stephen. "On Susan Sontag." *TriQuarterly* 7 (1966): 153-60.

Describes Sontag as a pragmatist of aestheticism. Notes that her discussions of aesthetic autonomy usually turn out to be disguised polemics on the subject of human liberty in general. Commends her for opening criticism to the needs of art and for using formalist arguments to open awareness to certain new modalities of expression.

Lewicki, Zbigniew. "Three Dimensions of Entropy: William Gaddis, Susan Sontag, John Updike." *The Bang and the Whimper: Apocalypse and Entropy in American Literature*. Zbigniew Lewicki. Contributions in American Studies 71. Westport: Greenwood, 1984. 103-16.

After developing the theme of entropy as central to Gaddis' *JR*, Lewicki describes the central metaphor of Sontag's *Death Kit* as that of "running down." Considers the running down and decay of Didi's personal life paralleled by the running down and decay of the exterior world depicted.

Madden, David. "*The Benefactor*." *Survey of Contemporary Literature*. Ed. Frank N. Magill. Rev. ed. 12 vols. Englewood Cliffs: Salem, 1977. 1: 637-42.

A standard reference article listing the principal characters and describing the contents, characters, themes, style, and symbolism of *The Benefactor*.

McCaffery, Larry. "*Death Kit*: Susan Sontag's Dream Narrative." *Contemporary Literature* 20.4 (1979): 484-99.

Argues that *Death Kit* does not employ the sort of highly self-conscious, blatantly artificial methods of structural innovation that force the reader to deal with the work primarily as an artifact. Claims that it belongs to the tradition of dream tale of Borges and Kafka, or the nightmarish works of Djuna Barnes, John Hawkes, or Anias Nin.

Mitgutsch, Waltraud. "Salvation or Annihilation?—The Theme of Regression in Contemporary Literature. (Susan Sontag, James Dickey, Theodore Roethke)." *Revue Des Langues Vivantes* 45 (1979): 64-77.

Recounts the frequency with which the myth of the underworld journey has informed literature before and after psychoanalytic theory was promulgated. Describes this journey Freud called regression as both a healing as well as a destructive journey. Notes that it can achieve the reintegration of an alienated and fragmented self. Argues that modern literature directs its aggressive, seemingly destructive tendencies not only against a civilization which is disintegrating, but also against itself. Traces this thesis through Sontag's fiction and criticism.

Mudrick, Marvin. "Susie Creamcheese Makes Love Not War." *Harper's* Feb. 1983: 62-65.

A stinging diatribe against Sontag's "seriousness" which discusses everything from her appearance to her political opinions, with special reference to *A Susan Sontag Reader*, the object of the essay. Denies Sontag is a novelist.

Pendleton, Dennis. *"Death Kit." Survey of Contemporary Literature.* Ed. Frank N. Magill. Rev. ed. 12 vols. Englewood Cliffs: Salem, 1977. 3: 1817-20.

A standard reference article discussing *Death Kit* in terms of its principal characters, themes, plot, style, symbolism, influences, and impact.

Tanner, Tony. "Interior Spaciousness—Car, Bell Jar, Tunnel and House." *City of Words: American Fiction 1950-1970.* Tony Tanner. London: Cape; New York: Harper, 1971. 260-72.

Discusses the subject of interior journeying on the postwar novel and Sontag's *The Benefactor*. A detailed account of the journey of Hippolyte. Traces the same journey in *Death Kit*.

Taylor, Benjamin. "A Centered Voice: Susan Sontag's Short Fiction." *Georgia Review* 34.4 (1980): 907-16.

Describes *I, etcetera* as a collection of short fiction which constructs a moral drama of antinomy. Notes that they are about the human longing for freedom from bondage, from the absolution from knowledge, for the completion of knowledge. Details the contents and thematic implications of each of the stories in turn, and concludes that Sontag has battled as strenuously as any writer of our time with the issues surrounding the embattled self and its problem of consciousness.

Reviews

Adams, Robert M. "Nacht und Tag." Rev. of *The Benefactor. New York Review of Books* 17 Oct. 1963: 19.

Calls *The Benefactor* an intricate post-Kafka monologue of private dreams masquerading as social reality disguised as private dreams. Claims that the book is done with great subtlety and with a style masked as anti-style, all infused with layered ironies. Suggests that, despite the shortcomings of the book, Sontag has not written the usual doughy first novel. Regards her scenes to be crisp, her prose hard, and praises resistance of romantic striving for effect. Concludes that this is a bold, flawed, impressive piece of work.

Aronowitz, Stanley. "Opposites Detract: Sontag Versus Barthes for Barthes's Sake." Rev. of *A Susan Sontag Reader. Village Voice Literary Supplement* Nov. 1982: 13.

Celebrates the simultaneous appearance of *A Roland Barthes Reader*, edited by Sontag, and *A Susan Sontag Reader*. Calls Sontag a major example of critic as star, the *enfant terrible* of the critical establishment, a passionate advocate of high art, and a defender of pop art. Commends her for framing Barthes's work in the categories of sensibility, beauty, style, and taste.

Bell, Pearl K. "Literary Waifs." Rev. of *I, etcetera. Commentary* Feb. 1979: 68-70.

Suggests that the eight stories in *I, etcetera* show language erecting a barrier between writer and reader which can only be surmounted by the supreme act of unriddling. Considers this less a work of fictional imagination than a miscellany of indiscriminate hypotheses about fiction, organized around an omnivorously conscious "I" in perpetual motion, driven by a fierce craving for the new. A detailed essay on the connection between Sontag's literary theory and this fiction.

Conrad, Peter. "Dark Lady of Letters." Rev. of *The Benefactor* and *Under the Sign of Saturn. Observer* 19 June 1983: 31.

Claims that in *Under the Sign of Saturn*, Sontag extols a gamey mental delight in Barthes, Benjamin, Goodman, Canetti, Syberberg, and others. Describes her views on Modernism, Romanticism, and criticism. Provides a detailed account of the contents of the book, and concludes that this is a parable of her own critical beliefs, influences, and agendas.

Cook, Bruce. "On Good Authority, A Tentativity." Rev. of *A Susan Sontag Reader. Los Angeles Times Book Review* 12 Dec. 1982: 2.

Describes *A Susan Sontag Reader* in the context of a short history of her life work. Considers Sontag to have more authority than most American critics, yet she wields greater care than before. Concludes that, considering her natural arrogance, this book reads with more humility, and comments that she has now grown so wise she even seems aware of her own ignorance.

Davies, Russell. "Members Only." Rev. of *I, etcetera. New Statesman* 11 May 1979: 689-90.

Claims that in *I, etcetera* we see Sontag's liberal intellect within which imagination and desire are perpetually restrained by conscience and fear of one's own inauthenticity. Notes that she hits a satirical vein now and then. Suggests that this whole restless book represents fifteen years of intermittent attempts to own up to this schizophrenic tangle. Details the contents of several of the pieces. Concludes, regrettably, that only members of the Sontag club of fans will read this book.

Davis, Douglas M. "Turning to the Novel, Miss Sontag Flits Between Dream and Reality." Rev. of *Death Kit. National Observer* 21 Aug. 1967: 21.

Claims that to call *Death Kit* "pregnant with meaning" is too pale a metaphor. Summarizes the ethos as "reality is whatever we say it is. Reality is beyond definition and logic affords us very little light on the subject." Calls reading the novel an experience beyond definition: part novel, part thriller, part philosophy, part dream.

Degnan, James. "The Empress' New Clothes." Rev. of *Death Kit. Critic* Oct.-Nov. 1967: 74-76.

Describes *Death Kit* in scathing terms as a banal exercise in the pure, sensuous, untranslatable immediacy of some of its images. Critiques Sontag's call for not an hermeneutics but an erotics of art, and ridicules the plot in which she demonstrates this erotics.

"Did He?" Rev. of *Death Kit. Time* 18 Aug. 1967: 86, 88.

Argues that *Death Kit* contains the blunted instruments of the *avant garde* movement and Freudian criticism. Sees it as studded with little messages to critics and "long hairs." Concludes that it is an arduously worked out novel with the author always at the reader's elbow pointing out why and how she wrote it.

"Diddy?" Rev. of *Death Kit. Times Literary Supplement* 25 Apr. 1968: 441.

Considers *Death Kit* as starting promisingly enough, but complains that the reader soon discovers Sontag does not wish to leave him or her smugly able to understand or guess, or be entertained. Suggests that this is an involved stylistic display, and only those very determined to see her as a high priestess of modern culture will cheerfully await the next weighty volume of her fiction. Details the contents.

Durrant, Digby. "Fatal Flaws." Rev. of *I, etcetera. London Magazine* July 1979: 93-94.

Briefly reviews the contents of *I, etcetera* and concludes that Sontag is obsessed by the need for freedom which she sees as markedly absent from the American way of life. She is often obscure and tiring, but equally often an exuberant and passionate moralist who fights absurdities and injustices by inflating them into huge balloons and then taking out a long, sharp needle and jabbing it in.

Enright, D. J. "On the Verge." Rev. of *I, etcetera. Listener* 26 Apr. 1979: 586.

Calls *I, etcetera* a collection of short stories much like debriefings of women and men suffering the ordeals and dilemmas of consciousness. Comments that one imagines the characters stumbling into the author's study, tearing off helmet, parachute, and flak jacket. Calls these stories unconventional, unusual, unorthodox, but not unreadable. Concludes that all are developed with passionless gusto and unspecific particularities.

Flint, Robert W. "Books in Review." Rev. of *The Benefactor. Commentary* Dec. 1963: 489-90.

Argues that *The Benefactor* is written with rapt thoroughness. Claims that Sontag has adapted her sources to her own temper, avoiding falling into the high vatic style of late nineteenth-century reactionary aestheticism. Calls this an intricate, ambitious fantasia or theme suggested by European literary modernism up to Simone Weil. A detailed account of the contents.

Frakes, James R. "Where Dreaming Is Believing." Rev. of *The Benefactor. New York Herald Tribune Book Week* 22 Sept. 1963: 10.

Suggests that *The Benefactor* is a very special book written with craft and daring, as well as certainty. Insists Sontag knows what she is trying to accomplish, avoids excess, and labors no point already made. Concludes that, above all, she respects craft. Details the contents of the book, and offers a plentitude of literary assessments.

Fremont-Smith, Eliot. "Diddy Did It—Or Did He?" Rev. of *Death Kit*.
    New York Times 18 Aug. 1967: 31.

Complains that *Death Kit* skips, shuffles, and snoozes over the same territory as *The Benefactor*. Wishes Sontag had stopped sooner to rethink
character development, craft, pacing, authenticity of tone, and other such
antiquarian matters. Argues that the persevering reader will earn what
answers they, with Miss Sontag's good-natured, earnest, and (too) occasionally brilliant help can deduce.

Furbank, P. N. "Two Hells." Rev. of *Death Kit*. *Listener* 25 Apr. 1968:
    548-49.

Comments that *Death Kit* reminds one of Sontag having some kind of
hitch in her relationship with enjoyment. Notes that with much effort,
she communicates joyless understanding. Sees this novel as an impressive exercise in motiveless irony. Considers it written in staccato syntax
with an irregular tense system and much stylistic invention. Details the
plot, and concludes that there is too much will in the writing.

Gitlin, Todd. "Sontag's Stories." Rev. of *I, etcetera*. *Progressive* Mar.
    1979: 58-59.

Notes that *I, etcetera* contains eight strange, uneven, hallucinatory pieces,
most of which are sketches and fragments. Describes several of these pieces.

Grumbach, Doris. "Book Reviews." Rev. of *Death Kit*. *America* 26 Aug.
    1967: 207.

Calls Sontag a unique kind of writer in that her original work is always
suffused with original and perceptive essays about fiction. Describes the
scenes as nightmarish, surrealistic, well-imagined, and somewhat like a
terrifying excursion. Commends it to the reader.

Halio, Jay L., Jr. "The Way It Is—and Was." Rev. of *Death Kit*.
    Southern Review 6.1 (1970): 258-60.

Calls *Death Kit* a suicide account drawing much from Sontag's interest
in Buber and D.H. Lawrence. Describes the plot and central characters
very briefly.

Hicks, Granville. "Guessing Game for Everyman." Rev. of *Death Kit*.
    Saturday Review 26 Aug. 1967: 25-26.

Argues that *Death Kit* bears some general resemblance to *The
Benefactor*, though in detail it is quite different. Suggests that it contains

distracting mannerisms and epithets, but maintains that the characters are powerful and the questions they raise important. Insists Sontag has a great gift and a talent with particular feeling for life and especially death, and a unique way of expressing it.

Hicks, Granville. "To Act, Perforce to Dream." Rev. of *The Benefactor*. *Saturday Review* 7 Sept. 1963: 17-18.

Calls Sontag a resolute explorer of that twentieth-century enigma: Reality. Provides a biographical sketch of her background, and recounts the contents of *The Benefactor*. Concludes that she eludes the reader at every corner, becoming arbitrary and even perverse at times.

Howard, Maureen. "Sontag's Surrender." Rev. of *I, etcetera*. *Saturday Review* 28 Oct. 1978: 46-47.

Calls *I, etcetera* a collection of short fiction showing Sontag's wit and her surrender to imaginative language—a taut, richly associative prose style. Describes many of the stories individually. Claims that Sontag is accurate and affectionate, and embraces our language as well as the accumulation of culture.

Howes, Victor. "Sontag's Ideas in Fiction Form." Rev. of *I, etcetera*. *Christian Science Monitor* 17 Jan. 1979: 19.

Suggests that *I, etcetera* contains characters who shift identities, long to interchange, keep their gender secret, live in a modern megalopolis, and speak like characters in Kafka's fiction. Comments that Sontag's stories of one decade impale a troubled time on a satiric, yet often sympathetic, ballpoint. Concludes that she is experimental, *avant-garde*, shrewd, witty, and creative.

"Identifiable as Prose." Rev. of *The Benefactor*. *Time* 13 Sept. 1963: 112-13.

Notes that *The Benefactor* is set in Paris and contains a series of fictional puzzles to be solved by the reader. Briefly describes the contents, and concludes that the prose sounds like a blurred translation from some other language.

Kauffmann, Stanley. "Interpreting Miss Sontag." Rev. of *Death Kit. New Republic* 2 Sept. 1967: 24, 45-46.

Describes *Death Kit* as soaring in and out of various levels of consciousness and reality. Notes that the anguish and terror lies in the very texture through an associative, daring, piercing prose. Describes the contents in detail. Complains that the characterization is uncompelling, and that, after a while the sensory evocations collapse into systems of symbols.

Kendrick, Walter. "In a Gulf of Her Own." Rev. of *A Susan Sontag Reader. Nation* 23 Oct. 1982: 404-06.

A brief essay discussing the appearance of *A Susan Sontag Reader* in which Kendrick criticizes Harwick's "Introduction" as smelling of formaldehyde and the selection of fiction as "overbalancing." Criticizes the inclusions from *The Benefactor*, and comments that the obvious omissions from *Illness as Metaphor* and *On Photography* are probably due to the fact both books demonstrate Sontag's inability to sustain an argument. Delineates the limits of her thought as aesthetic impressions. Makes brief and usually deprecating comments on the individual pieces in the reader, and concludes that Sontag is alternately brilliant and muddled.

Koch, Stephen. "Imagination in the Abstract." Rev. of *The Benefactor. Antioch Review* 24.2 (1964): 253-58.

Accuses Sontag of producing a very difficult book in *The Benefactor*. Claims that she uses this book to demonstrate the artistic impasse, and the degeneration of the relevance of art to experience and the reader to which she expects this development will lead. Describes the contents of the novel. Suggests that, ultimately, *The Benefactor* and its hero move in a distinctly aloof and unreal intellectual ether, failing to touch earth. Considers the prose lifeless, the whole effect impersonal and endlessly ironic.

Koch, Stephen. "Sontag: Shaking the Tree of Death." Rev. of *Death Kit. Nation* 2 Oct. 1967: 310-11.

Claims that *Death Kit* analyses what might be called the inside of a single moment and a single condition—a man's realization he is going to die. Suggests that the treatment of banality is in some ways the most surprising and original aspect of *Death Kit*. Provides a detailed account of the contents.

Kramer, Hilton. "The Passionaria of Style." Rev. of *A Susan Sontag Reader. Atlantic* Sept. 1982: 88-92, 94.

Celebrates the publication of *A Susan Sontag Reader*. Reviews her life and the impact of her early critical work which made criticism a medium of intellectual scandal. Critiques her ideas in *Against Interpretation* against the intellectual backdrop of criticism in the 1960s and the movement of radical aestheticism. A major introduction to Sontag's place in twentieth-century intellectual history.

Kriegel, Leonard. "The Soldiers of General McLuhan." Rev. of *Death Kit. Dimensions* (Wint. 1967-68): 48.

Argues that Sontag's public persona threatens to overwhelm her work. Describes *Death Kit* as original, and details its contents.

Kroll, Jack. "Diddy the Dead." Rev. of *Death Kit. Newsweek* 28 Aug. 1967: 78.

Calls Sontag a brilliant example of the "new sensibility." Yet claims that it is surprising she could read over *Death Kit* and not realize what a disaster it is. Suggests that its style is a jelly fish twitching, its characters shadowy, half materialized puppets, and its whole thrust and purport as muddled and mumbly as a village drunk. Provides a detailed account of contents.

Mednick, Liz. "Apres Moi, Etcetera." Rev. of *I, etcetera. New York Arts Journal* 13 (1979): 13-15.

Describes the contents of Sontag's collection of short stories, *I, etcetera*, as a pastiche of eight vignettes, chronicles, and monologues, six of them sandwiched between two travel pieces. Claims that all her characters look at the world through the index of personal gain meaning conceptual hoarding.

Merkin, Daphne. "Getting Smart." Rev. of *I, etcetera. New Leader* 18 Dec. 1978: 12-13.

Calls the eight stories in *I, etcetera* tricky, highwire acts of intellect— rather than tales of once-upon-a-time. Describes each piece in turn, and concludes that this is a work of complex, droll imagination, but that unfortunately, the fiction is also arid.

Miller, Jane. "Dissenting Voices." Rev. of *I, etcetera. Times Literary Supplement* 23 Nov. 1979: 41.

Comments that *I, etcetera* is an insistent, chattering collection of stories demanding a psychiatric ear. Notes that the narrative style is sometimes hectoring, and that it seems we are expected to interrupt these monologues in order to reply, to come clean, and confess something too. Details the contents of several of the stories.

Paulin, Tom. "Operatic Surfaces, Deep Politics." Rev. of *I, etcetera. Encounter* Aug. 1979: 57-58.

Argues that *I, etcetera* reads like jottings in a commonplace book. Notes that sometimes the absence of narrative is crossed by an intelligent observation of the life of the twilight of the 1970s, and that the mix of global bric a brac is reminiscent of Updike. Considers everyone in some sort of drag. Concludes that all too often Sontag attempts to tell the story and succeeds merely in being dull and brisk, like a poor Feiffer cartoon.

Phelps, Donald. "Form as Hero." Rev. of *The Benefactor. New Leader* 28 Oct. 1963: 24-25.

Notes that *The Benefactor* is a small, charming, comic book whose protagonist, Hippolyte, tries to encompass life with a Sontagesque sense of form, and whose hero is that sense of form. Notes that her world is one of metaphysical conceits and dreams, the substance of identity. Suggests that the atmosphere is one of hard-lit wakefulness. Concludes that this book, despite the fact that it does not press its limitations harder, is well worth reading.

Pickrel, Paul. "A Stegner, a MacLennan, and a Sontag." Rev. of *Death Kit. Harper's* Sept. 1967: 118, 120.

Describes *Death Kit* as being strung on the gimmick of the reader never knowing whether what is happening is real, or whether it is in Diddy's mind. Claims that it all takes place in some indeterminate zone between ordinary reality and hallucination. Considers much of the book excessively clever but Sontag's mannerisms annoying. Concludes that she writes most successfully when she sticks to the conventional methods.

"Proper Self Love." Rev. of *The Benefactor. Times Literary Supplement* 7 May 1964: 389.

Calls *The Benefactor* a gaunt phantasm in a quite vivid and convincing setting. Notes that the book never overcomes its preoccupation with fictional creation and what seems like an abstract creation. Yet suggests that this book marks the appearance of a genuine talent, even if the speculative side of it leaves one with a strong, general sense of the unexposed possibilities in life lying open to human freedom.

Reynolds, Stanley. "Dreaming." Rev. of *Death Kit. New Statesman* 26 Apr. 1968: 555-56.

Briefly reviews Sontag's publishing career, and then describes *Death Kit* as being in the puzzling genre of Vladimir Nabokov's *Invitation to a Beheading*. Describes her book as ruled by the unity of dream, the style as clear and blunt, and the contents as having force, momentum, puzzles, tricks, symbols, all based on the highly dubious theory that art that is composed of items of content violates art itself. Details the plot and characters.

Rosenthal, Raymond. "Death as a Middle-Class Hobby." Rev. of *The Benefactor* and *Death Kit*. *New Leader* 28 Aug. 1967: 14-15.

Suggests that *The Benefactor* contains less fruity prose, many shy ironies, and sharp thinking. But complains the novel concludes on every page, never quite arriving at a conclusion. Complains also, that the preoccupation with dreams is ambiguous, terrible, and intriguing. Concludes that, nevertheless, *Death Kit* is a book written by a top-heavy intelligence lacking even the slightest trace of sensibility. Contains a detailed plot summary.

Sage, Lorna. "Anti-Culture Vulture." Rev. of *I, etcetera*. *Observer* 22 Apr. 1979: 38.

Describes the style and contents of the eight pieces in *I, etcetera* as fictional by-blows of the last fifteen years. Notes that they are hardly stories but are full of invention, subversion, meditation, and conscience. Concludes that, for Sontag, literature is a society of witty cripples whose only hope of recovery lies in some unforeseeable miracle.

Sale, Roger. "Good Servants and Bad Masters." Rev. of *Death Kit*. *Hudson Review* 20.4 (1967-68): 667-69.

Argues that Sontag is not as good as Christina Stead, but certainly tries harder. Details the contents of *Death Kit*, and provides a brief history of the sources of her ideas. Admires the work for its frigidity and extraordinary belief in itself.

Sheed, Wilfrid. "Susan Sontag as Dandy Schoolmarm-Novelist." Rev. of *Death Kit*. *Commonweal* 20 Oct. 1967: 89-90.

Calls Sontag a philosopher-aesthete whose novel *Death Kit* is a fictional gloss on her critique of America in the *Partisan Review* (Winter 1967). Details character and contents. Concludes that Sontag is a fiendishly energetic writer who has put in the kind of work few novels get these days.

Sklar, Robert. "A Death in Theory." Rev. of *Death Kit*. *Reporter* 5 Oct. 1967: 52.

Calls *Death Kit* neither memorable nor especially good, but good enough to enjoy and forget. Concludes that it succeeds as an experiment principally because it tells a good story. Details the contents, and commends it to "symbol sniffers." Concludes that it is self-enclosed, leaving no emotional traces and no mental reverberations because ultimately it succeeds no better than the interpretive criticism she justly condemns in liberating fiction or clearing the air.

Solotaroff, Theodore. "Death in Life." Rev. of *Death Kit*. *Commentary* Nov. 1967: 87-89. Rpt. as "Interpreting Susan Sontag" in *The Red Hot Vacuum and Other Pieces on the Writing of the Sixties*. Theodore Solotaroff. New York: Atheneum, 1970. 261-68.

While providing an historical review of Sontag's reputation, Solotaroff comments extensively on *Death Kit* and *The Benefactor* as books illustrating Sontag's theories on interpretation. Calls both novels unusually interesting in their own right, and claims that their best qualities are those manifest in her best essays—intelligence, audacity, and creative bravura. Provides a detailed account of the contents of *Death Kit*. Calls *The Benefactor* an essentially analytic and technique-ridden work.

Stern, Daniel. "Life Becomes a Dream." Rev. of *The Benefactor*. *New York Times Book Review* 8 Sept. 1963: 5.

Describes *The Benefactor* as a carefully modern work full of characters who assume postures and a tone which is carefully detached. Describes the contents of the book, commenting on its cinematographic descriptions. Complains that the central analogies of the book remain abstract, unfleshed, and finally, unimportant.

Stone, Laurie. "Catching the Reluctant 'I'." Rev. of *I, etcetera*. *Ms*. Mar. 1979: 25-26, 28-29.

Comments that *I, etcetera* is composed of diary-like scenes and ruminations that progress in a seemingly nonsequential way. Notes that Sontag is interested in revealing human character and makes no points about life. Details the contents.

Taliafero, Frances. Rev. of *I, etcetera*. *Harper's* Jan. 1979: 90.

Considers these stories in *I, etcetera* to be cold. Notes that, like funeral baked meats, it is hard to work up an appetite for them. Calls them cerebrally gimmicky, heavy with allegory, and with virtues that do not justify their monochrome length. Concludes that they are passionless, unspontaneous, too unspecific, and finally disembodied.

Tanner, Tony. "Space Odyssey." Rev. of *Death Kit. Partisan Review* 25.3 (1968): 446-51.

Describes *Death Kit* as a novel about entropy and how the head gets rid of the world. Considers the energies of disburdenment—or the fatigues of relinquishment, very evident in both her novels. Claims that both explore interesting aspects of contemporary phenomenology and communications media, but, instead of containing relationships and people, they contain only diagrams of dispositions, schemes, and attitudes. Concludes that, to adopt two of her own chosen terms, her work is palpably "constructed" rather than "secreted."

Thomson, Ian. "Special Notices." Rev. of *A Susan Sontag Reader. London Magazine* July 1984: 103-06.

Argues that, with the publication of *A Susan Sontag Reader*, Sontag has finally been gift-wrapped into convenient consumerism. Describes the contents minutely, then describes her style, philosophy of criticism, "imaginationism," and theory of art. Concludes that Sontag is ultimately a broker in fads, writing for those who have a taste for the extreme in art or who enjoy the lunatic fringe.

Towers, Robert. "Verbal Constructs." Rev. of *I, etcetera. New York Times Book Review* 26 Nov. 1978: 10.

Calls *I, etcetera* a typically Sontagian collection of stories some of which are decidedly more successful than others. Details the contents of several of the pieces, and concludes that this is an eccentric, uneven, and nearly always interesting collection.

Tyler, Anne. Rev. of *I, etcetera. New Republic* 25 Nov. 1978: 29-30.

Describes the typical Sontag protagonist in these stories as intelligent, anxious, discontent, obsessed periodically by thoughts of freedom, and burdened by a body of fashionable knowledge that fails to solve any of his real problems. Suggests that, where the stories succeed, they succeed brilliantly. Concludes that, though this is not an easy book to read, it possesses its own kind of spirit and nerve.

Vidal, Gore. "The Writer as Cannibal." Rev. of *Death Kit. Chicago Tribune Book World* 10 Sept. 1967: 5, 34. Rpt. as "Miss Sontag's New Novel" in *Reflections Upon a Sinking Ship*. Gore Vidal. Boston: Little, 1969. 40-47; *Homage to Daniel Shays: Collected Essays 1952-1972*. Gore Vidal. New York: Random, 1972. 295-301.

Says the novel betrays such literary sources as Robbe-Grillet, Sartre, Kafka, and Sarraute. Calls the language rich and the plot elaborate. Details the contents and characters, and concludes that the flash of talent at the end of the book makes more annoying what precedes it. Considers Miss Sontag a didactic, Jewish-American writer who wants to be an entirely different sort of writer, not American but High-European, not Jewish but ecumenical, not naturalistic in style but allusive, resonant, ambiguous. Claims that she has been undone as a novelist by her training in comparative literature, but that, unfortunately, her intelligence is stronger than her talent.

Wain, John. "Song of Myself. 1963." Rev. of *The Benefactor*. *New Republic* 21 Sept. 1963: 26-27, 30.

Describes *The Benefactor* as European in character and a fairly standard exercise on that old European romantic theme, the relations between the night-self and the day-self. Details the contents of the novel. Concludes that this novel is evidence strange things are afoot in the American novel.

Wilding, Michael. "Selected Books." Rev. of *Death Kit*. *London Magazine* June 1968: 113-14.

Argues that *Death Kit* contains little originality, if any spirit of vitality. Notes that the tireless props and cliches sustain a mausoleum. Considers the contrivance insistent, the lumbering allegoric fantasy not even allowed autonomy, and the book arousing anger with its silly pretentiousness because the all-encompassing boredom it produces numbs our reactions.

Wilson, Frank. Rev. of *I, etcetera. Best Sellers* Apr. 1979: 10.

Describes the work as an unconventional set of eight stories with little plot, action, or characterization. Complains that it is deadpan serious and contains lots of wondering and depiction of the ordeals of modern consciousness weighted down with too much history, too much information, and too little wisdom. Concludes that this is "a good book to read in front of the fire. And nod off over. Or use as kindling."

Winegarten, Renee. "Innocence and Eccentricity." Rev. of *The Benefactor. Jewish Observer and Middle East Review* 8 May 1964: 18.

Describes *The Benefactor* as excessively cerebral, and complains that the joke palls a little before the end. Admits, however, that it is an extremely witty and disconcerting book. Details the contents.

Wood, Michael. "'This Is Not the End of the World'." Rev. of *I, etcetera*. *New York Review of Books* 25 Jan. 1979: 28-31.

Comments that, framed by two stories about journeys, this collection confronts and explores the life which is traveled rather than lived. Finds this an ideal metaphor for the unlived life, but complains that Sontag's epigrams sometimes get in the way of her compassion, keeping us at arm's length.

Interviews

Ableman, Paul. "Sontag in Interview." Rev. of *I, etcetera. Books and Bookmen* Apr. 1979: 34-35.

Reports Sontag's views on the centrality of American experimental writers, the bourgeois novel of the nineteenth-century, her favorite British and American authors, the relationship between television and the middle-class in America, the need for new forms, solipsism, and her own work.

Bellamy, Joe David. "Susan Sontag." *The New Fiction: Interviews with Innovative American Writers*. Ed. Joe David Bellamy. Urbana: U of Illinois P, 1974. 113-29.

In this interview, Sontag explains her harsh criticism of American fiction of the 1960s, and commends the writers who emerged after *Against Interpretation* for their daring innovations on the limiting traditions of the realistic novel—namely Iris Murdoch and Borges. Also discusses the influence of TV, advertising, and journalism upon form literature; the purposes of the novel as "intracranial" or to do with epistemology; and denies the existence of a common human experience in favor of multiple human perceptions. Claims that nature imitates art more than the other way around; art's job is to challenge accepted perceptions of human experience. Argues against the privileged position of certain kinds of realism, and asserts that every style embodies an epistemological decision. Argues for the simultaneity of intellectual and aesthetic experience. Describes the variety of meanings embedded in *Death Kit*. Talks briefly about her short stories and her filmmaking. Concludes with a theory of fictional character in the 1970s novel.

Benedict, Helen. "The Passionate Mind: Susan Sontag." *Portraits in Print: A Collection of Profiles and the Stories Behind Them*. New York: Columbia UP, 1991. 19-36. Rpt. in revised form from *New York Woman* Nov. 1988.

A profile of Sontag that focuses on her intellectuality, her writing, her upbringing, her relationship with her son, her future plans to write fewer essays to concentrate on writing "a more emotionally direct way," and other personal details. Includes commentary by the author on how she did the interview.

Berkley, Miriam. "PW Interviews Susan Sontag." *Publishers Weekly* 22 Oct. 1982: 6-8.

Begins describing Sontag's fascination with Wagner, opera, and classical ballet. Outlines her major works, critical and fictional, as well as her films. Also details her reading habits; her attachment to Poe and Hawthorne; her schooling in Arizona, Chicago, and California; her beginnings as a critic; her life in Europe as a filmmaker; and her latest set of political essays.

Beyer, Monika. "A Life Style Is Not a Life: An Interview with Susan Sontag." *Polish Perspectives* Sept. 1980: 42-46.

In this interview, Sontag queries the absence of a major literary genius of international status in America today, providing a cultural description of the intellectual status of American society. Suggests that it is the obligation of true writers to complain constantly. Condemns the failure of our educational system to produce a truly intellectual elite. Notes changes in form and style within the tradition of realism. Gives her views on her own novels, her support of the women's movement, her Jewishness, and her interest in Polish literature.

Boyers, Robert, and Maxine Bernstein. "Women, the Arts, and the Politics of Culture: An Interview with Susan Sontag." *Salmagundi* 31-32 (1975): 29-48. Rpt. in *A Susan Sontag Reader*. Susan Sontag. New York: Farrer, 1982; Vintage-Random; Harmondsworth: Penguin, 1983. 327-46.

In this extensive interview of Sontag about her ideas on various subjects, she discusses her essay writing, her views on Riefenstahl's Nazi propaganda films, the relationship of art to the moral sense, the tendency of some feminists to use second-hand militancy to serve their ends, her views on Ingmar Bergman as a filmmaker, the importance of the past to art, the falsity of concepts like the "cultural elite" and the "instinctual masses" to understanding our sick culture, her ideas on camp, the clash between sexuality and consciousness, her objections to Philip Rieff's definitions of teacher and student, and her view that our civilization—already overtaken by barbarism—is at an end and cannot be put back together.

Brennan, Paul. "Sontag in Greenwich Village: An Interview." *London Magazine* ns. Apr.-May 1979: 93-103.

In this interview Sontag describes: her recent bout with cancer, her attempts to fend off the media and interviewers, her recent book *Illness as Metaphor* as a political response to a society producing pollution and disease, her admiration for John Berger, her fear of becoming bored during her university career, her avoidance of such terms as "experimental" and *avant-garde* as tired and less meaningful, the confusion about literary standards, her espousal of old-fashioned seriousness, the loss of distance between high taste and mass taste, conventional sensibility and subversive sensibility, fascist rhetoric as student theatre, her delight in challenging historical insomnia, indifference as the real enemy of moral seriousness, her work habits, the writers she admires, the role of the university as cultural center, her attitudes toward capitalism, and her nonchalance about the commercial aspect of publishing.

Copeland, Roger. "The Habits of Consciousness." *Commonweal* 13 Feb. 1981: 83-87.

In this interview Sontag describes: her obsession with consciousness as a form of acquisition, the counter-projects of disburdenment and silence—the temptations of silence—as unifying positions in her fiction. Also describes her vast library and the role it plays in her life, what it means to be modern and how her ideas have changed over the last decade, how she has given the historicist approach a more central role in her reaction to things, and what it means to engage in eschatalogical thinking. Decries television as having heralded the death of Western Civilization, and yet maintains the importance of the relationship between high and pop cultures. Concludes with a tribute to Lionel Trilling and Kenneth Burke, the latter her more important mentor and teacher.

Eames, Elizabeth Ramsden. "Susan Sontag." *Papyrus* 1 (Spr. 1987): 51-61.

In this interview Sontag discusses: the relationship between her intellectual seriousness and her aesthetics, her transition from essayist to fiction writer, dealing with criticism of her work, the form-content split discussed in her critical theory, the United States and the arts, views on the press, and opinions on American film making of the decade.

Gordimer, Nadine, and Susan Sontag. "Even the Most Private Aspects of My Life Are Penetrated by Politics." *Listener* 23 May 1985: 16-17.

In this interview Gordimer and Sontag discuss the moral responsibility involved in being a writer, and their differing attitudes toward actually being published. Most of the discussion focuses on the respective socio-political visions of both writers.

Hitchens, Christopher. "Party Talk." *Observer* 20 June 1982: 27.

An early, anecdotal appraisal of Susan Sontag's anti-Communist ideas and attitudes toward Hanoi, Warsaw, and Moscow.

Holmberg, Arthur. "Susan Sontag." *Performing Arts Journal* 9.1 (1985): 28-30.

Reports Sontag's assessments of Kundera and Diderot, Kundera's roles for women, the differences between working with American and European actors, the influence on her of George Balanchine, her fascination with film, and her preference for the theatre as a genre.

Kent, Leticia. "Susan Sontag Speaks Up." *Vogue* 1 Aug. 1971: 88, 132.

In this brief interview Sontag objects to the terms "lady critic" and "lady novelist" used by Mailer. She discusses her attachment to feminist writers such as Simone de Beauvoir, Shulamith Firestone, and Germaine Greer. She also discusses her filmmaking and her experiences with theatre.

Ruas, Charles. "Susan Sontag: Past, Present and Future." *New York Times Book Review* 24 Oct. 1982: 11, 39-40.

Reviews *A Susan Sontag Reader*, and reports ideas obtained from an extended interview with Sontag.

Ruas, Charles. "Susan Sontag." *Conversations with American Writers*. Charles Ruas. New York: Knopf, 1985. 180-96.

In this interview Sontag discusses: the relationship between her critical work and her fiction, her bout with cancer, her career as a filmmaker, her identification with Europe, her favorite contemporary American writers, her shifting perspectives, the principles of selection in her *Reader*, attitudes towards women and women writers, her editors, her cultural essays, her belief in prose, and her essay on Barthes.

Toback, James. "Whatever You'd Like Susan Sontag to Think, She Doesn't." *Esquire* July 1968: 58-60, 114-16.

The report of an interview that took place in Sontag's New York apartment in which she discusses her son David, her book collection, personal appearance, reading tastes, American culture and politics, love of the opera, Vietnam, her predilection for Beckett and Kafka, attitude toward drugs, Timothy Leary, student impressions of her, her enemies, the responses of critics, and her work habits.

Biographical Sources

Hardwick, Elizabeth. "Knowing Sontag." *Vogue* June 1978: 184-85.
This brief article provides a summary of Sontag's life and work, along with Hardwick's assessment of her importance in American intellectual life and literary history. Interestingly, Hardwick accounts for the phenomenon of Susan Sontag by concluding that she is the most interesting woman of her generation and has entirely created herself.

Lacayo, Richard. "Stand Aside, Sisyphus." *Time* 24 Oct. 1988: 86-88.
Provides a literary biographical profile of Sontag's life, writing, reputation, critical views, and style. A brief, but useful introduction to her life. Contains a portrait of Sontag at 55.

Rowes, Barbara. "Author Susan Sontag Rallies from Dread Illness to Enjoy Her First Commercial Triumph." *People Weekly* 20 Mar. 1978: 74-76, 79-80.
Describes her present life, her recovery from cancer, her career, and her ideas about writing and life.

Sontag, Susan. "Pilgrimage." *New Yorker* 21 Dec. 1987: 38-48.
Describes her youth beginning at age fourteen, moving with her mother and new stepfather from Tucson to the San Fernando Valley, her eating habits, her feeling trapped in her prison of childhood, her reading, and her friends, particularly Merrill, to whom she introduced Mann's *The Magic Mountain*. The remainder of the article describes Merrill's calling to arrange a visit with Mann, who was then living in Pacific Palisades, and a detailed account of the visit and her reactions.

Dissertations

Holdsworth, Elizabeth McCaffrey. "Susan Sontag: Writer-Filmmaker." Diss. Ohio U, 1981.

Pestino, Joseph Francis. "The Reader/Writer Affair: Instigating Repertoire in the Experimental Fiction of Susan Sontag, Walter

Abish, Rejean Ducharme, Paul West, and Christine Brooke-Rose." Diss. Pennsylvania State U, 1986.

Rogers, Rita A. "Styles of Surrealism: Selected English and American Manifestations of Surrealism." Diss. U of Wisconsin, 1972.

Sayres, Sandra. "Susan Sontag and the Practice of Modernism." Diss. State U of New York at Buffalo, 1982.

Shinn, Thelma J. Wardrop. "A Study of Women Characters in Contemporary American Fiction, 1940-1970." Diss. Purdue U, 1972.

Richard G. Stern

1928 –

Primary Sources

Novels

The Chaleur Network. Sagaponack: Second Chance, 1981; London: Sidgwick, 1981. Publ. as *In Any Case.* New York: McGraw, 1962; London: MacGibbon, 1963; Harmondsworth: Penguin, 1971.

Europe: Or, Up and Down with Schreiber and Baggish. New York: McGraw, 1961; London: MacGibbon, 1962; Harmondsworth: Penguin, 1966. British eds. publ. as *Europe: Or, Up and Down with Baggish and Schreiber.*

A Father's Words. New York: Arbor, 1986; Chicago: Phoenix-U of Chicago P, 1990.

Golk. New York: Criterion, 1960; London: MacGibbon, 1960; Cleveland: Meridian-World, 1961; Harmondsworth: Penguin, 1963; Chicago: Phoenix-U of Chicago P, 1987.

In Any Case. New York: McGraw, 1962; London: MacGibbon, 1963; Harmondsworth: Penguin, 1971. Publ. as *The Chaleur Network.* Sagaponack: Second Chance, 1981; London: Sidgwick, 1981.

Natural Shocks. New York: Coward, 1978; London: Sidgwick, 1978; New York: Pocket, 1980; Arbor House Library of Contemporary Americana. New York: Arbor, 1986.

Other Men's Daughters. New York: Dutton, 1973; New York: Pocket, 1974; London: Hamilton, 1974; Arbor House Library of Contemporary Americana. New York: Arbor, 1986.

Stitch. New York: Harper, 1965; London: Hodder, 1967; London: Panther, 1969; Arbor House Library of Contemporary Americana. New York: Arbor, 1986.

Collected Works

1968: A Short Novel, an Urban Idyll, Five Stories, and Two Trade Notes. New York: Holt, 1970; London: Gollancz, 1971.

Contents: Veni, Vidi . . . Wendt; Ins and Outs; Milius and Melanie; East, West . . . Midwest; Idylls of Dugan and Strunk; Gaps; Gifts.

Noble Rot; Stories. New York: Grove, 1989.

Contents: Ins and Outs; The Ideal Address; Good Morrow, Swine; Mail; Wanderers; Gaps; Teeth; The Good European; East, West . . . Midwest; In Return; Gifts; Troubles; Dr. Cahn's Visit; Dying; Idylls of Dugan and Strunk; Gardiner's Legacy; In the Dock; A Short History of Love; Milius and Melanie; Losing Color; Lesson for the Day; A Recital for the Pope; Arrangments at the Gulf; The Girl Who Loves Schubert; Wissler Remembers; Orvieto Dominos, Bolsena Eels; Zhoof; Double Charley; Riordan's Fiftieth; The Sorrows of Captain Schreiber; La Pourriture Noble; Packages.

Packages. New York: Coward, 1980; London: Sidgwick, 1980.

Contents: Wissler Remembers; Mail; The Ideal Address; Packages; Troubles; Lesson for the Day; Double Charley; Riordan's Fiftieth; The Girl Who Loves Schubert; A Recital for the Pope; Dr. Cahn's Visit.

Teeth, Dying, and Other Matters. New York: Harper, 1964; London: MacGibbon, 1964.

Contents: Teeth; Assessment of an Amateur; Good Morrow, Swine; Wanderers; A Counterfactual Proposition; The Good European; Orvieto

Dominos, Bolsena Eels; Nine Letters, Twenty Days; A Short History of Love; Cooley's Version; Arrangements at the Gulf; Gardiner's Legacy; Dying.

Short Fiction in Anthologies

"Dr. Cahn's Visit." *Full Measure: Modern Short Stories on Aging.* Ed. Dorothy Sennett. St. Paul: Gray Wolf, 1988. 346-51.

"Dying." *Honey and Wax: Pleasures and Powers of Narrative.* Ed. Richard Stern. Chicago: U of Chicago P, 1966. 422-31.

"Present for Minna." *This Week's Short-Short Stories.* Ed. Stewart Beach. New York: Random, 1953. 165-69.

"Wissler Remembers." *The Best American Short Stories, 1981.* Eds. Hortence Calisher and Shannon Ravenel. Boston: Houghton, 1981. 293-302.

Short Fiction in Periodicals

"The Assessment of an Amateur." *Kenyon Review* 21.2 (1959): 250-59.

"Aurelia Frequenzia Reveals the Heart and Mind of the Man of Destiny." *Paris Review* 17.66 (1976): 117-22.

"Cooley's Version." *Kenyon Review* 16.2 (1954): 257-67.

"A Counterfactual Proposition." *Transatlantic Review* 14 (1963): 128-34.

"Dr. Cahn's Visit." *Atlantic* Oct. 1979: 80-82.

"The Ideal Address." *Harper's* Sept. 1976: 72-74, 76.

"In Return." *Encounter* July-Aug. 1988: 10-14.

"In the Dock." *TriQuarterly* 60 (1964): 177-212.

"Lesson for the Day." *Commentary* Aug. 1980: 50-53.

"Losing Color." *Antioch Review* 44.1 (1986): 40-41.

"Mail." *Encounter* June 1980: 3-8.

"Milius and Melanie." *Hudson Review* 21.3 (1968): 487-504.

"Orvieto Dominos, Bolsena Eels." *Harper's* June 1964: 68-70, 73-75.

"Riordan's Fiftieth." *Chicago* Apr. 1980: 188+.

"Teeth." *Partisan Review* 30.3 (1963): 327-41.

"Troubles." *TriQuarterly* 42 (1978): 191-202.

"Veni, Vidi . . . Wendt." *Paris Review* 13.49 (1970): 82-151.

"Wanderers." *Partisan Review* 31.3 (1964): 352-62; *Transatlantic Review* 17 (1964): 122-32.

"Wissler Remembers." *Atlantic* Sept. 1980: 65-69.

Secondary Sources

Articles and Chapters

Dembo, L. S. "Stern's Silent Monologue." *The Monological Jew: A Literary Study.* L. S. Dembo. Madison: Wisconsin UP, 1988. 35-43.
Characterizes Stern, the anti-hero of *Stern* as continually in flight from his Jewishness and a chronic rationalizer and fantasist driven by paranoia, anxiety, and a general sense of guilt. Claims that what should have been a *meeting* (in Buber's sense) is nothing more than a gathering of articulate though hopelessly monological solipsists who speak a low,

comic rhetoric and the dialogue through which it is expressed.

Fothergill, Charles E. *"Other Men's Daughters."* Survey of Contemporary Literature. Ed. Frank N. Magill. Rev. ed. 12 vols. Englewood Cliffs: Salem, 1977. 8: 5662-65.

A standard reference article on *Other Men's Daughters* covering principal characters, themes, social commentary, style, contents, plot, and impact.

Kulshrestha, Chirantan. "The Bellow Gyroscope: Letters to Richard G. Stern." *Saul Bellow Journal* 2.1 (1982): 38-43.

These letters from Bellow to Stern record many of Bellow's embryonic theories of the role of the artist, as well as showing the development of a warm, self-revealing relationship between them. Also records Bellow's responses to Stern's novels.

Sullivan, James. "Richard G. Stern." *Critical Survey of Long Fiction.* Ed. Frank N. Magill. 9 vols. Englewood Cliffs: Salem, 1983. Supplement: 360-68.

A standard reference article covering Stern's birthplace, principal long fiction, other literary forms, achievements, biography, analysis of major works, and a brief bibliography.

Reviews

Balliett, Whitney. "Books." Rev. of *Golk. New Yorker* 14 May 1960: 200-01.

Describes *Golk* as satirical, comic, full of Jewish dialect, and finally frozen-faced, like its prose. Suggests that the contest between Stern and his subject is unfortunately a draw.

Barnes, Julian. "Trick or Treat." Rev. of *Natural Shocks. New Statesman* 22 Sept. 1978: 377-78.

Describes *Natural Shocks* as having no desire to hector or bemuse. Calls it swift, elegant, witty, self-aware prose with an obstinate attachment to lucidity. Claims that Stern's intense intelligence discourages holiday skimmers. Discusses the central character, Wursup, and the plot. Concludes that this is a novel of the onset of doubt and quizzical sadness.

Bergonzi, Bernard. "Herzog in Venice." Rev. of *Stitch. New York Review of Books* 9 Dec. 1965: 26.

Describes *Stitch* as a book gracefully written, elegant, and a fetching conflation of dominant literary myths. Suggests, however, that none of this hides the fact that something went awry with the author's intentions: we are left with a certain unease.

"Bookmarks." Rev. of *Stitch. Prairie Schooner* 40.2 (1966): 186.

Calls Stitch of the novel *Stitch* a fictional Ezra Pound transmogrified into a sculptor. Claims that his thought and art mirror the fall of the world into fragments and chaos. Sees this as a skillfully constructed, crisply written novel which vividly renders the mental life of its characters. Considers Stern a writer of strong talent.

Borklund, Elmer. "A New Fictional Hero." Rev. of *Golk. Commentary* Aug. 1960: 177-78.

Discusses *Golk* as presenting an Augie March-type, middle-of-the road hero, or, a Goldian man of feeling sort of hero in Golk himself.

Bostwick, Joan. "Heritage of Treason." Rev. of *In Any Case. Saturday Review* 17 Nov. 1962: 30.

Describes the novel as fresh, subtle, and free of cliches. Notes that it contains economically stated flashbacks and perpetuates honest suspense. Shows how, with Sam, the reader progresses through a re-evaluation of people and situations, all the while developing the Kantian idea that reality can never be known.

Bowers, John. "Son of a Sad Sack." Rev. of *A Father's Words. New York Times Book Review* 15 June 1986: 15.

Sees *A Father's Words* as giving snapshots, through the eyes of Cyrus Reimer, of a comfortable middle-class man's divorce, his long suffering former wife, his girlfriend, and the world of gamey ads. Laments unfortunately that there is a flaw—Stern's prose glitters and shimmers and promises so much, yet it seldom lives up to that promise.

Braudy, Susan. "Man in the Middle." Rev. of *Other Men's Daughters. Ms.* Mar. 1974: 39-40.

Describes the contents of the novel, and calls it emotionally and intellectually profound with three vital, wonderfully drawn characters.

Brickner, Richard P. "The Secrets of Strangers." Rev. of *Packages. New York Times Book Review* 7 Sept. 1980: 13, 38.

Describes *Packages*, a collection of eleven stories, as told in fresh, alert prose, each story offering some originality. Details the contents of several of the stories, and concludes that the superior stories in the collection are the most structured and thorough, as opposed to the more spoken stories.

Brooke, Jocelyn. "New Fiction." Rev. of *In Any Case. Listener* 18 July 1963: 103.

Calls *In Any Case* a serious and important novel deserving judgment by the highest standards. Details the contents, and concludes that Stern's writing has firmness, an air of purpose, authority, and something of the style of Conrad and Kipling.

Broyard, Anatole. "Books: Novelists in Brief." Rev. of *Packages. New York Times* 12 Sept. 1980: C21.

Claims that *Packages* is filled with stories falling short of the usual grace and pleasure we associate with Stern. Concludes that here we are fascinated by gracelessness and downright ugliness.

Broyard, Anatole. "One Critic's Fiction." Rev. of *Natural Shocks. New York Times Book Review* 1 Jan. 1978: 12, 21.

Complains that *Natural Shocks* overstretches itself and fails to cohere. Thinks Stern has a lively mind, but a loose grip on this novel: there are too many themes for 260 pages and not all are interesting in their own right. Details the contents.

Broyard, Anatole. "Packages and World's End." Rev. of *Packages. New York Times* 12 Sept. 1980: C21. Rpt. in *Books of the Times* Nov. 1980: 546-47.

Calls Stern's collection in *Packages* well-named. Sees it as a collection of pleas by characters to "assume my burdens." Discusses the contents of several of the stories. Concludes that these stories are filled with grace and pleasure, but also with the fascinatingly ugly.

Buitenhuis, Peter. "Italy Can Be Boring, Too." Rev. of *Stitch. New York Times Book Review* 19 Dec. 1965: 14.

Identifies *Stitch* as written in stream-of-consciousness form and Poundian content. Argues that unfortunately it is shrouded in general gloom because for all the wide range of learning and sophistication that he shows, his lack of detachment has prevented him from giving expressive form to *Stitch*. Concludes that it remains a striking mass of fragments.

Buitenhuis, Peter. "A Pilgrimage of Self-Discovery." Rev. of *In Any Case. New York Times Book Review* 14 Oct. 1962: 5.

Calls *In Any Case* a pilgrimage of self-discovery as well as a search for a son, and a speculation about the meaning of love and espionage. Comments that it has a complex plot and a researched quality that recalls the novels of Zola. Concludes that the novel seldom flags in its narrative pace and excitement, although the experience is sometimes philosophized.

Butcher, Fanny. "Novel of French Underground Is Sparkling and Suspenseful." Rev. of *In Any Case. Chicago Sunday Tribune Magazine of Books* 7 Oct. 1962: 3.

Claims that *In Any Case* is excitingly written, full of allusions, and packed with overtones. Finds that, despite its suspenseful atmosphere of the French underground, it is full of cogent observations about life and the search for self, and it sparkles with descriptions of places. Concludes that despite its charm, most of the characters talk in the same knowledge-able, sophisticated manner though they are from many walks of life.

Caplan, Lincoln. "Books in Brief." Rev. of *Natural Shocks. Saturday Review* 21 Jan. 1978: 49.

Considers this novel sustained by the intensity of first encounters and by the spicy speculations accompanying them. Calls the prose erudite, inventive, flecked with insight, and indicative that Stern is in love with his own voice. Details contents, and concludes that finally we become weary of Stern's worldliness.

Cavell, Marcia. Rev. of *1968: A Short Novel, An Urban Idyll, Five Stories, and Two Trade Notes. Partisan Review* 38.1 (1971): 120-21.

Calls *1968* a funny and acerbic portrait of a contemporary Nero. Calls it a story about the radical isolation of the intellect from its own condition. Describes plot and characters.

Cook, Roderick. "Books in Brief." Rev. of *Stitch. Harper's* Jan. 1966: 99-100.

Describes *Stitch* as an intriguing book about American expatriates living in Venice. Comments that it is made up primarily of interior mono-logues, which document their lost souls through a very literate, funny, allusive, and provocative style.

Crews, Frederick C. "Domestic Manners." Rev. of *Teeth, Dying and*

Other Matters. New York Review of Books 22 Oct. 1964: 7-8.

Argues that *Teeth, Dying and Other Matters* would be the envy of any contemporary writer, but unfortunately, Stern holds his material at arm's length, thereby risking triviality. Concludes that he is too intellectually detached.

Davenport, Guy. "The Dust Witch, the Red October Moon." Rev. of *In Any Case. National Review* 31 Dec. 1962: 515-16.

Describes *In Any Case* as a story of a father whose son was a hero in British Intelligence during the German Occupation of France. Argues that for better or for worse, it is a novel in which what we are sure is bound to happen never does. Commends Stern's prose style.

Davenport, Guy. "Three Novels: Bland, Acerbic, Classical." Rev. of *1968: A Short Novel, An Urban Idyll, Five Stories, and Two Trade Notes. National Review* 28 July 1970: 796.

Considers *1968* a small Sternian library of short, compressed pieces he has declined to flatten out to fashionable size. Notes that his chief subject is the liberal arts and what is wrong with the academy. Generally commends the work and its robust prose.

"Death of Memory." Rev. of *Stitch. Newsweek* 22 Nov. 1965: 116.

Considers *Stitch* to be about fugitive Americans who go to Europe seeking regeneration that a moribund Europe can no longer give. Claims that *Stitch* becomes the super-expatriate giant emblem of the creative Europe of the American imagination. Admires the quick, clipped, but still emotive prose, and the exploding of the Stitch myth of Europe.

DeMott, Benjamin. "Couple Trouble: Mod and Trod." Rev. of *Other Men's Daughters. Atlantic* Dec. 1973: 126-27.

Calls this novel too detached, though stylish and always witty. Claims that vague nostalgia and melancholy are the central emotions. Concludes that Stern ends up with a dying fall of sad affection between new mates. Describes central characters.

DeMott, Benjamin. "Exclusive Interviewer." Rev. of *Natural Shocks. Atlantic* Mar. 1978: 128.

Comments that *Natural Shocks* is about an interviewer named Wursup who proves the meaning of the contemporary death fad and is drawn by a terminal cancer patient to examine his own life and emotional capacities.

DeMott, Benjamin. "Reviews." Rev. of *Golk*. *Hudson Review* 13.4 (1960-61): 609-11.

Calls *Golk* a book which is never oblique, and which answers every question it asks. Comments that, as a first novel, it is free from self-indulgence and has a surprisingly energetic command of its subject.

Donadio, Stephen. "The In Way Out." Rev. of *Teeth, Dying and Other Matters*. *Partisan Review* 32.2 (1965): 303.

Describes this as a collection of thirteen stories, a play, and an essay. Considers the play and the essay expendable. Claims that the stories are what count and are generally fine examples of economy, intelligence, and literary tact. Calls Stern a compassionate and careful writer, able to distinguish between his subjects, his limitations, and his intentions.

Elliott, George P. "The New Books." Rev. of *Teeth, Dying and Other Matters*. *Harper's* Apr. 1965: 112-13.

Argues that the thirteen stories in this collection are artfully constructed, elegant, comically intelligent, and unusual in subject matter.

Flower, Dean. "The Way We Live Now." Rev. of *Natural Shocks*. *Hudson Review* 31.2 (1978): 343-44.

Calls *Natural Shocks* a Herzogian meditation on death, heartache, and a thousand natural shocks that flesh is heir to. Describes the novel as hovering above the fatal discrepancy between the experience of suffering and writing about it. Concludes that the novel is searching, full of counter commentaries, and melancholy, without any Herzogian celebration to end it.

Frakes, James R. "Life and Sex in a Kibbutz and on a Campus." Rev. of *Other Men's Daughters*. *New York Times Book Review* 18 Nov. 1973: 4-5.

Claims that this novel is written with almost flawless technique and impeccable taste. Details the contents, and concludes that this is a story of Eros demythified and clinically articulated. Comments on the unusual use of time patterns, convolutions, and flashbacks as well as flash-forwards. Concludes that this is an unsparingly fine and resonant novel.

Fuchs, Daniel. "From Despair to Comic Wonders." Rev. of *Noble Rot: Stories 1949-1988*. *Chicago Tribune Books* 22 Jan. 1989: 1, 11.

Describes several of the stories and concludes that they enchant the reader and should not be missed. Considers Stern "a master, an event," and reiterates *Newsweek*'s statement that Stern is America's best kept secret.

Garrett, George. "American Publishing Now." Rev. of *The Position of the Body. Sewanee Review* 96.3 (1988): 517-18.

Describes the contents of the novel as quirky, eccentric, energetic, and profoundly oddball. Admires Stern's intellectualism, with-it-ness in reading, and general liveliness. Claims that he should be read not for information, but as Montaigne is.

Geismar, Maxwell. "The Week in Fiction." Rev. of *In Any Case. New York Herald Tribune Books* 28 Oct. 1962: 12.

Calls *In Any Case* an attractive and engaging novel at first, but which fails to maintain our interest. Calls it intelligent, well-written, heartless, cold, and slick. Comments that Stern writes so well about subjects he has no concern over.

Goodman, Walter. Rev. of *Natural Shocks. New Leader* 30 Jan. 1978: 20.

Calls *Natural Shocks* an uplifting model for journalism students. Details contents, and comments that this book is written in fast, big-city style crackling with energy, and studded with virtuoso turns and fine descriptions. Ultimately concludes, however, that the energy is dissipated by subcharacters and subplots.

Goodwin, Stephen. "Symbols, Spiels, and Strangeness." Rev. of *Packages. Washington Post Book World* 19 Oct. 1980: 4-5.

Describes *Packages* as a collection of pieces which aren't really stories at all but fat, ranging meditations delivered in an urgent, driving voice. Concludes that Stern is mad for his own spiels and learning.

Grigson, Geoffrey. "A Fly Like Thee." Rev. of *Golk. Spectator* 3 Feb. 1961: 158.

Calls *Golk* an American culture novel in which the culture satirized is more important, more actual than the people through whom it is presented. Concludes that finally, however, this novel substitutes an acquired quality for authentic vivacity.

Harris, Mark. "The Art of Being Brief." Rev. of *Packages. New Republic* 15 Nov. 1980: 32-34.

Calls *Packages* a book both unsentimental and artful. Considers Stern a rigorous monitor of his own aesthetic. Calls the stories short, economical, compressed literary jewels worked from character and anecdote. A useful introduction to Stern's style.

Hicks, Granville. "No Time for Satire." Rev. of *Europe: Or Up and Down with Schreiber and Baggish. Saturday Review* 16 Dec. 1961: 13.

Calls *Europe* a step backward from *Golk* and the short stories that preceded it. Considers it awkwardly constructed even though Stern seems to be developing his own kind of comedy. Details the contents and style.

Hicks, Granville. "A Witty Way with Life." Rev. of *Teeth, Dying and Other Matters. Saturday Review* 12 Dec. 1964: 35-36.

Describes this book as containing thirteen stories, a piece of political journalism, and a full-length play. Claims that Stern is not the master of the short story, but that all his tales are adroitly done and agreeable to read. Comments that his novels contain bizarre situations, ingenuity, and a certain sort of wryness. Concludes that his style is often sardonic and cruel, tender and compassionate.

Hollinghurst, Alan. "Making Up." Rev. of *Packages. New Statesman* 28 Nov. 1980: 24.

Suggests that *Packages* is about the frustrations and disappointments of middle age, among other things. Comments that many stories are about storymaking, while others show all the subtlety and sophistication of Stern's best work. Describes the effects of several of the stories.

Hope, Francis. "Second-Chance Continent." Rev. of *Europe: Or Up and Down with Schreiber and Baggish. Spectator* 13 Apr. 1962: 485.

Argues that *Europe* is made of the traditional materials of the American encounter with Europe, but that it is original, individual, and expert in its handling. Details the contents.

"Innocents Abroad." Rev. of *Stitch. Christian Science Monitor* 9 Dec. 1965: 19.

Calls *Stitch* ceremonial and deliberate in its casualness. Claims that Stern's interest lies in flawed character and that he offers no glib answers for people in conflict. Suggests that sometimes Stern shows off his knowledge and seems unable to pull all the necessary elements together, hence producing certain lapses in style and taste.

Jennings, Elizabeth. "New Fiction." Rev. of *Teeth, Dying and Other Matters. Listener* 2 July 1964: 28.

Calls *Teeth, Dying, and Other Matters* a collection of short stories full of perspicacity, drama, terseness, wit, and idiosyncratic slants on life. Decides Stern is assured, never slick, and always engaging.

Kelly, James. "Handbook on How to Trap People." Rev. of *Golk. New York Times Book Review* 1 May 1960: 34.

Suggests that *Golk* is an opportunity for Stern to sustain an eerie effect and unload pungent observations about topical mores, which he manages to do with considerable style and talent. Appreciates his good ear and clear eye. Concludes that most readers will not find this novel palatable or arresting.

Kemp, Peter. "Wet and Dry." Rev. of *Natural Shocks. Listener* 5 Oct. 1978: 455.

Calls *Natural Shocks* a book about facing up to death and about how intellectual perceptions of death are purely superficial. Comments on his female protagonist's failure to come alive, and claims that the book's central protagonist causes it to be rather low on emotional force.

Kendall, Elaine. "Collection of Stories with the Bouquet of Fine Wine." Rev. of *Noble Rot: Stories 1949-1988. Los Angeles Times* 17 Feb. 1989: sec. V: 10.

Describes several of the thirty-two stories that are set in locations all over the globe to show the breadth and variety of the collection. Notes that "there is hardly an aspect of human experience not confronted in one or another of these remarkable succinct and disciplined stories." Finds them dealing with the themes of love, death, work, and family and demonstrating Stern's maturity of style, form, and content.

Kenner, Hugh. "Stitch: The Master's Voice." Rev. of *Stitch. Chicago Review* 18.3-4 (1966): 176-80.

Asserts that *Stitch*, like the array of worked stones on the island, is itself concocted of self-sufficient fragments. Suggests that the book is an act of love testifying to the impact on its author's imagination of Stitch's "great original," who was old and nearly silent when Stern encountered him, but is yet capable still, long past his didactic years, of polarizing a novelist's vision.

Kenner, Hugh. "What the Boundary Between Fiction and Journalism Feels Like." Rev. of *The Books in Fred Hampton's Apartment. New York Times Book Review* 25 Mar. 1973: 6.

Describes *The Books in Fred Hampton's Apartment* as evidence of Stern's continuing taste for discontinuity, deft pratfall, good humor, a multiplicity of surface perceptions, economy, and fine eye. Details some of the incidents.

Klein, Marcus. "Pound Foolish." Rev. of *Stitch. Reporter* 21 Apr. 1966: 55-56.

Calls Stern a writer with a talented ear, and the equipment for a complicated comic apprehension, daring, and dedication. Sees *Stitch* as a book in which pathos has become almost a classical repose. Comments at length on the contents, their allusive qualities, and the book's style of humor.

Kubal, David. "Fiction Chronicle." Rev. of *Packages. Hudson Review* 34.3 (1981): 458-59.

Describes *Packages* as a book of eleven small stories or dramas about the perception of self's scope and its limitations imposed by nature and society. Sees them as works of artistic integrity which tell us of Stern's serious talent.

Lehmann-Haupt, Christopher. "Books of the Times." Rev. of *Natural Shocks. New York Times* 9 Jan. 1978: C29.

Says *Natural Shocks* moves easily and spontaneously, building a superstructure that is as solid and timeless as a folktale. Concludes that the characters are vividly realized and the prose energetic and muscular, intelligent and playful. Details the contents.

Lodge, David. "Talking Big." Rev. of *In Any Case. Spectator* 13 Sept. 1963: 325.

Describes the novel, and commends its cleverly wrought web of complex relationships showing betrayals, selfishness, and failure, as well as its skillfully plaited together themes and densely absorbing characters.

Lukacs, Paul. "Indirect Impression." Rev. of *Natural Shocks. National Review* 26 May 1978: 664-65.

Calls *Natural Shocks* a book in which the narrative perception is not sufficiently separated from the protagonist's. Notes that journalism as a profession is treated like a cancerous monster. Concludes that altogether, the novel fails to give a living impression of life because concept is too often substituted for event.

Maddocks, Melvin. "Harvard Square." Rev. of *Other Men's Daughters*. *Time* 5 Nov. 1973: 112.

Describes the novel in detail as a skillfully executed and extraordinarily touching story.

Maloff, Saul. "A Personal Quest." Rev. of *In Any Case*. *Commonweal* 14 Dec. 1962: 319-20.

Comments that this, like the earlier novels, is written in ample, supple, lively, vigorous narrative style with a sense of character, scene, place, person, and action. Notes that, at the center, lies a spy thriller based on the exploits of one Sam Curry. Describes the plot, and argues for its failure because it is not possible to dramatize ambiguity. Concludes that the roots of the action remain too hidden.

Maloff, Saul. "Sparks Fly, Wheels Turn." Rev. of *Teeth, Dying and Other Matters*. *New York Times Book Review* 27 Dec. 1964: 21.

Calls *Teeth, Dying and Other Matters* a collection of thirteen stories, an essay, and a play. Admires the essay, and argues that this book should not have been a grab bag swelled with whatever lies at hand. Considers some of the stories too slight to assert themselves, some as passing fancies, and others as exercises, others too oppressively bouncy and jazzy with willed gaiety, while some few are delicately calibrated and finely controlled.

Mellors, John. "Upward Paths." Rev. of *Packages*. *London Magazine* Feb.-Mar. 1981: 130-31.

Complains that the contents of *Packages* are not worth the trouble taken to provide them with fancy wrappings. Details the contents briefly, and then decides Stern's urbane geniality too quickly becomes folksy and whimsical.

Mellors, John. "Menopausal Man." Rev. of *Other Men's Daughters*. *Listener* 16 May 1974: 641.

Describes this as a novel about forty-year-old men who stray away from their wives and into the beds of women the same age as their daughters. Praises the volume for its glittering but credible dialogue, sympathy without sentiment, intellectual honesty, and tolerance of non-conformism.

Mitgang, Herbert. "Grab Bag After Golk." Rev. of *Teeth, Dying and Other Matters. Chicago Sunday Tribune Magazine of Books* 22 Nov. 1964: 11.

Characterizes *Teeth, Dying, and Other Matters* as a grab bag of pieces by a bright, restless novelist capable of dazzling style. Comments that the collection shows versatility and brilliance.

Monaghan, Charles. "New Traditions." Rev. of *Golk. Commonweal* 13 May 1960: 188-90.

Calls *Golk* an extraordinary novel written with a consistent and pleasant lightness of tone that never degenerates into frivolousness. Commends it for intriguing characterization and plotting, and for clean and efficient prose style. Describes the contents, and concludes that this novel shares certain characteristics with the finest writers of the time.

Morgan, Al. "Camera's-Eye View." Rev. of *Golk. Saturday Review* 23 July 1960: 37.

Considers that *Golk* may not be entirely successful, but concedes that it is ambitious and irritating. Thinks the satire seems to have been written with a blunt wet feather. Complains that this novel is all style and very little substance. Concludes that Stern's fuse sputters and goes out, smothered under a rather advanced case of delusions of allegory.

"Mounds of Comment." Rev. of *Teeth, Dying and Other Matters. Times Literary Supplement* 20 Aug. 1964: 741.

Comments that *Teeth, Dying, and Other Matters* contains stories uneven in quality, journalistic, and wordy. Calls Stern a narrowly interesting satirist of a narrow stream of American life, and says his work is over-priced for its marginality. Concludes that this is a grab bag, that reveals both his weaknesses and his strengths.

Nordell, Roderick. "Novel Probes Dilemmas of Journalists." Rev. of *Natural Shocks. Christian Science Monitor* 20 Jan. 1978: 23.

Describes *Natural Shocks* as being about the publishing world and its doings. Details the contents of the book briefly, and comments that newspapermen might learn the shortcomings of so-called objective reporting from this book.

Prescott, Peter S. "Good News." Rev. of *Natural Shocks. Newsweek* 2 Jan. 1978: 61-62.

Calls *Natural Shocks* refreshing because it presents, as its chief protagonist, a considerate, educated man who reads good books. Describes Fred Wursup and the plot. Concludes that Stern is a remarkably deft and witty writer who has produced a tightly wound novel of the Bellowvian school, taking as its central theme the retreat from human feeling and the reawakening to it. Advises that it may not be popular.

Prescott, Peter S. "Lonely Lives." Rev. of *Packages*. *Newsweek* 3 Nov. 1980: 88.

Considers *Packages* boring since most of its pieces center around the theme of loneliness, a theme better suited to the short story than the novel. Describes several of the pieces.

Prescott, Peter S. "When the Child Is Father of the Man." Rev. of *A Father's Words*. *Newsweek* 24 Mar. 1986: 74.

Considers Stern one of this country's best kept secrets. Calls this novel witty, wise, unfailingly humane, and well-written. Comments on the enjoyable wisecracks, literary homilies, and general erudition. Details the contents briefly.

Price, Martin. "New Books in Review." Rev. of *Other Men's Daughters*. *Yale Review* 63.4 (1974): 561-63.

Argues that this is a novel whose optimistic vision suffers because it is a self-justifying fantasy. Considers the milieu so dense and the characters so thin that the novel only has documentary interest. Concludes that there is not enough deep conflict in any of the lives portrayed.

Pritchard, William. "Broken Meats." Rev. of *The Books in Fred Hampton's Apartment*. *London Magazine* Aug.-Sept. 1974: 147-49.

Considers this a novel by a writer not quite of the first rank, less obsessed, and stylistically less bold than his best-selling contemporaries Bellow, Malamud, and Mailer. Calls his work intelligent, full of stylistic energy, and worthwhile. Describes the contents of the novel.

Raban, Jonathan. "Lullabies for a Sleeping Giant." Rev. of *Other Men's Daughters*. *Encounter* July 1974: 75-76.

Calls this a tamed, well-groomed, and strenuously inoffensive novel. Claims that there is not a page on which Stern does not display his considerable technical skill, his ear for academic dialogue, and his sprightly control of interior monologue. But considers these people just too urbane for fiction. Concludes that this is part of a fast-growing species of sophisticated sentimentality.

Rowley, Peter. "A Cloudy View of America." Rev. of *1968: A Short Novel, An Urban Idyll, Five Stories, and Two Trade Notes. Washington Post Book World* 2 Aug. 1970: 6.

Considers this work vibrant with Jewish humor and learned in the complexities of the middle-class intelligentsia. Claims that Stern needs to abandon those aspects of his style that signal the aspiring great writer, if he would achieve his objective. Calls the political references sharp and penetrating.

Scannell, Vernon. "New Novels." Rev. of *Europe: Or Up and Down with Baggish and Schreiber. Listener* 3 May 1962: 785.

Considers *Europe* to be about the flawed love of Americans for the moribund grandeur of Europe. Briefly describes plot, characters, and themes.

Scott, Paul. "New Novels." Rev. of *Golk. New Statesman* 27 Jan. 1961: 147.

Calls *Golk* a well-written novel whose characters are all variations of the main character. Describes contents briefly.

Sisk, John P. "Light on a Venal World." Rev. of *Europe: Or Up and Down with Schreiber and Baggish. New York Times Book Review* 12 Nov. 1961: 55.

Describes *Europe* as a fine second novel exploring the theme of fate in a comic manner. Comments that, though superficially a picaresque ramble, this collection gets by on its witty and stylish observance of exotic scenes.

Spacks, Patricia Meyer. "At the Outpost of Journalism." Rev. of *Natural Shocks. Nation* 11 Feb. 1978: 152-53.

Claims that this novel explores and demonstrates the imagination's current reliance on journalistic truth. Suggests that the overwhelming reality of public experience has drained authenticity from private suffering.

Spector, Robert Donald. "An Old Form, a Modern Tale." Rev. of *Golk. New York Herald Tribune Book Review* 15 May 1960: 9.

Considers *Golk* a modern picaresque using a candid camera rather than a journey motif to satirize not only TV but American life with its central focus on getting ahead. Commends Stern for his excellent portrayals, his ability to make the fantastic believable, and his sharp eye for detail. Concludes that the novel fails in handling point of view.

Spoliar, Nicholas. "Letters on Brown Paper." Rev. of *Packages. Times Literary Supplement* 21 Nov. 1980: 1342.

Asserts that *Packages* reduces vastness into something portable, and deals in sparked off memories. Details the contents of several of the stories, and concludes that this is an interesting collection—excellent, inventive, and economical.

Stern, Daniel. "Portrait of an Artist." Rev. of *Stitch. Saturday Review* 11 Dec. 1965: 80.

Finds *Stitch* full of mediocrities of characters with little to recommend. Describes the characters and story, and concludes that despite the book's basic failure, Stern writes well and builds scenes skillfully.

Straub, Peter. "Liberty Man." Rev. of *Other Men's Daughters. New Statesman* 10 May 1974: 668-69.

Suggests that *Other Men's Daughters* is a calm, measured novel with all Stern's characteristic music and wit. Claims that the slight, mundane story of a love affair between professor and student is done with tartness and an urgent feeling for private life and the shadings in human relationships. Calls this a male version of Lessing's *The Summer Before the Dark.* Comments that, as an expulsion myth, it is merciful, optimistic, and humane.

Van Vactor, Anita. "Minor Burghers." Rev. of *1968: A Short Novel, An Urban Idyll, Five Stories, and Two Trade Notes. Listener* 25 Mar. 1971: 387, 389.

Considers *1968* an impressive collection of stories. Describes the contents of several and states that his purpose is to show what counts, what is most demanding of imaginative response, and what lies closest to home, wasting out the shuffle of urban domestic life. Concludes that Stern confines himself to the daily getting on of the minor burghers of New York and Chicago.

Wasiolek, Edward. "Moralities and Ambiguities." Rev. of *In Any Case. Modern Age* 7.2 (1963): 218-19.

Argues that *In Any Case*, Stern's third novel, is by far his best. Comments that, in addition to the previously brilliant stylistic *tour de force*, this novel has form, sustained situation, and coherence. Details the contents, and concludes that the influence of Henry James on the novel is readily apparent, even though Stern does not manage James's acute penetration of moral experience.

Wilson, David. "Death Story." Rev. of *Natural Shocks. Times Literary Supplement* 27 Oct. 1978: 1264.

Claims that *Natural Shocks* is concerned with the effect of the dead on the living, or more precisely with the living dead. Laments that the subsidiary characters remain hollow, obstinately detached from emotions—they merely represent Worseg and most of them speak in the idiom of New York literati. Concludes that Mr Stern leaves his hero dangling, substantiating for the last time his view of himself as emotionally atrophied.

Yardley, Jonathan. Rev. of *Other Men's Daughters. Washington Post Book World* 28 Oct. 1973: 11.

Argues that *Other Men's Daughters* is at once witty and painful in its story of marital malaise and marital rejuvenation and the hard emotional burdens attendant to both. Finds that there is wit, sophistication, compassion, disruption of the heart, and exhalation in the novel. Concludes that its genius lies in its perception of marital anguish.

Interviews

Raeder, Robert L. "An Interview with Richard G. Stern." *Chicago Review* 18 (Aut.-Wint. 1965-66): 170-75.

In this interview Stern discusses: his theory of art, reviews of his books which charge him with lacking a center, his writing methods, character creation, his previous works, his reading and use of Nietszche, his defense of *Golk*, his use of narrative methods of indirection, and the stories in *Stitch*.

Rima, Larry. "An Interview with Richard Stern." *Chicago Review* 28.3 (1977): 145-48.

In this interview Stern discusses: the crisis in the genre of the novel; the place of experimental novelists; his belief in the survival of realistic fiction; his belief that art is more than sport and a toy; his low opinion of *Catch 22* and much "belly-aching" experimental fiction; his belief in an intelligent, even possibly a brilliant, reading public; Longinus on the sublime; the propensity of experimental novelists to comment on story; and the strength of literature as a silent medium minus lights, actors, and a stage.

Rosenberg, Milton, and Elliot Anderson. "A Conversation with Richard Stern." *Chicago Review* 31.3 (1980): 98-108.

In this interview Stern discusses: the effect of composition on personal material; his first ten to fifteen years of writing; his journalism; his character, Fred Wursup; his sense of duty; the recurrent theme of death in his works; his belief in the survival of personality; the function and nature of public books; popular writers; Jane Austen; and writing as the creation of the uniquely beautiful in the world that has never existed before.

Schiffer, Paul. "Q-and-A." *The Invention of the Real*. Richard Stern. Athens: U of Georgia P, 1982. 219-33.

Preceded by a brief portrait of Stern, Stern in this interview discusses classifications of contemporary literature, his Jewishness, his childhood, the governing principles of his work, *Moby Dick, Natural Shocks*, his character Wursup, contemporary conditions for the writing of a big work, Joyce, Philip Roth, literary coteries, and death as subject matter for the novel.

Biographical Sources

Rosen, Richard. "Heirs to Maxwell Perkins." *Horizon* Apr. 1981: 50-53.

Stern provides a series of insights into his relationships with his editors Roger Klein, Harold Scharlatt, and Joe Cannon and with Saul Bellow, Ezra Pound, and Philip Roth.

Ronald Sukenick

1932 –

Primary Sources

Novels

96.8. New York: Fiction Collective, 1975.

Blown Away. New American Fiction Series. Los Angeles: Sun & Moon, 1986.

Long Talking Bad Conditions Blues. New York: Fiction Collective, 1979.

Out. Chicago: Swallow, 1973.

Up. New York: Dial, 1968; New York: Delta-Dell, 1970; Los Angeles: Serendipity, 1970.

Collected Works

The Death of the Novel and Other Stories. New York: Dial, 1969.
Contents: The Permanent Crisis, Momentum, The Death of the Novel, Roast Beef: A Slice of Life, What's Your Story, The Birds.

The Endless Short Story. New York: Fiction Collective, 1986.

Contents: What's Watts, Aziff, Verticals and Horizontals, Fourteen, Divide, Dong Wang, 5 & 10, Boxes, This is the Part, Duck Tape, Bush Fever, End of Endless Short Story, Post Card.

Short Fiction in Anthologies

"The Birds." *Cutting Edges: Young American Fiction for the '70s*. Ed. Jack Hicks. New York: Holt, 1973. 473-93.

"The Endless Short Story: Verticals and Horizontals." *Statements: New Fiction from the Fiction Collective*. Ed. Jonathan Baumbach. New York: Venture-Braziller, 1975. 184-88.

"The Endless Short Story: Dong Wang." *Statements 2: New Fiction*. Eds. Johnathan Baumbach and Peter Spielberg. New York: Fiction Collective, 1977. 212-17.

"Momentum." *Innovative Fiction: Stories for the Seventies*. Eds. Jerome Klinkowitz and John Somer. New York: Dell, 1972. 177-214.

"What's Your Story?" *Superfiction: or the American Story Transformed*. Ed. Joe David Bellamy. New York: Vintage, 1975. 234-55.

Short Fiction in Periodicals

"Endless Short Story [Aziff]." *TriQuarterly* 35.1 (1976): 42.

"Endless Short Story: Five and Ten." *Criss-Cross Art Communications* 6 (1978): 36-41.

"Endless Short Story: What's Watts." *New Letters* 45.4 (1979): 177-79.

"Endless Short Story: Boxes." *Fiction* 6.2 (1980): 141-51.

"The Kite." *New American Review* 1 (1967): 200-11.

"A Long Way from Nowhere." *Epoch* (Fall 1964): 69-77.

"One Every Minute." *Carolina Quarterly* 13.2 (1961): 57-65.

"Palestine." *Partisan Review* 42.1 (1975): 23-29.

"What's Your Story." *Paris Review* 11.44 (1968): 33-51.

Secondary Sources

Books

Kutnik, Jerzy. *The Novel as Performance: The Fiction of Ronald Sukenick and Raymond Federman.* Crosscurrents/Modern Critiques. Third Series. Carbondale: Southern Illinois UP, 1986.

Sukenick, Ronald. *In Form: Digressions on the Act of Fiction.* Crosscurrents/Modern Critiques. Third Series. Carbondale: Southern Illinois UP, 1985.

Articles and Chapters

Adams, Timothy Dow. "Obscuring the Muse: The Mock-Autobiographies of Ronald Sukenick." *Critique* 20.1 (1978): 27-39.
Describes the critical positions of anti-self-reflexive fiction, and goes on to describe this trait in much earlier fiction, thus laying a foundation for defending Sukenick.

Brooke-Rose, Christine. "Where Do We Go from Here?" *Granta* ns 3 (1980): 161-88.
Reviews the attitudes of Ihab Hassan, Mas'ud Zavarzadeh, and Sontag on postmodern fiction, and reevaluates the work of Barth, Fowles, and Sukenick. Discusses Sukenick's *Up, Out,* and *98.6* as showing a steady progression in improving the balance between realism and stylization. Concludes with predictions on the future of the novel toward silence, exhaustion, or new beginnings.

Chabot, C. Barry. "Fiction, Truth, and the Character of Beliefs." *Georgia Review* 37.4 (1983): 835-46.

Details Sukenick's position that our beliefs about the world are the products of the imagination or mind. Describes his self-reflexive style and how this reflects on his assessments of Wallace Stevens in *Wallace Stevens: Musing the Obscure.*

Cheuse, Alan. "Way Out West: The Exploratory Fiction of 'Ronald Sukenick.'" *Essays on California Writers.* Ed. Charles L. Crow. Bowling Green: Bowling Green State U P, 1979. 115-121.

Discusses the regional quality of Sukenick's writing, its experimental nature, and its appeal to younger readers. Provides more detailed commentary on *Out* and *Up.*

Cowley, Julian. "Ronald Sukenick's New Departures from the Terminal of Language." *Critique* 28.2 (1987): 87-89.

Argues that Sukenick's fiction proceeds from his conviction stated in "Fiction in the Seventies," that "verbal art is the most conclusive escape into our birthright in the world beyond language from which language above all separates us, and which, therefore it has the power to restore." Elaborates this thesis showing how the conventions of literary realism must be jettisoned because the world is more mysterious than realism tells us with its persuasive likeness. Concludes that Sukenick's fiction retains the dream of getting "there" without neglecting his commitment to the actual, and that, through the tensions in the fiction, he has opened up the future by means of "new departures from the terminal of language."

Docherty, Thomas. "Characters, Religion, and Politics." *Reading (Absent) Character: Towards a Theory of Characterization in Fiction.* Oxford: Clarendon, 1983. 262-66.

Describes Sukenick's attempt to produce simultaneity in writing through breaking down regular syntax, running many phrases together, thus trying to negate gaps not between words and reality, but between the words themselves.

Glicksberg, Charles I. "Experimental Fiction: Innovation Versus Form." *Centennial Review* 18.2 (1974): 127-50.

A major historical description of the origins and philosophy of experimental fiction. Describes Sukenick as proceeding from the work of Samuel Beckett insofar as he breaks up the formal structure of the novel. Surmises that, instead of striving to achieve naturalistic fidelity of detail, thus creating a sustained illusion of reality, he refuses to play the game of realism.

Hornung, Alfred. "Absent Presence: The Fictions of Raymond Federman and Ronald Sukenick." *Indian Journal of American Studies* 14.1 (1984): 17-31.

Points out some of the characteristics of Federman's and Sukenick's texts, their similarities and differences. Also provides an in-depth account of the theories of narratology subscribed to by each and their particular uses of such terms as "surfiction" or "metafiction." Notes that the all-informing principle of the writing and reading process seems to be that of the "absent presence" of negative affirmation of fiction and life; consequently claims that the blank sheet of paper functions as a mirror for the self-reflexive constitution of reality and identity. Concludes that the text is the present mirror of the absent actual thing.

Imhof, Rudiger. *Contemporary Metafiction: A Poetological Study of Metafiction in English Since 1939*. Heidelberg: Winter, 1986. 81-83, 130-32, 213-14.

Provides a thorough description of the use of self-reflexive style in *Death of the Novel*.

Karl, Frederick R. "More Mid-1970s: Doctorow, Sukenick, Theroux." *American Fictions 1940/1980: A Comprehensive History and Critical Evaluation*. Frederick R. Karl. New York: Harper, 1983. 514-19.

Describes Sukenick's recurring themes of the failed English professor and his masturbatory fantasies as tired and retreaded. Calls *Up* no longer fresh, and *Out* a little more mature. A detailed assessment of both novels.

Klinkowitz, Jerome. "Getting Real: Making It (Up) with Ronald Sukenick." *Chicago Review* 23.3 (1972): 73-82.

Treats Sukenick biographically and critically. Primarily focuses on Sukenick's treatment of reality in the novels.

Klinkowitz, Jerome. "How Fiction Survives the Seventies." *North American Review* 258.3 (1973): 69-73.

An essay which distinguishes between several categories of seventies writers, and then comments on Sukenick's stardom in the unread but brilliantly innovative group. Praises him for bringing to American fiction the authority of modern French experience.

Klinkowitz, Jerome. "Ideology or Art: Women Novelists in the 1970s." *North American Review* 260.2 (1975): 88-90.

In the context of comments on several seventies writers, Klinkowitz comments that in *Up* Sukenick pushes sexuality to such imaginative limits that no one dare pull the old suspension of disbelief routine and read it as real life.

Klinkowitz, Jerome. "Literary Disruptions: Or, What's Become of American Fiction?" *Partisan Review* 40.3 (1973): 433-44.

Sees Sukenick's *Out* as the climax of the phenomenon of new methods in fiction and the solidifying of a tradition.

Klinkowitz, Jerome. "New American Fiction and Values." *Anglo-American Studies* 2.2 (1982): 241-47.

Discusses Sukenick's fiction and his ideas about fiction as indicators of a new style of fiction that perhaps "can create a world with a built-in perspective" as in primitive cultures that constantly create their world by day. Finds Sukenick's ideas agreeing with avant-garde thinking and the theories of language dominant in our century. Discusses Vonnegut's *Slaughterhouse-Five* as an example of the kind of work Sukenick was talking about, a work that became a metaphor of the new age. Concludes that Sukenick's *Long Talking Bad Conditions Blues* exemplifies the idea that "by discarding realist assumptions, the best of realistic conventions are saved, and both the novel and its surrounding culture live again."

Klinkowitz, Jerome. "A Persuasive Account: Working It Out with Ronald Sukenick." *North American Review* 258.2 (1973): 48-52.

A major article which attempts to make the case for Sukenick as the major talent since Barth, Jong and others declared the novel dead in the late 1960s.

Klinkowitz, Jerome. "Reflexive Fiction." *The Self-Apparent Word: Fiction as Language/Language as Fiction*. Jerome Klinkowitz. Carbondale: Southern Illinois U P, 1984. 78-83, 87-95, 128-31.

A thorough description of the self-reflexive writing techniques used by Sukenick.

Klinkowitz, Jerome. "Ronald Sukenick & Raymond Federman." *Literary Disruptions: The Making of a Post-Contemporary American Fiction*. Jerome Klinkowitz. Urbana: U of Illinois P, 1975. 119-153, 228-30.

Argues that these two writers question the entire premise of traditional fiction, publish the most straight academic fiction, and therefore offer the highest profile of the theory behind such works.

Klinkowitz, Jerome. "Ronald Sukenick." *The Life of Fiction.* Jerome Klinkowitz. Urbana: U of Illinois P, 1977. 17-29.

Provides a brief history of Sukenick's accomplishments and excerpts from Sukenick himself. Concludes with a useful description of his architectonics and stylistic devices.

Klinkowitz, Jerome, and Thomas Remington. "Science Fiction to Superfiction." *Granta* ns 2 (1980): 86-102.

Details the disruption of traditional literature during the 1970s by such things as science fiction. Describes Sukenick as a surfictionist who articulates most aptly the case of the "superfictionist" combining both science fiction and surfiction.

McCaffery, Larry. "The Fiction Collective." *Contemporary Literature* 19.1 (1978): 99-115.

An account of *The Fiction Collective*'s inception and history, as well as Sukenick's part in it.

Noel, Daniel C. "Tales of Fictive Power: Dreaming and Imagination in Ronald Sukenick's Postmodern Fiction." *Boundary 2* 5 (1976): 117-135.

Explores Sukenick's recent work in the context of "postmodernity," as tales of fictive power deriving some of their philosophical impact from his acquaintance with Don Juan, his recent fascination with Castenada, and his early study of Wallace Stevens. Suggests how fictive power is defined throughout the article as invention, composition, creative spirit, imagination, and sorcery.

Pearce, Richard. "Riding the Surf: Raymond Federman, Walter Abish, and Ronald Sukenick." *The Novel in Motion: An Approach to Modern Fiction.* Richard Pearce. Columbus: Ohio State U P, 1983: 118-30.

A major chapter in which the influence of Robbe-Grillet upon Walter Abish, Raymond Federman, and Ronald Sukenick is discussed in depth.

Putz, Manfred. "Ronald Sukenick: Connections Proliferate." *The Story of Identity: American Fiction of the Sixties.* Manfred Putz. American Studies: A Monograph Series 54. Munich: Fink, 1987. 176-93.

Provides a profound discussion of Sukenick's philosophy and aesthetic as a post-modernist writer.

Quartermain, Peter. "Trusting the Reader." *Chicago Review* 32.2 (1980): 65-74.

Describes the formation, publishing philosophy, and history of The Fiction Collective. Describes the participation in this publishing group of both Federman and Sukenick. Provides general descriptions of most of the work published, along with some critical appraisal.

Russell, Charles. "Individual Voice in the Collective Discourse: Literary Innovation in Postmodern American Fiction." *SubStance* 27 (1980): 29-39.

Argues that the postmodern aesthetic displays an alienated, if not antagonistic, response to the aesthetic, ethical, and spiritual concerns of bourgeios culture, and places Sukenick within this tradition. Comments further that in such a writer we see less anguish and less faith in one's assumptions of self-knowledge and mastery in one's perception and knowledge of the external world and the very means of expression.

Russell, Charles. "Postmodernism and the Neo-avant-garde." *Poets, Prophets, and Revolutionaries: The Literary Avant-garde from Rimbaud through Postmodernism.* New York: Oxford UP, 1985. 236-70.

Within the context of this major essay on postmodernism, Russell describes Sukenick as a writer whose literary techniques exemplify a large number of contemporary strategies, such as the unreliable nature of personal identity. Places him in context with Federman, Katz, Demby, and Major.

Russell, Charles. "The Vault of Language: Self-Reflective Artifice in Contemporary American Fiction." *Modern Fiction Studies* 20.3 (1974): 349-59.

In the context of this excellent article on contemporary fiction and its use of language, Russell uses Sukenick as a case in point for his taxonomy of language devices in contemporary *avant-garde* fiction.

Semrau, Janusz. "Flying a Kite: Ronald Sukenick's *Up* and *Out*." *Studia Anglica Posnaniensia: An International Review of English Studies.* 16 (1983): 255-63.

A major treatment of Sukenick's five novels dealing with voice, style, imagery, formal dimensions, preoccupation with self-begetting fiction, kite flying as central motif, poetic qualities, and general inventiveness.

Semrau, Janusz. "Ronald Sukenick." *American Self-Conscious Fiction of the 1960s and 1970s: Donald Barthelme, Robert Coover, Ronald Sukenick.* Seria Filologia Angielska 21. Poznan: Universytet IM. Adama Mickiewicza Poznanice, 1986. 99-151.

A major chapter which provides an excellent introduction to Sukenick's career, works, themes, stylistic characteristics, and contribution to American literature.

Sukenick, Ronald. "Experiment and Experience: My Life in Fiction." *American Book Review* 10.5 (1988): 3-4, 15.

Sukenick discusses his youth in Brooklyn and his writing to show that while his work has been labeled "experimental," it is more accurately "experiential." Discusses the difference between real life and the reality depicted in the novel, pointing out that even "Ronald Sukenick," the character in some of his novels, was an attempt to break through "the illusion of conventional artifice that has become so familiar we don't even realize that it's not real or even interestingly 'real'—to break through the artificial to the actualities of experience." He concludes by asserting that he is merely trying to "keep fiction as close as possible to the available data."

Trachtenberg, Stanley. "The Way That Girl Pressed Against You on the Subway: Ronald Sukenick's Real Act of the Imagination." *Journal of Narrative Technique* 12.1 (1982): 57-71.

A major treatment of Sukenick's novels and application of his own theories of novel writing. Pays particular attention to the shape of the author's imagination in relation to the structures embedded in the fiction.

Werner, Craig Hansen. "Homer's Joyce: John Updike, Ronald Sukenick, Robert Coover, Toni Morrison." *Paradoxical Resolutions: American Fiction Since James Joyce.* Craig Hansen Werner. Urbana: U of Illinois P, 1982. 68-96.

Argues that John Updike's *Centaur* and Ronald Sukenick's *98.6*, while sharing the desire for a constructive interaction between symbol and reality, veer off toward the ultimate irresolution. Suggests that Sukenick manipulates the myth of Frankenstein to probe the limits of conscious control and the nature of America.

Wilde, Alan. "Irony in the Postmodern Age: Toward a Map of Suspensiveness." *Boundary 2* 9.1 (1980): 15-20. Rpt. as "A Map of Suspensiveness" in *Horizons of Assent: Modernism, Postmodernism, and the Ironic Imagination.* Alan Wilde. Baltimore: Johns Hopkins UP, 1981. 136-41.

Discusses the views of Sukenick and Federman on the relationship between reality and the new fiction, and applies these views to their own fictional practices. Discusses Sukenick's *The Death of the Novel.*

Reviews

Bangs, Carol Jane. Rev. of *Out. Northwest Review* 14.1 (1974): 132-35.

Provides a brief history of the experimental novel, and classes Sukenick as an antimimetic writer. Describes the effects, and contents, primary themes, and tendencies of *Out.*

Bergmann, Linda S. Rev. of *Out. Chicago Review* 25.3 (1974): 9-12.

Calls the novel a bizarre fantasy of sexual brutality, violence in the streets, and fear in the guts. Details style and contents in the novel as well as characters, scenes, and descriptions.

"Celebration of Life." Rev. of *Up. Washington Post Book World* 21 July 1968: 10-11.

Calls *Out* tough, alive, in the lineage of Stephen Daedelus. Comments that this is a free-wheeling, discontinuous chronology and an undercutting of reality. Describes milieu, fictional antics, and contents.

Davis, L. J. "Two Novels, an Anthology and an Alphabet." Rev. of *Out. New York Times Book Review* 21 Oct. 1973: 49.

Considers Sukenick an exceptionally talented writer with purpose and sensitivity. Describes *Out*, finding it "precisely what it says it is, a novel that walks right out of itself, whose central character himself rejects all possible human pathways save that of total disappearance." Describes the story and some of the typographical innovations. Claims that Sukenick has taken the "devices of the literature of the id" and used them to find at the end "a brick wall, a blank page. There is no future in the id, only instinct, madness and ultimate death. The id cannot create, only destroy." Concludes that Sukenick has demonstrated that a literary movement that ends "screaming in a blind alley is going to do very little to increase the measure of a man. And that, in the last analysis, is the only thing that art is all about."

De Feo, Ronald. "Reviews." Rev. of *Out*. *Hudson Review* 26.4 (1974): 776-77.

Calls *Out* a wild experiment that does not work because of its moronic banter, glibness, and strange movements.

Federman, Raymond. "In." Rev. of *Out*. *Partisan Review* 41.1 (1974): 137-42.

Comments on the novel by mimicking and parodying its style. Calls it a rival act of fiction-making.

Goldberg, Gerald Jay. "In Short." Rev. of *Blown Away*. *New York Times Book Review* 15 Mar. 1987: 16.

Sees *Blown Away* as antiplot, anticharacter, and antiverisimilitude. Suggests that the book contains a large order of verbal playfulness and a small order of moral pique. Concludes that unfortunately this all results in a lethal loss of fictional energy.

Gordon, Lois. "Unboogalooable." Rev. of *The Endless Short Story*. *New York Times Book Review* 16 Nov. 1986: 37.

Describes *The Endless Short Story* as a beautiful poetic work, integrated into Sukenick's social and cosmic concerns and also full of word games. Suggests, however, that one or two of the shorter passages lack thematic or linguistic connection. Disapproves of the puzzling discontinuities.

Hassan, Ihab. "Reading *Out*." Rev. of *Out*. *Fiction International* 1 (1973): 108-09.

Locates Sukenick as a postmodern writer who does not deal with the human condition, uses no fixed points, and provides sudden and invisible waves of change. Claims that, as the paragraphs get shorter in this novel, we realize the novelist is rendering his perception of not only his artistic form, but also his destiny, in a projectile-like form escaping gravity, hurtling faster and faster. Concludes that Sukenick should be read.

Hill, Richard. "Expectations in the Ruins." Rev. of *The Death of the Novel and Other Stories*. *Village Voice* 8 Mar. 1973: 21.

Praises *The Death of the Novel* for its lack of self-conscious narcissistic analysis. Notes that although the stories are experimental in form and purpose, there is life and humor in them and a real commitment to making something of experience. Details the contents of several of the stories, and concludes that this is both an interesting and an important collection.

Hochswender, William. "The Way They Were in Greenwich Village."
     Rev. of *Down and In: Life in the Underground. Los Angeles Times
     Book Review* 18 Oct. 1987: 10.

Considers this an often solemn and vainglorious account of bohemianism
in Greenwich Village enabling one to relive the sixties. Briefly describes
the narrative experimentalism and literary effects of the book.

Howe, Irving. "First Novels: Sweet and Sour." Rev. of *Up. Harper's*
     May 1968: 85-86.

Describes *Up* as a book which really ought to have been great fun with
its exuberant outpouring of the banalities of the age and the pretensions
of the young, but which really fails in this agenda. Considers its satire
ineffective because effective satire cannot be written about a world
which is silly rather than evil, and in which characters are pipsqueaks
rather than ominous.

Inness-Brown, Elizabeth. "Reviews." Rev. of *98.6. Fiction International*
     4-5 (1975): 163-64.

Calls *98.6* a book without commas, question marks, exclamation points,
and a perfectly enigmatic, sorrowful, humorous, and fascinatingly complex combination of intense personal sensitivity and literary
game-playing. Suggests that it is about love of language, self-love, and
sexual, nationalistic, and scientific love.

Johnson, Tom. Rev. of *Out. Village Voice* 29 Nov. 1973: 29-30.

Warns that many women will be offended by the seduction scenes in
Out, as will casual readers out for a good, easy read. Describes the self-
reflexive experimental devices in the novel, and finally concludes that,
once we are captivated by the author's style, there is only one way out,
and that is to finish it.

Jones, D. A. N. "Lean Creatures." Rev. of *Up. New York Review of
     Books* 27 Feb. 1969: 16-17.

Calls *Up* a book of cruel fantasies, bad dreams of grotesquerie, guilty porn,
parody, and tearfulness. Describes individual scenes and passages, and concludes with admiration for Sukenick's fictional style and moral intentions.

Klawans, Stuart. "Hip and Square." Rev. of *Down and In: Life in the
     Underground. Nation* 19 Sept. 1987: 276-78.

Describes *Down and In* as a pub crawl record of counterculture and a lovely book deserving of thoughtful consideration. Sees it as an oral history full of wonderful stories wonderfully told.

Krupat, Arnold. Rev. of *Up*. *Catholic World* July 1968: 186-87.

Describes *Up* as a book one reads for pleasure, wisdom, and vision. Suggests that it is intelligently literate and very funny. Describes the experimental typography and the contents.

Lask, Thomas. "Making Their Way." Rev. of *Up*. *New York Times* 22 June 1968: 31.

Describes *Up* as a novel spinning its own form as it goes along, because it is full of color and life and, in fact, represents an action painting in words.

Lavers, Norman. "Some Parafictions: What Are, How Enjoyed, Where Next." Rev. of "Roast Beef: A Slice of Life." *American Poetry Review* Mar.-Apr. 1978: 44-47.

Wonders if this story is a psychoanalytic daydream since, in the interesting sex scenes which Sukenick writes, he has the capacity to turn erotic daydreams into instant gratification.

LeClair, Thomas. "New Fiction from the Fiction Collective." Rev. of *98.6*. *New York Times Book Review* 18 May 1975: 6.

Calls *98.6* Sukenick's reformulation of the Mosaic Law—the law of mosaics—a way of dealing with parts in the absence of wholes. Suggests that for narration and causation, Sukenick substitutes energy, the primacy of language, and inclusion.

Leonard, John. "The Death of the Review and Other Sorties." Rev. of *The Death of the Novel and Other Stories*. *New York Times* 25 Sept. 1969: 45.

Claims that *The Death of the Novel* is all about maintaining some interest in face of the void. Comments that, unfortunately, Mr. Sukenick enjoys himself too much to engender the proper amount of desperation into the task. Concludes that there is too much depersonalization and showing off.

Maddocks, Melvin. "Games Novelists Play." Rev. of *The Death of the Novel and Other Stories*. *Christian Science Monitor* 9 Oct. 1969: 12.

Complains that *Up* features little plot, less character, and practically no sense of chronology. Suggests that this is the aesthetics of chaos, an anti-manifesto of the arts.

McCall, Dan. "A Review." Rev. of *Up. Epoch* 34 (1968): 119-20.

Considers that *Up* has intelligence, intimacy, and insight. Comments that Sukenick doesn't so much look at the world, but touches it—keeps the lights on low, and gropes over distance to feeling. Notes that it has a careless abundance of energy and refuses to be a well wrought urn. Concludes that this is not a classical product, but rather a romantic process open to the creative participation of the reader.

McGlynn, Paul D. "Book Reviews." Rev. of *98.6. Southern Humanities Review* 11.1 (1977): 77.

Calls *98.6* a promising novel with weaknesses. Says it contains too much archness and a tendency to thump the reader over the head, but that, despite these weaknesses, the prose style is fast, nervy, and exciting. Concludes that the vision is genuinely universal.

O'Hara, Tim. Rev. of *Out. Best Sellers* 1 July 1973: 157-58.

In this account of *Out* O'Hara provides a visual and organizational description of the book, and concludes that medievalists best understand this kind of writing with its puzzles and conundrums. Comments that, ultimately, despite the apparent newness of all this touting and embroidering of the void, such writers as Sukenick are on a very old track leading through and beneath phenomenon to static truth.

Potoker, Edward M. "Class of '55 and How They Grew." Rev. of *Up. Saturday Review* 6 July 1968: 26-27.

Calls *Up* one of the most hilarious books of the season—an outburst of wild comedy that mocks the pretensions of the young, whether they involve "op, pop, or slop." Comments that, unconventional in the manner of *Tristram Shandy*, it asserts that its author is not required to follow the banality of chronology or conventional characters. Provides a detailed account of contents and characters.

Potoker, Edward Martin. "A Connoisseur of Chaos." Rev. of *98.6. Nation* 27 Sept. 1975: 282-84.

Discusses Sukenick's approach to the novel and reinvention of the form, since the realistic, chronological re-creating of life is no longer adequate to capture our experience. Describes the events of the novel; Sukenick's use of a series of "animated *fabliaux*" rather than coherent action"; the "demolition" of chronological time; the use of himself as a character; unusual spacing and page arrangements; and his ability, in spite of his falling into the "haphazard and banal," to maintain full control of his art. Concludes with Ihab Hassan that Sukenick should be read.

Potoker, Edward Martin. Rev. of *The Death of the Novel and Other Stories*. *Saturday Review* 1 Nov. 1969: 40-41.

Comments that this work is full of comedy, color, and wild parodies buried in filaments of plot. Sees its theme as the metacrisis of contemporary life and concludes that none of the pieces in this collection are revolutionary, but rather readable and hilarious. Describes several individual stories.

"Reservations." Rev. of *Out*. *Antioch Review* 32.4 (1973): 698.

Describes *Out* as a rueful dramatization of people's fears that their experiences are repetitious or insignificant, and extends the familiar fiction of the fragmented sensations outward in some amusing new ways.

Rivers, Larry. "Where Has All The Floating Energy Gone?" Rev. of *Down and In: Life in the Underground*. *New York Times Book Review* 1 Nov. 1987: 3, 31.

Discusses the contents and characters of *Down and In*. Questions some of the easy social criticism and formulas in the novel, and generally commends it as the best of a dubious set of novels of this kind.

Sale, Roger. "American Fiction in 1973." Rev. of *Out*. *Massachusetts Review* 14.4 (1973): 837-38.

Describes the typographical peculiarities of *Up*, its content, and its general tendency to have fallen to the theory of "the Novel is our Time."

Sale, Roger. "Reviews." Rev. of *Death of the Novel*. *Hudson Review* 22.4 (1969-70): 707-08.

Comments that, in the work of Sukenick, reality doesn't exist, time doesn't exist, and God was the omniscient author who died. Calls *Death of the Novel* the best programmatically experimental writing of the season.

Sokolov, Raymond A. "Ga-Ga-Ga-Gug." Rev. of *Up*. *New York Times Book Review* 14 July 1968: 34.

Calls *Up* a compendium of sly jokes about literature, and Sukenick's attempt to divest himself of the well-wrought urns and golden bowls of his graduate schooling—all with some success.

Tucker, Carll. "Failed Utopia." Rev. of *Searching for Survivors*. *Village Voice* 30 June 1975: 44.

Discusses *Searching for Survivors* as a radiant experiment in fiction which would never be published, sad to say, by a major publishing house. Describes several of the fourteen stories which make up the collection, and calls the failure of imagination at the end particularly sad since the author came so close to producing a masterpiece.

Tytell, John. "To Skewer McLuhan." Rev. of *The Death of the Novel and Other Stories*. *Catholic World* Feb. 1970: 237-38.

Claims that this collection of stories rejects the stultifying conventions of the Victorian novel and employs experimental techniques for conveying the illusion of control. Argues that readers, along with the writer, are able to seize the fantasy of the moment. Calls this a rigorously written, hilariously comic collection of fiction.

Interviews

Bellamy, Joe David. "Imagination as Perception: An Interview with Ronald Sukenick." *Chicago Review* 23.3 (1972): 59-72. Rpt. as "Ronald Sukenick" in *The New Fiction: Interviews with Innovative American Writers*. Joe David Bellamy. Urbana: U of Illinois P, 1974. 55-74.

In this interview Sukenick describes: his attempts at fantasy, myth in fiction, self-reflexiveness, autobiography as form in *Up*, the *bildungsroman*, past fiction as museum, present fiction as contemporary exhibit, the presence of the author in novels, the demise of conventional realism, the demise of characterization, Reichian analysis, writing about social taboos, and fiction as a normal epistemological procedure.

Bellamy, Joe David. "The Tape Recorder Records: An Interview with Ronald Sukenick." *Falcon* Apr. 1971: 5-25.

In this interview Sukenick discusses: language, writing and time, writing dialogue, the willing suspension of disbelief, ideas and meaning in experimental fiction, Joyce, Rabelais, books and wisdom, innocence and wisdom, editing literary magazines, humor, and the place of sex in his fiction.

Federman, Raymond, and Ronald Sukenick. "The New Innovative Fiction." *Antaeus* 20 (1976): 138-49.

A dialogue between Federman and Sukenick which took place in 1974 over KPFA, a Pacifica radio station, and which covers Federman's typographical idiosyncracies, his novel *Double or Nothing*, the concreteness of language, Sukenick's objections to this use of the visual page, the dynamics of the act of reading, their respective views on fiction as lying and fiction as truth telling, the loss of plot and characterization, the use of anecdote in their places, the relationship between form and content, the question of meaning and illusion, the cultural lag between Europe and America, the American cultural inferiority complex, official morality and the contemporary novel, the review process for experimental novels, and the use of writing as part of the search for freedom and liberation.

McCaffrey, Larry, and others. "Cross Examination." *In Form: Digressions on the Act of Fiction*. Ronald Sukenick. Crosscurrents/Modern Critiques. Third Series. Carbondale: Southern Illinois UP, 1985. 106-55.

In this interview with Larry McCaffrey and others Sukenick discusses his dislike of autobiography, using himself as a literary character, opinions of Barth, interpretation of data, language play, narrative methods, Pound's Bolingen prize, representation of sex, his characters, admiration for Henry James, metafiction, self-reflexive techniques, realism and art, views on abstract expressionism, pure linguistic invention, the differences in American and European culture, ideas about character, his uses of humor, the identity of the artist as inventor of experience, use of numbers for organizing experience, philosophy of form, views of postmodernism, improvisation and form, and fiction as a normal epistomological procedure.

McCaffrey, Larry. "An Interview with Ronald Sukenick." *Anything Can Happen: Interviews with Contemporary American Novelists*. Tom LeClair and Larry McCaffrey. Urbana: U of Illinois P, 1983. 279-97.

Sukenick discusses: his daily writing habits; fiction as a way of recreating his own life; his interest in capturing the data of reality; deconstruction as a writing strategy; language play and release of meaning; sex on the page; discovering Laurence Stern; influence of Wallace Stevens's poetry; the antiquatedness of the mimetic novel; the narcissistic playfulness of literature; using fiction to invent yourself; his use of improvisation as technique; his use of abstract impressionism and jazz forms; the secondary importance of characters; illusionism; and his admiration for Raymond Federman, Steve Katz, Clarence Major, George Chambers, and Walter Abish.

Meyer, Charlotte M. "An Interview with Ronald Sukenick."
Contemporary Literature 23.2 (1982): 129-44.

In this interview Sukenick discusses: his ideas about character; issues of
sexual repression and liberation in the 1960s; his comic sense; various
characters, novels and scenes; the experimental novel; his views on
Barth, modernism, the structural techniques of improvisation in his novels, and methods of revision.

Semrau, Janusz. "An Interview with Ronald Sukenick." *Studia Anglica
Posnaniensia: An International Review of English Studies* 18 (1986):
231-39.

In this interview Sukenick discusses his use of the tape recorder, photo-
realism, self-consciousness, postmodern form, his own life, the death of
the novel, realism, distinctions between art and life, use of time, framing,
closure devices, narrative, reinstitutionalization of the idea of the sacred,
language used for sacramental purposes, and the function of fiction in
predicting as opposed to recording.

Biographical Sources

Adams, Timothy Dow. "Ronald Sukenick." *Dictionary of Literary
Biography Yearbook: 1981.* Eds. Karen L. Rood, Jean W. Ross, and
Richard Ziegfeld. Detroit: Gale, 1982. 251-55.

More than details of his life, this is a career biography, tracing the development of the author's canon, describing the contents and themes of his
works, evaluating his reputation, and placing him in the larger context of
American literary history. Includes lists of primary and secondary
sources and illustrations.

Dissertations

Meyer, Charlotte Marie. "The Shell and the Wave: A Study of Narrative
Form in *Chimera* by John Barth and *98.6* by Ronald Sukenick." Diss.
U of Wisconsin—Madison, 1980.

Schroeder, Michael LeRoy. "Rhetoric in New Fiction." Diss. Kent State
U, 1986.

Winkelman, Aaron. "Authorial Presence in American Metafiction: The
Novels of Coover, Federman, Sorrentino, and Sukenick." Diss. U of
California, Los Angeles, 1986.

Harvey Swados
1920 – 1972

Primary Sources

Novels

Celebration. New York: Simon, 1974, 1975; New York: Dell, 1976.

False Coin. Boston: Little, 1959; Atlantic Press Book. Boston: Little, 1960.

Out Went the Candle. New York: Viking, 1955.

Standing Fast. Garden City: Doubleday, 1970; New York: Ballantine, 1971.

The Will. Cleveland: World, 1963; New York: Pocket, 1964; London: Hart-Davis, 1965; London: Panther, 1971.

Collected Works

Nights in the Gardens of Brooklyn: The Collected Stories of Harvey Swados. Atlantic Press Book. Boston: Little, 1961; London: Hart-Davis, 1962; Short Story Index Reprint Series. Freeport: Books for Libraries, 1970; Lifetime Library. New York: Books for Libraries, 1972; New York: Viking, 1986; New York: Penguin, 1987.

Contents: Nights in the Gardens of Brooklyn; A Glance in the Mirror; A Question of Loneliness; A Chance Encounter; A Handful of Ball-Points, a Heartful of Love; The Letters; Year of Grace; The Peacocks of Avignon; The Man in the Toolhouse; The Dancer.

On the Line. Atlantic Press Book. Boston: Little, 1957; London: Davies, 1957, 1958; New York: Bantam, 1960; New York: Laurel-Dell, 1978; Urbana: U of Illinois P, 1990.

Contents: The Day the Singer Fell; Fawn, with a Bit of Green; Joe, the Vanishing American; A Present for the Boy; On the Line; One for the Road; Just One of the Boys; Back in the Saddle Again; The Myth of the Happy Worker (The last story included in 1990 ed. only).

A Story for Teddy, and Others. New York: Simon, 1965; London: Hart-Davis, 1966.

Contents: A Story for Teddy, Something a Little Special, Bobby Shafter's Gone to Sea, Where Does Your Music Come From?, A Hot Day in Nuevo Laredo, Claudine's Book, Tease, The Hack, The Balcony, My Coney Island Uncle, The Tree of Life.

Short Fiction in Anthologies

"The Dancer." *Fiction of the Fifties: A Decade of American Writing.* Ed. Herbert Gold. Garden City: Doubleday, 1959. 356-83; Garden City: Dolphin-Doubleday, 1959. 363-92.

"Joe, the Vanishing American." *Identity: Stories for This Generation.* Ed. Katherine Hondius. Chicago: Scott, 1966. 217-33; *How We Live: Contemporary Life in Contemporary Fiction.* Eds. Penney Chapin Hills and L. Rust Hills. New York: Macmillan, 1968. 517-31.

"The Letters." *The Best American Short Stories, 1952.* Eds. Martha Foley and Joyce F. Hartman. Boston: Houghton, 1952. 305-30.

"The Man in the Toolhouse." *Best American Short Stories, 1959.* Eds. Martha Foley and David Burnett. Boston: Houghton, 1959. 274-310.

"A Story for Teddy." *The Best American Short Stories, 1964.* Ed. Martha Foley. Boston: Houghton, 1964; New York: Ballantine, 299-324; *The*

Human Commitment: An Anthology of Contemporary Short Fiction.
Ed. Don Gold. Philadelphia: Chilton, 1967. 20-51.

"Twelve O'Clock." *Stories from Epoch: The First Fifty Issues, 1947-67.*
Ed. Baxter Hathaway. Ithaca: Cornell UP, 1966. 351-58.

Short Fiction in Periodicals

"Bobby Shafter's Gone to Sea." *Kenyon Review* 24.1 (1962): 7-28.

"From the Unknown Constellations." *Michigan Quarterly Review* 21.1
(1982): 99-109.

"A Glance in the Mirror." *Hudson Review* 11.4 (1958-59): 522-36.

"Joe, the Vanishing American." *Hudson Review* 10.2 (1957): 201-18.

"Just One of the Boys." *Reporter* 8 Aug. 1957: 15-22.

"My Coney Island Uncle." *Saturday Evening Post* 17 Oct. 1964: 60-62,
64-66, 68, 70.

"Nights in the Gardens of Brooklyn." *Esquire* July 1960: 124, 126-30,
132-44.

"A Story for Teddy." *Saturday Evening Post* 23 Nov. 1963: 58-60, 64,
66, 69-70, 72, 74-75.

"The Tree of Life." *McCall's* June 1965: 84-85, 168, 170.

"A Very Human Story." *Playboy* July 1957: 15, 26, 69, 71.

Secondary Sources

Articles and Chapters

Boswell, William. *"Celebration."* *Survey of Contemporary Literature.* Ed. Frank N. Magill. Rev. ed. 12 vols. Englewood Cliffs: Salem, 1977. 2: 1149-52.

A standard reference article listing the novel's principal characters and describing its hero, themes, sources, plot, and characters.

Farrell, James T. "Harvey Swados: A Veblen of the Novel." *New Republic* 14 Oct. 1957: 17. Rpt. in *Literary Essays 1954-1974.* Ed. Jack Alan Robbins. Literary Criticism Series. Port Washington: Kennikat, 1976. 115-17.

Describes his discovery of *Out Went the Candle* as an exciting event because of its truth, revelation of the sensibility, technical and constructive skill, style, and the simplicity with which complex material is treated. Swados refuses melodrama and overwriting, while fusing dialogue, exposition, and description. Suggests that his objectivity is unmarred and unbroken. Concludes that by artistic re-creation, Swados has made emotionally comprehensible some of the best of Veblen's insights in *The Instinct of Workmanship.*

Goodman, Charlotte. "The Fiction of Harvey Swados." *Midstream* Nov. 1982: 45-49.

Reviews Swados's career, reputation, and death. Comments on his disappointment at never really receiving critical acclaim. Argues that his fiction, though not equally successful, deserves more recognition than it has had. Discusses his social philosophy of writing fiction, his devotion to an aesthetics of social commitment, his career after WWII, the contents of individual novels and short stories, and his final ability to see novels finer than his despite his inability to write that well. Sees his reputation resting primarily on his journalism, and suggests that he is likely to be forgotten, not having had someone like Saul Bellow to immortalize him the way Bellow immortalized Delmore Schwartz.

Gottfried, Alex, and Sue Davidson. "Utopia's Children: An Interpretation of Three Political Novels." *Western Political Quarterly* 15.1 (1962): 17-32.

Argues that novels track socio-political phenomena far in advance of

social scientists, as in the case of Hawthorne's *The Blithedale Romance,*
Mary McCarthy's *The Oasis,* and Swados's *False Coin.* Suggests that
each deals with utopian projects carried out in an American setting con-
temporaneous with the author's lifetime. Notes that each offers an
historical view of the American-dissident-idealist through the eyes of
gifted observers, and each examines the dynamism between a political
idea, and the individuals and culture in which it takes root. A major treatment of *False Coin.*

Hassan, Ihab. "Encounter With Necessity: Three Novels by Styron,
   Swados and Mailer." *Radical Innocence: Studies in the Contemporary
   American Novel.* Ihab Hassan. Princeton: Princeton UP, 1961. 124-52.

Describes the contents of *Out Went the Candle,* and complains that its
structure cannot be made to fit an ironic pattern without strain.
Comments that the management of time is largely conventional, the
action unified through the consciousness of Joe Burley, and that the character of Betsy remains unobservable. Complains that Morrow is
dramatized too late in the book, but concedes that this novel manages to
hold up an urban milieu as a powerful reflector of the relentless warfare
waged within a Jewish family.

Howe, Irving. "On Harvey Swados." *Massachusetts Review* 24.3 (1983):
   637-45.

Repeats the essence of his review, "War-Lost Souls." Adds that Swados
failed to experience the thrill of being part of the post-realist movement
and paid a large price. Claims that his earliest work shows the entangled
talent, the integrity, and the problems of self-definition as a novelist.
Concludes that often his voice shines out from the journalistic style
showing the shift in Jewish life from ghetto to suburb, and the floundering of young people in a chaos of vocation, style, and value.

Kramer, Hilton. "Harvey Swados." *New York Times Book Review* 23
   Mar. 1975: 43.

Describes Swados's last work, *Celebration,* as a private journal in form,
and an examination of the role of ideology in our lives. Provides mostly
a reminiscence about Swados's reputation in light of his recent death.

Marx, Paul. "Harvey Swados." *Ontario Review* 1.1 (1974): 62-66.

Describes Swados's socialist views, his major works and characters, his
final will that there be no funeral after his death, his reputation as a journal-

ist, his political stance up to and including the Nixon era, his relationship to middle-class America, and his attitudes toward the labor movement.

Shapiro, Charles. "Harvey Swados: Private Stories and Public Fiction." *Contemporary American Novelists*. Ed. Harry T. Moore. Crosscurrents/Modern Critiques. Carbondale: Southern Illinois UP, 1964. 182-92.

Begins by condemning modern readers and writers for being suspicious of commitment and traditional point of view in the novel—not to mention hostile to social criticism. Aligns Swados with Dickens, and defends his politics and aesthetics. Describes his political persuasion and comments on writing as an art. Provides a novel-by-novel account of Swados's career, quoting liberally from each work. Discusses his concern for his characters and his penchant for the short story. Also discusses his talents as a journalist, commending him for having a splendid creative imagination and political integrity.

Siegelman, Ellen. "A Battle of Wills: Swados' New Novel." *Critique* 7.1 (1964): 125-28.

Says *The Will* is a big, intensely plotted family novel. Its concerns are ambitious, but between the conception and the execution falls the shadow of the long-armed coincidence and the heavy-handed allegory. Describes the contents fully, and concludes that despite all, the novel comes off. Swados has an eye for telling offbeat detail, a largeness of vision, and a skilled apprehension of loves, hates, memories, and regrets that make up the knotted skein of the family.

Swados, Harvey. "The Image in the Mirror." *The Living Novel: A Symposium*. Ed. Granville Hicks. New York: Macmillan, 1957. 165-93.

A lengthy and important essay in which Swados makes an argument for putting aside the prejudices about the American novel the reader may have been accumulating for years, and for accepting in their place a willingness to grant the hospitality of his hearth to the American novelist with all his reputed eccentricity, tediousness, feebleness, and senility. Claims that he will demonstrate not only that American literary productivity is considerably less abysmal than might be thought, but that the contemporary novelist still has the power to speak, touch the heart, and open life for examination. Takes the critics and journals to task, along with the reviewers, and develops a large and erudite picture of contemporary American writing of his day.

Swados, Robin. Introduction. *Nights in the Gardens of Brooklyn: The Collected Stories of Harvey Swados.* New York: Viking, 1986. ix-xviii.

In this introduction, Robin Swados discusses his father's posthumous materials and collection of unpublished short stories. Describes the characters in the stories *Nights in the Gardens of Brooklyn,* the life of his father, the contents of individual stories, thematic continuities, and the impact of such materials today.

Wakefield, Dan. "Celebration Man." *Atlantic* Apr. 1975: 91-94.

Provides an overview of Swados's writing career, some biographical material, much commentary about Swados's marriage, and his financial sacrifices for the sake of writing. Calls *Celebration* Swados's inevitable "big novel," and commends the successes with which he made the fictional leap to encompassing the mind of an aging political radical.

Reviews

Abel, Lionel. "Our Time & The Left." Rev. of *Standing Fast. Commentary* Dec. 1970: 105-06, 109-10, 112.

Describes the content of *Standing Fast* with its emphasis on the supporters of Trotskyism. Complains at the lack of intellectual commitment to the movement on the part of Swados's characters, illustrating the point with reference to individual characters and situations. A lengthy review which turns into a political essay in its own right, and briefly returns to the politics of Swados's novel at the end.

Adams, Robert M. "Three Novels." Rev. of *The Will. New York Review of Books* 14 Nov. 1963: 12.

Describes *The Will* as a symphonic novel dealing with the House of Karamazov (so to speak) of a lakeside midwestern city. It has psychological depth and compelling social surfaces. For all its shortcomings, this is a massive and moving novel.

Balliett, Whitney. "The New Milquetoast." Rev. of *False Coin. New Yorker* 27 Feb. 1960: 138-39.

Argues that this novel bulges with tension, and seems to be an attempt to shake out the evils of the philanthropic foundations, the very rich, congressional committees, the arts, sociology, slick magazines, and the recording industry. Details the contents, and concludes that the prose is sticky, and the satire a freakish blend of symbolism and snickers.

Bemis, R. Rev. of *A Story for Teddy—and Others. National Review* 22 Feb. 1966: 178.

Calls *A Story for Teddy—and Others* a clever, deft, and mostly unexceptional group of eleven short stories written in bland, quotidian idiom of greater America, over which Swados has considerable mastery. Concludes, however, that these are honestly told, good, simple stories.

Brown, Rosellen. "After Such Knowledge, What Forgiveness?" Rev. of *Standing Fast. Northwest Review* 12.3 (1972): 86-87.

Calls *Standing Fast* a book one wants to like because one respects its premises. Claims that the characters are a set of feasible motives with arms, legs, and tongues attached. Concedes the book is a rock with fine angles here and there, but that it doesn't move because it is populated like a socialist mural or documentary. Claims that the language is nonexistent, and that, as a work of imaginative organization, it moves straight through its appointed decades, panning dutifully from one character to another, trying to create power by sheer mass.

Capouya, Emile. "The Writer as Subject." Rev. of *A Story for Teddy— and Others. Saturday Review* 14 Aug. 1965: 35.

Calls Swados an anachronism because he writes stories like *A Story for Teddy* that focus on family relationships that hark back to the 1930s. Concludes that, despite a certain gaucheness, the stories are very moving.

Cassill, R. V. "Allegory Unlimited." Rev. of *The Will. New York Times Book Review* 3 Nov. 1963: 58.

Calls *The Will* a book whose strategy is analogous to that of analytical cubism in painting where a number of points of view are fused into a single pictorial record. Concludes that the plot is little more than a scaffolding enveloping an allegory which soon curls up and lies down.

Cowan, Paul. "Books." Rev. of *Standing Fast. Village Voice* 22 Oct. 1970: 6, 37-38, 49.

Calls *Standing Fast* interesting and important. Relates the plot, situation, and characters. Applauds the lack of violence in the book, its old-fashioned realism, and beautiful people. Laments the fact that its publication was not the major event it should have been. Provides personal anecdote and social history as background to the politics described in the novel.

Craib, Roderick. "Art Down on the Farm." Rev. of *False Coin. New Leader* 4-11 July 1960: 29.

Describes *False Coin* as imbued with the idea that art is an individual matter, and concerned with theorizing about the function of art in American culture.

Crain, Jane Larkin. "New Books." Rev. of *Celebration. Saturday Review* 8 Mar. 1975: 25.

Suggests that this posthumous novel takes the form of a diary kept by a lifelong, radical crusader for children's rights and educational reform, who is now sitting back enjoying celebrity conferred on him by the liberal establishment. Concludes that the book is too much given over to ideological pontification; plus its self-indulgent and melodramatic attitudinizing seriously weaken the whole novel.

Curley, Thomas F. "The World of Foundations." Rev. of *False Coin. Commonweal* 25 Mar. 1960: 700.

Labels *False Coin* an interesting book which stays in the mind long after one's impatience with the mediocre prose has passed. Details the contents, and concludes that even if the reader ignores the quotations in the front of the book and refuses to identify with the narrator, it is well worth reading.

De Filipps, Anthony J. "Confirmed Promise." Rev. of *On the Line. Commonweal* 25 Oct. 1957: 109-10.

Discusses *On the Line* as a group of short stories about working men, assembly lines, freedom, choice-making, and not being mastered by machines.

Dupee, F. W. "Pieces of the Hour." Rev. of *A Radical's America. Commentary* Dec. 1962: 549-52.

Suggests that *A Radical's America* is informed by easy ironizing and the equally easy rhetoric of sociological expertise. Swados has little regard for logic, and is a very good defender of Marxist theory. Concludes that many of the stories are stunningly innocent, but that he is a persuasive writer.

Engle, Paul. "Three Brothers Inherit a Maelstom." Rev. of *The Will. Chicago Sunday Tribune Magazine of Books* 3 Nov. 1963: 4.

Claims that *The Will* is a novel of superb eccentrics wonderfully described. The book explores deeply and densely the lives of its people, and its conclusion is an ingenious one. Details the characters.

"Escape From Trivia." Rev. of *Out Went the Candle. Newsweek* 17 Jan. 1955: 88, 90.

Calls *Out Went the Candle* an excellent first novel probing the depths of financial mismanagement, family hatreds, human loneliness, and war. Concludes that when the story finally ends in what might be called tragedy, both the reader and the characters find new understanding.

"Fiction." Rev. of *Celebration. New Yorker* 21 Apr. 1975: 144.

Calls *Celebration* a doubtful novel but a very humane one. Provides an extensive plot summary.

Frankel, Haskel. "Tales of Disillusion." Rev. of *Nights in the Gardens of Brooklyn. New Leader* 29 May 1961: 28.

Describes this as a collection of ten stories, eight serious, one satirical, and one a farce. Suggests that Swados himself is obviously infected with disillusion at the corruption of American culture. Concludes that there is too much truth here to keep too many readers, despite Swados's talents.

Gelfant, Blanche H. "Fiction Chronicle." Rev. of *Celebration. Hudson Review* 28.2 (1975): 313-14.

Compares Rev. Marshfield from Updike's *A Month of Sundays* to Samuel Lumen in *Celebration*, and finds both characters celebrating their lives when they should feel shame because of the far-reaching extent of their treachery, destructiveness, and venality. Describes Lumen's destructive acts and concludes: "I am supposed to feel happy at the end . . . but I am distressed. I expect more from old age than 'good humor' and 'serenity.'"

Gill, Brendan. "Trials." Rev. of *Out Went the Candle. New Yorker* 15 Jan. 1955: 99-100, 102.

Describes *Out Went the Candle* as long, earnest, ambitious, and intelligent. Recounts the setting, plot, characters, and situations. Considers the attempt admirable, but in the final analysis, depressing and imperfect. Concludes, however, that Swados has not given himself an easy task like many similar authors who have failed.

Green, Martin. "Glimpses of Life in the Factory." Rev. of *On the Line. Dissent* 27.1 (1980): 115-16.

Reviews the novel in its reprint edition 23 years after its initial appear-

ance. Describes its initial reception, its location within the socialist literature of its day and type, and its present-day significance.

Greenfeld, Josh. "Yesterday on the Left." Rev. of *Standing Fast. New
York Times Book Review* 13 Sept. 1970: 59.

Calls this an old-fashioned panoramic novel operating like a Victorian
serial. Suggests that it is sprawling and flawed, sentimentally doctrinaire,
full of leftist cliches, and ultimately compassionate. Concludes that this
is a readable, important, and rewarding book.

Hayman, Jane. "Books." Rev. of *The Will. Hadassah Magazine* Dec.
1963: 18.

Claims that *The Will* lacks a distinguished style but insists that its timing,
narrative powers, and characterization are excellent. It awakens and
involves the reader in an old-fashioned sense. Describes contents.

Hayman, Jane. "Jews, Modern & Ancient." Rev. of *Standing Fast.
Hadassah Magazine* Jan. 1971: 20.

Calls *Standing Fast* a long, realistic novel which reflects on the lives of a
collection of Americans from the time of the Hitler-Stalin pact through to
the 1950s. Complains that it lacks the force and integration of *The Will*,
but judges it to be more a moral parable than a literary work, and essentially valuable because it gives an account of men, women, and events
through two important decades which have shaped the present era.

Hendin, Josephine. "The Costs of Living." Rev. of *Nights in the Gardens
of Brooklyn. New York Times Book Review* 21 Dec. 1986: 20.

Thinks *Nights in the Gardens of Brooklyn* continues Swados's championing of the embattled self against the damages of time and necessity.
Calls it a dense and beautiful tale about what one must exchange for the
cost of living. Outlines plot, themes, and characters. Concludes,
"Although its stories are sometimes flawed with too facile equations of
success and self-corruption, it bristles with revelations and returns us to
that humane economy Emerson had in mind when he wrote: 'The one
thing of value in the world is the active soul.'"

Hicks, Granville. "Heirs to the Family Misfortune." Rev. of *The Will.
Saturday Review* 26 Oct. 1963: 33-34.

Describes *The Will* as a story of three brothers struggling over an inheritance and making startling self-discoveries. Notes that Swados lacks the

skill of Updike or Flannery O'Connor with language or to characterize with a word or two, but that his own gifts and individual point of view make him an important writer.

Hicks, Granville. "The Importance of Being Honest." Rev. of *False Coin. Saturday Review* 9 Jan. 1960: 12.

Describes Swados as a writer who introduces us in this novel to the giants of the age. Describes and admires the vision of American democracy Swados dreams of, and concludes that he is a writer who knows how to clothe his vision in flesh and blood. Calls this his best novel thus far.

Hicks, Granville. "Some Good Fiction Which Won't Get the Popular Attention It Deserves." Rev. of *On the Line. New Leader* 7 Oct. 1957: 23.

Calls the stories in *On the Line* stories of frustration and defeat which are very uneven in quality. Claims that they read as if they were made on the assembly line. Describes several of the characters and situations.

Howe, Irving. "The Real World." Rev. of *The Will. Commentary* Apr. 1964: 80, 82-83.

Calls Swados an old-fashioned writer committed to the modes of realism who, nevertheless, has produced a book full of sick wisdom, comic nihilism, Hellerish fantasy, high-spirited nausea, Southern jokes, and Yiddish vaudeville. Calls him a writer free from public postures who has, through the decades, maintained a steady interest in and affection for his fellow human beings.

Howe, Irving. "War-Lost Souls." Rev. of *Out Went the Candle. Saturday Review* 22 Jan. 1958: 27-28.

Describes *Out Went the Candle* as a first novel with serious faults, which, nevertheless, remains extremely interesting. Details the contents of the novel, and concludes that it is an intelligent and sometimes powerful effort to look at what is puzzling and distinctive in American life, to measure the vast distance between generations torn apart by war, and to turn, modestly and without ideology, to the possibilities of human renewal. Concludes that he writes well enough, but that the books bear the sweat marks of too much concern with meaning and pattern.

Hutchens, John K. "A Determined Sermon by Novelist Swados." Rev. of *False Coin. San Francisco Chronicle* 19 Jan. 1960: 25.

Argues that *False Coin* sounds like axes grinding. Claims that this thesis novel, for all its fictional touches, turns out to be a rather determined sermon on the role of the artist in America today. The drama falls into conventional patterns of talk and action, but the thesis itself is lost in diffusion and irrelevancies.

Jones, D. A. N. "The Power of Positive Trotskyism." Rev. of *Standing Fast. New York Review of Books* 12 Aug. 1971: 28-29.

Calls *Standing Fast* a long, commonsensical chronicle of the lives of a score of American socialists over twenty-four years. Provides a very detailed account of the contents of the book, and concludes that Swados has tried to include too much historical material through allusions and parentheses in his characters' conversations.

Klein, Marcus. "Hatching a Brood." Rev. of *A Story for Teddy and Others. Washington Post Book World* 22 Aug. 1965: 9.

Claims that these stories in *A Story for Teddy and Others* run to shapelessness. They suffer a vertiginous tendency to end in bare-souled epilogues. Their sincerity is undermined by excursiveness, lack of sensation, and the voicelessness of Swados's prose. They consecrate youth and the theme of the necessity of compassion. Details the contents of several of the stories.

Kramer, Hilton. "Failures That Wear the Mask of Egregious Success." Rev. of *Standing Fast. Washington Post Book World* 20 Sept. 1970: 4.

Calls *Standing Fast* a novel about radical politics that is huge, clear-eyed, and explores the radical politics of the Thirties. Suggests that the novelistic machinery is distinctly mechanical after the modernist era of novels, but still finds this a remarkable achievement.

Kramer, Hilton. "The Odor of Gold." Rev. of *The Will. New York Herald Tribune Book Week* 3 Nov. 1963: 17.

Calls *The Will* a tightly plotted, swiftly paced novel dealing with a strange and yet representative family caught in a web of avarice, vengeance, and impossible aspiration. Details the contents, and concludes that in this novel the social meaning manages to transcend the psychology of the individual characters.

Kriegel, Leonard. "A Distinctive Literary Voice." Rev. of *Celebration. Nation* 10 May 1975: 565-67.

Provides anecdotal material about meeting Swados, reading his early fiction, and experiencing the news of his death as the loss of a writer who never really fulfilled his potential. Sees *Celebration* as a loss of power. Describes the journal contents of the book, and traces the familiar Swados themes and stylistic habits. Concludes with a tribute to the now dead author.

Larner, Jeremy. "Chuckling, He Squared His Shoulders." Rev. of *The Will. New Leader* 2 Mar. 1964: 22-23.

Sees *The Will* as another book of detailed radical reporting. Comments that the fiction is obsessive in its involvement with guilt and responsibility. Claims that Swados tries to explain human behavior by the application of hard fact to cerebral theory, the result being symbolic sociology rather than fiction.

LeClair, Thomas. "Mr. Samuel Lumen's Planet." Rev. of *Celebration. New York Times Book Review* 9 Mar. 1975: 4.

Calls *Celebration* a book which treats many of the familiar Swados themes, avoids sentimentality, and documents many of life's ironies. Considers this his most artful work, though the language is analytical, rather than presentational. Commends the work for its concentration of social themes into metaphor, attention to subtleties of character, and achievement of ironic complexity. Concludes that the journal form leads to weaknesses, but indicates Swados's attempt to try new forms of fiction.

Lemay, Harding. "Dreams Versus Realities in the Short Stories of Harvey Swados." Rev. of *Nights in the Gardens of Brooklyn. New York Herald Tribune Lively Arts* 29 Jan. 1961: 30.

Says *Nights in the Gardens of Brooklyn* is a collection of ten stories which pit the purity of dreams against the shabbiness of reality. They are tightly controlled stories done in simple prose which concentrate on love, marriage, parenthood, friendship and ambition.

Lemay, Harding. Rev. of *Standing Fast. Saturday Review* 10 Oct. 1970: 33.

Calls *Standing Fast* a laborious victory of content over craft in a literary age when craft disguises the absence of content. Concludes that all that intelligence, industry, and honorable intention can bring to fiction are found here. Describes the contents of the novel.

Leonard, John. "Keeping the Idea Alive." Rev. of *Standing Fast. New York Times* 15 Sept. 1970: 45. Rpt. as "Harvey Swados' *Standing*

Fast" in *This Pen for Hire*. John Leonard. Garden City: Doubleday, 1973. 28-30.

Complains that *Standing Fast* is written in flat prose and with a narrative machinery that creaks. The conversations are cliche-ridden. The love scenes are embarrassing, and the resolutions arrived at with a clumsy sort of inevitability. Details the contents, and concludes that, although the characters are real, the context smothers us and denies the innate integrity and compassion of the piece.

Levine, Paul. "Some Middle-Aged Fiction." Rev. of *A Story for Teddy— and Others. Hudson Review* 18.4 (1965-66): 588.

Thinks *A Story for Teddy* features visions of youth as viewed from the vantage point of middle age. Comments that he is always recollecting experience in tranquillity, and unfortunately, the stories are slight. Ultimately we believe the honesty of the author more than we believe in his tales.

"Loss of Innocence." Rev. of *A Story for Teddy—and Others. Newsweek* 9 Aug. 1965: 83.

Describes these stories as old-fashioned, no-nonsense stories set in a solid world. Claims that the best of the stories of nostalgia and regret, memory and art, and the self and the world portray movingly those moments of truth when the inert mass of the unformed spirit quickens and suddenly hardens into identity. Describes several of the stories.

Mills, Nicolaus. "Hold the Line." Rev. of *On the Line. Nation* 11 June 1990: 830-32.

Calls *On the Line* a collection of essays and stories about the plight of the blue-collar worker. Comments on assembly line life, and details the contents of several key pieces and the social issues they address.

Lowry, Robert. "Profiteer's Comeuppance." Rev. of *Out Went the Candle. New York Times Book Review* 9 Jan. 1955: 23.

Calls *Out Went the Candle* a book with a plot that is too loose-jointed to be compelling, and characters which are just real enough. Concludes that, with a harder-driving, more carefully pruned tale to tell next time, Mr. Swados may just look like the writer his earlier stories promised him to be. Details contents.

Malin, Irving. "Posterity Now." Rev. of *Celebration. New Republic* 22 Mar. 1975: 27.

Describes the hero Lumen of *Celebration*, and calls the book a wonderfully serene novel which accepts the conflict of generations as an inevitable fact of life. Concludes that because it acknowledges the need for liberation of fathers and sons, it refuses to flee from political, sexual, and educational strife. Deems it an appropriate testament—not only to Lumen, but to Swados himself.

Mirsky, Mark. Rev. of *Standing Fast*. *Partisan Review* 38.4 (1971-72): 483-84.

Considers *Standing Fast* as a fascinating encyclopedia of the non-Stalinist left, but as a novel—boring. Argues that all the characters have to bear the weight of Swados's leaning over their shoulder explaining. Abhors the noisy third person constantly giving us "quickly psychoanalytical insights, philosophical digressions, and journalistic roundups of the situations."

Mizener, Arthur. "Some Kinds of Modern Novel." Rev. of *False Coin*. *Sewanee Review* 69 (1961): 155-56.

Calls *False Coin* a book about the battle between organizational and individual values which leads Swados to select as a subject the experiment in the production and distribution of art to a mass public freed from commercial pressure. Suggests, however, that the sense of life beneath the surface of the novel is black and white, and that his characters, therefore, are somewhat lacking. Concludes, nevertheless, that this is a complex book and a considerable achievement.

Mudrick, Marvin. "A Warning To Optimists." Rev. of *False Coin*. *Hudson Review* 13.2 (1960): 309-10.

Calls *False Coin* a serious name-dropping novel, depending for effect on persuading the reader that most of the characters are straight out of weekly newsmagazines. Concludes that Swados, unfortunately, is not even cynical enough to be clever in the *New Yorker* profile, which is where his material belongs.

Neufeld, Alice. "Success At a Dead-End Price." Rev. of *Nights in the Gardens of Brooklyn: The Collected Stories of Harvey Swados*. New Leader 17 Nov. 1986: 16-17.

Reviews Swados's career, details the stories contained in *Nights in the Gardens of Brooklyn: The Collected Stories*, comments that Swados is often political but never doctrinaire, and concludes that his stories are full-blooded fictions that have one eye focused upon justice and the other upon love.

O'Connell, Shaun. Rev. of *Celebration. Massachusetts Review* 17.1 (1976): 190-91.

Describes the novel as "a morality play, a dialectical movement between yea and nay. Relates the novel to an essay, "The Coming Revolution in Literature" by Swados, in which he, like Bellow, complains about nay-saying novelists. Suggests that this novel attempts to impose order upon chaos, to seek out redemptive grace in a fallen world. Concludes that Swados praised works which normalize the abnormal, works which seek out in the wonderland of America justifiable cause for celebration.

O'Hara, Timothy. Rev. of *Celebration. America* 19 July 1975: 39-40.

Considers the ambitions of *Celebration* to be noble and the revelations in the book arranged in layers. But notes that their texture and delivery are, for the most part, flat and undistinguished. Sees that too often they sound like the dreary escape of wind from the standard talk show celebrity.

Ostermann, Robert. "Swados." Rev. of *Celebration. National Observer* 12 Apr. 1975: 21.

Describes the protagonist, Samuel Lumen, a 90-year-old advocate of unpopular causes who reveals through a diary, [the novel], sordid, shameful events and sexual excesses that lead him to conclude his private life was a gross betrayal of the public man. Concludes that it is a brilliant piece of characterization.

Peden, William. "Dissonant Notes at Harmony Farm." Rev. of *False Coin. New York Times Book Review* 10 Jan. 1960: 4-5.

Argues that *False Coin* is about the problem of the artist's need to be an artist, as well as one man's search for truth and self-realization. Comments that the book does not entirely succeed because of the unconvincing accumulation in contrivance of the climax. Sees Swados as a writer of integrity and talent who has produced an intelligent commentary on being torn between the material and the ideal.

Pomer, Belle. Rev. of *False Coin. Canadian Forum* June 1960: 69-70.

Considers the main theme in *False Coin* to be the danger to artistic freedom in the direction of, and administration of, the creative process. Details the contents, and concludes that this novel suffers from lack of depth and texture typical of the novel of ideas.

Poore, Charles. "Books of the Times." Rev. of *Nights in the Gardens of Brooklyn. New York Times* 24 Jan. 1961: 27.

Asserts that this collection contains an excellent variety of stories from an extremely talented writer. Sees them as wry, searching, passionate, and sociological. Describes contents in considerable detail.

Poore, Charles. "On the Wing and on the Make." Rev. of *A Story for Teddy—and Others. New York Times* 21 Aug. 1965: 19.

Calls this a collection of stories written retrospectively, discussing the problems of Americans on the make. Describes the contents of several stories.

Prescott, Peter S. "Antique Radical." Rev. of *Celebration. Newsweek* 31 Mar. 1975: 76.

Sees *Celebration* as an unusual novel because it deals with old age with compassion and insight. Provides a detailed character study of the major character. Concludes that Swados gives us only glimpses of Lumen's past, no sense at all of his former greatness, and far too tediously long a picture of a man who himself becomes tedious.

Price, Martin. "New Books in Review." Rev. of *False Coin. Yale Review* 49.3 (1960): 448-49.

Calls *False Coin* an inept book full of ludicrous characters treated implausibly. Suggests that they fail to move us, and often conform to stock figures like the mad scientist. Treats the contents scathingly.

Quinn, Patrick F. "Initiation into Defeat." Rev. of *Out Went the Candle. Commonweal* 14 Jan. 1955: 412-413.

Praises Swados for not writing an autobiographical first novel, or focusing it on initiation. Expresses pleasure in Swados's style of telling and the simplicity of the whole work. Expresses disappointment that some of the characters are made to walk on too often, and that there are too many coincidences.

Robbins, Richard. "The Strength of Memory." Rev. of *Standing Fast. Dissent* 18.3 (1971): 279-80.

Considers *Standing Fast* as a long, flowing novel about a small group of Old Left, Anti-Stalinist socialists tracing their paths from the 1930s to the weary 60s. Details the contents, and concludes that this is a good, honest, felt novel functioning as a farewell to the Old Left. Notes its structural problems. Comments on the plot sagging, but concludes that the read is worth it.

Robinson, Jill. "Uncle Sam, the Radical." Rev. of *Celebration. Village Voice* 24 Mar. 1975: 35-36.

Comments that *Celebration* is written in the form of a private journal written by Sam Lumen during the months preceding his 90th birthday. Sees this book as soft, rich and as understated as well-handled suede. The main character comes instantly alive; and as a social document it is more valuable than most non-fiction. Concludes that above all it is an acutely interesting statement on the state of our nation.

Rugoff, Milton. "Groping in the Wilderness of Our Time." Rev. of *Out Went the Candle. New York Herald Tribune Book Review* 9 Jan. 1955: 3.

Considers this novel about people groping through the wild places of trackless time, a bold mixture of action and speculation which moves swiftly and skillfully from scene to scene. Points out that most of the situations these characters create for themselves suggest that human beings are sometimes vicious, but generally frail, foolish, or pathetically self-destructive. Concludes, however, that they occasionally seem capable of courage, pity, and sacrifice.

Schott, Webster. "The Shrunken Vision." Rev. of *Celebration. Washington Post Book World* 23 Mar. 1975: 3.

Calls *Celebration* a work whose complexity makes for richness of concept and luxury of emotion. Suggests, however, that some of the richness cannot support its own weight because Swados seems to have been trying to put everything he had into this last novel. Concludes: "Swados seeks the bitterness of aging, the crookedness of achievement, and the mysteries of personal and social change in *Celebration.*"

Seager, Allan. "Inside the Machine." Rev. of *On the Line. Nation* 23 Nov. 1957: 393.

Calls *On the Line* a *roman a these* about intolerable life on assembly lines. Suggests that Swados is one of our few writers who cares about these men. Details contents.

Shapiro, Charles. "Political Fates." Rev. of *Standing Fast. Novel* 5.1 (1971): 87-88.

Describes *Standing Fast* as a political novel spanning the years between the days of the Hitler-Stalin Pact and the assassination of John F. Kennedy. Condemns the novel for its *agit-prop* qualities and failure to fall together, political ideology notwithstanding.

Sheppard, R. Z. "September Song." Rev. of *Celebration*. *Time* 24 Mar. 1975: 79.

Provides a detailed description of the character Sam Lumen, his concerns, and his view of the world. Comments that *Celebration* contains all the elements that should produce readability and substance in fiction, but that the clash of ideas between old and new radicals never reaches higher than Lumen's easy parodies of nihilistic rhetoric. Concludes that finally, Sam Lumen's eminence is never convincing.

Singer, Brett. "Title Page." Rev. of *Nights in the Gardens of Brooklyn*. *Los Angeles Times Book Review* 16 Nov. 1986: 4.

Calls this is a sad, poignant, old-fashioned collection of stories by a gifted and distinctly American writer. Concludes that by the end we mourn for a writer who died too soon.

Stevens, Elizabeth. "On Disciplined Passion." Rev. of *The Will*. *Books and Bookmen* Apr. 1965: 33.

Comments that *The Will* never fails to dig deep into the dark, unpleasant corners of people's desires because it is written with cool confidence, disciplined passion, and perception. Summarizes plot.

Szanto, Alison. "Original Mess." Rev. of *Standing Fast*. *Catholic World* Apr. 1971: 50.

Argues that almost everything in *Standing Fast* is about as mechanical as his sex scenes. Describes the great variety of characters in the American labor movement of the 1930s and the panorama of the past they inhabit. Claims that it is all a sort of fictionalized history of a contemporary phenomenon, and is quite authentic. Concludes, however, that in this book we are given a large chunk of nearly original mess that Swados has failed to find sufficient form to accommodate.

Talbot, Daniel. "Artists and Power Elite." Rev. of *False Coin*. *New York Herald Tribune Book Review* 17 Jan. 1960: 6.

Describes the contents of the novel, and labels its theme as being about the conflict between commercialism and art. Commends Swados for entering new territory, but notes the weakness in the purely realistic descriptions of the artists' community. Concludes that he should have used satire or panegyric to bring the characters to life.

Talbot, Daniel. "Grinding Prosperity." Rev. of *Nights in the Gardens of Brooklyn. New York Times Book Review* 29 Jan. 1961: 5.

Complains that *Nights in the Gardens of Brooklyn* is full of banal characters and dull images. Concludes that there are hundreds of stories like these. Suggests that since Swados is a writer with a fine morality and seriousness, we can surely demand more of him than this.

Taliaferro, Frances. "Fiction." Rev. of *Celebration.* May 1975: 55.

Calls *Celebration* an honest but tedious octogenarian's diary, with a point of view which is thoroughly refreshing. Concludes that this is not a great novel but a good one.

Vogler, Lewis. "A Successful Father Watches the Wrecking of His Family." Rev. of *Out Went the Candle. San Francisco Chronicle This World Magazine* 30 Jan. 1955: 16, 20.

Out Went the Candle is the story of the decline of a promiscuous, exceptional woman. Of most interest are the complex relationships, suggesting a cleavage of generations, all related through a series of intimate scenes. Notes that he hits hard at the bourgeois. Concludes that this is better than most first novels.

Wain, John. "American Victorian." Rev. of *The Will. New Republic* 16 Nov. 1963: 21-24.

Calls *The Will* a Victorian novel in modern dress, full of verse and coincidence. Gives a detailed account of plot and characters. Comments in detail on the unflagging pace and attack of the novel. Comments also on themes, narrative technique, and the Dickensian ending.

Interviews

Feinstein, Herbert. "Contemporary American Fiction: Harvey Swados and Leslie Fiedler." *Wisconsin Studies in Contemporary Literature* 2.1 (1961): 79-88.

Swados discusses with Feinstein American literature in the sixties, writers as characters, and several contemporary authors such as Mailer, Bellow, Paley, Herbert Gold. Also discusses American fiction of the fifties,

Nelson Algren, the writer's responsibility toward excellence, his own beginnings, and his view of the central themes in American literature.

Biographical Sources

Kramer, Hilton. "Remembering Harvey Swados." *Massachusetts Review* 14.1 (1973): 226-28.

A tribute to Swados on the occasion of his death. Discusses: their friendship, his publication of *A Radical's America*; the effect on its readership; Swados; his long novel, *Standing Fast*; and his personal qualities.

Shapiro, Charles. "Rebel with a Craft." *Saturday Review* 26 Oct. 1963: 34.

A brief biographical sketch that describes his work habits, reputation, and future plans. Provides a self-characterization of Swados as a novelist, a middle-class man of mid-century, a Jew, and a socialist.

Swados, Bette Beller. "Five Years Later." *New Letters* 44.3 (1978): 103-04.

A reminiscence by Swados's wife of a visit with a friend to the Shakespeare and Co. bookshop on the Left Bank where the owner, George Whitman, commented: "I loved Harvey Swados and everything he wrote. If there was a man who was true to himself and to his writing, it was he."

Walbridge, Earle F. "Harvey Swados." *Wilson Library Bulletin* Mar. 1961: 565.

Recounts his origins in Buffalo, his marriage, his professional career, and some of his early publications.

Lionel Trilling
1905 – 1975

Primary Sources

Novels

The Middle of the Journey. New York: Viking, 1947, 1975; London: Secker, 1948, 1975; Garden City: Anchor-Doubleday, 1957; Harmondsworth: Penguin, 1963, 1977; New York: Avon, 1966, 1976; New York: Harcourt, 1975, 1980; New York: Scribner, 1975; Oxford: Oxford UP, 1981.

Collected Works

Of This Time, of That Place, and Other Stories. New York: Harcourt, 1979; The Works of Lionel Trilling. Uniform ed. New York: Harvest/HBJ-Harcourt, 1980; Oxford: Oxford UP, 1981.

Contents: Impediments; The Other Margaret; Notes on a Departure; The Lesson and the Secret; Of This Time, of That Place.

Short Fiction in Anthologies

"Of This Time, of That Place." *Reading Modern Short Stories*. Ed. Jarvis A. Thurston. Chicago: Scott, 1955. 451-85; *The Short Story and the Reader*. Ed. Robert Stanton. New York: Holt, 1960. 266-99; *31 Stories*. Eds. Michael R. Booth and Clinton S. Burhans. Englewood Cliffs: Prentice, 1960. 288-316; *Stories of Modern America*. Eds.

Herbert Gold and David L. Stevenson. New York: St. Martin's, 1961. 59-94; *The Best Short Stories of the Modern Age.* Ed. Douglas Angus. Greenwich: Premier-Fawcett, 1962. 270-307; *The Forms of Fiction.* Eds. John Gardner and Lennis Dunlap. New York: Random, 1962. 395-429; *Modern Short Stories: The Fiction of Experience.* Eds. M. X. Lesser and John N. Morris. New York: McGraw, 1962. 337-73; *Fifty Best American Short Stories: 1915-1965.* Ed. Martha Foley. Boston: Houghton, 1965. 339-74; *The World of Modern Fiction: American.* Ed. Steven Marcus. 2 vols. New York: Simon, 1966. 1: 213-47; *The Rite of Becoming: Stories and Studies of Adolescence.* Eds. Arthur Waldhorn and Hilda Waldhorn. Cleveland: World, 1966. 240-72; *Identity: Stories for This Generation.* Ed. Katherine Hondius. Chicago: Scott, 1966. 52-86; *The Experience of Literature: A Reader with Commentaries.* Ed. Lionel Trilling. New York: Holt, 1967; Garden City: Doubleday, 1967. 755-81; *Stories from the Quarto.* Ed. Leonard Brown. New York: Scribner, 1968. 153-70; *The Survival Years: A Collection of American Writings of the 1940's.* Ed. Jack Salzman. New York: Pegasus, 1969. 311-42; *The Experience of Literature, Briefer Version.* Ed. Lionel Trilling. New York: Holt, 1969. 345-71.

"The Other Margaret." *The Best American Short Stories, 1946.* Ed. Martha Foley. Boston: Houghton, 1946. 464-96; *The Art of Modern Fiction.* Eds. Ray B. West and Robert W. Stallman. New York: Holt, 1949. 374-93; *Stories: British and American.* Eds. Jack B. Ludwig and W. Richard Poirier. Boston: Houghton, 1953. 109-31; *Fifty Modern Stories.* Ed. Thomas M. H. Blair. New York: Harper, 1960. 111-30; *The Short Story and the Reader.* Ed. Robert Stanton. New York: Holt, 1960. 236-56.

Short Fiction in Periodicals

"Chapter for a Fashionable Jewish Novel." *Menorah Journal* June 1926: 275-82.

"Funeral at the Club, with Lunch." *Menorah Journal* Aug. 1927: 380-90.

"Impediments." *Menorah Journal* June 1925: 286-90.

"The Lesson and the Secret." *Harper's Bazaar* Mar. 1945: 90, 136, 138, 140, 142-44, 146, 148, 150, 152; *Horizon* Aug. 1949: 111-22.

"Light to the Nations." *Menorah Journal* Apr. 1928: 402-08.

"Notes on a Departure." *Menorah Journal* May 1929: 421-34.

"Of This Time, of That Place." *Partisan Review* 10.1 (1943): 72-81, 84-105.

"The Other Margaret." *Partisan Review* 12.4 (1945): 481-501; *Life and Letters* Nov. 1949: 115-38.

Secondary Sources

Books

Boyers, Robert. *Lionel Trilling: Negative Capability and the Wisdom of Avoidance*. A Literary Frontiers Edition. Columbia: U of Missouri P, 1977.

Chace, William M. *Lionel Trilling: Criticism and Politics*. Stanford: Stanford UP, 1980.

Krupnick, Mark. *Lionel Trilling and the Fate of Cultural Criticism*. Evanston: Northwestern UP, 1986.

O'Hara, Daniel T. *Lionel Trilling: The Work of Liberation*. Wisconsin Project on American Writers. Madison: U of Wisconsin P, 1988.

Shoben, Edward Joseph, Jr. *Lionel Trilling*. Modern Literature Series. New York: Ungar, 1981.

Tanner, Stephen L. *Lionel Trilling*. Twayne's United States Authors Series 523. Boston: Twayne, 1988.

Articles and Chapters

Aaron, Daniel. "The Occasional Novel: American Fiction and the Man
of Letters." *Studies in American Fiction* 5.1 (1977): 127-41.

In the context of a discussion dealing with many novels written by
notable men of letters, Aaron singles out Trilling's *The Middle of the
Journey* for a more detailed treatment. Considers the novel mannered
and non-experimental, but not the least self-indulgent or memorializing.
Sees the work as Arnoldian in moral and political judgments. Details the
characters and plot, and discusses in detail its structural, stylistic, and fictional elements.

Allen, Walter. "The Thirties: American." *The Modern Novel in Britain
and the United States*. Walter Allen. New York: Dutton, 1964;
*Tradition and Dream: The English and American Novel from the
Twenties to Our Time*. Walter Allen. London: Phoenix, 1964;
London: Hogarth, 1986. 178-79.

Claims that the coda to the politically oriented fiction—in however
vague a sense—of the Thirties in America is a novel published when it
was all past: Lionel Trilling's *The Middle of the Journey*. Calls it an
intelligent work, a little too pat, yet capable of summing up the American
intellectuals' long love affair with Communism as no other novel has
done.

Anderson, Quentin. "On *The Middle of the Journey*." *Art, Politics, and
Will: Essays in Honor of Lionel Trilling*. Eds. Quentin Anderson,
Stephen Donadio, Steven Marcus. New York: Basic, 1977. 254-64.

Develops the thesis that *The Middle of the Journey* constituted an attack
so grave and conclusive on the pieties of middle-class radicalism that
what it made apparent simply had to be ignored. Claims that direct denial
would have been too painful. Concludes that the novel, though it has
made some inroads in England, is still largely unpalatable in America.

Blotner, Joseph. "Disillusionment and the Intellectual." *The Modern
American Political Novel, 1900-1960*. Joseph Blotner. Austin: U of
Texas P, 1966. 306-35.

A major chapter in which Blotner discusses the individual's gradual disillusionment with the revolutionary movement and his attempts to make
a life outside it during the 1930s. Deals with nine novels that express this
disillusionment or the intellectual politics. Devotes several pages to

Trilling, giving a detailed account of both the contents and the politics of *The Middle of the Journey*.

Boyers, Robert. "*The Middle of the Journey* and Beyond: Observations on Modernity and Commitment." *Salmagundi* 1.4 (1966-67): 8-18.

Argues that, while not a masterpiece, this novel speaks to us about matters it is no longer expedient for us to evade or suppress. Relates the contours of the novel for most of the article, and concludes that its message is that humanistic intelligence must not acquiesce in an oblivion-inducing logic, but must forge out of its despair a commitment to confront nullity with the hard facts of concern and intellect.

Bradbury, Malcolm. "Leaving the Fifties: The Change of Style in American Writing." *Encounter* July 1975: 40-51.

Describes *The Middle of the Journey* as a book which discusses the growing power and influence of intellectuals in the arts as well as the sciences, and the phenomenon of a nation opening itself to the pressures of the mind. Chronicles the nullifying effect that the flirtation with Communism has had on American intellectuals forged in the 1930s.

Bradbury, Malcolm. "Lionel Trilling: End of the Journey." *New Statesman* 14 Nov. 1975: 619.

A tribute to Trilling on the occasion of his death from cancer at age seventy. Briefly reviews his life and achievements as a critic and writer. Provides some personal anecdotal comments on the composition of *The Middle of the Journey*.

Casalandra, Estelle. "The Three Margarets." *Sewanee Review* 81.2 (1973): 225-36.

Discusses Trilling's short story "The Other Margaret" and its literary relationship to Hopkins' Margaret of *Spring and Fall*. Provides a detailed "new formalist critical" analysis of the story, and describes Trilling's probable use of the earlier source in writing it.

Chace, William M. "*The Middle of the Journey*: Death and Politics." *Novel* 10.2 (1977): 137-44.

Acknowledges the political content of the novel, and turns attention instead to themes concerning the ways in which death is approached and conceived in the modern era. Comes back to the idea that the novel is forever attached to history, despite its literary qualities. Concludes that it is "a glass through which we may darkly view American communism and anti-communism."

Cowan, S. A. "Parrington, Woolley, and Reality: A Note on Trilling's 'Of This Time, of That Place.'" *English Language Notes* 26.2 (1988): 56-59.

Discusses the autobiographical content of "Of This Time, of That Place," and comments that Frederic Woolley is built on V. L. Parrington, author of the classic *Main Currents in American Thought*. Traces the parallels between them in considerable depth, and concludes that there is convincing evidence that Parrington was the primary inspiration for Woolley."

Dembo, L. S. "Dissent and Dissent: A Look at Fiedler and Trilling." *Contemporary American-Jewish Literature: Critical Essays*. Ed. Irving Malin. Bloomington: Indiana UP, 1973. 134-55.

Describes the content of Trilling's *The Middle of the Journey*, and examines in detail Trilling's critique of bourgeois intellectuals and liberal responses to Stalinism.

Eisinger, Chester E. "Trilling and the Crisis in Our Culture." *University of Kansas City Review* 25.1 (1958): 27-35. Rpt. in revised form in *Fiction of the Forties*. Chester E. Eisinger. Chicago: U of Chicago P, 1963. 135-44.

Claims that in *The Middle of the Journey* four ideological positions may be distinguished: the Communist and the Christian are both embodied in Gifford Maxim; the fellow-traveler or leftist-liberal is represented by Arthur and Nancy Croom; and the new liberal appears as we finally understand John Laskell, the protagonist. Relates the philosophy of Trilling's "Manners, Morals, and the Novel" to the book. Articulates the essentially dialectical form of the novel, and concludes that Laskell's final position represents a midpoint between the leftist liberalism of the Crooms and the fanatic Christianity of Maxim. Discusses Trilling's critical perspectives at length, and examines the novel in this context.

Elledge, W. Paul. "The Profaning of Romanticism in Trilling's 'Of This Time, of That Place'." *Modern Fiction Studies* 29.2 (1983): 213-26.

Describes this work as one of architectonic elegance, with its shrewdly crafted network of thematically reinforcing symbols, wry wit, multi-layered ironies, stylistic grace, and haunting poignancy. Develops a close textual reading—a critique which illuminates the clash of romantic and classical values in the work which ultimately results in the profaning of romanticism.

Farrell, James T. "Literature and Morality." *Literature and Morality.* New York: Vanguard, 1947. 10-14. Originally published in *New International* 1945-46.

Provides a plot summary and discussion of "The Other Margaret."

Fergusson, Francis. "Three Novels." *Perspectives USA* 6 (1954): 30-44.

A general survey of *All The King's Men, Guard of Honor,* and *The Middle of the Journey,* lauding all three as having high intelligence and art, high moral seriousness, and representing the best novels published since WWII. Provides a detailed account of the contents of all three, and draws some casual comparisons.

Freedman, William. "*The Middle of the Journey*: Lionel Trilling and the Novel of Ideas." *The Forties: Fiction, Poetry, Drama.* Ed. Warren French. Deland: Everett/Edwards, 1969. 239-48.

Calls this Trilling's novel of the liberal crisis of re-orientation, a book that reads as if it had been serialized in *PMLA*. Comments that it is consciously intellectually impressive, full of acute understanding of middle-class manners and intricately structured flashbacks showing the consistent development of his hero, John Laskell. Explores the technique of the novel and the structure of its ideas in considerable depth.

Frohock, W. M. "Lionel Trilling and the American Reality." *Southwest Review* 45.3 (1960): 224-32.

In the context of discussing Trilling as a critic of American culture, Frohock sees *The Middle of the Journey* as dealing with the same matters as his criticism. Finds that while much of the novel is dated, Laskell's disorientation in Connecticut, where he is not in touch with the ways of the place, represents the plight of the intellectual in an anti-intellectual America who feels that his understanding of things is completely right, yet who does not understand that part of society outside his own experience.

Fuller, Roy. "Trilling at 70." *New Review* [London] Apr. 1975: 57-59.

Calls *The Middle of the Journey* a deeply intelligent and readable work. Suggests, however, that where it is vulnerable, is where the finally unadjudicated facts of history still cling to it. Claims that the historical in the novel seems pallid and a little contrived. Provides much detailed information on Chambers, the historical figure behind the central character.

George, Diana L. "Thematic Structure in Lionel Trilling's 'Of This Time, of That Place'." *Studies in Short Fiction* 13.1 (1976): 1-8.

Describes this as a story illuminating the sadness of passionate devotion to intellectual life by a person who is deranged. Claims that it was essentially to be the story of Tertan, the mad student, who gives the story its structure and thematic unity, not the story of the primary character whose story this becomes. Insists that it is Howe, narrator and professor, whose moral dilemma elevates the story to nearly tragic proportions.

Hagopian, John V. "A Reader's Moral Dissent from Lionel Trilling's 'Of This Time, of That Place.'" *American Literature in Belgium*. Eds. Gilbert Debusscher and Marc Maufort. Amsterdam: Rodopi, 1988. 227-38.

Objects to "Of This Time, of That Place," because rhetorically it subjects the reader to a form of ideological manipulation, which Hagopian finds oppressive. Details the story and then focuses on the narrator's position on all the crucial issues. Discusses mostly the issue of intentionality in the story and of who is speaking to what kind of implied reader.

Hagopian, John V. "The Technique and Meaning of Lionel Trilling's 'The Other Margaret'." *Etudes Anglaises* 16.3 (1963): 225-29. Rpt. in revised form as "Moral Realism." *Hibbert Journal* 63.2 (1965): 77-79.

Argues that the effect and substance of this short story is consistent with Trilling's philosophy of literature—to immerse the reader unremittingly in moral life and invite him to put his own motives under examination. Claims that in this story we see a man who, as a result of his contemplation of a work of art, is provoked into a ruthless examination of his own moral life and a rejection of the false values of his liberal education.

Hatfield, Henry. "The Journey and the Mountain." *Modern Language Notes* 90.3 (1975): 363-70.

This study concerns itself with comparisons and contrasts which both join and separate Thomas Mann's *The Magic Mountain* and Trilling's *The Middle of the Journey*. Points of comparison cited include setting, circumstances, disease, bourgeois status, training, and the character types of the two protagonists. Regards both books to be important political novels.

Howe, Irving. "On The Middle of the Journey." *New York Times Book Review* 22 Aug. 1976: 31.

Sees *The Middle of the Journey* as a rarity for its concentration on politics and their moral consequences. Claims that, though Trilling is a masterful critic, he has not yet mastered style in the novel. Sees Maxim as a brilliantly alive achievement among the other flatter characters. Concludes that the authorial voice is insufficiently novelistic.

Keech, James M. "Trilling's 'Of This Time, of That Place.'" *Explicator* Apr. 1965: 66.

A brief note identifying Wordsworth's *The Prelude* as the source for the title "Of This Time, of That Place." Concludes that Trilling must have intended a comparison between the character of Tertan and that of Wordsworth.

Kendle, Burton S. "Trilling's 'Of this Time, of That Place.'" *Explicator* Apr. 1964: 61.

Traces the many references to "The Ancient Mariner" and "Kubla Khan" in the story as the key to explicating the story's meaning.

Kubal, David. "Lionel Trilling: The Mind and Its Discontents." *Hudson Review* 31.2 (1978): 279-95.

Discusses the evolution of Trilling's ideas, particularly his feeling by the sixties that Modernism had lost the tension between the concept of individual will as opposed to that of necessary limit. Discusses Trilling's uneasiness about Modernism's demonstrated "tendency to nihilism" in *The Middle of the Journey*, particularly in the character of Maxim, who recognizes only the world's false image of strife without the true image of reconciliation, and who denies the virtues of human existence.

Kubal, David L. "Trilling's *The Middle of the Journey*: An American Dialectic." *Bucknell Review* 14.1 (1966): 60-73.

Argues that *The Middle of the Journey* dramatizes the author's principal critical ideas. Suggests that one can think of the novel as one more attempt on Trilling's part to clarify his thinking about the liberal imagination in society, certainly the underlying concern of all his prose. Suggests that, even in the longer books, those on Matthew Arnold and E. M. Forster, he focuses on the author's development in relation to the liberal tradition. Concludes also that in his short stories and essays, Trilling is intent on working out the inadequacies and assets of the liberal mentality.

McAfee. Tom. "A Note on 'The Other Margaret.'" *Western Review* 14.2 (1950): 143-44.

Calls "The Other Margaret" a story of realizations paralleling the author's own. Sees it as a Gerard Manley Hopkins story about growing older and growing more responsible.

Milne, Gordon. "The Doctrinal Barrage (1920-1964)." *The American Political Novel.* Gordon Milne. Norman: U of Oklahoma P, 1966. 127-52.

Calls *The Middle of the Journey* a convincing statement of the interplay between human experience and political idea in which Trilling enumerates the several approaches to liberalism made by a characteristic group of troubled intellectuals, all, in theory, wanting to improve the lot of those living in the confused thirties, but all offering different and conflicting ways to affect improvement.

Montgomery, Marion. "Lionel Trilling's *The Middle of the Journey*: A Good Book Gone Wrong." *Discourse: A Review of the Liberal Arts* 4.4 (1961): 263-72.

Claims that this book asks to what extent the individual must commit himself, body and soul, to humanity. Suggests that it is answered through the character of John Laskell and his antagonist, Gifford Maxim, a journey bracketed by an emotional climax in which Laskell is confronted by the necessity, the journey, and an intellectual climax in which he is perplexed by two branches of the road, those followed by Maxim on the one hand and the Crooms on the other. Yet, notes that the book is marred by a failure to handle adequately the external world of the novel and to adequately master dialogue, style, realism, and tone.

Prigozy, Ruth. "The Liberal Novelist in the McCarthy Era." *Twentieth Century Literature* 21.3 (1975): 253-64. A longer version of a paper presented at the December 1974 Modern Language Association meeting.

Begins with a definition of the political novel, and then proceeds to discuss *The Middle of the Journey*, along with several other novels, as dealing with the McCarthy period and delineating the dilemma of the liberal living in a nation which has lost faith in democracy. Claims that this novel studies the liberal's response to McCarthyism in which he fails, and illuminates the aesthetic, social and moral conflicts that arose in the post-WW II years.

Robinson, Jeffrey Cane. "Lionel Trilling and the Romantic Tradition." *Massachusetts Review* 20.2 (1979): 211-36.

Primarily a discussion of Trilling's "romantic aesthetics" as demonstrated in his interpretation of the Romantic period. Also discusses "Of This Time, of That Place" as a demonstration that identity is never simple and pure but rather, through the inevitable confrontation of self with intractable reality, becomes complex and shifting.

Scott, Nathan A., Jr. "Lionel Trilling's Anxious Humanism—The Search for Authenticity." *Three American Moralists: Mailer, Bellow, Trilling*. Nathan A. Scott, Jr. Notre Dame: U of Notre Dame P, 1973. 153-216.

A complete treatment of Trilling's *The Middle of the Journey*, placing it in the social context of Trilling's times. Argues that Trilling belongs with the long line of moralists and sermonizers who inhabit American literature.

Shoda, Wakiko. *"The Middle of the Journey:* A Commentary." *American Literature in the 1940s. Annual Report, Tokyo Chapter, American Lit. Soc. of Japan, 1975* (1976): 6-12.

Calls this a brilliant and absorbing novel in which we watch the process through which the protagonist discovers the errors and the limitations of both radicals and liberals and finds a new position. Concludes that the value and charm of the novel lies in the subtle, dramatic, even thrilling way in which the author develops it.

Stanton, Robert. "Reading 'The Other Margaret.'" *The Short Story and the Reader*. Ed. Robert Stanton. New York: Holt, 1960. 256-65.

Discusses theme, characterization, style, and point of view in the short story. Offers a new critical interpretation of the story, and concludes that it concerns the problem of human responsibility, not as an abstract idea, but as the complex experience of an intelligent, sensitive man. Identifies the focal point of the story as the conflict between wisdom and grief.

Tanner, Tony. "Lionel Trilling's Uncertainties." *Encounter* Aug. 1966: 72-77.

Sees in *The Middle of the Journey* a conflict between two systematic certainties: one, that all men are fully responsible and thus all are equally guilty (as Maxim insists); the other, that man cannot be blamed or held answerable since it is environment that is at fault (the position of the Crooms). Suggests that Laskell, going beyond ideology, adopts a position of honest uncertainty. Says Laskell's stance suggests the supple, probing, and unpolemical mind that Trilling brings to criticism.

Discusses Trilling's critical works to demonstrate that the most recurrent issue in his essays is really the question of the relationship between the self and the society around it.

Trilling, Lionel. "'Of This Time, of That Place.'" *The Experience of Literature.* Lionel Trilling. New York: Holt, 1967. 781-84; Rpt. in *Prefaces to the Experience of Literature.* Lionel Trilling. New York: Harcourt, 1979. 160-65.

Trilling's own introduction to and interpretation of his short story. Covers the origins, ideas, feelings, and strategies that went into the making of the story as well as the piece itself.

Wald, Alan. "The Politics of Culture: The New York Intellectuals in Fiction." *Centennial Review* 29.3 (1985): 353-69.

Discusses *The Middle of the Journey* and several of Trilling's short stories, along with the works of several other writers, to show that much of the imaginative writing of members of the New York intellectuals is unambiguously political in its intent. Notes that in the 1975 Introduction to the reissue of his novel, Trilling states, "From my first conception of it, my story was committed to history—it was to draw out some of the moral and intellectual implications of the powerful attraction to Communism felt by a considerable part of the American intellectual class during the thirties and forties."

Waldhorn, Arthur and Hilda Waldhorn. "'Of This Time, of That Place': More About this Story." *The Rite of Becoming: Stories and Studies of Adolescence.* Eds. Arthur Waldhorn and Hilda Waldhorn. New York: World, 1966. 270-72.

Provides a detailed analysis of the character of Howe as poet, compassionate teacher, and man of goodwill confronted by a student whose disconcerting presence threatens to upset the tidy balance of the professor's life.

Warshow, Robert S. "The Legacy of the 30's." *The Immediate Experience: Movies, Comics, Theatre, & Other Aspects of Popular Culture.* Robert S. Warshow. Garden City: Doubleday, 1962. 33-48.

Describes *The Middle of the Journey* as an explicit attempt to deal with the problem of Stalinism. Considers it less successful as art even though it is a profound expose of the problem of the American intellectual and the Communist liberal tradition of the thirties. Concludes that unfortunately, the Stalinism described in this novel was only a middle-class phenomenon because ultimately Trilling lacks Forster's detachment or Olympian disinterestedness.

Yudkin, Leon I. "From the Periphery to the Centre in America." *Jewish Writing and Identity in the Twentieth Century*. Leon I. Yudkin. London: Helm, 1982. 112-28.

Shows how the immigrant Jews have moved from the periphery of American life to its center, and discusses the works of several major novelists—Trilling, Bellow, Malamud, Mailer, Potok—as demonstrations of that movement. Sees Trilling's *The Middle of the Journey* as reflecting liberal ideas and abounding in moral commentary, but ultimately lacking in sufficient concreteness.

Reviews

Atlas, James. Rev. of *Of This Time, of That Place and Other Stories*. *New York Times* 9 July 1979: C15. Rpt. in *Books of the Times*. Vol. 2. New York: Times, 1979. 324-25.

Suggests that *Of This Time, of That Place* contains stories which are many hued but identical in their design. Claims that here Trilling's ideas are presented in a more formal manner and imbued with the quick-eyed life of fiction. Details the plots and characters of individual stories. Concludes that though they may lack art, they have a feeling of stamina, prose, and illumination.

Bayley, John. "Middle-Class Futures." Rev. of *The Middle of the Journey*. *Times Literary Supplement* 11 Apr. 1975: 399.

Calls *The Middle of the Journey* a true novel of ideas, compact, slightly enigmatic, and ideally powerful. Provides a very detailed account of the plot, characters, and politics of the novel.

Bayley, John. "The Way Towards Sanity." Rev. of *Lionel Trilling* by Robert Boyers. *Times Literary Supplement* 30 Dec. 1977: 1518.

Review of a book about Trilling that provides some useful historical and cultural context within which to view Trilling and *The Middle of the Journey*. Discusses several of his works, as well as general commentary on Trilling's life and work.

Belkind, Allen. "English Fiction." Rev. of *Of This Time, of That Place and Other Stories*. *World Literature Today* 55.1 (1981): 103-04.

Describes the stories in this collection as well as *The Middle of the Journey* published earlier. Claims that Trilling appears here as an impeccable stylist, somewhat mannered in the Jamesian sense, but with a moral sensibility sharply critical of stereotyped attitudes.

Caute, David. "Summer People." Rev. of *The Middle of the Journey*. *New Statesman* 11 Apr. 1975: 486.

Describes *The Middle of the Journey* in terms of its contents and characters. Provides a description of Trilling's critique of liberalism in the book. Sees the book partly as a *roman a clef.*

Cheney, Brainard. "Tenuous Moral Vision." Rev. of *The Middle of the Journey*. *Sewanee Review* 56.1 (1948): 152-55.

Describes the background to the novel, and gives a detailed account of its political vision, characters, settings, and outcome.

Cordell, Richard A. "Clash of Ideas." Rev. of *The Middle of the Journey*. *Saturday Review of Literature* 11 Oct. 1947: 25.

Calls *Middle of the Journey* an artistically conceived novel of ideas. Details the contents of the novel, and concludes that Lionel Trilling has chosen to write about a man whose dilemma is intellectual as well as emotional, and has done so with acumen and compassionate understanding.

Cox, C. B. "Trilling's Journey." Rev. of *Beyond Culture*. *Spectator* 15 Apr. 1966: 470-71.

This review of a collection of essays comments on Trilling's political climate, background, and the contents of *The Middle of the Journey*.

Flint, R. W. "From Vertigo to Tears: The Via Media in America." Rev. of *The Middle of the Journey*. *New Leader* 25 Oct. 1947: 10.

Calls *The Middle of the Journey* a remarkable first novel of the old-fashioned sort which addresses the alienation of the intelligentsia from the liberal tradition. Details politics, background, milieu, characters, plot, and ideas.

Furbank, P. N. "The Gravities of Grown-upness." Rev. of *Of This Time, of That Place and Other Stories*. *Times Literary Supplement* 21 Aug 1981: 951.

Comments on Trilling's *Of This Time, of That Place* that the stories are occasionally too literary, full of the stuff of ethical dilemmas, and indicative of Trilling's liberal humanism. Concludes that there is a place for intellectual debate in novels and plays, but, except for the purpose of irony, not in realistic ones.

Granetz, Marc. Rev. of *Of This Time, of That Place and Other Stories.* *New Republic* 7 & 14 July 1979: 36-38.

Describes the contents of the volume, the publishing history of each of the stories, and a brief synopsis of Trilling's life and career. Provides glimpses of the contents of a few of the stories. Concludes that what is unique about the collection is that it shows us Trilling the man before he became the eminent critic.

Halio, Jay L. "Reviews." Rev. of *Of This Time, of That Place and Other Stories. Studies in Short Fiction* 17.3 (1980): 354-55.

Observes that early in his career, Trilling thought of himself as a novelist and a writer of fiction. Comments that the stories in this collection all have a college setting and reflect the sensibility as well as the sensitivity to moral issues that characterize his major critical achievements. Concludes with a regret that he did not write any more fiction after his only novel.

Lainoff, Seymour. "Trilling's Jewish Persona." Rev. of *Of This Time, of That Place and Other Stories. Midstream* Dec. 1981: 54-56.

Describes Trilling's aloofness towards things Jewish and his own Jewishness, and then claims that *Of This Time, of That Place* reflects Trilling's preoccupation with Jewish identity. Examines "Impediments" in particular from this perspective. Then proceeds to examine several stories written in later life.

Lalley, J. M. "Two Journeys and a Pastoral." Rev. of *The Middle of the Journey. New Yorker* 25 Oct. 1947: 114, 116.

Suggests that this novel seems topical rather than aesthetic. Describes it in considerable detail, and complains that in three quarters of the novel there is no action, only long ideological conversations and philosophical analyses of political attitudes.

Mayberry, George. Rev. of *The Middle of the Journey. New Republic* 13 Oct. 1947: 29.

Considers the novel disappointing, not because it lacks distinction in the writing or that Trilling is not in charge of his subject, but that this is just another novel attempting to explore the sufferings of the contemporary intellectual. Complains that the characters are familiar to anyone and the influence of Forster and James is all too evident. Concludes, however, that it is a considerable cut above what passes for literature these days.

Morris, Lloyd. "Ideas and Intellectuals in Close Conflict." Rev. of *The Middle of the Journey. New York Herald Tribune Weekly Book Review* 12 Oct. 1947: 4.

Describes this novel as being about the plight of liberal and humanistic culture in America in a world increasingly given over to authoritarian societies and deterministic philosophies. Claims that its strongest effects lie in what is implied and suggested, rather than in what is directly represented. Concludes that it is sensitively written and loaded with implications of a larger significance than that actually expressed.

R. "Column." Rev. of *The Middle of the Journey. Encounter* June 1975: 34-36.

Describes *The Middle of the Journey* as a book which helped destroy some of the illusions by which Western intellectuals were infected before and after WW II. Claims that its purpose was to draw out some of the moral and intellectual implications of the powerful attractions to Communism felt by a considerable part of the American intellectual class before the 1940s. Commends the book for its literary merits, and describes its very different reception in England and the United States.

Rago, Henry. "Books of the Week." Rev. of *The Middle of the Journey. Commonweal* 14 Nov. 1947: 121-22.

Comments that *The Middle of the Journey* is a novel about ideas, and about the sufferings of the unsatisfied human being between and beneath those ideas. Concludes that this novel will make more demands on the reader than the popular novel.

Samet, Tom. "Reconsideration." Rev. of *The Middle of the Journey. New Republic* 23 Apr. 1977: 29-30.

Recounts the contents and politics of the novel. Claims that it is a story of recovery, renewal, resolution, and independence. Suggests that its strength lies in its refusal to acquiesce and in its assumption of moral responsibility. Concludes that it offers testimony to the rare and necessary virtues of the liberal imagination.

Schorer, Mark. "The Vexing Problem of Orientation." Rev. of *The Middle of the Journey*. *New York Times Book Review* 12 Oct. 1947: 4, 40.

Calls *The Middle of the Journey* literate, intelligent, lucid, and graceful. Identifies its subject as the problem of personal relations in the midst of the nonpersonal society. Suggests that while the novel is overschematized and directed to a notoriously thin-skinned audience, it is nevertheless occasionally blurred.

"Soul-Searcher." Rev. of *The Middle of the Journey*. *Time* 20 Oct. 1947: 106, 109.

Briefly reviews the plot, and notes both Trilling's clear grey style and his mishandling of the Dostoevskian character, Maxim. Feels the novel is good and honest, deals authentically with the period, and concludes that while Trilling is not yet a finished novelist, he writes beautifully about children and sometimes with gently dazzling insight about their elders.

Symons, Julian. "Liberalism and the Gods That Failed." Rev. of *The Middle of the Journey*. *Sunday Times* 9 Aug. 1981: 34.

Writes generally about Trilling's life and politics, with a brief pause to discuss the plot and characters of *The Middle of the Journey*. Characterizes Trilling as a man of common sense and rare moral concern.

Trilling, Lionel. "Whittaker Chambers and *The Middle of the Journey*." *New York Review of Books* 17 Apr. 1975: 18-24.

This important essay documents the historical roots of *The Middle of the Journey* at the time the reissue of the novel was about to occur in England. Responding to questions about what relation the novel bears to historical actuality after the book's initial appearance, Trilling has written this lengthy essay on the nature of his association with Whittaker Chambers.

Zabel, Morton Dauwen. "The Straight Way Lost." Rev. of *The Middle of the Journey*. *Nation* 18 Oct. 1947: 413-16. Rpt. in *Craft and Character: Text, Method, and Vocation in Modern Fiction*. Morton Dauwen Zabel. New York: Viking, 1957. 312-17.

Provides a detailed summary of the contents of the novel, and claims that it is keenly sustained and subtly arranged. Sees it as a novel of remarkable, almost unflinching austerity, where humor, incident, detail, byplay, and color are all pared to the quick. Concludes that it represents a new mode in fiction, one whose claim on the imaginative resources and personal responsibility of his generation the human faith evident in his pages demonstrates.

Biographical Sources

Trilling, Diana. "Lionel Trilling: A Jew at Columbia." *Commentary* Mar. 1979: 40-46. Rpt. in *Speaking of Literature and Society. The Works of Lionel Trilling*. Ed. Diana Trilling. Uniform ed. New York: Harcourt, 1980. 411-29.

Describes in detail Trilling's difficulty in becoming a professor of English at Columbia as well as the anti-Semitism that existed in academic departments of many universities. Also describes his upbringing and relations with his family.

Trilling, Lionel. "Under Forty: A Symposium on American Literature and the Younger Generation of American Jews." *Contemporary Jewish Record* Feb. 1944: 15-17.

In response to an invitation to discuss the relationship of his Jewish heritage to his writing, Trilling discusses his upbringing, his awareness of his Jewishness, his views on contemporary Jewish religion, Jewish cultural movements, the neurotic basis of Jewish assimilation, and his belief that the contemporry Jewish community can give no sustenance to a writer born a Jew.

Whitfield, Stephen J. "Lionel Trilling." *Twentieth-Century American-Jewish Fiction Writers*. Ed. Daniel Walden. Detroit: Gale, 1984. Vol. 28 of *Dictionary of Literary Biography*. 94 vols. to date. 1978- . 305-09.

More than details of his life, this is a career biography, tracing the development of the author's canon, describing the contents and themes of his works, evaluating his reputation, and placing him in the larger context of American literary history. Includes lists of primary and secondary sources and illustrations.

Bibliographies

Barnaby, Marianne Gilbert. "Lionel Trilling: A Bibliography, 1926-1972." *Bulletin of Bibliography and Magazine Notes* 31.1 (1974): 37-44.

A chronological listing of works by and about Trilling.

Robinson, Jeffrey. "Lionel Trilling: a Bibliographic Essay." *Resources for American Literary Study* 8.2 (1978): 131-56.

A review of the research and criticism on Trilling, including a list of primary sources.

Dissertations

Alspaugh, Elizabeth Norton. "The Formation of Lionel Trilling's Moral Dialectic: A Study of His Fiction and Criticism, 1939-1955." Diss. U of Maryland, 1979.

Grumet, Elinor Joan. "The Menorah Idea and the Apprenticeship of Lionel Trilling." Diss. U of Iowa, 1979.

Samet, Thomas Harold. "The Problematic Self: Lionel Trilling and the Anxieties of the Modern." Diss. Brown U, 1980.

Tsai, Yuan-Huang. "Men of Words and Ideas: Intellectuals in the Post-World War II American Novel." Diss. State U of New York at Binghamton, 1981.

Leon Uris

1924 –

Primary Sources

Novels

The Angry Hills. New York: Random, 1955; New York: Signet-NAL, 1955; London: Wingate, 1956; London: Hamilton, 1958; London: Corgi-Transworld, 1964, 1966; New York: Bantam, 1972; London: White Lion, 1973; London: Corgi, 1987.

Armageddon: A Novel of Berlin. Garden City: Doubleday, 1964; Toronto: Doubleday, 1964; London: Kimber, 1964; New York: Dell, 1965, 1985; London: Corgi, 1966, 1987.

Battle Cry. New York: Putnam, 1953; London: Wingate, 1953, 1955; New York: Bantam, 1954; London: Hamilton, 1958; London: Granada, 1985; London: Panther, 1987.

Exodus. Garden City: Doubleday, 1958, 1962; New York: Bantam, 1959, 1969, 1975, 1981, 1983; Toronto: Doubleday, 1959; London: Wingate, 1959; London: Kimber, 1959, 1968; London: Transworld, 1961; Franklin Center: Franklin, 1977; London: Corgi, 1987.

The Haj. Garden City: Doubleday, 1984; London: Deutsch, 1984, 1987; Large Print ed. Boston: Hall, 1985; Toronto: Bantam, 1985; London: Corgi, 1985, 1987; Large Print ed. Bath: Chivers, 1985.

Mila 18. Garden City: Doubleday, 1961; London: Heinemann, 1961, 1972; London: Transworld, 1965; New York: Bantam, 1970, 1981, 1983; London: Corgi, 1987.

Mitla Pass. New York: Doubleday, 1988; New York: Bantam, 1989; Large Print ed. Boston: Hall, 1990.

QB VII. Garden City: Doubleday, 1970; London: Kimber, 1971, 1987; New York: Bantam, 1972, 1980; London: Corgi, 1972, 1987; London: Transworld, 1972.

Topaz. New York: McGraw, 1967; Toronto: Bantam, 1968; London: Kimber, 1968, 1987; London: Corgi, 1969, 1987.

Trinity. Garden City: Doubleday, 1976; Franklin Center: Franklin, 1976; London: Deutsch, 1976; New York: Bantam, 1977, 1983; London: Transworld, 1977; London: Corgi, 1977, 1987.

Secondary Sources

Articles and Chapters

Darby, William. "'I Can't Leave My Outfit.'" *Necessary American Fictions: Popular Literature of the 1950s.* William Darby. Bowling Green: Bowling Green State U Popular P, 1987. 35-43.

Discusses *Battle Cry* along with several other novels as books which see the conflict of WWII as a necessary struggle against a discernible evil. Shows how *Battle Cry* uses all the cliches and dialogue one finds in WWII propaganda films. Judges Uris's marine corps, its veterans, its recruits, their love affairs, and social values to be taken from Hollywood.

Darby, William. "'The On-Going Thing That She Had Started. . . Was Now More Powerful Than She.'" *Necessary American Fictions: Popular Literature of the 1950s.* William Darby. Bowling Green: Bowling Green State U Popular P, 1987. 93-100.

Argues that in *Exodus,* Uris explores the idea that the individual derives meaning and identity primarily from his social setting, which in turn, is an amalgam of historical experiences grounded in religion and geography. Considers it a novel celebrating the tendency of popular writers in the 1950s to turn out epic tomes. Provides a thorough analysis of Uris's melodramatizing methods that threaten to wash away his idealistic themes, reducing his Arabians to cowardly ignoramuses and his Jews to ultimate heroes.

Downey, Sharon D., and Richard A. Kallan. "Semi-Aesthetic Detachment: The Fusing of Fictional and External Worlds in the Situational Literature of Leon Uris." *Communication Monographs* 49.3 (1982): 192-204.

Argues that the writing of Leon Uris represents a rhetorical/literary form wherein the contractual agreement binding writer and reader differs significantly from traditional literature. Shows how Uris's readers are required to assume a posture of semi-aesthetic detachment: they must weave between the fictional and external worlds Uris simultaneously presents. Concludes that only by integrating both worlds can readers serve Uris's ultimate purpose: insuring Israel's sovereignty.

Hall, Wayne. "*Trinity*: The Formulas of History." *Eire—Ireland* 13.4 (1978): 137-44.

Discusses the reception of *Trinity* in Ireland and the United States. Comments on his treatment of history as something which, having no past and future, simply repeats itself. Criticizes his use of fictional detail, the mechanical use of documentation, the stock characters, and his treatment of history.

Kuropatwa, Joy. "Leon Uris." *Beacham's Popular Fiction of America.* Ed. Walter Beacham. Washington: Beacham, 1986. 4: 1395-1402.

Contains the publishing history, critical reception, and analysis of *Exodus, The Haj,* and other titles.

McDowell, Edwin. "'Exodus' in Samizdat Still Popular and Subversive." *New York Times Book Review* 26 Apr. 1987: 13.

Describes Russian imprisonment of Jews for possessing *Exodus,* which has been banned for its subversiveness, its popularity in the U.S., and its impact on Russian Jews, who have found in it their first knowledge of Jewish efforts to create a national homeland and a sense of hope and pride in their Jewish tradition. Describes the methods by which the banned book was translated and circulated among the Russian Jews.

Munro, David A. "A Case ?—for 'Semi-Fiction'." *Trace* 48.2 (1963): 17-19.

Discusses *Exodus* as an historical novel masquerading as semi-fiction, propaganda, expose, and political commentary.

Roth, Philip. "The New Jewish Stereotypes." *Response* 5.2 (1971): 88-94. Rpt. from *American Judaism* (Wint. 1961).

Comments on *Exodus* as authorizing a new Jewish stereotype, the patriot-warrior-freedom fighter, a hero much more satisfying to the American public. Argues vociferously that this is a blatantly stupid reading of the Jew in history. Offers a lengthy essay on the historical remaking of the Jewish image.

Salt, Jeremy. "Fact and Fiction in the Middle Eastern Novels of Leon Uris." *Journal of Palestine Studies* 14.3 (1985): 54-63.

Comments on *Exodus* and *The Haj* from the perspective of whether they are good or bad history. Recounts descriptions of the cultures by nineteenth-century travelers to the Middle East, and then sets about systematically criticizing Uris's pictures of dirtiness, poverty, homosexuality, rape, violence, sexuality, hashish smoking, and promiscuity in Arab women. Objects vehemently to Uris' depictions of Palestinian self-destructiveness and self-annihilation, as well as his profoundly racist tendencies.

Uris, Leon. "About *Exodus*." *The Quest for Truth*. M. T. Boaz. New York: Scarecrow, 1961. 123-30.

Justifies his particular approach to historical writing and research. Condemns much current American fiction as an author's self-analysis palmed off as fiction. Contains much biographical information.

Reviews

Abrams, Garry. "Looking at *Exodus* Through Arab Eyes." Rev. of *The Haj*. *Los Angeles Times Book Review* 27 May 1984: 8.

Calls *The Haj* so unremittingly anti-Arab it causes one to wonder. Suggests that it gives evidence of scarcely being transposed from the notecards because the major characters are undeveloped and serve only as automatons for a morality play. Concludes that the lesson of this novel is that there are no limits to the Middle-East disaster.

Adams, Phoebe. "Warsaw Ghetto." Rev. of *Mila 18*. *Atlantic* Aug. 1961: 94.

Calls this novel five hundred pages of melodramatic hoopla about a small group of beleaguered ghetto fighters whose characters are celluloid, stringy and confused. Complains about the confusing geography, the dialogue, the interminable exchange of passwords, and the 1960s American prattle. Hopes that Uris's travesty of the achievements of these brave men and women will be quickly forgotten by the reading public.

Adler, Jerry. "Unchosen People." Rev. of *The Haj. Newsweek* 21 May 1984: 84.

Calls *The Haj* a five hundred page extended study in treachery, bigotry, obsequiousness, ignorance, and sheer malevolence among the Arabs. Suggests that Uris really believes all these vices come naturally to the Arabs and his story. Concludes that Uris is so totally out of sympathy with his Arabs that he scarcely troubles to put himself in their minds; hence, there is not a single convincing note in this vast symphony of sound.

"Appeal to Conscience." Rev. of *Mila 18. Times Literary Supplement* 27 Oct. 1961: 777.

Asserts that *Mila 18* is too long, too strained in style, and too documentary to be a good novel. Concludes that more discipline and economy were needed, though it is still a valuable historical document.

Arimond, Carroll. Rev. of *Mila 18. Extension* [Chicago] Sept. 1961: 15.

Describes *Mila 18* as fluent, virile, emotional, and too long. Asserts that it is frequently repetitive and sometimes poorly researched. Concludes that it finally becomes difficult for the detached reader to understand how these people can demonstrate such fatal devotion to lofty ideals while committing adultery and therefore transgressing the behavioral code of their faith.

"Back to *The Wall*." Rev. of *Mila 18. Time* 2 June 1961: 94.

Suggests that *Mila 18* reads like a Jewish Western where all the good guys are Zionist, and the bad guys are British and Arabs. Deplores the vicious stereotypes of the Arabs and Germans, the woes of sensuality instead of comic relief, and the celluloid cliches in each scene.

Barrett, William. "Big Canvas and Small." Rev. of *Armageddon. Atlantic* July 1964: 135-36.

Argues that *Armageddon* is not serious literature but journalism, entirely straightforward and unadorned. Notes that the characters are flat and one dimensional, as if already fabricated for Hollywood. Details the contents, and concludes that the story has the dimensions of a soap opera.

"Bestseller Revisited." Rev. of *Exodus*. *Time* 8 Dec. 1958: 110.

Calls this a sprawling novel with battle scenes that are clear and well done. Objects to the flag-waving Zionism of the book and the stereotypes of the Arabs, picturing them as witless dupes or the dregs of humanity. Concludes that even though this is the story of how the Jews won their homeland, the tepid love story of Kitty and Ari can be skipped.

Blocker, Joel. "Fantasy of Israel." Rev. of *Exodus*. *Commentary* June 1959: 539-41.

Describes *Exodus* as a sketch for a scenario rather than a book. Details the book as prose accretions, sentimentalized Jewish history, large doses of Zionist publicity, pamphlets ground down to fine pap, and cinematic possibilities. Mostly berates the book for its several gross distortions and details several of them.

Boland, Eavan. Rev. of *Trinity*. *Critic* 35.2 (1976): 82-84.

Laments the kind of research done on Ireland by Uris during preparation of this novel. Argues that the simplifications are chilling, the hero utterly implausible, the stock female characters appalling, and the accuracy and profusion of sheer detail amazing. Calls this a painstakingly-researched book, but complains that, for all its detail, it is not an enlightening book about Ireland, taking its force from only an approximation of a popular picture of Ireland.

Boroff, David. "Leon Uris as Novelist." Rev. of *Mila 18*. *Congress Bi-Weekly* 25 Dec. 1961: 21-22.

Provides a stinging denunciation of *Mila 18* as a piece of literary hucksterism, and belletristic trifling, with a coarsely pragmatic view, falsely reverberant prose, sentimentality, melodramatic instead of tragic.

Broyard, Anatole. "Books of the Times." Rev. of *The Haj*. *New York Times* 27 Apr. 1984: C25.

Asserts that in *The Haj* Uris makes no pretense at impartiality. Argues that we get sex, violence, panoramas, colorful details—but no perspective. Judges that Uris is not a natural storyteller, so whatever truth there may be in *The Haj* is lost in hyperbole and fails even at the level of propaganda.

Carmichael, Joel. "The Phenomenal Leon Uris." Rev. of *Mila 18*. *Midstream* 7.4 (1961): 86-90.

Expresses radical mistrust at the popularity that Uris's two books, *Exodus* and *Mila 18* have engendered, since both are repellent as prose and absurd as history. Produces a general essay on the events these novels chronicle, and the phenomena of Uris' immense popularity rather than a critical essay on the novels.

Christison, Kathleen. "The Arab in Recent Popular Fiction." Rev. of *The Haj. Middle East Journal* 41.3 (1987): 401-02.

Calls *The Haj* a book which runs through all the stereotypes among Arabs and Jews and glibly assigns poverty, lack of incentive, ignorance, violence, sexual deviance, and rape to the Arabs, while assigning noble qualities to the Jews. Concludes that this is a vile piece of anti-Arab propaganda masquerading as an attempt to understand them.

Coleman, John. "Proper Study." Rev. of *Exodus. Spectator* 10 July 1959: 44.

Describes *Exodus* as evidence of the booming of pseudo-science. Hates the black and white simplicity of the stories, and discounts the actual research behind the novel. Concludes that Uris has incredibly devalued such heroic material.

"Commercial—Just Barely." Rev. of *Topaz. Time* 29 Sept. 1967: 112.

Calls *Topaz* a contemporary spy thriller with wooden characters and unbelievable subplots. Concludes that with Uris's lack of talent with language, he should think twice about trying to put words into the mouth of Charles DeGaulle.

Connolly, Brendan. "Too Simple a View." Rev. of *Mila 18. America* 8 July 1961: 511.

Suggests that *Mila 18* is a blanket condemnation of nearly every group it deals with except the more devoted Zionist Jews. The history is of dubious quality, and the political views are monocular. Concludes that Uris needs to become less narrow and naive, at which point he may write a novel worthy of the story of the birth of Israel.

Cooney, Thomas E. "Love and Derring-Do in Greece." Rev. of *The Angry Hills. Saturday Review* 19 Nov. 1955: 46-47.

Describes the story of *The Angry Hills*, and then complains that the book relies too heavily on colorful action. Concludes, however, that it does contain a lyrically appreciative picture of remote, pastoral Greece conveyed with love and warmth.

Decter, Midge. "Popular Jews." Rev. of *Mila 18*. *Commentary* Oct.
1961: 358, 360; Rpt. in *The Liberated Woman and Other Americans*.
Midge Decter. New York: Coward, 1971. 177-20.

Comments that Uris has become not only a gifted writer of hardcore
trash, but a master chronicler and ambassador of Jewish aspiration to
both Jew and gentile. Predicts *Mila 18* will not enjoy the success of
Exodus, but that such a novel about Jewish fighters will be infinitely
palatable compared to one about analysis-ridden, Jewish couch riders.

Dempsey, David. "Unwitting Go-Between." Rev. of *The Angry Hills*.
New York Times Book Review 16 Oct. 1955: 32-33.

Describes *The Angry Hills* as a disappointment after *Battle Cry* because
this plot has all the limitations of an espionage novel. Details the story
and the characters.

Duffy, Martha. "Bestseller Revisited." Rev. of *QB VII*. *Time* 28 June
1971: 80.

Suggests that, for a Jew, *QB VII* is probably a gratuitous endurance test,
written in illiterate shorthand, and peopled by pasteboard characters.
Complains, furthermore, that it is full of sado-masochism and feckless
central characters.

"Fact Lift." Rev. of *Armageddon*. *Times Literary Supplement* 1 Oct.
1964: 903.

Delcares, that, in *Armageddon*, Uris has done the trick again: the head-
line history of the air lift is faithfully recorded, fact and fiction are
carefully balanced, and sex, pretty and ugly, is not overgenerously
rationed. Notes that Uris has difficulty only with the moral, and is a bit
short on optimism. Comments that all the characters are racial or national
stereotypes, and honesty gets lost. Concludes that: "if the blockade was
the last great battle before the German day of judgment, [readers] must
remain oblivious of what it was all about."

Farerty, Frederick E. "Turbulent Times, 16 Centuries Apart." Rev. of
Armageddon. *Chicago Sunday Tribune Magazine of Books* 7 June
1964: 5.

Asserts that *Armageddon* is not a great novel, but is instead an excellent
tract with no distinction of style, characterization, or storytelling. Judges
it to be a loose joining of several units and strictly one dimensional.
Paradoxically recommends the novel as non-fiction for those who want

to relive the good old days of Berlin's last stand when good and evil powers contended for mastery.

Farrell, Paul V. "U. S. Marines." Rev. of *Battle Cry*. *Commonweal* 8 May 1953: 128.

Describes the novel as a walloping five-hundred page book that reads at times as if Mickey Spillane and James Jones had collaborated to write *The Rover Boys*. Comments that Uris's best work is straight reporting as he skims the complex processes of characterization in favor of straight action. Concludes that *Battle Cry* is a corny but exhilarating yarn.

Feld, Rose. "Once More the Tragedy of Warsaw." Rev. of *Mila 18*. *New York Herald Tribune Lively Arts and Book Review* 4 June 1961: 28.

Notes that *Mila 18* is tightly packed with people, action, emotion, and tragedy, and unfortunately, unpolished prose. Wonders why Uris retold a story already so brilliantly told by Hersey.

"Fiction." Rev. of *The Haj*. *Kirkus Review* 1 Feb. 1984: 113.

Calls *The Haj* a cruel propaganda novel which blames 100% of the wrongs on the Arabs and the British. Comments that similar pictures about blacks would be unpublishable with their equation of violence and sexuality. Complains that there is no real characterization, the narration is rudimentary, the dialogue amateurish, the history lessons haphazardly thrown in, and the whole thing compounded of grossly-blurred fact.

Frank, Pat. "Tough Story of Transition from Hometown Boys to Men Trained to Kill." Rev. of *Battle Cry*. *New York Herald Tribune Book Review* 3 May 1953: 5.

Calls *Battle Cry* a big, sprawling novel whose best part is the first few hundred pages where the military training procedures are described. Objects to the shocking language, and admires many of the battle scenes. Calls this book more honest than *The Naked and the Dead*.

"Fresh Off the Assembly Line." Rev. of *Armageddon*. *Time* 12 June 1964: 118.

Calls *Armageddon* a money-making assembly line production, to which Uris has packed every stock figure and cliche. Suggests that it was dictated at Napoleonic speed to two secretaries at once, then corrected with glass in one hand, cigar in the other and no place to hold the blue pencil. Complains that even the title is a mindless piece of sensationalism.

Geismar, Maxwell. "Epic of Israel." Rev. of *Exodus*. *Saturday Review* 27 Sept. 1958: 22-23, 30.

Calls *Exodus* a fine if not great novel of Israel. Suggests that it is enlightening, horrific, heroic, and belongs to the same category as *The Wall* and *The Grapes of Wrath*. Faults the novel for its lack of literary qualities and stereotypes, but concludes that despite all, the narrative really holds up.

Gentry, Curt. "A Master Storyteller on the Warsaw Uprising." Rev. of *Mila 18*. *San Francisco Chronicle This World Magazine* 4 June 1961: 28.

Asserts that *Mila 18* is superior to both *Battle Cry* and *Exodus*, as the reader is rapidly involved in the story and continues to remain involved. Concedes Uris is not a great writer or craftsman, but adds that flashbacks over-used and exasperating in previous novels give way here to straight narrative that generates almost unbelievable intensity.

Gilroy, Harry. "The Founding of the New Israel." Rev. of *Exodus*. *New York Times Book Review* 12 Oct. 1958: 32.

Calls *Exodus* a passionate summary of the inhuman treatment of the Jews by the Arabs, the British, and a host of others. Describes the contents of the book.

Godsell, Geoffrey. "Cuba, Israel, and New Mexico in Novels by Greene, Uris and Eastlake." Rev. of *Exodus*. *Christian Science Monitor* 4 Dec. 1958: 21.

States that Uris is a skillful, lively writer who weaves a broad tapestry sufficiently colorful and vigorous to keep his reader's interest, even though the characters tend to be superficial. Comments that *Exodus*, however, is not careful history and that Uris is definitely convinced of the divine right of the Jews, offering the Arabs no rights at all.

Grusd, Edward E. "Berlin After the War." Rev. of *Armageddon*. *National Jewish Monthly* July-Aug. 1964: 34.

Describes the contents of *Armageddon* briefly, and comments that it is too long, too tedious, with too many characters, too much inserted historical background, all moving too slowly.

Hamill, Pete. Rev. of *Trinity*. *New York Times Book Review* 14 Mar. 1976: 5.

Suggests that Uris is a storyteller like those men who sat around the fire in the days before history and made the tribe more human. Says his subject is man and the story is all. Comments on his often barbarous and tragic writing. Details the contents of *Trinity*.

"Hard to Digest." Rev. of *Armageddon*. *Newsweek* 29 June 1964: 89.

Comments that, like a large cafeteria, *Armageddon* caters to a large group of people presumably without ill effect, but without distinction. Concludes that this is another reworking of a simple formula fiction folded into a simplified history.

Harounoff, David. "Reviews." Rev. of *The Haj*. *Books and Bookmen* Aug. 1984: 34.

Calls *The Haj* a kind of *Exodus* in reverse since it deals with the dispersal of the Jews. Complains that the book is propaganda and amounts to an indictment of those Arab states who today purport to buttress the Palestinian struggle. Notes that minor characters are inartistically drawn and that Uris endows his Arab characters with every conceivable vice and prejudice Westerners usually attribute to Arabs. Sadly concludes that this book is not in the same league with *Exodus*.

Hass, Victor P. "Kid Goes to War: Almost Another *Caine Mutiny*." Rev. of *Battle Cry*. *Chicago Sunday Tribune Magazine of Books* 26 Apr. 1953: 3.

Comments that *Battle Cry* has a discursive beginning, some rather absurd melodrama, and a certain straining for language effects. Suggests that the U. S. Marines will be proud to claim this book because it is first rank war fiction and by one of their own. Describes the contents briefly.

Hass, Victor P. "New Uris Novel Far Cry from *Battle Cry*." Rev. of *The Angry Hills*. *Chicago Sunday Tribune Magazine of Books* 20 Nov. 1955: 4.

Asserts that *The Angry Hills* is a descent from inspired chronicle (*Battle Cry*) to competent pot boiler. Says the characters are believable, the writing adequate, and the materials interesting. But it is only skin deep and barely plausible. Concludes that transferring this to the screen should be child's play.

Hass, Victor P. "Rich Novel of Israel's Birth." Rev. of *Exodus*. *Chicago Sunday Tribune Magazine of Books* 28 Sept. 1958: 3.

Concedes that *Exodus* is an exceptionally long book and a brilliant history of the dreaming, founding and making of Israel. Adds that this is the crystallizing of twenty years of dreams and struggles. Uris paints on an ample canvas and writes at white heat. Concludes that it is a richly detailed and enthralling book.

Hogan, William. "The Pursuit of a Dream Twenty Centuries Old." Rev. of *Exodus*. *San Francisco Chronicle* 18 Sept. 1958: 33.

Calls *Exodus* a book written with heart and considerable narrative talent. Says it reads well, is saturated with history, and is still entertaining. Especially applauds the minor characters and the emotional involvement of the novel.

Holland, Mary. "Rhapsody in Green." Rev. of *Trinity*. *Observer* 17 Oct. 1976: 33.

Asserts that *Trinity* is *Exodus* transferred to Ireland. Describes it as a wide blockbuster which moves with rattling pace, contains stock figures, and qualifies as melodrama, even by Watergate standards.

Hunter, Evan. "Palestine in Black and White." Rev. of *The Haj*. *New York Times Book Review* 22 Apr. 1984: 7.

Complains that *The Haj* is so dimmed by a severely biased, anti-Arab view point that the book loses all power and credibility as a work of fiction. Concludes that his assault leaves the reader battered and dumb.

Jackson, Joseph Henry. "The Story of a Marine Outfit—From San Diego to Saipan." Rev. of *Battle Cry*. *San Francisco Chronicle This World Magazine* 26 Apr. 1953: 16.

Says *Battle Cry* carries complete conviction as it tells the story of a bunch of kids who become marines. Comments that he is not a novelist but a storyteller, despite his lack of practiced novelistic technique. Describes contents in detail.

"John Who ?" Rev. of *Mila 18*. *Newsweek* 5 June 1961: 95-96.

Calls *Mila 18* badly written in a style totally unsuited for the subject of martyrdom in the Warsaw ghetto. Complains that the novel is partly a pogrom against the English language, a minor malfeasance compared to the razzmatazz melodrama he has made out of one of the most heart-rending episodes of modern history. Concludes that this Warsaw ghetto sounds like the OK Corral.

Kimber, William. "Follow the Leader." Rev. of *Topaz*. *Times Literary Supplement* 21 Mar. 1968: 285.

Describes *Topaz* as an odd hybrid of elaborately plotted, romantic tale of personal and national love, espionage, and the international power game. Asserts that it can be enjoyed as a smoothly inventive, romantic thriller.

Kupferberg, Herbert. "A Novel of Israel's Birth." Rev. of *Exodus*. *New York Herald Tribune Books* 28 Sept. 1958: 5.

Considers the task set in *Exodus* as an awesome, achievement, a swift, savage drama which is overwrought, but nevertheless searing and illuminating.

Lehmann-Haupt, Christopher. "How to Write a Leon Uris." Rev. of *QB VII*. *New York Times* 2 Dec. 1970: 45.

Calls *QB VII* a book which conceals its art, makes few demands of the reader, keeps us thoroughly absorbed as readers, and which has thoroughly mapped out its plot in advance. Concludes sarcastically, however, that the trouble with knowing where it will all come out is that you needn't bother to read it at all.

Levy, Alan. "War Is a Gold Mine." Rev. of *Armageddon*. *New Republic* 11 July 1964: 24-25.

Describes *Armageddon* as written in typical Uris style: epic dialogue, gratuitous sex data, lists, dozens of names, many speeches, and the whole thing sounding like a bad translation. Gives a scathing and scanty review of the contents.

Lowin, Joseph. "An Islamic Melodrama." Rev. of *The Haj*. *Jewish Frontier* Oct. 1986: 22-23.

Sees *The Haj* as a rewriting of *Exodus*. Judges that unfortunately Uris presents the historical background of his fiction without taking the trouble to give shape, contour, and texture to the material he has accumulated. Notes that the historic tends to become propagandistic and therefore interferes with the novelistic aspect of the text. Asserts that this is an earnest but pretentious discussion of the "Palestine" refugee problem. Concludes that Uris obviously has deep antipathy for the Arab culture and probably believes them decadent, savage people.

Macklin, F. A. Rev. of *Topaz*. *America* 6 Jan. 1968: 17.

Calls *Topaz* an outlandish novel wedding political propaganda and political paranoia. Complains that there is little character, plot, or mood, and that the whole thing is disturbingly naive, if not laughable.

Maddocks, Melvin. "The Uris School of Non-Fiction Fiction." Rev. of *Topaz*. *Life* 20 Oct. 1967: 8.

Calls Uris a novelist trying once more to pass as a historian. Calls him a second rank door-to-door troubadour with a knack for being simultaneously commonplace and imperishable in his latest novel, *Topaz*.

Marsh, Pamela. "You Can't Tell Fact from Fiction." Rev. of *Topaz*. *Christian Science Monitor* 16 Nov. 1967: 15.

Asserts that Leon Uris blindly plunges ahead, dabbling in half-truths to produce yet another example of the latest non-artistic form—his propaganda novel *Topaz*. Complains that the novel wanders confusingly between the USA, France, Spain, and Cuba. Concludes that it is a mixture of history, sensationalized torture, and rape; thus it is high on the best-seller list.

Martineau, Geoffrey. "Last World." Rev. of *Topaz*. *Washington Post Book World* 31 Mar. 1968: 12-13.

Describes this novel scathingly as built of jingoistic platitudes, big popular causes, big safe targets, big timely subjects, plot gimmicks, stereotypes, and no depth whatsoever. Ends with a lament that the public keeps on buying such books.

McGlinn, Ann. Rev. of *Trinity*. *Saturday Evening Post* Sept. 1976: 73, 105.

Describes the contents of *Trinity* as well as its background history, and concludes that Uris has drawn a picture of Ireland which has only a past it repeats over and over again.

McMillan, George. "Tension Never Eases." Rev. of *Battle Cry*. *New York Times Book Review* 26 Apr. 1953: 5.

Calls *Battle Cry* a novel using most of the conventions of the war novel as we have come to know it, but that this particular wartime setting he has used has pulled him out of the traces. Concedes it is the most intimate and accurate account of how marines operate, train, fight, and die.

Miller, Merle. "Backdrop Is Victory." Rev. of *Battle Cry*. *Saturday Review* 25 Apr. 1953: 16-17.

Calls *Battle Cry* a wonderfully different kind of war novel which writes the hitherto untold story of the marine corps. Condemns the foolishly stereotypical female characters, but concludes that most of the time Uris is superb.

Mitgang, Herbert. "Problem and Perils of the Berlin Airlift." Rev. of *Armageddon. New York Times Book Review* 28 June 1964: 22-23.

Describes *Armageddon* as another cliche-ridden, mass-cult, nonfiction novel with enough sex and real characters to spice it up. Suggests that this time the author waves Old glory against the Red Hordes and sounds like a Birch society lecturer, even pulling out his military strategist and political analyst cloaks.

Mulnix, Michael. "The Battle Cries of Leon Uris." Rev. of *Trinity. Writer's Digest* Nov. 1977: 26-27.

Cites *Trinity* as Uris's latest epic going into detail on his life and writing career. Contains first person interview material.

Parmentel, N. "Books in Brief." Rev. of *Mila 18. National Review* 21 Oct. 1961: 277.

Argues that *Mila 18* is by all odds the worst Uris book ever written. Complains that he seems to be pushing genocide for the Germans and Zionism for the Jews. Concludes that those who died valiantly in the Warsaw ghetto deserve better.

Pisko, Ernest S. "Warsaw Ghetto in Uris Novel." Rev. of *Mila 18. Christian Science Monitor* 22 June 1961: 7.

Regretfully, Uris has turned the tragedy of the Warsaw Ghetto into a melodrama. Complains that the characters are stock figures with their puppet strings showing, the sex scenes are liberally spread throughout, and the whole thing lacks the spirit of reverence for the tragedy.

Prescott, Orville. "Books of the Times." Rev. of *Mila 18. New York Times* 2 June 1961: 29.

Lacks the literary distinction of *The Wall* but is nevertheless quite good. Concedes that it is a huge, solid narrative, full of reportorial writing dramatizing the deeply moving material. Comments, however, that it badly needs compression and condensation. Adds that the dialogue seems too rhetorical, and many casual historical references are inaccurate.

Reynolds, Quentin. "In the Ghetto a Battle for the Conscience of the World." Rev. of *Mila 18. New York Times Book Review* 4 June 1961: 5.

Calls *Mila 18* a book fully worthy of a place with John Hersey's *The Wall*. Judges it to be an authentic book of history as well as a convincing fiction, and thinks it will be remembered as a fine and important novel.

Ribalow, Harold U. "A Look at the 'Israel Novel.'" Rev. of *Exodus*. *Congress Bi-Weekly* 25 Dec. 1961: 19.

Calls *Exodus* a book full of bumbling prose, cardboard characters, and stereotypes, which just happened to contain within it a three decade history of the Jewish people. Argues that thanks to this much maligned book, huge numbers of people actually know the Jewish story, who might not otherwise have paid it any attention. Admires Uris's belief and obvious enjoyment of his material and condemns the wise-guy mentality that would slight Uris's contributions.

Rogers, W. G. "Dr. Adam Kelno: Hero or Villain?" Rev. of *QB VII*. *New York Times Book Review* 15 Nov. 1970: 70.

Describes the characters and details, and generally applauds the book, with the exception of the trial scenes which, Rogers complains, drag and lose power if one already knows the ending of the story.

Rowan, Diana. "Uris's *Trinity*: Another Blockbuster of a Novel." Rev. of *Trinity*. *Christian Science Monitor* 21 Apr. 1976: 23.

Describes the epic proportions of the novel covering a long period of time in Irish history from the Elizabethans to the early 20th century, the amount of research required for the novel, its epic quality, the trinity of families, and some of the characters. Notes that such a massive panorama results in unnatural dialogue, unbelievable characterizations, and melodramatic strokes. But also finds unexpected strengths deriving from the material: political history brought into focus, a vivid picture of the horror of the Potato Famine, and gritty humor. Concludes that Uris creates a story told in much detail and serving a "socially useful function, after all."

Schott, Webster. "Pilgrims in the Promised Land." Rev. of *Mitla Pass*. *Washington Post Book World* 30 Oct. 1988: 6.

Details the contents of the novel, and concludes that the flashbacks and asides lie around as narrative decorations waiting for someone to give them meaning. Complains that out of nowhere come all the stories about his father and mother that have no discernible effect on his characters. Also complains that much of the material seems breathlessly written, reportial, or mere stereotyping without good dialogue or plotting.

Silverberg, David. "*Exodus* from the Arab Point of View." Rev. of *The Haj*. *Jewish Monthly* May 1984: 32, 34.

Calls Uris an inelegant and pedestrian writer, and *The Haj* an unheroic book with material too unfamiliar to him. Suggests that it is disappointing because it is a tale of cruelty, treachery, and torment with no joy to leaven these pages. Concludes that Uris is using them to gain revenge.

Spitzer, Jane Stewart. *"The Haj,* Uris' Richly Detailed Palestinian Portrait, Lacks Vitality." Rev. of *The Haj. Christian Science Monitor* 2 May 1984: 20.

Describes *The Haj* as confused, unsympathetic, and biased. Suggests that it reads like a treatise on the evils of Islam and conveys the distinct impression that there is no possibility for a peaceful solution in the Middle East. Comments that this pessimism, combined with Uris's prejudices, saps the novel of its appeal. Notes that there is too little plot, too much talk, too much pessimism, much stilted style, and major problems with the characterization.

Stabiner, Karen. "Storytellers: New in November." Rev. of *Mitla Pass. Los Angeles Times Book Review* 30 Oct. 1988: 12.

Calls this novel a book ostensibly about heroes with a subtext about an artist above government by mere mortals. Complains that Gideon, the protagonist, isn't an enthusiastic enough cad to make his reformation meaningful.

Stack, Kenneth G. Rev. of *Armageddon. Extension* [Chicago] Sept. 1964: 11.

Finds this novel like a western, having no plot subtleties, no problems telling the good guys from the bad, and without a deus ex machina ending. Expresses amusement at Uris's admission that a knowledge of the English language has nothing to do with good writing. Criticizes him for using such a slap-dash manner to chronicle such important events as the four-power occupation of Berlin. Gives him an A for effort, but barely passing for the product.

Stern, Daniel. "The Letdown After the Airlift." Rev. of *Armageddon. Saturday Review* 13 June 1964: 32.

Describes *Armageddon* as a book which reduces the reviewer to helpless, laughable historical paraphrase. Complains that the book is one great blob of sentimentality bolstered by exquisitely ferreted facts. Suggests that the continuing success of an author who takes the greatest themes of the time and treats them as a sort of Classics Illustrated comic book is a phenomenon with important cultural implications.

Strouse, Evelyn. "Book Section." Rev. of *The Haj. Hadassah Magazine*
    Apr. 1984: 24, 26.

Calls Ishmael a mouthpiece for Uris who is neither sympathetic to Arabs,
nor schooled in their customs and history. Calls the narrative dense and
war-ridden, peopled with a huge assemblage impossible to keep straight.
Notes that the problem here is that no character is evoked, no situation
informed with drama or authenticity, no point of view expressed except
contempt. Concludes that the entire production was fed from file cabinet
to typewriter.

Sullivan, Cecile. "Leon Uris' *Trinity*: 50 Years of Irish Woe, and Now
    This." Rev. of *Trinity. National Observer* 17 Apr. 1976: 18.

Notes that *Trinity* boasts a larger than life hero, a thousand violent skir-
mishes on the Rugby Field, and a host of peripheral characters, all utterly
depthless. Also notes that Ireland has inspired countless fine novels;
unfortunately, this is not one of them.

Wakefield, Dan. "Israel's Need for Fiction." Rev. of *Exodus. Nation* 11
    Apr. 1959: 318-19.

Describes the universal appeal of stories about Israel, and the contents of
the novel.

Ware, Cade. "The Good Guys Win." Rev. of *Armageddon. New York
    Herald Tribune Books* 14 June 1964: 16.

Calls *Armageddon* a vast panorama of people and places, both historical
and fictional. Admires the characterization, but criticizes the lack of
action and the fact that it turns out to be a surprisingly comfortable book
about a very discomforting subject. Judges this a heavily researched pre-
movie novel.

Weeks, Edward. "The Young Marines." Rev. of *Battle Cry. Atlantic*
    Aug. 1953: 82, 84.

Argues that *Battle Cry* represents a big, hard job of writing. Comments
that the novel is done in primary colors, and that the many scenes of violence almost preclude the elaboration of feeling. Notes that there is no
touch of the neurotic in this book, and that neither is it a tract for the
Marines or against the agonies of war because it is the story of fighting
men and the *esprit* they live by.

Weinstein, Mark A. "Book Reviews." Rev. of *Trinity*. *National Forum* 59.1 (1979): 47-48.

Claims that *Trinity* reveals a great deal about popular literary taste. Calls this an old-fashioned, nineteenth-century historical romance of epic proportions. Complains that the fictional creation and the historical situation are not well integrated, and the real weakness of the book lies in its hero, Conor Larkin, the major vehicle for the plot. Claims that this outrageous romanticizing of the central character casts an unreal aura of wish fulfillment over the bitter tragedy of Northern Ireland.

Woods, William C. "Fighting Irish." Rev. of *Trinity*. *Washington Post Book World* 25 Apr. 1976: G7.

Argues for *Trinity* as Uris's best book, despite his obvious partiality for the Republican cause. Suggests that again he is concerned with the record of vast events and demonstrates his passion for documentary. Claims that he has a self-evident passion for the material, and does extremely well with the literary, mythic, and symbolic dimensions of the Irish conflict.

Interviews

Hendrickson, Paul. "*Exodus* to *Trinity*: The Impact of Leon Uris' Runaway Epics." *Washington Post* 2 May 1978: B1, B3.

Reports an interview with Leon Uris in Baltimore, in which Uris gives his vita, his marriages, his reaction to critics, his own assessment of his place as a writer, his comparison of himself with Michener (admires his prolific research), his year's stay in Ireland, and the psychic drain exacted by writing.

Luther, Marylou. "Don't Let Education 'Sanitize' Talent—Uris. *Los Angeles Times* 10 Nov. 1960: B6.

Describes Uris' aesthetics and his philosophy that great themes make great books. Provides a series of random statements by Uris on the craft of writing.

Leroux, Charles. "Jill and Leon Uris: Looking at Ireland, Wars and All." *Chicago Tribune* 26 June 1976: 22.

Reports a chatty, anecdotal interview with Uris, and some brief commentary by Leon and Jill Uris about *Trinity*.

Peckham, Stanton. "PW Interviews Leon Uris." *Publishers Weekly* 29 Mar. 1976: 6-7.

Details Uris's life and writing career. Provides a brief discussion of the recently-published novel *Trinity*.

Biographical Sources

Kalb, Bernard. "The Author." *Saturday Review* 25 Apr. 1963: 16.

Provides a thumbnail sketch of Uris' life and writing career. Also contains interview material reported in first-person.

Uris, Leon. "What One Writer Likes—and Doesn't." *New York Herald Tribune Book Review* 16 Aug. 1959: 2, 11.

Describes his ideas about his writing—his hopes, his purposes, his writing habits, his assessment of its quality, and his reactions to reviews of his books. Also describes his personal habits, his business acumen, his hobbies, his tastes in music and art, his disdain for notoriety, his pet beef, and his grief over the loss of the pioneer spirit in America. Concludes: "Writing takes second place to me behind giving and receiving love from my family. With it, I'm a big man. Without it, no matter how big a book I write, I'm a bum."

Walbridge, Earle F. "Leon Uris." *Wilson Library Bulletin* Dec. 1959: 252.

Provides brief biographical details of his growing up, military service, marriage, and writing career. Briefly discusses the writing of *Battle Cry*, *The White Angry Hills*, and *Exodus*, and the critical responses.

Dissertations

Asbahi, Muhammad Muneer Salahi. "History and Ideology in *Exodus* and Other Novels." Diss. Bowling Green State U, 1973.

Edward Lewis Wallant

1926 – 1962

Primary Sources

Novels

The Children at the Gate. New York: Harcourt, 1964; New York: Popular Library, 1964; London: Gollancz, 1964; London: Sphere, 1970; New York: Harvest/HBJ-Harcourt, 1980.

The Human Season. New York: Harcourt, 1960, 1973; New York: Berkley, 1964; London: Gollancz, 1965; London: Sphere, 1970.

The Pawnbroker. New York: Harcourt, 1961; New York: Macfadden, 1962; New York: Manor, 1962, 1974; London: Gollancz, 1962; London: Pan, 1964; New York: Harvest/HBJ-Harcourt, 1978; Cutchogue: Buccaneer, 1979; New York: Woodhill [Cited in PBIP, 1982].

The Tenants of Moonbloom. New York: Harcourt, 1963, 1973; New York: Popular Library, 1963; London: Gollancz, 1964; Harmondsworth: Penguin, 1966.

Short Fiction in Anthologies

"I Held Back My Hand." *New Voices 2: American Writing Today*. Ed. Don M. Wolfe. New York: Hendricks, 1955. 192-201.

"The Man Who Made a Nice Appearance." *New Voices 3: American Writing Today.* Ed. Charles I. Glicksberg. New York: Hendricks, 1958. 336-53.

"When Ben Awakened." *American Scene: New Voices.* Ed. Don M. Wolfe. New York: Stuart, 1963. 94-100.

Secondary Sources

Books

Galloway, David. *Edward Lewis Wallant.* Twayne's United States Authors Series 319. Boston: Twayne, 1979.

Articles and Chapters

Alter, Robert. "The Novels of Edward Lewis Wallant." *Hadassah Magazine* Apr. 1964: 10, 21.

Writes a retrospective on Wallant's life and work after his death. Describes his milieu, style, works, and posthumously published final work, *The Tenants of Moonbloom.*

Angle, James. "Edward Lewis Wallant's 'Trinity of Survival.'" *Kansas Quarterly* 7.3 (1975): 106-18.

Argues that central to Wallant's novels is the attempt to answer the question of what remains for people who have lost through intelligence the hope for immortality. Suggests that the answer arrived at in *The Tenants of Moonbloom* is courage, dreams, and love. Discusses other Wallant novels.

Ayo, Nicholas. "The Secular Heart: The Achievement of Edward Lewis Wallant." *Critique* 12.2 (1970): 86-94.

Argues that, in the three year period before his death in 1962, Wallant wrote four novels and several short stories, all focusing on overwhelming accounts of human weakness and depravity, but all also showing an affirmation of life that is compelling because it develops out of the very misery. Concludes that, like a Phoenix rising in its own ashes, Wallant's hopeful vision, which is not a commonplace achievement among contemporary writers, is earned.

Baumbach, Jonathan. "The Illusion of Indifference: *The Pawnbroker* by Edward Lewis Wallant." *The Landscape of Nightmare: Studies in the Contemporary American Novel*. Jonathan Baumbach. New York: New York UP, 1965. 138-51.

Describes Wallant's novels and short stories as kinds of "pilgrim's progress about those blighted innocents, who, damned to disbelief, keep the vigil at the gate." Provides a general overview of plot, prose, characterization, and style in all of the novels.

Becker, Ernest. "*The Pawnbroker*: A Study in Basic Psychology." *Angel in Armor: A Post-Freudian Perspective on the Nature of Man*. Ernest Becker. New York: Braziller, 1969. 73-99.

Argues that Wallant's tragic death in his middle thirties was literally the result of squeezing insight out of his own living flesh as he developed his genius. Discusses the film version of *The Pawnbroker* and its examination of the elemental psychic condition, or basic psychology, for *homo sapiens* on the planet. Argues that, in both book and film, the cumulative force of the psychology developed was truly breathtaking. Suggests that it is reminiscent of Kierkegaard's work in its understanding of the limits of the human condition, the point of no return—since only in these conditions lie the possibilities for hope and growth. A major essay in formalistic and psychological analysis.

Beja, Morris. "Afterword: Contemporaries." *Epiphany in the Modern Novel*. Morris Beja. Seattle: U of Washington P, 1971. 211-33.

Argues that the modern writers beginning with Woolf and Joyce have rediscovered numerous literary techniques for presenting epiphany. Includes Wallant along with Bellow, Styron, and Malamud as one of the "consolidators" who use epiphany much more centrally than it was ever used in the eighteenth or nineteenth centuries. Treats several of the novels to illustrate this thesis.

Benson, Nancy A. "When This World Is Enough: The Vision of Edward Lewis Wallant." *Cross Currents* 34.3 (1984): 337-42.

Describes Wallant's novels as distinctively religious in voice and resonating with fresh lyrical power at each reading. Attributes this to Wallant's skill in opening up the interior lives of his characters and vividly rendering the quotidian worlds they inhabit. Deals with all the novels.

Berger, Alan L. "Symbolic Judaism: Edward Lewis Wallant." *Crisis and Covenant: The Holocaust in American Jewish Fiction*. Ed. Sarah

Blacher Cohen. SUNY Series in Modern Jewish Literature and Culture. Albany: New York State UP, 1985. 164-72.

Describes *The Pawnbroker* as one of the earliest works of Jewish fiction to bring the Holocaust into an American focus. Argues that, ostensibly treating the Jewish catastrophe, the novel portrays and subtly suggests an equation between two types of suffering: physical, psychic, spiritual, Jewish, Black, and Puerto Rican. Concludes that Wallant has thus trivialized and wrongly universalized the Holocaust while paying scant attention to physical detail.

Bilik, Dorothy Seidman. "Wallant's Reborn Immigrant and Redeemed Survivor." *Immigrant-Survivors: Post-Holocaust Consciousness in Recent Jewish American Fiction.* Dorothy Seidman Bilik. Middletown: Wesleyan UP, 1981. 81-100.

Singles out the characters who are immigrants, and provides an in-depth analysis of them and the contexts in which they appear. Demonstrates the epiphanic aspects of their experience and the religious dimensions of their solutions. Criticizes Wallant's unsympathetic treatment of Holocaust survivors in his fiction.

Casey, Bill. "Commitment, Compassion, and Cant: The Quality Fiction Formula." *Forum* [U of Houston] 4.4 (1964): 28-30.

Argues that *The Pawnbroker* is flawed because it provides an almost perfect example of the modern Sunday School formula of serious fiction with its depiction of realized evil and its subsequent justification—all of which results in demonic and therefore sentimental fiction.

Cunningham, Frank R. "The Insistence of Memory: The Opening Sequences of Lumet's *Pawnbroker. Literature/Film Quarterly* 17.1 (1989): 39-43.

Describes Lumet's film adaptation of *The Pawnbroker* in considerable detail. Considers that it might surpass the novel itself in its realistic and expressionistic representation of the personal costs of repression and self-delusion, of the harrowing prices that must be paid by human beings who attempt to become less than fully human. Discusses the variations from the novel, camera angles, sets, scenes, lighting, sequences, cutting, and additions.

Davis, William V. "Fathers and Sons in the Fiction of Edward Wallant." *Research Studies Washington State University* 40.1 (1972): 53-55.

Claims that the most complete treatment of father/son relationships in contemporary Jewish fiction lies in Wallant's work.

Davis, William V. "The Impossible Possibility: Edward Lewis Wallant's *The Tenants of Moonbloom.*" *Studies in American Jewish Literature* [Albany] 2 (1982): 98-114.

Argues that *The Tenants of Moonbloom* is a *tour de force* of existential fiction as well as a synthesis of Christian and Jewish themes. Notes that, through his superimposition of a Christian framework and a Christian set of symbols and metaphors on the Jewish base of his characters and setting, Wallant created a new genre.

Davis, William V. "Learning to Walk on Water: Edward Lewis Wallant's *The Pawnbroker.*" *Literary Review* 17.2 (1973-74): 149-65.

A generalized account of the four novels, their contents, themes, and characters. Focuses primarily on *The Pawnbroker* as the best expression of Wallant's exploration of the human growth toward love.

Davis, William V. "The Renewal of Dialogical Immediacy in Edward Lewis Wallant." *Renascence* 24.2 (1972): 56-69.

Argues that in *The Human Season,* Wallant details the religious process by which Berman seeks redemption and reconciliation through a season of grief, ritualistic behavior, and a mystical experience of death. A structuralist and thematic approach to the novel. Concludes that, while this is the least successful of the novels, it introduces the major themes examined in the remaining novels—the search for faith, the meaning of sorrow and grief, sonship, brotherhood, and the search for love.

Davis, William V. "A Snythesis in the Contemporary Jewish Novel: Edward Lewis Wallant." *Cresset* May 1968: 8-13.

Provides a brief biographical sketch of Wallant's life and writing career. Discusses the theme common to all the novels—the search for self-realization, the influence of Jewish (Buber) and Christian (Tillich) theology on his work, and his position as a Jewish writer between the two extremes of those who are concerned almost exclusively with Jewish characters and Jewish tradition, and those who saved Jewish writing in America from its innate provincialism. Concludes that "the Wallant hero will live in spite of the improbabilities of existence, because he looks to an essence beyond existence."

Davis, William V. "The Sound of Silence: Edward Lewis Wallant's *The Children at the Gate*." *Cithara* 8.1 (1968): 3-25.

Describes the contents of all four novels, and demonstrates Wallant's use of myth and symbol in each. Describes *The Children at the Gate* as a Christian type parable which becomes the source for the rest of the novels. Invokes the type of the Cain and Abel story, the Christ myth, and others.

Dembo, L. S. "The Tenants of Moonbloooo-ooo." *The Monological Jew: A Literary Study*. L. S. Dembo. Madison: Wisconsin UP, 1988. 44-53.

Calls *The Tenants of Moonbloom* virtually a comic anatomy of monologism in a dilapidated culture that concludes on a high note. Claims that the few instances of dialogue achieved suggest some kind of release from the monological lives in which the 'O's are bound up in a fixed name, just as the bearer of that name is bound up in the routine of rent collection.

Edlestein, Arthur. "*The Children at the Gate*." *Survey of Contemporary Literature*. Ed. Frank N. Magill. Rev. ed. 12 vols. Englewood Cliffs: Salem, 1977. 2: 1225-27.

A standard reference article listing the principal characters and discussing the background, sources, symbolism, themes, plot, style, and impact of *The Children at the Gate*.

Edlestein, Arthur. "The Novels of Edward Lewis Wallant." *Jewish Heritage* (Win. 1964-65): 35-40.

Considers the novels of Wallant as constituting a special strain in the literature of isolation. Sees that all his protagonists—exiles all—have achieved their loneliness by conscious design, usually in the form of willed apathy cutting them off from others. Describes each of the novels in order from this perspective.

Epstein, Seymour. "Edward Wallant's Literary Legacy." *Congress Bi-Weekly* 10 May. 1965: 8-10.

An essay describing Wallant as a person, his life and writing, and Epstein's personal acquaintanceship with him. Describes Wallant's characteristic themes and skill as a writer and storyteller, and his wrestle with such ancient themes as guilt and redemption. Provides lengthy pieces of his acceptance speech for the Wallant Memorial Book Award.

Fein, Richard J. "Homage to Edward Lewis Wallant." *Midstream* May 1969: 70-75.

A tribute to Wallant which recounts his upbringing, education, writing career, and the contents of his major works.

Galloway, David D. "Clown and Saint: The Hero in Current American Fiction." *Critique* 7.3 (1965): 46-65.

Discusses the concept of eclectic sainthood in *The Tenants of Moonbloom* and *The Children at the Gate*. Describes Moonbloom as a messianic character hooked on humanity. Considers Sammy a saint, clown, and criminal who profoundly influences the cynical Angelo.

Gurko, Leo. "Edward Lewis Wallant as Urban Novelist." *Twentieth Century Literature* 20.4 (1974): 252-61.

Recounts the history of the city as depicted in literature ranging from the Greeks to the American moderns. Locates Wallant as harsher than most American writers unsympathetic to the modern city. Suggests that his first novel sets the stage for all the others. Notes that the city depicted in all of the novels provides the appropriate backdrop for the human misery experienced by each of the protagonists.

Hoyt, Charles Alva. "The Sudden Hunger: An Essay on the Novels of Edward Lewis Wallant." *Minor American Novelists*. Charles Alva Hoyt. Carbondale: Southern Illinois UP, 1970. 118-37.

Recounts Wallant's published history and reception by the reading public. Details the contents, tone, style, structure, and themes of each of his novels. Argues for most of the essay that what lies at the heart of the fiction is Wallant's earnest desire to know what lies in the troubled hearts of others.

Karl, Frederick R. "The 1960s: The (Wo)Man Who Cried I Am." *American Fictions 1940/1980: A Comprehensive History and Critical Evaluation*. New York: Harper, 1983. 325-29.

Claims that what animates Wallant's fiction is a cry of pain and a yearning for love unsentimentalized. Recounts the basic thematic interests of the fiction and its identification as Jewish-American literature.

Karpowitz, Stephen. "Conscience and Cannibals: An Essay on Two Exemplary Tales—*Soul of Wood* and *The Pawnbroker*." *Psychoanalytic Review* 64.1 (1977): 41-62.

Treats Wallant's published and unpublished novels in order to provide a clearer picture of his development as a writer. Mostly deals with the development of technique and theme in each of the works in the order in which they were published.

Klein, Marcus. "Further Notes on the Dereliction of Culture: Edward Lewis Wallant and Bruce Jay Friedman." *Contemporary American-Jewish Literature: Critical Essays.* Ed. Irving Malin. Bloomington: Indiana UP, 1973. 243-47.

Sees both authors as lacking the imaginative will to create imposing fictions, but having the ability to create the shapes of a unitary common knowledge about the age. Provides a detailed description of the contents and the protagonists of each of Wallant's novels. Finds in them emblematically ordinary characters proceeding from a state of hermetic isolation to a vast conviction of the human community based on love.

Kremer, S. Lillian. "From Buchenwald to Harlem: The Holocaust Universe of *The Pawnbroker*." *Holocaust Studies Annual* 3 (1985): 59-78. Rpt. in *Witness Through the Imagination: Jewish American Holocaust Literature.* S. Lillian Kremer. Detroit: Wayne State UP, 1989. 63-80.

A literary and historical treatment of style and content in *The Pawnbroker* as a prototypical novel of American Holocaust fiction. Suggests that Wallant successfully removed the Holocaust from the shadowy realm of symbolism and allusion to the foreground of fiction, presenting it as a major component of theme, narrative, and character construct, hence making it the central focus of his survivor-protagonist's consciousness and experiences. Argues that, similarly, his use of a survivor-chorus and the evocation of the Holocaust era through voluntary and spontaneous recollection and dream have become the primary means of Holocaust re-creation in American fiction.

Lewis, Robert W. "The Hung-Up Heroes of Edward Lewis Wallant." *Renascence* 24.2 (1972): 70-84.

Describes Wallant as a writer whose symbolism is simple, and who, skirting the melodramatic, writes in the naturalistic tradition of Dreiser, concerning himself with the differences between appearance and reality. Considers Wallant a possible deterministic meliorist. Provides a general overview of the novels from this perspective.

Lorch, Thomas M. "The Novels of Edward Lewis Wallant." *Chicago Review* 19 (1967): 78-91.

Describes Wallant's growing up years, education, job as an art director, interest in themes of terror and suffering, aesthetics, and craftsmanship. Provides plot summary, background, and formalistic analysis for each of the four novels.

Lyons, Bonnie. "Seeing and Suffering in *The Pawnbroker* and *Mr. Sammler's Planet*." *Yiddish* 6.4 (1987): 114-21.

Recounts the difficulties which face the American writer who approaches the subject of the Holocaust without having experienced it firsthand. Asserts that both Wallant and Bellow are among the more successful, and that both employ the metaphor of seeing as the central, organizing principle of their respective novels. Describes their use of the variant metaphors related to seeing—insight, blindness, illumination, foresight, hindsight, and so forth.

Lyons, Joseph. "*The Pawnbroker*: Flashback in the Novel and Film." *Western Humanities Review* 20.3 (1966): 243-48.

Provides a comparative treatment of the novel and the film, focusing particularly on the technique of flashback.

Marovitz, Sanford E. "A Prophet in the Labyrinth: The Urban Romanticism of Edward Lewis Wallant." *Modern Language Studies* 15.4 (1985): 172-83.

Describes the novels as accounts of the hard-earned religious visions of their various "prophets" or central protagonists. Sees Wallant as immersed in the "New Romanticism" of the tradition of the urban novel—a romanticism which fits in well with the prophetic Judaic tradition. Suggests that Wallant actually relates the revitalization of the protagonists to the regenerative powers of the city itself.

Mesher, David R. "Con Artist and Middleman: The Archetypes of Wallant's Published and Unpublished Fiction." *Yale University Library Gazette* 56.1-2 (1981): 40-49.

Treats the published and unpublished novels to provide a clearer picture of Wallant's development as a writer. Mostly deals with the development of technique and theme in each of the works in the order in which they were published or written.

Miller, Gabriel. "Those Who Walk in Darkness." *Screening the Novel: Rediscovered American Fiction in Film*. Gabriel Miller. New York: Ungar, 1980. 167-91.

The first half of this article provides a standard, new critical, biographical treatment of the novels and Wallant. The second half provides an extensive treatment of Sidney Lumet's film version of *The Pawnbroker*.

Parks, John G. "The Grace of Suffering: The Fiction of Edward Lewis Wallant." *Studies in American Jewish Literature* [Albany] 5 (1986): 111-18.

Argues that while Wallant's fiction is affirmative, it faces squarely the enormities of our age. Sees each of Wallant's books as a kind of pilgrim's progress about those blighted innocents who are damned to keep vigil at the gate despite having been damned to disbelief. Concludes that to suffer, to feel pain, is to be at attention, to be able to notice things.

Petrie, Graham. "A Note on the Novel and the Film: Flashbacks in *Tristram Shandy* and *The Pawnbroker*." *Western Humanities Review* 21.2 (1967): 165-69.

Provides critical commentary and clarification on Joseph Lyon's article in the Summer 1966 issue of *Western Humanities Review* dealing with the technique of the flashback in both novel and film.

Ribalow, Harold U. "The Legacy of Edward L. Wallant." *Chicago Jewish Forum* 16 (1964): 325-27.

A historical account of Wallant's life, career, books, reviews, themes, and film adaptation of *The Pawnbroker*. Outlines the contents of each of his novels, and concludes that he has left us books slim, but powerful, that bear rereading and that help us understand our neighbors, fellow Jews, and contemporary life.

Rovit, Earl. "A Miracle of Moral Animation." *Shenandoah* 16 (1965): 59-62.

Discusses the posthumous publication of *The Children at the Gate*. Reviews Wallant's earlier works as "primitive" yet powerful, and notes that all four novels are coming-to-birth, coming-to-life, and learning-to-love stories. Describes the contents of this latest novel, and sees it as a parable against the backgrounds of Cain, Abel, and crucifixion stories.

Rubin, Louis D., Jr. "The Experience of Difference: Southerners and Jews." *The Curious Death of the Novel: Essays in American Literature*. Louis D. Rubin, Jr. Baton Rouge: Louisiana State UP, 1967. 268-71.

Describes the contents of *The Children at the Gate* and the character of
Kahan, concluding that this is a fine, posthumous novel.

Russell, Kenneth C. "The Devil's Contemplative & the Miracle Rabbi,
    Two Novels: Golding's *Spire* and Wallant's *Human Season.*" *Studia
    Mystica* 3.3 (1980): 52-64.

Recounts the teachings of St. John of the Cross and other spiritual masters with regard to faith, prayer, and the necessity of foregoing
"Consolations." Argues that *Spire* shows what happens when a self-centered human being mistakes the initial comforts of prayer for proof of
extraordinary spirituality, while *Human Season* describes the advance of
faith beyond images. An important treatment of the religious dimensions
of Wallant's work.

Schulz, M. F. "Wallant and Friedman: The Glory and the Agony of
    Love." *Critique* 10.3 (1968): 31-47. Rpt. as "Edward Lewis Wallant
    and Bruce Jay Friedman: The Glory and the Agony of Life" in
    *Radical Sophistication: Studies in Contemporary Jewish/American
    Novelists.* Max Schulz. Athens: Ohio UP, 1969. 173-97.

Illustrates the thesis that both Wallant and Friedman are concerned with
the theme of love, but, as illustrated by the passages selected for the article, they are poles apart in their treatment and understanding of the
subject. Notes that Wallant's handling of the material is often oppressive
with the tragic never wholly absent, while Friedman's is irreverent and
often indecorous, with the ludicrous ever present.

Silet, Charles L. P. "Edward Lewis Wallant." *Critical Survey of Long
    Fiction.* Ed. Frank N. Magill. 9 vols. Englewood Cliffs: Salem, 1983.
    7: 2758-66.

A standard reference article covering his principal long fiction, other literary forms, achievements, biography, analysis, and bibliography.

Sklar, Robert. "Edward Wallant's Jewish Novels." *Congress Bi-Weekly*
    30 Dec. 1963: 23-24.

Provides a general essay dealing with *The Human Season* and *The
Pawnbroker* as novels which deal with individuals cut off from their
very selves and having to find their way back to life through a faith born
of pain and sorrow. Concludes that these are average persons who live
unforgettably as they engage in the search for meaning, faith, and God.

Stanford, Raney. "The Novels of Edward Wallant." *Colorado Quarterly* 17.4 (1969): 393-405.

Provides a general tribute to Wallant extolling his virtues as both human being and novelist.

Reviews

Alter, Robert. "Affirmation of Human Solidarity." Rev. of *The Tenants of Moonbloom. Hadassah Magazine* Oct. 1963: 14.

Claims that *The Tenants of Moonbloom* distinctly reflects the sensitive and original talent the American reading public has now lost. Provides a detailed account of the contents, and concludes that tragic triumph over life through resolute laughter is realized brilliantly in the final scene of the novel. Comments that if Wallant had wanted to follow the old Jewish tradition of leaving a moral will, he could hardly have chosen anything finer than this.

Balliett, Whitney. "Lament." Rev. of *The Children at the Gate. New Yorker* 19 Sept. 1964: 210-13.

Calls Edward Wallant a melancholy, old-fashioned novelist who wrote combative, restorative, visionary books. A lengthy review essay discussing all the novels and concluding that Wallant has been ignored and underrated.

Baumbach, Jonathan. "The Locked and Lonely Hearts." Rev. of *The Children at the Gate. Saturday Review* 29 Feb. 1964: 33.

Considers *The Children at the Gate* a beautifully written, short novel of almost unbearable impact. Comments that, out of the final depths of depravity and horror, Wallant's children of darkness discover the terrible luxury of feeling that provides the price of pain and the redemptive possibility of love. Details the contents.

Bermel, Albert. "Frenzy in a Void." Rev. of *The Pawnbroker. Midstream* June 1965: 63-67.

Describes *The Pawnbroker* almost solely in terms of Sidney Lumet's screenplay of the same name. Mostly describes Lumet's vision of the character of Sol Nazerman and his personal history and psychopathology. Primarily an excellent essay in film criticism.

Boroff, David. "Abstainer from Life." Rev. of *Children at the Gate. New York Times Book Review* 8 Mar. 1964: 36.

Calls *Children at the Gate* a book about a solitary man who abstains from life by taking refuge in a small town drugstore. Details plot and characters, and concludes that, unlike earlier novels, the resolution here is not at all easily achieved. Suggests that this book published posthumously contains more ambiguity than his previous novels.

Boroff, David. "Rental Agent's New Lease on Life." Rev. of *The Tenants of Moonbloom*. *Saturday Review* 10 Aug. 1963: 27.
Suggests that *The Tenants of Moonbloom* is about disaffiliated sleepwalking through life. Remarks that Wallant's compassion for everyday derelicts seems bottomless, but that he is redeemed from sentimentality by a comic spirit giving a hard, firm edge to his feelings in this book. Describes his career, and laments his untimely death.

Boroff, David. "The Return of Feeling." Rev. of *The Pawnbroker*. *Saturday Review* 26 Aug. 1961: 16.
Argues that *The Pawnbroker* is utterly unsparing in its portrayal of the harsh, unyielding ugliness of Harlem life. Suggests that it is a far less lyrical and sentimental book than Malamud's *The Assistant*. Comments that, though its prose sometimes fails, and is often strained, Wallant is a gifted writer who probes with a kind of troubled tenderness into the pools of human darkness.

Corke, Hilary. "New Novels." Rev. of *The Human Season*. *Listener* 15 Apr. 1965: 573.
Sees *The Human Season* as a strong, but not cheerful book. Comments that, unfortunately, the author is cleverer than his characters, setting them up in order to knock them down. Concludes that this makes finishing the book a virtue rather than a pleasure.

"The Crucifixion of Sammy." Rev. of *The Children at the Gate*. *Times Literary Supplement* 29 Oct. 1964: 973.
Describes Wallant's *The Children at the Gate* as a posthumous novel which, though flawed, is serious, original, moving, and worthwhile. Comments on the problems inherent in the character of Sammy, the central protagonist.

"A Death in the Family." Rev. of *The Human Season*. *Time* 5 Sept. 1960: 76.
Describes the contents of *The Human Season*, and claims it to be brief, well-structured, and without abrasive bravura effects. Concludes that,

untainted by sentimentality, the novel is a *tour de force* accomplished with clarity and compassion.

Fuller, Edmund. "An Unworldly Young Man Touched by the Chaos in His Little Cosmos." Rev. of *The Tenants of Moonbloom. Chicago Sunday Tribune Magazine of Books* 11 Aug. 1963: 4.

Calls *The Tenants of Moonbloom* a story of comedy, pathos, and isolation in a community. Describes a melancholy, displaced Moonbloom unable to compete and engaged in fruitless disparate activities. Describes the contents.

Gilbert, Morris. "Without Hope or Illusion." Rev. of *The Pawnbroker. New York Times Book Review* 3 Sept. 1961: 14.

Describes the contents of *The Pawnbroker*, calling it an impressive critical comment on the Holocaust. Sees the Pawnbroker as an impressive flesh and blood poignant figure, while all the others in the cast are three-dimensional.

"Grace Among the Roaches." Rev. of *The Tenants of Moonbloom. Time* 16 Aug. 1963: 76.

Calls *The Tenants of Moonbloom* a horrifying human map of Manhattan's lower depths. Suggests that these characters are the unofficial dead of the affluent society. Describes the central characters and the plot.

Hass, Victor P. "Baffling, Compelling Tale of 'Little People.'" Rev. of *The Children at the Gate. Chicago Sunday Tribune Magazine of Books* 8 Mar. 1964: 3.

Asserts that *The Children at the Gate*, written just before his death, is Wallant's final comment on guilt and responsibility. Details the contents.

"Hell Let Loose." Rev. of *The Pawnbroker. Times Literary Supplement* 2 Mar. 1962: 141.

Calls *The Pawnbroker* a study in human desolation, and admires the wealth of accurate detail about pawnbroking. Concludes that, though the plot is neatly worked out, the godless universe depicted accomplishes very little.

Hugh-Jones, Stephen. "Worm's Eye View." Rev. of *The Human Season. Encounter* July 1965: 83.

Details the plot of Wallant's first novel, and speculates about his theology.

Johnson, B. S. "Tenement Symphony." Rev. of *The Tenants of Moonbloom. Spectator* 8 May 1964: 641.

Calls *The Tenants of Moonbloom* delightful to read, well-written, unsentimental, and competent. Details the contents.

Kaufman, Lenard. "Grieving Widower." Rev. of *The Human Season. New York Times Book Review* 11 Sept. 1960: 52.

Calls *The Human Season* a book which would hardly cause readers to say they had enjoyed it. Concludes that, despite excellent characterization, the book falls short of being credibly motivated.

"Lacerating." Rev. of *The Pawnbroker. Newsweek* 14 Aug. 1961: 70.

Calls *The Pawnbroker* solid and topical from end to end. Sees it as a lacerating portrait of Sol Nazerman done in strongly controlled prose utterly suited to its subject matter of the spiritual exhaustion of the many who faced the Nazi barbarisms of recent European history.

Lask, Thomas. "Books of the Times." Rev. of *The Pawnbroker. New York Times* 1 Sept. 1961: 15.

Argues that *The Pawnbroker* contains floating images of fear and violence and is filled with scenes of closeness and suffocation reminiscent of Dostoevski. Calls it a sharply edged series of sharply lit vignettes. Details the contents.

Mayne, Richard. "Messrs Universe." Rev. of *The Pawnbroker. New Statesman* 2 Mar. 1962: 309.

Calls *The Pawnbroker* more honest and more affecting than Duras's filmscript. Briefly describes the contents of the novel.

Mayne, Richard. "Technique." Rev. of *The Human Season. New Statesman* 16 Apr. 1965: 619.

Suggests that *The Human Season* is far more natural than *The Pawnbroker,* and is immensely skillful, well-observed, tender, profound, and in the end, heartening. Comments that the whole thing would be effortless if one did not sense the author's craftsmanship intruding.

Pine, John C. "The Novel of the Sixties." Rev. of *The Tenants of Moonbloom. 199 Ways to Review a Book: A Librarian's Readings in the Novels of the Sixties.* John C. Pine. Metuchen: Scarecrow, 1971. 66-67.

Comments that *The Tenants of Moonbloom* is surely one of the most powerful and disturbing novels with its compassionate, hauntingly sad, yet extravagantly funny tone. Details the plot.

"Rent Acts." Rev. of *The Tenants of Moonbloom. Times Literary Supplement* 30 Apr. 1964: 369.

Calls *The Tenants of Moonbloom* a brilliant performance, though not yet the height of Wallant's literary powers. Sees it as composed of a series of twenty dazzling set pieces about people of all colors and nationalities. Concludes that it has affinities with *Henderson the Rain King*, although occasionally the writing shows signs of hypertrophy. Comments that this author's death came all too soon.

Ribalow, Harold U. "A Jew in Harlem." Rev. of *The Pawnbroker. Congress Bi-weekly* 27 Nov. 1961: 14.

Describes *The Pawnbroker* as written in spare, controlled, emotion-charged prose and with great persuasion. Suggests that the book's qualities must be savored slowly, that the characterizations are carefully drawn, and that the human situation is sadly depicted. Concludes its scope to be considerable because it probes the hearts of more people than early work by Wallant.

Rubin, Louis D., Jr. Rev. of *The Children at the Gate. Southern Review* ns 2.3 (1966): 703-05.

Details plot and characters of the novel, Wallant's second posthumous work, and describes the central protagonist as a stereotype from Yiddish fiction.

Salvesen, Christopher. "Senior Citizen." Rev. of *The Tenants of Moonbloom. New Statesman* 8 May 1964: 734.

Describes the contents of this posthumously published novel, praising its power and social content. Suggests that the palpable message, if there is one, is in the conclusion which urges love one another or die.

Scannell, Vernon. "New Novels." Rev. of *The Pawnbroker. Listener* 22 Mar. 1962: 527.

Calls *The Pawnbroker* an outstanding, rich, and passionate book, informed by a real indignation at man's inhumanity to man and an unsentimental awareness of the truth that to cease loving is to cease living. Suggests that, occasionally, Wallant is guilty of overwriting, but that the ending is excellent because he has the gift of the image which is startling without being meretricious.

Schroth, Raymond A. "Prisoner of Time." Rev. of *The Pawnbroker. America* 23 July 1966: 98.

Calls *The Pawnbroker* an extremely important novel, and details Wallant's writing career. Discusses the movie and the reissue of the novel. Comments that both are very demanding on viewer and reader.

Scott, Winfield Townley. "Grieving Man and His Memories." Rev. of *The Human Season. New York Herald Tribune Lively Arts* 25 Dec. 1960: 34.

Details *The Human Season* as done in tones of gray with occasional blood splotches. Suggests that it is about the withdrawal into stricken loneliness. Concludes that, having started out on this level, Wallant has nowhere else to go except round and round; hence the book becomes a two-dimensional pasteboard until the whole thing feels like a literary exercise.

Sklar, Robert. "Wallant's Last Novel." Rev. of *The Children at the Gate. Congress Bi-Weekly* 12 Oct. 1964: 15-16.

Suggests that *The Children at the Gate* is the drama of the solitary man breaking through his shell of isolation. Details the contents, and concludes that this is the least satisfactory of Wallant's four novels because the style is bald and uneven, and we are not prepared for the raw melodrama of the conclusion, nor for its symbolic import. Argues that no inherent theology emerges from this novel, and that Wallant is concerned with afterlife rather than life. Comments that Wallant had only one story to tell, and he told it in *The Pawnbroker.*

Solotaroff, Theodore. "Suffering Was Better Than Nothing At All." Rev. of *The Children at the Gate. New York Herald Tribune* 5 Apr. 1964: 5, 19.

Claims that Wallant never became a truly competent writer, despite claims to the contrary. Suggests that his perception was largely psychoanalytic. Argues that his attempt to illuminate the inside human character with wonder and pity caused him to reach into the dark, marginal pockets of urban existence to find lost souls. Describes each of his works in this light. A useful, detailed overview of his life and writing.

Spector, Robert Donald. "Bitter Legacy of the Nazi Horror." Rev. of *The Pawnbroker. New York Herald Tribune Books* 20 Aug. 1961: 8.

Calls *The Pawnbroker* splendid, visionary, Dickensian, and somewhat sensational at its climax. Details the story.

Volpe, Edmond L. "The Landlord." Rev. of *The Tenants of Moonbloom*. *New York Herald Tribune Books* 11 Aug. 1963: 10.

Calls this is a realistic novel written in existential style. Details the plot, and concludes that Wallant does a better job with despair than with hope. Complains that he has not yet mastered his craft, but concedes that he is a serious artist groping beyond the confining strictures of realism.

Wall, Stephen. "New Novels." Rev. of *The Children at the Gate*. *Listener* 5 Nov. 1964: 732.

Claims that this novel reminds us we have lost an important American author. Details the plot, and concludes that Wallant's gift was the real thing.

Weintroub, Benjamin. "Books." Rev. of *The Pawnbroker*. *Chicago Jewish Forum* 21.1 (1963): 345-46.

Comments that *The Pawnbroker* is an exciting volume, with its central character vividly drawn. Claims that the story is powerfully told, but that the denouement is unconvincing though well supported with melodramatic detail. Concludes that this method is enigmatic and technically sound, but psychologically inadequate. Details the plot and characters thoroughly.

"Where the Ladders Started." Rev. of *The Human Season*. *Times Literary Supplement* 15 Apr. 1965: 289.

Calls Wallant a writer with a vision of ultimate grief, wounds so deep, and suffering so immense that the sufferer is scarcely human. Sees *The Human Season* as a first novel which gathers enormous strength and gets by through its intensity. Suggests that it is a typical apprenticeship novel in that the opening pages lack skill and there are no minor characters in the cast to provide relief.

"Who Will Not Go Away." Rev. of *The Children at the Gate*. *Time* 6 Mar. 1964: 100, 102.

Describes *The Children at the Gate* as Wallant's last novel in which he sears the reader's mind, leaving one with an agony of mocking. Deems it a fine work by a fine novelist. Details the contents.

"Within a Tower of Junk." Rev. of *The Pawnbroker*. *Time* 18 Aug. 1961: 75.
Says *The Pawnbroker* is not about a fresh theme, but that Sol Nazerman
is a fascinating complexity. Suggests that, as the centerpiece of a flawed
book, he is that literary rarity—the character whose sorrows seem as real
as the reader's own. Details the contents.

Bibliographies

Ayo, Nicholas. "Edward Lewis Wallant, 1926-1962." *Bulletin of
Bibliography* 28.4 (1971): 119.

Biographical Sources

Mesher, David R. "Edward Lewis Wallant." *Twentieth-Century
American-Jewish Fiction Writers*. Ed. Daniel Walden. Detroit: Gale,
1984. Vol. 28 of *Dictionary of Literary Biography*. 94 vols. to date.
1978- . 310-16.
More than details of his life, this is a career biography, tracing the development of the author's canon, describing the contents and themes of his
works, evaluating his reputation, and placing him in the larger context of
American literary history. Includes lists of primary and secondary
sources and illustrations.

Dissertations

Barmor, Yitzhak. "The Father Figure in Jewish-American Literature."
Diss. Kent State U, 1988.

Bernstein, Mashey Maurice. "The Individual as a Work of Art: Jewish
and Puritan Values in the Fiction of Norman Mailer and Edward
Lewis Wallant." Diss. U of California, Santa Barbara, 1977.

Davis, William V. "Sleep Like the Living: A Study of the Novels of
Edward Lewis Wallant." Diss. Ohio U, 1967.

Dell, Frances G. "From a Private Limbo to a World of Common Pain: The
Unity of Edward Lewis Wallant's Fiction." Diss. Fordham U, 1981.

Edwards, Lisa Ann. "Restoring Voices: Traditional Jewish Sources in
Post-Holocaust Jewish American Fiction." Diss. U of Iowa, 1984.

Greenberg, Hazel. "Cluster Imagery in the Novels of Edward Lewis Wallant." Diss. Southern Illinois U, 1972.

Krupat, Arnold. "The Saintly Hero: A Study of the Hero in Some Contemporary American Novels." Diss. Columbia U, 1967.

Mesher, David Ronald. "The Novels of Edward Lewis Wallant." Diss. U of Washington, 1978.

Ruddel, Joyce. "The Agony of Choice: Dialectic in the Novels of Edward Lewis Wallant." Diss. U of Wisconsin, 1971.

Woolf, M. P. "A Complex Fate: Jewish-American Experience in the Fiction of Leslie Fiedler, Edward Wallant, Chaim Potok and Jerome Charyn." Diss. U of Hull, 1981.

Zaitchik, Mark Barry. "Edward Lewis Wallant's *The Odyssey of a Middleman*: A Critical Introduction." Diss. U of Connecticut, 1977.

Jerome Weidman

1913 –

Primary Sources

Novels

Back Talk. New York: Random, 1963.

Before You Go. New York: Random, 1960; London: Heinemann, 1961; New York: Pinnacle, 1976.

The Center of the Action. New York: Random, 1969; New York: Pyramid, 1970; London: Bodley Head, 1970.

Counselors-at-Law. Garden City: Doubleday, 1980; London: Bodley Head, 1981.

A Dime a Throw. New York: Berkley, 1957.

The Enemy Camp. New York: Random, 1958; London: Heinemann, 1959; London: Pan, 1961.

A Family Fortune. New York: Simon, 1978; London: Bodley Head, 1978; New York: Pocket, 1979; Harmondsworth: Penguin, 1981.

Fourth Street East: A Novel of How It Was. New York: Random, 1970; London: Bodley Head, 1970; New York: Pinnacle, 1971; Large Print ed. Boston: Lanewood, 1972.

Give Me Your Love. Eton Pocket-Size Books. New York: Eton, 1952.

The Hand of the Hunter. New York: Harcourt, 1951; Toronto: McLeod, 1952; London: Cape, 1952; London: Consul-World, 1962; New York: Avon [1968].

I Can Get It for You Wholesale. New York: Simon, 1937; New York: Modern Library, 1937, 1959; London: Heinemann, 1938; London: WDL-World, 1959; Arbor House of Contemporary Americana. New York: Arbor, 1984; London: Bodley Head, 1985.

I'll Never Go There Any More. New York: Simon, 1941; Toronto: Musson, 1941; London: Heinemann, 1942.

I, and I Alone. N.p.: Pockettes, 1972.

Last Respects. New York: Random, 1972; London: Bodley Head, 1972; New York: Pinnacle, 1974.

Letter of Credit. New York: Simon, 1940.

The Lights Around the Shore. New York: Simon, 1943; London: Hale, 1948; New York: Popular Library [Cited in PBIP, 1969].

Other People's Money. New York: Random, 1967; London: Bodley Head, 1967; Crest-Fawcett World [Cited in PBIP, 1969].

Praying for Rain. New York: Harper, 1986.

The Price Is Right. New York: Harcourt, 1949; London: Hammond, 1950, 1956; Manchester: World, 1959; New York: Macfadden, 1964; New York: Manor, 1973, 1976; New York: Woodhill, 1976.

The Sound of Bow Bells. New York: Random, 1962; London: Heinemann, 1963; New York: Pinnacle, 1976.

The Temple. New York: Simon, 1975; London: Bodley Head, 1976; New York: Kangaroo-Pocket, 1977.

The Third Angel. Garden City: Doubleday, 1953; New York: Avon, 1954, 1966; London: Cape, 1954.

Tiffany Street. New York: Random, 1974; London: Bodley Head, 1974; New York: Pinnacle, 1975.

Too Early to Tell. New York: Reynal, 1946; New York: Popular Library, 1946.

What's in It for Me. New York: Simon, 1938; London: Heinemann, 1939, 1941; London: WDL-World, 1960; New York: Giant Cardinal-Pocket, 1963.

Word of Mouth. New York: Random, 1964; London: Bodley Head, 1965; Greenwich: Crest-Fawcett [Cited in PBIP, 1969].

Your Daughter Iris. Garden City: Doubleday, 1955; London: Cape, 1955; New York: Avon, 1956.

Collected Works

The Captain's Tiger. New York: Reynal, 1947; New York: Macfadden, 1964.

Contents: Monsoon, An Easy One, Examination, A Dime a Throw, Eyewitness, Philadelphia Express, Death in the Family, Dummy Run, The Third Alphabet, Joust, My Aunt From Twelfth Street, Gallantry in Action, Everybody and His Brother, Movable Feast, Houdini, The Neat Mexicans, A Lodging for the Night, The Pleasure of the President, Send Four Men to Hanoi, Something for Luck, The Bottom of the Mountain.

The Death of Dickie Draper, and Nine Other Stories. New York: Random, 1965.

Contents: The Death of Dickie Draper, The Three-Two Pitch, Wait for Me, The Love Philtre of Vittorio Adamello, A Knight Lay Dying, R. S. V. P., The City of Light, Tonight We Are Sharp, A Sense of Echelon, A Moment's Notice.

The Horse That Could Whistle "Dixie," and Other Stories. New York: Simon, 1939; London: Heinemann, 1941.

Contents: Thomas Hardy's Meat, The Explorers, My Father Sits in the Dark, Portrait of a Gentleman, Twice Blest, Home by Midnight, Let Me Explain You Something, You and Yours, Goodby Forever, Lions to a Lady, The Kinnehorrah, Dumb Kid, Old Clothes for Poland, The Tuxedos, Smart Dope, I Thought About This Girl, Everybody Wants to Be a Lady, Marriage Broker, —And Everything Nice, Chutzbah, Slipping Beauty, I Knew What I was Doing, Anything for a Laugh, On the Town, Good-Natured Slob, All I Survey, What Do You Know?, The Horse that Could Whistle "Dixie."

My Father Sits in the Dark, and Other Selected Stories. New York: Random, 1961.

Contents: And Everything Nice, My Aunt from Twelfth Street, The Bottom of the Mountain, Briefing Period, Chutzbah, The Clean Slate, Death in the Family, A Dime a Throw, Dumb Kid, Dummy Run, An Easy One, Everybody and His Brother, Examination, The Explorers, Eyewitness, Gallantry in Action, Goodby Forever, The Great Healer, The Half-Promised Land, The Hole Card, Home by Midnight, The Horse That Could Whistle "Dixie," Houdini, I Knew What I Was Doing, Invicta!, I Thought about This Girl, Joust, The Kinnehorrah, Let Me Explain You Something, A Lodging for the Night, Marriage Broker, Monsoon, Movable Feast, My Father Sits in the Dark, The Neat Mexicans, Off Season, Old Clothes for Poland, Pennants Must Have Breezes, Philadelphia Express, The Pleasure of the President, Portrait of a Gentleman, Send Four Men to Hanoi, Shoe Shine, The Third Alphabet, The Tuxedos, Twice Blest, The Waiting Game, Where the Sun Never Sets, You and Yours.

My Father Sits in the Dark, and Other Selected Stories. London: Heinemann, 1963.

Contents: My Aunt from Twelfth Street, Briefing Period, The Clean Slate, Death in the Family, Dummy Run, An Easy One, Examination, Eyewitness, Joust, My Father Sits in the Dark, Philadelphia Express, The Pleasure of the President, Shoe-Shine, The Third Alphabet.

Nine Stories; Selected from the Author's Retrospective Anthology, My Father Sits in the Dark, and Other Stories. New York: Cardinal-Pocket, 1963.

Contents: Briefing Period, The Great Healer, The Hole Card, Invicta!, Off Season, Pennants Must Have Breezes, Shoeshine, The Waiting Game, Where the Sun Never Sets.

Where the Sun Never Sets, and Other Stories. London: Heinemann, 1964.

Contents: A Dime a Throw, Gallantry in Action, The Great Healer, The Hole Card, Invicta!, A Lodging for the Night, Monsoon, Movable Feast, Off Season, Pennants Must Have Breezes, Send Four Men to Hanoi, Where the Sun Never Sets.

Short Fiction in Anthologies

"Cutzbah." *Short Stories from the New Yorker.* New York: Simon, 1940. 408-14.

"The Explorers." *Short Stories from the New Yorker.* New York: Simon, 1940. 193-202; *The Pocket Book of Modern American Short Stories.* Ed. Philip Van Doren Stern. New York: Washington Square, 1943, 1953; 3rd ed. 1972. Pag. not available.

"Good Man, Bad Man." *Best Detective Stories of the Year, 23rd Annual Collection.* Ed. Anthony Boucher. New York: Dutton, 1968; London: Boardman, 1968. 44-64.

"The Horse That Could Whistle 'Dixie.'" *Two and Twenty: A Collection of Short Stories.* Ed. Ralph H. Singleton. New York: St. Martin's, 1962. 277-84.

"I Thought About This Girl." *Tales of Our People: Great Stories of the Jew in America.* Ed. Jerry D. Lewis. New York: Geis, 1969. 177-80.

"Joust." *A Treasury of Jewish Sea Stories.* Ed. Samuel Sobel. New York: David, 1965. 164-69; *Jewish Sea Stories.* Ed. Samuel Sobel. Middle Village: David, 1985. 164-69.

"The Kinnehorrah." *This Land, These People*. Ed. Harold U. Ribalow. New York: Beechhurst, 1950. 115-22.

"The Man Inside." *This Week's Short-Short Stories*. Ed. Stewart Beach. New York: Random, 1953. 232-38.

"Monsoon." *55 Short Stories from the New Yorker*. New York: Simon, 1949. 279-87.

"My Father Sits in the Dark." *Jewish-American Stories*. Ed. Irving Howe. New York: Mentor-NAL, 1977. 118-21; *The Norton Book of American Short Stories*. Ed. Peter S. Prescott. New York: Norton, 1988. 460-64; *"The Safe Deposit" and Other Stories about Grandparents, Old Lovers, and Crazy Old Men*. Ed. Kerry M. Olitzky. New York: Wiener, 1989. 153-58.

"Slipping Beauty." *75 Short Masterpieces: Stories from the World's Literature*. Ed. Roger B. Goodman. New York: Bantam, 1961. 259-63.

"The Tuxedos." *Contemporary Short Stories*. Ed. Maurice Baudin. 2 vols. Indianapolis: Bobbs, 1954. 2: 204-10; *The Sense of Fiction*. Eds. Robert L. Welker and Herschel Gower. Englewood Cliffs: Prentice, 1966. 263-68.

"What Do You Know?" *New Stories for Men*. Ed. Charles Grayson. New York: Doubleday, 1941; Garden City: Garden, 1943. 587-603.

Short Fiction in Periodicals

"The Absolute Darlings." *McCall's* July 1965: 62-63, 144-48.

"All I Survey." *Collier's* 22 Jan. 1938: 9-10, 53-57.

"And Private Washroom." *Salute* Nov. 1946: 32-33, 63-64.

"Any Husband Can Have a Bad Day." *Saturday Evening Post* 16 Feb. 1952: 22-23, 101-02, 104, 106.

"Basket Carry." *Harper's* Aug. 1941: 313-20.

"The Blue Notebook." *Good Housekeeping* Oct. 1954: 54-56, 283-91.

"The Bottom of the Mountain." *Liberty* 16 June 1945: 20-21, 56, 60, 63-64.

"Charlotterussenik." *Accent* 1.1 (1940): 3-8.

"City of Light." *Good Housekeeping* Sept. 1948: 46-47, 88, 91-95, 97, 99-100, 102-04, 106, 109-15.

"Clean Slate." *Cosmopolitan* Aug. 1955: 56-67.

"The Decision." *Liberty* 30 Nov. 1946: 13, 54-56, 58-60.

"Diary." *Good Housekeeping* Nov. 1947: 36-37, 302-16, 318-23, 325-26, 328-30.

"A Dime a Throw." *New Yorker* 16 Aug. 1941: 13-15.

"Double Wife." *Today's Woman* Feb. 1949: 32-33, 48-53.

"Dummy Run." *New Yorker* 18 Dec. 1943: 24-28.

"An Easy One." *New Yorker* 6 Dec. 1941: 26-30.

"The Edges of a Nickel." *Today's Woman* Feb. 1948: 44-45, 147-52.

"Episode in Washington." *Today's Woman* Aug. 1946: 24-25, 107-09.

"Everybody Wants to Be a Lady." *Esquire* May 1937: 63, 244-45.

"Examination." *New Yorker* 30 Jan. 1943: 19-21.

"Exile." *College Humor* Sept. 1940: 6-8, 48-49.

"Eyewitness." *New Yorker* 8 Jan. 1944: 20-23.

"Fancy Seeing You Here." *McCall's* Mar. 1956: 40-41, 64, 68-69, 74, 76-77, 80.

"Fire Escape." *Yale Review* 32.1 (1942): 59-66.

"First Meeting." *Today's Woman* June 1946: 38-39, 136-39.

"Flowers for Judy." *Elks Magazine* Nov. 1940: 14-17, 37-38, 42-44.

"Foreign Exchange." *Esquire* Apr. 1954: 51, 113-15.

"Friends of Mary Fowler." *Redbook* July 1965: 58-59, 110, 119-21, 124-25.

"Gallantry in Action." *Story Digest* Oct. 1946: 78-83.

"A Girl to Leave Behind." *Collier's* 18 May 1940: 9-10, 49-50, 52.

"Gone Home." *Good Housekeeping* Nov. 1949: 44-45, 201-02, 204, 207-11.

"Good Man, Bad Man." *Saturday Evening Post* 1 July 1967: 48-53.

"Goodby Forever." *Collier's* 19 Feb. 1938: 25.

"The Greatest Man I Ever Knew." *Swank* Sept. 1941: 22, 54, 56.

"Half-Promised Land." *Harper's* Feb. 1955: 42-50.

"His Third Best Friend's Wife." *American Mercury* Apr. 1941: 450-58.

"Hole Card." *Cosmopolitan* May 1954: 74-87.

"Holiday on Lewis Street." *New Yorker* 22 Dec. 1945: 56-61.

"Home by Midnight." *American Mercury* Dec. 1938: 450-57.

"Home Is the Hero." *Collier's* 25 May 1946: 18, 85-89.

"Houdini." *New Yorker* 20 July 1940: 17-20.

"How to Move a Mountain." *Saturday Evening Post* 30 Nov. 1963: 46-52, 55-57.

"I Knew What I Was Doing." *American Mercury* Sept. 1936: 53-61; *Fiction Parade and Golden Book Magazine* Jan. 1937: 274-82.

"I Thought About This Girl." *Scholastic* 20 Nov. 1939: 27-28.

"I, and I Alone." *Good Housekeeping* Sept. 1952: 56-57, 139-42, 144, 146, 149-62, 164, 167-69; Oct. 1952: 58-59, 235-58, 260-61.

"The Invincible Miss Cranston." *Woman's Home Companion* Oct. 1949: 18-19, 41-42, 44, 47-48, 50, 53, 56, 59.

"Johnny Comes Marching Home." *American Magazine* July 1942: 48-50, 52, 110-13.

"The Kinnehorrah." *Fiction Parade* Sept. 1937: 610-14.

"A Knight Lay Dying." *Playboy* Dec. 1958: 30-34, 38, 44, 58, 68, 92.

"The Lady Who Gambled with Love." *Today's Woman* Oct. 1950: 38-39, 89-107.

"The Last Quarter." *This Week Magazine* 24 Oct. 1948: 6-7, 32, 34, 36.

"The Love Philtre." *Playboy* Jan. 1960: 21-22, 66, 78-80.

"The Man Inside." *This Week Magazine* 13 Mar. 1949: 22, 26.

"The Man Who Knew about Scarlet Things." *Today's Woman* Aug. 1949: 33, 110-24.

"Marriage Is No Honeymoon." *Cosmopolitan* Aug. 1948: 62-63, 100-04.

"Marriage on Location." *Collier's* 5 Aug. 1955: 56, 58-61.

"The Measure of the Man." *Good Housekeeping* Mar. 1950: 42-43, 284, 286-91, 293-308, 310-13.

"Monsoon." *New Yorker* 16 Feb. 1946: 29-33.

"Mrs. Gregory Is in Industrial Diamonds." *Cavalier* Aug. 1965: Pag. not available.

"Nest Egg." *Collier's* 4 Nov. 1944: 15, 50, 53-54.

"Never to Forget." *Good Housekeeping* Nov. 1948: 36-37, 157-58, 160, 163-71.

"Old Clothes for Poland." *Literary America* Feb. 1935: 126-31.

"Philadelphia Express." *New Yorker* 10 Oct. 1942: 16-20.

"Portrait of a Gentleman." *American Mercury* May 1936: 86-93.

"Prentiss." *Good Housekeeping* Sept. 1947: 34-35, 72, 74, 76, 79-80, 82, 84, 86, 88, 91, 93, 94, 96-98.

"Return Engagement." *Today's Woman* Nov. 1946: 42-43, 138-39, 142-46.

"The Rival." *Good Housekeeping* Jan. 1948: 34-35, 194-204.

"Second Breakfast." *Playboy* Feb. 1967: 83, 108, 150-51.

"Send Four Men to Hanoi." *New Yorker* 13 July 1946: 21-27.

"Sense of Echelon." *Collier's* 19 Oct. 1946: 14-15, 75-78, 81-83.

"She Wouldn't Stay Married." *Today's Woman* Oct. 1948: 31, 68-76.

"Shoe-Shine." *American Mercury* Feb. 1940: 210-27.

"The Sighing Sound." *Cosmopolitan* Sept. 1951: 29-31, 129-39; Oct. 1951: 64-65, 148-58.

"Smart Dope." *Collier's* 11 June 1938: 18.

"Something for Luck." *Good Housekeeping* June 1945: 30-31, 62, 64, 67-68, 71, 73, 75-76, 78-79.

"Something to Remember." *Good Housekeeping* Jan. 1950: 46-47, 175-82.

"Sometimes a Man Remembers." *Good Housekeeping* Nov. 1946: 24-25, 82, 85-86, 88, 90, 93, 95-96, 98, 100, 103-08, 110, 112, 114.

"That Other Woman." *Saturday Evening Post* 30 June 1956: 26-27, 76, 79.

"This Mysterious They." *Saturday Evening Post* 19 Aug. 1939: 16-17, 46, 48.

"Thomas Hardy's Meat." *Scribner's* July 1937: 36-40.

"The Tuxedos." *Encore* June 1946: 658-63.

"Wait for Me." *Good Housekeeping* Oct. 1951: 60-61, 122, 125-28, 131, 133-34, 136-39, 142, 145.

"Wanted: Poor Boy Who'd Like to Be Rich." *Good Housekeeping* May 1955: 52-53, 207-21.

"What Do You Know?" *Collier's* 19 Mar. 1938: 16-17, 66-69.

"What's in It for Me?" *Scribner's* Sept. 1938: 24-28, 38-44, 46-49.

"Who's a Jerk?" *Male Home Companion* Oct. 1942: 22, 59-60.

"Wife of the Man Who Suddenly Loved Women." *Ladies' Home Journal* June 1966: 72-73, 122, 124, 126-27.

"Woman of Experience." *Today's Woman* Jan. 1950: 22, 96-104.

"The Woman Who Married an Angel." *Today's Woman* Feb. 1950: 36-37, 139-48.

"Women Use Four-Letter Words." *Swank Magazine* Sept. 1945: 5, 34-35.

"You and Yours." *Collier's* 4 Sept. 1937: 9-11, 47-49.

"You're a Pal." *Saturday Evening Post* 23 Aug. 1941: 12-13, 35, 38, 40, 42-43.

Secondary Sources

Articles and Chapters

The Enemy Camp." Survey of Contemporary Literature. Ed. Frank N. Magill. Rev. ed. 12 vols. Englewood Cliffs: Salem, 1977. 4: 2264-65.

A standard reference article covering background, plot, style, themes, and characters in this novel.

Gertel, Elliot B. "Visions of the American Jewish Messiah." *Judaism* 31.2 (1982): 153-65.

Reviews Weidman's trilogy of novels, *The Enemy Camp, The Sound of Bow Bells*, and *The Temple,* for content and style. Suggests that in the last novel, he locates a messianic vision complete with rites of passage for the young messiah who must beat the Gentiles at their own game, and produce a program. Sees this as one of several important messianic novels in Jewish-American literature.

Glicksberg, Charles I. "When Is a Novel Anti-Semitic?" *Congress Weekly* 1 Nov. 1954: 11-13.

Discusses *I Can Get It for You Wholesale* and *What's in It for Me?*, and works by Budd Schulberg and Meyer Levin to develop his thesis that writers, Jew or non-Jew, must present the truth they see, no matter how unpleasant to some, so long as they present it with completeness and integrity. Suggests that, in order to do so, they must show the complex network of environmental forces and social conditions that influence the human soul and shape it in a given way for good or evil.

Haydn, Hiram. *Words and Faces.* New York: Harcourt, 1974. 215-21, 245-47.

In this article-interview Weidman discusses why he writes, his delight in writing, the problem of recognition, the issue of interpretation and meaning, rewriting, plotting, writing blocks, and writing as a way of life and as a compulsion.

Johnson, Clarence O. "Jerome Weidman." *Critical Survey of Short Fiction.* Ed. Frank N. Magill. 8 vols. Englewood Cliffs: Salem, 1981. 6: 2409-12.

A standard reference article covering principal short fiction, other literary forms, influence, story, biography, analysis, and bibliography.

Rascoe, Burton. "An Open Letter." *Newsweek* 2 Jan. 1939: 32.

Makes the argument in this letter that Simon and Schuster ought to republish *What's In It for Me?* despite complaints that it shows Jews in a poor light. Calls Weidman brilliant, sensitive, and extraordinarily talented. Draws a parallel between the criticism of the Episcopalians in Dreiser's *The Financiers* and other similar cases of censorship.

Sherman, Bernard. *"I Can Get It For You Wholesale* and *What Makes Sammy Run?" The Invention of the Jew: Jewish-American Education Novels (1916-1964).* Bernard Sherman. New York: Yoseloff, 1969. 176-78, passim.

Gives a brief account of the contents, Jewish themes, and style of *I Can Get It for You Wholesale.*

Weidman, Jerome. Introduction. *My Father Sits in the Dark and Other Selected Stories.* Jerome Weidman. New York: Random, 1961. ix-xvii.

A critical introduction by Weidman to his own stories. Provides a moving biographical account of his early life in 1932, family, prospects, the beginning of his writing career, and education as a writer.

Weidman, Jerome. Introduction. *Nine Stories*. Jerome Weidman. New York: Cardinal-Pocket, 1963. 1-11.

This is Jerome Weidman's critical introduction to his own collection of short stories. Mostly a biographical personal essay.

Weidman, Jerome. "Preface." Jerome Weidman. *The Horse That Could Whistle "Dixie" and Other Stories*. New York: Simon, 1939. ix-xvi.

A useful insight to Weidman's history as a writer, the evolution of the stories, his writer's credo, technical problems, views on the place of the story, composition methods, and choice of subject matter.

Reviews

Ackroyd, Peter. "Schmalzwerke." Rev. of *Tiffany Street*. *Spectator* 8 June 1974: 710.

Accuses Weidman of sentimentality, ethnic overkill, and nostalgic schmalziness. Also comments that he is too busy looking at the chip over his shoulder through a haze of regret and inaccuracy.

Altinel, Savkar. "Out of Court." Rev.of *Counselors-at-Law*. *Times Literary Supplement* 20 Mar. 1981: 304.

Says *Counselors-at-Law* takes in lawyers, financiers, show business people, politicians—all greedy, rich, and powerful people. Unfortunately there are too many shifts of tone and attitudes in the book for its message to emerge with anything like clarity. Weidman cannot extend to contemporary America the savage scorn with which Dickens viewed Victorian England in *Bleak House*.

Angoff, Charles. "Caricatures of Jewish Life." Rev. of *The Sound of Bow Bells*. *Congress Bi-Weekly* 4 Mar. 1963: 13-14.

Considers reading *The Sound of Bow Bells* a depressing experience because the book fails to leave an enduring impression and is full of "drug store" Jews. Calls them celluloid and sentimentalized.

Angoff, Charles. Rev. of *Before You Go*. *Chicago Jewish Forum* 19.1 (1961): 345.

Calls *Before You Go* the work of a facile, good, slick writer. Concludes: "there are nearly 195,000 words in this book and altogether they say virtually nothing. What a waste of effort, time, and labor! What a pity!"

Balliett, Whitney. "Happily Ever After, with Footnotes." Rev. of *The Enemy Camp. New Yorker* 6 Sept. 1958: 124-27.

Considers *The Enemy Camp* painstakingly mapped out, neatly written, but basically only an old-fashioned, nineteenth-century formula of persecuted, partly crippled heroine; strong, stubborn, dense hero; and arch villain. Describes the contents in detail.

Balliett, Whitney. "Pro." Rev. of *Praying for Rain. New Yorker* 8 Dec. 1986: 151-53.

Mostly recounts Weidman's publishing career and biography. Locates him with his contemporaries in the Jewish novel. Describes *Praying for Rain* as a neat, old-fashioned, realistic, canny, comic, moralistic, and narrated novel.

Boroff, David. "Jews in a Gentile World." Rev. of *The Enemy Camp. Congress Weekly* 8 Sept. 1958: 17-18.

Describes *The Enemy Camp* as Weidman's examination of just how much hatred, exclusion, and victimage Jews have perpetrated, not just experienced at the hands of others. Provides a very full account of the characters, situations, and plot. Condemns Weidman for his empty rhetoric, his frequent fuzziness of ideas, and sledgehammer prose. Claims that, ultimately, the novel strains our credulity.

Boroff, David. "Success by Chicanery." Rev. of *The Sound of Bow Bells. Saturday Review* 28 July 1962: 38-39.

Describes the contents of *The Sound of Bow Bells* as an East Side morality fable. Also contains a report of Boroff's personal acquaintance with the author. Considers Weidman's satiric sense deft, his descriptions masterful, the view of the publishing world fascinating, and the verve with which he manages ethnic materials remarkable.

Brewster, Dorothy. "Dog Eat Dog." Rev. of *I Can Get It For You Wholesale. Nation* 15 May 1937: 572.

Comments that in *I Can Get It For You Wholesale* Weidman has produced a creditable first novel. Describes the world it represents and the central character, Harry Bogan.

Brooks, John. "The Education of George Hurst." Rev. of *The Enemy Camp. New York Times Book Review* 15 June 1958: 5.

Calls this a large, rich novel about anti-Gentilism done with broad strokes. Notes that it is full of plot, exaggeration, and considerable passion held in fine restraint. Claims that this is a largely bitter tale brought to a provisionally happy ending. Concludes that it ends with final cosmic jest as Weidman leaves us to judge.

Brooks, John. "For Iris It's Not Cricket." Rev. of *Your Daughter Iris. New York Times Book Review* 3 Apr. 1955: 4.

Calls this novel a frothingly entertaining work that is really two stories. Suggests that the plot suffers from the weakness of the male protagonist who is no match for the two women. Details contents.

Brooks, John. "Hero's Widow." Rev. of *The Third Angel. New York Times Book Review* 27 Sept. 1953: 35.

Considers this a book full of creaking coincidence and hoary stylistic devices. Details plot and characters. Concludes that this novel seems to have gotten seriously away with Weidman and ended up as an overlong fustian, artificial, and rather humorous hassle.

Brooks, John. "Waiting In Limbo." Rev. of *The Hand of the Hunter. Saturday Review of Literature* 21 Apr. 1951: 17.

Describes the contents of *The Hand of the Hunter*, commends it for its interesting evocation of place and time, and laments that Weidman has not explored some aspects of character enough to make a really rich novel. Concludes, however, that many scenes are created with accuracy, tenderness, and intelligence.

Bull, Harry A. "Genre Pieces." Rev. of *The Captain's Tiger. Saturday Review of Literature* 30 Aug. 1947: 32.

Describes the plot and characters of the novel, and commends it for being moving, hilarious, and sharply detailed. Complains that both Weidman and his characters ultimately lack maturity.

Bullock, Florence Haxton. "J. Weidman in Connecticut." Rev. of *The Third Angel. New York Herald Tribune Book Review* 27 Sept. 1953: 12.

Commends *The Third Angel* for its solidity and value as a picture of the ins and outs of life in a small Connecticut town. Notes that the emotional lives of the major protagonists are done with brashness as well as subtlety.

Byrom, Bill. "The Utopian Kick." Rev. of *Word of Mouth. Spectator* 28 May 1965: 698-99.

Calls the novel remarkable, and details the plot.

Callahan, William M. "Fiction." Rev. of *I'll Never Go There Any More. Commonweal* 24 Oct. 1941: 28-29.

Describes the novel as sexually vulgar, the story as common, the characters as swell studies, and the hero as a person who matters not at all.

Chamberlain, John. "Weidman Novel Shows Worlds Within Worlds Social and Private." Rev. of *Enemy Camp. New York Herald Tribune Book Review* 15 June 1958: 1, 13.

Describes *The Enemy Camp* as a book about Jewish life in New York in which Weidman manages his overlapping flashback technique with consummate skill, piling story on top of story. Considers many of the caricatures Daumier-like pictures of New York law schools, accountancy firms, and theatrical worlds. Argues that Weidman shows us there is no such thing as the enemy camp for the free soul.

Chapel, America. "Adolescent's Coming of Age." Rev. of *The Lights Around the Shore. New York Herald Tribune Book Week* 30 May 1943: 2.

Calls this novel a top performance that provides immediate recall on the nostalgic pleasures of adolescence. Notes that Weidman is a sure-handed entertainer, who provides a charming, simple, and understanding tale.

Charyn, Jerome. "Novels and Stories." Rev. of *The Temple. New York Times Book Review* 22 Feb. 1976: 36.

Describes the contents of *The Temple*, and complains that although its psychology is primitive, and the writing often inept, the book seems to work, hopping between banalities and magic, and moving by sheer force of storytelling.

Cohen, Francis. "New World Symphonies." Rev. of *The Center of the Action. Tablet* 11 Apr. 1970: 359.

Calls *The Center of the Action* one of those American novels of considerable panache which relies on neatness of phrasing, fast narrative, and fashionable content rather than developing a moral center of its own. Concludes that it is all buoyed up with its own energy and crispness of style. Provides a plot summary.

Cook, Bruce. "For the Weidman Fans, Another Novel Pursuing a Familiar Theme." Rev. of *Other People's Money*. *National Observer* 29 May 1967: 19.

Claims that Weidman is about as consistently and competently professional as any other novelist in America. This and a well-made job is what we get in *Other People's Money*. It is a very funny book, but ultimately its plot is marred by weak motivations and afterthoughts, convenient coincidences, and other signs of poor construction.

Cook, Bruce. "Weidman Moves Knowingly in *The Center of Action*." Rev. of *The Center of Action*. *National Observer* 4 Aug. 1969: 19.

Says *The Center of Action* is fundamentally a tragedy, yet it is told with such gusto and relish by a character who is only by half the "conscience-less son of a bitch" he is called at the book's end. It is a book about the publishing history of Simon and Schuster, and largely inspired by the fate of Richard C. Simon. It is a kind of fingerless progress inspired by Runyan and O'Hara, an unlikely sort of poetry spun from the dross of human greed.

Cook, Bruce. "Weidman Reclaims Lower East Side for Literature." Rev. of *Fourth Street East*. *National Observer* 11 Jan. 1971: 23.

Claims that *Fourth Street East* is artfully done and the results satisfying. The mood is that of the memorist—elegiac. Sometimes he is discursive, sometimes relaxed, always reminiscing. He has taken material vulgarized by the Sam Levinsons and reclaimed it for literature—no little thing. Perhaps no other writer but Jerome Weidman could have managed it.

Coxe, Louis. "Unnecessary Books." Rev. of *Fourth Street East*. *New Republic* 30 Jan. 1971: 26-29.

Complains that *Fourth Street East* lacks a shaping spirit of imagination. Suggests that it has neither vision nor voice, and that strictly speaking, it is an unnecessary book.

Cromie, Robert. "Saga of a Smart Kid from the Bronx." Rev. of *The Center of the Action*. *Washington Post Book World* 29 June 1969: 4.

Gives a plot summary, and concludes that this is one of Weidman's best yet.

Cuddon, J. A. Rev. of *Fourth Street East*. *Books and Bookmen* June 1971: 40.

Describes the story of *Fourth Street East,* set in the 1920s in the ghetto, and all of the pains and trials of such a childhood. This is a plain and uncontrived tale written in beautiful, rhythmical prose. Characters are worked unobtrusively into the narrative, and Weidman has a fine ear for the subtleties of speech rhythms, and for deadpan, laconic humor.

Dempsey, David. "How It Went For Ben Ivey." Rev. of *Before You Go. New York Times Book Review* 31 July 1960: 5.

Comments that *Before You Go,* Weidman's twelfth novel, is full of breezy dialogue, improbable plot, humor, and just a tincture of social commentary. Considers the result acceptable summer fare that may, ultimately, seem a little thin. Details contents.

Dempsey, David. "A Trunkful of Old World Culture." Rev. of *My Father Sits in the Dark and Other Selected Stories. New York Times Book Review* 9 July 1961: 5, 26.

Describes *My Father Sits in the Dark* as a one-man omnibus, short story collection stitched together from other books. Concludes that this collection gathered together from the past thirty years does not escape this "nine-patch" method.

Dillon, George. "Hard Hitting Satire on OWI." Rev. of *Too Early to Tell. Chicago Sun Book Week* 15 Dec. 1946: 6.

Too Early to Tell is full of redundant types floating about with inflated egos. However, it is a readable, hard-hitting lampoon which drifts about for several chapters like a detective story, long on atmosphere and dialogue, and rather short on plot.

Du Bois, William. "Jitter and Fritter." Rev. of *Too Early to Tell. New York Times Book Review* 1 Dec. 1946: 9.

Calls *Too Early To Tell* a far too clinical report on the inanities of a psychological combat training school in wartime. Concludes that this is Weidman at the top of his form.

Fadiman, Clifton. Rev. of *I'll Never Go There Any More. New Yorker* 11 Oct. 1941: 84.

Sees this as another collection of laconic stories of people easy to dislike, who at the end are plunged into a James Cain, melodramatic finish. Considers Weidman enormously readable, and claims that when he has thought more about the business of construction, he will be top-notch.

Farrell, James T. "Improvisation." Rev. of *The Lights Around the Shore*. *New York Times Book Review* 16 May 1943: 6.

Argues that, unfortunately, *The Lights Around the Shore* substitutes mystery for toughness. Finds the story unmotivated and its attempt at a detective plot a failure. Concludes that, as an attempt to probe into subtle and unconscious human motivations, it is flat and unrewarding.

Feld, Rose. "A Tender, Bitter Growing-Up." Rev. of *The Lights Around the Shore*. *New York Herald Tribune Weekly Book Review* 16 May 1943: 6.

Claims that *The Lights Around the Shore* reveals Weidman as an excellent interpreter of a hard-boiled guy who has just written a bitter novel. This is a fine psychological study and an unusual story. It moves with the pace and suspense of a mystery novel. Details the contents.

Ferguson, Otis. "Success Story." Rev. of *I Can Get It For You Wholesale*. *New Republic* 9 June 1937: 136.

Calls *I Can Get It For You Wholesale* a slangy, wise novel written with unseen dramatic discipline and a fine, spare, working style. Concludes that the writing is never pretentious and that the whole thing reads like a *tour de force*.

Ferguson, Otis. "We Have Been Here Before." Rev. of *What's In It For Me*. *New Republic* 2 Nov. 1938: 371.

Considers this sequel to *I Can Get It for You Wholesale* inferior to the earlier novel, and a reader would be better off reading the first one again.

Ferguson, Otis. "What's In It For You." Rev. of *I'll Never Go There Any More*. *The New Republic* 20 Oct. 1941: 514.

Comments that *I'll Never Go There Any More* is exciting, if a bit self-conscious. Suggests that it loses its intensity in the end, and lacks a clear destination although there is good writing here. Commends Weidman for having a good ear, a clean, direct style, and a flinty imagination which throws sparks over the least thing touched in the most offhand way.

Ferguson, Otis. "A Writer on His Way." Rev. of *The Horse That Could Whistle 'Dixie' and Other Stories*. *New Republic* 7 June 1939: 137-38.

Calls *The Horse That Could Whistle* a collection of stories which indicate that Weidman is on his way to a literary reputation. Discusses the contents of the novel and its stylistic strengths and weaknesses.

"Fog, Finks, and Failure." Rev. of *The Sound of Bow Bells. Newsweek* 6
    Aug. 1962: 79.

Describes the contents of the novel and its themes as the recapturing of
Jewish heritage, the rediscovery of writing as an inward demand, and the
redemption of its central character. This is a novel full of feeling and insight
that turns wildly theatrical and implausible coming down the stretch.

Frankel, Haskel. "To Be or Not to Be." Rev. of *Word of Mouth. Saturday
    Review* 19 Dec. 1964: 42.

Suggests that this novel contains a solid plot idea and much talent. Notes
that the characterizations are of two types: theatrical or outrageous caricature while the rest is dull, flat portrayal. Concludes that this book will
not bring Weidman further honors.

Freedman, Richard. "Four Novels." Rev. of *Counselors at Law. New
    York Times Book Review* 26 Oct. 1980: 24.

Calls this a mystery novel with a Greek chorus of paralegal secretaries
gossiping about their bosses' colorfully unethical behavior, plus a good
deal of professional sleight of hand to keep the action moving.
Concludes that though a thin novel, it is still a thumping good read.

Fuller, Edmund. "Caught in Private Ghettos." Rev. of *The Enemy Camp.
    Saturday Review* 28 June 1958: 19.

Calls this a novel of depth, scope, and human sympathy because it has a
lively, crackling readability and concentrates on the immemorial hostility
between primitive cultures and their antagonists. Describes story and
characters.

Fuller, Edmund. "Weidman's Exciting but Complex Satire." Rev. of *The
    Third Angel. Chicago Sunday Tribune Magazine of Books* 27 Sept.
    1953: 4.

Argues that *The Third Angel* doesn't fully realize its intentions because its
story is not very believable. It reads best as broad satire with an accumulation of realistic detail. The build up of tension works, and the whole
thing finally becomes quite a yarn. Concludes: "One wishes he had kept
the book simpler, avoiding bad taste and subsidiary threads and tensions."

Gannett, Lewis. "A Man Who Was Born for Power." Rev. of *Before You
    Go. New York Herald Tribune Book Review* 24 July 1960: 1.

Describes the novel in detail, and commends it for its haunting power, ability to hold reader interest, and magnificent East Side scenes.

Gill, Brendan. "Small Towns." Rev. of *The Third Angel. New Yorker* 24 Oct. 1953: 151-52, 154, 157.

Argues that *The Third Angel* is based on a story that is better told than worth telling. Comments that for all of Weidman's skill, he has been acting out a trifle, and the reader is let down. Discusses the contents, providing a series of comments on style and plotting.

Goldberg, Mark F. "A Gallery of American Jews." Rev. of *Fourth Street East: A Novel of the Way It Was. Jewish Spectator* May 1971: 25-26.

Describes *Fourth Street East* as too plotted, too formulaic, and too thin. Finally, it is facile and emotionally and intellectually unsatisfying.

Haas, Joseph. "*Titanic* Orphan Becomes Tycoon." Rev. of *Other People's Money. Saturday Review* 20 May 1967: 43.

Accuses Weidman of functioning more like a tailor following patterns dictated by the customers than the author. Comments that in *Other People's Money,* he manipulates cardboard figures against an intricate tangle of plots, and to give them a semblance of reality, he catalogues all sorts of trappings from the years 1915 to the late 1940s. Concludes that sadly, this book is both not ambitious enough and too ambitious.

Healy, Robert C. "A Man Who Made It." Rev. of *The Sound of Bow Bells. New York Herald Tribune* 22 July 1962: 6.

Maintains that *The Sound of Bow Bells* is a book in which few authors could solve the technical problems posed. This is a fluent story—the telling is done with an incisive and direct narrative technique. Concludes that Weidman projects instant technicolor pictures of his characters to produce a rich, strong novel.

Hogan, William. "Weidman's Analysis of New York Jewish Life." Rev. of *The Enemy Camp. San Francisco Chronicle* 13 June 1958: 25.

The Enemy Camp is a rich, sprawling novel of New York life, masculine and powerful. It is honest, energetic, and curiously uneven. The plot is complex and detailed, and the storytelling quite superior.

Hughes, Riley. Rev. of *The Price Is Right. Commonweal* 25 Feb. 1949: 499.

Describes *The Price is Right* as dealing with New York and the advertising world, and using a heel for a hero. Concludes that, unfortunately, the book remains two-dimensional, achieving complacency and a clumsy touch minus the tang.

Hutchens, John K. "Book Review." Rev. of *Before You Go. New York Herald Tribune* 25 July 1960: 15.

Calls *Before You Go* a characteristically brisk piece of storytelling with some implausibly oratorical rhetoric and language that crackles in your ear when you read. Calls Weidman's wit brassy, New Yorkish, and, in its way, wicked. Finds the ending unconvincing.

"In Brief." Rev. of *Last Respects. New Republic* 12 Feb. 1972: 31.

Notes that Weidman's nineteenth novel is copious, energetic, perceptive, and abundantly inventive, but also rather unrestrained. Describes plot and characters.

Jackson, Joseph Henry. "Bookman's Notebook." Rev. of *Too Early to Tell. San Francisco Chronicle* 2 Dec. 1946: 12.

Weidman's *Too Early to Tell* is brutally wrathful and satirical. Describes the story, and comments that the reasonably sophisticated reader won't have much fun with the stereotypes. Still sees him as an extraordinarily capable writer who needed a tougher editor.

Jackson, Joseph Henry. "Drama in Country-Suburbia." Rev. of *The Third Angel. San Francisco Chronicle* 5 Oct. 1953: 19.

The Third Angel is a book in which Weidman observes and acutely controls his complicated material with dexterity and presents his people so that the reader is bound to feel kinship with them. It offers a warm, genuine understanding of American life. The characters are solidly painted and convincing, producing a first-rate picture gallery of recognizable flesh-and-blood people. Describes contents.

Jordan, Ruth. "Reversing the Masada Spirit." Rev. of *The Temple. Jewish Observer and Middle East Review* 31 Dec. 1976: 13.

Describes the contents of *The Temple,* and commends Weidman for his ability to tell a story, manage dialogue, and create character. Concludes, "For those who fall in with the conventions and who do not mind a layer of *schmaltz* to boot, *The Temple* is a good bedtime read."

Kazin, Alfred. "A Racketeer Among Fools." Rev. of *I Can Get It For You Wholesale*. *New York Herald Tribune Books* 9 May 1937: 2.

Describes *I Can Get It For You Wholesale* primarily in terms of its central character, Harry Bogan, who epitomizes an entire generation who grew up Jewish in New York City during the Depression, lacking heroes, being unsentimental about adolescence, elliptical, grim, politically radical, without idealism, and who felt the dilemmas of others were something to be avoided or exploited. Describes how, with the heart and mind of a gangster, Bogan becomes a lone symbol of a success in his generation. Commends Weidman for his acute knowledge of the culture, his morality, and his passion as a writer.

Kelly, James. "Coach on White House Sidelines." Rev. of *Before You Go*. *Saturday Review* 23 July 1960: 19-20.

Calls *Before You Go* another novel written in the long shadow of Harry Hopkins. Describes the story and characters. Concludes that this is a novel about the nature of leadership and its obligations. Complains that the form and motivation for this novel are not entirely clear, and suggests that, perhaps, it should have been shorter and more disciplined.

Kupferberg, Herbert. "Benny Kramer Is Back on the Make in *Tiffany Street*." Rev. of *Tiffany Street*. *National Observer* 9 Feb. 1974: 25.

Claims that *Tiffany Street* is full of warmth, humor, and sentimental affection for the past. With the skill of a natural storyteller, he moves swiftly back and forth between the various epochs and crises, peppering his narrative with sharp, sympathetic portrayals of interesting personages.

Lask, Thomas. "Books: Weidman's Saga of Immigrant Bootlegger." Rev. of *A Family Fortune*. *New York Times* 6 July 1978: C16.

Says *A Family Fortune* is written with craftsmanship and mastery. However, Weidman relies too much on skills , magnifies inessentials, provides unconvincing happenings, and substitutes melodrama for true conflict. There is a lot of highly polished veneer here. There is too much wiseacre-ish emphasis that makes all the characters sound the same, and he insists on spelling out the dialogue for the dim witted. This book is whipped cream—pleasant enough going down—but all air and no substance.

Leviant, Curt. "Weidman's East Side." Rev. of *Fourth Street East: A Novel of the Way It Was*. *Hadassah Magazine* Apr. 1971: 21.

Calls Weidman's novels generally facile, glib, and superficial. Describes

Fourth Street East, however, as a fine, warm book in which Jewish parents are not trodden on, and Jewish heritage is not viewed as a handicap.

Levin, Martin. "Reader's Report." Rev. of *The Center of the Action. New York Times Book Review* 13 July 1969: 40.

Complains that long before the end of the story, Weidman lets the steam out of the narrative through his windy style that embroiders peripheral matters at the expense of necessary tension. Concludes that this is a potpourri of period ingredients of the Jewish novel.

Ley, Murray Hickey. "Success Story." Rev. of *The Price Is Right. New York Times Book Review* 27 Feb. 1949: 24.

Calls the novel a fast moving story of cross and double cross. Sees it as a skilled delineation of people that shows an acute eye and ear at work. Comments also that it shows moral awareness as keen as a compass needle for where powerful pressure may eventually erupt and blow up the whole map. Concludes that mere contrivance has no place in this story.

Littell, Robert. "Outstanding Novels." Rev. of *I'll Never Go There Any More. Yale Review* ns 31.2 (1942): viii.

Describes the novel as less frenetic than his previous novels, less joyous, and less wallowing in a world of heels. Concludes that Weidman concentrates too much on cheap game, and never goes after wider problems and larger themes.

Little, Stuart W. "The Sissenwein Deal." Rev. of *The Center of the Action. Saturday Review* 12 July 1969: 58-59.

Considers this a book in which Weidman traces the most seemingly impersonal corporate decisions back to the very human factors that influence all such decisions. Concludes that he is a brilliant craftsman, and comments that the book is full of great one-liners.

"Madison Avenue Macbeth." Rev. of *The Price Is Right. Time* 21 Feb. 1949: 113-14.

Describes the story of *The Price Is Right*, and commends it for its satiric courage and verbal deftness in getting dialogue and character just right.

Maloney, Russell. "No Fuss, No Muss — and What Else?" Rev. of *The Captain's Tiger. New York Times Book Review* 10 Aug. 1947: 18.

Thinks that in *The Captain's Tiger* Weidman demonstrates his mastery of the short story form. Describes the *New Yorker* formula "no fuss, no muss" as the very formula these stories are based on.

March, Fred T. "Harry Bogan, the Bronx Hard Guy." Rev. of *What's In It For Me. New York Times Book Review* 30 Oct. 1938: 7.

Claims that *What's In It For Me?* demonstrates Weidman to be the best of our contemporary naturalists as he depicts the character of Harry Bogan in the Bronx. Suggests that there are three wisecracks to every page in what is a pretty hard cracking novel.

Marshall, Margaret. "Notes by the Way." Rev. of *I'll Never Go There Any More. Nation* 25 Oct. 1941: 403.

Describes *I'll Never Go There Any More* as containing bizarre characters, competent writing, and a passable plot. Suggests that it is time Weidman and other condescending hard-boiled novelists came off their perches and treated their characters as human beings, if only for the sake of their readers.

Mealand, Richard. "Mr. Weidman in Top Form." Rev. of *The Hand of the Hunter. New York Herald Tribune Book Review* 1 Apr. 1951: 4.

Claims that this novel shows Weidman at his most skilled, shrewd, entertaining, and profound. Provides a detailed account of the contents, and concludes that Weidman is really writing about all of us who may feel safe, prosperous, and untouchable by violence.

Mealand, Richard. "The Saga of a Feature Syndicate." Rev. of *The Price Is Right. New York Herald Tribune Weekly Book Review* 20 Feb. 1949: 4.

Calls *The Price Is Right* fast-paced, perceptive in its characterization, full of keen observation, original in humor and style, and just the last word in smartness. Concludes that it is well worth the price. Describes contents.

Morgan, Al. "A Versatile Story-Teller's Rich, Revealing Roundup." Rev. of *My Father Sits in the Dark and Other Selected Stories. New York Herald Tribune Lively Arts and Book Review* 2 July 1961: 21.

Describes several of the stories in this collection, and suggests that this is a rich collection by a master of this most difficult form. Concludes that it is Weidman at his best.

Morton, Frederic. "Jerome Weidman: Novel and Novelists." Rev. of *A Family Fortune. New York Times Book Review* 28 May 1978: 9.

Describes *A Family Fortune* as a book whose language is vintage Clifford Odets, without the poetic small talk to redeem it; whose juicy realism causes one to pause, and yet, whose total effect is to appall the reader with its truth.

"Now It Can Be Unloaded." Rev. of *Too Early to Tell. Time* 25 Nov. 1946: 114, 116.

Considers *Too Early to Tell* full of wonderful portraits of Vaudracour; malicious satire; and saucy, skillful scenes. Briefly summarizes plot.

Parker, Dorothy. "Book Reviews." Rev. of *Before You Go. Esquire* Sept. 1960: 40, 42.

Describes the novel as a masterful exercise in characterization through dialogue, despite the fact that this is a tale of almighty confusion with an all-time bore for a central character. Gives a full description of contents.

Parkinson, Richard N. "Life In Its True State." Rev. of *My Father Sits in the Dark and Other Selected Stories. Antioch Review* 21.4 (1961-62): 512-16.

Claims that *My Father Sits in the Dark* demonstrates Weidman's talent for making an incident which is so unpleasant, so well formed, and so seemingly attractive, the reader will be interested in it. Details contents of several of the stories.

Pickrel, Paul. "Jewish Families in Transition." Rev. of *The Sound of Bow Bells. Harper's* Sept. 1962: 100, 102.

Describes the novel in detail, commenting that the two sections differ widely in quality, the one being well done and the other, mere journalistic contrivance. Calls this mostly a slick commercial novel ironically concerning itself with the horrors of slick commercialism. Insists Weidman can do better.

Poore, Charles. "Books of the Times." Rev. of *Before You Go. New York Times* 26 July 1960: 27.

Claims that *Before You Go* is an outstanding success—heady and full of cheers and jeers. It is dramatically effective and full of commentary about passion, ambition, heartbreak, and revenge. All the material is fused in an immensely professional way into a picaresque hot lava flow of narrative.

Poore, Charles. "Books of the Times." Rev. of *My Father Sits in the Dark and Other Selected Stories. New York Times* 29 June 1961: 31.

Says *My Father Sits in the Dark* is a splendid retrospective exhibition done in the form of short stories. Details the content, and concludes that this is a skillful, humane, savagely brilliant performance.

Poore, Charles. "*I Can Get It For You Wholesale* and Other Recent Fictions." Rev. of *I Can Get It For You Wholesale. New York Times Book Review* 16 May 1937: 6.

Provides primarily a character study of Harry Bogan and a description of the contents of *I Can Get It For You Wholesale.* Commends the descriptions of the mother as some of the most moving in the book, as well as the wisecrack as the chief medium of speech.

Porter, John H. "With Malice Toward All." Rev. of *Too Early to Tell. The New Republic* 30 Dec. 1946: 928.

Complains that *Too Early To Tell* contains little except some shrill, rasping sounds as if the author felt himself strangling in red tape. Suggests that this is really a barrel house comedy full of bitter small talk and gossip. Concludes that there is no compassion or moral imagination here.

Portrait, Ruth. "Look Back in Nostalgia." Rev. of *Fourth Street East: A Novel of the Way It Was. Jewish Observer and Middle East Review* 4 June 1971: 19.

Calls *Fourth Street East* a heartwarming, sentimental book which provides a welcome antidote to today's piles of turgid or neurotic novels and depressing pornography. Concludes that it is beautifully and movingly conveyed.

Powell, Dawn. "Growing Pains." Rev. of *The Lights Around the Shore. New Republic* 7 June 1943: 771-72.

Calls this a book with no real foundation. The characters seem unreal, and the plot is wild. Argues that the idea of the book is far superior to its execution, which is blurred in the final chapter. Concludes that this is a better book than the previous one, but that the punch is still not there.

Rogow, Lee. "Money Talking." Rev. of *The Price is Right. Saturday Review of Literature* 19 Feb. 1949: 11.

Calls *The Price Is Right* a brisk, well-made work with a handy plot, well-tuned dialogue, a wide variety of characters, and a photographic appreciation for the fabric of contemporary life. Concludes that the story is deftly, and wittily told, and that each chapter ends with a cliff-hanging touch of suspense.

Rosenthal, Raymond. "What's in It for Weidman ?" Rev. of *The Enemy Camp. Commentary* Feb. 1959: 171-73.

Suggests that *The Enemy Camp* is that long-deferred moment of embarrassment because it is long-winded, uninspired, and patently illogical. But notes that this is a small matter compared to the author's spiritual and intellectual condition. Argues that Weidman's abhorrence of his despicable major character is so hedged, qualified, and camouflaged in the interests of popularity that he blunts all its passion. Concludes that this is a tawdry creation.

Rugoff, Milton. "Mr. Weidman Mellows." Rev. of *The Captain's Tiger. New York Herald Tribune Weekly Book Review* 17 Aug. 1947: 4.

Calls *The Captain's Tiger* a collection of stories surprising for an author with a reputation for hardness. Suggests that time and the war have given Weidman a chance to diversify his work. Concludes that the stories in this collection are consistently good reading.

Semple, Robert B., Jr. "Despite Some Touches of O. Henry, Mr. Weidman Belabors His Points." Rev. of *The Death of Dickie Draper and Nine Other Stories. National Observer* 24 May 1965: 21.

Word of Mouth is filled with nuances, moods, and depths and is a first class story. Yet it fails, largely because Weidman won't let the readers alone. Terrified that they will miss the point, he lays it all out in black and white like an editorialist pointing a deliberate moral, and the whole thing is suddenly more obvious than it has to be. This same tendency persists in his collection of stories *The Death of Dickie Draper.*

"Short Notices." Rev. of *Other People's Money. Time* 19 May 1967: 136, 138.

Describes this novel as based on an improbable situation, and writes it off as merely competent.

"Small Defeats." Rev. of *My Father Sits in the Dark and Other Selected Stories. Time* 7 July 1961: 69-70.

Claims that Weidman has an accurate ear, comes close to being a really good short story writer, and always presents the nubs of his stories neatly wrapped for the reader. Suggests, however, that while there is always something in the packages, it is never much. Details the contents of several of the stories, and concludes that Weidman's fiction suffers because he never takes risks.

"Smart Guy." Rev. of *I Can Get It For You Wholesale. Time* 10 May 1937: 93-94.

Describes the novel in detail, and recounts Weidman's story about meeting his classmate ten years after they had all graduated and wondering how they all turned into such sharp, little wise guys who have lost their idealism—hence the characters of the novel.

"Smart Guy's Fall." Rev. of *What's In It for Me? Time* 31 Oct. 1938: 57.

Complains that this novel contains Harry Bogan, the biggest heel in contemporary U. S. fiction. Details the contents, and concludes that when Harry makes his getaway, he will not be missed. Suggests that if author Weidman has any more like Harry Bogan up his sleeve, God help the good name of Manhattan's garment center.

Soskin, William. "Garment Center Photography." Rev. of *What's In It for Me?New York Herald Tribune Books* 30 Oct. 1938: 4.

Calls *What's In It for Me?* a realistic and horribly truthful story about the garment industry. Describes Harry Bogan in considerable detail, and describes the outcome of the story.

Soskin, William. "Sentimentality Reversed." Rev. of *The Horse That Could Whistle "Dixie" and Other Stories. New York Herald Tribune Books* 4 June 1939: 10.

The Horse That Could Whistle "Dixie" is a collection of short stories by a writer who is an excellent mimic, and writes his best when he is capturing the inflections of Jewish-American characters, or slinging the lingo of the buglers, salesmen, models, and entrepreneurs of the clothing industry. Unfortunately it is frequently his more serious writing that does not live up to its author's intentions.

"Sourball." Rev. of *The Horse That Could Whistle "Dixie" and Other Stories. Time* 29 May 1939: 80, 82.

Comments that this is a collection of short stories containing a wide variety of materials published in magazines over several years. Describes the majority as dealing with the Manhattan East Siders Weidman grew up with, while a good number show his range, human and geographical. Concludes that they also show that his sympathies can be as warm as his satire is cold.

Stegner, Wallace. "A New Weidman." Rev. of *The Lights Around the Shore. Saturday Review of Literature* 29 May 1943: 28.

Describes *The Lights Around the Shore* as an attempt to leave behind hard-boiled fiction and write another kind. Suggests that, unfortunately, the protagonist, Peter, never succeeds in being more than a sullen, bewildered youth and that Fini's mysteries remain unmotivated, either in terms of her character or the necessities of her case. Shows how, in the end, the book resolves itself into an experiment in mystery, the injections of artificial suspense into a slow plot full of bizarre characters and not-quite-likely coincidences. Concludes that the whole thing has too much glitter, surface skill, and slickness.

Sterne, Richard Clark. "SR: Books." Rev. of *Fourth Street East: A Novel of How It Was. Saturday Review* 9 Jan. 1972: 69.

Calls *Last Respects* a fictionalized memoir of life on the Lower East Side in 1927. Notes that, unlike *Fourth Street East*, the tone of this novel is relentlessly sour. Concludes that this book gives voice to the fears and resentments of middle-class city dwellers who are looking for scapegoats. Unfortunately it does not help us face these predicaments.

Sterne, Richard Clark. "SR Books." Rev. of *Last Respects. Saturday Review* 22 Jan. 1972:69.

Calls *Last Respects* a fictionalized memoir of life on the Lower East Side in 1927. Notes that, unlike *Fourth Street East*, the tone of this book is relentlessly sour. Concludes that this book gives voice to the fears and resentments of middle-class city dwellers who are looking for scapegoats. Unfortunately this book does not help us face these predicaments.

Stevens, George. "Double Exposure." Rev. of *I Can Get It for You Wholesale. Saturday Review of Literature* 15 May 1937: 11.

Calls this novel a realistic satire of an unscrupulous, young Jew done in a tough, ironic manner.

Stevens, George. "Good Ideas for Stories." Rev. of *The Horse That Could Whistle "Dixie" and Other Stories. Saturday Review of Literature* 3 June 1939: 7.

Calls this a book by a serious and talented writer. Considers it full of extended anecdotes that proceed from ideas rather than from a sense of life. Claims that they have more punch and point than the usual slice-of-life narratives, and carry more conviction than slick magazine jobs.

"The Tiger Scratches." Rev. of *The Captain's Tiger. Time* 11 Aug. 1947: 98.

Considers Weidman's talents noisy and devoted to proving that life in New York City is a rat race between the stinkers and the saps. Suggests that *The Captains's Tiger* will add little to Weidman's reputation because it shows that even tough guy fiction can be written to a formula as predictable as slick-paper romance.

Trilling, Diana. "Fiction in Review." Rev. of *Lights Around the Shore. Nation* 5 June 1943: 815-16.

Describes the contents of *Lights Around the Shore*, and comments that, though it is a failure, it has admirable intentions and an excellent idea. Considers the characterization often false, off-center and demoralizing.

Trilling, Diana. "Fiction in Review." Rev. of *Too Early to Tell. Nation* 14 Dec. 1946: 702.

Suggests that *Too Early to Tell* bears very little relation to earlier novels, and seems quirkily arresting and lacking in range. Concludes, however, that Weidman has been cast with his wicked characters and treated unfairly by critics.

Van Doren, Dorothy. "Modern Morality Play." Rev. of *What's In It for Me. Nation* 10 Dec. 1938: 636.

Sees *What's In It for Me* as an old-fashioned morality play where vice is punished and virtue rewarded. Comments on the plot of this novel and that of the novel which preceded it—*I Can Get It For You Wholesale*.

Van Gelder, Robert. "Max and Mary." Rev. of *I'll Never Go there Any More. New York Times Book Review* 19 Oct. 1941: 24, 27.

Claims that *I'll Never Go there Any More* reads like a Frankie and Johnnie folk ballad. Concludes that its scenes are undeniably authentic. Details plot and characters.

Van Gelder, Robert. "Mr. Weidman's Stories." Rev. of *The Horse That Could Whistle "Dixie" and Other Stories. New York Times Book Review* 28 May 1939: 7.

Describes *The Horse That Could Whistle "Dixie" and Other Stories* as a collection of wit-quickened morality stories about a vicious little Bronx bogeyman, Harry Bogan. Calls these original stories by a writer of marked talent which break through territory that popular fiction has hitherto ignored. Concludes that these are meaty, exciting, even disturbing stories.

"Virtuoso." Rev. of *My Father Sits in the Dark and Other Selected Stories*. *Times Literary Supplement* 25 Jan. 1963: 53.

Claims that *My Father Sits in the Dark* is a selection of short stories written naturally and skillfully. Weidman has dexterity and a sense of timing. His theme is exile and the darkness and power of America and modern New York. Concludes that his great weakness for one so endowed with fluency is a tendency to sometimes confuse hokum with the real thing.

Walsh, Chad. "Kindling Points." Rev. of *The Death of Dickie Draper and Nine Other Stories*. *Chicago Sunday Tribune Book Week* 30 May 1965: 14.

The Death of Dickie Draper and Nine Other Stories is described in terms of its wildly divergent settings, psychologically constructed characters and slickness, gimmicks, and fearful clarities.

Walsh, George. "Stage Lights on the Dark Past." Rev. of *Word of Mouth*. *Cosmopolitan* Nov. 1964: 27-28.

Claims that *Word of Mouth* is the mental dissection of a seemingly normal man done remorselessly and unpleasantly. Details the contents, style, and general effects on the reader.

Wiegand, William. "Upward, Ever Upward on a Red-Hot Typewriter." Rev. of *The Sound of Bow Bells*. *New York Times Book Review* 22 July 1962: 6, 7.

Provides a summary of the plot, and comments on the strengths and weaknesses of characterization. Finds the structure and the melancholy tone worthy of James Gould Cozzens, but suggests that Weidman is best when he taps his more natural vein. Comments on how fine and extravagant he is in his satiric moments, and how he can draw a villain as savagely as any writer around. Concludes that this novel, like most of his others, is a rags-to-riches story.

Winegarten, Renee. "From Belsen to Broadway." Rev. of *Where the Sun Never Sets and Other Stories*. *Jewish Observer and Middle East Review* 28 Feb. 1964: 19.

Says *Where the Sun Never Sets* is a collection of short stories whose slick expertise in dialogue, plotting, and technique is not to be despised, but which quite fail to disguise the fact that Weidman has nothing to say.

Woodburn, John. "School for Word-Warriors." Rev. of *Too Early to Tell. Saturday Review of Literature* 7 Dec. 1946: 34, 36.

Describes *Too Early to Tell* as full of venomous portraits, meticulous and repetitious, and failing to gauge the distance which furnishes the perspective of art. Suggests that, above all, it is unfair in that it actually describes the Vaudracour training school for psychological warfare at which Weidman taught during the war years, while at the same time he claims not to have built the characters on actual persons. Concludes that the book does have its high moments of comedy, passion, delicate emotion, and acute perception, but that when it comes to assassinating character through conversation, Weidman has few parallels.

Interviews

Bannon, Barbara A. "PW Interviews Jerome Weidman." *Publishers Weekly* 28 July 1969: 13-15. Rpt. in *The Author Speaks: Selected PW Interviews, 1967-1976.* New York: Bowker, 1977. 175-77.

Contains the reported conversation of Barbara Bannon and Jerome Weidman about his life and his latest novel, *The Center of the Action.* A general and discursive article.

Biographical Sources

Alsterlund, B. "Jerome Weidman." *Wilson Library Bulletin* May 1942: 696.

Briefly describes Weidman's upbringing and education, the development of his writing career, his approach to writing, and the account of a trip around the world in 1939 after Hitler invaded Czechoslovakia.

Blicksilver, Edith. "Jerome Weidman." *Twentieth-Century American-Jewish Fiction Writers.* Ed. Daniel Walden. Detroit: Gale, 1984. Vol. 28 of *Dictionary of Literary Biography.* 94 vols. to date. 1978- . 316-23.

More than details of his life, this is a career biography, tracing the development of the author's canon, describing the contents and themes of his works, evaluating his reputation, and placing him in the larger context of American literary history. Includes lists of primary and secondary sources and illustrations.

Shepard, Richard F. "Jerome Weidman: Novel and Novelist." *New York Times Book Review* 28 May 1978: 9, 14-15.

Recounts an interview with Weidman covering his forty-year writing career, his writing habits, his sources of ideas, his reactions to critics and reviewers, his literary output, his own evaluation of his success, and his treatment of Jewish characters and themes in what Meyer Levin called the "self-hating period of writing." Also discusses his latest novel, *Family Fortune.*

Weidman, Jerome. *Praying for Rain.* New York: Harper, 1986.

Herman Wouk

1915 –

Primary Sources

Novels

Aurora Dawn: The True History of Andrew Beale. Containing a Faithful Account of the Great Riot, Together with the Complete Texts of Michael Wilde's Oration and Father Stanfield's Sermon. A Venture Press Book. New York: Simon, 1947; New York: Eds. for the Armed Services, 1947; London: Barrie, 1947, 1948; Garden City: Doubleday, 1956, 1973; London: Cape, 1957; London: Four Square-Landsborough, 1959; London: Fontana-Collins, 1975; New York: Pocket, 1983.

The Caine Mutiny: A Novel of World War II. Garden City: Doubleday, 1951, 1954, 1961; Chicago: Sears Readers Club, 1951; London: Cape, 1951, 1952; Trade ed. Garden City: Doubleday, 1952; London: Reprint Society, 1953; Harmondsworth: Penguin, 1958; Abridged ed. London: Longmans, 1962; London: Pan, 1964; New York: Dell, 1966; London: Heron, 1972; New York: Pocket, 1973, 1975, 1979, 1983; London: Fontana-Collins, 1974, 1978; New York: Washington Square, 1975; Franklin Center: Franklin, 1977, 1978, 1980; Classics of Naval Literature. Annapolis: Naval Institute, 1987.

The City Boy: The Adventures of Herbie Bookbinder. New York: Simon, 1948; Garden City: Doubleday, 1952, 1969; London: Cape, 1956;

London: Brown, 1959; New York: Dell, 1964; New York: Pocket [Cited in PBIP, 1974]; New York: Pocket, 1980, 1983.

Don't Stop the Carnival. Garden City: Doubleday, 1965, 1973; New York: Pocket, 1965, 1966, 1983; London: Collins, 1965; London: Fontana, 1966; London: Fontana-Collins, 1974, 1979.

Inside, Outside. Boston: Little, 1985; London: Collins, 1985; New York: Avon, 1986; London: Fontana, 1986.

The Lomokome Papers. New York: Pocket, 1968, 1974; Spring Valley: Queens House, 1978; Publ. in full in *Collier's* 17 Feb. 1956: 69-84.

Marjorie Morningstar. Garden City: Doubleday, 1955, 1988; New York: Pocket, 1955, 1973, 1977, 1983; London: Cape, 1955; London: Four Square-Landsborough, 1958; New York: Signet-NAL, 1962; London: Fontana-Collins, 1973, 1979; Franklin Center: Franklin, 1981.

Slattery's Hurricane. New York: Permabooks, 1956; London: New English Library, 1965, 1975; London: Four Square, 1967; New York: Pocket, 1977.

War and Remembrance. Boston: Little, 1978; Franklin Center: Franklin, 1978; London: Collins, 1978; New York: Pocket, 1980, 1983; London: Fontana, 1980.

The Winds of War. Boston: Little, 1971; London: Collins, 1971, 1983; New York: Pocket, 1973; London: Fontana-Collins, 1974, 1978; Glasgow: Fontana, 1974; New York: Pocket [Cited in PBIP, 1974]; Text ed. New York: Pocket, 1977; T. V. Tie-in ed. New York: Pocket, 1983; Publ. with *War and Rembrance* as a boxed set. Boston: Little, 1978.

Youngblood Hawke. Garden City: Doubleday, 1962, 1988; London: Collins, 1962; London: Pan, 1964; New York: Signet-NAL [Cited in PBIP, 1969]; New York: Pocket, 1975, 1977, 1982. Serialized in *McCall's* Mar. 1962: 74-77+; Apr. 1962: 80-81+; May 1962: 98-99, 187-88, 190-205; June 1962: 92-93, 193-202; July 1962: 74-75, 134-41.

Short Fiction in Anthologies

"Herbie Solves a Mystery." *Feast of Leviathan: Tales of Adventure, Faith and Love from Jewish Literature.* Ed. Leo W. Schwarz. New York: Rinehart, 1956. 3-21.

"Irresistable Force." *Fireside Treasury of Modern Humor.* Ed. Scott Meredith. New York: Simon, 1963. 969-76.

Short Fiction in Periodicals

"Irresistible Force." *Esquire* Aug. 1952: 27, 96.

"Old Flame." *Good Housekeeping* May 1956: 68-69, 134, 136.

"Slattery's Hurricane." *American Magazine* July 1949: 52-59, 66-68, 70-72, 74-80.

Secondary Sources

Books

Beichman, Arnold. *Herman Wouk, the Novelist as Social Historian.* New Brunswick: Transaction, 1984.

Articles and Chapters

Bierstedt, Robert. "The Tergiversation of Herman Wouk." *Great Moral Dilemmas in Literature Past and Present.* Ed. R. M. MacIver. Religion and Civilization Series. New York: Inst. for Rel. and Soc. Studies, 1956. 1-14.

Describes the publishing history and reception of *The Caine Mutiny* and its subsequent play version. Recapitulates the plot, and then examines the moral question posed by the mutiny and subsequent trial. Believes Wouk belatedly tried to change the story from the way he had written it and botched it, with an unbelievable reversal at the end.

Bolton, Richard R. "*The Winds of War* and Wouk's Wish for the World." *Midwest Quarterly* 16.4 (1975): 389-408.

Describes this book as a phenomenon of popular culture—the shaping of a generation's perception of itself and its era. Argues that Wouk is not only re-creating and re-shaping our interpretation of WWII, but, like Tolstoy, advancing his own moral views of the society and world to which the war gave rise. Examines Wouk's stated purposes, methods, moral and philosophical attitudes toward WWII, and the comments on human will and destiny the book makes. A major treatment which views the novel primarily as an historical romance.

Brown, Spencer. "A Code of Honor For a Mutinous Era: Herman Wouk on the Problem of Responsibility." *Commentary* June 1952: 595-99.

Commends Wouk for the introduction of moral principles and issues into the business of writing about WWII. However, argues that he falls seriously short in each of the novels of the kind of moral seriousness found in *Billy Budd*. Argues that he narrows the tremendous gap between good and evil found in *Moby Dick*. Makes several comparisons with Melville, and finally complains that "two thirds of its length is a mixture of excellent adventure, a love affair about as exciting as tapioca with Scott Fitzgerald sauce. . . ." Concludes by analyzing the code of ethics in *The Caine Mutiny* and the pop formula employed in actually writing it.

Browne, James R. "Distortion in *The Caine Mutiny*." *College English* Jan. 1956: 216-18.

Concerns himself with the problematic ending of the novel which introduces the "Queeg as victim" problem, thus structurally distorting the book. Concentrates on Greenwald's defense of Queeg at the end of the novel as the author's view of him, and contrasts this with the other consistent picture of him built up throughout the novel.

Burgess, Anthony. "The Caine Mutiny." *Ninety-nine Novels: The Best in English Since 1939.* Anthony Burgess. London: Allison, 1984. 56.

Argues that no writer has worked harder at amassing the historical facts about WWII, and that this remains his best book, despite its non-literary qualities.

Carpenter, Frederic I. "Herman Wouk and the Wisdom of Disillusion." *English Journal* Jan. 1956: 1-6, 32; *College English* Jan. 1956: 211-15.

Details the history of Wouk's writing career, and relates the thematic and moral issues of *Aurora Dawn* to *The Caine Mutiny*. Discusses the shape, form, style, themes, and characters in *The Caine Mutiny*, and concludes that this is the best of his novels because it is the least moralistic.

Cohen, Joseph. "Wouk's *Morningstar* and Hemingway's *Sun*." *South Atlantic Quarterly* 58.2 (1959): 213-24.

Argues that Noel Airman is the Nick Adams of Hemingway's story "The Three Day Blow." Traces the parallels from one story to the other with regard to both protagonists' attitudes toward love and marriage. Describes the affinities in terms of characterization, plot, setting, and theme. The remainder of the article concentrates on *Marjorie Morningstar* in relation to the principal Hemingway source.

Darby, William. "I Can't Leave My Outfit." *Necessary American Fictions: Popular Literature of the 1950s*. William Darby. Bowling Green: Bowling Green State U Popular P, 1987. 43-55.

An extensive treatment of *The Caine Mutiny* which focuses on the understanding of war which the protagonist, Willie, develops as he passes through the course of the novel from being a spoiled, naive child, to being a responsible, reasonable adult.

Fiedler, Leslie A. "Clarissa in America: Toward Marjorie Morningstar." *Love and Death in the American Novel*. Leslie A. Fiedler. New York: Criterion, 1960. 248-53.

Claims that Wouk has profited by the collapse of hyper-genteel taboos in the bourgeois itself, while his literary forefather, Dreiser, could not write the pure Richardsonian drama of seduction like *Marjorie Morningstar*. Claims that only one major revision has been made in the myths of seduction between *Charlotte Temple* and *Marjorie Morningstar*—the newer genteel sentimentalism will not let the fallen woman die. Also discusses the shadow of Flaubert in this work.

Fitch, Robert E. "The Bourgeois and the Bohemian." *Antioch Review* 16.2 (1956): 131-45.

Argues that in *Marjorie Morningstar* Wouk is conducting a purge— "cleansing the temple and restoring the worship of the true god. So it is that he breaks down the Baalim and shatters the idols of heathen Bohemia." Names the idols as Marx, Freud, Sex, and Greenwich Village.

Frankel, Theodore. "The Anatomy of a Bestseller: Second Thoughts on *The Caine Mutiny*." *Western Humanities Review* 9.4 (1955): 333-39.

Decides to revalue the book because of its moral seriousness and social documentary nature. Considers it skillfully written, if a little prosaic, and claims that the plot and characters unfold throughout the action. Suggests, however, that they tend to become mechanical and rigid, moving with almost machine-like precision. Sees them as ambulatory case histories whose behavior is determined by class and individual neuroses. Believes, above all, that Wouk articulates the mentality of a middle class of the day which believes in authoritarian attitudes and which elevates the state as the "good" above all other special groups. Laments that Wouk's considerable talent should have been used in the service of political obscurantism.

Fuller, Edmund. "The Hipster or the Organization Man?" *Man in Modern Fiction: Some Minority Opinions on Contemporary American Writing.* Edmund Fuller. Random House, 1958. 133-48.

Considers Wouk the victim of an unfair type of criticism, and denies exclusivity to *The Naked and the Dead* or *From Here To Eternity* as normative views of the war. Examines the case against Wouk, and asserts that *The Caine Mutiny* discusses authority and the individual within a closed military system rather than civilian life at large. Examines the characters and situations within the theory of Whyte's *Organization Man* and finds the book profoundly aware of organizational dynamics and their effects on individuals and middle-class America.

Gordis, Robert. "Religion in One Dimension: The Judaism of Herman Wouk." *Midstream* 6.1 (1960): 82-90.

Considers Wouk's *This Is My God* a welcome introduction to the Jewish religion that will read well for Jew and non-Jew alike. Although this article explicates in great detail this non-fiction work, it is a useful background for students of Wouk's religious and social philosophy.

Grenander, M. E. "The Heritage of Cain: Crime in American Fiction." *Annals of the American Academy of Political and Social Science* 423 (1976): 47-66.

Argues that the treatment of crime in American popular fiction strokes the norms of the mass audience yet differs sharply from the depiction of crime in high culture literary art. Briefly mentions Wouk's quasi-serious philosophical depictions of crime in his several works.

Guttmann, Allen. "The Postwar Revival of Peoplehood." *The Jewish Writer in America: Assimilation and the Crisis of Identity.* Allen Guttmann. New York: Oxford UP, 1971. 120-25.

Describes the structures of *The Caine Mutiny* and *Marjorie Morningstar*, and identifies Wouk along with Cohen and Potok as novelists with a dramatic commitment to "peoplehood." Claims that the book provides a simple dramatization of moral death and resurrection.

Haley, Beverly. "The Caine Mutiny." *English Journal* Jan. 1976: 71-72.

Discusses the value of *The Caine Mutiny* in the high school English classroom because it is free of complexity of style, and because it fits various thematic units on war, prejudice, and growing up. Describes the contents and several of the major characters.

Hofstadter, Beatrice K. "Popular Culture and the Romantic Heroine." *American Scholar* 30.1 (1960-61): 98, 100, 102, 104, 106, 108, 110, 112, 114, 116.

In the context of a substantial article on the historical depiction of the romantic heroine of American fiction, Hofstadter identifies Marjorie Morningstar as a post-flapper Diana Mayo, who, after a brief rejection of her middle-class upbringing, finally immerses herself in conventional marriage. Concludes that this is a novel concerned not with individuality, but with the dangers of freedom.

Howard, Jane. "Herman Wouk Surfaces Again." *Life* 6 Nov. 1971: 53-54, 56.

Calls *The Winds of War* staggeringly earnest, uncontaminated by current literary fashion, and a tribute to the author's diligence, energy, and scholarly discipline. Describes the methods of Wouk's research, her own impression upon meeting him, his private charities, and his work habits.

Hutchens, John K. "Happy Success Story of Herman Wouk." *New York Herald Tribune Book Review* 4 Sept. 1955: 2, 10.

Discusses Wouk's success as a writer as evidenced by the success of *The Caine Mutiny*, and the advance sales of *Marjorie Morningstar*. Also discusses the relationship of his novels to the theater and his literary influences.

Hyman, Stanley Edgar. "Some Questions About Herman Wouk." *New Leader* 14 May 1962: 6-7. Rpt. in *Standards: A Chronicle of Books for Our Time*. Stanley Edgar Hyman. New York: Horizon, 1966. 68-72.

A satiric denunciation of *Youngblood Hawke* with its "Victorian-girlish" and "Tom Swiftian" prose, ridiculous similes, a "desperate contrivance" of a plot, and "cereal-box cut-out" characters. Claims that it is most fraudulent, and worthless. Concludes that Wouk has no subject left but his inexhaustible narcissism and that he stands for conventional American patriotism, old-fashioned morality: female chastity is right, adultery is wrong. Finally concludes that Wouk's morality is less interested in honesty and charity than it is in virtuous womanhood.

Jackson, Joseph Henry. "Bookman's Notebook." Rev. of *Aurora Dawn. San Francisco Chronicle* 21 Apr. 1947: 16.

Provides a plot summary of *Aurora Dawn*, calling it a classic of its kind. Concludes that this is a serious social commentary, and that Mr. Wouk's literary skills are not inconsiderable.

Karl, Frederick R. "The War Novel as Imitation." *American Fictions 1940/1980: A Comprehensive History and Critical Evaluation.* Frederick R. Karl. New York: Harper, 1983. 110-13.

Considers *The Caine Mutiny* superbly narrated and very indicative of the mood of the country in the 1950s. Claims that it is a good story told with a clear plot line and several varieties of character. Suggests that his ideological purposes were to do with the nature of responsibility, the limits of individuality, the question of command, and the role of the military in the life of the individual. Concludes that lying behind all this is the analogy of the state and its leaders while above all it is anti-intellectual and pro-Jewish.

Kramer, Maurice. "The Secular Mode of Jewishness." *Works* 1.1 (1967): 99-102, 104-08, 110-16.

Discusses the issues of Jewish identity having to do with both religious and secular positions. Comments that Wouk, an avowedly orthodox Jew, deftly skirts the issue of religion in *Marjorie Morningstar* though he writes with feeling about his grandfather in *This Is My God*. Concludes that Wouk cannot find holiness at all in his fiction.

Lester, Elenore. "*Marjorie Morningstar* Revisited." *Lilith* 1 (Fall 1976): 13-15, 42.

Argues that in this novel Wouk is interested in the woman protagonist as symbol of Jewish continuity. Sees her as a heroine whose decision for a middle-class existence is vital to the continuance of the Jewish community. Notes that the Jewish womb is the very house of Israel. Marjorie's defloration has cosmological implications because it occurs at the eclipse of the moon, resulting in nothing but shock and shame. Yet argues that this blueprint of female success is a problem in the novel because it begs the question of whether a happy marriage to Milton will turn a radiant woman into a suburban zombie by the time she is 40? Concludes that it would be better to blame the collapse of the Jewish family on the collapse of Jewish life.

Mandelbaum, Michael. "The Political Lessons of Two World War II Novels: A Review Essay." *Political Science Quarterly* 94.3 (1979): 515-22.

Calls these novels books that fall somewhere between fiction and history. Notes that the historical romance is an effective form in which to work out its central themes. Claims that Wouk gives better pictures of the principal leaders than military or political history could. Generally discourses on the war itself and Wouk's characters.

"Marjorie Morningstar." Survey of Contemporary Fiction. Ed. Frank N. Magill. Rev. ed. 12 vols. Englewood Cliffs: Salem, 1977. 7: 4769-71.

A standard reference article describing plot, character, themes, and style in the novel.

Mazzeno, Laurence W. "Herman Wouk." *Beacham's Popular Fiction in America.* Ed. Walton Beacham. 4 vols. Washington: Beacham, 1986. 4: 1483-89.

A standard reference article covering the publishing history, critical reception, and a complete analysis of *The Caine Mutiny, War and Remembrance,* and *Inside, Outside.*

McClean, Lydia. "The Incredible Voyage of the 'Caine.'" *Vogue* 1 Feb. 1953: 194-95, 222-24, 226.

Comments on the publishing history and describes the writing of *The Caine Mutiny.* Attempts to rectify the lukewarm reception *Saturday Review* gave to the book when it first appeared. Provides considerable plot summary, argues that the book can be read on several levels, and presents the characters as three-dimensional. Lauds the technical accuracy of the book, recounts Wouk's educational history, early jobs, and meeting with his first publishers and filmmakers.

McElderry, B. R., Jr. "The Conservative as Novelist: Herman Wouk." *Arizona Quarterly* 15.2 (1959): 128-36.

Disagrees with previous negative views on *The Caine Mutiny* and *Marjorie Morningstar.* Yet contends there are two common weaknesses in these two otherwise successful books. Sees the sudden reversal near the end of *The Caine Mutiny* as representing an injection of conservative values in such a manner that it is structurally weak and at odds with the character values established through nine-tenths of the novel. Also notes that the same injection of conservative values sends Marjorie Morningstar back into a lackluster, suburban existence at odds with the character she has become throughout the book. Concludes that it functions to warn youth to close their ears to the siren song of idealism, love, and ambition.

McInerny, Dennis Q. "Herman Wouk." *Critical Survey of Long Fiction.* Ed. Frank N. Magill. 9 vols. Englewood Cliffs: Salem, 1983. 7: 2961-73.

A standard reference article covering principal long fiction, other literary forms, achievements, biography, critical analysis, and bibliography.

Metraux, Rhoda. "*The Caine Mutiny.*" *Explorations* 5 (1956): 36-44.

Describes the theme of *The Caine Mutiny* as the development of reciprocal loyalty up and down the structure of authority with obedience as a necessary condition for responsible action. Claims that it is an American morality tale concerned chiefly with human relationships, structures of power, and responsibility.

Phillipson, John S. "Herman Wouk and Thomas Wolfe." *Thomas Wolfe Review* 12.2 (1988): 33-37.

Compares the character of Youngblood Hawke with Thomas Wolfe, pointing out both similarities and differences. Contains considerable biographical material on Wolfe and some material on style and contents of *Youngblood Hawke.*

Ribalow, Harold U. "From *Hungry Hearts* to *Marjorie Morningstar*: The Progress of an American Minority Told in Fiction." *Saturday Review* 14 Sept. 1957: 46-48.

Provides a brief history of Wouk's rise to fame and a history of how the Jew has been portrayed in fiction since the 1900s.

Rosenfeld, Isaac. "For God and the Suburbs." *Partisan Review* 22.4 (1955): 565-69; Rpt. in *An Age of Enormity: Life and Writing in the Forties and Fifties* . Ed. Theodore Solotaroff. Cleveland: World, 1962. 309-14.

Facetiously argues that the campaign managers of the New Orthodoxy have run through history, economics, sociology, political theory, psychology, theology, and mysticism, but that the only one to come up with a really new idea is Herman Wouk, who bases his case for God and the suburbs on Marjorie Morgenstern, a pretty Jewish girl with a talent for dramatics to preserve her virginity and bag a husband. A detailed, sarcastic analysis of the novel, concluding that the book is an artistic and moral failure.

Scott, Otto J. "Wouk's American Epos." *Chronicles of Culture* 3.3 (1979): 11-16.

Details Wouk's publishing career, discusses individual novels in passing, and spends most of its efforts on *The Winds of War* and *War and Remembrance*. Commends the pair for their careful plotting, fascinating description and lucid assessments of the world, war, and its people. Accounts for Wouk's lack of critical acclaim because of his refusal to accept counterculture mores and the fads of the contemporary novel—all attitudes which menace popular writing. Concludes with a structural, stylistic, and thematic examination of the book in an attempt to redeem it literarily.

Stuckey, W. J. "World War II as Entertainment and Moral Issue." *The Pulitzer Prize Novels: A Critical Backward Look.* W. J. Stuckey. Norman: U of Oklahoma P, 1981. 158-64.

Calls *The Caine Mutiny* a blend of popular entertainment and serious moralizing. Provides a detailed account of the contents and moral dilemmas of the novel, reviews its critical reception, and condemns the book for its unreasonable ending. Discusses Wouk's disturbing habits of using racial stereotypes, and delineates his attack on Freudian psychology and anti-intellectualism generally. Concludes that Willie's success is that of his predecessors. Sees Willie's and America's maturity as consisting of a willingness to blindly follow authority wherever it may lead. Wonders how the author reconciles this with his disapproval of Nazi abuse of authority.

Swados, Harvey. "Popular Taste and *The Caine Mutiny*." *Partisan Review* 20.2 (1953): 248-56. Rpt. in *The Scene Before You: A New Approach to American Culture.* Ed. Chandler Brossard. New York: Rinehart, 1955. 138-46; *A Radical's America.* Harvey Swados. Boston: Little, 1962. 235-44.

Details the emergence of a mid-cult audience of children of immigrants, who, bored with showgirl musicals and pulp fiction and imbued with leisure time in unprecedented quantities, have turned to Wouk's type of fiction to examine ideas, their own roots, and the culture in which they live. Assesses the popularity of *The Caine Mutiny* in light of this audience which believes in social pieties, admires racial stereotyping, engages in mass snobbery, hates intellectuals, enjoys pseudo-patriotic verbiage, and buys books which stoke their cultural biases.

Waldmeir, Joseph J. "Two Dissenting Voices." *American Novels of the Second World War*. Joseph J. Waldmeir. The Hague: Mouton, 1969. 125-37.

Considers Wouk a writer speaking loudly for a minority who dissented strongly from conventional literary treatments of war in WW II novels. Argues that *The Caine Mutiny* is a service-blasting, liberal, intellectual novel with a major twist in its ending in which Keefer, the reader of Proust, ends up being the villain of the piece. Calls this ending grossly sentimentalized, fantastic, and unprepared for.

Whipple, William. "Justice—the Phantom of the Literary Trial." *Ball State Teachers College Forum* 2.2 (1961-62): 33-38.

Discusses the traditional ways authors have used the central plot device of the trial to pit university against society. Then proceeds to explain how Wouk has both mastered and altered the formula in *The Caine Mutiny*. Questions the concepts of justice Wouk is advocating as he puzzles over the disposition of punishment at the end of the novel.

Wouk, Herman. "Gleanings from the Editor's Mail." *New York Times Book Review* 1 June 1947: 19.

Wouk responds to Maloney's review labelling him the "Dreyfus of the literary world" by arguing that the style of the novel is an eighteenth-century spoof, a sort of genial nose thumbing at the hairy-chested, four-letter-word school of composition.

Wouk, Herman. "On Being Put Under Glass." *Columbia Library Columns* 5 (May 1956): 3-9.

An address given by Wouk at the presentation of his manuscripts to Columbia University. He discusses the distinction between serious literature and literature written to entertain, placing his own work in the latter category, but pointing out that the best eighteenth- and nineteenth-century fiction was the best entertainment, and that he has followed those examples rather than Faulkner, Hemingway, Joyce, and contemporary models. Useful for its insight into Wouk's philosophy and theory of the novel.

"The Wouk Mutiny." *Time* 5 Sept. 1955: 48-50, 52.

An essay which jumps from accounts of the sales figures of *The Caine Mutiny* to Wouk himself and back to the upcoming publication of *Marjorie Morningstar*. Predicts that the public will object to its advocacy of marriage before sex, its orthodoxy, and its bourgeois values. Commends him for being a top-notch storyteller and for his integrity. Details the contents of the novel, and goes back to detailing Wouk's wartime experience. Much useful anecdote and biography.

Yidong, Zhang. "Two Panoramas About Great Wars." *Journal of Popular Culture* 19.1 (1985): 57-63.

Accounts for the recent popularity of Wouk in China. Describes Chinese critics as divided as to whether his work is realism or historical legend. Compares Wouk to Tolstoy, and goes through *The Winds of War* trying to decide about the justice and accuracy with which each of the major historical figures has been portrayed.

Reviews

Acken, Edgar L. "The War and Willie Keith." Rev. of *The Caine Mutiny*. *New York Herald Tribune Book Review* 18 Mar. 1951: 6.

Describes this as a novel about the seemingly eternal conflict of ethics between the military professional and the civilian. Sees it as an old problem set up in a dramatic and valid fashion. Concludes that it is provocative and full of authentic people and atmosphere.

"All at Sea." Rev. of *The Caine Mutiny*. *Times Literary Supplement* 9 Nov. 1951: 705.

Describes *The Caine Mutiny* as a brilliant act of virtuosity in its accuracy, plotting, pacing, and evocation of character. Claims that Wouk goes closer than anyone else in suggesting what life at sea might be like.

Angoff, Charles. "Mr. Wouk's Lusterless Morningstar." Rev. of *Marjorie Morningstar*. *Congress Weekly* 14 Nov. 1955: 21-22.

Comments that he is relieved upon reading the book to find it too trivial to do much damage to Jews despite its bestseller status. Describes several of the scenes that don't work, criticizes the characterization, and writes Wouk off as a skillful popular entertainer and manufacturer of soap operas.

"Art and Mammon." Rev. of *Youngblood Hawke*. *Times Literary Supplement* 2 Nov. 1962: 845.

Calls *Youngblood Hawke* a book by a gifted storyteller based loosely on the life of Tom Wolfe. Yet asserts that, though the book is fat, the characters seem only half at home. Suggests that money supplies the sole dramatic tension throughout these pages and that this is a Victorian novel about cash, negotiation, speculation, the plunge of failure, and the mirage of ultimate triumph.

Atkinson, Percy. "Advertising Lightly Lampooned." Rev. of *Aurora Dawn*. *Saturday Review of Literature* 19 Apr. 1947: 17-18.

Considers *Aurora Dawn* a light-hearted, pleasant satire on Madison Avenue, rather than a serious expose. Suggests that the effects of reading the book are of being in the entertaining, blithe company of the author himself.

Beichman, Arnold. "Jacob, Esau, and Nixon." Rev. of *Inside, Outside*. *National Review* 14 June 1985: 46-48.

Calls *Inside, Outside* an absorbing story of the Nixon White House, and a book full of interesting implications about the relationship of orthodoxy with the outside world of the *goyim*.

Beichman, Arnold. "Wouk's Wartime Epic Puts History Past Forgetting." Rev. of *War and Remembrance*. *Christian Science Monitor* 23 Oct. 1978: B14.

Considers this novel one of the great narratives of our time, and asserts that, just as we read Homer and Thucydides to learn about ancient Greece and Troy, our children will read Wouk. Describes the story, commenting on its authenticity.

Bell, Pearl K. "Good-Bad and Bad-Bad." Rev. of *War and Remembrance*. *Commentary* Dec. 1978: 70-73.

Commends Wouk for the prodigious amount of research and respect for facts that has gone into *War and Remembrance*. Sees the book as subliterary and therefore in the bin of Good-Bad books since it is aimed at a popular audience and makes no pretense of being literary. Concludes that, unfortunately, the book lacks any magic at all, being full of soap opera crudities and sentimentality. A detailed review which covers an impressive number of particulars in the book.

Bell, Pearl K. "Historical Whodunit?" Rev. of *The Winds of War*. *New Leader* 27 Dec. 1971: 14-15.

Claims that this is a Homeric-sized novel, a klutz of a book embarrassing for its pedestrian style; absurdly grandiose ambition; shameless sentimentality about patriotism, marriage, and children; and populated with creaky stereotypes for characters. Yet insists for all this, it is as readable as a well-honed detective story, even if we know how its main event, World War II, came out. Complains that Wouk shoehorns into it every scrap of information he knows about the war and throws discrimination and emphasis away. Concludes that for all his apparent seriousness, however, Wouk finally makes it clear he does not know how to take history seriously enough.

Bloom, Kathryn Ruth. Rev. of *Inside, Outside*. *Hadassah Magazine* Apr. 1985: 36-38.

Describes *Inside, Outside* as a wooden, tedious novel full of predictabilities and pop *Yiddishkeit*.

Boroff, David. "Hillbilly Literary Tycoon." Rev. of *Youngblood Hawke*. *Saturday Review* 19 May 1962: 36.

Calls this a kind of costume novel of the publishing industry that is clearly a fictionalized account of the life of Thomas Wolfe. Details the contents, and concludes that, to the sophisticated reader, this book will read like a sentimental fable of the Dionysian artist, soap opera unabashed and lachrymose except for a few redeeming interludes.

Brandel, Marc. "Little Boy Meets Girl." Rev. of *The City Boy*. *New York Times Book Review* 29 Aug. 1948: 10.

Sees *The City Boy* as a refreshing and thoroughly readable book which, though it gets away from its protagonist in the last quarter, nevertheless reveals her dream memorably.

Breit, Harvey. "Birthday." Rev. of *The Caine Mutiny*. *New York Times Book Review* 12 Apr. 1953: 8.

Describes *The Caine Mutiny* as a remarkable bestseller which caught on through spontaneous combustion. Details its printing history and statistics over a two year period.

Breit, Harvey. "Explication." Rev. of *Marjorie Morningstar*. *New York Times Book Review* 25 Sept. 1955: 8.

Describes the story as a picture of a modern girl in love for whom fate is either tragic or moral, depending on how one reads the novel.

Brennan, Thomas. "Ho, Hum, Herman!" Rev. of *Don't Stop the Carnival. Critic* Aug.-Sept. 1965: 85-86.

Describes *Don't Stop the Carnival* as the work of a novice humorist who has produced an "innocents abroad" trivia novel. Complains that his punch lines are telegraphed long before they arrive. The characters are eminently dull but believable. Concludes that the "goings-on" are written in a readable non-style, while the ending is abrupt and meaningless.

Buitenhuis, Peter. "Norman Was 'Horossed'." Rev. of *Don't Stop the Carnival. New York Times Book Review* 14 Mar. 1965: 47.

Argues that *Don't Stop the Carnival* is compulsively, clock-racingly readable, with a comic line that moves as fast as a Marx brothers movie. Claims that it is gay enough to divert the most sophisticated mind. Concludes, however, that the reader is left with a lingering uneasiness about the book's morality because if one stops the carnival and starts thinking, the book itself collapses.

Bullock, Florence Haxton. "Herman Wouk Spins a Tale in the Great Tradition." Rev. of *Marjorie Morningstar. New York Herald Tribune Book Review* 4 Sept. 1955: 1.

Calls this a novel of well-sustained suspense, lagging occasionally when side stories intrude on the main narrative. Concludes that this is a large, living picture of a modern American family.

"Caribbean Cream Puffs." Rev. of *Don't Stop the Carnival. Newsweek* 8 Mar. 1965: 92, 94.

Comments that *Don't Stop the Carnival* reads like a hit musical. Details the contents, and concludes that the book is ultimately creampuff, not steak.

Chamberlain, John. Rev. of *Youngblood Hawke. New York Herald Tribune Books* 20 May 1962: 4.

Calls *Youngblood Hawke* long, generously proportioned, daring, and perhaps insolently great. Comments on its characters, its portrayal of Thomas Wolfe, the style, and the narrative techniques of the book. Concludes that the non-literary reader will probably not care one bit that Hawke's imaginative life at the desk has been completely subordinated to the exigencies of lovemaking, beating the city slickers at their own multifarious games, and risking piles of royalty money on turns of fate in the market.

Chernofsky, Ellen. "Trade Reviews." Rev. of *Inside, Outside. AB Bookman's Weekly* 29 Apr. 1985: 3235-36.

Sees *Inside, Outside* as a painless instruction on the lifestyle, religious practices, history, and culture of the Jew which is woven into the central story. Calls it a book replete with well-drawn, lively characters, and marvelously entertaining scenes. Concludes that, unfortunately, it lacks depth and fails to deal with the issues it raises.

Christopher, Rita. "Plenty of Combat and Lots of Wind." Rev. of *War and Remembrance. Maclean's* 20 Nov. 1978: 63, 65.

Calls *War and Remembrance* a hefty tome which at times becomes altogether too confusing with its various subplots and geographic settings. Commends Wouk for his evocations of the horrors of the Nazi concentration camps. Concludes that Captain Queeg of the *Caine* has long mellowed; the ball bearings he rolls in his hands have rusted.

Clemons, Walter. "By the Numbers." Rev. of *The Winds of War. Newsweek* 29 Nov. 1971: 102, 104.

Claims that Wouk writes copiously and flatly in *The Winds of War*. He has done so much homework, his characters are inflicted with giving historical lectures. Sees Pug Henry as preposterous, and the rest of the book much like a massive treatise. Concludes that it is a farrago by a corny but likeable author.

Clemons, Walter. "A Harvest of Fiction." Rev. of *War and Remembrance. Newsweek* 9 Oct. 1978: 105-06.

Complains that the characters in *War and Remembrance* are predictable stick figures, and that the novel is generally cardboard, despite the fact that the author is a thorough professional whose two great obsessions are the Holocaust and naval operations. Concludes that it is a sage, trustworthy pop history of WWII, even if it is not great literature.

Corbett, Edward P. J. "Books." Rev. of *Youngblood Hawke. America* 26 May 1962: 318-19.

Calls *Youngblood Hawke* prolix, hefty, slick, and hypnotically fascinating. Details the contents.

Cornish, Sam. "Wouk's Latest Creates Its Own Category." Rev. of
Inside, Outside. Christian Science Monitor 7 June 1985: 81.

Sees *Inside, Outside* as one more Wouk book in Jewish history and identity. Claims that like Louis Auchincloss and John P. Marquand, Wouk is
an acute observer of one particular aspect of American society.

Davies, R. R. "Global Yarn." Rev. of *The Winds of War. New Statesman*
19 Nov. 1971: 706.

Claims that *The Winds of War* is shaped first by history and only second-
ly by the author, and that Wouk makes no pretense about it. Argues that
he intervenes occasionally with italicized chunks of political resume, or
more often, lapses into tactical analysis written by a fictitious German
general and translated in dazed retirement. Concludes that it is a well-
researched, global yarn adequately told.

Davis, L. J. "The Battle Hymn of Herman Wouk." Rev. of *War and
Remembrance. Washington Post Book World* 8 Oct. 1978: E1, E6.

Calls *War and Remembrance* implausible, whackingly popular, and
weakly plotted. Claims that if it were only a little less skillful, it would
be ridiculous. Describes the contents, and concludes that it indeed follows the formula of romance. Sees it finally as a layman's fictionalized
history, and an extremely good one at that.

Dempsey, David. "It Didn't Pay to Strike It Rich." Rev. of *Youngblood
Hawke. New York Times Book Review* 20 May 1962: 1, 38.

Calls *Youngblood Hawke* a book full of narrative talent, American types,
and formidable thematic power. Suggests that it is a stunning and merciless approach to a world Wouk knows well. Provides a lengthy description
of contents as well as a detailed discussion of the artistic failures of the
novel.

"Fiction." Rev. of *Inside, Outside. Kirkus Reviews* 1 Feb. 1985: 112-13.

Describes *Inside, Outside* as about the quintessential American Jew told
lovingly, and with leisurely, anecdotal material. Claims that frequently it
becomes tedious, platitudinous, sermonizing, complaining and "holier
than thou." Concludes that Jewish readers will be entranced and fortified,
and find fine, solid chunks of entertainment.

Fiedler, Leslie A. "What Makes Herman Run?" Rev. of *Marjorie
Morningstar. New Leader* 3 Oct. 1955: 21-25.

Provides a prefatory essay on the historical antecedents of the type of novel in *Marjorie Morningstar* as a vulgarized, latter-day form of the anti-anti-bourgeois novel.

Foote, Timothy. "Multitudes, Multitudes!" Rev. of *The Winds of War*. *Time* 22 Nov. 1971: 111, 113, E4.

Calls *The Winds of War* a book lying somewhere between the perspectives of history and the warmth of personal recollection. Claims that it is an upside down *bildungsroman* in which the author, rather than the characters, keeps growing. Provides good plot summary and some background information on Wouk.

Frankel, Haskel. "Land of Labels." Rev. of *Don't Stop the Carnival*. *Saturday Review* 13 Mar. 1965: 128.

Complains that *Don't Stop the Carnival*, despite its many themes, ultimately becomes wearying as disaster after disaster turns the protagonist's life into a hell on earth. Concludes, "if a novel can be thin and heavy, this is that novel—more Wouk than play, and that makes a dull buy."

Fuchs, Daniel. Rev. of *Inside, Outside*. *Los Angeles Times Book Review* 3 Mar. 1985: 2.

Calls *Inside, Outside* a jumbo novel about goodness, balance, kindliness, being rooted in traditions, and feeling contented, despite the evil that rages without. Details the contents.

Fussell, Paul. Rev. of *War and Remembrance*. *New Republic* 14 Oct. 1978: 32-33.

Calls the book a good popular history in the guise of a very bad novel. Claims that the characters and plot are strictly Metro-Goldwyn-Meyer 1950s, and the soap opera characteristics a tip-off that Wouk is about to "flog the whole thing off to the movies." Suggests, however, that when he turns from people to significant public environments and "things," he is wonderful because he is good at depicting what Himmler might have seen at an extermination, what the inmates saw at Theresienstadt, or what a naval officer would have seen at the White House during the war. Claims that he is without peer in presenting locales, and that he is serious about interpreting the war. Concludes that his romance of the Henrys compromises this admirable attempt to portray the Holocaust, and by proximity, demands his skillful historiography.

Gehman, Richard B. "Bronx Penrod." Rev. of *The City Boy. Saturday Review of Literature* 21 Aug. 1948: 10.

Calls Wouk a composite of Booth Tarkington and Sinclair Lewis in *The City Boy*, and cannot decide whether or not he is serious. Condemns the book as a total failure because of its fatuous, moralizing and boy's fiction sentimentality.

Geismar, Maxwell. "The Age of Wouk." *Nation* 5 Nov. 1955: 399-400. Rpt. as "The Age of Wouk: *Time, Life* and Art" in *American Moderns: From Rebellion to Conformity*. Maxwell Geismar. American Century Series. New York: Hill, 1958. 41-45; *A View of the Nation: An Anthology 1955-1959*. Ed. Henry M. Christman. New York: Grove, 1960. Essay Index Reprint Series. Freeport: Books for Libraries, 1970. 37-40.

Calls Wouk the house author of the American way at the middle of the twentieth century. Suggests that *The Caine Mutiny* affirms Wouk's belief in decency, discipline, authority, and hallowed institutions. Concludes that Wouk believes the final impact of the atomic age to have had the effect of a lobotomy upon the national spirit.

Geismar, Maxwell. "The Roots and the Flowering Tree." Rev. of *Marjorie Morningstar. New York Times Book Review* 4 Sept. 1955: 1. Rpt. as "The Age of Wouk: *Marjorie Morningstar*," *American Moderns: From Rebellion to Conformity*. Maxwell Geismar. American Century Series. New York: Hill, 1958. 38-40.

Describes *Marjorie Morningstar* as a novel lying curiously between the realms of art and entertainment, and dealing with the tragicomic meeting of traditional Jewish culture and the American success myth. Sees the larger issue as the denigration of all immigrant culture by a society that marks its children only with the stamp of material success, and that gave up its own religious orientation somewhere around 1870. Concludes that it is a story of false emancipation and sterile compliance.

Glassman, James K. "Wouk's Funny, Touching Novel of a Jewish Life." Rev. of *Inside, Outside. U.S.A. Today* 22 Mar. 1985: 3D.

Calls *Inside, Outside* a funny, touching, folkloric novel offering much more than just a series of cute ghetto stories.

Glick, Nathan. "Herbie." Rev. of *The City Boy. Commentary* Nov. 1948: 492-93.

Sees *The City Boy* as an admirable attempt to embrace, in the realm of the popular literature of childhood, the world of the Jewish ghettoes. Suggests that finally, the book fails because it is not serious enough about either comedy or sorrow. Notes also, that despite the fertile recall of early experience, there is an almost complete loss of its quality. Concludes that, unfortunately, Mr. Wouk has been content to trace just the platitudinous surfaces of this life.

Guidry, Frederick H. "Wouk's 'Doorstopper'." Rev. of *Youngblood Hawke. Christian Science Monitor* 24 May 1962: 7.

Calls Hawke a Wolfe-like hero on a roller coaster journey from obscurity to fame. Claims that though there are sensational elements in the book, it has serious artistic intentions.

Hicks, Granville. "If You Don't Know Who Fala Was, This Was Written for You." Rev. of *The Winds of War. New York Times Book Review* 14 Nov. 1971: 4-5, 52.

Finds this Wouk's most ambitious work, but only a mildly interesting, moderately informative novel. Claims that it reminds him of Sinclair's Lanny Budd series not only in subject matter and method, but also in the same indifference to quality, the same reliance on cliches and broad casual strokes. Suggests that the characters, historical and fictional, are treated mechanically, and that the failures of style betray the failures of imagination. Also discusses Wouk's failures and successes in some of his other works.

Hoffman, Marvin. "A Generation Between Two Worlds." Rev. of *Inside, Outside. New Leader* 22 Apr. 1985: 7-8.

Argues that a writer like Wouk acts like an anthropologist for the Jewish and non-Jewish reader. Suggests that his literary models are like David Goodkind in *Inside, Outside,* a Jewish mother's dream of a son inside the Nixon White House. Claims that while Bellow, Malamud, and both Roths have treated the inside/outside dichotomy with more sophistication, Wouk has appealed to a far larger audience, and is the only voice of an eroding heritage likely to reach it. Concludes that "His message may be thin but it is positive. For this generation, Out is In."

Horchler, R. T. "Life and the Dream." Rev. of *Marjorie Morningstar. Commonweal* 4 Nov. 1955: 123.

Considers *Marjorie Morningstar* less a romance than a strenuously didactic moral and sociological study. Sees the heroine as banal, unreal, and faintly pathetic. Claims that she is tiresomely imperceptive and a slow learner. States she is an unworthy subject for a novelist since she lacks intelligence, sensitivity, moral sense, or a regard for traditional religion. Concludes that this is a big book rich in minor treasures, serious in intentions, but not much more than slick fiction.

Kauffmann, Stanley. "Herzog, Schmerzog." Rev. of *Don't Stop the Carnival. New York Herald Tribune Book Week* 7 Mar. 1965: 1, 12, 14.

Describes the plot, setting, characters, and themes of the novel, and then comments that Wouk does not distill the aesthetic experience, but is overwhelmed by it, and reproduces this overwhelmingly as in colored postcards. Claims that Wouk is an honest merchant who researches adequately and keeps the whole thing humming along. Concludes that this book will for several hours kill time dead.

Kauffmann, Stanley. "Look Bankward Angel." Rev. of *Youngblood Hawke. New Republic* 11 June 1962: 24-25.

Argues that Hawke is a combination of Wouk and Wolfe. Claims that the pace is propulsive and uncomfortable, the sex is puritanically tinged, and the sincerity horribly suffocating.

Kempton, Murray. "The Coagulation of Herman Wouk"." Rev. of *Youngblood Hawke. National Review* 14 Aug. 1962: 105-06.

Argues that unlike previous bestsellers *Youngblood Hawke* moves at a gelatinous pace, and its vulgarities fail to amuse. Claims that it is a slovenly performance done in unchanging key. Suggests that this is Wouk with "Yomulka" on head writing his own "Lycidas" betrayed. Concludes that it is a book full of his hatred of publishers, critics, and gossip columnists, and that the story lacks curves.

Klaw, Spencer. "A Delightfully Fresh and Funny Satire." Rev. of *Aurora Dawn. New York Herald Tribune Weekly Book Review* 20 Apr. 1947: 3.

Describes *Aurora Dawn* as employing the technique of *Tom Jones*, never descending to burlesque, fat with charming eighteenth-century type digressions, and conceived in the mock heroic tradition. Concludes that the characters are displayed with affection and tolerance, not to mention good humored detachment.

Knickerbocker, Conrad. "Wouk's Cash-&-Cliche Trip to the Tropics." Rev. of *Don't Stop the Carnival. Life* 5 Mar. 1965: 8.

Argues that *Don't Stop the Carnival* is written with no more authority than a lace valentine, but that it is just this quality which has made Wouk rich and famous. Describes plot and setting in snide terms, and concludes that the images are manipulated to fit the requirements of media.

L., E. Rev. of *War and Remembrance*. *West Coast Review of Books* Jan. 1979: 29.

Calls *War and Remembrance* a vibrant, incandescent, and stunning piece—a profound interrogation of a deeply disturbing period. Concludes that Wouk's compassion and perspective on the triumph of good over evil—a 14 year literary project—is a massive continuation of *The Winds of War*.

Lehmann-Haupt, Christopher. "Barney Greenwald All the Way." Rev. of *The Winds of War*. *New York Times* 16 Nov. 1971: 43.

Describes the novel as dreary but redeemed somewhat by Wouk's story-telling ability. Claims that it does succeed in combining true history with fiction. Concludes that it is finally, however, superior *kitsch* with its advice to the U.S.A. to stay armed, stay vigilant, and heed the lessons of Munich.

Lehmann-Haupt, Christopher. "Books of the Times." Rev. of *Inside, Outside*. *New York Times* 7 Mar. 1985: C25.

Considers this novel rather implausible, a little tepid, and even smug. Claims that there is no moral ambiguity and little passion.

Lerner, Laurence. "New Novels." Rev. of *Youngblood Hawke*. *Listener* 18 Oct. 1962: 630.

Calls *Youngblood Hawke* long, complicated, contrived, informed, and penetrating. Sees Wouk as an entertainer who weaves his story skillfully. Likes the book as a documentary, but wonders why it can be read over with deepening delight. Notes that it does not grow beyond the common-place. Concludes that it deserves a kind of success, but no permanence.

Levin, Meyer. "Central Park West Revisited." Rev. of *Marjorie Morningstar*. *Saturday Review* 3 Sept. 1955: 9-10.

Sees Marjorie Morningstar as the classic American heroine who lives solidly through her middle-class Jewish background. Calls her the female counterpart of Augie March who realizes her folly and comes home to marry the nice Jewish attorney. Sees Noel, on the other hand, as ruined by his inability to respect his Jewish heritage. Considers this a fine novel.

Lewis, Anthony. "Wouk in the Pulpit." Rev. of *Marjorie Morningstar*.
   Nation 22 Oct. 1955: 347.

Argues that Wouk in *Marjorie Morningstar* continues the counterrevolu-
tion against promiscuity, social protest, and psychoanalytical
sermonizing. Waxes ironic over Wouk's formula for female happiness in
which he describes contentment as mother, wife, and ladies' auxiliary
member. Concludes that this book is comfortable, easy to read, and made
of lacquer-surface realism of one particular religious group.

Maddocks, Melvin. "Wouk at War in Slow Motion." Rev. of *The Winds
   of War*. *Life* 26 Nov. 1971: 16.

Finds Wouk antique and funny for trying to revive the subject of WWII
for the novel, and for writing a *War and Peace* epic at this point in time.
Claims that he huffs and puffs frantically from front to front and is as
reluctant to develop his ideas as he is his characters. Claims that he
thinks and feels as if he is still in the 1940s.

Magid, Nora. "The Girl Who Went Back Home." Rev. of *Marjorie
   Morningstar*. *New Republic* 5 Sept. 1955: 20.

Argues the moral of *Marjorie Morningstar* to be that if your fate is suburbia, there's no use trying to be an actress. Claims, however, that this is
only a masculine point of view, and Wouk should not push his luck too
far in reversing the formula. Concludes that it is really a rather banal love
story.

Maloney, Russell. "Another Soap Opera in Search of a Heroine." Rev. of
   Aurora Dawn. *New York Times Book Review* 20 Apr. 1947: 5.

Calls *Aurora Dawn* a soap opera which never finds its heroine. Claims
that its story and its language fail.

McCullough, David W. Rev. of *The Winds of War*. *Saturday Review* 27
   Nov. 1971: 55-56.

Claims that in *The Winds of War* Wouk is satisfactorily credible, and has
re-created a time on the brink of being forgotten. Calls this a crowded
and copious novel whose characterization is often purely functional and
the whole production curiously undramatic. Concludes that the result is
not an epic but a wooden novel of manners.

Metcalf, John. "New Novels." Rev. of *Marjorie Morningstar*. *Spectator*
   7 Oct. 1955: 470, 472.

Considers this an important novel for anyone interested in the development of transatlantic writing. Describes it as an analysis of the moral and social values of New York's Jewish bourgeois of almost *Middlemarch* length and certainly with all of Eliot's seriousness.

Michener, James. "Mr. Goodkind Goes to Washington." Rev. of *Inside, Outside. New York Times Book Review* 10 Mar. 1985: 1, 42.

Calls *Inside, Outside* an ambitious novel charting the spiritual and social adventures of Israel David Goodkind and delineating his dual personalities. Comments on style, form, and Wouk's all-out, freewheeling, scatological vocabulary.

Mohs, Mayo. "Multitudes II." Rev. of *War and Remembrance. Time* 16 Oct. 1978: 125-26.

Calls the novel an education as well as a drama. Considers the battles at sea the best parts in what is an uncommonly readable book. Does not recommend it for those who did not live through WWII.

Morgan, Edwin. "War Without Action." Rev. of *The Winds of War. Listener* 25 Nov. 1971: 738.

Argues that *The Winds of War* is written from an exclusively and naively American point of view, and has no depth, subtlety, or passion. Concludes that the best things are the rare moments when a whiff of action and danger is permitted to settle into the narrative.

Norman, Geoffrey. "Wouk on War." Rev. of *War and Remembrance. Esquire* 5 Dec. 1978: 96.

Commends Wouk for understanding the war as factuality, and in particular, for the description of the Battle of Midway in his *War and Remembrance*. Predicts the book will be accused of being prosaic and overlong, but approves of its scope and size anyway.

"Paper Man." Rev. of *Don't Stop the Carnival. Times Literary Supplement* 8 July 1965: 573.

Argues that in *Don't Stop the Carnival* Wouk has written a readable book about the Caribbean, but fails to make the reader take seriously his "hotel in the tropics" story. Concludes that he might perhaps have been better employed in writing about a factual travel book or journal about it.

Paulding, Gouverneur. "Central Park West." Rev. of *Marjorie Morningstar. Reporter* 22 Sept. 1955: 46-47.

A brief recounting of the plot followed by an examination of Wouk's Jewish moral stance in the novel. Claims that no matter what Wouk lets these young people say and do, he finally asserts that the older generation is right and brings Marjorie back to a conventional Jewish marriage in suburbia.

Pickrel, Paul. "Innocents in the Big City." Rev. of *Youngblood Hawke. Harper's* June 1962: 89-90, 92.

Describes *Youngblood Hawke* as discussing the ambiguous conflict between talent and the world as it is. Calls it a highly readable popular novel with a fine story, but claims that it lacks poetic feeling, wit, and irony. Concludes that instead we get sullen peevishness.

Pitt, Don. "Mutiny in a Manner Not So Grand." Rev. of *The Caine Mutiny. San Francisco Chronicle This World* 25 Mar. 1951: 19.

Calls *The Caine Mutiny* a sophisticated delineation of the narrow and tenuous threads upon which social relations hang, which also portrays the related effects of a personality triangle. Concludes that this is a saga—a highly superior web of days.

Podhoretz, Norman. "The Jew as Bourgeois." Rev. of *Marjorie Morningstar. Commentary* Feb. 1956: 186-88.

Argues that *Marjorie Morningstar* is obtusely doctrinal and negligible as a novel. Its prose is indigestible, the cultural commentary on Judaism negligible, and the dishonesty crucial. From the taste of the book, one has an image of Wouk as an old man with a twinkle in his eye asking us to accept him as a reliable witness. But the general appeal of the book is that it has a moral and treats American Jews as Jews, not exotics. Claims that its moral is that the Jewish personality can only disintegrate and wither away if it ventures beyond the moral and spiritual confines of a Judaic bourgeois style. Says the possibilities are greater than Wouk imagines here.

Prescott, Orville. "Books of the Times." Rev. of *Youngblood Hawke. New York Times* 18 May 1962: 29.

Traces Wouk's writing history, and then describes the contents, tracing the parallels between the life of Thomas Wolfe and Hawke. Concludes that, though this novel is expertly entertaining, it never achieves major stature.

Prescott, Orville. "A Comical Caribbean Carnival." Rev. of *Don't Stop the Carnival. New York Times* 5 Mar. 1965: 31.

Describes *Don't Stop the Carnival* as a book with an extremely sympathetic hero who is much beleaguered by events and other characters. Mostly describes the contents of the novel.

Pryce-Jones, Alan. "One Man's Family." Rev. of *The Winds of War. Washington Post Book World* 14 Nov. 1971: 3.

Sees *The Winds of War* as an attempt to establish the counterpoint between the events of WW II and the private lives of one American family. Provides extensive plot summary.

Putney, Michael. "After 885 Pages, Wouk Isn't Finished Yet." Rev. of *The Winds of War. National Observer* 1 Jan. 1972: 17.

Provides a description of the contents of *The Winds of War*, calling it mawkish and embarrassing. Claims that he has a slovenly tendency to fall back on cliches. Concludes that whatever the world holds for Victor Henry and his family will undoubtedly be contained in a sequel.

"Realism Without Obscenity." Rev. of *The Caine Mutiny. Time* 9 Apr. 1951: 110.

Describes *The Caine Mutiny* as avoiding the "crushed youth" school of American war novelists like Mailer, and providing sharply evoked, realistic scenes without obscenity, and a good humored acceptance of the situation. Concludes that the book is not only good reading, but also fine reporting.

Rogow, Lee. "Navy Regs to the Rescue." Rev. of *The Caine Mutiny. Saturday Review of Literature* 31 Mar. 1951: 17.

Talks of *The Caine Mutiny* as exciting and worthwhile with the exception of Willie's love affair with May Wynn. Wonders why Wouk writes with such professional skill and understanding on the one hand, and with such undigested immaturity on the other. Concludes, nevertheless, that as a modern sea adventure it is first-rate reading.

Roshwald, Miriam. "Wouk's *Inside, Outside*." Rev. of *Inside, Outside. Jewish Spectator* 50 (Fall 1985): 37-39.

Primarily explains the novel's contents from a Jewish perspective.

Samuel, Maurice. "Not Simply Rubbish." Rev. of *Marjorie Morningstar*. *Midstream* 2.1 (1956): 92-98.

Suggests that most bestsellers are relatively harmless, but argues that such is not the case with *Marjorie Morningstar*. Sees this book as not so much written as manufactured to specifications. Considers it full of dogged flatness and false sprightliness, with narrative and observation on the level of canasta table crackle, while the reader is carried along by the flattering self-consciousness of a cozy intellectual and spiritual equality with the author, achieved at no great cost to the gray cells. Concludes that it is all stable literalness and dreary cuteness.

Sheppard, R. Z. "Vicomte de Brag." Rev. of *Inside, Outside*. *Time* 1 Apr. 1985: 79-81.

Argues that this novel is told from the perspective of a Joycean Jew-as-outsider, a durable cliche in our national literature. Sees this as an amiable morality tale, long-winded, full of storytelling tricks, and scatological humor. Criticizes the depictions of women and Goodkind's amorous encounters, as well as the sermonettes on foreign policy and domestic relations.

Skolink, Norma. "Herman Wouk and War." Rev. of *The Winds of War*. *Jewish Spectator* May 1972: 28-29.

Describes *The Winds of War* in terms of plot, characters, and content, and concludes that much of the conservative morality of the novel has to do with Wouk's Jewish orthodoxy.

Smith, William James. "Slugging Along." Rev. of *Youngblood Hawke*. *Commonweal* 29 June 1962: 355.

Compares Wouk to Dickens and finds him the only living nineteenth-century novelist. Describes the story, and concludes that he "loved it, every mad, mad moment of it. . . . It would have stunned even Dickens."

Sugrue, Thomas. "Don Quixote from the Bronx." Rev. of *The City Boy*. *New York Herald Tribune Weekly Book Review* 29 Aug. 1948: 4.

Describes *The City Boy* in detail as a satire on growing up Jewish in Brooklyn, and on all summer camps. Calls this an excellent memoir done with a sharp sense of humor, maturity, light-heartedness, and accuracy. Calls it a good portrait of public schools of the day.

T., R. S. "Inside, Outside." Rev. of *Inside, Outside*. *West Coast Review of Books* May 1985: 34-35.

Calls Wouk a master storyteller who has turned inward at the age of seventy and produced a bittersweet, humorous, and provocative anecdote taking massive globs of his experiences and encasing them in a fiction like *Inside, Outside* which is both entertaining and revealing.

"Thinblood Wouk." Rev. of *Youngblood Hawke. Time* 18 May 1962: 96, 98.

Argues that *Youngblood Hawke* is about Thomas Wolfe, who becomes the victim of a literary act of violence. Claims that Wouk is not interested in Wolfe's life except as a scenario for exploring the agonizing problems of authorship. Suggests that this is an immoral use of Wolfe's life, distorted as the whole thing becomes.

Thomas, Ross. "Herman Wouk: The Bronx to Watergate." Rev. of *Inside, Outside. Washington Post Book World* 10 Mar. 1985: 1, 14.

Claims that *Inside, Outside* is David Goodkind's *kaddish* for his father—a sentimental big band number no one has heard until now. Asserts that it succeeds wonderfully well in parts, is often fascinating, frequently funny and usually moving. Details the contents.

Trilling, Diana. "Fiction in Review." Rev. of *Aurora Dawn. Nation* 24 May 1947: 636-37.

Calls *Aurora Dawn* a book full of eighteenth-century pretensions, absence of style, rosy anachronisms, sophomoric displays of learning, a reasonably neat story, and too many big gestures of the spirit.

Weeks, Edward. "The Gull Reef Club." Rev. of *Don't Stop the Carnival. Atlantic* Apr. 1965: 152.

Calls *Don't Stop the Carnival* a clever novel with carefully drawn and well-observed characters. Concludes, however, that Wouk lacks the superb sense of humor of a Noel Coward and is much more windy in achieving his effects.

Weeks, Edward. "Marjorie from Manhattan." Rev. of *Marjorie Morningstar. Atlantic* Oct. 1955: 86-87.

Provides a detailed account of the novel, and complains that it is one-third too long, that Noel's philosophizing is endless, and his racy talk tedious.

Weeks, Edward. "Outcast Ship and Crew." Rev. of *The Caine Mutiny. Atlantic* Aug. 1951: 79.

Describes the contents of the story and its three themes—life aboard ship with its community frictions and loyalty, an ironic scrutiny of the whole naval system, and the development of men at sea. Concludes that it is one of the best designed and best developed novels of the war yet published by an American.

Weeks, Edward. "The Peripatetic Reviewer." Rev. of *The Winds of War*. *Atlantic* Dec. 1971: 133.

Calls Wouk a compelling narrator who paints in big canvasses and avoids the fuss of symbolism and style while driving his story ahead with an infectious belief in the people he is writing about. Describes the contents of *The Winds of War*.

"Wind, Mostly." Rev. of *The Winds of War*. *Economist* 20 Nov. 1971: 70.

Comments that despite its lack of literary merits, this book will sell because of its popular formulas. Decries its interlarding with large extracts from the fictional Von Roon's *World Empire Lost* and presents a pugnaciously radical view of the key events of the war in Europe. However, the war has eluded Wouk and the book fails.

Yoskowitz, Herbert A. "Herman Wouk's Jewish Affirmation." Rev. of *War and Remembrance*. *Jewish Spectator* 44 (Fall 1979): 21-22.

Calls *War and Remembrance* a treatise on assimilation, condemns the shallowness of much of the characterization, but shows how Wouk has imbued much of the novel with his Jewish knowledge and commitment to live as Jew.

"You Must Go Home Again." Rev. of *Don't Stop the Carnival*. *Time* 5 Mar. 1965: 104, 106.

Calls Wouk's intelligence murky and antiromantic. Describes the novel as a book that finally makes its point—but clumsily. Describes plot and characters in detail.

Interviews

Bandler, Michael J. "Portrait of a Man Reading." *Chicago Tribune Book World* 26 Dec. 1971: 14.

An interview with Wouk in which he discusses *The Winds of War*, his reading interests, *City Boy*, magazine tastes, political and historical reading, and his love of Cervantes and Proust.

Bannon, Barbara A. "PW Interviews Herman Wouk." *Publishers Weekly*
    7 Feb. 1972: 44-45.

Details Wouk's educational background, first writing jobs, career in the
navy in WWII, early novels, Pulitzer Prize, his notetaking and reading
schedules, his attitudes toward the war and its historical significance,
combatting the antihero vogue in postwar literature, and his refusal to
read critics seriously.

Burger, Nash K. "Talk with Herman Wouk." *New York Times Book
    Review* 16 Sept. 1951: 16-17.

Provides general impressions from meeting Wouk, and comments briefly
on *The Caine Mutiny*.

Biographical Sources

Charney, Mark J. "Herman Wouk." *Dictionary of Literary Biography
    Yearbook: 1982.* Ed. Richard Ziegfeld. Detroit: Gale, 1983. 383-88.

More than details of his life, this is a career biography, tracing the development of the author's canon, describing the contents and themes of his
works, evaluating his reputation, and placing him in the larger context of
American literary history. Includes lists of primary and secondary
sources and illustrations.

Colby, Vineta. "Herman Wouk." *Wilson Library Bulletin* Mar. 1952: 500.

A biographical overview of Wouk containing reported comments from
him about his moral and professional goals in writing.

James, T. F. "Herman Wouk." *Cosmopolitan* Aug. 1958: 43.

Briefly reviews Wouk's writing career, the success in sales and dollars of
his early works, and his religious orthodoxy.

Kalb, Bernard. "The Author." *Saturday Review* 3 Sept. 1955: 9.

A brief biographical sketch describing aspects of his life incorporated in
his novels and his writing career.

Dissertations

Hudson, William Saxon. "Herman Wouk: A Biographical and Critical
    Study." Diss. George Peabody College for Teachers, 1969.

Anzia Yezierska

1885 – 1970

Primary Sources

Novels

All I Could Never Be. New York: Harcourt, 1932; New York: Brewer, 1932.

Arrogant Beggar. Garden City: Doubleday, 1927; London: Heinemann, 1927, 1928; New York: Grosset, 1929.

Bread Givers: A Struggle Between a Father of the Old World and a Daughter of the New. Garden City: Doubleday, 1925; New York: Persea, 1925; London: Heinemann, 1925; New York: Venture-Braziller, 1975; London: Women's Press 1984.

Salome of the Tenements. New York: Grosset, 1923; New York: Boni, 1923; London: Unwin, 1923.

Collected Works

Anzia Yezierska Reader. New York: Persea, 1979.
Contents: Not available.

Children of Loneliness; Stories of Immigrant Life in America. New York: Funk, 1923; London: Cassell, 1923.

Contents: Mostly about Myself, America and I, An Immigrant among the Editors, To the Stars, Children of Loneliness, Brothers, A Bed for the Night, Dreams and Dollars, The Lord Giveth, The Song Triumphant.

Hungry Hearts. Boston: Houghton, 1920; New York: Grosset, 1920; London: Unwin, 1922; The Modern Jewish Experience. New York: Arno, 1975; The Modern Jewish Experience. Salem: Ayer, 1984; New York: Persea, 1985; Virago Modern Classics. London: Virago, 1987.

Contents: Wings, Hunger, The Lost "Beautifulness," The Free Vacation House, The Miracle, Where Lovers Dream, Soap and Water, "The Fat of the Land," My Own People, How I Found America.

The Open Cage: An Anzia Yezierska Collection. New York: Persea, 1979.

Contents: The Miracle, America and I, Brothers, Where Lovers Dream, The Fat of the Land, The Lost "Beautifulness," The Lord Giveth, Children of Loneliness, Hester Street, Important People, My Last Hollywood Script, Bread and Wine in the Wilderness, A Chair in Heaven, A Window Full of Sky, Take Up Your Bed and Walk, The Open Cage.

Short Fiction in Anthologies

"The Fat of the Land." *Mothers: A Catholic Treasury of Great Stories.* Ed. Anne J. Fremantle. New York: Daye, 1951. 218-46; *Yisroel: The First Jewish Omnibus.* Ed. Joseph Leftwich. London: Heritage, 1933. 225-46; Rev. ed. London: Clarke, 1945. 180-97; Rev. ed. New York: Beechhurst, 1952. 180-97; Rev. ed. New York: Yoseloff, 1963. Pag. not available. Clarke ed. titled *Yisroel: The Jewish Omnibus.*

"Hunger." *These Your Children.* Ed. Harold U. Ribalow. New York: Beechhurst, 1952. 25-42.

"My Own People." *The Woman Who Lost Her Names: Selected Writings of American Jewish Women.* Ed. Julia Wolf Mazow. San Francisco: Harper, 1980. 3-15.

"The Open Cage." *"The Safe Deposit" and Other Stories About Grandparents, Old Lovers, and Crazy Old Men.* Ed. Kerry M. Olitzky. New York: Wiener, 1989. 225-31.

Short Fiction in Periodicals

"Brothers." *Harper's* Sept. 1921: 512-24.

"A Chair in Heaven." *Commentary* Dec. 1956: 550-57.

"Children of Loneliness." *Century Magazine* Mar. 1923: 700-09.

"The Fat of the Land." *Century Magazine* Aug. 1919: 466-79.

"The Free Vacation House." *Forum* Dec. 1915: 706-14.

"Hunger." *Harper's* Apr. 1920: 604-11.

"The Lord Giveth." *Menorah Journal* Feb. 1923: 33-44.

"To the Stars." *Century Magazine* May 1921: 65-79.

"Wild Winter Love." *Century Magazine* Feb. 1927: 485-91.

"A Window Full of Sky." *Reporter* 2 July 1964: 29-31.

Secondary Sources

Books

Carol B. Schoen. *Anzia Yezierska.* Twayne's United States Authors Series 424. Boston: Twayne, 1982.

Articles and Chapters

Auden, W. H. Introduction. *Red Ribbon on a White Horse.* Anzia Yezierska. New York: Scribner's, 1950. 11-19. Rpt. as "Red Ribbon on a White Horse." *The Dyer's Hand and Other Essays.* W. H. Auden. New York: Random House; London: Faber, 1962. 327-34.
Sees Yezierska's autobiography as her account of the pursuit of happiness, which was "her effort to discard fantastic desires and find real ones, both

material and spiritual." Compares life in America for the East European Jews with what they left behind and suggests that in America they probably found their poverty more intolerable, not because it was worse, but because here they were expected to extricate themselves from it if they were real men. Also discusses the paralyzing effect of being called to Hollywood on Yezierska and the drying up of her creative power, as well as her feeling of belonging as part of the W.P.A. Writers Project.

Avery, Evelyn Gross. "In Limbo: Immigrant Children and the American Dream." *MELUS* 8.4 (1981): 25-31.

In the context of a description of immigrant literature by Michael Gold, Mario Puzo, and Pietro Di Donato, Avery briefly discusses *The Bread Givers*.

Avery, Ellen. "Oh My 'Mishpocha!' Some Jewish Women Writers from Antin to Kaplan View the Family." *Studies in American Jewish Literature* [Albany] 5 (1986): 44-53.

Discusses the effects of Americanization on the structure of the family as reflected in the works of a variety of American-Jewish Writers. Of Antin and Yezierska she notes their depiction of Shtetl women as chained to housework, obligated to fathers and brothers, subjugated and deprived of an education. Details the contents of *The Promised Land* and *Bread Givers* as well as describing their respective heroines.

Brody, Alter. "Yiddish in American Fiction." *American Mercury* Feb. 1926: 205-07.

Discusses the problem in popular American fiction of "Yidgin" English. Criticizes Yezierska's use of it in her books and the attendant problems of precision, meaning, tone, and grammar. Considers Yezierska a horrible example of the worst uses and forms of "Yidgin."

Burstein, Janet. "Jewish-American Women's Literature: The Long Quarrel with God." *Studies in American Jewish Literature* [Kent State] 8.1 (1989): 9-25.

In this general article Burstein argues that, while some Jewish women writers cast Jewish tradition as an adversary, others see it as a source of nurturance, some ignore it, and still others tell of a search for substitute commitments. Concludes, nonetheless, that all seem to engage in a one-sided quarrel with God. Discusses briefly Jong, Kaufman, Shulman, Greenberg, Olsen, Rosen, Paley, Yezierska, and Broner.

Cooper, Anice Page. "Anzia Yezierska: A Pilgrim in Search of a Laugh."
Authors and Others. Anice Page Cooper. New York: Doubleday,
1927; Essay Index Reprint Series. Freeport: Books for Libraries,
1970. 103-06.

A chatty account of the plot of *Bread Givers* which concludes that the
writer finally taught herself the happy habit of laughter as an antidote for
the bludgeoning life gave her.

Drucker, Sally Ann. "Yiddish, Yidgin, and Yezierska: Dialect in Jewish-
American Writing." *Yiddish* 6.4 (1987): 99-113.

Commends Yezierska for her superior use of Yiddish-English dialect,
and traces its history on stage and in literature.

Duncan, Erika. "The Hungry Jewish Mother." *The Lost Tradition:
Mothers and Daughters in Literature.* Eds. Cathy N. Davidson and E.
M. Broner. New York: Ungar, 1980. 231-41.

Argues the thesis that the underside of the nag and Yenta of Jewish fiction, who devours the soul with every cup of chicken soup she gives, is a
woman who is asked almost from birth to give a nurturance she never
receives; consequently, she is starved for actual food she must turn over
to others and also for the stuff of self, soul, love and song. Demonstrates
this theme extensively in *Bread Givers.*

Garber, Frederick. "Scandals and Ironies." *Jewish Spectator* 42 (Sum.
1977): 26-29.

While discussing several books of interest to Jewish readers, Garber
praises the reprinting of *Bread Givers* and the book itself for its accurate
sociology. Details the plot and characters of the novel. States that
"Yezierska's passion does not usually burn itself out in vituperation, as
Linetcki's does. At its imaginative best it is patterned and guided into
clean and pure intensity." Describes the structure of the novel as a series
of juxtaposed scenes of confrontation, each rising to a climax and leading naturally into the other.

Girgus, Sam B. "'Blut-und-Eisen': Anzia Yerzierska and the New Self-made
Woman." *The New Covenant: Jewish Writers and the American Idea.*
Sam B. Girgus. Chapel Hill: U of North Carolina P, 1984. 108-117.

Claims that a double ideology consisting of a belief in America as a land
of hope, along with a passionate feminist consciousness, is what sustains
Yezierska's writing. Claims that she saw herself as a mediator between

two cultures, explaining each world to the other in terms related to her fight for identity, respect, and freedom as a woman. Claims that "the union of the American Way and feminism in the context of Jewish culture and the ghetto made Yezierska special to the tradition of the New Covenant." Suggests that the ideology of the individual self at the core of her writings represents basic American attitudes toward freedom, success, and culture.

Golub, Ellen. "Eat Your Heart Out: The Fiction of Anzia Yezierska." *Studies in American Jewish Literature* [Albany] 3 (1983): 51-61.

Describes a new revival of interest in Yezierska by feminists who see her as a visionary foremother, radicalized and politicized before her time. Suggests that, to students of the Jewish novel, she fattens the list of Russian-Jewish immigrant writers, and falls between the cheery optimism of Antin and the dour determinism of Cahan. Details her life and writings to illustrate this thesis.

Guttmann, Allen. "Interlude: Anzia Yezierska and Samuel Ornitz." *The Jewish Writer in America: Assimilation and the Crisis of Identity.* Allen Guttmann. New York: Oxford UP, 1971. 33-37.

Comments that Yezierska's contributions have been almost completely forgotten. Commends her books for their insights into the 1920s, and provides biographical insights. Deals primarily with *Bread Givers*.

Harap, Louis. *Creative Awakening: The Jewish Presence in Twentieth-Century American Literature, 1900-1940s. Contributions in Ethnic Studies* 17. New York: Greenwood, 1987. 46-49.

Describes her life and career briefly, noting that she was the first female East European immigrant to achieve prominence in American fiction and calling her a transitional figure in the twentieth-century acculturation novel. Notes that her autobiography published in 1950 revealed how closely her stories reflected her experience and the life around her. Describes some of her stories and her novel *Bread Givers*, particularly noting the father's male supremacism.

Henriksen, Louise Levitas. "Afterword About Anzia Yezierska." *The Open Cage: An Anzia Yezierska Collection.* Ed. Alice Kessler-Harris. New York: Persea, 1979. 253-62.

A personal reminiscence by Yezierska's daughter. Contains valuable biographical information and an excellent publishing history.

Hindus, Milton. "The Art of Anzia Yezierska." *Chicago Jewish Forum* 25.3 (1966-67): 136-41.

Describes Yezierska's rise to fame and money, and her plunge back into obscurity and poverty with the coming of the Depression. Describes the chronological relationship between Antin and Yezierska, and then describes each of Yezierska's major works.

Howe, Irving. "The East Side: Growing Up in the Ghetto." *The World of Our Fathers.* New York: Harcourt, 1978. 268-71.

Provides a brief sketch of Yezierska's life and a description of each of her books. Contains useful biographical information.

Inglehart, Babbette. "Daughters of Loneliness: Anzia Yezierska and the Immigrant Woman Writer." *Studies in American Jewish Literature* [University Park, PA] 1 (1975): 1-10.

Traces the history of immigrant women in literature from the turn of the century, and briefly describes their roles in the labor movement. Provides a sociological, political, and historical account of Yezierska's significance within this framework.

Kamel, Rose. "'Anzia Yezierska, Get Out of Your Own Way': Selfhood and Otherness in the Autobiographical Fiction of Anzia Yezierska." *Studies in American Jewish Literature* [Albany] 3 (1983): 40-50. Rpt. in rev. form as "'Anzia Yezierska, Get Out of Your Own Way.' Narrative Distance in Yezierska's Autobiographical Fiction" in *Aggravating the Conscience: Jewish-American Literary Mothers in the Promised Land.* Rose Yalow Kamel. American University Studies: Ser. 4, English Language and Literature 64. New York: Lang, 1988. 59-79.

Describes Yezierska's personal history and writing career. Provides accounts of the contents and styles of her various works, and traces through all this the theme of selfhood which binds together all her work. Discusses how *Hungry Hearts* was made into a film. Describes the kinds of Americans Yezierska worshipped and read, her protestant father surrogates, and the elegiac qualities about the waste of female talent her books contain.

Kaplan, Johanna. "Immigrant Into Person." Rev. of *The Open Cage: An Anzia Yezierska Collection. New York Times Book Review* 24 Feb. 1980: 14, 38.

Commends the publication of *The Open Cage*, Yezierska's selected collection, and eulogizes her contribution to American letters by reminding readers of her past reputation and the contents of the works extracted from or included in the collection.

Kessler-Harris, Alice. Introduction. *Bread Givers*. New York: Persea, 1975. v-xviii.

An excellent overview of Yezierska's life, publishing history, Jewishness, social philosophy, childhood in Europe, and place in American letters.

Kessler-Harris, Alice. Introduction. *The Open Cage: An Anzia Yezierska Collection*. Ed. Alice Kessler-Harris. New York: Persea, 1979. v-xiii.

Provides commentary on Yezierska's background, reputation, influence, world of origin, Americanization, early works, poverty, personal history, contents of the novel, its first reception, and the author's subsequent life.

Laufer, Pearl David. "Powerful and Powerless: Paradox in Vivian Gornick's *Fierce Attachments*." *Mother Puzzles: Daughters and Mothers in Contemporary American Literature*. Ed. Mickey Pearlman. Contributions in Women's Studies 110. Greenwood: Westport, 1989. 123-30.

Compares the young female life described in *Fierce Attachments*, set in the Bronx in 1940s and 50s, with that described in Yezierska's *Bread Givers* in the Bronx of the early 1900s.

Levenberg, Diane. "All She Could Never Be: Anzia Yezierska." *Midstream* Nov. 1981: 54-58.

Tries to discover what it was that, after so brief a rise to fame, plunged Yezierska into obscurity and personal unhappiness. Examines each of the novels in turn, and decides that it is her lack of courage in destroying her Anglo-Saxon cultural idols that caused her to give up fame, marriage, security, and her child.

Levenberg, Diane. "Three Jewish Writers and the Spirit of the Thirties: Michael Gold, Anzia Yezierska, and Henry Roth." *Book Forum* 6.2 (1982): 233-44.

Asks how artists such as Gold, Roth, and Yezierska perceived their roles in the 1930s at the great crossroads of political, economic, and social upheaval.

Provides a section on each writer which details the life, writing career, and political views. An article which places Yezierska in historical context.

Mintz, Jacqueline A. "The Myth of the Jewish Mother in Three Jewish, American, Female Writers." *Centennial Review* 22.3 (1978): 346-55.

A useful sociology of the Eastern European female roles and New World reversals. Challenges the fictional depiction of the stock Jewish mother prevalent in Jewish-American literature, and traces the evolution of this figure through examining the works of Yezierska, Tillie Olsen, and Susan Fromberg Schaeffer, writers who represent three generations of this "terrible burden."

Neidle, Cecyle S. *America's Immigrant Women.* Immigrant Heritage of America Series. Boston: Twayne, 1975. 264-67.

Provides some biographical information, but concentrates primarily on her literary works and achievements. Finds all her works, including her autobiography, harp on the same themes—hunger and loneliness. Considers her intense, passionate, and unrestrained and her stories sordid to the point of being repugnant. Concedes that she can stir one powerfully, because what she presents is lived life in all its horrors, but concludes that she has only partially transmuted real truth into artistic truth.

Regenbaum, Shelly. "Art, Gender, and the Jewish Tradition in Yezierska's *Red Ribbon on a White Horse* and Potok's *My Name Is Asher Lev.*" *Studies in American Jewish Literature* [Kent State] 7.1 (1988): 55-66.

Discusses *Red Ribbon on a White Horse* as a story of expulsion from Jewish home and community. Considers Yezierska an outcast artist creating art under a burden of guilt. Comments on her essential loyalty to the tradition, as well as the issue of female identity, self-doubt, and self-hatred.

Sachs, Susan Hersh. "Anzia Yezierska: 'Her Words Dance With a Thousand Colors.'" *Studies in American Jewish Literature* [Albany] 3 (1983): 62-67.

An historical overview of Yezierska's life and writing career which focuses critical attention on the quality of her descriptive prose in various of her books.

Salvatori, Mariolina. "Women's Work in Novels of Immigrant Life." *MELUS* 9.4 (1982): 39-58.

Traces numerous works in which the shock upon the human psyche and human relationships of the immigrant experience of the American work place is recorded. Describes several of Yezierska's works in this cultural context.

Schoen, Carol. "Anzia Yezierska: New Light on the 'Sweatshop Cinderella.'" *MELUS* 7.3 (1980): 3-11.

Notes the limitations of the biographical approach Yezierska took in most of her work. Traces the development of the Yezierska myth in the literary media, and provides many omitted facts, such as her seminal relationship with John Dewey. Traces the influence of Dewey on *Salome* and other works. Concentrates also on Yezierska as an educated and conscious craftswoman, and a writer who perpetrated inconsistencies in her public biographical record causing critics to miss important aspects of her life and the influences on her work.

Reviews

Adickes, Sandra. "Burned by a Matchmaker." Rev. of *Bread Givers*. *Village Voice* 27 Oct. 1975: 56.

Provides a brief history of Yezierska's life and a plot outline of *Bread Givers*. Calls the reissuing of the novel a step in providing one of the missing links in the literature of the struggle of women in this country.

"Child of Loneliness." Rev. of *All I Could Never Be. Christian Science Monitor* 8 Oct. 1932: 5.

Provides a brief introduction to Yezierska's previous work, and describes the contents of *All I Could Never Be*.

Field, Louise Maunsell. "Latest Works of Fiction." Rev. of *Salome of the Tenements. New York Times Book Review* 24 Dec. 1922: 22.

Primarily recites the plot and characterization of *Salome*. Recommends the book to educated, American-born patrons of charities to help them consider the effects their charities have on the immigrants in the Lower East Side like Salome. Commends the book for its sociology rather than its writing.

Gaer, Yossif. "Her One Virtue." Rev. of *Bread Givers. Menorah Journal* Feb. 1926: 105-08.

Describes this novel as redolent with Yiddishisms, the humor and irony of culture conflict, and a complete view of immigrant culture. Details the contents of the story without critical comment.

Goldreich, Gloria. "Striking Roots in the New World." Rev. of *Bread Givers*. *Hadassah Magazine* Feb. 1976: 21.

Calls *Bread Givers* a book written from harsh bitterness that does not flinch from describing the reality of the Jewish mothers and sisters. Briefly describes Sara Smolinski and her sisters.

Goodman, Henry. "What Anzia Yezierska Doesn't Know About East Side Fills Two Books." Rev. of *Salome of the Tenements* and *Children of Loneliness*. *Forward* 25 Nov. 1923: English Page.

Argues that this complaining essay mimicks the female voice of *Bread Givers,* and complains that in essence Yezierska is a turbid fountain of emotions, breaks all the laws of grammar, ploys, and literary conventions. Yet admits she touches worthwhile themes about racial variations in America and the whole secret of Anglo-Saxon poise and composure.

"A 'Hungry Heart' and $10,000." Rev. of *Hungry Hearts*. *Literary Digest* 24 Oct. 1925: 44, 46, 48.

Provides a description of the contents of *Hungry Hearts* as well as some interview material from Yezierska. Also contains biographical material.

Kreiter, Samuel. "Dusting off the Bookshelf." Rev. of *Children of Loneliness*. *Congress Weekly* 9 Apr. 1951: 12-13.

Describes *Children of Loneliness* in terms of its 1920s context in the larger national community, as well as that of the New York ghettoes. Describes the themes and settings common to Yezierska, and then comments that this novel is made up of seven pieces of autobiographical fiction about life on the Lower East Side.

"Latest Works of Fiction." Rev. of *Children of Loneliness*. *New York Times Book Review* 28 Oct. 1923: 9.

Describes *Children of Loneliness*, Yezierska's collection of short stories, as the work of a reporter rather than a talented writer. Calls her heroes and heroines all alike—passionate, emotional, unrestrained, intensely egotistical, and always living on the verge of hysteria. Commends the book for its color, dramatic qualities, and clear sociological picture of the people of the Lower East Side.

"Latest Works of Fiction." Rev. of *Hungry Hearts*. *New York Times Book Review* 5 Dec. 1920: 18.

Describes *Hungry Hearts* as a group of short stories which makes a strong appeal to the human heart. Briefly traces the ruling metaphor of hunger throughout the tales.

Mann, Dorothea Lawrance. "Anzia Yezierska Arrives in America." Rev. of *Bread Givers*. *Boston Evening Transcript* 12 Sept. 1925: 2.

Describes the plot, historical background, and characters in the novel.

Nearing, Scott. "A Depraved Spirit." Rev. of *Salome of the Tenements*. *Nation* 6 June 1923: 674, 676.

Finds the novel "a leaping, scorching, searing flame," but considers the comparison of Sonya Vrunsky with Salome a misnomer. Deems Salome a cat's paw in the hands of Herodias, while Sonya is a devouring monster. Cites several incidents to support his objection, and concludes that the book is vivid in places, and well done in others, but finally unwholesome.

"The New Books." Rev. of *The Arrogant Beggar*. *Saturday Review of Literature* 3 Dec. 1927: 405.

Fails to understand the adulation previous critics have expressed concerning Yezierska's books, and finds *The Arrogant Beggar* thin in plot, trite in characterization, and obvious in thought. Condemns her hostility to organized charity, and commends the lightning speed of the narration. Concludes, however, that, even though she is not Shakespeare or Cervantes, she is pleasant to listen to even when she has nothing to say.

Phelps, William Lyon. "The Heroine as a Woman of Letters." Rev. of *Bread Givers*. *Literary Digest International Book Review* Oct. 1925: 719, 722.

Provides a biographical portrait of Yezierska and an account of the contents of *Bread Givers*. Discusses style, background, religion, and sociology.

Popkin, Zelda F. "A New Adventure in the Promised Land." Rev. of *Hungry Hearts*. *American Hebrew* 3 Dec. 1920: 112-13.

An anxious Jewish reviewer's perspective on a Jewish writer pillorying Jews, and yet who admires *Hungry Hearts* as a book that takes its place beside Antin's *The Promised Land* and Cahan's *The Rise of David Levinsky*. Describes Yezierska's women as vibrant, full of stifled passion, hungry for love, and exuberant. Details contents of the story, and concludes that this is a book that will make the reader proud to be a Jew.

Rev. of *Children of Loneliness. Times Literary Supplement* 8 Nov. 1923: 748.

Discusses *Children of Loneliness* as a spiritual drama of the kind race contact must always produce: in this case the Americanization of the Russian immigrant. Details contents of the book.

Rivlin, Lilly. Rev. of *Bread Givers. Ms.* May 1976: 36-37.

Discusses the relevance of the feminist issues in the novel. Describes the contents of the book, and concludes that, schmaltzy as the ending might be, this is a powerful chronicle that needs to be shared.

Roberts, W. Adolphe. "Hungry Souls." Rev. of *Salome of the Tenements. New York Tribune* 17 Dec. 1922: 26.

Describes *Salome of the Tenements* as a novel, which, though shot through with genius, feels like organized chaos. Notes that the story is well-knit, yet the emotions are passionate. Admires the colloquial idiom, and yet criticizes the last chapter for its lack of artistry.

Robinson, James Harvey. "A Stormy Romance of the Ghetto." Rev. of *Salome of the Tenements. Literary Digest International Book Review* Feb. 1923: 14, 66.

Suggests that this novel should be required reading for sociologists, miscellaneous moralizers, and social psychologists so they would realize their academic generalizations do not catch the actual heartburnings of the people they pretend to explain. Describes the contents of the story, and commends the writer for feeling every word she has written about the ghetto as a crucible of privation. Considers the vivid color, style, and varied honesty rarely equalled in American fiction.

Smertenko, Johan J. "From the Ghetto Depths." Rev. of *Bread Givers. Saturday Review of Literature* 10 Oct. 1925: 192.

Sees *Bread Givers* as full of colorful personalities and strange, sordid scenes from the ghettos. Despite this fierce vitality, argues that this unharnessed and little-directed vitality is the author's undoing. Calls her egocentric after the fashion of her character, Sarah, and considers her dialogue a complete failure. Concludes that she failed to apprehend the novel's problems and is only concerned with a slice of life, not life itself.

"A Social Survey." Rev. of *Arrogant Beggar*. *New York Times Book Review* 6 Nov. 1927: 18, 20.

Describes the plot and characters of the story which is told in the first person by the heroine, Adele Lindner. Commends the characterization of Muhmenkeh as the most significant achievement of the book.

"Thwarted Love." Rev. of *All I Could Never Be*. *New York Times Book Review* 21 Aug. 1932: 11.

Argues that *All I Could Never Be* does not show much respect on the part of its author for art: she fails to create adequate characters and a sufficient plot. Claims that Yezierska is careless in typing up her material and in checking her facts.

"Turbulent Folkways of the Ghetto in a New Novel." Rev. of *Bread Givers*. *New York Times Book Review* 13 Sept. 1925: 8.

Provides a detailed account of characters and content in the novel, calling it a colorful and barbaric tapestry of the East Side. Claims that it has a raw and passionate poetry, and an amazingly strong self-assertion.

Van Doren, Carl. "Hungry." Rev. of *Hungry Hearts*. *Nation* 26 Jan. 1921: 121-22.

Accuses *Hungry Hearts* of sentimentalism, repeated formulas, and failure to capture larger realities. Praises it for its early and engaging portrait of this whole immigrant segment of American life. Describes its radiant aspiration and national wealth.

Interviews

Roberts, W. Adolphe. "My Ambitions at 21 and What Became of Them— Anzia Yezierska." *American Hebrew* 25 Aug. 1922: 342, 358.

An autobiographical piece about her early life, ambitions, habits as a writer, aesthetics, moral code, national identity as Polish Jewess, literary debut publishing *Hungry Hearts* and *Salome of the Tenement*, and love life. An early self-portrait also containing the text of her poem "I Am a Spendthrift in Love."

Browne, Edythe H. "A Hungry Heart." *Bookman* Nov. 1923: 269-71.

Summarizes an interview with Yezierska conducted in her home on the subject of *Hungry Hearts*. Recounts much biographical material.

Biographical Sources

Goodman, Charlotte. "Anzia Yezierska." *Twentieth-Century American-Jewish Fiction Writers.* Ed. Daniel Walden. Detroit: Gale, 1984. Vol. 28 of *Dictionary of Literary Biography.* 94 vols. to date. 1978- . 332-35.

More than details of her life, this is a career biography, tracing the development of the author's canon, describing the contents and themes of her works, evaluating her reputation, and placing her in the larger context of American literary history. Includes lists of primary and secondary sources and illustrations.

Henriksen, Louise Levitas. *Anzia Yezierska: A Writer's Life.* New Brunswick: Rutgers UP, 1988.

Yezierska, Anzia. *Red Ribbon on a White Horse.* New York: Scribner's, 1950; New York: Persea, 1981.

Yezierska, Anzia. "America and I." *Scribner's Magazine* Feb. 1922: 157-62.

Speaking as a voiceless immigrant Yezierska describes her coming to America, her first jobs, her efforts to learn English, her unrealized illusions of prosperity, and her final realization that America was still being created and that through her writing about the ghetto she finally found America.

Yezierska, Anzia. "The Struggles of an Immigrant Author." *Literary Digest International Book Review* Sept. 1923: 17-18, 21.

Describes her commitment to writing, her reactions to her published works, the influence of her childhood poverty on her development as a writer, her passion for beauty, and the opportunities America gives the writer—all illustrated by incidents from her life.

Weinberg, Helen A. "The Philosopher and the Poet." Rev. of *John and Anzia: An American Romance.* New Leader 19 Mar. 1990: 20-21.

Reviews a novel based on the secret affair between Yezierska and John Dewey that, according to contemporary scholars, occurred in 1917-18. Describes the contents of the novel, a combination of fact and fiction, that may be of interest to students of Yezierska.

Dissertations

Blustein, Bryna Lee Datz. "Beyond the Stereotype: A Study of Representative Short Stories of Selected Contemporary Jewish American Female Writers." Diss. Saint Louis U, 1986.

Demirturk, Emine Lale. "The Female Identity in Cross-Cultural Perspective: Immigrant Women's Autobiographies." Diss. U of Iowa, 1986.

Drucker, Sally Ann. "Anzia Yezierska: An Immigrant Cinderella." Diss. State U of New York at Buffalo, 1988.

Gartner, Carol Blicker. "A New Mirror for America: The Fiction of the Immigrant Ghetto, 1890-1930." Diss. New York U, 1970.

Gordon, Nicholas Karl. "Jewish and American: A Critical Study of the Fiction of Abraham Cahan, Anzia Yezierska, Waldo Frank and Ludwig Lewisohn." Diss. Stanford U, 1968.

Greenberg, Abraham Herbert. "The Ethnocentric Attitudes of Some Jewish- American Writers: Educational Implications." Diss. Yeshiva U, 1956.

Laufer, Pearl David. "Between Two Worlds: The Fiction of Anzia Yezierska." Diss. U of Maryland, 1981.

Meer, Esther Faygale. "The Polemics of the Heart: A Study of the Complete Works of Anzia Yezierska." Diss. City U of New York, 1987.

Neidle, Cecyle S. "The Foreign Born View America: A Study of Autobiographies Written by Immigrants to the United States." Diss. New York U, 1962.

Sullivan, Ralda Meyerson. "Anzia Yezierska, An American Writer." Diss. U of California, Berkeley, 1975.

Sol Yurick

1925 –

Primary Sources

Novels

The Bag. New York: Simon, 1968; New York: Trident, 1968; New York: Pocket, 1969; London: Gollancz, 1970; London: Panther, 1972; New York: Bard-Avon, 1974.

Behold Metatron, the Recording Angel. Foreign Agents Series. New York: Semiotext(e), 1985.

The Big Green-Out. New York: Arbor, 1983.

Fertig. New York: Simon, 1966; New York: Trident, 1966; London: Allen, 1966; New York: Pocket, 1967; London: Panther, 1968; New York: Avon, 1975.

An Island Death. New York: Harper, 1975.

Richard A. New York: Arbor, 1981, 1982; London: Methuen, 1982; New York: Avon [Cited in PBIP, 1983].

The Warriors. New York: Holt, 1965; London: Allen, 1966; Baltimore: Pyramid [Cited in PBIP, 1969]; London: Star, 1979.

Collected Works

Someone Just Like You. New York: Harper, 1972; London: Gollancz, 1973; New York: Manor, 1974.

Contents: The Annealing; The Child-God Dance; The Siege; The Before and After of Hymie Farbotnik, or The Sticking Point; The Passage; The Bird-Whistle Man; Tarantella; Someone Just Like Me; Not with a Whimper, But . . . ; Do They Talk about Genet in Larchmont?; The Age of Gold; And a Friend to Sit by Your Side; "And Not in Utter Nakedness . . . ."

Short Fiction in Anthologies

"The Siege." *Stories from the Transatlantic Review.* Ed. Joseph R. McCrindle. New York: Holt, 1970; London: Gollancz, 1970. 190-202; Harmondsworth: Penguin, 1974. 264-79.

Short Fiction in Periodicals

"'and Not in Utter Nakedness . . . .'" *Transatlantic Review* 23 (1966-67): 72-86.

"The Bird-Whistle Man." *Transatlantic Review* 31 (1968-69): 29-33.

"Not with a Whimper, But . . ." *Transatlantic Review* 25 (1967): 38-65.

"The Passage." *Transatlantic Review* 16 (1964): 129-36.

"The Seige." *Transatlantic Review* 14 (1963): 26-39.

"Tarantella." *Transatlantic Review* 31 (1968-69): 23-28.

"This Age of Gold." *Transatlantic Review* 37-38 (1970): 39-56.

Secondary Sources

Articles and Chapters

Graham, D. B. "Naturalism and the Revolutionary Imperative: Yurick's *The Warriors.*" Rev. of *The Warriors. Critique* 18.1 (1976): 119-28.

Argues that Yurick's *The Warriors* is a novel about street gangs, a subject of enduring significance in such naturalistic fiction. Shulman's classic naturalism presents the orthodox liberal view: gangs are sociological deviations and destructive alternates for youths dissatisfied for many reasons with home, family, and the restrictive, hypocritical values of their communities. Yurick creates a synthesis with latent ideological and covert political dimensions.

Jones, A. Wesley. "*Someone Just Like You.*" *Survey of Contemporary Literature.* Ed. Frank N. Magill. Rev. ed. 12 vols. Englewood Cliffs: Salem, 1977. 11: 7093-97.

A standard reference article covering background, influences, theme, style, character, and plot in the novel.

Reviews

Baker, Roger. "Their Own Bag." Rev. of *The Bag. Books and Bookmen* Mar. 1970: 23-24.

Suggests that *The Bag* is primarily about social problems facing modern, industrialized countries. Specifically it takes on the multi-layered aspects of poverty in New York City, creating remarkably realistic characters and a huge panoramic sense of the plight of forty million Americans living below the poverty line. Notes that this is all written in dazzling prose with a careful ear toward the language of the streets.

"Book Reviews." Rev. of *Richard A.. Southern Humanities Review* 17.3 (1983): 273-75.

Complains that *Richard A.* is full of nervous, paranoid energy. Suggests that Yurick hankers to write the prophetic novel, and has instead produced a political one where results have more in common with historical romance. Criticizes Yurick for his slangy diction and slender perceptions of people. Sarcastically compares the whole effect to the ABC Movie of the Week.

Cook, Bruce. Rev. of *Fertig. Commonweal* 14 Oct. 1966: 59-61.

Describes the novel as akin to *Crime and Punishment,* and Fertig himself as a sort of Raskolnikov. Describes the plot, the seven murders, and what Yurick seems to be doing by making the reader consider murder as a kind of sacred drama played out to provide society with both entertainment and emotional catharsis.

Crain, Jane Larkin. "Books." Rev. of *An Island Death. Saturday Review* 5 Apr. 1975: 27.

Calls *An Island Death* a powerful book marred by a few obviously contrived and declarative passages. It achieves a sustained intensity that justifies a bizarre and brutal climax. Still, Yurick fails to accommodate the complexity of the issues he himself raises, and this leaves his book much closer to the edge of inconsequence than it need have been.

Croman, Charlotte. Rev. of *Fertig. Catholic World* Aug. 1966: 314-15.

Argues that because of Yurick's many styles this novel lacks strength. Considers that some will find it interesting and provocative because it belongs to the "Jew-in-New York" and to "the-Jew-in-assimilation" school of Jewish fiction.

Davis, L. J. "A Footnote to a Voyage to the End of the Night." Rev. of *An Island Death. National Observer* 12 Apr. 1975: 21.

Describes *An Island Death* as a novel by a disquieting, solitary preacher. There is a kind of impassioned aphasia about his work, the stuttering intensity of a man who has seen too much. This is neither his best, nor his most important work, but rather an explanatory footnote to the rest of his work.

Elman, Richard. "Notes." Rev. of *Richard A. San Francisco Review of Books* Sept.-Oct. 1982: 27.

Calls *Richard A* a book about a particular evil, not a general despair. Considers the book hard to follow, informed by a historical imagination, and concerned for the survival of the human community. Considers the CIA and the KGB as enemies of all human enterprise—antimaterialist forces of negation warring within their own Apollonian ideologies like medieval templars.

Frank, Sheldon. "High-Tech Horrors." Rev. of *Richard A. Detroit News* 23 May 1982: 24.

Calls *Richard A.* an ingenious, compelling, and terrifying espionage guaranteed to make a reader distrust anyone he knows. Describes its structure as a chillingly intricate set of Chinese boxes. Describes the plot in detail.

Gold, Ivan. "Literary Switchboard." Rev. of *Richard A. New York Times Book Review* 18 Apr. 1982: 13, 13-34.

Says *Richard A.* is the work of an experienced, gifted writer and done as an engrossing, cerebral, political thriller. This is a skillful assault from somewhere on the apocalyptic left on the Le Carre turf. Details the plot and characters.

Grumbach, Doris. "As Ever, Sol Yurick." Rev. of *An Island Death. New York Times Book Review* 20 Apr. 1975: 5, 10.

Argues that Yurick is original, tricky, witty, complicated, and deadly accurate. But he is also ambiguous. Readers will delight in the suggestive language, the twin identities, and the palimpsestic meaning. Concludes, however, that the material is not memorable.

Harvey, David D. "Muddle-Browed Faction." Rev. of *Fertig. Southern Review* 5.1 (1969): 270.

Discusses *Fertig* as muddle-headed fiction because it details corrupt New York, social injustice, the inadequacy of the legal process, the criminal, and the motive behind the crime, but offers no ideas about how these problems might be solved. Concludes that we do not see the crime, the criminal, or the motivation in any clear, developed perspective.

Hatch, Robert. "Yurick's Way." Rev. of *The Warriors. Nation* 22 Nov. 1965: 394-95.

Says *The Warriors* is a novel of juvenile tribes that share out the territory of New York City. It is done with ingenuity and style. Yurick describes the steady soldier; the dreamer, sick with intimations of cowardice; the violent giant, half shield, half menace; the young recruit; the violent child. Argues that they are all living anachronisms. They are ignorant, lecherous, superstitious, and cruel by society's standards. Concludes that this is a blazing story.

Jordan, Clive. "Power Bag." Rev. of *The Bag. New Statesman* 9 Jan. 1970: 55.

Suggests that *The Bag* is about physical potency and political power. Says Yurick is not a social realist of the Dos Passos type, but rather more a realist-fantasist with a Gogol-like tendency to caricature. Describes several of the characters and the contents.

Kroll, Jack. "City of Dreadful Day." Rev. of *The Bag*. *Newsweek* 17 June 1968: 94.

Argues that *The Bag* reveals a first-rate writer for whom the novel is still a political-social weapon. Views this as a kind of urban mini-epic with a tight fabric of happenstance that reads like Nathanael West with the laughs turned to dry, chuckling gasps. Concludes that this is mostly a powerful, intelligent, balanced novel about our diseased, embattled, and explosive cities.

Lask, Thomas. "Relief." Rev. of *The Bag*. *New York Times* 4 June 1968: 45.

Calls *The Bag* a passionate, rolling, seething novel about the welfare system of a large industrial city. This is a clear-cut and psychologically convincing novel written in documentary style in quick, nervous prose, with a never-failing sense of the farcical and absurd. Concludes that this is a very rich book, another *Grapes of Wrath*.

Lehmann-Haupt, Christopher. "A Radical's Inventiveness." Rev. of *Someone Just Like You*. *New York Times* 1 Sept. 1972: 25.

Suggests that this is a collection of short stories fueled by a revolutionist's rage. Describes the political and psychological components of the stories as well as their Jewish content.

Leonard, John. "A Raw, High-Low Look at the City Now." Rev. of *The Bag*. *Life* 24 May 1968: 8.

Comments that *The Bag* is a novel written from the upper city by a novelist with appetite, intelligence, range, rage, and the moral commitment to skewer the denizens of both upper city and under city. Provides a detailed account of the contents.

MacManus, Patricia. "A Night to Dismember." Rev. of *The Warriors*. *New York Herald Tribune Book Week* 5 Sept. 1965: 12.

Calls *The Warriors* a masterly, stunning elucidation of worlds within worlds. Sees it as a stomach-gripping saga, dramatized almost entirely through direct action and shot through with a polemic that lies hidden within the reflections.

Miller, Thomas. Rev. of *The Bag. Commonweal* 4 Oct. 1968: 30-32.

Calls *The Bag* zany in the manner of *Catch 22* with its New Politics, whether black, white, establishment, anti-establishment, militant, or non-militant. Details the contents of the novel.

Morton, Brian. "Modern Superstitions." Rev. of *Behold Metatron, the Recording Angel. Nation* 1 Feb. 1986: 122-23.

Says *Behold Metatron, the Recording Angel* is about the myths that mask the relations of power and prevent a dominated population. This book also explores the emerging ideology of the information age. In Yurick's vision, modern capitalism is as deeply imbued with mysticism as any cargo cult. Concludes that every page of this novel is a provocation.

Nichols, Lewis. "Life Follows." Rev. of *The Bag. New York Times Book Review* 9 June 1968: 16.

Suggests that *The Bag* was written by Yurick while thinking that "fiction is drifting away from reality, and he would like to help bring it back." Briefly describes how Yurick obtained information for the book and his writing career.

Nightingale, Benedict. "Uptown and Downtown." Rev. of *The Bag. Observer* 18 Jan. 1970: 33.

Describes the novel as a persuasive description of convoluted power modes, as well as an imaginative achievement rich in ideas and vocabulary. Calls this an untidy, uneven, brilliant book full of vivid impressions.

"Novel Reading." Rev. of *Richard A. Washington Post Book World* 2 May 1982: 11.

Calls *Richard A.* a book with broad vision and scope, but comments that its ambitious attempt falls short. Describes the contents, and concludes that its incredible complexity surpasses richness until it confounds.

Oberbeck, S. K. "Blues Virtuoso." Rev. of *Someone Just Like You. Newsweek* 14 Aug. 1972: 82.

Suggests that *Someone Just Like You* has been whipped out of crackling anarchic prose as it describes the poor, the old, and the ethnics clawing upward in the ghetto. Calls this a virtuoso collection of stories that are so unified in theme and mood they read like a wild novel of the urban all-

American Marxist blues. Concludes that every story is unique and memorable with a precisely tooled social surface.

Oglesby, Carl. "Bagging It: Beyond Black Laughter." Rev. of *The Bag*. *Ramparts Magazine* 10 Aug. 1968: 53-54.

Suggests that *The Bag* attacks the idea of continuing, fixed serviceable social relations. Notes that its perceptions are ones of the despairing black ironist, supremely political in their thrust. Suggests that there is a fine anti-wisdom in this book, a sort of intellectualized blues. Describes some of the contents of the book.

Ostermann, Robert. "The Subject—No, the Protagonist—Is the City, Grim and Full of Devils." Rev. of *Someone Just Like You*. *National Observer* 30 Sept. 1972: 27.

Argues that *Someone Just Like You* is written out of an urban sensibility become maddened. Even as he portrays the demons that devil his characters, Yurick exorcises them and turns his enormous gifts of language and understanding and compassion against the city. Concludes that as grim as they are his stories are redemptive.

"Rubbing It In." Rev. of *The Bag*. *Times Literary Supplement* 15 Jan. 1970: 49.

The Bag is a huge, raw novel written with laborious, self-regarding care and turgid seriousness. Yurick has applied his intellectual prowess and personal experience to the task of assembling a sensationalist array of crudities which will neither contribute to the problem nor encourage the kind of social climate which will solve it. Concludes that this is a heavily repetitive and sententious work.

Seymour-Smith, Martin. "Murder Most Foul." Rev. of *Fertig*. *Spectator* 25 Nov. 1966: 697.

Calls *Fertig* a zany satire written with extraordinary gusto and skill. Details the contents.

Sukenick, Ronald. "Not My Bag." Rev. of *The Bag*. *New York Review of Books* 13 Mar. 1969: 40-41.

Calls *The Bag* a short novel about poverty in America, poverty programs, the New Left, welfare, and the Lower East Side. Suggests that there is much Joycean word-jamming and Faulknerian run-on, making it a novel made of subjects draped in words. Concludes that this is a rather hysterical book with vaguely surreal scenes and unconvincing revolutionary dialogue. Describes characters and plot in detail.

"The Trouble with Harry." Rev. of *Fertig*. *Newsweek* 9 May 1966: 106.

Calls *Fertig* a book in which Yurick's rage crackles in brutally funny prose that parallels the macabre, cynical humor of Nathanael West's *The Day of the Locust*. Suggests that it questions what society should accept in morals, medicine, law, and media. Concludes that this is a sharp and searing book by an author worth watching.

Tucker, Martin. "The Big Black Bag." Rev. of *The Bag*. *Nation* 8 July 1968: 28.

Claims that Yurick's talent and beauty of passion are magnificent. This novel is about people caught up in the blackness of New York City and its sick welfare system. Yurick rarely loses control—lyric, dramatic, rapacious, and numbing by turns. Concludes that it angers, frightens, entertains, and contains magnificent individual scenes.

Tucker, Martin. "Violence of the Dreamer." Rev. of *Fertig*. *Nation* 8 Aug. 1966: 128-29.

Calls *Fertig* a visionary protest novel with tremendous impact written in the nay-saying tradition of Melville and Dostoyevski. Concludes that this is a new American writer worth noting.

Dissertations

Haneline, Douglas Latham. "The Swing of the Pendulum: Naturalism in Contemporary American Literature." Diss. Ohio State U, 1978.

Harrison, Russell Tompkins. "Sol Yurick's Fiction in the Context of Marxist Critical Theory." Diss. State U of New York at Buffalo, 1983.